History of SOCIALISM

History of SOCIALISM

A Comparative Survey of Socialism, Communism, Trade Unionism, Cooperation, Utopianism, and Other Systems of Reform and Reconstruction

HARRY W. LAIDLER

Thomas Y. Crowell Company
ESTABLISHED 1834 NEW YORK

TO MY WIFE,
MY DAUGHTER ROSAMOND,
MY SON JOHN AND
HIS WIFE EUGENIE,
AND MY GRANDCHILDREN

This is an updated and expanded edition of *Social-Economic Movements* by Harry W. Laidler.

Manufactured in the United States of America

L. C. Card 67-29698

1 2 3 4 5 6 7 8 9 10

Preface

TODAY on every continent vast numbers of men and women are asking how their social, political, and economic institutions can be remolded so as to abolish poverty and war, assure full employment and high living standards to all, and lay the foundation for a co-operative order dedicated to equality of opportunity, democracy, and human dignity.

These aspirations, while voiced in greater volume today than in former generations, have constituted the warp and woof of the dreams and practical experiments of thinkers and doers for hundreds of years past. They have led to the rise of various schools of socialist thought—utopian, Marxist, Fabian, syndicalist, guildist, communist, Christian, humanist, and state socialist, among others.

They have led to the development of powerful consumers' and producers' co-operative movements, now conducting vast business and cultural ventures on a non-profit basis in every part of the world. They have supplied the main impetus for the organization and strengthening of great democratic labor and socialist parties—which, in the late sixties, constituted the governments or the chief opposition parties in Great Britain, Australia, Austria, Belgium, Denmark, Finland, France, Germany, Israel, Italy, Japan, New Zealand, the Netherlands, Norway, Sweden, Switzerland, and numerous countries in Asia, Africa, and Latin America.

They have profoundly influenced the vast communist movement and various progressive political groups. They have helped greatly to strengthen every phase of trade and industrial union activity and of the cultural, ethical, and international life of modern civilization.

In the days ahead these movements—economic, political, and cultural—are likely to transform, to a far greater extent than in the past, the social and industrial institutions of the peoples of the world. To be ignorant of them is to be ignorant of the world in which we live and of many of the most challenging proposals for future social change.

Thousands of volumes have been written on particular schools of social and economic thought and action. The present volume seeks to present a picture of practically all of the important movements for fundamental social reconstruction along co-operative lines.

It seeks to provide a history of these movements and systems of thought and describe something of the social environment which led to their development; to set forth their main principles, policies, and leadership and to compare them with other movements for social reconstruction. Within the limitations of space, an endeavor has been made, through the use of carefully selected quotations from the chief exponents of each school, to bring the reader into vital touch not only with the ideas, but with the spirit animating each movement.

History of Socialism, first published in 1944 as *Social-Economic Movements,* has, in this volume, remained intact, while many important political and ideological developments have taken place during the more than two exciting decades that have transpired since *Social-Economic Movements* appeared, have been included. New sections have likewise been added on the internationals of the labor, socialist, and communist movements.

The book should serve, as did its predecessor, as a handbook on social reconstruction for the general reader and as a text book and source book for courses in economics, labor, sociology, political science, and social ethics.

The author is greatly indebted to those who have generously supplied him with data on social movements here and in other lands and with the fine illustrations found in the volumes: to Professor Frank A. Warren, Professor of History, Queens College; to Sara Lowe and Rosamond Laidler for their secretarial assistance; to the staff of the Thomas Y. Crowell Company; to the League for Industrial Democracy for its aid in innumerable ways; and to my wife without whose constant encouragement this volume would not have been written.

HARRY W. LAIDLER

Introduction

ONLY the quest for religious transcendence has had a more permanent place in history than the quest for social justice. Indeed, in certain periods of history, the two have been connected. The constant search for social justice has given rise to the idea of socialism, though it would be false to equate the two. Yet, time and again throughout history, men who have cast critical glances at their contemporary societies and have offered possible alternatives to their "given" existence—alternatives which have had as a central element a personalized conception of social justice—have found this embodied in ideas that have been lumped together under the heading of socialism.

Since the idea of socialism has been present for such a long time, it is not surprising that it has been defined in so many different ways. And with so many definitions, it is not surprising that the public mind is often confused over the nature of socialism. To cite the most common example: a large segment of the American public continues to use the terms communism and socialism interchangeably despite the fact that most Socialists have insisted on the basic differences between the two philosophies and the Communists, although calling Russia a socialist country, have disparagingly labeled the Socialists "capitalist reformers."

One of the tasks of historical writing must be to straighten out this confusion by an examination and clarification of the various schools of socialism. In performing this task there are many valid approaches. There is the need for the specialized, scholarly study of restricted aspects of socialism or of a particularized school of socialism; there is also the need for the multi-volume, definitive approach, such as may be found in G. D. H. Cole's five-volume history of socialist thought: And there is the need for the introductory synthesis of the history of socialism—its ideas, its social and economic background, its political successes and failures. It is to this task—a thorough introduction to the history of socialism—that Dr. Harry Laidler, a veteran of the socialist movement in the United States, has addressed himself in *History of Socialism.*

Harry Laidler has long been known as one of the most prolific and authoritative writers on socialism in the United States. Like Norman Thomas, he entered the socialist movement as a young man and has devoted many years to its political and educational activities. While in high school, Laidler became interested in socialism, and in 1903, at the age of nineteen, while attending the American Socialist College in Kansas, he joined the Socialist Party. In 1904, he entered Wesleyan University, Connecticut, and, along with such young men as Upton Sinclair, Jack London, and Clarence Darrow, he helped found the Intercollegiate Socialist Society (I. S. S.). From 1910 until 1921 he served as executive head in the Society. During these early years in the movement, he also served as editor of the *Intercollegiate Socialist* (1913 to 1919) and the *Socialist Review* (1919 to 1921). In helping form the Intercollegiate Socialist Society, Laidler laid the foundations for the organization with which he has been associated most closely: the League for Industrial Democracy.

The I. S. S. was founded in 1905 with the desire "to promote an intelligent interest in socialism among college men and women." In 1921, it was reorganized as the League for Industrial Democracy, an organization which aimed at "education for increasing democracy in our economic, political and cultural life." The League, in its many activities, has sought to forward the ideas of democracy in industry, social planning, and public control and ownership; it has supported the labor movement, co-operatives, and civil liberties. Throughout the years, the League organized chapters for the study of social problems in hundreds of colleges and universities. The League has had many prominent officers including Norman Thomas and John Dewey, its one-time president; during most of its existence, it has been guided by the figure of Harry Laidler. When the League was formed in 1921, Laidler was chosen as Executive Director, a post which he held until 1957, part of the time sharing this task with Norman Thomas.

In addition to his work for the League, Laidler has served as member and officer in many other organizations, including the National Bureau of Economic Research, the Christian Social Action Commission of the Federal Council of Churches, and the National Housing Conference. His active role in these social organizations has been paralleled by an active role in political life. Laidler ran for public office many times as a Socialist candidate. He was the Socialist candidate for governor of New York in 1936, a candidate for United States senator from New York in 1938, and was elected to the New York city council under the then prevailing system of proportional representation, with the endorsement of labor, socialist, and civic groups.

At the same time that Laidler has carried on important organizational and political activity in the socialist and liberal movements, he has found time for voluminous writing—articles, pamphlets, and books. His many books on socialism and social problems include: *A History of Socialist Thought, Concentration of Control in American Industry, A Program for Modern America, Socializing Our Democracy,* and *The Road Ahead—A Primer of Capitalism and Socialism.* His pamphlets, many of them written under the auspices of the League for Industrial Democracy, include: *Public Ownership Here and Abroad, How America Lives, Unemployment and Its Remedies,* and *Incentives under Capitalism and Socialism.* In addition, he has edited *Socialist Planning and a Socialist Program* and co-edited, among others, *The Socialism of Our Times, New Tactics in Social Conflict,* and *Power Control.*

As a prolific author, Laidler has been concerned with the many problems involving the history and future of socialism. Time and again he has returned to the need for democratic social planning in industry. Most of these works have been written to describe contemporary social and economic conditions and to prescribe remedies for them. But throughout his life Laidler has also demonstrated a continuing interest in the history of socialism. And none of his works has been more ambitious than *Social-Economic Movements.* The book has grown as the man has grown. In 1927, Laidler wrote *A History of Socialist Thought,* an attempt to present the main systems of socialist thought and their historical results from pre-Christian times until the 1920's. Since then, under the title of *Social-Economic Movements,* the book has been updated, incorporating much of the earlier material from the pre-World War I period, revising much of the material on the Russian revolution and communism, and adding new material from the period between the wars. Now issued as *History of Socialism,* it contains once again the most recent developments in socialism in countries throughout the world, as well as new material on the Communist, Socialist, and Labor internationals.

History of Socialism is history in the "large" sense; it is designed as a single-volume survey of the history of socialism, and its purpose is to serve as an introduction to the main developments, the key issues, the basic ideas for which socialists have struggled in society and over which they have struggled among themselves. Such an introduction does not include an intensive diagnosis of Fourier's socialism or the Paris Commune or Clement Attlee's government, but, rather, presents a general exposition of the basic systems of socialist thought, the programs for which socialists have fought in and out of office, and the important socialist movements historically. In these terms, the book serves its purpose admirably in its description of Fabian and guild socialism in England, French syndicalism, the issues dividing Bernstein revisionism and Kautsky's attempt at defending orthodox Marxism, as well as in its examination of the ideas and concepts of the pivotal figure of Karl Marx himself.

The author's approach to his material is "evolutionary." It is not that he sees one form or school of socialism as *necessarily* evolving out of the previous form, but that, though he is aware of the basic differences between varieties of socialism and is especially concerned with distinguishing between democratic Socialism and the perversions of that ideal, the focus is on the contributions of each type of socialism. The result is an accumulation of historically evolving contributions to the quest for social justice. The author feels that the pre-Marxian utopian socialists, despite their inability to prescribe the means to their desired ends and their overly exuberant faith in all-wise philosopher kings, nevertheless, made an important contribution to society with a picture of an ideal state. Marxian socialism is portrayed as performing the necessary function of shifting socialism's emphasis from the abstract themes of the utopians to the arena of society and societal development. The Marxian economic interpretation of history; Marx's theory of the class struggle; Marx's views on concentration in industry, surplus value, and the growing misery of the proletariat are all shown to have contributed to the return of socialism to concrete reality; socialism's growth would now be part of the historical development of society–not the result of a reformation of society through reading and then imitating a utopian tract. After Marx, Laidler feels that both the revisionists of the left and the revisionists of the right made important additions to and corrections of Marxian theory. From the right, the Fabian socialists, led by the Webbs in England, and the "revisionists," led by Eduard Bernstein in Germany, stressed the necessity of appealing to the middle classes (not just the proletariat), the importance of gradualism in terms of socializing the economy, and the necessity of political victories on the path toward socialism. From the left, the syndicalists focused on the need for workers' control and the dangers that the political state might become oppressive even under a non-capitalist regime. The guild socialists, suspicious also of the state but less drastic than the syndicalists, called attention to the necessity for the consumers' voice to be heard, as well as to the necessity for workers' control in order to develop creative instincts.

In the period since World War I, the book discusses the promise of communism, and then its move toward political dictatorship; the ambiguous history of socialism between the wars, the dreadful impact of World War II, the re-emergence of socialist activity after the war; and the important ideas in the development of socialism and democracy that have been offered by such eclectic socialist thinkers as Harold Laski, Lewis Corey, and the contributors to the *New Fabian Essays*. All these movements, schools, and men are viewed as having made important contributions to the history of socialism and the possible shape that it will take in the future.

Although *History of Socialism* serves its purposes admirably, this does not imply that it serves them perfectly. In any large survey, there are errors of omission and commission. It may be wondered why Proudhon's anti-Semitism and racism are slighted, or if Proudhon, who wrote "do not forget that the despotism of the czar is necessary to civilization," can aptly be described as "an intense believer in liberty, in equality." There is the questionable assertion of a link between the socialist's commitment to equalitarian justice and Plato's vision of social justice, and the failure at least to mention the proto-totalitarianism in Edward Bellamy's socialism. To focus on such matters, however, only serves to divert attention from the importance of the book. Any historian is free to catalog his list of merits (interpretations with which he agrees) or demerits (interpretations with which he differs) in so large a framework. The importance of the book is not found in such a catalog (useful as it might be for certain scholarly purposes) but in the light it sheds on the historical schools of socialists and the classic problems of political, social, and economic organization. The state, centralization and decentralization, planning and democracy, efficiency and workers' control, depression and prosperity, poverty and affluence—these and many others are the problems with which men live and the problems over which socialists have fought and debated.

The debates have often been bitter and esoteric, but they have never been lacking in seriousness of purpose.

Modern problems, like the right amount of centralization and local autonomy in running society, are not recent concerns; guild socialists and Fabians argued over these issues fifty years ago. Will a socialist state necessarily become omnipotent and coercive? Socialists of many persuasions have offered solutions on how to prevent this development —what Marx labeled "barracks" socialism. It is because socialism has wrestled with such problems that the history of socialism forces itself on the attention of the modern reader. The earliest utopians sought to solve the problems of society by "example"; the Marxists and the Marxist revisionists, however much they debated tactics and ends, sought the correct solutions by direct confrontation with society. No other social movement has dedicated itself so seriously and arduously to the task of resolving the classic problems that have confronted man throughout history. Socialism has had its successes and failures; no movement has been composed of so many—often contradictory—trends and smaller movements. But the perpetuation of the ideals of socialism —the elimination of social and economic injustice, the end of exploitation, the creation of a fraternal society—point to the strength of the movement. Victim of many harsh setbacks and betrayals, socialism has constantly renewed itself. No single-volume history of socialism captures this large picture so well. There are those who may question certain aspects of the book's approach, which, except in the case of the communist dictatorships, is generous with regard to the contributions from the various currents within the over-all history of socialism. But what may appear at first glance as an overly generous forbearance in terms of criticism suggests the inner strength of the book: its ability to see the larger picture without carrying the doctrinal quarrels between socialists into the vast panorama of socialist history.

As Laidler charts the uneven course of socialism, one is reminded again of the man. He has been a socialist since the first few years of the century; he has remained faithful to socialism through the repressive days of World War I, through the lean years of the 1920's, and through the abortive enthusiasm of the 1930's. He has addressed himself to the post-war problems of the United States from a socialist perspective. Like socialism historically, he has seen dark years and the hopeful possibilities of a brighter future. In microcosm, his life has mirrored the ups and downs of the socialist movement.

Like Laidler's own socialism, the socialist movement, writ large, has prevailed. Reading this book, one will find many facts—points of difference between socialists, historical developments, socialist administrations—with which one may have been previously unfamiliar. In many of the later chapters, with their presentation of the developments in socialism throughout the world, it will be seen how parochial is the person who sees socialism only in terms of the major world powers with perhaps a passing glance at the Scandinavian countries. But finally, in addition to such factual information, one may also find, in the seriousness and dedication with which socialists of many varieties have faced the basic problems of society, a possible key to an understanding of *why* socialism has prevailed.

FRANK A. WARREN
DEPARTMENT OF HISTORY
Queens College

Contents

PART ONE
Utopianism and Its Precursors

PART TWO
Marxism

PART THREE
Other Schools of Thought (1880–1914)

PART FOUR
Communism

PART FIVE
Socialist Movements in Various Lands

PART SIX
Recent Socialist Thought

PART SEVEN
Consumer Co-operation and Miscellaneous Movements

PART EIGHT
Contributions of Various Social and Economic Movements

Acknowledgments

THE AUTHOR wishes gratefully to acknowledge the permissions granted by the publishers mentioned below to use in this volume selections from the pages of their publications as herein listed:

GEORGE ALLEN AND UNWIN: Kautsky, Karl, *The Labor Revolution*, pp. 100–1, 136, 137, 318, 163–4, 205–6, 266–7.

American Economic Review, December, 1943: Hoselitz, Bert F., Article on "Socialist Planning and International Economic Relations," pp. 849, 851.

BELL AND COMPANY: R. J. Tawney, *The Acquisitive Society*, pp. 7–8, 27, 30–1.

G. D. H. COLE: Cole, G. D. H., *Guild Socialism*, pp. 41, 42, 47–8, 108, 132, 165, 166, 167.

WILLIAM COLLINS SONS AND CO., LTD.: Wells, H. G., *A Modern Utopia*, p. 167.

FARRAR AND RINEHART: Hagen, Paul, *Germany after Hitler*, pp. 138, 146, 148.

HARCOURT, BRACE AND COMPANY: Beer, M., *History of British Socialism*, Vol. II, pp. 279–81; Mumford, Lewis, *The Story of Utopias*, p. 59; Russell, Bertrand, *Bolshevism in Theory and Practice*, pp 144–6; William, Albert Rhys, *The Russians*, pp. 88–9.

HARPER AND BROTHERS: Laidler, Harry W., *Socializing Our Democracy*, pp. 199–200; Schumpeter, Joseph A., *Capitalism, Socialism, and Democracy*, pp. 132–3; Yugow, A., *Russia's Economic Front for War and Peace*, p. 14.

HOUGHTON MIFFLIN COMPANY: McConnell, Donald W., and Others, *Economic Behavior*, p. 402.

UNIVERSITY OF KANSAS PRESS: Eldridge, Seba, and Associates, *Development of Collective Enterprise*, pp. 3–4, 549, 550.

KNOPF, ALFRED A.: Cole, G. D. H., *Economic Planning*, p. 253; Gide, Charles, *Consumers Co-operative Societies*, p. 79.

LONGMANS GREEN AND COMPANY: Webb, Sidney and Beatrice, *A Constitution for the Socialist Commonwealth of Great Britain,* pp. 101, 120, 147–8, 334–5; Webb, Sidney and Beatrice, *The Consumers' Co-operative Movement,* pp. 425–6, 432, 439–40, 463–4, 468.

THE MACMILLAN COMPANY: Cole, G. D. H. and Others, *What Is Ahead of Us?* pp. 109–10; Croce, Benedetto, *Historical Materialism and the Economics of Karl Marx,* pp. 50, 85; Florinski, M. T., *Toward Our Understanding of U. S. S. R.,* pp. 110, 179; Hobson, John A., *Free Thought and the Social Sciences,* pp. 149–50; Reckitt and Bechhofer, *The Meaning of National Guilds,* pp. XIII–XIV; Rauschenbusch, Walter, *Christianizing the Social Order,* pp. 322–3; Robson, William A., *The Relation of Wealth to Welfare,* p. 165; Wallas, Graham, *The Great Society* (quoted in Robson's volume above).

UNIVERSITY OF MINNESOTA PRESS: Lippincott, Benjamin E., *On the Economic Theory of Socialism,* pp. 4, 54.

W. W. NORTON: Borkenau, F., *World Communism,* pp. 27, 30, 37, 47, 387; Eastman, Max, *Marxism: Is It a Science?,* pp. 15, 194, 250; Russell, Bertrand, *Power, A New Social Analysis,* pp. 302–3, 319.

OXFORD UNIVERSITY PRESS: Andreae, J. V., *Christianopolis,* translated by Felix E. Held; Sweezy, Paul M., *The Theory of Capitalist Development,* pp. 361–2.

PRINCETON UNIVERSITY PRESS: Thomas, Norman, *We Have a Future,* p. 156.

CHARLES SCRIBNER'S SONS: Webb, Sidney and Beatrice, *Soviet Communism,* pp. 609, 997.

SIMON AND SCHUSTER: Davies, Joseph E., *Mission to Moscow,* pp. 49–50, 302–3, 402–3.

TWENTIETH CENTURY FUND: Corporate Survey Committee, *Big Business: Its Growth and Its Place,* p. 5.

VIKING PRESS: Corey, Lewis, *The Unfinished Task,* pp. 129, 141, 142; Laski, Harold J., *Reflections on the Revolution of Our Time,* pp. 224, 352, 407.

PART ONE

Utopianism and Its Precursors

CHAPTER I

The Social Prophets

For thousands of years those in control of political and industrial power in the nations of the world used that power to oppress the weak. For thousands of years, under every kind of industrial society, the great mass of the world's burden bearers were doomed to lives of poverty and want, while the few lived in luxury. The few declared the wars; the many went forth to battle and to death. The few made the laws, told the many under what conditions they should labor, what rewards they should obtain for that labor, what they should think, what they should believe. Until comparatively recent times, except for occasional rebellions, the many suffered in silence and obeyed.

And for these thousands of years, prophets and dreamers of the world—some from the heart of the common people, some from the privileged classes of society—agonized over this tyranny, this oppression, this injustice. They saw its results in the warped and starved and slavish lives of the multitudes, in the corrupt, the profligate, the arrogant lives of the few. Their hearts went out to the people in their suffering, their wrath to the oppressor. They contrasted the bitter realities of the present with a possible future where justice and brotherhood in the affairs of men would at last prevail. Some of the prophets appeared before the rulers of society, calling them to repentance and renunciation. Others made their appeal primarily to the common people, urging that they secure control of this sorry scheme of things, and transform it into a nobler social order.

Ethico-Religious Utopias[1]: Amos. The prophets who combined their denunciation of the conditions of their times with a picture of what to them appeared to be the state of the future may be grouped among the precursors of the utopians. One of the earliest of these in

[1] For a more complete account of the religious utopias, see Hertzler, J. O., *The History of Utopian Thought*, ch. II.

Old Testament history was Amos, a herdsman of Tekoa, and gatherer of sycamore fruit, born in the eighth century B.C. Amos lived at a time of comparative peace and prosperity, following the victory of Israel over Damascus. Corruption had eaten its way into public life. The privileged classes were thinking merely of their own enjoyment, wrung though it might be from the misery of the poor. To Amos this corruption and profligacy and oppression spelled ruin to his country. As a shepherd tending his sheep on the lonely hillsides, he pondered over the tragedy of it all, and his meditations moved him to interrupt the autumnal feast at Bethel with his warnings.

Amos is credited with showing nothing but scorn for those who "lie upon beds of ivory . . . and eat the lambs out of the flocks; that drink the best wines and anoint themselves with the finest ointments"; [2] who, while so doing, take bribes, sell inferior grain, give short weight, and "make the poor of the land to fail" that they "may buy the poor for silver and the needy for a pair of shoes." [3] He maintained, according to the Bible version, that the nation that tolerated these practices would surely die; [4] but that the righteous remnant would be saved and a kingdom arise in which the inhabitants would "build the waste cities and inhabit them; . . . plant vineyards, and drink the wine thereof; . . . make gardens, and eat the fruit of them." [5]

Hosea. A quarter of a century later—and nearer to the downfall of Israel—came Hosea to call attention to the evils of the day, particularly those of the religious oligarchy, and to proclaim a time when Jehovah would "betroth" Israel unto Him in righteousness, in judgment, in loving kindness, in mercies, and in faithfulness.[6]

Isaiah. Hosea was followed by Isaiah, a noble, a courtier, a councillor of Israel for fifty years, a man of strong personality and tremendous power.[7] The vision of Isaiah was far more vivid in its character than that of his predecessors. Like Amos and Hosea he bitterly denounced existing conditions and laid them chiefly at the door of the ruling class. "For ye have eaten up the vineyard," he told them. "The spoil of the poor is in your houses. What mean ye that ye beat my people to pieces, and grind the faces of the poor? saith the Lord of Hosts . . . Woe unto them that join house to house, that join field to field, till there be no place, they may be placed alone in the midst of the earth." [8]

[2] *Amos,* 6:4–6; some, however, doubt whether Amos made these statements ascribed to him or whether they were interpolated later. (See George Adam Smith, *Book of the Twelve.*)

[3] *Ibid.*, 8:4–6.

[4] *Ibid.*, 9:8.

[5] *Ibid.*, 9:14.

[6] *Hosea,* 2:19–20.

[7] His period of activity was between 740 and 700 B.C.

[8] *Isaiah,* 3:14–15; 5:8; 10:2.

He criticized the hollowness of much of the worship of the day, declared that worship consisted in service, not in the burning of incense, nor in silver and gold, nor in burnt offering of rams.[9] He believed, with Amos, that the doom of the nation was inevitable but with Hosea contended that the very small remnant who had faith would be saved and would help to build the Kingdom of God on earth, a kingdom where justice would be the rule and righteousness the standard.[10] In that kingdom there would be universal peace. Nations would "beat their swords into plowshares and their spears into pruning hooks." "Nation shall not lift up sword against nation, neither shall they learn war any more." [11]

In that kingdom there would be happiness. The people would come "with songs and everlasting joy and gladness," and sorrow and sighing would flee away.[12] Physical suffering would be a thing of the past.[13] There would be knowledge and understanding. "The eyes of them that see shall not be dim, and the ears of them that hear shall hearken. The heart also of the rash shall understand knowledge, and the tongues of the stammerers shall be ready to speak plainly." [14]

Wickedness and hypocrisy would cease. The effect of righteousness would be peace and security.[15] Nature would co-operate with man in making the Kingdom a joyous abode. The wilderness and solitary places would bear fruit. "The desert shall rejoice and blossom like a rose." "The parched land shall become a pool, and the thirsty land springs of water." [16]

Finally, the King (the prophets could scarcely imagine a country without a king) would be a righteous ruler possessing a spirit of wisdom and understanding, of counsel and might, of knowledge and the fear of God —He would protect the weak and crush the oppressor.[17]

OTHER OLD TESTAMENT PROPHETS. Among the social prophets of the Old Testament one might also mention Jeremiah, Ezekiel and Deutero-Isaiah. Jeremiah, born about 650 B.C., living at a time when Israel was passing through days of adversity, also prophesied the ultimate advent of a promised land in which the people would have abundance of the good things of life, their bonds would be broken, and their sorrows turned into joy; in which young and old would rejoice together and a righteous king would dispense justice.[18]

Ezekiel, the prophet of the captivity, who followed Jeremiah, en-

9 *Ibid.,* 1:11–13.
10 *Ibid.,* 28:17.
11 *Ibid.,* 2:4.
12 *Ibid.,* 35:10.
13 *Ibid.,* 35:5–6.
14 *Ibid.,* 32:4–5.
15 *Ibid.,* 32:17.
16 *Ibid.,* 35:1, 7.
17 *Ibid.,* 11:2.
18 *Jeremiah,* 30:8; 31:12, 13.

visaged a utopia in which land was distributed equitably among all of the people, both natives and strangers, and ideal princes dispensed justice and abandoned violence. His chief attention, however, was given to the portrayal of an elaborate system of religious ceremonials which he would have his ideal state adopt. The minuteness with which Ezekiel described these ceremonials reminds one of the detailed plans for community living laid down by some of the utopians of the nineteenth century.

Finally came Deutero-Isaiah, little known prophet, with his vision of a perfect society in which peace and tranquillity would reign, fountains would spring up in the midst of the valley, the wilderness would be made a pool of water, in which labor would receive its just reward, and life would be eternal.[19]

On the whole, "the prophets conceived of an earthly kingdom as a political organization inhabited by the select of Israel, governed by an idealized Davidic King, and permeated with the spirit of Jehovah. It was to be the rule of the world by the chosen people after their earthly enemies had been subdued." [20] With Deutero-Isaiah, on the other hand, salvation was extended to individuals of all races.

Apocalyptic Writers. During the period extending from 200 B.C. to A.D. 1300, but chiefly concentrated in the first four centuries of that era, came the Apocalyptic writers with their fantastic utopias, some earthly states, some supernatural commonwealths miraculously instituted by divine intervention in earthly affairs.[21] Perhaps the most famous of these was the vision of the New Jerusalem, where dwelt the spirits of the good in a city which had foundations of precious stones, walls of jasper, gates of pearl and streets of pure gold.[22] Few, if any, of these writers, however, came to grips with the life and struggle of their days in the same measure as did Amos and his fellow prophets.

Jesus. The summit of ethico-religious utopianism is to be found in the teachings of Jesus.[23] Throughout His teachings Jesus foretold the coming of the Kingdom of God on earth. Such a kingdom would, He believed, be brought about as a result of a gradual process of social and spiritual development. It would be both an earthly and a heavenly kingdom.[24] It would be founded on love. It would be free from Mammonism, from hypocrisy, from selfishness and oppression. The inhabit-

19 *Isaiah,* 41:18, 19; 43:19; 51:3; 60:20; 65:23.

20 Hertzler, *op. cit.*, p. 71.

21 *Ibid.*, pp. 50–66.

22 *Revelation,* 21:18–21.

23 See Hertzler, *op. cit.*, pp. 66–84.

24 *John,* 18:36; *Matthew,* 6:10; 7:21; *Luke,* 17:21.

ants of that kingdom would be imbued with the spirit of service, self-sacrifice, forgiveness, humility, cosmopolitanism.

ST. AUGUSTINE: *The City of God.* Among the remaining ethico-religious theocracies may be mentioned those of St. Augustine (A.D. 354–430) and of Savonarola (1452–1498). St. Augustine, in his *City of God,* written shortly after the barbarian hosts had swept over the Alps and captured Rome, a time of universal religious and political confusion, pictured a future city on earth and in heaven where men would be at peace with their Creator, and where they would do good to all within their reach.[25] His was a utopianism, however, which "despairing of self, cast all its hope on God." [26] St. Augustine's ideal was a perfect ecclesiastical organization. His concepts were greatly influenced by the political theories and practices of the Middle Ages and his utopia possessed few original elements.

SAVONAROLA. More than a thousand years after St. Augustine's death, we find Savonarola, foremost preacher of Florence, trying to superimpose a theocratic form of government—his ideal of a perfect state—upon his native city. The corrupt family of the Medicis had been driven out, and the citizens were trying to establish a republic. They were, however, without plan or compass; and their lack of leadership gave encouragement to the reactionary forces who were conspiring to return to power. Confusion and corruption followed. A dominant personality with a constructive scheme of government must take the helm. Savonarola assumed the spiritual leadership, introduced a Constitution modeled after that of Venice, and brought before the citizens of his city the concept of a theocracy in which vice would be suppressed, and men would be ruled by divine precepts. His proposals, expounded before great audiences who crowded the Duomo, met with enthusiastic response. The proposed Constitution was adopted. The whole aspect of the city changed. Women cast aside their jewels and finery. Merchants restored their ill-gotten gains. The churches became the most popular civic institutions. Philanthropy flourished. "Purity, sobriety, and justice prevailed in the city; and the Prior of San Marco (Savonarola) was everywhere hailed as the greatest of public benefactors." [27]

The Pope of Rome, reactionary politicians, and the populace itself, however, soon tired of the suppression to which they had been subjected under the rule of this dominant religious leader, and finally put an

[25] Hertzler, *op. cit.,* p. 89; St. Augustine, *City of God,* XIX.

[26] Hertzler, *op. cit.,* p. 90.

[27] Crawford, W. H., *Girolamo Savonarola,* p. 163.

end to his regime. Savonarola was later seized and hanged on the gallows, and the vision of his austere reign of righteousness gradually faded from men's eyes. With the death of this Italian preacher and reformer the long line of great ethico-religious utopians came to an end. But the influence of their teachings did not die.

Summary. Thus we find that, for many centuries, social prophets and dreamers in the religious field brought before their peoples the vision of a better, a more brotherly and equitable earthly abode which the righteous would inherit as a reward for their loyalty to their God. Generally these ethico-religious utopias, if they may be called such, were far from democratic in conception. It was hard for the prophets to visualize a worldly state without a king. The king was portrayed, however, not as an oppressor, but as a friend and guide to the people, and as a representative of God. Little attention was given in these visions to actual social or economic organization, and they thus differed widely from the accepted types of social utopias.

CHAPTER 2

Plato's *Republic*

Of a nature far different from the ethico-religious utopias of the prophets is the political utopia, *The Republic,* projected by the "broad-browed" philosopher of Greece. Plato (427–347 B.C.)[1] lived at a time when his country was passing through a death struggle. The age of Pericles (459–431), the most brilliant period in Grecian history, had just come to a close. In 404 B.C., when Plato was in his early twenties, the Spartans finally won their long struggle against Athens and leveled the long walls of the city to the ground. Then followed the arbitrary though short-lived rule of the thirty Tyrants, the re-establishment of the democratic constitution, and, in 399 B.C., the tragic execution of Plato's master, Socrates.

Witnessing both the corruption, extreme license, and grave dangers of tyranny, Plato became distrustful of all existing political institutions

[1] The date of Plato's birth is variously given as 430, 428, and 427 B.C., and the place as either Athens or Aegina. He was the son of rich parents and had every educational advantage. For eight years before the death of Socrates, Plato had lived in close intimacy with his master. Following Socrates' death, Plato withdrew to Megara, and thence traveled extensively through Cyrene, Egypt, Italy, and Sicily. While in Sicily, an unproved story has it that he was sold by Dionysius in slavery, but subsequently ransomed and returned to Athens.

On his return he pursued an even career as an illustrious philosopher for about forty years. He taught, like Socrates, who greatly influenced his life, chiefly by conversation, and received no fees for his instructions. His reputation was higher than that of any of the contemporary philosophers. His most illustrious pupil and his great rival was Aristotle.

His one attempt to apply his theory of political economy to an existing government was in Sicily after the death of Dionysius. The young Dionysius who succeeded to the throne was weak, and Plato was induced by Dion, Plato's friend and admirer, to visit Syracuse and act as his advisor. The attempt, however, was a complete failure. Dionysius banished Dion, and gave little heed to the advice of Plato. In Athens, Plato also remained aloof from governmental affairs. During the rule of the Thirty, when he was a young man, he was invited by his relatives to take some part in public affairs, but was alienated from public life by the corruption of the rulers and the injustices they heaped upon Socrates.

and of all philosophies which exalted the individual above society. He concluded that that state was most to be desired which embodied "in its laws and institutions the fundamental unity of the moral individual with the socialized state." [2]

He sought to impress his conclusions upon the public mind. To criticize present conditions directly was a dangerous procedure. For this reason, among others, it is declared, Plato resorted to the myth of an ideal republic in which mankind lived a life of supreme happiness.

The Republic. A QUEST FOR JUSTICE. *The Republic* begins with a conversation between Plato's revered master, Socrates, and the latter's companions. They are discussing the essentials of justice. Socrates remarks that the nature of justice can best be discovered by finding out what constitutes justice in an ideal state. His companions agree and he starts his journey to the new republic.

NEITHER POVERTY NOR RICHES. As Plato's utopia finally unfolds itself during the course of the Socratic dialogue, we begin to see a city-state inhabited by several thousand people, all of whom possess the necessities of life, but none of whom are wealthy. Plato argues for this equitable distribution of wealth on the ground that wealth "produces luxury and idleness and innovation," and poverty leads to "meanness and bad workmanship as well as innovation." Nor, he continues, can citizens of a state at one and the same time honor wealth and practice temperance.[3] Furthermore, as soon as the people seek luxuries, and "plunge into the unbounded acquisition of wealth," the demand for territory to accommodate new workers increases; the people seek to enlarge their territory at another people's expense, and war inevitably results.

Plato says, in picturing the simple life which the people of his utopia will lead: "I presume that they will produce corn and wine, and clothes and shoes, and build themselves houses. . . . And they will live, I suppose, on barley and wheat, baking cakes of the meal, and kneading loaves of the flour. And spreading these excellent cakes and loaves upon mats of straw or upon clean leaves, and themselves reclining upon rude beds of yew or myrtle-boughs, they will make merry, themselves and their children, drinking their wine, wearing garlands, and singing the praises of the gods, enjoying one another's society, and not begetting children beyond their means, through a prudent fear of poverty or war." [4]

[2] Hertzler, *The History of Utopian Thought,* p. 100.

[3] *The Republic of Plato,* translated by John L. Davies and David James Vaughan.

[4] *Ibid.,* pp. 63–4.

THE GUARDIANS. In this city-state there are three classes of men and women: (1) the artisans, who build the houses, make the clothes, and produce the food; (2) the warriors, who defend the city against attack; and (3) the guardians, who rule. All are necessary to the happiness of the state, although the guardians—the smallest of these classes—is the most important group. This group, therefore, should be most carefully selected and trained.

EDUCATION. Education of the guardians in the ideal republic should include thorough courses in music and in gymnastics. Supreme importance is attached to a musical education, "because rhythm and harmony sink most deeply into the inner recesses of the soul, and take most powerful hold of it, bringing gracefulness in its train, and making a man graceful if he be nurtured, but if not, the reverse." Such a one will also have "the keenest eye for defects, whether in the failures of art, or the outgrowths of nature; will commend beautiful objects, and gladly receive them into his soul, and feed upon them, and grow to be noble and good; whereas he will rightly censure and hate all repulsive objects, even in his childhood." [5]

The music taught, however, should be censored. Effeminate and convivial songs should be avoided, and an endeavor made to develop in the minds of the pupils a sense of beauty, harmony, and proportion.

In the early stages of their education, prospective guardians should be taught fables, but no fables derogatory to the dignity of the gods, and none which represent the gods as waging war upon one another, or breaking treaties, or inflicting misfortunes upon men. The stories told should breathe the spirit of truth, courage, and self-control.

Gymnastics should be taught with a view, not of gaining strength so much as of stimulating the spirited element in man's nature. The object of all education should be the development of "outward beauty of form" side by side with "moral beauty" of soul.[6]

Nor should any "trace of slavery" be found in the studies of the freeborn man. "In the case of the mind, no study, pursued under compulsion, remains rooted in the memory." Pupils must be trained in their studies "in a playful manner, without any air of constraint, and with the further object of discerning more readily the natural bent of their respective characters." [7]

Later, they are to be taught the mathematical sciences, to help them cultivate the habit of abstract thought, particularly the contemplation of the idea of good. Those possessing courage, but deficient in their capacity for science, are placed at the age of twenty in the ranks of warriors,

[5] *Ibid.*, pp. 105–6. [6] *Ibid.*, p. 106. [7] *Ibid.*, p. 289.

and the rest continue their studies until reaching thirty, during which time they strive particularly to discover the relationship between the various sciences. At thirty, the less promising are assigned to practical political positions. The more promising continue for five years longer "with the art of reasoning and perseverance and application," and from thirty-five to fifty years of age take an active part in the government of the Republic.

THE RULERS. After passing the half-century mark, the most intelligent and powerful of the guardians who have throughout their lives done only those things which they believed to be advantageous to the state [8] are selected as rulers. Those selected take turns as rulers, filling the highest offices of the state, and spending the remainder of their time in philosophic studies.

These rulers should, besides their other qualifications, have a retentive memory, be "quick at learning, lofty minded, and graceful, the friend and brother of justice, truth, fortitude, and temperance." [9]

"All private property, whether in houses or lands or anything else, must be forbidden to our guardians, who receive a maintenance from the rest of the citizens, as the wages of their office." This is essential if they are to be prevented from tearing the city asunder by applying the term "mine," each to a different object instead of all to the same, and by dragging to their several distinct abodes whatever they may acquire independently of the rest.[10]

"They should attend common messes and live together as men do in a camp; as for gold and silver, we must tell them that they are in perpetual possession of a divine species of the precious metals placed in their souls by the gods themselves, and therefore have no need of the earthly ore; that in fact it would be profanation to pollute their spiritual riches by mixing them with the possession of mortal gold, because the world's coinage has been the cause of countless impieties, whereas theirs is undefiled; therefore to them, as distinguished from the rest of the people, it is forbidden to handle or touch gold or silver, or enter under the same roof with them, or to wear them on their dresses, or to drink out of the precious metals.

"If they follow these rules, they will be safe themselves and saviors of their city; but whenever they come to possess lands and houses and money of their own, they will be householders and cultivators instead of guardians, and will become hostile masters of their fellow-citizens rather than their allies; and so they will spend their whole lives, hating and hated, plotting and plotted against, standing in more frequent

[8] *Ibid.*, pp. 120–1. [9] *Ibid.*, p. 220. [10] *Ibid.*, p. 190.

and intense alarm of their enemies at home than of their enemies abroad; by which time they and the rest of the city will be running on the very brink of ruin." [11]

Happiness of All. In reply to the accusation that under such conditions the guardians would not be happy, Plato makes Socrates reply that "our object . . . is not to make any one class pre-eminently happy, but to make the whole state as happy as it can be made." [12] Furthermore, they would have the satisfaction of knowing that their success carried with it the preservation of the state. While living they would receive "crowns and privileges from their country in the shape of maintenance and all that life requires, [for] themselves and their children," and when they died they would be admitted "to an honorable interment." [13]

Communism in Family Relations. But in addition to communism in property, Plato advanced the startling proposal that the guardians possess their wives in common. "No one," Plato had Socrates declare, "shall have a wife of his own; likewise the children shall be in common and the parent shall not know his child, nor the child the parent." [14]

The reason set forth by Plato for this unique proposal was the need for unity of purpose among the guardians, and the belief that when they rejoiced and grieved together at the same gains and the same losses, they were bound together much more closely. That city would be best conducted in which the largest proportion of its citizens apply the words "mine" and "not mine" simultaneously to the same objects.[15] Guardians would thus look upon everyone whom they met as either a brother or sister, a father or mother, a son or daughter, or as a child or parent of such relation.[16]

Moreover, such common ownership, observes Plato through Socrates, would make it possible for the state to develop the science of eugenics, "to bring together the best of both sexes as often as possible, and the worst as seldom as possible"; to abandon the inferior offspring and to prevent irregular alliances.[17] He goes into considerable detail regarding the relations which should be permitted and those which should be restrained "if the flock is to attain the first-class excellence." [18]

The Position of Woman. In his ideal republic, women occupy a far higher status than they did in Plato's day. Plato contended that woman was the weaker sex, and yet the difference between her abilities and those of man was a difference in degree, not of kind. "As far as

[11] *Ibid.*, pp. 126–7.
[12] *Ibid.*, p. 128.
[13] *Ibid.*, p. 192.
[14] *Ibid.*, pp. 179–80.
[15] *Ibid.*, pp. 186–7.
[16] *Ibid.*, p. 188.
[17] *Ibid.*, pp. 179–83.
[18] *Ibid.*, p. 183.

the guardianship of the state is concerned," he asserts, "there is no difference between the natures of the man and the woman, but only various degrees of weakness and of strength."[19] It is most desirable for the state that "it should contain the best possible men and women."[20] Both sexes, therefore, should be given the same education, and expected to share in all the duties of the state, military as well as civic, but with the women given the lighter tasks. To free the women from household tasks, the community would rear the children.

WHAT CONSTITUTES JUSTICE. Under the three-class system of the Republic, each class would perform the work for which it was best fitted.[21] Members born in one class would be promoted or demoted to another class, if their capacities made this shift desirable, but no one who was unfitted for a position in another group should shift from one to another, as such shifting "would inflict great damage on the state."[22] Such a transfer would be an injustice. "On the other hand . . . adherence to their own business on the part of the industrious, the military, and the guardian classes, each of these doing its own work in the state, is justice, and will render the state just."[23]

ATTAINMENT OF IDEAL STATE. When asked how the change to his ideal republic would be brought about, Plato intimated that its coming was a long way off: "Unless it happens that philosophers acquire the kingly power in states, or that those who are now called kings and potentates be imbued with a sufficient measure of genuine philosophy, that is to say, unless political power and philosophy be united in the same person, . . . there will be no deliverance." His republic, he declared, "exists in our reasoning, since it is nowhere on earth, at least, as I imagine. But in heaven, probably, there is a model of it."[24]

The Social Significance of *The Republic*. Plato thus pictured an aristocratic communism, a dictatorship of philosophic communists. The artisans were to have no share in the government of the city, because they were incapable of becoming philosophers and hence of directing the state to the highest ends. Nor does Plato propose that his communistic organization should include artisans. Their education would be primarily an education in their craft. Their status would be much the same as in other aristocracies. The warrior and guardian classes responsible for the well-being of the state, however, were to be far more self-sacrificing and selected in a far more scientific manner than in any empire before or since.

In his demand for a balanced education based on a recognition of the

[19] *Ibid.*, p. 177. [20] *Ibid.*, p. 178. [21] *Ibid.*, p. 173.
[22] *Ibid.*, p. 149. [23] *Ibid.*, p. 149. [24] *Ibid.*, p. 204.

more advanced groups, which gives proper regard for the free and harmonious development of the physical, intellectual, and moral qualities of men; in his emphasis on equal opportunity for men and women; in his suggestion that only those of marked intelligence and public spirit should be placed in the highest offices of state; and in his condemnation of gross economic inequalities, Plato set up ideals which have been a source of inspiration to later thinkers. And the world is beginning to give serious heed to the problems of eugenics and of the functional organization of society which Plato raised.

On the other hand, his fantastic ideas of communism in marital relations and in the rearing of children; his belief that a really beneficent rule by the few could be attained without the check of the many; and his advocacy of the iron control of the state in so many of the intimate relationships of life, indicate a surprising naïveté in so great a philosopher.

Plato's *Republic* indicates the truth of the contention that utopias are built up by the social dreamers out of the warp and woof of the social and economic institutions in which they live. Plato's picture of a future ideal state was inevitably limited by his environment. He could not possibly have envisaged a utopia with railroads, telephones, automobiles, aeroplanes, skyscrapers, steel mills, and ten-cent stores. The picture he had in mind could never come true in an age like this. Nevertheless, certain great principles of justice and social organization which he enunciated could well be applied, and with revolutionary effect, to our modern social structure.

CHAPTER 3

From Plato to Sir Thomas More

NINETEEN centuries intervened between Plato's *Republic* and the next great utopian work of a political nature—the *Utopia* of Sir Thomas More.

During these centuries, however, there were religious utopians, such as St. Augustine,[1] who portrayed a future religious order on earth or in heaven. There were likewise many social philosophers who condemned "this sorry scheme of things" and who yearned for a reversion to the communism which existed, at least in their imagination, in the "natural state" of primitive society.[2]

The Roman Writers. Thus philosophers, poets, and prophets of Rome in the early centuries of the Christian era were constantly bemoaning the class conflicts and corruption of their day, and pointing out the virtues of the primitive order of society, in which goods were held in common and covetousness, luxury, and poverty were unknown. A typical example is the paean to an idealized past of the poet Virgil in his celebration of the reign of Saturn, a reign which typified the state of nature:

[1] See *supra,* ch. I.

[2] For a description of the communistic tendencies during this period, see M. Beer, *History of British Socialism,* Vol. 1, chs. I to III.

"There is a span of nearly two thousand years," writes Lewis Mumford (*The Story of Utopias,* p. 59), "between Plato and Sir Thomas More. During that time, in the western world at any rate, utopia seems to disappear beyond the horizon. Plutarch's *Life of Lycurgus* looks back into a mythical past; Cicero's essay on the state is a negligible work; and St. Augustine's *City of God* is chiefly remarkable for a brilliant journalistic attack upon the old order of Rome. . . . Except for these works there is, as far as I can discover, scarcely any other piece of writing which even hints at utopia except as utopia may refer to a dim golden age in the past when all men were virtuous and happy."

Mr. Mumford points out that utopia for the first fifteen hundred years after Christ was transplanted to the skies, and called the Kingdom of Heaven, and was distinctly a utopia of escape.

No fences parted fields nor marks nor bounds
Divided acres of litigious grounds,
But all was common.[3]

Seneca (3 B.C.–A.D. 65) wrote in like vein in ardent admiration of the communism of the "natural state":

"The social virtues had remained pure and inviolate before covetousness distracted society and introduced poverty, for men ceased to possess all things when they began to call anything their own. The first men and their immediate descendants followed nature, pure and uncorrupt. When, however, vices crept in, kings were obliged to show their authority and enact penal laws. How happy was the primitive age when the bounties of nature lay in common and were used promiscuously; nor had avarice and luxury disunited mortals and made them prey upon one another. They enjoyed all nature in common, which thus gave them secure possession of the public wealth. Why should I not think them the richest of all people, among whom there was not to be found one poor man?" [4]

Similar sentiments are expressed in the writings of Horace, Tacitus, Juvenal, and Josephus.[5]

Influence of the Stoic Philosophy. This appeal for a return to primitive tribal society was based at least in part on an acceptance of the Stoic philosophy. According to Stoicism, the world was governed by a divine law of equity and goodness. This law was infinitely superior to man-made law, and applied to all human beings, for all men, as inheritors of the divine spirit, were free and equal. In the original society, the divine natural law governed men, but when corruption set in, man enacted his own law. Thus civil law was a debased substitute for the reign of God and nature, and, if social ills were ever to be remedied, mankind must abandon civil law and return to nature and a life in harmony with nature.[6]

***Jus Naturale* and *Jus Gentium*.** Most of the educated Romans who gave themselves over to philosophic speculations accepted this philosophy. The Roman lawyers undertook to incorporate it into their legal system as *Jus naturale,* combining with it, however, *Jus gentium,* the law which had developed out of the commercial and international relations of that time. In so doing they greatly diluted the original philosophy. *Jus naturale,* according to these lawyers, was that which

[3] Virgil, *Georg.* I, 125–8.
[4] Seneca, *Letters,* 90.
[5] Juvenal, *Satires,* 6 and 13; *Josephus, Antiq. Jud.,* l. 1, c. 2 (3).
[6] Maine, *Ancient Law,* ed. 1861, pp. 53–7, 70–2.

nature taught. Nature joined male and female, and taught procreation, and the need of educating one's offspring. It taught that all men were born free. From *Jus naturale* also came the doctrine that the air, water, public and religious edifices were common property. On the other hand, *Jus gentium,* the law of man, legalized private possessions, dominion and servitude, and neutralized much of the teachings of *Jus naturale* and of the Stoics. In the scholastic literature of the time, the doctrine of *Jus naturale* was preserved in full vigor, and was incorporated into the church law.[7]

This doctrine was further strengthened by the discovery of America and the primitive social organization of the aborigines. The romantic description of life in these tribes is due, to a considerable extent, to the acceptance of the concept of the primitive state—the state of nature. It had a far-reaching effect on the theologians of the time,[8] and its influence extended even to the nineteenth century socialists and social reformers of Great Britain.

Communism and the Peasants' Revolt. The first big crisis in English history in which the philosophy of natural rights and its communist implications played a conspicuous part was the Peasants' Revolt in 1381. New social forces had begun to be felt in England during the reign of Henry II, in the first part of the thirteenth century. By the middle of this century, dozens of towns had come into existence all over England, where once there was nothing but farming country. These towns demanded raw material from the country communities. Rural land thus became valuable, and with this increasing value the nobility began to encroach upon the land held in common for pasture and other community purposes.

The peasants at that time "were not propertyless proletarians, but partners of agrarian cooperative associations, imbued with traditions of their ancient liberties and with sentiments of communal life, and looking upon enclosures as private appropriations of what was common, and on the lords as usurpers." [9] And when the revolt broke out they demanded the return of their old charters of liberty and the restoration of their common lands.

Nor were the peasantry without leaders. Poor priests, friars, and monks were constantly touring the country expressing their indignation at the state of affairs, many of them preaching the gospel of communism as the ideal state of society. These monks and friars thus helped to form

[7] See Beer, *op. cit.,* p. 9.

[8] *Ibid.,* ch. II; see Aquinas, S. Thomas, *Summa,* 1, 2.

[9] Beer, *op. cit.,* p. 20; Walsingham, *Gesta Abbatum,* III, pp. 306, 308, 311.

"an alliance of an intellectual proletariat with the dissatisfied laboring masses. From Oxford as the intellectual and spiritual center the light was spread by the friars to the open fields." [10] All of them must have known St. Isidore's definition of natural law:

> They preach of Plato and prove it by Seneca,
> That all things under heaven ought to be in common.

John Wycliffe. Among these "intellectuals" was John Wycliffe (d. 1384), a "monarchical communist," if such there can be. Wycliffe's social teachings were based directly on the philosophy of *Jus naturale.* In the beginning of society, he contended, there was neither private property nor civil law. Men lived in an age of innocence and communism. After the Fall of Man, however, man's moral fiber became weakened, and he required artificial support. God therefore set up a civil government for the purpose of fostering love among men. The best form of government was government by Judges; where that was impossible, the next best was government by Kings. Civil government was thus of divine origin, although it would never have been instituted had it not been for the sinful nature of man. If combined with communism it would lead to the perfect state.

Communism, Wycliffe held, ought to be the actual state of society. For God grants everything to the righteous and makes them lords of the earth. All men ought to be righteous and thus lords of creation. But multitudes of men can not be heirs to the bounties of the earth unless everything is held in common. Communism is thus God-ordained, but man must constantly check his sinfulness if he is "to attain that degree of grace which would render him worthy of receiving the earth as a fief at the hands of the over-lord." [11] He disagreed with the contention of Aristotle that such an order of society would weaken a citizen's loyalty to his commonwealth. On the contrary, it would strengthen his loyalty. For the greater the number of people who have possession, the greater the sum-total of interest in social welfare and the greater the social unity.

Wycliffe's doctrine of the divine origin of the civil law, however, precluded sedition and violent revolt, and he gave no direct aid to the Peasants' Rebellion, though his teachings had a very considerable influence in bringing it about.

[10] *Ibid.*, p. 21; Little, A. G., *Gray Friars of Oxford*, pp. 63–4.

[11] Beer, *op. cit.*, p. 25; see also Trevelyan, *Age of Wycliffe;* Oman, *Great Revolt of 1381.*

John Ball. A follower of Wycliffe, but a man of a more aggressive type, was John Ball, rebel and communist. Ball, too, held the theory of the natural state. In the beginning, Ball declared, all men were created equal by nature. Servitude was introduced by the oppressors against the will of God. If God had willed it, He would have created both lord and serf. But

When Adam delved and Eve span
Who was then a gentleman?

The people should abolish the oppressors. They should fell the lords and all who do injury to the community. When these were gone, all would enjoy freedom.

A sample of Ball's exhortations is handed down by Froissart:

> My good people,—things cannot go well in England, nor ever will, until all goods are held in common, and until there will be neither serfs nor gentlemen, and we shall be equal. For what reason have they, whom we call lords, got the best of us? How did they deserve it? Why do they keep us in bondage? If we all descended from one father and one mother, Adam and Eve, how can they assert or prove that they are more masters than ourselves? Except perhaps that they make us work and produce for them to spend! They are clothed in velvet and in coats garnished with ermine and fur, while we wear coarse linen. They have wine, spices and good bread, while we get rye bread, offal, straw and water. They have residences, handsome manors, and we the trouble and the work, and must brave the rain and the winds in the fields. And it is from us and our labor that they get the means to support their pomp; yet we are called serfs and are promptly beaten if we fail to do their bidding.[12]

Ball took an active part with the Peasant Revolt, and, after the defeat of the insurrection, died on the gallows. Similar communistic sentiments are expressed in the exhortations of Jack Cade and his followers in the Kentish rebellion of 1449.[13]

Thus Shakespeare put into Cade's mouth:

> I have thought upon it; it shall be so. Away, burn all the records of the realm; my mouth shall be the parliament of England. . . . And henceforward all things shall be in common. (*Henry VI,* Part II, Act 4, Scene 7.)

[12] Froissart, *Collection des Chroniques,* VIII, c. 106.

[13] See Tawney, *Agrarian Problem,* 1912; Gonner, *Common Land and Enclosure,* 1912.

Despite these revolts, expropriation of the peasants proceeded apace. Dispossessed farmers flocked to the cities, and, concurrently with the breaking up of the old farmers' organizations, the guild system of the city was smashed into a thousand bits.

Faith and Reason. In the midst of this chaos in industrial life, the thinkers of the day began a quest for new truths and men began to rely on "knowledge as the regenerator of faith and society." Secular thought began to separate itself from theological dogma. "A rationalist element entered the life of the Christian. . . . Finally, reason was endowed with creative powers; right reason acting through great educators, legislators or king-philosophers could call into being perfect republics, virtuous and happy nations, and correct the fateful effect of the Fall of man." [14]

Summary. Thus we find that, for centuries from the age of Plato to that of Sir Thomas More, equality and common ownership were urged by philosophers, poets, theological writers, and agitators, in the belief that a communistic state of society was the first and "natural state" and that civil law, creating inequality, private ownership, and class divisions, had arisen as a debased substitute for the reign of God and nature. We shall now consider Sir Thomas More's *Utopia.*

[14] Beer, *op. cit.*, pp. 31–2.

CHAPTER 4

More's *Utopia*

IN THE MIDST of this social and philosophic ferment, within a generation of the Kentish rebellion, and some fourteen years before the discovery of America, was born the greatest of the utopian writers, the one who coined the term "utopia"—Sir Thomas More (1478–1535). Educated in the household of Archbishop Morton, the counselor of King Henry VII, More, at an early age, gave much attention to Greek literature and philosophy, and later worked on a dialogue in which he defended Plato's *Republic.* He also assiduously studied the pronouncements of the church fathers. As a young man he delivered lectures on the works of St. Augustine. As lawyer, arbitrator in trade disputes, and Lord Chancellor of England, he gained a wealth of knowledge regarding the national and international problems of his age. He was regarded as one of the foremost scholars of his time, and represented, as Lilly puts it, "the highest perfection discernible among the men of the Renaissance." [1]

Influences Affecting More's Writing. As has been stated, More was born just before great explorations began, and during his boyhood he heard countless tales of the lives of the natives of America and of the islands of the sea. Typical of these stories—some of them extremely fanciful—was that of a writer of the times, describing his voyage past the Canary Islands to Cape Verde:

"The people live according to nature, and may be called Epicureans rather than Stoics. . . . Property they have none, but all things are in common. They live without a king, without any sovereignty, and everyone is his own master. . . . Gold, pearls, jewels and all other such like things, which in this Europe of ours we count riches, they think nothing of, nay, they utterly despise them." [2]

[1] Lilly, *Renaissance Types,* p. 309; Erasmus also was in favor of communism. He asks Christians "to regard their goods as common property." Quoted by Roscher, *Geschichte der National-Oekonomie in Deutschland,* p. 42.

[2] Lupton, J. H., Introduction to his edition of *Utopia,* p. xxxviii.

More was greatly influenced by these accounts. He accepted the view that the state of nature was the state of innocence, and this viewpoint he incorporated in all of his writings. He was also influenced by the rising rationalism of the times, and came to feel that from learning the young "ought to derive the most sublime lessons—piety toward God, benevolence toward men, modesty of heart and Christian humility." However, to the fear of God he gave a more commanding place than to reason and philosophy.

The Story of *Utopia*. PURPOSE. More saw the old England casting off its feudalistic bonds and becoming a nation of merchants; changing from a rural to a money economy and from state regulation of labor and industrial activities to individual enterprise. He began to feel that an effort should be made to apply to this changing social organism the ethics and politics of the church fathers and the growing philosophy of Humanism, which enthroned reason with creative powers. His *Utopia* was written in pursuance of this conviction. More agreed with the early church fathers in their communist principles. His approach to communism, however, was different from theirs. The church fathers and the schoolmen favored communism as a logical application of abstract morality or of Scriptural teachings to society. More analyzed the defects of the industrial system as he saw them and concluded that social reform of a communistic type must be applied.

ADVENTURES OF RAPHAEL HYTHLODAY. In presenting his vivid word picture of the world of his imagination, More introduces to us a sailor and Portuguese scholar, learned in Greek, Raphael Hythloday by name. Hythloday has left his family possessions and his kinsmen and has gone forth with Amerigo Vespucci in search of high adventure.

And in this adventure he comes across the island of Utopia (meaning Nowhere). His experience leads him to describe the wonderful advances which the people of Utopia have made over the English way of living, and, by contrast, to condemn the many social injustices of the England of that day—injustices which appear doubly black against the white background of Utopia. This indictment is set forth in the first book of *Utopia*.

INDICTMENT OF ENGLISH SOCIETY. More, through the mouth of his spokesman, Hythloday, attacked the princes of his country who spent more time in studying how to enlarge their kingdoms by fair or foul means than how peacefully to rule.[3] He condemned the horrible punishments meted out to petty thieves, poor victims of circumstances,

[3] Sir Thomas More, *Utopia and the Dialogue of Comfort* (N. Y.: E. P. Dutton & Co.), p. 19. The references to More's *Utopia* are from this edition.

who were denied an opportunity to earn an honest living, and driven "first to steal and then to die." He denounced the spendthrifts who performed no useful work, but who carried around with them a "great flock of idle and loitering servingmen," [4] and abounded "in wealth and pleasure, when all about them were moaning and groaning," for this condition made the privileged one not a king but "a jailor." More protested against the maintenance of a large army, which must needs embroil the country in war, in order that the nation might continue to have "practiced soldiers and cunning manslayers," whose hands and minds might not wax dull through idleness and lack of exercise.[5] He also bemoaned the increase in the lands given over to the raising of cattle, the tragic condition of the tenantry, and the "corners" in cattle.

THE EVIL OF PRIVATE PROPERTY. Finally he attacked the institution of private property itself. "Where possessions be private . . . it is hard and almost impossible that there the commonwealth will be justly governed and prosperously flourish. Unless you think thus: that justice is there executed, where all things come into the hands of evil men, or that prosperity there flourisheth, where all is divided among a few; which few nevertheless do not lead their lives very wealthily, and the residue live miserably, wretched and beggarly. . . . And for the most part it chanceth that the latter sort is more worthy to enjoy that state of wealth, than the other be: because the rich men be covetous, crafty and unprofitable. On the other part, the poor be lowly, simple, and by their daily labor more profitable to the commonwealth than to themselves. Thus I do fully persuade myself that no equal and just distribution of things can be made, nor that perfect wealth shall ever be among men, unless this property be exiled and banished. But so long as it doth continue, so long shall remain among the most and best of men the heavy and inevitable burden of poverty." [6]

DESCRIPTION OF UTOPIA. In Book II the sunburnt traveler describes his land of Nowhere. It is two miles broad, shaped like a crescent, and is thus the better able to defend itself. It consists of fifty-four cities, some of which are within twenty-four miles' distance of another, and some separated by more than a day's walk. The chief city, Amaurot, is in the center. This, the Portuguese scholar describes.

The basis of industry in this city-state is agricultural. Every citizen must be acquainted with this art, and must spend at least part of his time in one of the great farm houses scattered throughout the country, each of which holds no less than forty men and women. Most of the workers divide their time between town and country, so that they may

[4] *Ibid.*, p. 22. [5] *Ibid.*, pp. 22–3. [6] *Ibid.*, pp. 43–4.

know both the trades and farming, and during the harvesting season thousands of extra hands are drafted from the city to aid in gathering the grain and other products of the soil. The amount of agricultural products needed by the city is nicely calculated in advance, and the citizens are allocated to farm work in proportion to these needs. Every person in Utopia has "a peculiar trade to which he applies himself, such as the manufacture of wool or flax, masonry, smith's work or carpenter's work," and no trade is held in any special esteem.

Eight hours are appointed for rest and six for work. The remainder of the day is put to the discretion of the citizens. The six-hour day without the use of improved machinery is possible because everyone does his share of useful work, and idleness is not permitted, neither among rich men, princes, nor beggars. The surplus labor—if there be any—is used to repair the highways. When all such work is completed, the hours of labor are lessened.

Communism in Distribution. Between city and country there is a monthly exchange of goods at festival time. And in the distribution of goods among the citizens a pure communism exists. Every month or so a representative of each family takes the goods that his family has manufactured to one of the four great public markets situated in different parts of the city. These goods in turn are carried to warehouses, and each commodity is placed by itself. "From hence the father of every family fetches whatever he and his have need of, and carries it away with him without money, without exchange. . . . For why should anything be denied unto him? Seeing that there is abundance of all things, and that it is not to be feared, lest any man will ask more than he needeth. For why should it be thought that that man should ask more than enough, which is sure never to lack? Certainly in all kinds of living creatures either fear or lack doth cause covetousness and ravine, or in man only pride, which counteth it a glorious thing to pass and excel others in the superfluous and vain ostentation of things.

"And though no man hath anything, yet every man is rich. For what can be more rich than to live joyfully and merely, without all grief and pensiveness: not caring for his own living, nor vexed nor troubled with his wife's importunate complaints, nor dreading poverty to his son, nor sorrowing for his daughter's dowry?"

Money and Precious Stones. It naturally follows that money is not needed, and the hoarding of gold and silver, which has led to such great evils in other parts of the world, is forbidden. In fact the utopians take special pains to bring these metals as well as precious stones into disrepute. They use them for the commonest of utensils and make chains of them for the slaves. When the children grow up, they are taught to throw them away as useless. This strange custom in the nature of the case has led to curious results when foreigners venture to the city. Thus, when certain Ambassadors from a certain strange country once visited Utopia, they bedecked themselves with costly jewels and rich raiment and went to see the officials. On their way they bowed low and reverently to the vilest citizens of Utopia, who were also adorned with gold decorations, but as badges of disgrace, and passed by the chief citizens —all plainly dressed—without so much as a nod. "Yea," observed Hythloday, "you should have seen the children that had cast away their own pearls and precious stones when they saw the like sticking upon the Ambassadors' caps, dig and push their mothers under the sides, saying thus to them: 'Look, mother, how great a lubber doth yet wear pearls and precious stones, as though he were a little child still.' But the mother, yea and that also in good earnest: 'Peace, son,' saith she: 'I think he be one of the Ambassador's fools.' " [7]

The people of Utopia are, moreover, continually marveling how it came to pass that such a worthless thing as gold should be so high in the estimation of the people of other countries, "insomuch that a lumpish, block-headed churl, who hath no more wit than an ass, nay, and as full of naughtiness as of folly, shall have nevertheless many wise and good men in subjection and bondage, only for this, because he hath a great heap of gold." [8]

They especially detest those who give almost divine honors to the rich merely because of their riches.

The Homes of the People. The streets of Utopia are "commodious and handsome." The houses are "of fair and gorgeous building," never locked nor bolted, "so easy to be opened, that they will follow the least drawing of a finger, and shut again alone. Whoso will may go in, for there is nothing in the houses that is private, or any man's own. And every tenth year they change their houses by lot. They set great store by their gardens. In them they have vineyards, all manner of fruit, herbs, and flowers, so pleasant, so well furnished, and so finely kept, that I never saw thing more fruitful, nor better trimmed, in any place." Each block competes against the other for beauty of gardens, "and verily you shall not find in any city anything that is more commodious, either for the profit of its citizens, or for pleasure." [9]

Families live in separate houses, but have common eating halls, pre-

[7] *Ibid.*, pp. 69–70. [8] *Ibid.*, p. 70. [9] *Ibid.*, p. 53.

sided over by magistrates, each of the halls utilized by some thirty families of from ten to sixteen persons each.

Utopia at Mealtime. At dinner and supper a trumpeter calls all families to their respective halls, which are provided with nurseries so that the mothers may not be inconvenienced during mealtime. The block stewards order the provisions from the common market at specified hours during the day, and the women aid in the preparation of the meal. They begin each dinner and supper by reading a short essay pertaining "to good manners and virtue."

The midday meal is informal. At the evening meal, however, music is provided, perfumes are burnt, and nothing is left undone "that maketh for the cheering of the company." [10]

Of course people are permitted, if they so desire, to eat alone in their own homes, but no one does this willingly, "as it were a folly to take the pains to prepare a bad dinner at home, when they may be welcome to good and fine fare so near at hand at the hall." [11]

Government. Each citizen is given a voice in the government. Every thirty families in the city elect a magistrate or Philarch. Each ten magistrates choose an Archphilarch, while the latter elect a Prince for life or until he is suspected of enslaving the people. But a matter of great importance is sent to the Philarchs who, after they have communicated it to the families that belong to their divisions and have considered it among themselves, make a report to the council, and upon great occasions the question at issue is referred to the council of the whole island. "The chief and almost the only office of the Philarchs is to see and take heed that no man sits idle: but that every one apply his own craft with earnest diligence and yet for all that not be wearied from early in the morning to late in the evening, with continual work, like laboring and toiling beasts, for this is worse than the miserable and wretched condition of bondmen." [12]

Many of the regulations observed in Utopia would seem indeed harsh to modern times. Any inhabitant desiring to visit the rest of the country must obtain a passport, and, if he tarries in any one place longer than a night, he must follow his occupation, while he who goes out of the city without leave is punished as a fugitive. Those who commit serious crimes are sentenced to a condition of slavery, and they it is who do the hard and disagreeable tasks of the community. Thus More solves the problem of "Who will do the dirty work?"

[10] *Ibid.*, p. 64. [11] *Ibid.*, p. 63. [12] *Ibid.*, p. 56.

Education. The education of the children of Utopia is of a practical nature. They devote themselves to exact sciences, such as arithmetic and geometry, and are given turns at learning agriculture. They are allowed to select their own trade. Children of marked ability are excused from labor in order that they may devote themselves to their studies. All are encouraged throughout life to spend their time in profitable reading.

The Aim Happiness. The aim of Utopia is the greatest happiness to the greatest number. The utopians believe that God has ordained happiness for mankind, and that if man follows nature he will be led to pleasures which have the approval both of his reason and his senses. He should be careful, however, that the lesser pleasure shall not interfere with the greater, and should realize that nothing is genuine pleasure which wrongs another or which brings in its wake displeasure, grief and sorrow. It should be one's pleasure to serve the commonwealth and to help others secure happiness.[13]

Furthermore, man should beware of the counterfeit pleasures which come from wearing a fine gown or precious stones, or from receiving vain and unprofitable honors. "For what natural or true pleasure dost thou take in another man's bare head, or bowed knees? Will this ease the pain of thy knees, or remedy the frenzy of thy head?" Likewise the vainglory of ancestry, the exhilaration which comes from hunting poor, helpless beasts or from playing dice is but sham pleasure. The contemplation of the truth, the study of art and literature, the enjoyment of good health, and rest and moderate eating and drinking are among the legitimate pleasures.

Conclusion. While many of More's suggestions were fantastic and impossible of application, throughout he strove to hold before men a commonwealth which honored its citizens neither for their wealth nor for their rapaciousness nor for their pride of ancestry, but for their service to society, which directed the attention of the people to useful work and to pleasures that developed body, mind, and soul; a commonwealth where neither idleness nor burdensome toil, neither poverty nor superfluous riches existed, but where the end was the good and happy life.

More's purpose in writing *Utopia* was probably a double one. He wished to emphasize certain principles of industrial organization which he felt that society should ultimately adopt. He desired at one and the same time to effect a number of immediate labor, agrarian, sanitary, penal, educational and religious reforms. And he undoubtedly felt

[13] *Ibid.*, pp. 73–5.

that Raphael Hythloday, the sunburnt sailor and scholar visiting an unknown land, could by indirection call to the attention of English royalty and statesmanship the need of these reforms more effectively and more safely than could Sir Thomas More, the politician and critic, by direct and blunt language.

CHAPTER 5

Bacon's *New Atlantis*

AFTER the death of Sir Thomas More, the conflict between the peasants and the possessing classes was vigorously waged for a number of years. The despairing cry of the farming population was thus vividly expressed by Robert Crowley, vicar, printer, and archdeacon:

"The great farmers, graziers, rich butchers, lawyers, merchants, gentlemen, lords, . . . men who have no name because they are doers of all things where gain is to be had . . . they take our houses over our heads, raise our rent, levy great (yea unreasonable) fines, they enclose our commons . . . and to go to the cities we have no hope, for we hear that these unsatiable beasts have there all in their hands."

To this indictment, the lord, accusing the peasants of communistic beliefs, replies:

"The peasant knaves . . . will have no gentlemen, they will have all men like themselves, they will have all things in common. . . . They will appoint what rent we shall take for our grounds. They will cast down our parks and lay our pastures open. We will teach them to know their betters; and because they would have all common, we will leave them nothing." [1]

In 1549, fourteen years after More's death, the peasants again rose in angry though unsuccessful revolt, the last such rebellion on a national scale staged in England against the crushing of the village communities.

Communist Loss of Caste. In defending these rebel peasants, the churchmen of the day made it clear that they had no sympathy with agrarian communism, for communism was losing caste with the Christian Church.

Thus Bishop Latimer, in urging leniency for the peasants, felt it necessary to quote Scripture against the communist tenets: For "if all things

[1] Robert Crowley, *Select Works* (1550), pp. 133–43; quoted in Beer, M., *History of British Socialism,* Vol. I, pp. 44–5.

were in common there could be no theft and so this commandment 'Thou shalt not steal,' were in vain. The laws of the realm make *meum* and *tuum,* mine and thine. If I have things by those laws then I have them. . . . Things are not so common that we ought to distribute them to the poor. . . . But we ought to help one another."

"On the whole," concludes Beer, "with the rise of Protestantism the clear Scriptural text of the Ten Commandments prevailed over the communistic traditions of Primitive Christianity, monastic orders and scholastic *Jus naturale.* . . . Communism lost its sanction in church and state, and took refuge with the extreme wing of nonconformity, revolutionary rationalism, and working class organizations, while society at large moved toward individualism, whose first manifestation was the Elizabethan age—an age of pioneers, men of keen initiative. Its great interpreters, Spenser and Shakespeare, were both anti-communist and anti-democratic." [2]

Communist agitation gave place to the movement for Poor Law Reform and similar legislation.

Bacon vs. More. Then came the accession of Elizabeth, the destruction of the Spanish Armada, the triumph of the Reformation. Men's minds turned to science, invention, exploration, and industrial production. It was in these times that the next great utopian, Francis Bacon, philosopher and natural scientist, lived and gave to the world—nearly a century after More's *Utopia*—at least a fragment of his utopia in the *New Atlantis.*[3]

More, a representative of the Humanist Period of the Renaissance, had advocated the recognition of equal social rights for all reasoning men, through the return to a primitive communism. On the other hand,

[2] Beer, *op. cit.,* p. 46.

[3] Francis Bacon, Baron of Verulam, and ranking only second to Shakespeare in the intellectual achievements of the sixteenth century, was born in London in 1561. He was the son of Sir Nicholas Bacon, Lord Keeper of the Great Seal, and, like More, was intended for the ministry, but actually was educated for the law. He was educated at Trinity College, and ultimately became one of More's successors as Lord Chancellor of England.

Bacon was a strange combination of a philosopher and an unscrupulous politician. So irregular were many of his activities that he was driven from the office of the Lord Chancellorship in 1621 on the charge of accepting bribes and other dishonest practices—which charges he admitted. He was fined 40,000 pounds and sentenced to life imprisonment, but later released by the king. In disgrace he retired to his home in St. Albans, and there devoted himself to science and philosophy. The *New Atlantis,* written in 1622, four years before his death, was the product of his final period of study and speculation. His writings embraced a wonderfully wide range of interests. He was at once historian, logician, philosopher, essayist. He was conversant with almost every science, and was one of the few really great scholars of his times.

Bacon, a representative of the Natural Science Period, believed that the salvation of the race and its ultimate perfectibility depended, not on reform of laws of property, but rather on increased productivity brought about by the progress of science and its application to human life. And so, in his *New Atlantis,* which described an imaginary island in the South Seas, he tells how a wise lawgiver had organized a kingdom of happy and prosperous men on the basis of applied science.[4]

The Story of *New Atlantis.* SALOMON'S HOUSE. The most important institution of this South Sea island was not, therefore, the communist form of property, but the great college called Salomon's House, wherein scientists were eternally engaged in discovering new scientific truths and principles—"the noblest foundation that ever was upon the earth, and the lantern of this kingdom."

The end of this foundation is "the knowledge of causes and the secret motions of things and the enlarging of the bounds of human empire, to the effecting of all things possible." [5] Here new metals are artificially made, great towers a half mile high aid in the observation of the weather and of the fiery meteors; strange new fruits and flowers are brought into being; deep caves are dug to be used in which men may conserve and regain their health; great lakes of salt and fresh water exist similar to our marine laboratories; medicines are discovered with wonderful healing qualities which banish diseases and prolong life, and an attempt is made to widen the gamut of human intelligence through scientific research in every sphere of human knowledge.

These researches are conducted by twelve endowed students who constitute the aristocracy of the island. A number of these are sent abroad every twelve years to observe the progress of science elsewhere. Thus trade with foreign lands is maintained "not for gold, silver or jewels, nor for silks, nor for spices, nor any other commodity or matter; but only for God's first creature, which was light; to have light, I say, in all parts of the world." [6]

MARRIAGE AND OTHER RELATIONS. Bacon did not advocate communism in property, but "communism in knowledge." Unlike More and Plato, he regarded the family as the unit of society, and his *New Atlantis* gave special place of honor to the father of large families. He bitterly attacked the loose marriage relations of the day and urged monogamous marriage, faithfully observed, as the ideal of any good society. His state was ruled by a king, but a king ruling through sheer ability. It per-

[4] See Hertzler, *op. cit.*, p. 147; Beer, *op. cit.*, p. 49.

[5] Morley, *Ideal Commonwealths*, p. 202.

[6] *Ibid.*, p. 191.

sistently kept out foreign influences, as tending to corrupt the population.

The Weakness in Bacon's Social Philosophy. Bacon's great defect was his refusal to see that the development of science, while necessary to any ideal society, was not sufficient. He failed to realize that the people of a nation must not only produce, but also must learn the art of social co-operation, and determine how every new invention and discovery may be applied to the broadest possible social ends. The history of civilization has since shown that science may not only be used as a great constructive force, but also as a great destroyer, unless guided by a correct social philosophy.

CHAPTER 6

German and Italian Utopias

Two other utopias appeared about the same time as the *New Atlantis,* one formulated by a comparatively obscure German traveler and social reformer, Johann Valentin Andreae, and the other, by an Italian monk, philosopher, and teacher, Thomas Campanella. Both these writers followed the communistic visions of Plato and More rather than the more individualistic teachings of Francis Bacon.

Andreae's *Christianopolis.* Andreae, who offers the more appealing utopia of the two, finds himself wrecked upon the shore of an island, dominated by the city of Christianopolis,[1] a clean, orderly city of 400 inhabitants, "a republic of workers, living in equality, desiring peace, and renouncing riches. The city is divided into zones for light and heavy industry. The workers consciously strive to apply science to production, thus introducing a sort of efficiency system. The men are not driven to a work with which they are unfamiliar, like pack animals to their task, but they have been trained before in an accurate knowledge of scientific matters."

The motto of this new utopia may be summed up in one of Andreae's sayings, "To be wise and to work are not incompatible, if there is moderation." The artisans are mostly all educated men. "For that which other people think is a characteristic of a few . . . , the inhabitants argue, should be attained by all individuals."

COMMUNISM OF CHRISTIANOPOLIS. All things produced are brought by the workers to a public booth, and every workman receives the things he needs for his work during the ensuing week. Production is thoroughly organized and those in charge "know ahead of time what is to be made, in what quantity, and of what form, and they inform the mechanics of these items. If the supply of material in the work booth

[1] Andreae, *Christianopolis,* translated in 1916 by Felix E. Held, Oxford University Press.

is sufficient, the workmen are permitted to indulge and give free play to their creative genius. No one has any money. . . . And no one can be superior to the other in the amount of riches owned, since the advantage is rather one of power and genius."

Other Institutions. The houses are inhabited by couples, rather than by patriarchal families, as in More's *Utopia,* and have ample light and air. There are covered walks in the streets, five feet wide, supported by columns twelve feet high, to shelter the citizens from the rain —an anticipation of Bellamy's *Looking Backward.* The furniture in the homes is very simple, so that the household work, performed by husbands as well as wives, will not be arduous, for the people of this city believe that "only those persons are rich who have all of which they have real need, who admit nothing else merely because it is possible to have it in abundance."

A special effort is made to obtain as teachers the very best available material in the community. The government is in the hands of a legislature and an executive, the latter consisting of a Minister, Judge, and Director of Learning. The administrative control of the city is thus delegated to representatives of religion, justice, and learning.

Campanella's *City of the Sun.* Of greater renown, though perhaps of less merit than Andreae's ideal commonwealth, was Thomas Campanella's *City of the Sun.*[2] Campanella's ideal state bears a distinct resemblance to those of Plato, More, and Andreae. A sea captain of Genoa is compelled to go ashore on a faraway island, and is led to the City of the Sun, which appears resplendent on a high hill overlooking an expansive plain. The communism in Campanella's ideal state is absolute—more absolute than that of any of his predecessors. Whatever the citizens "have, they receive from the community, and the magistrates take care that no one receives more than he deserves. Yet nothing necessary is denied to anyone."[3]

[2] Campanella was born in Calabria in 1568, seven years after the birth of Bacon. When but a boy he entered the Dominican order. While there he emphasized the need of studying nature through her own works, not through books. During the Calabrian revolt against Spanish rule, Campanella, who was an Italian patriot, was arrested and sent to prison. He was also attacked by the Spanish Inquisition, accused of writing books he had not written, and of holding opinions he did not hold. He was subjected to torture seven times, and suffered imprisonment for 27 years. The Pope himself interceded for him with the King of Spain.

Following his imprisonment, he went to Rome where he was protected by Pope Urban VIII, but was finally compelled to leave that city. In Paris, Richelieu became his friend. He received a pension of three thousand livres from the King of France while the Sorbonne vouched for his orthodoxy. He died in Paris in 1639 in the Convent of the Dominicans at the age of 71.

[3] Morley, *Ideal Commonwealths,* pp. 225–6.

No Riches or Poverty. They suffer neither poverty nor riches to exist, holding as they do that "grinding poverty renders men worthless, cunning, sulky, thievish, insidious, vagabonds, liars, false witnesses, etc., and wealth makes them insolent, proud, traitors, assumers of what they know not, deceivers, boasters, wanting in affection, slanderers, etc. . . . With them all the rich and poor together make up the community. They are rich because they want nothing, poor because they possess nothing; and consequently they are not slaves to circumstances, but circumstances serve them." [4]

Nor does communism stifle their incentive to action, as "they burn with so great a love for their fatherland as I could scarcely have believed possible." [5]

The Family. Communism enters even into family relations, as with the magistrates and soldiers in Plato's *Republic.* Campanella—after closely observing the work of destruction wrought by the great families of Italy during his lifetime—was convinced that devotion to the state and the desire to increase the prestige of family were not compatible. "For when we raise a son to riches and dignities, we become either ready to grasp at the property of the state, or avaricious, crafty and hypocritical, if any one is of slender purse, little strength and mean ancestry. But when we have taken away self love, there remains only love for the state." [6]

Honoring the Producer. The citizens of his ideal city honor only those who toil—there is no slave class—and the occupations that require the most labor are regarded as most praiseworthy.[7]

"Therefore they laugh at us in that we consider our workmen ignoble, and hold those to be ignoble who have mastered no pursuit; but live at ease and are so many slaves given over to their own pleasure." [8]

Four hours a day is the normal work day, for all engage in useful labor and no one needs to support another.

Visual Education. Campanella believed in new educational methods—methods centuries ahead of his time. He would have education presented to the growing youth by visual means. And so in the *City of the Sun* he had history, geography, mathematics, and botany presented pictorially on the seven great walls of the city, in such a way that the children could be taught "without toil and as if for pleasure." [9]

Aristocracy of Learning. The government in Campanella's city is in the hands of an aristocracy of learning, elected by the people, and the chief of the temporal and spiritual affairs of the state must be in-

[4] *Ibid.*, p. 238. [5] *Ibid.*, p. 225. [6] *Ibid.*, p. 225.
[7] *Ibid.*, p. 246. [8] *Ibid.*, p. 228. [9] *Ibid.*, p. 224.

formed concerning practically every branch of knowledge known to that day. So desirous are the people for the propagation of only the fit members of the race, that they give almost unbelievable powers of eugenic regulation to their magistrates.[10]

While the *City of the Sun* is in many respects a repetition of other utopias, as has been stated, it was, nevertheless, the most comprehensive scheme of social reform proposed in Italy since the days of Savonarola, a century before, and exerted a considerable influence over the disturbed political conditions of the times.

[10] *Ibid.*, p. 228.

CHAPTER 7

Social Thought through the Seventeenth Century

FOLLOWING the utopian visions of Bacon, Andreae, and Campanella, the old agrarian feudalism and communism throughout Europe and particularly in England began to crumble, and a new order began to emerge. English commerce was extended to hitherto unknown parts of the world; cities sprang up on every hand, and private property became firmly entrenched.[1]

Hobbes and the Social Contract Theory. With their growing power, the possessors of property sought to discover a philosophy which would justify the existence of private ownership and discredit the communist position. They formulated a theory known as the "social contract theory," originated by Hugo Grotius (1583–1645) and elaborated by Thomas Hobbes (1588–1679). Hobbes' thesis was essentially as follows: Communism, it is true, existed in the state of nature. Man, however, soon began to develop evil passions and lust for power, and these characteristics resulted in perpetual warfare and the survival of the strongest and craftiest. The laws of justice, of mercy and of modesty, which are nature's laws, were thus nullified. Mankind faced the alternative of seeking to preserve its natural liberty, as a consequence suffering from destructive warfare, or, on the other hand, subjecting itself to authority and gaining thereby a security and peace. Confronted with these hard alternatives, mankind chose authority and peace, because the desire for life and for self-preservation is fundamental.[2]

[1] Utopias based on communistic teachings continued to appear during that period. One was presented in a brief pamphlet, *Paradox,* in which the author portrays the people of Madagascar as the happiest people on earth, as they had no "inordinate desire for riches, which is the root of all mischief—a raging, famished beast that will not be satisfied, a bottomless gulf that cannot be filled." (*A Paradox, Harl. Misc.,* Vol. I, pp. 263–9; quoted in Beer, *History of British Socialism,* Vol. 1, p. 54.)

[2] Thomas Hobbes, *Leviathan,* ch. 14. John Selden worked out a somewhat similar philosophy during these days (Beer, *op. cit.,* p. 54).

After arriving at this decision, the people entered into a solemn contract to hand over their authority unconditionally to one man or to an assembly of men and pledged themselves to obey the laws of their sovereign. So binding was this pledge, according to Hobbes, that, "though a monarch, a sovereign, may in his passion pursue aims contrary to the laws of nature, no subject has a right to make war on him." [3]

With this transfer of power, the natural state ended, and the artificial state followed, with power over property, religion, and all the affairs of the commonwealth. "Inequality and the law of thine and mine" also arose; that is, "the right of a subject to exclude all other subjects from the use of things which he possesses." [4]

Thus Hobbes tried at one and the same time to defend the inviolability of private property and of absolute monarchy. But the England that beheaded King Charles did not take kindly to his monarchical arguments. As for his theory of social contract, that has long since been exploded by social thinkers.

John Locke and the Labor Theory of Value. In fact Hobbes' great successor, John Locke (1632–1704), refuted this social contract theory completely. In the first place he disagreed with Hobbes and Grotius in their contention that the state of nature was a state of communism. When the wild Indian gathered food and prepared it for his own use, it became his exclusive possession. This was legitimate, as the Indian "mixed with it his labor and joined to it something that was unquestionably his own." Moreover, things in their natural state have little value. Nine times their value is added to them through labor. As this labor, the creator of value, is a part of the Indian, in taking the food he was taking only that which was his own. Through labor, therefore, one acquires the title to property.

It follows that so much of land and other property as man can work and render useful belongs to him. This was acknowledged in the original state of nature. The one difference between the natural state and the civil state lies in the degree to which man appropriates property to himself. In the original state he secured only as much as he needed. Locke also took issue with Hobbes in his defense of absolute monarchy. The labor theory of value, which he developed, has done yeoman's work in the socialist movement.[5]

Revival of Communism in the Struggle against the Monarchy. In spite of these broadsides against communism and the increasing power

[3] Thomas Hobbes, *Leviathan*, ch. 16; ed. Toennies, I, ch. 14; II, ch. 1, *et seq.;* Beer, *op. cit.*, p. 55.

[4] Hobbes, *op. cit.*, ch. 15, ch. 16.

[5] See John Locke, on *Civil Government*, II, ch. 5; Beer, *op. cit.*, pp. 56–8.

of property owners, communistic ideals were revived with considerable enthusiasm in the middle of the seventeenth century during the bitter fight for supremacy between the monarch and Parliament. Many of the agitators of the day shifted their argument somewhat from that of the older communists. Communism, they claimed, did not cease with the Fall of Man, but continued even until the Norman Conquest, when the Englishman was defeated and the natural state was turned into a civil state. Thus Gerrard Winstanley, the leader of the small band of communist Diggers, pleaded with Oliver Cromwell that he cast out the "conquerors and recover our land and liberties . . . for when the Norman power had conquered our forefathers he took the free use of our English land from them and made them his servants." [6]

The Diggers' Utopia. In his new Law of Righteousness, Winstanley visualized a utopia in which "there shall be no buying and selling of the earth, nor of the fruits thereof. . . . If any man or family want corn or other provisions, they may go to the storehouse and fetch without money. If they want a horse to ride, they may go into the fields in summer or to the common stables in winter, and receive one from the keepers, and when the journey is performed, bring him back. . . . As every one works to advance the common stock, so every one shall have free use of any commodity in the storehouse for his pleasure and comfortable livelihood, without buying or selling or restraint from anybody." [7]

Family life, however, must be private and monogamous and "every man's house, furniture, and the provisions which he fetches from the storehouses are proper to himself, likewise the wife to the husband and the husband to the wife." [8] Throughout, Winstanley showed a devotion to the principle of common ownership equal to that of the great utopians of the past.

The Diggers, true to their name, soon began their peculiar propaganda of the deed by digging up and manuring one of the hills in Surrey in order to encourage others to "restore the creation to its former condition." The remedy for the present situation, they maintained, was to plow up the commons, parks, and other untilled lands. When others saw the blessings of this method, they would come to their communities. But their efforts were comparatively futile.

Harrington's *Oceana*. Contemporaneous with the communistic utopia of the leader of the Diggers was the political utopia *Oceana,* by the

[6] Winstanley, *Law of Freedom* (1652), p. 3; Beer, *op. cit.*, p. 60.

[7] From Winstanley, *op. cit.*, pp. 74–5, quoted in Beer, *op. cit.*, pp. 67–71; cf. Bernstein, *Sozialismus und Democratie,* 1905; Gooch, *Democratic Ideas,* 1898.

[8] Winstanley, *op. cit.*, p. 24.

gentleman-commoner James Harrington (1611–1677),[9] with its gospel of republicanism. Harrington's treatise was aimed primarily at the development under Oliver Cromwell of a sound and lasting political constitution.

INDUSTRIAL VS. POLITICAL CONTROL. The chief merit of this utopia lay in its clear analysis of the relation of industrial to political control. The property owners of society, Harrington contended, particularly those in possession of land, inevitably control the political life of the community. "As is the proportion or balance of dominion or property, such is the nature of the Empire." Where land is owned by one, there is monarchy; by a few, there is aristocracy; by the people generally, there is a commonwealth. Thus the commonwealth should enact a law forever "establishing and preserving the balance of dominion by such a distribution, that no man or number of men, within the compass of a few or aristocracy, can come to overpower the whole people by the possession of lands." [10]

DEMOCRATIC SAFEGUARDS. Thus Harrington was among the first to emphasize how completely those who control property may expect to control government and politics. As safeguards to democracy he urged, among other things, the secret ballot, rotation in office, and a two chamber legislative system. He undoubtedly stimulated the development of national forms of democracy. He also urged compulsory free education as the hope of democracy and religious toleration.[11]

Peter Chamberlen's Nationalization Program. Several other utopian writers and advanced social reformers appeared in England from the civil war to the end of the seventeenth century. Unique among these was the social reformer Peter Chamberlen, who argued that the wealth and strength of all nations was the propertyless workmen, who did all of the necessary work for society, made up most of the army, and possessed the same right to the earth as did the rich. The end of wealth,

[9] James Harrington, the son of Sir Sapcotes Harrington, was born in 1611, shortly after the birth of Milton. He was educated at Oxford, and later traveled extensively on the continent, where he became a keen student of government, and particularly interested in the governments of Holland and the municipality of Venice. It was during these studies that he became an advocate of the republican form of government. Returning to England, he lived the life of a student and wrote his *Oceana.* Following the downfall of the Commonwealth, he was committed to the Tower of London for holding republican opinions, and there became desperately ill. Though later liberated by Charles II, he never regained his health, and died at Westminster at the age of sixty-six.

[10] John Toland's *The Oceana and Other Works of James Harrington* (London, 1737), pp. 39, 40.

[11] See Hertzler, *op. cit.*, pp. 165–78.

he asserted, was the abolition of poverty. His teachings smacked of those of the modern socialist when he urged that poverty could only be abolished through the nationalization of the estates of the King, the bishops, the deans, and the delinquents, as well as the public ownership and development of the commons, the wastes, the forests, the mines, and the treasures in sea and land, and through taking possession of the unearned increments in value in agriculture, trade, and manufactures. Chamberlen also proposed the establishment of a national bank and the cultivation of land on a co-operative basis, but with farmers free to work individually if they so desired. The government should likewise be depended upon to furnish tools and raw materials to farmers and handicraftsmen.

"Let no man say that men were poor," Chamberlen declared, "because they were unworthy. Some of the greatest apostles, also Christ and the apostles, were poor. Besides, the poor would not be poor, if the rich were honest, so as to let the poor have their own; the riches of the rich are oftentimes but trophies of their dishonesty, of having robbed the poor or cozened the Commonwealth." [12]

[12] Chamberlen, Peter, *Poor Man's Advocate* (1649), p. 12; Beer, *op. cit.*, p. 72.

A utopia of minor importance was that of Samuel Hartlib, a German refugee from Poland, who wrote in 1641 a description of the Kingdom of Macaria, somewhat after the fashion of More's *Utopia*. No man in this imaginary government could hold more land than he could improve, and one-twentieth of the estate of each reverted to the state at his death.

The co-operative ideal was also emphasized by Peter Cornelius van Zurik-Zee of Plockhoy, a far less revolutionary writer than Chamberlen, in his pamphlet, *The Way to Make the Poor in These and Other Nations Happy* (1659). He declared that co-operative production and housekeeping and buying were far cheaper than private enterprise and would decrease the cost of necessities. He urged the organization of "Little Commonwealths" to carry out his schemes.

Much less millennial in its aspect was the scheme of social reform advocated by John Bellers (1655–1725), a member of the Society of Friends, and perhaps the most representative social reformer of that period. Bellers advocated the establishment by the rich—who would secure a fair rate of interest—of a series of co-operative agricultural colonies for the poor. Each colony was to contain about 300 persons able to perform all of the necessary work around the farm. Co-operative workshops for arts and crafts were to be established in all industrial centers. As these ventures would eliminate competitive wastes, a remunerative rate of interest would be ensured to the stockholders. Life in these colonies would be communistic, after the example of primitive Christianity.

Bellers anticipated Robert Owen and John Gray by his advocacy of *labor time as the standard of value*. The rich cannot live, Bellers maintained, but by the labor of others. As labor was the support of the rich, the rich should see that the poor worked under the most advantageous conditions, both from the standpoint of increasing wealth production and of elevating the condition of the poor.

There were other social writers who would not raise a finger for the elevation of the poor, such, for instance, as Bernard Mandeville, who, in his *Fable of the Bees,* maintained that in "a free nation, where slaves are not allowed, the surest wealth

Nor were men poor, he continued, because they were idle. If this were so, then it were a reason why rich men were not rich, since "Edel" man (gentleman) is idle-man. The poor have been accused of insolence. But there is no greater incitement to insolence than poverty face to face with flaunting wealth. The new order would lead to love of country, obedience to law and stability of government.

---

consists in a multitude of laboring poor . . . ignorant as well as poor." (Mandeville, *Fable of the Bees,* etc., edition 1724, pp. 328 and 280; Beer, *op. cit.,* p. 77.)

CHAPTER 8

The French Utopians

WITH the coming of the eighteenth century our scene shifts from England to France, for here lived the majority of the great utopians of the eighteenth and the beginning of the nineteenth centuries.

Social Forces and the French Revolution. The French utopians were a product of the forces that led to the French Revolution and its aftermath. The long reign of Louis XIV (1643–1715), with its unceasing wars of conquest, its profligate court, its burdensome system of taxation, its bankrupt finances, its weakened economic system, and its impoverished peasantry, had caused bitter resentment against the monarchical system. Resentment increased under the rule of Louis' dissolute successor, Louis XV (1715–1774), and was voiced by many Frenchmen, notably Voltaire and Rousseau. Voltaire (1694–1778) expressed his sympathy for the poor, but relied, for social salvation, on freedom of thought and individual self-culture rather than on revolutionary change. Jean Jacques Rousseau (1712–1778) followed with his criticism of the palliatives of the *intelligentsia,* and his advocacy of the total abolition of the reigning order. Private property, he contended, was plunder, and the Golden Age could be brought about only by its abolition and a return to nature.

These writings exerted a potent influence on the revolutionary movement of the day and gave encouragement to those who would sweep away rather than patch up monarchical institutions. The sentiment for the overthrow of French monarchy was increased by the stand of the ruling house against all reform measures. It was intensified by the American revolution. That which America had done, the Frenchmen should do. The belief in the need of revolutionary change was also constantly encouraged by growing commercial and industrial interests of the time desirous of wresting political power from the aristocracy. These were joined by the peasants and city workers, whose misery was extreme, and who were led to believe that an upheaval would mean for them liberty, equality, fraternity.

Disillusionment of the Revolution. The revolution came. The bourgeoisie wielded the power formerly possessed by the titled classes. Men were made equal before the law, but the relation of property had not changed, and when the common man began to ask what the revolution had meant to him, he discovered that the chief causes of economic and social inequality remained. The peasants and city workers were still the burden bearers of society. The lot of many had been made worse rather than better by the development of machine production, with its accompanying long hours, its low wages, and its unemployment. These conditions caused extreme pessimism on the part of many idealists. They turned the attention of others to constructive methods whereby equality, freedom, and brotherhood might become a reality. Among the latter group were the socialist utopians.

Appearance of the Utopian Socialists. These writers and prophets differed from one another. Some pictured a future condition of society in which the state would regulate in detail both industrial activity and individual behavior. Others pinned their faith to a system of free and voluntary co-operation. All tried, however, to visualize an industrial society wherein equality of economic opportunity would prevail and wherein no man would be able to live off the labor of his fellows. In general they believed with their predecessors that the institution of private property was brought about by a contract made in remote ages after the disappearance of the natural state and its communistic system of property. However, they argued, this social contract may be altered at any time by the individual members of society. It should be altered in such a manner that men—who are by nature good—shall be freed from vicious institutions and be permitted to develop according to the laws of nature. Their next question was, What social organization can be devised which will give nature's forces full play? It was in answer to this question that they elaborated their utopias, which differed so widely in concept from each other.

In working out their utopias they worried but little as to whether the great industrial forces at work in society would permit of the contemplated change. They scarcely thought in terms of social evolution. All that was necessary to do, the majority of them believed, was to present a plan for social salvation, begin to experiment on a small scale, interest powerful men in its development, and extend it to the masses. Such trifles as the state of industry and the preparedness of the masses disturbed them not at all.

Babeuf. A STORMY LIFE. The first of the school of utopian socialists, and an extreme product of the revolutionary period, is Francis Noel Babeuf (1764–1797). Babeuf, who represented the old communist conception of absolute equality rather than the socialist ideal of equal opportunity, was one of the stormy petrels of the Revolution.

Following a short career as a land surveyor and administrator of the Department of the Seine, he entered the revolutionary movement and founded *The Tribune of the People,* probably the first communist newspaper ever published. He launched violent attacks therein against the institutions of civilized society, and in particular opposed those who had terminated the Reign of Terror. For these activities he was arrested and imprisoned. On his release he formed a secret organization, with the object of overthrowing the Directory and of introducing the communist millennium. Considerable success attended his efforts, and it was said that in April, 1796, 17,000 men were prepared to join the insurrection. One of the inner circle, however, informed on the "Equals," as they called themselves, and Babeuf was again arrested and subsequently was sent to the guillotine (1797).

HIS PHILOSOPHY OF EQUALITY. The theoretical basis of Babeuf's communism was drawn largely from Morelly's *Code de la Nature.*[1] His philosophy is succinctly expressed in the dictum: "The aim of society is the happiness of all, and happiness consists of equality." "Nature," his followers asserted in the first article of the official declaration of rights of the secret committee, "has given to every man an equal right in

[1] Abbe Morelly, born about 1720, was the one writer of his time who did not content himself with criticizing the old society, but who formulated a scheme for a new order. Man, according to Morelly, is naturally good and naturally recognized the claims of others. Evil thus arises as a result not of the nature of man but of maladjustment of social forces. The remedy, therefore, is to be found in the eradication of those institutions which pervert human nature. The one institution which, more than any other, causes human misery is the institution of private property. The inroads of private property upon the primitive communism of the race are responsible for the evil and disorder of the times.

Morelly thus urged in his work of fiction, *Code de la Nature,* the common ownership of productive goods, private ownership being retained only in those things reserved for immediate use. Under the ideal society there would be no idlers. Each would labor for the community "according to his ability, and share according to his needs." (*Code de la Nature,* pp. 153–4; Guthrie, *Socialism before the French Revolution,* p. 266.) Nor would any man shirk labor if it were made attractive. To fit man for this state, Morelly urged compulsory education and a training in industrial arts. A unique plank in his program was his insistence that every man attaining his majority should be compelled to marry and that only those above forty years of age should be allowed to become celibates. "Festivals of marriage" should be instituted as an encouragement to the marriage state. Pleasure he conceived to be the end of human aspirations. All the human passions he regarded as essentially good.

the enjoyment of all goods." All wrongs, oppressions and wars have their origin in man's disobedience to this natural law.[2]

Gradual Nationalization. Babeuf, however, did not hope to bring about this state of absolute equality at once. It was to be established gradually. First, all the property of corporations and institutions would be nationalized. That of individuals would next be nationalized, on the death of each, for there was to be no inheritance. By the end of fifty years, all property would be in the hands of the nation. Production would then be carried on under officers elected by popular vote. These officers would determine the needs of individuals and divide the products of industry among the workers. They would receive the same reward as the ordinary workers, and rotation in office would prevent them from becoming intrenched in positions of power.

Further Details. The country, under Babeuf's utopia, would be divided into various regions, and, on orders of the government, workers would go from one region to another as required. The surplus products of a more prosperous region would likewise be sent to those districts in need. Only citizens performing labor considered useful by the government could exercise any political rights, a provision not dissimilar to that afterwards adopted by the Russian Soviet Republic.

Teaching would be regarded as useful only if undertaken by one who had declared his adherence to the principles of the community. Literature and fine arts would not be included in the category of useful occupations. All must eat alike, be dressed alike—allowances being made only for sex and age—and be educated in the practical sciences. Children were to be taken from their parents at an early age, brought up together, and taught the principles of communism, so as to prevent the growth of inequality.

Conclusion. While all of Babeuf's proposals cannot be dismissed as impracticable, the modern idealist will find his utopia on the whole cheerless and uninteresting, a fitting product of the age of terror and materialism through which its proposer was then passing, and in which he played so active a part.[3]

Cabet. His Career. Babeuf was one of the two Frenchmen included under the general title of utopian socialists who aligned themselves definitely on the side of absolute equality. The second of this

[2] See "Manifesto of the Equals," in Reybaud's *Études sur les Réformateurs,* etc., 1856, Vol. II, pp. 423–453.

[3] For a more extensive account of Babeuf's life and works see Ernest Belfort Bax on *The Last Episode of the French Revolution* (Boston, 1911); see also Ely's *French and German Socialism,* ch. II (N. Y., 1883); *Histoire de la Conspiration pour L'Egalité & dite de Babeuf,* 2 vols. (Brussels, 1828).

school, and a man of far greater idealism and poetic imagination than Babeuf, is Etienne Cabet.

Cabet was born in 1788 during the revolutionary period, received a good education, became a lawyer, was appointed in his early thirties attorney general of Corsica, which position he soon lost because of his opposition to the government, and was shortly afterwards elected a member of the Chamber of Deputies. Subsequently he became editor of *Le Populaire,* a journal of moderate communist principles, and was condemned to two years' imprisonment for an article appearing in this journal criticizing the king. He escaped, however, to England and while there became acquainted with Sir Thomas More's *Utopia.* It was from this book that he drew the inspiration which resulted in the writing of his social romance, *The Voyage to Icaria.*

ICARIA. In this book Cabet employs the familiar device of conversing with a traveler who had visited an ideal land. The traveler in this case was Lord William Carisdall, who had come across a second Promised Land, an Eden, an Elysium, a new terrestrial Paradise, Icaria, a land where peace and wisdom, joy and happiness, were universal. Lord William kept a journal of his observations in this Elysium.

According to the journal, Icaria is a well organized industrial machine on a national scale. The country is divided into a hundred provinces, and each province into ten communes. The capital cities are in the center of each district. Everything is symmetrical and follows the decimal system. The city of Icaria contains straight and wide streets and beautiful gardens. Each block has precisely fifteen houses, all of uniform size and construction. The city sees to it that the citizens are supplied with every sanitary convenience. Dust is collected by elaborate machines, and the sidewalks are roofed over with glass to protect the citizens against the rain.

Each citizen arises early for a six o'clock breakfast prepared according to scientific standards. The hours of work are seven in the summer and less in winter. The state owns all of the large industries, sees to the cultivation of the land, to the building of the houses, and to all other phases of production, and divides the product of industry equally among the workers. The inhabitants choose the officers, but these officers are given much power, and during their term of office, there is something akin to a dictatorship of technicians.

Every man, alas, has to wear the same kind of clothes, and all women and children are dressed alike, although variety is allowed in colors. Marriage is monogamous, a preliminary courtship of six months being provided for. Education begins at five, and is continued until eighteen for boys and seventeen for girls. Thereafter both sexes are put to the work for which they are best fitted. All can retire at 65 years of age. Women are held in high esteem. There are no newspapers and no way of crystallizing public sentiment, but there is the right of submitting proposals to public assemblies. Art and literature are encouraged, although books must be submitted to the state for approval before publication.

On the whole, while more idealistic than Babeuf's proposals, the utopia pictured by Cabet presents the same restrictions upon freedom of personal action and the same monotonous uniformity which are so deadening to initiative and so contrary to the modern socialist conception of a future state.

Efforts toward Realization. Cabet felt that a state similar to Icaria was in the realm of possibility, indeed, that it could be realized by society in the space of fifty years. In its realization, however, the teacher, not the soldier, would serve as the instrument. A beginning could be made by passing minimum wage laws, training the children in the doctrines of communism, and progressively taxing the rich and letting the poor go free.

He believed, furthermore, that the establishment of a sample colony in some undeveloped region would help to convince doubting Thomases of the virtue of his scheme. He secured a grant of land in Texas, started his band of followers there, but, with the development of yellow fever, transferred his colony to Nauvoo, Illinois, where some 1500 Icarians gathered. But Cabet was not a born leader. He dreamed of what he could do with 500,000, and failed to get his 1500 to work in harmony. Dissension finally broke up the colony. Some of the branches continued for years, but had no great significance, and the people of his day failed to see his vision and follow it.

Saint-Simon. His Youth. We now leave Babeuf and Cabet for Saint-Simon. We find in him a utopian whose aim was the development of a social system wherein man would be rewarded according to his deeds and equal opportunity rather than a mechanical equality would prevail.

Comte Henri de Saint-Simon was a personality unique in the history of social reformers. He was born in Paris in 1760, a younger brother in a noble family which traced its ancestry from Charlemagne. After losing an inheritance yielding an income of 500,000 francs, through a quarrel between his father and the Duke of Saint-Simon, he writes: "I have lost the fortune and the titles of the Duke of Saint-Simon, but I have inherited his passion for glory." That he might not forget the glorious destiny in store for him, he commanded his valet to awake him every morning with the words, "Arise, Monsieur le Comte, you have grand deeds to perform."

At nineteen he went to America, took part in the American Revolution, received official recognition for his gallant conduct in the siege of Yorktown, and was made colonel of a regiment on his return to France at the age of twenty-three. Military affairs, however, interested him but little and he soon resigned his post. He observed that he was far more interested in the political than in the military side of the American Revolution and that he had set before him in America the task of studying "the movements of the human mind, in order that I might then labor for the perfection of civilization. From that time forward I devoted myself to that work without reserve; to it, I consecrated my entire life." [4]

His Role in the French Revolution. During the French Revolution he took the side of the Revolutionists, became the president of a local commune, and proclaimed his intention to renounce the title of count, since he held the title of "citizen" in far higher esteem. His designation "comte," however, placed him under suspicion, and led to his imprisonment for eleven months as a dangerous citizen. Saint-Simon declared that while he was in prison his ancestor Charlemagne appeared to him and said: "Since the world has existed, no family has enjoyed the honor of producing a hero and a philosopher of first rank; this success has been reserved for my house. My son, thy success as a philosopher will equal mine as a warrior and politician."

As Student and Author. On his release he engaged in land speculation and accumulated a moderate fortune, then devoted himself to study. During this time he formulated the concept of a science of sciences from which Auguste Comte derived his idea of developing a universal science. Later he thought it necessary to add a training in experience to his training in theory, and undertook, with unfortunate results to himself, to live every kind of life from that of wealthy entertainer to that of profligate and pauper.

He began his career as author and social reformer in 1803 at the age of forty-three, and to it devoted his energies until his death in 1825. His money gone and his health broken, Saint-Simon suffered much during these days. He was sustained by his belief in the future of the race. "The golden age of humanity," he said, "is not behind us; it is to come,

[4] See Lettres à un Américain, deuxième Lettre in his *L'Industrie ou Discussions Politiques, Morales, et Philosophiques,* Vol. II, pp. 33–4 (Paris, 1817), quoted in Ely, *op. cit.,* p. 55.

and will be found in the perfection of the social order. Our fathers have not seen it; our children will one day behold it. It is our duty to prepare the way for them."

For a while he eked out an existence by working as copyist at $200 a year. He copied nine hours a day and weakened his health by his attempt, during hours that should have been given to sleep, to work out a social system. His former valet then came to his aid, but died in 1810. Saint-Simon continued with his labors, wrote two works, and appealed to scientists and other prominent men to aid in their publication. He wrote: "I am dying of starvation. For fifteen days I eat only bread and drink water; I work without a fire and I have sold everything except my garments to cover the expense of the copies. It is a passion for science and the public good, it is a desire of discovering the means of terminating in a peaceful manner the dreadful crisis in which I find the entire European society engaged, that has caused me to fall into this condition of distress; therefore, it is without blushing that I am able to confess my misery and demand assistance to enable me to continue my work."

His appeal met with small response, but was cherished afterwards by his disciples as indicative of the sacrifice made by their master for the common good. Later he received a small annuity from his family.

Just before his death he completed his three principal works, the *Industrial System*, the *Catechism of Industry*, and the *New Christianity*, the last being the most celebrated. Till his death he retained faith in the quick consummation of his plans. On his deathbed he bade his followers, Auguste Comte among them: "Remember that to accomplish grand deeds you must be enthusiastic. All my life is comprised in this one thought: to guarantee to all men the freest development of their faculties." He told of his plans for the projected publication, *Le Producteur*, and declared that forty-eight hours after the appearance of the second issue the party of labor would be formed. "The future is ours." [5]

HIS TEACHINGS. *Union of Knowledge and Industry.* The substance of Saint-Simon's contentions in his various works may be expressed as follows: The world is in need of some authority which will rule the inner life of man. The Catholic Church provided that authority up to the Middle Ages and the beginning of the Reformation, but its influence is waning and no agency has as yet taken its place. The present age is an age of destructive criticism. Its chief forces are producing disintegration, as is shown by the French Revolution. This period was necessary, as old obstacles to progress had to be cleared away. The time

[5] Reybaud, *op. cit.*, Vol. I, pp. 83–4; quoted in Ely, *op. cit.*, p. 61.

is now ripe, however, for constructive plans, for a new social system based on universal association.

A transition to this system can be brought about only through an advance in knowledge accompanied by a development from the feudal and theological to the industrial and scientific system. In the past, industry and warfare were united. In the society of tomorrow war must be eliminated. In the past, belief and faith were all potent. In the future this must be supplanted by knowledge, and industry and knowledge must unite to govern the world.

Peace and Co-operation. In bringing about this marriage between knowledge and industry, the thinkers in society should, first, see that peace was guaranteed. In earlier times the Catholic Church was able to act as mediator between nations. The hope today is a European parliament composed of real leaders whose function it is to arbitrate.

Second, there should be a united effort to establish universal association, which would guarantee labor for all, and would see to it that labor was rewarded according to its merits. A corollary to guaranteed work is that all should labor. The idler is a parasite, whether he is a rich idler or a poor beggar, and cannot be tolerated, for he eats that which others have produced and is thus no better than a thief.

Dependence on Persuasion. The future society should not practice the asceticism of early Christianity. The flesh is not evil. Both flesh and spirit should be united in an harmonious development. Reform should be brought about by persuasion, by the written and spoken word, not by means of violence.

To inaugurate this new order, Saint-Simon, during most of his life, appealed to the classes rather than to the masses, and even urged Louis XVIII to help in the transformation. He believed that the new state should be under the spiritual direction of the men of science. In his last days, however, he looked forward to the organization of labor as a means to his new order.

THE "NEW CHRISTIANITY." The Bible of Saint-Simonism is the *New Christianity*. In it the author held that God had founded the church, and that the fathers of the church should be honored. The only valid Christian principle, however, had been perverted, and this the new order would restore. "In the New Christianity," he declared, "all morality will be derived immediately from this principle: men ought to regard each other as brothers. This principle, which belongs to primitive Christianity, will receive a glorification, and in its new form will read: Religion must aid society in its chief purpose, which is the most rapid improvement in the lot of the poor." [6]

[6] Quoted in Ely, *op. cit.*, p. 66.

Socialist Proposals of the Followers of Saint-Simon. The followers of Saint-Simon were led to their socialistic conclusions by observing the discrepancy between merit and reward under the present economic system. The few were surfeited with riches, while the many, who worked ceaselessly, lived in poverty.

Their practical proposals included the transfer of industry from private to public ownership; the retention of private property in consumption goods, and the insistence that each shall labor according to his capacity and receive a reward according to services rendered.

Under their proposed plan production would be organized in somewhat the same way as the army is administered, with a gradation of authority and of ranks. The directing authorities would decide the value of the service of each to society and the reward which each should receive. The Saint-Simonians did not, however, make clear how these officers would be selected. The assumption seemed to be that the wise and the good would naturally gravitate to the top and voluntarily assume the positions for which their respective capacities fitted them, and that there would be no opposition to such an arrangement. Inheritance would be abolished, for it would interfere with the principle of reward according to merit. Their aim was, then, a co-operative commonwealth, ruled bureaucratically by an aristocracy of science. Their proposals for public ownership and their insistence on reward according to merit distinctly anticipated modern socialistic principles. On the other hand, their dependence on the classes rather than the masses to bring about the change and their plans for the bureaucratic administration of industry without proper democratic safeguards were greatly at variance with the ideals of the modern movement.

Denial of Communist Philosophy. The philosophy of Saint-Simon and his followers was admirably summed up in their brochure, published in 1830, replying to an attack on them in the Chamber of Deputies on the alleged ground that they advocated community of goods and of wives:

"Yes, without doubt the Saint-Simonians profess peculiar views regarding property and the future of women. . . . But these are very different from those ascribed to them. The system of community of goods means a division among all the members of society, either of the means of production or of the fruits of the toil of all.

"The Saint-Simonians reject this equal division of property, which would constitute in their eyes a more reprehensible act of violence than the present unequal division, which was effected in the first place by the force of arms, by conquest.

"For they believe in the natural inequality of men, and regard this inequality as the very basis of association, as the indispensable condition of social order.

"They reject the system of community of goods, for this would be a manifest violation of the first of all the moral laws which it is their mission to teach—*viz.*, that in the future each one should rank according to his capacity and be rewarded according to his works.

"But in virtue of this law they demand the abolition of all privileges of birth, without exception, and consequently the destruction of inheritance, the chief of these privileges, which today comprehends all the others, and the effect of which is to leave to chance the distribution of social privileges among a small number, and to condemn the most numerous class to privation, to ignorance, to misery.

"They demand that land, capital, and all the instruments of labor should become common property, to be so managed that each one's portion should correspond to his capacity and his reward to his labors. . . . Christianity has released woman from servitude but has condemned her to religious, political and civil inferiority. The Saint-Simonians have announced her emancipation, but they have not abolished the sacred law of marriage, proclaimed by Christianity. On the contrary, they give a new sanctity to this law.

"Like the Christians, they demand that one man should be united to one woman, but they teach that the wife ought to be the equal of the husband, and that, in accordance with the particular grace given to her sex by God, she ought to be associated with him in the triple function of temple, state, and family, in such a manner that the social individual which has hitherto been man alone should hereafter be man and woman." [7]

NEW ADHERENTS. The new faith gained a number of distinguished adherents, among them Buchez, president of the Constituent Assembly of 1830, DeLesseps, the famous engineer, and noted professors, writers, economists, lawyers, bankers, and members of other professions. The École Polytechnique, with its engineers, was the stronghold of this new order.

At first the fortunes of this group were placed largely in the hands of Enfantin, a strange leader of men, who combined a spirit of vanity and a delight in fantastic dress and ceremonies with noble and generous sentiments, self-confidence, and unusual enthusiasm and magnetic force. Of his influence upon his followers, Booth states: "He ruled despotically over their lives and thoughts; he induced them . . . to lead an ascetic life; he withdrew them from refined society, and forced them to

[7] See Reybaud, *op. cit.*, Vol. I, pp. 105–7.

share in the coarsest toil; he compelled them to undergo the humiliation of public confessions, and he received from them the reverence accorded to a divine teacher." [8]

The Sacred College of Apostles. Under the leadership of Enfantin, the Saint-Simonians established a "Sacred College of Apostles" consisting of six of their leaders, and a subordinate order of less influential members. They formed missions in various French cities and even abroad. Their members delivered numerous lectures, and they published a number of journals. They dressed in blue costumes, light blue being reserved for their leaders, royal blue for the lowest ranks. At times they wore a waistcoat which it was difficult for them to take off without the assistance of others. This symbolized man's dependence on his brother.

The Schism. Soon, however, Enfantin began to depart from his master's teachings in regard to love and marriage. His belief in the rightness of the impulses of the flesh led him first to advocate divorce and then practically a doctrine of free love. A violent controversy followed this departure from the faith, and, in 1831, after many all-night debates, during which some of his followers were borne from the room unconscious, the society divided, and Bazard, his co-leader, and many others—including all of the women—left the Enfantin faction.

Enfantin appealed to a priestess to come forward and occupy the seat left vacant beside his by Bazard, as only in that way could a perfect priesthood be formed. Though there were many applicants for this position, the right person, however, did not apply, and the perfect priesthood was not effected.

Enfantin's Retreat. Enfantin and those who remained loyal to him thereupon decided to retire from the world and to live a life of asceticism. Some forty or fifty of them moved to the leader's home at Ménilmontant, where they performed all of their own work as a religious duty—for the employment of servants was abhorrent to them. They continued their intellectual development by taking courses in astronomy, geology, physical geography, music, and civil engineering. Some of the teachers were men and women of rare eminence.

External persecution, intellectual differences, and financial difficulties finally led to the breaking up of this "monastery." The faith continued to prosper for a number of years, however, and the Saint-Simonians made a number of expeditions abroad to promote their faith and to serve mankind. Enfantin headed one expedition to Egypt, where he was a potent influence in urging the building of the Suez Canal.

[8] Booth, A. J., *Saint-Simon and Saint-Simonism* (London, 1871), pp. 102–3.

David, the opera composer, delighted the Alexandrians with concerts, while Barrault, an orator, fascinated them with his lectures. Enfantin on returning to France was appointed director of the Lyons Railway and became a wealthy man. He kept his faith, but took the position that the school had done its work and that the philosophy was slowly leavening the mass.

The Influence of Saint-Simon. In estimating his influence upon the future of the social movement, Booth maintains that Saint-Simon was a pioneer in noting the separation of the classes, in emphasizing the importance of labor and property in the development of man, in calling attention to the evil of inheritance, and in representing social reform as the true function of government. "Saint-Simonism is the first expression of the proletariat." Undoubtedly its ideas exerted a profound influence on the later socialist movement.

Fourier. FOURIER AND SAINT-SIMON. The teachings of Saint-Simon found their complement in many ways in those of a contemporary French utopian, Charles Fourier (1772–1837). The contrast between these two social philosophers was marked. Saint-Simon was a descendant of the nobility; Fourier, of the common people. Saint-Simon sought to find in history a clue to a new social order; Fourier withdrew within himself and sought deductively to discover the laws of progress. Saint-Simon presented a bold outline of a new social state which he hoped that society would adopt *en masse*. Fourier worked out in minute detail a social order for small communities and sought to demonstrate through experiments on a small scale the practical nature of his theories. Moreover, he based his system on logic and science rather than on feeling and impulse.

FOURIER'S LIFE. Fourier had a much less spectacular career than his fellow utopian. He was born at Besançon in 1772, the son of a cloth merchant. After distinguishing himself as a student, he entered business and became a traveling salesman, during which time he invested a small inheritance in cotton that he later lost completely during the Siege of Lyons. He was arrested and faced with the guillotine, joined the army on his release, and subsequently returned to business life and to his career as a reformer.

While a boy of five, young Fourier was severely punished by his father for telling a customer the truth about an article in his father's shop. At nineteen, while working for a business house at Marseilles, he was commissioned to throw overboard a quantity of rice which his employer had kept for speculative purposes until it spoiled. Prices were high, owing to a famine, and the rice had been withheld from the market for fear of a sharp decline in prices. These two instances of dishonesty and of waste in industry—instances which, Fourier believed, typified widespread evils in the industrial system—made an indelible impression on his mind, and ultimately counted heavily in turning the attention of the young merchant to the working out of a saner industrial order.

Career as Reformer. In 1808 Fourier published his first volume on social problems, but received practically no encouragement for his schemes for some five years. It must be said, however, that the chief support he craved was not that of the impecunious mass, but of the wealthy few who might subsidize some of his social experiments. Once he announced publicly that he would be at home every day at a certain hour to await any philanthropist who felt disposed to give him a million francs for the development of a colony based on Fourieristic principles. For twelve years thereafter he was at home every day punctually at noon awaiting the generous stranger, but, alas, no millionaire appeared. Most of the Saint-Simonians regarded his proposals with contempt.

During his life he tried but one experiment to test the value of his ideas. A member of the Chamber of Deputies offered him an estate at Versailles. Although it was occupied by his converts, it failed after a few years because of mismanagement. Thus he died without having witnessed any practical steps taken toward the realization of his dream. He had acquired, however, the warm support of a number of disciples. His life throughout showed a rare devotion to his convictions, honesty, integrity, and self-sacrifice.

FOURIER'S THEORIES. *Imaginings.* In connection with his social theories Fourier developed the strangest and crudest kind of world philosophy.[9] In his *Theory of Universal Unity,* for instance, he stated that the earth was just passing out of its infancy, and that upon its adoption of Fourier's plan of association it would enter upon a millennium of seventy thousand glorious years when the lions would become the servants of man, and draw men's carriages in a single day from one end of France to another; when whales would pull their vessels across the waters, and sea water would taste like a delicious beverage. Then would come an age of decline and a fourth brief era of dotage.

His Law of Attraction. But this and other theories are not a necessary part of Fourier's social concepts, though incorporated in the same work. The heart of Fourier's doctrine is the belief in the all-pervading

[9] His three most important works were the *Theory of the Four Movements and the General Destinies* (1808); *The Theory of Universal Unity* (1822) and *The New Industrial and Social World* (1829).

power of attraction: There is an ever present power in the world that draws men together in united action. Obstacles have hitherto been placed in the way of this law of attraction and, as a result, men have been led into anti-social paths. When these obstacles are removed, universal harmony will prevail, and the wealth of mankind will be increased many fold, for men will then love to labor, and the wastes of the present chaotic system will be eliminated.

The quest must be made for a social organization which will give free play to our passions, so that they may combine harmoniously. There are twelve of these passions: (1) the five senses; (2) the four "group passions" of friendship, love, the family feeling (familism), and ambition; and (3) the three distributive passions—which include the passions for planning, for change, and for unity. All twelve combine into one supreme passion of love for others, united in society.

The Phalanx. Obviously our present society does not lead to harmonious combination of these passions. There is here nothing but disharmony. Harmony can, however, be found if men and women come together into communities or phalanxes, from 400 to 2000 strong, in combinations of suitable numbers. In each phalanx all of the inhabitants should occupy a great central building, called a phalanstery—not unlike some of our modern apartment hotels. The industry should be largely agricultural.

Citizens in this community should unite in groups according to their tastes, which are determined by the character of their "passions." There are the small units of from seven to nine, called a "series," and the larger units, known as "groups." Each group undertakes to do a specific kind of work such as the caring for fruit trees, while a series in that group may take charge of the apple tree section of the work. Individuals may join any series or group as desired, and change from group to group at their will. They naturally choose those units whose work and tastes are congenial. Ordinarily one task gets somewhat monotonous at the end of a couple of hours, and the workers are then at liberty to change their occupation to a more pleasing one.

As a result of the joy that the members of the phalanx get out of their work under these conditions and of the healthy rivalry for quick and efficient results which naturally develops between the groups, the product of these workers will be far greater than at present. Labor here is relieved of the necessity of supporting soldiers, policemen, criminals, and lawyers, who are no longer needed in a society based on harmony. Nor will it have to build hundreds of separate houses equipped with separate stoves and maintaining separate kitchens, for the workers occupy apartments in the well-equipped phalanstery, have their food prepared in one great kitchen, and dine in a common hall. They also have central stables and central warehouses for the storing of their food. Under these conditions, Fourier held, productivity will increase fourfold or possibly fivefold, and a man will produce enough from his eighteenth to his twenty-eighth birthday to live in leisure and comfort during the remainder of his life.

Distribution of Product. Fourier was far less thoroughgoing in his demand for the abolition of unearned income than was Saint-Simon or our modern socialists. From the product of industry a sum is set aside for each member of the community. The surplus remaining is divided in a somewhat curious way between labor, capital, and talent. Five-twelfths of this surplus goes to labor, four-twelfths to capital, and the remaining three-twelfths to talent. Thus the motto of Saint-Simon is modified into the formula: from each according to his capacity and to each according to his labor, capital, and talent.

Fourier divided labor into three classes—necessary labor, useful labor, and agreeable labor. The first received the highest reward; the last, as it implied the least sacrifice, the smallest.

Government. Though there seems to be but little need of government under this system, officers are elected, the head of a phalanx being called an unarch, and the chief of the world phalanxes, an omniarch. The latter is to have headquarters at Constantinople.

The Family. Different gradations in society would necessarily remain, although Fourier believed that under his system the rich and powerful would be so filled with the spirit of co-operation that their presence would bring no disharmony. The communal life would be such, he contended, that every narrow affection in the family would be eliminated, and it would find its own interest in that of all. The Fourieristic philosophy rather implied that the family and marriage would gradually tend to disappear.

His Millennium Imminent. Fourier was for peace and against violence. He believed that one honest experiment in communal living according to the principles he laid down would be sufficient to convince the world of the correctness of his views. The millennium, he felt, would dawn within the space of ten years. Why, then, the need of a violent revolution? So near did this good time seem that Fourier urged his followers not to put their money into real estate, as a Fourieristic advance would cause it to lose value! How many times since then have leaders of socialist and communist thought made similar predictions!

Fourier's Contributions. Though Fourier's philosophy was fantastic at many points, he nevertheless did valuable service in calling attention to the wastes in the modern economic system, the unnecessary hardships of labor, and the need for devising some system which would make work pleasanter than it was in the France of his day. He also emphasized the value of machinery in doing the work of the world. His writings had considerable influence on factory laws and sanitary reforms.

Fourieristic Experiments. Following Fourier's death, many men of wealth and ability came to his standard, including some of the disgruntled followers of Saint-Simonism. His disciples finally formed The Society for the Propagation and Realization of the Theory of Fourier. Several communities were started along the lines he laid down. All of the French experiments in pure Fourierism failed, although one or more communities, founded by manufacturers in accordance with Fourier's idea of a phalanstery for the workers, which took good care to ignore many of his more fantastic suggestions, succeeded.[10]

In 1840 the Fourierist teachings were brought to America, and many of them secured the enthusiastic support of a brilliant group of thinkers, including Albert Brisbane, Horace Greeley, Charles A. Dana, and others. Some thirty-four experiments were tried, but all failed for various reasons. That at Brook Farm in Massachusetts was the most famous.[11] Through these writers and experiments Fourierism, however, contributed its share to the social thinking of the new world.

Louis Blanc. The first utopian socialist to attempt to use the political machinery of his own time to put his ideas into operation was Louis Blanc (1813–1882). Blanc was the first also to appeal to the workers rather than the privileged classes to effect the social transformation, and was in a sense a connecting link between the older utopians and the Marxian socialists. He was utopian in that he felt that the impossible of his generation could in that generation become a reality.

His Life. Blanc was born in Madrid, Spain, where his father had been sent by Louis Bonaparte as Inspector General of Finance. He passed his early years in Corsica, the home of his mother, studied in the College of Rodez, and continued his studies in Paris, earning part of his expenses by copying and teaching. After several years of editorial work he founded, at the age of twenty-six, the *Revue du Progrès,* which became the organ of the advanced democrats of his time. It was in

10 Godin, *Solutions Sociales,* Paris, 1871, p. 529.

11 See Noyes, *History of American Socialism,* Ch. XI.

this paper that his most important socialistic work, *Organisation du Travail,* appeared serially in 1840.

During the ensuing years he wrote excellent histories of the years 1830 to 1840 and of the French Revolution. He became a prominent member of the Provisional Government of 1848. As such, he demanded that the government guarantee work to everyone unable to obtain it elsewhere [12] and that it create a Ministry of Labor and Progress. He was afterwards forced to leave the country on account of alleged connection with an insurrectionary movement, and resided in England as a correspondent until the overthrow of Napoleon III in 1870. In 1871, on returning to France, he was elected to the National Assembly as a member of the extreme left, but during the rising of the Commune of Paris lost popularity with the revolutionists by opposing the insurrection. He even supported the 1872 law against the International Workingmen's Association. Blanc died in 1882, and was voted a state funeral by the Chamber of Deputies. He possessed a brilliant pen, and was noted for his simple, generous, and lovable disposition and for his fine integrity.

HIS TEACHINGS. *Development of Personality the Highest Aim.* Blanc was at one with many of his predecessors in emphasizing that human happiness and human development should be the goal of social effort. By development Blanc meant that everyone should have the requisite means for his highest mental, moral, and physical growth and that each individual should have an opportunity to develop a well-rounded personality. His thinking ran as follows: How can society guarantee this sort of opportunity? It is not now guaranteed. The present competitive system means *bellum omnium contra omnes* (war of all against all). It pits every man against his brother. It renders man "the sole and exclusive judge of that which surrounds him, gives him an exalted sentiment of his rights without indicating to him his duties, abandons him to his own powers, and proclaims *laissez faire* as the only rule of government." [13] The result is want and misery. Society must be transformed into a more brotherly system, modeled after the human body, which is the work of God. All men should be regarded as common members of one great family, and government should be based on common consent.

12 For description of this measure see John Stuart Mill's essay, *The French Revolution of 1848, and Its Assailants,* Dissertation and Discussions (Am. ed.), Vol. II, pp. 54–8.

13 Quoted from Louis Blanc, by H. Baudrillart in *Publicistes Modernes* (Paris, 1863), p. 308.

The Social Workshops. The first step in reaching the ideal society is to contrive some means whereby everyone shall be guaranteed work. This end can best be attained through the erection of social workshops by the state, "destined to replace gradually and without shock individual workshops." [14] The poor cannot at present produce commodities without the capitalist because they do not own tools and machines necessary in production. These instruments should be furnished by the state, which would thus become the banker of the poor. The state should lend to the workshops credit without interest, pass laws regulating their conduct, and see that they are administered for the common good. During the first year it should select the administrators on the basis of ability, but after that the workers, who will have become better acquainted with each other, should have the power of selection. Thus the principle of workers' control would be established. Money for this venture should be secured by the state from general taxation and from revenues derived from the railways—which must become public property—and from such other public undertakings as mines, banks, and insurance enterprises.

The workshops should be united into a great federation and form an insurance company to cover the losses of any individual workshop, a part of the profits of each concern being set apart for an insurance fund. Capitalists should be welcome in these shops. They should be paid interest on their capital investment, and receive a wage for their labor. Private workshops should not be forced to join the federation, but inability to compete against these enterprises would probably lead sooner or later to a merger. With the disappearance of these private concerns the socialistic state would come into being. Such a state would assuredly be conducive to the best interests of the rich as well as the poor, for who can gain any contentment from an order, like the present, in which so many are doomed to lives of misery?

Service According to Capacity. Blanc was not a believer in the equality of talents. He realized that great differences exist in the powers and abilities of men. In the development of social industry the ideal to be attained is the placement of each individual in such a position that he may be able fully to use his capacities. However, he should not use them for his own aggrandizement or for the exploitation of others. For God gave them to man as a measure of his obligation to society. "They are but the supreme indication of that which each one owes to the society of which he is a member. . . . If you are twice as strong as your neighbor it is a proof that nature has destined you to bear a double burden. If

[14] Blanc, *Organisation du Travail,* 9th Edition, p. 13.

your intelligence is superior, it is a sign that your mission is to scatter about you more light. Weakness is a creditor of strength; ignorance of learning. The more a man *can,* the more he *ought;*[15] and this is the meaning of those beautiful words of the gospel: 'Whosoever will be chief among you let him be your servant.' Whence the axiom, From every one according to his faculties; that is one's DUTY."[16]

Reward According to Needs. Man then should give according to his capacity. What should he receive? The Saint-Simonians declared that the reward of labor should be commensurate with the work performed; Fourier would make a division among labor, capital, and talent; Babeuf believed in absolute equality. Louis Blanc, however, rejected all of these formulae. They did not come up to a sufficiently high moral standard. The formula of the Saint-Simonians, he believed, would condemn the weak to extinction, and would give too great a handicap over their fellows to those who through no merit of their own, were born with superior ability.

Louis Blanc coined another formula: "From each according to his ability, to each according to his *needs.*" Each one should have that which he finds necessary to the development of his capabilities, limited of course by the ability of society to supply these needs.

"All men are not equal in physical force, in intelligence; all have not the same tastes, the same inclinations, the same aptitudes, any more than they have the same visage or the same figure; . . . but each one should be placed in a condition to derive the greatest possible advantage from his faculties, in so far as this can be done with due regard to others, and to satisfy as completely as possible, without injuring others, the needs which nature has given him. Thus there is no health or vigor in the human body unless each member receives that which is able to preserve it from pain and to enable it to accomplish properly its peculiar function. Equality, then, is only proportionality, and it exists in a true manner only when each one in accordance with the law written in some shape in his organization by God Himself, *produces according to his faculties and consumes according to his wants.*"[17] Thus Blanc contributes an ideal of distinct merit in the sphere of distributive justice.

Misery the Great Materialistic Force. Blanc, in defending his plan to guarantee employment and gradually to usher in a new order, expressed resentment at the charge that his proposal was a materialistic one. He claimed that, on the contrary, it was laying the foundation

[15] "We then that are strong ought to bear the infirmities of the weak." Rom. XV:1.

[16] Blanc, *Histoire de la Révolution de 1848,* Vol. I, pp. 147–8.

[17] Blanc, *Organisation du Travail,* p. 72.

for a nobler spiritual order by eliminating the materialistic influence of misery. "Misery," he declared, "restrains the intelligence of man in darkness, in confining education within shameful limits. Misery counsels always the sacrifice of personal dignity and almost always demands it. Misery places him whose character is independent in a position of dependence, so as to conceal a new torment in a virtue and to change into gall what there is of nobility in his blood. If misery creates long suffering, it engenders also crime. . . . It makes slaves; it makes of the greater part thieves, assassins and prostitutes." [18]

ORGANIZATION OF SHAM WORKSHOPS BY GOVERNMENT. While the complete socialist state which he pictured could be achieved only gradually, Blanc felt that a start, through the establishment of a number of national workshops, could be made immediately. So, as a member of the Provisional Government in 1848, he put forward this idea with great insistence. This was opposed by a majority of the politicians of the day, but they felt that some pretense at trying his scheme should be made in order to stop public clamor. Everything, however, they promised themselves, should be done to ensure failure. To make failure doubly sure, Emile Thomas, one of Blanc's worst enemies, was placed in charge. In appointing Thomas to his office, the Minister of Public Works wrote him that the experiment could not have anything but good results, "because it would demonstrate to the laborers the emptiness and falseness of these inapplicable theories and cause them to perceive the disastrous consequences flowing therefrom for themselves, and would so discredit Louis Blanc in their eyes that he should forever cease to be a danger." [19]

Under these conditions, the workshops of necessity had but a short existence, and during that time their achievements were greatly misrepresented. Thus all hopes of an immediate start toward production for service vanished. Blanc's social principles, however, have had an important influence in later social thinking. In particular they have had their share in inspiring a number of recent experiments with public work with a view to alleviate the unemployment problem.

Proudhon. HIS PLACE AMONG SOCIAL THINKERS. The last French revolutionary writer of this period is Pierre-Joseph Proudhon (1809–1865).[20] He is difficult to classify. His frontal attack on private property—the most direct made up to his time by any revolutionist—and his condemnation of the class of private proprietors put him in the

[18] *Ibid.*, p. 4.

[19] Quoted in Ely, *op. cit.*, p. 113; *Lorenz von Stein*, iii, S. 292; E. Thomas, *Histoire des Ateliers Nationaux.*

[20] For a complete edition of Proudhon's works, see Sainte-Beuve, *P. J. Proudhon, Sa Vie et Sa Correspondance* (Paris, 1875).

ranks of militant revolutionists, and men and women of all schools of thought have for generations drawn inspiration from his teachings. His bitter denunciation of all government and authority and his ridicule of the fantastic utopian plans of his predecessors seem to place him squarely, however, outside the school of utopian socialists and communists and into the ranks of anarchists. On the other hand, his belief in absolute equality smacks distinctly of the communist philosophy, and it is indeed doubtful whether such equality as Proudhon advocates could be carried out except under a pretty thoroughgoing authority armed with drastic power of interference in the affairs of men. It may be added that his concrete plan for initiating his system of free association appeared so utopian to the people of his day that it received but 2 out of 693 votes in the Assembly of 1848.

HIS LIFE. Proudhon was born in Besançon, the birthplace of Fourier, thirty-seven years after the birth of the great advocate of the phalanx form of human association. His parents were poor, and young Proudhon earned his way through school by taking care of cows, acting as a waiter in restaurants, and by other manual occupations. At school he earned numerous awards, and the story goes that he would arrive home loaded with prizes to find no dinner awaiting him. At nineteen he was obliged to leave college and became a printer, but continued his education, absorbing particularly the contents of volumes on theology printed by his firm. Subsequently he received a pension of 1500 francs from the Académie de Besançon, given to promising students in the field of literature and science.

In his letter to a distinguished literary man at that time, he complained that no one, in congratulating him on his honor, had come to him and said: "Proudhon, you ought before everything else to devote yourself to the cause of the poor, to the enfranchisement of the little ones, to the instruction of the people. You will perhaps be an abomination to the rich and powerful; pursue your way as a reformer regardless of persecutions, of calumny, of sorrow, and of death itself." On the other hand, all had felicitated him on the ground that he was almost certain to "obtain honors equal to those which the Jouffroys, the Pouillets, have obtained, and perhaps . . . even greater." [21]

In 1840, following a course of study in political economy, he wrote his famous book, *Qu'est-ce que la Propriété?* ("What is Property?") It is a pioneer work attempting to prove the iniquity of private property *per se;* it expounds the doctrine of labor time as a measure of value—a doctrine which subsequently did such service in the socialist movement

[21] Ely, *op. cit.*, pp. 126–7, quoted from Sainte-Beuve, *op. cit.*

—and provides a philosophic background for the anarchist movement.

Six years later he published his *Système des Contradictions Économiques ou Philosophie de la Misère,* in which he criticized socialist and communist theories, but failed to formulate a constructive philosophy.

He took no part in the Revolution of February, 1848, contending that, as all forms of government were bad, it did not matter which faction triumphed. When the political revolution had passed, he was elected by a large majority to the Constituent Assembly of the Department of the Seine, and urged his scheme for so organizing the credit of the country that all would be furnished with the instruments of production—a plan which, as has been stated, was defeated by an overwhelming vote. He then tried to develop the plan without state aid, and organized a private bank for that purpose, but, as he was able to raise only seventeen thousand francs out of the five million needed, the bank failed within a few weeks. Later Proudhon served three years in prison for breaking a censorship law, and upon his release was again sentenced to a prison term, this time for attacking the church. He escaped to Belgium, however, and returned to France in 1860, five years before his death.

Proudhon, while extreme in many of his statements and without mercy for his intellectual opponents, was the soul of sincerity. He lived a life of simplicity and of self-sacrifice. He was devoted to his family, and often rebuked some of the early utopians for their immorality. As the years went on, his early bitterness against individuals softened somewhat. "Perhaps I was sometimes wrong," he wrote in his letter to his pensioners at Besançon, "in confounding in my indignation persons and things; at present I only know how to despise and complain. In order to cease to hate, it is only necessary for me to understand." [22]

His Teachings. *"Liberty, Equality, Fraternity."* In approaching the social problem, Proudhon sought to discover the science of society based on liberty, equality, fraternity. A perfect state founded on these principles could, he felt, not be brought about overnight. The belief advanced by some of the utopian writers that society could be forced to adopt a ready-made scheme of social reform, he regarded as "the most accursed lie that could be offered to mankind."

Concept of a National Bank. Proudhon distinguished between the ultimate goal and the transition to that goal. As a step in bringing about his ideal society, he urged the organization of a great national bank from which the workers would be able to obtain the instruments of labor without price. The bank would issue paper money in the

[22] Preface to Proudhon, *Qu'est-ce que la Propriété?,* p. 5.

form of checks in exchange for commodities deposited therein. These checks would purchase anything else the production of which cost the same labor. The capital for the establishment of this bank was to be secured from taxation on property and a progressive tax on the salaries of government officials. The bank would organize branches in all parts of France and would furnish gratuitous credit to all comers.

Interest, Proudhon contended, had a tendency to fall. Its normal rate was zero. With the assistance of the bank its rate would actually become zero. It was then inevitable that rents and profits likewise would cease. As each one might obtain the instruments of labor from the National Bank without price, no one would pay interest to a private capitalist for their use. The laborer would receive all that he earned, and the products he bought would cost him no more than they were worth. All men would be associated with one another on terms of equality. This was the highest form of association.

Anarchism His Goal. Proudhon's ultimate society would possess several characteristics. In the first place it would be devoid of government, for, he believed, "the highest perfection is found in the union of order and anarchy." The control of man by man is oppression. "Anarchy —the absence of master or sovereign—such is the form of government which we approach every day, and our inveterate habit of taking man for a guide and his will for law makes us regard it as a heap of disorder and an expression of chaos. . . .

"No one is king. . . . Every question of internal politics ought to be solved according to the data of the Department of Statistics; every question of international politics is a question of international statistics. The science of government belongs by right to one of the sections of the Academy of Sciences, of which the perpetual secretary necessarily becomes the first minister; and since every citizen may address a *mémoire* to the Academy, every citizen is a legislator; but as the opinion of no one counts except insofar as it is demonstrated to be true, no one can substitute his will for reason—no one is king." [23]

"Property Is Theft." In the second place Proudhon's ideal society would contain no private property, which he regarded as theft. As he presented the case, economists try to justify the existence of private property on two grounds: first, that of occupation; second, that of labor. If we analyze both these arguments, we find that neither of them proves its case. According to the so-called occupation theory, that which belongs to no one becomes the property of him who takes possession of it. This theory thus makes private ownership depend on nothing more nor

[23] *Œuvres Complètes,* Vol. I, pp. 214–7.

less than the accident of birth. Your possessions depend on the number of people in a country, the extent of that country, and the time of your arrival on the scene. Late-comers, according to this theory, have no rights. The theory also defeats itself. It assumes that at one time property was held in common, for, if property occupied at one time belonged to no one, it must have belonged to society-at-large. But it is folly to think that all of society would or could renounce title to their common possession. Therefore, in taking it from the community, the occupier must have committed theft.

The second argument of the economists is that the basis of private property is labor. But in answer to this contention, it may be said that that only is mine which I produce. The earth is mine only so long as I cultivate it. The moment another labors thereon, it becomes his private property. "Again, labor presupposes the instruments of labor, and where is one to obtain these in a system of private, personal property, provided one does not already possess them? The theory of labor demands the abolition of property, in order that everyone may have free access to the soil and to the instruments of labor." [24]

Labor Theory of Value. Not only is property theft, but the proprietor is a thief. This conclusion Proudhon arrived at as a result of his labor theory of value. The worth of goods, he maintained, was measured by the time and labor put into their production. If a capitalist or landlord added ten per cent to the cost thereof, the goods were thus made to cost more than they were worth, and the proprietor thus became a robber.

Private Possession of Property. While Proudhon condemned private property, he was not opposed to private possession, providing it was secured by labor. But one should not rob another by charging for the use of the instruments of labor, by exacting rent, profit, or interest. In his emphasis on private possession, he opposed communism whereby the community was "proprietor not only of goods, but of persons and wills" and labor, which ought to be a condition imposed by nature, became "a human command, and thereby odious."

He took issue with communists on the ground that their system would lead to the oppression of the strong by the weak. His aim was not primarily to bring to men equality of compensation, but equality of means for producing wealth. And yet, where each one possessed the instruments of labor, he seemed to be of the opinion that each would labor equally and that the products, being measured by labor time, would

[24] Quotation of Ely, *op. cit.*, p. 133.

be equal in value. Furthermore, he opposed giving higher remuneration to superior brains, providing society had contributed to the worker the means of doing his work. On this point he observed:

"When the astronomer produces observations, the poet verses, the savant experiences, they consume instruments, books, travels, etc.; now, if society provides for this consumption, what other proportionality of honors can the astronomer, the savant, the poet demand? Let us conclude, then, that in equality, and in equality, alone, the adage of Saint-Simon, 'to each one according to his capacity, to each capacity according to its works,' finds its full and complete application." [25]

Proudhon also, ignoring the teachings of heredity, looked forward to a time in which "the present inequality in the talent and capacity of men would be reduced to an inappreciable minimum." [26]

His Theories of Anarchy and Equality Inconsistent. In advocating both anarchy and absolute equality, Proudhon confronted himself with a dilemma and failed to answer it. Suppose that each cultivated the fields as he wished under Proudhon's non-authoritarian system, without any outside interference. "Can anyone suppose," asked Professor Ely, ". . . that all would derive the same products from the same instruments? . . . What is to prevent my accumulating labor receipts if my production exceeds my consumption? Or shall the state or some outside body prevent my taking more than I consume from the magazines or banks, whatever they are called? If so, do we not have all the interference and control of the hated community? It is thus seen that Proudhon is inconsistent as well as paradoxical." [27]

Summary. A social organization without government, without private property, without inequality, was therefore negatively Proudhon's ideal. His philosophy was nearly devoid of positive, constructive elements. He did not think that anyone was capable of working out a future state in any detail. He believed primarily in enunciating general principles, and in trying to apply those principles to concrete steps. He was an intense believer in liberty, in equality. He did not show us how each of these principles could be worked out systematically without interfering with the other. But his ideal of free association, his desire to give scope to the development of human personality are as a breath of fresh air in contrast to the myriad of state regulations of individual conduct which many of the pictured utopias imply.

25 Proudhon, *Qu'est-ce que la Propriété?*, p. 157.
26 Quoted in Kirkup, *History of Socialism*, p. 55.
27 Ely, *op. cit.*, p. 140.

After Proudhon the scene in revolutionary thinking and action shifts from France to other parts of the world, and it is some time before the French socialist or communist movement contributes anything of note to the world's revolutionary thinking.

CHAPTER 9

The Forerunners of Robert Owen

As we have seen in the preceding chapter, it was revolutionary France of the late eighteenth and the early nineteenth centuries that produced the greatest of the utopian socialists. France, however, was not alone in contributing to this important school of social thought. England followed, with Robert Owen as its most conspicuous example.

But between the end of the seventeenth century, where we left England earlier in our book, and the days of Robert Owen, many men of fine social idealism and far-reaching social vision appeared in England and added their contributions to the communist and socialist philosophies of their day. The appearance of these men was inevitable, for while France was passing through its spectacular and bloody revolutionary period, a revolution of even greater importance to social life—the great Industrial Revolution—had been going on steadily, relentlessly, grimly, in the British Isles.

The England of the eighteenth century necessarily inherited much from the social philosophies of the preceding centuries. Among other things it became the heir to the controversy regarding the relative advantages of the state of nature and the state of civil law. This, in the nature of the case, carried with it the discussion of communism *vs.* individualism.

Pope, Reconcilor. One of the first to oppose communist conceptions was the poet Alexander Pope (1678–1744). In his *Essay on Man* (1734), Pope tried to reconcile the two states of society and to show that the unrestrained character of man's nature made an ordered society under civil law a necessity. Man, he declared, should take a lesson from the ants, "how those in common all their wealth bestow, and anarchy without confusion know." They learned

Order is heaven's first law; and this confessed,
Some are, and must be, greater than the rest,
More rich, more wise.[1]

Edmund Burke. Edmund Burke (1729–1799), thoroughly alarmed at the growing discontent of his period, also entered the lists of combatants against communism. In his *Vindication of Natural Society* (1756), which was supposedly written by Lord Bolingbroke, an upholder of the natural state, Burke attempts through his superb irony to demonstrate the absurdity of the arguments advanced in behalf of the natural state and the communist form of society, and to bring home to social reformers that their agitation was bound to lead to revolution. But he presented the indictment which was then being brought against the society of the day with such force and incisiveness that the book produced a most disturbing effect on many conservatives of the time.

Blackstone and Adam Smith. Other noted opponents of the natural state were the great legal authority William Blackstone (1723–1780) and the classical economist Adam Smith (1723–1790). Blackstone, presupposing a primitive communism, declared that private property was demanded to guard individuals in their peace and security. The economist Smith, though holding that "in the original state of things . . . the whole produce of labor belongs to the laborer," took the position that the improvements in production stimulated by private ownership sufficiently justified its existence. It likewise justified the guardian of such ownership—the civil government.[2]

Wallace, Forerunner of Malthus. While distinguished economists, statesmen, and lawyers were calling attention to the virtues of private property, moralists were busy pointing out its iniquities. One of these was Robert Wallace, the progressive preacher of the royal chapel of Edinburgh. In his *Various Aspects,* Wallace drew a strong indictment against private property, on the ground that it rendered great numbers of poor the slaves and the beasts of burden of the rich; that, on the one hand, it led to overwork, and, on the other, to idleness; and that it did nothing to advance morality. These evils, he maintained, could only be remedied by the abolition of private property.

However, it must be admitted that there were a number of obstacles to the attainment of a communist state. The powerful minority would oppose any radical change, and only in time of revolution could men be lifted to a state of enthusiasm and a spirit of sacrifice sufficiently great

1 Pope, *Essay on Man* (1734), Epistle 3, ch. 4–6; Epistle 4, ch. 2.
2 Adam Smith, *Wealth of Nations,* Bk. 5, ch. I, Pt. II.

to bring about the transition. Or a new order would have to be introduced by means of small, successful communistic experiments led by men of exceptional ability and demonstrating the truths of communism. But the chief obstacles to a communist state would be the problem of over-population. Under communism, men would incur no inconveniences in bringing up large families. The main check to the growth of population in the past would thus be thrown aside, and the population would then press so hard on the means of subsistence as to produce again a state of poverty. In this argument Wallace laid the foundation for the Malthusian doctrine, a doctrine which was utilized extensively by the conservative forces of the country.

The Parable of Archdeacon Paley. More vigorous than Wallace in his criticism of individualism was Archdeacon William Paley (1743–1805). In his picturesque indictment of the immorality of private property, the archbishop declared:

"If you should see a flock of pigeons in a field: and if (instead of each picking where and what it liked, taking just as much as it wanted, and no more) you should see ninety-nine of them gathering all they got into one heap, reserving nothing for themselves but the chaff and the refuse, keeping this heap for one, and that the weakest, perhaps worst, pigeon of the flock; sitting round and looking on all the winter, whilst this one was devouring and throwing about and wasting it; and if one pigeon more hardy or hungry than the rest touched a grain of the hoard, all the others instantly flying upon it and tearing it to pieces; if you should see this, you would see nothing more than what is every day practised and established among men." [3]

He agreed, however, with Adam Smith that private ownership possessed certain counteracting advantages, among them the increase of productivity, and improvement in the conveniences of life.

Effect of the Industrial Revolution on England. Archbishop Paley was the last outstanding social thinker in England who wrote in terms of the conditions before the industrial revolution. While the noted clergyman was setting forth the misery of the British people, great and impressive changes were taking place as a result of the significant inventions of the period 1760 onward. Factories were springing up in every part of England, and wealth was accumulating "beyond all credibility," . . . "and there," as Wordsworth puts it,

> Where not a habitation stood before,
> Abodes of men irregularly massed

[3] Paley, William, *Moral and Political Philosophy*, 1785, Book 3, Part I, chs. 1–4.

Like trees in forests—spread through spacious tracts,
On which the smoke of unremitting fires
Hangs permanent, and plentiful as wreaths
Of vapor glittering in the morning sun.[4]

Until 1806 wages were high and employment plentiful. Then came unemployment and deterioration in the condition of labor. To adjust society to the great changes in the economic structure, "peace, watchfulness, and social reform were necessary, instead of which came war, repression of the discontented elements, suspension of the Habeas Corpus Act, high treason trials, indiscriminate poor relief, and Malthus' population theory as a salve to the agitated conscience of the nation." [5]

Influence of Locke and Bentham. The industrial revolution and its immediate aftermath inevitably gave rise to a group of socialist and communist thinkers. Some of them based their radical conclusions on the philosophic premises laid down by Locke in his treatise *On Civil Government*. Others argued from the premises laid down by Bentham. Locke, declared his socialistic followers, showed that common possession was natural. From this it follows that private property is unnatural, and should be abolished. Locke stated that labor was the title to property or wealth. If this be so, all deductions from the produce of labor in the form of rent, interest, and profit are contrary to natural law. Nature, including human nature, is governed, maintained Locke, by divine laws. Therefore all reform should be directed to the restoration of, or be in harmony with, natural law.

The socialist followers of Bentham, who for a time supplanted Locke, argued from a somewhat different angle. Bentham had held that the real test of governments or other social institutions was: Do these institutions lead to the greatest good to the greatest number? The system of private property, the socialists stated, does not pass this test, for under it the mass of people are doomed to misery. It does not lead to security, for the worker is never secure in his product, but is compelled constantly to divide it up with the capitalist and the landlord. Common ownership is the only alternative.

Spence: Single Taxer. The progressive thinkers of the period of the industrial revolution may be divided, roughly speaking, into the agrarian reformers, forerunners of our single taxers, and the communist and socialist writers. Of the former group, Thomas Spence (1750–1814), William Ogilvie (1736–1813), and Thomas Paine (1737–1809) were the principal figures.

[4] Wordsworth, *Excursion*, Book 8.

[5] Beer, *History of British Socialism*, Vol. I, p. 100.

Spence, a Scotch schoolmaster, originator of the single tax theory, was the first of this group. While he was an obscure schoolteacher, the corporations of Newcastle, Durham, and other cities enclosed the commons, rented them out for agricultural purposes, and divided the rent between the members of the corporation to the exclusion of the freemen. The latter brought action against the corporations, demanding their share of the rent. It was this controversy that decided Spence to fight for a fundamental change in land ownership, a plan of which he submitted to the Newcastle Philosophical Society in 1775. Spence assumed the existence of common land in the natural state. It is contended, declared Spence, that private property originated in agreement. But an agreement, to be binding, must be renewed with each successive generation. Had it been thus renewed? Neither he nor anyone else was aware of any such renewal. Besides, civil society came into existence to free man from burdens, not to impose new burdens upon him. Locke had defended private property on the ground of labor. The argument might hold true in the case of the manufacturer, but not in the case of the landholder, for no one could argue that the aristocracy had created the land. The land should be restored to its natural heirs, the people. It should be transferred to the parishes, and the latter should rent it out to farmers at a moderate rental, this rental to be the only form of taxes.

The real struggle of the people, he added some years later, was not about certain forms of government, but for "a system of society capable of delivering us from the deadly mischief of great accumulations of wealth, which enable the few rich, unfeeling monsters to starve whole nations." [6]

Spence sold his tracts on the streets, shocking the good members of the Philosophical Society thereby and scaring away his pupils. He was frequently arrested and imprisoned for his attacks on the government, but unmindful of his own comfort he kept constantly at his propaganda up to the time of his death in the hope that through his panacea the time would soon come when mankind would be virtuous, happy, and wise.

Ogilvie and Doctrine of Land Improvements. Far keener but also more cautious in his practical suggestions than Spence was William Ogilvie, professor of humanity at Aberdeen University. Ogilvie declared that by the operation of land monopoly "the happiness of mankind had been for ages more invaded and restrained than by all the tyranny of kings, the imposture of priests, and the chicane of lawyers

[6] Thomas Spence, *Restorer of Society to its Natural State* (1801), Letter 14.

taken together, though these are supposed to be the greatest evils that afflict the societies of human kind." [7]

From natural law he gained two maxims, the first, that every man had an equal share in land; the second, "that every one by whose labor any portion of the soil has been rendered more fertile, has the right to the additional produce of that fertility, or to the value of it, and may transfer this right to other men." And "whoever enjoys any revenue not proportioned to such industry or exertion of his own or of his ancestors, is a freebooter who has found means to cheat or rob the public. . . . The hereditary revenue of a great landlord . . . is a premium given to idleness." [8]

However, the Aberdeen professor believed that "great changes, suddenly accomplished, were always pregnant with danger and evil," and the immediate legislation suggested was of a mild nature. The land would be left in private possession under his plan, but the rent would be determined by arbitrators.

Proposed Inheritance Tax of Thomas Paine. The third member of this school was Thomas Paine, who in his *Rights of Man* distinguished between land and its improvements. The land itself, he maintained, belonged to the community. On the other hand, the value of land improvements belonged to the cultivator who created it. The community, as the owner of the land, must reclaim the ground rent in the shape of a ten per cent inheritance tax, and divide the national fund thus obtained among the propertyless to compensate them for the loss of their natural rights! For this proposal he was accused by Spence in his *Rights of Infants* (1797) of selling the people's birthright for a mess of pottage.

William Godwin and the Intellectuals. The doctrines of Spence, Ogilvie, and Paine may have appealed to certain elements among the masses, but in the fervid days of the French Revolution they left the radical intellectuals cold. These had read the flaming words of Rousseau and of the Encyclopaedists, and "nothing else satisfied them than political anarchy, abolition of private property, absolute reign of reason, universal benevolence, and joyful devotion to social duty and justice." [9]

This demand was eloquently expounded by William Godwin, unfrocked preacher of a journalistic turn of mind, who arose one morning in 1793, after writing his *Enquiry Concerning Political Justice,* to find himself famous.

Godwin's Attack on Government. Throughout, Godwin's social views were based on abstract theory. Man, he held, had no innate ideas

[7] Ogilvie, *Essay on the Right of Property in Land* (1781), Pars. 28, 29.

[8] *Ibid.,* Pars. 10, 39.

[9] Beer, *op. cit.,* p. 114.

of an either good or bad nature. He had but the passive capacity to receive sensations and the active capacity to reason. Reason turned sensations into thoughts. On thought depended moral action. If social institutions were based on justice, man's impressions, thoughts, and motives would be good, and evil would be eliminated. Man would thus steadily improve. But government, originating in force and violence, strengthens evil by defending institutions that are based on injustice. It perpetuates inequalities and binds men with the chains of authority. Government is evil, society is natural; government springs from our vices, society from our needs. Government can be abolished by equity and the common deliberations on general welfare, which is the law of reason.[10]

INSISTENCE ON ABOLITION OF PRIVATE PROPERTY. Government, however, is not the only institution that must be abolished if justice is to reign. Private property must also be eliminated, for it develops an inequality which fosters vanity and depravity among the rich and a slave status and immorality among the poor. It deprives the worker of leisure to cultivate his mind, and leisure is the real wealth of the nation. Economic justice would work a rare transformation:

"If justice reigned, a state of equality would prevail. Labor would become so light as rather to assume the appearance of agreeable relaxation and gentle exercise. Every man would have a frugal, yet wholesome diet; every man would go forth to that moderate exercise of his corporeal functions that would give hilarity to his spirits. None would be made torpid with fatigue, but all would have leisure to cultivate the kindly and philanthropical affections and to let loose their faculties in the search of intellectual improvements. How rapid would be the advance of intellect, if all men were admitted into the field of knowledge! And the moral progress would be as great as the intellectual. The vices which are inseparably joined to the present system of property would inevitably be eliminated in the state of society where all shared alike the bounties of nature. . . . No man would be an enemy of his neighbor, for they would have no subject of contention, and, of consequence, philanthropy would assume the empire which reason assigns her." [11]

"EACH ACCORDING TO HIS NEEDS." Godwin had no patience with the theory afterwards enunciated by Saint-Simon that each should be recompensed in accordance with his capacity. It is not just, he held, that one should receive a hundred times more than he needs, simply because he performs greater service. For no one has a right to superflui-

[10] Beer, *op. cit.*, p. 116; see Godwin's books on *Political Justice.*
[11] Quoted in Beer, *op. cit.*, pp. 117–8.

ties. If one has ten loaves of bread and another has none, common justice demands that the hungry should obtain from the well-to-do enough to appease his hunger. He approved, on the other hand, the formula afterwards adopted by Louis Blanc, "to each according to his needs." Godwin did not project a future utopia. He advocated no close communist society, but a community of free individuals bent on the development of their personality. He did not share the anxiety of Wallace regarding the over-population of the globe. Mind, he believed, was perfectly capable of controlling matter in this respect.

In his later editions Godwin, doubly convinced by the French Revolution of the futility of force, made it clear that he depended on reason and persuasion as the sole instrument for bringing in the new order. He even approved of the repressive measures which Mr. Pitt had introduced against some of his followers accused of inciting to violence in order to attain their ends.

The Poets' Dream of Liberty: Wordsworth. When Godwin's *Enquiry Concerning Political Justice* first appeared in 1793, William Wordsworth, Samuel Taylor Coleridge, and Robert Southey were young men of twenty-three, twenty-one, and nineteen years of age, respectively. The book profoundly influenced the ideas of all of them.

Wordsworth had just returned from a trip to France, where he had become acquainted with the French revolutionists. He felt that the travails of the time presaged the moral rebirth of humanity, and hoped to see the establishment of utopia not on "some secret island, but in the very world, which is the world of all of us—the place where, in the end, we find our happiness or not at all." Of the period he writes:

> Bliss was it in that dawn to be alive,
> But to be young was very heaven!
> I had approached, like other youths, the shield
> Of human nature from the golden side,
> And would have fought, even to the death, to attest
> The quality of the metal which I saw. . . .
> I began
> To meditate with ardor on the rule
> And management of nations, what it is
> And ought to be; and strove to learn how far
> Their power or weakness, wealth or poverty,
> Their happiness or misery, depends
> Upon the laws and fashion of the State.

And when the terror of the revolution began to raise doubts in his mind regarding the quick realization of liberty and equality, Godwin's book came and taught him "to look through all the frailties of the world, and with a resolute mastery . . . build social upon personal liberty." [12]

Coleridge and Southey. Both Coleridge and Southey, students at Cambridge and Oxford, felt the same thrill, wrote dramas, hymns, and odes to the new age. Thus Southey in Wat Tyler had the hero describe the early communism under natural law:

> No fancied boundaries of mine or thine
> Restrain our wanderings! Nature gives enough
> For all; but Man, with arrogant selfishness
> Proud of his heaps, hoards up superfluous stores
> Robb'd from his weaker fellows, starves the poor,
> Or gives to pity what he owes to justice!

Coleridge was not satisfied, however, with poetic imaginings. He wanted to try the experiment in a higher liberty at once, and in 1794 he proposed to Southey the organization of a communist colony, "Pantisocracy," where all-equality would reign. "Oh! shall I have such a scheme of it! My head, my heart, are all alive. I have drawn up my arguments in battle array." [13]

Southey, the one who had property, decided, however, not to enter the partnership with Coleridge, who retorted, "You are lost to me, because you are lost to virtue." [14]

Alas, however, Coleridge's ardor also soon cooled with the depressing reports from France, and the poets returned to a faith in the institutions of government. Southey remained anti-capitalist in spirit and strongly denounced the manufacturers as the cause of the people's misery.[15] Wordsworth, to the end of his life, expressed his sympathy with the masses, though Coleridge developed into a conservative.

Charles Hall. HIS ANALYSIS OF CLASS STRUGGLE. As we round the eighteenth century and begin the nineteenth, we find increasing emphasis laid on the struggle between the working and capitalist classes.

[12] William Wordsworth, *Prelude,* Book II; cf., Leslie Stephens, *The English Utilitarians,* II, pp. 368–73.

[13] Coleridge, *Letters,* 1895, I, p. 81.

[14] Coleridge, *Letters,* 1895, I, pp. 137–51.

[15] Southey, *Letters from England* (1807), I, pp. 306–8; II, pp. 139–44; III, pp. 114–9, 132–4.

"If religion were out of the question," Southey wrote later in 1807, "it would have been better for them [the lower classes] to have been born among savages than in a civilized country, where they are in fact the victims of civilization. If the manufacturing system continues to be extended, increasing as it necessarily does the number, the misery, and the depravity of the poor, I believe that a revolution must come and in the most fearful shape." (See *Letters I,* pp. 306–8, II, p. 157, III, pp. 132–3.)

This emphasis is especially marked in the writings of Charles Hall, a British physician. Hall was the first to attempt to demonstrate by statistics the great injustice of the profit system and to interpret the growing discontent of labor. In his *Effects of Civilization* (1805) he criticized so-called civilization for the division of society into rich and poor. The life of the poor was a short and difficult one, devoid of proper physical or mental care. Wealth possessed more than kingly power over the lives of the many. "The situation of the rich and the poor, like the algebraic terms of plus and minus, are in direct opposition to and destructive of each other." [16] Eight-tenths of the population receive one-eighth of the wealth, while two-tenths who produce nothing, receive seven-eighths. In other words, a workingman labors seven days for the capitalist to one for himself, his wife, and children.[17] As the Latin verse goes, "You make the honey, but not for yourself, bee; you make the land fruitful, but not for yourself, oxen." [18]

ECONOMIC CAUSES OF WAR. Hall's economic analysis of the causes of war sounds as if it had been made but yesterday. Wealth, he contended, is one of the most potent causes of international warfare, for the object of war is to increase trade and territory and to repress internal revolutionary movements provoked by the lust of the rich for power. The rich see that the poor are taught the so-called glories of war, not its seamy side of suffering and death. What power the wealthy must possess, that they are able to stifle reason and morality and induce man to murder his fellow man!

Hall, however, took no stock in the belief that the present order resulted from any conscious conspiracy. It resulted logically, he felt, from the division of land into great estates. Such division led to inequalities and to subsequent investment in manufacture and commerce. With the rise of the factory system the poor became even poorer than formerly. The remedy was the nationalization of land, its occupation by small farmers, and the making of agriculture the basic industry. It was the critical analysis of Hall, however, rather than his constructive proposals, which made his work significant. We find in him a connecting link between revolutionism based on natural law, and proletarian socialism.

Colquhoun on "Who Gets England's Wealth?" Two other writers who, although not radicals, influenced the thought of the incipient socialist movement of the day, were Patrick Colquhoun and David

[16] Hall, *Effects of Civilization,* pp. 53–4.

[17] *Ibid.*, pp. 94–6.

[18] "Sic vos non vobis mellificatis, apes;
Sic vos non vobis fertis aratra, boves."

Ricardo. Colquhoun, jurist, municipal administrator, and business man, was the first to describe to England of what its economic life consisted. In 1814 he published his *Treatise of the Wealth, Power, and Resources of the British Empire,* in which he told statistically the story of the wealth of the British Isles and how that wealth was distributed. After analyzing the official documents to which he had ready access, he concluded that the higher and lower nobility received from 200 to 400 pounds a person per year, while, on the other hand, the agricultural and industrial workers and their families obtained on the average about 11 pounds a person per year. These figures were used extensively by socialists and others to prove the inequity of the existing order.

Ricardo: Theories of Value and Wages. Ricardo, though a staunch upholder of things as they were, elaborated in his abstract system of distribution two theories at least which proved grist for the socialist mill. One was his labor theory of value. According to this theory the exchange value of a commodity arises from labor and is measured by the quantity of labor necessary to produce the commodity, or rather the quantity necessary under the most unfavorable circumstances of production. The second was his theory of wages, according to which wages are not determined by the product of the worker, but by the amount of food, clothing, shelter, and certain conveniences which the worker must have in order to live and to perpetuate his race without increase or diminution.[19]

Socialistic writers for years accepted these theories as correct statements of economic relationships under the capitalistic regime, but protested that if labor was the basis of wealth, and if the workers received under the most favorable circumstances only enough to keep them alive and to produce the next generation of workers, there was something fundamentally wrong with the system.

Shelley. It was in this spirit of protest that Shelley (1792–1822), the young revolutionary poet of the period, addressed the people:

> The seed ye sow, another reaps;
> The wealth ye find, another keeps;
> The robes ye weave, another wears;
> The arms ye forge, another bears.

Reaction from French and Industrial Revolution. The revolution in France and the industrial revolution in England gave rise not only to the protest of occasional social reformers, but to those of numerous groups of working men, the forerunners of the modern labor move-

[19] Beer, *op. cit.,* Vol. I, pp. 155–9.

ment. These groups came into constant clashes with the government, who, terrorized by the French Revolution, decided to put down with a ruthless hand any signs of a violent upheaval in England.

THE LONDON CORRESPONDING SOCIETY. Among the first of these working class groups was The London Corresponding Society (L. C. S.). The program of this society was democracy and social reform; the leaders were Thomas Hardy (1752–1832), a Scotch shoemaker, and John Thelwall (1764–1844), orator and poet. The L. C. S. was formed in 1792 and at once began its agitation among the masses. Its connection with the French Convention and its insurrectionary activities soon brought down on it the strong arm of the government. The leaders were arrested and tried for high treason, but, thanks to the defense of Erskine, they were acquitted. In his undelivered speech prepared for his own defense, Thelwall presented the challenge of his organization:

"If, once in every year, the poor man's vote were as important as the employer's, the poor could not be forgotten. But it is property, we are told, that ought to be represented, because by property government is supported. What? Does property man the navy or fill the ranks of the army? . . . Property is nothing but human labor. The most inestimable of all property is the sweat of the poor man's brow; the property from which all other is derived, and without which grandeur must starve in the midst of supposed abundance. . . . Man and not immovables is the object of just legislation. All, therefore, ought to be consulted where all are concerned, for not less than the whole ought to decide the fate of the whole. . . . The few are . . . the owners of the life and liberty and possessions of the many." [20]

Universal suffrage, to be used in obtaining economic justice, was thus among the chief demands of the society. The organization continued its work for several years longer. However, by the Corresponding Act of 1799, which prohibited all communication between political societies—so panicstricken had the ruling class become at the time as a result of the French Revolution—the Society was finally suppressed.

PROPHETS OF COMING REVOLUTION. The government knew how to suppress the discontented, but not how to eliminate the evils which produced discontent. The effects of unrestricted individualism under the developing manufacturing system became so tragic for great masses of the people as to lead to frequent prophecies of revolution. In 1807 Southey prophesied: "If the manufacturing system continues to be extended, increasing as it does the number, the misery, and the depravity

[20] Quoted in Beer, *op. cit.*, pp. 124–5; see Cestre, Charles, *John Thelwall*, 1906.

of the poor, I believe that a revolution must come, and in the most fearful shape." [21]

Declared the *Edinburgh Review* three years later: "The great body of the nation appear to us to be divided into two violent and most pernicious factions: the courtiers, who are almost for arbitrary power; and the democrats who are almost for revolution and republicanism. . . . If the Whig leaders do not first conciliate and then restrain the people . . . the Constitution itself, the Monarchy, and the Whig aristocracy will, in no long time, be swept away. . . . The nation is on fire at four corners." [22]

Revolution did not take place, but the cities seethed with protesting groups. At first, the workers organized groups bent upon the wholesale destruction of machinery. Groups of workers, known as Luddites, embittered at the misery which came in the wake of machinery, felt that the remedy lay in its destruction and in the return of the good old days of the past. Their sabotaging led only to the passage of severe laws against the destroyers and, in 1813, to the execution on the gallows of nearly a score of workers.

Demand for Suffrage and Further Repressive Measures. Many social reformers endeavored to show the futility of these destructive tactics. Among the most prominent of these was William Cobbett, the democratic editor of the popular weekly *The Register*. Nothing, he declared, can be achieved by smashing the instruments of production. The only remedy for oligarchic rule, heavy taxation, debased currency, and the Corn and Combinations Acts passed against the workers is a popularly elected Parliament. This belief took root. Universal suffrage became the demand of increasing groups among the middle class and the workers, who made their demands heard through numerous weeklies, public meetings, and societies.

The spirit of the agitation of that period may be indicated by the resolutions of the Female Reform Association at Blackburn in 1818:

"By means of the improvement of machinery, the means of producing most articles of agriculture and manufacture has been increased in an astonishing degree; it necessarily follows that the industrious laborer ought to have a far greater quantity of the produce than he had previous to those improvements; instead of which, by means of taxation and restrictive laws, he is reduced to wretchedness. . . . No man can have a right to enjoy another man's labor without his consent. And we con-

[21] See Southey, *Letters* II, p. 157; III, pp. 132–3.
[22] *Edinburgh Review,* 1810.

template with horror the number of placemen and pensioners, whilst at the same time we live in poverty, slavery, and misery. We protest against those unjust and unnatural regulations—the Corn laws and the Combinations Acts. We demand universal suffrage, annual Parliaments and the ballot." [23]

But the government considered agitation for suffrage as dangerous as the smashing of machinery, and on the excuse of rioting at St. Peter's Field, Manchester, in August, 1819, it passed the Six Acts which put a stop for some time to public agitation in England. Demonstrations, however, continued in Scotland, where a number of unions were organized in the manufacturing districts. "The devil seems to have come among us unchained," wrote Sir Walter Scott, concerning the agitation and organization of these days. "In Glasgow, Volunteers drill by day and radicals by night, and nothing but positive military force keeps the people under." [24]

In 1820 the leaders of the agitation posted proclamations on the walls of many Scotch houses in manufacturing towns, calling on the people to stop work until universal suffrage was granted. "Equality of rights" (but not of property) was the shibboleth. Many struck. Some took up arms and were arrested or wounded in skirmishes with the military. Andrew Hardie, forbear of James Keir Hardie, and two others were convicted of high treason and executed.

Followers of Spence. In the meanwhile other groups were conducting propaganda along different lines. One was the Spencean Philanthropists, as the followers of Thomas Spence were called. They were divided into four groups of ten persons each, and gave the impression through their activities that they controlled the working class movement. They urged that the land be returned to the people. They denounced the Napoleonic Wars on the ground that they but served the interests of Russia. They organized demonstrations, some of which led to rioting. As in the case of the London Corresponding Society, the Luddites, and the advocates of universal suffrage, laws were enacted against the Spenceans on the ground that they were aiming at the confiscation and division of the lands, and the repudiation of the national debt. Most of the Spenceans dropped active agitation. Five of them, embittered by the governmental policy of ruthless suppression, abandoned peaceful methods of reform, and with the help of government spies, organized the so-called "Cato Street Conspiracy" of 1820, only to pay for their agitation with their lives. Thus was closed "one of the

[23] *Black Dwarf*, July 14, 1819.
[24] Sir Walter Scott, *Familiar Letters*, II, p. 78.

most agitated and terrible and at the same time mentally most active and prolific decades in British history." [25] Stirred by the spirit of the time, Shelley contributed *Queen Mab, Poems of the Times,* and *Prometheus Unbound.* These conditions produced also a new reformer of exceptional ability and understanding, Robert Owen.

[25] Beer, *op. cit.*, p. 142.

CHAPTER 10

Robert Owen

IN THE previous chapter we have indicated something of the setting of the activities of Robert Owen, manufacturer, utopian, co-operator, "father of British socialism." The industrial revolution had completely transformed British industry, greatly increasing the wealth of England and heaping high the coffers of the manufacturers. For the workers, however, it meant unemployment, misery, and starvation. Child labor in a most pernicious form had increased many fold. The old personal relations between master and worker had been dissolved, labor was being brought together in large masses in factories and mills, and, in consequence, economic and political labor groups were springing up on all sides.

These organizations, in turn, were causing grave anxiety within the governing classes, who had visions of a repetition of a French Revolution on British soil. Resort was made to severe repressive, rather than to remedial legislation as the best method of preventing open revolt.

"At this juncture," wrote Friedrich Engels, "there came forward as a reformer, a manufacturer, a man of almost sublime and childlike simplicity of character, and at the same time one of the few born leaders of men." [1]

Owen's Early Life. Robert Owen was born May 14, 1771, in North Wales, the son of a saddler and ironworker. Though an eager student he had little schooling, and at ten years of age became an apprentice to a Stamford clothier. His employer fortunately had a well-selected library, and young Owen spent much time in reading. At the end of his apprenticeship he connected himself with several concerns in London and Manchester, where he did exceptionally well, and at the age of nineteen became superintendent of a large Manchester cotton mill, which employed some five hundred men. The goods manufactured by

[1] Quoted in Lockwood, *The New Harmony Movement* (Appleton, 1905), p. 46.

the mill soon commanded a fifty per cent advance over regular market prices, and Owen rose rapidly among the spinners of the country. "Indeed there is no reason to doubt that at this early age he [Owen] was the first cotton spinner in England, a position entirely due to his own capacity and knowledge of the trade."

Owen was soon taken into partnership, but later resigned and associated himself with another well-established Manchester house. It was while on a business trip for this firm that he met his future wife, Miss Dale, and was induced by her to visit her father's cotton mill in New Lanark, Scotland. He and his partners afterwards bought this mill for $300,000.

Transformation of New Lanark. Following the purchase of this mill and his marriage to Miss Dale, Owen moved to New Lanark, and, on January 1, 1800, he started his work as superintendent of the newly bought mill. In the town of New Lanark there were thirteen to fourteen hundred families and several hundred pauper children. Theft, drunkenness, and other vices were prevalent among the mill hands. Most of the families lived in one room, under most unsanitary conditions. Children worked long hours and had no opportunity for education.

Owen, spurred on by his former success, decided to give attention not only to the technical equipment of the mill but also to its human equipment. He enforced strict sanitary rules. He established stores from which the workers could get their supplies at cost—a reduction of twenty per cent from the prices previously charged. He built decent houses. He kept a record of the conduct of his employees, which was used as a basis for promotion. He restricted drinking. He established kindergartens for the children of the operators and developed a general educational system.

During the depression of 1806, when the United States had placed an embargo on cotton from America and his mill had to close down, Owen established the startling precedent of paying the wages of his workers in full. As a result of these reforms, a remarkable transformation took place in the life of the workers, and the New Lanark community soon gained fame for its temperateness, cleanliness, and intelligence. It became a mecca for students of social problems, statesmen, and even for royalty, among them Nicholas, afterwards Czar of Russia.

Nor did the business suffer as a result of these innovations. The mills made more money for the owners than ever before. However, many of Owen's proposals required a considerable outlay. The partners complained of this, and a new partnership was formed. Further disagreement arose, and in 1813 Owen, backed by William Allen, Quaker, Jeremy Bentham, the philosopher, and other stockholders who were willing to take five per cent on their investment, bought the firm out at auction for nearly $800,000. When the books of the second partnership were balanced, it was found that the firm had made a profit during the previous four years, excluding five per cent paid on capital stock, of approximately the selling price.

Owen brought to completion his educational plans for his mill operatives with the opening of the New Lanark institute in 1816. Twelve years later, after further dissension in the ranks of his company on account of his unorthodox religious views, Owen finally left the business. Of the results of Owen's social experiments in this mill town, Mr. Griscom, an American traveler, who spent some time there, wrote:

"There is not, I apprehend, to be found in any part of the world, a manufacturing community in which so much order, good government, tranquillity, and rational happiness prevail." [2]

His Philosophy. Happiness the Goal of Society. Shortly after Owen assumed charge of the New Lanark mills, he began to show an interest in the larger social problems. In 1813, the year his new partnership was formed, he published the first of the essays which contained his social philosophy, *Essays on the Formation of Character*. He elaborated his views in further essays published during the succeeding two years.[3]

In these and other essays Owen took as the basis for his social philosophy the thesis of his friend and business associate, Jeremy Bentham, that the aim of human society is the greatest happiness of the greatest number. Each individual should strive for happiness, both individual and collective.

"The primary and necessary object of all existence," he declared, "is to be happy. . . . But happiness cannot be obtained individually; it is useless to expect isolated happiness; all must partake of it, or the few will never enjoy it; man can, therefore, have but one real and genuine interest, which is to make all of his race as peaceful in character and happy in feeling as the original organization of nature of each will admit; . . . then will they be occupied in promoting to the greatest limit, their own individual happiness, . . . and the only contest among men then will be, who shall the most succeed in extending the happiness of his fellows." [4]

[2] Quoted in Lockwood, *The New Harmony Movement*, p. 52.
[3] Reprinted in *Life of Robert Owen* (Autobiography), 1857, Vol. I, pp. 257–332.
[4] *The Book of the New Moral World*, Part IV, p. 54.

In the coming age, "to produce happiness will be the only religion of man; the worship of God will consist in the practice of useful industry; in the acquisition of knowledge; in uniformly speaking the language of truth; and in the expression of the joyful feeling which a life in accordance with nature and truth is sure to produce." [5]

CHARACTER A PRODUCT OF ENVIRONMENT. At present there are now but few happy individuals, and happy nations are unknown. What is the cause of this condition? Owen was a rationalist and, as such, declared that the cause of the unhappiness of his day could not be found in the human will—since reason, not will, was the prime mover in human action—but in some error of belief. And the belief that is in error is that which teaches that man makes his own character. This is utterly false, for a man's character is a product of the circumstances in which he is born, lives, and works. Evil conditions breed evil men; good conditions develop good men. Today man is surrounded by conditions that breed selfishness, ignorance, vice, hypocrisy, hatred, war. If a new world is to be born, the first thing that must be done is to spread the truth concerning the formation of character, namely, that man's character is made for him, not by him. The acceptance of this truth will lay a foundation for a change in circumstances that will produce good characters.[6]

In fact, Owen claimed that "any general character, from the best to the worst, from the most ignorant to the most enlightened, may be given to any community, even to the world at large, by the application of proper means; which means are to a great extent at the command and under the control of those who have influence in the affairs of men." [7]

POWER OF EDUCATION. By education the inhabitants of a community could be trained to live a perfect life. Education, according to Owen, should be universal and compulsory. It should begin by teaching children the principles of brotherhood, industry, and character building. Being so trained, the child would realize the folly "of being angry with an individual for possessing qualities which, as a passive being during the formation of these qualities, he had not the means of preventing." [8] He would be filled with fine tolerance and good will and would desire to do good to all men.

NEED FOR AN ABUNDANCE OF WEALTH. An abundant supply of wealth was also a necessity to a proper environment, for without a surplus of

[5] *Ibid.*, Part II, p. 33.
[6] See Podmore, *Robert Owen*, 2 vols. (N. Y., 1917), Vol. II, p. 648.
[7] *Life of Robert Owen, Written by Himself*, Vol. I, p. 226. [8] *Ibid.*, Vol. I, p. 273.

wealth, the many must live in poverty, and poverty is a fertile field for many social and individual ills.[9] Fortunately the truth regarding the development of character was now being widely disseminated, he declared, and for the first time in history wealth was being produced at a rate that could lift all above the poverty line.

Need for Guaranteed Employment. The first step in the attainment of this ideal was the establishment of a labor bureau which would provide for the worker "perpetual employment of real national utility in which all who apply may be immediately occupied," [10] for, through continuous employment, "some of the circumstances which tend to generate, continue, or increase bad habits," would be eliminated.[11]

Owen during these days believed that great changes were in progress. "See the whole mass of men in full motion," he writes, "behold it momentarily increasing in vigor, and preparing, ere long, to burst its confinement." [12]

First Aim Ameliorative. When Owen first undertook the task of creating a better environment for his countrymen, he did not have in mind any revolution in the relations of property. The evils he wished abolished were chiefly those of sweating, ignorance, and enmity. He depended on private initiative, legislative action, and education to eliminate social maladjustments. In 1813 or 1814, in his address to his fellow manufacturers, he called attention to the superior productivity of clean, well-kept, well-oiled machinery. "If, then," he declared, "due care as to the state of your inanimate machines can produce such beneficial results, what may not be expected if you devote equal attention to your vital machines, which are far more wonderfully constructed?" [13]

Campaign for Labor Legislation. From 1815 to 1818 he devoted much of his energy and money to the promotion of legislation to alleviate some of the worst evils of the factory system. In 1815 he organized a conference of employers in Glasgow to protest against the heavy import duties on cotton and to consider means of improving conditions of labor.

In his speech before this gathering Owen drew a dark picture of conditions among the workers and declared that he would oppose with all his faculties every attempt to extend the cotton trade which is "more

[9] See Owen's pamphlets on *Observations on the Effect of the Manufacturing System, Report on the Poor, Memorial to the Allied Powers,* and *Report to the Country of Lanark,* written 1815–20.

[10] *Essays on the Principle of the Formation of Human Character,* p. 329.

[11] See Beer, *op. cit.,* Vol. I, p. 164 from *First Essay on the Principle of the Formation of Character.*

[12] See *Third Essay on the Principle of the Formation of Character.*

[13] *Life of Robert Owen, Written by Himself,* Vol. I, pp. 260–1.

injurious to those employed in it than is the slavery of the West Indies to the poor Negroes," unless something is done at the same time to correct the evils it creates. He concluded: "Perish the cotton trade, perish even the political superiority of our country, if it depends on the cotton trade, rather than that they shall be upheld by the sacrifice of everything valuable in life." [14]

But Owen's plea was coldly received. Only his protest against the import duty on cotton found a responsive ear. During the next few years he issued literally tons of literature, urging that Parliament limit the number of hours in mills to twelve a day, including an hour and a half for meals; prohibit the employment of children under ten, and limit the workday of those less than twelve years of age to six hours a day. He also proposed the establishment of schools where reading, writing, and arithmetic should be taught. Sir Robert Peel was chosen to introduce a bill embodying these demands. In 1819 the measure passed, but in such an emasculated form that it had little effect on labor conditions.[15]

His Turn to Utopianism. It was in 1817 that Owen placed himself squarely in the ranks of utopian writers by his proposals for the solution of the problem of unemployment. At the end of the previous year, England for the first time in its existence had passed through a crisis which resulted not from scarcity but from overproduction. The demands for relief became so great that the House of Commons was finally forced to appoint a Committee on Poor Laws. Owen wrote a report for this committee,[16] and the succeeding year addressed another memorial to the Allied Powers assembled in a congress at Aix-la-Chapelle.[17]

In these and other statements, Owen declared that, as a result of the introduction of machinery, the world was now being saturated with wealth. Machinery was also displacing manual labor. The wage bill of the country was being diminished, and the workers were unable to buy much of that which they produced. Commodities thus remained unsold in barns and warehouses. Only when consumption kept pace with production would unemployment and industrial crises be elimi-

[14] Quoted in Lockwood, *op. cit.*, pp. 54–5.

[15] Owen always believed that he had been the main driving power behind that Act. On the other hand, Alexander Ure, whose knowledge of the history of the factory system was considerable, ascribed this law to the "strikes and turmoils" of the Lancashire cotton spinners in the years 1817–1818. Beer, *History of British Socialism,* Vol. I, p. 168.

[16] *Life of Robert Owen, Written by Himself,* IA., pp. 53–63.

[17] *Ibid.*, pp. 212–22.

nated. However, this was not possible so long as private profit rather than social welfare was the goal of industry. If something radical was not done, he added, the workers would be goaded into fury and despair.

"We resemble individuals," he said, "standing upon the narrow causeway of a narrow abyss." And the tragic fact was that large masses of workers were being brought face to face with starvation because they had produced too much wealth!

"Owen's Parallelograms." The remedy, Owen maintained, was communism, but this must be applied gradually. A beginning should be made in the formation of villages of "unity and co-operation" for the unemployed. These villages were to have about one thousand to fifteen hundred acres of land and accommodate between five hundred and two thousand persons, who were to engage both in agriculture and manufacturing. They were to live in large buildings (quadrangles) built in the form of a square, situated in the center of each community and containing common dormitories, dining rooms, libraries, reading rooms, and schools. Attractive gardens and playgrounds should be located within and without the quadrangle, and laundries, factories, and farm buildings would be built beyond the outside gardens. Each family would live in a separate apartment. It would have entire charge of its children until three years of age, when the latter would be given over to the community to be educated. After that, the parents would be permitted to see their offspring at meal-times and at other proper intervals.

There would be within each community a large variety of occupations, chiefly agricultural, partly manufacturing, and the latest and best machinery would be used throughout. All except the children would be compelled to work at some useful task, and each community would be supervised by a qualified technician.

The communities could be established by individuals, parishes, counties, or the state. They would be self-contained, independent economic units combining the advantages of city and country, and in technical efficiency, economy of living, education, and distributive justice would be far superior to the industrial communities of Owen's day. Although independent units, they would not, however, be isolated, but, "as the townships should increase in numbers, unions of them, federatively united, should be formed in circles of ten, hundreds, thousands, until they should embrace the entire world." Naturally the present states would become useless and would be sloughed off. Poverty and exploitation would be unknown, and all would then work in the spirit of brotherhood and co-operation.

As Podmore reminds us, the whole picture which Owen painted of his ideal state was necessarily limited "by his nature, his personal experience, his environment, the whole circumstance of his times." [18] It was in all probability the basis of Fourier's phalanxes, conceived several years later by the great French utopian.

Owen's scheme, jocularly called Owen's Parallelograms, did not make any wide appeal. Even the London workingmen voted against the proposal at two public meetings held in 1817 on the ground that it was too paternalistic and would too greatly restrict individual action.

His Attack on Religion. Owen regarded its defeat as due to the conspiracy of the churches and the political economists. In August, 1817, in the City Hall Tavern he denounced as gross errors all religions as then taught and accused them of preventing mankind "from knowing what true happiness really is." This attack on a belief so firmly rooted in the lives of the people alienated from him many of his followers, particularly among the middle and upper classes, and from this time onward his influence as a social reformer declined.

His Appeals to Labor. In 1819 he worked in London with untiring energy to raise enough money to start his experiments, but his efforts were unavailing. The same years he issued an *Address to the Workmen,* offering them his assistance in their efforts to emancipate themselves from poverty and ignorance, with the proviso, however, that they would accept his doctrine regarding human nature and renounce all violence and all hatred against the ruling classes. The rich and the poor, the governors and the governed, he told them, had common interests, nor did the upper classes desire to keep the workers in subjection. The latter had within their grasp all of the means to emancipate themselves, but the knowledge of these means must be withheld from them until they realized that all classes were alike creatures of circumstances and that all bitterness was folly. Finally, they must realize that the past belonged to the era of irrationality, but that the future belonged to reason. Occupied as they were with Parliamentary reforms, the workers did not heed this appeal.

Notes on Labor. Owen then returned to Scotland, where he twice ran for Parliament, but was defeated. In 1820 the County of Lanark asked him to recommend a remedy for unemployment. In his report to this county he reiterated his views on communism and in addition, being influenced by the currency discussions of the time, attacked the old form of circulating medium as one of the causes of misery. The remedy, he declared, lay in the adoption of human labor as the standard of value. A certain quantity of labor should constitute a unit of value,

[18] Podmore, *op. cit.,* p. 646.

and those performing labor should obtain a paper note signifying the units of value they had produced. With this they could obtain other goods costing similar amounts of labor.

There was much confusion in his thinking on these questions. He believed that money and the standard of value were identical, whereas money but expressed the standard of value. He regarded gold and silver as artificial, not real values. "A discordant character was hereby imparted to his social economic reasonings which made itself felt in the course of development of the Owenite Movement."

His Communist Stand. In 1821 Owen wrote his *Social System*, published a few years later, in which he took a completely communist position that did not allow for any admixture of private property. In it he bitterly attacked the political economists who regarded the object of society as the accumulation of riches alone, and men as inanimate machines. Their praise of individualism and competition had led to the degradation of labor. They were unable to solve the question of distribution—the main problem before society. The main object of society should be the happiness of all, to be attained by the establishment of communities wherein both labor and distribution were equal. "With means thus ample to procure wealth with ease and pleasure to all, none will be so unwise as to have the trouble and care of individual property. To divide property among individuals in unequal proportions or to hoard it for individual purposes will be perceived as useless and injurious as it would be to divide air or light into unequal quantities for different individuals, or that they should hoard them." [19]

His "New Harmony" Colony. Anxious to put some of his ideas into practice, he bought in 1824 for 30,000 pounds the Rappist community at Harmony, Indiana, which contained 30,000 acres of land, and called it "New Harmony."

"I am come to this country," declared Owen in his opening address to the colony, "to introduce an entire new state of society; to change it from an ignorant, selfish system to an enlightened social system which shall gradually unite all interests into one, and remove all causes for contest between individuals." [20] However, after three years of struggle, the experiment, which had taken most of Owen's money, failed. The adoption in the second year of the experiment of the principles of absolute equality of compensation, irrespective of effort or productivity, was one of the factors in this failure. In 1825 a similar venture started by a follower of Owen in Orbiston, near Glasgow, met a similar fate.

[19] *The Book of the New Moral World*, 1836, Introduction xxi.
[20] Lockwood, *op. cit.*, p. 83.

Labor Exchanges. But the failure of this and other colonies established after the Owenite pattern did not dampen Owen's ardor for social change. He returned to England, and we next find him fighting for a system of labor exchanges as a means of alleviating the wretched condition which prevailed in England during the early thirties. To these exchanges producers could take their goods and receive in return vouchers or labor notes, stating the amount of labor time, in the form of commodities, that they had left on deposit. In return for these vouchers they could obtain at any time goods valued at a like amount of labor time. The labor bureau would ask a small commission for overhead expenses, but the exploiting middlemen would be entirely eliminated. He also urged the establishment of labor exchange banks in connection with these exchanges.

An organization was formed to agitate for this idea, headquarters were established in Gray's Inn Road, and the institute, as it was called, for some time met with considerable success, although its activities did not reach the very poor. It was in this institute that the Third Co-operative Congress was held in April, 1832, in which for the first time the political socialists clashed with the non-political, co-operative socialists of whom Owen had become a moving spirit. Other branches of the institute were established, and "for a whole year Owen lived in a state of ecstasy," as the apparent success of this venture and the rapid growth of the co-operative and trade union movements during these months "were all considered harbingers of the imminent emancipation of the world from error and injustice." [21]

Plan to Combine Trade Unions and Co-operatives. Touring England, he conceived the idea of uniting the trade unions and co-operative societies into a single organization "and of transforming them in a communistic sense so as to place the whole country on a co-operative basis." [22]

In October, 1833, at the conclusion of this tour, a conference of trade unions and co-operatives was held in London at his request to consider his plan for unity. Owen, full of enthusiasm, addressed the convention. He maintained that the workers would be won over to the truths of co-operation within six months, and added: "I will only briefly sketch the outlines of the great revolution in preparation, which will come upon society as a thief in the night." [23]

The Owenite plan was simple. The trade unions would be made into co-operative societies, and would exchange their goods through

[21] Beer, *op. cit.*, p. 325. [22] *Ibid.*, p. 326.
[23] *Ibid.*, p. 330.

labor exchanges. A general congress to sit in London would supersede Parliament and conduct the business of the country. All would be accomplished without violence or disorder.

Dream of a New Society. The delegates worked harmoniously at this convention, and considerable progress was made toward the unity idea. *The Poor Man's Guardian* (October 19, 1832) was jubilant. A grand national organization of producers was in process of formation, it declared, with the sublime object of establishing "for the productive classes a complete dominion over the fruits of their own industry. Heretofore these classes wasted their strength in fruitless squabbles with their employers or with one another. They have never sought any grand object, nor have they been united in that which they sought. To obtain some paltry rise, or to prevent some paltry reduction in wages, has been the general aim of their turn-outs; and the best result of the best combinations, even when successful, was merely to secure their members against actual want in the day of sickness or of superannuation.

"These and the like objects were only worthy of slaves; they did not strike at the root of the evil; they did not aim at any radical change; their tendency was not to alter the system, but rather to perpetuate it, by rendering it more tolerable. . . . But far different from the paltry objects of all former combinations is that now aimed at by the congress of delegates. Their reports show that an entire change in society—a change amounting to the complete subversion of the existing 'order of the world'—is contemplated by the working classes. They aspire to be at the top rather than at the bottom of society—or rather that there should be no bottom and no top at all!"

Morrison, editor of the *Pioneer,* a trade union organ, declared that they had "now macadamized the road to success or, rather, we have laid a railroad to prosperity. . . . The crisis of our condition is at hand—close upon it. The contest affects all alike; and woe unto the man who deserts his post. The question to be decided is: Shall labor or capital be uppermost?" [24]

Labor's Demand for a General Strike. The convention was followed by feverish activity on the part of the labor unions, and by the end of the following year it was estimated that 800,000 operatives had become members of the unions. Many of these members, however, took little stock in the methods advocated by Owen for improving their conditions. A large number were captivated by the idea of the general strike. For instance, we find the Glasgow workers, on October 5, 1833,

[24] *Pioneer,* October 12, 1833.

enthusiastically endorsing a general strike resolution. Their discussion at this meeting reads like a modern syndicalist manifesto:

"There will not be insurrection; it will simply be passive resistance. The men may remain at leisure; there is and can be no law to compel men to work against their will. They may walk the streets and fields with their arms folded, they will wear no swords, carry no muskets; they will present no multitude for the riot act to disperse. They merely abstain, when their funds are sufficient, from going to work for one week or one month; and what happens in consequence? Bills are dishonored, the *Gazette* teems with bankruptcies, capital is destroyed, the revenue fails, the system of government falls into confusion, and every link in the chain which binds society together is broken in a moment by this inert conspiracy of the poor against the rich." [25]

Reaction. This turn in events greatly displeased Owen, who regarded the salvation of the country as dependent on the co-operation of laboring and propertied classes. Capital, he insisted, was also a producer and deserved to be approached in a friendly spirit. As a means of bringing capital and labor together in a common effort at reform, he formed, on November 25, 1833, still another organization—the National Regeneration Society—and planned to have both employers and operators unite the following March in the introduction of the eight-hour day. A fight ensued between the Owenites, with their message of peaceful co-operation, and the syndicalistic group who emphasized the inevitability of class warfare and who urged a general strike. This and other controversies within the movement and renewed opposition from a nervous employing class led to the temporary collapse of the trade union movement, however, and for some years it sank into relative unimportance, with the general strike and labor supremacy an unrealized dream.

Last Days. During the last years of his life Robert Owen was less in the public gaze. He was, however, far from inactive. He republished many of his earlier writings. He was active in the co-operative movement. He restated his views on national education, maintaining that "the great want of the world was a good training from birth, and a sound, practical education for all, based on true principles." And he gave considerable attention to international affairs and urged a federation between Great Britain and the United States to which all other nations should be admitted, and which should recognize it as a duty

[25] *Glasgow Liberator* (*Trades Union Gazette*), Feb. 1, 1834; quoted in Beer, *op. cit.*, p. 333.

to terminate war "and live in the abundance of peaceful industry and friendly exchange." [26]

In his eighty-sixth year he read a paper on the *Human Race Governed without Punishment* before the Social Science Association of Great Britain, and the next year, while attempting to deliver another paper before the same association at Liverpool, broke down, was taken to his native town of Newton, and soon after died.

An Estimate. The concrete achievements of Robert Owen during his lifetime did not make an impressive showing. His most important practical experiment in improving labor conditions was that undertaken during his days as superintendent of the New Lanark mills, an experiment that attracted world-wide attention. But when he lost touch with the industrial world and as an unattached reformer made wholesale proposals for social changes, his efforts met with failure. His colonies did not succeed. The labor legislation that he and others were finally able to force through Parliament was comparatively ineffective. His labor exchanges did little practical good. His appeal to capital and labor to co-operate for the attainment of the eight-hour day and the reconstruction of society met with little response. He made the old mistake of thousands of social idealists before and since, in believing that the great changes of which he dreamed were right at hand. He inherited and propagated the fallacy, taught freely in his day, that reason was the prime mover in human action. He gave too little consideration to the forces of heredity in the formation of human character. And so little of an organized following had he gathered around him a decade before his death, that when the poet Emerson asked this most amiable, sanguine, and candid of men: "Who is your disciple? how many men possessed of your views, who will remain after you, are going to put them in practice?," Owen candidly replied, "Not one." [27]

And yet, despite his errors in judgment and the failure of many of his plans, the great-hearted and lovable cotton manufacturer and communist did exert a profound influence on the social thinking of the world. His indictment of the present order of society for its waste, its injustices, its tragedy of unemployment; his emphasis on social happiness as the ideal of human progress; his insistence that character was profoundly influenced by social environment; his urgent plea that all co-operate for the common welfare in the production and distribution of wealth, all these left their imprint on future generations. And his life of untiring devotion and sacrifice proved one of the great sources of in-

[26] Quoted in Lockwood, *op. cit.*, pp. 311–2.
[27] Quoted in Lockwood, *op. cit.*, p. 310.

spiration to those who followed later in the socialist, co-operative, and trade union movements, as well as those who worked in behalf of child training, of labor legislation, of prison reform, and of similar causes.[28]

[28] We cannot leave this portion of our history without mentioning the effect on the social thinking of the times of the writings of Thomas Carlyle (1795–1881), George Sand (1804–1872), Charles Dickens (1812–1884), John Ruskin (1819–1900), and Matthew Arnold (1822–1888), among others. While none of these may be classed as socialists, they did much to draw to the attention of the people of England the ugliness of the then industrial system and arouse in many a desire for social change (see Carlyle's *Sartor Resartus,* Dickens's *David Copperfield,* Ruskin's *Unto These Last, A Crown of Wild Olives,* and *Ethics of the Dust*).

CHAPTER 11

Utopianism in America

AMERICA was the happy hunting ground for the experiments of the utopian socialists—Cabet, Owen, Fourier. The philosophy of these utopians also secured the adherence of a brilliant group of America's mid-nineteenth century intellectuals. Chief among these was Albert Brisbane, father of the journalist, Arthur Brisbane.

Albert Brisbane. Brisbane was born in 1809 in Batavia, N. Y., the son of a well-to-do landowner. He received a thorough education, traveling and studying extensively in Europe. While there he became acquainted with the works of Saint-Simon and devoted much of his time and money to the propagation of his views. Shortly after Fourier's *Treatise on Domestic and Agricultural Association* was published, Brisbane obtained a copy. He became enthusiastic about it. "For the first time," he writes,[1] "I had come across an idea which I had never met before—the idea of *dignifying and rendering attractive* the manual labor of mankind, labor hitherto regarded as a divine punishment inflicted on man."

He went to Paris in 1832, studied the details of the system under the personal direction of Fourier, and on his return to the United States worked quietly in behalf of Fourierism until 1840, when he published his *Social Destiny of Man*. The book was a reprint of the striking passages from Fourier's works, accompanied by Brisbane's comments and illustrations.

Horace Greeley and Fourierism. It met with instant success. Incidentally it proved one of the means of converting the famous newspaper man Horace Greeley to Fourieristic principles. Following his conversion, Greeley, as editor of the New York *Tribune,* entered into an arrangement with Brisbane whereby the latter was to edit a column each

[1] Brisbane, Redelia, *Albert Brisbane, A Mental Biography,* Redelia Brisbane, Boston, 1893; see also Hillquit, *op. cit.,* p. 80.

day on the theories and practice of Fourierism. This column, together with editorial comments, did much to advance the ideas of the French utopian. Greeley, who was long regarded as the foremost editor of his time, also gave unstintingly of his energy and means to forward this movement. His interpretation of Fourieristic principles is contained in the famous debate with Henry J. Raymond, then editor of the *Courier and Enquirer,* and later editor of the New York *Times.* The debate was printed in some 24 issues of the *Tribune* from November, 1846, to May, 1847. The earth and all natural products, contended Greeley, were, in the beginning, intended for the use of all. But "civilized society, as it exists today, has divested the larger portion of mankind of the unimpeded, unpurchased enjoyment of their natural rights. That larger portion may be perishing with cold, yet have no legally recognized right to a stick of decaying fuel in the most unfrequented morass; or may be famishing, yet have no legal right to pluck and eat the bitterest acorn in the depths of the remotest wilderness.

"The only solid ground on which this surrender of the original property of the whole to a minor portion can be justified is that of the public good—the good not of a part, but of the whole." But the misery of mankind indicates that this dispossession of the people of their rights has not been for the common good. Tens of thousands are far worse off today than they would have been "if nature's rule of allowing no man to appropriate to himself any more of the earth than he can cultivate and improve had been recognized and respected by society. . . . But those who have been divested of an important, a vital natural right, are also entitled to compensation.

"The Right of Labor, secured to them in the creation of the earth, taken away in the granting of the soil to a minor portion of them, must be restored. . . . But the right to labor—that is, the constant employment with a just and full compensation—cannot be guaranteed to all without a radical change in our social economy. . . . The ultimate and thorough remedy I believe is Association.

"By Association I mean a social order which shall take the place of the present township, to be composed of some hundreds or some thousands of persons, who shall be united together in interest and industry for the purpose of securing to each individual the following things: (1) an elegant and commodious house; (2) an education, complete and thorough; (3) a secure subsistence; (4) opportunity to labor; (5) fair wages; (6) agreeable social relations; (7) progress in knowledge and skill. As society is at present organized, these are the portion of a very small minority. But by Association of capital and industry they might become the lot of all; inasmuch as Association tends to *economy* in all departments, economy in lands, fences, fuel, household labor, tools, education, medicine, legal advice, and commercial exchanges. . . .

"The property of an Association will be vested in those who contribute the capital to establish it, represented by shares of stock, just as the property of a bank, factory, or railroad now is. Labor, skill, and talent will be remunerated by a fixed proportion of their product, or of their proceeds, if sold. Men will be induced to labor by a knowledge that its rewards will be a certain and major portion of the product, which, of course, will be less or more, according to the skill and industry of each individual. The slave has no motive to diligence except fear; the hireling is tempted to eye-service; the solitary worker for himself is apt to become disheartened; but men working for themselves, in groups, will find labor not less attractive than profitable. Moral offenses will be punished by legal enactment, and they will be rendered infrequent by plenty and education. . . ."

In reply to Raymond's contention that there was little difference between his proposed communities and the present form of ownership, and that "Association would be merely a plan for extending the relation of landlord and tenant over the whole arable surface of the earth," Greeley declared:

"By no means. The capital of a mature association would be, perhaps, half a million dollars; of an infant association, fifty thousand dollars; and this increase of value would be both created and *owned* by labor. In an ordinary township, however, the increase, though all created by labor, is chiefly owned by capital. The majority of inhabitants remain poor; while a few—merchants, landowners, mill-owners, and manufacturers—are enriched. . . . In Association those who furnish the original capital are the owners merely of *so much stock* in the concern—not of all the land and other property. Suppose that capital be fifty thousand dollars. At the end of the first year it is found that twenty-five thousand dollars have been added to the property by labor." For this amount new stock is issued in such a way "that when the property of the Association is worth half a million, capital will own about one-fifth of it. . . .

"Under the present system, capital is everything, man nothing, except as a means of accumulating capital. Capital founds a factory, and for the *single* purpose of increasing capital, taking no thought of the human beings by whom it is increased. The fundamental idea of Association, on the other hand, is to effect a just *distribution* of products among capital, talent, and labor."

In answer to the contention that individual reform must precede social reform, Greeley again replies: "I am as well aware as you are that the mass of the ignorant and destitute are, at present, incapable of so much as understanding the social order I propose, much less of becoming efficient members of an association. What I say is, let those who *are* capable of understanding and promoting it, *begin* the work, found associations, and show the rest of mankind how to live and thrive in harmonious industry. You tell me that the sole efficiency agency of social reform is Christianity. I answer that Association *is* Christianity; and the dislocation *now* existing between capital and labor, between the capitalist and the laborer, is as atheistic as it is inhuman." [2]

Greeley on Slavery. Greeley's every speech contained some reference to the need for emancipation of labor, and he frequently urged the members of the typographical union of which he was first president to develop a larger social vision. Though he fought vigorously against chattel slavery in the South, he ever made clear that he considered that there were other kinds of slavery in the United States. *"I understand by slavery,"* he wrote in an anti-slavery convention in 1845, *"that condition in which one human being exists mainly as a convenience for other human beings*—in which the time, the exertions, the faculties of a part of the human family are made to subserve, not their own development, physical, intellectual, and moral, but the comfort, advantages, and caprices of others. . . . If I am less troubled regarding the slavery prevalent in Charleston or New Orleans, it is because I see so much slavery in New York, which appears to claim my first efforts."

Parke Godwin, associate editor of the New York *Post,* and son-in-law of its editor, William Cullen Bryant, was also brought into the inner circle of Associationists. In his *Democracy, Pacific and Constructive,* published in 1844, he urged that the existing townships be gradually transformed into Fourierist communities. In this pamphlet he showed a recognition of class divisions which brought him near to the position of the later socialists. He drew a strong indictment against the capitalist system. "Blind competition," he contended, "tends to the formation of gigantic monopolies in every branch of labor; it depreciates the wages of the working classes; it excites an endless warfare between human arms and machinery and capital—a war in which the weak succumbs; it renders the recurrence of failures, bankruptcies and commercial crises a sort of endemic disease; and it reduces the middle and lower classes to a precarious and miserable existence."

[2] See Southeran, Charles, *Horace Greeley and Other Pioneers of American Socialism.* N. Y.: Mitchell Kennerley, 1915. Ch. V.

He drew frequent analogies from Greek mythology. The masses, he declared, "provoked by all that can gratify desire—yet unable to catch one jot or tittle of it—offer a terrible exemplification of Tantalus, tormented by an external hunger and thirst after fruits and water, always within his reach, yet perpetually eluding his grasp. Was the penalty of Sisyphus, condemned to roll his stone to a summit, from which it was forever falling, more poignant than that of many fathers of families, among the poorer classes, who, after laboring to exhaustion during their whole lives, to amass somewhat for their old age or for their children, see it swallowed up in one of those periodical crises of failure and ruin which are the inevitable attendants of our methods of loose competition? Or the story of Danaides, compelled incessantly to draw water in vessels from which it incessantly escaped, does it not with a fearful fidelity symbolize the implacable fate of nearly two-thirds of our modern societies, who draw from the bosom of the earth and the workshops of production, by unrelaxing toil, floods of wealth, that always slip through their hands, to be collected in the vast reservoirs of moneyed aristocracy?"

But while pessimistic about his own times, he felt that a happier day was at hand; that the world was "travailing in the birth-throes of a mighty and better future." [3]

Channing and Others. William Ellery Channing, the great Unitarian minister, also showed sympathy during the last years of his life for the Associationists, and strongly denounced the existing order, the natural fruits of which were "contempt of others' rights, fraud, oppression, a gambling spirit in trade, reckless adventure, and commercial revulsions, all tending to impoverish the laborer and to render every condition insecure." [4]

Charles A. Dana, afterwards editor of the New York *Sun;* George Ripley, later literary editor of the *Tribune* and editor of the *American Encyclopaedia;* and John S. Dwight, poet and music lover, were a few of the other Fourierites to join the inner circle.

During the early forties numerous periodicals sprung up, devoted to this new social philosophy, extensive lecture trips were arranged, and Fourierism became the subject of public discussion among increasing thousands. The industrial crisis of that time and the general humanitarian agitation that surrounded the anti-slavery movement also gave impetus to these teachings.

Formation of National Organization. As a result several societies were formed to propagate the idea in the East and Middle West, and on

[3] *Ibid.*, p. 140.

[4] *Ibid.*, p. 121.

April 4th, 1844, a National Convention of these societies was called at Clinton Hall, New York. George Ripley was elected president and among the vice-presidents were Horace Greeley, Albert Brisbane, Parke Godwin, and Charles A. Dana. The Convention indorsed the phalanx as the one form of organization calculated to solve social problems, but warned against starting phalanxes with insufficient preparation or funds. A National Confederation of Associations was agreed upon, and the *Phalanx* was made the official organ of the movement. Albert Brisbane was appointed a committee to get into closer touch with the international movement.

The Brook Farm Experiment. Of the experiments at this time Brook Farm was the most famous and spectacular. In the thirties an informal group, called by their enemies a "Transcendental Club,"[5] met at irregular intervals in Boston for the purpose of discussing social and philosophical problems. George Ripley, William Ellery Channing, John S. Dwight, Margaret Fuller, Ralph Waldo Emerson, Henry D. Thoreau, Nathaniel Hawthorne, and Elizabeth P. Peabody were among its members. From religious matters they turned to social problems, and many of them urged the claims of the utopian socialists and advocated the establishment of colonies which might prove the truth or falsity of these claims. Of this literary circle Emerson wrote to Carlyle, "We are all a little wild here with numberless projects of social reform; not a reading man but has a draft of a new community in his waistcoat pocket."

Ripley, then a Unitarian minister and an ardent devotee of the new doctrines, was particularly anxious to submit his views and those of the group to a test. So in 1840 he resigned his post as Unitarian minister and chose a 200-acre milk farm at West Roxbury, near Boston, for his proposed experiment. A group of about twenty—including Mr. and Mrs. Ripley, Dwight, Hawthorne, and William Allen—went there to live, and called it "The Brook Farm Institute for Agriculture and Education." Their ideal was a noble one. They desired to substitute "a system of brotherly co-operation for one of selfish competition; to secure for our children and to those who may be trusted to our care, the benefits of the highest physical, intellectual, and moral education which, in the present state of human knowledge, the resources at our command will permit; to institute an attractive, efficient, and productive system of

[5] The interpretation placed on the word transcendental by the group was expressed by Ripley, "We are called Transcendentals because we believe in an order of truth that transcends the sphere of the external senses. Our leading idea is the supremacy of mind over matter." (Quoted in Hillquit, *op. cit.,* p. 96.)

industry; to prevent the exercise of worldly anxiety by the competent supply of our necessary wants; to diminish the desire for excessive accumulation by making the acquisition of individual property subservient to upright and disinterested uses; to guarantee to each other the means of physical support and of spiritual progress, and thus to impart a greater freedom, simplicity, truthfulness, refinement, and moral dignity to our mode of life." [6]

In pursuance of these aims they maintained a uniform rate of compensation for all labor; a maximum workday of ten hours; free support of children under the age of ten years, of old persons, and of the sick; and free education, medical care, and use of the library and bath. They furthermore stipulated that all persons be provided with employment according to their taste and ability.

The community's administration was entrusted to four departments: General Direction, Agriculture, Education, and Finance. In its school an unusually wide range of sciences and arts were taught. While the working hours were many and leisure was scarce, the residents enjoyed an attractive social life. Dances, music, and literary and scientific discussions were provided for the leisure hours, and such visitors as Greeley, Brisbane, the Channings, and Theodore Parker paid frequent calls.

In 1844, following the National Convention of Associations, Brook Farm became a full-fledged Fourieristic experiment, was renamed the "Brook Farm Phalanx," and came to be the very center of Fourieristic activity in the United States. The official organ of the Fourierists, *The Harbinger,* was transferred to the Farm, in editorial charge of Ripley, Dana, and Dwight. Lowell, Whittier, George William Curtis, Parke Godwin, Higginson, Storey, Channing, Greeley, and others contributed to it. And from this center journeyed many a distinguished lecturer to tell the good tidings to other parts of the land.

In 1846 the Farm was beginning to prosper financially, and the residents were living in anticipation of the completion of the unitary phalanx building, the most pretentious of their edifices. But just as the structure was nearing completion, an accidental fire broke out, and the building was burned to the ground. Coming as this misfortune did at a time when the movement was waning in other parts of the country, it proved fatal to the experiment, and in the autumn little of Brook Farm remained but a memory of noble ideals and self-sacrificing devotion.

Other Communal Experiments. In some ways the most important of the Fourieristic experiments was the North American "Phalanx," de-

[6] Quoted in Hillquit, *op. cit.*, p. 97.

veloped by a number of idealists of New York at Red Bank, New Jersey, in 1843. The Phalanx dwellers, to the number of ninety, built a three-story mansion and a grist mill and developed a seventy-acre orchard, investing in the property some $8,000. At first, success seemed to crown their efforts, and by 1852 the community's property was inventoried at $80,000.

The colony established the unusual custom of paying the highest wages—though the scale was a very low one—to those doing the hardest and most disagreeable work, and of giving an extra reward for special skill and talent. The social life, as in the case of Brook Farm, was pleasant, and to the outsider the members appeared to be a genial band. For twelve years the experiment endured, but the waning of the movement without and dissensions within had their effect, and after a loss from fire amounting to $12,000, the members voted to dissolve.

Many other experiments were tried by the followers of Fourier, Owen, and Cabet, but sooner or later they failed. More fortunate were several religious colonies. The Oneida Community was among the most prosperous. Communism in these latter groups, however, was an incidental feature, and they had little social significance.

Causes of Failure. The failure of the American communities was due to several factors. They were often founded with little preparation and with little or no capital. The members were usually a heterogeneous group of mere adventurers who possessed scant knowledge of farming or of the other trades which must be successfully pursued in order to prosper. Small attention was given to the selection of members, and when the fundamental principles of the colonies were under discussion, the absolutely diverse points of view among the colonists led to bitter clashes. An endeavor was often made to work out in detail certain rather fantastic plans of social theorists living in another country, unacquainted with the difficulties their followers were compelled to face and possessed of an inadequate philosophy of human activity. Above all was the difficulty of conducting isolated social experiments on principles directly at variance with those of the outside world.

These failures caused dismay among the followers of Owen, Cabet, and Fourier, for the Owenites had regarded their colonies as nuclei for a world federation of associations that would ultimately supplant the present political and economic structure, and the followers of Fourier believed that the phalanxes, founded here and there, would soon demonstrate the soundness of the master's principles and lead to their universal adoption. With their disappearance the Owenite and Fourierist wave gradually ebbed and finally disappeared from American life.

But despite the fact that the American communistic experiments did not adapt themselves successfully to their industrial environment, the communities possessed, during their lifetime, many social advantages.

"No one who visits a communistic society which has been for some time in existence," says Nordhoff, "can fail to be struck by the amount of ingenuity, skill, and business talent developed among men from whom, in the outer world, one would not expect such qualities. . . . The communists are honest. They like thorough and good work and value their reputation for honesty and fair dealing. Their neighbors always speak highly of them in this respect."

"It is the unanimous testimony of all observers," declared Hillquit, "that the communists were, as a rule, very industrious, although no compulsion was exercised. . . . Disease was a rare occurrence among them, and they are not known to have had a single case of insanity or suicide. And, finally, it must be noted that the communists invariably bestowed much attention upon the education of their children and their own culture. . . . On the whole, the communistic mode of life proved to be more conducive to the physical, moral, and intellectual welfare of man than the individualistic regime." [7]

Wilhelm Weitling. Connected partly with the American radical movement and partly with the German is another utopian writer, Wilhelm Weitling, a tailor by trade, and advocate of a utopia controlled by a dictatorship of men of genius. Weitling was born of humble parentage in Magdeburg in 1808. He received little schooling, but through his unusual native ability, his wide reading, and his extensive travels during his days of apprenticeship as a tailor he acquired a vast store of knowledge. At an early age he embraced the theory of communism and became an organizer and propagandist among German workingmen living in other countries. He established restaurants for traveling tailors in Paris and Switzerland and a workers' educational society in London, and in 1846 joined the German Workingmen's Society in Brussels, of which Marx and Engels were leading figures. At one time he was regarded as the most influential figure among the German workingmen's colonies in Switzerland, Belgium, France, and England.[8]

Dictatorship by Men of Genius. In 1838 Weitling wrote his first book, *The World As It Is, and Should Be,* and two years later, his second, *Guarantees of Harmony and Freedom,* which attracted wide attention.

In common with other utopians, he based his plea for a new social

[7] See *Ibid.*, pp. 128–31.
[8] See *Ibid.*, 1910, pp. 43–50.

organization on moral grounds. The ideal state he pictured contained elements drawn from both Saint-Simon and Fourier. Like Saint-Simon, he would have the management of affairs in his highly centralized republic given over to men of knowledge and genius.

"In the first place," he said, "I adopted a principle which is admitted as an axiom in the learned world, that philosophy must bear rule. I then thought out the meaning of philosophy, and discovered that it stands for the sum total of all knowledge. . . . What steps should be taken to hand over the social order to knowledge?" Weitling answers this question by asserting that men of learning should be asked to apply for the position and should send in their scientific dissertations. These should be examined by members of the academies, and "the writer who is adjudged the best shall be appointed to that branch of government where his natural gifts may be of the greatest possible utility to society. I should advocate the following arrangement for the government of societies. At their head should be placed a triumvirate composed of great philosophers who are at the same time the highest authorities respectively in the sciences of healing, of physics and of mechanics." [9]

Appeal to Earth's Mighty. In the conclusion of his *Guarantees of Harmony and Freedom,* Weitling thus appeals to the "mighty ones of the earth": "You have the means of winning greater fame than an Alexander or a Napoleon. You have the means of removing all the evils of society in a way that is agreeable both to you and to us. If we are forced to undertake the work in our own rough and ready way, it will be a weary and painful process both for us and for you. Consider, therefore, and choose!"

On the other hand, he did recognize class distinctions between employer and employee, and his views on the rôle of social classes came rather close to those held by modern socialists.

Later Life. Weitling was exiled from his native land for his connection with secret organizations. In Brussels he became involved in a controversy with Marx and Engels over his advocacy of violence and of secret conspiracies to attain his ends. He at one time urged that the workers, 20,000 strong, should go armed to European capitals and terrify the propertied classes into a recognition of the principles of justice. Ultimately he journeyed to America, where he became particularly enthusiastic about the possibilities of labor exchange banks somewhat after the model of Owen, and helped to establish communist colonies. With the failure of these ventures, however, he ceased his activity in the labor movement and passed his last days in the prosaic occupation of a clerk in the Bureau of Immigration, New York City.

[9] Quoted in Sombart, *Socialism and the Socialist Movement,* p. 34.

CHAPTER 12

The Significance of Utopianism—Modern Utopian Writers

In the foregoing pages we have obtained a bird's-eye view of that distinguished group of thinkers in France, England, Germany, and America during the first half of the nineteenth century who were known as utopian socialists. We have noted many points of difference between them. What is their point of agreement with later socialists? What is their point of agreement with each other?

Agreement of Utopian Socialists with Other Schools. Utopian socialists are at one with socialists of other schools in their indictment of the system of private property, with its economic wastes and social injustices; in their belief that the remedy for existing conditions is to be found in some form of social ownership of industry, under which mutual aid would supplant competition as the law of social well-being. They also voice the sentiment of all schools of socialism in their advocacy of a society which should afford each individual a full opportunity for physical, intellectual, and moral development; in their recognition of work as a necessity, and their demand that all should participate therein; and in their insistence on the importance of environment in the molding of human character.

Their Philosophy. They differ materially from the later schools of socialists, however, in their philosophic and historical approach to a new industrial order and the methods whereby they hope to bring about this new order.

Their philosophy drew its inspiration from various sources, including the old Stoical school with its doctrines of *Jus naturale,* the early Christians, and the later Humanists and Rationalists.

Out of these various streams of philosophic thought the utopian socialists developed in substance the following line of reasoning: God or nature is good. Since God made the world, the world also is good, for a beneficent God could not have made anything which was not goodness and harmony.[1] Human society is a part of the world. Therefore God must have made it also a realm of peace and harmony, where all should be happy. Man is by nature good, and is capable of developing to the highest perfection.[2]

However, an analysis of society shows only misery and suffering. How has this come about? There is but one answer: Man has tampered with the original, perfect constitution of human society, which was in essence communistic, and by such artificial devices as private property has destroyed its natural harmony and, as a consequence, the happiness of the individual. There are therefore two orders of society: the natural order, which leads to happiness; and the unnatural or artificial order, which leads to disharmony and suffering. Those who love mankind have but one duty to perform, that of bringing back the "natural order" among men.

CHANGE THROUGH KNOWLEDGE. As a first step in this direction, men must discover the reason why mankind departed from the natural state. Investigation will show that this departure was due not to wickedness, but to error, to short-sightedness. The truth about the laws underlying the "natural order" must therefore be sought. Reason will lead us to the discovery of this truth, and once it is known, the path to a better state is open.

Since the changes in society will be brought about as a result of knowledge, the main need, as soon as truth is discovered, is to make it known, for the knowledge of it will insure its practical application. For how can a man who knows the truth fail to change conditions? "The complete change which is necessary," proclaimed Godwin, "can hardly be thought of as something to be done. It is rather a vision that men must see. They need but to understand their condition, and their chains will disappear like shadows from the dawn. When the decisive hour strikes, there will be no need to draw a sword or even move a finger. Our opponents will be too weak to withstand feelings common to all humanity." [3]

Nor will the change be brought about through class struggle. All men suffer as a result of the existing "irrational" conditions. Therefore all men, when once they know the truth, will naturally assist in the change. Thus the new doctrines should not be taught to the work-

[1] "All that God made is good." Fourier, quoted in Sombart, *Socialism and the Socialist Movement,* p. 31.

[2] "As God or nature has made all the qualities of humanity, they must be good and of necessity such as they are" (Owen), quoted in Sombart, *op. cit.,* p. 32.

[3] Quoted in *Ibid.,* p. 36.

ers alone. They should be preached to the rich as well as the poor. Indeed, special effort should be made to convert the rich and the powerful, for their conversion would help materially in reaching the masses. "Must we not first convert the rich?" asks Cabet. "Certainly, to commence with them is the best policy, for the rich and educated will have great influence in converting others of their class, and even the poor. . . . But can we hope that the rich will be converted? Why doubt it? Are there not among the rich cultivated, just, and generous men?" [4]

Thus the utopian socialists—whom Sombart prefers to characterize as rationalist socialists—believed that the way to salvation was propaganda by word and example. Many held that examples of successful colonies organized according to the principles they advocated constituted the most effective form of propaganda.

Violent means of bringing about their dream states were generally tabooed. Most of the utopians felt that little could be gained by political action or by trade union organization.

Some Defects of the Utopians. The utopians failed to appreciate the moving forces in society in the past and in the present. They overlooked the fact that many who realized the conditions of the times had no desire for change, since these conditions, bitter for the masses, meant for them definite economic advantage and power. In view of this, small, powerful minorities were ready to do all that in them lay to oppose social changes. "In other words, they [the utopians] did not see that all social conditions are the expression of the prevailing division of power among the different classes of society. And to think that the possessors of power would be prevailed upon by preaching to give up their position, was hopelessly to underrate their strength." [5]

Furthermore, they thought too highly of their own power to bring about a future society; their power of discerning the exact truth regarding social principles; their power of spreading knowledge; their power of conversion, of actually transforming society, and of conducting industry after the great change.

They also lacked historical perspective. They failed to consider, as did later socialists, the historical mission of capitalism in increasing productivity, in developing the basis for concerted action on the part of the workers, and in rendering labor ever more capable of taking charge of its industrial affairs. Social change was regarded by them as largely a result of the social discoveries of brilliant men. If someone in society five hundred years before their time had discovered the truths which they were proclaiming, and had explained these truths to their fellow

[4] *Ibid.*, p. 37.

[5] *Ibid.*, p. 39.

men, misery and suffering, they felt, would long since have disappeared. For "absolute truth is independent of time, space and of the historical development of man," and it is thus "a mere accident when and where it is discovered." [6] They also had the mistaken notion that it was possible for social thinkers to cut out a pattern of a future order in all of its details, and that mankind could be induced to follow faithfully every detail of that pattern. Nor, after their perfect state had been achieved, did they conceive that there would be perpetual change and continual readjustments thereto. And, unfortunately, their patterns for a future society and the absolute truths which they "discovered" were "different with the founder of each different school." And as each one's special kind of absolute truth, reason and justice was conditioned "by his subjective understanding, his conditions of existence, the measure of his knowledge and his intellectual training, there is no other ending possible in this conflict of absolute truths" than that they were bound to be mutually exclusive of the other." [7]

Differences among Utopians. The characters of their utopias differed widely. They differed in the extent of common property advocated. They differed in their attitude toward equality. Some, as Babeuf and Cabet, advocated absolute equality in all things; Fourier and Saint-Simon allowed for a difference in compensation, dependent on capacity; whereas Louis Blanc would have the relative needs of the workers in his ideal republic determine their compensation. They differed in their concept of the future state. On the one extreme was Owen, who felt that the state would gradually become obsolete; on the other, Louis Blanc, who went to the National Assembly and pleaded with it to begin the construction of his social workshops, nuclei of a new order.

They were "keenly critical, ingeniously suggestive, and contagiously enthusiastic." But their dreams were incapable of realization, and they had to give way to others whose schemes for social change bore some relation to reality. While, during their lifetime, they could show few tangible results, their exposure of social ills, their demand for a worthier civilization, and their faith in human development have had no small influence on later socialist thought and on social improvement.

Modern Utopian Writers. Although the school of utopian socialism virtually ended with the middle of the nineteenth century, writers of renown have continued even to the present to publish to the world their visions of new social systems which, they hoped, might evolve from

[6] Engels, *Socialism, Utopian and Scientific,* ch. I.
[7] *Ibid.,* ch. I.

the existing order. The modern writers differ from the older utopians in their realization of the ever-changing character of industrial society. They do not regard the utopia they have drawn as the last word on social development, but write largely as a means of bringing before the people the possibilities of a more equitable social order and, to some extent, of helping themselves to discover the kind of social order which would satisfy their ideals of justice and brotherhood. These portraits, although still defective in many ways, are far less fantastic and more realistic than are the "genuine utopias."

In this connection H. G. Wells declares in *A Modern Utopia:* "The utopia of a modern dreamer must needs differ in one fundamental aspect from the Nowheres and Utopias men planned before Darwin quickened the thought of the world. Those were all perfect and static states, a balance of happiness won for ever against the forces of unrest and disorder that inhere in things. One beheld a healthy and simple generation enjoying the fruits of the earth in an atmosphere of virtue and happiness, to be followed by other virtuous, happy, and entirely similar generations, until the gods grew weary. Change and development were dammed back by invincible dams for ever. But the modern utopia must be not static but kinetic, must shape not as a permanent state but as a hopeful stage, leading to a long ascent of stages. Nowadays we do not resist and overcome the great stream of things, but rather float upon it. We build now not citadels, but ships of state. For one ordered arrangement of citizens rejoicing in an equality of happiness safe and assured to them and their children for ever, we have to plan a flexible common compromise, in which a perpetually novel succession of individualities may converge most effectually upon a comprehensive onward development.' That is the first, most generalized difference between a utopia based upon modern conceptions and all the utopias that were written in the former time." [8]

BELLAMY'S "LOOKING BACKWARD." Perhaps the most popular of these "pseudo-utopias" was *Looking Backward,* written in 1887 by Edward Bellamy, an American author.[9] Within ten years this volume sold over a million copies and was translated into more than a dozen languages. Bellamy has his hero, Mr. Julian West of Boston, fall asleep

[8] Wells, H. G., *A Modern Utopia,* pp. 16–17.

[9] Bellamy was born in 1850 in Chicopee Falls, Mass., the son of a Baptist minister. He studied for some time in Union College, Schenectady, N. Y., spent a year in Germany, and later became a member of the bar. Journalism, however, attracted him, and he became a member of the *New York Post* and later of the *Springfield Union.* He was of a retiring disposition, and ever shunned the limelight. He died in 1898, at the age of 48.

under the efforts of a mesmerist on Decoration Day, 1887, and wake up in the year 2000, to discover not the squalid, shabby Boston of old, but a city beautiful, without politicians, without corruption, without riches or poverty, but with peace and plenty and equal opportunity for all based on the development of a co-operative system of production and distribution developed in every phase of industrial life.

Some of the pictures of social changes considered quite fantastic in 1887 are commonplaces today, as, for instance, when Julian West, sitting comfortably in the house of his friend, listens to the beautiful strains of the opera played in the central music hall of the city.

A few years after the publication of *Looking Backward,* Bellamy wrote *Equality,* a more scientific, but less popular piece of utopian writing. William Dean Howells' *Traveler from Altruria* was another utopian novel which attracted considerable attention during that period.

HERTZKA'S "FREELAND." On the continent of Europe, Dr. Theodor Hertzka, a Viennese economist of note, created quite a profound impression through the publication in 1890 of *Freeland—A Social Anticipation.* The publication of this book led to the organization of nearly 1000 societies in Austria and Germany whose members were determined to put the ideals expressed in the book into practice. A central committee was organized and a piece of land in British East Africa was purchased as an experiment station for Hertzka's ideas, but the difficulties in the way of the proposed colony proved to be too great. Dr. Hertzka maintains in *Freeland* that, with the development of the arts and sciences, "a moderate amount of labor ought to produce inexhaustible abundance for every one born of woman," and yet that this advance has hitherto been unable to ameliorate one human woe. Throughout his book Hertzka endeavored to portray society based on social production—co-operative associations organized by whole industries—in which the workers enjoyed the product of their own industry and thus secured a direct, economic incentive to the best endeavor.

WILLIAM MORRIS' "NEWS FROM NOWHERE." The outstanding modern English Utopias are William Morris' [10] *News from Nowhere* and H. G. Wells' *A Modern Utopia.*

[10] William Morris was born on March 24, 1834, in a small village near London. His early schooling was of no great importance. He was a voracious reader and spent much of his childhood ranging around the fields and woods. At 14 he went to Marlborough College, a preparatory school, and later to Exeter College, Oxford. In the vacations he traveled through the continent, visiting the art galleries and churches. During one of these visits he decided to abandon theology—for which he had matriculated in college—and to serve the world through the medium of art.

"England," declared Hammond in Morris' *News from Nowhere,* "was once a country of clearings amongst the woods and wastes, with a few towns interspersed, which were fortresses for the feudal army, markets for the folk, gathering places for the craftsmen. It then became a country of huge and foul workshops and fouler gambling-dens, surrounded by an ill-kept, poverty-stricken farm, pillaged by the masters of the workshops. It is now a garden, where nothing is wasted and nothing is spoilt, with the necessary dwellings, sheds, and workshops scattered up and down the country, all trim and neat and pretty. For, indeed, we should be too much ashamed of ourselves if we allowed the making of goods, even on a large scale, to carry with it the appearance, even, of desolation and misery." [11]

Morris visualizes a utopia from which big cities have disappeared. London is again a collection of villages, mingled in great woodlands and meadows, where the school children have their recreation. There are shops from which one takes the necessities of life for the asking, and great common halls, where one eats—picturesque, spacious, and beautiful. And people work for the joy of it, and all labor for useful ends.

H. G. Wells' "Modern Utopia." H. G. Wells' [12] *Modern Utopia* was written in 1905, partly with the aim of clarifying the author's own

---

After leaving Oxford, he went into an architect's office and later tried painting, modeling, embroidery, and the designing of furniture. In 1861 the firm of Morris and Company was organized. As a partner of the firm, he learned one technique after another, and the firm gained increasing fame throughout England.

In the meanwhile Morris began to write verse, and during the sixties published *The Earthly Paradise* and other poetical works. Morris became interested in the social movement through his agitation in the late seventies to prevent the war in the East which sprang, he believed, from the intention of the ruling classes to extend the field of commercial exploitation. He traveled up and down England telling of his hope in the masses. He spoke at street corners, in public parks, at political meetings. He wrote social poems and plays and romances of reform. In his *Signs of Change, Dream of John Ball, News from Nowhere,* etc., he wrote more as a poet than as a scientist. He joined the Social Democratic Federation in the early eighties and was active in the socialist movement until his death in 1896.

[11] Morris, William, *News from Nowhere* (Chas. H. Kerr edition), p. 91.

[12] H. G. Wells was born September 21, 1866, in Bromley, Kent, England, the son of an unsuccessful storekeeper who had attained some fame as a cricket player. At the age of fifteen, Wells became a clerk in a dry goods store. He ran away from this occupation, however, and later became assistant in the Midhurst Grammar School, studied at a Normal School of Science, and obtained his B.S. degree at the Royal College of Science of the University of London. He first went into teaching, but his health broke down, and he entered the field of journalism. In 1895 he published his first book of fiction. His first attempts in literature from 1895 to 1900 consisted chiefly of fantastic romances. From 1900 to 1908 he wrote a number of sociological essays, including his *Anticipations* (1901), *The Discovery of the Future*

conception of future development. In this book the great English author insists that a modern utopian must think in terms of a world economy and not, as in the older utopias, confine his imaginings to an isolated spot on some strange planet. The cornerstone of a modern utopia should be freedom. "To have free play for one's individuality is, in the modern view, the subjective triumph of existence, as survival in creative work and offspring is its objective triumph." [13] However, "no one but a despot can be perfectly free to do everything he likes," and in the state of the future society must step in to delimit those freedoms that infringe on the freedom of others, "those spendthrift liberties that waste liberty," in order to attain the maximum happiness for all. Of equal importance is that of sustenance and work.

The world state of H. G. Wells is the sole landowner of the earth, with the local governments holding it, as it were, feudally as landlords. The state or its subsidiaries hold all sources of food and power energy and develop these through tenants, farmers, and agents.[14]

These "pseudo-utopias," although more scientific than their predecessors, have many flaws from the standpoint of economic science. Appealing, however, as they have, to the imaginative and emotional side of human nature, they have furnished a powerful drive to many thousands to join the labor movement and to sacrifice their time and strength in the cause of "human emancipation."

(1901), *Mankind in the Making* (1903), *A Modern Utopia* (1905), *This Misery of Boots* (1907), *New Worlds for Old* (1908) and *First and Last Things* (1908). Later he began his series of sociological novels which brought him such fame. During the World War he wrote extensively on international problems and following the war branched out as an historian, with his *Outline of History*. He was a member of the Fabian Society during the early part of the century and in 1922 ran for Parliament as candidate of the British Labor party. See H. G. Wells' *Social Anticipation*, edited by H. W. Laidler (N. Y.: Vanguard Press, 1927).

13 Wells, H. G., *A Modern Utopia*, p. 20.

14 Among other utopias of recent years may be mentioned W. H. Hudson's *A Crystal Age*.

PART TWO

Marxism

CHAPTER 13

Beginnings of Marxism

UNTIL the middle of the last century, the school of social thought which held the center of the stage, as we have elsewhere observed, was that of *utopianism.* During the thirties and the forties, however, the concepts of the utopians were subjected to merciless criticism by a group of able writers committed to fundamental social change.

The Advent of Marxian Socialism. Among these critics of utopianism was a brilliant young Doctor of Philosophy of the University of Jena, Karl Heinrich Marx, and a young German businessman residing in England, with a bent for economics, Friedrich Engels. Their *Communist Manifesto,* issued in the revolutionary year 1848 at the behest of a small international workingmen's organization, was at once an interpretation of the rôle of the working class in past and future history and a clarion call to labor to unite for the purpose of securing its emancipation and, through that emancipation, the freedom of all mankind. It marked the definite decline in the leadership of the utopian school of thought among the advocates of a new social order. It marked at the same time the advent of Marxian, or "scientific," socialism, a social philosophy which has exerted such a powerful influence on the political, social, economic, and cultural thought of the last half century and which seems destined to play a still larger rôle in future historical developments.

Early Life of Karl Marx. The real author of "scientific" socialism was, of course, Karl Marx. The career of this remarkable student and leader of men—the outstanding working class theorist of the nineteenth century—was a striking one. Marx was born in Treves, the Rhineland, Germany, on the fifth of May, 1818. His father was a Jewish jurist, and his grandfather a German rabbi. His mother was descended from a Dutch rabbi's family, which had emigrated from Hungary to Holland in the seventeenth century.

When Karl, one of several children, was six years of age, his family embraced Christianity. In the grammar school of Treves and at the home of L. von Westphalen—his future father-in-law, and a government Privy Counsellor of a literary turn of mind—Karl received his early education. To this cultured friend, Marx afterwards dedicated his doctor's thesis, describing him as one "who welcomes every progressive movement with the enthusiasm and sober judgment of a lover of truth, and who is a living proof that idealism is no imagination, but the truth." [1]

Marx's University Days. Following his elementary education, Marx at the age of seventeen entered the University of Bonn, with the object of taking up the study of law, in deference to the wishes of his father. The next year, 1836, however, he transferred his undergraduate study to Berlin University, where he threw himself into his work with great intensity, applying himself to a wide variety of subjects, including philosophy, jurisprudence, history, literature, and art.

"Giving up social intercourse," writes Beer, "he worked night and day, making abstracts of what he read, translating Greek and Latin, working at philosophical systems, setting down a considerable number of his own thoughts, and drafting outlines of philosophy and jurisprudence, as well as writing three volumes of poems." [2] His intellectual studies during 1837, when he was still but nineteen years old, led him to reject the abstract idealism of Kant and Fichte and to seek refuge in Hegel. "From the idealism which I had cherished so long," he wrote to his father, "I fell to seeking the ideal in reality itself. . . . I had read fragments of Hegel's philosophy, the strange, rugged melody of which had not pleased me. Once again I wished to dive into the midst of the sea, this time with the resolute intention of finding a spiritual nature just as essential, concrete, and perfect as the physical, and, instead of indulging in intellectual gymnastics, bringing up pure pearls into the sunlight." [3]

His Study of Hegelian Philosophy. The Hegelian philosophy finally took possession of him. He became ill, burnt his poems and material for short stories, and during his illness and his subsequent rest at Stralau acquainted himself with Hegel's philosophy and that of his followers from beginning to end. Later he became an ardent member of the Graduates Club of the University in which he held long arguments on philosophical questions.[4]

[1] Beer, *Life and Teaching of Karl Marx*, p. 2.

[2] *Ibid.*, p. 4. [3] *Ibid.*, p. 7.

[4] Until the end of the eighteenth century, the universe and social organizations were conceived for the most part as fixed, constant, and eternal. With the coming

His father admonished him against such intellectual dissipation and urged him to follow the example of other students who attended their lectures regularly and had an eye to a future career.

---

of the nineteenth century, however, this concept gradually began to give way to a concept of eternal change, endless evolution. All things were in a flux, a state of becoming and disappearing. The new philosophy demanded a new logic. It was G. W. H. Hegel (1770–1831) who made a careful attempt to formulate this new logic. The essence of the logic which he formulated was the dialectic. Hegel's dialectic method conceived that change took place through the struggle of antagonistic elements and the resolution of these contradictory elements into a synthesis, the first two elements forming a new and higher concept by virtue of their union.

Hegel obscured his meaning by the use of a rather difficult phraseology. The *thing* or *being* against which the contradiction operated he called the positive. The antagonistic element, or antithesis, was the negation. To Hegel the contradiction, antithesis, or negation was the "source of all movement and life; only insofar as it contains a contradiction can anything have movement, power, and effect." A continued operation of the negation led to the negation of negation or synthesis.

The dialectic method of Hegel colored all of Marx's social thinking. He was always on the outlook for a negation, an antithesis, in the belief that progress began with its appearance.

In his *Holy Family,* written in 1844, Marx used the Hegelian dialectic, for instance, in describing the class struggle. There is the positive—private property—Marx maintains, and the negative, or antithesis—the proletariat. As a result of the conflict between the rising proletariat—the antithesis—and private property—the thesis—we might expect to see the emergence of a new form of society—a synthesis—under which the proletariat does not "become the absolute side of society, for it triumphs only by abolishing itself and its opposite. In this way both the proletariat and its conditioned opposite, private property, are done away with." (In Mehring, *Collected Works and Literary Remains of Marx and Engels,* Vol. II, p. 132.)

Hegel himself failed to apply his dialectic method to the social relations, his nationalistic sentiments being definitely reflected in his philosophic system, disagreeing as he did with the view that the universe arose out of pure reason, out of the logical idea.

Although Marx was an ardent follower of the philosophic method of Hegel, he took issue with the Prussian state. Many differences of opinion developed among Hegel's disciples, chiefly in regard to the doctrines of the Deity, immortality, and the personality of Christ. The "Young Hegelians" took the unorthodox point of view. In politics many of them were mild liberals. Karl Marx, the youngest of the "Young Hegelians," was the first to apply the dialectic method to the social sciences.

In commenting on the value of Hegel's philosophy to the revolutionary thought of the day, Engels declared: "Just there lay the true significance and the revolutionary character of the Hegelian philosophy . . . in that it gave the *coup de grace* to finiteness of results of human thought and action. Truth . . . was no longer . . . a collection of ready-made dogmatic statements, which, once discovered, must be thoroughly learned; truth lay now in the process of knowledge itself, in the long historical development of learning, which climbs from lower to ever higher heights of knowledge, without ever reaching the point of so-called absolute truth. And just as little as knowledge can history find a conclusion, complete in one completed ideal condition of humanity. A completed society, a perfect state, are things which can only exist in phantasies. On the contrary, all successive historical conditions are places of pilgrimage in the endless evolutionary progress of human society from the lower to the higher." (Friedrich Engels, *Feuerbach, The Roots of the Socialist Philosophy,* pp. 41–3.)

"Indeed," the elderly Marx declared in a fatherly letter to his restless son, "these men sleep quite peacefully except when they now and then devote a whole or part of a night to pleasure, whereas my clever and gifted son Karl passes wretched, sleepless nights, wearying body and mind with cheerless study, forbearing all pleasures with the sole object of applying himself to abstruse studies; but what he builds today he destroys again tomorrow, and in the end he finds that he has destroyed what he already had, without having gained anything from other people. At last the body begins to ail and the mind gets confused, whilst these ordinary folks steal along in easy marches, and attain their goal if not better at least more comfortably than those who contemn youthful pleasures and undermine their health in order to snatch at the ghost of erudition, which they could probably have exercised more successfully in an hour spent in the society of competent men—with social enjoyment into the bargain."[5]

But Karl was bent on seeking the truth, and abjured an easy life. Nor did an official career have any appeal for him. He wrote:

Let us not in base subjection
  Brood away our fearful life,
When with deed and aspiration
  We might enter in the strife.

Completion of Doctorate and Entry into Journalism. Karl's ambition soon turned toward a lectureship at the University of Bonn, where his friend Bruno Bauer hoped to be appointed professor. He gave up the study of law, became completely engrossed in philosophy, and in 1841 at Jena at the early age of twenty-three received the degree of Doctor of Philosophy, after defending his dissertation on the *Natural Philosophies of Democritus and Epicurus.* He applied for the lectureship, but the Prussian universities were not free centers of thought and turned down the applications of both Bauer and Marx on the ground that they were too non-conformist in their attitude.

Thereupon young Marx turned to free-lance journalism. In doing so he resolved to employ the weapon of the Young Hegelians of that period—the weapon of criticism—for the purpose of sweeping away old dogmas and of bringing about the spiritual freedom of Germany, by which he understood freedom in religion and liberalism in politics.

His Study of Economics. About that time a group of liberals in the Rhine-provinces founded a newspaper. Marx, a friend of the editor,

[5] Beer, *op. cit.*, pp. 9, 10.

was asked to contribute to it. His contributions were so trenchant that on the resignation of the editor in October, 1842, young Marx was asked to take his place. It was at that time that he was first forced to begin a serious study of economic problems. In his *Critique of Political Economy* (1859) he writes:

"As editor of the *Rheinische Zeitung,* in 1842 and 1843, I came up, for the first time, against the difficulty of having to take part in the controversy over so-called material interests. The proceedings of the Diet of the Rhine provinces in regard to wood stealing and parceling out of landed property, and their action towards the farmers of the Moselle districts, and lastly debates on free trade and protection, gave the first stimulus to my investigation of economic questions. On the other hand, an echo of French socialism and communism, feebly philosophical in tone, had at that time made itself felt in the columns of the *Rheinische Zeitung.* I declared myself against superficiality, confessing, however, at the same time that the studies I had made so far did not allow me to venture any judgment of my own on the significance of the French tendencies." [6]

Conversion to Socialism. Marx soon retired from the paper in order to have more leisure to devote to these studies. His retirement came at a time when he was contemplating marriage with Jenny von Westphalen, the charming and cultured daughter of Marx's fatherly friend, the Privy Councillor. During his reading and thinking in the years 1843 and 1844 he delved as deeply into the socialist literature of the times as he had some six years before into the philosophical writings of Hegel. He emerged from his reading at the age of twenty-five or twenty-six a convinced socialist.

In the following two years he laid the foundation for the historical theories with which his name is associated. In a letter from Cologne in May, 1843, he remarked:

"This system of acquisition and commercialism, of possession and of exploitation of mankind, is leading even more swiftly than the increase of population, to a breach within the present society, which the old system cannot heal, because indeed it has not the power either to heal or create, but only to exist and enjoy." [7]

His Belief in the Importance of Labor. In a letter in September, 1843, he showed his acquaintance with the writings of the utopian socialists, Fourier, Proudhon, Cabet, and others, and asserted that his task did not consist in the setting up of utopias, but in the criticism of exist-

[6] *Ibid.*, pp. 13–4; Marx, *Critique of Political Economy* (Kerr Edition), p. 10.
[7] Beer, *op. cit.*, p. 15.

ing social and political conditions, "in interpreting the struggles and aspirations of the age."

By the winter of 1843 he had come to the conclusion that if any revolutionary change was to be brought about in industrial conditions it was to come through the efforts of labor, not of the owners of industry. In his introduction to Hegel's *Philosophy of Law*, for instance, he maintained that the positive conditions for the German revolution and liberation were to be found "in the formation of a class in chains, a class which finds itself in bourgeois society, but which is not of it, of an order which shall break up all orders. . . . When the proletariat proclaims the dissolution of the existing order of things, it is merely announcing the secret of its own existence, for it is in itself the virtual dissolution of this order of things. When the proletariat desires the negation of private property, it is merely elevating as a general principle of society what it already involuntarily embodies in itself as the negative product of society." [8]

His Function Criticism, Not Dogma. The foregoing was written in Paris, whence Marx had gone with his young wife in October, 1843, to take up the editorship of the *Franco-German Year Books*. He declared that the aim of these books was "the fearless criticism of all existing institutions—fearless in the sense that it does not shrink from its logical consequences, or from the conflict with the powers that be. I am therefore not with those who would have us set up a standard of dogmatism; far from it; we should rather try to give what help we can to those involved in dogma, so that they may realize the implications of their own principles. So, for example, communism as taught by Cabet . . . and others is a dogmatic abstraction. . . . We do not then proclaim to the world in doctrinaire fashion any new principle: 'This is the truth, bow down before it!' We do not say: 'Refrain from strife, it is foolishness!' We only make clear to men for what they are really struggling, and to the consciousness of this they must come whether they will or not." [9]

Beginning of Friendship with Engels. But one number of the *Franco-Prussian Year Books* appeared in the spring of 1844. This number contained among other contributions an article by Friedrich Engels, then a young businessman of Manchester, aged 24, which condemned the economic system in the name of justice, though refusing to accept the socialist utopias of Owen and other utopians. The contact afforded by this article led to an enduring and quite beautiful friendship between Marx and Engels, a friendship which made it possible for Marx to continue his literary career, although at times amid great hardship,

[8] *Ibid.*, pp. 16, 17.

[9] *Ibid.*, p. 18.

and without which "Marx, with his unpractical, helpless, and, at the same time, proud and uncompromising disposition, would most probably have perished in exile." [10]

[10] *Ibid.*, p. 20. Engels was born in Barmen, November 28, 1820, two and a half years after the birth of Marx. He was the son of a wealthy manufacturer and was brought up in an extremely conservative environment. On graduating from Barmen high school he went to the gymnasium of Elberfeld, but entered his father's business a year before his final examination. In 1841 he served in the Guard Artillery in Berlin and became quite an authority on military science. Following this experience he went to Manchester as an agent of the spinning mill of Ermen and Engels, of which his father was a partner. For a number of years prior thereto he had been interested in the newer developments in philosophy and social thought, and on his way to England dropped in at the editorial office of the *Rheinische Zeitung*, where he met Marx for the first time. At that time Marx and Engels failed to see eye to eye, and Engels' reception was cool. In England he connected himself with the Chartist, the utopian socialist, and the trade union movements, and became intimately acquainted with the newer developments in the capitalist industry. He gathered material at this time which formed the basis of his *Condition of the Working Classes in England in 1844*, a powerful indictment of the capitalist order.

On returning to the continent, Engels collaborated with Marx in writing *The Holy Family*. In 1845 he gave up the mercantile business, which he greatly disliked, and went to Brussels, where Marx was then doing his work. The two were busy during the remaining two years in research, writing and organization. Engels visited London in the summer of 1847 as a representative of the Paris group, to formulate a new program for the Communist League, and helped in writing the *Communist Manifesto*.

In 1849 he joined a volunteer corps in the Palatinate, which was demanding a constitution for the whole German Empire, and on his return to London collaborated with Marx on the revolutionary movements of 1848–50. In 1850 he re-entered business in order to earn enough to permit Marx to continue his literary work.

For the following twenty years Marx and Engels saw little of one another, but were nevertheless in almost daily correspondence. They exchanged freely their every new economic discovery and published their articles only after each had been submitted to the other for criticism. Engels also aided Marx extensively in his work for the *New York Tribune*. He was particularly helpful to Marx in supplying actual data from industrial life. "Without you," wrote Marx, "I could never have brought the work [*Capital*] to a conclusion, and I assure you that a load like a mountain has always lain on my mind; that chiefly on my account you have allowed your splendid powers to go to waste and to grow rusty in commerce."

In 1860 Engels' father died, and he became partner in the business. In writing to Marx later about his desire to get out of the commercial field, he said: "I long for nothing so much as to get free from this dastardly commerce, which, with all the loss of time involved, is completely demoralizing me. So long as I am in it, I am useless for anything; particularly since I became partner, it has become worse, because of the greater responsibilities. Were it not for the larger income, I should really prefer to be a clerk again."

In 1869 he sold out his partnership, and obtained a large sum of money in return for his promise not to open up business in the same trade on his own account. Through this deal he was able to pay Marx some 350 pounds a year for a number of years. From September, 1870, when Engels moved to London, to the death of Marx, the two kindred spirits worked side by side. Marx devoted himself chiefly to the working out of systematic social and economic theories, while Engels dealt more largely with the discussion of current questions of the day in the light of these theories.

The Germs of Historical Materialism. Following the discontinuance of the *Year Books,* Marx spent much time in the study of English and French systems of political economy, of socialism, and of history.[11] In the autumn of 1844 he published *The Holy Family,* an attempt to force the Young Hegelians to enter the field of social criticism. The book contains the germs of the materialist conception of history and of the theory of the class struggle. Marx criticized his friend Bruno Bauer for not realizing that it was impossible to understand any period "without having studied, for example, the industries of that period, the immediate means of production of life itself." He maintained that *ideas were potent in the development of society only as they represented the interests of the masses.* "Otherwise the ideas might indeed stir up enthusiasm, but they could not achieve any results. . . . Ideas have only had effective results insofar as they correspond to mass interest. The enthusiasm to which such ideas gave birth arose from the illusion that these ideas signified the liberation of mankind in general."

Marx's Forced Departure from France. During this time Marx became acquainted with Heine, Proudhon, and other reformers, and contributed frequently to the Paris *Vorwaerts.* In 1845, at the instigation of the Prussian government, he was forced to leave Paris and went, bag and baggage, to Brussels. There he remained until the outbreak of the European revolution of February, 1848, reading avidly the many works on political economy that Engels had placed at his disposal and embodying his researches in his *Misère de la Philosophie,* a polemic against Proudhon, published in 1847, which embodied many of the doctrines of social conflict and social change stated more popularly in the *Communist Manifesto* of the following year.

On Marx's death, Engels translated, completed, and secured the publication of many of Marx's works. He died on August 6, 1895, at the age of 75. His chief works were *Socialism, Utopian and Scientific*—one of the two or three foremost classics on scientific socialism; *Condition of Working Class in England in 1844; Origin of the Family;* and *Feuerbach, The Roots of the Socialist Philosophy.*

Engels is described as tall, slender, erect in bearing, quick and witty in speech, and a man of unusual intellectual grasp. He shunned the limelight and was constantly belittling his work in comparison with that of his co-worker. He was a born optimist and was, especially in the early part of his life, constantly viewing the revolution as but a few years ahead. (See the *Life and Works of Friedrich Engels.* By Zelda Kahan Coates, 1920. London.)

[11] Writing of the literary atmosphere of Paris at the time (1840–43), Louis Reybaud, a contemporary French writer, observed: "For some time there has arisen a great concert of recriminations and anathemas against society. Every day a new champion appears in the arena to challenge the existing order; now in the name of literature, now in the name of science. The detractors raise such a noise that few writers dare defend it." (*"Etudes sur les reformateurs ou socialistes Modernes,"* Vol. II, p. 1, Paris. 1843.)

The Communist Manifesto. Since 1836 German workers living abroad had been organized into the League of the Just, which had correspondents in various centers and since 1840 had its headquarters in London. Hearing about this able student from its Paris and Brussels members, the League sent one of its members to Brussels in January, 1847, to learn more about Marx. The League subsequently became the League of Communists and held its first Congress in London in the summer of 1847, attended among others by Engels. At the second Congress in December, 1847, Marx also appeared, and he and Engels were commissioned to prepare a new program. The program prepared was the now famous *Communist Manifesto*.[12]

History One of Class Struggles. Although the joint production of Marx and Engels, the *Manifesto* undoubtedly owed more to Marx, then a young man of twenty-nine, than to his co-worker, then in his twenty-seventh year.

"I consider myself bound to state," declared Engels, "that the fundamental proposition which forms the nucleus belongs to Marx. That proposition is: *that in every historical epoch the prevailing mode of economic production and exchange, and the social organization necessarily following from it, form the basis upon which is built up, and from which alone can be explained the political and intellectual history of that epoch; that consequently the whole history of mankind (since the dissolution of primitive tribal society, holding land in common ownership) has been a history of class struggles, contests between exploiting and exploited, ruling and oppressed classes; that the history of these class struggles forms a series of evolution in which, now-a-days, a stage has been reached where the exploited and oppressed classes (the proletariat) cannot attain its emancipation from the sway of the exploiting and ruling class (the bourgeoisie) without, at the same time, and once for all, emancipating society at large from all exploitation, oppression, class-distinction and class struggles.*

"This proposition which, in my opinion, *is destined to do for history what Darwin's theory had done for biology,* we, both of us, had been gradually approaching for some years before 1845." (Italics ours.)[13]

12 Marx was also the author of the preamble to the rules of the Communist League: "The object of the League," the rules read, "is the overthrow of the bourgeoisie, the rule of the proletariat, the abolition of the old bourgeoisie society which is based on class antagonism, and the establishment of a new society without classes and without private property."

13 *Communist Manifesto* (Rand School Edition, 1919), Preface, p. vii.

CHAPTER 14

The Communist Manifesto and the Revolutions of 1848

"A SPECTRE is haunting Europe—the spectre of communism," runs the opening sentence of the *Communist Manifesto*.[1] "All the powers of old Europe have entered into a bold alliance to exorcise this spectre; Pope and Czar, Metternich and Guizot, French Radicals and German police spies." In view of the growing power of communism it behooves the communists to publish openly, in the face of the whole world, "their views, their aims, their tendencies, and meet this nursery tale of the spectre of communism with a manifesto of the party itself." [2]

Scope of the Communist Manifesto. CLASS STRUGGLES. The *Manifesto* is roughly divided into four sections. Part One considers the rise and development of the bourgeoisie, that is, the class of modern capitalists, owners of the means of social production and employers of wage labor; and of the proletariat, wage-earners who, having no means of production of their own, sell their labor power in order to live.

The history of recorded society, it maintains, is a history of class

[1] The question has often arisen as to why the *Manifesto* was called "communist," rather than "socialist," although Marx and Engels are regarded as the fathers of scientific socialism. Friedrich Engels, in his Preface to the 1888 edition, gives the following explanation:

In 1847 socialists were commonly regarded, on the one hand, as adherents of the various utopian systems and, on the other, as social reformers who, "by all manner of tinkering, professed to redress, without any danger to capital and profit, all sorts of social grievances; in both cases men outside the working class movement, and looking rather to the 'educated classes' for support." On the other hand, "Whatever portion of the working class had become convinced of the insufficiency of mere political revolutions, and had proclaimed the necessity of a total social change, that portion then called itself communist. . . . And as our notion from the very beginning was that 'the emancipation of the working class must be the act of the working class itself,' there could be no doubt as to which of the two names we must take."

[2] Marx and Engels, *Communist Manifesto* (Rand School Edition), p. 11; to avoid confusion, due to the existence of numerous editions of the *Manifesto,* we will not refer to particular pages in further references in this chapter.

struggles. Under slavery and feudalism these struggles were carried on, sometimes openly, sometimes secretly, between oppressor and oppressed, and ended "either in a revolutionary reconstruction of society-at-large, or in the common ruin of the contending classes."

Capitalism appeared with the discovery of America, the opening up of Asia, and the consequent development of world markets. Under the feudal regime industrial production was monopolized by closed guilds. These guilds were able to supply a limited local market, but were, in the nature of the case, unable to adjust themselves to international commerce. The guilds were succeeded by the manufacturing system. At first goods were manufactured by hand. Hand power, however, was soon superseded by steam power and the small tool by steam-driven machinery. The appearance of steam and machinery revolutionized industrial production and made it possible to send a steady stream of goods to distant parts of the earth. A world market in turn gave a great impetus to communication by land and sea.

THE REVOLUTIONARY RÔLE AND DEVELOPMENTS OF CAPITALISM. The capitalist class during the last hundred years has played a most revolutionary part. Wherever it has obtained the upper hand, it has torn asunder all of the old feudal relationships and has "left no other nexus between man and man than naked self-interest, than callous 'cash payment.' It has drowned the most heavenly ecstasies of religious fervor, of chivalrous enthusiasm, of Philistine sentimentalism in the icy water of egotistical calculation. It has resolved personal worth into exchange value, and in place of the numberless indefeasible chartered freedoms, has set up that single, unconscionable freedom—free trade. In one word, for exploitation veiled by religious and political illusions, it has substituted naked, shameless, direct, brutal exploitation. The bourgeoisie has stripped of its halo every occupation hitherto honored and looked up to with reverent awe. It has converted the physician, the lawyer, the priest, the poet, the man of science, into its paid laborers."

On the other hand, its achievements have been vast. "It has accomplished wonders far exceeding Egyptian pyramids, Roman aqueducts, and Gothic cathedrals; it has conducted expeditions that put in the shade all former exoduses of nations and crusades. . . . Constant revolutionizing of production, uninterrupted disturbance of all social conditions, everlasting uncertainty, and agitation distinguish the bourgeois epoch from all earlier ones. . . . All fixed, fast, frozen relations, with their train of ancient and venerable prejudices and opinions, are swept away, all new formed ones become antiquated before they can ossify. All that is solid melts into the air, all that is holy is profaned, and man is at last compelled to face, with sober senses, his real conditions of life, and his relations with his kind."

Capitalism and World Interdependence. The need for constantly expanding markets impels the capitalist class to advance all over the globe. Production and consumption become cosmopolitan in their character. There develops a universal interdependence of nations. Intellectual creations also become international and we begin to develop a world literature. The most barbarian nations are drawn into civilization. "The cheap prices of its commodities are the heavy artillery with which it batters down all Chinese walls. . . . It compels all nations, on pain of extinction, to adopt the bourgeois mode of production. . . . In a word, it creates a world after its own image."

Centralization under Capitalism. "The capitalist class has agglomerated population, centralized means of production, and has concentrated property in a few hands." It has at the same time accelerated political centralization. "The bourgeoisie, during its rule of scarce one hundred years, has created more massive and more colossal productive forces than have all preceding generations together. Subjection of nature's forces to man, machinery, application of chemistry to industry and agriculture, steam-navigation, railways, electric telegraphs, clearing of whole continents for cultivation, canalization of rivers, whole populations conjured out of the ground—what earlier century has even a presentiment that such productive forces slumbered in the lap of social labor?"

The modern capitalist regime, which has sprouted from the ruins of feudal society, has not abolished class struggles, but has created new classes, and at the same time has simplified the class antagonisms. "Society as a whole," the *Manifesto* reads, "is more and more splitting up into two great hostile camps, into two great classes directly facing each other: bourgeoisie and proletariat."

The Appearance of a World Market. The development of world markets through the discovery of America, the opening up of Asia, etc., the *Manifesto* continues, dealt a death blow to the feudal system of industry under which industrial production was monopolized by close guilds. The guilds were succeeded by the manufacturing system, and this system was soon revolutionized by the appearance of steam and machinery. Modern industry has established the world market. This market has given a great impetus to commerce and communication by land and sea.

Increased Power of the Capitalist. With the development of capitalism the capitalist class as such continually increased in industrial power, an increase which was accompanied by increased political power. "The executive of the modern state is but a committee for managing the common affairs of the whole bourgeoisie."

Industrial Crises—"Seeds of Destruction." Feudal society gave birth to forces that it could no longer control. At a certain stage in its development feudal property relations became fetters binding the developing commerce and industry of that time. The fetters had to be burst asunder. A similar situation is beginning to confront bourgeois society. "A society that has conjured up such gigantic means of production and exchange is like a sorcerer, who is no longer able to control the powers of the nether world whom he has called up by his spells." For many decades past the history of industry has been a history of the revolt of the modern productive forces against modern conditions of production.

"It is enough to mention the commercial crises that by their periodical return put on its trial, each time more threateningly, the existence of the entire bourgeois society." In these crises there breaks out an epidemic of over-production. Industry and commerce seem to be destroyed, because there is too much civilization, too much means of subsistence, too much industry, too much commerce. The conditions of bourgeois society are too narrow to comprise the wealth created by them. The bourgeoisie overcomes each crisis by mass destruction of productive forces, by the conquest of new markets and the more thorough exploitation of the old ones, that is to say, by paving the way for more extensive and more destructive crises, and by diminishing the means whereby crises are prevented. "The weapons with which the bourgeoisie felled feudalism to the ground are now turned against the bourgeoisie itself."

The Development of the Working Class. "But not only has the bourgeoisie forged the weapons that bring death to itself; it has also called into existence the men who are to wield those weapons—the modern working class—the proletarians." The modern working class is developed in the same proportion as is the bourgeoisie. "Owing to the extensive use of machinery and the division of labor, the work of labor has lost its individual character and its charm. The worker becomes an appendage of the machine, and it is only the most simple, the most monotonous and most easily acquired knack that is required of him. Hence, the cost of production of a workman is restricted almost entirely to the means of subsistence that he requires for his maintenance, and for the propagation of the race. . . . In proportion as the use of machinery and division of labor increases, in the same proportion the burden of toil increases, whether by prolongation of the working hours, by increase of the work exacted in a given time, or by increased speed of the machinery."

Modern industry has converted the small shop into the great factory. The workers are crowded together, enslaved by the capitalists and by the machines alike, continues the *Manifesto.* With the development of machinery, women's labor gradually supersedes men's labor. As soon as the worker receives his wages in cash, he is set upon by other members of the bourgeoisie—the landlord, the shopkeeper, and others.

DISAPPEARANCE OF MIDDLE CLASS. The lower strata of the middle class—the small tradesmen, the shopkeepers, the handicraftsmen, the peasants—all sink gradually into the proletariat, partly because they cannot compete with their small capital against the large capitalists, and partly because their specialized skill is rendered worthless by new methods of production. "Thus the proletariat is recruited from all classes of the population."

ORGANIZATION OF WORKERS. The working class goes through various stages of development. From its birth it carries on a struggle with the capitalist class. At first that struggle is conducted by the individual worker, then by the work people in the factory, then by the operatives in one trade, in one locality. The contest is at first waged against the machinery as such, and much is destroyed. The workers are enlisted by the bourgeoisie in the beginning of their career in a fight against absolute monarchy. Machinery tends to obliterate distinctions of labor and nearly everywhere reduces wages to the same low level. Their livelihood becomes ever more precarious. Collisions between them and the capitalists assume increasingly the character of collisions between two classes. "Thereupon the workers begin to form combinations (trade unions) against the bourgeoisie; they club together in order to keep up the rate of wages; they form permanent associations in order to make provision beforehand for these occasional revolts. Here and there the contest breaks out in riots."

The workers have occasional victories. Their unions become more expansive. Their growth is aided by the increased means of communication. The struggle becomes a national one. It also becomes political in its nature.

EMERGENCE OF LABOR PARTIES. The proletarians form a political party. The party is continually upset as a result of competition between the workers themselves. "But it ever rises up again, stronger, firmer, mightier. It compels legislative recognition of particular interests of the workers by taking advantage of the divisions among the bourgeoisie itself." The capitalists, involved in contests with other capitalists of their own and other countries, are often compelled to appeal to the workers for help. In so doing the ruling class "supplies the proletariat with its own elements of political and general education; in other words, it furnishes the proletariat with weapons for fighting the bourgeoisie."

Proletarization of Other Classes. Further, entire sections of the ruling classes are precipitated into the working class, or at least the conditions of their existence are threatened. "These also supply the proletariat with fresh elements of enlightenment and progress.

"Finally, in times when the class-struggle nears the decisive hour, the process of dissolution going on within the ruling class—in fact, within the whole range of an old society—assumes such a violent, glaring character that a small section of the ruling class cuts itself adrift and joins the revolutionary class, the class that holds the future in its hands. Just as, therefore, at an earlier period, a section of the nobility went over to the bourgeoisie, so now a portion of the bourgeoisie goes over to the proletariat, and in particular a portion of the bourgeois ideologists who have raised themselves to the level of comprehending theoretically the historical movement as a whole."

Labor the Only Revolutionary Class. Of all the classes that face the capitalists, the proletariat alone is the really revolutionary class. Other classes, such as the small manufacturer and the peasant, finally disappear, fighting the while against the bourgeoisie to save themselves from extinction. They are reactionary, as they try to roll back the wheel of history. If revolutionary, they are so on account of their impending transfer to the proletariat. They defend not their present but their future interests. "The social scum, that passively rotting mass thrown off by the lowest layers of old society, may, here and there, be swept into the movement by a proletarian revolution; its conditions of life, however, prepare it far more for the part of a bribed tool of reactionary intrigue."

Movement of Immense Majority. The proletarian is without property. Modern subjection to capital has stripped him of every trace of national character. "Law, morality, religion, are to him so many bourgeois prejudices, behind which lurk in ambush just as many bourgeois interests." When other classes get the upper hand, they seek to subject society to their domination. The workers, however, "cannot become masters of the productive forces of society, except by abolishing their own previous mode of appropriation. They have nothing of their own to secure and fortify. . . . All previous historical movements were movements of minorities, or in the interest of minorities. The proletarian movement is a self-conscious, independent movement of the immense majority. The proletariat, the lowest stratum of our present society, cannot stir, cannot raise itself up without the whole superincumbent strata of official society being sprung into the air."

The struggle of the worker is at first a national struggle. "The proletariat of each country must, of course, first of all settle matters with its own bourgeoisie." It later becomes international. "We traced," write the authors, "the more or less veiled civil war, raging within existing society, up to the point where that war breaks out into open revolution, and where the violent overthrow of the bourgeoisie lays the foundation for the sway of the proletariat."

INCREASING MISERY OF LABOR. The serf, under serfdom, raised himself to membership in the commune. The petty bourgeois under feudalism managed to develop into the bourgeois. "The modern laborer, on the contrary, instead of rising with the progress of industry, sinks deeper and deeper below the conditions of his own class. He becomes a pauper, and pauperism develops more rapidly than population and wealth. And here it becomes evident that the bourgeoisie is unfit any longer to be the ruling class in society, and to impose its conditions of existence upon society as an over-riding law. It is unfit to rule, because it is incompetent to assure an existence to its slave within his slavery, because it cannot help letting him sink into such a state that it has to feed him, instead of being fed by him."

CAPITALISTS' PRODUCTION OF THEIR OWN GRAVE DIGGERS. The essential condition of the existence of the capitalist class is the formation and increase of capital. The condition for capital is wage labor. Wage labor cannot exist without competition between laborers. The development of modern capital brings labor together into combinations, therefore cutting "from under its feet the very foundation on which the bourgeoisie produces and appropriates products. What the bourgeoisie therefore produces, above all, are its own grave diggers. Its fall and the victory of the proletariat are equally inevitable."

RELATION OF COMMUNISTS TO WORKING CLASS. After thus prophesying the downfall of capitalism and the supremacy of the producing class, Marx and Engels turn to the second section of the *Manifesto,* a section devoted to the relation of the workers to the communists or socialists. The authors insist that the communists or socialists are part of the working class and decry any idea of isolation:

"The communists do not form a separate party opposed to other working-class parties.

"They have no interest separate and apart from those of the proletariat as a whole.

"They do not set up any sectarian principles of their own, by which to shape and mold the proletarian movement.

"The communists are distinguished from other working class parties by this only: 1. In the national struggles of the proletarians of the different countries, they point out and bring to the front the common interests of the entire proletariat, independent of all nationality. 2. In the various stages of development which the struggle of the working class against the bourgeoisie has to pass through, they always and everywhere represent the interests of the movement as a whole. They are the most advanced and resolute section of the working classes of every country, that section which pushes forward all others; on the other hand, theoretically, they have over the great mass of the proletariat the advantage of clearly understanding the line of march, the conditions, and the ultimate general results of the proletarian movement.

"The immediate aim of the communists is the same as that of all the other proletarian parties: formation of the proletariat into a class, overthrow of the bourgeois supremacy, conquest of the power by the proletariat."

The conclusions of the communists are not based on ideas discovered by a universal reformer, but spring from an historical movement going on under our very eyes.

ANSWER TO CHARGES AGAINST COMMUNISTS. The remainder of the section takes up one by one the charges hurled at communists. Communism does not intend to deprive any man of the power to appropriate the products of society, but merely "of the power to subjugate the labor of others by means of such appropriation." The capitalist bemoans the loss of culture resulting from a producer's regime, but capitalist culture for the enormous majority "is a mere training to act as a machine." The communists are accused of desiring community of women, but their whole point is merely the abolition of "the status of women as mere instruments of production. For the rest it is self-evident that the abolition of the present system of production must bring with it the abolition of the community of women springing from that system, i.e., of prostitution both public and private."

DISAPPEARANCE OF NATIONAL ANTAGONISMS BETWEEN PEOPLES. Communists are reproached for desiring to abolish countries and nationalities. "The working men have no country. We cannot take from them what they do not possess. Since the proletariat must first of all acquire political supremacy, must rise to be the leading class in the nation, it is, so far, itself national, though not in the bourgeois sense of the word. National differences and antagonisms between peoples are daily more and more vanishing, owing to the development of the bourgeoisie, to freedom of commerce, to the world market, to uniformity in the mode of production and in the conditions of life corresponding thereto. The supremacy of the proletariat will cause them to vanish still faster. . . . In proportion as the exploitation of one individual by another is put an end to, the exploitation of one nation by another will also be put an end to. In proportion as the antagonism between classes within the nation vanishes, the hostility of one nation to another will come to an end."

THE COMMUNIST PROGRAM. The *Manifesto* then turns to the communist program. It maintains that "the first step in the revolution by the working class is to raise the proletariat to the position of ruling class, to win the battles of democracy. The proletariat will use its political supremacy to wrest, by degrees, all capital from the bourgeoisie, to centralize all instruments of production in the hands of the state, i.e., of the proletariat organized as the ruling class; and to increase the total productive forces as rapidly as possible."

In the beginning this cannot be accomplished except by measures "which appear economically insufficient and untenable, but which in the course of the movement outstrip themselves, necessitate further inroads upon the old social order, and are unavoidable as a means of revolutionizing the mode of production."

IMMEDIATE DEMANDS. The *Manifesto* thereupon enumerates some of these immediate measures. They include the abolition of property in land and application of all rents of land to public purposes; a heavy progressive or graduated income tax; abolition of all right of inheritance; confiscation of the property of all emigrants and rebels; centralization of credit in the hands of the state by means of a national bank with state capital and an exclusive monopoly; centralization of the means of communication and transport in the hands of the state; extension of factories and instruments of production owned by the state; the bringing into cultivation of waste lands, and the improvement of soil generally in accordance with a common plan; equal liability of all to labor; the establishment of industrial armies, especially for agriculture; combination of agriculture with manufacturing industries; gradual abolition of the distinction between town and country by a more equitable distribution of the population over the country; free education of all children in public schools; abolition of children's factory labor in its present form; combination of education with industrial production, etc. A number of these immediate demands have since been secured by the workers. Other demands labor is still trying to achieve.

Abolition of Own Supremacy by Working Class. The Second Section concludes that when, in the course of development, class distinctions have disappeared and production is controlled by the whole people, political power will lose its political character. "Political power, properly so-called, is merely the organized power of one class for oppressing another. If the proletariat during its contest with the bourgeoisie is compelled, by the force of circumstances, to organize itself as a class, if, by means of a revolution, it makes itself the ruling class, and, as such, sweeps away by force the old conditions of production, then it will, along with these conditions, have swept away the conditions for the existence of class antagonisms, and of classes generally, and will therefore have abolished its own supremacy as a class.

"In the place of the old bourgeois society, with its classes and class antagonisms, we shall have an association in which the free development of each is the condition for the free development of all."

Criticism of Utopian Socialism. A terse criticism of various forms of so-called socialism follows in Section III. "The attacks of the utopian socialists on every principle of existing society," declared Marx and Engels, "were full of the most valuable material for the enlightenment of the working class." On the other hand, the proletariat, yet in its infancy, offered to the utopians "a spectacle of a class without any historical initiative or any independent political movement. . . . Historical action is to yield to their personal inventive action, historically created conditions of emancipation to fantastic ones, and the gradual, spontaneous class organization of the proletariat, to an organization of society especially contrived by these inventors. Future society resolves itself, in their eyes, into the propaganda of the practical carrying out of their social plans. . . . They habitually appeal to society-at-large, without distinction of class; nay, by preference, to the ruling class. For how can people, when once they understand their system, fail to see in it the best possible plan of the best possible state of society? Hence they reject all political, and especially all revolutionary action; they wish to attain their ends by peaceful means, and endeavor, by small experiments, necessarily doomed to failure, and by the force of example to pave the way for the new social gospel. . . ."

Co-operate with Other Democratic Forces. The communists fight, we are told in the final section, "for the attainment of the immediate aims, for the enforcement of the momentary interests of the working-class; but in the movement of the present they also represent and take care of the future of that movement." In France they ally themselves with one party, the Social Democracy; in Switzerland, Poland, and Germany with other parties.

"In Germany, they fight with the bourgeoisie whenever it acts in a revolutionary way against the absolute monarchy, the feudal squirearchy, and the petit bourgeoisie," at the same time showing the masses the antagonism that exists between the bourgeoisie and the proletariat. They turn their attention chiefly to Germany, "because that country is on the eve of a bourgeois revolution" that is bound to be carried out under more advanced conditions than in England or France, and that will be but the prelude to an immediately following proletarian revolution. In short, the communists everywhere support every revolutionary movement against the existing social and political order of things. "Finally, they labor everywhere for the union and agreement of the democratic parties of all countries."

FOR FORCIBLE OVERTHROW. Marx and Engels declared that the communists refuse to conceal their aims. They insist that "their ends can be attained only by a forcible overthrow of all existing social conditions. Let the ruling classes tremble at a communistic revolution. The proletarians have nothing to lose but their chains. They have a world to gain.

"Working men of all countries, unite!"

An Estimate of the Manifesto. The *Manifesto,* as Harold J. Laski has pointed out,[3] "gave direction and a philosophy to what had been before little more than an inchoate protest against injustice. It began the long process of welding together the scattered groups of the disinherited into an organized and influential party. It freed socialism from its earlier situation of a doctrine cherished by conspirators in defiance of government and gave to it at once a purpose and an historic background. It almost created a proletarian consciousness by giving, and for the first time, to the workers, at once a high sense of their historic mission and a realization of the dignity implicit in their task. It destroyed at a stroke both the belief that socialism could triumph without long preparation and the hope that any form of economic organization was possible save that which was implicit in the facts of the time. It insisted upon no natural rights. It did not lay down any metaphysics. It was, on the contrary, a careful and critical historical survey of the institutional process regarded as a whole. It is a book of men who

[3] Laski, Harold J., *Karl Marx: An Essay,* with the *Communist Manifesto* by Karl Marx and Friedrich Engels, pp. 16–18.

have viewed the whole process of history from an eminence and discovered therein an inescapable lesson. It is at once an epilogue and a prophecy—an epilogue to the deception from which the workers suffered in the Revolution in 1789, and a prophecy of the land of promise they may still hope to enter."

The Revolutions of 1848. THE CONDITIONS IN EUROPE. The spirit and contents of the *Communist Manifesto* can only be understood when studied in relation to the condition of the times—the ruthless exploitation of men, women, and children by the rising capitalists, described so vividly in Engels' *Condition of the Working Class in England in 1844;* the startlingly revolutionary effects of machine production on all relationships during the preceding fifty or seventy-five years; the economic crises, increasingly severe; the utter lack of organization on the part of the worker, either on the industrial or the political field, except in scattered instances; the widespread disfranchisement of the working class in most European countries; and, finally, the many signs of rebellion and violence which were then in evidence.

THE FEBRUARY REVOLUTION IN FRANCE. A few weeks after the manuscript of the *Communist Manifesto* was sent to the printer the French Revolution of February 24, 1848, broke out. During the previous eight years Guizot, who was constantly urging the King, Louis Philippe, to assume real power, ruled France as its Prime Minister. The political machinery was hopelessly corrupted. Power was concentrated in a few hands. Suffrage was denied to all except a few hundred thousand of the population. Open protests against social conditions were not tolerated. Discontent increased in volume to such an extent that Guizot was forced to resign. This resignation failed to satisfy the people. A formidable demonstration was organized on the night of February 23 before the Foreign Office in Paris. Shots were exchanged. Several were killed. Before the dawn of the twenty-fourth the eastern part of the city was covered with barricades and the entire city was in a state of insurrection. Louis Philippe abdicated in favor of his grandson, and that afternoon the republic was proclaimed, subject to ratification by the National Assembly. Many workers welcomed this revolution as the forerunner of a social revolution when labor would be the dominating force.

Spread of the Revolution. On hearing of the February revolt in Paris, Metternich, the Austrian statesman, declared: "Europe finds itself in the presence of a second 1793." As Metternich suspected, the revolt was not confined to France. On March 13, a few weeks after the Paris *coup d'état,* the students of Vienna marched to the assembly hall with cries of "Down with Metternich," forcing that statesman to resign and flee. In Austria the people had for long suffered under a cruel despotism, a despotism where laws were passed and taxes exacted without consulting the people; where peasants could not go from village to village without permission; where all newspapers and books were under strict police surveillance; and where the powerful Metternich was able to boast that he had kept the scientific spirit out of even the universities. Two days after Metternich's resignation the Hungarian Diet dispatched delegates to the Emperor to request a responsible government, and under the influence of Kossuth established their own ministries of finance, war, and foreign affairs, and freed the peasants without compensation. The Czechs followed with their demands for civil liberty and the abolition of serfdom.

These upheavals, in turn, provided the impetus in Italy for countless revolts. In a few days Italy, as a result of these uprisings, had caused the Austrian troops to evacuate a large portion of Lombardy and had set up a number of city republics.

There were simultaneous uprisings in Baden, in Württemberg, in Bavaria, and in Saxony. In Berlin the populace demanded that the King grant Prussia a constitution. The King replied by calling a national assembly, chosen by popular vote, for the purpose of drafting one. About the same time the Swiss people were occupied in sweeping away their old constitution of 1814, and the British Chartists were engaged in an attempt to wring from Parliament the right to vote. The revolution seemed to be on in earnest, and many thought that the people, obtaining the suffrage, would soon go forward to economic emancipation. But the pendulum was not then destined to swing in that direction.

THE JUNE DEFEAT. In Paris the Provisional Government decreed immediately after the February revolution that the national workshops, advocated by Louis Blanc, should be established, that employment should be guaranteed to all, and that a committee should be set up in Luxemburg Palace to look after the interests of the working class. Blanc and Albert, at the head of this committee, saw in this gesture a new day for the workers. They convened a labor parliament made up of delegates from the various trades, and, on the opening day of this parliament in Luxemburg Palace on March 10, Blanc enthusiastically remarked:

"On these same seats, glittering with embroidered coats, what do I see now? Garments threadbare with honorable toil, some perhaps bearing the marks of recent conflict."

The business elements in the Provisional Government, however, in voting for its various decrees, had no intention of conceding Blanc's program to the workers. They passed these measures as a means of allaying unrest until the conservative rural population could be heard from and could elect their representatives to the National Assembly. While voting formally for labor measures, they failed to make appropriations to carry them out. The work offered to the unemployed consisted largely of the digging of ditches and the building of forts at two francs a day. In May the National Assembly was elected by universal suffrage. It was chiefly representative of the more moderate republicans, who had little sympathy with socialistic legislation. On meeting, it closed the national workshops and gave the discharged workers the alternative of joining the army or quitting the city. The people rallied to the cry of "bread or lead," and from Friday, June 23, to the following Monday they engaged in most terrific fighting against government troops on the Paris streets. Half-starved and poorly equipped, the workers were easily defeated by General Cavaignac with his well-disciplined troops. In defeat, they were treated with severity. Four thousand of them were transported without trial; the leaders were imprisoned and their papers suppressed.

The June defeat was followed by the election of Louis Bonaparte to the presidency and the transformation in 1852 of the republic into the Second Empire.

REACTION IN OTHER EUROPEAN COUNTRIES. In the Austrian Empire the republicans also suffered defeat. Race rivalry among them in Bohemia led to a division which gave to General Windischgrätz a chance to bombard Prague and defeat the rebels. Flushed with success, he proceeded to Vienna, gave new courage to the monarchy, marched to Hungary, dissolved the Hungarian parliament, and took a terrible revenge on the rebels. He also assisted in restoring Austria's power over Italy.

In Berlin the assembly, proposing, from the standpoint of the monarchy, a too liberal constitution, was dissolved, and a constitution finally adopted which gave little power to the people. The radicals found the country a difficult place for them, and many thousands of them sought in America a refuge from political persecution.

Dissolution of Communist League. The defeat of the European insurrections drove into comparative obscurity the revolutionary movements of the European working class. For years thereafter, the struggle was one between various sections of the owning class. "The working class fight," as Engels has it, "was reduced to a fight for political elbow room, and to the position of the extreme wing of the middle-class radicals. Wherever independent proletarian movements continued to show signs of life, they were ruthlessly hunted down." [4]

The members of the Central Board of the Communist League, located in Cologne, were arrested by the Prussian police and subsequently imprisoned for terms varying from three to six years. Immediately following the sentence the League was dissolved, and it looked for a time as if the influence of the *Communist Manifesto* would cease with the burial of the League. It was yet destined, however, to play a powerful part in the labor movement of the world.

[4] *Communist Manifesto* (Rand School Edition), p. 5.

CHAPTER 15

Marx's Career after 1848

THE European upheaval, followed by the reaction, had a profound effect on Marx's future career. The first result of the February revolt on his personal fortunes was his banishment from Belgium by a government fearful that the revolution might spread northward. The French Revolutionists, however, at that time extended a cordial invitation to him to visit Paris.

"Brave and Faithful Marx," writes Ferdinand Flocon of the Provisional Government, in a letter dated March 1, 1848, "the soil of the French Republic is a place of refuge for all friends of freedom. Tyranny has banished you; France the free opens to you her gates—to you and to all who fight for the holy cause, the fraternal cause of all the people. In this sense shall every officer of the French government understand his duty."[1]

From France to Germany. In France Marx gathered together some of the members of the League of Communists and assisted them in returning to Germany to take part in the German revolution. Marx and Engels also proceeded to the Rhineland, and the former became editor in June, 1848, of the *Neue Rheinische Zeitung,* a paper which passed through a stormy career during the next year or so.

In his *Rheinische Zeitung* articles, feeling that a peaceful path to the revolution was closed to the workers (they had not at that time created any powerful agencies in the political and economic field through which to express themselves) and that labor was ripe for another revolt in the not distant future, Marx advocated the disarming of the bourgeoisie, the erection of revolutionary terrorism "to abridge and concentrate the hideous death agonies of society," and the creation of a revolutionary army.

In his last issue, in May, 1849, he showed his anticipation—despite

[1] Quoted in Beer, *Life and Teaching of Karl Marx,* p. 49.

reaction then prevailing—of a speedy victory for the workers. "Already in the east," he declared, "a revolutionary army composed of warriors of all nationalities stands confronting the old Europe represented by and in league with the Russian Army; already from Paris looms the Red Republic." [2] His hopes, however, were not then to be realized.

Engels' Reflections on Early Tactics. Years after, in 1895, six months before his death, Friedrich Engels thus acknowledged the mistake made by Marx and himself in judging the time of the revolution and the tactics that the workers should adopt in bringing about the great change:

"History proved us in the wrong and revealed our opinion of that day (1848–50) as an illusion. History went even further; not only did it destroy our former error but also transformed the conditions under which the proletariat will have to battle. The fighting methods of 1848 are today obsolete in every respect. . . .[3]

"History has made clear that the status of economic development on the Continent was then by no means ripe for the abolition of capitalist production; it has proved this by the economic revolution which, since 1848, has affected the entire continent and has introduced large industry in France, Austria, Hungary, Poland, and, more recently, in Russia, and has made of Germany an industrial nation of first rank—all this upon a capitalist basis which, reckoning from 1848, implies great expansive capacity." [4]

THE FRANCHISE. Continuing, Engels declared that the workers were learning how to change the ballot from a means of duping into an instrument of emancipation. The franchise had increased the feeling of the certainty of victory and had permitted the workers to ascertain their own strength and that of their enemies. It had furnished the workers, during election times, with a means of getting into touch with the masses, of forcing all parties to defend their views. It had supplied their representatives with a tribune from which they could address their opponents in Parliament and the masses outside with freedom. "And so it came about that bourgeoisie and government feared far more the legal than the illegal action of the workers' party, more the successes of the elections than those of rebellion." [5]

THE BARRICADES. Engels declared that barricade fights had by 1895 become antiquated. "Let there be no illusions about this: the real victory over the military in a street battle, a victory as between two armies, belongs to the greatest rarities. . . . The utmost the insurrec-

[2] *Ibid.*, p. 50.
[3] *Class Struggles in France* (N. Y. Labor News Co.), pp. 7–8.
[4] *Ibid.*, pp. 10–11. [5] *Ibid.*, p. 19.

tion can accomplish in a tactical action is the proper erection and defense of a single barricade."

On the side of the military, he continued, is the control of large ordnance and of fully equipped and thoroughly trained engineering troops. Already by 1849 the chances of success were small. The bourgeoisie had gone over to the side of the government. The barricades had lost their charm. The soldiers saw behind them no longer the "people," but rebels. The officers had become familiar with the tactical forms of street fighting. Since then all had been in favor of the military. Armies had become larger. By means of railroads, garrisons might be doubled within twenty-four hours. The armament of the enormously augmented troops had become incomparably more effective. Solid projectiles and case shots of the artillery had given place to the percussion shell that sufficed to shatter the best barricades.

"The time is past," he continued, "for revolutions carried through by small minorities at the head of unconscious masses. . . . The irony of history turns everything upside down. *We, the 'revolutionists,' the 'upsetters,' we strive much better with legal than with illegal means in forcing an overthrow.* The parties of order, as they call themselves, perish because of the legal conditions set up by themselves." [6] (Italics ours.)

Marx on the Revolution. So Engels wrote forty-five years after he and Marx sounded their clarion calls to immediate revolt in the columns of the *Rheinische Zeitung.* The workers failed, however, to heed the call of the young editors and the paper suspended after a year and a half of struggle. Following suspension, Marx paid out of his own pocket no less than 7000 thalers, to obtain which he sold practically all his possessions. With his paper gone he traveled to Paris to witness the Red Revolution, but instead came face to face with the counter-revolution. In 1849 he was banished from Paris and went to London, where he spent practically the remainder of his life.

Marx spent the first few months in London writing on the European revolutions, preparing the *Eighteenth Brumaire of Louis Bonaparte* on the French revolt, and writing his brilliant articles on the German situation for the *New York Tribune,* later published under the title, *Revolution and Counter-Revolution.* The real cause of the February and March revolts, he maintained, was the world commercial crisis. The cause of the reaction, on the other hand, was the industrial prosperity that gradually arrived during the summer of 1848 and developed full bloom in 1849–50.

His articles on the German revolution brought out the folly of blam-

6 *Ibid.,* pp. 22–7.

ing the failure of a revolution upon the betrayal of any one individual. They also emphasized how difficult of success is the *coup d'état* method of revolution in a country which, like Germany, had not one, but many important centers that must be taken before the ground won could be retained. Marx declared:

"When you inquire into the causes of the counter-revolutionary successes, there you are met on every hand with the ready reply that it was Mr. This or Citizen That who betrayed the people. Which reply may be very true or not, according to circumstances, but under no circumstance does it explain anything—not even show how it came to pass that the 'people' allowed themselves to be thus betrayed. And what a poor chance stands a political party whose entire stock-in-trade consists in a knowledge of the solitary fact that citizen So and So is not to be trusted." [7]

In Germany, Marx pointed out, the mass of workers were employed by small tradesmen, whose entire manufacturing system was a mere relic of the Middle Ages. Industrial workers were in a minority. There were large numbers of peasantry—small freeholders, feudal peasants, and agricultural laborers. There was thus an unsubstantial foundation for a successful revolution. He added:

"When the interests so varied, so conflicting, so strangely crossing each other, are brought into violent collision; when these contending interests in every district, every province, are mixed in different proportions; when, above all, there is no great center in the country, no London, no Paris, the decisions of which, by their weight, may supersede the necessity of fighting out the same quarrel over and over again in every single locality; what else is to be expected but that the contest will dissolve itself into a mass of unconnected struggles in which an enormous quantity of blood, energy, and capital is spent, but which, for all that, remain without any decisive results." [8]

Life in London. For years while in London Marx was an almost daily visitor to the British Museum and could be seen there from the opening time in the morning until the attendants sent the readers home, poring over books on economics, history, and political and social science, gathering material for his great book, *Capital.*

During those days he and his family were in dire want. They lived in a two-room apartment in Dean Street, London, near Soho, in the humblest style. In 1852 the story goes that he sent his last coat to the pawnshop in order to buy paper for the pamphlet on the Cologne Com-

[7] *Revolution and Counter-Revolution,* pp. 2–3.
[8] *Ibid.,* p. 11.

munist trial. During the years 1851–60 his only regular source of income was a sovereign an article from the *New York Tribune.*

In the sixties, however, the fortunes of Marx were improved by a small legacy of 800 pounds from his friend Wilhelm Wolff and by Engels' annual contribution of about 350 pounds. Wolff's legacy enabled him to write his first volume of *Capital.*

The Critique of Political Economy. Marx in 1859 published the *Critique of Political Economy,* originally intended as the first instalment of a complete treatise on political theory. This plan was finally abandoned. The value of the book lies chiefly in its formulation of the economic interpretation of history and of the Marxian theory of value, and partly in its historical sketches of money and value theories.

The Sixties. The sixties were Marx's happiest years. He was a genial host and spent countless Sunday evenings with his family and friends. His wife was a helpmate in the best sense of that word. Despite her early aristocratic surroundings and the hardships and persecutions suffered at the side of her husband, she never regretted her alliance with him.

"Heinrich Heine, the relentless satirist," wrote Paul Lafargue, "feared Marx's scorn; but he cherished the greatest admiration for the keen, sensitive mind of Marx's wife. Marx esteemed so highly the intelligence and critical sense of his wife that he told me in 1866 that he submitted all of his manuscripts to her and that he set a high value upon her judgment." [9]

Marx had six children, four girls and two boys, of whom three survived—Jenny, afterwards the wife of Charles Longuet; Laura, the wife of Paul Lafargue; and Eleanor, who married Dr. Edward Aveling.

Marx's Address to the First International. In 1863 a gigantic protest meeting was arranged in London, directed against Russia's attack on Poland. Odger, a trade-union leader, suggested regular international meetings. A conference was finally arranged in London from September 25 to 28, 1864. Marx was asked to be present as a representative of the German workingmen. The conference gave birth to the International Working Men's Association at St. Martin's Hall, London—the First International of labor.

Marx wrote the "Inaugural Address" and the declaration of principles. The address gives a history of the English workers from 1825 to 1864 and deals with the tremendous growth in trade and commerce during the period from 1848 to 1864, maintaining that "the intoxicating augmentation of wealth and power is entirely confined to the propertied

[9] Beer, *op. cit.,* p. 53.

classes."[10] Concentration in land had increased from 1851 to 1861. The workers were sinking to a lower depth of misery, while those above them were rising in the social scale.

However, some constructive measures had been forced on society by the working class. One of these was the Ten-Hour Day. Economists had heretofore argued that such a measure would sound the death knell of British industry, that industry could live only by the blind rule of supply and demand. "The Ten-Hour Bill was, therefore," Marx affirmed, "not only a great practical measure; *it was a victory of a principle; it was the first time that in broad daylight the political economy of the middle classes succumbed to the political economy of the working class."* (Italics ours.) It had also contributed "immense physical, moral, and intellectual benefits to the factory operatives."

"But there was in store a still greater victory of the political economy of labor over the political economy of property. We speak of the co-operative movement, especially the co-operative factories raised by the unassisted efforts of a few bold 'hands.' The value of these great social experiments cannot be overrated. By deed instead of by argument they have shown that production on a large scale and in accord with the behests of modern science may be carried on without the existence of a class of masters employing a class of hands; that to bear fruit, the means of labor need not be monopolized as a means of dominion over, and of extortion against, the laboring man himself; and that, like slave labor, like serf labor, hired labor is but a transitory and inferior form, destined to disappear before associated labor playing its part with a willing hand, a ready mind, and a joyous heart."[11]

Nevertheless, "if kept within the narrow circle of the casual efforts of private workmen" co-operation "will never be able to arrest the growth in geometrical progress of monopoly, to free the masses, nor even perceptibly to lighten the burden of their miseries. It ought to be developed to national dimensions and, consequently, to be fostered by national means. . . .

"To conquer political power has become the great duty of the working classes . . . one element they possess—numbers; but numbers weigh only in the balance if united by combination and led by knowledge." The fight for a foreign policy based on the morals and justice which should govern the relations of private individuals, is also a part of the general struggle for the emancipation of the working class.

[10] *Address and Provisional Rules of the International Working Men's Association*, London: The Labor and Socialist International, 1924.

[11] *Ibid.*, p. 10.

This *Address to the Working Classes* was delivered before the International in 1864. The following year Marx sent to the Workingmen's International Association another communication embodying his theory of value, published as *Value, Price, and Profit* after his death, and considered one of the clearest expositions of the theory of value made by Marx.[12]

Capital. Three years after his Inaugural Address, in 1867, Marx published the first German edition of his monumental work, *Capital*. As the subtitle indicates, this volume of some 800 pages is intended as a "critical analysis of capitalist production." In his Preface Marx apologizes for the long lapse between the *Critique of Political Economy* (published in 1859) and *Capital,* "due to an illness of many years' duration" that again and again interrupted his work. He has taken England as his chief illustration of modern industry, he declares, because it is the classic land of capitalism. Moreover, the more highly developed capitalist country "shows to the less developed, the image of its own future." [13] Perhaps the most striking passage in the Preface is that which sets forth Marx's concept of the character of the future trend of social developments:

"As in the eighteenth century, the American War of Independence sounded the toscin for the European middle class, so in the nineteenth century the American civil war sounded it for the European working class. In England, the progress of social disintegration is palpable. When it has reached a certain point, it must react on the Continent. *There it will take a form more brutal or more humane, according to the degree of development of the working class itself. Apart from higher motives, therefore, their own most important interests dictate to the classes that are for the nonce the ruling ones, the removal of all legally removable hindrances to the free development of the working class.*

"For this reason, as well as others, I have given so large a space in this volume to the history, the details, and the results of English factory legislation. One nation can and should learn from others. *And even when a society has got upon the right track for the discovery of the natural laws of its movement*—and it is the ultimate aim of this work to lay bare the economic law of motion of modern society—*it can neither clear by bold leaps, nor remove by legal enactments, the obstacles offered by the successive phases of its normal development. But it can shorten and lessen the birth pangs.*" (Italics ours.) [14]

[12] See pp. 164–69.

[13] Marx, *Capital* (London: Sonnenschein), p. xvii.

[14] *Ibid.*, pp. xviii–xix.

The last-named passage has been quoted frequently by non-bolsheviks in support of their contention that an attempt to jump stages of economic development is impossible of accomplishment. Marx concludes his Preface with an expression of his belief that a radical change is in evidence in the relations between capital and labor in England, on the Continent, and in America. After mentioning a few indications of such a change, he adds:

"These are signs of the times not to be hidden by purple mantles or black cassocks. They do not signify that tomorrow a miracle will happen. They show that, within the ruling class themselves, a foreboding is dawning, that the present society is not solid crystal, but an organism capable of change, and is constantly changing." [15]

The book itself treats of the nature of commodities, money, capital, and their interrelations. It explains at length the author's theory of surplus value. It shows the revolutionary effect of machinery upon the life of the worker and upon society as a whole and calls attention to the results obtained by the Factory Acts up to that time. It finally develops "the general law of capitalist accumulation."

Law of Capitalist Accumulation. As capitalist production grows apace, Marx maintains, capital concentrates in fewer and fewer hands. The productiveness of labor increases, the demand for additional labor decreases, and, with this decrease, the army of the unemployed constantly enlarges. "But the greater this reserve army in proportion to the active labor army, the greater is the mass of a consolidated surplus population. The more extensive, finally, the lazarus-layers of the working class and the industrial reserve army, the greater is official pauperism. *This is the absolute general law of capitalist accumulation.* Like all other laws it is modified in its working by many circumstances." [16] (Italics ours.)

Accumulation of Misery. The accumulation of capital is thus accompanied by an accumulation of misery. In letters of fire Marx sets forth the tragic condition of the workers under machine production.

"Within the capitalist system . . . all means for the development of production transform themselves into means of domination over, and exploitation of, the producers; they mutilate the laborer into a fragment of a man, degrade him to the level of an appendage of a machine, destroy every remnant of charm in his work and turn it into a hated toil; they estrange from him the intellectual potentialities of the labor process in the same proportion as science is incorporated in it as an independent power; they distort the conditions under which he works, subject him

[15] *Ibid.*, p. xx.

[16] *Ibid.*, p. 660.

during the labor process to a despotism the more hateful for its meanness.

"They transform his life time into working time, and drag his wife and child beneath the wheels of the Juggernaut of capital. But all methods for the production of surplus-value are at the same time methods of accumulation; and every extension of accumulation becomes again the means for the development of those methods. *It follows therefore that in proportion as capital accumulates, the lot of the laborer, be his payment high or low, must grow worse.* (Italics ours.)

"The law, finally, that always equilibrates the relative surplus population, or industrial reserve army, to the extent and energy of accumulation, this law rivets the laborer to capital more firmly than the wedge of Vulcan did Prometheus to its rock. It establishes an accumulation of misery, corresponding with accumulation of capital. *Accumulation of wealth at one pole is, therefore, at the same time accumulation of misery, agony of toil, slavery, ignorance, brutality, mental degradation, at the opposite pole, i.e., on the side of the class that produces its own product in the form of capital.*" [17] (Italics ours.)

This passage expresses the Marxian "increasing misery theory," which has been so frequently challenged during these later years.

In support of this theory of capitalist accumulation, Marx marshals as witnesses the statesmen and economists of England. He quotes Gladstone as saying in 1843 that "while there was a decrease in the consuming powers of the people and while there was an increase in the privations and distress of the laboring class and operatives, there was at the same time a constant accumulation of wealth in the upper classes and a constant increase in capital." [18]

Twenty years later (1863) Gladstone described the "intoxicating augmentation of wealth and power" on the part of the propertied classes, at the same time expressing uncertainty as to whether the condition of the worker had improved. Marx also quotes Professor Fawcett's statement that "the rich grow rapidly richer, whilst there is no perceptible advance in the comfort enjoyed by the industrial classes. . . . They [the laborers] become almost the slaves of the tradesman, to whom they owe money." [19] He follows these quotations with statistics after statistics, laying bare the utter misery of the masses of the people and the increasing army of the unemployed.

Capitalism Digging Its Own Grave. This contradiction in capitalist society, he maintains, is forcing capitalism to dig its own grave. "Along

[17] *Ibid.*, pp. 660–1.
[18] *Ibid.*, p. 667.
[19] *Ibid.*, p. 669.

with the constantly diminishing number of the magnates of capital, who usurp and monopolize all advantages of this process of transformation, grows the mass of misery, oppression, slavery, degradation, exploitation; *but with this, too, grows the revolt of the working class, a class always increasing in numbers, and disciplined, united, organized by the very mechanism of the process of capitalist production itself.* The monopoly of capital becomes a fetter upon the mode of production, which has sprung up and flourished along with it and under it. Centralization of the means of production and socialization of labor at last reach a point where they become incompatible with their capitalist integument. This integument is burst asunder. The knell of capitalist private property sounds. The expropriators are expropriated, and the capitalist era gives birth to an industrial society based on the possessions in common of the land and of the means of production." [20] (Italics ours.)

CHANGE LESS VIOLENT THAN FORMER REVOLUTION. Let no one think, Marx continues, that this change will bring with it the same misery as did the industrial revolution that heralded in capitalism.

"The transformation of scattered private property, arising from individual labor, into capitalist private property is, naturally, a process incomparably more protracted, violent, and difficult than the transformation of capitalistic private property, already practically resting on socialized production, into socialized property. In the former case, we had the expropriation of the mass of the people by a few usurers; in the latter, we have the expropriation of a few usurers by the mass of the people." [21]

Reception of *Capital*. In describing the reception of the first edition of his book, Marx afterwards remarked that "the learned and unlearned spokesmen of the German bourgeoisie" tried first to kill it by silence, as they had managed to do with his earlier writings, but that as they found that these tactics no longer fitted in with the conditions of the times, they wrote, under pretense of criticizing his book, prescriptions for the "tranquillization of the bourgeois mind." [22]

The book ultimately assumed the place of honor among all working-class classics, and has time without number been referred to as the "Bible of the working class." [23]

Marx's Activities in the First International. For the next several years after the publication of *Capital* Marx gave much thought and energy to the development of the First International, which he looked

[20] *Ibid.*, pp. 788–9. [21] *Ibid.*, p. 789. [22] *Ibid.*, p. xxv.

[23] The second and third volumes of *Capital* were not published until after Marx's death. The years of publication were 1885 and 1894 respectively.

upon with high hopes. "Things are moving," he wrote to Engels in 1867 with his usual optimism, "and in the next revolution, which is perhaps nearer than it seems, we (i.e., you and I) have this powerful machinery in our hands." [24] From the first there was a fierce struggle among various elements to control the International, which Marx regarded as an agency paving the way to revolution. Roughly speaking it was controlled by the followers of Proudhon from 1865 to 1867, by Marx from 1868 to 1870, and by the Bakunists from 1871 to its downfall a year or so later. Only the Marxian group favored political action. The others strove for the federative economic form of social organization. The Bakunists were communists, whereas the Proudhonists bitterly opposed the communist program. The International was divided not only on theoretical lines, but on racial and national lines. Marx was denounced as dictatorial and as a Pan-German. In the midst of these controversies came the Franco-Prussian war and the Commune of 1871.

The Franco-Prussian War and the French Commune. During the Franco-Prussian War Marx strongly urged the German workers to prevent the war from becoming a war of aggression. "If the German working class allow the present war to lose its strictly defensive character and to degenerate into a war against the French people," he wrote prophetically in behalf of the General Council of the International Workingmen's Association, July 23, 1870, "victory or defeat will prove alike disastrous. All the miseries that befell Germany after her War of Independence will revive with accumulated intensity." [25]

A few days after the defeat of the French at Sedan on September 3, 1870, Marx addressed another letter to the General Council, asking that the French workers stand by the Provisional Government and against any revolutionary action to bring about an immediate working-class commune. "Any attempt to overthrow the new government, when the enemy is already knocking at the gates of Paris," he wrote in this address, "would be a hopeless piece of folly. The French workers must do their duty as citizens. . . . Let them quietly and with determination make the most of the Republican freedom granted to them, in order to carry out thoroughly the organization of their own class. That will give them new Herculean strength for the rebirth of France and for our common task—the emancipation of the proletariat." [26]

[24] *Correspondence of Marx and Engels,* Vol. III, p. 406.

[25] Marx, Karl, *The Civil War in France,* pp. 4–5 (London: Labor Publishing Co., 1921).

[26] See Marx, *op. cit.,* Second Address, quoted in Beer, *op. cit.,* p. 60.

The French workers, however, fearful of the monarchical tendencies of the National Assembly and suffering keenly from unemployment and from hunger, paid little heed to Marx. The Paris Commune was proclaimed on March 18, 1871. Seven weeks thereafter it was overthrown with bloody massacre. Despite his letter advising against the uprising Marx later defended the workers with great energy for their part in the Commune.

Removal of First International. Following the fall of the Commune, the First International found that its field for practical action had been cut off for some time to come. The sectarian and revolutionary conspiracies within the International found a fertile field. As general secretary of the International, Marx, who was crowded more and more by work, and was extremely anxious to finish his *Capital,* suggested a transfer of the Association to New York. At the Hague Convention of 1872 the majority, following his advice, resolved to move the headquarters to the American metropolis.

Marx's Belief in Different Types of Transition. In a notable speech on tactics made at the Hague Convention Marx took the position that the methods of revolution could not be the same in all countries, and that in England and America the revolution might be attained by peaceful means. He said:

"The worker must one day capture political power in order to found the new organization of labor. He must reverse the old policy, which the old institutions maintain, if he will not, like the Christians of old who despised and neglected such things, renounce the things of this world. But we do not assert that the way to reach this goal is the same everywhere. We know that the institutions, the manners, and the customs of the various countries must be considered, and *we do not deny that there are countries like England and America, and, if I understood your arrangements better, I might even add Holland, where the worker may attain his object by peaceful means.* But not in all countries is this the case." [27] (Italics ours.)

After its removal to America, the International lingered on awhile, and in 1876 finally went entirely out of existence. With the passing of the First International and the downfall of the Commune, the working class movement gradually as a whole rid itself of the idea of progress through secret conspiracies and the *coup d'état* methods. The idea of violent change did not gain any great number of adherents again until the Russian revolution nearly a half century later.

[27] See Kautsky, *Dictatorship of the Proletariat,* pp. 8 and 9.

Marx and the Gotha Program. Following the virtual demise of the International, Marx continued his literary work. In 1875 he locked horns with the social democratic followers of Lassalle over the Gotha Program on several points and defined his position toward the state, socialism, and capitalism. In his criticism of the Gotha Program [28] he denied the complete validity of Lassalle's "iron law of wages"; brought to task those who failed to believe that "nature was just as much the source of use-values as labor"; attacked the proposal of state aid to producers' co-operatives; and scoffed at the assumption that in the mere formulation of programs lies the salvation of the workers. *"Every real advance step of the movement,"* he declared, *"is more important than a dozen platforms."* (Italics ours.)

It was in this famous document that Marx's brief allusion to the "dictatorship of the proletariat" appeared. It reads:

"Between the capitalist and the communist systems of society lies the period of the revolutionary transformation of the one into the other. This corresponds to a political transition period, whose state can be nothing else but the revolutionary dictatorship of the proletariat." [29]

The interpretations of this short paragraph have since been legion.

Marx on Compensation. Marx's statement regarding remuneration under a socialist form of society is of interest to those who would immediately institute a system of compensation according to needs:

"In the higher phase of communist society, after the enslaving subordination of the individual under the division of labor has disappeared, and therewith also the opposition between manual and intellectual labor; after labor has become not only a means of life, but also the highest want in life; when, with the development of all the faculties of the individual, the productive forces have correspondingly increased, and all the springs of social wealth flow more abundantly—only then may the limited horizon of capitalist right be left behind entirely, and society inscribe on its banners: 'From everyone according to his faculties, to everyone according to his needs.' " [30]

Marx's Last Days. From 1875 until his death in 1883 Marx suffered incessantly from bodily ailments. During his enforced leisure he made special studies of American and Russian agricultural conditions and busied himself with many other subjects. He visited Karlsbad in 1877–78 to recover his health and there got together material for the second

[28] Marx, Karl, *The Gotha Program* (N. Y.: Socialist Labor Party, 1922), p. 19.
[29] *Ibid.*, p. 48.
[30] *Ibid.*, p. 31.

volume of *Capital*. Karlsbad and other watering places, however, failed to effect a cure, and on March 14, 1883, he died.

"Mankind is less by a head," wrote Engels to his American friend, Sorge, "and indeed by the most important head it had today. The working-class movement will pursue its course, but its central point, to which French, Russians, Americans, and Germans turned of their own accord in decisive moments, always to receive that clear, unambiguous counsel which genius and perfect mastery alone can give, is gone." [31]

On Saturday, March 17, 1883, Marx was buried at Highgate Cemetery, London. Friedrich Engels and William Liebknecht, who had hurried from Germany to attend the funeral, spoke, among others, at the grave of Marx.

"Just as Darwin discovered the law of the evolution of organic nature," declared Engels, "so Marx discovered the evolutionary law of human history—the simple fact, hitherto hidden under ideological overgrowths, that above all things men must eat, drink, dress, and find shelter before they can give themselves to politics, science, art, religion, or anything else, and that therefore the production of the material necessaries of life and the corresponding stage of the economic evolution of a people or a period provides a foundation upon which the national institutions, legal systems, art, and even the religious ideas of the people in question have been built and upon which, therefore, their explanation must be based." [32]

"He has raised social democracy," declared Liebknecht, "from a sect, from a school, to a party which now already fights unconquered, and in the end will win the victory."

An Appraisal. The years that have intervened since his death have shed new luster on his name, and have given him a secure place as one of the great economists, social scientists, historians, and leaders of the working-class movement of all time. He made his mistakes in calculating the speed with which the great change was to be brought about but he prophesied with remarkable insight the general direction of that change. "He put in the forefront of social discussion," declares Harold J. Laski, "the ultimate question of the condition of the people. And he performed the incalculable service of bringing to it a message of hope in an epoch where men seemed to themselves to have become the hapless victims of a misery from which there was no release. In every country of the world where men have set themselves to the task of social im-

[31] Beer, *op. cit.*, p. 62.
[32] *Ibid.*, p. 63.

provement, Marx has been always the source of inspiration and prophecy." [33]

"Where he was also irresistibly right," continues Laski, "was in his prophecy that the civilization of his epoch was built upon sand. And even the faults of his prophecy may be pardoned to an agitator in exile to whom the cause of the oppressed was dearer than his own welfare."

[33] Laski, *Karl Marx,* etc., N. Y.: League for Industrial Democracy, pp. 47–8.

CHAPTER 16

Theoretical Foundation of Marxism

THE three cornerstones of Marxian theory are the materialist or economic interpretation of history, the doctrine of the class struggle, and the theory of value.

THE ECONOMIC INTERPRETATION OF HISTORY

The materialist or economic interpretation of history, a term to which we have referred elsewhere, means that in any given epoch the economic relations of society, the means whereby men and women provide for their sustenance, produce, exchange, and distribute the things they regard as necessary for the satisfaction of their needs, exert a preponderating influence in shaping the progress of society and in molding political, social, intellectual, and ethical relationships.[1]

Marx nowhere formulated that theory in a comprehensive manner,

[1] Edward Aveling in his *Charles Darwin and Karl Marx* (Twentieth Century Press, 1897, pp. 10–11) thus defines this theory:

"The materialistic conception of history is that the chief, the fundamental factor in the development of any nation or any society, is the economic factor—that is, the way in which the nation, or the society, produces and exchanges its commodities. . . .

"Now, whilst it [the economic factor] appears to be the fundamental one, there are others developed from it and reflexes of it, that also play their parts, acting and reacting upon their parent, the economic factor, and one another. The art, the science, the literature, the religion, the legal and juridical formulae of a country, although they all spring directly from the economic conditions of the country, have to be reckoned with."

"We understand by the theory of economic interpretation of history," writes Professor E. A. R. Seligman (*Economic Interpretation of History*, p. 67), "not that all history is to be explained in economic terms alone, but that the chief considerations in human progress are the social considerations, and that the important factor in social change is the economic factor. Economic interpretation of history means, not that the economic relations exert an exclusive influence, but that they exert a preponderant influence in shaping the progress of society."

although he referred to it in many portions of his writings, particularly in the *Communist Manifesto* and the Preface to the *Poverty of Philosophy*. A projected book on *Logic,* in which he planned to examine the theory in detail, was never written. His aim had been not to discover origins of things, but the causes of social change and development. He searched for the "dynamic law of history."

Pre-Marxian Interpretations. Predecessors of Marx had found the explanation of the great changes in history in "great men," in the development of ideas, in religious beliefs, in the change of political systems, or in the physical environment—in climate, food, and soil.[2]

Suggestions of the theory were found in the works of a number of the utopian writers, but, as Professor Seligman puts it, "if originality can properly be claimed only for those thinkers who not alone formulate a doctrine but first recognize its importance and implications, so that it thereby becomes a constituent element in their whole scientific system, there is no question that Marx must be recognized in the truest sense as the originator of the economic interpretation of history." [3]

From his study of Hegel the young social scientist had become a firm believer in the idea of *process,* the belief that all that exists is destined some day to pass out of existence, and that growth and change occur as a result of the conflict of opposites. He was also strongly influenced by the naturalistic interpretation of Feuerbach, and "the naturalism of Feuerbach, combined with the conception of process in the dialectic of Hegel, led him finally to the theory that all social institutions are the result of a growth and that the causes of this growth are to be sought not in any idea, but in the conditions of material existence. In other words it led him to the economic interpretation of history." [4]

Marx's Explanation of His Theory. In his Preface to the *Critique of Political Economy* Marx explains how, in revising Hegel's *Philosophy of Law,* he was led to the conclusion that "legal relations as well as forms of state could neither be understood by themselves, nor explained by the so-called general progress of the human mind, but that they are rooted in the *material conditions of life.*"

"The general conclusion at which I arrived and which, once reached, continued to serve as the leading thread in my studies," he added, "may be briefly summed up as follows: In the social production which men carry on they enter into definite relations that are indispensable and independent of their will; these relations of production correspond to a definite stage of development of their material powers of production.

2 See Seligman, *Economic Interpretation of History,* Ch. I.

3 *Ibid.,* pp. 52–3.

4 *Ibid.,* p. 23.

The sum total of these relations of production constitutes the economic structure of society—the real foundation on which rise legal and political superstructures and to which correspond definite forms of social consciousness. *The mode of production in material life determines the general character of the social, political, and spiritual processes of life.*" [5] (Italics ours.)

"In changing the modes of production [Marx maintains in his *Misery of Philosophy* (1847) [6]], mankind changes all its social relations. The hand mill creates a society with the feudal lord; the steam mill a society with the industrial capitalist. The same men who establish social relations in conformity with their material production also create principles, ideas, and categories in conformity with their social relations. . . . All such ideas and categories are therefore historical and transitory products."

Marx and Engels in 1848 pointed out in the *Communist Manifesto* how the bourgeoisie, in revolutionizing the means of production, change, in so doing, the entire character of society. Following the *Manifesto,* Marx made several attempts to apply his theory to the existing political situation. In his work on *Capital,* published in 1867, he nowhere formulates his theory, but continually takes it for granted. Continental writers in general failed to grasp the real significance of the theory until the publication in 1894 of the third volume of *Capital,* with its great amount of historical interpretation.

THE ECONOMIC NOT THE ONLY FACTOR. Much of the criticism aimed at the economic interpretation of history is based on the assumption that Marx and Engels utterly denied the influence of any except the economic factor. This they did not do, although at times, in the rough and tumble of debate, they failed sufficiently to safeguard themselves against that charge.

"Marx and I," wrote Engels to a student in 1890, "are partly responsible for the fact that the younger men have sometimes laid more stress on the economic side than it deserves. In meeting the attacks of our opponents it was necessary for us to emphasize the dominant principle, denied by them; and we did not always have the time, place and opportunity to let the other factors, which were concerned in the mutual action and reaction, get their deserts." [7]

In another letter he elaborates this same point of view:

[5] Marx, *Critique of Political Economy,* p. 11.

[6] Quoted in Seligman, *op. cit.,* p. 35-6.

[7] Seligman, *op. cit.,* p. 142; letter printed in *Der Sozialistische Akademiker,* October 1, 1895.

"According to the materialistic conception of history the factor which is *in the last instance* decisive in history is the production and reproduction of actual life. More than that neither Marx nor I have ever asserted. But when anyone distorts this so as to read that the economic factor is the sole element, he converts the statement into a meaningless, abstract, absurd phrase. The economic condition is the basis, but the various elements of the superstructure—the political forms of the class contests, and their results, the constitution—the legal forms, and also all the reflexes of these actual contests in the brains of the participants, the political, legal, philosophical theories, the religious views . . . all these exert an influence on the historical struggles, and in many instances determine their form." [8] (Italics ours.)

While Marx and the "orthodox" Marxians are materialists in the philosophical usage of that term, the economic interpretation of history does not necessarily involve a materialistic theory of the universe and of man's nature.

Spread of Theory. Marx saw in his theory grounds for hope of future development from the present economic system to a socialist order, as is indicated in his analysis of social development in the *Communist Manifesto* and in his later works. Most modern historians are now following Marx in emphasizing the importance of the economic factors in past and present history, although many of them are somewhat agnostic concerning a like influence of economic factors in the life of the future and the application of this theory to future social changes. The revolutionizing effect of Marx's pioneer work on the interpretation of historical events, past and present, however, can hardly be overestimated.

THE DOCTRINE OF CLASS STRUGGLE

Importance of Class Struggles. We have already had occasion in our discussion of the *Communist Manifesto* and in the later account of Marx's career to bring into the foreground the Marxian conception of the historical rôle of the class struggle. Marx believed that the part played by this struggle between owner and worker had been a fundamentally important one in the society of the past "since the dissolution of primitive tribal society holding land in common ownership." He contended likewise that class struggles would take place in society until such time as the workers should become the controllers of society. All would then be transformed into producers, and once for all society would be emancipated "from all exploitation, oppression, class-distinction, and

[8] *Ibid.*, pp. 142–3. *Der Sozialistische Akademiker* (Oct. 15, 1895), p. 251.

class struggles." This "fundamental proposition, which forms the nucleus" of the Marxian theory needs, perhaps, no further elaboration at this point.

THEORY OF VALUE

The economic interpretation of history and the theory of the class struggle form what are regarded as the sociological bases of the Marxian system. The theory of value, on the other hand, constitutes the economic base. Although all three are interwoven, many socialists who have accepted the sociological teachings of Marx are prone to maintain that his labor theory of value and his theory of surplus value are inadequate and not necessary parts of the modern socialist philosophy.

Labor Theory of Value. During a century and a half preceding the writings of Marx, English and French economists had gradually evolved a theory that the value of a commodity, that is to say, the quantity of any other commodity for which it will exchange, depends on the *relative quantity of labor necessary for its production.*[9] The development of this theory, as Marx brings out, begins with such economists as William Petty in England and Boisquillebert in France, and ends with Ricardo of England and Sismondi of France.[10]

In brief outline, the value theory which Marx took from the classical economists and which he elaborated somewhat further is as follows:

"The common *social substance* of all commodities is *labor* . . . A commodity has a *value* because it is a *crystallization of social labor.* The *greatness* of its value or its relative value depends upon the greater or lesser amount of that social substance contained in it; that is to say, on the relative mass of labor necessary for its production. The *relative values of commodities* are, therefore, determined by the *respective quantities or amounts of labor, worked up, realized, fixed in them.*"[11] (Italics ours.)

LABOR ENTERING INTO A COMMODITY. In estimating the amount of labor embodied in a commodity, Marx argues that it is not only necessary to consider the quantity of labor *last* employed, say, in producing the finished article, but that one must take into consideration that labor previously put into the raw material and employed on the tools, machinery, and buildings. "For example, the value of a certain amount of cotton yarn is the crystallization of the quantity of labor added to the cotton during the spinning process, the quantity of labor previously realized in the cotton itself, the quantity of labor realized in the coal, oil,

[9] Ricardo, *Principles of Political Economy* (N. Y.: Macmillan, 1909).
[10] Marx, *Critique of Political Economy,* p. 56.
[11] Marx, *Value, Price and Profit* (Chicago: Kerr), p. 57.

and other auxiliary substances used, the quantity of labor fixed in the steam engine, the spindles, the factory building, and so forth." [12]

Socially Necessary Labor. Nor must it be inferred, Marx continues, that, under his theory, the lazier or clumsier the man, the more valuable his commodity, since the time required by a lazy man to produce a commodity is greater than that required by the more skilled. "In saying that the value of a commodity is determined by the *quantity of labor* worked up or crystallized in it, we mean the *quantity of labor necessary* for its production in a given state of society, under certain social average conditions of production, with a given social average intensity, and average skill of the labor employed. (Italics ours.)

"When in England the power loom came to compete with the hand loom, only one half the former time of labor was wanted to convert a given amount of yarn into a yard of cotton or cloth. The poor handloom weaver now worked seventeen or eighteen hours daily instead of the nine or ten hours he worked before. Still the product of twenty hours of his labor represented now only ten social hours of labor, or ten hours of labor socially necessary for the conversion of a certain amount of yarn into textile stuffs. His product of twenty hours had, therefore, no more value than his former product of ten hours. If, then, the quantity of socially necessary labor realized in commodities regulates their exchangeable values, every increase in the quantity of labor wanted for the production of a commodity must augment its value, as every diminution must lower it." [13]

Price. Price, of course, must not be confused with value. It is but the monetary expression of value. To the extent that it is merely the monetary expression of value, price has been called *natural price.* But besides the *natural price,* there is the *market price,* which now rises, now sinks, under the value of the natural price, depending upon the fluctuations of supply and demand. "The natural price," as Adam Smith put it, "is the central price to which the prices of commodities are continually gravitating. Different accidents may sometimes keep them suspended a good deal above it, and sometimes force them down even somewhat below it. But whatever may be the obstacles which hinder them from settling in this center of repose and continuance they are constantly tending toward it."

It follows that if supply and demand equal each other, the market price will correspond with the natural price. For longer periods supply and demand do tend to compensate each other, "so that *apart from the effect of monopolies and some other modifications* . . . all descriptions

[12] *Ibid.*, p. 60.

[13] *Ibid.*, pp. 62–3.

of commodities are, on the average, sold at their respective *values* or natural prices." [14] (Italics ours.)

Labor Power. Like every other commodity, *labor power*, which is bought and sold, has a value, and that value is determined by the *quantity of labor necessary to produce it*. The laborer needs a certain number of necessities to grow up and maintain his life. But, like the machine, he sooner or later wears out, and must be replaced by another man. Thus, besides the necessities desired for his own maintenance, "he wants another amount of necessaries to bring up a certain quota of children that are to replace him on the labor market and to perpetuate the race of the laborers."

Furthermore, to develop his laboring power and acquire a given skill, another amount of values must be spent. Thus "*the value of laboring power* is determined by the *value of the necessaries* required to produce, develop, maintain, and perpetuate the laboring power." [15] (Italics ours.)

Surplus Value. Suppose that the average amount of daily necessaries of a laboring man requires six hours of average labor to produce. Suppose that this six hours of average labor is realized in a quantity of gold equal to $3. Then $3 would be the price, or the expression of the daily value of that man's laboring power.

The man in question is a wage laborer. He must sell his labor to a capitalist. If he sells it at $3 daily, he sells it at its value. If he works at the job six hours daily, he will add to the cotton a value of $3 daily. But this $3 would be the exact equivalent of his wages, and in this case no *surplus value* or *surplus produce* would go to the capitalist.

But in buying the use of the laboring power, the capitalist has acquired the right to use or consume it the same as any other commodity purchased. He can make that laboring power work, within certain limits, during the whole day or week. "The *value* of the laboring power is determined by the quantity of labor necessary for its maintenance and reproduction, but the *use* of that laboring power is only limited by the active energies and physical strength of the laborer. The daily or weekly value of the laboring power is quite distinct from the daily or weekly exercise of that power." [16] (Italics ours.)

Over and above the six hours required to replace his wages, the laborer is likely to have to work several more hours, say six hours, which may be called hours of surplus labor, which surplus labor will realize itself in a *surplus value* or *surplus produce*. If, for instance, the spinner works twelve hours, he will be advanced $3 for wages, while the

[14] *Ibid.*, pp. 67–8. [15] *Ibid.*, p. 76. [16] *Ibid.*, p. 79.

capitalist will pocket the other $3 in the form of surplus value for which the capitalist pays no equivalent. "*The rate of surplus value,* all other circumstances remaining the same, will depend on the proportion between that part of the working day necessary to reproduce the value of the laboring power and the *surplus time* or *surplus labor* performed for the capitalist." [17] (Italics ours.)

PROFIT. A profit is made by selling a commodity not over and above its value, but at its value. Suppose that twenty-four hours of average labor, valued at $12, were embodied in the production of a piece of cloth (including raw materials, machinery, etc.). Suppose that Mr. Jones, clothing manufacturer, paid this $12 for the cloth; suppose the worker in Mr. Jones' clothing establishment added to the cloth twelve hours of value, realized in an additional value of $6. Then *the total value of the product* would amount to thirty-six hours of realized labor and be equal to $18. But as the value of labor, or the wages paid to the workman would be but $3, no equivalent would be paid to the laborer by the capitalist for the six hours of surplus labor worked by him and realized in the value of the commodity. By selling the commodity, therefore, for its value of $18, the capitalist would gain a surplus value or profit of $3.

DIVISION INTO RENT, PROFIT, AND INTEREST. Of course the whole of the profit is not pure gain for the capitalist. Part of the surplus is taken by the landlord under the name of rent; part goes to the money-lending capitalist as interest, so that there remains to the capitalist as such only *industrial* or *commercial profit.* "Rent, interest, and industrial profit are only different names for different parts of the surplus value of the commodity, or the unpaid labor enclosed in it, and they are equally derived from this source and from this source alone. They are not derived from *land* as such, or from *capital* as such, but land and capital enable their owners to get their respective shares out of the surplus value extracted by the employing capitalist from the laborer. For the laborer himself it is a matter of subordinate importance whether that surplus value, the result of his surplus labor, or unpaid labor, is altogether pocketed by the employing capitalist, or whether the latter is obliged to pay portions of it, under the name of rent and interest, away to third parties. Suppose the employing capitalist is to use only his own capital and be his own landlord; then the whole surplus value would go into his own pocket." [18] (Italics ours.)

VALUE OF LABOR POWER—PHYSICAL AND SOCIAL. Returning to the value of labor power, Marx maintained that there are some peculiar

[17] *Ibid.,* p. 81.

[18] *Ibid.,* pp. 90–1.

features which distinguished the value of laboring power or the value of labor from the values of all other commodities. "The value of laboring power is formed of two elements—the one merely physical, the other historical or social. The ultimate limit is determined by the *physical element,* that is to say, to maintain and reproduce itself, to perpetuate its physical existence, the working class must receive the necessaries absolutely indispensable for living and multiplying. . . .

"Besides this mere physical element," Marx continues, "the value of labor is in every country determined by the *traditional standard of life.* It is not mere physical life, but it is the satisfaction of certain wants springing from the social conditions in which the people are placed and reared up. This historical or social element, entering into the value of labor, may be expanded or contracted, or altogether extinguished, so that nothing remains but the *physical limit.* . . . By comparing the standard of wages or values of labor in different countries, and by comparing them in different historical epochs of the same country, you will find that the *value of labor* itself is not a fixed but a variable magnitude, even supposing the values of all other magnitudes remain constant." [19] (Italics ours.)

THE RATE OF PROFIT. On the other hand, there exists no law determining the minimum of profit. The maximum of profits is limited by the minimum of wages and the physical maximum of the working day. An immense scale of variation is thus possible in the *rate of profits.* The actual rate of profits is only settled "by the continuous struggle between capital and labor, the capitalist constantly tending to reduce wages to their physical minimum and to extend the working day to its physical maximum, while the working man constantly presses in the opposite direction. The matter resolves itself into a question of the respective powers of the combatants." [20]

WAGES AND THE LAW OF SUPPLY AND DEMAND. The law of supply and demand must also be taken into account in determining the kind of wage settlements actually made. The greater the demand for labor on the part of the capitalist in proportion to the supply of available labor, the more favorable will be the wage settlements. However, as capitalist industry progresses, the demand for labor fails to keep pace with the accumulation of capital. This development tends to turn the scale against the worker and in favor of the capitalist. The general tendency of capitalist production is, therefore, to push the value of labor more or less toward the *minimum limit.* Some might argue that, in view of this tendency, the workers should remain passive and fail to

[19] *Ibid.*, pp. 116–9.

[20] *Ibid.*, p. 120.

resist the encroachments of capital. However, this does not follow. If they did this, they "would be degraded to one level mass of broken wretches past salvation . . . and disqualify themselves for the initiating of any larger movement." [21] (Italics ours.)

On the other hand, they should not forget that in resisting such encroachments, they are fighting effects rather than causes, "that they are retarding the downward movement, but not changing its direction; that they are applying palliatives, not curing the malady. They ought, therefore, not to be exclusively absorbed in these unavoidable guerrilla fights. . . . Instead of the conservative motto 'A fair day's wages for a fair day's work,' they ought to inscribe on their banner the revolutionary watchword, *'Abolition of the wages system!'* " (Italics ours.)

Marx thus connects up his value theories with his demand that the system which creates a surplus value should be eliminated.

Summary. The theories of Marx heretofore presented have furnished much of the theoretical basis for the modern socialist movement. By many millions they have been accepted as truths which should not be disputed. By many others, they have been subjected to severe critical analysis, and to a considerable modification in the light of more recent economic developments.

But, as Professor E. R. A. Seligman remarks:

"Whether or not we agree with Marx's analysis of industrial society, it is safe to say that no one can study Marx as he deserves to be studied —and, let us add, as he has heretofore *not* been studied in England and America—without recognizing the fact that, perhaps with the exception of Ricardo, there has been no more original, no more powerful, and no more acute intellect in the entire history of economic science." [22]

[21] *Ibid.*, pp. 125–6.

[22] Seligman, *Economic Interpretation of History*, p. 56.

PART THREE

Other Schools of Thought (1880-1914)

CHAPTER 17

Forerunners of the Fabians

SINCE the middle of the nineteenth century, Marxian socialism, somewhat modified, has remained the most vital and dominant school of socialist thought despite the many attacks made upon it by friend and foe alike. A number of other schools, however, have played their part in the molding of socialist thought and action. Some of these have aimed to supplement the Marxian school; some have endeavored to revise it; others have sought to carry out to what was felt to be their logical conclusion one or more portions of Marx's teachings.

A few months after the death of Marx, in March, 1883, a small group of young people met in a bare room somewhere in Chelsea, London, to listen to an American, Thomas Davidson, expound his ideas of a Fellowship of a New Life. Out of that meeting developed the English Fabian Society, actually born on January 4, 1884, a society which has exerted a profound influence over the economic and social thinking of that country.

Engels' Prediction of Revolutions. A great change in Britain and in Continental Europe had taken place during the thirty-six years between the issuance of the *Communist Manifesto* and the birth of the Fabian Society. In the forties, Engels anticipated the complete collapse of the capitalist system within the next decade or so as a result of economic crises and the spirit of revolt in the working class as manifested in the Chartist movement:

"I think the people will not endure more than another crisis," he said. "The next one in 1846 or 1847 will probably bring with it the repeal of the Corn Laws and the enactment of the Charter. What revolutionary movements the Charter may give rise to remains to be seen. But by the time of the next following crisis which, according to the analogy of its predecessors, must break out in 1852 or 1853, the English people will have had enough of being plundered by the capitalists and left to starve when the capitalists no longer require their services. If up to that time the English bourgeoisie does not pause to reflect—and to all appearances it certainly will not do so—a revolution will follow with which none hitherto known can be compared." [1]

Engels' Description of Commercial and Industrial Development. The revolt, however, did not occur. British industry, far from collapsing, expanded by leaps and bounds. Particularly in the first part of the period, from 1850 to 1866, when Britain held what was virtually a monopoly of the world market, was this development in evidence.

"The revival of trade after the crisis of 1847," wrote Engels years later in explaining the reason for his failure of his prophecy to materialize, "was the dawn of a new industrial era. The repeal of the Corn Laws and the financial reforms subsequent thereto gave to English industry and commerce all the elbow room they had asked for. The discovery of the Californian and Australian gold fields followed in rapid succession. The colonial markets developed at an increasing rate their capacity for absorbing English manufactured goods. In India millions of hand weavers were finally crushed out by the Lancashire power-loom. China was more and more being opened up. Above all, the United States—then, commercially speaking, a mere colonial market, but by far the biggest of them all—underwent an economic development astounding even for that rapidly progressive country.

"And, finally, the new means of communication introduced at the close of the preceding period—railways and ocean steamers—were now worked out on an international scale; they realized actually what had hitherto existed only potentially, a world market. This world market, at first, was composed of a number of chiefly or entirely agricultural countries grouped around one manufacturing center—England—which consumed the greater part of their surplus raw produce and supplied them in return with the greater part of their requirements in manufactured articles. No wonder England's industrial progress was colossal and unparalleled and such that the status of 1844 now appears to us as comparatively primitive and insignificant." [2]

Breakdown of British Monopoly. Following the Civil War and the Franco-Prussian War, England began to feel the competition from the United States and Germany, while its monopolistic grip over world markets was distinctly loosened. "Even while that monopoly lasted," observed Engels in 1885, "the markets could not keep pace with the in-

[1] Engels, *Condition of the Working Class in England in 1844* (London, Sonnenschein), 1892 edition, p. 296.

[2] *Ibid.*, Preface, p. vi.

creasing productivity of English manufacturers; the decennial crises were the consequence. [Thus there arose the crisis of 1866 and the extended period of depression from 1876.] And new markets are getting scarcer every day, so much so that even the Negroes of the Congo are now to be forced into the civilization attendant upon Manchester calicoes, Staffordshire pottery, and Birmingham hardware." [3]

He added, with keen historic insight: "How will it be when Continental, and especially American, goods flow in in ever-increasing quantities—when the predominating share, still held by British manufacturers, will become reduced from year to year? Answer, Free Trade, thou universal panacea.

"I am not the first to point this out. Already in 1883, at the Southport meeting of the British Association, Mr. Inglis Palgrave, the President of the Economic section, stated plainly that 'the days of great trade profits in England were over, and there was a pause in the progress of several great branches of industrial labor.' *The country might almost be said to be entering the non-progressive state.*" [4] (Italics ours.)

Improvement among Sections of Workers. The revival of trade during the early part of the period, the great increase in exports and imports, and the astounding increase in productivity through mechanical inventions, while benefiting chiefly the capitalist class, did reflect itself in improved conditions among certain sections of the workers. Engels maintained in 1885 that the mass of the workers had been *temporarily* improved, although this improvement "was reduced to the old level by the influx of the great body of the unemployed reserve, by the constant superseding of hands by new machinery, by the immigration of the agricultural population, now, too, more and more superseded by machinery." [5]

On the other hand, there had been a more *permanent* improvement among "two 'protected' sections" of the working class. "Firstly, the factory hands. The fixing by Parliament of their working day within relatively rational limits has restored their physical constitution and endowed them with a moral superiority, enhanced by their local concentration. They are undoubtedly better off than before 1848. . . . Secondly, the great trade unions. They are the organization of those trades in which the labor of *grown up men* predominates, or is alone applicable. Here the competition neither of women or children nor of machinery has so far weakened their organized strength. The engineers, the carpenters and joiners, the bricklayers, are each of them a

[3] *London Commonwealth,* Mar. 1, 1885; quoted in Engels, *op. cit.,* p. xvi.

[4] Engels, *op. cit.,* p. xvii.

[5] *Ibid.,* p. xiv.

power, to the extent that, as in the case of the bricklayers and bricklayers' laborers, they can even successfully resist the introduction of machinery. That their condition has remarkably improved since 1848 there can be no doubt, and the best proof of this is in the fact that for more than fifteen years not only have their employers been with them, but they with their employers, upon exceedingly good terms. They form an aristocracy among the working class; they have succeeded in enforcing for themselves a relatively comfortable position, and they accept it as final. They are the model working men of Messrs. Leone Levi and Giffin, and they are very nice people indeed nowadays to deal with, for any sensible capitalist in particular and for the whole capitalist class in general." [6]

"The truth is this," Engels continued, "during the period of England's industrial monopoly the English working class have, to a certain extent, shared in the benefits of the monopoly. These benefits were very unequally parcelled out among them; the privileged minority pocketed most, but even the great mass had at least a temporary share now and then. *And that is the reason why, since the dying out of Owenism, there has been no socialism in England.* With the breakdown of that monopoly, the English working class will lose that privileged position; it will find itself generally—the privileged and leading minority not excepted—on a level with its fellow workers abroad. And that is the reason why there will be socialism again in England." [7] (Italics ours.)

Ebb of Revolutionary Spirit. As Engels' statement implied, the revolutionary idealism found among the workers during the Chartist movement had largely disappeared by the beginning of the eighties, due largely to the change in the industrial situation. Thomas Cooper, the old Chartist, after a visit to the North of England during 1869 and 1870, noted the difference in attitude toward radical change:

"In our old Chartist time, it is true," he said, "Lancashire working men were in rags by thousands, and many of them lacked food. But their intelligence was demonstrated wherever they went. You could see them in groups discussing the great doctrines of political justice . . . or they were in earnest dispute respecting the teachings of socialism. *Now,* you will see no such groups in Lancashire. But you will hear well-dressed working men talking of co-operative stores, and their shares in them, or in building societies. . . . Working men had ceased to think, and wanted to hear no thoughtful talk; at least, it was so with most of them. To one who has striven, the greater part of his life, to

[6] *Ibid.*, p. xv.

[7] *Ibid.*, pp. xvii–xviii.

instruct and elevate, and who has suffered and borne imprisonment for them, all this was more painful than I care to tell." [8]

Development of Trade Unions. As was heretofore indicated, the third quarter of the nineteenth century saw a distinct development of the trade-union movement. In 1851 the Amalgamated Society of Engineers was established. This was followed by the organization of the Carpenters and Joiners in 1860, of the Miners National Union in 1863, the Tailors in 1866, and the Amalgamated Society of Railway Servants in 1872. In 1868 the workers held their first Trade Union Congress at Manchester.

In 1848 all strikes were regarded as illegal, and as a consequence, in the first part of the period, the activities of the trade unions were of an exceedingly mild character. Trade-union restrictions were, however, gradually removed through a series of acts culminating in the Conspiracy Acts of 1875, by which not only strikes but also picketing and other activities not involving violence were taken out of the scope of the criminal law.

Period of Protective Legislation. Since the late forties the Ten-Hour Law had been enacted, the truck system had been suppressed, and a number of secondary reforms had been introduced "much against the spirit of the Free Trade and unbridled competition, but quite as much in favor of the giant-capitalist in his competition with his less-favored brother." [9]

Attitude of Employing Class. Engels insists that both the development of trade unions and the enactment of factory laws were in line at that time with the interests of the larger capitalists, although such labor organizations and legislation were fought vigorously by many groups in the employing class. "The fact is," he maintained, "that all these concessions to justice and philanthropy were nothing else but means to accelerate the concentration of capital in the hands of the few, for whom the niggardly extra extortions of former years had lost all importance and had become actual nuisances; and to crush, all the quicker and all the safer, their smaller competitors, who could not make both ends meet without such perquisites. Thus the development of production on the basis of the capitalistic system has of itself sufficed—at least in the leading industries, for in the more unimportant branches this is far from being the case—to do away with all those minor grievances which aggravated the workman's fate during the earlier stages. And thus it renders more and more evident the great central fact that

[8] Thomas Cooper, *Life,* 1897, pp. 393–4.
[9] Engels, *op. cit.,* p. vii.

the cause of the miserable condition of the working class is to be sought, not in these minor grievances, but *in the Capitalist system itself.*[10]

"Again, the repeated visitations of cholera, typhus, small pox, and other epidemics have shown the British bourgeois the urgent necessity of sanitation in his towns and cities, if he wishes to save himself and his family from falling victims of such diseases." [11]

It might be added that throughout the period the landed proprietors were often found on the side of legislation protecting the worker against unrestricted exploitation by the manufacturer, whereas the manufacturer frequently expressed his deep and abiding sympathy for agricultural workers and others victimized by the landed proprietors.

Growth of Co-operation. The workers had not only organized in these years as producers in the trade unions, but as consumers in the co-operative movement. The Rochdale co-operative, started in 1844 by twenty-eight flannel weavers in Rochdale, outside of Manchester, was given a great impetus during the revolutionary days of 1848–9 and was greatly encouraged by the passing, in 1852, of the "Magna Carta of Co-operators," the Industrial and Provident Societies Act. By 1862 the number of societies had grown to 450 and the members to 90,000. In 1864 the English Co-operative Wholesale was organized. During the succeeding twenty years the movement went steadily forward.

Extension of Franchise. Side by side with the organization of labor on the economic field went the increased enfranchisement of labor on the political field. Although the Chartist agitation had failed, the demand for the suffrage did not cease. Measures for an extension of the franchise were proposed from time to time in the House of Commons, but each time were easily defeated. The agitation, however, gradually gained in influence. The American Civil War, the Polish Insurrection, and the work of the International Working Men's Association, all had their effect in stirring the workers to demand greater democracy at home.

In 1864 a Suffrage Association, afterwards the Reform League, was formed in London to fight for a more liberal suffrage. In a debate on parliamentary reform in 1864 the agitation soon assumed practical political importance. Gladstone maintained that the burden of proof remained on those "who would exclude forty-nine fiftieths of the working classes from the franchise." [12] In 1866, when elevated to the leadership of the lower house, he proposed a moderate extension of the franchise, based, however, on property qualifications. The measure was

10 *Ibid.*, p. vii. 11 *Ibid.*, p. viii.

12 See Robinson and Beard, *Outline of European History,* Part II, p. 388.

displeasing to some of Gladstone's followers because it went too far, and to others because it did not go far enough. The ministry resigned and was succeeded by a Conservative cabinet represented in the House of Commons by Benjamin Disraeli (afterwards Lord Beaconsfield).

Disraeli, against the opposition of some of his fellow-Conservatives, forced through the Reform Law of 1867. This law granted the franchise to every adult male in the larger towns who occupied for twelve months a dwelling within the borough and paid the local poor tax; also to lodgers who paid ten pounds a year for unfurnished rooms. In the country it permitted those owning a certain minimum of property or paying not less than twelve pounds' rent a year to vote. The law doubled the number of voters. Suffrage was further extended in 1884, the date of the birth of the Fabian Society, so as to include the agricultural laborers. With the growth of the franchise the workers began to give increased attention to political activity, and in 1874 returned two workingmen—Alexander Macdonald and Thomas Burt—to the House of Commons.

Mill and the Economists. The increasing influence of the working class led the economists of the day to consider with renewed interest the relation of labor to property. Among the most prominent of the progressive economists were Cliffe Leslie, David Syme, and John Stuart Mill. Mill was the economist of the transition period. He first showed a quite heretical attitude toward the "sacredness" of private property in land. The right to private property in land, he maintained, was not "sacred," "for no man made the land; it is the original inheritance of the whole species."[13] Rent was the effect of a natural monopoly. It was a fit subject for taxation.

"Suppose," he said, "there is a kind of income which constantly tends to increase, without any exertion or sacrifice on the part of the owners; those owners constituting a class in the community, whom the natural course of things progressively enriches, consistently with complete passiveness on their part. In such a case it would be no violation of the principles on which private property is grounded, if the state should appropriate the increase of wealth or part of it, as it arises. This would not properly be taking anything from anybody; it would merely be applying an accession of wealth, created by circumstances, to the benefit of society, instead of allowing it to become an appendage to the riches of a particular class. This is actually the case with rent. The ordinary progress of a society which increases in wealth is at all times tending

[13] J. S. Mill, *Principles of Political Economy*, Book II, ch. 2, Par. 6. Mill was born in 1806 and died in 1873.

to augment the incomes of landlords. . . . They grow richer, as it were, in their sleep, without working, risking, or economizing. What claim have they, on the general principle of social justice, to the accession of riches?"

These teachings and those of others gave birth to the organization of the Land Tenure Reform Association, which claimed "the unearned increase of the land and the produce thereof for those who are the real authors," society, and which urged the nation to control the land. This society, founded by Mill in 1870, contained such prominent theorists as Professor Thorold Rogers, John Morley, Sir Henry Fawcett, Professor Cairns, and Alfred Russel Wallace. So great was the interest of labor in the land question that Mill maintained that "an active and influential portion of the working classes have adopted the opinion that private property in land is a mistake." [14]

Mill's Inclination toward Socialism. In the latter part of his life Mill leaned more and more toward the socialist point of view. In the 1852 edition of his *Principles of Political Economy* he said:

"If, therefore, the choice were to be made between communism with all its chances and the present state of society with all its suffering and injustices; if the institution of private property necessarily carried with it as a consequence that the produce of labor should be apportioned as we now see it, almost in an inverse ratio to the labor—the largest portions to those who have never worked at all; the next largest to those whose work is almost nominal, and so in a descending scale, the remuneration dwindling as the work grows harder and more disagreeable, until the most fatiguing and exhausting bodily labor cannot count with certainty on being able to earn even the necessaries of life; if this or communism were the alternative, all the difficulties, great or small, of communism would be but as dust in the balance." [15]

Later he wrote of the beliefs of his wife and himself:

"While we repudiated with the greatest energy that tyranny of society over the individual which most socialistic systems are supposed to involve, we yet looked forward to a time when society will no longer be divided into the idle and the industrious; when the rule that they who do not work shall not eat will be applied not to paupers only, but impartially to all; when the division of the product of labor, instead of depending, as in so great a degree it now does, on the accident of birth, will be made by concert on an acknowledged principle of justice; and when it will no longer either be, or be thought to be, impossible for

[14] Mill, *Programme of the Land Tenure Reform Association,* London: 1871, pp. 6–7.
[15] *Principles,* Book II, ch. 3.

human beings to exert themselves strenuously in procuring benefits which are not to be exclusively their own, but to be shared with the society they belong to. The social problem of the future we considered to be how to unite the greatest individual liberty of action with a common ownership of the raw material of the globe, and an equal participation of all in the benefits of combined labor." [16]

In the last year of his life Mill planned a book on socialism, but only completed the first four chapters. These were published in the *Fortnightly Review* in 1879. Here he maintained that the arrival of manhood suffrage would sooner or later lead to a thorough discussion of the foundations of the system of private property, and that, in fact, this discussion was already taking place. The socialists, in attacking competition, have pointed to a great evil, and "one which grows and tends to grow with the growth of population and wealth." Though feeling that they exaggerated these evils in certain instances, he nevertheless admitted that "the intellectual and moral grounds of socialism deserve the most attentive study, as affording in many cases the guiding principles of improvements necessary to give the present economic system of society its best chance."

Realizing that there must be a change in the attitude of the state to property, if a new social order were to be brought about, Mill concluded:

"A proposed reform in laws and customs is not necessarily objectionable because its adoption would imply not the adaptation of all human affairs to the existing idea of property, but the adaptation of existing ideas of property to the growth and improvement of human affairs. . . . Society is fully entitled to abrogate or alter particular rights of property which, on sufficient consideration, it judges to stand in the way of the public good. And assuredly the terrible case which . . . the socialists are able to make out against the economic order of society, demands a full consideration of all means by which the institution may have a chance of being made to work in a manner more beneficial to that portion of society which at present enjoys the least share of its direct benefits." [17]

Cairns on the Idle Rich. During the same period other economists were pointing to the injustices in the social system and suggesting some form of co-operation as a remedy. Thus Professor Cairns bitterly assailed the idle rich then existing in society:

"It is important on moral no less than on economic grounds to in-

[16] *Autobiography*, p. 133.

[17] See also West, Julius, *John Stuart Mill*, Fabian Tract 168, pp. 20–1.

sist upon this, that no public benefit of any kind arises from the existence of an idle rich class. The wealth accumulated by their ancestors and others on their behalf, where it is employed as capital, no doubt helps to sustain industry; but what they consume in luxury and idleness is not capital, and helps to sustain nothing but their own unprofitable lives. By all means they must have their rents and interest, as it is written in the bond; but let them take their proper place as drones in the hive, gorging at a feast to which they have contributed nothing."[18]

Or again:

"If workmen do not rise from dependence on capital by the path of co-operation, then they must remain in dependence upon capital; the margin for the possible improvement of their lot is confined within narrow barriers, which cannot be passed, and the problem of their elevation is hopeless. As a body they will not rise at all. A few, more restless, or more energetic than the rest, will from time to time escape, as they do now, from the ranks of their fellows to the higher walks of industrial life, but the great majority will remain substantially where they are. The remuneration of labor as such, skilled or unskilled, can never rise much above the present level."[19]

The writings of Mill, of Cairns, of other economists, had a considerable effect on the social thought of this period, as did likewise the indictment of the capitalist order from the pens of Ruskin, Carlyle, Kingsley, Maurice, and others.

Summary. The early eighties, therefore, found conditions of industry and the physical and psychical conditions of the working class far different from those in the late forties, when the great *Manifesto* of Marxian socialism was formulated. Contrary to the expectations of the brilliant young authors of the *Manifesto,* capitalist industry had survived and expanded in England. The workers had passed through a number of crises, but had not revolted. Conditions had improved for numbers of them as a result both of the economic organization of the workers and of the enlightened selfishness of the employing class. The workers had achieved many of the political forms their predecessors, the Chartists, had demanded. Great numbers of them had received the franchise. They were able to effect changes through the ballot. They had created for themselves such economic agencies for peaceful progress as trade unions and co-operative societies. They had seen some of their worst evils ameliorated through social legislation. Their demand for immediate and violent change had largely given way to a struggle for

[18] Cairns, *Some Leading Principles of Political Economy,* p. 32.
[19] *Ibid.,* p. 348.

improvement through the ballot, through legislation, through the strengthening of labor unions and of co-operatives. Nor did they see so clearly as some of their predecessors seemed to see the imminent breakdown of the capitalist system.

CHAPTER 18

Fabianism

IT WAS in an England undergoing the changes discussed in the preceding chapter that Fabian socialism developed, as a flexible school of socialist thought. It therefore differed in a number of respects from Marxian socialism, formulated during the revolutionary period of the late forties. Adapting itself to these changed conditions, Fabian socialism regarded the transition from capitalism to socialism as a gradual process; looked forward to the socialization of industry by the peaceful economic and political agencies already at hand; saw in the middle class a group that could be utilized in developing the technique of administration in behalf of the new social order, and felt that an important step in the attainment of socialism was the arousing of the social conscience of the community in favor of the socialist ideal.

Difference between Marxists and Fabians. M. Beer, the British socialist historian, thus clearly describes the differences between the tactics prescribed by the early Marxian and the early Fabian schools—a difference which has, however, not wholly persisted:

"Between the years 1865 and 1885 Great Britain had entered on a period of change. . . . The rise of the working classes could no longer be denied; their influence on legislation and the wage-contract was visibly on the increase. They had obtained the franchise and the legalization of trade unionism. The British Constitution was turned into a democracy. . . . A democratic state which was prepared to take upon itself social reform duties, a working class with economic influence and power, a nation with a growing social conscience, could not be treated from the standpoint of revolution and class struggle. The fundamental socialist concepts required a new basis and new methods more in harmony with new conditions. . . .

"Rightly understood, the pre-democratic socialists of the Chartist or Marxist type could not but think of a revolution, since they had first to sweep away the old state in order to create a political mechanism for a collectivist reorganization of society. In a democratic society, and in a state which acknowledges the duty of carrying legislation, there was no need of a revolution in order to create a new political mechanism, for it was in existence and needed but to be used. The real question therefore was, How was this state to be used in order to get systematic social reform?

"The Owenites went outside the state for the purpose of building up a co-operative commonwealth, and they elaborated its general outline, and even its detail, by pen and pencil. The Marxists scorned all sketches and all questionings for the details of the future state, but urged upon the working class to fight against the existing order, to obtain political power, to seize the state for the purpose of the abolition of the capitalist system which obstructed the birth of the new order . . . ; this constituted the real mission of the socialists. Webb [representing the Fabians] investigates the particular evils of society, points out the remedy for each of them in accordance with the general principles of socialism, and endeavors to persuade the nation that these remedies are practicable and suitable for legislation. The mission of the socialist was, therefore, to acquire knowledge by means of specialized research into the various manifestations of economic and social life, to acquaint themselves with the machinery of legislation and administration, and to put their knowledge and experience at the disposal of all political agencies.

"There was no reason for socialists to wait for the social revolution. The realization of socialism had begun from the moment when the state became accessible to social reform ideas, and the employers of labor admitted collective bargaining and submitted to state and trade union intervention. . . .

"The key to Owenism is the doctrine of circumstances in relation to the formation of human character. The philosophy which served Marx in his analysis of capitalist society and in the mobilization of the working class for socialism consists of the labor theory with class struggle as the dynamic force. The socialism of Webb is based on the extension of the theory of rent and on the growth of the social conscience of the nation." [1]

Marxism in England in the Early Eighties. While Fabian socialism was England's distinct contribution to socialist thought during the

[1] M. Beer, *History of British Socialism,* Vol. II, pp. 279–81. The Fabians took as the cornerstone of their economic doctrine, as will be explained later, the Ricardian theory of rent, and declared that the private appropriation of rent was unjustifiable.

eighties, Marxian socialism in those days rallied around it the first organized group of British socialists. Marx's doctrines, up to 1880, had been accessible only to those Englishmen who read German and French. In that year two articles appeared in English monthly magazines, one for and one against the Marxian theories. In June, 1881, Henry Hyndman,[2] a patrician by temperament, who had become imbued with the socialist philosophy, published *England for All.* This book embodied Marx's main doctrines on the relationships of capital and labor. Knowing, however, the prejudice of Englishmen against foreigners, Hyndman did not mention Marx in the volume. He merely stated in his Preface, "for the ideas and much of the matter contained in chapters two and three, I am indebted to the work of a great thinker and original writer," whose works he hoped would soon be accessible to the majority of Englishmen! This failure on his part to give public credit to Marx caused an estrangement between Marx and Hyndman that was never healed. In his later works he did much to bring the teachings of Marx, Engels, Lassalle, and other socialist writers to the attention of the English-speaking world, but the original slight was never altogether forgiven by Marx's friends.

THE SOCIAL DEMOCRATIC FEDERATION. In June, 1881, Hyndman and others organized the Democratic Federation, afterwards the Social Democratic Federation, with the aim of creating a working-class movement to carry on the "great work of Spence and Owen, Stephens and Oastler, O'Connor and O'Brien, Ernest Jones and George J. Harney." [3]

Hyndman had discussed with Marx the advisability of resuscitating the Chartist movement. Marx was interested in the idea, but doubted its feasibility. Hyndman, however, went ahead and worked for the organization of the Federation. The program he formulated was largely one for greater political rights. Its most radical industrial plank advocated the nationalization of land.

At first the Federation spent much of its energy on mere protests against the coercive policy toward Ireland of the Gladstone cabinet, then in power. In behalf of that country it held a number of remarkable demonstrations. Under the stimulating influence of Henry George, whose *Progress and Poverty,* written in 1879, was then being read throughout England, its members also did much propaganda work in behalf of the socialization of the land.

In the autumn of 1883 it came out with a full-fledged socialist platform. Hyndman's pamphlet *Socialism Made Plain* (1883), which de-

[2] See Hyndman, Henry M., *Record of an Adventurous Life* (N. Y.: Macmillan, 1911).
[3] *Justice,* April 19, 1884.

manded the socialization of the means of life, made a deep impression. The Federation's official statement in advocating extensive social changes, adopted in October, 1884, read:

"Labor is the source of all wealth, therefore all wealth belongs to labor. The object of the Social Democratic Federation is the establishment of a free society, based on the principles of political equality, with equal social rights for all and complete emancipation of labor."

Then followed a list of immediate demands, including universal suffrage, the elimination of a standing army, free education, free justice, home rule for Ireland, "the production of wealth to be regulated by society in the common interests of all, the means of production, distribution, and exchange to be declared collective property."

The Federation in its early days included, besides Hyndman, the poet William Morris, Ernest Belfort Bax, Eleanor Marx, daughter of Karl Marx, Walter Crane, the artist, Henry H. Champion, Harry Quelch, editor of their paper, *Justice,* Helen Taylor, step-daughter of John Stuart Mill, and other notables. Morris was among the most enthusiastic and active. He helped to finance the Federation's publications. He delivered lectures on socialism on street corners and before working men's clubs, played the part of a newsboy in distributing literature, and wrote pamphlets, books, and poems, calling upon the masses to align themselves with the movement. Typical of these poems were the following:

Come, shoulder to shoulder, ere the earth grows older!
The Cause spreads over land and sea;
Now the world shaketh and fear awaketh,
And joy at last for thee and me.

and

Come, then, let us cast off all fooling,
  And put by ease and rest,
For the Cause alone is worthy
  Till the good days bring the best.

Come, join in the only battle
  Wherein no man can fail,
Where whoso fadeth and dieth,
  Yet his deed shall still prevail.

Ah! come, cast off all fooling,
  For this, at least, we know:
That the Dawn and the Day is coming
  And forth the banners go.

In 1884 some of the Federation's more prominent members broke away and formed the Socialist League, which, coming under anarchist control, soon began to disintegrate. The Social Democratic Federation remained intact, however, and was, until the breaking out of the First World War, the most pronounced Marxist organization in England.

Organization of the Fabians. In the fall of 1883, some two years after the organization of Hyndman's Federation, a small group of earnest students started a series of meetings which resulted in the formation of the Fabian Society.

The occasion for the first gathering was the visit of Thomas Davidson from America. Davidson was a descendant of the utopians of Brook Farm and the Phalanstery, "and what he yearned for was something in the nature of a community of superior people withdrawn from the world because of its wickedness, and showing by example how a higher life might be led." [4]

The group that met were divided between those who emphasized individual regeneration and those who felt that their main emphasis should be laid on social, rather than individual, progress. The latter group sympathized with the work that was being done by the Social Democratic Federation. They stayed outside this organization, however, partly because "it assumed that a revolutionary change affecting the very bases of society could be brought about at once; second, it appeared to ignore what may be called the spiritual side of life and to disregard the ethical changes necessary to render a different social system possible." [5]

At the November 7 meeting of the group, after much discussion regarding the efficacy of moral and social reforms, the following resolution was passed:

"The members of the Society assert that the competitive system assures the happiness and comfort of the few at the expense of the suffering of the many and that Society must be reconstituted in such a manner as to secure the general welfare and happiness." [6]

Naming the Society. On January 4 the society was formally organized as the Fabian Society, and for a convenient motto took the following:

"For the right moment you must wait, as Fabius did, most patiently, when warring against Hannibal, though many censured his delays; but when the time comes you must strike hard, as Fabius did, or your waiting will be in vain and fruitless."

[4] Pease, *History of the Fabian Society,* p. 26.

[5] Clarke, William, in *The Fabian Essays in Socialism,* p. xiii.

[6] Pease, *op. cit.,* p. 32.

(Left) Sir Thomas More (1478–1535), author of *Utopia,* the most noted of the British utopian writings. (Copyright, the Frick Collection, New York.) (Right) Charles Fourier (1772–1837), the French utopian writer and initiator of Fourieristic colonies in Europe and America. (Courtesy Donald Macbeth, London)

(Left) Robert Owen (1771–1858), British utopian businessman, philanthropist, and co-operator. (Right) Horace Greeley, famous American editor of the New York *Tribune* and follower of Fourier. (Courtesy New York Public Library)

(Left) Friedrich Engels (1820–1895) and (right) Karl Marx (1818–1883), the two founders of Marxian or "scientific" socialism. Marx was the greater scholar and leader. Engels, businessman and student, contributed invaluable financial, intellectual, and moral aid to Marx during his years of research and writing.

(Left) Ferdinand Lassalle (1825–1864), brilliant founder of the German social democracy. (Courtesy New York Public Library) (Right) Karl Kautsky (1854–1938), chief protagonist of the Marxian point of view in Germany.

Left to right: George Bernard Shaw, Mrs. Sidney (Beatrice Potter) Webb, Sidney Webb, and Graham Wallas, four of the leading spirits in the development of the school of Fabian socialism, sketched at an outing in the early days of the Fabian Society. *(The Sketch,* July, 1895)

(Left) Eduard Bernstein (1850–1932), German socialist, founder of the school of revisionists. (Right) G. D. H. Cole, one of the most prominent leaders of the guild socialist school, economist, writer, and chairman in the early forties of the reorganized Fabian Society.

Karl Seitz-Hof in Vienna, one of the many attractive apartment houses owned by the city for which, before the Dollfuss *coup d'état,* the socialist administration was justly famous.

(Left) Guy Mollet, Socialist Prime Minister in French coalition government, January, 1956–May, 1957; General Secretary, French Socialist party, first elected 1946. (Courtesy French Embassy, Press & Information Division) (Right) Willy Brandt, Social Democratic Vice-Chancellor and Foreign Minister in coalition government of West Germany, 1966– ; Mayor of West Berlin, 1957–66. (Courtesy German Information Center)

H. G. Wells afterwards pointed out, however, that Fabius never did strike hard.

The Fabian Society's Basis. In 1887, a few years after the formation of the society, it hammered out its Basis which, with slight modification, remains the Basis of the present day:

"The Fabian Society consists of socialists.

"It therefore aims at the reorganization of society by the emancipation of land and industrial capital from individual and class ownership, and the vesting of them in the community for the general benefit. In this way only can the natural and acquired advantages of the country be equitably shared by the whole people.

"The Society accordingly works for the extinction of private property in land and of the consequent individual appropriation in the form of rent, of the price paid for permission to use the earth, as well as for the advantages of superior soils and sites.

"The Society, further, works for the transfer to the community of the administration of such industrial capital as can be conveniently managed socially. For, owing to the monopoly of the means of production in the past, industrial inventions and the transformation of surplus income into capital have mainly enriched the proprietary class, the worker being now dependent upon that class for means to earn a living.

"If these measures be carried out, without compensation (though not without such relief to expropriated individuals as may seem fit to the community), rent and interest will be added to the reward of labor, the idle class now living on the labor of others will necessarily disappear, and practical equality of opportunity will be maintained by the spontaneous action of economic forces with much less interference with personal liberty than the present system entails.

"For the attainment of these ends the Fabian Society looks to the spread of socialist opinions, and the social and political changes consequent thereon, *including the establishment of equal citizenship for men and women.* It seeks to achieve these ends by the general dissemination of knowledge as to the relation between the individual and society in its economic, ethical and political aspects." [7]

The Society attracted some of the most brilliant of the younger men of England. George Bernard Shaw [8] joined it in September, 1884.

[7] *Ibid.*, p. 269. The words in italics were added in 1907.

[8] George Bernard Shaw, who is generally regarded as the foremost dramatist of the English-speaking world, was born July 26, 1856, in Dublin, Ireland. He was the son of an ex-civil servant, turned merchant. His mother, daughter of a country gentleman, became a teacher of singing late in life in London to support her son. George attended Wesley College, Dublin, and other schools. At the age of 15 he entered the office of an Irish land agent; in 1876 he went to London, and three years later

He later wrote in the minutes of the first meeting he attended in May of that year: "This meeting was made memorable by the first appearance of Bernard Shaw."

Sidney Webb,[9] who was destined to become the Society's most important figure, joined in 1885 along with his Colonial office colleague, Sidney Olivier. Graham Wallas, Annie Besant, Hubert Bland, H. W. Massingham, Edward R. Pease, H. H. Champion, Percival Chubb, and William Clarke were among the early signers, later followed by H. G. Wells, Beatrice Potter Webb,[10] Ramsay Macdonald, Pethick-Lawrence, Sir Leo Chiozza-Money, Keir Hardie, G. D. H. Cole, and a host of others.

---

wrote his first novel, *Immaturity*. In London he became successively a member of the reviewing staff of the *Pall Mall Gazette*, art critic of the *World*, musical critic of the *Star* and of the *World*, and dramatic critic of the *Saturday Review*. One of the earliest members of the Fabian Society, he was a member of its Executive continuously from 1884 to 1911 and chairman of the Labor Research Department for several years. He spoke extensively for socialism, edited the *Fabian Essays* and a number of other volumes, was the author of *The Impossibilities of Anarchism, Socialism for Millionaires, The Common Sense of Socialism*, etc. Later in his career, he came to the conclusion that he could be of more use to the socialist movement by writing plays than by writing economic essays. The series of brilliant plays which have given him the reputation of the foremost dramatist of modern times followed. Mr. Shaw, however, has kept up his connection with the socialist movement and has remained one of the mainstays of the Fabian Society. On the occasion of his 70th anniversary, he stated that he was more proud of his socialist faith than of his literary achievements. He has always believed that under socialism, workers should be paid equally irrespective of their product. (See *The Socialism of Shaw*, N. Y.: Vanguard Press, 1927.)

[9] Sidney Webb was born in London in 1859. He was educated in Switzerland and Germany. In 1878 he became a member of the British civil service. In 1881 he was elected a member of the London County Council, and was active in this Council for the next eighteen years. In the meanwhile he received his LL.B. degree from the University of London and became a barrister in 1885. He also served on many government commissions. From 1894 to 1925 he was co-author, with his wife, of more than 20 volumes, including the *History of Trade Unionism, Industrial Democracy, English Local Government*, 6 volumes; and *Consumers' Co-operative Movement*. During the nine months of the Macdonald cabinet in 1924 he was head of the Board of Trade. Since 1912 he has been Professor of Public Administration of the University of London, and since 1895 lecturer of the London School of Economics. In 1922 he was elected member of Parliament on the Labor party ticket. He and his wife have been the most prominent members of the Fabian Society and among the most prominent and prolific writers on economics in England.

[10] Beatrice Potter Webb was born in 1858, daughter of a financier, at one time chairman of the Western Railway and of the Grand Trunk Railway of Canada. She was privately educated and received an Honorary LL.D. degree from Edinburgh and an Hon. D.Lit. degree from Manchester. One of her first contributions was *The Co-operative Movement in Great Britain* (1891). She served on several Royal Commissions, and, as member of the Poor Law Commission, 1905–1909, submitted with others the famous minority report. She collaborated with her husband in most of his important works. A fascinating account of her life is contained in her autobiography, *My Apprenticeship* (1926). She died in 1943.

The Society developed a pamphlet literature which has secured an international reputation for its high scholarship and literary style. It prepared and introduced many legislative measures; encouraged its members to enter legislative bodies; aided in the organization of the Labor party; and arranged for thousands of lectures by its members before groups of all sorts. In speaking of his early days as a member of the Society, Bernard Shaw wrote:

"My own experience may be taken as typical. For some years I attended the Hampstead Historic Club once a fortnight, and spent a night in the alternate weeks at a private circle of economists which has since blossomed into the British Economic Association—a circle where the social question was left out, and the work kept on abstract scientific lines. I made all my acquaintances think me madder than usual by the pertinacity with which I attended debating societies and haunted all sorts of hole-and-corner debates and public meetings and made speeches at them. I was President of the Local Government Board at an amateur Parliament where a Fabian ministry had to put its proposals into black and white in the shape of parliamentary bills. Every Sunday I lectured on some subject which I wanted to teach to myself; and it was not until I had come to the point of being able to deliver separate lectures, without notes, on rent, interest, profits, wages, toryism, liberalism, socialism, communism, anarchism, trade-unionism, co-operation, democracy, the Division of Society into Classes, and the Suitability of Human Nature to Systems of Just Distribution, that I was able to handle social democracy as it must be handled before it can be preached in such a way as to present it to every sort of man from his own particular point of view. . . . A man's socialistic acquisitiveness must be keen enough to make him actually prefer spending two or three nights a week in speaking and debating or in picking up social information even in the most dingy and scrappy way, to going to the theatre, or dancing or drinking, or even sweethearting, if he is to become a really competent propagandist—unless, of course, his daily work is of such a nature as to be in itself a training for political life; and that, we know, is the case with very few of us indeed. It is at such lecturing and debating work, and on squalid little committees and ridiculous little delegations to conferences of the three tailors of Tooley Street, with perhaps a deputation to the Mayor thrown in once in a blue moon or so, that the ordinary Fabian workman or clerk must qualify for his future seat on the Town Council, the School Board, or perhaps in the Cabinet." [11]

[11] Pease, *op. cit.*, pp. 77–8.

THE FABIAN ESSAYS ON THE BASES OF SOCIALISM

The most comprehensive statement of the early Fabian approach to socialism is contained in the *Fabian Essays,* edited by Bernard Shaw and based on a series of lectures delivered by prominent members of the Fabian Society before London audiences in the year 1888. There are seven of these lectures. Four of them deal with the Basis of Socialism —Historic, Economic, Industrial, and Moral. Two depict the socialist society of the future, and one is devoted to the transition to socialism. Bernard Shaw, Sidney Webb, William Clarke, Sydney Olivier, Graham Wallas, and Annie Besant are the authors.

The Fabian Society never had a president and no person or group of persons ever claimed to act as its authoritative spokesman. Nevertheless the *Fabian Essays* are so representative of the general point of view of the members of the Society in the early days as to warrant a careful summary of them.

Webb on "The Historic Basis of Socialism." To Sidney Webb, "Barrister of Law and Lecturer of Political Economy at the City of London College," was given the task in these essays of dealing with the Historic Basis of Socialism. Webb's treatment of this phase of the subject was in essence as follows:

"The historic ancestry of the English social organization during the present century stands witness to the irresistible momentum of the ideas which socialism denotes. The record of the century in English social history begins with the trial and hopeless failure of an almost complete industrial individualism, in which, however, unrestrained private ownership of land and capital was accompanied by subjection to a political oligarchy. So little element of permanence was there in this individualistic order that, with the progress of political emancipation, private ownership of the means of production has been, in one direction or another, successively regulated, limited, and superseded, until *it may now fairly be claimed that the socialist philosophy of today is but the conscious and explicit assertion of principles of social organization which have been already in great part unconsciously adopted. The economic history of the century is an almost continuous record of the progress of socialism.*" [12]

Socialism, Webb continued, has also an internal history of its own. Until the present century its form was largely utopian, and its advocates offered "an elaborate plan with specifications of a new social order from which all contemporary evils were eliminated. Just as Plato had his

[12] Shaw and Others, *Fabian Essays* (Boston: The Ball Publishing Co., 1908), pp. 26–7.

Republic and Sir Thomas More his Utopia, so Babeuf had his Charter of Equality, Cabet his Icaria, St.-Simon his Industrial System, and Fourier his ideal Phalanstery. Robert Owen spent a fortune in pressing upon an unbelieving generation his New Moral World; and even August Comte, superior as he was to many of the weaknesses of his time, must needs add a detailed Policy to his Philosophy of Positivism." [13]

Society Dynamic. The difficulty with all of these proposals was that they regarded society as static. "The ideal society was represented as in perfectly balanced equilibrium, without need or possibility of future organic alteration. Since their day we have learned that social reconstruction must not be gone at in that fashion. Owing mainly to the efforts of Comte, Darwin and Herbert Spencer, we can no longer think of the ideal society as an unchanging state. The social ideal from being static has become dynamic. The necessity of the constant growth and development of the social organism has become axiomatic. *No philosopher now looks for anything but the gradual evolution of the new order from the old, without breach of continuity or abrupt change of the entire social tissue at any point during the process.* The new itself becomes old, often before it is consciously recognized as new; and history shows no example of the sudden substitution of utopian and revolutionary romance." [14] (Italics ours.)

Progress toward Socialism. Webb contended that the main stream that bore European society toward socialism during the previous hundred years was the irresistible progress of democracy. De Tocqueville, Webb continued, drove home this truth to a reluctant world two generations ago. Some there are who imagine that democracy is merely the substitution of one kind of political machinery for another. It is now, however, becoming increasingly recognized that political changes bring with them corresponding changes in social and economic relations.

"Advocates of social reconstruction have learned the lesson of democracy, and know that it is through the slow and gradual turning of the popular mind to new principles that social reorganization, bit by bit, comes. All students of society who are abreast of their time, socialists as well as individualists, realize that *important organic changes can only be (1) democratic, and thus acceptable to a majority of the people, and prepared for in the minds of all; (2) gradual, and thus causing no dislocation, however rapid may be the rate of progress; (3) not regarded as immoral by the mass of the people, and thus not subjectively demoralizing to them; and (4) in this country at any rate, constitutional and peaceful.* . . . There is every day a wider consensus that the in-

[13] *Ibid.*, p. 27. [14] *Ibid.*, p. 27.

evitable outcome of democracy is the *control by the people themselves,* not only of their own political organization, but, through that also, *of the main instruments of wealth production; the gradual substitution of organized co-operation for the anarchy of the competitive struggle;* and the consequent recovery, in the only possible way, of what John Stuart Mill calls the enormous share which the possessors of the instruments of industry are able to take from the produce. *The economic side of the democratic ideal is, in fact, socialism itself.*[15] (Italics ours.)

FEUDALISM AND THE INDUSTRIAL REVOLUTION. Western Europe, in the middle of the eighteenth century, was still organized on a feudalistic basis. For the mass of the people there was nothing but obedience. "Even in England the whole political administration was divided between the king and the great families; and not one person in 500 possessed so much as a vote. As late as 1831, one hundred and fifty persons returned a majority of the House of Commons. The Church, once a universal democratic organization of international fraternity, had become a mere *appanage* of the landed gentry. The administration of justice and of the executive government was entirely in their hands, while Parliament was filled with their leaders and nominees. No avenue of advancement existed for even exceptionally gifted sons of the people; and the masses found themselves born into a position of lifelong dependence upon a class of superior birth.

"The economic organization was of a similar character. Two-thirds of the population tilled the soil, and dwelt in lonely hamlets scattered about the still sparsely inhabited country. . . . It was a world still mainly mediaeval in political, in economic, and in social relations; a world of status and of permanent social inequalities not differing essentially from the feudalism of the past." [16]

This system was rudely shaken by the industrial revolution, brought about by the inventions of Watt, Crampton, Arkwright, Hargreaves, and others. The manor gave way to the mill, the mine, the factory. "The mediaeval arrangement, in fact, could not survive the fall of the cottage industry; and it is, fundamentally, the use of new motors which has been for a generation destroying the individualist conception of property. The landlord and the capitalist are both finding that the steam-engine is a Frankenstein which had better not have been raised; for with it comes inevitably urban democracy, the study of political economy, and socialism." [17]

THE DEMOCRATIC TRIUMPH IN ENGLAND. The French Revolution brought to a head the influences making for political change. It

[15] *Ibid.*, pp. 30–1. [16] *Ibid.*, p. 33. [17] *Ibid.*, p. 33.

brought a violent reaction in England. The mildest agitation was put down by a strong hand. But the old order was doomed. Measures of repression gave place to measures of reform, culminating in the Reform Act of 1832, "by which the reign of the middle class superseded aristocratic rule." The people, however, were no more enfranchised than before. "Democracy was at the gates; but it was still at the wrong side of them. Its entry, however, was only a matter of time. Since 1832 English political history is the record of the reluctant enfranchisement of one class after another, by mere force of the tendencies of the age . . . The virtual completion of the political revolution is already in sight; and no more striking testimony can be given of the momentum of the new ideas which the Fall of the Bastille effectually spread over the world than this democratic triumph in England, within less than a century, over the political mediaevalism of ten centuries' growth.

"The full significance of this triumph is as yet unsuspected by the ordinary politician. The industrial evolution has left the stranger [the worker] a landless stranger in his own country. The political evolution is rapidly making him its ruler. Samson is feeling for his grip on the pillars." [18]

Brutal Reign of Individualism. The first result of the industrial revolution was that of unrestrained license to appropriate the means of production for private gain. "Ignorant or unreflecting capitalists speak of those terrible times with exaltation. 'It was not five per cent or ten per cent,' says one, 'but thousands per cent that made the fortunes of Lancashire.'

"Mr. Herbert Spencer and those who agree in his worship of individualism apparently desire to bring back the legal position which made possible the 'white slavery' of which 'the sins of legislators' have deprived us; but no serious attempt has ever been made to get repealed any one of the Factory Acts. Women working half naked in the coal mines; young children dragging trucks all day in the foul atmosphere of the underground galleries; infants bound to the loom for fifteen hours in the heated air of the cotton mill, and kept awake only by the onlooker's lash; hours of labor for all, young and old, limited only by the utmost capabilities of physical endurance; complete absence of the sanitary provisions necessary to a rapidly growing population; these and other nameless iniquities will be found recorded as the results of freedom of contract and complete *laissez faire* in the impartial pages of successive blue book reports. But the Liberal mill owners of the day, aided by some of the political economists, stubbornly resisted every at-

[18] *Ibid.*, pp. 34–5.

tempt to interfere with their freedom to use 'their' capital and 'their' hands as they found most profitable, and (like their successors today) predicted of each restriction as it arrived that it must inevitably destroy the export trade and deprive them of all profit whatsoever." [19]

Webb maintained that this emphasis on individual freedom was partly a result of the blundering interference with economic laws by the kings in preceding decades—their debasing of the currency and then their surprise, for instance, that, in spite of stringent prohibitions, prices skyrocketed and many fled the country. So the political economists joined with the utilitarians in the belief that every man must fight for himself and the "devil take the hindmost."

A revolt against this doctrine and its tragic results soon began to show itself. The first revolt came from the artistic side. Coleridge, Owen, Carlyle, Maurice, Kingsley, and Ruskin, were its leaders. It was furthered by the conception of the social organism elaborated by Comte, Mill, Darwin, and Spencer.

ADVANCE OF STATE OWNERSHIP. Practical men were forced to seek a remedy for the ills of individualism. Numerous factory, drainage, mine, and public health laws were passed. The liberty of the property owner to oppress the propertyless began to be circumscribed, obstructed, and forbidden. "Slice after slice has gradually been cut out from the profits of capital, and therefore from its selling value, by socially beneficial restrictions on its user's liberty to do as he liked with it. Slice after slice has been cut from the incomes from rent and interest by the gradual shifting of taxation from consumers to persons enjoying incomes above the average from the kingdom. Step by step the political power and political organization of the country has been used for industrial ends, until *today the largest employer of labor is one of the ministers of the Crown (the Post Master General); and almost every conceivable trade is, somewhere or other, carried on by parish, municipality or the national government itself without the intervention of any middle man or capitalist.*

"The theorists who denounce the taking by the community into its own hands of the organization of its own labor as a thing economically unclean, repugnant to the sturdy individual independence of Englishmen, and as yet outside the sphere of practical politics, seldom have the least suspicion of the extent to which it has already been carried out. Besides our international relations and the army, navy, police, and the courts of justice, the community now carries on for itself, in some part or another of these islands, the post-office, telegraphs, carriage of small

[19] *Ibid.*, pp. 36–7.

commodities, coinage, surveys, the regulation of the currency and note issue, the provision of weights and measures, the making, sweeping, lighting, and repairing of streets, roads and bridges, life insurance, the grant of annuities, shipbuilding, stockbrokering, banking, farming, and moneylending.

"It provides for many thousands of us from birth to burial—midwifery, nursery, education, board and lodging, vaccination, medical attendance, medicine, public worship, amusements, and interment. It furnishes and maintains its own museums, parks, art galleries, libraries, concert-halls, roads, streets, bridges, markets, slaughterhouses, fire-engines, lighthouses, pilots, ferries, surfboats, steam tugs, life boats, cemeteries, public baths, washhouses, pounds, harbors, piers, wharves, hospitals, dispensaries, gasworks, waterworks, tramways, telegraph cables, allotments, cow meadows, artisans' dwellings, schools, churches, and reading rooms. It carries on and publishes its own researches in geology, meteorology, statistics, zoology, geography, and even theology.

"In our colonies the English government further allows and encourages the communities to provide for themselves railways, canals, pawnbroking, theatres, forestry, cinchona farms, irrigation, leper villages, casinos, bathing establishments, and immigration, and to deal in ballast, guano, quinine, opium, salt, and what not.

"*Every one of these functions, with those of the army, navy, police, and courts of justice, were at one time left to private enterprise, and were a source of legitimate individual investment of capital.* Step by step, the community has absorbed them, wholly or partially; and the area of private exploitation has been lessened." (Italics ours.)

ELIMINATION OF PERSONAL ELEMENT IN BUSINESS MANAGEMENT. "Parallel with this progressive nationalization or municipalization of industry, there has gone on the elimination of the purely personal element in business management. The older economists doubted whether anything but banking and insurance could be carried on by joint stock enterprise: now every conceivable industry, down to baking and milk-selling, is successfully managed by the salaried officers of large corporations of idle shareholders. More than one third of the whole business of England, measured by capital employed, is now done by joint stock companies, whose shareholders could be expropriated by the community with no more dislocation of the industries carried on by them than is caused by the daily purchase of shares on the Stock Exchange." [20]

INCREASE IN PUBLIC REGULATION. In addition to state ownership during the past decades there has developed an increasing amount of

[20] *Ibid.*, pp. 42–3.

regulation of private enterprise by the state. "The inspection is often detailed and rigidly enforced. The state in most of the larger industrial operations prescribes the age of the worker, the hours of work, the amount of air, light, cubic space, heat, lavatory accommodations, holidays, and mealtimes; where, when, and how wages shall be paid; how machinery, staircases, lift holes, mines, and quarries are to be fenced and guarded; how and when the plant shall be cleaned and repaired. . . .

"Even in the fields still abandoned to private enterprise, its operations are thus every day more closely limited, in order that the anarchic competition of private greed, which at the beginning of the century was set up as the only infallible principle of social action, may not utterly destroy the state. All this was done by 'practical' men, ignorant, that is to say, of any scientific sociology, believing socialism to be the most foolish of dreams, and absolutely ignoring, as they thought, all grandiloquent claim for social reconstruction. Such is the irresistible sweep of social tendencies, that in every act they worked to bring about the very socialism they despise; and to destroy the individualistic faith which they still professed. They builded better than they knew." [21]

These reforms have not, of course, been effected without the conscious efforts of individual reformers, but these reformers would have been powerless had not the social tendencies of the times been working with them and making it expedient for legislators to heed the demands for improvement. Nor, declared Webb, is there any apparent prospect of the slackening of the pace away from individualism.

The Socialist Trend among Economists. Accompanying these newer developments a change is evident in the attitude of economists toward the social organism. Numbers are realizing that "without the continuance and sound health of the social organism no man can now live or thrive; and its persistence is accordingly his paramount concern. This new scientific conception of the social organism has put completely out of countenance the cherished principles of the political scientist and the philosophic radical. We left them sailing gaily into anarchy on the stream of *laissez faire*. Since then the tide has turned." The publication of John Stuart Mill's *Political Economy* in 1848 marks conveniently the boundary of the old individualist economics. Every edition of Mill's book became more and more socialistic. After his death the world learned from his personal history, penned by his own hand, of his development from a mere political democrat to a convinced socialist.

Webb concludes: "The change in tone since then has been such that

[21] *Ibid.*, p. 44.

one competent economist, professedly anti-socialist, publishes regretfully to the world that all the younger men are now socialists, as well as many of the older professors. . . . Thirty years ago Herbert Spencer demonstrated the incompatibility of full private property in land with the modern democratic state; and almost every economist now preaches the same doctrine. . . . The steady increase in government regulation of private enterprise, the growth of municipal administration, and the rapid shifting of the burden of taxation directly to rent and interest mark in treble lines the statesman's unconscious abandonment of the old individualism, and our irresistible glide into collectivist socialism.

"It was inevitable that the democracy should learn this lesson. With the masses painfully conscious of the failure of individualism to create a decent social life for four-fifths of the people, it might have been foreseen that individualism could not survive their advent to political power. If private property in land and capital necessarily keeps the many workers permanently poor (through no fault of their own), in order to make the few idlers rich (from no merit of their own), private property in land and capital will inevitably go the way of the feudalism which it superseded. . . . *So long . . . as democracy in political administration continues to be the dominant principle, socialism may be quite safely predicted as its economic obverse,* in spite of those freaks and aberrations of democracy which have already here and there thrown up a short-lived monarchy or a romantic dictatorship. Every increase in the political power of the proletariat will most surely be used by them for their economic and social protection. In England, at any rate, the history of the century serves at once as their guide and their justification." [22] (Italics ours.)

Webb thus saw socialism coming in England, at least, not as a result of a cataclysmic change, but as a result of the development of political democracy, the changed conceptions of economists and the people generally respecting the relation of the individual to the commonwealth, and the gradual absorption by the municipalities, by the state and nation, of industrial and social functions. The evolution toward socialism most to be desired was an evolution of a democratic, gradual, ethical, and peaceful character.

Clarke on "An Industrial Basis for Socialism." In his contribution to the *Fabian Essays* Sidney Webb deals with the general historical trend toward a co-operative system of industry; William Clarke was assigned the task of appraising the more specifically industrial forces leading in that direction.

[22] *Ibid.*, p. 52–5.

Socialistic Trends in Factory Legislation. Mr. Clarke begins his analysis with a careful survey of the effects of the industrial revolution on the working class and the absolute need of factory legislation to save the workers from utter demoralization under the capitalist system. The development of such legislation, he contends, destroys the *laissez faire* regime. Further it proves:

"(1) That, with private property in the necessary instruments of production, individual liberty as understood by the eighteenth-century reformers must be more and more restricted, i.e., in our existing economic condition, individualism is impossible and absurd. (2) That even hostile or indifferent politicians have been compelled to recognize this. (3) That unrestrained capitalism tends as surely to cruelty and oppression as did feudalism or chattel slavery. (4) That the remedy has been, as a matter of fact, of a socialistic character, involving collective checking of individual greed and the paring of slices of the profits of capital in the interest of the working community. These four propositions can scarcely be contested." [23]

Capitalist's Surrender of Functions as Manager. Capitalism has also led to other developments of significance to socialists. Among these developments has been the growing distinction between the capitalist and the entrepreneur. In the beginning of the capitalist regime the capitalist was "a manager who worked hard at his business, and who received what economists have called 'the wages of superintendence.' As long as the capitalist occupied that position, he might be restrained and controlled in various ways, but he could not be got rid of. His 'wages of superintendence' were certainly often exorbitant; but he performed real functions; and society, as yet unprepared to take those functions upon itself, could not afford to discharge him. Yet, like the King, he had to be restrained by the legislation already referred to; for his power involved much suffering to his fellows. But now the capitalist is becoming absolutely useless. Finding it easier and more rational to combine with others of his class in a large undertaking, he has now abdicated his position as overseer, has put in a salaried manager to perform his work for him, and has become a mere rent or interest receiver. The rent or interest he receives is paid for the use of a monopoly which, not he, but a whole multitude of people, created by their joint efforts." [24]

Rise of Joint-Stock Company. It was inevitable, declares Clarke, that the functions of manager should, with the progress of events, be separated from those of capitalist. As competition led to waste, it also led to the cutting of profits. To prevent this, it became necessary for

[23] *Ibid.*, pp. 70–1. [24] *Ibid.*, p. 76.

some of the rival firms to mass their capital in order that they might be able to produce more cheaply and undersell their smaller competitors. Thus arose the joint-stock company or corporation, which pooled many small capitals into one massive capital.

"Through this new capitalist agency," continues Clarke, "a person in England can hold stock in an enterprise in the Antipodes which he has never visited and never intends to visit, and which, therefore, he cannot 'superintend' in any way. He and the other shareholders put in a manager with injunction to be economical. The manager's business is to earn for his employers the largest dividends possible; if he does not do so he is dismissed. The older personal relation between the workers and the employer is gone; instead thereof remains merely the cash nexus." [25]

To secure high dividends the manager endeavors to lower wages, and this in turn often means a strike or lockout, the importation of cheap labor, and, perhaps, intimidation by the capitalist-controlled state.

Development of Trusts. The joint-stock company in many industries develops into trusts and combines, the "ultimate effect of which must be the destruction of that very freedom which the modern democratic state posits as its first principle. Liberty to trade, liberty to exchange products, liberty to buy where one pleases, liberty to transport one's goods at the same rate and on the same terms enjoyed by others, subjection to no *imperium in imperio:* those surely are all democratic principles. Yet by monopolies every one of them is either limited or denied. Thus capitalism is apparently inconsistent with democracy as hitherto understood. The development of capitalism and of democracy cannot proceed without check on parallel lines. Rather they are comparable to two trains approaching each other from different directions on the same line. Collision between the opposing forces seems inevitable." [26]

However, both the trusts and democratic forces are inevitable growths of an evolutionary process. Combinations are "the most economical and efficient methods of organizing production and exchange. They check waste, encourage machinery, dismiss useless labor, facilitate transport, steady prices, and raise profits—i.e., they best effect the objects of trade from the capitalist's point of view." [27]

The trust thus places the individualist either in the dilemma of accepting the terms dictated by the capitalist and of submitting to combination, or of advocating the socialist remedy of social ownership. For the capitalist will not turn back.

[25] *Ibid.*, p. 77. [26] *Ibid.*, p. 89. [27] *Ibid.*, p. 90.

Need for Elimination of Capitalist. The socialist has the logic of the situation. He declares that the capitalist is no longer a necessity to the industrial process; "that society can do without him, just as society now does without the slaveowner or feudal lord, both of whom were regarded as necessary to the well-being and even the very existence of society. In organizing its own business for itself, society can employ, at whatever rate of remuneration may be needed to call forth their powers, those capitalists who are skilled organizers and administrators. But those who are mere dividend receivers will not be permitted to levy a contribution on labor, but must earn their living by useful industry as other and better people have to do." [28]

Immediate Steps. It may be said that society is not as yet ready for socialism. But it looks as if society is rapidly approaching an *impasse* necessitating some very definite extension of the collective authority, which, among other things, will lead to a general reduction of the hours of labor and an attempt on the part of the community to absorb a greater portion of those social values which society creates.

"As regards the great combinations of capital," writes Clarke, "state action may take one of three courses. It may prohibit and dissolve them; it may tax and control them; or it may absorb and administer them. In either case the socialist theory is *ipso facto* admitted, for each is a confession that it is well to exercise a collective control over industrial capital." [29]

If the first course is taken, there will be a retrogression to the chaos of "free competition" and a yielding of the undoubted benefits which combinations secure. Such a policy would also signify "the forcible prevention of acquisition of property, the very thing dearest to the individualist" and would put the state in the position of saying: "You shall carry your privileges of acquisition just up to the point where competition is likely to ruin you; and there you shall stop. Immediately you and your friends combine to prevent waste, to regulate production and distribution, to apply new methods of manufacture, we shall absolutely prevent you or restrain you by vexatious regulations." [30]

Public Control Probably First Step. If we were sensible we would bring these combinations under common ownership immediately. "But the human race generally contrives to exhaust every device which stupidity can suggest before the right line of action is ultimately taken. I think therefore that some probably inefficient method of taxation and public control over combination will, as a matter of fact, be

[28] *Ibid.*, p. 90. [29] *Ibid.*, p. 91. [30] *Ibid.*, p. 91.

adopted. Such legislation will immensely restrict individual liberty in certain directions, will produce much friction, and may possibly hamper production; until by a long series of experiments men shall discover what is the most reasonable way of acquiring for the community as a whole the wealth which it produces. But in any case individualism or anything whatever in the nature of *laissez faire* goes by the board." [31]

Need for Continued Progress. As for the socialists, they should support every measure, however small, which is a genuine step forward; but they cannot support any effort to call back the past. They may help to build a new bridge across the gulf that separates us from the co-operative commonwealth; but they cannot repair the old, broken-down structure which leads back to individualism. Instead, therefore, of attempting to undo the work which capitalists are unconsciously doing for the people, the real reformer will rather prepare the people, educated and organized as a true industrial democracy, to take up the threads when they fall from the weak hands of a useless possessing class. By this means will the class struggle, with its greed, hate, and waste, be ended.

Shaw on *The Economic Basis of Socialism*. The Fabians, it is thus seen, regard socialism as the logical development from the present-day social and industrial situation.

During the early days of the Society, with the exception of Bernard Shaw and Sidney Webb, they gave comparatively little attention to economic theory in its relation to socialism. When some of them did direct their attention to the more theoretical aspects, they were inclined to take as their starting point the theory of economic rent, as expounded by the classical economists, rather than, as in the case of the Marxists, the theory of value.

Bernard Shaw, a close student of the economic theories of the classical school, describes the situation among the Fabians during the eighties:

"By far our most important work at this period [during the eighties] was our renewal of that historic and economic equipment of social democracy of which Ferdinand Lassalle boasted, and which had been getting rustier and more obsolete ever since his time and that of his contemporary, Karl Marx. In the earlier half of the century when these two leaders were educated, all the socialists in Europe were pouncing on Ricardo's demonstration of the tendency of wages to fall to bare subsistence, and on his labor theory of value, believing that they constituted a scientific foundation for socialism; and the truth is that since

[31] *Ibid.*, p. 92.

that bygone time, no socialist (unless we count Ruskin) had done two-pennyworth of economic thinking, or made any attempt to keep us up to date in the scientific world.

"In 1885 we used to prate about Marx's theory of value and Lassalle's iron law of wages as if it were still in 1870. In spite of Henry George, no socialist seemed to have any working knowledge of the theory of *economic rent;* its application to skilled labor was so unheard of that the expression 'rent of ability' was received with laughter when the Fabians first introduced it into their lectures and discussions; and, as for the modern theory of value, it was scouted as a blasphemy against Marx." [32] (Italics ours.)

ECONOMIC RENT. In an effort to correct this defect in economic thinking among the socialist intellectuals, and to satisfy his curiosity, Shaw, for several years, regularly attended the fortnightly meetings of the Hampstead Historic Club, which devoted itself to the study of Marx and Proudhon, among others, and, on alternate weeks, visited a circle of economists which later blossomed into the British Economic Association—a circle "where the social question was kept out and the work kept on abstract lines." [33]

He became fascinated with Jevons' theory of marginal utility and adopted it as his theory of value. He accepted Ricardo's law of rent and was likewise greatly influenced by the economic writings of Henry George, whose *Progress and Poverty* "beyond all question had more to do with the socialist revival of that period in England than any other book." [34]

In the meanwhile, Webb studied John Stuart Mill with great assiduity, accepted Mill's law of rent, and applied it to movable capital as well as to land.

INJUSTICE OF PRIVATE APPROPRIATION OF RENT. To Shaw was given the task in the *Essays* of presenting the economic theories of the early Fabians. Naturally, he began with an analysis of the law of rent. He took as his definition the widely accepted one that rent in substance was "the difference between the fertility of the land for which it is paid and that of the worst land in the country." The workings of this law under private ownership, he contended, led to grave injustices. For illustration: Adam owns a piece of primeval land. This land is fertile and well situated. It yields 1000 pounds a year. Others appear on the earth and seek land. They spread the area of cultivation into the wilderness until

32 Shaw, Fabian Tract 41, *The Fabian Society,* p. 15.

33 *Ibid.,* p. 16.

34 Pease, *History of the Fabian Society,* p. 260.

they begin the farming of land which yields but 500 pounds annually.

When this occurs, the rent of Adam's land is 500 pounds a year, the difference between the yield of his land and the yield of the marginal land. Adam rents his land at that price—500 pounds—to a tenant. Adam retires and obtains from the mere ownership of land, without a stroke of work, 500 pounds, an amount equal to that retained by his tenant, who labors from morning until night.

Suppose that other people appear on the earth and demand more land. The margin of cultivation is pushed still further, until marginal land is reached which yields, say, but 100 pounds a year. When this happens, the rent of Adam's land goes up still further. It now becomes the difference between 1000 pounds and 100 pounds, or 900 pounds. Suppose that the tenant on Adam's land has a long-term lease. He may then sublet it to a laborer for 900 pounds a year. In this case, the laborer, who does all of the work, keeps 100 pounds as his share—the amount which he would earn if he worked for himself on the marginal land—and hands over 900 pounds to the tenant. The tenant, who has by this time become a country gentleman, keeps 400 pounds, and hands over 500 pounds to Adam, who continues to enjoy his leisure and his generous income of 500 pounds.

"It has, in fact, come to this," writes Shaw, "that the private property in Adam's land is divided between three men, the first doing none of the work and getting half of the produce; the second doing none of the work and getting two fifths of the produce; and the third doing all of the work and getting only one tenth of the produce. Incidentally, also, the moralist who is sure to have been prating somewhere about private property leading to the encouragement of industry, the establishment of a healthy incentive, and the distribution of wealth according to exertion, is exposed as a futile purblind person, starting *a priori* from blank ignorance, and proceeding deductively to mere contradiction and patent folly." [35]

APPEARANCE OF THE PROLETARIAN. But this condition, under which every man is a proprietor, if even only of a tenant right, is "freedom and happiness" compared with the world as it is. For there finally comes a time when no more land is to be had, and at this point there appears one "who wanders from snowline to seacoast in search of land, and finds none that is not the property of someone else." This is the proletarian. The proletarian soon discovers that the tenant proprietors have not time or energy enough to exhaust the productive capacity of their holdings. If they could buy men in the market for less than the labor of these

[35] *Fabian Essays*, pp. 5–6.

men would add to the product, then the purchase of such men would be sheer gain. It would indeed be only a purchase in form; the men would literally cost nothing, since they would purchase their own price, with a surplus for the buyer. Never in the history of buying and selling was there so splendid a bargain for buyers as this. Aladdin's uncle's offer of new lamps for old ones, was in comparison a catch-penny. The result is that the worker sells himself into bondage. His lot becomes different from his forerunners—the buyers of tenant rights—for he renounces not only the fruit of his labor, "but also the right to think for himself and to direct his industry as he pleases." [36]

This selling of labor power becomes ever more frequent until this new traffic soon takes the place formerly held by traffic in tenant rights.

Exchange Value. From this discussion of rent, Shaw turns to the analysis of the exchange of commodities, including labor power. Here he takes issue with Marx. The exchange value of a commodity, according to Shaw, depends not on the quantity of labor embodied therein, but on its utility. "No moral exertion can make a useless thing exchangeable, nor is it exchangeable if it is limited in supply." Exchange value is fixed by the utility, not of the most useful, but of the least useful part of the stock.

Should much profit be obtained from their sale, the tendency is for the commodities to be so increased in amount that the price secured for them is brought down to the cost of their production, or, at least, the cost of production on the margin of cultivation. This means a very considerable profit to those who produce more economically, "as commodities produced well within the margin of cultivation will fetch as high a price as commodities produced at the margin with much greater labor. Under these conditions, individuals are constantly striving to decrease the supply so as to force the value of the commodities they handle to the highest possible point."

Labor Power and Wages. The proletarian has a commodity to sell. That commodity is labor power. Over this commodity he has practically no control. He is himself driven to produce it by an irresistible impulse. So plentiful has this commodity become in England that it can be had for the asking. "The proof of this is the existence of the unemployed who can find no purchasers." [37]

What is the explanation of wages, the price received by the worker for this commodity? The wage of the worker is not the price of himself. He is worth nothing. It is his keep. "For bare subsistence wages you can get as much common labor as you want."

[36] *Ibid.*, p. 9. [37] *Ibid.*, p. 15.

And the more the workers are degraded and robbed of all artistic enjoyment, the more they are thrown back on the gratification of their instinct to produce fresh supplies of men. They breed like rabbits. Their poverty breeds filth, ugliness, dishonesty, disease, and murder. "You withdraw in disgust to the other side of the town from them; you appoint special carriages on your railways and special seats in your churches and theatres for them; you set your life apart from them by every class barrier you can devise; and yet they swarm about you still; your face gets stamped with your habitual loathing and suspicion of them; . . . they poison your life as remorselessly as you have sacrificed theirs heartlessly. You begin to believe intensely in the devil. Then comes the terror of their revolting; drilling and arming bodies of them to keep down the rest; the prison, the hospital, paroxysms of frantic coercion, followed by paroxysms of frantic charity." [38]

Riches vs. Wealth. It is often said that wealth is increasing side by side with poverty. Riches are increasing, which is a different thing. "In the things that are wanted for the welfare of the people we are abjectly poor; and England's social policy today may be likened to the domestic policy of those adventuresses who leave their children half-clothed and half-fed in order to keep a carriage and deal with a fashionable dressmaker. But it is quite true that *whilst wealth and welfare are decreasing, productive power is increasing; and nothing but the perversion of this power to the production of socially useless commodities prevents the apparent wealth from becoming real. The purchasing power that commands luxuries in the hands of the rich would command true wealth in the hands of all.* Yet private property must still heap the purchasing power upon the few rich and withdraw it from the many poor. . . . With all its energy, its 'self help,' its merchant princely enterprise, its ferocious sweating and slave driving, its prodigality of blood, sweat, and tears, what has it heaped up, over and above the pittance of its slaves? Only a monstrous pile of frippery, some tainted class literature and class art, and not a little poison and mischief.

"This, then, is the economic analysis which convicts private property of being unjust even from the beginning, and utterly impossible as a final solution of even the individualist aspect of the problem of adjusting the share of the worker in the distribution of wealth to the labor incurred by him in its production." [39] (Italics ours.)

Social Appropriation of Economic Rent. Shaw maintains that the private appropriation of land is the source of the unjust privileges against which socialism is aimed. Socialism, however, does not involve

[38] *Ibid.*, p. 18.

[39] *Ibid.*, pp. 19–20.

at present a literal restoration of the land to the people. "The land is at present in the hands of the people: its proprietors are for the most part absentees. The modern form of private property is simply a legal claim to take a share of the produce of the national industry year by year *without working for it. . . . Socialism involves the discontinuance of the payment of these incomes, and addition of the wealth so saved to incomes derived from labor.* As we have seen, incomes derived from private property consist partly of economic rent; partly of pensions, also called rent, obtained by the subletting of tenant rights; and partly of a form of rent called interest, obtained by special adaptations of land to production by the application of capital; *all these being finally paid out of the difference between the produce of the worker's labor and the price of that labor sold in the open market for wages, salary, fees, or profits.*[40] *The whole, except economic rent, can be added directly to the incomes of the workers by simply discontinuing its exaction from them. Economic rent,* arising as it does from variations of fertility or advantages of situation, *must always be held as common or social wealth,* and used, as the revenues raised by taxation are now used, for public purposes, among which socialism would make national insurance and the provision of capital matters of the first importance." [41] (Italics ours.)

Fabian Application of Law of Rent to Capital. As may be gleaned from the above analysis, Shaw was greatly influenced by Henry George in placing the law of economic rent in the center of the stage in the discussion of the economics of socialism. However, Shaw, Webb, and the other Fabians went beyond George, Ricardo, and Mill, and applied this law to capital as well as to land. They claimed that the world of business enterprise was as diverse in its productivity as were the various classes of soil. The differential advantages of sites, of machinery, of the more favored businesses, consisted of great industrial rents, which did not result from the mental and bodily efforts of the capitalists.

Taking the contention of Henry George and the Single Taxers that, unlike land, capital is created by labor, and therefore the proper subject of private ownership, Shaw and the rest of the Fabians first insist that much of the value of land is also due to labor. It is true, they admit, that nature bestows on land certain "natural capabilities"—climate, virgin soil, and mineral elements. But these qualities are of no value unless the land is found in accessible positions "and *their advantage to*

[40] "This excess of the product of labor over its price," writes Shaw in a footnote, "is treated as a single category with impressive effect by Karl Marx, who called it 'surplus value.' "

[41] *Ibid.*, pp. 22–3.

the proprietor of the land increases rapidly as human society develops in their neighborhood; whilst in all advanced societies we find large areas of town lands whose usefulness and value have nothing to do with their soils, but are due entirely to the social existence and activity of man. . . . 'Prairie value' is a fiction. Unpopulated land has only a value through the expectation that it will be peopled. The 'natural' capabilities of land are thus increased, and, indeed, even called into existence, by the mere development of society. But, further, every foot of agricultural and mining land in England has been improved as an instrument of production by the exercise of labor."[42] (Italics ours.)

Exercise of Labor on Land and Capital. This labor is exercised, first of all, not on the land itself, but by the clearing of forests, the draining of swamps, the making of canals, roads, and railways in the neighborhood of the land, the building of villages and towns, the development of scientific agriculture, of manufacture and foreign commerce. In the second place, "every farm or garden, every mine or quarry, is saturated with the effects of human labor. Capital is everywhere infused into it and intermixed with land. . . . Who distinguishes from the farm, the lanes, the hedges, the gates, the drains, the buildings, the farm houses?"[43]

Of course socialists do not overlook that there are differences between land and capital, "but they deny, on the grounds already partly stated, that any distinction can be founded on them sufficiently clear and important to justify the conclusion drawn."

Capitalist and Landlord. Suppose, however, the Fabians continue, that the assumption is granted that land is not the product of labor and that capital is, "*it is not by any means true that the rent of land is not the product of labor and that the interest on capital is.* Nor is it true, as land nationalizers frequently seem to assume, that capital necessarily becomes the property of those whose labor produces it; whereas land is undeniably in many cases owned by persons who have got it in exchange for capital, which may, according to our premises, have been produced by their own labor. Now since private ownership, whether of land or capital, simply means the right to draw and dispose of a revenue from the property, why should the landlord be forbidden to do that which is allowed to the capitalist in a society in which land and capital are commercially equivalent?

"In England, industrial capital is mainly created by wageworkers—who get nothing for it but permission to create in addition enough subsistence to keep each other alive in a poor way. Its immediate ap-

42 Fabian Tract No. 7, *Capital and Labor* (Revised 1908), pp. 3–4.
43 *Ibid.*, p. 4.

propriation by idle proprietors and shareholders, whose economic relation to the workers is exactly the same in principle as that of the landlords, goes on every day under our eyes. The landlord compels the worker to convert his land into a railway, his fen into a drained level, his barren sea-side waste into a fashionable watering place, his mountain into a tunnel, his manor park into a suburb full of houses let on repairing leases; and lo! he has escaped the land nationalizers: his land is now become capital and is sacred." The position is glaringly absurd.[44] (Italics ours.)

Olivier on "The Moral Basis of Socialism." We have now seen how the Fabians approach socialism from the historic, the industrial, and the economic angle. To Sidney Olivier, afterwards Lord Olivier and Secretary for India under the Labor government, was left the exposition of the Moral Basis.

Individualism and Socialism. Olivier maintains that so far from socialism being the antithesis of individualism, it is "the offspring of individualism, . . . the outcome of the individualist struggle, . . . the necessary condition for the approach of the individualist ideal." The opposition commonly assumed between individualism and socialism is based on the confusion between *personality* and *personalty,* "between a man's life and the abundance of things that he has. Socialism is merely individualism rationalized, organized, clothed, and in its right mind. Socialism is taking form in advanced societies, and the social revolution must be brought to its formal accomplishment through the conscious action of innumerable individuals seeking an avenue to rational and pleasant existence for themselves and for those whose happiness and freedom they desire as they do their own." [45]

Present System Immoral. The present system of private ownership is immoral, Olivier declares. Most of our opinions regarding social morality are adapted to a system in which every citizen is contributing active service. The most ancient and universal judgments of mankind as to the virtues of industry, of honesty, of loyalty and forbearance between man and man, point to societies composed of free and equal individuals dependent for their subsistence upon the exercise of each one's abilities. In the present society the livelihood of the typical workingman is earned by the exercise of his faculties for useful activity. On the other hand, that of the typical capitalist, or owner of property, "is obtained without any contribution of his or her activity, in the form of a pension called rent, interest, or dividend, guaranteed by law out of the wealth produced from day to day by the activities of the proletariat." [46]

[44] *Ibid.,* p. 5. [45] *Fabian Essays,* p. 96. [46] *Ibid.,* p. 105.

Under such conditions the parasitic class, while preaching thrift and industry, becomes interested not so much in productive endeavor, but in agreeable and exciting methods of passing time. And this parasitism leads to snobbery, lying, hypocrisy, and a laudation of useless endeavor as opposed to honest toil.

EFFECTS OF CAPITALISM ON CHARACTER. No class can live in idleness except by the double labor of another class or classes. The exploited class remains generally industrious and kindly, "thus exhibiting the two most important qualifications for social life. It remains to a great extent honest, though competition and capitalism are directly antagonistic to honesty." But the capitalist order is constantly engaged in thrusting workers from their occupations to unknown fields. Thousands of them suffer from unemployment. The strong survive, but the weak invariably become outcasts and paupers, unprofitable and hopeless. Their children become street Arabs. This situation is leading to an increasing demand that society shall re-establish a moral social order in which each individual has an opportunity to earn a living, and there is a compulsion upon him so to do.[47]

Under present conditions the average worker lacks intelligence in his amusements and refinement in his tastes. "But when society has insured for man the opportunity for satisfying his primary needs—once it has insured him a healthy body and wholesome life—his advance in the refinements of social morality, in the conception and satisfaction of his secondary and more distinctly human desires, is solely and entirely a matter of education. . . . But education in the sense alluded to is impossible for the lad who leaves school at fourteen and works himself weary six days in the week ever afterwards." [48]

NEED OF EDUCATION. Social morality is fostered by means of various forces. One is the educational system. The ideal of the school implies leisure to learn, "that is to say, the release of children from all non-educational labor until mind and physique have had a fair start and training, and the abolition of compulsion on the adult to work any more than the socially necessary stint. . . . The schools of the adult are the journal and the library, social intercourse, fresh air, clean and beautiful cities, the joy of the fields, the museum, the art gallery, the lecture-hall, the drama, and the opera; and only when these schools are free and accessible to all will the reproach of proletarian coarseness be done away with." [49]

INDUSTRIAL CO-OPERATION AND SOCIAL MORALITY. Yet the most important influence in the changing of social morality may be found in

[47] *Ibid.*, pp. 112–3. [48] *Ibid.*, p. 113. [49] *Ibid.*, p. 115.

socialist forms of property. "Nothing so well trains the individual to identify his life with the life of society as the identification of the materials of his material sustenance with those of his fellows, in short, as industrial co-operation. . . ." The individual worker under machine production earns his living not by direct personal production, "but by an intricate co-operation in which the effect and value of his personal effort are almost indistinguishable. The apology for individualist appropriation is exploded by the logic of the facts of communist production: no man can pretend to claim the fruits of his own labor; for his whole ability and opportunity for working are plainly a vast inheritance and contribution of which he is but a transient and accidental beneficiary and steward; and his power of turning them to his own account depends entirely upon the desires and needs of other people for his services. The factory system, the machine industry, the world commerce, have abolished individualist production; and the *completion of the co-operative form towards which the transition stage of individualist capitalism is hurrying us, will render a conformity with social ethics,* a universal condition of tolerable existence for the individual." [50] (Italics ours.)

The morality of socialism is only that which the conditions of existence have made necessary. "It is the expression of the external passion of life seeking its satisfaction through the striving of each individual for the freest and fullest activity."

Wallas' Forecast of a Socialist Society. Thus, according to the Fabians, social and industrial developments are leading to socialism, and at the same time sound economic and moral principles demand that the system of social ownership be substituted for the present industrial order. The Fabians do not stop with the analysis of trends toward socialism. They give much attention to the character of the social system that socialists should strive to attain. In doing this, they attempt to avoid the errors of the early utopians in depicting in detail their ideal social state, irrespective of social trends, and endeavor to trace to their logical conclusion social tendencies definitely observable in the body politic.

PROPERTY UNDER SOCIALISM. Graham Wallas, a political scientist, undertook the task of envisioning property relationships under socialism. In the days of the utopian socialists, he declares, socialists were tempted to exaggerate the influence of the ideal, "to expect everything from a sudden, impossible change in men's hearts." [51] Conditions in the eight-

[50] *Ibid.*, p. 116.

[51] *Ibid.*, p. 120.

ies, however, are entirely reversed. "Nowadays we are tempted to undervalue the ideal—to forget that even the Time spirit itself is only the sum of individual strivings and aspirations, and that again and again in history changes which might have been delayed for centuries or might never have come at all, have been brought about by the persistent preaching of some new and higher life, the offspring not of circumstance, but of hope."

Problems of Associated Production and Consumption. In describing the socialist ideal, he declared that, in substance, socialists "work for the ownership of the means of production by the community, and the means of consumption by individuals." That generalization, however, does not prevent the community, at its will, from using property for direct consumption, as when a piece of common land is used for a public park, or when the profits from a municipal water-works are applied to the upkeep of a municipal library. Nor would socialists prevent an individual from working on his possessions in such a way as to make them more valuable. "But men are as yet more fit for association in production, with a just distribution of rewards, than for association in the consumption of the wealth produced." [52] It is true indeed that the economies of associated consumption promise to be quite as great as those of associated production; and it was of these that the earlier socialists mainly thought. "But experiments have since proved that, in spite of the economies of associated consumption, any complete scheme of such is distasteful to most men as they are.

"Our picture galleries, parks, workmen's clubs, or the fact that rich men are beginning to live in flats looked after by a common staff of servants," Wallas continues, "do indeed show that associated consumption is every year better understood and enjoyed; but it remains true that pleasures, chosen by the will of the majority, are often not recognized as pleasures at all. . . . Each family now insists on having a separate home, and on cooking every day a separate series of meals in a separate kitchen. Waste and discomfort are the inevitable result; but families at present prefer waste and discomfort to that abundance which can only be bought by organization and publicity." [53] It is true that the land on which houses are built could immediately become the property of the state, but people would "certainly insist on having their own crockery and chairs, books and pictures, and on receiving a certain proportion of the value they produce in the form of a yearly or weekly income to be spent or saved as they pleased."

[52] *Ibid.*, p. 121.

[53] *Ibid.*, pp. 121–2.

NATIONAL AND LOCAL OWNERSHIP. There would remain to be owned by the community the land in the widest sense of the word, and the materials for those forms of production, distribution, and consumption which can conveniently be carried on by associations wider than the family group. In the case of the principal means of production and distribution, where the larger the area covered, the more efficient the management, ownership would reside in the nation, as in the case of the postal and railway industries and probably others of the larger industries. Ultimately, perhaps, such ownership would be transferred to a federation of nations.

On the other hand, land might often better be held by smaller social groups. At the same time those forms of natural wealth which are considered necessary by the whole nation, including the monopolies of certain districts, such as mines, harbors, or sources of water supplies, should be nationalized. Even where land was owned by local bodies, those bodies should contribute to the national exchequer some proportion of the income. Voluntary associations should persist, as in the editing of journals of opinion, but perpetual rights should not be given to any association not co-extensive with the community.

In his writing Mr. Wallas also endeavored to present solutions for various other problems that would arise under a socialist society.

Annie Besant on Industry and Incentives. Annie Besant, later famous as the advocate of Indian reform, discusses the problem of industry under socialism. Among the most interesting portions of her discussion is that which deals with future incentives. The first general stimulus to labor under socialism, she maintains, is the starvation which follows the cessation of labor. Generally men will prefer short and well-paid work to starvation. "The individual shirker will be dealt with much as he is today: he will be warned, and, if he prove incorrigibly idle, discharged from the communal employ. The vast majority of men now seek to retain their employment by a reasonable discharge of their duty: why should they not do the same when the employment is on easier conditions? The next stimulus would be the appetite of the worker for the result of the communal toil, and the determination of his fellow-workers to make him take his fair share of the work of producing it. . . . If there is one vice more certain than another to be unpopular in a socialistic community, it is laziness. The man who shirked would find his mates making his position intolerable, even before he suffered the doom of expulsion." [54]

[54] *Fabian Essays,* pp. 151–2.

Reasons for the Gold Hunger under Capitalism. But there would be more compelling motives for doing one's best than the negative motive of fear. "Under our present social system, the struggle for riches assumes an abnormal and artificial development; riches mean nearly all that makes life worth having, security against starvation, gratification of taste, enjoyment of pleasant and cultured society, superiority to many temptations, self-respect, comfort, knowledge, freedom, as far as these things are attainable under existing conditions. In a society where poverty means social discredit, where misfortune is treated as a crime, where the prison or the workhouse is a guerdon of failure, and the bitter carking harassment of daily wants unmet by daily supply is ever hanging over the head of each worker, what wonder that money seems the only thing needful, and that every other thought is lost in the frenzied rush to escape all that is summed up in the word poverty?

Non-Profit Incentives under Socialism. "But this abnormal development of the gold hunger would disappear upon the certainty for each of the means of subsistence. Let each individual feel absolutely secure of subsistence, let every anxiety as to material wants of his future be swept away; and the longing for wealth will lose its leverage. The daily bread being certain, the tyranny of pecuniary gain will be broken; and life will begin to be used in living and not in struggling for the chance to live. Then will come to the front all those multifarious motives which are at work in the complex human organism even now, and which will assume their proper importance when the basis of the physical life is assured.

"The desire to excel, the joy in creative work, the longing to improve, the eagerness to win social approval, the instinct of benevolence; all these will start into full life, and will serve at once as the stimulus to labor and the reward of excellence.

"It is instructive to notice that these very forces may already be seen at work in every case in which subsistence is secured, and they alone supply the stimulus to action. The soldier's subsistence is certain and does not depend on his exertions. At once he becomes susceptible to appeals to his patriotism, to his *esprit de corps,* to the honor of his flag; he will dare anything for glory, and value a bit of bronze, which is the 'reward of valor,' far more than a hundred times its weight in gold. Yet many of the private soldiers come from the worst in the population; and military glory and success in murder are but poor objects to aim at.

"If so much can be done under circumstances so unpromising, what may we not hope from nobler aspirations? Or take the eagerness, self-denial, and strenuous effort, thrown by young men into their own games! The desire to be captain of the Oxford eleven, stroke of the Cambridge boat, victor in the foot-race or the leaping, in a word, the desire to excel, is strong enough to compel the exertions which often ruin physical health." [55] (Italics ours.)

Bland on "The Outlook." The *Fabian Essays* close with a summarizing chapter or "Outlook" by Hubert Bland. Bland, expressing the sentiments of most of the Fabians, sees no hope in revolution by physical force. "The physical force man, like the privileged tory, has failed to take note of the flux of things, and to recognize the change brought about by the ballot. Under the lodger franchise the barricade is the last resort of a small and desperate minority, a frank confession of despair, a reduction to absurdity of the whole socialist case." [56]

Assume that the process toward trustification goes on. Changes must follow in the political field. The extension of the suffrage has done more than make the working class articulate. It has given them consciousness. They will henceforth be heard clamoring for relief. Thus the coming struggle between the "haves" and the "have nots" will be a struggle of political parties, each conscious of the goal and the life and death character of the struggle. Political progress has, however, generally lagged far behind economic progress. We must therefore not be surprised if the progress in the future has no proper relation to the rate at which we are traveling toward socialism in the spheres of thought and industry.

PRINCIPALITIES ON SIDE OF SOCIALISM. Nevertheless "those who resist socialism fight against principalities and powers in economic places. . . . The continuous perfecting of the organization of labor will hourly quicken in the worker the consciousness that his is a collective and not an individual life. . . . The intensifying of the struggle for existence, while it sets bourgeois at the throat of bourgeois, is forcing union and solidarity upon the workers. And the bourgeois ranks themselves are dwindling. The keenness of competition, making it every year more obviously impossible for those who are born without capital ever to achieve it, will deprive the capitalist class of the support it now receives from educated and cultivated but impecunious young men whose material interests must ultimately triumph over their class sympathies. . . . Inquiry proves that socialism is built upon a triple rock, historical, ethical, and economic. . . . By the light of the socialist ideal he sees the evil—yet sees it pass. Then and now he begins to live in the cleaner,

[55] *Ibid.*, pp. 152–3. [56] *Ibid.*, p. 185.

braver, holier life of the future; and he marches forward, steeled and stimulated, with resolute step, with steadfast eye, with equal pulse."

Summary. Thus the Fabians of the eighties concluded their survey of economic trends toward a co-operative commonwealth, and their picture—based on developing tendencies—of the socialist society. With the Marxians they saw socialism coming as a result of great economic and social forces. As has been elsewhere brought out, they had more faith than did the early Marxians in gradual, peaceful progress, following from the steady extension of the functions of the state, more effective political action, the development of education, and the arousing of the moral forces of the community. They had little faith in a violent revolution as a result of cataclysmic changes. They emphasized in economic theory the iniquities following from the private appropriation of economic rent rather than from surplus value. They sought to inspire devotion to the cause by visualizing the possibilities of associated production, while avoiding the impossible imaginings of the utopians. On the other hand, having as their chief objective the conversion of the middle class, they failed to arouse the worker as the Marxians aroused him, by a clarion call to action through emphasis on the class struggle. On the whole, however, they made an important contribution to socialist thinking not only in England, but throughout the world.

Webb's Later Critique of *Fabian Essays*. In the 1920 edition of the *Fabian Essays,* Webb attempted to trace the changes in thought within the Fabian Society since the publication of the first edition, a generation before. The economics of the essays, he maintained, were essentially sound. The historical portion, however, was more vulnerable.

Neglect of Trade Union Movement. Referring to the omissions in the first formulation of Fabian thought, Webb declared that the early Fabians did not realize the importance of the trade-union movement.

"We evidently," writes Webb, "attached quite insufficient importance to trade-unionism, which the book never mentions as a political force, or as constituting any essential part of the social structure. It is clear that we had little notion, in 1889, of the enduring value and indispensable social function of vocational organization of any sort; and we had no anticipation that it was to be, as is nowadays commonly accepted, a permanent part of social organization, destined, in the state of tomorrow, for important public functions. We very soon set about remedying this particular gap in our knowledge; and the publication, in 1894, of the *History of Trade-Unionism,* and, at the end of 1897, of the comprehensive analysis of the whole structure and function of the workmen's organizations, entitled *Industrial Democracy,* effectively brought the trade-union movement into our common consciousness. We may perhaps say that it did more than this. It laid the foundation for, and possibly contributed to promote, in a younger generation, the whole series of studies of different aspects of vocational organization, and its place in the society of the future, which, whatever we may think of their elaboration into what is called guild socialism, constitute, perhaps, the most important addition that this century has yet made to socialist thought." [57]

UNDERESTIMATE OF CO-OPERATIVE MOVEMENT. "We were similarly unappreciative of the co-operative movement," continues Webb. "We did not recognize in the working-class co-operative store any part of the social structure of the future. Hence we did not, in our constructive forecasts, make any use of the very important discoveries in practical organization that the co-operators had, from 1844 onward, stumbled upon; we did not realize the extent to which these would render practicable the social advantage of producing, not in the mere anticipation of profit but in order to satisfy an ascertained demand; and how they would demonstrate the success, in the extensive business of household supplies, of the supersession of the profit-making capitalist by an essentially collectivist organization. Our omission was made good by the publication, in 1890, of *The Co-operative Movement in Great Britain,* by one who presently joined our group." [Beatrice Potter, afterwards Beatrice Potter Webb.]

IMPORTANCE OF MUNICIPAL SOCIALISM. Webb furthermore declares that, at the date of the writing of the essays, the Fabian group did not realize what an extensive sphere must necessarily be assigned, in any highly organized and populated community, to municipal socialism, and the important part to be played in the socialist state by its various democratically organized and practically autonomous local governing bodies. Later the group "came very vividly to appreciate the significance of their manifold functions in ridding us from the hypothetical tyranny of a single national employer, inevitably 'bureaucratic' in character, no less than from the incubus of an all-pervading uniformity of social life. In the State of Tomorrow, as we realized, those who did not like the arrangements of Hampstead would always be able to move to Highgate and live under a different local government. We accordingly saw our way to a vast increase in the consciousness of personal freedom, a vista of endless diversity, the practical opportunity for an

[57] This and the following quotations are from the Introduction to 1920 Edition of *Fabian Essays,* published by the Fabian Society.

indefinitely varied development of human personality, under the most complete and all embracing collectivism. We threw ourselves with energy into the study and the propaganda of 'municipal socialism,' the steady increase of which has resulted not merely in greatly widening the available experience of collectivism, and in placing, by 1919, of literally thousands of members of the Labor party on local governing bodies, but also in considerably filling out the visions of the organization of the socialist state."

Inadequate Concept of Unemployment Solution. The Fabian writers of the eighties, Webb continues, were better informed concerning the national government, although they were very vague and general in regard to practical proposals for nationalization. They were wholly speculative regarding the future of agriculture. They understood little about ways and means of grappling with the problem of unemployment. They "erred, in common not only with other socialists, but also with the ordinary economists and politicians, in assuming that recurrent periods of widespread unemployment could not in practice be prevented under any system short of a completely organized collectivism," and they were speculating about the organization of the unemployed as such. They failed to realize that under socialism, as under the present system, provision should be made for the nurture and maintenance of the "non-effectives" in society.

The Fabian International Position. Webb contended that a more general shortcoming of the Fabians was their failure "to think internationally." None of the Fabians, with the partial exception of William Clarke, had any real knowledge either of the Continental socialist movements or of international relations.

"Except for our studies of Proudhon, Lassalle, and Karl Marx, and some slight personal acquaintance with socialist exiles in London, we knew practically nothing of what was happening in the socialist world outside of our country. But here, too, we quickly improved our qualifications. The Fabian Society was represented at the next International Socialist Congress at Brussels in 1891, and has ever since taken its share in international relations. But we had our own view of internationalism. We had little sympathy with the ideal of a universal cosmopolitanism which some socialists and many liberals more or less consciously cherished, as an exaggeration, if not a perversion, of the teachings of Mazzini on the one hand, and Cobden on the other. What we aimed at was, literally, an organized 'inter-nationalism,' in which national characteristics among the manual-working wage-earners no less than among governments, far from becoming obliterated or straightened out with a mechanical uniformity, would be not only separately developed, but also differentiated even further than at present. We counted on each racial group or national state pursuing its own evolution, and shaping its own destiny, uninterrupted in its own way, intensifying thereby its characteristic faculties, and thus increasing the special services that it could render the world; in order to enrich the common future, not only by exchange but actually by the continuous increase of a desirable variety in qualities and achievements, even in such secondary matters as costume and language. We held that, whilst profiting to the utmost by what we could learn from each other, and without imagining or seeking a superiority which it is between combinations of qualitative differences, always impossible to measure, it behooves the British to be as good Britons as they can possibly make themselves and the Frenchmen as good Frenchmen. This, at any rate, was the synthesis between patriotism and internationalism that we evolved for ourselves; and to these tenaciously we held; yielding neither to 'imperialism' on the one hand, nor to 'Little Englandism' on the other; and seeking always to replace the ignorant pride of pre-eminence of race or dominance of Empire by a recognition, among all states and peoples—to use a phrase of John Stuart Mill—of 'that best kind of equality, reciprocal superiority'; always prompt to recognize and acknowledge, for the common service of all, every feature in which any race differs from, and thereby in that particular excels another, even if that be our own!"

THE PSYCHOLOGY OF FREEDOM. The early Fabians, Webb declares, made a mistake in not giving enough thought to the conditions of a "generally diffused consciousness of social freedom." "We did not allow for the psychological fact that no man is free who does not think himself free; and that no one is benefiting by the responsibilities of governing unless he is aware that he is governing. . . . And whilst we were strong on liberty and fraternity, as essentials of democracy, we were apt to forget equality, as a no less indispensable element in socialism. We presently acquired something of what we lacked from our nearer acquaintance with co-operation, municipal government, and, above all, trade unionism, but much had to be learned from the studies subsequently made in what may be called social psychology, to which some of us contributed."

THE POLICY OF PERMEATION. Taking up the Fabian Society's policy of "permeation," Webb declares that the society believes with all its might in that policy—that is to say, the policy of inculcating "socialist thought and socialist projects into the minds not merely of complete converts, but of those whom we found in disagreement with us—and we spared no pains in these propagandist efforts, not among political liberals or radicals only, but also among political conservatives; not only among trade unionists and co-operators, but also among employers and financiers. I do not suppose that, nowadays, anyone would question that this was a powerful and successful propaganda at a period when no other form of political action was open to us."

Independent Political Action. However, adds Webb, the Fabian Society at the same time realized that "not much progress could be made toward socialism without the formation, and the entry into British politics, of a definitely Socialist party putting itself in opposition to both the Liberal and Conservative parties. . . . We were . . . striving persistently to get on foot an independent political party, which would hold socialist views and adopt a definitely socialist program. We recognized—as events have proved, accurately—that for such a party, in this country in this generation, the only practicable basis was the wage-earning class, and the only available machinery was the trade union organization." The Fabians gladly took part in the formation of the Independent Labor party in 1893, and participated in the first meeting of the Labor Representation Committee, the predecessor of the British Labor party. The program of this party adopted in 1918 corresponds closely with the ideals held aloft by the Fabian writers thirty years before.

DEVELOPMENTS OF FABIAN SOCIETY SINCE 1920

During the twenties and thirties there were numerous controversies within the Fabian Society regarding socialist and labor tactics and many of the younger intellectuals left the Fabian Society to join the guild socialist movement and the New Fabian Research Bureau, formed in 1931 during the period of office of the second Labor Government.

During the thirties, the Webbs became intensely interested in the Soviet experiment, visited Russia, and subsequently prepared a two-volume treatise on Russia under the title of *Soviet Communism,* in which they praised many aspects of the Soviet system.

In 1939, a union of the New Fabian Research Bureau and the Fabian Society was effected. Mrs. Sidney Webb became president of the reorganized Fabian Society, from which position she resigned in 1941. Two years later, she passed away. G. D. H. Cole was elected chairman, Margaret Cole, honorary secretary, and John Parker, secretary. Under its new set-up the society continued with vigor its lectures, conferences, summer school, pamphleteering, and research work.

During the Second World War it increased its membership, the number of members standing at over 3,600 in March, 1943, the highest in its existence—this in addition to members of its three-score local Fabian Societies scattered over the country. Included in this membership were 18 members of the House of Lords, 75 members of the House of Commons, and numerous leaders in the labor, business, and professional world. In the forties, through its Research and Publication Departments, its Colonial and International Bureaus, its Socialist Propaganda Committee, its Industrial Advisory Committee, its Women's and other groups, it conducted educational and propaganda activities along many lines.

In a restatement of the nature of the Fabian Society, G. D. H. Cole declared in 1942: "We believe there is need, somewhere in the socialist movement, for a body which is entirely free to think out and to give publicity to new ideas, even where they run counter to socialist orthodoxies inherited from the past. Socialism is not a set of fixed dogmas, always ready to be applied irrespective of time and place. It is a set of principles that need continual re-interpretation in the light of changing needs and conditions. There is always a danger of mistaking dogmas for principles, and of allowing policies and programs to become ossified; and this danger can be held off only by continual fresh thinking of an essentially objective sort." The Fabian Society is "organized for thought and discussion," Cole continued, "and not for electoral action, which it leaves to other bodies, though it encourages its members, in their individual capacities, to play an active part in the work of these other bodies."

In 1943 Cole expressed the opinion that as long as the Independent Labor party remained within the Labor party as a socialist propaganda group it was fitting that the Fabians should specialize in their chosen task of writing and research. "But now," he contended, "that no one is doing this wider job [of socialist propaganda within the party] Fabian tract-making and research . . . are unable to make their needed impact on the party as a whole. . . . The Fabians will have to go out and preach socialism far and wide, if no one else will." [58]

[58] G. D. H. Cole, *Fabian Socialism*, p. 164.

CHAPTER 19

Beginnings of German Social Democracy

THE scene shifts from Great Britain, where we have been surveying Fabian socialism, to Germany, and from the Fabian school of socialist thought—if the Fabians can be regarded as having developed a separate school of thought—to revisionism.

Before, however, discussing the revisionists, who, as their name implies, are bent on the revision of the Marxian philosophy, we might glance briefly at the socialist movement in Germany, as it developed up to the early nineties, when the revisionist movement made its appearance.

The German socialistic movement had its beginnings during the revolutionary days of 1848. Although King Frederick IV failed to redeem the promises he made when his throne seemed about to totter, the general agitation of 1848–1850 gave a tremendous impetus to the democratic movement. "Socialism," writes W. H. Dawson,[1] "emerged from the convulsions and the ferment of these years as a fresh goal of popular aspirations. It was socialism which remained after the earthquake, the tempest, and the fire had passed away."

Restrictive Legislation. As a result of these agitations, the working classes began to feel for the first time that they had some place in the constitutional system of the country. Workingmen's associations of various kinds came into being. Such organizations greatly worried many in the upper classes and there soon followed a flood of restrictive legislation. In 1851 several of the states passed laws for the expulsion of political suspects and for the elimination of workers' groups. One of the resolutions passed by the Diet in July, 1854, read: "In the interest of the common safety all Federal Governments should undertake further to dissolve, within two months, the workingmen's associa-

[1] *German Social Democracy and Ferdinand Lassalle,* p. 33.

tions and fraternities existing in their territories which pursue political, socialistic, or communistic purposes, and to forbid the resuscitation of such organizations under penalty." [2]

The stringent Press Law passed that year made it necessary to obtain a special personal license before one could become a printer, and most democratic papers were driven to extremities through the application of this law. The right to hold public meetings was likewise greatly restricted. A report to a Federal Diet soon thereafter maintained that Frankfort, the seat of the revolutionary element, had been delivered from the hands of the democracy, whose literature was no longer on sale. Certainly the movement disappeared temporarily from the surface.

The Co-operative Movement. During the next few years the chief manifestation of liberalism in Germany was the moderate co-operative movement of Schulze-Delitzsch, which aimed to inculcate in the working class the doctrine of "self-help" as opposed to "state help." The movement gained headway, organized co-operative associations to assist merchants to secure raw material, and developed loan associations. It appealed primarily to small tradesmen and members of the artisan class, but had little effect on the workers. In 1860 it reached its high water mark with an estimated membership of 200,000, and a business of nearly $30,000,000.

German Political Parties. In 1860 the most important political parties in Germany were the Conservatives and the National-Liberals. The Conservative party, known as the Great German party, desired retention of Austria in the Federal system. The National-Liberal party, which, it is interesting to note, refused to admit workers as regular members, wanted Austria excluded. It represented the middle and upper classes. The Democrats had little effective organization. In 1861 a Progressist party was formed to represent a more liberal policy. It soon became a strong and vigorous organization, and in 1862 it controlled most of the large cities of Germany.

The Workingmen's Association. About that time a Leipzig Workingmen's Association appointed a committee to take steps for the establishment of labor associations in all parts of Germany.

The first meeting was held in Berlin in October, 1862. The proceedings of the meeting revealed great confusion of aim among the delegates. Some favored a non-political platform. Others desired to make the association a mere appendage of the Progressist party.

In the midst of this chaos of thought came Ferdinand Lassalle, one

[2] Dawson, *op. cit.*, p. 134.

of the most brilliant and picturesque figures in the entire socialist movement.

Ferdinand Lassalle. Born in Breslau in 1825, son of a wealthy wholesale merchant, Lassalle specialized in philology and philosophy at the universities of Breslau and Berlin. His career at the university was exceptionally brilliant. Wilhelm von Humboldt, one of the great men of that time, called him "Das Wunderkind" (The Miraculous Child).[3]

Following Lassalle's university career, he became acquainted with the poet Heine and interested himself in the question of an inheritance that was troubling the poet. Heine became a close friend of Lassalle, and in a letter of introduction wrote: "My friend, Herr Lassalle . . . is a young man of the most distinguished intellectual powers. To the most thorough scholarship, the widest knowledge, and the greatest penetration that I have ever known, he adds the fullest endowment of imaginative powers, an energy of will, and a dexterity of action which simply astonish me." [4]

Lassalle's first book was *The Philosophy of Heraclitus the Obscure.* His second book, *The System of Acquired Rights,* published in 1861, was pronounced by the jurist Savigny the ablest legal treatise written since the sixteenth century.

His remarkable championship of the Countess von Hatzfeldt, the mistreated wife of a brutal husband, in a trial for separation and alimony, lasted from 1846 to 1854, and his victory over the Count, after arguing the case before 36 tribunals, made him a unique figure in public life. The trial was undoubtedly one of the most dramatic and picturesque episodes in modern legal history.[5]

[3] Lassalle at an early age showed a keen interest in public affairs. At fifteen he wrote in his diary: "Two opposed principles struggle within me for the mastery. Is expediency or honesty to guide my life? Shall I spread my cloak to the breeze, flatter the great, intrigue to gain advantage and reputation, or shall I cling to truth and virtue with republican obstinacy, and fix my gaze upon one sole object—to deal a death-blow to aristocracy? . . . I will proclaim freedom to the nations, though I shall die in the attempt." (Brandes, George, *Ferdinand Lassalle,* p. 14.) His father for a while opposed his democratic idealism. "My son," he wrote, "I am well aware of the truth of your words, but why should you, of all people, become a martyr? You, our only hope and support? Freedom must be gained by struggle, but it will be gained even without your help." Lassalle replied in his diary: "If every one said as much and withdrew with like cowardice, when would a warrior be forthcoming?" He declared that he would not deceive God in the use of his strength which should be used for definite ends.

[4] Brandes, *Ferdinand Lassalle,* p. 20.

[5] Countess von Hatzfeldt married, at the early age of fifteen, her cousin Count Edmund von Hatzfeldt, the richest member of the powerful Hatzfeldt family, who possessed all the privileges of the high Prussian nobility. He ill-treated her from the outset, confined her in his castles on the Rhine, secretly abducted her children

During these years he showed a keen interest in revolutionary movements. In 1848 he became acquainted with Marx and contributed to a paper edited by him. The following year he was arrested on the charge of urging the people to armed resistance against the autocratic Prussian state, and sentenced to six months' imprisonment.

He dropped out of public life during the fifties, devoting himself to philosophic and literary studies and, in the beginning of that decade, to the trial of the Countess.

His Entrance into Labor Politics. Lassalle joined the Progressist party for a while, but soon left, declaring that the party lacked both courage and enterprise.

In 1862 he was asked to address a Berlin Liberal Club. He accepted and chose as his subject, "The Nature of Constitutions." He declared that constitutions were based on power and that if the Progressists wished to defeat the reactionary Prussian monarch and government with its medieval constitution they must not rely merely on arguments setting forth the injustice of the present situation. They must act. The printed address was confiscated by the police, but no action was taken against its author. This speech led to an invitation to address an artisan's association in Berlin, April 12, 1862, a date sometimes referred to as "the birthday of the German Social Democracy." The talk before this group, published afterwards as the "Workers' Program," had in it a number of elements found in the *Communist Manifesto*. Its economic view of history and its conception of the proletariat as the class that would dominate in the future were pure Marxism.

However, Lassalle departed from Marx in his insistence that the true

---

and deprived her of the means of existence, while he squandered his patrimony in debauchery. The Countess had no parents, and her relations, who held high official posts, were anxious to avoid a scandal. Only one course appeared to be open—an appeal to the law. About this time Lassalle was introduced to the Countess. The handsome bearing of the young man and his unusually beautiful dark eyes made a very favorable impression on her. Angered at the story of her ill-treatment, he challenged the Count, but the high-born Junker laughed in the face of the "silly Jewish boy." Then it was that Lassalle seriously resolved to undertake the cause of the Countess. He knew nothing of law, but nothing could restrain him. He brought the case of the Countess before thirty-six courts from 1845 to 1854. Before the revolution of 1848, decisions in his favor were, on the whole, favorable. When the counter-revolution was triumphant, hardly a week passed in which some one of the large number of cases he set on foot was not lost. At length, in August, 1854, his opponent, the Count, was exhausted, his strength was broken, and Lassalle dictated terms of peace under conditions most humiliating to the Count. Lassalle secured for the Countess a princely settlement. He had shared with her during the trial his small allowance from his parents, but stipulated that, should he be successful, he should secure a definite yearly income of 4000 thalers. Henceforward he was relieved from anxiety concerning his daily wants.

function of the state is "to help the development of the human race towards freedom." Such a state can be attained, he asserted, only through rule by the majority, based on universal and equal suffrage. The growth of the factory system had made the workers potentially the most powerful force in the state. The next necessary step was to make them legally the most powerful by instituting complete democracy. The next revolution was that which would place the proletariat in power. This would mean a victory for all mankind.

The publication of this address led to Lassalle's arrest for "exciting the non-possessing classes to hatred and contempt of the possessing classes."

The Leipzig Workingmen's Association, followers of Schulze-Delitzsch, formerly referred to, was the next group to invite Lassalle to appear before it. Lassalle accepted this invitation with eagerness and with his reply to them on March 31, 1863, begins the actual socialist agitation leading to the formation of the Social Democratic party of Germany.

His Appeal for Producers' Co-operatives. He declared that such groups as credit unions and co-operative societies are mere palliatives and do not get below the surface. The kernel of the social problem is found in the "iron economic law," established by Ricardo, namely that "the average wages of labor always remain reduced to the necessary subsistence which is conformable with the prevailing standard of life of a nation, requisite to the prolongation of existence and the propagation of the species." [6]

The credit proposals of Schulze, he declared, would hardly be of much benefit to people who were scarcely able to live. Credit and raw material were of value to the small merchants, who possessed some capital, but were a mockery to others. Similarly co-operative societies were of little use to workers who were suffering as producers and not as consumers. "As consumers," he declared, "we are in general all equal already. As before the gendarmes, so also before the sellers, all men are equal—if they only pay." [7]

There is only one solution. The laborer must be his own producer. The working classes must organize with productive organizations, so that they may secure the full value of their toil—and the state must provide the necessary capital.

The path to the organization of these productive societies is an easy one. "The working class must constitute themselves an independent political party and must make universal, equal, and direct suffrage their watchword. The representation of the working classes in the legislative

[6] *Offenses Antwortschreiben,* p. 13. [7] See Dawson, *op. cit.,* pp. 139–41.

bodies of Germany—that alone can satisfy their legitimate interests in a political sense."

The majority of the committee of the workers' association adopted Lassalle's viewpoint. Others were shocked at this position, and the membership was divided into two rival camps, one supporting Lassalle, and one, Schulze.

FOUNDING OF UNIVERSAL WORKINGMEN'S ASSOCIATION. In May he and Schulze were invited to state their respective positions before the workers' congress in Frankfort-on-Main. Parliamentary duties prevented Schulze from attending. Lassalle, with his eloquence and fire, swept the great majority of his audience before him. Should his point of view be rejected, he told his audience in his final appeal, he would say to Herr Schulze, "You are right—these people are not yet advanced enough to be helped"—and he would stretch himself out in the Gulf of Naples and let the soft breezes of the South blow over him. "I should spare myself a life full of torment, exertion, vexation, and worry . . . but you would lose one of the best friends of your class."

After some of his opponents had left the meeting, the vote was taken and showed 400 to 1 in favor of Lassalle.

Lassalle found himself at the head of the democratic movement and formed the Universal German Workingmen's Association. The statutes of the Association were adopted May 23, 1863. The first section read:

"With the name Universal German Workingmen's Association the undersigned found for the German Federal States an association which, proceeding from the conviction that the adequate representation of the social interests of the German working classes and the real removal of class antagonism in society can alone be secured by universal, equal, and direct suffrage, has as its purpose the acquisition of such suffrage by peaceable and legal means, and particularly by gaining over public opinion."

All German workingmen were eligible to join the association on nominal payments. Agents were appointed throughout Germany.

DEFENSE OF UNIVERSAL SUFFRAGE AND PRODUCERS' ASSOCIATIONS. In justifying his program, Lassalle declared that universal suffrage was necessary, for without this practical way of realizing its claims, "we may be a philosophical school, or a religious sect, but never a political party. Thus, it appears that universal suffrage belongs to our social demands as the handle to the axe." [8]

He did not regard his idea of productive associations as final. He felt, however, that mere abstract principles of economics would fail to touch

[8] Letter of April 20, 1863.

the masses, and that some tangible, simple, yet fundamental proposition must be placed before them if their imagination was to be captured. A final solution, he declared in his letters to Rodbertus (April 28 and May 26, 1863), might require 500 years for accomplishment, but his proposal was a step in the right direction.

From the formation of the association until his death Lassalle worked ceaselessly and with wonderful effectiveness for the building up of a powerful political party. He set his heart on 100,000 members.

At first the press ignored the movement, though later it was compelled to break its silence. A number of papers finally came to his position, as did many distinguished publicists, and in less than a year Lassalle found himself one of the most talked-about public men in Germany.

TRIUMPHAL MARCH. The next winter was spent in bitter controversies. In the spring of 1864 Lassalle began his "glorious review of the army," held great gatherings in Cologne and elsewhere, and on May 22 reached the climax, when, at Ronsdorf, he was hailed as a great prophet of the workers, deluged with flowers thrown in his pathway by working girls, escorted by a joyful group of workers under triumphal arches, and given a wonderful ovation during the delivery of his address. "I had a feeling," he wrote afterwards to the Countess, "that such scenes must have been witnessed at the founding of a new religion."

DEATH OF LASSALLE. It was after these ovations that Lassalle, at Rigi, again met Fräulein von Donniges, with whom he had become acquainted in one of the fashionable circles of Berlin. They became greatly devoted to each other and decided to marry. The father of the young woman, a Bavarian diplomat, was indignant, however, when he heard of the proposed match. The girl finally, under questionable pressure, renounced Lassalle in favor of a Wallachian, the Prince von Racowitza. Lassalle immediately challenged the successful suitor to a duel. At Carouge, near Geneva, the fateful event took place on August 28, 1864. Lassalle was wounded and died three days later.

Of unbounded energy and brilliancy, Lassalle nevertheless lacked the saving grace of common sense and too easily became diverted by personal passions from the cause he held so dear. He had, however, given much of inspiration to the movement of the workers.

"Until Lassalle entered public life," writes Dawson, "the working classes had been without organization, and had wandered about like sheep without a shepherd. He it was who drew the masses together and formed for the first time a true workingmen's party." [9]

[9] Dawson, *op. cit.*, p. 183.

Program of Bebel and Liebknecht. The membership of Lassalle's party came chiefly from Prussia. At his death it amounted to scarcely more than 5000. The movement was unfortunate in the selection of a successor, one Bernherd Becker, who, vain and incapable, made himself ridiculous with his self-imposed title of "President of Mankind." In 1867, after several changes, Schweitzer, able and well educated, was elected president. In the first year of his presidency universal suffrage was granted as far as election of members of the North German Reichstag was concerned. This concession had a profound influence on the whole movement.

Prior to Lassalle's death other associations had been organized among the workers of Saxony and South Germany. These latter groups united at Frankfort in 1863. In general they were for supporting Schulze-Delitszch and opposing Lassalle. Although generally regarded as merely progressive in its tendency, this union contained a number of radical spirits. One of these was Wilhelm Liebknecht, descendant of Luther, who had been raised in a family of education and refinement. Liebknecht had been exiled after the revolutionary outbreak of 1848 and in Paris had been introduced into the circle of Marx and Engels. Of prominence also was August Bebel, a turner by trade, who had drunk the bitter cup of abject poverty and was the incarnation of the spirit of working-class revolt.

Under the guidance of these men the union became more radical in its nature. As early as August, 1866, Liebknecht and Bebel drew up at a Congress of workers at Chemnitz political demands which in their opinion should constitute the immediate objectives of German labor: the unrestricted right of people to self-government, universal, direct, and equal suffrage with the secret ballot, the abolition of the standing army and the substitution of the militia, a sovereign Parliament with power to decide questions of peace and war, the unity of Germany as a democratic state, the abolition of the privileges of position, birth, and profession, and legislation tending toward the furtherance of the physical, intellectual, and moral improvement of the people.

In the autumn of 1867 Bebel was elected president of the League of Workingmen's Associations. In 1868 the radicals succeeded in persuading the congress to accept the main tenets of the International. In 1869 the League dissolved, and the Social Democratic Workingmen's party was formed at Eisenach. The party sent representatives to the International Congress at Basle.

Socialists Secure Parliamentary Representation. This party and the party of Lassalle had for a time seven representatives in the North German Diet. The tactics of the two parties differed. Schweitzer, the leader of the Lassalle organization, regarded the North German Confederation as a necessary evil, which the socialists should make the best of. Liebknecht, on the other hand, believed that the Confederation was a reactionary state which spelled the servitude of Germany and that the socialist representatives should further none of the practical legislative measures proposed in the Diet, but should use it merely as a platform from which to proclaim their message to the people-at-large. The Lassalle party was nationalistic in its outlook; the Liebknecht group, international.[10]

Socialist Attitude on Franco-Prussian War. During the Franco-Prussian War Liebknecht and Bebel refused to vote for the war loan, objecting as they did to the policies of both Bismarck and Napoleon. Schweitzer and the other socialist representatives, on the other hand, supported the budget, at first on the ground that the success of France would mean the overthrow of the French workmen, the ascendancy of Napoleon, and the disintegration of Germany. Following the fall of the Empire, however, the entire socialist delegation refused to vote for a further loan, and urged a speedy peace. They furthermore opposed the annexation of French territory. Many of the leaders at this time were thrown into prison for their peace activities.

In 1871, during the uprisings attending the Commune of Paris, the German socialists held mass meetings in many of the large cities to express their sympathy with the Parisian workers. Bebel, at that time, delivered his memorable speech in the Reichstag. He said:

"Be assured that the entire European proletariat, and all that have a feeling for freedom and independence in their hearts, have their eyes fixed on Paris. And if Paris is for the present crushed, I remind you that the struggle in Paris is only a small affair of outposts, that the main conflict in Europe is still before us, and that ere many decades pass away, the battle-cry of the Parisian proletariat, war to the palace, peace to the cottage, death to want and idleness, will be the battle-cry of the entire European proletariat."

Gotha Congress of 1875. Though temporarily weakened by the war, the socialist movement soon regained its former strength; and in 1874,

[10] Paul Kampffmeyer in *Changes in the Theory and Tactics of the Social Democracy* (Chicago: Kerr), describes at length the various changes in the attitude of the German socialists toward participation in the elections and in parliamentary activity. At first their attitude was a purely negative one, and they urged the use of politics merely for agitational purposes. They finally became convinced that their representatives should do all they could to put legislation on the statute books favorable to the workers.

following the speculation and industrial depression, the vote rose to 340,000 (as compared with 102,000 in 1871), and nine socialists were returned to the Reichstag. The resignation of the old leader of the Lassallean group now cleared the way for fusion between the two wings of the socialists. This was effected in 1875 at the Gotha Congress, when the Social Democratic Workingmen's party of Germany, with a membership of 25,000, was formed. As usual, the program was a compromise, and Marx strongly condemned its demand for state-aided productive organizations.

Anti-Socialist Legislation. By 1877 the socialists boasted a half million votes and a dozen members in the Reichstag. This increase alarmed the bureaucracy. Something had to be done to stop its progress. An excuse came. Two unsuccessful assaults had been made in 1878 on the life of the Emperor. Neither assailant had any official connection with the party.

Bismarck immediately pressed upon the Emperor and the Reichstag the need for anti-socialist legislation. Wilhelm I yielded, but the Reichstag balked and was dissolved. The next election brought a majority favorable to Bismarck's demands. In the ensuing attack on the socialists the Chancellor declared that he had great respect for Lassalle, one of the cleverest and most amiable men he had met. But the speech of Bebel in the Reichstag lauding the Paris Commune had convinced him that the socialists were a dangerous element. Anti-socialist laws resulted, which placed the ban on socialist meetings and the distribution of socialist literature.

For a number of years thereafter free speech was enjoyed only in the Reichstag. It was freely predicted that the end of the socialist movement had come. The socialists, however, soon began to publish in Switzerland *The Social Democrat,* edited by Eduard Bernstein. Each week they sent thousands of copies over the border, distributing them in the homes of German workers.

In the meanwhile the socialist vote mounted. In 1881 it numbered 312,000. In 1890 it totaled 1,427,000, an increase of 300 per cent. Enormous gains were shown in practically every industrial city, and after 1885 considerable headway was noticeable even among the rural population. Evidently suppression was not the way to crush socialism. The laws were repealed. In commenting upon the part played by the social democrats during these trying days, Kirkup truly says:

"The struggle had proved the extraordinary vitality of the movement. The social democrats had shown a patience, resolution, discipline . . . which are unexampled in the annals of the labor movement since the beginning of human society. They made a steady and unflinching resistance to the most powerful statesman since the first Napoleon, who wielded all the resources of a great modern state, and who was supported by a press that used every available means to discredit the movement; and, as a party, they had never been provoked to acts of violence. In fact, they had given proof of all the high qualities that fit men and parties to play a great rôle in history." [11]

Bismarck and the "State Socialists." Bismarck, during the years of suppression, was too wise to confine his activity to mere suppression. He sought to compensate the working class for their loss of liberty by granting moderate social reforms. In 1882 the government introduced two bills providing for accident and sickness insurance. These bills went into effect in 1885. These measures were supplemented, after the accession of Kaiser Wilhelm II, by an old-age insurance law, which provided an annual pension for the worker after he had reached the age of seventy, and before that time in case of incapacity. In undertaking social reform measures Bismarck admitted that he was but renewing the old Brandenburg policy of paternal interest in the welfare of the people with a view of increasing the power and prosperity of the state.

He was also influenced by the philosophy of the "state socialists," the new school of economists, who maintained that the government should make the employment of the workers more steady, improve their sanitary and moral conditions, restrict the labor of women and children, equalize the distribution of wealth through taxation, nationalize the means of communication and transportation, protect the workers against accidents and sickness, and otherwise aid in improving their lot.

The Erfurt Program. During the period of the restrictive laws it was natural that the party should be divided on the question of tactics. The extreme wing demanded militant tactics and accused the leaders of cowardice for counseling moderation. Following 1890, however, after conferences were again held on German soil, a frank discussion of the situation led to a complete vindication of the tactics of the leaders, Bebel, Liebknecht, and Singer.

In 1891 the party reconstructed their program, and adopted the Erfurt program, which eliminated all demands for state-aided productive enterprises, and pledged the party to the Marxian program.

The Erfurt program of 1891 was Marxian in its conception. It maintained that the means of production were concentrating in the hands of the few; that an ever-increasing number of the population were being

[11] Kirkup, *History of Socialism,* p. 222.

hurled into the ranks of the working class; that the lot of these workers was becoming increasingly worse; that the chasm between exploiter and exploited was being widened by the periodic crises that plague capitalist society; that only the transformation of the means of production could solve the social problem and that this transformation could be effected as a result of the international solidarity and organization of the working class. The statement of principles, which recalls the *Communist Manifesto,* is as follows:

"The economic development of the bourgeois society leads by a necessity of nature to the downfall of small production, the basis of which is the private property of the workman in his means of production. It separates the workman from his means of production, and transforms him into a proletarian without property, whilst the means of production become the monopoly of a comparatively small number of capitalists and great landowners.

"This monopolizing of the means of production is accompanied by the supplanting of the scattered small production through the colossal great production, by the development of the tool into the machine, and by gigantic increase of the productivity of human labor. But all advantages of this transformation are monopolized by the capitalists and great landowners. For the proletariat and the sinking intermediate grades—small tradesmen and peasant proprietors—it means increasing insecurity of their existence, increase of misery, of oppression, of servitude, degradation, and exploitation.

"Ever greater grows the number of the proletarians, ever larger the army of superfluous workmen, ever wider the chasm between exploiters and exploited, ever bitterer the class struggle between bourgeoisie and proletariat, which divides modern society into two hostile camps, and is the common characteristic of all industrial lands.

"The gulf between rich and poor is further widened through the crises which naturally arise out of the capitalistic method of production, which always become more sweeping and destructive, which render the general insecurity the normal condition of society, which prove that the productive forces have outgrown the existing society, that private property in the means of production is incompatible with their rational application and full development.

"Private property in the instruments of production, which in former times was the means of assuring to the producer the property in his own product, has now become the means of expropriating peasant proprietors, hand-workers, and small dealers, and of placing the non-workers, capitalists, and great landowners in the possession of the product of the workmen. Only the conversion of the capitalistic private property in the means of production—land, mines, raw material, tools, machines, means of communication—into social property, and the transformation of the production of wares into socialistic production, carried on for and through society, can bring it about that the great production and the continually increasing productivity of social labor may become for the hitherto exploited classes, instead of a source of misery and oppression, a source of the highest welfare and of all-sided harmonious development.

"This social transformation means the emancipation, not merely of the proletariat, but of the entire human race which suffers under the present conditions. But it can only be the work of the laboring class, because all other classes, in spite of their mutually conflicting interests, stand on the ground of private property in the means of production, and have as their common aim the maintenance of the bases of the existing society.

"The struggle of the working class against capitalistic exploitation is of necessity a political struggle. The working class cannot conduct its economic struggle, and cannot develop its economic organization, without political rights. It cannot effect the change of the means of production into the possession of the collective society without coming into possession of political power.

"To shape this struggle of the working class into a conscious and united one, and to point out to it its inevitable goal, this is the task of the Social Democratic party

"In all lands where the capitalistic method of production prevails, the interests of the working classes are alike. With the extension of the world commerce and of the production for the world market, the condition of the workmen of every single land always grows more dependent on the condition of the workmen in other lands. The emancipation of the working class is therefore a task in which the workers of all civilized countries are equally interested. Recognizing this, the Social Democratic party of Germany feels and declares itself at one with the class-conscious workers of all other countries.

"The Social Democratic party of Germany therefore contends, not for new class privileges and exclusive rights, but for the abolition of class rule and of classes themselves, and for equal rights and equal duties of all without distinction of sex and descent. Proceeding from these views it struggles in the present society, not only against exploitation and oppression of the wage-workers, but against every class of exploitation and oppression, whether directed against class, party, sex, or race."

Immediate Demands of Social Democrats. Proceeding from these principles to the immediate demands, the party urged universal, equal, and direct suffrage; direct legislation; a people's army in place of a standing army; freedom of speech and the right of free assembly; equality between the sexes; separation of the church from the state; compulsory secular education; free administration of justice; free medical treatment; progressive income and inheritance taxation; abolition of direct taxes; and such protective labor legislation as the fixing of an eight-hour normal working day, prohibition of night work and child labor, guarantee of a rest period of 36 hours a week, legalization of labor combinations, the granting of equality of remuneration as between industrial and agricultural workers, and the establishment of a system of social insurance, with effective co-operation of the working class in its administration.

The Erfurt Program represented a triumph of the Marxists, led by Liebknecht and Bebel, over the Lassallean group. It reflected the feelings of the Prussian socialists, confronted as they were by the autocratic, militaristic Prussian state, with its undemocratic constitution, its uncompromising opposition to the rights of the workers, and its highly organized industrial system.

CHAPTER 20

Eduard Bernstein and Revisionism

A GRADUAL opposition developed in Germany to the Marxian point of view. It was the opposition of the revisionists. The center of the opposition was in southern Germany—Saxony and Bavaria—where capitalist industry had not developed as rapidly as in Prussia and where the state was more democratic. George von Vollmar, the leader of the Bavarian social democrats, always refused to accept the dogma that capital and land—particularly the latter—were being concentrated in fewer and fewer hands. He urged that increasing attention be given by socialists to immediate reforms, and maintained that this was necessary in order to obtain the support of the farming population who would be alienated if the socialists insisted that aid could come to the present proprietors only through the evolutionary process leading to the concentration of farming and to ultimate socialization.

The Life of Eduard Bernstein. The cause of the revisionists was greatly aided by the publication of Bernstein's *Die Voraussetzungen des Socialismus und die Aufgaben der Sozialdemokratie* (translated under the title *Evolutionary Socialism*) in 1899.[1]

Bernstein was born in Berlin in 1850, the son of a locomotive engineer. After being educated in a German gymnasium, he became a clerk in a bank at the age of sixteen. In 1872 he joined the Social Democratic party and from that time was actively identified with the German socialist paper, *Die Zukunft*.

In 1878 Bernstein gave up his banking position to become private secretary to the well-to-do secretary of *Die Zukunft*, Karl Hochberg. In that year, the year of the anti-socialist Act, he left Germany and was an exile from that country for the next twenty-odd years. Until 1888 he acted as editor of the Zurich edition of the *Social Democrat*, which de-

1 Eduard Bernstein, *Evolutionary Socialism* (N. Y.: B. W. Huebsch, 1909).

spite the stringent laws was distributed widely and regularly in the cities of Germany. The German authorities eventually brought pressure to bear on the Swiss government to deport Bernstein, and in 1888 he left for London, where he served as London correspondent of the Berlin *Vorwaerts* and as an historian and theorist of the socialist movement.

While in England, Bernstein came into close contact with the British socialist movement, although taking no active part therein. For years he was a close and loyal friend of Friedrich Engels and spent many an evening at the latter's London home. Indeed, his friendship for Engels deterred him for some years from giving publicity to his criticisms of the Marxian economic structure.[2] He also knew intimately the leaders of the Fabian Society, and their point of view must have greatly influenced his writings.[3]

As Marx elaborated his theories during his residence in London, so it was in London that Bernstein wrote his criticisms of Marxism. These criticisms appeared in a series of articles—among others, in the *Neue Zeit*—during the late nineties and led to a vigorous controversy within the German party. Later he set forth his views in a letter to the Convention of the Social Democratic party meeting at Stuttgart in October, 1898. This letter was followed a few months later by his book *Voraussetzungen des Socialismus.* The Hanover Congress of 1899 spent more than three days discussing the conclusions reached in this book, passing a resolution at the end indicating their dissent from these views.

When Bernstein again returned to Germany about the year 1900, he became the leader of the school of thought known as revisionism, which, despite the official opposition of the Social Democratic party, gained a large following among the younger men.

From 1900 until the outbreak of the World War the controversy between the revisionists and the Marxists, the latter led by Karl Kautsky, received much attention in the socialist press. The revisionist leader died in 1932.

Revisionists' Critique of Marxism. Six Main Contentions. Bernstein's contentions, as set forth in a letter written in October, 1898, to the Social Democratic party, meeting in Stuttgart, were in brief as follows:

1. *The collapse of the capitalist system is not imminent.* It is therefore a mistake for the party to adopt tactics which presuppose the immediate development of a great, social catastrophe.

[2] See Eduard Bernstein, *My Years of Exile,* esp. Chs. IX, X.

[3] Pease, *History of the Fabian Society,* p. 239.

2. The theory of social evolution set forth in the *Communist Manifesto* was correct in so far as it characterized the *general tendencies* of that evolution. However, it was incorrect in its estimate of the *time* the evolution would take. Friedrich Engels unreservedly acknowledged this in his preface to the *Class War in France.*

3. *Social conditions have not developed to so acute an opposition in classes* as was depicted in the *Manifesto.* "The enormous increase of social wealth is not accompanied by a decreasing number of large capitalists, but by an increasing number of capitalists of all degrees. *The middle classes* change their character, but they *do not disappear from the social scale.*" [4]

4. *The concentration of productive industry is not being accomplished even today in all its departments with equal thoroughness and at an equal rate.* In a great many branches the forecasts of the Marxists have been justified. In agriculture, however, concentration proceeds more slowly. There exists today an extraordinarily elaborated graduation of enterprises in this respect.

5. Under the pressure of the working-class movement a *social reaction has set in against the exploiting tendencies of capital.* "Factory legislation, the democratizing of local government, and the extension of its area of work, the freeing of trade unions and systems of co-operative trading from legal restrictions, the consideration of standard conditions of labor in the work undertaken by public authorities—all these characterize this phase of the evolution. But the more the political organization of modern nations is democratized the more the needs and opportunities of great political catastrophies are diminished." [5]

Is the conquest of political power by the proletariat simply to be by a political catastrophe? Marx and Engels in 1872, in the preface to the new edition of the *Communist Manifesto,* announced that the Paris Commune had exhibited a proof that "the working classes cannot simply take possession of the ready-made state machinery and set it in motion for their own aims"; whereas Engels in 1895 declared that the time of "revolutions of small conscious minorities at the head of unconscious masses" was at an end. And yet Engels, even in 1895, overestimated the rate of the process of evolution.

6. *A greater security for lasting success lies in a steady advance rather than in the possibilities offered by a catastrophic crash.*

Holding these views, Bernstein laid the greatest value *"on the next tasks in social democracy,* on the struggle for the political rights of the working man, on the political activity of the working men in town and

[4] Bernstein, *Evolutionary Socialism,* p. xi. [5] *Ibid.,* p. xii.

country for the interests of their class, as well as on the work of the industrial organization of the workers." [6]

In that sense, Bernstein maintained, *the movement meant everything*, the final aim of socialism, nothing. He could not express indifference concerning the final carrying out of socialist principles, but only indifference—or better, carelessness—"as to the form of the final arrangements of things. I have at no time had an excessive interest in the future, beyond general principles; I have not been able to read to the end any picture of the future. My thoughts and efforts are concerned with the duties of the present and the nearest future, and I only busy myself with the perspectives beyond as far as they give me a line of conduct for suitable action now. . . . The conquest of political power necessitates the possession of political *rights;* and the most important problem of tactics which German social democracy has at the present time to solve appears to me to be to devise the best ways for the extension of the political and economic rights of the German working class.[7]

"Unable to believe in finalities at all," he continues, "I cannot believe in a final aim of socialism. But *I strongly believe in the socialist movement, in the march forward of the working classes, who step by step must work out their emancipation by changing society from the domain of a commercial landholding oligarchy to a real democracy which in all its departments is guided by the interests of those who work and create.*" [8]

THE ECONOMIC INTERPRETATION OF HISTORY. Bernstein then proceeds to take up in greater detail the fundamental concepts of Marxian socialism. First of all, he deals with the materialist conception of history, or, as it has been more generally referred to of late, the economic interpretation of history. This interpretation he does not deny. He merely objects to the narrowness of the theory as originally set forth by Marx and Engels and calls attention to the statements contained in their later writings that other factors besides the economic factor must be taken into account in explaining past history and in forecasting future developments.

"He who today employs the materialist conception of history," the author contends, "is bound to employ it in its most developed form—that is, he is bound, in addition to the development and influence of the productive forces and conditions of production, to make full allowance for the ideas of law and morals, the historic and religious traditions of every epoch, the influences of geographical and other circumstances of nature —to which also the nature of man and his spiritual disposition belong.

[6] *Ibid.*, p. xv. [7] *Ibid.*, pp. xv–xvi. [8] *Ibid.*, pp. xxii–xxiii.

This must be kept quite particularly in view when it is a question no longer of simple research into earlier epochs of history, but of foretelling coming developments, if the materialist conception of history is to be of use as a guide to the future. The purely economic causes create, first of all, only a disposition for the creation of certain ideas, but how these then arise and spread and what form they take, depend on the co-operation of a whole series of influences." [9]

Moreover, with the progress of society, non-economic factors, Bernstein argues, tend to become increasingly important in determining future changes. "Modern society is much richer than earlier societies in ideologies which are not determined by economics and by nature working as an economic force. Sciences, arts, a whole series of social relations are today much less dependent on economics than formerly, or, in order to give no room for misconception, the point of economic development attained today leaves the ideological, and especially the ethical, factors greater space for independent activity than was formerly the case. The fundamental idea of the theory does not hereby lose in uniformity, but the theory itself gains in scientific character." [10]

It must be admitted, maintains Bernstein, that it is not an easy task to prophesy the future when one acknowledges the influence of other than economic factors, since it is difficult to give proper weight to all of the factors that affect the situation. Nevertheless, one who oversimplifies the situation and concentrates only on the economic factor is bound to prove a false prophet. Bernstein also objects to the use of the phrase "materialist conception," on the ground that the theory is not based upon philosophic materialism.

It is thus seen that Bernstein's criticism of the Marxian theory, known as the economic interpretation of history, is not so much a criticism of the more mature position taken by Marx and Engels, as a criticism of the original statement of their position, which the socialist leaders confess to have been at times too extreme. This criticism cannot, therefore, in any real sense, be regarded as a revision of this foundation stone of Marxian socialism.

THE THEORY OF VALUE. The next of the Marxian doctrines to come under the scrutiny of the revisionist leader was the Marxian theory of value and the theory of surplus value. These, Bernstein declares, are general and abstract concepts remote from the actual conditions. His contention is that "the theory of surplus value can only be grasped as a concrete fact by thinking of the whole economy of society. Marx did not succeed in finishing the chapter on the classes that is so important

[9] *Ibid.*, pp. 12, 13.

[10] *Ibid.*, pp. 15–6.

for his theory. In it would have been shown most clearly that labor value is nothing more than a key, an abstract image, like the philosophical atom endowed with a soul—a key which, employed by the master hand of Marx, has led to the exposure and presentation of the mechanism of capitalist economy as this had not been hitherto treated, not so forcibly, logically, and clearly. But this key refuses service over and above a certain point, and therefore it has become disastrous to nearly every disciple of Marx." [11]

Furthermore, Bernstein maintains, the theory is misleading, "in that it appears again and again as the measure of the actual exploitation of the worker by the capitalist. . . . The theory of value gives a norm for the justice or injustice of the partition of the product of labor just as little as does the atomic theory for the beauty or ugliness of a piece of sculpture. We meet, indeed, today the best-placed workers, members of the 'aristocracy of labor,' just in those trades with a very high rate of surplus value, the most infamously ground-down workers in others with a very low rate.

"A scientific basis for socialism or communism cannot be supported on the fact only that the wage worker does not receive the full value of the product of his work. 'Marx,' says Engels, in the preface to the *Poverty of Philosophy,* 'has never based his communistic demands on this, but on the necessary collapse of the capitalist mode of production which is daily more nearly brought to pass under our eyes.' " [12]

Bernstein also maintains, however, that whether the Marxist theory of value is correct or not is quite immaterial to the proof of the existence of surplus value. Surplus value is an empirical fact, demonstrable by experience, and needs no deductive proof. Experience shows that a part of the community enjoys an income, though living in idleness, out of all proportion to the ratio of its number to that of the total number of workers.[13] This fact needs no proof.

Wealth Concentration. Coming to the distribution of wealth in the modern community, Bernstein asks whether Marx was right in describing the trend of capitalist production as leading to greater centralization of capital, greater concentration of enterprises, an increased rate of exploitation. He answers, Yes and no. It is true as a tendency. The forces are at work in a given direction. "The fall of the profit rate is a fact, the advent of over-production and crises is a fact, periodic diminution of capital is a fact, the concentration and centralization of

[11] *Ibid.*, pp. 38–9.
[12] *Ibid.*, p. 39.
[13] *Ibid.*, p. 35.

industrial capital is a fact, the increase of the rate of surplus value is a fact." [14]

But a number of counteracting tendencies, he declares, are ignored in the Marxian analysis. Unfortunately complete statistics are not available regarding concentration of ownership. But analysis will show that the most modern and crass form of capitalist concentration—the trust—has in fact quite a different effect on the distribution of wealth from what it seems to outsiders to possess.

The average trust is not owned by a few, but by thousands of stockholders. Not all shareholders deserve the name capitalists, and often one and the same great capitalist appears in all possible companies as a moderate shareholder. But with all this, the number of shareholders and the average amount of their stockholdings have been of rapid growth. If we analyze the trend in income distribution in Great Britain from 1851 to 1881, for instance, we will discover, if the British *Review* is correct, that, while the population increased by 30 per cent, the number of families in receipt of incomes ranging from 150 pounds to 1000 pounds increased 233⅓ per cent.[15]

After analyzing such statistics of income as were available in France and Germany, Bernstein concludes:

"It is thus quite wrong to assume that the present development of society shows a relative or indeed absolute diminution of the number of the members of the possessing classes. Their number increases both relatively and absolutely." [16]

This failure of the middle class to disappear, however, according to the revisionist, does not have a deterrent effect on the movement toward socialism. "If the activity and the prospects of social democracy were dependent upon the decrease of the wealthy, then it might indeed lie down to sleep. But the contrary is the case. The prospects of socialism depend not on the decrease but on the increase of social wealth.

"Socialism, or the social movement of modern times, has already survived many a superstition. It will survive this, that its future depends on the concentration of wealth or, if one will put it thus, on the absorption of surplus value by a diminishing group of capitalist mammoths.

"Whether the social surplus produce is accumulated in the shape of monopoly by 10,000 persons or is shared up in gradual amounts among half a million men makes no difference in principle to the nine or ten million heads of families who are worsted by this transaction. Their struggle for a more just distribution or for an organization which

[14] *Ibid.*, p. 42. [15] *Ibid.*, p. 46. [16] *Ibid.*, p. 48.

would include a more just distribution is not on that account less justifiable and necessary. On the contrary, it might cost less surplus labor to keep a few thousand privileged persons in sumptuousness than half a million or more in wealth." [17]

Absorption of Surplus Goods. Bernstein next takes up the question as to what group absorbs the surplus product. Modern industry, he contends, is characterized by a great increase in the productive power of labor. Where have these riches gone? Not primarily to the capitalist class. Even though this class could consume ten times as many commodities as they do, "their consumption would only be a feather in the scale against the mass of yearly national product—for one must realize that the capitalist great industry means, above all, production in large quantities." [18]

The argument may be advanced that these goods are exported. This, however, is no answer, for other capitalist countries must pay, in general, for the goods received not in money but in the form of other commodities. We must thus look in other directions for the consumption of surplus goods. Who consumes them? Through a process of elimination, they must either go to the proletarians, or they must be taken up by other classes.

"Crises and unproductive expenses for armies, etc., devour much, but still only a small part of the surplus product. If the working class waits till 'capital' has put the middle classes out of the world it might really have a long nap. 'Capital' would expropriate these classes in one form and then bring them to life in another. It is not 'capital' but the working class itself that has the task of absorbing the parasitic elements of the social body." [19]

Industrial Combinations Not Uniform. After dealing with the distribution of wealth, Bernstein considers the problem of centralization of industrial establishments. Although large industrial establishments have grown to ever greater proportions, he points out that thousands of small and medium-sized establishments still survive, that the greatest diversity in size exists, and that no class of any size disappears from the scale. After reviewing the situation in Great Britain, Germany, France, Switzerland, and the United States, he concludes:

"If the continual improvement of technical methods and centralization of businesses in an increasing number of branches of industry is a fact whose significance scarcely any crazy reactionaries can hide from themselves, it is a no less-established fact that in the whole series of branches of industry small and medium-sized undertakings appear quite

[17] Bernstein, *Evolutionary Socialism*, pp. 48–9. [18] *Ibid.*, p. 50. [19] *Ibid.*, pp. 50–1.

capable of existing beside the large industries. In industry there is no development according to a pattern that applies equally to one and all its branches." [20]

As in industry, so in commerce and agriculture. In fact, in the latter industry there is a distinct standing still or a direct retrogression in regard to the size of holdings. "There can, then, be no doubt that in the whole of western Europe, as also in the eastern States of the United States, the small and medium agricultural holdings are increasing everywhere, and the large and very large holdings are decreasing. There can be no doubt that the medium holdings are often of a pronounced capitalistic type. The concentration of enterprises is not accomplished here in the form of annexing an ever-greater portion of land to the farm, as Marx saw in his time, but actually in the form of intensification of the cultivation, changes in cultivation that need more labor in a given area, or in the rearing of superior cattle." [21]

INDUSTRIAL CRISES. The fourth question raised by Bernstein is whether the present economic system will inevitably result, as Marx at first believed, in a series of crises "whose crowning point is the universal crisis." [22]

In analyzing this problem, Bernstein first examines what he considers to be the most popular socialist explanation of economic crises, namely that they result from under-consumption. Despite the popularity of this theory Bernstein points out that both Marx and Engels in their later writings did not regard "under-consumption" as the main cause of crises. Engels, for instance, in the third chapter of his treatise against Dühring, although admitting that under-consumption on the part of the masses may "also be a condition of crises," asserted that it explained their presence at that time just as little as it explained their former absence.[23] "To explain the present stagnation in the sale of cotton yarns and textile fabrics by the *under-consumption* of the English masses and not by the *overproduction* of the English cotton manufacturers," Engels maintained, in dealing with the crisis of 1877, was rather stretching facts to fit a preconceived theory. The theory of under-consumption, he declares in a footnote,[24] originated in the writings of Sismondi, from whom it was borrowed by Rodbertus. "It is pure

[20] *Ibid.*, p. 59. The smaller industrial units, he asserts, are particularly persistent in wood, leather and metal work, etc., where the home industry offers distinct advantages; in the bakery, the shoe shop, the tailor shop, etc., where the customer demands a certain accessibility to his home and in the production of novelties which have not become popular as yet with the masses.

[21] *Ibid.*, p. 71.

[22] See Preface to the second edition of *Capital*.

[23] Bernstein, *op. cit.*, p. 73.

[24] Quoted in *Ibid.*, pp. 73–4.

tautology," wrote Marx about 1878 in the second volume of *Capital,* "to say that crises arise from the want of consumers able to pay. Crises are each time preceded by a period in which the workers' wages rise and the working classes actually receive a relatively greater share than usual of the yearly produce destined for consumption." [25]

In contradistinction, however, to this position, Marx, more than a decade earlier, in the sixties, in the second edition of *Capital,* gives as "the last reason for all social crises the poverty and limitation of consumption of the masses as opposed to the impulse of capitalist production to develop the productive forces, as though only the absolute capacity for consumption of the community formed their limit." In this passage, under-consumption on the part of the masses is emphasized even as opposed to the anarchy of production. To this earlier conception Bernstein voices his objection.

Will Crises Lead to Economic Collapse? Bernstein next challenges the Marxian thesis that economic crises tend to become ever more violent in their nature, finally ending in the complete collapse of the system. Engels, he declares, goes so far as to maintain that such devices as trusts and combines for preventing the recurrence of crises conceal in themselves "the seeds of a more powerful future crisis." The alternative seems to be either "a new world crash of unheard-of violence," or a chronic rotation of crises with a relatively shorter and feebler improvement of trade, and a relatively long, indecisive depression. In answer to this position, Bernstein declares:

"Signs of an economic world-wide crash of unheard-of violence have not been established, nor can one describe the improvement of trade in the intervals between the crises as particularly short-lived. Much more does a third question arise which after all is partly contained already in the second—namely: (1) whether the enormous extension of the world market, in conjunction with the extraordinary shortening of time necessary for the transmission of news and for the transport trade, has so increased the possibilities of adjustment of disturbances; and (2) whether the enormously increased wealth of the European states, in conjunction with the elasticity of the modern credit system and the rise of industrial cartels [or combines], has so limited the reacting force of local and individual disturbances, that, at least for some time, general commercial crises similar to the earlier ones are to be regarded as improbable." [26]

Credit, Speculation, and Crises. Such critics of Bernstein as Rosa Luxemburg argue that the credit system but accelerates foolhardy specu-

[25] See *Ibid.*, p. 74.

[26] *Ibid.*, pp. 79–80.

lation and crises. In endeavoring to prove her case, she concentrates, however, declares Bernstein, on the destructive, not the constructive, functions of the credit system. Marx realized the mixed character of credit when he spoke of it as "half swindler, half prophet." It is not true that speculation grows greater with the advance of capitalism. The maddest outbursts of speculation come at the dawn of the capitalistic era, "and speculation celebrates its wildest orgies usually in the countries where the capitalistic development is youngest. In the domain of industry speculation flourishes most luxuriantly in new branches of production. The older a branch of production is, under modern forms, with the exception of manufacture of mere articles of fashion, the more does the speculative momentum cease to play a decisive part. The conditions and movements of the market are then more exactly foreseen and are taken into consideration with greater certainty." Increasingly rapid means of communication from one industrial center to another, increasingly close relationships between manufacturers, and the influence of the trusts, all modify the intensity of crises. The failure of a world crisis to materialize, in fact, led Engels, in 1894, to question whether the world was facing a new enlargement of the cycle, and to warn his readers against the abstract deduction that these crises must repeat themselves in the old form.[27]

"There remains," concludes Bernstein, "only so much, that the capacity for production in modern society is much greater than the actual demands for products determined by the buying capacity; that millions live insufficiently housed, insufficiently clad, and insufficiently nourished, in spite of abundant means at hand for sufficient housing, nourishment, and clothing; and that out of this incongruity, overproduction appears again and again in different branches of production, so that either actually certain articles are produced in greater amounts than can be used—for example, more yarn than the present weaving mills can work—or that certain articles are produced not indeed in a greater quantity than can be used, but in a greater quantity than can be bought; that, in consequence of this, great irregularity occurs in the employment of the workers, which makes their situation extremely insecure, weights them down in unworthy dependence, brings forth overwork here and want of work there; and that of the means employed today to counteract the most visible part of this evil, the cartels represent monopolist unions—on the one side against the workers, and, on the other, against the great public."

[27] NOTE: In questioning the possibilities of the catastrophic crisis, Bernstein, however, excluded from consideration the political crises due to war and threatened war, to widespread failure of crops, etc.

Bernstein declares that the great danger of trusts is not that they breed more extensive crises, but that they "virtually bear within themselves the possibilities of a new and more hopeless serfdom for the working classes." He concludes:

"The problem of crises cannot be solved by a few well-preserved catchwords. We can only investigate what elements of modern economy work in favor of crises and what work against them. It is impossible to prejudge *a priori* the ultimate relation of these forces to one another, or their development. Unless unforeseen external events bring about a general crisis—and as we have said that can happen any day—there is no urgent reason for concluding that such a crisis will come to pass for purely economic reasons. Local and partial depressions are unavoidable; general stagnation is not unavoidable with the present organization and extension of the world market, and particularly with the great extension of the production of articles of food." [28]

It is seen that here Bernstein comes to direct grips with the over-simplified theory of crises propounded by the early scientific socialists, as he carries to their logical conclusion some of the earlier declarations of Marx and Engels. Since he fails to see a general crisis as the inevitable result of economic forces, his suggested tactics for ushering in the co-operative commonwealth are necessarily different from those advocated by persons who are firmly convinced of the truth of the cataclysmic theory. The possibility of a collapse due to political events, however, Bernstein nowhere denies.

Revisionists' Theory of Political and Social Progress. Turning to the question of the industrial and political agencies which are destined to bring about socialism, Bernstein has a number of strictures to make upon the older Marxian concepts. He first analyzes the doctrine that capitalist society has advanced industry from individual to social production and that it is now ripe for social ownership and management. While concentration has taken place in many industries, still there are hundreds of thousands of separate businesses in existence. It would be impossible to socialize all of these industries at once and to run them efficiently.

And if one considers only the larger industries, the task of socialization, he contends, is a colossal one. Should Germany and the individual states wish to take over only the larger industries (this refers to the nineties of the last century), it would be a question, in industry and commerce together, declares Bernstein, of about a hundred thousand businesses with five or six million employes, and, in agriculture, of

[28] Bernstein, *op. cit.*, p. 93.

over 300,000 holdings with over five million workers. "What abundance of judgment, practical knowledge, talent for administration, must a government or a national assembly have at its disposal to be even equal to the supreme management or managing control of such a gigantic organism!" [29]

Conquest of Political Power. After dealing with the first preliminary condition, the ripeness of industry for socialization, he analyzes the second condition, namely, the conquest of political power by the proletariat. There are still many obstacles in the way of this conquest. It is true that the proletariat is in the majority "if one counts in it all persons without property, all those who have no income from property or from a privileged position." [30] But this group is an extraordinary mixture of different groups, and the difference of occupation, education, and social position has prevented any great spirit of solidarity from developing. When we come to the industrial proletariat, we find that they are in a minority. In Germany some 7,000,000 out of 19,000,000 earning incomes at the time of his writing were industrial wage-earners. As far as the agricultural workers are concerned, but a small number of them can look much beyond the immediate amelioration of their economic conditions. "To by far the greatest number of them the socialization of agricultural production cannot be much more than empty words. Their ideal is in the meanwhile to get their own land." [31] Meanwhile the desire of the industrial working classes for socialistic production is for the most part more a matter of assumption than of certainty.

Bernstein adds that the great increase in socialist votes indicates a steadily increasing interest in socialism, although it cannot be said that all of the votes come from socialists. In case of a socialist victory, he concludes, it can be taken for granted that "there would be no question of an immediate taking over by the state of the total manufacture and distribution of products. The state could not even take over the whole amount of medium and large enterprises." The local authorities too, as connecting links, could not do so very much. They could socialize at most those businesses which produce, or which perform, services locally. As for the large manufacturing and commercial businesses, the communes would either have to leave them in the hands of the former proprietors, "or, if they wanted to expropriate these absolutely, they would be obliged to give them over to associations of workmen on some leasing conditions." [32]

[29] *Ibid.*, p. 100.
[30] *Ibid.*, p. 103.
[31] *Ibid.*, p. 107.
[32] *Ibid.*, p. 108.

Co-operative Enterprises as a Preliminary to Socialism. Many of the older socialists, Bernstein continues, put too much faith in productive co-operative enterprises as a preparation for socialism; too little faith in consumers' co-operative undertakings. The history of productive co-operation, he declares, has thus far been a history of failure. The tendency of an association of producers and sellers is to become exclusive and individualistic and to engage in an intense hunt for profits.

Furthermore, hitherto productive co-operatives have split on the rock of control. It is difficult to have an efficient organization where the workers elect their own immediate officers and have the right to remove them. "Where day by day and hour by hour prosaic decisions are to be taken which always give an opportunity for friction, it is simply impossible that the manager should be the employe of those he manages, that he should be dependent for his position on their favor and their bad temper." [33]

On the other hand, as Beatrice Webb brings out, a co-operative association of consumers, as in the Rochdale co-operative movement, tends constantly to broaden out and become more inclusive. The British co-operative movement has become a powerful factor in economic life, and consumers' co-operatives on the continent have grown rapidly.

One of the great problems is the development of agricultural co-operatives which will lead to a co-operative tilling of the land. Co-operative societies for the buying and selling of commodities have succeeded among the farmers, but not for co-operative production. Many difficulties will have to be overcome before the co-operative principle wins out in this line of effort.

Democracy and Socialism. Bernstein relies on the methods of democracy rather than on proletarian dictatorship, for the attainment of socialism. Among the democratic forces in the community he gives a prominent place to the trade unions. They tend to destroy "the absolutism of capital, and to procure for the worker a direct influence in the management of industry. . . . There are socialists in whose eyes the union is only an object lesson to prove the uselessness of any other than political revolutionary action. As a matter of fact, the union today—and in the near future—has very important social tasks to fulfill for the trades, which, however, do not demand, nor are even consistent with, its omnipotence in any way." [34]

To Sidney and Beatrice Webb and other English writers he gives the credit for bringing forcefully before the world the fact that the trade

[33] *Ibid.*, p. 119.

[34] *Ibid.*, p. 140.

unions are indispensable organs of democracy and not merely passing coalitions. That does not mean that the trade union should be the controlling monopolist of industry under a democracy. The trade union, "as mistress of a whole branch of production, the ideal of various older socialists, would be only a monopolist productive association, and, as soon as it relied upon its monopoly or worked upon it, it would be antagonistic to socialism and democracy, let its inner constitution be what it may." [35]

Universal Suffrage and Democracy. Bernstein defines democracy as an absence of class government, though it does not yet involve the absolute suppression of classes. "The right to vote in a democracy makes its members virtually partners in the community, and their virtual partnership must in the end lead to real partnership. With a working class undeveloped in numbers and culture, the general right to vote may long appear as the right to choose the 'butcher.' With the growing number and knowledge of the workers, it is changed, however, to the implement by which to transform the representatives of the people from masters into real servants of the people.

"Universal suffrage in Germany could serve Bismarck temporarily as a tool," continues Bernstein, "but finally it compelled Bismarck to serve it as a tool. . . . In 1878 it could bring Bismarck into a position to forge the weapon of socialistic law, but through it this weapon became blunt and broken, until by the help of it Bismarck was finally beaten. . . . Universal franchise is . . . the alternative to a violent revolution. But universal suffrage is only a part of democracy, although a part which in time must draw the other parts after it as the magnet attracts to itself the scattered portions of iron. It certainly proceeds more slowly than many would wish, but in spite of that it is at work. And social democracy cannot further this work better than by taking its stand unreservedly on the theory of democracy." [36]

Dictatorship Antiquated. Bernstein asserts that social democracy in Germany has always in practice taken such a stand. However, many socialist theorists have adopted phrases used by socialists in the days when political privilege ruled throughout Europe, and have treated them as though the progress of the movement depended on these phrases rather than on an understanding of what can and should be done. "Is there any sense, for example, in maintaining the phrase of the 'dictatorship of the proletariat' at a time when in all possible places representatives of social democracy have placed themselves practically in the arena of parliamentary work, have declared for the proportional representa-

[35] *Ibid.*, p. 141.

[36] *Ibid.*, pp. 144–5.

tion of people, and for direct legislation—all of which is inconsistent with a dictatorship?

"The phrase is today so antiquated that it is only to be reconciled with reality by stripping the word dictatorship of its actual meaning and attaching it to some kind of weakened interpretation. The whole practical activity of social democracy is directed toward creating circumstances and conditions which shall render possible and secure a transition (free from convulsive outbursts) of the modern social order into a higher one. . . . The dictatorship of the classes belongs to a lower civilization, and apart from the question of the expediency and practicability of the thing, it is only to be looked upon as a reversion, as political atavism." [37] If the thought is generated that the transition is to take place by means of agencies utilized in an age which knew little or nothing of the present methods of passing and enforcing laws, a reaction is sure to take place.

Socialism a Logical Development from Liberalism. Finally Bernstein believes that the socialists should use moderation in their attacks on liberalism. Socialism is the legitimate heir of liberalism. Socialists have always stood four square for civil liberties. In fact "the security of civil freedom has always seemed to it [socialism] to stand higher than the fulfillment of some economic progress.

"The aim of all socialist measures, even of those which appear outwardly as coercive measures, is the development and the securing of a free personality." A careful examination of socialist measures will indicate that the coercion involved in the application of these measures is far less than the liberty which they make possible. Thus the sum total of liberty in society is vastly increased.

"The legal day of a maximum number of hours' work, for example, is actually a fixing of a minimum of freedom, a prohibition to sell freedom longer than for a certain number of hours daily, and, in principle, therefore, stands on the same ground as the prohibition agreed to by all liberals against selling oneself into personal slavery." [38]

There is, in fact, no liberal thought which is not also found in the ideology underlying the socialist philosophy. Take the question of economic personal responsibility. Without responsibility there is no freedom. A healthy social life is impossible unless the personal economic responsibility of all those capable of work is assumed. The recognition of individual responsibility is the individual's return to society for services rendered or offered him by society. Critics of socialism have accused socialists of giving little consideration to responsibility. Indeed some socialists have assumed that society under the new

[37] Bernstein, *Evolutionary Socialism*, pp. 146–7. [38] *Ibid.*, p. 150.

order would give an absolute guarantee of employment to all of its members. Under socialism society would indeed do far more than at present to see that the individual obtained and kept positions suitable to his abilities and tastes.

"But a right to work, in the sense that the state guarantees to everyone occupation in his calling, is quite improbable in a visible time, and also not even desirable. . . . In such great and complicated organisms as our modern civilized states and their industrial centers an absolute right to work would simply result in disorganization." [39]

Socialism and Freedom. Socialism will create no new bondage whatever. The individual is to be free, not in the metaphysical sense of the anarchists—free from all duties toward the community—"but free from every economic compulsion in his action and choice." Such freedom is only possible by means of organization. In this sense socialism may be regarded as organized liberalism, for "when one examines more closely the organizations that socialism wants and how it wants them, he will find that what distinguishes them above all from the feudalistic organizations, outwardly like them, is just their liberalism, their democratic constitution, their accessibility. If democracy is not to excel centralized absolutism in the breeding of bureaucracies, it must be built up on an elaborately organized self-government with a corresponding economic, personal responsibility of all the units of administration as well as of the adult citizens of the state. Nothing is more injurious to its healthy development than enforced uniformity and a too abundant amount of protectionism and subventionism." [40]

Both Marx and Proudhon agreed, declares Bernstein, in that they favored decentralization and federalism in their new social order, a democratic organization from the bottom up. Thus here they meet again in liberalism.

The growth of liberalism, Bernstein believes, makes possible a peaceful transition not to be attained in former days. "Feudalism, with its unbending organizations and corporations, had to be destroyed nearly everywhere by violence. The liberal organizations of modern society are distinguished from those exactly because they are flexible and capable of change and development. They do not need to be destroyed, but only to be further developed. For that we need organization and energetic action, but not necessarily a revolutionary dictatorship." [41]

Immediate Tasks. Bernstein then gives his attention to the immediate tasks before the social democracy—the task of working out a peas-

[39] *Ibid.*, p. 153.
[40] *Ibid.*, pp. 153–5.
[41] *Ibid.*, pp. 164–5.

ants' program, of encouraging co-operation and municipal ownership, of formulating a foreign policy, of removing the existing class franchise, of "emancipating itself from a phraseology which is actually outworn," and of making up its mind to appear as what it is in reality today, "a democratic socialistic party of reform," "a party that strives after the socialist transformation of society by the means of democratic and economic reform." [42]

VIOLENCE VS. LEGISLATION. In conclusion he warns the party that a theory that does not permit a movement at every stage of development to give its consideration to the actual interests of the working classes will always be cast aside.[43]

In Marx's writings he finds a dualism, resulting from the fact that his works aim both at scientific inquiry and at proof of a theory laid down long before the inquiry is started. There is, he contends, a real residue of utopianism in the Marxian system. Nowhere in the writings of Marx do we find a systematic investigation of what may be expected from legal, and what from violent, revolutionary action. In general it may be said that the violent method is quicker, in so far as it deals with the removal of obstacles which the privileged minority places in the path of social progress; that the strength of this method lies on the negative side. Constitutional legislation, on the other hand, works more slowly in this respect. Its path is a path of compromise. "But it offers greater advantages where it is a question of the creation of permanent economic arrangements capable of lasting; in other words, it is best adapted to positive social-political work." [44]

"In legislation intellect dominates over emotion in quiet times; during a revolution, emotion dominates over intellect. But if emotion is often an imperfect leader the intellect is a slow motive force. Where the revolution sins by overhaste, the every day legislator sins by procrastination. Legislation works as a systematic force, revolution as an elementary force.

"As soon as the nation has attained a position where the rights of the propertied minority have ceased to be a serious obstacle to social progress, where the negative tasks of political action are less pressing than the positive, then the appeal to a revolution by force becomes a meaningless phrase." [45]

In conclusion Bernstein makes a plea for thinkers in the socialist movement who base their principles on ascertained facts, not on dogmas handed down to them from above.

[42] *Ibid.*, p. 197.
[43] *Ibid.*, p. 205.
[44] *Ibid.*, p. 218.
[45] *Ibid.*, p. 218.

"Today the movement needs, in addition to the fighting spirit, the co-ordinating and constructive thinkers who are intellectually enough advanced to be able to separate the chaff from the wheat, who are great enough in their mode of thinking to recognize also the little plant that has grown on another soil than theirs, and who, perhaps, though not kings, are warm-hearted republicans in the domain of socialist thought." [46]

Summary. Bernstein thus suggested a revision of Marxian doctrines at many points, although many of his criticisms were directed against the crude statements of Marxian principles, rather than against their more mature elaboration. He criticized the exclusive emphasis laid by some socialists on the economic factor in history. He maintained that, although surplus value existed as an empirical fact, the Marxian doctrine of surplus value was an abstraction. He maintained that Marx was wrong in holding that the middle class was decreasing and that the lot of the workers was becoming ever more miserable. Industrial combinations, he asserted, had not developed in a uniform fashion in the various industries, and in agriculture concentration in the generally accepted sense of that word had hardly taken place at all. Economic crises there were, but they gave no indication of leading to the world catastrophes which Marxists predicted, although cataclysms due to political events were at any time possible.

Bernstein also put his hope in the evolutionary processes of democracy. He saw socialism as the logical carrying out of certain liberal principles and put much faith in the efficacy of the co-operative and trade union movements as means of progress. He agreed with the social democrats of his day in most of the immediate demands contained in their program, and for which they so ardently worked, although he insisted that a number of these immediate demands were likely to ward off the cataclysm which many socialists regarded as the necessary forerunner of an industrial revolution. Therefore, he insisted, there was a certain inconsistency between the declaration of principles in the Erfurt Program and the demands for social reform which followed this statement. However, Bernstein's criticisms of Marx in no way interfered with his support of the social democratic movement, but merely led him to the belief that tactics proposed by Marx for the attainment of a co-operative commonwealth, during the early days, should be changed to meet the realities of the situation.

Though many of Bernstein's contentions were vigorously assailed by Marxists under the leadership of Kautsky, they had quite a profound

[46] *Ibid.*, p. 224.

influence on the movement of his day and it must be admitted that many of the prominent social democrats prior to 1914 who still officially proclaimed their belief in the Marxian formulae, acted in their day-to-day agitation for practical, peaceful measures of social reform as though they had accepted in essence the teachings of the revisionist school.[47]

[47] Benedetto Croce, the well-known Italian philosopher, took a somewhat different point of view regarding the Marxian system of thought from that of Bernstein, in his *Historical Materialism and the Economics of Karl Marx* (N. Y.: Macmillan, 1914). Marx's doctrines in many instances, he declared, do not correspond with the realities of the capitalist system. But Marx was conducting a scientific investigation regarding the laws of the capitalist system, and it is legitimate in such an investigation to deal with abstractions. In fact "all science deals with abstractions . . . and it is fatal to confuse the system of abstractions which science builds up with the concrete, living reality" (p. 57).

"*Das Kapital* is without doubt an *abstract* investigation [Croce declared]. The capitalist society studied by Marx is not this or that society, historically existing, in France or in England, nor the modern society of the most civilized nations, that of Western Europe and America. It is an ideal and formal society, deduced from certain hypotheses, which could indeed never have occurred as actual facts in the course of history. It is true that these hypotheses correspond to a great extent to the historical conditions of the modern civilized world." But "nowhere in the world will Marx's categories be met with as living and real existences simply because they are abstract categories, which, in order to live, must lose some of their qualities and acquire others" (p. 50).

The concept of labor-value, he contended, is true for an ideal society whose only goods consisted in the products of labor and in which there was no monopoly and there were no class distinctions (p. 135).

The Marxian theory that history is class war is true, Croce was inclined to believe, "(1) where there are classes, (2) when they have antagonistic interests, (3) when they are aware of this antagonism, which would give us, in the main, the humorous equivalence that history is a class war only when it is a class war. In fact sometimes classes have not had antagonistic interests, and very often they are not conscious of them, of which the socialists are well aware when they endeavor . . . to arouse this consciousness in the modern proletariat" (p. 85).

Croce concluded (1) That Marxian economics finds its justification, not as a general economic science, but as "comparative sociological economics, which is concerned with a problem of primary interest for historical and social life."

(2) That the economic interpretation of history, freed from all traces of the *a priori* standpoint, had validity as "a simple, albeit a fruitful, canon of historical interpretation."

(3) That the "appraisement of social programs must be a matter of empirical observations and practical convictions, in which connection the Marxian program cannot but appear one of the noblest and boldest and also one of those which obtain most support from the objective conditions of existing society." At the same time, the Marxian social program or any other program could not be deduced from the propositions of pure science.

(4) That the legend of the intrinsic immorality and the intrinsic anti-ethical character of Marxism must be abandoned (p. 117).

For a good description of the issues at stake on the Marxian and revisionist controversies, see Blake, *Marxian Economic Theory*, ch. XXXIII, and Hughan, *American Socialism of the Present Day*, chs. IV–VIII.

CHAPTER 21

Marxists' Reply to Revisionists

FROM the time of the publication of Bernstein's criticisms in the late nineties until the First World War began, a battle royal was waged between the upholders of the revisionist point of view and the Marxists. Various critics within and without the social democratic ranks joined forces with Bernstein in their attacks on certain phases of the Marxian philosophy. These included Tugan-Baranowsky, Jean Jaurès, Werner Sombart, T. G. Masaryk, first president of Czecho-Slovakia, Paul Barth, and Franz Oppenheimer.

The chief protagonist of the Marxian point of view in Germany was Karl Kautsky. Henry Hyndman in England, Louis B. Boudin, and I. M. Rubinow in America, and a host of others also arose to the defense of Marx. Kautsky and others were careful to take the position, however, that the orthodox Marxian was not he who thoughtlessly followed Marx, but he who applied the Marxian method in order to understand the facts.[1]

Marxists' Admission of Error on Time Element. Marx and Engels, the Marxists admitted, were fallible and erred in numerous analyses. Although they were correct in their prophecies concerning the *direction* of social progress, they were wrong in foretelling the *time* when the social revolution in various countries would take place. It was a rare thing, it is true, for them to set down in black and white the exact year when a particular crisis would occur. Nevertheless, it cannot be denied that "Marx and Engels expected a far-reaching and violent revolution in Germany in 1847 similar to the great French upheaval that began in 1789. Instead of this, however, there was but a wavering uprising that served only to frighten the whole capitalist class so that it took refuge under the wing of the government. The result was that

[1] Kautsky, *The Social Revolution,* p. 61.

the government was greatly strengthened and the rapid development of the proletariat was stifled." [2]

Forty years later, in the eighties, Engels looked forward to a revolution in Germany, which did not materialize. "Marx and Engels," declared Kautsky, in 1902, "were able to determine the *direction* of economic development for many decades in a degree that the course of events has magnificently justified. But even these investigators would strikingly err when it came to the question of predicting the *velocity* and *form* of the development of the next month," for, in the final analysis, in determining great social developments, "geographical peculiarities, racial individualities, favor and disfavor of a neighbor, the restraint or assistance of great individualities," all these and many other things have had their influence. Many of these cannot be foreseen, "but even the most recognizable of these factors operate upon each other in such diverse ways that the result is so extremely complicated as to be impossible of determination from a previous stage." [3]

And yet, despite the errors of Marx and Engels, an extraordinary number of prophecies have come true in whole or in large part.

The Rejoinder of Marxists on the Theory of Value. The revisionist attacks on the labor theory of value and the theory of surplus value have been met variously by Marxists. Kautsky, as late as 1924, in dealing with the labor theory of value, maintained that it has "stood the test, inasmuch as it has afforded us a closer insight into the laws of capitalist enterprise than any other theory. We may therefore regard labor-value as a reality."

"All the same," he continued, "it remains merely a tendency. It is real, but not tangible and exactly measurable. Measurements are only possible in the case of temporary phenomenal form, price. All attempts are doomed to failure which aim at 'constituting' the value of each separate commodity, that is, at determining exactly the quantity of labor contained in it." [4]

Although not rejecting the theory of final utility accepted by many economists as a more adequate theory of value, Kautsky maintained that "the subjective value of the final utility theorists is something quite different from value in the sense of a Ricardo or a Marx. The former is a relationship of an individual to the commodities that surround him, while the latter is a phenomenon which, under given conditions of production, is the same for all persons, who find it already in existence,

[2] Kautsky, *Road to Power* (Block, 1909), p. 8.

[3] Kautsky, *Social Revolution,* pp. 84–5.

[4] Kautsky, *The Labor Revolution* (George Allen and Unwin, 1925), p. 266.

however varied their subjective needs, inclinations, or circumstances may be.

"These two kinds of value have therefore nothing in common except the name, which is not precisely an aid to clear thinking.

"The value which Marx had in mind arises from and reacts upon specific conditions of production. It forms the starting point for the comprehension of these conditions. Subjective value, on the other hand, is a relation of a single individual to the things which surround him, whether they are produced by human labor or not; it contributes absolutely nothing to the knowledge of definite social conditions of production." [5]

On the other hand, Dr. Rubinow in his defense of the general Marxian thesis affirmed that all socialist students admit that commodities or even services were not actually exchanged in direct and exact proportion to the amount of socially necessary labor. Nor could the Marxian formula permit of a proof, as "the amount of labor represented in any one commodity cannot be measured, let alone the amount of socially necessary labor."

The time consumed in producing a certain commodity, he continued, seems to offer a convenient measure of labor quantities, but "the admission by Marx that 'skilled labor counts only as simple labor intensified, or, rather, as multiplied simple labor,' [6] altogether destroys the utilization of *time* as a method of measuring values, for, instead of the objective measure, 'time,' there is substituted a subjective measure of comparative valuation of direct different kinds of human effort. This alone, entirely irrespective of the famous 'Marxian puzzle,' makes impossible the proof that commodities do exchange proportionately to the amount of labor, for the one mechanical method of measuring labor falls away."

But the impossibility of proving this theory, Rubinow declared, does not affect the socialist movement one way or the other. Marx's demand for social justice, as some critics maintain, never depended on the ability to prove the correctness of his theory of value. "The *demand* of the hand and brain workers for the ownership of what they create is very much more important socially than any logical, mathematical or metaphysical proof of the economic accuracy of the theory." [7]

Although the labor theory of value cannot be proved, Rubinow continued, it is easy to realize its popularity with the masses, irrespective

[5] *Ibid.*, pp. 266–7. See also Sachs, A. J., *Basic Principles of Scientific Socialism*, Chs. V–VIII.

[6] Marx, *Capital*, Vol. 1, Kerr Edition, 1908, p. 51.

[7] Rubinow, *Was Marx Wrong?*, p. 17.

of the criticisms of the economists. In this connection it must be realized, concluded the author, that every theory of value is a class theory. "That is why it is so easy to criticize the numerous theories of value and so hard to prove any one of them."

Boudin, on the other hand, defended the labor theory of value *in toto* against its critics, maintained that the "Great Contradiction" between Marx's explanation of value in the first and third volumes of *Capital* was no contradiction at all and that the law of value was a vital and integral part of the Marxian structure. Nor did he regard it as an objection to this law that it did not show the formation of prices and was no guide to the *actual* prices paid for commodities. "A theory of value need not show that," he maintained, "and, as a matter of fact, could not." He quoted Professor Carl Diehl, an opponent of Marx, as saying, "The price of a commodity is a concrete, quantitative determination: it shows us the quantity of goods or money which must be given in return for this commodity. *Value,* on the other hand, is an *abstraction.* When we speak of the value of commodities, we mean the regulative principle which lies at the bottom of the formation of prices." [8] (Italics ours.)

Marxists and Concentration. However, the keenest controversy between the revisionists and the Marxists prior to the First World War did not take place over Marx's philosophy of history or his abstract economics, but over his sociological doctrines regarding the future development of the capitalist system and the transition to the co-operative commonwealth.

As has been stated, Bernstein saw the movement toward concentration of ownership and control of industry as slow and extremely irregular. As illustrative of this slow development, he called attention to the persistence of many small businesses in manufacturing and distribution. In reply to this, the Marxians maintained that the important thing was not the number of small, struggling concerns that continued to live, but the relative amount of the product of the small and of the large undertakings. When the subject was approached from that angle, a very great amount of concentration is indicated. The process toward concentration might be slower than Marx anticipated, but the tendency was there. That could not be denied.[9]

[8] Boudin, *Theoretical System of Karl Marx,* p. 108; see Chs. V and VI. See also Hughan, *American Socialism,* etc., p. 76. For a more recent discussion of the Marxian Theory of value, see H. W. Laidler, Editor, *The Socialism of Our Times,* Chs. XIV (1929). In this discussion, Algernon Lee and Louis B. Boudin defend the theory and Dr. N. I. Stone criticizes it.

[9] Rubinow, *op. cit.,* Ch. IV.

THE CORPORATION AND CENTRALIZATION. Bernstein, as will be recalled, maintained that the appearance of the corporation, far from centralizing ownership and wealth, was an agency for the diffusion rather than for the concentration of wealth. To this point of view Kautsky replied that the corporation in no way hindered the growth of great fortunes. "On the contrary, the corporation not only makes the control of production by a few banks and industrial combines possible; it also furnishes a means by which the smallest fortunes can be transformed into capital and thereby be made to contribute to the centralizing process of capital.

"Through the corporation the savings of even the poor are placed at the disposal of great capitalists, who are enabled to use those savings as if they were a part of their great capitals. As a result the centralizing of their own great fortunes is increased still more." [10]

Boudin approached the subject from a somewhat different angle. According to the American author, "the Marxian analysis of the capitalist system and his deductions as to the laws of its development proceed upon the assumption of the absolute reign of the principle of competition. It was on the basis of that assumption that Marx declared that during the progress of capitalist development 'one capitalist kills off ten,' thereby centralizing all wealth in the hands of a steadily diminishing number of persons, eliminating the middle class, and leaving society divided into two classes only." [11]

But what if competition should be checked? What if the capitalists should decide not to compete with one another, or to restrict the area and intensity of such competition and divide profits amicably instead of fighting with each other over their division?

The result would be to retard the progress toward concentration predicted by Marx. This is what has happened with the advent of the corporation. The primary purpose of the corporation is to blunt the edge of competition. There are but two legitimate reasons for organizing corporations. One is to enable those with insufficient capital to remain in the field by combining their several insufficient capitals into a capital sufficient to meet the newer requirements of the industrial process. The second is to enable those whose capital is sufficient to split up their large capital into many parts and to invest in many small undertakings. In the first case it is an effort "by those whom competition has forced out of the economic arena to stay in, by *representation* at least. In the second case it is an effort to limit the effects of competition in the future by dividing up and limiting its risks and liabilities

[10] Kautsky, *Road to Power,* p. 28. [11] Boudin, *op. cit.,* p. 177.

(it should be remembered that the essence of the corporation is limited liability) and by providing a sort of mutual insurance between capitalists and capitals." [12] This new development necessarily requires the revision of the Marxian formula of centralization.

"It is, therefore, not a refutation of the Marxian analysis of the capitalist system to show that tendencies in the development of that system which Marx said would continue to exist as long as capitalism lived, disappeared in whole or in part when the basic principle of that system (competition) was abolished or modified." [13]

Boudin on the Disappearance of the Middle Class. In discussing the Marxian prediction regarding the disappearance of the middle class, Boudin declared that Marx in no sense considered the complete disappearance of that class essential, as some of the revisionists intimated, but only the disappearance of a particular middle class of which he treated. The middle class undoubtedly had failed to disappear. And yet the statistics introduced by Bernstein in his attempt to show the increase in that class were unconvincing. They merely showed that the group obtaining what Bernstein maintained were "middle class incomes" were increasing. In the first place it may be said that his classification into lower, middle, and upper class incomes was an arbitrary one. Such a classification had its dangers, since a stated sum of money had a different purchasing power in different countries, in different parts of the same country, and at different periods of time. But what was of more vital importance, "income as such is no index whatever of either social or economic position." The question was, or should be, not *what* was a man's income, but *what did he derive it from?* When one investigated that question he would find that many included in the middle-class income group were in reality members of another economic group. They came partly from salaried employes of large corporations and partly from former members of the employing class who were thrust out of the ranks of capitalists, but who lived on their wits and refused to become members of the working class. The salaried workers in the corporations who made up the bulk "are in reality just as much a part of the proletariat as the merest day laborer." [14]

Nor was this group which lived on its wits, and which might be regarded as the "new middle class," a real obstacle to the advance of socialism. In fact the members of this group hardly constituted a social class, since they performed as a group no social-economic function. As a group it "has no veneration for property or property rights, no love

[12] *Ibid.*, p. 178. [13] *Ibid.*, p. 179. [14] *Ibid.*, p. 206.

of economic independence, and consequently no constitutional abhorrence of 'paternalism' or of socialism." [15]

Nor could the small stockholding capitalists be said to have the same anti-socialist make-up as the old bourgeois group. While this group owned shares of stock, it did not control property. "Robbed of its economic independence, deprived of the control of its property and of the opportunity of individual enterprise, it has no other aspiration except to preserve its comforts, its incomes. If it has any ideals at all, its ideals may be said to be just the reverse of those of the old bourgeois middle class. By the very nature of its way of managing its affairs the propriety, effectiveness, and, above all, the necessity of socialization, is brought home to it. Furthermore, being minority stockholders, the members of this class naturally look upon the general government, the social organization as a whole, as the protector of its rights against the unscrupulous methods and the rapaciousness of the big capitalist sharks. . . . The ideology of this class, like that of the new middle class, is a curious mixture of old and new ideas, but one thing is clear in the midst of all this confusion, that its antagonism to socialism is not a matter of principle, but of convenience. . . . Whatever, therefore, has been saved of the middle class by the corporation with regard to *numbers,* has been destroyed, and very largely, by this agency, as to *character.* What was saved from the fire has been destroyed by water. The result is the same: the *middle class,* that middle class which Marx had in view, the middle class which was a factor obstructing the way toward socialism, is *doomed.*" [16]

It has likewise been pointed out that technical progress requires an increasing variety of specialists, and that this is a material factor in the growth of the middle class, in so far as its professional groups are concerned.

Boudin Answers Bernstein on Crises. It will be remembered that Bernstein also made a number of strictures on the Marxian position regarding economic crises, which, in his opinion, were becoming less, rather than more, acute. Boudin admitted the contention of Bernstein that crises depending on "anarchy of production" might disappear with the development of the trust and combine. However, he asserted, if the trust eliminated the crisis due to that cause, it would not abolish the most important crises. For the chief cause of crises was not anarchy. Crises resulted from "the dual position of the laborer, as a seller of his labor power and the purchaser of the products of his labor power, and

[15] *Ibid.,* p. 211.

[16] *Ibid.,* pp. 211–2.

the creation of a surplus flowing therefrom which must result in an overproduction of commodities, quite apart from the 'anarchy of production.' "[17] Trusts and combinations, therefore, could only affect the form taken by the crises, whether they be short and acute, as formerly, or mild and drawn out. But the disappearance of the acute crisis did not alter the revolutionary significance of the crisis, did not lessen the mass of misery produced by it, nor indicate any lessening in the contradictions of the capitalist system. *The real question was whether the economic contradictions which produced crises had lost any of their acuteness.* It was a question of the adaptability of the capitalist system.

Capitalism had undoubtedly obtained a new lease on life by embarking on imperialistic ventures, continued Boudin. An imperialistic program, however, could not abolish the contradiction within the system. For "by the very processes with which it creates its new customers for its goods, it makes of them competitors in the business of producing these goods."[18] During the period when the colonies were being developed, some relief was afforded to the mother country, anxious to get rid of its surplus product. Besides furnishing a market for surplus goods and for means of production, such development led ordinarily to the building up by the mother country of a large army and navy. It led to a withdrawal of thousands of workers from productive enterprise and to their absorption in the colonies as civil employes; to the feverish construction of railroads, factories, roads, etc., in many instances far beyond the requirements of the situation. Through imperialism, waste, and wars, the surplus product which threatened to clog the wheels of business was thus disposed of and capitalism continued on its way.

How long will it be possible to maintain capitalism by these means? It is difficult to tell. Marx never contended, of course, that there would have to be an utter collapse of capitalism before a social revolution was possible. It is, according to his theory, sufficient that production becomes "fettered." "The knell of capitalist private property sounds," he asserted, when "the monopoly of capital becomes a *fetter* upon the mode of production which has sprung up and flourished along with it and under it."[19] Or, in other words, a system of production could only last so long as it helped, and did not hinder, "the unfolding and full exploitation of the productive forces of society," and must give way when it became a *fetter* to production. Such a system, maintained Boudin, had become a fetter to production when it could only exist by preventing production and by wasting what had already been produced.

[17] *Ibid.*, pp. 238–9. [18] *Ibid.*, p. 241. [19] *Ibid.*, p. 254.

Its duration was limited, "quite irrespective of the purely mechanical possibility or impossibility of its continuance." [20]

Kautsky on Reform vs. Revolution. Is capitalism imperceptibly to grow into socialism as a result of the enactment of an infinite number of reforms or as a result of a revolution? Are class antagonisms softening or becoming ever sharper? Is the revolution to be a peaceful or a violent one?

It is on these questions that there were in the days before the First World War sharp differences of opinion between the revisionists and the Marxists.

Kautsky was emphatically of the opinion that socialism would be brought about as a result of a revolution, rather than, as Bernstein seemed to feel, a series of reform measures. It must be added that revolution to him was not necessarily a violent upheaval, but any kind of change which placed in control of government a hitherto oppressed class.

VIOLENCE. In fact Kautsky felt that violence was a weak weapon for the workers to use, and that peaceful methods were likely to prove much more effective. In the first place, he claimed, the great superiority of the weapons possessed by the standing armies to those owned by civilians practically doomed to failure any resistance of the latter from the beginning. On the other hand, it should be realized, the revolutionary sections of the population possessed far better weapons for economic, political, and moral resistance than did the revolutionists of the eighteenth century, prewar Russia being the only exception to this rule. These weapons included freedom of organization and of the press and universal suffrage.[21]

DEMOCRACY AND REVOLUTION. Kautsky believed that political democracy with universal suffrage could not in itself abolish revolution, "but it can avert many premature, hopeless revolutionary attempts, and render superfluous many revolutionary uprisings. It creates clearness regarding the relative strength of the different parties and classes." It prevents the workers from attempting to accomplish the impossible, and the governing classes from refusing to grant concessions that it no longer possesses the strength to withhold. "The direction of development is not thereby changed, but its course becomes steadier and more peaceful." [22]

Peaceful methods, including parliamentarism, strikes, and press propaganda, stood a greater chance of success in the more democratic

[20] *Ibid.*, p. 254.

[21] See Kautsky, *Roads to Power*, pp. 50 ff.

[22] *Ibid.*, p. 52.

countries, and among those groups who had the greatest faith in themselves and their cause. He added: "The political situation of the proletariat is such that it can well afford to try as long as possible to progress through strictly legal methods alone." [23] The great fear was that the capitalist class, realizing their ultimate defeat, would try to incite the workers to violent acts in order thereby to create a reaction. Violence in the past had time and time again assisted in setting back the labor movement.

THE VALUE OF REFORMS. In their endeavor to prove the necessity for a revolution the Marxists did not deny the ameliorating influence of those agencies mentioned by Bernstein—trade unions, co-operatives, labor legislation, nationalization of certain public utilities. Kautsky wrote:

"The slightest reform or organization may be of great significance for the physical or intellectual *rebirth of the proletariat* that, without them, would be surrendered helpless to capitalism and left alone in the misery that continuously threatens it. But it is not alone the relief of the proletariat from its misery that makes the activity of the proletariat in Parliament and the operation of the proletarian movement indispensable. They are also of value as a means of practically familiarizing the proletariat with the problems and methods of national and municipal government and of great industries, as well as to the attainment of intellectual maturity which the proletariat needs if it is to supplant the bourgeoisie as ruling class. . . . Democracy is to the proletariat what light and air are to the organism; without them it cannot develop its powers."

However, Kautsky and others felt that it was impossible to obtain a correct picture of social progress by concentrating attention only on these advances. It was necessary to study also the development of opposing forces. Kautsky thus warned the optimists:

"To be sure, the co-operatives are increasing, but simultaneously and yet faster grows the accumulation of capital; to be sure, the unions are growing, but simultaneously and yet faster grows the concentration of capital and its organization in gigantic monopolies. To be sure, the socialist press is growing but simultaneously grows the partyless and characterless press that poisons and unnerves ever wider popular circles. To be sure, wages are rising, but still faster rises the mass of profits. Certainly the number of socialist representatives in Parliament is growing, but still more sinks the significance and efficaciousness of this institution, while simultaneously Parliamentary majorities, like the gov-

[23] *Ibid.*, p. 54.

ernment, fall into ever greater dependence on the powers of high finance.

"So beside the resources of the proletariat develop also those of capital, and the end of this development can be nothing less than a great, decisive battle that cannot end until the proletariat has attained the victory." [24] Nor is this battle to be waged by a degraded, "slum" proletariat. "The emancipation of the laboring class is not to be expected from its increasing demoralization, but from its increasing strength." [25]

Boudin and Rubinow on Increasing Misery. One of the doctrines of capitalist development advanced by Marx and most severely criticized by the revisionists was that prophesying the "increasing misery" of the working class. As we have seen, the revisionists vigorously attacked this doctrine. The workers, they maintained, were steadily improving as capitalism progressed. Boudin's answer to this contention is of interest. "Marx," he maintained, "does not speak of the growth of the *poverty* of the working class. This omission is very significant and alone would be sufficient warrant for us in assuming that Marx did not consider the growing poverty of the working class as a *necessary* result of the evolution of capitalism, all revisionist assertions to the contrary notwithstanding." [26] This was clearly seen in his statement that, with the accumulation of capital, the lot of the worker must grow worse, *no matter whether his wages are high or low.* Poverty was not the same as misery. Poverty in general depended on the amount of wages or other income a person received. Misery, on the other hand, was a psychological, rather than a material condition.

The workers were increasingly miserable, as compared with the well-to-do, whose incomes had increased by leaps and bounds. Marx declared that there was a growing degradation among them. Degradation accompanied insecurity of tenure. The fact that the jobs of the workers were so insecure gave the capitalist a far greater power over the life and liberty of the "free workingmen than was ever enjoyed either by feudal baron over his serf or by the slave holder over his chattel-slave." [27]

Moreover, Marx predicted not only the tendency toward increasing misery, but also the development within the capitalist system of an organized, disciplined working class, fighting for immediate relief and for ultimate emancipation. The working-class struggle, predicted by Marx, has undoubtedly led to better labor conditions. Present conditions were "not merely the result of the *tendencies* of capitalistic accumulation, but of the tendencies of capitalist accumulation as *modified*

24 Kautsky, *Social Revolution,* pp. 82–3.
25 *Ibid.,* p. 38.
26 Boudin, *op. cit.,* p. 221.
27 *Ibid.,* p. 224.

by the struggle of organized labor against them." [28] It is this struggle which is the most important factor from the Marxian point of view in the final overthrow of capitalism. In its advance, labor develops steadily in economic power and independence in the sense that it takes possession of more and more responsible positions in the economic life of the nation.

Some Marxists do not attempt to defend the theory of increasing misery. They feel that Marx meant that the workers tended to become increasingly poverty stricken as well as mentally more miserable. But whether Marx "only meant to state the tendency of uncorrected capitalism, and not the historic law," wrote Rubinow, or whether he had in mind "relative poverty" rather than absolute poverty, "is important for students of history of economic thought, but not for the socialist movement. . . . The important decisive fact is that the theory of increasing misery has been gradually abandoned by the socialist movement, and the movement still survives." [29]

Rubinow took to task those critics who felt that capitalism automatically led to constant improvement of the laborer's condition. After an examination of the trend of real wages, he maintained that "the capitalist system does not at all produce any marked improvement in the condition of the wage worker and that wherever such improvement has taken place, it may be easily explained by the obstinate struggle of the working class, of which struggle the socialist movement is the most comprehensive expression. That under the influence of the rising price level, which benefits the property owner primarily, the tendency, unless corrected by an aggressive labor movement, seems to be the other way." [30]

Kautsky with the revisionists scouted the idea of the revolution as a sudden *coup d'état,* declaring that Marxists were not disguised Blanquists, "who expect by a *coup d'état* to make ourselves dictators." He considered the revolution an historical process that might easily draw itself out into a decade of hard battles.

Kautsky on the New Social Order. The early Marxists hesitated to depict a future social order based on proletarian control. All such pictures seemed to them too utopian. Kautsky, however, ventured a brief outline of the probable developments of a proletarian state "the day after the revolution," or, to be more exact, during the decade or two after a working-class government came into power. These developments, which he presented in a simplified form, would, he believed, be

[28] *Ibid.,* p. 228.
[29] Rubinow, *op. cit.,* pp. 46–7.
[30] *Ibid.,* p. 57.

the logical outworking of economic necessity. In the first place a proletarian government would sweep all remnants of feudalism away. "It would extend universal suffrage to every individual and establish freedom of press and assemblage. It would make the state completely independent of the church and abolish all rights of inheritance. It would establish complete autonomy in all individual communities and abolish militarism."[31] It would dissolve the army though it would see that the people were armed. It would make fundamental reforms in taxation, and would cover the governmental expenses through the imposition of the graduated income tax and a property tax. It would increase and improve the schools and raise the pay of teachers. It would see to it that all children were equally well nourished and clothed and had equal school facilities, while at the same time insisting that education be adapted to varying mentalities.

PROGRAM OF SOCIALIZATION. A proletarian government would give immediate attention to the unemployed, as "enforced idleness is the greatest curse of the laborer." It would begin the purchase of private enterprises. "The political domination of the proletariat and the continuation of the capitalist system of production are irreconcilable. A portion of the factories, mines, etc., could be sold to the laborers who are working them, and could henceforth be operated co-operatively. Another portion could be sold to consumers' co-operatives and still another portion to the communities or to the states. Its most extensive purchasers, of course, would be the states and municipalities.

"The industries that are most prepared for nationalization," according to Kautsky, "are the national means of transportation, railroads and steamships, together with those which produce raw material and partially produced goods; for example, mines, forests, iron foundries, machine manufactures, etc. These are also the very spheres where the great industries and trustification are most highly developed. The manufacture of raw material and partially produced articles for personal consumption as well as small trading have many local characteristics, and are still largely decentralized." In these spheres the municipality and co-operatives will come more to the front, leaving the national industries to play a secondary rôle. Money capital and land used for exploitation will also be socialized.

Kautsky on Incentives. After the revolution the successful proletariat will have the gigantic task of keeping industry going. What incentives will be brought into play? "Certainly not the whip of hunger and still less that of physical compulsion. If there are people who think

31 Kautsky, *Social Revolution*, p. 108.

that a victory of the proletariat is to establish a prison regimentation where each one can be assigned his labor by his superior, then they know the proletarian regime very poorly. The proletariat which will then make its own laws has a much stronger instinct for freedom than any of the servile and pedantic professors who are crying about the prison-like character of the new state.

"The victorious proletariat will never be satisfied with any prison or barrack-like regulations. Moreover, it has no need of anything of the kind since it has other means at its command to hold the laborer to his labor." [32] Custom can be depended upon to keep large masses of people at their work. "I am convinced that when once labor loses its repulsive character of over-work and when the hours of labor are reduced in a reasonable degree, custom alone will suffice to hold the great majority of workers in regular work in factories and mines." [33]

A much stronger motive is the *discipline* of the proletariat. "If the union once recognizes the necessity of the unbroken regular progress of labor we may be sure that the interest of the whole is so great that scarcely a single member will leave his post. The same force that the proletariat uses today to destroy production will then become an effective means to secure the regular continuance of social labor. The higher the economic organization develops today the better the outlook for the undisturbed progress of production after the conquest of political power by the proletariat." [34]

However, it must be realized that the discipline of the proletariat is not military discipline. It is self-imposed, democratic discipline, a free submission to self-chosen leadership and to the decisions of the majority of their own comrades. A democratic regime would from the beginning seek to organize production democratically. The maintenance of social discipline can only be achieved in that manner. Of course industries differ a good deal in their make-up and require varying forms of democratic organization. In some instances the workers would elect delegates who would constitute a sort of parliament for the purpose of adjusting labor conditions and controlling the government of the machinery. In other instances the union undoubtedly would maintain control, and in still other industries there would be co-operative management.

A socialist regime may more and more also depend on the attractive power of labor. Labor should be made a pleasure rather than a burden, and as the proletarian regime develops, with shorter hours, more hy-

[32] *Ibid.*, p. 124–5. [33] *Ibid.*, p. 125. [34] *Ibid.*, p. 126.

gienic surroundings, and a more friendly atmosphere, the labor process will gradually lose its repulsive side.

Labor would be paid in money. Many advocate the abolition of money. But money "is the simplest means known up to the present time which makes it possible, in as complicated a mechanism as that of the modern productive process with its far-reaching division of labor, to secure the circulation of products and their distribution to the individual members of society."

Increase of Production. One of the first tasks of a proletarian regime would be to increase production in order to satisfy the enormous demands that would be made upon it. Production could be increased by concentrating the total production in the most perfect industrial plants and throwing all those out of operation which do not attain a definite standard, and, in the second place, by utilizing such aids as the best labor-saving devices and by-products. Revisionists have criticized those who believe that industry is ripe for socialization, on the ground that in many industries the number of private plants is very great, and it would take a considerable time for competition to destroy the smaller plants. The answer to this is that while society might expropriate all of the plants at once, it would operate only the best-equipped large industries. In the textile industry in Germany, for instance, of the 200,000 textile establishments there are only 800 plants employing more than 200 laborers. For the state to operate these 800 is not an impossibility.

"Here again there is another significant point of view. Our opponents and the pessimists in our own ranks measure the ripeness of our present society for social production by the number of ruins which are strewn around it and of which it is incapable of ridding itself. Over and over again the great number of little industries that still exist is triumphantly pointed out. But the ripeness of socialism does not depend on the number of little industries that *yet* remain, but upon the number of great industries which *already* exist. Without a developed great industry socialism is impossible. Where, however, a great industry exists to a considerable degree it is easy for a socialist society to concentrate production and quickly to rid itself of the little industry." [35]

Production would also be increased as a result of the increase in wages, for "the raising of wages in industry would set free a large number of labor powers whose existence today is merely parasitic. They maintain a wretched existence today in their little shops, not because these shops

[35] *Ibid.*, pp. 144–5.

are a necessity but because their possessors are in despair of finding their bread in any other place or because they cannot earn enough by wage labor and seek a supplementary occupation." [36]

Kautsky on Production Under Socialism. AGRICULTURE. Under a labor government many of the functions now undertaken by middlemen would largely be assumed by co-operatives or municipalities. Bakeries, milk and vegetable production, and the erection of buildings would also fall to co-operatives and municipalities. It is, however, not to be expected that all small private industries would disappear. Much of the agricultural industry, for instance, would probably remain private for a long time to come. To be sure, the large agricultural plants would fall with the wage system and be transformed into national, municipal, or co-operative businesses. Many of the small farmers would undoubtedly go into industry or into large agricultural enterprises in order to secure a respectable existence. "But we may be sure that some farmers would always remain with their own family, or at the most with one assistant or maid that will be reckoned as part of the family, and would continue their little industry. . . . The proletarian governmental power would have absolutely no inclination to take over such little businesses. As yet no socialist who is to be taken seriously has ever demanded that the farmers should be expropriated, or that their goods should be confiscated. It is much more probable that each little farmer would be permitted to work on as he has previously done. The farmer has nothing to fear from a socialist regime." [37]

Indeed, continued Kautsky, it is probable that these agricultural industries would be considerably strengthened through the new regime. As a result of the abolition of militarism, the reduction of taxation, the growth of self-government, the improvement of schools and roads, and the lightening of mortgage burdens, the demand for agricultural products on the part of the workers would be further increased. The community would also assist the farmers in obtaining machines, fertilizers, and other needed materials. It would at the same time encourage the formation of farmers' co-operatives and societies. "So here the private industry would continually recede before the social, and the latter would finally transform the agricultural industry itself and permit the development of such industries through the co-operative or municipal co-operative into one great social industry. The farmers will combine their possessions and operate them in common, especially when they see how the social operation of the expropriated great industry proves that with the same expenditure of labor perceptibly more can be produced, or

[36] *Ibid.*, p. 140.

[37] *Ibid.*, p. 159.

that with the same number of products the laborers can be granted more leisure than is possible in the small industry. If the small industry is still able to assert itself in agriculture, this is due not a little to the fact that it can pump more labor out of its laborers than the great industry." [38]

THE SMALL INDUSTRY. Nor will the small industry in business completely disappear. There will always be branches in which the machine cannot compete successfully with hand labor or cannot accomplish what the latter can. The small industry, however, will still remain "as islands in the ocean of great social business." [39]

"In this as in every other relation, the greatest diversity and possibility of change will rule. Nothing is more false than to represent the socialist society as a simple, rigid mechanism whose wheels, when once set in motion, run on continuously in the same manner.

"The most manifold forms of property in the means of production—national, municipal, co-operatives of consumption and production, and private—can exist beside each other in a socialist society; the most diverse forms of industrial organization, bureaucratic, trade union, co-operative and individual; the most diverse forms of remuneration of labor, fixed wages, time wages, piece wages, participation in the economies in raw material, machinery, etc., participation in the results of intensive labor; the most diverse forms of the circulation of products, like contracts by purchase from the warehouses of the state, from municipalities, from co-operatives of production, from producers themselves, etc. The same manifold character of economic mechanism that exists today is possible in a socialistic society. Only the hunting and the hunted, the struggling and resisting, the annihilated and being annihilated of the present competitive struggle are excluded and therewith the contrast between exploiter and exploited." [40]

INTELLECTUAL PRODUCTION. Finally, Kautsky took up the question of intellectual production under socialism. The general educational system and the system of scientific research, requiring, as they do, an immense volume of capital, will be largely social in their nature. The least that a proletarian regime can do is so to adjust the educational system that "each genius will have within his reach all the knowledge that the social educational system has at its disposal." It will free scientists and educators from the present domination by the capitalist class which so demoralizes science. The intellectual worker will breathe more easily.

In painting and sculpture, requiring individual production, there

[38] *Ibid.*, p. 161. [39] *Ibid.*, p. 165. [40] *Ibid.*, pp. 166–7.

will be much private effort. "Just as little as the needle and thimble, will brush and palette, or ink and pen belong to these means of production which must under all conditions be socialized." The number and artistic quality of public buildings will greatly increase. "Instead of accumulating statuettes and pictures that will be thrown into a great impersonal market whence they finally find a place utterly unknown to the artist and are used for wholly unthought of purposes, the artist will work together with the architect as was the case in the Golden Age of art in Athens under Pericles and in the Italian Renaissance. One art will support and raise the other and artistic labor will have a definite social aim so that its products, its surroundings and its public will not be dependent on chance."[41] On the other hand the necessity of producing artistic works for sale as commodities will cease.

Intellectual production will flourish as a result of the increased leisure on the part of the working class. "It is by no means fantastic to conclude that a doubling of the wages and a reduction of labor time to half of the present one is possible at once, and technical science is already sufficiently advanced to expect rapid progress in that field." [42]

Free Unions and Organs of Opinion. At present a third group of intellectual workers, among them, writers and actors, are mercilessly exploited by big capitalistic concerns. Such exploitation will cease under a proletarian regime. It has been argued that the substitution of state ownership of organs of opinion would mean intellectual stagnation. Socialists, however, do not propose centralization of these organs of opinion in the hands of the state. There will be much municipal control. "Through these alone all uniformity and every domination of the intellectual life by central power is excluded." [43]

As another substitute for capitalist industry there will also be found "*free unions* which will serve art and science and the public life and advance production in these spheres in the most diverse ways or undertake them directly as even today we have countless unions which bring out plays, publish newspapers, purchase artistic works, publish writings, fit out scientific expeditions, etc. The shorter the hours of labor in material production and the higher the wages the more will these free unions be favored. . . . Freedom of education and of scientific investigation from the fetters of capitalist dominion; freedom of the individual from the opposition of exclusive, exhaustive physical labor; displacement of the capitalist industry in the intellectual production of society by the free unions—along this road proceeds the tendency of the proletarian regime in the sphere of intellectual production." [44]

[41] *Ibid.*, pp. 173–4. [42] *Ibid.*, p. 174. [43] *Ibid.*, p. 178.
[44] *Ibid.*, pp. 178–9.

"May we not expect," concluded Kautsky in an eloquent passage, "that under such conditions a new type of mankind will arise which will be far superior to the highest type that culture has hitherto created? An overman, if you will, not as an exception but as a rule, an overman compared with his predecessors, but not as opposed to his comrades, a noble man who seeks his satisfaction not by being great among crippled dwarfs, but great among the great, happy among the happy—who does not draw his feelings of strength from the fact that he raises himself upon the bodies of the downtrodden, but because a union of his fellow men gives him courage to dare the attainment of the highest tasks.

"So may we expect that a realm of strength and of beauty will arise that will be worthy the ideal of our best and noblest thinkers." [45]

Summary. Following Bernstein's attacks on the Marxian system, the apologists for Marx made certain admissions regarding the imperfections of the Marxian theories and put forth certain defenses. They also sought to carry forward the Marxian theories into new fields of thought. On various questions they were divided among themselves in their interpretations.

Universally they defended the economic interpretation of history, admitting, however, the contention of Bernstein that the complexity of human relationships made extremely difficult the task of exact prophecy. They split over the validity of the Marxian theory of value and its importance in the Marxian system. They admitted the mistakes of the fathers of scientific socialism as far as the *time element* was concerned, though maintaining that the Marxian analysis of social tendencies was correct. They admitted that concentration did take place more rapidly in some industries than in others, but pointed out that many of Bernstein's figures in his chapter on concentration were quite meaningless. The important thing was not the number of small industries that survived, but the proportion of the output produced by small and large concerns. They pointed out that, while the corporation permitted small capitalists to become part owners in industry, it put enormous power in the hands of small groups on the inside. The corporation, furthermore, interfered with the free play of competition; and, inasmuch as Marx's predictions were based on the assumption that free competition would continue, the growth of the corporation necessitated the revision of the Marxian formulae of concentration.

While the group receiving "middle-class incomes" was increasing in modern society, a "middle-class income" did not make a middle-class person, within the meaning intended by Marx. Artisans working for others still remained members of the proletariat though their wages were

[45] *Ibid.*, pp. 188–9.

raised. Much of the proof advanced by Bernstein in support of his argument that the middle class was increasing was no proof at all. Further, the new middle class did not present the same obstacle to socialism as did the old, small employing class.

While many of the Marxists of the period preceding the First World War still maintained that crises could not be eliminated under capitalism, they were not quite so sure of their ground as were their predecessors, and insisted that the social revolution did not depend on the utter collapse of the capitalist system as a result of acute crises, but might be brought about through the mere "fettering" of the system.

Kautsky and other Marxian authorities saw class antagonisms increasing, rather than softening. And yet the revolution they visualized was not the violent revolution, resulting from a *coup d'état,* predicted by the early Marxians, but a change in control of government from the capitalist to the working class brought about by the ballot and by economic action. They agreed with the revisionists that social reforms were desirable, where these reforms made for the physical, mental, and ethical development of the working class. They put no faith in the "slum proletariat" as inaugurators of social change, and abandoned the theory of the increasing "poverty" of the working class, though some of them insisted that the "increasing misery" theory of Marx must be interpreted in the psychological sense, and that in such a sense it was true.

Finally, they began to visualize the future social state, as it would be developed by a working class in control of the powers of government and ever more conscious of its goal. In that task they sought to avoid dogmatism, and to see the new social order under labor control, not as a static, simple organism, but as an organism of infinite complexity and variety, continuously adjusting itself to its ever changing environment, to the end that personality might be developed and exploitation and oppression be a thing of the past.[46]

[46] For a far more comprehensive analysis of the attacks on Marx's economic theories and a more detailed exposition of these attacks than space here permits, see William J. Blake's *Marxian Economic Theory,* esp. chs. XXXIII–XXXVIII.

See also text ch. 40.

CHAPTER 22

French Syndicalism

FROM Germany we proceed to France and from the revisionist to the syndicalist phase of socialist thought; to syndicalism, with its *positive* emphasis on the trade and industrial union movement as the basis of the new industrial structure, on the producer rather than the consumer as the controlling factor in industry, and on the general strike and other forms of "direct action" as the means of social transformation; with its *negative* emphasis on the need for abolishing the political state and on the impotency of political action as a means of working-class emancipation.

DEVELOPMENT OF FRENCH LABOR ORGANIZATIONS

Struggle of Workers for Right to Organize. The syndicalist philosophy was the product of the French labor movement. The French working class, as was the case with the working class in practically all industrial countries, found it no easy task to gain a foothold in the national life. Although the French Revolution was ostensibly fought in behalf of the ideals of "liberty, equality, fraternity," it brought but little liberty to the workers, redounding primarily to the advantage of the commercial and manufacturing classes who took control of the reins of government.

In fact, no sooner was the Republic established than laws were passed forbidding the workers from combining for the improvement of their condition. One anti-combination law passed at that time went so far as to declare gatherings of artisans riotous and to provide that such gatherings be dispersed by force and that the artisans holding them be punished with all the severity which the law permitted.[1]

An 1803 statute declared that those involved in coalitions to cease work were punishable by imprisonment of from one to three months,

[1] *Les Associations Professionelles,* Vol. I, pp. 13–14.

and that the leaders of such coalitions were subject to terms of from three to five years.[2] The law of 1834 prohibited associations of even twenty persons, if such associations were connected with larger unions.

Despite these laws, however, trade unions gradually developed in different parts of the country and strikes became ever more frequent. The Revolution of July, 1830, resulted in considerable labor agitation and in frequent demands for the right of collective bargaining. Small groups here and there began to urge the complete reorganization of industrial society as the only solution of the labor problem. The writings of Saint-Simon, Fourier, and the utopian socialists made a deep impression on many thousands of workers at this period.

In the late forties and the early fifties enthusiasm for co-operative societies ran high among the French workers, and over 300 producers' co-operative organizations were formed in Paris and a considerable number in the provinces. Encouragement was temporarily given to these associations by the subsidy of 3,000,000 francs granted by the Constituent Assembly. The Revolution of 1848, in which the socialist idea of the "Organization of Work" gained considerable headway, left a tradition emphasizing the possibilities of social transformation and gave a strong impetus to the trade-union movement. The revolution was followed by a period of persecution, and this in turn by renewed agitation for the legalization of the unions, culminating in the law of 1864, granting the right to strike, and the law of 1884, legalizing the formation of syndical chambers.

The French Co-operative Movement during the Sixties. During the sixties interest in the co-operative movement was renewed, and credit and savings organizations flourished for some time. From 1863 to 1868 the *Credit au Travail* became the center of this movement. The council of the bank subsidized co-operative journals, furnished the co-operatives with credit, and advised them in regard to their management. The bankruptcy of the *Credit au Travail* in 1869, as a result of the extension of too many long-term loans, dealt a heavy blow to the movement and turned the activity of the workers into other channels.

The French Section of the First International. While many of the French workers were experimenting with co-operatives, others were becoming interested in the political organizations of the workers, and, in particular, in the activities of the International Workingmen's Association—the First International [3]—organized in London in 1864 by French, English, and German socialists.

[2] See Levine (Lorwin), Louis, *Syndicalism in France,* p. 23.

[3] See text pp. 149–51, 154–56.

The French section of the International during the first years of its existence was composed mainly of followers of Proudhon, and went by the name of *mutuellistes.* The mutuellistes believed in a peaceful change in social relations; in progress through education and mutual insurance, and through syndicats, co-operative societies, and similar organizations. They gave much attention to credit societies and popular banks. Through such financial institutions, they believed, cheap credit would be placed at the disposal of all, and co-operative societies of production and consumption could then be organized in large numbers. Like the Marxists, they believed that the emancipation of the working class must be the work of labor. "Their ideal was a decentralized economic society based on a new principle of right—the principle of mutuality." [4]

From 1864 to 1868 the International met with but little success in France. The association was persecuted by the government, and by 1868 it seemed completely to have disappeared. The following years, however, it revived again, this time under the leadership of those who accepted the ideas of collectivism and communism. One wing in this revived movement was led by Blanqui, who urged the organization of secret societies and the seizure of political power through a revolutionary upheaval, and denounced the tactics of the co-operators and mutuellistes. During the last days of the Second Empire the Blanquists numbered something like 2500, chiefly among the republican youth.[5]

The International and Industrial Workers. The other wing of the revived movement followed the socialist ideals of Caesar de-Paepe and Marx. This wing was strengthened by the action of the International in 1868 and 1869 in favoring the socialist proposal of ownership of industry by the community. In the latter year the members of the French section succeeded in obtaining financial support for the strikes that were then sweeping the country. This direct assistance to the workers on the industrial field so increased the popularity of the French section that it was reputed to have grown during that year to a membership of about 250,000.

This keener interest of labor in the work of the International led the French leaders to change their attitude toward the strike as a radicalizing influence, and they now declared it to be "the means *par excellence* for the organization of the revolutionary forces of labor." [6]

To several the idea of the general strike suggested itself. Many dur-

[4] See Levine, *op. cit.,* p. 41. See also Proudhon, *De la Capacité Politique des Classes Ouvrières.*

[5] Thomas, A., *Le Second Empire,* p. 363. [6] *Ibid.,* p. 363.

ing these years began to speculate regarding the possibilities of a future social order based on the trade-union structure rather than on the state. At the International Conference at Basle in 1869, for instance, we find one of the French delegates advocating the necessity of organizing syndicats both as a means "of resisting exploitation of capital in the present" and as a means of organizing, out of the grouping of different trades in the city, "the commune of the future." In the latter event "the government will be replaced by federated councils of syndicats and by a committee of their respective delegates regulating the relations of labor—this taking the place of politics." [7]

Organization of Conservative Unions. Local trade unions were organized by the dozen during the next year, followed by the creation of a federation in Paris of numerous syndicats. These, however, were largely swept away by the Franco-Prussian War, the Proclamation of the Republic, and the Commune. In 1871 the work of organization had to begin over again, and for some time thereafter the workers avoided centers of syndical activity for fear of arrest.

The work of resuscitating the trade-union movement was, curiously enough, finally undertaken by Barbaret, a republican journalist, who looked upon the syndicats as agencies for the elimination of strikes, which he regarded as fatal to the workers and dangerous to the republic.[8]

Barbaret, in this work of reorganization, specified a number of things which he felt the trade unions should strive to do. They should organize employment bureaus, create boards of conciliation, establish libraries and courses in technical education, purchase raw materials and instruments of labor, and, finally, "to crown these various preparatory steps," develop co-operative workshops, "which alone would give groups of workingmen the normal access to industry and to commerce" and which would in time equalize wealth.[9]

During the following years numerous syndicats were organized. This renewed activity culminated in the organization of the first French Labor Congress in Paris in 1876. This congress included over 400 delegates from syndicats, co-operative, and mutual aid societies. The resolutions of this congress were of a mild order. They favored the peaceful solution of industrial questions, pronounced the strike an unsatisfactory weapon, affirmed the efficacy of co-operation as a path leading to working-class emancipation, and repudiated the ideals of socialism.[10]

[7] Guillaume, James, *L'Internationale, Documents et Souvenirs* (Paris, 1905), Vol. I, p. 205.

[8] See Barbaret, J., *Monographies Professionelles* (Paris, 1886), Vol. 1, p. 16.

[9] Barbaret, *op. cit.*, pp. 20–5.

[10] *Séances du Congrès Ouvrier de France, Session de 1876.*

The Socialist Trend in the Trade Unions. The second congress was similar to the first. The third, on the other hand, held in Marseilles in 1879, showed a distinctly more militant spirit. It repudiated the leadership of Barbaret, accepted the title of "Socialist Labor Congress," and favored the collective ownership of the means of production and the formation of a workingmen's political party.

This change in attitude was attributable to several things: the feeling that the republic was no longer in danger since the election of President Grevy and the resignation of MacMahon, and that its cause would not be jeopardized by workers who took an advanced position on economic questions; the failure of the co-operative movement to bring about any considerable improvement in working-class conditions; and the activities of the socialists. The logical step was to take the socialist position.

Jules Guesde as Socialist Leader. A group of collectivists, inspired by the ideals of the International, had existed in Paris since 1873. It was only, however, from 1877, when they secured a dynamic leader in the person of Jules Guesde, that they began to develop strength. Guesde was one of the most remarkable figures in the French socialist movement and more responsible than any other one individual for the actual organization of the movement. As a result of his editorship of *Les Droits de l'Homme* in 1870–1871, which expressed sympathy for the Commune, he was sentenced to a term in prison. During a subsequent stay in Switzerland he came into contact with the ideals of the International and of Marx. On his return to France he became the chief exponent of Marxian socialism. In 1877 he founded a weekly, *L'Egalité* the first number of which outlined the policy the paper proposed. "We believe," declared the paper, "with the collectivist school to which almost all serious minds of the working class of both hemispheres now belong, that the natural and scientific evolution of mankind leads it irresistibly to the collective appropriation of the soil and of the instruments of labor." In order to achieve this end it is necessary for the proletariat to constitute itself into a distinct political party which will aim to conquer the political power of the state.[11]

In 1878, the year following the establishment of this paper, a proposal was made to hold an international congress of workingmen in Paris. The government issued an order prohibiting such a gathering. Some of the moderates bowed to the governmental decree. Guesde refused, however, to heed the government order and went ahead with arrangements. The meeting was held but dispersed at its first session. Guesde

11 *L'Egalité,* Nov. 18, 1877.

was arrested and with others sent to jail. While in jail the socialists issued an appeal for the organization of a labor party, which secured wide circulation and helped to popularize the labor party idea.

The advocacy by the Marseilles Congress of 1879 of independent political action was undoubtedly largely brought about by the action of the government in breaking up the gathering of the International. "When the International Congress," writes the Committee on Organization, "was brutally dispersed by the government, one thing was proved: the working class had no longer to expect its salvation from anybody but itself. . . . The suspicions of the government in regard to the organizers of the congress, the iniquitous proceedings which it instituted against them, have led to the revolutionary resolutions of the congress which show that the French proletariat is self-conscious and is worthy of emancipation." [12]

Prior to the congress, furthermore, a committee appointed at Lyons had called on several of the more liberal deputies in behalf of labor legislation. They had found these deputies opposed to the limitation of hours of work in the name of liberty, and to liberty of association in the name of the superior rights of the state. "The remedy to this state of affairs," conclude the committee, "is to create in France a workingmen's party such as exists already in several neighboring states." [13]

The Marseilles Congress carried out with precision the desires of the socialists. It took the position that co-operative societies could not be regarded as agencies sufficiently powerful to bring about the freedom of the workers. It favored "the collectivity of soil and of sub-soil, of instruments of labor, of raw materials—to be given to all and to be rendered inalienable by society to whom they must be returned." [14] It also constituted itself a distinct political party under the name of the "Federation of Socialist Workingmen of France."

Thus the leadership of the syndical movement passed to the collectivists. Unfortunately, this caused considerable discussion in the ranks of the trade unionists, and at the next congress at Havre in 1880 the "moderates" and "co-operators" separated from the revolutionary collectivists. They formed a separate organization, which, however, soon passed out of existence. As soon as they were rid of the more moderate elements, the collectivists also began to dispute among themselves. One branch consisted of parliamentary socialists, who emphasized the political machinery as a means of social change, and another branch, of the

[12] Blum, Léon, *Les Congrès Ouvriers et Socialistes Français* (Paris, 1901), pp. 33–4.
[13] *Ibid.*, p. 36.
[14] de Seilhac, Léon, *Les Congrès Ouvriers de France* (Paris, 1899), p. 47.

communist-anarchists, who rejected the idea of the state and felt that the first act in the social revolution should be the destruction of this instrument of working-class oppression. Parliamentary action the latter denounced as a "pell-mell of compromise, of corruption, of charlatanism, and of absurdities, which does no constructive work, while it destroys character and kills the revolutionary spirit by holding the masses under a fatal illusion." [15]

"The anarchists," writes Levine, "saw only one way of bringing about the emancipation of the working class: namely, to organize groups, and at an opportune moment to raise the people in revolt against the state and the propertied classes; then destroy the state, expropriate the capitalist class, and reorganize society on communist and federalist principles. This was the social revolution they preached." [16]

[15] *Pourquoi Guesde n'est-il pas anarchiste?* p. 6.

[16] Levine, *op. cit.*, p. 84. On the anarchist theory see Paul Eltzbacher, *Anarchism* (N. Y.: Benj. R. Tucker, 1908); P. A. Kropotkin, *Anarchism* (in *Ency. Brit.*, 1910); Bertrand Russell, in *Proposed Roads to Freedom*, pp. 32–55; P. Kropotkin, *Conquest of Bread* (N. Y.: Putnam, 1906); Bernard Shaw, *Impossibilities of Anarchism* (London. Fabian Society, 1893); Benj. R. Tucker, *Individual Liberty* (N. Y.: Vanguard Press, 1926); Hunter, Robert, *Violence and the Labor Movement* (N. Y.: Macmillan, 1914), Part I; Russell E. Westmeyer, *Modern Economic and Social Systems* (N. Y.: Farrar and Rinehart, 1940), ch. XX; Earl R. Sikes, *Contemporary Economic Systems* (N. Y.: Holt, 1940), ch. VII; Alexander Berkman, *What is Communist Anarchism?* (N. Y.: Vanguard Press, 1929).

Anarchists differ from the socialists in their opposition to *all forms* of the political state; in their belief that *all* social coercion can be dispensed with; in their refusal to rely on parliamentary action as one of the means of reorganizing industrial society in their insistence that industry must be run entirely by voluntary autonomous groups and in their general lack of plan for the operation of a new society. To the extent that they urge terrorism to achieve their ends—the violent anarchists have always however, been in the small minority—they also differ from the socialist school of thought.

Anarchists urge the abolition of the political state. They are in general of two schools—the individualist-anarchists and the communist or syndicalist-anarchists The individualists would not disturb present property relations. Their desire is merely that the state be eliminated, so that all may mold their lives as they see fit. There is the anarcho-communist and anarcho-syndicalist, on the other hand who would substitute for private ownership a system of community or producers ownership and operation of land and capital without the interference of the political state. Most anarchists urge the development of loosely federated autonomous co operative industrial groups organized on a voluntary basis and accept syndicalism as the expression of the anarchist principle in the economic field. Under anarcho syndicalism there would not only be no state, but there would be no compulsion to work and all things would be shared in equal proportion. Reliance would be placed on the possibility of making work so pleasant that practically everyone would prefer work to idleness; under anarchism, work would not involve either overwork or slavery, or the excessive specialization that industrialism is bringing out, but merely an enjoyable activity for certain hours during the day, giving an outlet to man's spontaneous constructive impulses. "There is to be no compulsion, no law,

Socialists' Defense of Political Action. The socialists, on the other hand, maintained that to ignore political action was neither helpful nor possible. The workingman believes, they declared, in utilizing his right to vote and if he is not given an opportunity to support working-class candidates, he will vote for the bourgeoisie. Moreover, there is no other way of social transformation than through the capture of the state. The state, as an instrument of class rule, will disappear as soon as socialism is established, but during the transition period it must be used by the socialists, representing the working class, for the purpose of effecting the change.

Guesdists' Revolutionary Program. While all socialists emphasized the need for political action, they were divided on the kind of political action that was most desirable and on the effectiveness of immediate measures of social reform.

In the Congress of St. Etienne in 1882, the socialist forces split, one portion of the delegates following Guesde and taking the name *Parti Ouvrier Français,* and another group pledging allegiance to Paul Brousse and designating themselves by the name *Parti ouvrier socialiste révolutionnaire Français.* Later, this group dropped the word *révolu-*

no government exercising force; there will still be acts of the community, but these are to spring from universal consent, not from any enforced submission of even the smallest minority."

Anarchism is not merely an economic-political program, but is a philosophy of social arrangements applying to every activity of human beings—education, marriage, religion, as well as work and "order." Proudhon, Bakunin, and Kropotkin have been among its greatest advocates.

The leading members of the movement aim to realize their ideals through education, leaving "indiscriminate killing and injuring to the government—to its statesmen, its stockbrokers, its officers, and its law" (L. S. Bevington in Russell, *op. cit.,* p. 53). The movement, however, has contained a considerable number who have been impatient with educational methods and have preferred violent means.

The strongest support for the movement has been found in the Latin countries —Spain, Italy, France—and to some extent in Russia before the bolshevik revolution.

Socialists, like the anarchists, desire to see the state shorn of much of the coercive power that it exercises today. They believe, however, that, if it ceased to be a class instrument, the need for organized compulsion would be greatly reduced. They urge the opinion that, at least for generations, organized society must have at its disposal some means of enforcing its decrees, democratically arrived at, against an anti-social or non-social minority—decrees against violence, against thefts, laws for the protection of the health, the safety, the education, and the industrial development of the community.

Nor do socialists agree with anarchists that enforcement of decrees necessarily limits community freedom. Such laws are often the means of protecting the weak against the strong and of adding to, not subtracting from, the sum total of human liberty.

As for the difference between the socialist and the anarchist industrial organization, a comparison between the socialist conception as heretofore given and the ideal of voluntary communism here outlined will be immediately revealing.

tionnaire from the title. The party of Guesde emphasized its revolutionary and Marxian character. It denied the efficacy of immediate reforms under the capitalist system, and insisted that it was necessary to seize the political power of the state in a revolutionary fashion. "In multiplying reforms," writes Guesde, in *Le Socialisme au jour de jour,* "one only multiplies shame, for all rights granted to the workers in the capitalist regime will always remain a dead letter." The entrance of the socialists into politics is not, therefore, to carve out seats of councillors or deputies, but to grasp the remarkable opportunity for reaching the masses with the party's educational propaganda. The main object of the *Parti Ouvrier* is to be "a kind of recruiting and instructing sergeant preparing the masses for the final assault upon the state, which is the citadel of capitalist society." [17] Only a revolution, they insisted, would permit the working class to seize the political power and socialize industry. No party could, of course, create the revolution, but once the revolution was created as a result of national and international crises, the socialists would be in a position to direct it.

The party adopted a strongly centralized plan of organization and became in time the most active socialist party in France. It was especially strong among the textile workers in the north.

Broussists' Evolutionary Program. The Broussists were called "possibilists" and "opportunists" by the Guesdists, because they believed that social reforms were desirable and that it was necessary "to split up our program until we make it finally possible." [18]

They permitted greater differences of opinion within their ranks and a larger amount of local autonomy than did their rivals. The conquests of political power appeared to them to be a rather peaceful and gradual process of infiltration into municipal, departmental, and national legislative bodies. Like the Guesdists their final aim was collectivism, and they were committed to the class struggle. They had a considerable following among the workers of Paris and among the lower section of the middle class.

The Broussists, however, failed to remain intact. A considerable section of the membership soon became disaffected from the leadership on the ground that it was too absorbed in politics and too little interested in the building up of the party and in socialist propaganda. In 1890 this group, under the leadership of J. Allemane, separated from the main body and formed a socialist party of their own. They took with them a number of the most effective leaders in the larger syndicats.

[17] *Le Programme du Parti Ouvrier,* p. 52.
[18] Blum, *op. cit.*, p. 75.

Other Political Groups. Two smaller groups active during that period were the Blanquists and the independent socialists. The Blanquists, also known as the *Comité Révolutionnaire Central,* were held together by their loyalty to their former leader, Blanqui. For the most part they had been active in the Commune, returning to France when amnesty was granted in 1880. Though regarding themselves as the inheritors of Blanqui, they no longer practiced the secret tactics advocated by their former leader, but formed another legal political party. Their aim was the capture of political power, and they approved all means that would bring about that end.

The independent socialists, the group that produced Jean Jaurès, Millerand, Viviani, and others of great prominence in later years both in socialist and non-socialist ranks, were the outgrowth of the Society for Social Economy, founded in 1885 by Malon, a former member of the International. This society was organized for the purpose of formulating legislative projects of a general socialist character, which were published in a monthly, *La Revue Socialiste.* Gaining adherents among the republicans and radicals, the society finally entered into politics, put forth measures for the gradual socialization of industry, for the democratization of the communes, and for the protection of labor, and became an influential factor in the political life of France.[19]

All of these political groups coveted the control of the syndicats. They urged their members to join syndicats where they existed, to help in the creation of trade unions, and, incidentally, to draw the syndicats into politics. The result was that many of the syndicats were torn asunder by political dissensions, and the differences between the various socialist political groups found their expression on the floor of the conventions. At times the control of a syndicat by one section of the movement led to the organization of rival syndicats in the same trade and locality.

Trade-Union Unity. Economic conditions, however, were forcing the unions to come together. The industries of France had been growing apace during these years, and the employers were presenting a united front against the workers. Small, insignificant, isolated unions were unable to resist the demands of the employing class. The law of 1884 legalizing syndicats compelled the unions to hand in the names and addresses of their officers to governmental officials; in Paris, to the Prefect of Police. The workers considered this a move on the part of the gov-

[19] For further analysis of the socialist groups during that period, see Seilhac, *Le Monde Socialiste* (Paris, 1896) and Paul Louis, *Histoire du Socialisme en France* (Paris: Librairie des Sciences Politiques et Sociales, 1936).

ernment and the employers to penalize active unionists. A general congress of syndicats was called in October, 1886, at Lyons.

"Slaves of the same master, . . . suffering from the same evils, having the same aspirations, the same needs and the same rights," reported the Committee on Organization, "we have decided to set aside our political and other preferences, to march hand in hand, and to combine our forces against the common enemy. The problems of labor have always the power of uniting the workingmen." [20]

The congress resulted in the formation of a National Federation of Syndicats. The *Parti Ouvrier* was not slow in gaining control of the Federation, and during the next few years both the federation and the Guesdists met at the same time and place, welcomed, to a large extent, the same delegates, and passed similar resolutions.

The Bourses (Labor Exchanges). A rival to the federation soon appeared in the Federation of Labor Exchanges of France (*Fédération des Bourses du Travail de France*). Labor exchanges had been in existence for many years in French cities as centers where workers and employers could meet each other and arrange for jobs. Following the passage of the law of 1884, their functions enlarged, and they were conceived as centers where all syndicats of a locality could "have their headquarters, arrange meetings, give out information, serve as bureaus of employment, organize educational courses, have their libraries, and bring the workingmen of all trades into contact with each other." [21] The municipalities were to assist in their creation and subsidize them. The first such bourse was opened in Paris in 1887, and others sprang up all over the country. The Allemanists obtained the control of most of them. The Federation of *Bourses du Travail* followed in 1892.

Labor's Discussion of General Strike. About the time of the formation of the league of bourses the French labor movement became agitated with the concept of the general strike. The general strike idea was not a new one. It had been discussed in England during the thirties, and later at the Congresses of the International.[22] Its first French propagandist appears to have been an anarchist workingman, Tortelier, a member of the carpenters' union.

The general strike idea was hailed with enthusiasm by the syndicats. During the sixties and seventies many of the workers regarded the strike as a necessary evil which never really compensated labor for the sacrifices

20 *Séance de Congrès Ouvrier, Session de 1886,* pp. 18–19.

21 Levine, *op. cit.*, p. 63.

22 Beer, *History of British Socialism,* Vol. II., pp. 81–91; Dr. E. Georgi, *Theorie Praxis des Generalstreiks in der Modernen Arbeiterbewegung* (Jena, 1908).

involved. The general strike seemed to repair the defects of a strike in one trade, to insure a successful outcome, and to be an admirable means of social revolution. "The conquest of political power," said Levine, "the method advocated by Guesdists and others, seemed vague and indefinitely remote; a general revolt, such as advocated by the anarchists, seemed impossible in view of the new armaments and of the new construction of cities that made barricades and street-fighting a thing of the past. These two methods eliminated, the general strike seemed to present the only and proper weapon in the hands of the workingmen for the realization of their final emancipation." [23]

In this sense, the idea of the general strike was favored in the congress of the National Federation of Syndicats in 1888. The Allemanists adopted it in 1891; in 1892 Fernand Pelloutier defended it with marked success before a socialist congress, and Aristide Briand appeared the same year as its eloquent sponsor at the National Federation at Marseilles. The Blanquists naturally adopted it as one of the means to the realization of their aims. The Guesdists alone frowned on it and in their Congress at Lille (1890) declared that it was impossible.

At that time the general strike was regarded as a peaceful weapon. The strike in one industry was legal. Even if it should spread to other industries not originally involved, it would not lose its legal character. This peaceful strike of folded arms would therefore permit the workingmen to carry out the revolution through legal means and in an easy manner. It must mean revolution because it would paralyze life and reduce the ruling classes to famine. During the few days in which it would be waged, its advocates contended, it would be able to compel the government to capitulate and would carry the workers into political power.

The French workers of that day seemed to feel that it might begin at any moment and that it therefore assured the speedy coming of the co-operative commonwealth. At first its advocates felt that it might be decreed for a particular day. Afterwards they took the position that it must be spontaneous and could be brought about only through educational propaganda.

Guesdists Oppose General Strike. Of course the acceptance of the concept of the general strike implied that one regarded the economic as superior to the political weapon. The Guesdists bitterly attacked this position. No real social revolution, they asserted, could be brought about in the way indicated. The idea was puerile. By the time that the capitalists felt the pangs of hunger, the workers would be starved.

[23] Levine, *op. cit.*, pp. 65–6.

Besides, no peaceful general strike was possible. One side or the other would be sure to make it the occasion for violence. It could not succeed without a high degree of organization and discipline, which, if attained, would make the strike unnecessary. Finally, the workers could not hope to win on the economic field, for there the capitalists were far stronger than their opponents. Labor, through its numbers, had superior strength only on the political field.

The general strike concept thus raised a definite issue between the socialists in control of the Federation and the trade unionists who placed chief reliance on the economic weapon. The passage of the general strike resolution in the 1892 congress of the National Federation of Syndicats at Marseilles was a disastrous blow at socialist leadership in the trade-union field. In 1894 a combined congress of this Federation and the Bourses was held at Nantes. Here the question of the general strike was the main issue on the agenda. The strike was favored by a large majority. The Guesdists, thereupon, withdrew and held a separate congress of their own. The organization they fostered, however, was soon absorbed in the *Parti Ouvrier.* A year later, in 1895, the elements gathered at Nantes laid foundations for a new organization, the General Confederation of Labor (the C. G. T.), at the congress at Limoges. The C. G. T., in its regulations, pledged itself to remain independent of all political schools and incorporated the general strike as part of its program. "The creation of the General Confederation of Labor," writes Levine, "may be considered the first important revolutionary tendency in the syndical movement in France." [24]

The formation of the C. G. T. was a distinct victory for those who asserted the superiority of economic action over political and who wanted to keep the syndicats independent of political parties. The ideas formulated by this group contained the germs of revolutionary syndicalism.

The syndicalist idea grew at first chiefly through the bourses of the various cities. The organization of local bourses, as has been said, finally led to the formation of the *Federation des Bourses du Travail* in 1892. Though organized first as a political measure against the Guesdists, the federation of bourses soon began to devote its main energies to economic functions, due largely to the efforts of Fernand Pelloutier, who was secretary of the organization from 1894 to his death in 1901.

Fernand Pelloutier. Pelloutier (1867–1901), a member of a well-to-do family, received his early education in the Catholic schools. At an

[24] *Ibid.*, p. 71.

early age he entered political life and soon became an advanced republican, later joining the *Parti Ouvrier.* He defended the general strike before the congress of the Guesdist party in 1892 and later broke with the party over this question. In 1893 he went to Paris, came under the influence of the anarchist-communists there, and accepted their point of view. His selection as secretary of the Federation assured its political neutrality, as it was his dream "to oppose a strong, powerful economic action to political action." [25]

To the federation Pelloutier devoted all his energies. He regarded the bourses as the nuclei of the society of the future and syndical activity as the means of enhancing the power and initiative of the workers and developing their administrative abilities. He would have the workers free themselves from every institution which had not for its essential purpose the development of production.

From 1894 to 1902 the *Fédération des Bourses du Travail* was the most important trade union organization in France. Until 1902, when an amalgamation took place, it had frequent clashes with the General Confederation of Labor, since both organizations were appealing to local syndicats for membership. The *Fédération des Bourses du Travail* finally joined the C. G. T. in 1902 and was soon lost in the other organization.

Revolutionary Position of the Confederation. In the years following its organization at the Congress at Limoges in 1895 the General Confederation of Labor gradually assumed an ever more revolutionary position. It repeatedly endorsed the general strike, regarding it as synonymous with the revolution. In the Paris Congress of 1900, five years after its organization, the sentiment prevailed that a general strike might take place at any moment, and that its success depended not on money, nor on the conscious effort of a majority of workers, but on a daring, revolutionary minority conscious of its aims. The delegates did not at this time exclude the idea of political action, although they displayed a definite mistrust of politicians as betrayers and intriguers. The delegates had also apparently come to the belief that the general strike would probably take on a violent character.

When the delegates met in 1901 at the Congress of Lyons, the miners were threatening a strike, and the report of the committee maintained that "the moment had come to try the general strike with strong chances of success." The aim of such a strike, the motion adopted read, "can

[25] P. Delessale, *Temps Nouveaux*, 23 Mars, 1901; see also Maurice Pelloutier, *F. Pelloutier, sa Vie, son Œuvre* (Paris, 1911).

be only the complete emancipation of the proletariat through the violent expropriation of the capitalist class." [26]

The Confederation likewise went on record during these years in favor of *sabotage,* boycotts, and other forms of "direct action." It urged that the revolutionary spirit be instilled in the army. It maintained that the idea of "fatherland" had been utilized to protect the strong against the weak and that the workers should develop the spirit of internationalism.[27]

Labor Legislation and the Confederation. The delegates at the congresses also hotly discussed the attitude workers should assume toward the labor laws that were then being enacted. The Waldeck-Rousseau government was in power during the years from 1899 to 1902. This was the period of the Dreyfus affair, when all the liberal elements united to secure the vindication of the Jewish army officer, falsely accused of treason. Republicans, radicals, socialists, and anarchists were fighting hand in hand against monarchists, nationalists, anti-Semites, and clericals. The Waldeck-Rousseau ministry constituted itself a "Cabinet of Republican Defense." It sought by every possible means to obtain the support of all the republican elements. It invited the socialist Millerand to enter the cabinet as a Minister of Commerce and Industry. It proposed a series of protective labor laws "as the best means of bringing back the working masses to the government." [28] It passed a ten-hour law as "a measure of moralization, of solidarity, and of social pacification." It gave to the workers a representation of 22 out of 66 on the Superior Council of Labor, a consultative body in matters of labor legislation. Fifteen of these 22 labor representatives were allotted to the Confederation of Labor. The Prime Minister urged the workers to join the syndicats, helped to secure for them additional rights, and introduced into the Chamber a bill for the regulation of strikes and for arbitration.

The Congress of Lyons was asked to define its attitude toward these measures.

The delegates, by a small majority, approved the principle of the Superior Council of Labor. On the other hand, by an almost unanimous vote, they rejected the proposal of regulation of strikes. In debating the labor laws, the speakers denounced the Prime Minister as a "clever defender of the interests of the bourgeoisie," who desired

[26] *XII Congrès National Corporatif* (Lyons, 1901), pp. 170, 179.

[27] *XII Congrès National Corporatif* (Paris, 1900), p. 205.

[28] Lavy, A., *L'Œuvre de Millerand* (Paris, 1902), p. 2.

merely to stop the offensive movement of the workingmen. The acceptance of these laws, they declared, would but "reinforce a power they wanted to destroy." [29]

The revolutionary element did not, however, deny the possibility or desirability of reforms, but desired only those reforms that would "undermine the foundations" of existing society and strengthen the forces and organization of the workers, and that could be obtained independently of parliamentarism. The syndicats, they felt, should carry the struggle not only against the employers by strikes, *sabotage,* and boycotts, but against the state, and not only the state appearing as the enemy of labor, but the state posing as its protector and benefactor.

The Confederation and the Socialists. The Congress of Lyons also took a stand against socialist political action. The socialists had had their first big success in 1893, when they obtained 600,000 votes and elected over 50 deputies to Parliament. In the Chamber they constituted a parliamentary group, the *Union Socialiste,* for common action. This union of necessity strengthened the general tendency toward unity among the various socialist parties. There was much talk of unity during these days, and, naturally, as the differences between the parties were becoming less and less. Following the year 1892, when the Guesdists obtained a number of seats in municipal councils, they turned their attention in considerable part to immediate municipal reforms and had less energy left to preach the ultimate revolution. In their Congress at Nantes in 1894 they elaborated a detailed program of reforms that would appeal particularly to the agricultural population and increasingly emphasized the necessity of securing changes through universal suffrage and other legal means. This approach did not differ much from that of the Broussists and the independent socialists. On numerous occasions the Guesdists revealed their growing moderation. In 1896, at a banquet of all parties to commemorate the victory of socialists during the municipal elections, all factions applauded the remarks of Millerand, when he maintained that they all now relied for social advance on universal suffrage. The Dreyfus affair brought the socialist groups into still closer relations. A Committee of Harmony was formed in which all socialist parties participated. The cry for unity was beginning to be heard throughout the socialist press, and Jean Jaurès outlined a plan whereby all of the rival groups were to be absorbed in one unified party. The hope of unity was general.

Millerand's Acceptance of Cabinet Post. The acceptance by Millerand of a post in the Waldeck-Rousseau ministry was a shock to

[29] *XII Congrès,* p. 112.

many. The Guesdists, Blanquists, and others denounced this act as a betrayal of the working class. On the other hand, the independents and Broussists insisted that socialists must take part in the general life of the country and assume increasing responsibility. The problem was thrashed out in two general congresses, but no compromise could be reached and a definite rupture in relations followed. The Guesdists, Blanquists, and several regional groups formed the *Parti Socialiste de France,* and the independents, Broussists, and Allemanists, the *Parti Socialiste Français,* the latter supporting the Waldeck-Rousseau ministry. The old organizations, however, remained intact within each group.

In view of this political turmoil the syndicats were more anxious than ever to keep politics out of the union. The result was the passage of resolutions that syndicats remain independent of politics and permit the individual to go his own way.

Trend away from Political Action. While criticizing Millerand for his decision, many of the Guesdists began to lose faith in their own party. M. Briand, in the party congress of 1899, thus upbraided the party officials for their moderate tactics:

"You became interested in these [electoral] struggles which gave immediate results, and little by little our militant comrades also became interested in them, took a liking for them to such a degree that they soon came to believe that in order to triumph definitely over the capitalist society nothing was necessary but to storm the ballot boxes."

Millerand's action, he maintained, was but a natural result of such teachings. Briand himself was soon to follow the same course.

Feeling that there was little chance of revolutionary action through political parties, many socialists joined with the communist-anarchists in an effort to permeate the unions with revolutionary ideals. This development led to a still further growth of revolutionary sentiment within the trade unions, and many came to regard the unions as the chief instrument for the transformation of society. This belief was confirmed by the action of the delegates at the Congress of Lyons.

THE PHILOSOPHY OF SYNDICALISM

Syndicalism and the Class Struggle. The various revolutionary forces centering in the General Confederation of Labor soon began to formulate a distinct philosophy known as syndicalism. The main tenets of this philosophy have already been indicated. The fundamental idea of revolutionary syndicalism, as of Marxian socialism, is that of the class struggle. Society is divided into two classes, the workers, who own nothing but their labor power and who live by selling it, and the employers, who own the instruments of production. Between these two classes constant struggle is being waged. This struggle is not a fact to be deplored, but a creative force leading to the emancipation of the working class. It is the class struggle that is unifying the workers in their fight to end exploitation, that is making them rely on their own ability, that is developing their self-consciousness, their intellectual and moral nature, and that is creating forms of organization proper to them.

The Syndicat the Germ of Social Organization. The unit of social organization, according to the syndicalist, is the syndicat or trade union. Dr. Levine thus states the syndicalist case: "The task of the syndicalists is to organize the more or less class-feeling of the workingmen and to raise it to a clear consciousness of class interests and of class ideals. This aim can be attained only by organizing the workingmen into syndicats. The syndicat is an association of workingmen of the same or of similar trades, and is held together by bonds of common interest. In this is its strength. Of all human groupings it is the most fundamental and the most permanent, because men in society are interested above everything else in the satisfaction of their economic needs. . . .

"Political parties, groups of idealists, or communities possessing a common creed are associations which cannot but be weak and transient, in view of their heterogeneous composition and of the accidental character of their bond of union. Political bodies, for instance, are made up of men of various interests grouped only by community of ideas. Only in groupings of real and fundamental interests, such as the syndicats, are men of the same conditions brought together for purposes inextricably bound up with life. . . .

"A workingman enrolling in a syndicat is not entering a party, not subscribing to a platform, nor accepting a creed. He is simply entering into a relation which is forced upon him by his very position in society, and is grouping himself with his fellowmen in such a way as to derive more strength for himself in his struggle for existence, contributing at the same time to the strength of his fellowmen. These conditions make the syndicat peculiarly fit to serve the interests of the workingmen. The syndicat is a sphere of influence which by the volume of its suggestion and the constancy and intensity of its action shapes the feelings and ideas of the workingmen after a certain pattern. . . .

"The syndicats should prefer industrial unionism to craft or trade unionism. The separation of workingmen into trades is apt to develop in them a corporate spirit which is not in harmony with the class-idea. The industrial union, on the other hand, widens the mental horizon of the workingman and his range of solidarity with his fellow workers and thus serves better to strengthen his class consciousness."[30]

Direct Action. Furthermore, through the syndicat, the workers can enter into a "direct" struggle with their employers. "Direct action" is the only means, claims the syndicalist, of educating the worker and of preparing him for his final struggle for freedom. "Direct action," explains Levine, "is action by the workingmen themselves without the help of intermediaries; it is not necessarily violent action, although it may assume violent forms; it is the manifestation of the consciousness and of the will of the external agent; it consists of pressure exerted directly for the sake of obtaining the ends of view."[31]

The Educative Power of Strikes. Direct action may be of various kinds. The principal forms of such action, however, are the strike, the boycott, the label, and *sabotage*. Of these types of action, the most important is the strike. The syndicalist attitude toward the strike is thus represented by Dr. Levine, who, however, does not, in interpreting this attitude, commit himself to it: "The strike brings the workingmen face to face with the employers in a clash of interests. A strike clears up, as if by a flash of lightning, the deep antagonism which exists between those who employ and those who work for employers. It further deepens the chasm between them, consolidating the employers on the one hand, and the workingmen on the other, over against one another. It is a revolutionary fact of great value."[32]

All strikes, the syndicalists hold, have some revolutionary influence. The extent of that influence, however, depends on the way in which the strike is conducted. "If the workingmen rely only on their treasury, the strike degenerates into a mere contest between two moneybags—that of the employer and that of the syndicat—and loses much of its value." Conciliation and arbitration should also be avoided. Strikers should endeavor to win their battles through *Sturm und Drang*, through quick and energetic pressure on the employers. The financial strength of the workers while on strike should be regarded as unimportant. Money, of course, is necessary. But money should be secured for the conduct of the strike, whenever possible, from other trades and industries. Thus given it helps to develop class solidarity. Sympathetic strikes are often a means of winning a victory for the workers.

The label, on the other hand, helps to show labor its power as consumer. In wielding the boycott, workingmen mobilize their power both as consumers and producers.

[30] Levine, *op. cit.*, pp. 124–6.
[31] *Ibid.*, p. 126.
[32] *Ibid.*, pp. 126–7.

Sabotage. *Sabotage,* a weapon given much prominence in the syndicalist philosophy, consists "in obstructing in all possible ways the regular process of production to the dismay and disadvantage of the employer." It may mean "loafing on the job," following the Scotch principle of *Ca Canny* (giving slow work for slow wages), or the French principle, *a mauvaise paye mauvais travail* (bad work for bad pay). It may be seen in the practice of railway workers in Austria, Italy, and France of carrying out to a nicety all of the rules and regulations of a railroad, and of refusing to apply discretion and common sense to a job. It may consist in misdirecting commodities. It may involve deliberate damage or temporary disarrangement to machinery or to a commodity. On the other hand, syndicalists as a rule condemn any act which results in the loss of human life.

The Syndicalist Attitude toward the State and Politics. As previously indicated, the syndicalists object to the state as such, whether monarchical or republican. They regard all states, as many Marxians regard them, as instruments of class rule. Workers, they declare, thus cannot succeed unless they destroy the power of the state. The struggle for the overthrow of the state must be carried on directly by the workers themselves. This excludes the participation of syndicats in politics. The parliamentary system cannot be trusted to emancipate labor from the wage system. It is particularly suited for manipulation by the bourgeoisie and has even a corrupting influence on the representatives of labor parties, whose policy "degenerates into bargaining, compromising, and collaboration with the bourgeois political parties," thus weakening the class struggle.

Opposition to Democracy. The workers, therefore, claim the syndicalists, if not hostile to working-class political parties, should remain indifferent to them. They should force the state to yield to the will of the workers through external pressure on public authorities. They should agitate in the press, through public meetings, parades, and other forms of demonstrations. Only reforms gained and upheld through force are real. All others are illusory and tend to deceive the workers. An analysis of democratic reforms, the syndicalists assert, will show that those of value have been wrested by force. Too many reforms granted by legislators are devised to weaken the revolutionary movement by developing class harmony. The doctrine of class harmony blinds the worker "to the real facts of inequality and of class-distinctions which are the very foundations of existing society." [33]

[33] *Ibid.*, p. 131.

Anti-Patriotic. In attacking the state, the syndicalist attacks the idea of patriotism. "Our country," they maintain, has no meaning for the workers. The workingman's country is where he works. He has no fatherland in the real sense of that term. "Ties of tradition, of a common intellectual and moral heritage do not exist for him." The only real ties are economic interests which bind him to the workers of the world and, by the same token, separate him from the capitalists. International solidarity and anti-patriotism are necessary corollaries of the class struggle.

The capitalist state does not rely on sweet reason alone in its task of keeping the workers in their place. It relies on force—the force of the judiciary, the police, the military. The military are the most effective force. They should be reached by the workers. A strong propaganda should be started among the army and navy in the workers' behalf, and a general anti-militarism campaign should be conducted. The soldiers should be urged not to use their arms against the workers in case of strikes, and to refuse to bear arms in time of war. Syndicalists also should refuse to take part in international warfare.

EFFECTIVENESS OF DIRECT ACTION. It might be said that direct action which forces improved conditions from the state and the employing class tends to take the edge off of the revolutionary spirit of the workers. This, however, is not the case, according to the syndicalists, as such reforms do not fundamentally alter conditions, but do fortify the workers in their preparation for the final struggle. "Every successful strike, every effective boycott, every manifestation of the workingmen's will and power is a blow directed against the existing order; every gain in wages, every shortening of hours of work, every improvement in the general conditions of employment is one more position of importance occupied on the march to the decisive battle, the general strike, which will be the final act of emancipation." [34]

THE GENERAL STRIKE. The general strike, the syndicalists declare, is the weapon that can be depended upon to abolish classes and bring about the new order. It will not come from the clouds, but will be the logical outcome of the syndicalist movement gradually prepared for by the daily struggles of the workers. It might fail today, but today's failure is a preparation for tomorrow's success.

Structure of Syndicalist Society. Following the syndical revolution, what? Shortly after the congress of the Confederation in 1901 a questionnaire was sent to the locals of the syndicats throughout the country,

[34] *Ibid.*, pp. 132–3.

asking the members of the organization to give their conception regarding the structure of the syndicalist order. The reports received differed in detail. In general they agreed that the syndicat should constitute the cell of the new society. The syndicat under syndicalism, they maintained, will group together the workers of one and the same trade, who will control the means of production. No one syndicat, however, will be the exclusive owner of any portion of collective property. It will merely use such property with the consent of society. The syndicat will be connected with the remainder of society through membership in the *Bourse du Travail* and the General Confederation of Labor. The relations of the local syndicats with the national federations of their respective trades will be technical and special, and the rôle of the national trade union will not be a great one. "With the General Confederation relations will be indirect and mainly by mediation of the *Bourse du Travail.* Relations with the latter will be of permanent importance, as the *Bourses du Travail* will be the centers of economic activity." [35]

THE BOURSE DU TRAVAIL. The *Bourse du Travail,* or the city trade-union council, "will concentrate all local interests and serve as a connecting link between the locality and the rest of the world. In its capacity as local center it will collect all the statistical data necessary for the regular flow of economic life. It will keep itself informed on the necessities of the locality and on its resources, and will provide for the proper distribution of products; an intermediary between the locality and the rest of the country, it will facilitate the exchange of products between locality and locality and will provide for the introduction of raw material from the outside." It will thus, in a word, combine the organization of local and of industrial autonomy. "It will destroy the centralized political system of the present state and will counterbalance the centralizing tendencies of industry." [36]

The General Confederation will take charge only of such national services as railways. Its function will consist chiefly in furnishing general information and in exerting a controlling influence. It will also serve as an intermediary in international relations.

DISAPPEARANCE OF STATE. Under syndicalism the political state as we know it will disappear. It is true that there will be local and national organizations which might be designated a state. Syndicalists, however, maintain that a state presupposes an organization in which a delegated minority centralizes in its own hands the power of legislation over all matters. "The essential character of the state is to im-

[35] *Ibid.*, p. 135.

[36] *Ibid.*, p. 135.

pose its rule *from without.* The legislative assemblies of the present state decide upon questions which are entirely foreign to them, with which they have no real connection in life, and which they do not understand. . . . The state is, therefore, arbitrary and oppressive in its very nature." [37]

The syndicalists, on the other hand, maintain that the discipline they exact is that from within, decided upon by those whose duty it is to carry on the processes in question. "The syndicats, the delegates of the syndicats to the *Bourses du Travail,* and so on, only they can properly deal with their respective problems. The rules they would impose would follow from a knowledge of the conditions of their social functions and would be, so to speak, a 'natural' discipline made inevitable by the conditions themselves." [38]

Furthermore, many of the functions of the existing state would be found unnecessary under a co-operative system. The necessary local functions could be carried on by the *Bourses du Travail.*

However, most modern syndicalists have given little attention to the problem of the future state, maintaining that the necessary forms can be worked out by labor when necessity arises. The main need, they maintain, is that of preparing the workers for the change. Where they still seek to picture their future society, they tend to give to the national labor organizations greater power, and deprive the local bourses of some of the functions formerly allotted to them.

THE MILITANT MINORITY. The syndicalist lays great emphasis on the importance of the small, conscious, militant minority as the leaders of the revolution. The great mass of workers, they maintain, are inert and are moved only as the result of the most vigorous efforts by the minority. "Every strike, every great demonstration is generally started by a small and daring group with a vision. The conscious minority, however, can succeed only by carrying with them the mass of the workers and by inducing the mass to participate in the struggle. This conscious minority works in a far different manner from that of the parliamentary representatives of the people. The latter wish to do all themselves and are thus intent on keeping the masses quiescent and submissive. The conscious minority, on the other hand, who realize that their only chance of success comes through the solid support of the great mass of the workers, strive necessarily to stimulate the energy and intelligence of their fellows."

The Syndicalist and Democracy. The idea of control by the conscious minority is, of course, opposed to the democratic principle, func-

[37] *Ibid.*, p. 136. [38] *Ibid.*, pp. 136–7.

tioning through universal suffrage. While the majority is supposed to rule, the minority, according to the syndicalists, generally get into control and exploit the majority for their own interest. "Universal suffrage is a clumsy, mechanical device, which brings together a number of disconnected units and makes them act without proper understanding of the things they are about. The effect of political majorities, when they do make themselves felt, is to hinder advance and to suppress the progressive, active, and more developed minorities." [39]

The syndicats do not arise out of universal suffrage and do not represent the majority in the generally accepted sense of that term. They group together but a minority of the workers, and never expect to take in all. The more sensitive, the intellectually more able, the more active workingmen come together and constitute themselves a syndicat. They discuss their special problems, and when they have demands to make, they enter into a struggle without finding out what the so-called "general will" has to say. In so doing, the members of the syndicats are convinced, however, that they are expressing the feelings of all. The syndicat constitutes the leading conscious minority. Its self-leadership is justified on the ground that it is not striving for selfish ends. Its victory will mean better conditions for many outside the organization. "If the general mass of workingmen do not enter the syndicats, they themselves renounce the right of determining conditions for the latter. Benefiting by the struggles of the minority, they cannot but submit to its initiative and leadership." Furthermore, it must be said that syndicats are open to all. Those in charge of a syndicat are also, it is claimed, necessarily disinterested, and within the group a sense of solidarity and devotion to community interests are encouraged. The syndicats "are gradually undermining the existing structure of society, and building a new structure, and when the time is ripe they will sweep away the undermined edifice and erect a new society born from their own midst." [40]

The Theorists of Syndicalism. The theorists of revolutionary syndicalism may be divided into two groups: members of the working class and those completely identified with them, on the one hand, and "intellectuals" outside of the labor movement, on the other. The most prominent in the former group were Fernand Pelloutier, the secretary of the Federation of Bourses from 1894 to 1902; Emile Pouget, assistant secretary of the Confederation and editor of the *Voix du Peuple* from 1901 to 1908; V. Griffuelhes, secretary of the General Confederation of Labor from 1901 to 1908; George Yvetot; Louis Niel; and others, all

[39] *Ibid.*, pp. 138–9.

[40] *Ibid.*, p. 140.

active officers of the Confederation. Pouget and Yvetot came to syndicalism from the anarchist movement; Pelloutier started as a socialist and then became a convert to the anarchist faith; Griffuelhes came from the Allemanists. These "working-class theorists," active in the day-to-day struggle of the unions, were less interested in the mere speculative side of syndicalism, more in the methods that should be adopted in the industrial struggle if the revolution were to be brought about more speedily.

The principal figures in the "intellectual" group were Georges Sorel, Hubert Lagardelle, and Edouard Berth. Their organ was *Le Mouvement Socialiste,* founded in 1899 by Lagardelle, a member of the Socialist party. Sorel, Lagardelle, and Berth, through *Le Mouvement Socialiste,* endeavored to supply a philosophic and sociological basis for syndicalism.

Sorel's Approach to Syndicalism. Sorel was the most prolific writer. He saw syndicalism as a further development of the fundamental ideas of Karl Marx. Syndicalists were "neo-Marxists," accepting as they did the spirit of Marx, though rejecting a number of the current interpretations of the great socialist thinker. The syndicalist philosophy was in a sense "revisionism of the left." Revision of Marxian theories was essential "because, on the one hand, Marx was not always 'well inspired,' and often harked back to the past instead of penetrating into the future; and because, on the other hand, Marx did not know all the facts that have now become known: Marx knew well the development of the bourgeoisie, but could not know the development of the labor movement which has become such a tremendous factor in social life." [41] The new school, Sorel continued, did not feel that it was bound to admire "the illusions, the faults, the errors of him who has done so much to elaborate the revolutionary ideas." [42]

Syndicalism, according to this writer, retains from Marx the idea that each social system contains the germs of a new system that is to be developed gradually within the bosom of the old and is to be liberated from its outworn integument when the time is ripe.

Sorel conceived the main task before syndicalists as that of training the working class to behave in the "workshop created by capitalism," of developing the proper capacities of the workers.[43]

He regarded the syndicats as the best place to obtain this training, for from the syndicats the workers could exclude "the dictatorship of the intellectuals" who had conquered the world of politics.

[41] *Ibid.,* p. 143; Sorel, *Réflexions sur la Violence* (Paris, 1910), pp. 246, 249.
[42] Sorel, *op. cit.,* p. 249.
[43] Sorel, Preface to Pelloutier's *Histoire des Bourses du Travail.*

The General Strike a Social Myth. It was primarily in his conception of the general strike that he made his contribution—a contribution not altogether accepted by his friends—to the syndicalist philosophy. The idea of the general strike, he maintained, was the greatest organizing and educative force in the possession of the workers. Not that the general strike was ever likely to take place. That was not necessary. "Social myths" play a very large part in social development. How powerful a factor in early Christianity was the myth of the second coming of Christ! Myths are indispensable to every revolutionary movement. They make it possible for those believing in the day of deliverance to keep up their courage and enthusiasm. They concentrate the forces of a rising class and intensify it to the point of action. Social myths generally have utopian features connected with them. But these features are not essential. The essentials are the hope which the acceptance of the myth brings and the ideals strengthened by the myth.

The general-strike idea is the social myth most needed by the modern working class in their struggle for emancipation. The masses who hold the image of the final general strike before them are encouraged to fight in the intermediate struggles, regarding them as skirmishes before the great, decisive battle. On account of the idea of the general strike, "socialism remains ever young, the attempts made to realize social peace seem childish; the desertion of comrades who run over into the ranks of the bourgeoisie, far from discouraging the masses, excites them still more to revolt; in a word the rupture (between the bourgeoisie and the working class) is never in danger of disappearing." [44]

This rupture, according to Sorel, should be developed by every possible means, for progress through democracy which is based on the fiction of the "general will" cannot be depended upon. The working class must break with this idea.

Sorel on Violence. This rejection of the democratic method leads Sorel to lay much emphasis on the application of proletarian violence as the way out. This does not mean wholesale brutality but that the "social struggles must assume the character of pure struggles similar to those of armies in a campaign." [45] Such violence will indicate to the capitalists that social peace is impossible. They will then turn their attention to their economic interests, and the development of the forceful, inventive captains of industry will be the result.

Violence has the additional effect of stimulating the class consciousness of the workers, of bringing vividly before them their sublime mis-

[44] Sorel, *Réflexions sur la Violence,* p. 179.
[45] Sorel, *op. cit.,* pp. 256–7.

sion in history and, as a result, of incorporating their aspirations in the idea of the general strike.

The catastrophic character of the general strike heightens its moral value. The workingmen are stimulated by it to prepare themselves for the final combat by a moral effort over themselves, for only in such unique moments of life "when we make an effort to create a new man within ourselves" "do we take possession of ourselves" and become free in the Bergsonian sense of the term. The general strike, therefore, raises socialism to the rôle of the greatest moral factor of our time.

Sorel and Marx. "Thus M. Sorel," remarks Levine, "having started out with Marx, ends up with Bergson. The attempt to connect his views with the philosophy of Bergson has been made in all his later works. But all along M. Sorel claims to be true to 'the spirit of Marx.' . . . It is doubtful, however, whether there is an affinity between the 'spirit' of Marx and that of Professor Bergson. It appears rather that Professor Sorel has tacitly assumed that affinity because he interprets the 'spirit' of Marx in a peculiar and arbitrary way." [46]

In fact, as Levine points out, Sorel differed from Marx in his emphasis on the mystical and subconscious factors, as contrasted with the economic factors in social development; in his utter skepticism as to the possibility of determining the future course of history and in his belief that the new social order would arrive—if it came at all—through a possible or probable general strike, rather than as a result of necessary economic and social changes. From Proudhon, the anarchist, Bergson, Nietzsche, and Renan; Sorel received perhaps more of his inspiration than from the socialist thinker.

It might be added that the actual influence of Sorel on the syndicalist movement has often been overestimated. Many of his philosophical interpretations, notably that on the general strike, received scant consideration among the rank and file of the movement. Later he broke off relations with syndicalism and at one time was a collaborator with a group publishing a "neo-monarchist" journal.

Other Theorists. Lagardelle's writings were far more systematic than were those of Sorel. He confined his attention to the economic and political and acknowledged the value of democracy in making socialism possible and of the Socialist party in dealing with problems not included within the domain of industrial activities. Hervé's contribution was chiefly in the domain of the movement's relations to militarism and the army of which he was a bitter opponent until France's participation in the World War.

[46] Levine, *op. cit.*, pp. 150–1.

The philosophy of revolutionary syndicalism was influenced vitally not only by the foregoing influences, but by many anarchist thinkers and writers as well as by the left wing socialists who entered the movement.

Later History of French Syndicalism (1902–1914). So much for the theory of syndicalism. From 1902 to the outbreak of the First World War a constant battle took place within the Confederation between the revolutionary branch of the movement and the reformists. During 1905 and 1906 the French unions conducted a vigorous campaign for the eight-hour day during which several of the leaders of the Confederation were arrested, and the government, under the premiership of Clemenceau, sent numerous troops to Paris to protect it against the so-called "coming revolution" that the C. G. T. was supposed to be setting loose on society.

SOCIALISTS UNITE; SYNDICALISTS DISCUSS RELATIONSHIP. At the Congress of Amiens in September, 1906, the question of the affiliation of the trade-union movement with the Socialist party again came up for discussion. The question had by that year taken on a different aspect from that manifested in previous congresses. The International Socialist Congress in Amsterdam in 1904 had urged the French socialists to come together if possible into a unified movement. As a result of this action, a Congress of Unification was held in April, 1905, and the *Parti Socialiste de France* and the *Parti Socialiste Français* formed the *Parti Socialiste Unifié*. At its first congress in October, 1905, the unified party claimed a dues-paying membership of 35,000 members in 2000 groups. In the elections of 1906, 54 socialists belonging to the party were elected to Parliament. With this union of socialist forces, one of the reasons for the action of the Confederation in originally holding aloof from political organizations of workers thus disappeared. M. Renard, secretary of the Federation of Textile Workers, urged, at the instigation of his union, that permanent relations be established between the two groups. Side by side with the economic struggle, the political struggle, Renard asserted, should be carried on for the purpose of securing labor legislation for the workers. The Socialist party had always proposed and voted for laws having as their object the amelioration of the working class as well as their emancipation, and was therefore the logical party to support.[47] If a revolution were to occur today, he added, the syndicats, with their present organization, would not be able to carry on industry without the use of the governmental machinery, and from this point of view also, the Socialist party was useful to the economic

[47] *XV Congrès Corporatif* (Amiens, 1906, pp. 135–6).

wing. M. Renard declared that he had no intention of introducing politics into the union. Politics had already been introduced. Whenever an anti-militarist resolution was urged before the syndicats, when electoral abstention was preached, there was politics.[48]

Both reformist and revolutionary elements, however, fought the resolution. The Textile Federation was defeated by a vote of 724 to 371, and the C. G. T. declared itself "independent of the political schools." In the declaration of principles adopted at the congress, it came out for a day-to-day struggle for better conditions and maintained that the syndicats were preparing the way for the emancipation of the workers to be realized only by the expropriation of the capitalist class. The congress again commended the general strike as a means to that end and declared that it regarded the syndicat as the future basis of social organization. Every syndicalist was free to participate outside of his organization in any political movement he deemed best, but he was not to introduce his ideas into the union.

THE 1910 STRIKE AND ARISTIDE BRIAND. Strikes and rumors of general strikes and frequent arrests characterized the years of 1907 to 1909. On October 10, 1910, a railway strike started on the system Paris-Nord. The following day the strike committee ordered a general railway strike, and on the twelfth the Western division went out. Briand, former ardent advocate of the general strike, then in the ministry, arrested the members of the committee and placed the railway men under the colors, thus establishing a condition of martial law. Although a second strike committee took the place of the first, the back of the strike was broken. The new committee failed to function energetically, and there was little response to the strike appeal from the workers on the eastern and southern railway divisions. By the end of the week the strike was practically abandoned, and on October 18 the committee ordered that work be resumed.

The revolutionary members of the Confederation attributed the defeat to the hesitating tactics of the reformist leaders, whereas the latter maintained that the action of the left wing in ordering the strike on the northern railways was too hasty. The defeat was a definite blow to the prestige of the Confederation, although it had not been directed by this body.

During the succeeding years before the First World War the Confederation conducted a campaign against the inadequate old-age pension act, against the wave of militarism and nationalism that swept the country following the Agadir incident in the summer of 1910, and for

48 *Ibid.*, p. 165.

shorter hours. The growth of the national unions during the decade far outdistanced that of the bourses, and at the end of the period the national unions were consequently far more powerful in the Confederation than were the bourses.

During these years the syndicalists' philosophy also gained adherents among the workers in some of the other countries, notably in Italy and Spain. In the United States the Industrial Workers of the World held a general syndicalist point of view.

The war of 1914–18 put a temporary quietus on the syndicalist movement. Hervé, the militant anti-patriot, and other leaders of French syndicalism became a part of the war machine, and following the War there developed a sharp cleavage between the communists who gave their adherence to Moscow and the pure and simple syndicalists who refused to have a political party, no matter how revolutionary, dictate their policies. Many of the old syndicalists, formerly regarded as the revolutionists, were now attacked as conservatives. Undoubtedly the communist movement deprived the syndicalists of some of their most active spirits, and captured many of the younger men who would otherwise have joined their ranks.

Reasons for Syndicalism in France. Many reasons have been given for the remarkable growth of syndicalism among the workers in France during the last years of the nineteenth century and the opening years of the twentieth century.

The youth of the trade-union movement in France (it had only been rendered a legal movement in 1884); the small scale on which industry is conducted in France as compared with other industrialized countries; the French tradition of insurrection and of change by quick, sudden revolt, centering in the capital city; the historic demand—found in much of French literature for generations—for an economic freedom based on the very considerable influence of the anarchist philosophy and their concept of a society of free groups or communes; absence of tyranny in the workshop; the conspicuous betrayals of the workers by brilliant leaders who began their careers in parliament as socialists (among them Briand, Millerand, and Viviani) and ended as opponents of labor; the dominating place occupied by "intellectuals" in the political working-class movements and proletarian reaction against this domination; the poverty of the trade unions and their inability to finance long, drawn-out strikes; the psychology of the French workers—the fact that, on the one hand, they "lack method, persistence, and foresight," and, on the other, "they are sensitive, impulsive, and combative"; [49] and the pen-

[49] *X Congrès National Corporatif,* p. 203; *XII Congrès National Corporatif,* pp. 15, 29, 44.

chant of the French for finding a fundamental philosophic justification for their actions which the necessities of the moment dictate—all these elements have undoubtedly played their part in the adoption of syndicalist tactics and philosophy by such a large proportion of French trade unionists.

Socialist Criticism of Syndicalists. NEED FOR PARLIAMENTARY ACTION. Socialists criticize syndicalists both on the ground of tactics and of ultimate ideal. They maintain that, while independent working-class political action has its dangers, economic action has also its dangers, but that both, taken by and large, can be used with very powerful effect by the workers. It is said that parliamentary leaders of working-class parties become compromisers; so do leaders of trade unions, declare socialists, if they desire to retain their leadership. In fact, with thousands of followers on strike, faced with starvation, more pressure, they maintain, can often be brought to bear on a trade-union leader to compromise in the settling of disputes than on a political leader advocating a particular law in a legislative chamber. While political leaders have deserted the working class, the trade-union leaders who have betrayed the interests of labor are not few in number, and as much "politics" can be observed in the average union as in a political party. Representatives of socialist parties in the legislative chambers, socialists assert, can generally be depended upon at the least to fight for labor freedom of action during trade disputes. They can be relied upon to favor labor legislation which protects particularly the weaker elements among the working population; to utilize the power of taxation to lessen the inequalities of wealth; to support public services for the social well-being; and to work for the socialization of important industries.

Socialists have never relied, however, on parliamentary action alone for social advancement. They have ever sought to organize the workers in trade and industrial unions and in co-operative organizations and to educate the workers regarding their fundamental problems, as well as to mobilize them in political movements. All legitimate agencies, they believe, should be used by the workers in their struggle for a better life. The economic weapon, they admit, has certain advantages over the political. On the other hand, the hard-won political weapon has advantages over the economic. For one thing, under universal suffrage, workers and capitalists are put on a par as far as actual voting is concerned. Each has one vote and one vote only. As the workers are in a majority, they can by proper co-operation ultimately gain control of the legislative assemblies. There are, to be sure, many obstacles in their path, but the task of winning a majority is not an impossible one. Furthermore, it costs in time, effort, and physical discomfort far less to vote than it does to strike for better conditions. In each case sacrifice is required, but as a general rule not such great sacrifice in the political as in the industrial field.

Intellectuals, it is true, have been excluded more from syndicats or trade unions than from working-class political parties. But, declare socialists, they have a distinct contribution to make to the movement for the emancipation of the workers, and the working class is the gainer if it provides some agency through which the brain workers can effectively serve labor. Many of the most important leaders in working-class thought and action have been the so-called "intellectuals," and a very large proportion of the attacks hurled against domination by the "intellectuals" as such have come not from the workers but from lesser "intellectuals" striving to gain popularity among the workers. Besides, with the evolution of trade unions, "intellectuals" are being called upon to an ever-increasing extent to serve labor in numerous capacities.

As for the defects of universal suffrage, two schools of thought have developed—the socialist and the communist. Many socialists admit the present defects of the democratic method as now operated. They believe, however, that a number of these defects can be remedied by "more democracy"—the application of the initiative, referendum, recall, and other democratic safeguards; greater educational opportunities, a more careful discrimination as to which problems should be settled by experts, and which by the mass of voters, etc.

Sabotage and the General Strike. Various points of view have been held in the socialist movement regarding the use of *sabotage* and the general strike. Individual socialists have severely condemned the use of *sabotage* as a working-class weapon on the ground that the secret and underhanded methods of warfare and the constant effort at deceit entailed in certain forms of *sabotage* have a vitiating effect upon the morale of the workers, and that practice of *sabotage* against employers is likely to lead to the use of the same weapon between various factions of the working-class movement. J. Ramsay MacDonald urges this position:

"Society is in process of change, and the workers who are toiling for greater justice are only retarding progress by following the wrongdoing of which they are victims, rather than strengthening the social tendencies which make for their emancipation. The creative vitality of society is neither expressed nor strengthened by *sabotage,* riots, destruction of industrial capital, or any one of the other minor violences of the syndicalist program." [50]

[50] MacDonald, *Syndicalism* (Chicago; Open Court Publishing Co.), pp. 52–3.

While believing in the strike as an important means of working-class progress, socialists do not feel with the syndicalists that every strike is of positive value to labor. Many a strike, entered upon at an unstrategic moment, with inadequate preparation and for unwise ends, has had a profoundly depressing effect upon the labor movement. It is true that, in the early stages of a union, when the organization has little or no money, it is often better to strike and to depend upon financial support from other labor groups and the general public than not to strike at all. However, most socialistic unions of the present day will agree that a large "war chest" is often a powerful aid both in securing a settlement before a strike is declared, and in winning a victory after the men have stopped work; that, while other organizations might generously aid a union without money in their treasury, such aid cannot be depended upon and should be regarded merely as a desirable supplement to financial assistance given strikers by their own organization. The spectacular tactics worked out by syndicalists to attain their end in the French unions, furthermore, are more adapted to unions located in Latin countries than in countries where the workers come from the less emotional northern stocks. Furthermore, with the development of large-scale production and the pitting of labor against vast aggregations of capital, the guerrilla warfare methods of the syndicalists are not likely to prove effective. A different kind of industrial statesmanship is required.

Socialists frankly differ as to the efficacy of the general strike in bringing about the revolution. The difficulty they see in such a strike is that, in attempting to paralyze industry and starve the capitalists, the working class is likely to starve itself first. Such a strike is also likely to alienate many outside the immediate ranks of organized labor, to split up, rather than to solidify, the ranks of labor, to bring the whole weight of the capitalist state to bear on those in leadership, to develop into violent combat, and, if not successful, to lead to a violent reaction.[51] In capitalist countries where the chief power is not concentrated in one or two industrial centers and in countries where the industrial system is highly developed and complex, its success is likely to be considerably less than in other lands. At least the hope of the revolution should not be based on the success or failure of the general strike. Rather, the workers should put their reliance on the development of economic forces, the increasing power of the workers in municipal, state, and national councils, the ever more effective organization of trade and industrial unions, the assumption of increasingly important functions by labor

[51] *Ibid.*, Ch. VIII.

in the workshops and in the field of co-operative distribution, the growth of public services at the expense of private enterprise, and the development of the socialist way of looking at things among an ever-larger circle of the population. The general strike may be utilized as a deliberate effort or as a more or less spontaneous movement, to supplement these other forces, and may, at the critical moment when other forces are ripe for a change, be exceedingly effective. But the workers are likely to be sorely disappointed if it is regarded as the one means of social salvation.

Since the general strike failed to materialize in France at various periods when the syndicalists confidently expected its occurrence, the French syndicalists after the First World War began to view it as a less immediate means of salvation than in the days before the war. On the other hand, the effectiveness of a stoppage of work in strategic industries in Russia during the revolutionary crisis, the use of the strike in portions of Germany during the attempted *coup d'état* engineered by Kapp, in preventing the return of the monarchy to power, and the 1926 strike in Great Britain in aid of the miners, among other partial or complete general strikes, led in the twenties to renewed interest in the general strike as a weapon to be reckoned with.

Defects of the Syndicalist Ideal. Socialists criticize the syndicalist picture of the future social orders, as far as syndicalists have sought to depict a new order. Too much attention, socialists maintain, has been given to the rights and responsibilities of producers; too little, to those of consumers. Too much emphasis has been put on control by the local bourses; too little on control by national units. That the syndicalists began to realize this immediately after the First World War was indicated by the resolution at their Congress in 1919, favoring the "industrialized *nationalization* of the great services of modern economy: land and water transport, mines, water power, and credit organizations," and defining *nationalization* as the transfer of national property to the control of interested parties, namely, the associated producers and *consumers*. This pronouncement brought the syndicalists much nearer to the socialist position than in former years. Yet, despite this pronouncement, the general tendency of syndicalism has been to ignore the consumer and to favor the smallest unit at the basis of social organization. MacDonald also calls attention to the fact that it is the craft and not the workshop that under syndicalism is regarded as the social unit in control. He points out that the workshop today is not the scene of the activity of one craft, but of many. Self-governing crafts can never be "unless the shadow of Time is to wander back reversely over the dial, and the middle age come again." [52] Even should the control be centered in the workshop, rather than in the craft, the social problem would not be solved, as the workman cannot be depended upon to keep the national or international interests constantly before him when working under conditions which make decisions in his own interests easy.

The socialist, as has been indicated, believes that an all-inclusive political organization is necessary—whether it is called a state, a commune, or what not—for the conduct of functions that must be performed for all the people as residents of a community—functions involving the health, education, and recreation of the community, the prevention of crime, the raising of taxes, the adjusting of relations with other countries, etc. Furthermore they contend that no adequate provision is made for the successful performance of such functions under a syndicalist society. Socialists also seriously question the moral value of violence praised so highly by Sorel, the desirability of laying so great an emphasis upon the negative side of the class struggle and the primary need of action, rather than upon thought, in the onward march toward a new order.

Influence of Syndicalism. The syndicalist movement of the early twentieth century, however, had a very great stimulating influence on socialist thinking and was of service in calling attention to the weaknesses of parliamentarism, the inadequacies of a type of bureaucratic "state socialism," the possibilities of the trade union movement, the numerous weapons at the disposal of labor during trade disputes, and the importance of the producers sharing in the control of a new social order. It stimulated the development of a new school of socialist thought, guild socialism, as a compromise between the older socialism and syndicalism, and undoubtedly its imprint can be seen in the early bolshevik movement, with its emphasis on the importance of the militant minority, with its scorn for democracy, its faith in the *coup d'état* methods of social change, and its insistence upon control by soviets of workers.

French Syndicalism After First World War. Following the war of 1914–18, the C. G. T., center of syndicalist activity, ceased its purely negative attitude toward parliamentary action. It supported the organization of the International Labor Office in Geneva. It likewise urged the public ownership in large sections of French economic life, maintaining that whenever capitalist concentration made it possible for industry to charge unreasonable prices, then "state monopoly must be

[52] *Ibid.*, p. 59. (Italics ours.)

imposed as a means of restoring equilibrium and the proper rate of production." [53]

"Economic reorganization," declared the Confederation, "will not be able to produce its full valuable results unless the nation now takes up and establishes its due social authority over collective wealth and the means of producing and exchanging it, and unless it increasingly hands over managerial autonomy—subject to control—to the Departments, to co-operative communes, and, above all, to new collective bodies, having the legal privileges of incorporation, and administered by qualified representatives of producers and consumers."

To help to effectuate this program, the C. G. T. urged that the government appoint a Grand Council of Production, to be composed of workers, employers, technicians, and government officials, this council to make a survey of the nation's resources and needs.

ESTABLISHMENT OF ECONOMIC COUNCIL. After the rejection of this proposal by the government, the trade unions set up an Economic Council of their own, composed of representatives from the C. G. T., the federations of civil servants and of consumer co-operatives, and of Astica, a federation of technicians in industry, commerce, and agriculture. This Council rendered its report in January, 1920, and urged a program similar to that demanded by the trade-union movement the year before, a program which included a demand for the nationalization of "natural monopolies," transportation and electricity, and their management by a board of 18, one-third workers and technicians, nominated by their respective unions, one-third consumers, and one-third representatives of the community, the last nominated by the state. Various other councils were suggested for the regulation of other industries. The program was a far cry from the anti-state proposals of the prewar syndicalists.

SPLIT IN FRENCH LABOR MOVEMENT. The French syndicalist movement, however, had little time to agitate for the enactment of this program and was soon divided into a number of warring groups. Many of its members went along with this program and with other policies of the majority. Others began to place their hope in Russia as the country "in which the workers have found social salvation," and decided to support the policies that were then being formulated by the French Communist party. This group broke away from the C. G. T. in 1922 and formed the *Confédération Générale du Travail Unitaire,* or C. G. T. U.

At the first congress of the C. G. T. U. in Etienne three trends began

[53] See Marquand, *Organized Labor in Four Continents,* p. 11.

to appear in this left-wing trade-union organization. There was the group of orthodox communists, headed by Frossard, later a Radical Minister; the revolutionary syndicalists, who retained their old anarchistic loyalties; and a third group of conciliators, who favored contacts with the Communist International, but who desired to maintain trade-union independence.

After the C. G. T. U. joined the Red International, bitter controversy regarding communist domination flared up within the new federation; a number of trade-union groups were expelled; and others seceded over the issue of communist control. Some of the seceding unions, among them the building trades, formed a third organization, the *Confédération Générale du Travail Syndicaliste Revolutionnaire,* which sought complete independence from outside controls.

During the ensuing years the left-wing C. G. T. U. showed a readiness to rush into industrial controversies for the purpose of communist political advantage, even where the chances of success were slim. At this same time the C. G. T. exhibited an increasing moderation in its policies, frequently asking public authorities to become mediators or arbitrators of disputes. It also brought constant pressure on legislators to pass labor legislation and on administrators to enforce the labor laws enacted. During the thirties it advocated another plan similar to that urged in the twenties under which much of the economic life of the nation would be brought under the control of a Supreme Economic Council.

Reunion of Labor Federations. Support of Popular Front Governments. As the fascist threat in France appeared to be ever more menacing, there developed within both federations an increasing demand for a unified labor movement, and in the fall of 1935 the two federations—the C. G. T. and the C. G. T. U.—were fused, and their fusion was followed by a Congress of Unification in February, 1936. This congress provisionally approved the general C. G. T. policy, urged retention of membership in the International Federation of Trade Unions, with headquarters in Amsterdam, and approved close co-operation with the International Labor Office. It urged numerous immediate reforms, including the establishment of a national unemployment fund, the forty-hour week, minimum wage laws, and extensive public works. It likewise reaffirmed the traditional stand of the French movement in favor of trade-union independence of political parties, although permitting industrial federations freedom to decide for themselves their policy on this question.

The congress resolutions, however, permitted collaboration with political parties for the achievement of the C. G. T. program and pledged renewed allegiance to the *Front Populaire*. When the Popular Front government came into power in 1936, C. G. T. organizations took the leadership in the strikes that swept the nation, the unions gaining at that time millions of new members. During the succeeding months they spent much effort in support of the social reforms initiated by the Blum government. These included the Collective Contracts Act of June, 1936, under which the government acted as mediator in the settlement of disputes. Under this act the syndicats, members of the C. G. T., were usually called upon to act as arbitrators for the workers. As a result of these various developments one of the secretaries of the C. G. T. was able to declare: "French trade unionism is no longer in opposition; it is no longer an outlaw; social reforms no longer seem unclean to it; it submits to arbitration; it seeks to make collective agreements; it places itself under the power of the law." [54] In other words, the C. G. T., as the chief expression of French labor, was no longer thinking during the late thirties in syndicalist terms.

Under the governments of the right following the resignation of the Popular Front government, French labor became engaged in numerous controversies over attempts to restrict its power. It attempted a general strike against the decree of the Daladier government on Novem- 27, 1938, which repealed much of the recent anti-strike legislation, but this strike was a failure. Following the nazi invasion, the labor movement in France virtually ceased to exist as an independent force.

Syndicalism in Other Countries. In other countries the syndicalist labor movement was destroyed either as a result of dictatorial suppression, as in the case of fascist Italy, or as a result of unfavorable economic and social conditions, as in the case of the Industrial Workers of the World (I. W. W.) in the United States, which had its period of greatest activity between 1905 and 1914.

In Spain the movement was crushed by the government, particularly under the Rivera dictatorship, but began to flourish again following the revolution of 1931. In a short time its membership grew to an estimated total of 1,000,000, and it became the most important anarcho-syndicalist movement in the world. An attempt at a syndicalist revolution in Spain in 1933 proved abortive.

The syndicalist movements that survived the First World War were affiliated for some time with the International Working Men's Association founded in Berlin in 1922. Between 1923 and 1932, most of the

[54] Marquand and others, *Labor on Four Continents*, pp. 51–2.

theoretical work in connection with the movement was carried on by German, Swedish, and Dutch members of the labor movement.

Following the access of Hitler to power in 1933, the I. W. M. A. was transferred from Berlin to Holland and thence to Madrid. Its membership in 1933 probably totaled at the outside limit no more than 1,100,000, most of whom were members of the Spanish C. N. T. With the coming of Franco to power in Spain, the Spanish movement as an independent entity ceased to exist.[55]

[55] For a comprehensive analysis of the history of general strikes, one of the main weapons of labor urged by syndicalists, see Crook, *The General Strike.* Dr. Crook deals particularly with the British General Strike of 1926 and the Seattle, Washington, and Winnipeg, Manitoba, Canada, general strikes in 1919.

In the United States the Industrial Workers of the World—the I.W.W.—was the body that most nearly embraced the principles of syndicalism. It was formed in Chicago in 1905 and prior to and during the First World War conducted spectacular drives for the organization of workers along industrial lines. Of late years it has been comparatively inactive. (See Brissenden, *The I.W.W.;* Gambs, *The Decline of the I.W.W.;* Levine, *The Development of Syndicalism in America;* Saposs, *Left-Wing Unionism;* Westmeyer, *Modern Economic and Social Systems*, ch. XXII.

CHAPTER 23

Guild Socialism

IN GREAT BRITAIN, in the days immediately before the First World War, a somewhat new and fascinating phase of socialist thought began to take root. It went by the name of guild socialism. During the period between the early eighties when the members of the Fabian Society were first formulating their theory of socialism and the socialist state and the definite launching of the propaganda of guild socialism about the year 1912, the socialist movement had become a vital factor in the life of the community.

Formation of the Independent Labor Party. The formation of the Social Democratic Federation and the Fabian Society in the eighties had been followed by the election in 1892 of Keir Hardie, a British miner, to the House of Commons as an independent labor candidate. The latter event was followed by the formation one year later by Hardie and others of the Independent Labor party, organized with a view to bringing the socialist message before the people in a manner which they could understand. The aim of the Independent Labor party was the collective ownership and control of the means of production; to be achieved through parliamentary action, social reform, pressure of labor, and democracy in local and central government. Its platform did not differ to any extent from that of the Social Democratic Federation, but its attitude toward the trade unions was more sympathetic, and in its active work among the unions its speakers usually avoided mention of revolution, class warfare, and Marxian concepts in general, and approached the problem more from the ethical, nonconformist, and democratic points of view which appealed to the British workmen.

Organization of the British Labor Party. J. Ramsay MacDonald soon joined the Independent Labor party, and during the remainder of the nineties the party devoted its chief efforts to winning the trade unionists for independent political action. It made headway, and in 1899, through an executive of the Railway Workers, secured the passage of the following resolution in the Trade Union Congress:

> This Congress, having regard to the decisions of former years, and with a view of securing a better representation of the interest of labor in the House of Commons, hereby instructs the Parliamentary Committee of the Trade Union Congress to invite the co-operation of all the co-operative, socialist, trade union, and other working-class organizations jointly to co-operate on lines mutually agreed upon in convening a special congress of representatives from such of the above-named organizations as may be willing to take part, to devise ways and means for the securing of an increased number of labor members to the next Parliament.

This resolution, passed by a vote of 546,000 to 434,000, laid the foundation for the British Labor party. A committee was appointed in pursuance of the resolution, consisting of four members of the Parliamentary Committee—a liberal, a radical and Fabian, a social democrat, and a fourth with socialist leanings. Two members each were also selected from the Independent Labor party, the Social Democratic Federation, and the Fabian Society. They were Keir Hardie, J. Ramsay MacDonald, Harry Quelch, H. R. Taylor, George Bernard Shaw, and E. R. Pease (secretary of the Fabians). The socialists, who were in the majority on the committee, were far superior to the trade unionists in intelligence, knowledge, and energy.

The committee decided to call a conference to consider what future action should be taken, and on February 27 and 28, 1900, the conference met in London, with 120 delegates present representing over a half million workingmen belonging to trade-union and socialist organizations. The conference favored the support of candidates for Parliament who belonged to the organizations represented on the committee. Before adjournment it appointed a Labor Representation Committee of seven trade unionists, two members of the Independent Labor party, two of the Fabian Society, and two of the Social Democratic Federation. Ramsay MacDonald was elected secretary and immediately set to work to enlist the sympathies of the trade unionists in the work of the Labor Representation Committee. In September, 1900, at a general election, the Labor Representation Committee placed fifteen candidates in the field, of whom two, Keir Hardie and Richard Bell, were successful.

The Labor Party Victory of 1906. Interest in the work of the committee increased due, to no small extent, to the influence of the Taff Vale decision, which permitted the courts to levy upon trade-union budgets for damages caused to employers by strikers during trade disputes. In 1902 David Shackelton, a trade unionist, was elected to

Parliament at a special election, and the following year Arthur Henderson and William Crooks joined the ranks of Labor M. P.'s. In 1903 the railway union paid to the Taff Vale Company under a court decision 23,000 pounds, and judgment was delivered against the South Wales miners for 50,000 pounds. This created further unrest in the ranks of labor, who felt that their treasuries might be entirely wiped out if this precedent were followed. The Conservative government, absorbed in discussions over tariff reforms and the Anglo-German situation, made no attempt to amend the trade-union law.

In January, 1906, came the next general election. The Labor Representation Committee placed fifty candidates in the field and, to the surprise of England, elected twenty-nine out of the fifty, polling a total vote of 323,000. The Miners' Federation was the only one of the larger unions which remained outside the folds of the Labor Representation Committee, although it came in a few years later and increased labor's forces in Parliament to 40. The committee thereafter went by the name of the British Labor party.

The Achievements and Failure of the Labor Group (1906–14). The labor election was the sensation of the year, and as a result the interest in socialism increased enormously. No sooner did Parliament meet than the Labor party forced through the Trades Disputes Act, often called the *Magna Carta* of British labor, extending to labor, as it did, the right of picketing and boycotting and freedom from collective responsibility for damages incurred during a trade dispute. This quick result led the labor and socialist forces to cherish high hopes that the labor group would force through other legislation in behalf of the worker. However, these hopes were doomed to disappointment, and from that time until the beginning of the First World War few fundamental reforms were achieved.

This failure of great accomplishment was due in considerable part to circumstances beyond their control. The months following the passage of the Trades Dispute Act were months of economic depression. Unemployment was widespread and prices were rising. England was feeling the results of the inflation following the Boer and Russo-Japanese wars, the increased world production of gold, and the competition with Germany. The Labor group was in a small minority, and its more radical proposals had no chance of passage. Parliament ignored its efforts to relieve the unemployment problem, and labor's efforts in this direction were not so constructive as they might have been. The party was handicapped in a sense by having no legislative program to which it had been definitely committed. The viewpoint of many members of the group was more liberal than socialist. The Irish Home Rule, the Suffrage, and the Welsh Disestablishment Bills were before Parliament for several years, having been regularly vetoed by the House of Lords, and the Labor Parliamentary group was anxious for the time being to keep the Liberal party in power in order to secure final passage of these bills. The Labor group likewise supported several other Liberal bills and worked at times in close co-operation with the Lloyd George group. This situation led to growing criticism from the socialist wing of the labor movement, and among many a growing skepticism as to the value of political action. A definite swing of the pendulum toward industrial action took place, and in the trade union field a veritable strike fever waged, in attempts to secure wage raises proportionate to the increase in the cost of living.

Forces Contributing to Guild Socialism. It was during this period that the guild socialist movement, with its ideal of a social order midway between syndicalism and the older socialism, its emphasis on producers' control, and its criticism of programs favoring too great a development of state functions, began to take root.

The guild socialist school of thought was a resultant of the political and industrial situation just outlined and of various other forces. These others included:

1. In the nature of the case, the general socialist movement, with which most of the guildsmen had been closely identified. The socialist attack on the wage system and its advocacy of a system of production not based on profit were fundamental to the guild philosophy.

2. The influence of John Ruskin, Thomas Carlyle, William Morris, and others who detested the ugliness and monotony of machine production and who regretfully looked back to the time when the independent guildsmen of the Middle Ages took pride in creative work and produced the great art for which the Middle Ages were famous.

3. The French syndicalist movement and the theories of the American Industrial Workers of the World, with their bias against the state and against political action and their shibboleth of "all power to the producer."

4. The writings of such anti-collectivists as Gilbert K. Chesterton and Hilaire Belloc, who saw in much of the recent collectivist legislation in Great Britain the beginnings of a "servile state," and who proposed as their ideal a "Distributive State" largely composed of peasant proprietors, where the "instinct of ownership" would be satisfied. These writers maintained that much of the collectivist legislation, by making the workers physically comfortable, was rendering capitalism en-

durable, and that it was at the same time restricting the freedom of trade-union action. Would a strike, they asked, be permitted in a state-owned industry? This question was given special point in 1907 by the attitude of the Fabian Society in approving the treaty which Lloyd George "imposed upon the railroad industry" in his attempt to settle a threatened railroad strike. "In the case of the nation's principal means of land transport," declared the Fabians, "resort to the characteristic trade-union weapon of the strike" was "such a national calamity that no responsible statesman could nowadays treat it as a private matter. . . . The nation can no more afford to let the railway industry be interrupted by the claims—however just—of the railway workers, than by the obstinacy—however dignified—of the railway directors." [1]

5. The school of anti-state political philosophers, led by the Reverend J. N. Figgis, who was engaged in exploding the "myth" of the sovereignty of the state.

In his writings Father Figgis maintained that there were certain associations residing in the state—churches and trade unions among them—whose interests were independent of the state and whose personalities were inviolable by state authority.[2] The state "could recognize and guarantee . . . the life of these societies—the family, the club, the union, the college, the church; but it no more created life than it created the individual, though it orders his birth to be registered." Consequently, "the theory of sovereignty, whether proclaimed by John Austin or Justinian, or shouted in conflict by Pope Innocent or Thomas Hobbes, is in reality no more than a venerable superstition. . . . As a fact it is as a series of groups that our social life presents itself, all having some of the qualities of public law and most of them showing clear signs of a life of their own, inherent and not derived from the concession of the state." [3] Political authority, in brief, is "an association, not a lordship."

In this view Father Figgis followed the historian Maitland, who had maintained the thesis that other groups than the state possessed legal personalities. It was not a far cry to the conclusion that associations residing in the state should not only be able to preserve their personalities inviolate from state encroachment, but also should be permitted to assume new duties at the expense of the state. The guild socialists attempted to prove the justice of this contention. Figgis' lectures, appear-

[1] Letter in *New Age*, Dec. 7, 1907.

[2] A series of articles in the *New Age*, afterwards appearing in book form, in *Churches in the Modern State* (London: 1914).

[3] *Ibid.*, p. 224.

ing at the time that the guildsmen were finally formulating their doctrine, had a distinct influence on guild thought.

6. Guildsmen, following the first formulation of their theory, were also influenced by the "functional principle" theory enunciated by the Spanish journalist, Señor Ramiro de Maeztu, a theory which maintained that there are no natural rights, but only "objective rights," conditional upon performing some useful function by the individual or group claiming them.[4] R. H. Tawney later elaborated on this theory in his *The Acquisitive Society*,[5] insisting that property should be "functional" and that industrial control should pass out of the hands of functionless owners into those of the workers who rendered actual service.

7. We might mention also the influence on later guildsmen of J. M. Paton's theory of "encroaching control," with its demand that the employer be gradually pushed out of the control of industry through aggressive trade-union action and of Major Douglas' credit scheme for the acquisition by labor of the credit resources of the country.

Reckitt and Bechhofer thus succinctly summarized these various currents which went into the making of the guild movement:

"We should find the craftsmen's challenge and the blazing democracy of William Morris; the warning of Mr. Belloc against the huge shadow of the servile state and, perhaps, something also of his claim of the individual's control over property; the insistence of Mr. Penty on the evils of industrialism and its large scale organization, and his recovery and bequest to us of the significant and unique word 'guild.' We should find something of French syndicalism, with its championship of the producer; something of American industrial unionism, with its clear vision of the need of industrial organization; and something of Marxian socialism, with unsparing analysis of the wage-system by which capitalism exalts itself and enslaves the mass of men." [6]

The Guild Leaders. Four personalities stood out above the others in the formulation of guild theory. The first of these was A. J. Penty, architect, called by some the "original guildsman," designer of garden cities, a former Fabian and I. L. P. member, who came to the social reform movement by means of the road of John Ruskin and William Morris, who sought with them the restoration of the architectural beauties of the Middle Ages, and whose *Restoration of the Guild System* in

[4] See de Maeztu, *Authority, Liberty and Functions in the Light of the War* (London: 1916).

[5] Tawney, R. H., *The Acquisitive Society*, London: Bell, 1924.

[6] Reckitt and Bechhofer, *The Meaning of National Guilds* (N. Y.: Macmillan, 1919), pp. xiii–xiv.

1906 foreshadowed many of the characteristics of the guild socialist theories.

In the second place there was A. R. Orage, a fellow of Penty's in the socialist movement, editor of the *New Age,* the brilliant "center of educated revolutionary activity," and collaborator with S. G. Hobson of the articles on national guilds appearing in the journal, which placed the theory of guild socialism in the forefront of discussion. A third personality was S. G. Hobson, the "veteran" of the movement, journalist and socialist propagandist of many years' standing, who largely formulated the guild socialist theory and provided it with its Marxian economic basis. Fourth, and by no means the least, was that *enfant merveilleux,* as he has been often called, G. D. H. Cole, the keen-minded Oxford fellow, who, while not joining the movement until 1913, proved to be its most effective and prolific thinker and popularizer.[7]

The Aims of Guild Socialism. The first attempt to conduct propaganda work for the general idea of guild socialism, then in a rather nebulous stage, may be said to have started with the organization of the Guilds Restoration Movement in 1906. The appearance of the Hobson-Orage articles on the subject in 1912 officially launched the idea; and the formation of the National Guilds League in 1915, which followed Cole's unsuccessful attempt to commit the Fabian Society to guild socialism, and his organization of the Guild Socialist Propaganda Society, translated the idea into an effective movement.

The objects of the League were stated as "the abolition of the wage system, and the establishment of self-government in industry through a system of national guilds working in conjunction with the state." The words "a democratic state" were afterwards inserted, and at the 1920 conference of the League the word "state" was omitted altogether, and the phrase "other democratic functional organizations in the community" substituted therefor. According to its constitution the League propaganda was to be conducted by means of lectures, meetings, and publications.

In brief, the guildsmen urged wholeheartedly the Marxian demand that the wage system should be abolished. To them the wage system was bad economically, morally, psychologically, aesthetically, and spiritually. It meant dishonest and inartistic work. It produced a slave state of mind, which the worker carried over with him into his social and political life. It suppressed the creative instinct in labor, the worker's instinct to own and control, and for the system of production for service it substituted a system designed to grind out profits for the absentee

[7] See Niles Carpenter, *Guild Socialism* (N. Y.: Appleton, 1922), pp. 81–90.

owners, irrespective of the desires of the consumers or the needs of the producers.

Positively the guildsmen aimed at "self-government in industry," a self-government for the worker which would give him an opportunity to develop his personality and which would at least assure to him as a minimum:

1. Recognition and payment as a human being, and not merely as the mortal tenement of so much labor power for which any efficient demand exists.

2. Consequently, payment in employment and in unemployment; in sickness and in health alike.

3. Control of the organization of production in co-operation with his fellows.

4. A claim upon the product of his work, also exercised in co-operation with his fellows.[8]

Application of the Functional Principle to Industry. Many also sought to incorporate the "functional principle" of society into the industrial structure. Men, Cole and others contended, organize various groups to carry out particular functions in which they are interested. They establish churches, trade unions, clubs of various sorts, co-operative societies, municipalities. These should not be regarded as subordinate to an omni-competent state, but should remain relatively independent of each other, co-operating with, but not under the authority of, any so-called sovereign entity. Only through such co-operation can the best results be attained. To be sure, the state or the commune has certain functions to perform, including that of police and fire protection, functions which affect all men equally as they reside in a community. But this fact gives it no claim to primacy over other functional groups. It follows from this reasoning that true democracy does not begin and end with voting on election day, but resides in the functioning of every organization which vitally affects the life of the citizen. It follows that the state is not in a position to dictate to a trade union, a guild, or any other economic organization, but that each is sovereign within its own sphere; and that the worker should participate in the election of the officials in his industry in the same way as in the election of city officials. As we shall see later, this principle was not adhered to universally by the guildsmen, but seemed to have the majority support.

The Guild Commonwealth. While the guildsmen disclaimed any desire to build a utopia, they nevertheless drew up rough outlines of their future guild system to give their theory more definiteness. As

[8] Cole, *Self Government in Industry*, p. 155.

there was considerable difference of opinion regarding many of the desirable features of a guild society among the leaders of the guild movement, and as these leaders themselves changed their concept of an ideal society somewhat frequently, no complete picture of the guild ideal of those early days can be here portrayed.

CHARACTERISTICS OF A GUILD; *Inclusiveness, Responsibility, Monopoly.* Practically all guildsmen, however, were agreed that the unit in the guild socialist society should be the guild. The guild was defined as "a self-governing association of mutually dependent people organized for a responsible discharge of a particular function of society." [9] The guild, within the definition of the guildsman, had several important characteristics. It included *all of the workers* in an industry, trade or profession, in so far as such was "guildized"—the managerial and technical staff as well as the manual workers, the salariat as well as the proletariat.

It would be *responsible* and be given virtual autonomy within its own sphere, so long as it performed its functions satisfactorily. On this point the guildsman was insistent. Those who were doing the actual work should be responsible for its direction, if waste was to be avoided and work was to be done well. Standards of "ethics" and "honor," the guildsman believed, could be maintained in industrial effort, as they were in part in the teaching and other professions, if industry should "cease to be conducted by the agents of property owners for the advantage of property owners, and should be carried on instead for the service of the public" and if "the responsibility for maintenance of the service should rest upon the shoulders of those, from organizer and scientist to laborer, by whom, in effect, the work is conducted."

A third characteristic of the guild, in the eyes of the majority of guildsmen, was *monopoly,* although in some cases the guild socialists provided for a "fringe" of enterprises free from guild control.

Democracy in the Guild. Furthermore, the guild should be *democratically run.* Democracy did not mean, according to Cole, that mass votes would be taken on every move in the productive process. "A mass vote on a matter of technique understood only by a few experts would be a manifest absurdity, and even if the element of technique is left out of account, a factory administered by constant mass votes would be neither efficient nor at all a pleasant place to work in." [10]

As for the leaders under the guild system, they would of course be

[9] Orage, *An Alphabet of Economics,* p. 53.

[10] Cole, *Guild Socialism* (N. Y.: Stokes, 1920), p. 41.

elected by the guild itself. "But this does not mean that every type of leader must be chosen by a mass ballot of the whole guild." Officials employed to perform a function essentially technical would not be leaders but rather consultants and advisers, and their appointment would not raise the issue of democratic control. On the other hand, for those who were to direct their fellows, "the only right principle is that the person who is to perform it [the function] should be chosen by those in co-operation with whom it is to be exercised. That is to say, the governing principle in the choice of guild leaders will be election 'from below,' by those whom the leaders will have to lead." [11]

However, added Cole, there should be certain safeguards. Whenever a position required, in addition to ability to lead, certain qualifications of skill or technique, the possession of those characteristics could be made a condition of eligibility for the position. "A shipowner today can only appoint as captain of his ship a man who holds a master's certificate. The seamen of the future guild will only be able to choose as their captain a man who is similarly equipped."

While Cole was of the opinion that, as a rule, the actual group which an official was to direct should usually choose him, he admitted the possibility of other workers in the same calling assisting in the choice. In factories he favored direct elections, whereas in larger units election by delegates might, he conceded, be the better course. The guild socialists admitted the enormous difficulties in the way of democratic control, and realized that it must come gradually, but felt that there was in the long run no alternative but to try it, "for the old idea of leadership by the imposition of will is breaking down with the old industrial system." [12]

Managers of the Guild Regime. This democratic regime, according to Cole, should make a special appeal to the manager and technician. It was true that under it the manager would not have the uncontrolled power to "fire" a worker, for the guildsman "would insist that a man threatened with discharge should be tried by his peers, and every man would surely have behind him a considerable measure of economic security." Nor would he be able to ignore public opinion in the factory or the guild as a whole. On the other hand, there would be counteracting advantages. He would have a good prospect—if he did his work well—of having the public opinion of his factory decidedly on his side, in his attempt to make things move smoothly and efficiently. He could look to the workers to co-operate with him in accomplishing

[11] *Ibid.*, p. 42.

[12] *Ibid.*, p. 46.

the best results. At the worst he would not be in the anomalous position in which he finds himself under the profit system as the nominee of a capitalist employer.

"I strongly suspect," Cole added, "that the managers in such a guild factory would have no cause to complain of lack of power. If they wanted authority, they would find ample scope for it; but I believe most of them would cease to think of their positions mainly in terms of power, and would, instead, come to think of them mainly in terms of function. Only under the free conditions of democratic industry would the leader find real scope for leadership, and he would find it in a way that would enable him to concentrate all his faculties on the development of his factory as a communal service, instead of being as now constantly thwarted and restrained by considerations of shareholders' profits. There is no class of 'industrious persons,' as the Chartists would have said, to whom the guild idea ought to have a stronger appeal than to the managers and technicians of industry; for it alone offers them full opportunities to use their ability in co-operation with their fellow workers and for the service of their fellow men.

"The guild factory, then, would be a natural center of self-government, no longer, like the factories of today, a mere prison of boredom and useless toil, but a center of free service and associative enterprise. There would, of course, be dull and unpleasant work still to be done in the world; but even this would be immeasurably lightened if it were done under free conditions and if the right motives were enlisted on its side." [13]

As for the tenure of the manager, should he prove unsatisfactory to the workers, he should have the right, before he could be deposed, to appeal to his peers—his fellow managers. Should they hold that he was in the right, but should the workers still desire his dismissal, the case could go to a higher tribunal of the guild. Should, however, there be a sustained desire to have him go, that would prove the incompatibility of his temperament for democratic leadership in that particular factory, and the workers should have their way.

Types of Guilds. Guilds, according to the guild socialist, would be divided into industrial and civic guilds, and, some added, into distributive guilds as well. There would be industrial guilds for transit, agriculture, mines, buildings, printing, textiles, clothing, food, etc. One writer suggested nine or ten great industrial guilds to administer the economic activities of the community.

[13] *Ibid.*, pp. 47–8.

The Agricultural Guild. The various industrial guilds would have practically the same structure, with the possible exception of the agricultural guilds. The latter would probably admit into their membership non-farmers in the small farming villages engaged in small-scale operations ministering to rural needs. Under the guild regime farming on a small scale would probably continue to supplement large-scale agriculture. Many of these small farms would probably remain outside of the guild system, subject in certain respects to guild regulations, and, perhaps, using the guild in part as an agency for purchase and sale, "but otherwise on their own." [14]

The guild system would not interfere with such independent farming, except to see to it that the land was being properly utilized and to prevent ruthless exploitation of labor on the farm. In an endeavor to do this, a system might be worked out requiring that labor be supplied only through the guild and under conditions which the guild laid down.

Civic and Distributive Guilds. Most guildsmen advocated, in addition to the industrial guilds, the organization of civic guilds. These would include, in a general way, the professions of today—the medical or health, the educational, the legal, the dramatic, and others. The distributive guild proposed by Hobson would have charge of much of the retail trade, and would contain on its council representatives of the consumers, of the municipal bodies of the area covered by the guilds, and of the productive societies whose goods it distributed. Cole would substitute for the distributive guild a producers-consumers' organization associated with his proposed "commune."

Local, Regional, and National Guilds. The guildsmen seemed generally agreed that the guild unit should be the national guild, highly decentralized. Penty and his followers favored the local guild as the unit, on the ground that the basis of the medieval guild was local and that only by restoring local autonomy in industry could the tyranny of machine production be overthrown. The majority of guildsmen, on the other hand, pointed to the economies of production on a national scale, as in the purchase and marketing of goods; to the fact that trade unions, which might be regarded as the basis of their ideal system, were national; to the improbability of a return to the localized economy existing at the time of the supremacy of the medieval guilds, and to the fact that one should not be fearful of the domination of the machine as such, but of the control of the machine by absentee owners.

The national guild would have under its control such matters as the

[14] *Ibid.*, p. 151.

purchase of raw materials, the securing of markets, the laying down of general policies, as in the setting of standards of workmanship and safety, the conduct of research and the representation of the guild industry in its outside relationships. In actual matters of administration, on the other hand, the local unit, ordinarily the factory, would have very large discretion.

There would likewise be regional guilds to look after the interests of industry in different parts of the country. The local guild would elect representatives to the regional or district guild, and the district guild, to the national organization. The local guild would thus be represented indirectly, not directly, in the national council.

Members of particular trades, furthermore, would be able to express themselves not only through the guilds but through craft organizations, which might cut across guild borders and have special representation, particularly in the national guilds. Provision might also be made for shop committees for "rank and file" suggestions and criticisms, within the various factories.

In regard to membership in the guilds and expulsion of recalcitrant members therefrom the guildsmen had little to say. They gave more consideration, however, to the method of paying the members of the guild for their services. Hobson suggested that at the beginning of each year an amount be placed aside as the total wage budget of the year for the members of all of the guilds and that a wage fund be allotted to each guild in proportion to its membership, thus applying the *principle of equality in wage payments as between the guilds.* However, that would not necessarily mean that each guild member would receive the same reward. The guild would have full authority to pay unequal amounts to various categories of workers, and would probably do so for some time. Ultimately, it would be the hope of the guild leaders that the principle of equality in payments should be fairly generally applied. As has already been observed, the guildsmen advocated payments in sickness, and during slack times, as the needs of the workers did not cease when, through no fault of their own, they found themselves out of work.

INTER-GUILD RELATIONS. There would, of course, be a great many business transactions between the guilds. For instance, the clothing guild and the textile guild stood in the relation of buyer and seller. Business relations could be adjusted between guilds partly by means of a system of "interlocking directorates"—that is, the clothing guild could permit the textile guild to appoint a few representatives to sit on its local, regional, and national councils—and partly through the holding of numerous inter-guild congresses in which knotty problems of inter-guild relationships would be decided.

THE GUILDS AND THE COMMUNITY. It was in the relation of the guilds to the community that there was the greatest difference of opinion between guildsmen. This difference was owing in large part to the fundamentally different political and social theories held by the various schools of guildsmen. Hobson and his followers, who believed that the state should be the final arbiter, were greatly at variance with Cole, who would eliminate the state, the sovereignty of which he denied, and substitute a "commune" in its place.

INDEPENDENT CRAFTS. There were, however, a few miscellaneous relationships between guilds and the community on which the guildsmen were fairly well agreed. They were agreed, for instance, that there would probably be a number of occupations that would not be "guildized," but regarded as independent. These would include journalism, the ministry, the arts, invention. Members of these professions would be largely engaged in free lance work, receiving voluntary support from individual citizens or groups or, as in the case of certain inventors, subsidized by guilds.

Guildsmen were also agreed that private enterprise would probably continue to exist in certain industries, notably in connection with small workshops or handicraft industries. However, the vast proportion of workers would be included in the guild system, and occupations outside of the system would be so regulated as to compel the observance of certain guild standards.

RETENTION OF RIGHT TO STRIKE. Guildsmen agreed that under guild socialism the workers should retain the right to strike. The possibility of losing that right was one of the considerations which drove many of them to the guild movement. However, the guild community, through its control over the means of production and distribution, would be in a position to institute an economic boycott against any guild whose workers "ran amuck." This possible means of retaliation would, the guildsmen believed, tend to prevent the unwise use of the strike. Besides, most of the causes for striking under capitalism would be eliminated under a guild regime.

FUNCTIONS OF THE STATE OR COMMUNE. In general the guildsmen believed that somebody, representative of the entire community, either the state or a commune, should have charge of such communal functions as the preservation of order, international relations, and defense, though some were inclined to the belief that such functions as the consular service carried on should be left to the guilds. Little was said by those outside of the Orage-Douglas credit group regarding currency. Hobson favored labor notes based on labor time and the dropping of the gold standard except, perhaps, in foreign exchange.

Power of Taxation. Guildsmen were also pretty much agreed that the state, the commune, or the guild congress should exact from them for the common good any surplus they might have after paying the expenses of the guild and laying aside a sufficient fund for such needs as depreciation, improvements, and insurance. Such a levy would kill two birds with one stone: it would provide sufficient revenue for community purposes and it would discourage any tendency on the part of the guild to charge exorbitant prices, for what incentive would there be for high prices, adulteration, bad work, restricted output, and the stimulation of demand in illicit ways, if any profits above what was necessary for present and future needs were automatically absorbed by the community?

The Civic-Sovereignty Theory. Agreeing thus far, the guildsmen tended to disagree as to the kind of agency which would look after the civic interests. Hobson and others adhering to the *civic-sovereignty* theory believed that the state should still exist; that it should be relieved, however, of most of its active administrative functions—the guilds taking over these—and thus be able to concentrate on its civic interests. It should act as the representative of the individual, in other words, not as consumer or producer, but as *citizen*. According to Hobson, the "sense of nationality operating in the individual consciousness" was the greatest fact in the life of a democratic people. As the greater contained the less, so citizenship contained and comprehended the lesser motives and interests. These motives and interests, important though they might be, must ultimately merge into the will of citizenship, realizing in it the sovereign power. "It is not mere rhetoric when we counter 'the sovereign will of the monarch' with the 'sovereign will of the people.' It is a declaration of democracy. It envisages no balance of power; it knows no checks or counterpoises; it is an ultimatum that the will of the citizens, in their civic capacity, shall prevail over every sectional interest, economic or functional. Its decision is the greatest of national sacraments." [15]

Thus the state, accorded the sovereignty power, would hold the final authority over industrial affairs. It would be the owner of the tools of production, and would hand over its property to the guilds as *trustees*, but could require at any time an accounting of the trusteeship. It would also be the final court of appeals in a dispute arising between

[15] Hobson, *National Guilds and the State*, pp. 102–3.

two or more guilds or between the national guild congress and the community.

On the other hand, the guilds would have complete freedom of action as long as a deadlock did not develop between different guilds. The guilds would be free "to make what goods they pleased, charge what prices they pleased, pay what wages they pleased, and make what provisions for capital they pleased—or could" [16]—except be it repeated, and it is a big exception, that the state would have the power to impose a tax levy directly on the guilds, and thus prevent the exploitation of the community. The guilds would even be able, according to the program of Hobson, to set up their own bank.

THE GUILD-COMMUNE THEORY. The guild-commune theory, on the other hand, denied the sovereignty of the state, and almost denied it any function at all. In place of the state, it set up a "commune" which it placed in closer relationship with the guilds than Hobson's citizen state. The commune would be organized locally, regionally, and nationally. Each type would be closely connected with the corresponding type of guild.

As outlined by Cole, the commune could in no sense be regarded as an extension of the present political state. The present state, Cole maintained, following Marx and Lenin, "is definitely an organ of class domination, not merely because it has been perverted by the power of the capitalist, but because it is based on coercion, and is primarily an instrument of coercion. Its essential idea is that of an externally imposed 'order.' "

In the second place, Cole continued, the state "is based essentially on a false idea of representative government, which assumes that one man can represent another, not *ad hoc,* in relation to a particular purpose or group of purposes, but absolutely." [17]

But "Smith can not represent Brown, Jones, and Robinson as human beings; for a human being, as an individual, is fundamentally incapable of being represented. He can only represent the common point of view which Brown, Jones, and Robinson must hold in relation to some definite social purpose or group of connected purposes. Brown, Jones, and Robinson must therefore have, not one vote each, but as many different functional votes as there are different questions calling for an associative action in which they are interested." [18]

Not even as an instrument of co-ordination would Cole have anything to do with the state, for, he contended, the co-ordination of func-

[16] Carpenter, *op. cit.,* p. 181.
[17] Cole, *op. cit.,* pp. 108–9.
[18] *Ibid.,* p. 24.

tion was not in itself a function. "Either co-ordination includes the functions it co-ordinates, in which case the whole of the social organization comes again under the domination of the state, and the whole principle of functional organization is destroyed; or it excludes them, and in this case, it cannot co-ordinate them." [19]

Thus some other form of organization must be substituted. That organization, for lack of a better name, would be called the commune. The commune would be thoroughly representative of both producer and consumer. To its councils would come representatives from the industrial and civic guilds, representing the producer. To them also would come representatives of the consumers' viewpoint, who had organized for their protection, as Cole suggested, in co-operative societies —"collective utilities councils"—having to do with the supply of electricity, gas, water, and the like; and councils concerned with health, education, drama and music, art galleries, museums, libraries, and similar institutions. In addition there might be representatives from certain territories, organized, say, on a ward basis.

Functions of the Communes. This method of representation would apply to the local commune. The regional commune would be of a similar nature, except that it might give special representation to agricultural guilds. The national commune would be made up of "the representatives of the national guilds, agricultural, industrial and civic, of the national council, economic and civic, and of the regional communes themselves."

The communes should be given important duties. These duties might be grouped into five categories:

(1) Financial problems, especially the allocation of national resources, provision of capital, and, to a certain extent, regulation of incomes and prices;

(2) Differences arising between functional bodies on questions of policy;

(3) Constitutional questions of demarcation between functional bodies;

(4) Questions not falling within the sphere of any functional authority, including several questions of external relations;

(5) Coercive functions.[20]

Most of these functions are self-explanatory. A number of them are co-ordinating functions. In the final analysis the community should have a say over the prices charged. Under the plan as proposed, should the price of milk be under consideration, the distributive guild, in

[19] *Ibid.*, p. 108.

[20] *Ibid.*, p. 125.

consultation with the co-operative society representing the consumer, should set the price. If these groups were unable to come to a satisfactory arrangement, the matter would be brought for final settlement before the commune.

The community would also be greatly interested in the capital outlay of the various guilds, for every outlay of new capital means the diversion of productive labor forces from one field to another. It was essential at all times, therefore, for the community to preserve a balance between production for immediate use and production for use in further production, such as the making of machines, the building of railways, and the like. And this balance was a matter for civic organizations to decide as well as those representative of consumers and producers. For "if more is spent on economic services, there will be less to spend on education, which needs both incomes for the teachers and labor for buildings, books, and equipment of all sorts." [21]

The procedure for determining future improvements and budgets, according to Cole, would be somewhat as follows: Each guild would make out a tentative budget in consultation with other guilds and with the various consumers' councils; the matter would then go before the finance committee of the commune, which would have before it all of the other budgets. This committee would then make suggestions on the basis of the available capital for all industries and the needs of the various guilds and of the community at large, and the final decision would be made by the commune, instead of, as at present, being left "to the blind play of economic forces and the machinations of financiers." [22] Provisions for social services which would be undertaken at the common expense, according to Cole and his followers, would likewise be determined by the commune. As for the commune's power of taxation, that would be exercised by levying the sum approved by that body "in the form of an agreed claim on the labor-power of the guilds." Moreover, any surplus realized by a guild in its annual working would, if Cole's proposal carried, "pass to the commune for its allocation, or be set off against the claim of communal services on the productive guilds as a whole. . . . The commune would clearly control the currency, and the general banking system would also be communal." [23]

In deciding questions of demarcation of functions arising between various guilds, Cole continued, the commune would have to formulate a set of rules or a *constitution* and would in effect become the *constituent assembly or the constitutional legislature of the guild democracy.* It would also have to create a *judicial system* to interpret these laws, but

[21] Cole, *Guild Socialism,* p. 129. [22] *Ibid.,* p. 131. [23] *Ibid.,* p. 132.

would make sure that this system subordinated itself to the commune itself. The national commune would have the power not only of passing laws, but, in disputed cases, of interpreting them, which interpretation would be binding on the judges. "In a sense the guilds and other functional bodies would also legislate, . . . but they could only do so within the powers conferred by the communal constitution, and any law of a functional body involving coercion should, I think, only become enforceable in the communal courts after ratification by the commune," unless such coercive power had been definitely assigned it by the communal constitution.

The commune would have power of war and peace. It would have control over the military forces. It would serve as supreme representative of the nation abroad, although the trade, commercial, civic, and cultural relations would be largely taken charge of by the various guilds and councils. It would, in the last analysis, have power of coercion over individuals and groups, but its aim would be to use that power only as a last, desperate resort, and to create a society "of free service, in the belief not that men must be driven, but that they are capable of leading themselves." Cole acknowledged that the society he had described seemed quite complicated, but maintained that it was in reality much less so than the capitalist society in which groups were organized not so much to fulfill a social function, but to get the best of one's fellow men.

The advocates of the civic-sovereignty theory maintained that Cole, in advancing his proposals for a commune, had merely destroyed a state in order to build a state, for this elaborate structure would be a joint body representative of all the major interests of society. If it were in a position to reach an agreement on problems presented before it, "it would have the substance, if not the form, of sovereignty, including the sanction of coercion, and would, further, through its share in the financial operations of the guilds, have an opportunity of wielding this power in such a way as to exercise a very large degree of control over the most important features of guild administration and policy."[24] Thus the effect of Cole's scheme might be to grant the commune far greater possibilities of interference with group autonomy than would be that of Hobson's scheme, which sought to endow the state with final sovereignty, but provided few opportunities for its exercise upon the guilds.[25]

Guild Tactics. As they differed regarding the details of the future state, so guildsmen likewise differed as regards the best tactics to be pursued in ushering in the guild state. They were generally agreed,

[24] Carpenter, *op. cit.*, p. 189.

[25] See also Hobson, *op. cit.*, p. 126.

however, that the main organization that must be depended upon to inaugurate the guild state was the trade union. Like the syndicalists, they put little stock in parliamentary action as a means to that desired end.

Political Action Inadequate. Constitutional political action, declared Cole, could not be relied upon to bring the revolution, "because, in the first place, there is no chance under capitalism of the whole working class voting together, or of a really 'class conscious' majority returning to power a really 'class conscious' government; because, in the second place, this government, if it could exist, would find the change impossible to achieve in less than a century of parliamentary methods; because, in the third place, the existing state organization is quite unsuited to the execution of any purpose involving fundamental structural changes in society; and because, in the fourth place, the attempt to bring about the transformation by political means alone would almost inevitably, long before its completion, provoke a counterrevolutionary movement by the governing classes, based on their power in the economic sphere. The period required to convert, in opposition to the whole force of money-directed education, propaganda, and pressure, a majority of the people to a habit of sound political thinking is a sufficient reason against the practicability of social transformation by these means; for long before the culmination of the process the present economic system would have fallen in ruins owing to the operation of other causes." [26]

The fundamental reason why political methods would not bring about the social transformation, he added, was that transformation was not political but economic, and under the capitalist system economic power preceded political power. On the other hand, the guildsmen did not declare that political action should be eschewed altogether. In the 1920 Conference of the National Guilds League, the delegates, by a large majority, declared for "the use of the political weapon to hamper the operations of capitalism and to educate the workers."

Need for Reorganization of Trade Unions. If the chief responsibility for bringing about the social transformation was to devolve upon the trade unions, they should equip themselves for this high mission, declares the guild socialist, by a thorough reorganization and a unification of their forces. They must be more than mere trading organizations aiming at an improvement of their conditions under the capitalist system. They must aim at the complete abolition of the wage system.[27]

[26] Cole, *Guild Socialism*, pp. 160–1.
[27] Hobson, *Guild Principles in Peace and War*, pp. 15, 28.

They must organize the unions on the basis of *industries, rather than of crafts.* Under modern industrial conditions the complex of craft organizations was utterly unsuited to the task of reconstructing the industrial society.

They must also follow the lead given by the shop steward movement during the war, and form *shop committees,* since such organizations were far more effective in grappling with the problems of industry than were locals organized on the basis of residence.

They must, furthermore, develop a far greater unity than in the past. Trade unions should in fact "be linked up in a *single body* with internally autonomous sections for the various industries and services, with provision for the full representation of the various classes of workers by hand and brain, and with the workshop or similar economic unit, as the basis of the whole system of administration and direction of policy." [28] Finally, the unions should seek to expand until they virtually possessed a monopoly of the labor market, both among men and women, and among manual and brain workers. On these points there was little dissent among guildsmen.

Encroaching Control. Following this reorganization, what next? Encroaching control, declared some. For one thing, unions should strive through the "collective contract" to supply all of the workers to the employer as needed; to see to it that no worker was dismissed for misconduct except by the judgment of his peers; to appoint their own foremen and be responsible for shop discipline; to induce the employer to turn over to the trade unions or the works committee a lump sum, to be distributed to the men as wages in any manner the workers saw fit; in short, to take the organization and management of the shop out of the hands of the employers and his nominees and to transfer it to the workers and to those whom they appoint. This theory of encroaching control was the distinct contribution of the guildsmen to the theory of working-class tactics.

In addition to encroaching control, many guildsmen had also advocated that trade unions, once they obtained a labor monopoly, should seek to encroach ever more on the profits of industry, appropriating an ever-larger share of these profits to themselves, utilizing the threat of the strike to obtain concessions.

Such control would not bring about the "great transformation," nor would it "give any assurance that profits would be diminished by a single penny." But it would weaken capitalism and "strengthen the

[28] Resolution of the National Guilds League, published in supplement to *The Guildsman,* June, 1920. See also pamphlet.

workers' hand for that further frontal attack on capitalism without which its destruction is impossible." Having secured complete control in the workshops and learned how to run the workshops for themselves, the workers would be in a far better position than they now are to tell the capitalist that they are "able to manage industry for themselves, and that they do not propose to allow him to go on drawing dividends at the expense of the community in return for no service at all." [29]

NATIONALIZATION. Some guildsmen advocated as another transitional measure the nationalization of certain industries, on the ground that national ownership substituted a unified control for control by a large number of employers, and thus tended to make the fight of the workers not so much a fight, as under decentralized private ownership, to bring the worse employer to the level of those who are better, as a fight for workers' control. When, as in the case of the miners, a movement for nationalization was actually on foot, they urged its support "where it includes the concession to the workers of a preponderant control," but only advocated it "in those industries in which it appears to be suitable and convenient." [30] They insisted, however, that the road to guild socialism did not necessarily lie through a program of nationalization, and some guildsmen were unalterably opposed to state ownership as a transitional step.[31]

Furthermore, they favored the establishment of guilds of a character similar to the building guilds organized immediately after the war, which incorporated the spirit of guild socialism. The success of such ventures would prove a valuable object lesson to the workers and would open up a "field in which the workers can, without the need for expropriating the present owners, hope to supersede them." [32]

DIRECT ACTION AND THE GUILDSMEN. How should actual transfer of ownership be effected? On this point, again, there was considerable disagreement. A group of the guildsmen favored the use of "direct action," following the syndicalist method. Cole and others, however, were exceedingly skeptical of this method, unless it were resorted to after many more years of education, organization, and discipline on the part of the working class. It was not the job of the guildsman, declared Cole, to work for "an early revolution, but the consolidation of all forces on the lines of evolutionary development with a view to making the 'revolution,' which in one sense must come, as little as possible a civil war and

29 Cole in *The Guildsman*, July, 1920, p. 4.
30 Pamphlet, *The Policy of Guild Socialism* (May, 1921), p. 18.
31 Douglas and Orage, *Credit-Power and Democracy*, Ch. VI.
32 *The Policy of Guild Socialism*, p. 19.

as much as possible a registration of accomplished facts and a culmination of tendencies already in operation." [33]

He held that direct action depends for its success "on the power of the workers, by means of their industrial organization, without first starving themselves out, to hold up the economic mechanism of society for a long enough time to cause the political and economic structure of the present system to fall to ruins." [34]

This, Cole declared, would not be possible except at an exceptionally favorable moment, such as occurred in Russia in 1917. "To overthrow by this means the far stronger capitalism of Great Britain or America would require a very much stronger and more fully awakened labor movement than now exists in either country." The movement must have carried the evolutionary processes of democratic control, which were the necessary precursors of a successful revolution, much farther than they had gone, for during a revolutionary crisis, the workers "would be confronted with the immediate and imperative necessity of occupying simultaneously many thousand strategic points—not merely of seizing power at the center and improvising a provisional government, but of seizing thousands of local civic bodies, of taking over and improvising administrations in many thousands of factories—of learning in a day a thousand lessons of self-mastery and communal service. I do not say that it could not be done; but I say that its doing would be a miracle." [35]

These difficulties, he continued, would be less insuperable the further the workers could carry the evolutionary process without sacrificing their ultimate ideal. "Trade-union membership, organization, and education extends and improves the fighting force; development of co-operation improves the rationing facilities; conquest of power in local government simplifies the administration transition and places important economic services in the workers' hands; the extension of trade-union control weakens the capitalists' hold of the factories, and helps to teach the workers how to run industry themselves. He who wishes revolution to succeed should hasten toward it slowly, and prepare the way for it by detailed conquests." [36]

Recent Progress of Guilds Movement. The National Guilds League never had a larger membership, its numbers for several years having approximated about 500 members, chiefly in London and its environs. However, its influence at home and abroad was far greater than that membership would seem to indicate. It exerted for several years a considerable influence both over intellectual thought in Great Britain

[33] Cole, *op. cit.*, p. 168.

[34] Cole, *Guild Socialism*, p. 165.

[35] *Ibid.*, p. 166.

[36] *Ibid.*, p. 167.

and over the trade union movement, particularly among the miners, the engineers (machinists), the teachers, railroad workers, and post-office workers. The Church Socialist League and many of the clergy of Great Britain were also at times ardent supporters of the guild idea.

One of the most distinctive features of the guild movement was the organization of building guilds during the period immediately following the First World War. The guilds built successfully large numbers of houses, and, during times of full employment, the workers in the guilds showed greater efficiency than those working for private contractors. However, they were unable to survive the period of severe industrial depression that followed and finally disbanded.[37]

During the twenties the National Guilds League was greatly weakened by the differences of opinion regarding the relation of the guild socialist movement to the Russian Soviet experiment, on the one hand, and the Douglas-Orage credit-control scheme, on the other, and gradually became extinct.

While it failed to survive as a separate organized movement within the socialist movement, its vigorous propaganda and penetrating analysis continued to exert for years after the death of the National Guilds League a decided influence on the general movement of socialist thought.

Objections to Guild Socialism. Leading socialists took exception to many features of the guild plan. They pointed to the difficulty, if not the impossibility, of superimposing the guild structure of the Middle Ages on modern industry. They particularly criticized Mr. Penty's advocacy of the revival of the old guilds with their handicraftship, as opposed to machine production, and their local unit of organization. In the face of international trade, of capitalist enterprise and the division of labor, and of modern political institutions, this attempt at restoration, they maintained, was chimerical.

Furthermore, the critics of guild socialism asserted, the guilds of the Middle Ages should not be over-idealized. Before their dissolution they fell increasingly into the control of cliques; their journeymen came to be regarded as inferiors rather than as associates in the industry; and the regulations they imposed were often arbitrary and monopolistic. They were destroyed through their own failures as much as through any anti-social institutions emerging at that time.[38]

As we have seen, Mr. Cole differed from Penty in striving to re-establish the *spirit* of the guilds, though not necessarily their structure.

[37] See article by Alex. Bing in *Survey*, Jan. 1, 1924; Carpenter, *op. cit.*, pp. 118–37, 314–6.

[38] See Carpenter, *op. cit.*, pp. 246–7.

Far from being a believer in local industry, he would, indeed, accelerate present-day economic concentration. But "as well talk," said Carpenter, "of applying the general organization and spirit of St. Francis to a modern Charity Organization Society." The guild system and modern industrialism "are cast of entirely different metal. The one was built around highly skilled, small scale handicrafts, rigidly restricted, strongly traditional, fiercely local. The other takes for granted unskilled, minutely divided labor; large-scale machine production; remorseless change and innovation; national and even international organization." [39]

Many socialists questioned the need of destroying the state as Cole proposed, for the purpose of again building up the commune, with its potentially great industrial and economic power. Others maintained that with the checks and balances proposed for the commune it would be unable to reach decisions on many questions presented to it for consideration.

They were inclined to agree with Professor Carpenter that the guild commune "would organize people upon the basis of their different and divergent interests; would give them an opportunity to thwart each other; and would give nobody—not even the population as a whole—a chance to make them compose their differences. The omnicompetent state admittedly works badly at times; but it *does* work, which is more than the impotent 'commune' would be likely to do." [40]

Guild critics also saw the danger under guild socialism of concentrating too much attention on the organization of production, thus lessening the workers' interest in and leisure for, matters of greater importance. For it was "as consumer in the widest sense of the word," they claimed that the worker "will realize his individuality and enjoy his freedom." [41] The mass of socialists failed to share the guildsmen's prejudice against political action. Many socialists also questioned the advisability of barring consumers from the boards of administration of an industry, and favored joint control, rather than an exclusive producers' control, for they felt that there is a danger that must be guarded against, under too exclusive workers' control, of seeking to maintain existing processes unchanged, of discouraging innovations, and of developing vested in-

[39] *Ibid.*, p. 249.

[40] *Ibid.*, p. 273; see also Field, *Guild Socialism*, ch. 5. "The danger is not," argues MacIver, "that particular interests will not be focused and asserted, but rather that the general interest may suffer domination through their urgency. Against this danger the general bulwark is the state, because its organization presupposes and in some degree realizes the activity of the general will." MacIver, R. M., *The Modern State*, p. 465.

[41] Philip Snowden in *The Socialist Review*, April–June, 1919.

terests opposed to other sections of the community of workers. Nor did they all see the need from the democratic point of view of the workers directly electing foremen and superintendents who were to be given the power of direction. They maintained with the Webbs that this "relationship set up between a manager who has to give orders all day to his staff, and the members of that staff who, sitting as a committee of management, criticize his action in the evening, with the power of dismissing him if he fails to conform to their wishes, has been found by experience to be an impossible one." [42] As there was a great difference of opinion among those who classified themselves definitely as "guild socialists" regarding these positions, so, naturally, there were many shades of opinion in the general movement.

Guildsmen's Contribution to General Socialist Thought. Though objecting to certain phases of the guildsmen's message, socialists outside the guild movement nevertheless expressed gratitude to the guild socialists for pointing out in such an effective manner the possibilities of industrial action, and for emphasizing the dangers of bureaucratic collectivism, the desirability of producers' participation in the management of the workshop, and the value of the functional principle as applied to politics and industry. Many of these suggestions were, in fact, incorporated in their proposals for social reorganization. Thus Sidney and Beatrice Webb, the Fabians, proposed that an industry under socialism be administered by a national board, the *"large majority of which would be either engaged as principal officers in service or would be representative of the vocations to which the bulk of the employes* belonged; with a minority representing the interests of the remainder of the public." [43] (Italics ours.)

While this was not guild socialism, it suggested a far larger amount of workers' control than the Webbs in the earlier days were wont to advocate.

Later Developments of Guild Socialist Movement. G. D. H. Cole continued throughout the thirties to write extensively on the labor, co-operative, and socialist movements and on various theories of social reform. He was likewise instrumental in forming in 1931 the New Fabian Research Bureau following the demise of the National Guild League, and in the later thirties in merging the New Fabian Research Bureau with the old Fabian Society.

In his writings in those days Cole acknowledged that in an era of

[42] Sidney and Beatrice Webb, *Constitution of a Socialist Commonwealth of Great Britain*, p. 161. (N. Y.: Longmans, 1920.)
[43] *Ibid.*, pp. 176–7.

mass production the conduct of industry was "necessarily a highly technical matter" and that it was more difficult than in the past for the ordinary manual or clerical worker to pass a worth-while judgment on many. phases of industry. On account of these developments the case against "workers' control" was "far more formidable" than he had admitted when he wrote his guild socialist books. However, Cole declared that he remained an "unrepentant guild socialist" and that he "refused to accept the plausible conclusion that all hope of 'workers' control' must be abandoned, and that we must content ourselves with the safeguard of ultimate political control over the technical autocrats of industry." [44]

As far as the introduction of guild socialism was concerned, however, Cole came to the belief by the mid-thirties that the socialization he envisaged "must come as a political measure, rather than as a product of direct action in the industrial field."

The reason for this change in his program arose from his recognition of the continued comparative weakness of the trade-union movements. In many industries labor unions were non-existent; in many, workers were organized in company-controlled unions. In others, a definite shift had taken place from union to non-union plants, as a result of mechanization. In the United States, Cole maintained, the unreadiness of labor for an aggressive campaign for "workers' control" was even more marked than in Great Britain.[45]

Nor did Cole in his later writings lay the stress which he formerly did on the substitution of a commune for the present state. He would retain the guilds in each industry and have the guild workers elect a national council for an industry—a council which would appoint the industry's manager and lay down general policies for its conduct. He would have the guilds make their plans for output, prices, and terms of employment, and present their suggestions to a national Planning Commission, with the understanding, however, that to Parliament would be reserved "the final authority for approving the economic plan." [46]

He, moreover, made it crystal clear in the mid-thirties that all of his detailed plans were formulated not as final blueprints, but as illustrations of how a genuine industrial democracy could be attained.

"I do not profess to be able to forecast with any confidence," wrote Cole in 1935, "precisely how a planned socialist economy would decide

[44] Cole, G. D. H., *Economic Planning,* 1935, p. 342.
[45] Cole, *op. cit.,* pp. 346–8.
[46] Cole, *The Simple Case for Socialism,* pp. 154–5.

to organize the machinery of production, and both the few words I have said here and the many detailed proposals which I have given elsewhere [*Principles of Economic Planning* (1935) and *Self-Government in Industry* (1917)] are intended rather to illustrate principles than to lay down dogmatically how they can best be applied." [47]

[47] Cole, *The Simple Case for Socialism*, p. 156.

PART FOUR

Communism

CHAPTER 24

Russia to the Bolshevik Revolution

WHILE the guildsmen were theorizing regarding the future state of society in England, the bolsheviks, now known as communists, were putting their theories into operation in Russia. The Russian revolutionary movement is the result of many decades of struggle on the part of minorities in Russia, as well as of the peculiar economic, social, and political developments in that country.

Beginnings of Revolutionary Agitation. Democratic movements have appeared in Russia since the days following the Napoleonic wars, when returned officers gathered in the Senate Square of St. Petersburg (now Leningrad) and demanded a constitution.

Prior to 1861, however, the date when the serfs were emancipated, there was little socialist activity. In fact from the years 1855 to 1870 agitation among the workers was given over almost wholly to that of the nihilists, who accepted no principle on faith and bitterly denounced all existing institutions.

This nihilist agitation, while crude and violent, led many of the brightest young minds of Russia to inquire into the causes of unrest, and hundreds of them went abroad to study in the universities of Western Europe, chiefly in Switzerland. They were brought there under the influence of Herzen, Bakunin, and the Marxist, Peter Lavrov, and became enthusiastic over the new teachings. Fearing the effect of these doctrines on the Russian youth, the Czar issued a *ukase,* calling them back to Russia in January, 1874. They returned, but not with the old veneration for Czardom. They went into the rural districts by the hundreds, as teachers, carpenters, and shoemakers, helped to educate the peasants, imitated their customs, learned their opinions, their living conditions, and at the same time taught them something of the new faiths. The activities of these educators were soon discovered. They were hounded by the police, arrested, often imprisoned, exiled, executed without semblance of trial. From 1873 to 1877 large numbers were arrested and imprisoned, and this phase of educational propaganda temporarily ceased.

Reign of Terrorism. Frustrated in their legitimate educational work, some of them resorted to violence. At this juncture, Vera Zasulich, a young woman, assassinated General Trepoff, prefect of the police in St. Petersburg, because of his brutal treatment of a political prisoner. The girl was arrested, tried, and acquitted by a jury, and escaped to Switzerland amid the plaudits of large numbers of sympathetic Russians. Her success fired the more militant of the revolutionists; and, while the peaceful educators of former days dropped out of the movement, a new terroristic group took their place, and for the next three years terrorism reigned in many parts of Russia. General Mezentseff, chief of police, was stabbed in broad daylight. Prince Kropotkin, relative of the revolutionist, was shot, as were numerous others.

The Czar, Alexander II, was the next object of attack. Finally, on March 13, 1881, a successful attempt was made on his life by Sophia Perovskaia. The subsequent uprising of the populace which the revolutionists had looked forward to, failed to occur. Industrial evolution had not developed sufficiently. What did happen was the denial by the government of the most elemental rights. Workers were forbidden to hold public meetings or to publish or distribute socialist periodicals; and "The Will of the People," the name of the terrorist organization partly responsible for the assassinations, was crushed. In 1883 Plekhanov, who had been with "The Will of the People," broke with this group and founded, with Axelrod, Deutsch, and Vera Zasulich, a "Society for the Liberation of Labor," for the purpose of keeping before the workers the problems of socialism.

Formation of Parties. During these days of comparative quiet, however, masses of people were being influenced by the writings of the Russian novelists and essayists—Turgeniev, Dostoievsky, Prince Kropotkin, Count Tolstoi, Maxim Gorki, and others; by the underground propaganda of socialist and anarchist groups; and by the oppressive policy of the government. Russia also was gradually becoming industrialized. Factories were appearing; workers were gathering into groups, were realizing their identity of interests, were organizing. In 1895 Lenin with Martov founded in St. Petersburg the "Union of Struggle for the Liberation of the Working Class." A year later a gigantic strike broke out in this city, and the modern proletariat for the first time exhibited their will to power. It was also about this time that the Social Democratic Labor party organized, and sent delegates to the International Congress in London. The central committee was soon arrested, but the movement made considerable headway during the next few years. This group felt that little could be done until economic conditions were ripe, and had little hope of reaching the peasants until the great landlords had expropriated their lands.

The more radical of the workers also began to organize, and, in 1901, the Social Revolutionary party was formed. This party believed that an active campaign should be made against the Czar and his followers and that the time was now ripe for aggressive work among the peasants. Nor was it opposed to the use of violence. Other groups sprang up among the Lithuanians, Poles, and Jews. University students became active, and many of the participants in revolutionary outbreaks were drafted into the army. These drafts led to further rioting, in which the students and workingmen joined. Count Witte, the Premier, seeing the signs of the times, began to take initial steps toward a constitutional government. Because the Czar disapproved of this procedure, the Count was dismissed and Von Plehve appointed in his stead.

Contest between Bolsheviks and Mensheviks. In 1903 the Social Democratic Labor party held its second congress, first at Brussels and later at London. The congress was largely attended. It set before itself the task of fixing the rules and statutes of party organization and of working out a political program. It formulated as its chief demand the creation of a democratic republic and the summoning of a Constituent Assembly.

The gathering, however, revealed radical differences of opinion. One party, headed by Lenin, demanded more thorough centralization of power in the hands of the executive committee, a more vigorous suppression of all independent activities, and a severer code of rules. The other group, led by Martov, defended the ideal of a more democratic party organization and urged that the local groups be permitted wide freedom of action. It proposed that "anyone who adheres to its program, supports it by material means, and furnishes it assistance under the direction of one of its organizers will be considered a member of the party." The first group developed into the bolsheviks; the second, into the mensheviks.

In their 1904 congress the bolsheviks and the mensheviks proposed for discussion the question: "In case of political revolution in Russia: what attitude should the party adopt?" The mensheviks took the position that victory would be decisive if the revolution should result in the creation of a Constitutional Assembly under the direct pressure of the people in revolt.

"The problem of the revolution," they maintained, "is essentially that of liquidating the monarchical regime . . . the socialist party ought not propose cornering the power by eliminating the other liberal parties from the provisional government, but should itself continue as the opposition and the extreme revolutionary party."

On the other hand, the bolsheviks declared that the establishment of a democratic republic was possible only through the victorious uprising of the people and the establishment of a revolutionary provisional government. A bourgeois revolution, they declared, would try to wrest from the revolutionary proletariat the largest part of the gains of the active revolutionary period. Therefore the workers must seek to place into the revolutionary provisional government representatives of the Socialist party to organize a merciless struggle against counterrevolutionary efforts of the bourgeoisie and to defend the special interests of the working class. They urged a "struggle for the revolutionary dictatorship of the proletariat and the peasants, aiming at a complete social transformation on the basis of the bolshevik platform." This was before the 1905 revolution, and their point of view gained a majority support. The victorious group in the party was given the name, bolshevik, meaning majority; and the defeated group, menshevik, the minority.[1]

The 1905 Revolution. In 1904 came the war against Japan. With every defeat in that war, strength was added to the democratic forces in Russia. Revelations of inefficiency and graft in official Russia increased the discontent against the monarchy. Strikes were prevalent. In July, 1904, a member of the Fighting Organization of the socialist-revolutionists assassinated the Minister of the Interior, Von Plehve. Nicholas II, fearing further outbreaks, appointed a liberal Minister of the Interior in his place, and for a while freedom of speech and press was enjoyed. A Congress of Zemstvos met in St. Petersburg and drew up a resolution demanding reforms on "eleven points." Soon thereafter, however, the government reversed its liberal policy, the press was forbidden to discuss reform measures, and all public meetings were declared unlawful.

On Sunday, January 9, 1905, an intensely cold and snowy day, tens of thousands of workers, carrying ikons and singing "God Save the Czar,"

1 Antonelli, Étienne, *Bolshevik Russia* (N. Y.: Knopf, 1920), pp. 60–2; *Bolshevik Aims and Ideals.* Reprinted from the *Round Table* (N. Y.: Macmillan, 1919).

marched to the Winter Palace to present a petition to the Czar and to demand the reforms urged by the Zemstvos and other groups. At their head was Father Gapon, a leader of the Union of Russian Workingmen, an organization existing under the sanction of the Minister of the Interior, who had encouraged it as a counter-force to socialism.

The previous day, in announcing their coming, Father Gapon had urged the Czar to meet them and accept their petition, and had pledged to hold the life of the monarch inviolable.

The petition they planned to offer recited their wrongs: "We have become beggars," it said in part. "We have been oppressed; we are burdened by toil beyond our powers; we are treated as slaves who must suffer their bitter fate and must keep silence. We suffered, but we are pushed farther into the den of beggary, lawlessness, and ignorance. We are choked by despotism of ignorance and irresponsibility. . . . The limit of patience has been reached." Time and again, they maintained, they had been turned down by their masters, when seeking to redress their wrongs. "There is not recognized any human right, not even the right of speaking, thinking, meeting, discussing our needs, taking measures for the improvement of our conditions. . . . All the people—workingmen as well as peasants—are handed over to the direction of the officials of the government, who are thieves of the property of the state."

They urged the monarch to hear them and thus to preserve the unity between him and the people. "Art thou not placed there for the happiness of thy people? But this happiness the officials snatch from our hands."

They came to their principal demand. "National representation," they asserted, "is indispensable. . . . Order immediately the convocation of representatives of the Russian land from all ranks, including representatives from the workingmen. . . . Let everyone be equal and free in the right of election, and for this purpose order that the elections for the Constituent Assembly be carried on under conditions of universal, equal, and secret suffrage. . . . This is the principal and only plaster for our wounds." They also urged the release of political and religious prisoners, freedom of speech and free press, compulsory education, separation of the church from the state, freedom of labor organization, and similar reforms.

When they approached the palace, the Czar failed to appear. In his stead, the Grand Duke Vladimir, uncle of the Czar, ordered the troops who had surrounded the palace in readiness for the demonstration, to fire on the unarmed workers, and to shoot until the crowd was completely dispersed. The soldiers obeyed orders, and after the carnage was over, 1500 men and women, boys and girls, remained dead or wounded on the streets.

"Bloody Sunday," as the day was afterwards called, was the signal for uprisings in Warsaw, Odessa, the fleet of the Czar on the Black Sea, and, indeed throughout Russia.

The Establishment of the Duma. On August 3 a manifesto was issued, announcing the establishment of the Imperial Duma. But it was evident that the members thereto were to be elected according to a very undemocratic law and that it was to have only consultative, not legislative powers. A second Congress of Zemstvos was called and demanded a constitutional government. A general strike followed, leading to almost complete stoppage of work in St. Petersburg and other cities. Nicholas II, now thoroughly scared, dismissed his reactionary Minister, appointed Count Witte Premier of Russia, and in a manifesto on October 30 granted the people "inviolability of person, freedom of thought, speech, assemblage, and organization." He also granted the electoral right to many classes not permitted representation in the Imperial Duma by the previous manifesto.

There was much rejoicing, but it was short-lived, for the Czar's associates soon instituted a series of horrible massacres of Jews and "intelligentsia" throughout the country. In Odessa alone no less than a thousand were killed and many thousands were wounded in a massacre that lasted four days.

Appearance of the Soviets. The revolution continued to spread, and in St. Petersburg soviets of delegates from the factories, elected by the workers, later to play such an important part in history, made their appearance. Soviets sprang up among the workers in other cities, and even the peasants, and, in some cases, the soldiers, organized their councils of soviets, for active propaganda in their behalf. "Pressed in the iron vise of the general political strike of the Russian proletariat," declared the St. Petersburg soviet, "the Russian autocratic government has granted concessions. . . . But the Russian revolutionary proletariat cannot lay down its arms until the time when the political rights of the Russian people are established on firm foundations."

Unity among the revolutionists, however, finally began to disappear. The constitutional democrats, known as the Cadets, and representing the liberal element, became nervous regarding the actions of some of the extremists. The government saw this weakness. It began cautiously to try its strength and arrested the president of the St. Petersburg soviet. The soviet passed a vigorous resolution of protest and elected Leon Trotsky its next president, but was unable to arouse the people to militant revolt. Other arrests followed, and finally the revolutionary movement was for the moment crushed, and every effort was made to secure the punishment of its promoters.

Meeting of the Duma. The first Duma was convened in May, 1906. Before the election the Czar's government still further limited the power of the Duma, and the socialists decided to boycott it. Despite this action, however, 107 peasants and workers were elected to the labor group. The forces opposed to the government were in the majority, with the constitutional democrats in the lead.

Amnesty was one of the most important questions before it. As the working-class representatives passed the prisons on the way to the Tavrichesky Palace, the political prisoners from behind the bars called out to them and urged that everything be done for their release. Throughout Russia some 70,000 to 80,000 were said to be in jail for political offenses.

One of the first acts of the Duma was to draw up a demand for amnesty and other reforms. The Czar, however, disapproved of their attitude, and when the Duma decided to demand action on the agrarian question, seventy-two days after they first met, he had the troops surround the palace and the Duma dissolved.

Armed revolt was again urged, but the response was weak. New elections were finally held for the second Duma.

The socialists decided to run for office in these elections and when the next Duma opened its sessions in the spring of 1907, the social democrats and the social revolutionists were represented each with about 130 representatives out of a total of 524. This second Duma was dissolved in June, 1907, following the declaration of the premier that he would arrest 16 of the socialist deputies and indict 55 others for spreading revolutionary propaganda in the army and navy.

Reaction of 1907–1908. Following the dissolution, the autocracy promulgated a new electoral law without constitutional sanction, whereby the electorate was divided into five parts. One representative was allotted to each 230 of the landed nobility, one to every 1,000 of the larger capitalists, one to every 60,000 peasants and one to every 125,000 of the artisan class.

In spite of this procedure, the November, 1907, election resulted in again electing 14 socialists and 14 members of the Labor party. A policy of repression was promptly adopted. Hundreds of newspaper editors were sent to Siberia, 26 socialist members of the second Duma were imprisoned with hard labor, 163 members of the first Duma were sentenced to 3 months' imprisonment and loss of political rights for signing in 1905 the Viborg Memorial calling on the people passively to resist the government as a reply to the dissolution of the first Duma, and 600 Polish schools established by voluntary funds were closed. During 1908 the regime of reaction prevailed: no less than 70,000 persons were banished for political offenses and 782 executed, while the persons in exile numbered no less than 180,000.

In 1909 came the astounding revelations in the Azev Case. Azev pretended that he was a revolutionary leader, but was in reality an *agent provocateur* in the employ of the Russian police. Many of the assassinations of the eight previous years, it was shown, were instigated by him in order to cause the arrest of the leading revolutionists and to justify the reactionary policy of the government. In some of the cases plans had been made to save the officials from assassination at the last moment, but these had miscarried.

The funerals of Tolstoi and of Professor Muromitzev, President of the first Duma, in 1910, which brought together hundreds of thousands from all parts of the country, were the occasion of a revivified revolutionary movement. The 1912 Duma refused to approve the budget, largely because of the persecution of the business interests by the autocracy, partly, no doubt, because of the rise of the socialist vote among the working and middle classes. In the fourth Duma the socialists divided into the "liquidators," a group of 7 who believed that the underground method in politics would no longer accomplish results, and the left-wing group of 6 who believed that this was the only way out of the difficulties. The socialists lost no opportunity to speak on every subject that came up before Duma, and as their speeches were reported verbatim in the press of the country, in accordance with custom, they exerted considerable influence. In the meanwhile the peasants were getting increasingly restive under a system of land tenure which placed in the hands of some 130,000 landlords no less than 86,000,000 dessiatines of land, whereas more than 100,000,000 peasants possessed but 138,-000,000, or 1.4 dessiatines per head. (A dessiatine is 2.7 acres.)

One of the most dramatic events before the Duma convened was the republican demonstration in June, 1914. Tchcheidze, the leader of the socialist group, had previously delivered a speech in the Duma in which he declared that the only workable reform would be the establishment of a democratic republic. The howls of the Black Hundred Deputies prevented him from finishing his address. Several days afterwards indictments were brought against him and against Deputy Kerensky of the Labor party for violation of section 129 of the code relating to treason and sedition. The charge led to a vigorous discussion in the

Duma, not only among the socialist and labor deputies, but among the conservatives, many of whom claimed the right to express their view on any subject under consideration. The socialist and labor deputies during the debate that followed were finally excluded from the Duma. The event was followed by a remarkable general strike in St. Petersburg and elsewhere. Then suddenly came the First World War.

The First World War. Most of the elements of Russian life supported the war, including a majority of the socialists, who believed that a defeat of Russia in her struggle with Germany would mean her defeat in her struggle for freedom. Nicholas Lenin and a small following of Russian socialists, on the other hand, in their paper, the *Social Democrat,* published in Switzerland, propagated the idea of the necessity of Russia's defeat from the standpoint of her democratic progress.

The war brought to Russia intense suffering and increasingly fanned the flame of discontent. The manner of living of the Czar's family; the inefficiency and corruption in military and governmental circles; the imperialistic aims of the government; the terrible loss of human life on the western front; the breakdown of the economic machinery—all steadily increased the spirit of revolt among the masses.

All of the liberal groups, excluding the socialists, joined together in the summer of 1915 in demanding a responsible government, which demand led to an indefinite suspension of the Duma. In the following Duma, convened in November, 1916, vigorous opposition to the government was again voiced.

In January, 1917, the progressive members of the Duma were dismissed and conservatives were substituted. The reopening of the Duma was postponed. Prices soared. The people faced starvation. The army was put on short rations.

The March Revolution. On February 27, 1917, several thousand workers in St. Petersburg went on strike. The strike spread. Increasing demands arose for bread and peace. The government sent out Cossacks to break up the strikes, but, instead, they smiled approval. The Duma became rebellious. It went so far as to state that it ceased relations with a government which had covered its hands with the blood of the people. This led to a further dissolution.

On Sunday, March 11, the streets of St. Petersburg were black with people. The officialdom was frightened. The police were ordered to fire on the crowd; they obeyed, but one of the famous regiments, upon receiving a similar order, joined the masses instead, amid the applause of the populace.

The government seemed impotent. It sent a message to the Czar, stating that anarchy was rampant. The Czar made no reply. The people turned for leadership to the liberal group. It seemed unable to unite on a course of action. It was then that the socialists assumed the leadership and proceeded immediately to organize the workers into soviets of workmen's delegates, after the example of the revolution of 1905. The following morning, March 12, the revolt was thoroughly organized. The revolutionary forces were augmented by the Guards regiment, closest to the Czar. Arsenals were occupied, the police silenced, fortresses captured, and inmates released.

In the meanwhile the Duma was undecided regarding its course of action. That night Tchcheidze, the social democrat, was made president of the soviet of workmen's delegates; and Kerensky, laborite, afterwards of the social revolutionists, vice-president. They issued a declaration demanding political democracy for Russia and declared for a Constituent Assembly on the basis of universal, equal, direct, and secret suffrage.

Abdication of the Czar. The Duma still felt that a constitutional monarchy was the way out and that the Grand Duke Michael might be called to the throne. The delegates from the Soviet of Workers and Soldiers opposed this compromise. On March 15, Miliukov, one of the leaders of the constitutional democrats, finally announced that the Duma had agreed to depose the Czar, to form a provisional government, and to issue a call for a Constituent Assembly. On hearing that decision, the Czar signed his abdication papers, and named his brother, Grand Duke Michael, his successor. The Grand Duke, however, agreed to accept this honor only if this "be the will of our great people, who, by plebiscite organized by their representatives in a Constituent Assembly, shall establish a form of government and new fundamental laws of the Russian state." With this declaration the old monarchy drew its last breath.

Russian Political Parties. This first victory of the March revolution over Czarist reaction can be attributed, as has been indicated, largely to the leadership of the socialists constituting then a strong minority of the population. The leadership during these days was united. Prior to the revolution the socialists had been divided into two large groups, the social democrats and the social revolutionists. The social democrats, led by Plekhanov, the great Marxian scholar, Leo Deutsch, and others, emphasized their Marxian character, made their appeal to the city workers primarily, and showed little faith in the potential revolutionary character of the peasants. The social revolutionists, on the other hand, felt that the peasantry must be reached if socialism was to be attained in Russia, and did most of its propaganda among that group. Their principal demand was the abolition of private ownership in land. At first they advocated compensation, but later urged a policy of confiscation. A considerable section of the social revolutionists, including the revered Katherine Breshkovskaya, advocated terroristic methods as a means of advancing the revolution. The more moderate section contained a rather nondescript group as far as social philosophy was concerned. Kerensky, a member of the Labor party, joined the social revolutionists about the time of the revolution. Offshoots of the social revolutionists were the maximalists and minimalists, the former demanding, as their name indicated, the immediate adoption of the maximum program.

MENSHEVIKS AND BOLSHEVIKS. In 1903 two groups, as we learned earlier, appeared within the Social Democratic Labor party—the bolsheviks (meaning majority) and the mensheviks (the minority). From 1905, after the unsuccessful revolution, to 1917 the mensheviks, however, were the real majority in the movement and the bolsheviks, the minority. The contention of the mensheviks was that Russia must pass through the stage of capitalist development before it was ready for socialism and that the next stage in the development of Russia would be the stage of political democracy.

Marx taught, they maintained, that capitalism had an historic mission to perform, which was the development of natural resources and of production. Only when a state is highly developed industrially, when production is so concentrated that a small group of private capitalists practically controls the economic interests of the nation, and when the working class is educated, disciplined, and organized as a result of this development, can a democratic government step in and take control of economic life. The natural resources of Russia are undeveloped; its masses are uneducated; its industrial working population comprises only four or five per cent of the Russian people. Surely the hour for social revolution in Russia has not as yet struck; a bourgeois republic must follow absolutism, and socialism must follow a bourgeois republic.

On the other hand, the bolsheviks, led by Lenin, maintained that it was possible for Russia to jump from its primitive industrial development into socialism without necessarily passing through the capitalist stage. This was partly due to the fact that other countries in Europe had advanced capitalistic systems, and a social revolution starting in Russia was likely to light a flame which would spread throughout Europe. The advent of socialist republics in other parts of Europe as a result of a revolution would make it possible for Russia to adapt itself speedily to the requirements of a socialist society. Furthermore, it could for a season act as the agricultural storehouse for the more industrialized part of Europe.

This difference in belief regarding the immediacy of the social revolution led inevitably to a difference in tactics advocated by the two groups, a different attitude toward parliamentary government, toward peaceful methods of progress, etc.—a difference which is discussed at greater length in a later section.

Besides these groups in the Social Democratic party was the small Internationalist group of which Leon Trotsky was formerly a member, a group which was opposed to any coalition with the propertied classes, but which was unwilling to break with the mensheviks. In addition there was the Unified Social Democratic International party, which included Maxim Gorky, a group which refused to tie itself up with either of the two great factions of the social democrats, but which otherwise resembled in social outlook the menshevik internationalists.

The Bourgeois Groups. The leading bourgeois party in the Duma was the Octobrist party, which represented the feudal landlords and the great capitalists. It contained Rodzianko, the leader of the Duma at the outbreak of the revolution, and Guchkov, the Moscow banker, and Minister of War in the Provisional Government. Next to this group came the constitutional democrats, known as Cadets, which consisted of the more liberal capitalists, professional workers, and landowners, and had as their ideal a bourgeois republic or a constitutional monarchy of the British type. This group, led by Miliukov and Lvov, later assumed leadership in the Provisional Government. The Octobrists and other monarchical and conservative parties practically disappeared in the March revolution.

The Provisional Government. The Provisional Government, which was immediately formed, was dominated by the constitutional democrats, with Lvov as Premier and Paul Miliukov, Minister of Foreign Affairs. Its Minister of Finance was a sugar king; its Minister of Trade and Commerce, a wealthy manufacturer; and its Minister of War and Navy, a Moscow banker. Its one socialist was Alexander Kerensky, Minister of Justice. It represented a Duma elected under the Czarist regime. Unfortunately the Ministry failed to recognize the economic significance of the revolution and regarded it primarily as a political revolt. It announced a program of political reform, including universal suffrage, amnesty, and freedom of speech. It confiscated the holdings of the imperial family and the monasteries and enacted an excess profits tax. It failed, however, to tackle the industrial problem. It postponed the question of land distribution until the calling of the Constituent Assembly. It did little to revise Russia's war aims. In fact Miliukov declared that he regarded the possession of Constantinople as a necessary step in the economic evolution of Russia. Although Lvov maintained that Miliukov's statement in no way represented the opinion of the cabinet, the government was severely criticized.

The Rise of the Soviets. During this period soviets, made up of representatives from trade unions, shop committees, professional, industrial, and peasant groups, and delegates from the army, were continually increasing in strength. At first they were controlled by the moderate socialists, the social democrats, and the social revolutionists.

On April 16 these groups called a national congress of the Council of Workers' and Soldiers' Delegates. This congress urged the Russian people to support them as the center of progressive forces that could be relied upon to combat counterrevolutionary activities. It warned the people against possible reaction and asked support of the Provisional Government as long as the government continued to consolidate and develop the conquests of the revolution and did not pursue an imperialistic policy.

Following this congress, the Provisional Government announced its agreement with the soviets and on May first issued a manifesto urging the Allied Government to restate their war aims. Its accompanying note, however, to the effect that it would maintain strictly Russia's agreement with the Allies, was interpreted by some to indicate that the Allies could, if they wished, ignore the manifesto. Huge demonstrations followed. The government declared that it had been misunderstood, and the soviets, by a small majority, passed a vote of confidence. The incident, however, strengthened the parties of the left.

Nicholai Lenin. In late April this trend to the left became more pronounced on the arrival in Petrograd (later Leningrad) of Nicholai Lenin, who had been closely watching developments from Switzerland. Lenin had been one of the great figures in Russian revolutionary life for many years past. Vladimir Ilyich Ulianov, his real name, was born on April 10, 1870, the son of a councillor of state of the government of Simbirsk.[2] A Greek Catholic by upbringing, he was educated at the Simbirsk gymnasium where he was first in all of his classes. In 1887

[2] Lenin's father, Ulianov Lenin, was born of a middle-class family. He received a good education at the University of Kazan, and became a teacher of mathematics and physics. Later he became director of the rural schools of Simbirsk government, received a decoration of St. Vladimir, and was raised to the rank of a nobleman.

he entered the University of Kazan, from which he was soon expelled for revolutionary activities, and after which he was exiled from Kazan and placed under police surveillance. The execution of his brother in 1886 for complicity in an attempt on the life of Alexander III both stimulated Lenin's activities and caused those activities to be under close surveillance. He entered the University of St. Petersburg, devoted himself to literary work, and in 1892 was admitted to the bar. During this time he organized working-class groups in the city in the "Union of the Struggle for the Emancipation of Labor" and rallied around him a number of Marxist intellectuals. He lived in the working-class quarters of the city. He led a number of strikes and was constantly hunted by the police. He bitterly attacked the populists, who made their main appeal to the peasant, and became an ardent follower of Marx and Plekhanov. He repeatedly declared during these years that only the working classes could bring freedom to Russia and that their organization should be started immediately.

At the age of 25 Lenin left Russia and aided in the organization of a service aiming at the introduction of revolutionary literature into his country. Upon his return he edited *Labor's Work,* an underground journal. The police followed his movements, and on January 29, 1897, he was exiled to Siberia by an imperial ukase because of his activity in connection with a social democratic circle in Leningrad. There he remained for three years under close guard, and for the following three years was forbidden to return to industrial or university centers. In exile he wrote his great work, *The Development of Capitalism in Russia,* in which he proved that Russia was being rapidly drawn into the maelstrom of capitalism. In 1900 he went abroad and soon attained a prominent place among Russian political refugees, becoming co-editor in 1901 of a revolutionary journal, *Iskra* (the *Spark*), in which he expounded the initial development of the theory of bolshevism, and attacked "legal" Marxism and the social revolutionaries. His wife acted as his secretary and was an able collaborator in all his activities.

When the bolshevik group made itself felt within the Social Democratic party in 1903 at the third congress of the party, he led the attack against Martov, Plekhanov, and other mensheviks and later established the first bolshevik paper, *Forward.* At the first Congress of the bolsheviks in 1905 he observed for the first time that the Russian workers in their revolution should not stop with a bourgeois republic, but should carry it through to a socialist commonwealth. He began his bitter attacks against social democratic parliamentarism.

He returned to Russia during the revolution of 1905 and observed the soviets at work, although he obeyed the orders of the party and remained for the most part in hiding. His influence as adviser on the movement during those days was considerable. Later he worked out a possible technique for the revolution of the future and urged that, in the next revolutionary crisis, the proletariat should gain the adherence of the peasants and raze to the ground the monarchy, landlordism, and all the survivals of the Middle Ages. This portion of the revolution, characterized by co-operation with the peasants as a whole, would be the bourgeois phase. When this phase was completed, the proletariat should then ally themselves with the semi-proletariat and overthrow the bourgeoisie. This would be the socialist revolution, as distinguished from the bourgeois revolt.

Following the revolution of 1905 he lived in Finland, Switzerland, and France, editing socialist journals and conducting exhaustive researches into the works of Marx and Engels and other revolutionary writers. For two years he worked early and late at these researches in the Paris National Library.

During this time he wrote much concerning the rôle of the soviets during the next revolutionary crisis. In 1912, when the bolsheviks were permitted to publish a legal paper in St. Petersburg, he traveled to Galicia, and from there advised constantly with his followers in Russia regarding the best tactics to pursue.

The war found him in Austria, where he was at first imprisoned as an enemy alien. He was finally released and went to Switzerland. Here he urged that the Russian workers should take advantage of the chaos of the war to prepare for the revolution. He participated actively in the Zimmerwald Conference, the first conference of the socialists in Allied and Central Powers following the outbreak of the war, called for the purpose of securing working-class action in behalf of peace.[3]

Upon returning to Russia, Lenin demanded that immediate peace negotiations be undertaken and that a restatement of war aims be obtained from the Allies. In the middle of May, Guchkov, the Premier, resigned as a result of growing criticism, and a few days later Miliukov presented his resignation.

Leon Trotsky. On May 17 Leon Trotsky returned to Russia, giving additional impetus to the left-wing movement. In many ways Trotsky was the very opposite of Lenin. Whereas Lenin gave the appearance of great calm and reserve, and usually held the crowd by the sheer

[3] See Levine, Isaac Don, *The Man Lenin;* Williams, A. R., *Lenin, the Man and His Works;* Trotsky, Leon, *Lenin.* Lenin died Jan. 21, 1924.

logic of his statements and with no attempt at oratory, Trotsky was a man of impulsive, emotional temperament, a fiery and eloquent orator. Lenin was a Catholic of the orthodox church, a descendant of the nobility. Trotsky was a member of a race which had long been subjected to brutal persecution by the Czarist government.

On his return to Russia in 1917 Trotsky was about forty years of age. Leaving the University of Odessa in the late nineties, he had thrown himself into revolutionary work in behalf of the Russian masses. His first period of work was of short duration. Arrested for his activity, he was placed in solitary confinement in Odessa. As in the case of most revolutionists, he took advantage of his imprisonments to devour book after book. After two and a half years of confinement he was exiled to Eastern Siberia, where he seized the first opportunity to escape.

During the following years he devoted much energy to uniting the revolutionary groups into one strong Social Democratic party. His first pamphlet in 1903 dealt with the controversies between the two factions of the Social Democratic party that later became the bolshevik and the menshevik, and attempted to effect a reconciliation between these two groups that professed the same Marxian theory and the same revolutionary aim. These attempts failed, but Trotsky for years did not give up hope of success.

By 1905, the year of the first revolution, he had already become popular as a pamphleteer. He looked forward in Russia to a violent rising of the masses, headed by organized labor, which should forcibly overthrow the bureaucracy and establish an era of democratic freedom. Prior to the revolution he urged a general political strike. He hailed the 1905 revolution as a means of lifting "the people over scores of steps, up which in times of peace we should have had to drag ourselves with hardships and fatigue." [4]

It was also during this great upheaval that Trotsky framed his theory of the immediate transition from monarchism to socialism. His line of reasoning was as follows: The working class is the only real revolutionary power. The capitalists are weak and incapable of effective resistance. The intellectual groups are of little account. The peasants are politically primitive, and yet they have a consuming thirst for land. "Once the revolution is victorious, political power passes into the hands of the class that has played a leading rôle in the struggle, and that is the working class." [5] To ensure permanent control, the working class must win over the peasants. This would be possible by recognizing the agrarian changes brought about by the peasants during the revolution-

[4] Trotsky (edited by Olgin), *Our Revolution* (N. Y.: Holt, 1919), pp. 9, 10.
[5] *Ibid.*, pp. 10–11.

ary crisis and by developing a radical agrarian legislative program. "Once in power, the proletariat will appear before the peasantry as its liberators." To imagine the social democrats playing a leading rôle in the revolution and the provisional government, "only to step aside when the democratic program is to be put into operation, to leave the completed building at the disposal of the bourgeois parties and thus to open an era of parliamentary politics where social democracy forms only a party of opposition—to imagine this would be to compromise the very idea of a labor government." Moreover, "once the representatives of the proletariat enter the government not as powerless hostages, but as a leading force, the divide between the minimum program and the maximum program automatically disappears, collectivism becomes the order of the day," because "political supremacy of the proletariat is incompatible with its economic slavery." [6]

In 1905 Trotsky felt that the hour may have struck. When a soviet was formed in St. Petersburg, Trotsky became one of its leading spirits. At this time he showed his great ability as an administrator, speaker, and writer of short, stirring articles, comprehensible to the masses. "The soviet," he afterwards wrote, "was the organized authority of the masses themselves over their separate members. This was a true, unadulterated democracy, without a two-chamber system, without a professional bureaucracy, with the right of the voters to recall their representative at will and to substitute another." [7]

Following the break-up of the soviets by the government, Trotsky was arrested and imprisoned. In prison he continued writing. After twelve months of solitary exile he was sentenced to life imprisonment in Siberia. In January, 1907, he started his trip to Northern Siberia. Crowds gathered at every station to see him and the other "workingmen's deputies." In Tiumen he left the railroad train to take a sleigh to his destination. Watching his chance, he managed to escape and on a sleigh drawn by reindeers crossed a wilderness of snow and ice 500 miles in extent. He finally left the country and established his home in Vienna, where he lived until the outbreak of the First World War, working for the social democracy and editing a revolutionary magazine which was smuggled into Russia. Visiting the Balkans during the Balkan war as a war correspondent, he became more of an internationalist than ever. He was finally forced as an enemy alien to leave Vienna for Switzerland. He wrote vigorously against war, moved to Paris, was compelled to leave France for Spain, and finally journeyed to the United States, where he wrote for radical journals.

[6] *Ibid.*, pp. 11–12.

[7] *Ibid.*, p. 14.

When the March revolution took place, he hastened to Russia, believing that it would be but the beginning of a European revolt. "If the first Russian revolution," he wrote, "brought about revolutions in Asia—in Persia, Turkey, China—the second Russian revolution will be the beginning of a momentous social revolutionary struggle in Europe. Only this struggle will bring real peace to a blood-stained world."

The Kerensky Government. In the meanwhile during the spring of 1917 the Russian military front was becoming ever more demoralized. The resignation of Miliukov and Guchkov led to the organization of a new ministry with six socialists thereon, as against nine non-socialists. The bolsheviks opposed this ministry, Trotsky urging that everything be done to transfer power to the revolutionary proletariat. The peasants became ever more insistent on a solution of the land question, a peasant congress meeting about that time urging the abolition of private property in land and natural resources, without compensation. On June 22 the All-Russian Congress of Soviets met. Kerensky at this congress urged the continuance of the war, but Lenin characterized such continuance as "an act of treason against the socialist international." The congress, however, supported the coalition ministry and expressed its belief that the passing of all power to the soviets would alienate elements still capable of serving the revolution.

The defeat of the July offensive on the western front and delay in land and industrial reforms led in mid-July to a great demonstration against the coalition Ministry, and to its resignation. Kerensky became Premier. The soviets supported him against the opposition of the bolsheviks. Trotsky, Kollontay, and others were arrested for alleged collusion with German authorities in organizing the July revolt. A new government was formed, with four socialist and two liberal parties represented.

But the war continued to go badly on the Russian front. Kornilov, asked by Kerensky to give up command of the army, moved instead on Petrograd. The soviets constituted the chief defense of the city. Through the power of numbers and oratory they persuaded Kornilov's soldiers to lay down their arms. Kerensky was appointed commander-in-chief, but his power was weakened and the bolshevik argument against a coalition government strengthened.

The November Revolution. During the summer and the fall the Provisional Government lacked a definite policy on the land, war, and industrial questions. At the same time the bolsheviks were demanding that full power be given to the soviets, that land be immediately distributed without compensation, that industries be socialized and workers' committees be formed, and that immediate negotiations be started for a general, democratic peace. These proposals struck a popular chord. Russia swung more and more to the left.

Under pressure from the bolsheviks an All-Russian Congress of Soviets was called for November 7. The calling of this assembly was a signal to the bolsheviks to prepare for the capture of the governmental machinery. They felt that the congress would approve their aim, but they desired to be backed by force. They brought to their side the Petrograd garrison. On November 4, 1917, they announced "Petrograd Soviet Day." Great crowds demonstrated against the Kerensky Government. The Semyonovski regiment, by a large majority, decided to cast their fortunes with the soviets. The insurgents occupied the Fortress of Peter and Paul and during the next two days took charge of railroad depots, through their Military Revolutionary Committee, and occupied telegraph stations, the state bank, and similar institutions. On the night of November 6 many strategic points were captured by the bolsheviks without struggle or bloodshed. On November 7 the Winter Palace, the headquarters of the Provisional Government, was surrounded, and at one o'clock in the afternoon Trotsky announced that the government of Kerensky had ceased to exist. The Winter Palace was taken that night. Kerensky fled, and other ministers were arrested and imprisoned in the Fortress of Peter and Paul.

With the taking of the Winter Palace, power passed immediately to the Military Revolutionary Committee. The next night the social revolutionists and mensheviks were asked to participate in the establishment of a Soviet government. They hesitated on the ground that all parties, anti-soviet as well as soviet, should be asked to form the cabinet. The bolsheviks thereupon assumed control and selected an all-communist government. Lenin was elected President, and Trotsky, the Minister of War.

Opposition to the bolsheviks immediately developed, and hundreds of opponents to Soviet Government, socialist and non-socialist, were imprisoned on account of this opposition. Kerensky and others secured the support of Cossacks, who, however, were decisively defeated by the bolsheviks.

"All Power to the Soviets." During these days one of the burning questions was whether the soviets should take supreme charge of governmental affairs, or whether power should be left to the Constituent Assembly, elected by the vote of the Russian people. The bolsheviks raised the shibboleth, "All Power to the Soviets." They claimed that:

(1) A republic of the soviets was a higher form of democracy than

the ordinary bourgeois republic with a Constituent Assembly, and "the only form capable of securing the most painless transition to socialism";

(2) The Russian people had gone far to the left in their social thinking between the elections for the Constituent Assembly and January, 1918, the time fixed for its sessions. The Constituent Assembly therefore did not fairly represent the people when it came together in January.

(3) The civil war which the rebellion of the Kaledinites started "against the soviet authority, against the workers' and peasants' revolution, . . . destroyed all chances of settling in a formal democratic way the acute problems raised by history before the peoples of Russia and more particularly before the Russian working class and peasantry."

(4) The reactionaries were striving for the retention of power by the Constituent Assembly in an effort to defeat the aims of the November revolution, and only a complete victory over the capitalist and landlord group would preserve the fruits of the revolution.

(5) The soviets more nearly represented than did the Assembly the most recent point of view of the Russian people on the need for peace.[8]

On January 9, after the Assembly had agreed to the demands of the soviets, with the exception of that for the transfer of power to them, the Assembly was dissolved. Following the dissolution came the negotiations of the Soviet Government for peace at Brest-Litovsk, the ending of Russian participation in war, and the final adoption of the Soviet Constitution on July 10, 1918.

[8] See *Pravda,* January 8, 1918; reprinted in Lenin's *Proletarian Revolution* (London: B. S. P.).

CHAPTER 25

Principles and Tactics of Communism

AS EXPOUNDED IN THE COMMUNIST MANIFESTO OF THE THIRD INTERNATIONAL (1919)

ON WHAT concepts were based the communist tactics in promoting the November revolution and establishing the soviet form of government? The communist point of view was most authoritatively stated in the Manifesto issued by the First Congress of the Communist International held in Moscow, March 2–6, 1919, and signed by Lenin, Trotsky, Zinoviev, Rakovsky, and Fritz Platten, the last-named of the Swiss Socialist party.[1]

This Manifesto begins by recalling the fact that seventy-two years had passed since the issuance of the *Communist Manifesto,* written by Marx and Engels in 1847; that during the seven intervening decades the revolutionary movement had undergone many successes and many defeats; but that, "in spite of all, the development at bottom went the way forecast by the Manifesto of the Communist party. The epoch of the last decisive battle came later than the apostles of the social revolution expected and wished. But it has come."

Communist Indictment of Capitalist Society. The communists, representing the revolutionary proletariat of the countries of the world, "consider ourselves followers and fulfillers of the program proclaimed seventy-two years ago. It is our task now to sum up the practical revolutionary experience of the working class, to cleanse the movement of its admixtures of opportunism and social patriotism, and to unite the forces of all the true revolutionary proletarian parties in order to further and hasten the complete victory of the communist revolution."

IMPERIALIST WAR AND INCREASING MISERY. For many years, the Manifesto continued, socialism predicted the inevitability of an imperialist war. It perceived the essential cause of the First World War "in the insatiable greed of the possessing classes in both camps of capitalist

[1] Given in full in Appendix of Postgate, *Bolshevik Theory.*

countries. . . . The contradictions of the capitalist system were converted by the war into degrading torments of hunger and cold, epidemics and moral savagery, for all mankind. Thereby the academic quarrel among socialists over the theory of increasing misery, and also of the undermining of capitalism through socialism, is now finally determined. Statisticians and teachers of the theory of reconciliation of these contradictions have endeavored for decades to gather together from all countries of the earth real and apparent facts to prove the increasing well-being of the working class.

"But we are faced today with the harrowing reality of impoverishment, which is no longer merely a social problem, but a physiological and biological one. This catastrophe of the imperialist war has with one sweep swept away all the gains of experts and of parliamentary struggles."

Militarization of Finance-Capital. Finance-capital, which had flung mankind into the abyss of war, had also suffered. The complete deterioration of paper money reflected the general deadly crisis of capitalist commodity exchange. The war had taken the regulating rôle out of the hands of monopolies, which replaced free competition, and had given it directly to the military power. "Finance-capital has, through this mass slaughter, completely militarized, not the state alone, but itself also. It can no longer fulfil its essential economic functions otherwise than by means of blood and iron."

The opportunists who, before the war, preached moderation, and, during the war, submission to the Fatherland, were now urging the workers to self-abnegation. If these preachings were listened to, "capitalism would build out of the bones of several generations a new and still more formidable structure, leading to a new and inevitable world war. Fortunately for humanity this is no longer possible." The absorption by the state of economic life had already become a fact. The main question now was, "what shall be the future mainstay of state production, the imperialist state or the state of the victorious proletariat?" In other words shall the working class "become the feudal bond-servants of the victorious Entente bourgeoisie, which, under the name of the League of Nations . . . here plunders and murders, there throws a crumb, but everywhere enchains the proletariat? . . . Or will the working class take into its own hands the disorganized and shattered economic life and make certain its reconstruction on a socialist basis?"

National State too Narrow. Only the dictatorship of the proletariat could shorten the period of the present crisis. To this end it would mobilize its forces, introduce the universal duty to labor, and establish the regime of industrial discipline. The national state, which was given a tremendous impetus by capitalist evolution, had become too narrow for the development of the productive forces. The big states were now trying to dominate the small ones and to make the backward countries their slaves. The war had brought these backward countries by force into the capitalist whirlpool. The battle would go on for their liberation and socialist Europe would come to the aid of the liberated colonies with its technique and spiritual forces in order to facilitate their transition into the orderly system of socialist economy.

Bourgeois Democracy Undemocratic. The whole bourgeois world accused the communists of destroying liberty and political democracy. "That is not true. Having come into power the proletariat only asserts the absolute impossibility of using the methods of bourgeois democracy and creates the conditions and forms of a higher working-class democracy. The whole course of capitalist development undermined political democracy, not only by dividing the nation into two irreconcilable classes, but by condemning the numerous petty bourgeois and semi-proletarian elements, as well as the slum proletariat, to permanent economic stagnation and political impotence."

In countries where the opportunity had permitted, the working class had utilized the regime of political democracy for its organization against capitalism. But whole layers of the population on the farm had remained stagnant. Those who had been thus thrust aside from the main road of development by capitalism were nominally permitted under the regime of political democracy to take part in the administration of the state. In reality, however, the finance-oligarchy decided all important questions which determined the destinies of nations behind the back of parliamentary democracy. Particularly was this true of the war question.

"If the finance-oligarchy considers it advantageous to veil its deeds of violence behind parliamentary votes, then the bourgeois state has at its command, in order to gain its ends, all the traditions and attainments of former centuries of upper-class rule, multiplied by the wonders of capitalist technique: lies, demagogism, persecution, slander, bribery, calumny and terror. To demand of the proletariat in its final life and death struggle with capitalism that it should obey lamblike the precepts of bourgeois democracy would be the same as to ask the man who is defending his life against robbers to follow the artificial rules of a French duel that have been set by the enemy but not followed by him."

Need for Creation of Soviets. The proletariat must create its own apparatus to serve as a bond of unity. This apparatus was the workers' soviets. The institution "embraces the entire working class, without distinction of vocation or political maturity, an elastic form of organization capable of continually renewing itself, expanding, and drawing into itself ever new elements, ready to open its doors to the working groups of village and city which are near to the proletariat. This indispensable autonomous organization of the working class in the present struggle and in the future conquests of different lands tests the proletariat and represents the greatest inspiration and the mightiest weapon of the proletariat of our time. . . . By means of these soviets the working class will gain power in all countries most readily and most certainly when these soviets gain the support of the majority of the laboring population. By means of these soviets the working class once attaining power will control all the fields of economic and cultural life."

The Manifesto declared that the denunciation of civil war by the bourgeoisie is sheer hypocrisy, since there would have been no civil war in Russia had the capitalists not brought the workers to the verge of ruin. Communists were trying to shorten the duration of civil war as much as possible. "This makes necessary the disarming of the bourgeoisie at the proper time, the arming of the laborer, and the formation of a communist army as a protector of the rule of the proletariat and the inviolability of the social structure."

The Failure of the Second International. Conscious of the world character of the movement, the communists were forming another international. The First International organized in 1864 was undermined by the Franco-Prussian War. The Second International arose in 1889. During its existence "the center of gravity of the labor movement rested entirely on national ground, confining itself within the realm of national parliamentarism to the narrow compass of the national state and national industries. Decades of organizing and labor reformism created a generation of leaders, most of whom gave verbal recognition to the program of social revolution but denied it in substance. They were lost in the swamp of reformism and adaptation to the bourgeois state. The opportunist character of the leading parties of the Second International was finally revealed—and led to the greatest collapse of the movement in all history—when the events required revolutionary methods of warfare from the labor parties. Just as the war of 1870 dealt a death-blow to the First International by revealing that there was not, in fact, behind the social revolutionary program any compact power of the masses, so the war of 1914 killed the Second International by showing that above the consolidated labor masses there stood labor parties which converted themselves into servile organs of the bourgeois state." The leaders of the Second International appeared as before the war with proposals of compromise and reconciliation, thus lengthening the period of crisis and increasing the misery of Europe. "War against the socialist center is a necessary condition of successful war against imperialism."

Elaboration of Communist Tactics. This statement indicates the spirit of the new communist force which came into control as a result of the November revolution and something of its theories and tactics. It was followed by a more concrete program which will be referred to later. It is seen that the communists differed from Kautsky and other Marxians who led the movement prior to 1914, not so much in ultimate ideals as in the tactics which should be pursued in getting control of government and industry and in retaining control during the transitional period.

Revolution by Force. In the first place, communists had no faith in the achievement of a social revolution through the peaceful means of the ballot, aided by economic, co-operative, and general educational activity. During times of peace, while the proletariat was preparing itself for the crisis, it was legitimate, they maintained, to use parliamentary methods, to go into election campaigns, and to send representatives to parliament, for political campaigns gave to the communists an opportunity "to speak to the working class, pointing out the class character of the state and their class interests as workers. They enabled them to show the futility of reforms, to demonstrate the real interests which dominate the capitalist—and 'yellow' socialist—political parties, and to point out why the entire capitalist system must be overthrown." They also prepared the people, the communists believed, to accept communist leadership more readily during a revolutionary crisis. If communists were elected to parliament, they were in a position ceaselessly "to expose the real nature of the capitalist state," and "against the sounding board of the nation," to "show up capitalist brutality and call the workers to revolt." [2]

However, they should regard the parliamentary struggle of only secondary importance,[3] as the "parliamentary struggle is only a school, a fulcrum, for the organization of the extra-parliamentary struggle of

[2] Zinoviev's letter to I. W. W. in Postgate, *The Bolshevik Theory*, p. 234.
[3] See Program of *Communist Manifesto* of 1919.

the proletariat. . . . The essential questions of the labor movement within the capitalist order are settled by force, by open struggle, the general strike, the insurrection of the proletarian masses." [4]

LIMITATIONS IN CONTROL THROUGH BALLOT. It is true that the workers in many countries had the vote, and could elect to office those representing them. But, as the Manifesto declared, "finance-capital decides all important questions . . . behind the back of parliamentary democracy."

Moreover, as Lenin asserted, "if we look more closely into the mechanism of capitalist democracy everywhere—in the so-called petty details of the suffrage (the residential qualifications, the exclusion of the women, etc.); in the technique of the representative institutions, in the actual obstacles to the right of meeting (public buildings are not for the poor); in the purely capitalist organization of the daily press, etc., etc.—on all sides we shall see restrictions upon restrictions of democracy. These restrictions, exceptions, exclusions, obstacles for the poor, seem light—especially in the eyes of one who has himself never known want, and has never lived in close contact with the oppressed classes in their herd life, and nine tenths, if not ninety-nine hundredths of the bourgeois publicists and politicians are of this class! But in their sum these restrictions exclude and thrust out the poor from politics and from an active share in democracy. Marx splendidly grasped the *essence* of capitalist democracy, when, in his analysis of the experience of the commune, he said that the oppressed are allowed, once every few years, to decide which particular representatives of the oppressing class are to represent and repress them in politics." [5] This situation made it exceedingly difficult for the workers, even though in a majority, to obtain a majority control of representatives in the various legislative bodies, and thus to accomplish a change of the economic system through parliamentary action.

COMMUNIST TECHNIQUE OF REVOLUTION. Granting that the seizure of political power was not coming through the ballot box, through the election of a majority of representatives to office, but through a violent upheaval, what should be the nature of that upheaval? The communists who promoted the November revolution declared that that depended on circumstances. They pointed to the methods pursued in the Russian revolution. Before the crisis which, in their opinion, would make the situation ripe for the revolution, they would, as has been indicated, make use of elections and parliamentary action for propaganda purposes. They would educate and agitate among the city

[4] Stalin, *Leninism*, p. 23.

[5] Lenin, *op. cit.*, p. 89.

workers, the peasantry, and other groups. They would organize "communist cells" in trade unions. Where possible they would work openly; where that was impossible, secretly and illegally. They would place chief reliance not upon the workers in general, but upon a conscious, militant, revolutionary minority of the workers in city industries. For "only the proletariat—on account of its economic rôle in production on a large scale—is capable of leading *all* the toiling and exploited masses, who are exploited, oppressed, crushed by the capitalists even more, not less, than the town proletariat, but are unable to carry on the struggle for freedom unaided." [6]

As the crisis drew near, they would organize soviets or councils of workers, of peasants, of soldiers, as in the Russian revolution, as centers for revolutionary activity. At opportune moments, they would organize street demonstrations to show each other and the people their strength, to arouse the revolutionary enthusiasm of their fellows, to put fear in the hearts of their opponents. They would inaugurate general strikes, so as to paralyze economic life, create chaos, and demonstrate the spirit of solidarity. They would agitate with might and main among the soldiers, and urge insurrection in the army and navy, so that at the strategic time the armed forces might be on their side. And at a concerted moment they would arm the proletariat, seize strategic positions in the economic and political life of the country—munition plants and arsenals, the press, the means of communication and transportation, the sources of light and power, and the public buildings—and proclaim their control of the nation.[7]

Ripeness for the Social Revolution. Of course the question of the opportune, the ripe time, for a *coup d'état* leading to the conquest of political power was of supreme importance. For if the time were unripe, the attempted revolt might lead to a counterrevolution and to the setback of the revolutionary movement for decades.

What was the criterion of ripeness, from the communist point of view? Negatively, it was not the criterion put forth by some of the opponents of communism, namely, the knowledge that the majority of the people were on their side. For the communists argued that it was impossible to tell beforehand when a majority was with the revolters, "for in no capitalist state would the democracy be left free by the capitalists to convince itself that it had a majority of people at its back." Furthermore, it was difficult, if not impossible, for the militant minority to convince the inert majority by mere agitation before the revolution that a revolution should take place. For the majority had a great dis-

[6] Lenin, *State and Revolution,* p. 28. [7] See Stalin, *Leninism,* p. 97.

trust of their own powers, and "it is only during the revolution that the more advanced and self reliant of the working class can carry with them the big masses." [8]

Russia Ready for Revolution. The communist leaders of the November revolution maintained that, contrary to the belief of most socialists, it was not necessary for a country in which a social revolution was planned to have a well-developed capitalist system and a proletariat which constituted a majority of the population and which had been trained, educated, and disciplined under highly industrialized conditions. "The day and the hour when political power shall pass into the hands of the working class, is determined not directly by the degree of capitalistic development of economic forces," declared Trotsky shortly after the revolution when he was still a bolshevik leader, "but by *the relation of the class struggle, by the international situation, by a number of subjective elements, such as tradition, intuition, readiness to fight. . . . To imagine that there is an automatic dependence between the dictatorship of the proletariat and the technical and productive resources of a country, is to understand economic determinism in a very primitive way.* Such a conception would have nothing to do with Marxism." [9] (Italics ours.)

"The front of capital will not be necessarily pierced where industry is most developed," declared Stalin. "It will be broken where the chain of imperialism is the weakest, for the proletarian revolution is the result of the rupture of the chain of the imperialist front at its weakest point. So then it is possible that the country which begins the revolution, which makes a breach in the capitalist front, may be less developed from the capitalist point of view than others which remain, nevertheless, within the framework of capitalism."

In 1917 the chain was weakest in Russia, Stalin continued, "for in Russia there unfolded a great popular revolution led by the proletariat which had for itself so important an ally as the peasantry, oppressed and exploited by the landed proprietors." Moreover, "the revolution had czarism as its opponent, the most hideous representative of imperialism, deprived of all moral authority and hated by the whole people." [10]

Positively, the communists would choose a time for the decisive *coup* and the insurrection, when the crisis had attained its highest pitch, or when the vanguard, sure of the support of the reserves, was ready to engage in battle to the bitter end, or when the disorder was

[8] Radek, *op. cit.*, pp. 20–1.
[9] Trotsky (edited by Olgin), *Our Revolution*, pp. 84–5.
[10] Stalin, *Leninism*, pp. 35–6.

worst in the ranks of the enemy.[11] No insurrection should be started if it had to be left unfinished, the communists asserted.

"When all the forces of classes hostile to us are sufficiently wasted in internecine quarrels and weakened in their mutual strife," said Lenin, "when all the intermediate elements which are hesitating and unstable (i.e., the petit bourgeoisie) are sufficiently unmasked, and their prestige lowered by their failure in practice; when the mass of the proletariat begins to applaud the most revolutionary acts against the bourgeoisie, then the time is ripe for revolution. Then if we have been keeping good account of all the conditions enumerated above, and have well chosen the moment, our victory is assured." [12]

It followed that, when the workers had a chance to succeed in gaining control and administrating industry in their own interest, "they have no right to let their fellows sink into the capitalist bog only out of fear that the young proletariat would not be able to control the forces which had been combined together by capitalism." [13]

It was better, they asserted, for the workers to seize control, and, after control, learn the technique of administration under conditions favorable to the development of the proletariat than to remain outside of the administrative machinery until, under unfavorable conditions, the workers would have learned the technique of management.

Furthermore, it must be realized that capitalist countries were now so interrelated that a revolution in a backward country was likely to draw into the vortex of revolution the more advanced lands of the Continent, which would then be in a strategic position materially to assist the less developed country in its industrial advance. Most of the revolutionary leaders in Russia, it might be said, were firmly convinced that a revolutionary conflagration in Russia would encompass Europe and "then the revolutionary impulse in Europe" would react upon Russia and reduce the duration of the revolution to a few years.[14]

Shattering the State Machine. Assuming that the time was ripe for an insurrection, and the workers obtained control of the political machinery, what then? Should they *use* or *shatter* the state machine? The communists maintained that the latter should be done. The "conquest of political power," they contended, meant "not merely a change in the personnel of ministries, but annihilation of the enemy's machinery of government: disarmament of the bourgeoisie, the counter-revolutionary officers, of the White Guard; the arming of the proletariat, the revolutionary soldiers, the Red Guard, the workingmen; displace-

[11] *Ibid.*, p. 98. [12] See *Ibid.*, pp. 98–9. [13] Radek, *op. cit.*, p. 13.
[14] See quotation of Lenin (1905) in Stalin, *Leninism*, p. 39.

ment of all bourgeois judges and organization of all proletarian courts; elimination of control by reactionary officials and substitution of new organs of management of the proletariat. The victory of the proletariat consists of shattering the enemy's organization and organizing the proletarian power; in the destruction of the bourgeoisie and upbuilding of the proletarian state machinery. Not until the proletariat has achieved this victory and broken the resistance of the bourgeoisie can the former enemies of the new order be made useful, by bringing them into accord with its work." [15] Prior to the November revolution, Lenin urged as of prime importance in the work of "shattering the bourgeois state," the lowering of the salaries of the state officials to the "ordinary pay of the workers," after the practice in the Paris Commune, for this would do much to wipe out the old privileged bureaucracy, one of the greatest bulwarks of the old political state.[16]

Following the revolution, he expressed his regrets that the soviet was forced "to make use of the old bourgeois method and agree to a very high remuneration for the services of the biggest of the bourgeois specialists. . . . It is clear that such a method is a compromise, that it is a defection from the principles of the Paris Commune and of any proletarian rule, which demands the reduction of salaries to the standard of remuneration of the average workers—principles which demand that 'career hunting' be fought by deed, not by words." [17] The abolition of the standing army and the substitution of the citizen army, and the transformation of officials into elective and removable agents of the state were also suggested by Lenin in August of 1917 as among the measures which a proletarian government should enact, if it were to break down the old machine.

Transitional State. THE PROLETARIAN DICTATORSHIP. While the communists of the days of the November revolution believed ultimately in the abolition of the state as a class organ, they were convinced that, for some time, they should retain a state of the workers, a proletarian dictatorship, "an authority resting on the armed force of the masses, in order that the resistance of the bourgeoisie may be broken, that the reactionaries may be inspired with fear,[18] and that the great mass of the population—the peasantry, the lower middle class, the semi-proletariat—may be properly guided in the work of economic socialist reconstruction." [19]

[15] From the Program of the *Communist Manifesto* of 1919.
[16] Lenin, *The State and Revolution,* pp. 43–5.
[17] Lenin, *Soviets at Work,* pp. 14–5.
[18] See Lenin, *The Proletarian Revolution,* p. 35.
[19] Lenin, *The State and Revolution.*

Iron and steel works at Magnitogorsk, Russia. (Courtesy Sovfoto)

View of the Gorki Central Park of Culture and Rest in Moscow. (Courtesy Sovfoto)

Voroshilov Red Army Sanatorium, Sochi. (Courtesy Sovfoto)

Meeting of the Communist International in Moscow in 1935. At this Seventh Congress of the Third International the communists of the world officially launched their drive for the "united front." The International was dissolved in 1944. (Courtesy Sovfoto)

(Left) A photograph of V. I. Lenin (1870–1924) in Gorki, near Moscow, in 1922. (Right) Several of the leaders of the Soviet Union on their way to a parade in Red Square, 1938. In the foreground are J. V. Stalin, K. E. Voroshilov, and V. M. Molotov. (Photos courtesy Sovfoto)

(Left) Harold Wilson, Prime Minister of Labor Government of Great Britain, 1964–
(Courtesy British Information Services) (Right) Clement R. Attlee, Labor Prime Minister of Great Britain, 1945–51, created Earl Attlee, 1955. (Courtesy Wide World Photos)

(Left) Professor Harold J. Laski, political scientist, writer, and member of the Executive Committee, British Labor party, 1893–1950. (Right) Ernest Bevin, trade-union official, Laborite, and Minister of Labor and National Service during the Second World War, 1884–1951. (Photos courtesy Wide World Photos)

Quarry Hill Flats, public apartment houses in Leeds, England. The British Laborites in Leeds city council have furnished much of the drive for the construction of public apartments for working class families.

London public housing development. Some of the 1212 houses on the London County Council's estate at Roehampton, in southwest London, a "garden city" at the city's outskirts, which, supported by Laborites and others, supplements the large public apartment projects in the city's center. (Photos courtesy British Information Services)

While it was possible to *defeat* the exploiters at one blow, Lenin maintained, it was not generally possible to *destroy* them or their influence at once. It was impossible to expropriate at once the landlords and the capitalists of a large country and to substitute a working-class management of the factories and estates. There was no equality between the exploiters who, for generations, had enjoyed the advantages of education and of prosperity, and the exploited, the majority of whom, even in an advanced country, were cowed, frightened, ignorant, unorganized. For a considerable period after the revolution, the old bourgeoisie would continue to enjoy a considerable advantage. They would have some money, some movable goods, social connections, knowledge of management, the friendship of the technicians, and an incomparably greater understanding of military affairs and international connections than had the workers. They would never submit to the decision of the workers without utilizing every one of these advantages in one or more desperate battles. And, of course, all elements of decay of the old order could not fail to "show up" during this period, with a resulting "increase of crime, ruffianism, bribery, speculation, and other indecencies. It takes time and *an iron hand* to get rid of this." [20]

The power of resistance of the capitalist class, he declared in another connection, "increases tenfold after its overthrow, even though overthrown only in one country. The power of the bourgeoisie rests not alone upon international capital, upon its strong international connections, but also upon the force of habit, on the force of small industry of which, unfortunately, there is plenty left, and which daily, hourly, gives birth to capitalism and the bourgeoisie, spontaneously, and on a large scale. Victory over the bourgeoisie is impossible without a long, persistent, desperate, life-and-death struggle; a struggle which requires persistence, discipline, firmness, inflexibility, and concerted will action." [21]

The exact nature of the dictatorship would, of course, depend entirely on the conditions of the country in which the revolution was taking place. In could not be determined in advance. Its necessary condition was the forcible suppression of the exploiters as a class, and, consequently, "an infringement of 'pure democracy,' that is, of equality and freedom, in respect to that class." [22] In Russia it first involved disfranchisement of the bourgeoisie, but this was not a necessary element of proletariat dictatorship. In fact, in Russia, immediately after the Revolution, the dictatorship was less violent in character than later.

[20] Lenin, *Soviets at Work.*

[21] Lenin, *Left Wing Communism,* p. 10.

[22] Lenin, *Proletarian Revolution,* p. 40.

The political parties of various sorts continued to exist and bourgeois newspapers to circulate, capital punishment was abolished, and the army demobilized. Then the opposition began to mobilize, the Czecho-Slovaks seized railway stations, anti-bolshevik governments were formed in the East, and at Kiev the Cossacks began their counterrevolutionary attacks, the European countries began to undertake their military enterprises, Lenin and others were violently attacked, and the Red Army, the reign of terror and further limitation of political liberty followed.[23]

NATURE OF THE SOVIET FORM OF GOVERNMENT. The dictatorship of the proletariat during the transitional period, the communists of those days maintained, expressed itself through the soviet form of government. This form, under which the workers selected delegates to the soviets or councils to represent them as industrial as well as political groups, was a better form of proletarian democracy, Lenin and his followers claimed, than was the parliamentary form. For the soviets, they contended, reflected and expressed the moods and changes of view of the masses much more rapidly, much more fully, and much more faithfully than other institutions.[24]

They "are the direct organization of the laboring and exploited masses themselves, which enables them to organize and administer the state by their own efforts in their own manner. The city proletariat, the advance guard of the toiling and exploited, enjoys under this arrangement a position of advantage, due to its being best organized by the large industrial concerns, which enables it best to hold elections and to control the elected."

The bolsheviks until 1936 advocated indirect elections to the non-local soviets, declaring that such type of elections rendered "the entire apparatus cheaper, more elastic, more accessible to the workers and peasants at a time when life is overflowing and it is necessary rapidly to recall a delegate or to send him to the general congress of soviets." [25]

Stalin's contention immediately after the revolution was that the soviet organization of the state, "uniting legislative and executive power in a single organ and replacing territorial divisions by divisions (factories and workshops) based on the principle of production, . . . directly connects the workers and laboring masses with the governmental apparatus and teaches them how to administer the country." It was the only power that could "withdraw the army from bourgeois command and transform it, the instrument for oppressing the people, into an instrument for freeing it from the yoke of the native and foreign

[23] See Kamenev, *The Dictatorship of the Proletariat,* p. 9 ff.

[24] Lenin, *op. cit.,* p. 56.

[25] *Ibid.,* p. 30, see also *Soviets at Work.*

bourgeoisie." It was the only power that could destroy the old bourgeois judicial and administrative apparatus. While "allowing the constant participation of the organizations of the workers in the management of public affairs," it "is able to prepare that gradual disappearance of the state toward which the development of a communist society naturally tends." Although the soviet state as organized in Russia was not pure democracy, the communists argued, it was more democratic than was bourgeois democracy, the veiled dictatorship of the bourgeoisie, for the bourgeois dictatorship was a dictatorship of a minority, aiming at the exploitation of the majority, while the proletarian dictatorship "directs its attacks against the exploiting minority in the interest of the exploited majority." [26] The bourgeois dictatorship aimed to keep the great mass separated from the control and administration of political and economic life; the aim of the proletarian dictatorship was to arouse the masses to ever greater participation in industry and politics.

Socialization of Industry. Once the communists were in power, they should not only endeavor to suppress the bourgeois elements; they should begin the construction of the socialist state; they should adopt a program of socialization. Social ownership did not mean, of course, the "dividing up" of the means of production and exchange, but "the centralization of production and its subjection to a systematic plan." As a first step, declared the 1919 Manifesto, communists should promote the socialization of the great banks, the country's utilities, all communal enterprises, and trustified as well as other industries where the degree of centralization rendered social ownership technically practicable.

"As far as the smaller enterprises are concerned [the Manifesto continued], the proletariat must gradually unite them, according to the degree of their importance. It must be particularly emphasized that small properties will in no way be expropriated and that property owners who are not exploiters of labor will not be forcibly dispossessed. This element will gradually be drawn into the socialist organization through the force of example, through practical demonstration of the superiority of the new order of things and the regulation by which the small farmer and the petty bourgeoisie of the city will be freed from economic bondage to usurious capital and landlordism and from tax burdens, especially by annulment of the national debts, etc."

After socialization, the program of the Manifesto asserted, the proletariat should create centralized organs of management and workers' control. In the field of distribution, the following methods were to

[26] Lenin, *Soviets at Work,* p. 35.

be considered: "the socialization of wholesale establishments; the taking-over of all bourgeois state and municipal apparatus of distribution; control of the great co-operative societies, which organizations will still have an important rôle in the production epoch; the gradual centralization of all these organizations, and their conversion into a systematic unity for the rational distribution of products."

All qualified technicians, in the nature of the case, should be utilized, providing they were still capable of adapting themselves to the new economic system. "Far from oppressing them, the proletariat will make it possible for them for the first time to develop intensive creative work. The proletarian dictatorship, with their co-operation, will reverse the separation of physical and mental work which capitalism has developed, and thus will science and labor be unified. Besides expropriating the factories, mines, estates, etc., the proletariat must also abolish the exploitation of the people by capitalist landlords, transfer the large mansions to the local workers' soviets, and move the working people into the bourgeois dwellings."

The Attainment of Communism. THE "WITHERING AWAY" OF THE STATE. While the workers needed a state as an instrument for enforcing their will over the "exploiting minority" during the transitional stage from capitalism to socialism or communism, the communist ideal, at least in the beginning, was the elimination altogether of a state which, to them, as has been stated, stood as a representative of one class for the suppression of another class.

"With the final triumph of the soviet revolution," wrote Trotsky, "the soviet system will expand and include the whole population, in order thereby to lose the characteristics of the form of state, and melt away into the mighty system of producing and consuming co-operation." [27]

"We set ourselves, as our final aim," declared Lenin, "the task of the destruction of the state, that is, of every organized and systematic violence against man in general. We do not expect the advent of an order of society in which the principle of the submission of the minority to the majority will not be observed. But, striving for socialism, we are convinced that it will extend further into communism, and, side by side with this, there will vanish all need for force, for the subjection of one man to another, of one section of society to another, since people will *grow accustomed* to observing the elementary conditions of social existence *without force and without subjection.*" [28]

[27] Trotsky, *Dictatorship* vs. *Democracy,* p. 106.
[28] Lenin, *The State and Revolution,* pp. 84–5.

"In order to destroy the state [Lenin declared in another place] it is necessary to convert the functions of the public service into such simple operations of control and bookkeeping as are within the reach of the vast majority of the population, and, ultimately, of every single individual." [29]

Again Lenin wrote:

"When all, or be it even only the greater part of society, have learnt how to govern the state, have taken this business into their own hands, have established a control over the insignificant minority of capitalists, over the gentry with capitalist leanings, and workers thoroughly demoralized by capitalism—from this moment the need for any government begins to vanish. The more complete the democracy, the nearer the moment when it ceases to be necessary. The more democratic the 'state' consisting of armed workers, which is 'no longer a state in the ordinary sense of the term,' the more rapidly does every form of the state begin to decay, for when all have learnt to manage, and really do manage, socialized production, when all really do keep account and control of the idlers, gentlefolk, swindlers, and such-like 'guardians of capitalist traditions,' the escape from such general registration and control will inevitably become so increasingly difficult, so much the exception, and will probably be accompanied by such swift and severe punishment (for the armed workers are very practical people, not sentimental intellectuals, and they will scarcely allow anyone to trifle with them), that very soon the *necessity* of observing the simple, fundamental rules of any kind of social life will become the habit. The door will then be wide open for the transition from the first phase of communist society to its second and higher phase and along with it the complete withering away of the state." [30]

How long it would be before the state "withers away" after the conquest of political power by the proletariat was another question. Some were of the opinion that it would take in every country at least a generation, others believed that the period of dictatorship would be shorter. They conceded, however, that the social revolution would be a lengthy process; that it could not be regarded as a twenty-four-hour happening.

"To Each According to His Needs." Under an ideal communist commonwealth Lenin declared that the principle of "from each according to ability, to each according to his needs" should prevail. Until that stage was reached, the principle of equal work and equal pay, he contended, would have to be made effective. Such formal equality of com-

[29] *Ibid.*, p. 80. [30] *Ibid.*, p. 105.

pensation, however, would not mean *actual* equality, inasmuch as workers had varying responsibilities and needs. During the period of formal equality "the state will be necessary, in order to preserve the equality in labor and equality in the distribution of products." [31]

The need principle could be made operative when men "have become accustomed to observe the fundamental principles of social life," and their labor will have become "so productive that they will voluntarily work *according to their abilities.* 'The narrow horizon of bourgeois law,' which compels one to calculate, with the pitilessness of a Shylock, whether one has not worked half an hour more than another—this narrow horizon will then be left behind. Then will there be no need for any exact calculation by society of the quantity of products to be distributed to each of its members; each will take freely 'according to his needs.' " [32]

Communism and Marxism. In all of their writings, the communists during and immediately after the Russian revolution sought to prove that they were but following out the proposals of Marx and Engels. Marx and Engels, they maintained, felt that the violent overthrow of the state was, for the most part, inevitable; that the bourgeois state machine should be shattered; that a dictatorship of the proletariat should prevail during the transitional period, and that, when classes disappeared, the state itself should wither away.

If Marx and Engels failed to point out the way completely, they declared, it was because the fathers of modern socialism lived "in a prerevolutionary epoch, when imperialism was still in an embryonic condition, when the proletarians were only preparing themselves for the revolution, when the proletarian revolution was not yet a direct, practical necessity." [33] And in all of their writings, the communists laid great stress on the lessons of the Paris Commune of 1871, "the first, though still pale dawn," as Lavrov would have it, "of the proletarian revolution." [34] For it was the Commune of Paris which suggested a proletarian state machinery different from that of the capitalist state, a machinery after which, in part, the soviets were patterned; it was the Commune which showed to the communists the need for the use of force against the counterrevolution, and it was the final downfall of the Commune which convinced the communists, among other things, that the proletariat, when they obtained control of the government,

[31] Lenin, *The State and Revolution,* p. 97.
[32] *Ibid.,* p. 99.
[33] J. Stalin, *The Theory and Practice of Leninism,* p. 10.
[34] Quoted in Trotsky, *Dictatorship* vs. *Democracy,* p. 69.

should be prepared to use sufficient force to suppress all attempts at reaction.[35]

Communist tactics have changed in many ways since the November Revolution in 1917, but the general point of view of communists in regard to the need for a dictatorship during the period of transition remains essentially the same.

It is seen that the communists who supported the November, 1917, revolution held before them as an ultimate ideal a socialist society, that they differed from socialists primarily on tactics. They saw the revolution coming as a result of a violent change. They believed that the workers, once in control, should establish a proletarian dictatorship, break up the capitalist state and organize a soviet government; and gradually, with the overthrow of the bourgeoisie, permit greater freedom of expression and increasing democracy.

[35] Lenin's *State and Revolution* and his *Proletarian Revolution,* particularly the former, for quotations from Marx and Engels on revolutionary tactics.

CHAPTER 26

Soviet Russia through the Five-Year Plans

FROM THE REVOLUTION TO THE RISE OF STALIN

SINCE the November revolution the communists in Russia have been engaged in trying to carry on as a communist dictatorship. On January 19, 1918, the communists, controlling the Soviet, dissolved the Constituent Assembly and immediately began a drive for peace in order that they might "have a breathing space for internal stabilization and for an increase in the Russian power of resistance," and on March 16, 1918, signed the "Tilsit" peace.

The 1918 Soviet Constitution. On the tenth of the following July they adopted the Russian Constitution, the Constitution of the first Socialist Federated Soviet Republic in the world. Article One of this Constitution was largely a repetition of the "Declaration of Rights of the Laboring and Exploited People" submitted to the Constitutional Assembly on the eve of the revolution and approved by the All-Russian Congress of Soviets in January.

It declared that (a) "all private property in land is abolished, and the entire land is declared to be national property and is to be apportioned among agriculturists without any compensation to the former owners, in the measure of each one's ability to till it. (b) All forests, treasures of earth, and waters of general public utility, all equipment, whether animate or inanimate, model farms, and agricultural enterprises, are declared to be national property."

It provided for the transfer of all banks to the ownership of the government and for the government control of factories, mills, railways, and mines. It proclaimed a universal obligation to work, decreed that all workers be armed, authorized the abrogation of secret treaties, and adhered to the policy of concluding a general democratic peace without annexations or indemnities. It also maintained that "exploiters should not hold a position in any branch of the Soviet government" and that "power must belong entirely to the toiling masses."

Article Two declared that the fundamental aim of the constitution, in view of the present transitional period, was the establishment of "the dictatorship of the urban and rural proletariat and the poorest peasantry in the form of a powerful All-Russian Soviet authority, for the purpose of abolishing the exploitation of men by men and of introducing socialism, in which there will be neither a division into classes nor a state of autocracy." It proclaimed as its motto, the motto of St. Paul, "He shall not eat who does not work." It provided for the introduction of universal military training. It declared against the oppression of national minorities. It gave the right to vote to men and women who had completed their eighteenth year and were performing labor useful to society, and denied the vote to persons employing "hired labor in order to obtain from it an increase in profits" or who had an income from property without doing work, and to merchants, clergy, etc.

THE BASIS OF REPRESENTATION UNDER THE SOVIET GOVERNMENT. The basis of representation the communists made partly occupational and industrial, partly geographical. Under its constitution and that of the Union of Russian Republics (adopted in July, 1923), each village elected its own soviet, which in turn selected an executive committee that exercised administrative powers. Delegates from the various village soviets in a township (Volost) assembled in a township soviet, and the various township soviets in a province (Gubernia) sent delegates to a provincial soviet.

Delegates to town or city soviets came from the various productive groups in the community—from the factories, mills, mines, co-operative societies, etc. From the local or productive units the soviets pyramided to the Congresses of Soviets representing the constituent republics and the entire Soviet Union.

THE GOVERNMENT STRUCTURE. The supreme authority was the All-Union Congress of Soviets, composed of delegates from town and township soviets and from provincial Congresses of Soviets.

During the interval between the Congresses of the Soviet Union, authority was placed in the Central Executive Committee. This Committee consisted of the Council of the Union and the Council of Nationalities. The Congress met once a year, and the Central Executive Committee four times a year. During the interval between meetings of the C. E. C., the Presidium of the Committee, with its half dozen chairmen, was the supreme legislative, executive, and administrative power.

The executive and directive organ of the Central Executive Committee was the Council of People's Commissars. Members of this Council were elected for one year. The Council consisted of a President, Deputy Presidents, the chairman of the Supreme Economic Council, and the Commissars.

In the administrative scheme of the Soviet there were three types of Commissariats: those representing the entire Union alone; those representing both the Union and the Constituent Republics; and those representing the Constituent Republics alone.

A pyramidal representative form of government was found not only in the Union but likewise in each of the Constituent Republics.

Period of Workers' Control. From 1917 to 1926 the communists in Russia several times varied their policy in regard to industrial ownership and control to meet critical situations. The first period, from the November Revolution to the middle of 1918, has been referred to as a period of "Workers' Control." The decree of November 14, 1917, established a strict control over industrial production and distribution and over the finances of trade and industrial organizations, but did not actually nationalize the general run of industries, as the communists were not at first prepared to issue a measure so sweeping in its application. They assumed that the owners of the industrial enterprises would continue to administer them under public regulation. The government was anxious to concentrate on the management of railroads and other key industries. There was, however, a good deal of sporadic confiscation throughout these months, many times against the orders of the national government.[1]

"What was fatal and irremediable in giving the management of each factory to the persons employed therein, whether to a majority or to the whole aggregate of them, . . ." declared the Webbs, commenting on this first period of industrial control, "was that each factory under such control—deprived of the automatic checks and warnings which the capitalist system supplies to the profit-maker in the relations of wages cost to selling prices, and of these to customer demands—necessarily judged and decided its policy exclusively from the standpoint of its own wishes and interests. Each factory was without knowledge alike of what the whole community of consumers needed or desired, or of how much all the other factories were simultaneously producing. . . . What stood revealed to every intelligent person, when the experiment was tried, was that the function of each producing unit in the com-

[1] See Zimand, Savel, *State Capitalism in Russia* (N. Y.: Foreign Policy Association, 1926), pp. 30–1; Heller, *Industrial Revival in Russia,* p. 81; British Trade Union Delegation to Russia, *Report,* 1924, p. 42.

munity was to produce, *not what that unit might prefer to produce, but what the community needed or desired.*" [2]

As a result of the failure of this type of control to produce satisfactorily for the market, the experiment was soon discontinued. Lenin induced his colleagues to insist, by a decree of June 28, 1918, that each industrial plant be put under the control of a single manager, appointed by and responsible to the government itself. Further, to co-ordinate the production of individual plants and plan from week to week, a new government department was set up under a committee charged to direct manufacturing and mining throughout the country, "with the dominant object of getting produced, not what the workmen in each factory thought fit, or even what the manager might decide, but what the community needed and desired in due order and proportion. It had, in fact, been discovered by painful experience that the 'liquidation of the employer' necessarily involved the governmental planning of production." [3] The development of the Supreme Economic Council of Public Economy, empowered to organize the national economy and the finances of the state, followed.

Period of Military Communism. The second period in the history of the Soviet government was that of "Military Communism." This was the period of civil war, of the struggle with the Czecho-Slovaks, with Kolchak, Denikin, Yudenich, and Wrangel; the period of the economic blockade, of the war with Poland, of the intervention of French, Japanese, German, American, and other military forces. This period extended from the middle of 1918 to the end of 1920. With the outbreak of civil war many of the old factory owners and managers left Russia altogether, and many who remained practically sabotaged their plants. Military necessity compelled a more systematic policy of nationalization, much as the First World War led to an extension of collectivism on the part of the warring powers. The result was the decree of June 28, 1918, ordering a systematic nationalization of large industries. It was not, however, until November 29, 1920, at the height of War Communism that nationalization was decreed in the case of all plants operated by machinery and employing more than five workers as well as in the case of handicraft industries employing ten or more workers. The same decree legally abolished private property in small industry.

In explaining this policy of nationalization Leo Kamenev, President of the Moscow Soviet, afterwards wrote:

[2] Sidney and Beatrice Webb, *Soviet Communism,* p. 608.
[3] *Ibid.,* p. 609.

"We see . . . that the exigencies of the direct and immediate struggle with the bourgeoisie, which was working underground and using its industrial position as an instrument of political and economic struggle—that this purely political situation was at the bottom, for the most part, of our nationalization policy. Purely economic reasons, which should have given to the nationalization policy a systematic character, received secondary consideration. Political considerations compelled us to place in the hands of the proletarian government a greater number of enterprises than we could administer in the interests of the national economy as a whole." [4]

The state administration was successful in its main aim of supplying the army with enough clothes and munitions to win the civil war. But "from a business standpoint . . . it left much to be desired. Debts were contracted without regard to the credit side of the ledger; bureaucracy exerted an unfavorable influence upon industrial development; the lack of trained business executives was often painfully felt." [5] The control of each industry by a "Head Center" under the direction of the Supreme Council of National Economy, with little co-ordination between the various industries, made for waste and inefficiency. This situation, plus the terrible heritage of the First World War, the ravages of the blockade and the civil war, which cut the factories and transportation system away from their necessary fuel and raw material, and the refusal of the peasants to pay their requisitions, made for economic chaos. The workers were suffering because of the lack of food and raw material, and the peasants, from the lack of the manufactured product. A vicious circle was thus established.

Dissatisfaction against the drastic nationalization decrees and their operation steadily increased during the fall of 1920 and the spring of 1921. But the leaders for some time ignored the protests and continued to elaborate far-flung plans for industrial reconstruction. Many of them were confident that labor armies, by a series of successful drives on the railroads, mines, and key industries, could put the productive machinery of the nation into proper condition within a comparatively short time, and that after this was accomplished the peasant situation and the production of commodities for nation-wide consumption could be given due consideration. They failed to realize "that a predominantly agricultural country like Russia cannot be industrialized overnight. Such a transformation must proceed slowly and naturally; it must come in response to the country's growing needs; and it cannot

[4] Quoted in Heller, *op. cit.*, p. 82.

[5] *Ibid.*, p. 82.

be arbitrarily imposed from above, although, of course the government can facilitate the process." [6]

In March, 1921, the sailors of Kronstadt started a revolt. Other revolts occurred along the Volga. When the Congress of Soviets met in March, 1921, they were confronted with a practical breakdown of the economic system. The only escape lay in the adoption of a new policy. The policy adopted was in the nature of a revolution. Under it the government substituted a regular tax system for food requisitions and gave to the peasants the liberty to dispose of all surplus remaining after the payment of the levy. It reorganized many of the state industries, and began a policy of state leasing. It reopened its state bank and authorized it to resume loan and deposit operations with private individuals. It restored to the individual the right to buy and sell articles of prime necessity in the open market. It did away with many of the restrictions surrounding co-operative enterprises and re-established credit co-operation and the Consumers' Co-operative Bank.

The government in the nature of the case did not abandon the principle of nationalization of industry, but in its decree of July 7, 1921, exempted from future nationalization or municipalization all small enterprises employing less than twenty persons, and recognized the right of all citizens of eighteen years and over freely to engage in home industry and to establish small industrial enterprises. No person, however, was supposed to engage in more than one enterprise. The state also ceased to supply with raw materials, fuel, and foodstuffs many of the state enterprises other than the coal, iron, metallurgy, transportation, and other heavy industries. Henceforth these were expected to secure their material in the open market.

"For three years, up to the spring of 1921," wrote Lenin in November, 1921,[7] "our plan was to revive our large-scale industries and to organize a system of exchanging their products with the peasants, while endeavoring to socialize agriculture." In pursuit of this, "we proposed to take from the peasants a certain amount of foodstuffs and raw materials as a sort of loan by means of requisitions."

"We are no longer attempting to *break up* the old social economic order, with its trade, its small-scale economy and private initiative, its capitalism, but we are now trying to *revive* trade, private enterprise, and capitalism, at the same time gradually and cautiously subjecting them to state regulation just as far as they revive."

Lenin's defense of this change of policy is given in his pamphlet, "Con-

[6] *Ibid.*, p. 91.

[7] *Pravda*, Nov. 7, 1921.

cerning the Food Tax." As early as 1918, he was convinced that, in view of the chaotic condition of Russian life, state capitalism would be a step forward, not backward. "There is not a communist, it seems to me," he wrote, "who would deny that the expression, 'Socialist Soviet Republic' means the determination of the soviet power to realize the transition to socialism, and does not by any means signify that the present economic order is regarded as socialistic."

Many forms of economic life, he declared, from patriarchal peasant economy to socialism, existed side by side in Russia. It was not correct to say that the struggle in Russia was at this time a struggle between socialism and capitalism, for the greatest part of Russia had not reached the highest form of capitalist development. Despite the fact that the November Revolution did not usher in socialism, it played an essential rôle in wresting political power from the bourgeoisie and in making it possible to direct the whole administrative apparatus of the state toward the objective of socialism.

The revival of small industries, he maintained, was a necessity of the hour. For these could flourish, as large scale industry could not flourish, without large reserve stocks of fuel, food, and raw material. And such reserve stocks did not then exist in devastated Russia.

Facing the realities of the situation, Lenin continued, socialized industry at this time affected but a smaller number of the population. The vast majority of the people were peasants. With few exceptions they retained the psychology of small capitalists. Under the circumstances the only sensible course was to "refrain from prohibiting and preventing the development of capitalism and strive to direct it in the path of *state* capitalism."

The granting of concessions to private corporations for the operation of mines, factories, etc., Lenin felt, would strengthen advanced as against backward industrial methods and would provide the soviet industries and peasant farmers with needed materials. He urged that the cooperatives be utilized for trade and exchange with the peasants. Cooperatives, he argued, eliminate the wastes of competition and help to organize large masses of people.

"We are too fond of saying, 'capitalism is an evil, socialism is a blessing,' but such an argument is incorrect, because it leaves out of consideration all the existing social and economic strata and takes in only two of them.

"Capitalism is an evil in comparison with socialism, but capitalism is a blessing in comparison with medievalism, with small industry, with fettered small producers thrown to the mercy of bureaucracy."

The pamphlet closed by affirming optimistically that "there is nothing really dangerous in this policy for a proletarian government, so long as the proletariat fully retains the administrative power, the means of transport, and large-scale industry."

The Third World Congress of the Communist International in June-July, 1921, approved the policy as a necessary one for Russia at that time. The New Economic Policy, or NEP, as it was called, led, as was expected, to a very distinct revival of Russian trade.

The New Economic Policy. Under the New Economic Policy, which was confirmed by a decree published August 9, 1921, concessions were granted to private capitalists in Russia and abroad to operate mines and factories. The state bank was reopened and was permitted to receive deposits from private individuals and to grant loans to them. Co-operatives and private stores were allowed to carry on retail trade, and in place of requisitions a regular tax was collected from the peasants. The latter were allowed to sell their produce for the price they could command on the open market and after paying the tax to keep the surplus. As for the workers, the government sanctioned overtime and piece-work payments.

Under the NEP, foreign money came into the country. Foreign trade rapidly increased. Exports more than doubled from 1922 to 1923. The depreciated Soviet money was replaced by the stabilized chervonetz ruble. Agriculture began to revive and with it the peasant demand for manufactured goods. Industry began to seek raw materials and to aim at large-scale production. Prewar specialists began to devote themselves to the reconstruction of industry, and improved technological methods were introduced into many industries. The output of large industry began to show a considerable increase. Important services began to be rendered, retail stores reopened, and a great change was evidenced in the outward appearance of cities.

One of the most radical changes involved in the NEP was the restoration of the whole internal currency of the country to a straight money basis. Instead of the vague system of accounting prevalent under military communism, every state enterprise was required to render a balance sheet which showed profit and loss as in private industry. Employees received wages in cash rather than in commodity cards. Housing committees were required to charge rent on a graduated scale, taking due consideration of the social position and the earnings of the tenant.

As the New Economic Policy developed, industrial control was decentralized, industry being divided into "trusts"—the Oil Trust, the Coal Trust, and the like. Associated with the trusts, which were agencies of production, were syndicates, which were organs of purchase and sale, handling both domestic and foreign trade. As a means of coordinating the activities of the trusts, the Supreme Economic Council was expanded so as to include representatives of the trust sections, thus forming a kind of Industrial General Staff.

The New Economic Policy did much to save Soviet economy from collapse. The situation among the peasants, however, was anything but satisfactory. In the autumn of 1923 the prices of agricultural products fell to 60 per cent of the prewar level. On the other hand, urged on by the necessity of showing profits required under the NEP, trusts and other industrial enterprises had raised the prices of manufactured goods to 80 per cent above that level. The disproportion between these prices was so great that the peasants began to refuse to sell grain or to buy manufactured goods. Warehouses became glutted and industrial stagnation was threatened.

The gap between these two sets of prices had to be closed. The disparity was largely wiped out in a period of six months by the sale of goods below cost—a sale which eliminated most of the paper profits of the trusts—and by a steady increase in the prices of food products. These actions made it possible to overcome this developing crisis, but the question of keeping this gap closed still remained one of the major problems of the Soviet economy.

During these years the private merchants, traders, and small manufacturers, called the Nepmen, grew in strength and wealth, and many of the old bolsheviks began to fear that if the Nepmen became stronger they might soon obtain the upper hand. As a means of preventing their continued acquisition of power, those in control of the state in 1924 began to impose upon the Nepmen heavy taxes and many restrictions.

In May, 1924, the congress of the Communist party approved the establishment of a Commissariat of Home Trade, with power to supervise private trade and "to suppress all attempts by private capital, whether overt or otherwise, to injure the trade and industry of the state or the co-operative movement." About the same time other decrees were passed giving complete autonomy to the co-operatives, and the government established a "united front" with these organizations against the private trader. While many private traders were forced out of business under this policy, others continued to operate, and by the end of 1924 about 60 per cent of the retail trade was said to be in the hands of private traders.[8]

[8] *Economicheskoye Obozreniye,* July, 1925, pp. 147 ff.

On account of its lack of capital the state was unable to function effectively in the trading field, and in 1925 the Soviet Congress decided that the policy of suppression should be discontinued, that private traders should be encouraged, and that the co-operatives should constitute the principal link between the state economic authorities and the small rural producer. A short time thereafter, however, the private traders were, for the most part, liquidated.

In the early twenties, despite the increase in private industry under the New Economic Policy, the state furnished four fifths of the industrial production in the domestic market. Railroad transportation was one hundred per cent in the state's hands, ninety-five per cent of the foreign trade was carried on by the state, and credit institutions were a centralized national monopoly. On the other hand, in the mid-twenties, agriculture was operated by 22,000,000 peasant establishments, "thus constituting," in the words of Leon Trotsky, "the principal social problem of a socialist construction" of the country.[9]

The Death of Lenin. During this period in which the Soviet government was striving to meet these economic conditions, Lenin ceased to guide the destinies of the republic. In 1922 he suffered a paralytic stroke and had to take a temporary rest from his post in Moscow. He later returned to his task as head of the government, but was soon forced to retire again and died on January 21, 1924. His remains were interred in a dark-red granite mausoleum in the Red Square of Moscow, which is backed by the Kremlin wall. Three-quarters of a million people waited in line to view his remains for an average of five hours in an arctic cold of 30 degrees below zero before they were able to take their turn in passing through the hall where he lay in state.

The Rise of Stalin to Power. No sooner had Lenin passed away than a bitter struggle for party leadership ensued between the faction in the party led by Trotsky and that headed by Stalin, who had been chosen the secretary of the party, and who, from the early twenties to his death in 1953, was destined to be the chief figure in Soviet political life and the virtual dictator of the Soviet Union.

Joseph V. Stalin—his real name is Joseph Vissarionovich Djugashvili—was born on December 21, 1871, in Gori, Georgia, a mountain town on the railway leading down to the Black Sea. He was a son of Vissarion, a shoemaker. His father died when he was a young boy, and his mother earned the family bread with her needle. To obtain an education, he entered the Orthodox Seminary in Tiflis, which trained its students for the priesthood.

[9] Trotsky, *Whither Russia?* (N. Y.: International Publishers, 1926), pp. 10, 43.

While at the Seminary, however, young Stalin became convinced that "existing conditions were wrong and unjust," and that "Russian capitalism was the most atrocious and bestial in the world; the government of the Czar the most corrupt, cruel, and inefficient." He resolved to do what he could to remedy conditions and "turned from the Fathers of the Church to the fathers of scientific socialism." [10] At eighteen years of age, charged with propagandizing among his fellow students in behalf of the Marxian philosophy, he renounced the priesthood and became a bookkeeper by day and a revolutionist by night.

Following a large street demonstration, he fled from Tiflis to Batum to escape the Russian police. Here he was arrested on the charge of fomenting a strike and sent to jail for twenty months. Following his imprisonment, he was sentenced to exile in Siberia for three years. Escaping after a few weeks, Stalin was soon back on his home ground in charge of an illegal paper, *Fight of the Proletariat.* Later he took a prominent part in labor and revolutionary struggles, helped to organize the oil workers in Baku, to promote a general strike as an overture of the revolution of 1905, and to direct raids on government institutions. "By bombing in daylight a carriage that under Cossack convoy was carrying funds to the State Bank, 150,000 rubles came into the party coffers." [11]

During the next decade, young Stalin was constantly hounded by the Russian police and soldiers, and finally was jailed and sent into exile, only to escape. For a while he lived abroad, preparing a book on the question of nationalities. Returning to Russia, he directed in St. Petersburg the publication of the *Star* and the *Pravda.* Trapped in March, 1913, as a result of information given by an *agent provocateur,* he was sent to Turukhansk in northern Siberia, and there remained as fisherman, hunter, and trapper until the fall of the Czar in 1917. At that time he returned to St. Petersburg and was elected to numerous revolutionary committees and helped chart the course of the November (1917) Revolution. As a member of the Supreme War Council he was active in the fight against the armies of Yudenitch, of Denikin, and of the Poles.

In the early twenties Stalin was elected secretary of the Communist party, and while holding this position during the twenties and thirties, he became the most powerful figure in Russia. During these years he served as a member of the Polit-Bureau and the Presidium of the Third International, and held numerous positions in the Soviet government.

[10] Williams, Albert Rhys, *The Soviets,* p. 96; see also Souvarine, *Stalin: A Critical Survey of Bolshevism,* chs. I, II.

[11] Williams, *op. cit.;* Souvarine, *op. cit.*

On May 6, 1941, the Supreme Council appointed him President of the Council of People's Commissars, the chief administrative position in the Soviet government. He continued to retain also his positions as a Commissar for People's Defense and head of the National Defense Council.

The Stalin-Trotsky Controversy. In the controversy between the followers of Stalin and those of Trotsky, the "old bolsheviks" (members of the Communist party prior to the revolution), who were aligned with Stalin, contended that Europe was not ready for the social revolution and that the most effective way for the time being of propagandizing for communism was to make a success of the Soviet system in Russia. They maintained that the Soviet system would never succeed until it had assured an adequate supply of food to the working population and that this necessitated concessions to the peasants.

The Trotskyites, on the other hand, contended that the Third International should seek more vigorously than it had been doing to sow the seeds of social revolution throughout Europe; that, far from doing this, the Communist party through its New Economic Policy was favoring the peasants over the city population, and at the same time was encouraging small merchants and bringing about the return in Russia of the capitalist system. Preobrazhensky, the economist of the left communist opposition, argued that sooner or later "one system must devour the other." He declared that it was impossible to build a socialist state without obtaining the funds from non socialized forms of the national economy, including agriculture, and that it was a sign of a reactionary spirit to think otherwise.[12] "The more economically backward and petty bourgeois a country which enters upon the socialist organization and the smaller the amount of accumulated wealth which the proletariat receives from the revolution," Preobrazhensky asserted, "the more is such a socialist state obliged to depend upon the exploitation of presocialist economic sources." [13]

The Stalin-Zinoviev-Kamenev forces won out in the fight over communist policy, and in 1924 the Trotskyite program was decisively re-

[12] After the death of Lenin, Stalin at first, and as late as April, 1924, expressed in print the view that the victory of socialism in one country only was impossible. He then suddenly reversed himself, advancing the doctrine that "socialism in a single country" was quite feasible, provided the country in question had a large territory, a large population, and all essential natural resources. However, he maintained, to build communism in one land did not constitute a "final victory" of socialism, for there is always the danger of intervention by the capitalist nations. (Florinski, *Toward an Understanding of the USSR,* pp. 93–4.)

[13] Manya Gordon, *Workers before and after Lenin,* p. 377; Preobrazhensky, *Vyestnik Kommunisticheskiy Akademi* (Journal of the Communist Academy), 1923, Vol. 8.

jected by the Communist party. Trotsky refused to consider the verdict final and in the fall of the year issued propaganda material interpreted as an attack on the party leadership. For this alleged violation of discipline he was removed from the position of Commissar of War and sent on a prolonged vacation to the Caucasus.

Soon thereafter another controversy broke out between Stalin, on the one hand, and the two other members of the triumvirate, Zinoviev and Kamenev, on the other. In the summer of 1926 a good crop had strengthened the national food resources of the country, and led Zinoviev and others to believe that the country could do without the "village capitalists," or "kulaks." Stalin disagreed with this position, maintaining that the peasants should be given further concessions. The congress backed Stalin, but the two "old bolsheviks" refused to conform and joined the forces of Trotsky.

After a year or so of heated debate, Trotsky, Zinoviev, and Kamenev, at the Communist party Congress in December, 1927, were expelled from the party and sent into exile. The two latter finally recanted their communist "heresy" and were reinstated in the party ranks, but Trotsky began to organize an underground opposition movement from his Russian Turkestan residence. A few years later, in 1929, he was expelled from the country. He later became the center of revolutionary activity in Turkey, was forced out of that country, and made his residence successively in France, Norway, and Mexico. In Mexico two attacks were made on his life, the second on August 20, 1940, by a man whom Trotsky alleged to be an agent of the Russian OGPU. His injuries were so serious that he died the next day.

While Trotsky and his followers were being denounced for economic heresy, Stalin incorporated many of their proposals in his own program. The "kulak" was becoming too strong, and many of the communists were beginning to feel that they could do without them. The government greatly increased the taxes imposed on the agricultural population and urged the speeding up of the industrialization of the country. The measures thus adopted caused Professor Kondratiev, one of the moderate bolshevik economists, to write in 1927: "We have undertaken much too high a pace in industrialization, and in the hunt for money for capital investments we are compelled to extract our resources from the village by means of an unsatisfactory relation between agricultural and industrial products." [14]

[14] Gordon, *op. cit.*, p. 377.

In June, 1928, Stalin, convinced that the peasantry should be asked to bear increasing burdens, declared: "We have no colonies, credit, or loans. They [the international capitalists] will not give to us; consequently our basis must be taxing the peasantry." (Gordon, *op. cit.*, p. 382.)

THE FIVE-YEAR PLANS

The First Five-Year Plan. ORIGIN. In 1928 the desire to increase the pace of industrialization led to a demand by the Soviets for some kind of economic plan. A significant economic plan had been suggested for Russia in 1919 by Professor V. I. Grinevetsky in his book, *Postwar Perspective of Russian Industry*. Professor Grinevetsky's volume briefly outlined Russian prewar industry and drew up a blueprint for postwar reconstruction based on electrification. The book presupposed the continuance of the capitalist system and contained numerous uncomplimentary remarks regarding the communists. Nevertheless Lenin saw in this volume many valuable suggestions that could be applied to the Soviet economy, and the communists had a second edition of this work published in 1922. On the question of economic planning, the communist V. Sarabyanov wrote, "We have only one book, Professor Grinevetsky's."

The reading of this book led Lenin to consult with a group of engineers regarding ways and means of adapting the plan to Russia's needs. He decided to create a commission of specialists to plan the reconstruction of industry with due regard to Grinevetsky's plan. In February, 1920, he organized the National Commission for the Electrification of Russia. A staff of 200 persons was organized, including the leading professors and engineers of the country. With the exception of the chairman it contained no communists. Some bolsheviks at first criticized the domination of the commission by those outside of the communist ranks, but these critics were reprimanded by Lenin, who declared, "Regarding this commission it is the business of the communist to command as little as possible, more correctly not to command at all. Of such communists we have a great many, and I would give dozens of them for one conscientious, experienced bourgeois specialist who had learned his business." [15]

The commission published its report in 1920. The report outlined a plan for the expansion over a period of from 10 to 15 years of the coal, peat, petroleum, iron, and electrical industries, among others, giving special attention to the electrical industry. The plan was later ratified by the Congress of Soviets.

CONTENT OF FIRST FIVE-YEAR PLAN. In February of the next year the State Planning Commission, the Gosplan, was organized within the Council of Labor and Defense. The Gosplan and the Supreme Soviet of National Economy set to work to plan in detail for all industry. A draft of the plan was published in 1928. It became known as the

[15] *Ibid.*, p. 380; *Encyclopaedia Britannica,* Vol. XXVI, p. 124.

Piatiletka, or Five-Year Plan. Its initial task was the restoration of the national economy which had suffered so severely as a result of wars and revolution and "its reconstruction along lines of increased industrialization." At first the plan was supposed to guide industry with mere suggestions, but, with the progress of the years, the proposals for increased productivity were regarded more and more as commands.

There was no phase of the social and economic life of the country which the plan did not cover. Specifically, it dealt with such activities as (1) electrification, (2) light and heavy industry, (3) agriculture, (4) transport, (5) mail, (6) telephones and telegraphs, (7) consumers' co-operatives, (8) labor, (9) public instruction, (10) scientific research, (11) health protection and social life, (12) housing, (13) finance. For each of these phases of activities it proposed considerable advances, which many specialists declared were beyond human attainment.

As is indicated by the activities listed above, the plan did not confine itself to the industrial sphere. It grappled also with the educational and cultural phases of Russian life. It mapped out proposals for the fight against illiteracy, for compulsory school education, and for the construction of school buildings. It made estimates regarding the number of students who should be admitted to different types of educational institutions and who should be trained for various trades and professions. It presented proposals for health resorts, for rest houses for workers, for physical culture training, for educational and recreational tours, for housing, and for many other forms of social welfare services. The goals it set related not only to the nation as a whole but to various regions and localities, to specific trusts and factories, and to varying periods of time of from five days to five years.

PREPARATION AND ENFORCEMENT OF PLAN. The broad policies underlying these Five-Year Plans were set forth first not by the Gosplan but by the Communist party and the Soviet government, the general aim being that "of constructing a socialist society on the basis of the maximum development of productive force and the systematic improvement of the condition of the workers." [16] The government indicated to the commission its general policies regarding wages, prices and consumption, investment production, and priorities in industrial development.

[16] V. V. Obolensky-Ossinsky in *World Social Economic Planning* (International Industrial Relations Institute), 1932, p. 330; Yugow, A., *Russia's Economic Front for War and Peace,* ch. I. The Fifth Congress of the Soviets and the Sixteenth Communist Party Conference adopted the maximum variant of the Gosplan projects (minimum and maximum drafts were considered) on April 23 and May 28, 1929.

The government memorandum, however, did not contain detailed figures, nor did it lay down specific tasks for individual sectors of the national economy or individual industries.

The Gosplan took the government directions and worked out from the information acquired from various parts of the nation detailed blueprints of production. It passed on these blueprints to all the departments of the Soviet government and to all republics and districts. From there they were distributed to corporations, trusts, and social groups and discussed by them. "Counterplans" were returned to the Gosplan, which considered the suggestions from the country at conferences of workers from planning and scientific institutions. The final draft was then submitted by the Gosplan to the government for its approval.

After this procedure the government announced the plan to the country, to induce the workers of the country to carry out this plan. It distributed prizes to individuals and groups of workers. It increased wages and reduced hours. It employed "shock troops" and various techniques of "socialist competition."[17] It conducted an extensive propaganda within the educational system of the country. It sought to stimulate new inventions, hired hundreds of foreign technicians, and employed in behalf of the plan all of the coercive machinery of the state.

The plan investment for the first five years amounted to nearly 20 billion rubles, exclusive of the amount invested in transportation, commerce, and many other national necessities. Under the First Five-Year Plan the government proposed to increase production in heavy industry by 231 per cent and in light industry by 144 per cent.

INDUSTRIAL RESULTS OF FIRST FIVE-YEAR PLAN. At the end of the five years it was possible for the initiators of the plan to show a number of positive results. The country witnessed a remarkable development in the electrical industry.[18] The mechanized production of coal increased. The petroleum industry was reconstructed. Advances in the

[17] Under "socialistic competition," workers in factories—or departments of factories—mines, schools, on ships, etc., declared themselves to be "shock," or industrial troops and challenged each other or their fellows in other establishments to beat old records, "to make new ones, to lift them as high or higher than in America," etc. Often prizes or special privileges were conferred on those who excelled in such competition. (Williams, *The Soviets,* p. 266.) As a means of assuring a rapid rate of industrialization it had been decided to invest a large part of the national income in the construction of capital goods. "Even the First Five-Year Plan was to a great extent permeated by the idea of 'autarchy,' i.e., the aim of making Soviet economy independent of the rest of the world both industrially and with respect to raw materials." (A. Yugow, *Russia's Economic Front for War and Peace,* p. 11.)

[18] Gordon, *op. cit.,* p. 395.

metal, chemical, and the machine-manufacturing industries were very considerable. The railroad plant improved somewhat and several thousand miles of new line were constructed. The country became dotted with a network of new factories and electrical plants, some of them the largest of their kind in the world.

These results, however, were attained at great cost. The government paid out great sums to import machines, engineers, and technicians. "In 1927–28 industry contributed to the national budget 288 million rubles and received from the government 783 million; for every ruble it gave it obtained in return three rubles. In 1932 the entire revenue from industry amounted to 943 million rubles and in return industry received from the government 15,357 million rubles, sixteen rubles for every ruble it paid." [19]

THE DRIVE TOWARD FARM COLLECTIVIZATION. The Five-Year Plan had provided for the expansion of state and collective farms, and soon after its adoption the government began a drive against the "kulaks," who had expanded their production steadily since the introduction of the NEP. This drive was resented by the new right opposition, led by Rykov, Bukharin, and Tomsky, who described the treatment of the kulaks as "military feudal oppression" and warned the government that its agrarian policy would alienate the peasants and result in a grain crisis. The 1929 harvest, however, showed considerable expansion of collective farming and improvement in agricultural production; the right opposition thereupon recanted their "heresy." On January 6, 1930, the government began its campaign for complete collectivization of farms. On February 1, 1930, a decree for the liquidation of the kulaks as a class was formally issued.[20]

[19] Gordon, *op. cit.*, pp. 395–6. "The First Five-Year Plan," according to Florinski, "called for an increase of 110 per cent in the production of labor. The actual average increase, according to official estimates, was 41 per cent." The result was that, while the planners had expected to increase the number of wage-earners from 11.3 million to 15.8 million, this number by 1932 reached 22.8 million. (Florinski, *Toward an Understanding of the USSR*, pp. 162–3.)

[20] The "kulaks" were the more well-to-do peasants, who "exploited" others, and the owners of brick kilns and of other small village enterprises. They were regarded by the government as opposed to collectivization. Their "liquidation" involved confiscation of their property and banishment to forced labor.

In the twenties, the socialized sector consisted of state farms established by the government on lands seized by it in the revolution of 1917, and collective or co-operative farms of various types which by 1927 contained but 1,100,000 peasants. The state and collectivized farms together supplied only about 1.5 per cent of the total grain produced and only 3 per cent of the total marketed grain. (Vera Micheles Dean, *Soviet Russia, 1917–1936*, p. 27.) The First Five-Year Plan was cautious about taking the path toward collectivization of agriculture. It proposed a gradual absorption of individual farms, and at first its authors declared that the privately owned sector of agricultural economy would prove to be the basic producer of agri-

As a result of this drive, it is estimated that by March 1, 1930, 55 per cent of all peasant farms had been collectivized. However, in many regions collectivization had been effected on paper only. Many of the bolshevik organizers had consulted only the poorer peasants with little or no assets, who were unable to establish a collective without the assistance of their more well-to-do neighbors. In many of the more backward districts the peasants had joined the collectives only after the use of military and economic pressures and in the fear that failure to do so would only lead to confiscation and exile. So drastic had been some of the methods in this campaign that Stalin felt it necessary on March 2, 1930, to warn his followers against "dizziness from success," and denounced the formation of collectives in regions unprepared for collectivization. He maintained that the organizers should strive to consolidate existing collectives and win the voluntary co-operation of the peasants.[21]

During the next few years, working morale and efficiency on the collective farms were low. The livestock of the country, moreover, was decimated, partly as a result of the lack of fodder and the spread of infectious diseases and partly because the peasants, who in the beginning had been called on to give up their animals to common ownership, slaughtered their stock by the wholesale. Figures cited by Stalin at the Communist party Congress in 1934 reflected the disastrous results of peasant and governmental activities in this field:

---

cultural products. Later there began a mass confiscation of the property of all well-to-do peasants. (A. Yugow, *Russia's Economic Front,* 1942, ch. III.)

[21] Albert Rhys Williams, a writer sympathetic to the Soviet regime, thus describes the treatment of the "kulaks" who, by various means, had resisted the drive toward collectivization: "In thousands the kulaks were marched to the stations where under OGPU guards they were deported to the lumber-camps in the North and new settlements in the faraway steppes and tundras. This in turn brought those who remained up in arms with ax and knife and sawed-off shotguns. In scores the communist officials perished—waylaid in ambush, clubbed to death, or hacked to pieces. And, throughout the land . . . the torch was applied to barns and houses of the collectives . . .

"According to the plan some twenty per cent of the small individual farms were to be united in the collectives. But so irresistible was the first drive that over half the peasants were swept into them. The abuses and excesses with which this was accompanied brought from Stalin the famous article of March 2, 1930, 'Dizziness from Success.' He pointed out that by zealots, intoxicated with the idea of creating communism in one jump, large numbers had been forced into the new farms against their will, middle peasants had been hounded like kulaks. He declared that joining or remaining in the collectives must henceforth be a voluntary act. The result was a stampede of millions back to the old way of farming, but the class war went on unabated. . . . In many regions opposition took the form of passive resistance. The fields went unsown or unweeded, crops were ungathered or left to rot on the ground. . . . In the wake of this followed what has been controversially called the 'acute food shortage' and the 'famines' of 1932. In any case undoubtedly many perished of hunger and disease." (Williams, *The Soviets,* pp. 180–1.)

	(millions omitted)		
	1916	*1929*	*1933*
Horses	35.1	34	16.6
Large horned cattle	58.9	68.1	38.6
Sheep, goats	115.2	147.2	50.6
Pigs	20.3	20.9	12.2

This great reduction in livestock, the sub-average harvests in 1931 and 1932, the heavy requisitions at fixed prices of grain, meat, milk, and other food products carried out by the Soviet authorities—not to speak of the unfavorable climatic conditions—combined to produce a disastrous famine in the first half of 1933, a famine which led to the death from hunger of millions of the Russian people.[22]

The Second Five-Year Plan. The First Five-Year Plan, despite its many shortcomings, had started the country well on the road to industrialization and at the same time had advanced the movement toward the collectivization of agriculture.[23] The Second Five-Year Plan, launched during the Russian famine, was to run from 1933 through 1937.

In view of the changed situation, the framers of the Second Five-Year Plan decided to give more attention than was given during the period of the first plan to the improvement of living standards. When the plan was initiated, it was announced that the emphasis would be shifted from industrial expansion to production of goods that would meet the daily needs of the people. In his report to the Seventeenth Conference of the Communist party on the Second Five-Year Plan in February, 1932, Kuibishev, chairman of the National Planning Department and member of the Politburo, said: "During the Second Five-Year Plan

[22] See *Encyclopaedia Britannica,* 1940 Edition, Vol. 19, pp. 744–5; Gordon, *op. cit.,* p. 400. Miss Gordon declares that "between the harvests of 1932 and 1933 it is estimated that perhaps nine million people died of hunger or its sequels." Other estimates vary anywhere from one to nine million. No official figures are available. During the famine not a word was printed in the Soviet press and no effort was made to obtain relief from abroad. It was officially denied that a famine existed and foreign journalists were refused permission to travel in the area. (For full information on the peasant problem and the famine see Webb, Sidney and Beatrice, *Soviet Communism,* pp. 358–94 and 561–72; Dean, Vera Micheles, "Industry and Agriculture in the USSR," *Foreign Policy Reports,* June, 1938, pp. 70–4; Chamberlin, William H., *Russia's Iron Age,* pp. 66–92; Yugow, A., *Russia's Economic Front,* etc., 1942, ch. III; Davies, Joseph E., *Mission to Moscow,* p. 390. Former Ambassador Davies gave the estimates of deaths of peasants during these days as between two and three millions.

[23] In 1935 it was estimated that about three fourths of the peasant homesteads, organized in 240,000 collective farms, cultivated nine times as much land as the decreasing number of peasants working along individualistic lines.

production of consumers' goods will increase two or three times and the level of consumption with respect to the most important articles of personal use will establish the position of the Soviet Union in 1937 as the most advanced country in the world." [24]

Under the Second Five-Year Plan, levy in kind upon the peasants was fixed for each region instead of being left to the arbitrary discretion of the grain-collecting authorities. Peasants were encouraged to develop, in addition to their collective farms, small individual homesteads, with a cow, pigs and chickens, and garden plots. There was an effort to insure that the payments given to farmers be more definitely related to the quantity and quality of work which each individual performed.

Under the plan there was less attempt to force exports in order to keep up imports, and the value of Soviet exports in gold rubles sharply declined. More foodstuffs remained within the country, and, as a result of this and the improvement of peasant morale and production, ration cards introduced for bread in 1929 were abolished toward the end of 1934 and the rationing of other food products ceased in October, 1935.

During this period there was an increasing emphasis on the necessity of unequal wages and salaries for work of unequal quality and responsibility. A new note of Soviet nationalism began to be emphasized, and a tendency to insist on the social desirability of stable family relationships appeared.

Soviet Purges. The Second Five-Year Plan, however, received far less attention from the people of the country than did the first plan, and its character was not fully known by many Russians until its completion in 1937. The chief reason for this was that the economic developments in the country were largely obscured by the many political changes of that period. It was during those days that numerous technicians and industrial managers were placed on trial on the charge of sabotage and "wrecking." Sergei M. Kirov, a member of the Politburo in Leningrad and a close political friend of Stalin, was assassinated in December, 1934, by an opposition communist named Nikolaev. This assassination was the signal for wholesale arrests and for a series of treason trials in the Hall of Columns of the Nobles' Club of Moscow

[24] Gordon, *op. cit.*, p. 401; *Ekonomicheskaya, Zhizn*, Feb. 9, 1932. According to the authors of the Second Five-Year Plan, its basic contention was "to liquidate completely all exploiting classes, to destroy forever the causes which breed the exploitation of man by man and the division of society into exploiters and exploited, i.e., to liquidate private ownership of the means of production." "Actually," as A. Yugow maintained, "the main task of the Soviet government was the completion and consolidation of the collectivism of Soviet agricultural economy" and the liquidation of the peasant opposition. (A. Yugow, *Russia's Economic Front*, etc., p. 11.)

between August, 1935, and March, 1938, which led to the extermination of practically all of the old bolsheviks. The list of accused read like the "Who's Who" of the Russian Revolution. One of the chief charges against those placed on trial was that they had conspired to wreck the Second Five-Year Plan and that they were influenced in their activities by Leon Trotsky, the former communist war leader.[25]

The second plan was officially completed in 1937, but its results were not published until 1939. Between the time of the completion of the plan and the official announcement of results Soviet papers were filled with stories of alleged sabotaging. *Pravda,* the official Soviet paper, on January 2, 1938, denounced the "fascist wreckers of the Trotsky-Bukharin bandit gang," who "worked their way into the fishing industry," and brought about a lag between the catching and the canning of fish. The February 9th issue condemned those saboteurs who "did not hesitate to employ the most criminal methods to wreck the monopoly of foreign commerce and hand over the Soviet Union into the vassalage of the fascist grabbers." Other issues denounced alleged sabotaging in the woolen, flour, electrical, machinery, clothing, forestry, cotton, housing, food, and other industries.

Even the military forces, according to the government, had become infested with "wreckers," the March 22, 1938, issue of *Pravda* announcing, "For a number of years the administration of the Red Army and the Navy was under such enemies as Marshal Tukhachevsky and General Gamarnik, Yakir, Uborevich, Orlov, Kork, Eideman, Sivkov. This military-fascist gang worked silently, selling and betraying their fatherland."

As a result of the liquidation of the old bolsheviks and others accused of sabotage and other crimes against the government, few of the veterans of the bolshevik revolution were in evidence at the Communist party Congress of 1938. Stalin was the only prominent bolshevik left of those active in 1917 on the Central Committee, on the Politburo, or among the People's Commissars.[26]

[25] "Three years after the assassination of Kirov," writes Souvarine, "Stalin declared that the principal assassin was Yagoda, his closest colleague, the chief of the GPU, the man Stalin had appointed Commissar of the Interior. He had ordered 117 executions after the crime, the imprisonment of 97 former representatives of the old bolshevik opposition to Leningrad which had been dissolved—with Zinoviev and Kamenev at their head—the condemnation of the 12 Stalinist chiefs of the local police, and finally the deportation to Asia of some 100,000 inhabitants of Leningrad." (Souvarine, *Stalin,* p. 598.) See also Florinski, *Toward an Understanding of the USSR,* p. 103; Pares, *Russia,* p. 134, 180.

[26] The Central Committee of the party, elected at the party convention in August, 1917, consisted of 24 members. Of these, seven—Lenin, Sverdlov, Uritzky, Dzerzhin-

To overcome this alleged sabotage and to stimulate the average worker to put forward his maximum efforts, piecework was made the order of the day; and Stakhanovism appeared upon the scene. Under Stakhanovism, especially competent workers were placed in plants, often under particularly favorable conditions, and urged to produce to the maximum, as pacemakers in the industry. Their high records of productivity were publicized, and the workers throughout industry were urged to emulate their examples. The results attained were applauded by the government, and the pacemakers were made the heroes of the day. The system, on the other hand, was condemned on the ground that it often forced an abnormal rate of speed, led to emphasis on quantity rather than quality, and resulted in a large destruction of machinery. Thus *Industry,* official organ of the movement, complained on December 1, 1937, that "Stakhanovism produces defective goods and destroys machines and tools." [27]

Some Results of the Second Plan. Despite the promise made by the economic planners that main emphasis under the Second Five-Year Plan would be placed upon consumption goods, the greatest progress made from 1932 to 1937 was, in general, in the heavy industry and particularly in those branches which were hardly in existence in prewar days—electric power, automobiles, tractors, airplanes, and the like. On account of the international situation, much attention was given to military preparedness, and a shift was made in many industries from the western borders to the Urals and the East. Few realized during

---

sky, Nogin, Shomian, and Artem—died a natural death. (Nogin was branded a traitor years after his death.) Six—Rykov, Bukharin, Zinoviev, Kamenev, Krestinsky, and Smilga—were executed. Sokolnikov at the time of the 1938 Communist Congress was in prison, Bubnov and Stassova had been branded traitors and had disappeared, and four—Lomov, Berzin, Muranov, and Milliutin—had disappeared without a trace. Trotsky was in exile, and Joffe had committed suicide in protest against the treatment accorded Trotsky. Madame Kollontai, though envoy to Sweden, was not politically active. Only Stalin was left.

The original Politburo, elected in October, 1917, consisted of seven members—Lenin, Zinoviev, Kamenev, Trotsky, Sokolnikov, Bubnov, and Stalin. One died a natural death, two were executed, one was in jail, one had been branded a traitor and had disappeared, one was in exile, and only Stalin was left.

"Practically the only original bolshevik leaders now left," wrote Ambassador Joseph E. Davies in February, 1937, "are Stalin, Kalinin, and Voroshilov. All the others have been banished or are dead, many 'liquidated' or shot." (Davies, *Mission to Moscow,* p. 46.)

[27] Gordon, *op. cit.,* p. 406. On July 10, 1940, the Supreme Soviet promulgated a decree providing "criminal responsibility of the heads of industrial undertakings and of the technical personnel for turning out products of poor quality" where such production had taken on a mass character. (See A. Yugow, *Russia's Economic Front,* etc., 1942, p. 23.)

those years the tremendous strides that the Soviet government was making in the development of defense industries.[28]

The Third Five-Year Plan. As the Second Five-Year Plan came to an end, the Soviet authorities began the formulation of the Third Five-Year Plan (1938–1942), the task of which, officially stated, was "to complete the construction of a classless socialist society and to accomplish the gradual transition from socialism to communism." In view of the increasingly tense international situation, the third plan was directed especially to the problem of strengthening the defenses of the nation. At the same time, like the preceding plan, it contained "a gigantic program for raising the material and cultural level of the laboring masses." [29] Its promoters aimed during the five years in which the third plan was to operate greatly to expand the production of various industrial commodities and services, to increase the productivity of labor, to lower manufacturing costs, and to improve the quality of goods in all branches of industry. Gross agricultural yield was to increase by over 50 per cent, and the aim of new construction schemes was "to bring industry closer to its raw materials and to consumption areas, so as both to rationalize transport problems and to develop the economically backward regions."

For the year 1939 the greatest increases in production were registered in the defense industries. In 1939, 1940, and the years immediately following, the aim of the government became that of achieving maximum production within a minimum of time in the defense industries while tightening discipline and seeking to reduce production costs.[30] The Third Five-Year Plan was interrupted by the outbreak of the Russo-German War.

Soviet Planning during the Second World War. With the outbreak of the Second World War, as has been said, attention was directed primarily to production for military purposes. "In 1937 defense expenditure amounted to less than one fifth of total budget expenditure, and in 1940 to about one third of the budget or one fifth of the national income." [31]

Not only did the distribution of resources shift more and more to

[28] See Albert Rhys Williams, *The Russians.*

[29] *New Republic,* Nov. 17, 1941, p. 652; A. Yugow, *Russia's Economic Front,* etc., 1942, p. 12. In submitting the Third Five-Year Plan, Molotov defined it as "the gigantic program of raising the level of national economy, of culture, of the general welfare. The Third Five-Year Plan is a program for a gradual transition from socialism to communism." (V. Molotov, *The Third Five-Year Plan,* 1939, p. 5.)

[30] See "Union of Socialist Soviet Republics," in *Britannica Books of the Year.*

[31] "Soviet Planning in War-Time," *Planning,* No. 196 (Nov. 17, 1942), p. 6.

armament plants and to the output of munitions of war but the Soviet government devoted much effort to the shifting of industry to the east, with the view of allocating it nearer to its actual and potential sources of supply and of decreasing the danger of the conquest of industrial plants by foreign invaders from the west. The government likewise conducted an intensive drive for more productive efficiency, the diminution of waste, the reduction of administrative staffs, and the drawing of increasing numbers of women into industry.

As the war progressed, the relative importance of the centers of production in the Urals and in Asiatic Russia increased enormously, especially during 1942 when the area lost to the Germans included three fifths of the prewar production of coal, iron ore, iron, pig iron, steel, and aluminum.

Basing his estimates, as is necessary, on the figures furnished by the Soviet government, Mr. A. Yugow, author of *Russia's Economic Front for War and Peace,* presents the following table indicating the growth of the gross output of industry in Russia from 1913 to 1940, and particularly under the First and Second Five-Year Plans and the first years of the Third Plan.[32]

GROSS OUTPUT OF INDUSTRY [33]

(In billions of rubles of 1926–27 price level)

	1913 *	1928	1933	1937	1940	1941	1942	1940	1940
						Planned		Times Greater Than	
								1913	1928
All industries	16.2	18.3	43.3	95.5	137.5	162.0	180.8	8.5	7.5
Output of Producers' Goods	5.4	6.0	23.1	55.2	83.9	103.6	112.0	15.5	14.0
Output of Consumers' Goods	10.8	12.3	20.2	40.3	53.6	58.4	68.0	4.9	4.4
Per cent of Producers' Goods in Total	33.3	32.8	53.3	57.8	61.0	63.9	62.2		
Per cent of Consumers' Goods in Total	66.7	67.2	46.7	42.2	39.0	36.1	37.8		

* For the territory of the USSR.

32 Mr. Yugow, an economist who participated actively in the planning and administration of Soviet industry at the outset of the Soviet regime, declares that Soviet figures are frequently inaccurate and biased, but that they are the only figures available. He measures the gross output of Soviet industry in rubles in terms of the 1926–27 price level. He declares that this method of measurement has its shortcomings, since the make-up of commodities in 1940 was no longer what it was in 1926–27; and that the prices of 1926–27 have not been maintained in the case of many commodities.

33 A. Yugow, *Russia's Economic Front,* etc., p. 14.

Results of Plans, 1928–1940 Summarized. Social developments in Russia since the First World War, and particularly since the beginning of the First Five-Year Plan, appear from the figures of the above table and from other sources.

1. Industrial Output. The industrial output increased in the twelve-year period from 1928 to 1940 under the five-year plans seven-and-one-half times. During the entire 27-year period from 1913 to 1940, that increase was eight-and-one-half fold.

2. Annual Increases in Production. During the first five-year period of planned production, the annual increase in gross product fluctuated from 11 to 27.3 per cent; in the second five-year period, the average annual increase was 17.1 per cent; and during the first three years of the third period, from 1938 to 1940, the average annual increase was 13 per cent.[34] These rates of growth were much higher than in pre-Soviet Russia and higher than in other lands. They were in part the result of the fact that the Soviet government had "extracted from the population a larger share of the national increase than had been attempted in any country in Europe or America." [35]

3. Producers' Goods versus Consumers' Goods. The chief advance in production was found in the producers' goods industries. The output of producers' goods increased during the dozen-year period of the plans fourteen-fold, but consumers' goods production multiplied during the same period only 4.3 fold.

The relative position of the consumers' and the producers' goods industry in the national economy changed radically since 1913. In this prewar year, producers' goods constituted but one third of the total output, and consumers' goods, two thirds. In 1940, on the other hand, producers' goods took up over three fifths (61 per cent) of the total industrial output, leaving less than two fifths (39 per cent) for consumers' goods.[36]

4. Industrial Workers. There was a great increase in the number of industrial workers during that period. By 1940 the number of such

[34] Yugow, *op. cit.*, pp. 15, 31–3; *Economics of Socialist Industry*, pp. 40, 92, Academy of Science, Moscow, 1940 (in Russian).

[35] Yugow, *op. cit.*, pp. 32–3. Mr. Yugow estimates that, in the Five-Year-Plan periods, long-term investments in the USSR were equal to between 22.6 per cent and 28.3 per cent of the national income.

[36] The production of coal increased from the prewar period about sixfold; of metals, fourfold; of electric energy, twentyfold; of chemicals, fifteenfold. On the other hand, the growth of consumers' goods was a much more moderate one, in some instances falling behind in proportion to the increase in the population during that period. This was the case in the cotton and woolen industries, which produced less in 1932 than in 1928.

workers had risen to over 30 millions. Although in 1930 only 3.4 per cent of the gainfully employed population were employed in large scale industry, in 1937 over 30 per cent were so engaged.

5. *Agriculture.* A revolution, as has been said, took place during the twelve-year period in agriculture. Instead of 26 million individual farms, mostly small, there were, by the early forties, 242,000 kolkhozes, embracing over 93 per cent of the peasant farms and 99.3 per cent of all land under cultivation.[37]

6. *Industry versus Agriculture.* Industry during those years became more important than agriculture in the national economy. While in 1913 60 per cent of the national income was derived from agriculture and only 40 per cent from industry, by 1940 the ratio was virtually reversed: 70 per cent of the income came from industry and about 30 per cent from agriculture.[38]

7. *Labor Conditions.* On the eve of the Second World War, labor conditions had considerably improved over the beginning of the First Five-Year Plan and over prerevolutionary days. The proportion of children working in the Soviet Union had decreased. The Soviet law prohibited all child labor below the age of 16.

The number of working hours had been considerably reduced. Before the Revolution the normal workday was usually 10 hours in length. This had been reduced in 1917 to 8 hours, and in 1929 to 7. White-collar workers had long before obtained a 6 hour day. The working day was again increased with the coming of the Second World War.

8. *Social Insurance.* From the Revolution to the Second World War there had been an expansion of the system of social insurance. In 1929 a decree was issued providing for old-age pensions. Toward the end of the Third Five-Year Plan this type of social insurance covered all persons employed in the cities. The worker in Russia had been for years covered by a system of health insurance. In 1931, however, this system was limited so as to apply only to workers who had been employed in a plant for at least two years, and non-members of unions were paid only 50 per cent of their wages. "This decree was motivated by the desire to bind workers to plants, but in practice it has deprived a considerable part of the workers of the right to relief in case of illness or injury." [39] A step backward, however, was taken in 1930 in connection with unem-

[37] *The Socialist Agricultural Economy of the USSR,* Moscow, 1939, p. 15; Yugow, *op. cit.*, p. 46.

[38] *USSR, The Land of Socialism,* Gosplan, 1939. *The Economics of Socialist Industry,* 1940, Report to the 18th Conference of the Communist Party, 1941.

[39] Yugow, *op. cit.,* pp. 166–7.

ployment insurance which was abolished by the Soviets "in view of the disappearance of mass unemployment in the USSR." [40]

9. Living Standards. Before the Second World War the standard of living, according to Yugow, was "undoubtedly higher than in pre-Soviet days" and during the late thirties rose steadily. In 1938, however, the Soviet workman was still more poorly fed than the French or German or even than the Bulgarian. "Compared with the Swedish workman," declares Yugow, "the Soviet worker, though he ate much more bread, had one third the meat, two fifths the fats, one third the milk, one tenth the sugar, and one fifteenth the eggs, not to speak of vegetables, fruit, and so on." [41]

10. Quality of Goods. While the quantity of goods turned out was much greater than before the First Five-Year Plan, the quality of the civilian goods produced was frequently poor. In steel and machine-making plants, for instance, rejections amounted to 2 billion rubles in 1940. "Tens of thousands of tons of metals are rejected," declared the report of Voznesensky in 1941, "on account of poor workmanship in the steel and metal-working plants." [42] The quality of purely military goods seems to have been far superior to that of many other commodities.

11. Efficiency. Much waste, carelessness, and inefficiency existed throughout the period in many of the plants which lacked a trained personnel. In submitting the Third Five-Year Plan, Molotov declared that "we still suffer from much mismanagement, wasteful expenditures, abominably great waste of raw materials, and squander much fuel and electric energy; keep our plant equipment idle for shamefully long periods, all of which means that there is no real effort to reduce costs of production and construction." [43]

[40] Decree of the People's Commissariat of Labor, October 11, 1930.

[41] Yugow, *op. cit.*, p. 212. Florinski, commenting on the results of the Second Five-Year Plan, declares that failure to accomplish the proposed lowering of consumers' goods necessitated an increase of wage rates for the five-year period of 151 per cent, instead of the estimated 55 per cent. "The absence of an index in the cost of living," he added, "makes it impossible to determine whether the increase in monetary wages has brought about an increase in wages." (Florinski, *Toward an Understanding of the USSR*, p. 163.

[42] *Pravda*, Feb. 19, 1941; quoted in Yugow, *op. cit.*, p. 21.

[43] See Yugow, *op. cit.*, p. 23. In his report to the 18th Congress of the Communist party Stalin spoke scornfully of some of the assignments under the Second Five-Year Plan as "fantastic, if not worse." The plans were over-fulfilled in some respects, under-fulfilled in others, thus making proper co-ordination impossible. As a result, Florinski believes "the practical usefulness of the plan very slight except as a slogan." (Florinski, *Toward an Understanding of the USSR*, p. 164.)

12. Cost of Production. The cost of production in Soviet industry at the outbreak of the Second World War was higher than that of foreign countries, and the productivity of labor was still low as compared with that of workers in other industrialized countries.[44]

13. Attendant Suffering. The plans for industrialization were carried out by the sternest decrees of the dictatorship and at the cost of great suffering.

[44] Yugow, *op. cit.*, p. 59. "The cost of production of manufactured goods is 30–50 per cent higher than in European countries, and their selling price in Russia is 100–200 per cent higher." Mr. Yugow maintained that high prices were determined by a high mark-up of the gross profit at every link of the chain and by a special sales tax added by the government to the price in its monopolistic control of trade. As for production per worker, in 1937 the average production of coal per worker in the USSR was 370 tons, whereas in France it was 195 tons, in Germany 435 tons, and in the United States 844 tons. Yugow, *op. cit.*, p. 184.

CHAPTER 27

The 1936 Soviet Constitution-Communist Party Controls

IN THE mid-thirties, while the Second Five-Year Plan was in the process of completion, the Soviet government, after having made numerous amendments to its 1924 Constitution, decided on the drafting of a new and more democratic constitution. The definite decision to change the constitution "in the direction of further democratization of the electoral system" was made on February 6, 1935, at the Seventh Congress of Soviets.

Adoption of the 1936 Constitution. A commission of 31, made up of economists, historians, and political scientists, was appointed under the chairmanship of Joseph Stalin to draft this new instrument. In June, 1936, the draft drawn by the Constitutional Commission was approved by the Presidium of the Central Executive Committee of the USSR and published. Following widespread discussion, the constitution was presented for adoption at a special congress and on December 5, 1936, following a ten-day session, was finally proclaimed the law of the land.

Socialized Property in the USSR. Maintaining that the Union of Soviet Socialist Republics was "a socialist state of workers and peasants," the 1936 Constitution declares that "the economic foundation of the USSR consists of the socialist economic system and the socialist ownership of the tools and means of production."

The term "socialist property," the Constitution reads, includes both state property ("the wealth of the entire people") and co-operative-collective property ("the property of separate collective farms and co-operative organizations").

EXTENT OF STATE OWNERSHIP. The 1936 Constitution is much more specific as to what constitutes state, co-operative, and private property in the Soviet Union than was the Constitution of 1918. Under the

Soviet form of government, the Constitution states, the main portion of the economic structure is state property. This includes "the land, mineral deposits, waters, forests, mills, factories, mines, railways, water and air transportation, banks, means of communication, and large state-organized farm enterprises (state farms, machine tractor stations, etc.), as well as municipal enterprises and the basic housing facilities in cities and industrial localities."

Co-operative Ownership. A considerable amount of the socialized property, however, belongs to co-operative enterprises in the farms and villages, and in these collectives such wealth as the machinery, livestock, and public buildings are the property of the group as a whole. "Every collective farm household [declared the Constitution], in addition to its basic income from the public collective farm enterprise, has in personal use a plot of land attached to the house and, as personal property, the subsidiary husbandry on the plot, the house, productive livestock, poultry and small farm tools—according to the statutes of the farming artel [co-operative productive society]." As for the land occupied by collective farms, that "is secured to them without payment and without time limit, that is, forever."

Private Enterprise. Alongside the socialist system of economy which is the dominant form of economy in the USSR, Article 9 of the Constitution affirms that "the law allows small-scale private enterprise of individual peasants and handicraftsmen based on their personal labor, provided there is no exploitation of the labor of others." [1]

Article 10 of the Constitution assures the right to a certain amount of personal property and of restricted inheritance. It declares: "The right of citizens to personal property in their income from work and in their savings, in their dwelling houses and auxiliary husbandry, in

[1] Dealing with the extent of socialized property a year after the adoption of the 1936 Constitution, Dr. Florinski declares: "At the end of 1937, the closing year of the Second Five-Year Plan, 98.7 per cent of all the means of production in the Soviet Union were officially stated to be 'socialist property,' that is, they were controlled either by the state or by the collective farms. Of the gross production of industry, 99.8 per cent came from state-owned enterprises, 98.6 per cent of agricultural production was supplied by state farms or by collective farms, and commerce was 100 per cent in the hands of socialist distributing agencies." (Florinski, *Towards an Understanding of the USSR,* p. 173.)

While governmental organizations employed nearly thirty millions of employees who were essentially servants of public authorities, there "are also in the USSR," declared the Webbs during the late thirties, "several millions of independent individual producers—handicraftsmen; inventors; free lance journalists and authors, who simply sell their copy to any public authority; unsalaried artists of every kind paid by fees; prospectors of minerals; hunters and fishermen on their own account; and even a remnant of isolated peasant agriculturists. More interesting are the (possibly) ten or twenty millions of members of *artels,* or co-operative productive societies, them-

household articles and utensils, and in objects of personal use and comfort, as well as the right of inheritance of personal property of citizens, are protected by law."

WORK AND PLANNING. "The economic life of the USSR," the 1936 Constitution adds, "is determined and directed by a state plan of national economy in the interest of increasing the public wealth, of steadily raising the material and cultural standard of the working people, and of strengthening the independence of the USSR and its capacity for defense." Work in the USSR is a duty and a matter of honor for every able-bodied citizen. In the USSR, the Constitution maintains, the principle of socialism is realized: "From each according to his ability, to each according to his work."

Government of USSR. Further, the 1936 Constitution declares that the USSR is a federal union based upon the federation of eleven republics. The union possesses many specified powers necessary for the joint operation of the eleven republics, all other powers being reserved to the constituent bodies. Each constituent republic has its own constitution and possesses the right to secede from the USSR.

Seven-odd years after the adoption of the 1936 Constitution, on February 1, 1944, the Soviet government adopted an important amendment to the Constitution which grants each of the 16 republics then composing the union permission to have independent international relations and to convert the Red Army into 16 federated republican armies.

LEGISLATIVE BRANCH OF THE SOVIET REPUBLIC. As in the former Constitutions, the highest body in the USSR is the Supreme Soviet, which possesses the exclusive legislative power of the country. It consists of two chambers: the Soviet of the Union and the Soviet of Nationalities. The Soviet of the Union is elected by electoral districts on the basis of one deputy for every 300,000 of the population. Thus the old system of indirect elections was abolished. The Soviet of Nation-

---

selves making in partnership every kind of household requisite or article of clothing; the members thus working in textiles, leather, wood, iron, and lacquer, and occasionally even working their own small mines of lead or coal. Even more numerous are the members of the quarter of a million collective farms or fisheries (*kolhozes*), in which nearly twenty-five millions of households unite in co-operative partnerships for their main crop or product, whilst conducting as independent individual producers their subsidiary enterprises in pig and poultry, dairy and garden products, beehives and winter handicrafts. . . . As a matter of fact, more than one half of all the adult inhabitants of the Soviet Union find themselves outside the ranks of public employees, even in the widest sense of that term" (Webb, Sidney and Beatrice, *The Future of Soviet Communism*, pp. 109–10. See also Williams, *The Russians*, p. 135.)

alities, on the other hand, is elected by constituent republics, autonomous republics, autonomous provinces, and national regions on the basis of 25 deputies from each constituent republic, 11 deputies from each autonomous republic, five deputies from each autonomous province, and one deputy from each national region.

The Supreme Soviet is elected for four years. The two chambers have equal rights and a law is considered adopted if passed by a majority of each. The sessions of the Soviet are held twice a year, and special sessions are convened at the call of the Presidium. In the case of disagreement between the two bodies, the question is referred to a conciliation commission composed of an equal number of members of both houses. If the conciliation commission does not arrive at an agreement, or if the agreement reached does not satisfy both houses, the question is considered a second time by the two Chambers. In case of failure to agree then, the Presidium of the Supreme Soviet dissolves the Soviet and the country is called upon to elect new representatives.

The Presidium referred to is a body elected at a joint sitting of the two Chambers, consisting of a Chairman, 11 vice-chairmen, the secretary, and 24 members. It is accountable to the Supreme Soviet and has power to convene the sessions of the Soviet, to interpret laws, to fix new elections, to hold consultations of the entire people on important matters, to rescind decisions of the People's Commissars, to exercise the right to pardon, to appoint and replace the high command of the armed forces of the country, and to declare a state of war in case of an armed attack upon the USSR or "in case of the need of fulfilling international treaty obligations of mutual defense against aggression."

The Presidium likewise possesses the authority to declare general or partial mobilization, to ratify international treaties, and to appoint and recall the country's representatives abroad. Eight days after the nazi invasion in 1941, all government power was concentrated in a single "War Cabinet" of five, then of eight, with Stalin as Chairman, known as the State Defense Committee.

The Constitution provides likewise for Supreme Soviets in each of the constituent republics elected by the citizens for four-year terms and a Presidium of the Supreme Soviet of the individual republic.

Executive Branch-Councils of People's Commissars. We have now covered the organization and powers of the legislative branches of the Soviet Republics. As for the administrative functions, those reside, under the 1936 Constitution, in the Councils of People's Commissars, appointed by the Supreme Soviet.

The Union of Socialist Soviet Republics possesses such a Council, as did also the individual republics. The Council of the Union is strictly subordinate to the Supreme Soviet, and the Councils of the republics are likewise subordinate to the republics' legislative branch. They are similar to cabinets in the western parliamentary governments.

The duties of the Council of the USSR are important and various. They include power to:

(1) Co-ordinate and direct the work of the corresponding commissariats of the republics and of the other economic and cultural institutions subordinate to it.

(2) Take measures to carry out the national economic plan and the state budget.

(3) Adopt measures "to secure public order, to defend the interests of the state, and to safeguard the rights of citizens."

(4) Exercise general supervision in the sphere of foreign relations.

(5) Fix the annual number of citizens to be called for active military service and direct the general organization of the armed forces of the land.

(6) Set up special committees and central administrations for economic, cultural, and defense reconstruction.

(7) Suspend resolutions and orders of the Councils of People's Commissars of the constituent republics and to annul their orders and instructions.

The Councils are made up of their chairmen and vice-chairmen, the heads of the State Planning Commission, of the Soviet Control Commission, of the Committees on Agricultural Products, on Arts, and on Higher Education, and, in addition, of the Commissariats of Defense, Foreign Affairs, Finance, Home Affairs, Justice, Health, Agriculture, which correspond roughly to government ministries in capitalist governments, and a somewhat longer list of commissariats connected with the management of many of the economic affairs of Russia. These include the Commissariats of Heavy Industry, Defense Industry, Light Industry, Food Industry, Timber Industry, State Grain and Livestock Farms, Railways, Water Transport, Communications, Foreign Trade, and Home Trade.

The State Planning Commission, as its name suggests, formulates the economic plans for all the industry, farming, trade, and transport of their country, and the Soviet Central Commission acts as "efficiency expert"' to investigate their operation.

Under the 1936 Constitution the heads of the various departments in Russia perform a different function from that of the Cabinet members in non-socialist and non-communist republics. They actually direct the operation of the industries of the country instead of applying rules and regulations for them to follow. The executive heads of the government are not elected for a fixed term of office, but may be removed at any time by the Supreme Soviet or its Presidium which appointed them. Theoretically at least, under the Constitution, the executive branch of the government is clearly subordinate to the legislative branch.

The Council of People's Commissars of the constituent republics contain a group of commissariats somewhat similar to that of the Union, except that, quite logically, they do not include Commissars for Defense, Foreign Affairs, Foreign Trade, Transportation, and Communication. In addition, however, the Councils for the individual republics include Commissars for Municipal Economy and Social Welfare.

The 1936 Constitution provides also for "soviets of working people's deputies of territories, provinces, regions, districts, cities, and rural localities, to be elected by the working people in the respective localities, and to serve for two years." Here, as in the case of elections of members of the Soviets of the Union and of the Constituent republics, elections are direct, the old pyramidal form of elections held under the former constitutions having been discarded.

THE SOVIET SYSTEM OF JUSTICE. The relationship of the Soviet judiciary to the Supreme Soviet is somewhat different from that of the executive. The Supreme Court of the USSR is elected, as is the executive, by the Supreme Soviet, but it is not, as is the executive, under the constant control of the legislature or removable by the Soviet at will. Judges are declared by the Constitution to be subject only to the law. They are independent of the executive branch and are elected by the Soviet for a term of five years, longer than the life of the Soviet. Lower courts in the country are likewise elected by the Supreme Soviets of the territories they serve; the "people's courts," or courts of first instance, being elected by popular suffrage for a term of three years.

A unique feature of the Soviet system of justice is that court cases are tried with the participation of "associate judges"—laymen selected from a panel of names and submitted by social and professional organizations, "except in cases provided by law." All judicial activity is supervised by the Supreme Court of the USSR. This court, however, does not have, as in the United States, the power to declare laws by the Supreme Soviet unconstitutional.

Perhaps the most independent office in the Soviet under the 1936 Constitution is that of the Procurator, an office similar to that of the Attorney General of the United States, but which has more power. He possesses "the highest supervision over the strict observance of laws by all the People's Commissariats and institutions subordinate to them, as well as by individual officials and also by citizens of the USSR." He is appointed by the Supreme Soviet for a term of seven years—longer than any other official. The Attorney General is not only given great powers of investigation and prosecution, but also has the appointment of all the lower state and district attorneys.

The government of all the smaller territorial units in the Soviets is, as has been indicated, similar to that of the All-Union government. The local officials have a twofold responsibility—to the local authorities who appointed them and to the commissariat in the higher government which corresponds with their type of work. "Thus a city health official is responsible both to the 'executive committee' of the city and also to the health officials of the province, while provincial health officials are responsible both to the provincial executive committee and to the All-Union Commissariat of Health. Conflicts between executives in any territory are resolved through the executives immediately superior to the complainants."

Rights and Duties of Citizens of the Soviet Republic. Chapter 10 of the 1936 Constitution defines the rights and duties of the Citizens of the Soviet Republic. The first of the rights guaranteed, according to the provisions of the Constitution, is the right to work. "Citizens of the USSR," Article 18 declares, "have the right to work, that is, the right to guaranteed employment and payment for their work in accordance with its quantity and quality. The right to work [the Constitution continues] is ensured by the socialist organization of the national economy, the steady growth of the productive forces of Soviet Society, the elimination of the possibility of economic crisis, and the abolition of unemployment."

The second right officially attributed to the citizens of the country by the revised Constitution is the right to leisure and rest. "The right to rest [the Constitution states] is ensured by the reduction of the working day to seven (7) hours for the overwhelming majority of the workers, the institution of annual vacations with pay for workers and other employees, and the provision of a wide network of sanitaria, rest rooms and clubs serving the needs of the working people."

Citizens in the third place, according to the Section on "Basic Rights and Duties," have "the right to material security in old age and also in case of sickness or loss of capacity to work. This right is ensured by the wide development of social insurance of workers and other employees at state expense, free medical service for the working people, and the provision of a wide network of health resorts at the disposal of the working people."

The fourth right set forth in this article is the right to education. "This right is ensured by universal compulsory elementary education, by education free of charge including higher education, by a system of state stipends for the overwhelming majority of students in higher schools, by instruction in schools in native language, and by the organization in factories, state farms, machine-tractor stations, and collective farms of free industrial, technical, and agricultural education for the working people."

The Constitution likewise declares the equal right of men and women in economic, cultural, social, and political life, and the special right of women to state protection in the interest of mother and child. The state shall provide a wide network of maternity homes, nurseries, and kindergartens and shall see to it that women in pregnancy have leave from work with pay.

According to the Constitution, equal rights are also to be accorded to all citizens irrespective of nationality or race, and "Freedom of religious worship and freedom of anti-religious propaganda" are recognized.

Civil Rights. Dealing with the question of civil rights, the Constitution of 1936 reads:

"In accordance with the interests of the working people, and in order to strengthen the socialist system, the citizens of the USSR are guaranteed by law: (a) Freedom of speech; (b) Freedom of the press; (c) Freedom of assembly and meetings; (d) Freedom of street procession and demonstrations." "These rights of citizens," Article 125 of the Constitution reads, "are ensured by placing at the disposal of the working people and their organizations printing shops, supplies of paper, public buildings, the streets, means of communication, and other material requisites for the exercise of these rights."

Citizens likewise are accorded the right "to unite in public organizations—trade unions, co-operative associations, youth organizations, sport and defense organizations, cultural, technical, and scientific societies; and the most active and politically conscious citizens from the ranks of the working class and other strata of the working people unite in the All-Union Communist party, which is the vanguard of the working people in their struggle to strengthen and develop the socialist system and which represents the leading nucleus of all organizations of the working people, both social and state."

The Constitution further maintains that "no person may be subject to arrest except by an order of the court or with the sanction of the state attorney"; that the homes of citizens and the secrecy of correspondence shall be respected; and that the right of asylum shall be granted to foreign citizens.

Civic Duties. As for the duties of Soviet citizens, they are set forth in Articles 131 to 133 inclusive, as follows:

> Article 131: It is the duty of every citizen of the USSR to safeguard and strengthen public socialist property as the sacred and inviolable foundation of the socialist system, as the source of the wealth and might of the fatherland, as the source of the prosperous and cultural life of all the working people. Persons making attacks upon public socialist property shall be regarded as enemies of the people.
>
> Article 132: Universal military duty shall be the law. Military service in the Workers' and Peasants' Red Army represents an honorable duty of the citizens of the USSR.
>
> Article 133: The defense of the fatherland is the sacred duty of every citizen of the USSR. Treason to the homeland—violation of the oath, desertion to the enemy, impairing the military might of the state, espionage—shall be punished with the full severity of the law as the gravest crime.

The Soviet Electoral System. Chapter XI of the 1936 Constitution deals with the electoral system. It maintains that the election of deputies to all soviets shall be effected by the voters "on the basis of universal, equal, and direct suffrage, by secret ballot . . . All citizens who have reached the age of 18, irrespective of race and nationality, religion, educational qualifications, residence, social origin, property status, or past activity shall have the right to take part in the elections of deputies and to be elected, with the exception of insane persons condemned by court with the deprivation of electoral rights. The election of deputies shall be equal; every citizen shall have one vote; all citizens shall take part in the elections on an equal basis. Women shall have the right to elect and be elected on equal terms with men. Citizens who are in the ranks of the Red Army shall have the right to elect and to be elected on equal terms with all citizens."

The election of deputies to all the Soviets, moreover, as has been before indicated, is to be effected under the Constitution by citizens through direct elections and the voting at elections is to be secret.

As for the nomination of candidates, the 1936 Constitution provides that "the right to nominate candidates shall be ensured to public organizations and societies of working people; Communist party organizations; trade unions; co-operatives; organizations of youth; cultural societies." And after election, "every deputy shall be obliged to report to the electors on his work and on the work of the soviet of working people's deputies and may at any time be recalled by decision of a majority of the electors in the manner prescribed by law."

Amendments to Constitution. The Constitution provides that amendments can be made by a majority of not less than two thirds of the votes of each of the Chambers of the Supreme Soviet of the USSR.

Changes in 1936 Constitution from Previous Constitutions. The 1936 Constitution differs from the earlier instrument in a number of important respects. In 1918, the government was officially regarded as a dictatorship of the proletariat organized for the purpose of suppressing the bourgeoisie, abolishing exploitation, and ushering in a socialist society. In 1936 the makers of the Constitution regarded this task as having been accomplished, and, in the Constitution, refer to Russia as having become "a socialist state of workers and peasants."

As for the governing body in Russia, the 1924 Constitution gave supreme power to the All-Union Congress of Soviets composed of some 2000 members elected indirectly and convening once a year. Between the sessions of this Congress, power was vested in a Central Executive Committee of somewhat more than 400 members sitting in two Chambers. This Committee convened twice a year and in turn elected a Presidium which possessed "supreme legislative, executive, and administrative" power between the Executive Committee's sessions.

The 1936 Constitution, on the other hand, vests the power of the government in the Supreme Soviet, a body composed of slightly more than 1000 members meeting twice a year and organized in two chambers roughly equal in numbers. The Soviet is elected directly by the voters rather than indirectly by the members of the next highest Soviet. The 1936 Constitution, on the other hand, eliminates the Central Executive Committee and vests limited functions between sessions in a Presidium of 36 members. These functions do not include the power to legislate.

The 1936 Constitution substitutes eight All-Union Commissariats, ten Union-Republic Commissariats, and five Chairman of Commissions—a total of 23 main departments—for the five All-Union Commissariats and six Unified People's Commissariats of 1924. The former All-Union Commissariats included Foreign Affairs, War and Marine, Home and Foreign Trade, Transport, Posts and Telegraphs. These, in general, are retained, except that Transport is divided into Railways and Water Transport, and Home and Foreign Trade have become two separate departments.

The six former Unified Commissariats included the Supreme Economic Council, Agriculture, Labor, Finance, Workers' and Peasants'

Inspection, and the Central Statistical Department. In the 1936 Constitution, the Supreme Economic Council is succeeded by the Commissariats of Heavy Industry, Defense Industry, Food Industry, Light Industry, Timber Industry. Agriculture is supplemented by State Grain and Livestock Farms; Labor is abolished, its functions being given over to the trade unions. Finance remains. The Central Statistical Department is replaced by the State Planning Commission. The Commissariats of Justice and Health are organized with a view of centralizing the functions formerly performed in localities. The OGPU, formerly an independent body, is included in the Commissariat of Home Affairs. The Committees on Agricultural Products, Art, and Higher Education are added as completely new departments.

As far as the judiciary is concerned, the 1936 Constitution gives greater independence to the Courts, and greater power to the Attorney General.

The earlier constitution had a somewhat different list of "basic rights and duties," and "the honor of bearing arms" was "granted only to the workers." The leisured members of the population, the pre-1936 constitutions declared, would fulfill other military duties.

According to the provisions of the previous constitution, deputies to the town and rural soviets were elected by the voters by a show of hands at meetings. Congresses of Soviets governing larger areas were elected by the lower soviets. The city population was given a distinct advantage over the rural population, one delegate being elected to the All-Union Soviet for every 25,000 electors in the cities and for every 125,000 electors—five times as many—in the provinces. The 1936 Constitution makes elections direct in the case of both local and central governments on an equal basis of representation and by secret ballot.

In previous Constitutions, several groups in the population were declared to be excluded from the ballot, including those who employed others with a view to profit, clergy, and former Czarist officials. The 1936 Constitution, as has been shown, grants suffrage to all except the mentally deficient.

As for amending the Constitution, in previous documents the All-Union Congress of Soviets could change the Constitution by a majority vote. Since 1936, however, it takes a two-thirds vote in each of the Chambers of the Supreme Soviet to pass an amendment.

1936 Constitution and Democracy. What is the significance of this Constitution from the standpoint of democratic development in Russia? There is a wide difference of opinion. Millions of communist sympathizers hailed this Constitution as signalizing the end of dictatorship and the beginning of a genuine democracy in Soviet Russia. Stalin praised what he termed "the consistent and fully sustained democracy" of the 1936 Soviet Constitution.

"Democracy in capitalist countries [Stalin went on], where there are antagonistic classes, is in the last analysis the democracy for the strong, democracy for the propertied minority. Democracy in the USSR, on the contrary, is democracy for all. But from this it follows that the principles of democracy are violated not by the draft of the new Constitution of the USSR but by the bourgeois constitutions.

"That is why I think that the Constitution of the USSR is the only thoroughly democratic constitution in the world." Yet almost in the same breath Stalin said: "I must admit the draft of a new Constitution really does leave in force the regime of the dictatorship of the working class, and also leaves unchanged the present leading position of the Communist party of the USSR." [2]

While, at first sight, Chapter 10 of the Constitution seems to guarantee civil liberty to all citizens, critics maintain that "no full civil rights are likely to be enjoyed by the people unless the secret police are abolished." [3]

In the years immediately following the adoption of the 1936 Constitution, while Russian citizens could speak freely within the limits prescribed by the party line, they were not supposed to criticize Stalin, the state, or its institutions. On political subjects in the broader sense there could be but one opinion, while, if the government expressed a particular point of view on any subject, be it art, poetry, or education, that opinion was usually the official opinion of Russians who desired to keep out of trouble. Of open criticism of governmental practices under this Constitution there was a great deal, but that criticism was largely confined to details. A network of government secret agents covered the country. Commenting on the work of these agents, Harold Denny of the *New York Times,* declared in 1937: "Persons have been sent to prison or to exile for some remark, made at a private party, that a secret agent there among the guests construed as disloyal. When the people speak at all on any touchy subjects they speak in whispers." [4]

Although the 1936 Constitution accorded to citizens the right to join "public organizations," no organization is allowed in the Soviet Union unless it is officially sanctioned. Only one political party and one group of unions are permitted. All organizations meet, furthermore, under

[2] *Stalin on the New Soviet Constitution,* pp. 22, 23; Norman Thomas and Joel Seidman, *Russia—Democracy or Dictatorship?,* p. 10; Florinski, *op. cit.,* p. 140.

[3] Thomas and Seidman, *op. cit.,* p. 15.

[4] *New York Times,* September 15, 1937.

party control. The Communist party group prepares or approves the agenda of such meetings and the important decisions made at the meetings are usually prepared in advance by higher authorities.

Article 126 specifically declares that the Communist party "represents the leading nucleus of all organizations of the working people, both social and state." In view of this provision, the question was soon raised: "Can real freedom exist if the Communist party is by law made the leading nucleus of all other organizations, particularly if, as has been so often maintained, there is no real freedom within the Communist party?" The ordinary member, it was contended, might, under these conditions, safely vote only for the proposals advanced by or with the approval of the party nucleus.

THE RUSSIAN PRESS. Even though the 1936 Constitution proclaims the freedom of the press, critics have pointed to the fact that only official or approved bodies, following the adoption of this Constitution, as before its enactment, may publish papers, and little or no deviation from governmental and party policies is permitted. Members of official boards are invariably party members, who may forfeit both membership in the party and their freedom if they refuse to follow party dictates. The editors of the papers receive news of events in Russia and outside of the country from government news agencies, and the news released by these agencies is that which the government desires to be read by the Russian people. Important news items are often suppressed for long periods.

The Russian press, in other words, is looked upon primarily as a propaganda agency for the Soviet government. Much more than being a purveyor of news, declared Albert Rhys Williams, a warm sympathizer with the Soviet government, in 1937, the press is an instrument for mobilizing the people's minds and energies for concrete tasks. "On all major issues," he wrote, "it [the press] presents a solid, unserried front. Occasionally its columns are open to hot discussions on most questions of the day. But when the debate is closed, or any crisis arises, every organ, from the biggest in Moscow down to the tiniest sheet in a mountain village, speaks in a single voice." [5] As for books, every volume, before publication, must bear a permit from the censor and "no book which seems to the censor hostile to Soviet ideology will be accepted." [6] With the shifting of the party line, a book which is accepted one day may be banned the next.

Freedom of movement after the adoption of the Soviet Constitution

[5] Albert Rhys Williams, *The Soviets,* p. 352.
[6] Williams, *op. cit.,* p. 378.

of the mid-thirties continues to be restricted, internal passports being necessary for those traveling from one part of the country to another—a regulation observed since the end of 1932.[7]

Worship in the Soviet Union. While freedom to worship is officially guaranteed, the Soviet government continued for many years to prohibit religious teaching to persons under 18 in groups larger than three. Religious schools were not allowed. However, following 1936, civil rights were restored to the clergy, school manuals were revised, with omission of the former vigorous attacks on religion, the vast publishing project of the Godless Union was suspended, a theological institute was established in Moscow, and, in September, 1943, during the Second World War, Metropolitan Sergius was elevated to the Patriarchate. Other trends toward the re-establishment of traditional religious rights are in evidence, while an increasing number of people attend church services.[8]

Education. In the field of education, increasing numbers of the population in the thirties, as the Constitution provided, were able to enjoy educational facilities. Illiteracy was being wiped out, and "higher education was fostered in a manner never dreamt of under the Czars."

On the other hand, political orthodoxy was being constantly required of the teachers in the schools and universities, and many teachers were dismissed, imprisoned, and shot for the lack of it. Sidney and Beatrice Webb, ardent champions of the Soviets, declared that, within and without the educational institutions, Soviet thought was in danger of reverting to the doctrinal rigidity of the Orthodox Church. "There is at present," they wrote, "too frequently an attempt to deal with problems, not by scientific investigation of the facts, but by the application of phrases culled from the writings of Marx and Engels, and now also from those of Marx and Stalin. Any conclusion in other terms is often not demonstrated to be scientifically incorrect, but summarily denounced as being either a 'left deviation' or a 'right deviation'; that is to say, as unorthodox." [9] The same was true in drama and in the arts.

[7] Thomas and Seidman, *op. cit.*, pp. 22 *et seq.*

[8] Moscow dispatch from Harold Denny in the *New York Times*, October 24, 1938; Pares, *Russia*, p. 148 *et seq.*

[9] Sidney and Beatrice Webb, *Soviet Communism*, p. 997; Thomas and Seidman, *op. cit.*, pp. 28–31; *The Annals of American Academy of Political and Social Science*, Nov. 1938, pp. 254, 259; *Information Service*, Federal Council of Churches, Dec. 11, 1943; *Soviet Russia Today*, Oct., 1943.

Ambassador Joseph E. Davies (*Mission to Moscow*, p. 396), dealing with the expansion of educational facilities under the Soviets, declared that while, in 1913, it was estimated that 67 per cent of the population was illiterate, by 1940, it was

FREEDOM FROM ARREST AND THE SECRET POLICE. The 1936 Constitution, as has been said, guaranteed the inviolability of the person and the home and freedom from arrest except by order of the court or sanction of a state attorney. However, as many critics have pointed out, the secret police are not bound by these provisions. Article 103 of the 1936 Constitution provides that "cases in all courts shall be tried with the participation of people's associate judges, except in cases especially provided for by law." The difficulty lies in the fact that other provisions are made for political offenses and that any offense may be construed as political.

The 1936 Constitution does not provide for the right of *habeas corpus* nor does it grant to a citizen the right to demand a prompt and open trial or a trial by jury. In the years following the adoption of the Constitution, as in previous years, the accused has had no right to know the charges against him until twenty-four hours before the trial. He possesses no right to have witnesses summoned in his behalf, nor to have his relatives notified that he is under arrest. He can hire counsel, but defense counsel seldom has the courage to deny charges pressed by the state. Sometimes the counsel for the defense considers it his duty to outdo the prosecution in affirming the guilt of the accused.[10]

Under the Constitution of the thirties, the Russian secret police still continue to function. They are no longer known as the Cheka or OGPU, but are controlled by the Commissariat of Internal Affairs, the NKVD. This Commissariat has been described as "a state within a state, with its own police, its own laws, its own courts, and its own army, . . . answerable only to the Politburo and Stalin. . . . The secret police are omnipresent, and every important train, every large station, every large factory, every hotel, every town, almost certainly has its agent or agents." [11]

---

claimed that illiteracy had been wiped out. The number of colleges and higher technical schools had increased from 91 in 1915 to 592 in 1936. The number of children attending schools was estimated at 3½ times the number prior to the First World War.

[10] Speaking of the conduct of the Moscow trials, Joseph E. Davies declared: "If any demonstration of the wisdom and desirability of the principles of Anglo-Saxon jurisprudence for the protection of the accused by the presumption of innocence, the right of counsel, the right of refusal to testify against one's self, the writ of habeas corpus, and the soundness of Anglo-Saxon law from the Magna Charta to the Bill of Rights, were required, it would be found in this proceeding." (Davies, Joseph E., *Mission to Moscow*, pp. 49–50.

[11] Thomas and Seidman, *op. cit.*, p. 33. "The Terror here," wrote Ambassador Joseph E. Davies in April, 1938, "is a horrifying fact. There are many evidences here in Moscow that there is a fear that reaches down into and haunts all sections of the community. No household, however humble, apparently, but what lives in constant

To the secret police are given the political offenders. Trials are usually secret. The accused are arrested, often in the middle of the night, without any formality. The trials are not concerned with ordinary court procedures. Political offenders cannot demand counsel as a right. The verdicts are purely administrative affairs. The family may never be told of the verdict arrived at.

THE SUFFRAGE. The 1936 Constitution provides for universal, equal, and direct suffrage by secret ballot. However, Soviet critics have brought out the fact that this type of suffrage may mean little when there is no right of organized opposition at the polls.

In the elections to the Supreme Soviet of the USSR in December, 1937, and in the elections to the Supreme Soviets of the constituent and of the autonomous republics in June, 1938, "only one candidate was submitted to the voters in each electoral district, although several candidates had been nominated by various organizations during the preliminary discussions." [12]

To bring about the withdrawal in each district of all the candidates but one, declared Rose Somerville, "some machinery must have been in operation which is not revealed by the public record. Some influence, probably the Communist party, made the several nominees aware of the desirability of avoiding public contest." [13]

In both elections the nomination of candidates was by the showing of hands, the secret ballot being used only in the final voting. No registration of voters was required, the list being prepared by the local soviets. Authorities took check on those who did not vote. Before the elections of December 12, 1937, *Pravda* gave full instructions as to how to vote. It declared that each elector would receive ballots containing the names of candidates for membership in the Soviet of the Union and the Soviet of Nationalities; that he must not write anything

---

fear of a nocturnal raid by the secret police (usually between one and three in the morning). Once a person is taken away, nothing of him or her is known for months —and many times never—thereafter. . . . It is commonly alleged that the secret police of this proletarian dictatorship are as ruthless and as cruel as any during the old Czarist regimes. It seems to be an old Russian custom." (Joseph E. Davies, *Mission to Moscow,* pp. 302–3; see also pp. 400–1.)

[12] Florinski, *op. cit.*, p. 141; see also Albert Rhys Williams, *The Russians,* pp. 84–6. "In practice," declared Williams, "all candidates are approved by the [communist] party."

[13] Rose Somerville, "The New Soviet Elections," in *The American Quarterly on the Soviet Union,* October, 1938, pp. 71–2. In the Supreme Council elections in December, 1937, about 20 per cent of the candidates in the Council of the Union and about 30 per cent in the Council of Nationalities were "non-party" people. (W. H. Chamberlin, *The Russian Enigma,* pp. 152–3; see also Sir Bernard Pares, *Russia,* p. 180.)

upon these ballots, but merely hand them in except that, if there were more than one candidate for a particular office, he must cross out the names of the candidate whom he disapproved. "May the elector," *Pravda* asked, "write new names in the ballot?" The answer given was "No, he may not." Thus to write in a name was to render a ballot invalid. After seeing that the ballots given him were in order, the voter put them in an envelop, sealed them, and placed them in a box.

The Communist Party. The government was thus, in the years immediately following the adoption of the 1936 Constitution, as prior to the Constitution, the government of the Communist party. Of the total membership of 569 in the Council of the USSR in the late thirties, 81 per cent were members or candidates of the Communist party and of the total membership of 574 in the Council of Nationalities, 71 per cent were drawn from the ranks of the party. The remainder was made up of people described as "non-party bolsheviks." [14]

In the twenties, Stalin maintained that control of the government was centralized in the Communist party. "In the Soviet Union, in the land where the dictatorship of the proletariat is in force, no important political or organizational problem is ever decided by our soviets and other mass organizations without directives from our party. In this sense, we may say that the dictatorship of the proletariat is substantially the dictatorship of the party, as the force which effectively guides the proletariat." [15]

Addressing on November 25, 1936, the congress of the Soviets which adopted the text of the 1936 Constitution, Stalin declared, as we have stated earlier, that the draft of the new Constitution actually leaves in force the regime of the working class as well as it preserves unchanged the present leading position of the Communist party.[16]

The nature of the Communist party control of government, as he saw it, was thus described in the early forties by Albert Rhys Williams in his book, *The Russians:*

> Though distinct from the government the communists largely control it. The party openly admits, says Stalin, that it guides and gives general direction to the government.
>
> This is putting it modestly. As the only legal party the communists enjoy a complete monopoly in the political field. Almost automatically the party decision of today becomes the Soviet law of tomorrow. Almost exactly as the Five-Year Plans are outlined by the party, they are adopted by the government.
>
> Control is achieved, not by arbitrary imposition of the party's will, but

[14] Florinski, *op. cit.*, p. 143. [15] Stalin, J., *Leninism,* Vol. 1, p. 23, 1928.
[16] See quotation from *Stalin on the New Soviet Constitution* on text page 423.

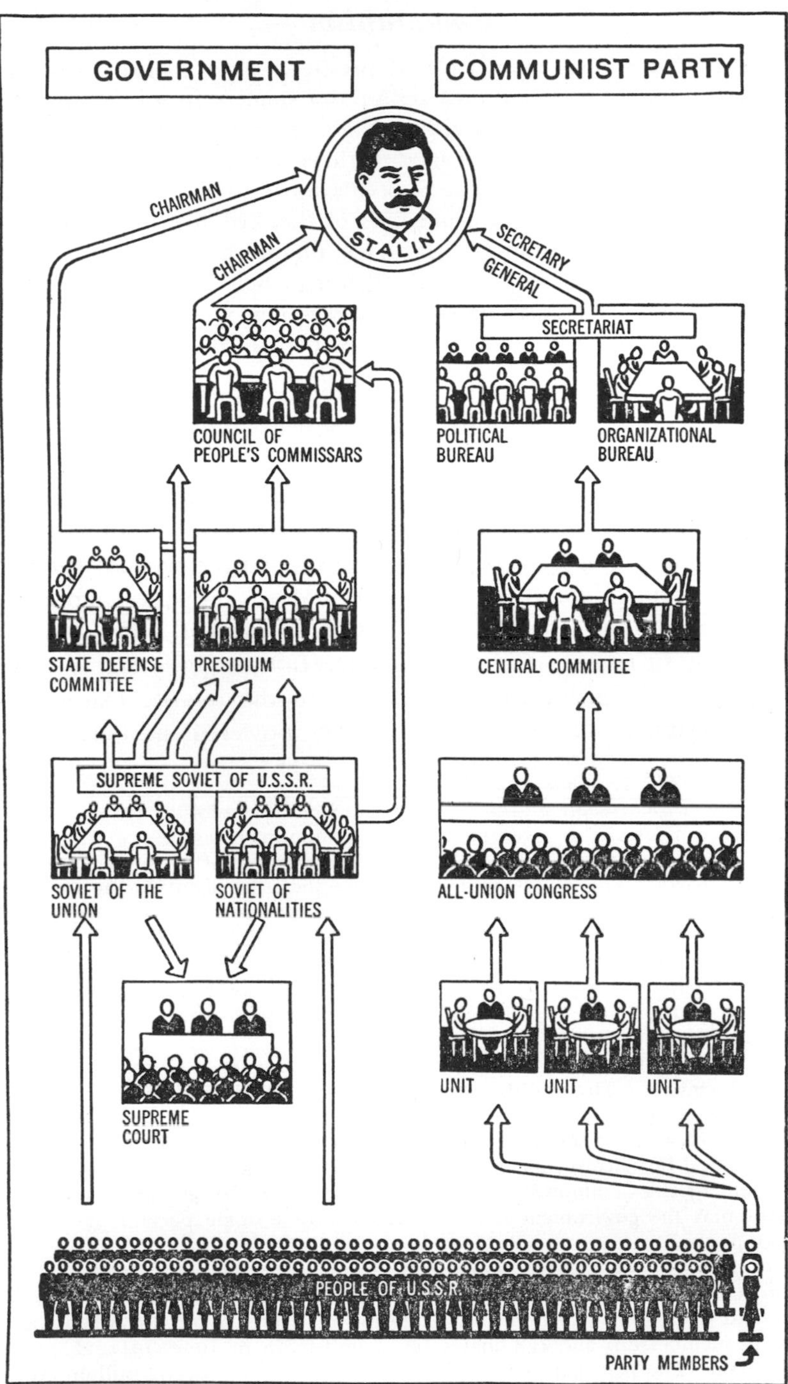

Chart paralleling the structure of the federal government of the USSR and that of the Communist party. Only party members elect party officials, but all Soviet voters can vote for government deputies. (Courtesy ***Life*****)**

by using its tremendous influence and prestige. As a compact, disciplined body with all its parts moving into action as a single unit, presenting a solid front on every issue, it carries decisive weight in every council. Members of the party, pledged to carrying out its directions, are commissars in every cabinet, make up three fourths of the Supreme Soviet, head most of the trusts and universities, staff the high commands of the Red Army. They likewise hold most of the key positions in the labor unions, co-operatives, and press. Upon its members in these organizations, using 'their influence and all their arts of persuasion,' the party depends for carrying out its policies. If they do not, it straightway discredits, demotes, or deposes them.[17]

Mr. Williams quotes Lenin's saying about the Russian people that "we are a drop in the sea and we can govern only if we adequately express what they feel." [18]

The All-Union Communist party membership varied from 1905 to 1939 from less than ten thousand to about two and a half million as follows: beginning of 1905, 8,400; beginning of 1917, 23,600; beginning of 1920, 431,400; January, 1929, 1,532,300; March, 1939, 2,479,000.[19]

In criticizing the above concentration of control, the student of Russia must, of course, give due consideration to the social, economic and political background of Russia and to the intense fear that the Soviet government had of attack by other powerful nations.

[17] Williams, *The Russians*, pp. 88–9.

[18] In June, 1938, Joseph E. Davies, then U. S. Ambassador to Russia, wrote regarding the control of the government by the communists, as he saw it, as follows:

"The government in fact consists of a very small group of men, who control the Communist party. The government is no more than the agent of the Communist party, and takes orders from it. Realistically, the government is in fact one man —Stalin, the 'strong' man, who survived the contest, completely disposed of all competitors, and is completely dominant. He appears to be the type of 'easy boss,' quiet, self-effacing, but nevertheless a real power. The government is a dictatorship not 'of the proletariat,' as professed, but 'over the proletariat.' It is completely dominated by one man.

"The Communist party is governed by a Central Committee of approximately one hundred members. The Politburo, consisting of eleven members, is a kind of board of directors. It runs the party and the government. These organizations do the will of Stalin. There is obviously no 'opposition.' " (Davies, *op. cit.*, pp. 402–3.) Sidney and Beatrice Webb, on the other hand, while admitting control of Russian government by the Communist party to an extent "it would be hard to exaggerate," maintain that the government is not controlled by a single person. (*Soviet Communism*, p. 429.)

[19] Florinski, *op. cit.*, p. 110; figures include members and candidates. They are from article by A. Bubnov (figures to 1930), *History of Communist Party of Soviet Union*, and (1934 and 1939) from 18th Congress of party. Albert Rhys Williams put the party membership and candidates for membership in June, 1942, at 4,500,000. (See Williams, *The Russians*, p. 88.) Besides these there are several million members of the Comsomol—the All-Union Leninist Communist League of Youth—and several million Young Pioneers—members of the children's organization from 10 to 16 years of age.

CHAPTER 28

Soviet Economic and Social Institutions and Policies

As THE Russian political state in the inter-war years underwent numerous changes, so with the industrial structure of the Soviet Union. We have already commented on the various changes in public, private, and co-operative industry in Russia before, during, and following the New Economic Policy, and the shift, in the early years of the Soviet government, toward and away from workers' control of individual industries and plants.

Following the days of workers' control the pendulum swung toward a rather rigid supervision of industry by the Supreme Council of National Economy. Under the NEP the situation again changed, and control was again, to some extent, decentralized.

Industrial Organization. In the late thirties the People's Commissariat of the USSR constituted the highest administrative organ for each branch of industry. Within the Commissariat were contained a number of departments. Each department had under it industrial boards or commissions, known as trusts or combines,[1] which grouped together factories, mines, and mills in specified industries and territories, under one Commissar.

The directors of the boards, or combines, were "trustees" of the state property entrusted to them. They were appointed by the People's Commissars and were removable at the end of any year at the will of the higher authorities. Usually the board consisted of a president, a secretary, and from three to twelve members, all of whom gave their en-

1 The term *trust* is usually employed in USSR, according to the Webbs, to designate what may be regarded as a "horizontal" combination, in which factories and other establishments producing similar commodities are united for management and sales. The term *combine* or *combinat,* on the other hand, seems to be used to describe "vertical" trusts, in which establishments are included which produce for each other, as when coal and iron mines produce for steel mills and automobile plants.

tire time to their duties. The Commissars aimed to secure among the members of each trust or combine a "Red" or political director—as a direct representative of the Communist party—a technical director, a factory director, a commercial director, and a general director. But there was no rigid uniformity as to their make-up.

Each trust or combine, after consultation with the People's Commissar and with the workers in their several trade unions, appointed a manager for each factory or plant, and frequently assigned specialist technicians to it. The general plant manager, after consultation with the directors, appointed the staff of the factory, and, together with heads of the departments, directed all of the plant's operations, including such auxiliary sections as the medical department, restaurants, and consumers co-operatives. In each plant, besides the manager, could usually be found a representative of the trade unionists of the plant and of the Communist party nucleus, who advised with the manager on problems of production and labor relations, assisted in stimulating the workers to greater productivity, and helped in the conduct of the educational, recreational, and co-operative organizations of the workers.

The trusts in the large- and middle-sized state industries numbered in 1940 over 600. Half of these—the big trusts—covered about 80 per cent of the total state industries.[2]

The departments in the People's Commissariat had large powers during the thirties in dealing with the production of the trusts, combines, and enterprises. They provided technical and financial guidance and controlled the sale of goods produced and the supply of raw materials. They called likewise on special councils within the Commissariat to furnish information and advice on various technical and scientific questions.

Under the industrial plan as evolved, every industrial enterprise and every trust received a definite assignment which specified the volume of goods to be produced, the price and quality of the goods, and the cost of production. The latter consisted of the cost of raw materials and

[2] A small number of trusts, called monopoly trusts, combined all the enterprises of a given branch of industry in the whole union. Such, for instance, were the Rubber Trust, the Silk Trust, and the Urals' Asbestos Trust. In some industries there were several trusts. Thus the oil, cement, and a few other industries had four trusts each, but in the vast majority of the industries in the Soviet Union there were a number of separate trusts in the various parts of the union. On January 1, 1936, the USSR possessed 574,064 industrial enterprises, which included 61,428 large enterprises. (*Statesmen's Year Book,* 1941.) The smaller enterprises are controlled by the People's Commissariats of the constituent republics and other subordinate organs. Trends during the thirties were in the direction of greater differentiation and specialization. See also Williams, *The Russians,* p. 133.

fuel supplied at fixed prices, labor costs, taxes, and other necessary expenses. In order to calculate costs the actual cost of production of the preceding year was first estimated, and from this figure a certain percentage prescribed in the plan was deducted. If the enterprise kept its costs within the prescribed limits without a reduction in the quality of its goods, the income and outgo of the enterprise was so balanced as to produce a "planned profit." [3]

Before the Second World War it was the aim of the Soviet government to make practically every branch of industry self-supporting. The device adopted for the purpose of achieving this aim was to fix the price of every commodity at a figure representing the average cost of production. The losses in some of the enterprises under this plan were made up by the gains of other undertakings in the same industry. In carrying out its function of producing and distributing its particular product, each trust was given power to enter into contracts, and to borrow money on the security of its working capital, but not of its fixed capital. In practice it contracted for the purchase of raw materials, paid wages on the basis of collective contracts with the trade unions, and entered into contracts with trading organs for the disposal of its finished product.[4]

When an enterprise had fulfilled its task and made a "planned profit," it retained four per cent of the profits, which were paid into the "director's fund" (consisting of contributions from profits). If the profits exceeded those planned, half of the surplus profits was turned over to the "director's fund." This fund was used in building houses for the employees and for cultural activities, bonuses, and technical improvements.

Domestic and Foreign Trade. We have already dealt with the development of retail trade in the early years of the Soviet government.[5] In the early forties, the vast proportion of retail trade in the cities was conducted in state stores mainly operated directly under the Commissariat of Home Trade. Some of these, however, were run under the supervision of city soviets or other city units, others were operated by state-owned trusts or enterprises as an outlet for their particular products, or by the Central Co-operative organization. But in all cases the Soviet government controlled their policies.[6] By 1937 the state stores

[3] Florinski, *op. cit.*, p. 182.

[4] "If it desires to renew or extend its plant or to erect new factories, it can do this either by capitalizing its reserve fund, by raising a loan, or by securing a direct grant from the state for that purpose." (Maurice H. Dobb, in *Encyclopaedia Britannica,* 14th Edition, Vol. 19, p. 708.)

[5] See text, pp. 392–93.

[6] Sikes, *Contemporary Economic Systems,* p. 292.

carried on over two thirds of the total retail trade. Consumers' co-operatives in the cities had been liquidated two years before, although the rural co-operatives continued in operation on an extensive scale.[7]

At the end of the period of rationing in 1935 a rather complicated system of open and closed stores at which prices greatly varied was superseded by open commercial stores. Uniform prices were established for all stores within each of eight zones. Prices differed as between various zones, the price differentials, with one exception, being based on difference in costs. In one zone, prices were kept low to attract workers to the region with a view to its industrial development. Following the new system, the stores became more attractive, and greater initiative was evidenced in the displaying and selling of goods.

Under this new-set-up, the retail stores purchase from wholesale enterprises at a price which covers costs, and sell the goods to the customer at the wholesale price plus the retailing expenses. The state wholesale establishment purchases goods from the manufacturing or processing undertaking at cost of production plus a turnover tax which may vary from 2 to 90 per cent, depending on whether the state wishes to encourage or discourage the use of an article. The tax paid is, of course, passed on to the retail store and customer.

As for foreign trade, that is a government monopoly under the jurisdiction of the Commissariat of Foreign Trade, which controls the volume of trade and its general character. The actual task of importing and exporting goods is left to various state trusts, which obtain special licenses issued by the Commissariat of Foreign Trade and its respective departments. As in other nations, the Soviet government maintains trade delegations in each country with which it has normal trade relations. These delegates have the right to purchase goods for importation and to sell Russian exports. By special decrees various government departments select those state and co-operative enterprises which are authorized, under the control of trade delegations, to engage in foreign trade. The Soviets look upon the import aspect of foreign trade as the more important, the goods that are exported merely serving as means of paying for imports.

Banking. The state virtually monopolizes the banking and credit system of the country. The Soviet banking system includes the State Bank, or *Gosbank,* the Savings Bank, the Bank of Foreign Trade, the Bank of State Trading Enterprises, or *Torgbank,* and four long-term investment banks. The latter include (1) a Long-term Bank for Industry, or *Prombank,* (2) a Central Bank for Municipal Economy and

7 See Harry W. Laidler and Wallace J. Campbell, *The Consumer Co-operative Movement* (L. I. D., 1937), pp. 35–38.

House Building, or *Tzekombank,* (3) the All-Russian Co-operative Bank, or *Vsekobank,* and (4) the Agricultural Bank, or *Selkhozbank.* All banking institutions are agencies of the state and are closely connected with the People's Commissariat of Finance.

The Gosbank (State Bank) is the one source of short-term credit. It was formed in 1921 and two years later was named the State Bank of the USSR. Its functions are similar, in many respects, to those of the central banks of other countries. Although the bank has its own capital subscribed by the state and is a separate legal unity, operating independently on a commercial basis, it is, in actual practice, little more than a department of the Commissariat of Finance.

The directors of the Gosbank are all state officials. The chairman of the board of directors is the Commissar of Finance. Other board members are the chairman of the four long-term banks, the chairman of the Bank for Foreign Trade, one representative from each Federated Republic, and members appointed by the government to represent different branches of the national economy.

The Gosbank has the sole power of issuing bank notes and, with minor exceptions, is the depository of free cash reserves of all credit institutions. If the bank makes any profits, half of them go to the Treasury as revenue; 5 per cent to staff welfare; not more than one fourth of one per cent to the bonus fund, and the remainder to reserves.

The bank's principal department is devoted to general credit planning, the department being divided into subsidiary sections for every branch of the national economy. An important section of the bank is the foreign department.[8]

Every quarter each enterprise presents to the branch of the Gosbank with which it has an account estimates of its credit and cash requirements. The special planning board of the bank, on receipt of these estimates, decides whether the enterprise needs the funds requested. The proposals for the extension of funds by the local banks then go to the regional and finally to the central bank at Moscow for consideration. A consolidated credit plan is formulated and sent to the State Planning Commission, which body fits all of the various requests for funds into the general plan for the period. The credit to be extended is then allocated among the various administrations, trusts, and enterprises, and each enterprise receives from the branch bank instructions as to the credit supply available to it for the ensuing quarter and the purpose for which the credit is given. The interest rates charged in-

[8] For a detailed description of the banking system, see L. E. Hubbard, *Soviet Money and Finance.*

dustry following 1936 varied from 2 to 4 per cent—4 per cent on planned and unplanned loans; 2 per cent on loans on goods in transit.

The collective farms secure some credit from the Gosbank, but obtain most of their credit from the state agricultural collective organizations, which supply loans of seeds and fertilizer, and from the machine tractor stations, which maintain a tractor and machinery service.

The Gosbank closely supervises the use of the loans made and, should the loans be inefficiently or dishonestly handled, may stop further credit extensions while an investigation is made. Unplanned loans are also given in cases of emergency.

As for the banks organized for the extension of long-term credit, the Prombank (Long-term Bank for Industry) supplies funds to enterprises coming under the Commissariats of Heavy, Light, Timber, Food, and Local Industries, and also to those under the Departments of Civil Aviation, Roads, and Cinema.[9] Though called a bank, the Prombank is, in reality, a department of the Finance Commissariat charged with the carrying out of the planned capital development of the country. Most of the funds supplied since 1932 are in the nature of non-payable grants rather than loans. The Tzekombank (Central Bank for Municipal Economy and House Building) finances the construction of dwelling houses, scientific, social, educational, and health buildings, and municipal enterprises. The Selkhozbank (Agricultural Bank) deals with long-term capital investments of agricultural enterprise, and the Torgbank supplies funds to state trading enterprises, to the committee for the storing of agricultural products, and to the Departments of Workers' Supplies.

The deposits of private individuals are kept in the Savings Bank. In the late thirties over 20,000,000 depositors had accounts in approximately 60,000 branches of this bank, operated under the supervision of the Commissariat of Finance. The depositors consist of individuals and of organizations, such as trade unions. Individual and collective farms receive 3 per cent on their deposits, whereas other depositors receive but 1 per cent. The deposits are placed at the disposal of the government through the purchase of bonds. The branches of the banks are also used for the selling of bonds to the public.

Agriculture. We have already discussed some of the changes that took place in Russian agriculture during the twenties and early thirties. At the beginning of the Second World War, as a result of these changes, there were three clearly defined types of farms in Soviet Russia—state

[9] A. Z. Arnold, *Banks, Credit and Money in Soviet Russia*, p. 464. Columbia University Press, 1937; Sikes, *op. cit.*, p. 322.

farms, collectives or co-operatives, and individually owned and operated farms.

The state farms were under the control of the Federal People's Commissariat of State Grain and Livestock Farms. They were managed by appointed directors clothed with full authority. Each laborer was permitted to keep as his private property one cow and one calf or goat, but was specifically debarred from owning draft animals—horses, oxen, and camels.[10] For each farm a directors' fund was established which functioned in a similar fashion to those in the industrial sector of Russian economic life.

During the late twenties and early thirties the Soviet government invested large sums of money in farm equipment and had high hopes of greatly increased productivity as a result of the large size of the farm and the capital investment. Many of these hopes, however, were doomed to disappointment. In the 1934 Congress of the Communist party, Stalin complained of the "great discrepancy between the vast investments made and the results obtained." Beginning in 1935 the government proceeded to disband many of the state farms and to transfer the lands to collective farms. The sown area of state farms declined as a result.[11]

Following World War II, however, there was a rapid growth in the number of state farms and their share in agricultural production. While in 1940 the state farms accounted for a mere 9 per cent of the crop area, a quarter of century later this figure had increased to about 50 per cent. This was the result of the setting up of newly developed lands as state farms and of farmers' decisions at *Kolkhoz* meetings. State farms produced over two fifths of all the grain procured by the state, over half of the vegetables, and a fifth of the raw cotton.[12]

Side by side with the state farms were the collective farms, or *Kolkhoz*. The rise of the collectives dated almost entirely from 1927. In 1965 there were 37,100 collective farms as contrasted with 12,196 state farms. Individual farms were practically nonexistent.

Each collective has it own charter, which follows closely the "model charter." The land occupied by the collective is technically public property, but the collective has the use of the land in "perpetuity." The land cannot, however, be sold or leased.

The agricultural land, buildings used for communal purposes, agricultural machines, and the more important implements, draft animals, and stocks of seed are regarded as "public socialist property" of the col-

10 Decree of September 30, 1938. 11 Florinski, *op. cit.*, p. 199.
12 Moisei Green, *At the Map of the U.S.S.R.*, p. 35.

lective farm. On the other hand, members of the collective retain their individual homesteads, an adjoining lot of from a quarter to one hectare, small implements, and some live stock.

Membership in the *Kolkhoz* is open to all citizens reaching the age of 16. Each pays an admission fee of 20 to 40 rubles. From a quarter to a half of the property the newcomer brings into a collective farm is added to the "indivisible fund" of the farm, and the remainder is credited to him as his contribution to the share capital.

The administrative committee is elected by the members. The members carry on the cultivation of the farm collectively, organized into brigades under the supervision of an appointed brigadier, also a member of the farm. Each brigade, usually from 40 to 60 strong, is given supplies and equipment and put in charge of a definite area of land. Each member is assigned specific tasks by the brigadier. They are paid in cash or in kind, their earnings being computed on the basis of "labor days." [13]

Trade Unions. Prior to the revolution of 1905 trade unions in Russia were declared illegal. Subsequent to this revolution unions were for a time permitted and even encouraged, but later suppressed and driven underground.

When the 1917 revolution broke out, the trade unions were used as a revolutionary force. Following the March revolution, the union forces were divided, the June, 1917, Congress showing a majority against class war. After the November *coup d'état,* however, the First Trades Union Congress, meeting in January, 1918, voted for war communism. At first factory committees took over the management of many of the industries from the owners and the technical staff. As time passed these committees began to feel that they were the owners of the industry, and to favor a syndicalist, rather than a socialist control. The government thereupon appealed to the trade unions to assist it in enforcing nationalization and in protecting production. It likewise reduced the representation of the factory committee on the management committees to one third, the other two thirds to consist of representatives of the Supreme Economic Council and of the trade unions. Later on,

[13] The "labor day" is an abstract unit comprising the element of physical exertion, skill, and "social usefulness" of the work. Each collective can devise its own schedule of the value of different grades of work, but usually follows the official models. In 1933 a government decree divided the work into 7 categories, declaring that the work of the president of a collective and that of a tractor driver were worth two "labor days," but that a day's work in the lowest class was accounted as worth only a half of a "labor day." Premiums are given to those individuals and brigades exceeding their quota. At the end of the year the net earnings of the farm both in kind and cash are distributed among the members.

as a result of the inefficiency of the committee head, Lenin substituted the "single management."

The unions soon reorganized along the lines of One Factory, One Union, and compelled a worker in a factory of whatever kind to join the union to which the factory belonged. They at the same time suppressed the movement among the factory committees to form central councils as competitors against the regular trade-union movement.

The January, 1920, congress of the trade unions voted to become a part of the state machine with responsibility for the management of industry and the protection of labor.

Three views of the function of a trade union under a workers' republic began to emerge. One, expressed by Shliapnikov, was that, as the soviet system suffered from bureaucracy, the supervision of production should be turned over to the trade unions. On the other extreme was Trotsky, the administrator, with the thesis that the greatest need of the hour was production; that, under a state where the workers constituted the government and owned the principal industries, the trade unions had no reason for a separate existence and should be merged with the working-class state. Between these extreme views came those of Lenin, who felt that the trade unions had a useful function to perform in combating bureaucracy in state industries and in representing the interests of the workers as distinguished from those of the peasants. "Comrade Trotsky," Lenin declared, "talks of a 'workers' state.' But this is an abstract idea. When we wrote about a workers' state in 1917, it was quite justified. But when you say: 'Why and against whom defend the working class, if there is no bourgeoisie, if we have a workers' state?' then we reply: 'Not quite a workers' state.' As a matter of fact our state is not of the workers, but of the workers and peasants. This is the first thing. And this means a good deal. But it is not all. The very program of our party shows that we have a workers' state with too much bureaucracy. It was a disagreeable necessity for us to put this label on our state. This is the reality of the transition period. Now would you say that there is no need for the trade unions to defend the material and spiritual interests of the working class in this bureaucratic state?" [14]

The New Economic Policy, which increased the number of privately managed plants, had the effect of relieving the unions of much of their responsibility for management and of making them an independent opposition group, for the protection of matters such as wages and hours. The Fifth Trade Union Congress in September, 1922, formally ac-

[14] Heller, *Industrial Revival in Russia,* pp. 98–9.

claimed this independent status. The joining of the union ceased to be compulsory in its nature and became voluntary, and the state ceased to finance the unions. On the restoration of the union as a voluntary institution, the membership decreased from 8,500,000 to 4,500,000, but later increased again, and in 1926 was estimated at more than 7,000,000, or over nine tenths of the industrial workers.

State Control of Unions. With the liquidation of the New Economic Policy and the further extension of government and co-operative employment, the situation again changed, and a demand was made that the trade unions cease laying chief emphasis on their function as an independent opposition group.

The introduction of the Five-Year Plan again brought to the forefront of discussion the question of what the function of the trade union should be. At the Eighth All-Union Congress of Trade Unions in 1928–29 a bitter controversy took place. Tomsky, who had been president of the All-Union Central Council of Trade Unions, maintained that the unions should assume a position substantially similar to that in capitalist states. He urged complete freedom of unions to press for improvements in the material conditions of their members. On the other hand, he maintained that it was not the duty of the unions to work for improvements in factory techniques, even though such improvements would lead to increased productivity.

Against Tomsky's view, the whole weight of the Communist party was thrown. The party leaders contended that steadily increased productivity of labor was essential both for the future of the country and for increasing the living standards of the workers. It was thus the duty of labor to do what it could to increase industrial production.

The Eighth Congress, which sponsored this discussion, elected to its presidium L. M. Kaganovich, assistant secretary of the Communist party, and during the next two years he and others did much to bring the Communist party point of view before the Trade Union Congress and initiated a purge of dissenting elements. The 1930 meeting of the All-Russian Congress of the Communist party declared that it was the duty of the trade unions to take a leading part in promoting "socialist competition," and also to organize "shock brigades," in order to raise to the uttermost the production of the entire community, and, when the Ninth All-Union Congress of Trade Unions met in 1931, the party line was definitely followed. Tomsky in the meanwhile retired from leadership in the movement and, denounced as a traitor for his economic views, committed suicide during the great purge.

On Russia's entrance into the Second World War, the trade unions formed a vast organization, with the shop committees elected in each industrial enterprise at its base, and at its top the All-Union Central Council of Trade Unions elected by the All-Union Congress of Trade Unions. While membership in the unions was not compulsory, almost nine tenths of the workers were enrolled as members. All the workers in one plant from the unskilled worker to the technical staff were in one union. No craft unions existed. There were in the late thirties 192 unions embracing about 25 million members.

The unions in the early forties were engaged in a number of activities:

(1) They were the administrative agency for social insurance and relief, this function having been turned over to them in 1933 by the former People's Commissariat of Labor.

(2) They retained, as one of their official duties, the signing of collective bargain contracts, although many authorities felt that there was little necessity for their assuming this duty, "since wages, labor conditions, and hours of labor are regulated by the state, and the trade unions never question the wisdom of official decisions." [15] In fact, the trade unions had often neglected to conclude such agreements and in 1937 were specifically directed "to resume the practice of collective contracts" by the plenary session of the Central Council of Trade Unions.

(3) In addition to these functions trade unions provided for the educational, recreational, and other needs of the workers; helped to improve housing conditions; co-operated with the management in promoting labor discipline and in increasing productivity through the encouragement of "socialist competition," and strove for the fulfilment of the Gosplan. They were controlled, as were every other important organization in Russia, by the "leading nucleus" of the Communist party and "were a hardly more than another vast agency for fostering the general objectives of the socialist state." [16] After the outbreak of the Second World War their chief function became that of promoting labor efficiency and discipline.[17]

Rewards and Regulation of Labor. WAGES. While in the advanced communist society the bolsheviks have maintained that men and women would be rewarded for their labor on the basis of their needs, the Soviet

[15] Florinski, *Toward an Understanding of the USSR*, pp. 190–1.

[16] Florinski, *op. cit.*, p. 191.

[17] At the sixth plenary of the Central Council of Trade Unions in 1937, the alleged laxity of trade unions was strongly denounced. According to the resolutions general meetings of unions were seldom summoned, and when summoned, were poorly organized and merely formal-declarative. The 1938 congress continued criticism along many of these lines, avowing that there existed "a bureaucratic heartless attitude toward the vital needs and requirements of the members among presidents and secretaries of unions." (Florinski, *op. cit.*, pp. 191–3.) For a more optimistic view of the activities of the Russian trade unions, see Albert Rhys Williams, *The Russians*, pp. 142–9.

Constitution provides that, in the measurable future in Russia, the principle applicable to the compensation of workers will be, "from each according to his *ability,* to each according to his *deeds.*"

In the early days of the Soviet Republic, the differences of income among Soviet workers, on the basis of work rendered, were comparatively slight, especially when consideration is given to the lower charges made to the poorer paid workers for rent and other services and commodities, and to the free educational, health, and other services received by such workers. The primary appeal made during these early days in behalf of increased efficiency and productivity was based largely on the desirability of improving the living standards of the workers of the Soviet Union as a whole.

As the years went on, however, Soviet leaders became increasingly dissatisfied with the results obtained and began to advocate methods of compensation more directly related to the productivity of the individual workers. In 1924 the Sixth Trade Union Congress declared that "in order to increase the personal intensity of labor, an extensive application of stimulative forms of wages is necessary." Piece wages were resorted to in numerous instances, and growing differences in wages and salaries began to prevail in the Soviet economy.

Such differences, however, were still not sufficient to produce the desired results, and in 1931 Stalin felt it necessary to call vigorous attention to the larger turnover that was constantly occurring as a result, in his judgment, of too great equality in wage scales, particularly between the skilled and the unskilled worker. "In a host of businesses [he declared] the wage scale makes practically no distinction between the skilled and the unskilled laborer. The effect of this equality is that the unskilled workman has no interest in making himself skilled; he has no incentive to improve himself. He feels himself, so to speak, a 'passing guest' in the factory where he is employed. As a result of wage equality the skilled worker goes from one factory to another in search of one which will pay him a wage proportionate to his skill. Both Marx and Lenin have declared that the distinction between skilled and unskilled labor must continue even under socialism, when class distinctions have been abolished, and can only disappear under communism; that therefore even under socialism payment must be measured by the work accomplished, not by the recipient's needs." [18]

Stalin's address was followed by a great extension of the piece-work form of compensation and by 1934, approximately 70 per cent of the

[18] Address of June 23, 1931, reported in *Pravda,* July 5, 1931. See Waldemar Gurian, *Bolshevism, Theory and Practice,* p. 321; see also Florinski, *Toward an Understanding of the USSR,* p. 89.

total hours of work in manufacturing industry was paid for on a piece-work basis. This system was even used in the remuneration of members of the collective farms, although there the payments made were in part on the basis of results obtained by group effort.[19]

The Stakhanov Movement. Beginning in the middle of 1935, the government conducted a vigorous campaign in behalf of increased productivity through what was popularly known as the Stakhanov movement. This movement was named after a Don Basin miner, Alexey Stakhanov, who in August, 1935, knocked down several times as much coal as the average miner. He did this by more effectively organizing the work of himself and his fellow miners. In his mine the individual coal-driller had performed a variety of tasks, such as stopping his pneumatic hammer frequently to fetch props, clear the debris away, load the coal, or shore up the veins. Stakhanov suggested that these tasks be divided among the members of the brigade and that one miner be left free to keep the drill incessantly in action. He did the drilling. The results were that, instead of mining seven tons each during the day, the miners increased the number of tons mined to 35. For this exploit he received a wage of 225 rubles.

The story of these results was flashed throughout the country, and Stakhanovite groups appeared among the oil-drillers, engine-drivers, gold-diggers, sales-girls, and the workers in a host of other trades, all intent on increasing their productivity through a more scientific use of their tools and of the labor force, and of obtaining increased wages and other rewards. Old norms of productivity were shattered. Stakhanov became a national hero. Whole enterprises set out to excel themselves on special Stakhanov "days," and finally 1936 was declared a Stakhanov year for the whole country.[20]

Increasing Inequalities. By the beginning of the forties, as a result of these various developments, differences in income scarcely imagined by the bolsheviks at the time of the Russian Revolution prevailed in Russia. In 1943 the *Economist* of London described these differences as follows:

"Judged by the wages paid in a number of big metal factories, the lower categories of earnings have been in the order of 330 rubles a

[19] Sikes, *op. cit.*, p. 289. See also Harry F. Ward, *The Place of Profit,* pp. 30 ff.

[20] Prior to this movement there was a movement known as "Saturdaying" during the Civil War, when workers volunteered to donate their time off to needed work, and a movement in 1928 known as the "shock-brigade" movement, started by a squad of Leningrad Comsomols, who volunteered to increase their output by pledging not to miss a day or let their machines stand unnecessarily idle. See Williams, *The Soviets,* pp. 222–3; 258–69.

month. Some 8 to 10 per cent of the workers in these factories earn more than 1200 rubles, whereas the earnings of some Stakhanovites amount to more than 4000 rubles. The salaries of the technical staff in the same groups of factories vary from 1000 to 5000 or 6000 rubles." [21]

Besides the increased wages, Stakhanovites often secured, before the Second World War, returns in the form of automobiles, scholarships, nameplates on seats in the opera, or cruises to Europe. Artists, authors, and playwrights also obtained royalties on their works, and many of them as well as the leading actors were men of considerable means.[22] Public honors were also bestowed on workers and professionals for outstanding achievement.

Supplementing wage differentials, bonuses, prizes, and honors as a means of securing efficient work, the Soviet government has provided, particularly in times of crisis, for the arbitrary allocation of labor. During periods of public crises, all men between 16 and 45 and all women between 18 and 40, except during certain periods of pregnancy and after childbirth, may be called upon to take part in any work required by the government. Members of the Communist party and of the Young Communist League must, of course, stand ready to undertake any task assigned to them in any part of the republic.

To keep workers on the job and prevent large turnover, the Soviet government also provides certain rewards for continuous employment in one factory. Those in enterprises for more than two years receive such gains as longer vacations, social insurance advantages, bonuses, and the privileges of going to rest homes or sanitaria.

GOVERNMENT COERCION. The government has likewise sought by various decrees to restrain an employee from leaving his employment. On March 4, 1933, a government *ukase* provided that the reason for the change of employment and the date thereof be stated on special labor cards issued to workers, pronouncing it a criminal offense for a manager to employ any worker whose record did not appear on his card.[23]

Four years later, on October 17, 1937, the government provided for the eviction of workers who voluntarily gave up their jobs or were dismissed for a breach of labor discipline or were convicted of a crime.

[21] *Economist*, July 3, 1943; *New York Times*, Aug. 9, 1943. The large surplus permitted at times to collective farmers is indicated by the gift of 1,000,000 rubles to the Red Army fund by a Kirghiz farmer.

[22] Williams, *The Soviets*, p. 449 ff.; see Laidler, *Socializing Our Democracy*, pp. 195 ff.

[23] Florinski, *Toward an Understanding of the USSR*, p. 185.

A person so evicted, according to the decree, was not entitled to the allocation of "living space" elsewhere.

On June 27, 1940, during the war crisis, the Presidium of the Supreme Soviet issued a decree declaring that "workers and employees who, by their own will, leave state, co-operative, and/or public enterprises, shall be handed over to the Courts and, by sentence of the People's judges, condemned to imprisonment"; and for idleness [staying away from work] workers shall likewise be brought before the Courts and, "by sentence of the People's judges, condemned to forced penal labor at their places of employment up to a term of six months and have withheld up to 25 per cent of their wages." [24]

The government during the Second World War provided somewhat similar punishment for peasants who failed to report for work. In a decree in the spring of 1942 it prescribed that the number of "work days" for the collective farm must be increased from 60–100 to 100–150. (The workday, as a unit of labor, may be longer or shorter than one working day.) Any peasant who failed to show up for work on the collective farm when most needed, in the press of harvest, was subject to a term of six months at hard labor without pay. On March 22, 1942, *Izvetsia* observed: "All the force of organized persuasion must be directed against the people who don't want to participate in *social* production." [25]

Summary. The Soviet government is thus seen to have gone through numerous economic, social, and political changes since its foundation. In the first decade of its existence it passed through a period of workers' control, of military communism, and of the so-called New Economic Policy. In the second decade it made a tremendous effort to industrialize the country, increase productivity, and advance living standards through the introduction of a series of Five-Year Plans, the wholesale collectivization of the farms, the application of efficiency techniques to production, the increased utilization of money, and other incentives to the skilled worker, technical, and other groups, the purging of those accused of sabotage, and the use of coercive methods in preventing labor turnover.

In this period most of the old bolsheviks were liquidated and power was still further centralized in the hands of the inner circle of the Communist party, particularly in those of the leader of the party, Joseph Stalin.

24 "The Silent Soviet Revolution," *Harper's Magazine,* June, 1941, p. 11, by Bertram D. Wolfe.

25 "The Sources of Russia's Strength," *Harper's Magazine,* March, 1943, p. 400, by William Henry Chamberlin.

Accompanying these developments were the revision of the Soviet Constitution, carrying with it among other things the abolition of the indirect method of legislative elections; the large increase in educational, recreational, and cultural facilities for the masses; the further development of a system of social insurance; and the building up of a strong military machine. In the early forties attention was concentrated chiefly on the war and the attempt of the Russian people, following the Nazi invasion, to resist the German armies and to defeat the forces of nazism and fascism.

In dealing with the first twenty years of the Soviet government, Norman Thomas and Joel Seidman set forth the following positive achievements:

"Unquestionably a vast amount has been achieved within a comparatively short space of time. A primitive agricultural society is being transformed into a modern industrial nation. Greater production has been achieved, and the basis laid for a higher living standard in the future. Unemployment has been eliminated, and some measure of general economic security provided. A huge increase in literacy has been attained, higher education encouraged, science fostered, and health service vastly improved. Scientists, musicians, and artists enjoy economic security, free from the whims of wealthy patrons. The persecution of national or racial minorities has been stopped, and the national minorities placed on a level of equality with the Russians. Race or color has been made no bar to high office; women have been raised legally to a level of equality with men. The worker is honored, and a privileged class based on ownership or birth no longer exists. Above all, Soviet Russia has demonstrated that the private capitalist is not necessary to production, that government ownership does work, that national planning is of enormous value." [26]

On the other hand, these writers criticize the continuing dictatorship in the Soviet Union and the principles and tactics of the communist movement. The criticisms by many non-communists of the underlying philosophy and the current practices of communism are discussed in the succeeding chapter.

[26] Thomas and Seidman, *Russia, Democracy or Dictatorship*, p. 7.

CHAPTER 29

Criticisms of Early Communist Principles and Tactics

IN THE previous chapters we have described the rise of communism, the principles and tactics employed by the Communist party in attaining power, the economic and social aims, and the achievements of the Russian Soviet government from its birth until the early forties. During these days communists were active in many parts of the world and, following the "line" laid down by the Communist International until that organization's demise in 1943, endeavored to mobilize, wherever possible, public sentiment in behalf of communist theory and tactics.

The chief criticisms of the tactics employed by communists in countries outside of Russia were based upon the fact that, particularly in the early days after the Russian Revolution, members of the Communist parties and their "fellow travelers" [1] advocated the application to Western countries of tactics which had led to the assumption of power by the bolsheviks of Russia. The early bolsheviks, as has been indicated, believed that, while parliamentary institutions should be used in the early stages of the struggle for power, the labor movement should ever keep in mind that the essential questions of labor within the capitalist order were "settled by force, by open struggle, the general strike, the insurrection of the proletarian masses." [2] This point of view was expressed by the Communist party of the United States in its first convention in 1919,[3] and was reiterated during the thirties by the Communist

[1] The phrase "fellow travelers" has for many years been widely applied to non members of the Communist parties who faithfully followed "the communist line, or, in other words, who shifted their theories and tactics coincidentally with the shifts made by the Communist parties in their respective countries.

[2] *The Theory and Practice of Leninism* (British Communist Party edition), p. 23 see also text, pp. 371–73.

[3] The Communist party of the United States in the program adopted by it in its first convention in Chicago in early September, 1919, declared, among other things "The Communist party shall keep in the foreground its consistent appeal for prole

party's candidate for President of the United States, William Z. Foster, in a statement in which he declared: "In all parliamentary activities, the Communist party makes it clear to the workers that the capitalist democracy is a sham and that there must be no illusion about peacefully capturing the state for the working class. . . . The capitalists will never voluntarily give up control of society and abdicate their system of exploiting the masses . . . , nor can they be talked, bought, or voted out of power. To believe otherwise would be a deadly fatalism, disarming and paralyzing the workers in their struggle. No ruling class ever surrendered to a rising subject class without a last-ditch open fight. To put an end to the capitalist system will require a consciously revolutionary act by the great toiling masses, led by the Communist party; that is, the conquest of the state power, the destruction of the state machine created by the ruling class, and the organization of the proletarian dictatorship. The lessons of history allow no other conclusion." [4]

These tactics adopted by communists outside of Russia were attacked on the ground, among others, that they were based largely on a number of false assumptions.

---

tarian revolution, the overthrow of capitalism, and the establishment of a dictatorship of the proletariat. . . . Participation in parliamentary campaigns, which, in the general struggle of the proletariat, is of secondary importance, is for the purpose of revolutionary propaganda only. Parliamentary representatives of the Communist party shall not introduce or support reform measures. Parliaments and political democracy shall be utilized to assist in organizing the working class against capitalism, and the state parliamentary representatives shall consistently expose the oppressive class character of the capitalist state, using the legislative forum to interpret and emphasize the class struggle; they shall make clear how parliamentarism and parliamentary democracy deceive the workers. . . . The uncompromising character of the class struggle must be maintained under all circumstances. The Communist party, accordingly, in campaigns and elections, and in all its other activities, shall not co-operate with groups or parties not committed to the revolutionary class struggle, such as the Socialist party, Labor party, Non-partisan League, People's Council, Municipal Ownership Leagues, etc. . . . The Communist party shall participate in mass strikes, not only to achieve the immediate purposes of the strike, but to develop the revolutionary implications of the mass strike. . . . In mass strikes under conditions of concentrated capitalism there is latent the tendency towards the general mass strike which takes on a political character and manifests the impulse towards proletarian dictatorship" (*The American Labor Year Book*, 1919–20, p. 418).

[4] Foster, *Toward Soviet America*, pp. 213, 255. In 1934, the Communist party, U. S. A., at its April National Convention, maintained again that it was "the central task of the party to organize and lead the fight against the offensive of the capitalist class, against developing fascism, and the threat of imperialist war, and to develop these struggles, on the basis of the fight for the immediate partial demands of the workers, into general class battles for the overthrow of capitalist dictatorship, and the setting up of the Soviet government . . . Only the establishment of the dictatorship of the proletariat, of the Soviet power, can free the millions of toilers from the bondage and misery of the capitalist system" (*The Communist*, May 1934, pp. 443, 453).

False Communist Assumptions. *1. Russian Tactics Suitable to Western World.* One assumption prevalent in the communist movement in the twenties was that a type of tactics that succeeded in Russia at the time of the bolshevik revolution would be most likely to succeed in the countries of the Western world. However, the revolution in Russia occurred in a country where the prestige of the ruling class had been greatly weakened by a prolonged and costly war and where this class had shown its utter inability to rule; where the masses were desperately in need of bread; where industry had completely broken down and the industrialists were without strength or leadership; where the majority of the people were illiterate and where political democracy was practically unknown; where the soldiers were anxious to lay down their arms and return to their homes; and where a well-directed appeal by a strong and determined minority based on the promise of bread, land, and peace was all that was needed to make possible a successful bolshevik coup. To assume that similar *coups d'état* could be successfully attempted in Western countries where there are traditions of parliamentary and democratic government, where the industrial machine is still intact, where strong middle-class, capitalist, and military groups are utterly opposed to violent revolutionary changes, is a social assumption of a thoroughly unscientific nature—an assumption, by the way, which time and again proved its invalidity during the twenties and the thirties, and which the communists themselves declared to be without validity when they decreed the end of the Third International in late May, 1943.

2. *Only Minority Group Capable of Applying Revolutionary Techniques.* Communists based their original tactics on other assumptions. They took for granted that, when preparing for a violent revolution in a democratic country, they would be the *only* minority actively engaged in the development of such tactics, and that other minority or majority groups would remain passive.[5] They were, however, doomed to tragic disappointment in this assumption. The tactics of violent change by determined minority groups were closely studied by other minorities. The fascists and nazis in Italy, in Hungary, in Austria, in Germany, and in other countries proved to be apt pupils, and many of the techniques which communists had taught their followers for preparing the soil for violent, extra-legal change were adopted bodily by the dictators of the right and used by them to get into power and ruthlessly to crush the communist movement and every working-class agency that stood in their path.

[5] Bertrand Russell, *Bolshevism in Theory and Practice,* pp. 146–7.

3. Power of Capitalist Propaganda. Akin to the above assumptions was that of the early bolsheviks that, in a democratic country, capitalist propaganda was so powerful that it could prevent the majority from voting at elections for the program of the bolsheviks and could prevent communists from assuming power, but that capitalist laws and police forces could not prevent the communists, while still a minority, from acquiring a supremacy of military power. In answer to such an assumption, Bertrand Russell asked, "Is it not as clear as noonday that in a democratic country it is more difficult for the proletariat to destroy the government by arms than to defeat it in a general election? Seeing the immense advantage of a government in dealing with rebels, it seems that rebellion could have little hope of success unless a very large majority supported it. . . . What seems to emerge from these considerations is that a revolution in favor of communism would have no chance of succeeding unless it were supported by a larger majority than would be required for the election of a communist government by constitutional methods. It is possible that, if such a government came into existence and proceeded to carry out its program, it would be met by armed resistance on the part of capital, including a large proportion of the officers in the army and navy. But in subduing this resistance it would have the support of that great body of opinion which believes in legality and upholds the constitution. Moreover, having, by hypothesis, converted a majority of the nation, a communist government could be sure of loyal help from immense numbers of workers, and would not be forced, as the bolsheviks are in Russia, to suspect treachery everywhere. Under these circumstances, I believe that the resistance of the capitalists could be quelled without much difficulty, and would receive little support from moderate people. Whereas, in a minority revolt of communists against a capitalist government, all moderate opinion would be on the side of capitalism." [6]

4. Bolshevik Tactics Successful in Attaining Socialist Goal. A fourth communist assumption of the twenties and thirties was that the tactics adopted by the communists of Russia had actually demonstrated a successful method, in at least one country—Russia—of establishing a socialist economic order. While Lenin and other leaders of the communist movement were often at pains to deny this assumption, it nevertheless was ever present in the minds of many active communists, who were pointing to the "superiority" of communist tactics to the slow-

[6] Bertrand Russell, *Bolshevism in Theory and Practice,* pp. 144–6; Morris Hillquit in *From Marx to Lenin,* pp. 94 ff., emphasized the poor strategy, outside of any other question, of fostering among the masses the hypothetical necessity of violent revolution during a preparatory stage.

moving tactics of democracy. However, what communists had established in Russia during the twenties and thirties, declared their critics, was not democratic socialism, but a communist dictatorship with government ownership. This is a far cry from socialism. Socialism is impossible without democracy. It involves both collective ownership of industry and democratic control of the economic, the political, and the cultural life of a nation. "We understand by modern socialism," as Karl Kautsky maintained, "not merely social organization of production, but democratic organization of society as well." [7]

In the days of Lenin, communists assumed that such democratization would take but a comparatively short time once the nation had eliminated the power of the private capitalist. They did not, however, take sufficiently into account that the love of power might be as strong a motive and as great a source of injustice as love of money and that under a system of public ownership those in control of the government might seek to continue for long periods to exercise their power to their own advantage over both industry and the state machinery. In private industry, as Berle and Means have pointed out, the directors of large corporations own but a small per cent of the stock. And yet they are the controlling group and are constantly seeking the maintenance and strengthening of their power. So in public industry, as Bertrand Russell maintains, "those who control economic power can, without owning anything, have palatial residences, the use of the best cars, a princely entertainment allowance, holidays at the public expense in official holiday resorts, and so on and so on. And why," he asks, "should they have any more concern for the ordinary worker than those in control have now? There can be no reason why they should have, unless the ordinary worker has power to deprive them of their positions. . . . While, therefore, public ownership and control of all large-scale industry and finance is a *necessary* condition for the taming of power, it is far from being a *sufficient* condition. It needs to be supplemented by a democracy more thoroughgoing, more carefully safeguarded against official tyranny, and with more deliberate provision for freedom of propaganda than any purely political democracy that has ever existed.[8]

[7] Kautsky, *Dictatorship of the Proletariat*, p. 24.

[8] Russell, *Power, A New Social Analysis*, pp. 302–3; see also Eduard Heimann in *Communism, Fascism, or Democracy?*, pp. 141–3. Heimann declares that power in itself is not bad, but that what is objectionable is "the flat denial of its existence and the problems it raises." One of the main issues in Russia, he contends, is that "such tremendous power creates a social position for its holders, regardless of their salaries, and gives rise to their having a group interest in defending and developing this position." He quotes Bukharin, when official spokesman of the Soviets, as estimating that the Russian dictatorship would be needed for another two or three

Under a system of public ownership, furthermore, it is absolutely necessary to safeguard freedom of propaganda as the communists have not thus far done. That it is possible to combine freedom of propaganda with government monopoly is indicated by the British Broadcasting Corporation which, in ordinary times, represented different points of views, as nearly as may be, in proportion to their numerical strength.

Finally, if undue power is to be tamed, the people of the country must be educated in the scientific attitude of mind—which is not yet the case in Russia—in tolerance, in ability to form independent judgments, while they are at the same time assuming their responsibilities as members of a free community. "It is," declares Russell, "the task of liberal education to give a sense of the value of things other than domination, to help to create wise citizens of a free community, and, through the combination of citizenship with liberty in individual creativeness, to enable men to give to human life that splendor which some few have shown that it can achieve." [9]

5. *Ruling Class Surrender Only after Use of Violence.* A fifth invalid communist assumption of the original bolsheviks was that "no ruling class ever surrendered without a last-ditch open fight." A study of revolutions indicates, however, that, while some past revolutions have been sudden and violent, others have been gradual and peaceful. Revolutionary struggles have occurred in England since the seventeenth century without a violent revolt. "The history of the Reform Bill agitation, the broadening of the franchise in the nineteenth century, and finally the prewar Irish struggle," declared E. F. M. Durbin, "all seem to me to shake to the foundation the doctrine that social classes cannot rise or fall, that privileged groups cannot be dispossessed of power, without an appeal to force." [10]

In a number of countries the status of slavery was abolished by the stroke of a pen. The slave traffic was ended in the Danish possessions in 1902 by a royal order. The last remnant of the dying slave system was swept away in the thirties of the last century in England by acts of Parliament, Parliament appropriating 20 million pounds sterling as compensation to the planters. The immediate emancipation of slaves in the French colonies was decreed in 1848 by the Provisional Government. In 1858 the Portuguese government issued an edict that every

generations. "If one adds the past years of this dictatorship to this calculation, the total period is about a century, a period approximating the whole duration of Western capitalism until the [First] World War."

[9] Russell, *op. cit.*, p. 319.

[10] Durbin, *The Politics of Democratic Socialism*, pp. 191–205.

slave belonging to a Portuguese subject should be free twenty years from that date. The Dutch emancipated their slaves in 1863, and several Spanish-American states, on declaring their independence, adopted measures for the discontinuance of slavery within their limits. By an act of September, 1871, the Brazilian Chamber brought an end to the slave system. In America, it is true, the abolition of slavery was effected only after a tragic Civil War, but many students of the subject believe that if that war had been averted for the time being, slavery would have disappeared as a result of its increasing unprofitableness. In some countries slavery was abolished during a revolutionary period, whereas in others this step was taken during comparatively peaceful times.

As for serfdom, it was abolished in France during the turbulent days of the French Revolution. In Prussia it was wiped out by the famous Edict of Emancipation at Memel in 1807, and in Russia, by a series of imperial decrees beginning in July, 1858.[11]

Nor was there any violence to speak about during the Industrial Revolution of the late eighteenth and early nineteenth centuries. "Yet that was probably the greatest social revolution which has ever occurred on this planet." [12] As for counterrevolutions, that engineered by Hitler in Germany was carried out within the legal framework of the country, Hitler having been given dictatorial power by the Reichstag majority following the elections of March 5, 1933, in which the Nazis won 44 per cent of the seats, and their supporters, the nationalists, 8 per cent.

In fact, such an authority on revolutionary movements as Raymond Postgate, after a careful analysis of such movements in contemporary history, goes so far as to say that "the student of revolutionary technique must (subject of course to the appearance of extraordinary circumstances) conclude that armed revolt, as a method, direct or indirect, by a revolutionary elite or by a discontented army is now totally impracticable." [13]

Moreover, as Soule brings out, a true revolution is not usually sudden

[11] See Laidler, *Socializing Our Democracy,* p. 105. Professor Lyford P. Edwards, in *The Natural History of Revolution* (p. 7) declared that "the overthrow of the monarchy and feudal system in France was not caused by the French Revolution. The revolution simply made evident the fact that the real power in France had passed into the hands of the middle class."

[12] Edwards, *The Natural History of Revolution,* pp. 7–8.

[13] Postgate, *How to Make a Revolution,* p. 162. See also Professor Morris Cohen in *Meaning of Marx,* by Bertrand Russell and Others, p. 93. "The idea that armed rebellion is the only or always effective cure for social ills [declares Cohen] seems to me no better than the old superstition of medieval medicine, that bloodletting is the only and the sovereign remedy for bodily ills." See also Laski, *Reflections on the Revolution of Our Time,* p. 221.

and violent, but one which "takes many years, even generations, in the making. . . . The transfer of power is often quick and comparatively painless, because the old regime has been so weakened and has lost so much of its self-confidence that it vanishes almost without resistance. Its most trusted supporters abandon it." [14] The most serious violence occurs after the transfer of power. On this account, declared Hillquit, "a proletarian regime must at all times maintain an efficient and adequate organization to protect its conquests, and must be particularly alert and determined in the early period of its existence, when counter-revolutionary capitalist attacks are likely to be most frequent and dangerous." [15]

The history of interwar years, furthermore, points to the possibilities of peaceful change in many of the world's democracies. During the twenties and thirties, labor and socialist parties, as a result of successes at the polls, were able to organize labor, socialist, or coalition governments at varying periods in Great Britain, France, Denmark, Norway, Sweden, Belgium, Australia, New Zealand, and other countries. In most instances those in office did not have the support of a majority of legislators, nor did they possess a mandate from the large majority of voters to establish a socialist society. In the case of the smaller European countries, even if that definite mandate had been given, it would have been difficult, on account of the fascistic character of some of the large European countries, to have carried out that mandate in the unsettled thirties. But the point is, many students maintain, that labor and socialist governments were not prevented, when voters decreed it, from peacefully taking over the reins of government. From this experience, they contend, the chances are that if labor had assumed office as a majority government in these countries, it would have been able to proceed peacefully with its program of socialization, provided, at least, that it compensated the owners of the property taken over, confined its early efforts to specified groups of industries, and worked out a co-operative arrangement with the agricultural and middle classes.

It should also be realized, declare the believers in peaceful and democratic change, that in the United States, before it would be possible to elect a government dedicated to the socialization of industry, many changes would have occurred in the social fabric, tending to render the owning class in the community weaker economically, politically, and psychologically than at present—among these changes being higher taxes, stricter regulation, smaller net profits, a more extensive system

[14] George Soule, *The Coming American Revolution,* pp. 17 ff.
[15] Hillquit, *From Marx to Lenin,* p. 106.

of public ownership, expanded co-operative and labor movements, and shifts in the functions of the owning and managerial groups in the operation of industry and in the moral prestige of those groups.[16] The loss of prestige of the owners and managers of industry during the depression of the thirties was a marked one.

However, if those advocating fundamental change refuse to take advantage of the peaceful and democratic agencies of social change provided by democratic political institutions; if they are constantly undermining the faith of the masses in political democracy; and are constantly urging the establishment of a proletarian dictatorship under which the non-communist would be at least temporarily denied his civil rights, peaceful progress toward a co-operative social order, even in democratic countries, will be made increasingly difficult; perhaps impossible.[17]

Other Criticisms of Communist Tactics. SPLIT THE WORKING CLASS. The tactics of the communists during the twenties were also condemned on the ground that they led, outside of Russia, to the splitting of the labor movement; to bitter conflicts between the communist and non-communist elements in the labor movement. Following the formation of the Third International, the communists in various countries of Europe formed a left wing within the socialist parties. They strove to capture the party machinery, and when they failed to do this, they split the parties and formed communist organizations. They heaped bitter denunciation upon social democratic leaders of the political and trade-union sectors of the labor movement and upon the democratic form of government. By these means, many contended that they greatly weakened the working-class political and economic movements, and prepared the soil for the rise of fascism.[18] "I think it probable," de-

16 See Laidler, *Socializing Our Democracy*, ch. IV, "Undermining Capitalism in America"; Schumpeter, *Capitalism, Socialism and Democracy*, ch. XII; Corey, *Decline of American Capitalism.*

17 See Kautsky, *Dictatorship of the Proletariat*, p. 7; Angell, *Must Britain Travel the Moscow Road?*; Hillquit, *From Marx to Lenin*, pp. 132–6. Mr. Hillquit maintained that in democratic countries liberty of the press, speech, and meeting, the right of organization, and the franchise were practically indispensable to the development of a movement toward a better social order, but that these rights were likely to be seriously curtailed if demands for the observance of such freedoms were coupled "with the cheerful assurance that when the 'times change' and the working class gains political power, it will use it to 'crush once and for all' these same liberties of the bourgeois."

18 See Heimann, *Communism, Fascism, or Democracy?* p. 187. Heimann calls attention to the joint political enterprises of the communist and fascist movements in Germany "which culminated in the big traffic strike in Berlin less than three months before fascism came into power. It was a political action of the first order in size and success, organized by a strike committee which consisted of an equal

clares Professor Harold J. Laski, "that had Lenin not precipitated the fatal split in the working-class forces implied in the foundation of the Third International, certainly not Hitler, and perhaps not Mussolini, would have attained power. But the preliminary conditions of their success was that, through communist fanaticism, the organized forces of the working class were divided and hesitant when they could have been united and strong." [19]

"Ends Justify the Means" Philosophy. A still further criticism of communist tactics has been made by non-communists on ethical grounds.[20] In country after country many communist leaders have maintained in their dealings with other groups, as well as with other factions within the communist movement, that "the ends justify the means"; that all means are justifiable, so long as they promise to advance communists nearer to their goal. In criticism of this point of view, Dr. John Dewey declares:

"Fair play, elementary justice in the presentation of facts and especially of the opinions of others, are something more than bourgeois virtues . . . The systematic, persistent and seemingly intentional disregard of these things by the communist spokesmen in speech and press, the hysteria of their denunciations, their attempts at character assassination of their opponents, their misrepresentation of the views of the 'liberals' to whom they also appeal for aid in their defense campaigns, their policy of 'rule or ruin' in their so-called united front activities, their apparent conviction that what they take to be the end justifies the use of *any* means if only those means promise to be successful—all these, in my judgment, are fatal to the very end which official communists

number of official delegates from the communist and fascist parties, and designed to stir up the population against the Republic on the occasion of the approaching elections for Parliament—the last election under the Republic. Of course, each side hoped not only to destroy the Republic with the aid of the other, but to win over the adherents of the other side at the same time." Stalin, declared Heimann, "had officially declared that the principal enemies of world communism were the social democrats and the Christian trade unions of Germany and that one had to take into the bargain a "temporary rule of fascism in Germany because its historical mission would be to do away with those worst enemies of communism." After dealing with the activities of communists in Germany, England, and other countries, Raymond Postgate in *How to Make a Revolution,* p. 184, declared, "Communist propaganda has induced the workers to distrust their political and economic leaders; communist activity has caused them to dislike the communists. The net result has been to produce that disillusioned and cynical state of mind (most of all favorable to fascism) where the working class is imbued with a belief that all action must necessarily fail." See also John Dewey in *The Meaning of Marx,* by Bertrand Russell and Others, pp. 88–9.

19 Laski, *Reflections on the Revolution of Our Time,* p. 84.

20 See Laidler, *Socializing Our Democracy,* p. 97.

profess to have at heart." [21] And, it may be added, these tactics have been in many countries a far greater barrier to co-operation with other groups than have been the ultimate goals of the communist movement.

COMMUNISM AND DICTATORSHIP. Over and above these criticisms have been the criticism of the dictatorship established by the communists in Russia. Making due allowance for the ignorance of the Russian people during and immediately after the revolution; for the fact that Russia had never enjoyed a democratic form of government and had never known any other form of government than a dictatorship, as well as for the fact that Russia was faced with many actual and potential enemies abroad, critics of bolshevism still maintain that there was little or no justification for the centralization of power in the hands of the inner group in the Communist party such as the world witnessed in the first quarter century of the Soviet regime; nor was there justification for the iron discipline imposed upon members of the Communist parties throughout the world by the Communist International directed, for so many years, by the ruling group in the Russian Communist party. In fact, many of the costly mistakes made by the Russian communists and the leaders of communist groups in other countries could be attributed to this centralization of power in Moscow.[22]

[21] John Dewey in *The Meaning of Marx,* by Bertrand Russell and others, p. 89.

"The most disastrous mistake of the communists in their efforts to convert the Western workers," declared G. D. H. Cole, "was their attempt to discard 'bourgeois morality' in favor of a hard-boiled, 'scientific' attitude. For the Western workers were not hard-boiled; and the hard-boiling they received in the Communist parties of the Western countries was as apt to convert them into fascists as anything else. If there were no morality, but only science, why not? It could not be more 'moral' to be on one side rather than on the other"(Cole, *Europe, Russia, and the Future,* p. 222).

Former Ambassador Joseph E. Davies made a vigorous criticism of the members of the Russian Communist party in his *Mission to Moscow* (p. 402): "The philosophy of communism," he maintained, "justifies all acts if done in its name. There are no considerations of honor or loyalty which control as against duty to the party. The result is that there can be no confidence or faith between these men in leadership. No man can trust another. It is a serious and basic weakness and a constant threat to existing government."

[22] See Laski, *Reflections on the Revolution of Our Time,* p. 85; see also pp. 459–60. Max Lerner in *It Is Later than You Think* (pp. 67–72), criticizes the communists from the standpoint of errors of emphasis and calculation. The six errors cited include (1) an underestimate of the strength of capitalism; (2) an overestimate of the revolutionary character of the proletariat; (3) an underestimate of the strength of the middle class and the misreckoning of its direction; (4) an underestimate of the strength of the nationalist idea; (5) a faulty theory of human nature in politics; and (6) the misreckoning on proletarian dictatorship. Of the latter, he says: "From the past decade of Soviet history we have begun to understand that political power may have its inner structure and its life history fully as much as economic power; that the problems of group conflict and tyranny are not automatically solved

when the means of production are socialized; and that the need of proletarian dictatorship must be minimized, its time-span shortened, and channels found for the expression of political opposition in the socialist states of the future" (p. 71).

John L. Childs and George S. Counts, in *America, Russia, and the Communist Party* (Chapter IX), declare that occurrences in the interwar years challenged the validity of the following dogmas held by the communists in the twenties and thirties:

(1) That all of the so-called capitalist powers would inevitably combine to destroy the Soviet Union; (2) that the working people of the world would in all crucial matters exhibit a first loyalty to their class rather than to their nation or people; (3) that the state in all capitalistic societies is, by its very nature, not a neutral agency, but the perfected tool of the owning and exploiting class; (4) that the capitalist system, after the First World War, was in the last stages of decay and that the Russian Revolution was the spark that would ignite world revolution—a point of view later modified, although this modification failed for some years to bring about the necessary changes in the tactics of the Communist movement in democratic countries.

Childs and Counts also express criticism of the centralized structure and the tactics of the American Communist party during the twenties and thirties:

"The pattern of organization and procedure [communist]," they declare (p. 65), "was developed for the most part in Czarist Russia and was designed to enable a small group of deeply devoted revolutionaries to operate amid conditions of blackest tyranny and oppression, where secrecy and absolute solidarity were essential to survival. This pattern concentrated authority and power of decision in a central bureau or committee, which acted as the directing head, formulated all important policies, developed the conception of a 'party line,' and imposed obedience and military discipline upon all members. When the original Russian party came into power and sought to build an international organization this pattern was adopted not only by the Third International but also by all national branches of the Communist party."

The authors likewise upbraid the communists for "Machiavellian" tactics and maintain that they have "spread confusion and created division in the ranks of organized labor and of all liberal, social, and political movements" (p. 71). At the same time they urge close and friendly co-operation between the United States and Russia in the building of the postwar world as well as during the Second World War.

CHAPTER 30

Changes in Communist Tactics; Their Significance

THE FOREGOING criticisms of communist principles and tactics were directed primarily against the philosophy and tactics of the communists as formulated during the November Revolution of 1917 and the years immediately following. Many of these criticisms have continued to be valid in the early forties. Some of them, on the other hand, have had to be modified as a result of the changes which took place in the twenties and the thirties in the theories and practices of the communists both in Russia and elsewhere.

Shift from Emphasis on World Revolution. Most of the shifts in communist tactics had to do with the changed attitude of the communists in Russia and in other lands regarding the immediate possibilities of world revolution. At the time of the Russian Revolution Lenin and the communist leaders felt that the establishment of the republic would be the signal for revolutionary outbreaks in other lands. Doubtful of being able successfully to defend the revolution in Russia from within or from without unless it spread to the industrialized countries, Lenin and others regarded the primary task of the Communist International as that of creating a fertile field for armed revolt outside of Russia and the establishment of the dictatorship of the proletariat. To prepare the ground, it would be necessary to build up separate communist parties and economic groups in capitalistic countries directed by the central committee of the Comintern, with headquarters in Moscow, and to make these parties the spearheads of revolt when the time was ripe.

The result was the organization of communist parties and communist-controlled trade unions in country after country and the splitting of the working classes of these countries into warring factions, along the line discussed earlier.

The World Revolution, however, did not materialize. Soviet republics were established in Hungary and Bavaria, but their communist governments were soon crushed. Instead, fascist movements sprang up in Italy and in Hungary during the early twenties, and communist movements lost strength in many European countries.

As a result, the Russian communists increasingly came to the conclusion that they should concentrate their best efforts on the building of communism in Russia, rather than on the fomenting of communist revolutions elsewhere. Within the Soviet Republics, as has been seen, the controversy over communist revolutionary policies came to a head with the expulsion from Russia of Trotsky, advocate of the "permanent revolution," and the rise of Stalin to the position of undisputed head of the Russian dictatorship.

With the expulsion of Trotsky, the first phase of the Communist International as an organization dedicated to world revolution came to an end. From 1928 to the rise of Hitler, the Comintern, according to Franz Borkenau, historian of the movement, passed through a second stage, one which was utilized by the Russian Soviet leaders to assist them in winning their fight for the achievement of their domestic policies.

During this stage the alleged danger of imperialistic aggression on the part of Great Britain, France, the United States, and other countries was broadcast by Communist parties. This scare, declared Borkenau, "belonged essentially to the atmosphere the Russian rulers thought fit for the execution of the First Five-Year Plan, for the destruction of every opposition, notably the opposition of the right wing, and for the establishment of a fully totalitarian regime. The Comintern during these years, as so often since 1923, had been made the instrument not so much of Russian foreign policy, as of the dominating Russian faction in its struggle with other factions." [1]

With the advance of the thirties, however, came the triumph of Hitler, the rise of fascism in Austria, the fascist currents in Spain, and the menace of nazism throughout all of Europe, with its grave threat of aggressive warfare on the part of the fascist states against Soviet Russia.

The Russian leaders decided that something must be done to avert this danger, and that the Comintern and the various Communist parties throughout the world must be utilized to the full not for world revolution or for internal Russian political controls, but for the fight against fascism and the threat of war resulting from nazi aggression.

1935 Congress of Comintern. United Front Against War and Fascism. In August, 1935, the Comintern held its Seventh Congress in Moscow. At this congress the entire system of communist tactics was

[1] Franz Borkenau, *World Communism—a History of the Communist International*, pp. 387–8.

revised. The congress stated the dangers of fascist and nazi control. It condemned certain sections of the International which, "by overestimating the degree of revolutionizing of the masses, by creating the illusion that the path to fascism had already been barred while the fascist movement was continuing to grow, actually fostered passivity in relation to fascism." It likewise denounced them for "adopting stereotyped tactics and slogans for all countries without taking into account the special features of the concrete situation in each particular country." [2]

It proposed, on the basis of the world situation, that the communists throughout the world endeavor to unite their forces in the war against fascism with other working class and communist groups. Georgi Dimitrov, secretary of the Comintern, at this congress, explaining the position of the International, declared:

"We communists have other ultimate aims than these parties [other parties fighting against fascism], but in struggling for our aims we are ready to fight jointly for any immediate tasks which when realized will weaken the position of fascism and strengthen the position of the proletariat.

"We are ready to do all this because, in countries of bourgeois democracy, we want to block the road in the way of reaction and the offensive of capital and fascism, prevent the abrogation of bourgeois-democratic liberties, forestall fascism's terroristic vengeance upon the proletariat, the revolutionary section of the peasants and the intellectuals, save the young generation from physical and spiritual degeneration." [3]

The congress thus set before the Communist parties the task in their respective countries of trying to bring about a single mass political party and of uniting Social Democratic partics or individual organizations with the Communist parties. At the same time, the directions from the congress declared, communists must explain "to the workers without fail that such unity is possible only under certain conditions: under the condition of complete independence from the bourgeoisie and the complete severance of the bloc between social democracy and the bourgeoisie, under the condition that *unity of action* be first brought about, that the necessity of the *revolutionary overthrow of the rule of the bourgeoisie and the establishment of the dictatorship of the proletariat in the form of Soviets be recognized,* that support of one's own bourgeoisie in *imperialist war* be rejected, and that the party be constructed on the basis of *democratic centralism* which ensures unity of will and

[2] Resolutions of the Communist International, Seventh Congress, 1935, p. 36.
[3] *Ibid.*, p. 7.

action and has been tested by the experience of the Russian bolsheviks." [4] (Italics ours.)

PROLETARIAN DICTATORSHIP ULTIMATE AIM. The resolutions likewise made it plain that, while the immediate task of the proposed united fronts was that of fighting fascism, the more far-flung aim was that of putting the communists in a position of leadership among the workers of various countries so that they might be able to lead labor through a revolutionary crisis and to a proletarian dictatorship when the capitalist system had reached a critical stage.

"The establishment of the united front of the working class [a congress resolution maintained] is the decisive link in the preparation of the toilers for the forthcoming great battles of the second round of proletarian revolution. Only the welding of the proletariat into a single mass political party will ensure its victory in the struggle against fascism and the power of capital, for the dictatorship of the proletariat and the power of the Soviets.

" 'The victory of revolution,' declared Stalin, 'never comes by itself. It has to be prepared for and won. And only a strong proletarian revolutionary party can prepare for and win victory.' " [5]

PROPOSED TACTICS FOR CAPITALIST CRISIS. The congress laid down specific directives regarding ways and means of organizing resistance to fascism and war.

"While preparing the working class for rapid shifts in the forms and methods of struggle as circumstances change [the resolution on the fight against fascism stated], it is necessary to organize, in proportion as the movement grows, the transition *from the defensive to the offensive* against capital, steering toward the organization of a *mass political strike,* in which it is indispensable that the participation of the principal trade unions of the country should be secured." [6] (Italics ours.)

"In the circumstances of a *political crisis,* when the ruling classes are no longer in a position to cope with the powerful sweep of the mass movement [the resolution continued], the communists must advance *fundamental* revolutionary slogans (such as, for instance, control of production and the banks, the disbandment of the police force and its displacement by an armed workers' militia, etc.) which are directed toward still further shaking the economic and political power of the bourgeoisie and increasing the strength of the working class, toward isolating the parties of compromise, and which lead the working masses right up to the point of the revolutionary seizure of power." [7]

[4] Resolutions of the Communist International Seventh Congress, p. 37.
[5] *Ibid.*, p. 39. [6] *Ibid.*, p. 27. [7] *Ibid.*, p. 30.

"The struggle for the establishment of the united front [the resolution added] charges every communist party to wage an irreconcilable struggle against any tendency to gloss over the differences in principles between communism and reformism" as well as against "the illusion that it is possible to bring about socialism by peaceful, legal methods." [8]

As for the fight against war, every effective means should be used to prevent war. Should, despite the opposition of a united front against war, a new imperialist war break out, despite all efforts of the working class to prevent it, "the communists [maintained the resolution] will strive to lead the opponents of war, organized in the struggle for peace, to the struggle for the transformation of the imperialist war into civil war against the fascist instigators of war, against the bourgeoisie, for the overthrow of capitalism." [9]

Following the 1935 Congress, the communists returned from Moscow to their respective countries with the message of the united front, offering the olive branch to socialists (whom they had formerly designated "social fascists"), to trade unionists, and to various progressive groups, and urging united front activities against fascist aggression.[10]

Change of Communist Tactics in United States. In the United States, in the 1936 campaign, in response to the changing policy of the Comintern, the Communist party sought an alliance with socialist and progressive groups, its spokesman, Earl Browder, declaring that, as a future socialist system was supported by only a small minority of the population, communists considered it to be "the duty of adherents of socialism to join hands with all progressives not ready for socialism, on the basis of such a platform of democratic and progressive measure, which will guarantee our country from the horrors of fascism and war, and make the future social transformation less difficult and painful." [11] While he did not publicly support the Democratic candidate for President, Franklin D. Roosevelt, Browder declared that Roosevelt's reelection would "be a rebuke to the worst reactionaries." [12] Instead of pronouncing capitalist democracy "a sham," as did the party's standard bearer in 1932,[13] Mr. Browder time and again maintained that com-

[8] *Ibid.*, p. 37.

[9] *Ibid.*, p. 47.

[10] "Instead of class struggle, co-operation with the bourgeois [declared Borkenau, in describing the changed attitude of Communists as he saw it]. Instead of the Soviet system, eulogy of democracy. Instead of internationalism, nationalism . . . Hundreds of responsible communist leaders, a few months before, had denounced everybody as a Trotskyist traitor who spoke of co-operation with the socialists and the necessity of defending democracy, now not a single one of these leaders rose against the change" (Borkenau, *op. cit.*, p. 387).

[11] Browder, *The People's Front*, p. 85.

[12] *Ibid.*, p. 103.

[13] Foster, *Toward Soviet America*, p. 255.

munists were ardent believers in democracy. "It is a popular superstition," he declared before the National Press Club,[14] "that the communists are anti-democratic. This arises out of a vulgar interpretation of our slogan of the dictatorship of the proletariat as the means of the transition to socialism. The communists are not and never have been anti-democratic. The communists' program is only realizable through the fullest possible extension of democracy, and the realization of democracy on a scale which has not been dreamed of in our country before."

As for violence, Browder maintained, "The Communist party is not and has not been the advocate of force and violence."

Two years later, at the Communist party's convention in 1938, the party completely revised its Constitution and further maintained its allegiance to democratic principles, declaring that the party upholds the achievements of democracy and "defends the United States Constitution against the reactionary enemies who would destroy democracy and all popular liberties." At the same time, however, it pledged itself to strive to bring about socialism "according to the scientific principles enunciated by the greatest teachers of mankind, Marx, Engels, Lenin, and Stalin, embodied in the Communist International."

In 1940, a year when the Soviet-Axis pact was still in force, the party vigorously opposed support of the Democratic administration and urged the people to "combat the imperialist policies and acts of the President . . . to spread the war and involve the United States in it."[15] "Not a cent, not a gun, not a man," its platform read, "for war preparations and the imperialist war."

Following the German invasion of Russia on June 22, 1941, however, the communists of the United States threw their support to many candidates of the Democratic party who were backing "President Roosevelt and the government's win-the-war policies."

The Death of the Third International (1943). As the Second World War advanced, the Russian communists became increasingly of the opinion that the continued existence of the Communist International was proving a stumbling block to the Soviet government in its relations with other governments composing the United Nations. On May 22, 1943, the Presidium of the Communist International proposed to the constituent Communist parties the Comintern's dissolution. In issuing this proposal, the Presidium maintained that the International had outlived its usefulness.

[14] Speech of August 26, 1936; Browder, *The People's Front,* p. 209.
[15] See *New York Times,* June 2, 1940.

"Long before the war," the Presidium's pronouncement declared, "it became more and more clear that, with increasing complications in international relations of various countries, any sort of international center would encounter insuperable obstacles in solving the problems facing the movement in each separate country.

"Deep differences of the historic paths of development of various countries, differences in their character and even contradictions in their social orders, differences in the level and tempo of their economic and political development, differences finally in the degree of consciousness and organization of workers, conditioned different problems affecting the working class of the various countries."

Following the dissolution of the Communist International in 1943, the Communist party of the United States continued its support of many Democratic party candidates who favored President Roosevelt's foreign policies, including Mayor Frank Hague of Jersey City, who had been for years denounced by the communists as an American "dictator." It opposed any attempt to form labor parties which might take support away from the Roosevelt wing of the Democratic party. At the plenary session of the Communist party National Committee held in New York, January 7–9, 1944, Browder announced that the Political Committee of the party had recommended that the Communist party be disbanded and that some such organization as the American Communist Political Association be formed. In announcing this decision, Mr. Browder declared that communists in the United States, during and immediately after the war, were in no sense aiming at the transformation of the United States into a communist or a socialist economic order, but were of the belief that "any plans for American postwar reconstruction which are based on the introduction of socialism are in effect a repudiation of the aim to unite the majority of the nation behind the Teheran policies." "It is my considered judgment," he declared, "that the American people are so ill-prepared, subjectively, for any deep-going change in the direction of socialism that postwar plans with such an aim would not unite the nation, but would further divide it. . . .

"Whatever may be the situation in other lands, in the United States this means a perspective in the immediate postwar period of expanded production and employment and the strengthening of democracy within the framework of the present system—and not a perspective of the transition to socialism. . . . Marxists will not help the reactionaries by opposing the slogan of 'free enterprise' with any form of counter-slogan . . . We will choose our associates first and above all according to whether they are for or against the Teheran policy, and the effectiveness of their support, regardless of class differences or past political divisions."

"The whole development of events in the last quarter of a century and the experience accumulated by the Communist International convincingly showed that the organizational form of uniting workers chosen by the First Congress of the Communist International answered conditions of the first stages of the working-class movement, but it has been outgrown by the growth of this movement and by the complications of its problems in separate countries, and has even become a drag on the further strengthening of the national working-class parties."

The declaration maintained that the Second World War had "still further sharpened these differences in the situation of the various countries and has placed a deep dividing line between those countries that fell under the Hitler tyranny and those freedom-loving people who have united in a powerful anti-Hitlerite coalition." In the former countries the foremost task of the workers was the development of an armed struggle which would eventuate in a national war of liberation against Hitlerite Germany. In the United Nations, the task of the workers was to give their whole-hearted support to the war against Hitler.[16]

On May 20, 1944, the Communist party of the United States, at a convention in New York, dissolved as a political party and reorganized as the Communist Political Association with a view of achieving collaboration with the "broader circles" of American life. It opened its membership to any resident of this country over 18 years old interested in "the advancement of the interests of the nation and its people. It provided also for the expulsion from its ranks of any one who seeks to "subvert, undermine, weaken or overthrow any or all institutions of American democracy." Earl Browder was elected president of the new organization. He made it clear in his convention addresses that the association stood four square upon the "principles of scientific socialism" and recognized socialism's "character as an international movement." He likewise declared that socialism for America was "something which will and must be realized in characteristic American terms, when it is practical to speak of a democratic choice of the American people which will decide the transition to socialism in our country." On the other hand, he maintained, the communists' own program had "not the slightest suggestion of confiscation of wealth" and was "consistent with the fullest possible expansion of consumption by the wealthy

[16] Browder, *Teheran and America*, pp. 19, 20, 24, 41.

and the accumulation of their private incomes above their consumption level in whatever form they see fit." [17]

Summary of Communist Shift in Policy. Thus by the early forties the communists had shifted their tactics and philosophy of social change in several particulars from those enunciated in 1919, largely as a result of the changed position of the Soviet government, the relative lack of success of the communist movement outside of Russia, the rise of fascism, and the emergence of the Second World War. These shifts involved:

The abandonment of the attempt of the Soviet government to serve as an instrument of world revolution—utilizing the Third International as its foreign arm for that purpose—and the concentration of the government on the task of constructing communism in Russia.

The abandonment, as a consequence, of a highly centralized Communist International and the freeing of "the sections of the Comintern from their obligations arising from the statutes and resolutions of the Congresses of the Communist International."

The abandonment of the concept that social change in all countries is likely to follow the same pattern as in Russia.

The abandonment of the policy of refusing to co-operate with non-communist groups on the economic and political fields in countries outside of Russia.

The abandonment of the policy of denouncing socialists as "social-fascists," and of denouncing all "bourgeois democracy" as sham.

The abandonment of communist advocacy of indirect pyramidal representation in Russia as an essential characteristic of a Soviet form of government.

The abandonment of communist advocacy, in the official pronouncements of their parties in democratic countries, of force and violence as the only means to the achievement of power.

Comments on Communist United Front Policies. Critics of the communist movement have made a number of comments on the significance of these changes:

They point out that, despite the Third International's contention that communist tactics should differ in each country, and despite the freedom of the Communist party of the United States from official connection with the Communist International from 1940 to 1943, the tactics of the American party during these years were attuned to the

[17] *New York Times,* May 21–4, 1944; *World Telegram,* May 24, 1944; *Daily Worker,* May 21–4, 1944.

changing policies of the Soviet government, rather than to the changing needs of the American people.

They maintain that communist united-front tactics in the past constituted a mere temporary expedient, with the primary aim of strengthening the hold of the communist movement on the masses and placing communists in a more effective position of leadership in the battle for proletarian dictatorship, with the resulting division of the workers into bitterly antagonistic communist and non-communist camps.

They contend that, while communists have now publicly come to the defense of democracy, it is anything but clear what is their definition of democracy, especially when they eulogize the dictatorship in Russia as having "shown the way to the final and complete guarantee of democracy and its fullest development." [18]

Further, they question the sincerity of the use by communists of democratic slogans, when such slogans have been used in the past with the view of destroying "bourgeois democratic institutions." [19]

However, while still aiming at a dictatorship as a transitional stage of development, many communists during the last decade or so have come to the conclusion that, in some democratic countries, power may be attained through parliamentary means, this to be followed by dictatorial control.[20]

[18] Browder, *The People's Front,* p. 346.

[19] Such use of slogans was described by Georgi Dimitrov, secretary of the Communist International, in the debate over the change in tactics in the 1935 Congress of the Comintern. Dimitrov declared in this debate that the communist "attitude toward bourgeois democracy is not the same under all conditions." At the time of the October Revolution, for instance, "the Russian bolsheviks engaged in a life and death struggle against all political parties which opposed the establishment of the proletarian dictatorship *under the slogan of the defense of bourgeois democracy.*"

"The bolsheviks fought these parties because the banner of bourgeois democracy had at that time become the standard around which all counterrevolutionary forces mobilized to challenge the victory of the proletariat. The situation is quite different in the capitalist countries at present. Now the fascist counterrevolution is attacking bourgeois democracy in an effort to establish a most barbaric regime of exploitation and suppression of the toiling masses. Now the toiling masses in a number of capitalist countries are faced with the necessity of making a definite choice, and of making it today, not between proletariat dictatorship and bourgeois democracy, but between bourgeois democracy and fascism" (Executive Committee of the Communist International, *Report of the Seventh World Congress,* p. 116). (Italics ours.)

"As long as we cannot replace bourgeois democracy by the dictatorship of the proletariat," declared Pigck, in his official report on the work of his committee, "the proletariat is interested in retaining every scrap of bourgeois democracy in order to use it to prepare the masses for the overthrow of the power of capitalism, and to achieve proletarian democracy" (Executive Committee of the Communist International, *Report of the Seventh World Congress,* p. 28).

[20] Durbin, *The Politics of a Democratic Socialism,* p. 224.

Socialists' Stand in Regard to Co-operation with Soviet Government. These criticisms of communism in theory and practice, however, in no way prevented socialists in various of the United Nations from acknowledging the real achievements of the Soviet government along industrial, social, educational, and other lines,[21] nor from urging close co-operation between the Soviet government and other countries in the prosecution of war against nazism, in the framing of the peace, and in the development of world co-operation for the maintenance of permanent peace and the attainment of the Four Freedoms. In fact, such socialist students as Professor Laski contend that such co-operation by non-communist democratic nations is a necessary preliminary to the gradual weakening of dictatorship in Soviet Russia. "So long," he maintains, "as there is widespread conviction that the capitalist powers are prepared to attack the Soviet Union, so long the dictatorship will persist; for so long will it be able to utilize national sentiments on its own behalf." When, on the other hand, the Russian people can look expectantly forward to adequate assistance in case of attack by aggressor nations, "the demand for democratic concessions from the dictatorship will follow rapidly." [22]

Summary. It is thus seen that, while socialists and communists envisage, in general, a society in which production is carried on for use and not for profit, they differ on many questions of principle and tactics.

The communists maintained in their Manifesto of 1919 that violence and civil war were necessary and well-nigh inevitable in the ushering in of the new society. Socialists, on the other hand, maintained, that, while violence might attend the change to a co-operative society, every effort should be made to introduce socialism in a peaceful fashion through parliamentary victories, industrial organization, co-operative action, and educational propaganda; that, if force were to be used, it should be resorted to primarily for the purpose of defending the gains of the labor government against counterrevolutionary attacks, and that the force employed should be the minimum required to safeguard the gains of the co-operative order which the masses of the people supported.

The communists insisted that, during the transitional stage, the workers should establish a dictatorship of the proletariat, which virtually

[21] See Laski, *Reflections on the Revolution of Our Time,* pp. 44 ff.

[22] Laski, *op. cit.,* p. 77.

In describing the communist position we have dealt in this text with the policies of the official communist movement of the Stalinists. The position of the followers of Trotsky and of the Fourth International, which existed for some years, hewed more closely to the original bolshevik line and emphasized the alleged need of an International that would continue to work for world revolution.

means a dictatorship of the Communist party; should, in many countries, exclude non-producing classes from voting or holding office; should maintain a strict censorship of the press and of speech, and should concentrate all power in the hands of the dictatorship. They also urged the soviet form of government as the most efficient type of government during the period of transition.

The socialists, on the other hand, while realizing the defects of capitalist democracy and advocating a number of changes in the parliamentary structure, still hold that dictatorship both in theory and practice contains gravely dangerous implications from the standpoint of the working class and of society-at-large, and that the democratic procedure, so modified as to adjust itself to the complexities of our times, is wiser.

Since the issuance of the *Communist Manifesto* of 1919, however, communist tactics, as has been indicated, have changed in several respects. In the early years, the Communist International bent its every energy toward dividing the working class in Western European countries into socialist groups, on the one hand, and communist nuclei, on the other, which should incite the working class to armed rebellion against their respective governments.

With the failure of the communists to gain political power in other countries of Europe, and the rise of fascism, these tactics were definitely modified and an attempt made to co-operate with democratic forces in the fight against fascism. The Third International, first utilized by Soviet leaders in their effort to foster world revolution, then in their struggle against dissenting forces at home, and finally in their fight against fascism abroad, was abandoned in the midst of the Second World War. Upon its liquidation, the Soviet leaders paid their acknowledgment to the great social, political, and cultural differences existing in various countries, necessitating differences in tactics and policies.

The communists have recently changed their attitude toward democratic institutions in countries outside of Russia and have made definite changes in the Soviet constitution looking toward democracy. In practice, however, they have centralized power increasingly in the Communist party and its leadership in Russia. Some of the communists now visualize gaining power through democratic means, as did the nazis in Germany, and then using their power democratically gained to establish a temporary dictatorship, with a view to effecting the social change they desire.

How much of the change in tactics is temporary and how much is permanent is difficult to tell. In the 1935 Congress of the Communist International, communist leaders maintained that the changed tactics urged did not mean the final abandonment of former communist tactics, but their temporary postponement. Many non-communists contend that the permanence or temporary character of the changes depends largely on the sense of security from outside attack felt by the Russian communists after the Second World War, and on the type of international co-operation that is developed between Soviet Russia and the important democracies of the world.

PART FIVE

Socialist Movements in Various Lands

CHAPTER 31

Labor and Socialism in Great Britain and Western Europe

WHILE the Russian communist movement was the most conspicuous in its activities in the years during and following the First World War, other movements have had interesting and important developments.

In our chapter on "Guild Socialism," we have described in brief the early history of the British labor party.[1] Prior to the First World War, the British Labor party, while looking in the direction of socialism, never officially committed itself to the socialist position. During the war, however, its membership swung to the left, and in 1918 it adopted the now-famous program known as "Labor and the New Social Order" to which it has since adhered.

BRITISH LABOR SINCE THE FIRST WORLD WAR

1918 Program on Labor and the New Social Order. "We need," declared the document in which this new labor program was set forth, "to beware of patchwork. The view of the Labor party is that what has to be reconstructed after the war is not this or that government department, or this or that piece of social machinery; but, so far as Great Britain is concerned, society itself. . . . The individualist system of capitalist production, based on the private ownership and competitive administration of land and capital, with its reckless profiteering, with the monstrous inequality of circumstances which it produces and the degradation and brutalization, both moral and spiritual, resulting therefrom may, we hope, indeed have received a death blow. . . . If we in Britain are to escape from the decay of civilization itself . . . we must ensure that what is presently to be built up is a new social order, based not on fighting but on fraternity—not on the competitive struggle for the means of bare life, but on a deliberately planned co-operation in production and distribution for the benefit of all who participate by

[1] See text, pp. 316–19.

hand and by brain—not on the utmost possible inequality of riches, but on a systematic approach to a healthy equality of material circumstances for every person born into the world—not on an enforced dominion over subject nations, subject colonies, subject classes, or a subject sex, but, in industry as well as in government, on that equal freedom, that general consciousness of consent, and that widest participation in power, both economic and political, which is characteristic of democracy."

The party declared that it did not in any sense believe that the new social order could be brought in within a year or two of feverish reconstruction but that what it intended to satisfy itself about was that each brick that it helped to lay should go to erect that structure and no other.

The B. L. P. held that its main point of cleavage from the parties of capitalism was its desire to build up the community as a whole rather than to magnify individual fortunes. Abroad it sought constant progress in democratic self-government of every part of the British Alliance. The four pillars of the house which it hoped to erect, resting upon the common foundation of the democratic control of all of society in all of its activities were:

First, The Universal Enforcement of the National Minimum, the minimum which would ensure to each member of the community all the requisite leisure, health, education, and subsistence. That program would involve such provisions as minimum wage legislation, better provision for education and health, unemployment insurance, and systematic planning of public works.

Second, The Democratic Control of Industry. This change would include the immediate nationalization of mines, railways, and electrical power and the generation and distribution of such power on a national scale. Industrial insurance should be brought under community control and municipalities should not only control their water, gas, electricity, and trolley lines, but should extend their enterprises in town planning and housing, parks and public libraries, the provision for music, and the organization of recreation. They should also undertake, according to this program, the retailing of coal and other services of common utility, particularly the local supply of milk, wherever this was not already fully and satisfactorily organized by a co-operative society.

Third, A Revolution in National Finance, and the paying off of the war debt by the imposition of steeply graduated income and inheritance taxes and the conscription of wealth.

Fourth, Surplus Wealth for the Common Good. The income from the taxes listed above and from the municipal and federal services should be used for the sick and for the provision of such educational opportunities as would overcome all differences of material circumstances. "From the same source will come," the platform reads, "the greatly increased public provision that the Labor party will insist on being made for scientific investigation and research, in every branch of knowledge, not to say also for the promotion of music, literature, and fine art, which have been under capitalism so greatly neglected, and upon which, so the Labor party holds, any real development of civilization depends."

The First Labor Government (1924). During the "khaki election" of December, 1918, British Labor increased its representation from 38 to 59. In 1922 this was increased to 144, and, in late 1923, to 192, out of 640, or about 30 per cent of the members of the House. Following the latter election the King asked Ramsay MacDonald, chairman of the Parliamentary Labor group, to take office. A labor cabinet was formed with MacDonald as Premier, and Arthur Henderson, Philip Snowden, Sidney Webb, Sir Sidney Olivier, James Thomas, Lord Haldane, Sir Charles Trevelyan, and others as members. The party served as a minority government—a government backed by only a minority of the members of Parliament—for nine months. The administration during these months gave chief attention to the cultivation of a more peaceful spirit in Europe. It recognized Russia, limited army and naval expenditures, and outlined a progressive housing, educational, and unemployment policy. It was finally forced to resign on a minor issue—that of refusing to prosecute a communist leader—and, in the ensuing election, lost some 40 seats, electing 142 members. Its popular vote increased, however, more than a million, to 4,500,000. The decrease in parliamentary representation was due in part to the publication of a letter alleged to have been sent to MacDonald by Zinoviev, although proof of its authenticity has never been made public, and, in larger part, to the unification of the opposition and the concentration of antilabor votes in the Conservative party. The great decline at this election of the Liberal party—it elected only 36 members—however, placed the Labor party securely in the position of His Majesty's opposition.

During the spring of 1926 occurred the nine-day general strike in support of the miners, led by the British Trade Union Council. The collapse of the strike and the consequent chaos in the mining industry led, among other things, to increased interest in political action.

The Labor Government of 1929. In 1928 the Labor party issued another manifesto, "Labor and the Nation," which again committed the party to the socialization of coal, land, transport, power, the Bank of England, and life insurance, among other industries and services.

In the elections of 1929, Labor elected 288 representatives, only 20 less than a majority. MacDonald was again chosen Prime Minister; Arthur Henderson was appointed Foreign Minister. As was the case with the 1924 Labor government, Labor had to obtain the support of the Liberals for any legislation the government hoped to pass. This situation precluded the introduction of much legislation of a socialistic character. The MacDonald government therefore contented itself in the domestic field with urging a public-works program to reduce unemployment and with reforms in housing, education, health, transportation, and mining.

On the international field the ministry carried through the British evacuation of the Rhineland; liberalized Britain's policy in Palestine, Iraq, and Egypt; ratified the Washington eight-hour convention; suspended, for the most part, cruiser building; resumed diplomatic relations with Soviet Russia; and prepared for the disarmament conference. Mr. Henderson showed marked ability as Britain's Foreign Minister.

The cabinet was frequently attacked for its alleged overcaution. Among the dissidents was Sir Oswald Mosley, later the fascist leader, who resigned as Chancellor of the Duchy of Lancaster because of the failure of J. H. Thomas, then Minister of Employment, to give heed to Mosley's plan for dealing with unemployment. The I. L. P., on the other hand, criticized the government for failing to adopt a policy looking toward "socialism in our time."

As a means of satisfying some of the cabinet's critics, the government constituted an Experts' Commission, headed by Sir George May, to recommend a way out of the financial dilemma. The commission, in July, 1931, submitted a conservative report, in which it urged that the government's expenditures be reduced by nearly a hundred million pounds, this reduction to be effected largely by cutting unemployment benefits, by reducing the pay of teachers and civil servants, and by contracting social service activities.

MacDonald's Desertion of Labor Party (1931). The commission's recommendations were rejected by the trade-union movement and the Labor party, which insisted upon an increase in taxation and in unemployment insurance benefits. MacDonald was empowered by labor bodies to present his resignation to the King.

When the time came to submit his resignation, MacDonald resigned —August 24, 1931—as Labor party Prime Minister. However, after an interview with the King, to the astonishment of Labor, he thereupon formed a National government which embraced Conservatives, Liberals, and such Laborites as Philip Snowden, J. H. Thomas, and Lord Sankey.

The desertion of MacDonald, the party's most prominent leader, at this critical moment, together with those of the brilliant socialist and financier, Philip Snowden, and the powerful, right wing trade-union leader, J. H. Thomas, was a heavy blow to the party.

On August 28 MacDonald was deposed as leader of the Labor party's parliamentary group. Arthur Henderson was chosen in his place by a vote of 274 to 6. MacDonald was also repudiated in his home constituency of Seaham Harbor, but was later re-elected by the voters of that district.

Labor as Opposition, 1931–1935. On reconvening on September 8, 1931, Parliament gave to the new Coalition government a vote of confidence (309 to 250), and the Cabinet undertook the task of carrying out a program of economy along the lines suggested by the May Commission. On October 7, Parliament was dissolved.

In the ensuing elections Labor urged various measures of socialization, but the Conservatives denounced Labor's program as "bolshevism gone wild." The Conservatives were overwhelmingly elected, winning 471 out of 615 seats. The Liberals won 67 seats; the Liberal opposition, 4; Labor, 52; National Labor, 13; the Independents, 8. Despite its small parliamentary representation Labor received a popular vote of 6,363,000 as compared with 11,871,000 for the Conservatives and 2,003,000 for the Liberals.

During the next few years Labor fought in Parliament as "His Majesty's Opposition," with George Lansbury as parliamentary leader. Arthur Henderson, secretary of the party, continued his work in 1932 as President of the World Disarmament Conference, though without result. Because of ill health, he was forced to resign his secretaryship of the party in 1934, and, on October 20, 1935, passed away. Through his death the party lost its most effective organizer and most trusted leader, and Europe one of its outstanding labor statesmen. He was succeeded as secretary by James Middleton.

The National Laborites, as time went on, gradually dwindled in numbers and influence. MacDonald, owing to failing health, resigned from the premiership in June, 1935, becoming Lord President of the Council, and was succeeded by Stanley Baldwin. Philip Snowden severed his relation with the government in September, 1932, because of strong disagreement with its tariff policy, and died the following year.

Labor's 1935 Campaign. In October, 1935, Parliament was dissolved, and on November 14 new elections were held. Prior to the dissolution, Labor's vigorous stand in favor of a policy of collective security led George Lansbury and Lord Ponsonby, noted pacifists and Labor's leaders in the House of Commons and House of Lords, respectively, to hand in their resignations. Labor fought its campaign on the basis of a program of action formulated the previous year, under the general title, "For Socialism and Peace," a companion manifesto to "Labor and the New Social Order," its 1918 proclamation, and of "Labor and the Nation," its 1928 pronouncement.

In this manifesto, Labor attacked the National government for its conservative domestic policy and its timid foreign policy. Democracies in Austria and Germany, it maintained, had been destroyed without a word of protest from the British government. The government's high-tariff system and its domestic policy of contracting public expenditures had made the failure of the World Economic Conference inevitable. Headstrong Japanese Imperialism in the Far East had been assisted by the "timid and supine attitude, not to say the tacit connivance" of Great Britain. "A feeble and disingenuous policy on disarmament and security" had helped to frustrate the attempts to achieve a reduction in armaments and had stimulated the arms race to which Far Eastern events gave the initial impulse.

"In every field [the manifesto continued] the government presents a spectacle of moral and political bankruptcy . . . Its members are united on nothing except their desire to prevent the coming of socialism. . . .

"The choice before the nation is either a vain attempt to patch up the superstructure of a capitalist society in decay at its very foundations, or a rapid advance to a socialist reconstruction of the national life." There is no halfway house between a society based on private ownership in the means of production, with the profit of the few as a measure of success, and a society where public ownership of the means of production makes possible the deliberate planning of the nation's resources with a view of attaining the maximum of general well-being.

In the campaign the Conservative party attacked Labor on the alleged grounds that its policy would lead the nation into war, whereas the Conservative government could be depended upon to preserve the peace. The Independent Labor party, for the first time in its history, found itself in opposition to some of the candidates of the Labor party and conducted a separate campaign in 16 districts. The communists, in accordance with the new line laid down by the Communist International, supported Labor candidates except in two districts where they thought that they could make a good showing. The British Union of Fascists ran no candidates, but prominently displayed the slogan during the campaign, "Blackshirts watch this futile farce and say 'Fascism Next Time.' "

The November 14 balloting resulted in the election of 154 Labor candidates, and an increase in popular votes for the Labor party from 6,363,000 to 8,326,000. The Conservatives, however, while electing 84 representatives less than in 1931, still retained a majority, winning 387 seats. The "National" Liberals elected 33; "National" Labor, 8; "National," 3; Liberals, 17; Independent Liberals, 4; and all others, 9. The following table indicates the position of Labor as a result of the 1935 elections, as compared with other years:

General Elections	*Members Returned*	*Labor Vote*
1900	2	62,698
1906	29	323,195
1910 (Jan.)	40	505,690
1910 (Dec.)	42	370,802
1918	57	2,244,945
1922	142	4,236,733
1923	191	4,348,379
1924	151	5,487,620
1929	287	8,364,883
1931	46	6,362,561
1935	154	8,326,131

Following the 1935 election and until Britain's entrance into the Second World War, the British Labor party, as the official Opposition, attacked, within and without Parliament, the domestic and foreign policy of the Conservative party, advocated a constructive program of its own, and worked energetically toward the strengthening of its party organization.

Labor's Immediate Program (1937). At its 1937 conference the party adopted "Labor's Immediate Program" as a basis for its propaganda before and during its next electoral campaign and as a guide to its governmental activity, should it win the succeeding election. As in previous manifestoes, the party pledged the use of the resources of the nation for the service of all and maintained that a Labor government would prove that "while preserving freedom and respecting the rights of minorities, the democratic system can work swiftly and effectively. The Labor party [it continued] when the electors give it power, will, without hesitation or delay, take the first steps to reorganize the economic life of our country. As a means to this end, the community must command the main levers which control the economic machine. These are finance, land, transport, coal, and power."

In the 1937–38 session of Parliament, besides presenting numerous bills for immediate reforms before Parliament, the party introduced a sweeping proposal that legislative effort be directed "towards the substitution of an industrial and social order based upon public ownership and democratic control of the instruments of production and distribution." The proposal was rejected by a small vote of 153 to 117.

Labor's Attack on Chamberlain's Foreign Policy. During these days the party representatives denounced the government's failure to lift the Spanish embargo so as to permit the Loyalist Spanish government to obtain arms, and attacked the government's lack of effective action in the Ethiopian crisis and in connection with the invasion of China by Japan and of Austria and Czechoslovakia by Germany.

In September, 1938, the Labor party joined with the trade unions in urging Great Britain to join with the French and Russians in pronouncements which left no doubt in the minds of the German government that they would resist any attack on Czechoslovakia. Later the National Council of Labor bitterly denounced the action of the Chamberlain government in permitting the dismemberment of Czechoslovakia as "a shameful betrayal of a peaceful and democratic people." It urged the reconvening of Parliament, held great demonstrations in behalf of Czechoslovakia in various parts of the country, and issued an appeal to the German people to restrain their government "from plunging Europe once more into the horrors of wholesale slaughter."

In the summer of 1939 the party issued a further appeal to the people of Germany to insist that all issues between the nations of Europe be settled by reason and not by war. "Far from wishing to encircle your country with a view of crushing it," the National Council of Labor declared, "we invite you to come into the circle yourselves, to join up with a world-wide combination of nations so that the great abilities of the German people may make their contributions to the establishment of a friendly world in which mankind may prosper." [2]

Labor's Support of War: Criticism of Conduct. Following the signing of the Nazi-Soviet Pact in late August, the National Council urged that the obligation undertaken by Britain in defense of the independence of Poland be honored to the full. After the invasion of Poland the party declared that it was prepared to support the fulfilling of the treaty with Poland, but would not accept any invitation that might be extended to it to join the government.

During the next few months the Labor party, while vigorously sup-

[2] *Report of the 39th Annual Conference of the Labor Party,* 1940, pp. 6–7.

porting the war, severely condemned the conduct of many governmental departments. Its spokesmen urged that the trade unions be brought into active consultation on questions of production, denounced war profiteering, and declared that national factories were "absolutely essential." "The labor movement," asserted Arthur Greenwood, "cannot be regarded as a sort of helot class whose grievances about labor conditions may be settled so that they will make better slaves in munitions factories and mines. I ask that labor in this problem of production be treated on a basis of equality."

The party also urged the organization of an economic general staff with the view to the mobilization of the whole of the country's national and human resources. It likewise proposed a capital levy as a means of raising money for defense. It urged the government to make some definite pronouncement in favor of a policy which would expedite progress toward Dominion Home Rule in India, and attacked several of the acts of government as menacing the legitimate liberty of the individual.

Labor and the Peace. The peace aims of Labor were set forth in February, 1940, in the party's pronouncement on "Labor, the War, and the Peace." The peace settlement, according to Labor's manifesto, should establish "a new Association or Commonwealth of states, the collective authority of which must transcend, over a proper sphere, the sovereign rights of separate states. This authority must control such military and economic power as will enable it to enforce peaceful behavior between its members and thus secure the all-around reduction of national armaments to the level required for the preservation of international order. . . . Labor will be no party to imperialist exploitation, whether capitalist or other. . . . Colonial peoples everywhere should move forward as speedily as possible towards self-government. . . . There must be equal opportunity of access for all peaceful peoples to raw materials and markets in these colonial territories."

"A new world order, which applies these principles," the statement continues, "can only be securely founded on socialism and democracy. . . . There must be bold economic and financial planning on a world-wide scale," [3] in addition to national policies of reconstruction, in order to avoid mass unemployment following the war.

As the spring of 1940 advanced, the Labor party's representatives continued their attacks on the Chamberlain government—attacks which were redoubled with the invasion of Norway.

[3] *Labor Aims in War and Peace,* pp. 89–95.

Entry of Labor into Churchill Cabinet (1940). On May 11, 1940, Prime Minister Chamberlain resigned, and Winston Churchill was asked to form a new cabinet. Labor was asked to become a part of the reconstructed cabinet and accepted.

In the new government Labor was represented by many members. Clement R. Attlee, parliamentary leader, became Lord Privy Seal; Arthur Greenwood, Minister without Portfolio; A. V. Alexander, First Lord of the Admiralty; Herbert Morrison, Minister of Supply; Ernest Bevin, Minister of Labor and National Defense; Hugh Dalton, Minister of Economic Warfare; D. R. Grenfell, Secretary of Mines; and Sir William Jowitt, Solicitor General. Attlee and Greenwood constituted two of the five members of the War Cabinet.

When the approval of the new cabinet was sought, James Maxton and Campbell Stephen of the I. L. P. voiced the only opposition. As they were designated tellers and could not vote, the balloting ended with a vote of 381 to 0. At the May Conference of the Labor party, the entrance of party representatives into the cabinet was approved by a card vote of 2,413,000 to 170,000. Three other resolutions presented were defeated. One demanded a socialist government as a precondition of labor's support of the war. Another presented by a delegate from Edinburgh, described the war as imperialistic and called for the establishment of a workers' government, and a third deplored the policy of a fight to the finish and urged a negotiated peace.

When the government introduced the Emergency Powers Defense Act of May 22, 1940, under which the whole resources of the community, according to the law, might be "rendered available when required for purposes connected with the defense of the realm," the Labor party supported the bill. The I. L. P., following its passage, urged that the powers be applied with a view to the conscription of wealth.

In early October, when Mr. Chamberlain resigned from his position of Lord President of the Council, the cabinet was further reconstructed, and Ernest Bevin was appointed a member of the War Cabinet, and Herbert Morrison was promoted to the position of Minister for Home Security. Bevin became one of the cabinet's most powerful figures. For the following months the Labor party gave unstintingly of its support to the war, while endeavoring to maintain labor standards and preserve civil liberties.

In the Annual Conference in the spring of 1942 the party again urged "the socialization of the basic industries and services of the country, and the planning of production for community consumption as the only lasting foundation for a just and prosperous economic order in which political democracy and personal liberty can be combined with a reasonable standard for all citizens." [4] Further, the Independent Labor party urged that steps be taken immediately toward the ushering in of a socialist society.

In the 1943 Conference the Labor party once again turned down the application of the British Communist party for affiliation. It reaffirmed its support of the party's electoral truce and the party's participation in the War Cabinet.

During the war the Common Wealth party, headed by Sir Richard T. D. Acland, gained considerable impetus and elected several members to Parliament. In its manifesto it demanded the transfer to common ownership of all the land of Great Britain, as well as the common ownership of all credit and investment institutions, public-service enterprises, mines, factories, and large-scale distributive trading enterprises. Its program called for "reasonable" compensation to the owners, starting with 100 per cent to small holders and small remuneration to the largest. Other demands included self-government for the colonies, immediate independence for India, and a postwar world council to control shipping, civil and military aviation, and international trade. The party asked for the support not only of labor, but "of every possible kind of people," maintaining that "the salaried manager, the engineer, the scientist, the technician of every kind, the black-coated office worker, has exactly the same *economic* interest to struggle against this [the capitalist] system as has the miner or the engine driver." [5]

In 1944 the National Executive Committee of the Labor party prepared for a party conference a report on "The International Postwar Settlement," which urged the creation of a world organization with power to suppress aggressive war; the disarmament of Japan and Germany after their defeat; the government manufacture of arms in Great Britain; a colonial policy aimed primarily at "the well-being and education of the native inhabitants . . . and their preparation for self-government without delay"; the strengthening of the International Labor Organization as a powerful instrument for understanding among the workers of all lands and for raising living standards especially in backward countries; and the creation and strengthening of international

[4] See pamphlet on *British Labor on Reconstruction in War and Peace* (published by The League for Industrial Democracy and by British Labor party); and criticism of the Labor party on the ground of lack of sufficient militancy, by Harold J. Laski in *Marx and Today.*

[5] *The People's Year Book,* 1943, p. 12.

institutions "to plan relief and rehabilitation, to organize abundant world-wide food supplies and to regulate international trading, transport and monetary relationships."

The Executive Council's report reiterated the party's socialist goal. "The Labor party," it maintained, "works for a socialist future. It does so because twice in our own lifetime, we have seen that war is inherent in the nature of a capitalist society. Capitalism means everywhere the protection of the privileges of the few by the sacrifice of the well-being of the many, and in the relations between states, capitalism means a power-politics which is even more ugly and brutal. This is why the Labor party is convinced that, only as the framework of our civilization is socialist can we hope both for the assurance of economic plenty and a peace which it is to the interest of all states to preserve."

In 1944 the Labor party, as a result of various elections since the mid-thirties was represented by 167 members of Parliament. Other party representatives were as follows: Conservative, 365; Liberal National, 26; Liberal, 18; National Labor, 7; National, 4; Independent, 23; Independent Labor, 3; Communist, 1.

In Parliament during the war Labor members pressed for the presentation by the government of comprehensive postwar plans on housing, education, social security, and other services. Arthur Greenwood, leader of the Parliamentary party, in the Spring of 1944, contended that England and Wales alone needed, after the war, on any reasonable standard, 5,500,000 new houses, and pointed out that in northern England there were still many semi-slums built three-quarters of a century ago when there were no housing standards. The problem of how far the Labor party was obligated to support the government in civil matters as well as in the war effort was vigorously debated throughout the war years.

THE FRENCH MOVEMENT

In the chapter on "Syndicalism" [6] we have told something of the history of the French socialist movement up until the time of the First World War. When the war broke out the French Socialist party was represented by slightly more than 100 members in the House of Deputies, under the leadership of Jean Jaurès, one of the most brilliant orators of modern times. The party was dealt a severe blow in the assassination of Jaurès on the eve of the war in 1914. During the war most of the socialists, regarding the conflict as a war of defense, supported the French government. Later, however, opposition developed, and a large section in the latter days of the war fought for the cessation

[6] See text, p. 277.

of hostilities and a democratic peace. After the Russian revolution a majority of its members joined the Third International and formed the Communist party, capturing the chief party organ, *L'Humanité.*

Split in Socialist Movement; Rise of Communists. The years following the First World War were a period of much dissension within the socialist movement regarding the part played by the leaders in the world conflict, the party's attitude toward Coalition governments, and the rôle which French socialists should assume toward Russia and the communist movement. These dissensions resulted in the expulsion of the extreme right wing, who advocated continued socialist participation in capitalist ministries, and in the development of a new left wing, the growth of which helped to swell the party membership to 180,000. In the first postwar elections in 1919, the party, largely on account of these conflicts, elected only 68 representatives to the Chamber of Deputies as compared with over 100 prior to the war.

The left wing continued to increase in numbers following these elections, and in the Congress of Tours in 1919 took control of the congress and demanded affiliation with the Third or Communist International. Léon Blum, Jean Longuet, Paul Fauré, and other moderate leaders refused to accept the decision of the congress and re-established the Socialist party, making Longuet's paper, *Le Populaire,* the party's official organ. *L'Humanité,* the influential journal founded by Jean Jaurès, and the general party machinery became the possession of the left wing group who later organized the Communist party of France.

The re-established Socialist party began with a membership of about one third that of the Communist party. However, 55 of the 68 socialist deputies in the Chamber remained loyal to the party.

Rise of Léon Blum to Socialist Leadership (1923). In 1923 Jules Guesde and Marcel Sembat died, and the leadership of the party passed, in considerable part, to Léon Blum. Blum was one of the leading intellectual socialists in France. He was born in Paris on April 9, 1872, son of a silk merchant who had developed the most successful ribbon house in France.

In the École Normale Supérieure young Blum fell under the influence of Lucien Herr, the school's librarian, an ardent socialist, who helped to introduce him to socialist literature and later to bring him into contact with Jean Jaurès, eighteen years his senior. He became an active Marxist in 1896, at the age of 24. In 1899 he joined a group engaged in promoting unity among the socialist forces of the country. The efforts of this group, among others, led in 1905 to the formation of the Unified Socialist party.

In 1904 Blum became one of the editors of *L'Humanité,* but retired a year later to devote himself to literary criticism, a field in which he did distinguished work. When, a decade later, Jaurès was assassinated, Blum made a vow to re-enter political activity.

During the war the socialist leader became, at the age of 42, *chef de cabinet* to Marcel Sembat, Minister of Public Works. At that time he made a thorough study of the parliamentary system and published a book, at first anonymously, on the representative system.

At the close of the war Blum took a somewhat centrist position between that of Renaudel, leader of the right wing, and Marcel Cachin, leader of the left. When Cachin received a mandate from the majority to affiliate the party with the Third International, Blum refused to follow the majority action and helped to reorganize the Socialist party. He soon became the leader of the party, and, under his leadership, the party became an increasingly influential force in French politics. In 1924 the Socialist party formed a *Carter des Gauches* with the radicals. The elections of that year resulted in the winning by the socialists of 105 seats in the Chamber of Deputies, a little more than one sixth of the total. During the next few years, when government after government was formed and dissolved, Socialist party deputies continued to fight for improved social legislation and in behalf of a more liberal international policy.

Socialists' Gain through Second Balloting (1928). In 1928 a new system of elections was introduced under which a second balloting was held in any district in which no candidate received a majority of votes. In the second election the candidate obtaining a plurality of votes was declared the winner. Socialists voted for their own candidates on the first ballot, but, in order "to keep out the reactionary," agreed to withdraw their favorite at the second election in behalf of the most favored left-wing candidate. As a result of the new agreement, the Socialists elected 112 candidates, the Radical Socialists (a mild social reform group), 109; the Communists, 15; and the Dissident Communists, 5. Four years later, in 1932, Socialists increased their representation from 112 to 129, and received the largest popular vote in their history. The Communist representation increased to 27; the Radicals, to 157.

Following the elections, the Socialists declared that they would cooperate with the Radicals in forming a government on the basis of a program which included stricter government control of banks, the forty-hour week, the immediate control and nationalization of the munitions industry, reduction of military expenditures, unemployment insurance, and nationalization of railways and insurance companies. Édouard

Herriot, leader of the Radicals, despite his party's pre-election agreement, refused to co-operate under these terms, fearful that the social reforms advocated would lead to an unbalanced budget and that the proposed reduction of armaments would lay France open to attack, particularly in view of the advent in Germany of the Von Papen government.[7]

Divergence over International Policy. With the emergence of the Hitler regime in Germany great differences arose within the party regarding the wisest international policy for the party to advocate. Marquet, Deat, and others of the party's right wing declared that it was folly "to think internationally," and that socialists should substitute for their international slogans the slogan of "Order, Authority, and Nation." In April, 1933, when the question of military credits was presented to the Chamber, a majority of 90 deputies out of 129 voted the credits, reversing the party's traditional policy. Eleven, including Léon Blum, however, opposed the measure, and 28 abstained from voting.

Following the balloting, Blum resigned from the party's leadership. The party, in turn, moved a vote of censorship on those who approved the credits. In July, 1933, a part of this latter group—43 deputies—left the organization and later formed the Neo-Socialist party, a group which sought to make a special appeal to the middle class.

Socialists' Attack on Fascistic Forces. During these days the Socialist deputies engaged in many clashes in the Chamber with the Daladier and Chautemps governments over the budget, and caused, at one time, the overthrow of the Daladier Cabinet. However, following the great anti-government demonstration engineered by *Action Français, Croix de Feu, Jeunesses Patriotes, Solidarité Français,* and other fascistic and veteran groups and in which communists participated, the socialists, as a challenge to those who, in their opinion, were endeavoring to overthrow the government by unconstitutional means, voted for the continuance of the Daladier government.

On February 9 Socialists participated in an anti-fascist meeting initiated by communists and other anti-fascist groups, and helped to organize a further vast demonstration initiated by the trade unionists on February 12. The first demonstration was fired on by the police and resulted in several deaths. These days witnessed the beginning of a type of co-operation among Radicals, Socialists, and Communists, which developed later into the Popular Front.

During the next year Socialist party deputies bitterly denounced the demands of M. Gaston Doumergue, the new Premier, who maintained, in late 1934, that the most urgent thing needed by France under the

[7] Alexander Werth, *Which Way France?* p. 42.

circumstances was "an authoritative government" and who urged several measures which Blum declared would, if carried out, place France well on the way to fascism. The Radicals supported Blum in these criticisms of the Doumergue cabinet and handed in their resignations. The government was overthrown, and Doumergue returned in anger to his country estate.

Flandin, the successor of Doumergue, shelved the latter's constitutional proposals, but, in turn, gave way to the pressure of the "200 families" controlling the Bank of France and to the advocates of a big military budget. Blum and his followers fought against the bill providing for two years of military training, in the belief that the General Staff had "Napoleonic ambitions" and that, if Hitler were to attack France, the working class would arise like one man to defend their country. At the same time, Blum maintained that France could not hope to win an armament race against Germany and that the only way to stop the German menace was to obtain unanimous agreement among the other powers on the question of disarmament and to force on Germany the program thus agreed upon. The Socialists likewise opposed Flandin's program for the reduction of state services and his request for plenary powers, and attacked the extreme demands for emergency powers.

In the meanwhile the continued activities of fascistic forces in France and the attempt of "the street" to dominate French politics led the Socialists, on August 24, 1934, to sign a United Action Pact with the Communists.

Under the Laval ministry the fascistic forces in France continued to grow, and in the summer of 1935 giant *Croix de Feu* and *Front Paysan* demonstrations were staged in France, giving rise to fears of a fascist *coup d'état.* Both Socialist and Radical deputies denounced Premier Laval—whose regime extended from June, 1935, to late January, 1936—for his friendly attitude toward fascist groups. They finally forced through an anti-fascist bill which gave the government power to dissolve by decree any groups found guilty of provoking armed demonstrations on the streets, of organizing in private militias, or of conspiring to make an armed attack on the republican form of government. During that period Blum and his followers denounced Laval for his refusal to oppose the Italian invasion of Ethiopia. The strife between the progressive and reactionary forces of the country became increasingly bitter, resulting in frequent physical assaults and riots. One of the most spectacular of the personal attacks of that period was that upon Léon Blum on February 13, 1936, by a group of royalists, who stopped his car on the

Boulevard St. Germain, dragged him out of it, and struck him savagely on his head and neck before he could be rescued by the police and some nearby workers.

Organization of the Popular Front (1936). In the May, 1936, elections, Socialists joined with Radicals, Communists, the two trade-union federations, and several other left-wing groups in the famous Popular Front. The members of the Popular Front agreed on an extensive domestic and foreign program. On the international front, they urged a system of collective security, automatic concerted application of sanctions in case of aggression, the rationalization of war industries, and limitation of armaments, followed by simultaneous and controlled armament reduction. In the domestic field, the *Front Populaire* urged a shorter work-week, an efficient public works program, adequate pensions, public control of the Bank of France, the revision of the tax system, agricultural reforms, and a civil liberties program which would provide for a general amnesty, the dissolution of fascist organizations, freedom of the press, and the recognition of the rights of labor.

During the ensuing campaign the candidates of the Popular Front tickets gave chief attention to their planks on banking, shorter hours, armament rationalization, bank control, and the revision of Laval's economic decrees. The left wing, in the elections of April 26 and May 3, 1936, scored a distinct victory. After the final balloting it was announced that the Socialist party had increased its parliamentary representation from 101 to 148 and the Communist party, from 10 to 73. The Dissident Communist party remained stationary (10 as compared with 11), and the Radical Socialist party deputies dropped from 159 to 108 and the Socialist Union and other small left-wing parties, from 66 to 36.

Formation of Blum Cabinet (1936). In general. the left-wing parties elected 380 deputies as compared with 238 for the center and right. Prior to this election the left claimed 346 deputies. In popular votes the Socialists obtained 1,922,000, or about the same as in 1932 before the party split, whereas the Communists secured about 1,500,000 as compared with 800,000 in 1932. The Radicals received slightly less than the Communists, a drop of a third of a million from the 1932 level. The victory of the left-wing forces was taken as a clear verdict against fascism, against deflation, against the '200 families,' against the *marchands de canons,* and against the "National government." It was a vote for the maintenance of political democracy and moderate, peaceful, economic change.

Léon Blum, who had been raised to the position of a national hero after the assault upon him on February 13, 1936, was asked to form a cabinet. The Communists refused to enter the government, but declared that they would give it their support, "while continuing to minister to the masses." The Radicals formed the cabinet with the Socialists, who were represented by 19 out of 35 members.

Blum assumed office on June 4, 1936, when over a million workers were out on strike. He refused to interfere with the "stay-in strikes" throughout the country. He declared, however, that it was the duty of the government to see that no disturbances occurred in the public services or the food supply, that the cabinet utilize to the full the machinery of arbitration and conciliation, and that the bill for the forty-hour week, for holidays with pay, and for collective bargaining be prepared without delay.

On June 7 the Matignon Agreement was formulated in the Hôtel Matignon by representatives of the C. G. T. and the employers' organization. This agreement provided for the immediate establishment of collective bargaining, for the right of workers to belong to any legally constituted trade union, for a policy of non-discrimination against trade unionists, for an increase in wages of from seven to fifteen per cent, and for the appointment of workers' delegates to submit the claims of the workers to management. *Le Peuple* characterized the agreement as the "greatest victory of the workers in their history."

The Matignon Agreement was confirmed by the Collective Contracts Act of June 24, 1936, which provided in detail for the method of arriving at collective bargaining. Under this law, the Ministry of Labor was authorized to set up mixed commissions, whenever requested to do so by workers' or employers' organizations, to serve as mediators. This law was supplemented by legislative enactments providing for holidays with pay, for the forty-hour week, for the stabilization of wheat prices, and for greater governmental control of the policies and administration of the Bank of France.

Other important laws passed during Léon Blum's premiership authorized the government to take over plants engaged in the manufacture of armaments or in armament trade, increased the compulsory school age to 14, lowered the age of retirement of governmental employes, regulated the price of mineral products, enlarged the public works program, revised the tax system, subsidized small businesses, declared a moratorium on farm mortgages and rents, and devalued the franc. In the field of international relations, the Blum government observed, at least in its official actions, strict neutrality toward the Spanish Civil War, justifying this stand as the only means of averting a European conflagration.

In the early months of 1937 the Chamber passed Blum's defense program, which doubled the 19 billion franc appropriation already voted for that year. In the spring of 1937 Blum decided to concentrate on a few important reforms and, because of the continued decrease of gold stocks in the Bank of France, asked the Chamber in mid-June for emergency financial powers "to protect the franc, the savings of the people, and public credit against speculative attack."

Resignation of Blum and Formation of Second Cabinet (1937). The Chamber, however, refused to grant Blum these powers, and, on June 21, 1937, Blum resigned. A Popular Front Cabinet was then formed under Radical leadership. Following the installation of the new cabinet, a controversy arose between the Radicals, on the one hand, and the Socialists and Communists, on the other, regarding the nationalization of the railways. A compromise plan was finally agreed upon, and on August 31, 1937, the cabinet set up a National Railway Company for the eventual fusing of the six big railway systems of the country. A further dispute between various elements on the Popular Front government developed over the Chautemps strike and social legislation policy, and on January 14, 1938, the nine socialist members of the cabinet resigned from the ministry. A reconstituted Chautemps cabinet again carried on for a while, but resigned on March 10, 1938, a date which coincided with Hitler's annexation of Austria; and Blum, for the second time, became head of the cabinet.

Upon becoming Premier, Blum introduced a plan of financial reform which included proposals for a graduated capital levy as a means of raising the required revenue and for the centralization of exchange operations. The Senate, by a vote of 214 to 47, refused to go along with the Lower House, and, on April 8, 1938, the cabinet resigned after a short term of 28 days.

Pivert's New Party (1938). The socialists refused to accept places in the succeeding Daladier cabinet. This refusal and the constitution by Daladier of the "Government of National Defense" marked the virtual end of the Popular Front.

At the June, 1938, Congress of the Socialist party three factions fought for control. The largest section, consisting of the followers of Léon Blum, supported the policies pursued by the party in the Popular Front governments. The second largest group, followers of Jean Zyromski and A. D. Bracke—the "Socialist Battle" faction—while urging an international policy of "collective security," opposed further support of the Daladier government and favored union with the communists. A third group, the "Revolutionary Left," led by Marceau Pivert, former head of the Seine Federation of the party, and Lucien Herard, voiced vigorous opposition to any government headed by a non-socialist and to any National Union cabinet with a socialist Premier. It further opposed any credits and any aid to a war that was not primarily a class conflict.

The Pivert group were refused seats in the Congress, on the ground of violation of party discipline and later formed a new party, the Workers' and Peasants' Social party. This new party, which took from the main organization a membership of from 5000 to 10,000 out of a membership of 286,000, failed to attract to its ranks any deputies. After a heated debate at the Congress between the Blum and Zyromski followers, the delegates voted by a large majority in favor of the policies of former Premier Blum.

Socialists during Second World War. When the Second World War broke out in September, 1939, the French Socialist party voted its support of the war. It opposed attempts to suppress parliamentary activity and to abolish essential reforms and urged a progressive policy in the country's North African possessions.

The Communist party, following the signing of the Russian-German pact, opposed France's entrance into the war and was later outlawed, its deputies being excluded from Parliament. In early 1940 the socialists were represented in the war ministry and were active in urging a more vigorous prosecution of the war. With the defeat of France and the rise of the Petain government, the Socialist party was outlawed and Blum and other socialists put on trial at Riom, accused of responsibility for France's defeat. Many socialists were placed in concentration camps. Many were executed. The trials of Léon Blum and other socialists were called off following Blum's eloquent defense of his stewardship while Prime Minister of France. In 1943 Blum and other socialists were removed from France to the Reich to prevent them from taking part in a possible revolt against Hitler. Both socialists and communists conducted from 1941 to the occupation of France by the United Nations a widespread underground movement. When the French Provisional Consultative Assembly met in November, 1943, it contained five former members of the socialist delegation in the French House of Deputies and three representatives of the reconstituted French Socialist party.

THE BELGIAN LABOR PARTY

Rise of Labor Party. Trade-Union Co-operation. In Belgium the Labor party from its inception until the Second World War closely united the political, the trade-union, the co-operative, and the educational wings of the labor movement. The Labor party was formed at Brussels on April 15, 1885 and adopted a socialistic program. As organized, it was an amalgamation of trade-union, co-operative, and other groups. During the decade following its formation more than 400 co-operatives and 7000 mutual aid societies were formed largely through its help, while the membership of the trade unions steadily increased.

On the political field the party, during the days before the First World War, gave much attention to the establishment of universal suffrage, in 1893, 1902, and 1912 calling general strikes in behalf of more liberal suffrage laws. It likewise agitated vigorously for social and labor legislation.

While in general fighting against the drift toward war, the socialists after the declaration of war took an active part, as did other European socialist movements, in the defense of their country. Vandervelde, leader of the party and Anseele, the famous Belgian co-operator, entered the Coalition ministry.

Socialist Activities (1919–1932). In the elections of 1919 the government finally acceded to the socialists' demands and granted votes to males 21 years old and over, though denying votes to women. In the succeeding elections in 1919 the socialists increased their parliamentary representation from 34 to 70, receiving a popular vote of 644,000, or over 36 per cent of the total.

The Catholics in this election were deprived of the majority they had enjoyed since 1884. The Catholic party, however, was again asked to form a cabinet, which it did in co-operation with the Labor party. Taking advantage of the fact that they possessed the balance of power, the socialists in this cabinet were able to secure legislation providing for the graduated income, inheritance taxes, the eight-hour day, and old-age pensions, and to obtain the repeal of the law prohibiting picketing. After gaining this minimum program, they resigned from the coalition. They came back in the succeeding election with 68 Labor party representatives, but refused during the next few years to take any part in the Coalition government.

Four years later, in 1925, when its representation in the House had increased to 78, the party again decided to enter the ministry, accepting five posts in the cabinet, the Catholics five, and the Liberals two. In this cabinet the party's representatives took part in the government's attempt to stabilize the franc. They also demanded the reduction of military service to six months. Upon the government's refusal to accede to this demand, the Labor members resigned, and the party continued as an opposition movement until 1932.

In the elections of 1932 the Labor party gained three seats, the party electing 73 deputies as compared with 79 for the Catholics. Its popular vote was 37 per cent of the total, that of the Communists, 2.8 per cent. The majority of the seats were retained by the right-wing bloc.

The succeeding Theunis government was unable to deal effectively with the existing crisis. During this period of depression the fascist groups first began to exercise their influence in Belgium, functioning through a brownshirted organization, which was at one and the same time anti-Walloon, anti-French, anti-Marxist, and anti-Semitic.

Plan of Economic Transformation. As a means of combating fascism, the Belgian Labor party during the next few years urged, on the one hand, the organization of workers' defense corps and, on the other, the adoption by the country of a *Plan du Travail* formulated by Henri De Man. This "plan of economic transformation" called for the nationalization of the key industries and the banking system, but proposed that most non-monopolistic industries be left for the time being in the hands of private owners. Every effort should be made by the socialists, maintained De Man, to win the middle class to socialism and away from fascist groups. Socialists must seek to give immediate employment to labor and the middle class and to overcome the crisis while building for socialism.

The party agitated for the plan during the next two years. On March 16, 1935, the Theunis government resigned and was replaced by the Van Zeeland Cabinet of National Union. The Labor party at first refused to join the coalition on the ground that the new government would not accept the Labor plan, but the King finally induced them to accept. In order to secure the co-operation of the left wing of the party, Paul-Henri Spaak, its leader, was given the office of Postmaster General. According to De Man the alternative presented to the party was either "to join the concentration government at once or be sent to the concentration camp within two months."

The cabinet, as finally constituted, consisted of six Catholics, five Socialists, and four Liberals, and three additional ministers without portfolios. The government was granted emergency powers because of the fascist threat in the country, and began what was called a "New Deal" for Belgium. Currency was devalued and a program for raising prices was put into effect.

Labor Party Largest Belgian Party (1936). In the following year, 1936, the Labor party opposed the extension of power to the government, and a general election was called. In the 1936 elections a fascistic organization, the Rexist party, participated for the first time. It received 271,000 votes and elected 21 deputies, most of its votes being taken from the Catholic party. The Labor party in this election won 70 seats and again became the largest party in the Lower Chamber, the Catholic representation declining from 79 to 63. In that year, the Communist party increased its strength, receiving 155,000 votes, as compared with 64,000 four years before and 758,000 for the Labor party, and electing nine deputies.

As the Labor party won the highest number of seats, its leader, Émile Vandervelde, was asked to form the government. The King, however, insisted that the cabinet be a National Union cabinet and contain members of the right, as well as of the center and left. Vandervelde found the organization of such a cabinet an impossible task, and Van Zeeland managed with difficulty again to form a Liberal-Catholic-Socialist Coalition. The Labor party at a special convention, by a vote of five to one, approved the action of their leaders in joining this cabinet.

The new government took office in the midst of a strike wave which paralleled that in France at the beginning of the Blum government. At its height some half million workers were out on strike. The labor conflict was finally settled, the men receiving their basic demands—a 40-hour week, vacations with pay, a minimum wage of 32 francs for eight hours of work for able-bodied workers, the liberalization of unemployment insurance provisions, and an increase in unemployment insurance benefits.

In the new cabinet Paul-Henri Spaak was given the post of Minister of Foreign Affairs instead of Vandervelde, who had been the socialists' most prominent intellectual and political leader for over a generation. Upon his assumption of office Spaak deserted the left wing and later went over to the right.[8]

A few months after assuming office Spaak negotiated a non-aggression pact with Germany as a means of preserving the peace of Belgium. In late 1936 and early 1937 marked differences emerged within the party over Belgium's attitude toward Spain. Vandervelde took the position that Belgium had the right and duty to permit the Loyalist government to buy war materials. The ministry took issue with the veteran socialist and sent a sharp note to Spain over its request to purchase military

[8] Spaak was the grandson of Paul Janson, the Belgian nineteenth-century Liberal and nephew of Paul Van Zeeland, the man whom he afterwards succeeded as Premier. He was born in 1899, studied law at the University of Brussels, and immediately took an active part in the socialist movement. He was elected to Parliament in 1932, and, while there, edited a left-wing paper which was continually taking to task the "reformist tendencies" within the party. In 1935 he was appointed Minister of Transport in the Van Zeeland government. Three months later he was appointed Foreign Minister.

equipment. Vandervelde took exception to the tone of this note and on January 27, 1937 resigned, in protest, from his post as Minister of Health and Vice-Premier. The Labor party decided not to make this resignation a signal for the withdrawal of all party ministers, and, for the time being, Spaak remained as Foreign Minister, De Man as Minister of Finance, but Arthur Wauters took Vandervelde's place in the ministry.

In the electoral fight of Premier Van Zeeland in the spring of 1937 against Léon Degrelle, Rexist leader, the socialists supported the Prime Minister, who received five votes for every one for his opponent. The Labor party was to no small extent responsible for Degrelle's crushing defeat. The party during that year demonstrated its hostility not only to fascism but to communism, refusing in the fall of 1937 to accept the Communist party as an autonomous section of the Belgian Labor party. Throughout that year the Laborites gave much aid to the Spanish Loyalists and urged the League of Nations and the countries constituting the League to use their influence to assist the Spanish government "to recover its political and territorial independence."

Spaak as Prime Minister (1938–39). Early in 1938 Spaak became Prime Minister, retaining his portfolio as Foreign Minister and heading a Coalition government. The Labor party showed a good deal of opposition to the action of the government in sending an official representative to the Burgos fascist government in Spain and to Belgium's subsequent recognition of that government.

On Christmas Day, 1938, the Belgian Labor party lost through death its leader of many years' standing, Émile Vandervelde, former chairman of the Labor and Socialist International.[9]

In 1939 the Belgian socialists continued their participation in the Belgian cabinet. On January 21 Premier Spaak re-formed his cabinet, appointing to the new ministry five Socialists, five Catholics, three Liberals, and a member without party affiliations.

In the elections of that year the Catholics won 73 seats and supplanted the Labor party again as the country's largest political group. The Labor party retained 64 seats. In the Senate the Socialists returned 62 Senators, a decrease of five. The Rexist party lost 17 of its 21 seats

[9] Vandervelde was born on January 25, 1866. He studied law at Brussels University and took his doctor's degree in social science. He joined the Labor party at the age of 20 and for half a century devoted himself to that movement. He was Minister de l'Intendance Civile et Militaire, 1916–18; Minister of Justice, 1918–21; Minister of Foreign Affairs in the Socialist-Catholic Coalition, 1925–37; Minister without Portfolio, 1935–36, and Minister of Public Health during the next two years. Vandervelde was for many years Professor of Political Economy of the University of Brussels, an orator of distinction, an author, historian and economist of note and one of the most prominent statesmen in the international labor movement.

in the Lower House and cast but 4.4 per cent of the votes, as compared with 11.5 per cent in 1936. The Communist party elected nine deputies, the same as in 1936, although it obtained only slightly more than 5 per cent of the popular vote as compared with 6.6 per cent in 1936.

Following these elections Spaak, who was succeeded by Hubert Pierlot, Catholic, as Premier, became Minister of Foreign Affairs; Henry De Man served without portfolio; and the Labor party held the Ministries of Information, of Education, and of Labor. On January 5, 1940, a new cabinet was again formed with Spaak, Soudan, and Matagne, members of the Labor party, without Wauters and De Man. On February 9 the Spaak government resigned following a long, drawn-out struggle over the party's relations with Adrian Maerteus.[10]

Second World War. Another cabinet was formed in February by M. Pierlot, this one composed of Catholics, Socialists, and Liberals. Six days later, on February 27, 1940, the cabinet resigned over Labor party protests against the cut in government salaries and the social services.

A new election was called by King Leopold. The campaign was a bitter one. The Catholics again emerged as the largest single party. After the elections Pierlot first included in the cabinet the three main parties, but on April 17, 1940, the Labor party refused to permit its members to participate and the Labor members resigned. The following day a Catholic-Liberal coalition was formed. The nazi invasion took place a short while later in May. Most of the leaders of the Belgian Labor party, including Paul-Henri Spaak, former Labor Prime Minister, left Belgium and affiliated with the Belgian Government in Exile in London. Arthur Wauters, former Minister of Labor, was appointed chairman of the Post-War Reconstruction Committee of the Belgian Government in Exile. Only Henri De Man, elected shortly before the war the head of the Labor party, remained behind.

De Man, on June 28, 1940, issued a so-called *Manifesto of the Belgian Labor Party,* without consulting with any other leaders, urging the workers to consider the political rôle of the Labor party as finished and "prepare to enter the cadres of national resurrection."

During the next few years many former members of the Labor party and the trade-union movement engaged in sabotaging the work of their nazi conquerors, many, in so doing, making the supreme sacrifice.

[10] Maerteus had been convicted after the First World War for dealing with the enemy. He had subsequently been pardoned upon the extension of amnesty to war-offenders. Under pressure from the Flemish inhabitants of Belgium, Spaak had nominated him as a member of the Royal Academy. This appointment and other selections had caused intense opposition from many French sections.

HOLLAND'S SOCIAL DEMOCRATS

Early Years of Socialists. The socialist movement in Holland may be said to have been initiated in 1878 with the formation of the Dutch Social Democratic Union under the leadership of Romela Nieuwenhuis. The Union made slow but steady gains and in 1888 succeeded in electing Nieuwenhuis to the States General. In Parliament the socialist leader met with bitter opposition, became discouraged with parliamentary action, and soon joined the anarchists.

In 1894 the anarchist group made a clean break with the socialist movement. In that year the Social Democratic Labor party was formed under the leadership, among others, of Pieter J. Troelstra. On January 1, 1895, this party claimed a membership of 700.

From the middle of the nineties until the First World War, the movement spent much of its energy in the fight for universal suffrage and labor legislation. In 1909, following the action of the party in throwing its weight in Parliament in favor of the more liberal of the two parliamentary factions, a small Marxist group left the party and formed a movement of their own—the Social Democratic party.

Pre-First World War Growth. During the nineteen years between its formation and 1913 the Social Democratic Labor party gradually grew in membership and in parliamentary representation.

Dutch Social Democratic Party, 1897–1913

Year	*No. of Votes*	*Parliamentary Representatives*
1897	13,000	3
1901	38,279	8
1905	65,743	7
1910	82,494	7
1912	144,000	19

In 1913 the S. D. L. P. had 52 representatives in the provincial legislatures and 247 in the municipal assemblies. Two representatives were in the Upper House, and a number of Dutch Mayors were members of the party.

The electoral campaign of this prewar year resulted in the seating of 55 Liberals and Socialists in a House of 100 members. Following this election, the Social Democratic Labor party was asked to enter a Coalition cabinet, which, its members were assured, would immediately introduce a constitutional amendment providing for general and equal suffrage. The proposal to enter a coalition was, however, turned down by the party congress by a close vote of 375 to 320, on the ground that "a party like the Social Democratic Labor party, which . . . is diametrically opposed to the political domination of the capitalist class, is under no obligation to join a capitalist ministry." The resolution declared that socialists were doing their full duty in their fight for universal suffrage and old-age pensions by promising to support any government which sought to establish these reforms.

The party leaders during the First World War were instrumental in forestalling attempts to align Holland on the side of Germany and in keeping the country neutral. The Hague, the capital of Holland, housed the International Socialist Bureau during the latter part of the war.

A group of Dutch socialists—critical of the fact, among other things, that the party voted appropriations for defense during the war—joined the Third International after the war. Despite this split the party emerged from the war a force of increasing influence in the nation's life, with a membership of 43,000, as compared with 16,000 prior to the conflict, and its national vote about 300,000, double the 1912 total.

Program of Socialization (1920). In 1920 the party adopted a program for the socialization of industry which served its members as a guide for years. This program urged the socialization both of industry and land. The transfer of industry to public ownership should begin, it maintained, with monopolies and other highly concentrated industries. The industries to be socialized last should be the small competitive industries and services producing such necessities as food, clothing, and shelter. Reasonable compensation should be given to the owners of the industries taken over, the money for these payments to be raised largely through income and inheritance taxes.

The party gave much attention during the twenties to social legislation, the agrarian and colonial problems, disarmament, and international organization. After the First World War it voted to remain in the Second International and urged affiliation with the League of Nations.

The death of Pieter J. Troelstra in 1930, at the age of 70, deprived the party of one of its most powerful personalities. Prior to Troelstra's death the party had become the second largest political party in the country, its votes having increased from 568,000 in 1922 to 707,000 in 1925 and to 805,000 in 1929 (23.8 per cent of the total). The 1929 elections resulted in the seating of 24 socialist deputies out of a total of 100. The Catholic State party, the leading political group, elected that year 30 deputies; the Communist party, two. The party membership in 1930 was 70,000 as compared with 37,000 in 1920. The Communist party during the previous decade split into two groups—the Stalin group and the Wynkoop party.

Development of Left Wing. In the early thirties a left wing developed in the S. D. L. P. under the leadership of Edo Fimmen of the International Transport Workers Federation and others, who felt that the capitalistic system was about to collapse and that extra-parliamentary means should be employed in the conquest of political power. Following attempted restriction of the propaganda activities of this group, the left-wingers withdrew from the party and organized an Independent Socialist party with Fimmen as President. Fimmen later withdrew from the I. S. P. and the party played but a small rôle in the political life of the country.

In 1933 the social democrats carried on one of their most vigorous campaigns, but the political atmosphere of the country was surcharged with a super-patriotism as a result of a disturbance in the navy, and the socialist vote was decreased by 6,000. The Communist party seated four deputies, as compared with 22 Social Democrats and two members of the Revolutionary Socialist party.

Campaign against Fascism. In 1935 the party conducted a vigorous campaign against a new fascist group in the provincial elections, winning 21.9 per cent of the total votes, as compared with 9.1 per cent for the National Socialists. A short time before these elections the Independent Socialists amalgamated with the Revolutionary Socialist party, a semi-syndicalistic group, and formed the Revolutionary Socialist Labor party. This party in 1935 secured 1.39 per cent of the total votes and the Communists, 3.42 per cent. In the succeeding municipal elections the S. D. L. P. won 1,451 seats in city councils, a gain of 154. Nearly two fifths of the councillors elected in Rotterdam and one third of those in Amsterdam were Socialists. In that year the party congress approved a "Plan of Action" formulated by the party to meet the economic crisis.

On account of the seriousness of the unemployment situation, the increase of fascist propaganda in the country, and the gravity of the international crisis, the party gave ever greater thought during these days to possible collaboration with other parties in the formation of a cabinet. Party leaders in the 1935 congress declared their willingness to have the party enter a coalition ministry if a guarantee were offered for a constructive program for combating the crisis and defending democracy.

For Collective Security and Defense of Democracy. In the late thirties the party campaigned in behalf of a system of collective security under the League of Nations, the revision of the peace treaties (though not under the threat of military force), and the arming of the democratic nations to prevent treaty revision by Germany and Italy under the threat of war. They opposed unilateral disarmament, but favored international disarmament. During these days they refused proffered co-operation with the Dutch communists.

As a result of the 1937 elections, in which the party urged democratic socialism, the S. D. L. P. secured 23 seats in the Lower House and 12 out of 50 in the Senate. Its popular vote increased by nearly 100,000 to 891,000. Mussert's Nazi party, said to have been largely financed from Berlin, increased its representation from zero to four in the Lower Chamber and from two to four in the Senate, but its popular vote fell by over 40 per cent to 171,000. The vote of the Communist party, on the other hand, advanced to 288,000, but its parliamentary representation decreased to three.

Lower Chamber, Holland

Elections of May, 1937 (for four years)

Parties	*Representation*
Catholic	31
Social Democratic Labor	23
Anti-Revolutionary	17
Christian Historical	8
Liberal Democratic	6
Liberal	4
National Socialist	4
Communist	3
Minor Parties	4
Total	100

In the provincial elections of 1939 the party conserved its electoral strength. From 1935 to 1939 its membership fluctuated between 82,000 and 89,000.

Entrance of Social Democrats into Cabinet (1939). In August, 1939, Social Democrats entered the cabinet for the first time in the country's history. J. S. Albarda, President of the Labor and Socialist International and the party's leader, was appointed to the Ministry of Waterways, but died shortly afterwards. Dr. J. van den Tempel was chosen Minister of Social Affairs. Other parties in the coalition were Catholics, Christian Historical, and Liberal Democrats.

Occupation of Holland. On May 10, 1940, the German military forces suddenly invaded the Netherlands despite the fact that the German government had repeatedly declared that it would respect the neutrality of that state. Three days later, the Queen and all of the members of the cabinet transferred the seat of government to London. The London government assumed control, through royal decree, of the territories of the kingdom outside of Europe, and the German controlled territory in Holland was declared enemy country until the German occupation ended. On May 29, 1940, Dr. Seyss-Inquart was appointed as Reich Commissar of Holland, with supreme authority over the civilian population. With the invasion of Holland, the socialist and other antifascist movements were completely suppressed. All possessions of the trade unions and the party were seized and utilized by the nazis. During the next few years the German army of occupation was confronted with much rioting and disorder which resulted in the imprisonment and execution of many laborites as well as other members of the population.

CHAPTER 32

Socialism in Central Europe

In the days between the First and Second World Wars the labor, socialist, and communist movements in the six important countries of Central Europe—Germany, Austria, Hungary, Czechoslovakia, Poland, and Switzerland—whose proponents had faced the early postwar years, for the most part, with high hopes of continually increasing strength, fell victim sooner or later, with the exception of Switzerland, to the machinations of the forces of fascism and nazism. By the beginning of the forties, five of these six nations were ruled by Hitler and his followers; the labor and radical forces had been completely suppressed as a legal force. Where the latter existed at all, they operated only through refugee organizations outside of the borders of their respective countries or through scattered underground groups ready, with the defeat of Hitler, to resume their important role in the economy of their respective countries.

GERMAN SOCIALISM AFTER 1914

The German Revolution. We have already described the rise of German socialism during the nineteenth and the early part of the twentieth centuries.[1] The German socialists entered the First World War with a representation of 110 in the Reichstag and a vote of four and a half million, about one third of the total vote. During the years before the war they had followed a middle-of-the-road policy and had concentrated most of their energy on immediate social reform measures. In August, 1914, to the surprise of many, they voted in support of the war budget, but opposition to the war gradually developed, and in December, 1915, on the passage of the fourth budget, some twenty members of the Reichstag, including Kautsky, Bernstein, Ledebour, and Haase, formed a group which afterwards became the Independent Social

[1] See chs. 19–21, "Beginnings of German Social Democracy," "Eduard Bernstein and Revisionism," and "Marxists' Reply to Revisionists," respectively.

Democratic party. Others, including Liebknecht, Mehring, the historian, Rosa Luxemburg, and Clara Zetkin, organized a more pronounced left-wing International group, which, for a time, co-operated with the Independents. In October, 1918, fearful of the anti-war opposition which was constantly increasing, the government invited some of the majority socialists into the cabinet; they entered on condition that the government would repudiate any policy of annexations and indemnities.

On November 9, 1918, the Kaiser was forced to flee the country. That same morning the Workers' and Soldiers' Council of Berlin, composed of representatives of the social democrats and the independents, issued a call for a general strike. The workers laid down their tools, and by the afternoon motor cars were rushing through the streets proclaiming the "bloodless revolution," the abdication of the Kaiser, and the appointment of Ebert as Imperial Chancellor. Shortly thereafter Scheidemann appeared on the balcony of the Reichstag and announced the change of government, and Prince Max handed over the chancellorship to Ebert. The next day the majority and minority socialists formed a coalition government, which later included a few non-socialists.

On November 10 the Workers' and Soldiers' Council urged an armistice and immediate peace, and this policy was proclaimed next day by the coalition government. The Council also urged the rapid and consistent socialization of the privately owned means of production, declaring that in view of the development of the country this change could be attained without any serious disturbance, and that it was the only means of averting economic enslavement.

The program of the Provisional Government, issued the following day, was of a more conservative nature. It declared that elections would be carried out "according to equal, secret, direct, and universal franchise on the basis of proportional representation of all males and females of not less than 20 years of age." It proclaimed the various democratic safeguards of free speech and press, restored prewar labor legislation, and declared for the eight-hour day and for a better system of insurance. In its later message to the soldiers it expressed its approval of the socialization of those industries that were ready for it. "Your country," it asserted, "is also to become your possession and your inheritance in an economic way, in that no one shall any more, without your consent, exploit and enslave you."

The workers' councils soon began to assert themselves and urge that power be vested in them. Three groups among the radicals began to emerge: The majority socialists, who demanded that a Constituent Assembly be convoked on the ground that the Allies would not recognize any but a responsible government formed as a result of such an assembly; the left-wing, or Spartacus group, who declared that such an assembly would rob the workers of their power, and urged a dictatorship; and the independents, who favored an Assembly as an accelerator of peace, but believed that such an Assembly should be postponed until the government had time to socialize industry. Kautsky, a member of this latter group, however, felt that a postponement of the Assembly would "give an impression of insincerity, of hesitation, and of lack of faith in one's own strength," and that socialization could not be carried out with the then governmental machinery.

The Congress of Councils of Workmen's and Soldiers' Deputies, meeting on December 18, 1918, however, despite the agitation of the left wing, adopted a moderate position and called for the speedy convocation of the Constituent Assembly. Its chief argument was that the present government might crumble and that peace negotiations might be broken off unless a competent German government were formed.

After the meeting of the Congress, the Spartacans continued their attacks on the government, which began a campaign of ruthless suppression. This campaign caused the independents to resign from the government. At about the same time the Spartacans separated from the independents because of the failure of the latter to oppose the calling of the Constituent Assembly. Early in January the Spartacans revolted, but were crushed by the government forces, and during the struggle Liebknecht and Rosa Luxemburg were killed.

The elections for the National Assembly resulted in a plurality vote for the majority social democrats, who obtained 39.3 per cent of the vote cast. The independents secured less than 8 per cent. The Spartacans refused to take part in the election.

Election of Ebert to Presidency. In early February Herr Ebert, a saddle maker, who was a member of the majority Socialists, was elected president. The government, in outlining its program, advocated the socialization of industries which had attained the character of monopolies. The German, or Weimar constitution, promulgated August 11, 1919, followed the lines of the western republics, rather than those of Russia. It provided for the election of a president for a term of seven years by the popular vote of electors and for a bicameral legislature. The legislature, by the terms of the constitution, was given authority to legislate regarding socialization of natural resources, manufacture, and distribution.[2] Provision was made for the initiative and referendum and for the creation of a system of industrial councils in each industry.

On account of the growing conservatism of the government, the independents decided on a general strike in July, 1919, and in Berlin the stoppage of work was complete. The lack of any definite plans of socialization, the fear that the Allies would take active steps against a

[2] In the nature of the case the question of the socialization of German industry occupied a very large place in the socialist thought and agitation of these years. On November 24, 1918, about two weeks after the revolution, *Vorwaerts,* official organ of the Social Democratic party, published a letter from the prominent economist, Professor Robert Wilbrandt, urging a socialization program. On February 2, 1919, it published as a special supplement Kautsky's "Suggestions for a Program of Socialist Action."

"As soon as peace is concluded," wrote Kautsky, "and it is ascertained to what extent the German people can dispose of its state and imperial property, nothing will stand in the way of declaring forthwith that all large properties in mines, forests, and large landed estates (over 100 hectares) as well as all landed urban properties (excluding the houses erected thereon) be the property of the state, in consideration of compensation to be determined. Revenues from land originated from the feudal period, that is, mining royalties and landed possessions generally derived from feudal times, such as most fiefs and princely domains, which have not been acquired by way of purchase, do not require to be compensated.

"The undertakings erected on the urban lands will remain for the time being private businesses, leased from the state. They would be socialized gradually. Forests would be socialized forthwith. So far as possible, whole branches in industry, and not isolated undertakings, should be socialized.

"In accordance with the demand contained in the scheme for socialization, put forward by the Austrian socialists, each of such branches of industry shall be administered by a committee, of which one third of the members shall be the representatives of the state. The second third shall be the representatives of the workers in this branch of industry, and the last third shall be the representatives of those who use the products of the industry" (see Stroebel, *Socialization in Theory and Practice,* p. 173).

At the first Congress of the Workers and Soldiers' Councils, December 20, 1918, it was urged "that a beginning be made forthwith with the socialization of the industries which were adapted for this change, in particular the mining industry."

The independent social democracy urged that a systematic policy of socialization should be immediately carried out. *Die Freiheit,* November 19, 1918, in urging such a program, declared that "the war economy has brought into existence a series of organized institutions, which need only to be slightly extended in order to provide a useful basis for nationalization. Prompt action is necessary in the interests of the community."

On November 21, 1918, a Socialization Committee was appointed by the People's Commissaries "to make a report as quickly as possible."

According to *Deutsche Allgemeine Zeitung,* some time later, the Commission, after considering the question, felt that it had to proceed slowly. For the present there would be no interference with the export industry, foreign trade, and the supply of foodstuffs. "On the other hand, the Commission is of the opinion that socialization should be applied, in the first place, to those spheres of national economy in which conditions of capitalist monopoly have developed. In particular, the community must assume absolute control over the most important raw materials, such as coal and iron."

socialistic program, the crowding in of immediate tasks, the bitter fight against the Spartacans, and the hesitation on the part of the party leaders to have the state take over a broken-down economic machine, all combined to prevent the government from transferring industry from private to state ownership.

Loss of Socialist Strength (1920–1928). In June, 1920, the parties of the left failed to obtain a majority of votes, and a non-socialist cabinet was formed with Fehrenbach, the leader of the Catholic party, as Chancellor, and five Catholics, three Democrats, and three members of the German People's party as members of the cabinet. The following May, in 1921, there was another shift of Chancellors, and socialists were included again in the cabinet. From that time on, the cabinets were composed largely of non-socialist groups with a sprinkling of socialists. Herr Ebert, Social Democrat, remained President until his death on February 28, 1925.

In the succeeding elections the Social Democrats at the beginning supported Otto Braun, the socialist Prussian Prime Minister, but labor

---

Otto Hué, the veteran miners' leader, appointed to the Socialization Committee, was, however, skeptical even regarding this step. "There are no differences of opinion as regards the necessity of socializing the mines and associated industries, so as to deprive capitalism of its strongest support. But today the question arises as to whether the time is ripe for the socialization of our extraordinarily complicated industry, which in our opinion, has become necessary. Our old master, Marx, envisaged the transference to the community only in a time of surfeit of the means of production. This period is not the present. The socialization of such powerfully developed undertakings as the mines and iron and steel industries cannot be carried out according to the dictates of the minority, but only at the right time and for the benefit of the community." Ebert and Otto Braun also uttered warnings against too precipitate action. Braun, according to the *Berliner Tageblatt* of December 1, 1918, declared: "For socialization generally no time could be more unfortunate than the present. Germany is starving, raw materials are lacking, machines are defective. Any upheaval may discredit socialism for years."

"A strong united section representing democratic and Marxian socialism," remarks Stroebel, "could have conducted the campaign for democracy and socialization with calm energy, in spite of the furious attempts of the right and the left. Divided, social democracy, one section violently struggling with the other, was obliged to deviate from its path, and to expose itself to the temptation of a policy of coalition and concessions. Thus the independents fell into the orbit of the Spartacists and communists, while the social democrats, freed from the restraint of their former left wing, fell more and more under the influence of the middle-class parties and middle-class ideology, certainly not to the advantage of socialization" (*ibid.*, p. 178).

One great difficulty was that the leaders of the German social democracy were "completely in the dark as to the stages to be traversed and the details of a socialization scheme." "It was calamitous for German socialism," writes Stroebel, "that the discussion of a socialist policy of transition had been so completely neglected that there was not the slightest agreement as to the measures and changes that would be necessary after the seizure of political power . . . all was left to the happy inspiration of the hour and the true instinct of the masses" (*ibid.*, pp. 6, 14–6).

had been greatly weakened during the inflation period of the early twenties, the middle class was in the saddle, and the first elections ended in a stalemate. Thereupon the Social Democrats united with the other Weimar parties in voting for the Conservative Center leader, Wilhelm Marx, opponent of Hindenburg. But Hindenburg's popularity and the support of the Nationalist party carried the day. The Communist candidate Thaelmann obtained 2,000,000 votes; the Nazi candidate, General Ludendorff, less than 300,000. "Conservatives hostile to the Republic and the military clique now controlled the position of the chief executive of the Republic."

Rise of Social Democrats as Strongest Party (1928). In the May, 1928, elections, however, the Social Democratic party increased its representation in the Reichstag from 135 to 153 and its popular vote to 9,111,-438. The Communists polled 3,000,000 votes and secured 54 seats; the German People's party—the second largest party—86. The Social Democrats, as the strongest party, provided the Chancellor, in the person of Hermann Müller, together with three other ministers, the German People's party and the Democrats each supplied three ministers, and the Center party, one.

The year 1928, in which socialists secured their greatest victory since 1918, was a year of comparative economic stability. Unemployment was at a low ebb. Wages, profits, and industrial production were rising. Soon after the elections, however, the economic sky became clouded again. Foreign credits decreased. Interest and reparations payments became burdensome. Industrial expansion began to slacken. Unemployment began to increase. The Social Democrats in the cabinet unfortunately failed to present and dramatize an effective program for meeting the growing crisis, confining themselves largely to efforts to maintain unemployment benefits. When non-working-class elements began to press for the cutting down of unemployment benefits because of the mounting tax rates, Rudolf Hilferding, Social Democratic Finance Minister, urged the reduction of such benefits as the only means of avoiding a crisis which would force the socialists out of the government into what he believed would be ineffectual opposition. The left groups within the Social Democratic party joined with the trade unions in opposing a compromise which had been devised among the various government parties, and the parliamentary group decided almost unanimously to vote against the proposed compromise if it were submitted to the Reichstag.

WITHDRAWAL OF SOCIAL DEMOCRATS FROM CABINET (1930). Immediately thereafter the cabinet met under Müller's chairmanship and resigned. With this action ended the last German government in which the Social Democratic party was represented and at the same time the last strictly parliamentary government in Germany.

Rise of Nazism. Brüning succeeded Müller as Chancellor in March, 1930. Six months later, on September 14, 1930, the nazis won the first in a series of election victories and, by increasing their Reichstag representation from 12 to 107, secured the second largest representation in that body.

From that date until the rise to power of Hitler the Social Democrats waged a largely defensive warfare, with the view of keeping the nazis out of the control of the government. In pursuance of that aim they voted for a considerable number of conservative measures, rather than witness the defeat of the Brüning government. Brüning finally resorted to Article 48 of the Constitution, which permitted the President, in case of an emergency, to govern by presidential decree. In May, 1932, he proposed to President Hindenburg the breaking up of the large estates in East Prussia to make small farms on which the unemployed could settle. But Hindenburg and his friends were large landowners. He refused. Brüning resigned and was succeeded by Colonel Franz von Papen. Von Papen dissolved the Reichstag and called a new election for July 31, 1932.

Ousting of Socialist Government of Prussia (1932). On July 20, 1932, the socialists suffered a mortal blow in the ousting of the Socialist government in Prussia. On this day Otto Braun, Social Democratic Prime Minister, and Karl Severing, Minister of the Interior, were deposed.

Since the dismissal of Brüning, the Prussian government had constituted a stronghold of the anti-nazi forces. Here, under socialist leadership and with anti-nazi middle-class support, the Prussian cabinet controlled the police of the large German state. When the Prussian coup took place, socialist leaders were presented with the question as to whether they should order the Prussian police to resist, should order a general strike, or should submit to the coup. After consultation, the socialist leaders came to the conclusion that should the Prussian police resist, they would be annihilated by the Reichswehr—the army of the Reich. Should they call a general strike, the strike would gradually dwindle in strength and lead to bitter fighting between the employed and the large body of unemployed. The socialists decided, therefore, to yield under protest.

Hitler's Rise to Powfr (1933). A few days after this coup—on July 31, 1932—the new elections were held. Hitler's National Socialist party secured in the election more than a third of the total number of seats (230 out of 608). No Reichstag majority could be formed without his support. Hitler was thereupon offered by Von Papen a seat in the Cabinet as Vice-Chancellor. He declined and, as the head of the largest party, demanded the chancellorship itself—"all or nothing." President Hindenburg refused to grant this demand. Von Papen called for a new election in November, 1932, in which elections the National Socialists lost slightly, but still won a third of the votes and were strong enough to defeat the coalition cabinet. Von Papen, like Brüning, proposed the breaking up of the large East Prussian estates. Upon Hindenburg's refusal, Von Papen resigned. Kurt von Schleicher was then appointed Chancellor. He met with the same difficulties as his predecessor and resigned on January 28, 1933. He was succeeded as Chancellor by Adolf Hitler.

Two days later the Hitler cabinet, composed of National Socialists and Nationalists, was formed. Hitler announced the new Reichstag elections for March 5, 1933. On the evening of February 27 the central part of the Reichstag building was destroyed by fire. The fire was made the pretext for the arrest of communists and the suppression of their newspapers, so that they could play no part in the new elections. As a result of this and strong-arm methods, the Nazis won 44 per cent of the votes and, with 8 per cent of their Nationalist Coalition allies, had a clear majority of 52 per cent. On March 23 the Reichstag majority virtually set aside the Weimar Constitution, and thereby placed dictatorial power in Hitler's hands. The Social Democrats vigorously protested, but to no avail. From then on, the socialist, free trade-union, and independent co-operative movements as legal entities were over for the duration of the nazi regime. Socialists functioned merely as an underground movement.

Factors in Success of Nazism. Many factors contributed to the dominance of nazism. These included the terms of the Versailles treaty; the failure of the Allied governments to give proper encouragement to the internationally minded in the German ministries of the twenties and early thirties; the continuance after the 1918 revolution of the enemies of democracy in important governmental posts; the failure of German Social Democracy to stir the imagination of the masses with a program that would deal fundamentally with the problem of unemployment; the gulf existing between labor and the middle-class and agricultural population; the bitter fights among the many German parties; the difficulty of forming a majority government; the continual conflicts between communists and social democrats and the strong communist attacks on democracy and democratic institutions. Communists insisted during many years that "there are no distinctions between democracy and fascism" and that in "social fascism," as they termed the social democratic movement, not in fascism, "lay the greatest danger to the workers." The workers were constantly hearing from both the nazis and the communists that the source of their trouble lay in the democratic system and that they must rid themselves of "such bourgeois prejudices" as freedom, justice, and democracy. The Weimar Republic, the communists maintained, was "bankrupt" and the "revolutionary proletariat" was mobilizing its forces against it. It was not until February, 1933, when Hitler had already become Chancellor, that the communists accepted, though in a non-committal way, the socialist invitation to discuss joint resistance to the nazis. The first meeting was arranged for the very same evening that the Reichstag went up in flames. The meeting could not be held. Hitler was the primary beneficiary of the working-class divisions and suppressed all opposition groups.

AUSTRIAN SOCIALISM: ITS RISE AND DECLINE

Socialism before and during the First World War. In Austria a unified Social Democratic party was formed in 1888. In 1897 the proletariat of the country was, for the first time, permitted to send representatives of the workers to Parliament, and four years later the Socialists elected 10 members. Their next step was to fight for universal suffrage, which they gained in 1907. The following May they accounted for about one third of the vote cast and out of a total of 516 sent 87 members to Parliament.

During the next few years preceding the outbreak of the First World War the socialists fought vigorously within and without Parliament for social legislation and democratic political measures. On the threshold of war they protested against Austria's declaration of war on Serbia, but, when war was declared, the party maintained that it was its duty to defend the country against Russian despotism, and the majority threw their support to the government.

As in other countries, with the progress of the war, the anti-war minority gradually increased, and in July, 1915, the party issued a manifesto expressing the earnest desire of the people for peace. At the national Conference of the Austrian Social Democracy in Vienna, March 25–28, 1916, in a sharp debate between Dr. Victor Adler, prominent leader of the party, and his son, Dr. Friedrich Adler, the militant party secretary, the elder Adler declared that the Socialist party must set the interests of its own proletariat above all other interests, striving the while for a union of the proletariat of the world. Friedrich Adler, on the other hand, declared that this position was responsible for the disunity among the workers of the world and maintained that socialists should recognize as binding decisions of the international congresses on all international questions. The position of the elder Adler won out by a large majority.

Socialists' Protest of Continuance of War. As the war advanced and conditions became worse, the government refused to convene Parliament, ruthlessly suppressed socialist and radical papers, and imprisoned hundreds of radical agitators while the masses suffered tragically because of the lack of the necessities of life.

Socialist officials in September, 1916, demanded that steps be taken immediately toward peace negotiations. A few days later, after the Premier, Count Stuergkh, had refused to attend a conference called by the leaders of all parties for the purpose of restoring constitutional government, Friedrich Adler shot and killed the Premier.

The assassination and following trial caused a great uproar throughout the empire. The Social Democratic party declared that it had nothing to do with this act and was opposed to all individual acts of vengeance. Friedrich Adler declared that he thought that it would be a grave error if the party resorted to terroristic methods, but that, in peculiar cases, where the party had lost its revolutionary spirit, "an individual act may revive this spirit." He declared that he was opposed to all killing and always regarded the killing of a human being as something inhuman, but that they were living in a barbaric age. Adler was sentenced to death. On the ground that the trial was illegal, the death penalty was finally commuted, and in the fall of 1918 Adler was released.

Three weeks after Stuergkh's death, the government decided on a convocation of the Parliament. Until the end of the war, socialists continued their attacks on the government's reactionary measures. On October 5 the Hussarek Ministry resigned and was succeeded by one under Professor Lammasch, a peace advocate. Riots followed. On November 3 the Emperor abdicated, and the royalty began its flight to Switzerland.

Socialists in and outside the Government (1919–1920). In the elections of February, 1919, for the Constituent National Assembly, the Austrian Social Democrats won 69 seats out of a total of 159, and thus became the strongest Austrian party. The Socialists allied themselves with the Christian Socialists (the Catholic reform party) and formed a government in which Socialists predominated. Of the Social Democrats, Karl Seitz was elected President, Karl Renner, Chancellor, and Otto Bauer, Foreign Secretary. Social Democrats also controlled the Ministries of War and Interior. A democratic constitution was adopted, and important reforms were soon after carried through.

The growing reaction in Italy, Hungary, and Bavaria, however, weakened the socialist influence in Austria. The Allies forbade the Austro-German *Anschluss,* and Otto Bauer resigned from the cabinet. Other socialists remained with the coalition for some time, but no longer had controlling influence. Placed in a compromising position, the remaining socialists resigned in June, 1920.

In the succeeding elections the Social Democratic party lost 200,000 votes, and the Christian Socialists, who increased their vote by 150,000, assumed control of the government. Socialists, however, continued in office in Vienna and some of the other larger cities of Austria and in the capital city, until the Dollfuss *coup d'état.* In these cities they won the admiration of the world for their constructive achievements in the fields of housing, education, health, and recreation.

Socialists as Government Opposition (1920–1927). During the early twenties Social Democrats constituted a vigorous opposition in the National Chamber, and in April, 1927 they polled 42 per cent of the votes at a general election, and in Vienna they held a two-thirds majority. In the meanwhile reactionary elements grew in strength, as Austria was increasingly surrounded by countries hostile to democracy.

In 1927, following the acquittal of a defendant accused of killing a socialist war invalid, a great crowd congregated in the Ringstrasse, in Vienna, to protest against what they considered to be a miscarriage of justice in this case and in many previous cases. The crowd was attacked by armed forces and, goaded to anger, stormed and burned the law courts. The police, fearing further violence, shot into the crowd. There was a demand among the crowd, initiated in part by the communists, that this event be turned into a civil war. The Social Democrats, while proclaiming a one-day general strike, feared the violent reaction to a civil war of the type witnessed in Italy, Hungary, and Bavaria, and insisted that such civil conflict be avoided.

Rise of Austrian Fascism. Following the July 15, 1927 riots, the fascist danger began to take shape in Austria. The reactionary Heimwehren, a private army consisting mostly of sons of well-to-do peasants, and led by officers of the Imperial army and German Free Corps leaders, began to grow. It gained the support of the government, of big business and of the Catholic Church. The Heimwehren, encouraged by Father Seipel, Chancellor of Austria, began a campaign for the establishment of a fascist dictatorship in Austria. They saw to it that conservative youth became increasingly dominant in the military and police forces. They organized and armed their private army. They sought to show their strength in impressive parades, and the Social Democrats, on their part, organized parades participated in by the Schutzbund, labor's military force. Repeatedly the Social Democrats urged that an agreement be entered into for the disbanding of the private armies of both the right and the left, but in each instance Chancellor Seipel, thinking that victory over the "reds" was in sight, refused to answer the socialist proposals.

Soon there appeared on the political scene other fascist-minded leaders, among them Prince Ernst Rudiger von Starhenberg, who had participated in nazi activities in Germany and who used his large fortune to arm a private corps integrated into the Heimwehren. He was surrounded by officers of the Imperial Army, among them Major Fey, business men of the type of Herr Mandl, big munitions producer, and various adventurers.

In the elections of 1930, however, the Heimwehren forces, which had been urging the government to effect a *coup d'état,* suffered an electoral defeat, the Social Democrats winning 72 seats out of a total of 165 and again becoming the strongest party in Parliament, the Heimwehren obtaining but 8 seats, and the Christian Socialists losing heavily. Not a single nazi entered the Austrian Parliament.

Dollfuss' Assumption of Chancellorship (1932). A middle-class government was thereupon formed under democratic leadership and with the Heimwehren excluded. With the growth of nazism in Germany, however, the demand for an Austrian dictatorship increased in strength. Provincial elections in 1932 gave the Nazis one sixth of the votes in Vienna, 18 per cent in Lower Austria, and 22 per cent in Salzburg. Most of these advances were at the expense of the Christian Socialists. The government had a majority of but one over a combination of the two opposition parties, the Social Democrats and the Pan-Germans. Dr. Engelbert Dollfuss, former secretary of the Chamber of Agriculture in Lower Austria, and a devout Catholic, who had become Chancellor, took advantage of the resignation of Dr. Karl Renner as President of the Lower House to declare that only the president could convene the House and that, since there was no longer any president, Parliament could not meet.

From that time on, Dollfuss ruled by emergency decrees. Socialists were pushed increasingly in the background. Dollfuss looked forward to an arrangement with the nazis which would preserve the independence of the country and the domination of the Catholic Church.

The socialist defense corps was dissolved. Socialist Vienna was deprived of much of its income. Socialist workers were ordered to join the "Patriotic Front," which was to supersede all parties. Dollfuss in the meanwhile announced his plan to abolish democracy forever and build Austria as a Christian, corporate, and federal state, to be ruled according to the ideals of the Pope. The Nazi party was also officially outlawed, but nazi atrocities, encouraged by the followers of Hitler in Austria, continued.

Socialists were faced with two foes: Dollfuss and the Heimwehren, on the one hand, and the nazis, with their German loyalties, on the other. They felt that if they came to blows with Dollfuss, the country would be overridden by the nazis. On the other hand, there might be a chance for a compromise with Dollfuss.

On March 15, 1933, one of the vice-presidents called a meeting of Parliament. Chancellor Dollfuss announced that he would prevent Parliament from convening—by armed force, if necessary. The Social Democrats declared that they would go ahead with the meeting. But Parliament convened a half hour earlier than announced and was closed by the vice-president immediately after opening. Police arrived too late to prevent the meeting. Both sides claimed victory. But Parliament continued in recess, and the workers were not called on to resist. Democracy was the loser. Dollfuss, believing that he was the victor in this first battle, went to Rome to consult Mussolini and received a promise of Mussolini's protection, with Austria becoming an Italian protectorate. Backed by Mussolini, Dollfuss was in a position to destroy the Social Democrats. Upon his return he issued new decrees, which were used primarily against the Social Democrats.

The Social Democrats realized that an out-and-out battle with Dollfuss was inevitable. They ordered their followers to resist in case of certain overt acts against them and the trade unions. But Dollfuss proceeded with caution to undermine the party by a series of small measures, none of which individually was regarded as important enough to warrant open resistance.

Austrian Civil War (1934). Then on February 6, 1934, came the crisis in French democracy when fascism made its first assaults against the republic, and Dollfuss felt that the democracy of the last great western power on the continent was about to collapse. With the events of February 6 came the end of the government to which Austria had pledged its word to preserve Austrian democracy as a means of securing French credits. When the civil war in Austria began on February 12, 1934, France was in the midst of a general strike waged to combat the fascist peril.

A short time prior to the fascist threat in France, on January 30, 1934, the Heimwehren in Tyrol marched into the provincial capital, Innsbruck, and demanded, among other things, the dissolution of the Social Democratic party. These demands were repeated in other cities and provinces. On February 11 Vice-Chancellor Fey announced that Dollfuss had been won over to the plans of the Heimwehren. The next morning the police began their search for arms in the socialist headquarters in Linz. Workers in the house resisted. Firing began. Three hours later electrical workers in Vienna struck—a signal for a general strike. Firing thereupon began in Vienna. The civil war had begun.

The civil war lasted four days. Many Social Democrats took up arms, but many secret stores of arms could not be found, as the leaders who knew the hiding places had been arrested. The party was unable to send out an official call for a general strike, as it had forgotten to make arrangements with the electrical workers for the use of socialist printing presses. Socialist group after socialist group was finally overpowered by machine guns and cannons. The revolt was soon over and many of its leaders fled to Czechoslovakia. Others were hanged. The Austrian labor movement was driven underground.

The underground movement, "revolutionary socialists," commonly referred to as "R. S.," succeeded in bringing together many small socialist groups, and four years later, in February, 1938, when Hitler issued his ultimatum to the Chancellor, von Schuschnigg, socialists were again a strong force in Austrian politics. When Hitler demanded that Schuschnigg release all nazis from prison, Schuschnigg went further and released all imprisoned socialists and communists.

Nazi Invasion of Austria (1934). Several weeks later Schuschnigg, realizing the seriousness of the situation and knowing that Austria had been abandoned by Italy, met representatives of this underground movement. These working-class leaders declared that they would be willing to fight for Austrian independence, but on condition that they were given something worth fighting for. Their demands included freedom to profess socialist ideas, self-administration of the trade unions, and permission to publish a trade union paper. Schuschnigg declared that he accepted these demands in principle, and on March 7, 1938, the illegal, anti-fascist, trade-union leaders met openly for the first time since February 12, 1934. The communists held that Schuschnigg should be supported unconditionally, but the large majority at the meeting voted that the government should first give definite evidence that it had changed its policy toward the workers. Arrival at an agreement with Schuschnigg's negotiators proved difficult, and no agreement had been reached when a plebiscite on Austria's independence, to be held on March 13, was announced. However, the revolutionary socialists decided to vote for Schuschnigg. "Sunday," the underground paper declared, "is the day for showing our bitter hostility to Hitler's fascism. On that day therefore the whole working class must vote 'Yes.' " The workers' representative was to see Schuschnigg's representative on March 12 and broadcast to the people that evening. But that day the radio brought Schuschnigg's farewell to Austria. The nazi troops invaded Austria and the workers' movement was again driven underground. Many Austrian socialists escaped the country and continued their agitation for a democratic Austria from other lands. Socialist resistance to the dictatorship inside Austria steadily increased as the Second World War advanced.

SOCIALISTS IN CZECHOSLOVAKIA

The Socialist Movement in Bohemia. Another strong European socialist movement in the interwar years was that in Czechoslovakia. While the Czechoslovakian Republic dates back only to the fall of 1918, the Czech labor movement on the political field may be said to have begun with the birth in Bohemia, then under Austrian-Hungarian control, of the Social Democratic party, in the year 1896, the year that suffrage was extended to the workers of Bohemia. In 1907, following the electoral reform of that year, the Social Democratic party secured its first significant victory. In this election the party obtained 40 per cent of the total vote in Bohemia and elected 24 deputies to the Austrian-Hungarian Reichsrat. From that date until the First World War the socialist deputies waged a vigorous fight for social legislation and equal rights for minority groups.

Socialists' Fight for Independence. During the war a sharp division arose between different groups of socialists on the question of the future relations between Bohemia and the Austrian-Hungarian Empire.[3] As the war advanced, a powerful campaign was launched for the realization of independence, the leader in the movement being Thomas G.

[3] In the Middle Ages the King of Bohemia had been a powerful one among European potentates. In the sixteenth century the nation lost its autonomy and became a part of Austria. As a result, Czech cultural life and language were almost extinguished. In the eighteenth century a strong movement developed in Bohemia in behalf of the revival of Bohemian culture and of political autonomy.

Masaryk, professor of philosophy at Prague and a scholar with strong socialistic sympathies. The majority of socialists joined with Masaryk in the fight for independence and in January, 1919, the three socialist groups then in existence effected an amalgamation for the purpose of working for the achievement of a free Bohemia, although Dr. Smeral and a number of other socialists opposed the majority policy of collaboration with "bourgeois" elements and urged the party to conduct an independent fight.

Following the armistice, the Czechs of Bohemia joined with the Slovaks and other groups to form the Czechoslovakian Republic. The first cabinet contained, among others, three Czechoslovak (national) Socialists [4] and three Social Democrats—Soukup, Huberman and Winter. The unified Socialist parties agitated during the spring of 1919 against military intervention in Russia and demanded from their own government immediate withdrawal of Czechoslovak troops from Siberia. They led the fight for the abolition of feudal institutions and for the enfranchisement of women.

Tusar, Social Democrat, as Premier (1919). In the municipal elections of June, 1919 the Social Democrats and the Czech Socialists received 46 per cent of the votes cast. As a result of their demand, a new cabinet was constituted in July with Vlastmil Tusar, a Social Democrat, as Premier. The German Social Democrats in Czechoslovakia, however, refused to participate in the government, and Tusar formed a cabinet composed of the Social Democrats, with four cabinet seats; the Czech Socialists, with three; the Agrarians, with four; the Slovaks, with two; and with Beneš, an independent, retaining his position as Foreign Minister.

During the ministry of Premier Tusar the rights of minorities in Czechoslovakia were guaranteed, the great landed estates were expropriated, the legal eight-hour day was enacted, social insurance legislation introduced, a levy on capital imposed, and the new constitution adopted.

In the elections of April, 1920, the first elections after the adoption of the constitution, the votes were divided about half and half between the socialist parties and the "bourgeois" groups. In the nation as a whole, the socialist parties received a combined vote of 2,870,000 as compared with 2,966,000 for the bourgeois parties. Of the 199 seats in the Chamber of Deputies, the Social Democratic party won 74 and the Czech Socialists, 24. Tusar again received the mandate to form a

[4] The Czechoslovakian National Socialist party should not be confused with the nazi movement. It advocated social reforms, but was opposed to extreme Marxist principles.

cabinet, and his new one included seven Social Democrats, three Czech Socialists, three Agrarians, and two non-party members.

Party Split; Formation of Communist Party (1919). As a result, however, of bitter attacks against the majority leadership on the part of left-wing groups within the party, who had temporarily seized the party press, the Tusar cabinet resigned in September, 1920, the better to oppose the attempted domination of the party by these leftists. Soon thereafter the party executive expelled the left-wingers, who had participated in a separate convention and had started negotiations with the Third International. Those excluded later formed the Czechoslovakian Communist party. Twenty-four Social Democratic deputies joined the new party which, for some time, promised to outrank the Social Democrats in numbers and vitality. Similar cleavages took place in the country's German and Slovak minorities.

In 1921 the Social Democrats rejoined the government as a part of the Beneš cabinet and, later, of the Svehla cabinet. During the next few years they conducted an aggressive fight for the reduction of military expenditures and the expansion of expenditures for the social services.

In the 1925 elections the Communist party won 41 parliamentary seats, the representation of the Czech Social Democrats being reduced to 29, and that of the German Social Democrats to 14. Four years later the Czech Social Democrats again increased their parliamentary membership, this time to 39, and the German Social Democrats increased to 21, the Communist representation shrinking to 30. As a result of the 1929 elections a coalition cabinet under the premiership of Malypetr was formed of five bourgeois and three socialist parties, and the German Social Democracy voted to become a part of the coalition for the first time.

Rise of Henlein Party (1935). During the thirties the socialists gave constantly increasing attention to the relief of the unemployed and to the fight against the fascist groups in the population which the rise of the Dollfuss and Hitler regimes in Austria and Germany, respectively, had greatly stimulated. The government suppressed several out-and-out fascist groups which refused to swear allegiance to it, but most of the followers of these groups joined the Sudeten Deutsche Front of the Henlein party, followers of Conrad Henlein, a former gymnastic instructor, who was called *The Fuehrer* by his followers.

In the 1935 elections, taking advantage of the insecurity caused by the world depression and backed by reactionary groups in Czechoslovakia and by the Hitler government, Henlein's group secured two thirds of the German vote in Czechoslovakia and won 44 seats in the Chamber of Deputies, as compared with 45 for the Agrarians, 38 for the Czech Social Democrats, 11 for the German Social Democratic party, and 30 for the Communists, out of a total of 300. Shortly after the election in December, 1935, President Masaryk resigned from his office at the advanced age of 86 and was succeeded by Eduard Beneš, his closest collaborator. Masaryk died September 14, 1937. On November 5, 1935, Dr. Milan Hodza, a Slovak and member of the Agrarian party, became Prime Minister.

German Occupation of Czechoslovakia. During the next few years the socialists co-operated with other elements in the government in endeavoring, through the extension of additional rights to the German and other minorities, to prevent the dismemberment of Czechoslovakia. In this, owing to the determination of Hitler to annex the Sudeten portion of the Czech territory, they failed. The fate of the country was sealed on September 20, 1938, in the signing of the Munich Pact. The Hodza cabinet and President Beneš soon resigned, and in early November, 1938, under General Syrovy's ministry, a transition was effected from a democratic state to a fascist state within the German axis. On March 14, 1939, using as an excuse the charge that Germans had been mishandled, German troops entered Bohemia and Moravia, dissolved the Czechoslovak Republic, and incorporated Bohemia and Moravia in the German Reich. Soon thereafter all democratic organizations were wiped out, and there followed years of destitution, terrorization, and wholesale execution of those protesting against the dictatorship.

REVOLUTION AND REACTION IN HUNGARY

The Soviet Regime in Hungary (1918). In the neighboring country of Hungary, where the Social Democratic party was virtually disfranchised prior to the First World War, a political revolution was effected without bloodshed on the night of October 31, 1918. The supreme power was vested in a National Council, consisting of the Karolyi party, the Social Democrats, the bourgeoisie, and the radicals, and on November 16 a republic was officially declared, with Count Karolyi as president. The general disorganization of industry, however, led to increasing discontent. This was crystallized by the communists, headed by Dr. Bela Kun, into a formidable movement. Karolyi endeavored to secure the co-operation of the Allies in the stabilization of the country, but they failed to assist his government. In the meanwhile, Rumanian, French, and Czech troops were trying to get a foothold in the country. The situation becoming desperate, the Karolyi cabinet resigned in favor of the communists. The reins of government were turned over to the Workers', Soldiers', and Peasants' Deputies, and Bela Kun was selected Foreign Minister. The Bela Kun council immediately decreed "the socialization of large estates, mines, big industries, banks, and transport lines," declared complete solidarity with the Russian Soviet government, and offered to contract an armed alliance with the proletariat of Russia. It nationalized all retail businesses employing more than ten workers. It proclaimed "all houses used for residential purposes" to be the property of the soviet republic and began the organization of agriculture on an extensive scale. However, the Allies did everything possible to destroy the revolution. The Rumanian and Czech armies invaded the country, and under the wing of a French command a royalist White Guard, a counterrevolutionary army, was formed in the occupied territory. After three months of fighting, the Rumanians, under French command, marched to within twenty miles of Budapest.

Coming of Horthy Dictatorship (1919). In the meanwhile the Peace Conference promised the trade unions that it would give a moderate labor and socialist government its support if such were set up. Labor forces thereupon brought pressure to bear upon Bela Kun to resign. On their plea, he did so, giving over the government to the moderate elements. A Social Democrat succeeded as Premier. The Rumanians, however, refused to stop their advance and on August 4, 1919, entered Budapest, arrested some of the members of the new government, and issued an ultimatum in contravention of the terms of the armistice and the pledges of the Allies. At the expiration of the ultimatum they seized live stock, farming implements, rolling stock, and food, and proceeded to send them back to Rumania.

During these days Archduke Joseph, member of the House of Hapsburg, had been plotting a royalist *coup d'état,* and on August 6 a number of gendarmes, led by the chief of police, surrounded the palace in which the new government was sitting and forced the cabinet to resign. Archduke Joseph thereupon took over the government and was invested with supreme powers. The Supreme Council of the Allies, however, demanded his resignation, and a new reactionary cabinet was formed, which immediately proceeded to imprison and kill hundreds of communists and socialists. Later Admiral Horthy established a virtual dictatorship in Hungary, which during the thirties and early forties was "a dictatorship of a clique . . . a fascist regime without a fascist philosophy of its own, screened by a sham constitutionalism." In 1939 five Social Democrats were elected to the Lower Chamber, out of a total of 323.

THE SOCIALIST MOVEMENT IN POLAND

Socialist Groups to the First World War. The Polish socialist movement may be said to have had its origin in 1878, with the founding that year of the organization, "Proletariat." During the next four years a number of the members of the Proletariat engaged in conspiratorial activities which in many cases led to imprisonment and execution. In 1892 the Polish Socialist party (P. P. S.) was formed. As an exponent of the nationalist idea among the masses, the party was distinctly antagonistic to the Russian and German socialists. It regarded the First World War as a means of liberation, first from Russia, then from Germany and Austria. Pilsudski, afterwards dictator of Poland, and Dashinski were once active workers in its ranks. These two helped to form the Polish Legion and urged that the war be waged to the bitter end.

This party was opposed to Rosa Luxemburg, who organized the Social Democracy of Russian-Poland to combat the "social patriotic" attitude of the P. P. S. After the Russian Revolution the Social Democracy joined with the communist forces.

Socialists Oppose Pilsudski Dictatorship. Following the First World War, socialists participated in the cabinet, but later resigned. In 1926 Pilsudski assumed the dictatorship as a result of a *coup d'état*. The Socialists, at first undecided on the best course, finally united in opposition to him. In 1928 they elected 63 deputies to the Lower Chamber, but in the elections of 1930, where terroristic methods were employed by the followers of Pilsudski, this number fell to 23. During the following years they were in the forefront of the forces seeking to bring about a democratic regime. Their attempts to achieve this objective led to the arrest and conviction of many of their leaders, who were accused of plotting to overthrow the government by force. In 1933 the Socialists had increased again their representation in the House of Deputies to 41 out of 444. The communists, regarded as an illegal party, were represented by 2, elected as members of the Workers' and Peasants' party.

Two years later, in 1935, Parliament was dissolved. In the new Parliament under the constitution of that year, members were elected as representatives not of parties, but of the districts from which they came. Outside of Parliament the P. P. S. and the Polish Bund, which had often denounced the P. P. S. for alleged opportunism, continued their strong opposition to governmental policies, and their vigorous support of programs for regional self-government, for racial minorities, and for social and agrarian reforms.

Socialist Fight against Nazism. Members of the Socialist party took an active part in the defense of Poland against German and Russian forces in September, 1940 and, following the subjection of Poland, in the underground movement against German rule. Thousands of socialists paid for their opposition with their lives. The execution in 1942 by the Russian government of Henry Ehrlich and Victor Alter, two prominent Polish socialists who had organized widespread resistance to the nazis after the Polish government had fled and had served two years in prison when the Soviet government entered Poland, led to world-wide protests.

During the Second World War representatives of the Polish Socialist party and the Polish Peasant party submitted to the Polish National Council, Poland's Parliament in Exile, a postwar program for Poland calling, among other things, for a democratic constitution, a just redistribution of income, and an economic order in which public utilities, natural resources, and banking would be collectively owned, and in which farmers' and consumers' co-operatives would play an important part in the economic life.[5]

THE SOCIAL DEMOCRACY OF SWITZERLAND

The Grütli Union. The socialist movement in Switzerland was one of the few movements among the democracies of Europe which, until the Second World War, had been unrepresented in the cabinet of the country.

The Grütli Union claims the distinction of being the oldest political organization of the working class in that country, having been in existence since 1838. While at first merely a progressive party, in 1878 it declared in favor of socialism and in 1901 joined the Marxian Social Democratic party, in which it became the opportunistic wing. The following year this party polled 55,000 votes and elected seven members of the National Council. The vote steadily increased, and by the fall of 1914 the Social Democrats were represented in the National Council by 18 out of 200, and in the Cantonal Councils by 212 members.

Relations of Social Democrats with Internationals. During the First World War, the party took a vigorous stand against international warfare. After the war, the party veered to the left, and at the party convention held in early 1919 the delegates voted to withdraw from the Second International and join the Third, or Communist, International. They refused, however, to repudiate parliamentary activities, and this

[5] *Program for People's Poland,* published by Polish Labor Group.

action caused a number of extremists in the party to withdraw and form the Communist party of Switzerland.

But these steps proved to be too radical for the rank and file of the party, who, in two referenda votes, defeated the motion for union with the Third International. Following the second rejection, a second group split from the party and formed another communist political organization. In March, 1921, this second splinter group merged with the already existing Communist party.

Clear of Moscow affiliations, the Swiss party then joined the International Working Union of Labor and Socialist parties, afterwards referred to as the Second-and-a-Half International. Later, in 1926, it became a member of the reconstructed Labor and Socialist International.

Growth in Social Democratic Party Strength. After the First World War the party sent 19 of its members to the National Council. This number increased to 41 deputies in 1919, at the time of the introduction of proportional representation, out of a council of 187 members.

During the twenties the party gradually grew in strength, obtaining in 1928, a vote of 220,000, 27.6 per cent of the total, and electing 50 members of the Lower House. The votes obtained by the Communist party totaled between 15,000 and 17,000, and its representation in Parliament, from two to three.

Program and Policies of Social Democrats. Modification of Position on Military Defenses (1935). In the 1935 Congress the Swiss Social Democratic party carried on a vigorous campaign against militarism and for total disarmament. At the Luzerne Conference, after the Hitler triumph in Germany and the Dollfuss *coup d'état,* the delegates modified their attitude on national defense, declaring that the party recognized the necessity for armed defense of the frontier which "must be sustained by the will of an anti-capitalist community, if it is to fulfill its task with success."

At a subsequent conference in June, 1935, in Zurich, the party delegates refused to sanction a vote for military appropriations, however, unless the surplus over $235,000,000 be used for "internal national defense"—particularly to give work to the unemployed. Later 21 Social Democrats supported the credits, 12 abstained, 8 were absent, and 8 voted against them.

Formulation of Plan for Employment. In the mid-thirties the party formulated what it termed a Labor Plan, which was aimed at the maintenance of the consuming power of the people, the protection of wages, the reduction of unemployment, the expansion of export trade, and the regulation of the financial market and of trusts and cartels. The plan was submitted to the Swiss people in a referendum vote, but, receiving the approval of only 43 per cent of those voting, was defeated.

In the following elections of 1935 the party won 50 seats in the Lower House and became the largest party in Parliament. The Radical Democrats followed close behind the 49 deputies. The Communists elected two deputies. The Radicals again formed a cabinet in a coalition with the Catholics. During the thirties the party, time after time, refused to engage with the Communist party in united-front activities.

Battle against Fascist Trends. In the late thirties the Swiss Social Democracy was compelled to give a tremendous amount of energy to an aggressive fight against the development of the nazi and fascist forces in the country. In 1938 the party became a member of the "Movement of Guiding Principles," an anti-fascist movement consisting of the Social Democracy, the Swiss Trade Union Federation, the Young Peasants' movement, and organizations of white collar workers and other groups. In the same year, the party took the initiative in securing 300,000 signatures in behalf of a large public-works program.

Referendum on Direct Elections. In December, 1938, following the resignation of Dr. L. F. Meyer of the Federal Council, a body of seven chosen by Parliament, the Social Democrats made a vigorous effort to secure the election of one of their own number, Dr. Emil Kloeti, mayor of Zurich, to the Council, "as an act to secure equality for an important section of the population which fully and honorably bears the burden of the state." The majority of Parliament, however, remained adamant to the Socialists' plea and by a vote of 117 to 98 elected a representative of the financial interests instead of Kloeti. This defeat gave a further impetus to the Socialists' proposal for a referendum on the direct election of members of the Federal Council.

In the December 13, 1939, elections, following the outbreak of the Second World War, the representation of the Social Democratic party decreased, the party electing 45 deputies compared with 51 for the Radicals and 43 for the Catholic Conservatives. After the elections, however, Charles Rosselet, a Social Democrat, was elected speaker of the Lower House.

Activities during Second World War. During the Second World War the social democrats took a conspicuous part in strengthening the defense of the country with a view to resisting any attempt on the part of the forces of Germany to invade one of the last strongholds of democracy on the Continent. The Nazi and Communist parties in late 1940 were outlawed. Socialists continued in control of Zurich and several other important Swiss cities in which their administration had long been outstanding for integrity and social vision.

On January 25, 1942, the party suffered a defeat when its proposal that the Federal Council be elected directly by the people instead of by Parliament was turned down by the electorate. In 1943, under stress of the war crisis, the party was given one representative in the Federal Council, Ernest Nobs being appointed Minister of Finance and Customs.

In the elections of October, 1943, the Social Democrats again increased their representation to 56, with the Radical Democratic party electing 47, and the Catholics, 43.

CHAPTER 33

The Socialist Movement in Northern Europe

SOCIALISM IN DENMARK

Danish Socialism Prior to First World War. We have thus far considered some of the outstanding developments in the socialist movements of Great Britain, France, Germany, Austria, Hungary, Russia, Belgium, Switzerland, and Czechoslovakia. The labor and socialist movement has, in addition, played a rôle of very considerable significance in a number of other countries. Of outstanding importance before the Second World War was the movement in the three Scandinavian countries—Denmark, Sweden, and Norway.

The Danish socialist movement was one of steady growth from its inception to the invasion of Denmark by the forces of nazi Germany on April 9, 1940. The social democratic movement in Denmark may be said to have had its beginning on May 21, 1872, when the Danish Section of the First International called a meeting on the Copenhagen Commons in behalf of some striking bricklayers. The meeting was dispersed by the police, and several of the organizers of the meeting were arrested. The chief of police assured the Minister of Justice that socialism had been crushed in Denmark.

A few years later, in 1876, a conference of trade unionists and socialists was called, and this meeting resulted in an organization that combined trade-union and political activities. Two years later, on February 12, 1878, an independent Social Democratic party was formed. In 1884, six years after its formation, the party obtained its first parliamentary victory, returning to the Folketing, the Lower House of Parliament, two of its representatives.

From that date until the nazi invasion in 1940, the Social Democratic party grew steadily in influence and power. In 1884 it secured 6,805 votes in the parliamentary elections, 3.5 per cent of the total vote cast.

By 1935 its vote had increased to 759,102, 46.1 per cent of the total, and its representation in the Lower House to 68 (out of 149 members), 45.7 per cent of the total. Four years later, 1939, the proportion of its votes decreased to 46 per cent and the number of its parliamentary members to 64, the first decrease in any election since 1926. From 1884 to 1939 the dues-paying membership in the party had grown from a mere handful to around 200,000.

Prior to the First World War the party consistently refused to enter a coalition cabinet with non-socialists, though it lent its support to progressive cabinets which it refused to enter. In 1916, however, when the international situation for Denmark had become particularly critical, the party accepted the proposal that one of its members join the Radical cabinet. Thorvald Stauning, president of the party and later Prime Minister, became Minister without Portfolio. Shortly thereafter he was appointed Minister of Labor.

Social Democrats in Power. STAUNING AS PRIME MINISTER (1924). The party emerged from the international crisis of 1914–18 with increased prestige and in the elections of September, 1920 sent to Parliament 48 of its members as contrasted with a representation of 32 in 1913. Four years later, in 1924, following a severe economic depression, it elected 55 representatives to the Folketing, 10 more than the Farmers, its nearest competitor, and formed a wholly Social Democratic cabinet, with Stauning, for years leader of the party, as Prime Minister.[1]

In 1926, after two years in office, the Social Democratic party lost two seats, and the right-wing parties, who won a majority, formed a cabinet under Liberal leadership. The widely differing groups in the coalition cabinet of the right, however, began soon to disagree over industrial and military policies, and the cabinet resigned in 1929.

In the following campaign the Social Democrats urged the repeal of recent anti-strike legislation, the substitution for the army and navy of a system of customs patrol and frontier guards, the abolition of the Upper House, and labor and agrarian legislation. As a result of the campaign the Social Democrats made considerable gains, winning 61 seats, as compared with 44 for the Liberals, and again undertook to form

[1] Premier Thorvald Stauning was born on October 26, 1873. At an early age he became a cigar-sorter and, at the age of 23, the chairman of the cigar-sorters' union. In 1906, two years before resigning from this position, he was elected to Parliament and, in 1913, to the Copenhagen City Council. He served from 1916 to 1920 in the Radical ministry. His honesty, integrity, devotion to the cause of labor, and his common-sense approach to the problems of the day won him the confidence of the masses, and for years he was regarded as their outstanding leader. He died in 1942.

a cabinet, which this time included three Radical Ministers. From that day until after the nazi invasion, the Social Democrats remained in office, with Stauning as Prime Minister.

SOCIAL DEMOCRATS AS MAJORITY PARTY (1935). The party's 1935 campaign, which led to a greater success at the polls than ever before, was waged on the issues of public ownership of the central bank of issue, of the insurance companies, and of certain monopolized industries; a program of agricultural relief; improved social and labor legislation; more rigorous control of the banking system and of prices and industrial profits; a constitutional amendment for a one-chamber Parliament; an equitable system of proportional representation; and the modernization of the school system. The program likewise pledged the party to a continuous and vigorous struggle for democracy and continued co-operation with other democratic countries, particularly those in Scandinavia. In view of the nazi menace, the party reversed its former policy of urging sharp reductions in military expenditure.

Several months after the Folketing election the country elected members of the Upper House—the Landsting. In this election the Social Democrats increased their representation from 28 to 31. As a result, the left-wing parties were for the first time in the history of Denmark represented by a majority in both Houses. This revolution to a Socialist-Radical-controlled legislature made possible the passage of a long list of progressive laws on a scale hitherto unheard of in Danish history.

Two years later, in the municipal field, the party elected a majority of members in 50 out of 80 large and small towns in the country. In Copenhagen, the socialist vote was 64.6 per cent of the total.

1939 ELECTIONS. The 1939 elections for members of the Lower House resulted in the following representation of the various Danish parties, as compared with those of 1935:

Danish Parties	*No. of Seats Won in Folketing Elections*	
	1939	*1937*
Social Democratic	64	68
Liberal (Farmers)	30	29
Conservative	26	26
Radical	14	14
Free People's (Agrarian)	4	5
Justice League	3	4
Communist	3	2
National Socialists	3	0
Faroe Representative	1	0
Slesvig	1	1
Total	149	149

Opposition to Dictatorship. The Social Democratic party throughout its career was known as one of the most moderate of the European socialist movements. It refused to have any dealings with the Communist party, even in opposition to the nazis. In spurning the appeal of the communists to unite with them in a fight against nazism, the Social Democrats in 1936 declared: "The disciples of Moscow are utterly mistaken if they suppose that we are fighting against one dictatorship only to clear the way for another. We shall fight against every dictatorship because we respect the spiritual and political freedom of our people and mean to defend it."

Denmark in Second World War. German Invasion of Denmark. As the nazi menace became greater in the late thirties, the Danish socialists gave ever more attention to the defense of their country. Realizing, however, that Denmark would be unable, despite its best efforts, to withstand an invasion from Germany, the government sought to avoid entanglement in war, and, through treaties and daily conduct, did all within its power to remain neutral. The destiny of Denmark, however, was not within its own hands. Hitler had resolved to control the rich agricultural land of little Denmark and in April, 1940, on the excuse that the military resources of Denmark were insufficient to repulse the alleged Allied attempts against this democracy, saw fit "to proceed with the occupation of certain strategically important points in Danish territory." A "memorandum" to that effect was handed to the Danish Foreign Minister on the morning of April 9. King Christian, believing that resistance to the German army would be futile, appealed to the people of Denmark to refrain from such resistance on the ground that it would mean annihilation of his small kingdom. The German troops occupied all of the country, and although the Germans permitted the government to remain in office, they deprived it of most of its power and made the country a virtual feudal estate of the German Reich.

A few months after the German occupation, on July 3, 1940, the leaders of the five principal parties issued a joint statement declaring that Danish political parties will "abandon all points of disagreement and unite to make secure the independence and integrity promised our country, which is the Danish people's dearest desire." The signers pledged themselves to decrease unemployment, speed up work, practice economy, and work closely in co-operation with nations with which collaboration is still possible. Several demonstrations were made during these days against the invaders to whom the Danish people were bitterly hostile, but they were broken up by the German soldiers and many arrests made.

In the following years of war the German government brought continuous pressure on the Danish government to become a puppet of the Reich. Many of the demands were successfully resisted, though many had to be conceded. The Stauning government remained in office, and the free trade unions kept intact and even increased in membership. As the war advanced, however, the Reich forced the cabinet to accept Eric Scavenius, a collaborationist, as foreign minister. Following the death of Prime Minister Stauning in May, 1942, the nazis forbade any popular demonstrations in honor of the nation's late leader, and after a few months of the premiership of Vilhelm Buhn, successor to Stauning, the nazis compelled (November 8, 1942) the reorganization of the cabinet with Scavenius as Premier.

1943 ELECTIONS. On March 23, 1943, at the elections for members of Parliament, the Social Democrats obtained 45.5 per cent of the total (894,636 votes as compared with 729,619 in 1939), and more than the two next largest parties—the Conservatives and the Liberals—combined. The pro-nazi Farmers' and Nazi parties received a total of only 67,977 votes, or less than 3.5 per cent of the total, and the distinctly German Nazi party, but a little over one per cent of the votes cast. The municipal elections in May, 1943, showed similar results.

In the summer of 1943 the Danish social democrats urged a considerably broadened policy of postwar political and economic co-operation for Scandinavia, but not an isolated, armed, defensive union. The common policy, they declared, "should not be directed against anyone, but should be a part of an international system for peace and security."

RESISTANCE TO NAZI CONTROL. The Social Democrats in 1943 stiffened their resistance to nazi demands and forbade any party member to attend any meeting arranged or attended by anti-democrats or opponents of parliamentary government. The "underground" press reported in 1943 a circulation of 120,000. Many cases of sabotage were reported throughout Denmark, and the demand was made that those accused of sabotage be turned over to the German authorities for trial. This demand was refused by Parliament, whereupon the Reich authorities declared martial law and arrested thousands of anti-nazis. Riots took place throughout the country. Many were killed; others fled the country. To prevent the fleet from falling into the hands of the Germans, many vessels were scuttled, and others made their way to neutral or United Nations' ports. Much ammunition and numerous fortifications were also destroyed to prevent their use by the invaders. In the meanwhile the cabinet resigned, and a number of members of the government were able to escape to other lands.

THE SWEDISH SOCIAL DEMOCRATS

Branting, Early Socialist Leader. The Swedish socialist movement began to develop somewhat later than its brother movement in Denmark. In 1889 the Social Democratic party was organized, with Hjalmar Branting, later the first socialist Prime Minister, as its leading figure.[2]

Branting was elected the first Social Democratic representative in Parliament in 1897, but it was not until 1920 that the party began to gain any great momentum. In that year it increased its parliamentary representation to four. Three years later its representation advanced to 17; in 1908, to 33; in 1911, to 64; and, in the two elections in 1914, to 73 and 87, respectively—one of the most remarkable advances in the history of labor parties in Europe. The Social Democratic party increased its votes during those years from 8,751 in 1902 to 265,000 in September, 1914.

Party Opposition to War. During the First World War, the socialists opposed Sweden's entrance on the side of Germany and urged strict neutrality. It was largely through their activity that Sweden refused to join forces with the Central Powers. In their efforts in behalf of peace, the social democrats sent delegates to the anti-war Zimmerwald Conference in 1915 and endorsed the Stockholm Peace Conference in 1917.

Prior to that war, the party, as in Denmark, persistently refused to join in a coalition cabinet. As the war increased the tenseness of the Swedish situation, however, socialist leaders were more and more inclined to co-operate with other parties and in November, 1914, the delegates

[2] Branting was born in Stockholm on November 23, 1860. He was a student of science at Stockholm and Uppsala. At the age of 24 he joined the staff of *Tiden*, radical newspaper, and soon became its editor. Two years after his affiliation with this paper, he became editor of the *Social Demokraten*, remaining the head of this paper until 1917.

When the Social Democratic party was formed, Branting threw himself with enthusiasm into its work of organization and in 1907 became the party leader. He was elected a member of the Second Chamber of Parliament in 1897 and for the next five years was the only socialist member of that body.

When Norway demanded its freedom from Sweden, Branting, backed by the Social Democratic party, demanded that Norway be permitted peaceably to separate from the Swedish Crown. From 1914 to 1918, when there were strong forces in Sweden working on the side of Germany, Branting urged a policy of strict neutrality, though himself sympathizing strongly with the Allies. He was appointed delegate to the Paris Peace Conference in 1919 and, when Sweden entered the League of Nations, became the country's first representative in the League's Assembly and, in 1922, a member of the League's Council. In 1921 he was awarded the Nobel Peace Prize for his long years of peace activity. He died in 1925.

at the Social Democratic Congress by a vote of 90 to 58 expressed their willingness to join with other parties after the war in the formation of a Swedish cabinet. This decision, among other things, led to a cleavage between the left wing of the party and the administrative forces, and in May, 1917, the radicals split away from the party and formed the Swedish Socialist party. Fifteen members of Parliament, including Mayor Lindhagen of Stockholm, joined this new political alignment.

In the September, 1917 elections, the socialist movement, despite the split, won 98 seats, of which the Social Democratic party won 86. The socialists emerged as the strongest group in the country.

Socialist Entrance into Cabinet (1918). The result was the formation of a new cabinet containing seven Liberals and four Social Democrats—the first cabinet in which the socialists were represented. Hjalmar Branting became in this cabinet the Minister of Finance, but a few months later resigned. It was not long before the Swedish Socialist party divided into two sections. One of these, which refused to accept unconditionally the terms laid down by the Third International for affiliation with it, retained the name "Swedish Socialist party." The other wing, which swore unconditional allegiance to the policies of the Communist International, formed the Swedish Communist party.

In the meanwhile the Social Democratic party continued to function as the principal political agency of the workers of Sweden and, upon the resignation of Premier Eden, the liberal leader, Branting formed an all-socialist cabinet. In the following September, however, the Social Democrats, whose program for the democratization of industry had been bitterly attacked by the opposition, lost 10 of their 86 seats, and the Swedish Socialists, 4 of their 11. Branting thereupon resigned, and another Liberal cabinet was formed.

The country, however, failed to take kindly to the Liberal policies, and in September, 1921, the Social Democrats returned 99 of their representatives to the Lower House and 49 to the Senate, as contrasted with 19 three years before. Branting, thereupon, organized his second all-Socialist cabinet. The Socialists, however, were still in a minority in both Houses, and in a violent struggle in Parliament over the granting of relief to workers involved in a big lockout in the country in 1923 were defeated in their attempt to aid the workers. The Socialist government again came to an end, and a new government emerged, with Lord Justice Ernest Trygger, a director of one of the lumber and saw firms, as Premier.

Social Democrats as Opposition Party (1923–1924). This defeat, as former defeats, gave the Social Democratic party an opportunity to mend its fences as an opposition party. It sent its organizers throughout the country urging the government to spend a larger proportion of its budget on social services, a smaller proportion on armaments, and in the 1924 elections, as a result of their campaign of organization and propaganda, won 104 seats in the Lower House and 52 in the Senate.

Death of Branting; Sandler Prime Minister (1925). On October 14 of this year the third all-Socialist cabinet was formed. Unfortunately, however, Hjalmar Branting, Prime Minister and the leading intellectual figure in the movement, became seriously ill, and was forced to resign. On February 24, 1925, he passed away at the age of 64. He was mourned not only as the outstanding labor statesman of Sweden, but as one of the great leaders of the European labor movement. Branting was succeeded by Richard J. Sandler, who had served as Minister of Commerce.

In 1924, the Swedish Communist party split into two sections, the dissenters objecting to the centralism of the Third International and the discipline to which Swedish communists were subjected by this body.

Socialists As Opposition (1926–1932); Communist Activity. Sandler's cabinet continued for two years until the fall of 1926, when it fell, again on the question of relief measures for the unemployed. In 1928 the Social Democrats waged their campaign partly on the program of heavier inheritance taxes. Their proposals were attacked by the conservatives as a program of confiscation. The attacks by the forces to the right had their effect, and in the elections the Social Democrats lost four seats, returning 90 to the Lower House. The popular vote, however, increased from 725,407 to 872,500.

The Communists in this election increased their representation to 8. The following year the Communists again split over the expulsion from their organization of two communist deputies for refusing to wage a more vigorous war against Swedish capitalism and particularly against their "arch-enemies," the Social Democrats.

Socialists in Power (1932–1939). Election of Hansson as Prime Minister. The socialist chance again came in 1932. The conservative government had failed to grapple, with any degree of success, with the problem of unemployment. In the 1932 campaign the Socialists put forward their program for relieving unemployment, the reduction of the tariff, and the defense of democracy. Their campaign struck fire. In the September elections the Social Democrats polled 1,400,000 votes, and elected 104 to the Lower House, 58 to the Senate; the Communists retained their representation of 8 in the Lower Chamber; and the two parties combined fell short of possessing the majority by only three seats.

The popular vote of these two parties exceeded the combined votes of all the other parties in the country. After the votes were counted, the King requested Per Albin Hansson to become Prime Minister.[3]

Upon taking up the reins of office, the Hansson government began an inquiry into the desirability of government ownership of the country's chief munitions factory. Faced with an army of unemployed aggregating 150,000, it also began a many-sided attack on the unemployment problem. It instituted a comprehensive program of public works and increased its expenditures in connection with state enterprises, such as the post offices, telegraph communications, water-power plants, and railways. Partly as a result of this program and partly because of increased iron and other exports and general business conditions, the number of the nation's jobless steadily decreased from 164,000 in 1933 to 35,000 in 1936.

The government also gave much attention to an improvement in the social insurance system and to a study of the possibilities of the socialization of key industries. In its fight against fascism, it likewise initiated legislation for the prohibition of organizations whose objects were to act as defense corps for political parties.

After four years in office, Hansson finally resigned in 1936 after the Chamber had refused to plug the holes in the old-age insurance system and to raise pensions with the increase in living costs.

SOCIALIST TRIUMPH OF 1936. In the fall of 1936 another parliamentary election was held. The Social Democrats went before the country on their record of achievement in meeting the unemployment situation. Their appeal proved to be a popular one. The followers of Per Albin Hansson increased their popular vote by 20 per cent, and won 112 seats in the Lower Chamber, 45.9 per cent of the total and five more seats than the number secured by the three bourgeois parties combined. The Independent Socialists sent 6 members to the Lower Chamber and the Communists 2. The three labor parties thus possessed 53.6 per cent of the 230 seats in the *Andra Kammaren,* as this Chamber is called. Thus,

[3] Hansson was widely hailed as the incarnation of the spirit of the Swedish workers. He was born on September 10, 1885, a son of a mason, and began his career as a clerk in a co-operative store. He early became chairman of the socialist youth of Sweden and editor of the socialist paper *Fram,* and in 1911 was elected to the Lower House. Nine years later he was appointed Minister of National Defense in the Branting government and remained in the succeeding Branting ministries.

After the death of Branting, Hansson became the acknowledged leader of the Social Democratic party. Beginning his socialist career as an extreme anti-militarist, he later modified his policies and as Premier was usually regarded as one of the moderate members of the movement. Vigorous in debate on problems of immediate importance, he took little part in the discussion of abstract socialist economics.

"for the first time, the working class in a European country obtained a clear majority by democratic methods both among the electorate and in [the Lower Chamber of] Parliament." [4]

Following this election, King Gustav again asked Per Albin Hansson to form a cabinet, and Hansson again assumed the rôle of Prime Minister and appointed to his cabinet eight Socialists and four Agrarians. On returning to the premiership, he promised to continue his program for the elimination of unemployment, heavier taxes on large incomes, and the socialization of industry.

Coalition War Government. FORMATION IN 1939. After the outbreak of the Second World War, the Social Democrats, as a means of preserving unity, asked for the resignation of their cabinet and on December 13, 1939, organized a new coalition government consisting of six representatives of the Social Democratic party, three Agrarians, two Conservatives, and two members of the People's party. The Socialists, in the new setup, retained the premiership and the Ministries of Foreign Affairs, of Finance, of Social Welfare, of Defense, and of National Economy—six of the thirteen members—thus placing the party in the minority in the cabinet for the first time in many years.

During the ensuing months the question arose within the Social Democratic party as to whether, in view of the international crisis, the 1940 election should be postponed. The decision was made, however, to hold the elections as usual, and, in September, 1940, the Social Democrats won 134 out of 230 seats—as compared with 115 in 1936.

PREPARATIONS FOR DEFENSE. The aim of the government following the election was that of preserving neutrality and the country's independence against the pressures from without. Much of the federal budget following the beginning of the nazi invasion of Poland was spent on strengthening the defenses of the country. The social democrats gave generous assistance to the Finns in their fight in 1939 against Russian invasion and to the Norwegians, when attacked by the nazis. In 1940 and 1941 the Hansson government was compelled, on threat of more drastic measures, to permit the transit of nazi troops through Swedish territory to Norway.

In the city and county council elections of 1942, the Social Democrats won 54 per cent of the seats as against 17.4 per cent for the Conservatives and 2.8 per cent for the Communists. Their popular vote was 50.7 per cent of the total.

In June, 1943, the Riksdag requested the government to make a comprehensive study of postwar problems. In the fall of 1943 the govern-

[4] *International Information,* Sept. 23, 1936.

ment refused longer to permit the Germans to send their furloughed soldiers and war matériel through Sweden on their way to and from Norway. It protested to Germany against several of the latter's outrages against the peoples of Denmark and Norway and proposed closer co-operation after the war with other northern countries and Russia.

NORWEGIAN LABOR IN POLITICS

Unlike the Danish and Swedish Social Democratic parties, the Norwegian Labor party (at first called the Social Democratic party) was for years regarded as one of the left-wing Socialist parties of Europe and for some time worked rather closely with the Communist International. As in the case of the other Scandinavian working-class parties, it was in power for several years prior to the Second World War. With the nazi invasion, however, it was wiped out as a functioning party on the Norwegian soil. Following this invasion, the Labor government moved to London and continued to direct the great Norwegian shipping fleet from that capital.

The Norwegian Labor party was the successor of the Social Democratic party, formed in Christiana in 1887. The party participated in elections for the first time in 1894, polling in that year a small vote of but 732. At first it gave much attention to the formation of trade unions, but in 1899 handed over this function to the purely economic organization of workers.

In 1903 the party entered a national political campaign as an independent force and elected four members of Parliament. Two years later, when Norway broke away from Sweden, the party was without representation, but in 1906 it came back with a parliamentary deputation of 10. By 1912 this had grown to 23.

The Swing to the Left. During the First World War, the party took an extreme anti-militarist position and went on record against every kind of military preparedness, supporting a program of disarmament, permanent neutrality, and the submission of every kind of international dispute to an international tribunal of arbitration. It took an active part in the anti-war conference at Zimmerwald, Switzerland, in 1915.

After the Russian Revolution many members of the party veered to the left, and the 1919 Congress committed the party to affiliation with the Third (Moscow) International and to a belief in the dictatorship of the proletariat. In the 1918 elections the party vote increased from 196,000 to 297,000. The granting of the suffrage to women, however, was responsible for from 25,000 to 30,000 of this increase.

Three years later, after the new executive of the Labor party decided to accept, with a few modifications, the twenty-one points laid down by the Third International, the moderate group of socialists who disagreed with the communistic turn taken by the party decided to sever relations with the Labor party and form the Norwegian Social Democratic Labor party. Two months after this split the Labor party moved to accept the executive's recommendation and applied for affiliation with the Communist International on the basis of the conditions laid down by Moscow. In the following elections the Labor party elected 29 members to Parliament, and the Social Democratic Labor party, 8.

Controversy within the party over the International, however, would not down. The Labor party, without consulting the executive in Moscow, had expelled individual communists from the party for alleged violations of the rules laid down by the Norwegian section. Moscow took the position that no member of the party should be ousted without the International's consent. Many of the delegates took exception to this position and in the next Congress, by a vote of 169 to 103, denounced Moscow's communication. Martin Tranmael, the secretary and leader of the party, declared at the convention that the Labor party was under the supreme authority, not of Moscow, but of the Norwegian workers. The Russian delegates who had been sent to the congress thereupon declared that the minority, composed of communists, would henceforth be regarded as the Norwegian Section of the Third International. The minority left the convention and formed the Communist party.

Formation of All-Socialist Cabinet (1929). In 1927, a few years later, the Social Democratic Labor party severed its connection with the Labor and Socialist International and united with the Norwegian Labor party. The united party, in the elections of the following October, won no less than 59 seats in the Storting, as Norway's one Chamber is called, out of a total of 159, and polled 367,000 votes, or 36.9 per cent of the total cast. The Communist party, in the same election, cast a vote of but 40,000, 4 per cent of the total, and elected but three representatives.

In the following January, 1928, as the country's largest party, the Labor party was called upon for the first time in its history to form the government. It accepted and organized an all-Socialist cabinet. A few days after the formation of the cabinet, Christian Hornsrud, the socialist Premier, introduced a bill for the redistribution of wealth. This measure met with the violent opposition of the other parties; the government was overthrown, and a cabinet of the right was substituted in its place.

Norwegian Labor as Country's Opposition (1930–1932). In the October, 1930, elections the party was attacked on the ground that it was aiming at the "bolshevization" of Norway. The party had previously overwhelmingly rejected a motion to include in the party platform a plank favoring the dictatorship of the proletariat and vehemently denied the charges hurled against it. It increased its popular vote slightly, but obtained a smaller proportion of the total—31.6 per cent—and its parliamentary representation decreased from 61 to 47. The Communist party lost the one seat it had left after the desertion of two of the three deputies elected in the 1927 elections. From 1930 to the nazi invasion of Norway the Communist party had no representation in Parliament.

During the next few years, as opposition party, the Norwegian Laborites urged a program for grappling with the economic crisis and with the growing militarism in the country. Their campaign proved a popular one, and in the 1933 elections they received 40 per cent of the votes cast and sent to Parliament a delegation of 69, 46 per cent of the total. Although it was generally assumed that the Labor party, with its huge representation, would be called upon again to form the government, the party found itself confronted with a combined opposition who feared the destruction in Norway of the capitalist economy. These groups united on Johan L. Mowinckel as the "Savior of Norway" in the crisis. Mowinckel became Norway's next Premier.

During the next two years the Labor delegation introduced many measures for social control of credit for the employment of the unemployed and for assistance to farmers and the population generally. By virtue of the measures they sponsored, they drove a wedge between various parties of the right. The Mowinckel government finally fell, following its refusal to adhere to the demands of the Labor and Agrarian parties for increased emergency expenditures.

Nygaardsvold as Prime Minister (1932). With the fall of the Conservative cabinet, labor was called to form the government. This time it secured the support of the Agrarian party, though it effected no coalition with this group. Johan Nygaardsvold, a former worker on the railroads of the United States, and long a leading figure in the trade-union movement and the party, was elected Premier.

Upon their assumption of office, the Labor party representatives immediately launched an extensive public-works program with the result that, at the end of 18 months, unemployment was declared to be lower than in any period since 1931. The party likewise secured the passage of an old-age pension law, extended the unemployment insurance law, passed a new factory act, and repealed the laws disfranchising those on relief. It rescinded an anti-picketing law, banned the wearing of distinctive uniforms and badges—a blow to the nazis—and enacted in a modified form a proposal for a State Industrial Bank. It also promoted several other social measures.

The Labor administration met with popular support, and in the elections of 1936, 70 Laborites were elected to Parliament. In the next few years the party continued its fight against unemployment, placed housing in the very forefront of needed social services, and worked for the use of direct taxation and a credit and monetary system which favored the development of public enterprise. In 1938 it applied for affiliation with the Labor and Socialist International.

Program for Planned Economy (1939). In 1939 the party presented to the electorate a new declaration of principles. The declaration maintained, among other things, that "the economic conditions of capitalism will increasingly render necessary organized effort in the direction of a planned economy and a gradual socialization of big industry, foreign trade, the large private banks, and the means of transportation." It reiterated its solidarity with the other socialist parties of the world. Although it disassociated itself "from the policies of the Communist International which are conditioned by Russian circumstances and determined by the national interests of the Soviet Union," it viewed with sympathy the work of the Russian people in constructing a new and better society. It attributed to capitalism and fascism the armament race and the threat of war. It continued its support of the League of Nations, but declared that only the conquest of power by the workers and the establishment of socialism "can secure lasting good relations between the nations and guarantee the further peaceful and harmonious development of the whole of humanity and of the civilization of the world." [5]

Norway under Nazi Rule. When the Second World War broke out, the party strove vigorously for the strengthening of the country's defenses. When the forces of the German Reich invaded the country, the members of the Labor party were among the chief of the country's defenders. On April 9 the government met at Elverume and decided to include in the cabinet members of the Labor, Conservative, Liberal, and Agrarian parties. Many of the heads of the Labor government later escaped from Norway and established in London on June 10, 1940, the "official Norwegian government," which assumed control of the power-

[5] *International Information*, L. S. I., March 9, 1939.

ful Norwegian merchant marine. Inside the country, where civil liberties were crushed, large numbers of Norwegians conducted a persistent sabotage of the German forces who occupied the country. Many were arrested and sent to concentration camps; others were executed. On February 1, 1942, Major Vidkun Quisling received from Reich Commissar Joseph Terhoven the title of Prime Minister of Norway, but obtained the willing support of scarcely one per cent of the population. Throughout the occupation all the non-Quisling political groups acted as a united movement. Much sabotage against the invaders took place. In early 1943 the Norwegian Government in exile issued from London a decree depriving in the postwar period Axis collaborationists of their citizenship and the right to carry on business.

FINNISH SOCIAL DEMOCRATS

Beginnings of Labor Political Action. The Finnish socialist movement may be said to have had its origin in 1895 with the establishment of the *Työmies* (The Worker), following much propaganda on the part of Finns upon their return from visits to other European countries. The organization of this group was followed by a demand for a political party of labor. In 1898 two workers in Helsingfors organized a local Labor party, and in 1899 at a trade-union convention at Åbo the Labor party of Finland was launched.

The Labor party was at first reformist in character. In 1903, however, it adopted a definitely socialist program along the lines of the Austrian Social Democracy, changed its name to the Social Democratic party of Finland, and joined the International Socialist Bureau.

Advance of Socialist Forces; Russian Suppression. In the fall of 1905 the socialists took an active part in the general strike declared in behalf of the liberties Finland had lost under Russian rule. In 1906 Finnish suffrage was extended to include all men and women 24 years of age and over, and a one-Chamber Parliament was established.

In the succeeding election labor elected 80 deputies out of the total of 200, including nine women, and the workers began to organize in every part of the country. The Social Democrats in the Diet introduced social and labor legislation and sponsored bills for universal municipal suffrage and other reforms. However, the Czar refused to sanction most of the progressive legislation passed, and in 1911 the Russian Duma transferred the right of decision in all of the most important questions to the Imperial Duma. Workers' organizations were suppressed, social legislation came to a standstill, and burdensome customs duties were imposed on the country.

Opposition to First World War. When the First World War broke out, the Czar attempted to dissolve the Finnish regiments and to draft the troops to serve in the interior of Russia. The Finnish Constitution, however, provided against the use of the Finnish army outside of its own borders. The troops went on strike, and thousands of young men, when called, refused to appear at the enlisting stations. Many migrated to America. The strike was successful, but the Czar later retaliated by destroying Finland's autonomy and suppressing its liberties.

Electoral Triumph (1916). Despite the Czar's repressive measures, however, the forces of Finnish labor increased in influence, and in 1916 the Social Democratic party elected a majority of deputies (103 out of 200) to Parliament. This election marked the first time in the history of a European labor movement when a Labor or Socialist party elected a majority to its national legislature.

Within a year after this victory came the March, 1917, Revolution in Russia. In Finland this revolution resulted in sweeping the reactionary Russian officials out of office and in the inauguration of a new government with a cabinet in which half of the ministers were Social Democrats, headed by the socialist, Tokoi, the President of the Senate. The Finns thereupon asked the Kerensky government to grant them a number of reforms. Russia made no reply, and many Finns came to the conclusion that complete independence provided Finland's only solution. The Social Democrats, in their convention, accepted that point of view, but urged that independence be obtained as a result of friendly negotiations, not of military action. A number of reactionary industrial groups close to Germany urged, on the other hand, the use of military force, aided by German troops.

As the months advanced, the Finnish population grew further apart on this issue. The dissolution of the Finnish Parliament by the Kerensky government, the presence of Russian soldiers in Finland engaged in bolshevik propaganda, and the tragic economic conditions in Finland weakened the position of the socialists with their more moderate proposals, and in the October elections the latter secured but 96 out of 200 seats and the socialist ministers resigned from the cabinet.

The Revolutionary Government: Its Rise and Defeat. The November Revolution in Russia was followed by the recognition of Finnish independence. Attention was thereupon turned to the domestic scene. Extremists among the workers began to form into Red Guards; activists, to organize into Defense Corps. On January 25, 1918, the conservative forces attacked the Red Guards. Two days later the workers in Helsingfors elected a revolutionary government and took possession of the state buildings. The social democrats, who had opposed violence, cast their lot with the revolutionary movement. The new government, however, was short-lived. The Red army was attacked by the Defense Guards, many of whom had obtained their military training in the Russian and German armies, and was defeated. In April, 1918, an Imperial German army occupied Helsingfors. The revolutionary government fled from the capital and the war soon came to an end.

The defeat of the Red Guard was followed by wholesale arrests and executions. The Finnish Parliament, in the meanwhile, functioned without the Social Democratic members. Parliament rescinded progressive legislation and suppressed civil liberties. In October, 1918, they went so far as to elect a German Prince King of Finland.

Adoption of New Constitution (1919); Dissolution of Communist Party. The next month, however, the German forces were defeated and the First World War was over. Labor again began to organize. In the March, 1919 elections, the Social Democrats elected 80 representatives. The old cabinet was forced to resign, and a new government was formed. A liberal constitution was adopted, and significant advances were made in social legislation. Big business interests, however, began an active campaign to align the farmers on their side and against the city workers. A campaign of persecution against the communists ensued, leading to a dissolution of the Communist party.

Formation of Government under Tanner. In 1926, with the overthrow of the conservative government, the Social Democrats, supported this year by a parliamentary group of 60, formed a socialist government under the premiership of the famous co-operator, Väinö Tanner. This minority Socialist government accomplished a number of reforms, passing, among other things, a liberal amnesty law and old-age pension and health insurance legislation, and reducing customs duties on foodstuffs. Lacking, as it did, a majority, it found itself unable to secure the passage of fundamental social legislation and was finally defeated in December, 1929, and succeeded by an Agrarian government under Kallio.[6]

The Lapuan Movement. In the late twenties increasing bitterness developed among the population against the communists. In November, 1929, the communists decided to combine their fight for the capture of the trade-union movement with an anti-religious campaign. They organized an anti-religious demonstration at Lapua, the stronghold of a Lutheran religious denomination. A volunteer vigilante group prevented the holding of meetings, organized into a permanent movement, and demanded the suppression of the communists and, like-

[6] In the 1929 elections the Social Democrats elected 59 members to Parliament.

wise, of the socialists until the latter "dropped their Marxist doctrines." This vigilante group became known as the Lapuan movement.

The government passed legislation enlarging its powers over the formation and the dissolution of the country's political organizations but as a result of social democratic opposition refused to favor legislation for the control of the press. When the Lapuans realized that legal suppression could not be expected under the Kallio coalition government they began to stir up violence. Together with members of the Lock movement—a movement reactionary in its economic doctrines—they started a march on Helsingfors. Before they reached the Finnish capital, however, Parliament passed a bill permitting the government to suppress communist newspapers, and a more inclusive cabinet was formed headed by Senator Svinhufvud. Svinhufvud met the Lapuans when they reached Helsingfors, received their demands, and proceeded to enact many of them into legislation, after depriving the communists of their seats.

Parliament was then dissolved and new elections were called. Between the dissolution and the elections, socialist and communist leaders were kidnapped and a campaign of terror was waged against radicals of various schools. The elections resulted in the seating of 66 Socialists and were followed by the passage of further sweeping anti-communist laws.

Entrance of Socialists into Cabinet (1937). Socialists remained as an opposition force in the country until 1937, in the meanwhile supporting measures for civil liberties and social reform. In the latter year, following the election of Kyosti Kallio, member of the Agrarian party, as President, socialists joined the cabinet, assuming the Ministries of Finance, Commerce, Communications and Public Works, Transport, and Social Affairs. Väinö Tanner, as Minister of Finance, was one of the cabinet's most powerful figures.

In the July, 1939 elections, Social Democrats won 80 seats in Parliament, and the Socialist Dissenters 5, whereas the Patriotic National Movement, the fascistic party of the country, won but 8 seats, a decrease of 6.

The constitution of Parliament as a result of this election was as follows:

Parties.	*Members*
Social Democratic	80
Agrarian	56
National Coalition	25
Swedish People's	18
Patriotic National Movement	8
National Progressive	6
Socialist Dissenters	5
Small Farmers	2
Total	200

The Social Democrats during Second World War. The socialists retained important positions in the new cabinet. Tanner became Minister of Foreign Affairs and, later, Minister of Food Supplies. Social democrats took a leading part in the task of national defense in the following months until the outbreak of the Second World War and were among the staunchest defenders of the country when Russia invaded Finland in the fall of 1939. They likewise assisted greatly in the rehabilitation of the country following the war and in the conflict against Russia in 1941.

As the Second World War with Russia continued, social democrats brought increasing pressure upon the government to find some satisfactory way of ending it lest it lead to territorial aggrandizement. "In Finland," declared the Social Democratic daily, "the problem of Lebensraum has never existed. The Workers' Lebensraum is freedom." K. Wiik, former secretary of the party, was arrested in 1942 for agitating against certain of General Mannerheim's military policies.

In late February, 1943, Risto Ryti was again elected President by the presidential electors following a short campaign in which the discussion of vital national problems was forbidden. Following his inauguration, President Ryti asked Väinö Hakkila, Social Democratic speaker of Parliament, to form a cabinet. After an unsuccessful attempt to secure the co-operation of the Agrarian party, however, Hakkila declined the premiership. During 1943 the Social Democrats remained the largest single party, with a representation in Parliament of 85 out of 200. The parliamentary elections, scheduled for 1943, were postponed until 1944. Opposition within the Social Democratic party to the continuance of the war with Russia became stronger during early 1944. This opposition, under the leadership of Professor Väinö Voionmaa, chairman of the Foreign Affairs sub-committee, commanded a majority vote of the party, although not of its representatives in the Riksdag.

CHAPTER 34

Labor's Struggle against Dictatorship in Italy and Spain

IN THE two Latin countries on the European continent—Italy and Spain—the socialist movement, after achieving a position of prominence, was gradually overwhelmed by the forces of fascism during the twenties and thirties.

ITALIAN SOCIALIST MOVEMENT

Socialist Separation from Anarchists. The restriction of the franchise, the large class of illiterate workers, the strong anarchistic elements in the Italian population, and the backwardness of industrial development were among the causes of the comparatively late development of the socialist movement in Italy.

Italy was represented in the old International, but chiefly by the anarchistic groups supporting Bakunin. In 1892 the movement definitely separated itself from the anarchists and formed a distinct party under the leadership of Philipo Turati, a brilliant Italian lawyer and editor. In the following election the party elected six members to the House of Deputies. In 1906, after an acrimonious debate, Labriola, the well-known social scientist, and his syndicalist following resigned and formed a syndicalist group.

Increase in Socialist Strength (1913). Until 1913 only 7 per cent of the Italian people was permitted the franchise. In that year, however, all literate male citizens over 21 years and all illiterate males over 30 years of age were given the vote. The vote for 1913 consequently increased to 960,000 for the Socialist party and to 200,000 for the Socialist Reformist party, formed the previous year by a group of deputies expelled from the Socialist party for their compromise position on the Tripoli war. The official Socialist party won 51 seats in Parliament; the Reformist party, 23; the Independent Socialists, 8—a net increase of 40 seats for the Socialists who, with the 70 Radicals and 24 Catholics, formed the opposition to the Giolitti government.

Opposition of Mussolini to Socialist Party. The Socialist party opposed Italy's participation in the First World War. Later, Mussolini, editor of the *Avanti,* resigned, established a paper of his own, and henceforth became a bitter opponent of the Socialist party.[1]

Forces to Right and Left following the First World War. Following the war, the returned soldiers and war workers found it difficult to obtain jobs. Hungry and discontented, they loafed around the streets ready to become revolutionists of the right or of the left, as occasion of-

1 Benito Mussolini entered the fascist movement after a long record of activity as a socialist. He was born July 29, 1883 at Dovia. His mother was a woman of deep religious spirit. His father was a blacksmith, an atheist, and a follower of Bakunin who believed that the political system should be overthrown by violence.

At eighteen he taught school. He became involved soon thereafter with the law—some said that he smashed a ballot box—and left the country, striking out for Switzerland. There he worked at odd jobs, seeking out a precarious existence, and studying at the Universities of Lausanne and Geneva. Wilfred Pareto was among his teachers. He assisted while in Switzerland in the organization of labor, promoted several strikes, and was expelled from one canton after another and finally from the country itself. The legal bar to his entry into Switzerland was not removed, interestingly enough, until he became Prime Minister.

In 1908 Mussolini participated in Italian agrarian conflicts and was at one time jailed for ten days. Shortly thereafter he became editor of *Popolo,* published in Austria, from which country he was expelled after he had contributed an article in which he declared: "The Italian frontier does not end at Ala."

In 1910 Mussolini was invited to the editorship of another paper, *La Lotta di Classe,* a socialist publication. While editor he opposed the military expedition of the Italian government to Tripoli, even to the extent of urging the people to resist the authorities, and received for this another jail sentence, this time for five months. His last socialist assignment was the editorship of the *Avanti,* the official socialist paper of the country.

Until the outbreak of the First World War, Mussolini was generally to be found on the extreme left wing of the socialist movement. On occasions, breaking with the traditions of socialism and leaning toward anarchism, he often gave approval to outrages committed by individual anarchists. Thus when in March, 1912, the anarchist Alba made an attempt on the life of the King of Italy and a group of socialists congratulated the king on his escape, Mussolini, at the next socialist congress, censured this group severely and had them expelled from the party.

When the First World War broke out, Mussolini, then the editor of the socialist paper, *Avanti,* maintained in his editorials for two months that the workers should not permit themselves to be swept into the "bourgeois war," but should prepare themselves to be ready to bring about the social revolution as soon as the war had precipitated the "crisis of the capitalist society."

As the European conflagration continued, however, Mussolini suddenly shifted his position following visits from the French radical, afterwards communist leader, Marcel Cachin, and, in October, 1914, declared himself in favor of Italy's entrance into the war on the side of the Allies. Resigning from the editorship of *Avanti,* he was soon expelled from the Socialist party. In November, 1914, "without a penny in his pocket," Mussolini founded a daily paper, *Il Popolo d'Italia,* which vigorously

fered. Some of these became members of the socialist movement; others, in 1919 and 1920, formed the first nuclei of the Fascist party.

During these years, many syndicalists, on the one hand, and bolsheviks, on the other, began to propagandize among the workers, urging strikes, the occupation of factories, and the seizure of the land—striving to prepare the way for the dictatorship of the proletariat. Added to all this confusion was that engendered by Italian generals and members of the Foreign Office who contended that Italy had not obtained the territorial gains to which it was entitled. Thus was generated the state of mind that eventually resulted, among other things, in D'Annunzio's raid on Fiume.

The socialists were greatly influenced during these years by the general Italian situation and by the Russian revolution. In March, 1919, the party's national Executive Committee endorsed the manifesto of the Third International, and the party's November, 1919 elections were waged on an anti-war and revolutionary program that included unqualified support of the Soviet government. Socialists received 3,000,000 votes, or more than one third of the votes cast, and their representation in the Chamber increased to 156.

During the year much discussion arose within the party regarding the movement's continued relation with the Communist International. In January, 1921, at the national party congress all sections declared their adherence to the Third International and acceptance of the 21 points laid by that organization as conditions for affiliation. But the right and center groups claimed national autonomy in the interpretation and application of the conditions. A representation of the Third International at the Congress, however, demanded complete acceptance of the 21 points and the expulsion of the so-called reformist elements. On January 20 the convention, by a large vote, decided against the acceptance of the Moscow conditions. The minority seceded and formed the Communist party of Italy.

In May, 1921, following months of violence on the part of fascist groups, the government called new parliamentary elections. Many conservatives hoped that, as a result of these elections, the socialist delegation in Parliament would be wiped out. In spite of a reign of terror in many districts, however, the Socialist party returned 123 deputies, and the Communists, 15.

Radical Character of Early Fascist Appeal. Following these elections, in which no party secured a majority, widespread disorders con-

espoused the cause of the Allies. A Milanese weekly paper, *L'Italia del Popolo*, in its issue of March 3, 1919, accused Mussolini of "having cashed patriotic cheques from the French government," and challenged him to bring the matter into court (see Salvemini, *The Fascist Dictatorship in Italy*, p. 12).

tinued in the country—both in the army and in civilian life. The fascist movement became increasingly destructive and increasingly powerful.

Fascism in Italy dated officially from the foundation in March, 1919, by Mussolini, then editor of *Il Popolo d'Italia,* of the first *Fascio di Combattimento* in Milan. At first the fascists started a vigorous agitation for economic and political reforms. They demanded that a National Constituent Assembly be called, to be the Italian section of the International Constituent Assembly of the Peoples. They urged the proclamation of an Italian republic, universal suffrage for both men and women; the abolition of the Senate and of all titles of nobility; the end of compulsory military training; international disarmament; an elected magistracy; the confiscation of unproductive capital; the transference of land to the peasants and of the management of industry to syndicates of technicians and workers; the suppression of the stock exchange; and the dissolution of limited liability companies and banks.

When the socialists urged the eight-hour day, the fascists declared that this was too mild a reform and a betrayal of the proletariat. They encouraged food riots, whereas the socialist organizers did their best to restrain rioting. "It is not the Socialist party which has promoted and directed these demonstrations," declared Mussolini in his newspaper on July 4, 1919. "It [the S.P.] lacks the will to lead a movement which will disrupt the parliamentary game of trickery, past and present. For our part we explicitly affirm the fundamental justice of the popular protest." The next day he declared, "A few food-hogs hanging from the lampposts would be a good example."

While welcoming these disturbances, Mussolini urged the masses to overthrow their "weak and useless government" and to aid the defeated nations in a new war against the so-called capitalist nations—France, England, and the United States. The United States, he maintained, had prevented Italy from becoming the master of Fiume, Dalmatia, Asia Minor, and other territories suitable for colonies necessary for her development, and should be dealt with accordingly.

Seizure of Italian Factories (1920). The year 1920 witnessed numerous seizures of factories, a half-million workers occupying factories from August 21 to September 3. Mussolini declared his sympathy with these disorders and maintained that they should be stepping stones to social upheaval. The more moderate members of the General Confederation of Labor and the Socialist party opposed the efforts of the fascists, the communists, and the anarchists to give the crisis a definitely revolutionary turn, and on September 11 this moderate point of view won out in the labor federation.

As the days of the factory occupation continued, the workers began to realize that without technical assistance, raw material, or foreign markets, the possession of a factory meant little. They finally became tired of remaining in the shops, and by September 25, 1920, most of the workers had gone home.

However, during the remainder of 1920, disturbances continued. These led to much controversy among the radicals and in January, 1921, to a split between socialists and communists.

During these days an increased feeling of discouragement was evidenced among the masses, and the conservatives among the industrialists, shopkeepers, civil employees, ex-service men—all with grievances of one kind or another—became ever more articulate and began to look around for leadership to represent them. They found it in the fascists, who started to rally around them these diverse elements to "put an end to the communist menace."

Fascists Swing to Right (1921). Although the fascists had for years mouthed revolutionary phrases, numerous industrialists, small shopmen, and landowners began to take the view that, if they gave extensive enough aid, if their sons and followers became enrolled in the fascist bands, they would be able to control the fascist policies and mold fascist programs. The resulting influx into the movement of the conservative and wealthy bewildered many of the "fascists of the first hour," among them thousands of poverty-stricken youth.

Mussolini sensed this trend and soon was found launching an attack against the socialists not from the left, but from the right. Instead of calling socialists "ineffectual revolutionists," he declared that their revolutionary program was fraught with danger. From then on Mussolini appealed now to one group, now to another, for support, with arguments wholly inconsistent one with the other. He was particularly successful in stirring the nationalist youth to a state of hysteria.

From the latter part of 1921 the fascist forces sought to feel out their strength in preparation for their invasion of the Italian capital. They marched on Ravenna in September, 1921. The march demonstrated that many of the military were on their side. Later they invaded other cities. During the months before the "March on Rome" the communist forces were steadily weakening. The economic crisis was being gradually overcome and greater unity was being developed among the democratic political forces governing the country. The way was being made clear for a stabilization of the parliamentary groups. Many fascists began to fear that, unless the *coup d'état* was soon staged, it would become an impossibility.

The March on Rome (1922). The "March on Rome" took place on October 28, 1922. It could have been stopped by the military if they had been so disposed. It was not participated in, some authorities maintain, by more than 8000 fascists. But the King refused to proclaim martial law and the fascists entered Rome unresisted. From that moment Italy was under a dictatorship.

Mussolini became Premier with the support of the King and appointed himself Minister of the Interior, of War, of Marine, and of Aviation. At first the regime was not totalitarian. The Fascist party entered the election campaign as a part of a bloc instead of as a totalitarian ruler. At these elections, in spite of fascist terror, the government was in a minority in all industrial centers. Socialists and communists together polled more than a million votes. In cities and countryside combined, the opposition parties were almost as strong as the government. Mussolini, however, evolved a plan to centralize control in fascist hands. He forced through a law by which the votes given to all parties were added together in a national total. The majority receiving the highest number of votes in the nation was given two thirds of the seats in all of the regional districts. The remaining third of the seats was distributed in proportion to the votes which each party received.

In the elections of 1924 the opposition parties were unable to reach an understanding and each went to the polls with its own list, whereas the fascists and their sympathizers presented a united front. Of the total vote, estimated at 7,500,000, the Fascist party (including the Nationalists) received 4,500,000 and was assigned 375 seats in the Chamber, and the opposing parties were given 160 seats.[2]

Murder of Matteotti (1924). Following the election, on May 30, 1924, the Socialist deputy Giacomo Matteotti delivered an address in the new Chamber in which he contested the validity of the fascist majority. He maintained that the voters had not been free to express themselves and that the government had prejudiced the outcome of the election by declaring that, whatever the outcome, it would stay in power. He described many alleged violations of the election law and ended his speech—which had been subjected to constant interruption—by demanding that the elections be annulled.

The speech led to bitter replies from the fascists, and Mussolini's or-

[2] The opposition seats were divided as follows: 25 to followers of Giolitti and other small independent groups; 40 to Popularists; 25 to Unitary Socialists; 14 to Maximalists; 19 to Communists; 8 to Republicans; and 25 to Democrats. The Communist deputies, together with the other opposition parties, abstained, in general, from participation in Parliament.

gan, *Il Popolo d'Italia,* on June 1, 1924, declared: "The honorable Matteotti has made a monstrously provocative speech which would merit something more tangible than the epithet 'ruffian' [which had been applied to him by a fascist deputy.]" Addressing the Chamber on June 6, Mussolini praised the example of Russia where, he said, "There are magnificent teachers. . . . We made a mistake not to imitate them fully, because at this hour you would no longer be here, you would be in prison. . . . You would have had lead in your back. But we have the courage, and we will prove it to you." The day following, Mussolini declared that he would see to it that Parliament functioned and that if the opposition continued to show political indifference, it would be condemned to "perpetual exile from history."

On June 10 Matteotti suddenly disappeared. Police investigation revealed that he had been kidnapped by five fascists and had subsequently been murdered. The investigation implicated Finzi, Under-Secretary of the Interior, and Cesare Rossi, chief of the Press Department. Other prominent fascists were involved, and it was even rumored that Finzi and Rossi had implicated Mussolini in their confessions. The five men accused were brought to trial in 1926, the Secretary-General of the Fascist party acting as counsel for the defendants. Two of the defendants were acquitted and three others were condemned to imprisonment but were released two months later under the terms of an amnesty granted in 1925.[3]

The murder greatly aroused public opinion. The historian Ferrero described the elections of 1924 as a "strangulation of the country." The opposition parties, as a sign of protest, withdrew from the Chamber of Deputies and became known as the *Aventine.* The elder statesmen, Giolitti, Orlando, and Salandro, who, while maintaining a somewhat independent position in the Chamber, had sympathized with the fascists, now joined the opposition. The opposition, however, failed to arouse the country against fascism, which many observers felt was then seriously in danger of downfall.

The fascists, supported by propertied interests, who wanted "public order" above all things, and by numerous elements from various non-fascist groups, began a new era of repression and intransigeance. Mussolini, in a speech which may be said to have inaugurated this new era in fascist development, challenged the Chamber to impeach him for the murder of Matteotti and declared that he accepted full responsibility for the Matteotti affair. "If fascism has been nothing more than castor oil and cudgels and not a magnificent passion of the best youth of

[3] For details of this trial, see Salvemini, *The Fascist Dictatorship in Italy,* ch. V.

Italy," he declared, "then the responsibility is mine. If fascism has been a criminal association, well, I am its chief and I am responsible." Mussolini declared that his new watchwords to the fascists were, "Absolute intransigeance, theoretical and practical" and "All power to all fascism." He denounced the *Aventine* as seditious and unconstitutional. The opposition parties replied that the *Aventine* was a "resolute and irrepressible protest against the most atrocious crime of the regime."

Increase in Fascist Suppression. The fascists had now gained the upper hand and began to strengthen their position by the passage of numerous repressive laws dealing with the press, secret societies, the civil service, and public safety. There was little discussion in the Chamber when these laws were presented, as it was then composed only of fascists and their sympathizers.

Meanwhile, the opposition gradually drifted apart, and after July, 1925, the *Aventine* ceased to function as an organized group. The continued abstention of the anti-fascists from parliamentary activity deprived them of the last semblance of power, and the repressive legislation concerning the right of association and of the press took from them all means of effective expression and action.

The government, on its part, had no intention of permitting the return of its opponents to effective participation in the control of the government, and when members of the Popular party tried to return to the Chamber in January, 1926, Mussolini declared that their presence would be "tolerated" on one condition only—that they undertook to separate themselves from anti-fascist activities in Italy and abroad.[4]

In the meanwhile, on January 31, 1925, a commission of 18 Senators, deputies, and experts had been appointed for the purpose of reforming Italy's political institutions. As a result of its recommendation, the law "on political representation of May 17, 1928," was passed by the Chamber acting as "a constituent assembly."

Reorganization of Chamber of Deputies by Law of May 17, 1928. The law of May 17 established a single electoral district—the nation. According to this law 800 candidates for the Chamber were to be designated by fascist syndicates and 200 by "the legally constituted bodies and by associations, the scope of which is cultural, educational, charitable, or propagandist, and which exist owing to the fact that they are of national importance." Candidates were to be assigned to the various

[4] Scores of headquarters of labor and socialist groups had long since been destroyed. Opposition individuals were compelled to live in restricted districts. Many socialists fled to Paris and, under the leadership of Filippo Turati, Claudio Treves, and others, conducted anti-fascist activities. Later they sought other centers for their activities.

organizations in accordance with their relative importance in the eyes of the government to the productive life of the nation. The candidates were to be men of competence in their professions capable "of furthering the historical aims of the nation."

None but fascists could be expected to be selected. This was made plain by Mussolini in his farewell address on December 8, 1928, to the old Chamber of Deputies: "If the Chamber which is about to conclude its labors today has been, from the point of view of numbers, eighty-five per cent fascist [he declared], the Chamber which will assemble for the first time on Saturday, April 20 of Year VII (1929), will be a one hundred per cent fascist Chamber." [5]

To insure the fascist character of the Chamber, the Grand Chamber was to receive the list of 1000 candidates prepared by the syndicates and the approved societies, and from this list the Council was to select 400. This latter list was then to be submitted to the voters for a "plebiscite."

As for the voters, under the 1928 law their right to vote was conditioned upon their active participation in national life, whether as producers or taxpayers. All male citizens who had reached the age of 29 (or of 18, if they were married and had children) might vote (1) if they paid syndicate contributions or 100 lire in taxes; (2) if they received pensions from the state; or (3) if they belonged to the clergy. The voters were asked one question: "Do you approve of the list of deputies designated by the National Grand Council?" and their sole function as members of the electorate consisted in giving an answer, "Yes" or "No." In other words, the voters were invited to express their views, not in regard to individual candidates, but in regard to the program of the government as a whole.

If, by any chance, the country should reject the list of deputies drawn up by the Grand Council, all the associations would be asked to draw up lists of candidates, and the voters would be requested to make a choice among these lists. All of the candidates on the lists that obtained the largest number of votes would be declared to be elected and the seats reserved for the minority would be distributed among the remaining lists. This provision, however, was regarded by the fascist leaders as of little or no importance, since the rejection of the list prepared by the Grand Council was regarded as outside of the realm of possibility.[6]

[5] *Corriere della Sera,* December 9, 1928. The year 1922 is regarded as year I of the fascist era, and all public documents bear a double date.

[6] *Il Popolo d'Italia,* April 24, 1929. On April 23, 1929, Achille Starace, vice-secretary of the Fascist party, declared in a speech: "If the twelve million votes 'yes' should transform themselves into twenty-four million 'noes,' Mussolini would still

The new electoral law met strong opposition in the Senate. Forty-two Senators signed a resolution declaring that this law deprived the Italian people of the most essential of its rights, but the law was finally adopted.

The first test of the new electoral law was made on March 24, 1929. The same number of candidates was assigned to the federations of employes and those of employers in each branch of the national economy. This gave little or no opportunity to present their views. The voters were warned by their respective syndicates, and frequently by their employers, that they might be deprived of various privileges, and even of their jobs, if they failed to appear at the polls or if they cast a negative vote. The president of the National Confederation of Fascist Syndicates of Industry issued a circular declaring that "industrial workers must go to the polls perfectly organized and demonstrate their acceptance of the regime." The Catholics, pleased by the conclusion of the Lateran accord on February 11, 1929, urged a vote for the government. Finally, the tenth anniversary of the *Fascio di Combattimento* was celebrated the day preceding the elections and was made the occasion of public demonstrations of loyalty to the government.

Fascists in Complete Control of New Chamber (1929). At the polls the voters could choose one of two ballots. The pro-fascist ballot was decorated with the tricolor and was inscribed: "Do you approve of the list of deputies designated by the national Grand Council? Yes." The tricolor was visible after the ballot was folded. The other ballot was plain and inscribed with but one word, "No." There was thus no secrecy in the casting of the ballots, and those attempting to cast a negative vote were intimidated, it is claimed, in numerous ways. When the votes were counted, it was found that 8,519,559 voted "yes" and only 135,761 "no."

The new Chamber of Deputies, elected for a five-year term, was inaugurated on April 20, 1929. Under the rules of the Chamber as elaborated by Augusto Turati, then Secretary-General of the Fascist party, no questions not already on the agenda could be discussed by the Chamber, except on the initiation of the government. In practice, bills were submitted by the head of the government to the Grand Council of the party, then passed along to the Council of Ministers for examination, and only then were they submitted to the Chamber for action. The Chamber, in the words of Mussolini, might at any time "freely discuss

---

remain at Palazzo Venezia and the revolution of the Black Shirts would not thereby have suffered any check."

the work of the government, not, of course, for the purpose of overthrowing it, but for the purpose of criticism and collaboration." From that time until the Second World War, fascists had a virtual monopoly of all avenues and agencies of public discussion and socialist, communist, and other non-fascist groups existed in Italy only as scattered underground organizations.

Opposition to Continuance of Second World War. With the coming of the Second World War, socialist and communist groups secretly distributed much literature denouncing Italy's participation in the war on the side of Germany. In 1942 the underground Socialist party inaugurated an anti-war week throughout Italy on April 1–7, with the shibboleth, "Enough of war! enough of fascism." From the fall of 1942 it urged the workers of Italy to civil disobedience.

With the forced resignation of Mussolini the socialists collaborated with communist and other anti-fascist groups in organizing demonstrations throughout Italy in behalf of peace and a democratic government in Italy. When the United Nations occupied Italy, the Socialist party joined with the Communists and four other groups to form the Committee of National Liberation. This Committee in June, 1944, selected Ivanoe Bonomi, a former socialist, as the next Premier of Italy. Socialists continued to urge the abdication of the House of Savoy.

SPANISH SOCIALISTS' RISE AND FALL

Spanish Socialists in First International. The Spanish socialist movement, which was temporarily in power during the early thirties, had its beginnings in 1869, when a small branch of the First International was formed. This organization, however, subsequently fell into the hands of the anarchists, and it was not until 1879 that the Social Labor party was formed, partly through the influence of Pablo Iglesias.[7]

Socialists' Opposition to Dictatorships. Following the First World War, in the elections of 1923, the Socialist party gained its first spectacular success, winning seven seats in the lower house of the Cortes—the national legislature—, a success attributed by the socialists to their strong opposition to the war in Morocco.

[7] Pabli Iglesias was born October 15, 1850. On the death of his father, he was placed in a foundling asylum, where, despite repeated attempts to escape, he remained for several years. In 1871 he became secretary of the International Proletarian Federation, and in 1872 founded the Typographical Societies, of which in 1885 he became president. He helped found the first socialist group, became editor of *El Socialiste* in 1886, Deputy in 1910, and, when in 1923 de Rivera dissolved the party, he was the chief of the Parliamentary Socialist group. He died December 8, 1925.

(Left) Levi Eshkol, Prime Minister of Israel, 1963– ; leader of the Mapai, a moderate socialist party. (Courtesy Israel Information Services) (Right) Giuseppi Saragat, Socialist President of Italy, 1964– ; former Deputy Prime Minister, Minister of Foreign Affairs, and leader, Social Democratic party. (Courtesy Italian Information Center)

(Left) Einar Gerhardsen, Norwegian Labor Prime Minister, 1945–1951, 1955–1965. (Courtesy Norwegian Embassy Information Service) (Right) Jens Otto Krag, Social Democratic Prime Minister and Minister of Foreign Affairs of Denmark, 1962–1968. (Courtesy Danish Information Office)

Swedish political leaders of many parties parade for "Sweden's Liberty and Independence" on May Day, 1966. (Courtesy Swedish Information Service)

(Left) Tage Erlander, Social Democratic Premier of Sweden, 1946– ; President, Social Democratic party of Sweden. (Courtesy Swedish Information Service) (Right) Paul-Henri Spaak, former Socialist Prime Minister and Foreign Minister of Belgium; Secretary General, N.A.T.O., 1957–61; President of Consultative Assembly of Council of Europe. (Courtesy Belgian Information Service)

The Eight-Hours Monument of the Victoria Labor movement in Melbourne, Australia, commemorating an important victory of Australian labor, prior to formation of Labor government. (Courtesy Australian News and Information Bureau) (Right) Walter Nash, Labor Prime Minister of New Zealand, 1957–1960; President of the International Labor Organization, 1945. (Courtesy Wide World Photos)

(Left) Jawaharlal Nehru, Prime Minister of India, 1946–1964, with his daughter Indira Gandhi, elected Indian Prime Minister in 1966. Both designated themselves democratic socialists, though their party, the Congress party, has never been affiliated with the Socialist International, as has the Praja Socialist party. (Courtesy Information Service of India) (Right) Tetsu Katayama, elected Socialist Premier of Japan in coalition government, 1947, seated with his wife outside his Tokyo home. (Courtesy Wide World Photos)

(Left) E. G. Whitlam, Q. C., leader of the Australian Labor party and leader of the Federal Opposition, February, 1967– ; Member of the Australian House of Representatives. (Courtesy Australian News and Information Bureau) (Right) Philibert Tsiranana, President and Chief of Government, Malagasy Republic (Madagascar), elected President of Social Democratic Government, 1959; re-elected, 1965. (Courtesy Madagascar Republic Mission to the United Nations)

Two Labor prime ministers, John Curtin of Australia (seated right) and Peter Fraser of New Zealand (standing right), at No. 10 Downing Street with Prime Ministers Winston Churchill of Great Britain, Jan Christian Smuts of South Africa, and Mackenzie King of Canada. (Courtesy British Information Services)

Following the *coup d'état* of Primo de Rivera in September, 1923, and the establishment of his military dictatorship, the Socialist party conducted a vigorous campaign for a republican form of government. When de Rivera resigned on January 28, 1930, and gave over the reins of government to General Damaso Berenguer, many were hopeful that the dictatorship might disappear. Berenguer, however, soon began to pursue the same policies of suppression as had his predecessor. When convinced that they could expect little from the new dictator, several socialist leaders, among them Francisco Largo Caballero, general secretary of the General Union of Workers, and Indalecio Prieto, agreed with some republican chiefs, among them Niceto Alcala Zamora, former minister of war, upon the setting up of a republic by revolution. But premature attempts at revolt that year were crushed, many thousands were imprisoned, labor-union offices were closed, and martial law proclaimed.

Socialist Entrance into Zamora Government (1931). The following year discontent increased, and organized labor and the Socialist party led a practically bloodless revolution that forced King Alfonso XIII, on April 14, 1931, to quit the throne and make way for the installation the same day of a Provisional Republican government headed by Alcalá Zamora and participated in by several Socialists.

In the June 28, 1931, election of the new Cortes, the Socialists won 117 seats and the Socialistic Radicals, 54, in a body totaling 470. When the Cortes met, Julian Besteiro, a prominent Socialist, was elected its presiding officer. In December, Zamora, as the first constitutional President, selected a cabinet headed by Don Manuel Azaña, former minister of war, and containing Fernando de los Rios, Socialist, Minister of Education; F. Largo Caballero, Socialist, Minister of Labor; Indalecio Prieto, Socialist, Minister of Public Works, and seven members of other republican parties.[8]

The New Constitution (1931). The Constitution, promulgated by the Cortes, defined Spain as "a democratic republic of workers of all classes," with authority "emanating from the people" and "no official religion." Titles of nobility were abolished. Freedom of expression was guaranteed to all. Men and women reaching the age of 23 were permitted to vote. All property and wealth were to be "subordinated to the interests of the national economy." A number of constitutional

[8] De los Rios and Caballero had been in prison and Prieto a refugee in France following the failure of the December, 1930, revolution. Communists, after the inauguration of the new government, devoted much energy to the promotion of strikes, agrarian uprisings, and other movements aimed at the overthrow of the republican regime and the setting up of a workers' and peasants' dictatorship.

clauses drastically limited the power of the church. The church was to be disestablished and the state payment of clergy was to cease in December, 1933.

Reforms under Azaña Government. One of the first measures of the Azaña government provided for the expropriation of certain large estates with varying degrees of indemnification for their owners, based on the value of the land as assessed for taxation. The indemnity was to be made in government bonds.

The new government granted a considerable amount of autonomy to Catalonia. The government gave much attention to education. By the end of 1932 it had opened 10,000 new elementary schools. It reformed educational teaching in the university, organized traveling schools to country districts, set up in the first year 1500 new village libraries, and developed extensive systems of adult education, old-age pensions, and public assistance and public health services.

As the year 1933 advanced, church, business, and other forces began to mobilize their followers in opposition to the Azaña government. The municipal elections of the year indicated a strong conservative drift. In the autumn of 1933 Azaña resigned. Lerroux, the Radical leader, attempted unsuccessfully to form a cabinet. The Cortes was dissolved.

Cancellation of Azaña Reforms by Right-Center Government (1933–1936). The following elections of November, 1933, in which 6,500,000 women were first allowed to vote, resulted in a decrease in the left representation to 99, as compared with a right representation of 207 and a center group of 167. A government controlled largely by the center was set up. The new government held up much of the left-wing legislation, postponing the substitution of lay schools for religious schools, restoring to the clergy part of their state-paid stipends, passing an agrarian law more favorable to the large landed proprietors, and postponing the autonomy of Catalonia.

Following a revolt, many Catalonians were imprisoned. Azaña, sent to jail on suspicion of aiding this revolt, became a national hero. Opposition to the center-right government grew. The President dissolved the Cortes and set new elections for February 16, 1936.

Formation of Popular Front Government (1936). During the ensuing campaign a group of parties and trade unions (Republican Left, Republican Union, Socialist, Communist, Trotskyite, Syndicalist, and Anarchist) banded together under the name of "Popular Front" with a view to winning a victory for the progressive forces of the nation. They won 256 seats, against 165 captured by the right and 52 by the center party.

Civil War against Government. The announcement of these results was a signal for many disorders. Upon the convening of the Cortes, Azaña was elected President by an almost unanimous vote. Casares Quiroga was made Prime Minister. The government set itself to the tasks of new measures of reform. The Prime Minister threw down a challenge to fascism, declaring that, "in its relations with fascism, the government is a belligerent." The fascist forces began to mobilize. Soon thereafter an army mutiny, led by General Francisco Franco, broke out in Spanish Morocco. The movement spread to the mainland and within 48 hours the country was involved in a civil war. Most of the army joined Franco.

A bitter struggle began between the well-trained army under Franco and the army of the government—the "Loyalist" army—which was mostly untrained. By the end of 1936, Italy and Germany began to supply military and technical aid to the Franco Nationalists on a large scale.

Following the fall of Irein to the Nationalists, a government under Don Francisco Largo Caballero, including Socialists, Republicans, and Communists, was formed. Later, when Madrid was threatened, anarcho-syndicalists were included. Madrid was finally left in charge of a Defense Council, and the government moved to Valencia. President Azaña had left some weeks before for Barcelona.

On October 1, 1936, Franco assumed the headship of Nationalist Spain. He proposed a "broadly totalitarian" government, in which popular suffrage and regional autonomy were abolished, communistic contacts were to be avoided, and preferential treatment given to "nations of related race, language, or ideology." On April 19, 1938, the two main Nationalist groups—Phalangists and Traditionalists—were merged into a single party and all other political parties were dissolved. Vertical syndicates containing employers and workers were later created. In August, 1937, a National Council of 50 members was created.

Faced with a common foe in control of a large part of Spain, those composing the Loyalist government co-operated on many fronts, though there were many disagreements on policies. The most serious dissension occurred when anarcho-syndicalists staged an uprising in Barcelona (May 3–10, 1937) followed by a major political crisis in the Valencia government. After this outbreak, anarcho-syndicalists were eliminated from the new cabinet headed by Dr. Negrin, who succeeded Caballero and held office until nearly the end of the civil war. Anarcho-syndicalists remained unrepresented until April, 1938.

Triumph of Franco; Suppression of Socialist Movement (1939). The Nationalist army, with the continuous aid of Italy and Germany, finally overcame the desperate resistance of the Loyalists. The Loyalist government moved from one capital to another. On February 28, Azaño resigned his office, but Dr. Negrin and his cabinet returned to Madrid, once more the capital of Republican Spain. On March 5, 1939, all parties but the Communist formed a Council of Defense, under General Miaja, ousting Dr. Negrin and his cabinet. Forty-eight hours later the communists and the late Premier's supporters revolted against the Council. In a week the revolt was put down, but the Council set to work to prepare a surrender. On March 28, 1939, 200,000 National troops marched into the capital, and by the next day all of Spain had surrendered. Wholesale arrests and imprisonment of the Loyalist leaders followed, with many executions. A fascistic regime was inaugurated throughout Spain; all socialist and radical groups were suppressed and all political groups were merged into one government party, the Falange Española, under the control of General Franco.

CHAPTER 35

Labor and Socialism in Australasia

Australian Labor in Politics. For many years socialistic experiments in Australia and New Zealand have attracted the attention of students of government and economics throughout the world. Prior to the First World War, as a result of the need for the development of the country and the fact that it was difficult to obtain large sums of money for such development from private sources, the government, without any conscious attempt to follow a socialistic plan, engaged in vast governmental undertakings from the building of railways to such services as the export of butter, apples, and other products.

AUSTRALIAN LABOR PARTY

Labor first expressed its demands in the country primarily through its trade-union organization, which concentrated largely on the question of wages, hours, the exclusion of Chinese immigration, and labor legislation. In Victoria, however, as early as 1859, a labor representative was sent to the Victorian legislature.

In 1885 William Lane, a cultured Englishman, who had settled two years earlier in Queensland, started a socialist paper, *The Boomerang*, which scored a success. Through the pages of this paper Lane sought to convert the trade-union movement of the country to socialism. He was assisted by other immigrants from Great Britain, among them Tom Mann.

It was not, however, until after the unsuccessful strike of sheepherders and shearers, shipworkers, and others in 1890 that labor began to turn in numbers to political action. In that year a Labor Electoral League was formed in New South Wales. The following year the League surprised even its own friends by winning 35 of the 125 state legislative seats. The Laborites would have wielded much influence had they not split over the question of protection. This division destroyed their effectiveness, but, in turn, led the party to exact in future years a "solidarity pledge" from each of its parliamentary candidates in which the candidate pledged to vote with the majority of the parliamentary party. In 1894 the number of Labor members shrunk to 19, but these presented a united front, with consequent increased effectiveness.

Establishment of Labor Governments in Australian States. Labor parties spread after 1890 from New South Wales to other Australian states. Their growth was steady, and by 1911 they had instituted Labor party governments in four of the states. In Queensland a Labor coalition ran the government from 1903 to 1907 and from 1908 to 1912. West Australia followed with a Labor ministry from 1904 to 1905, and from 1911 to 1917. South Australia came next with Labor governments during portions of 1905 and 1906 and from the middle of 1910 to February, 1912. Finally came New South Wales, in which state the Labor party was in control from 1911 to 1916. In the years immediately prior to the First World War the Labor party held a majority in three of the Australian state legislatures.

After the First World War, Labor controlled the governments at various times of each of the Australian states and effected much social legislation. Queensland, during the fourteen year period 1914–1929, was headed successively by Labor party members Ryan, Theodore, Gillies, and McCormack. During that time a system of state insurance was introduced, coal mines were made state property, and the state organized and successfully ran butcher shops, fish supply produce agencies, canneries, restaurants, hotels, and other services.

Throughout these years, however, a growing schism had been developing between the lefts and the rights. These differences were made plainly evident during a railway strike on the Queensland State Railways. The Queensland railwaymen, in sympathy with striking sugar-workers, refused to handle sugar sent to railroads for transportation while the strike was going on. Following several suspensions of railroad workers for such refusal, Premier McCormack proclaimed a lockout of the railroad workers affecting 11,000 men, and in the ensuing struggle the men were defeated. As a condition of their return to work, those locked out were later compelled to sign a pledge to observe in the future the rules of the railway administration.

Although the Premier was upheld by Parliament in this action, much bitter resentment was aroused against him among the workers. As a result of this resentment, Labor's representation in the 1929 elections fell from 43 to 29 and that of the two other parties increased to 43.

Formation of First Labor Government in Commonwealth of Australia (1904). The chief struggles of labor in the political field in

Australia, however, occurred in the Commonwealth of Australia. A Labor party was formed in 1901, the year when the Commonwealth came into existence, under the leadership of J. C. Watson,[1] a remarkable public figure in that country.

In 1904 Watson had the honor to be chosen Labor's first Prime Minister in the world. However, he retained the premiership for only four months, at the end of which the opposition parties combined to bring about his overthrow.

Fisher as Prime Minister (1907). In 1907, at the third election, the Labor party again increased its representation. It gave its support to the protectionist party until the settlement of the tariff problem, which was then a much-mooted question. Watson in that year retired from the party leadership, his place being taken by Andrew Fisher.[2]

Fisher's premiership, like that of Watson, lasted less than a year, from November 1908 to June 1909. In the general election of 1910, Labor was returned for the first time with a working majority, both in the Senate and the House of Representatives. Fisher was again asked to head the government. His second ministry lasted from May, 1910 to June, 1913.

One of the important questions before the country at that time was that of defense. Under Fisher's premiership Parliament passed a measure establishing universal military training and laid the foundation for an Australian navy.

In 1911 the government submitted to the people a number of proposed amendments to the Constitution, which, among other things, sought to give to the Federal legislature power to deal with labor conditions, labor disputes, and corporations and monopolies, and to acquire certain industries. The proposed amendments, however, failed of passage, the Labor government thus being seriously handicapped in any effort on its part to make any fundamental changes in the economic system of the country.

In 1912 the government took an important step toward collective control by the creation of a Commonwealth Bank. Under the law es-

[1] Watson was born in 1867 of poor Scottish parents who were at that time emigrating to Australia. He received little schooling, but possessed much inborn tact and wisdom and became a tower of strength in the Australian Labor party.

[2] Fisher, like Watson, was of Scottish parentage. He was born in Crosshouse, Kilmarnock, in 1862. At the age of 14, he entered the mines, and for some years worked side by side with the Scottish socialist leader, Keir Hardie. In 1885 he migrated to Australia and eight years later became a member of the Queensland legislature. In 1899 he became Minister of Railways; in 1901 he was elected a member of the Commonwealth Parliament; and in 1904 he was made Minister for Trade and Customs in the Watson Ministry.

tablishing the bank, half of the profits were to be added to various reserves, and the other half were to be used in behalf of the liquidation of the Australian national debt. During these years, the government passed laws establishing systems of compulsory arbitration, nationalizing monopolies, and effecting social reforms of a somewhat nationalistic nature.

In the 1913 elections Labor lost its majority control of the House of Representatives to the Liberals, though it retained its majority in the Senate. Shortly before the outbreak of the First World War the Governor-General dissolved Parliament, and Fisher, Laborite, again became Prime Minister. He resigned, however, in 1915 to become the High Commission in London. In 1926 he retired and died two years later.

Formation of War Cabinet by Hughes. Following Fisher's resignation, William Hughes [3] became leader of the Labor party and Prime Minister and formed a war cabinet. In 1917 Hughes failed of re-election to the leadership of the party because of his strong advocacy of conscription. He resigned from the Labor party, but effected a coalition with the Liberal party leader, and remained as the head of the cabinet. Soon thereafter, he became a member of the British Imperial War Cabinet. While thus serving, he was frequently accused of "playing to the London galleries."

In 1919, Hughes' coalition, then called "The Country Party," defeated Labor at the polls. Four years later—after eight years as Premier—he resigned from the office, greatly dissatisfied, many claimed, with his rôle as opponent of Labor. Under his leadership Australia had temporarily shifted its attention from a program of socialistic reform to one of national defense.

Labor as Opposition and as Government (1924–1931). From 1924 to 1929 the Australian Labor party constituted the country's chief opposition. In the October elections of 1929 the Coalition government, under the leadership of Prime Minister Bruce, was beaten, the Labor party winning 43 out of 75 seats in the Lower House. Mr. Bruce resigned, and James Scullin, Laborite, became Prime Minister on October 21.[4]

Curiously enough, one of the new government's first acts was to introduce a higher tariff, partly to secure revenue to meet the heavy

[3] Hughes was a Welshman who migrated to Australia at the age of 20. In 1895 he was elected to the New South Wales Parliament and later became a member of several of the Labor ministries.

[4] Scullin was born in 1876. He became deputy leader of the party in 1927 and leader in 1928. He was an effective debater and, unlike many members of the party, had been in close contact with the international labor movement.

deficit, partly to stop the "flood of overseas imports" and thus to increase Australian employment. The new tariff schedules were severely criticized in England where several industries found Australian markets virtually closed to them. The government likewise took steps to reduce defense expenditures and to expand public works.

Formation of Labor Government under Curtin (1941). In the early thirties the Labor party again became the government opposition, and it was not until October, 1941, after occupying the opposition benches for ten years, that the Labor party, under the leadership of John Curtin, formed the government. The government committed itself to the maximum war effort, with war burdens distributed as equitably as possible over the whole community.

The government invited the opposition to participate in the Advisory War Council, on which it had an equal number of representatives with the government. Following its accession to office, the Labor government increased the pay of the military forces, raised old-age and invalid pensions, and expanded the Australian defense forces. It increased direct taxation, centralized the collection of income taxes, controlled prices, limited profits and interest, and worked for a constitutional amendment permitting the use of conscripted men outside the Commonwealth and the territories controlled by it. The party in 1942 had 36 members in the Lower Chamber out of 75 and 17 members of the Upper Chamber out of 36. The objective of the party is socialist, but in practice its socialism has not gone beyond "a tendency toward using governmental controls as a means of dealing with immediate problems, and toward expanding social services for the mass of the Australian people." The party convention of 1942 resulted in the establishment of a Department of Postwar Reconstruction.

1943 Election Victory. In the August, 1943 elections, the Labor party won a sweeping victory, winning 49 out of 75 seats, a clear majority, and all of the 19 seats in the Senate for which elections were held. Following July, 1944, 22 of the 36 members of the Senate were Laborites. This was the first time that the Australian Labor party had been reelected after going to the country following its term of office, and the first time that the party had a majority of seats in both the Senate and the Lower House of Parliament. The vote in this election was interpreted by many as an indication that the voters preferred a Labor party government to a national government made up of representatives of the various parties of the Commonwealth.

Of the general program sponsored by the Australian Labor party during these years, Lloyd Ross, labor leader and member of the New

South Wales Executive Committee, declared: "The Labor party program is a mixture of long-range ideals and immediately obtainable reforms. . . . No labor leader would repudiate the socialist objective; but none could honestly argue that in practice his socialism had gone beyond a tendency toward using governmental controls as a method of dealing with immediate problems, and toward expanding social services for the mass of the Australian people. We have accepted socialism as a goal, but we have seldom planned a legislative program of rapid and widespread steps toward socialism." [5]

THE NEW ZEALAND LABOR PARTY

Labor in Coalition with Liberals. A Labor party in New Zealand was formed in the eighties of the last century, followed soon after, in 1890, by a Liberal-Labor Alliance under the leadership of W. Pember Reeves. Three years later this alliance came into power with Richard Seddon, a miner from Lancashire, as leader. For the next 13 years this liberal government was in office, during which time women were given the franchise, railways and coal mines were nationalized, landed estates were broken up, social and labor laws introduced, and a system of compulsory arbitration and of state insurance started. The government was re-elected in seven successive elections.

In 1906 Seddon died. There followed a lull in progressive legislation. Labor became increasingly dissatisfied and began to demand political action independent of other parties. Some labor leaders joined the syndicalist school of thought. In the meanwhile a Social Democratic party had come into being.

Union of Labor Political Forces. In 1913 a conference sponsored by the trade unions and participated in by members of the United Labor party and the Social Democratic party was called to work out a plan for political unity. It passed the following resolution: "Recognizing that political action is necessary and inevitable in the working-class movement, we agree to the formation of a political party for the enacting of legislation to better the conditions of the working class and ultimately to achieve its economic emancipation."

The passage of this resolution laid the foundation for the New Zealand Labor party. Its program was social democratic in character, its objective, as written on the membership card, being the socialization of the means of production, distribution, and exchange. A complete change in the social system, it believed, could be brought about by legislative action.

[5] Ross, *Labor in Australia*, p. 17.

Progress of Labor Party. During the succeeding years the Labor party steadily increased in numbers and influence, as shown in the following table.

PROGRESS OF NEW ZEALAND LABOR PARTY

Year	*Votes Obtained*	*Seats Won*
1914	49,577	6
1919	132,715	8
1922	145,148	17
1925	184,616	12
1928	196,382	19
1931	241,991	24
1935	392,972	53
1938	530,810	51

Labor Party in Power (1935). In the 1935 elections the Labor party elected 51 out of 80 representatives in Parliament, defeated the Coalition government, and came into power for the first time, with Michael J. Savage as Prime Minister. The new government immediately proceeded to enact into law a number of advanced social and economic measures. It made provision for nationalizing the reserve bank and the mortgage corporation, organizing a state marketing system for New Zealand produce sent abroad, adjusting farm mortgages, and guaranteeing a reasonable price to dairy farmers. It introduced the 40-hour week, established a minimum wage and compulsory unionization of workers, restored wages that had been cut, enlarged its public-works program, and undertook an extensive housing program. In the late thirties its principal measure was the Social Security Act, which "ensured that in the future no individual, whether because of age, widowhood, invalidity, sickness, unemployment, or any other normal hazard of life, need ever lack an income sufficient to provide a reasonable standard of comfort and financial independence." [6]

In the 1938 election the party urged the continuation of the progressive legislation of the previous three years, the strengthening of the defense forces, the support of the League of Nations, and collective security.

Labor in the Second World War. At the outbreak of the war the party strongly supported the United Kingdom in its war effort. A few months afterwards the Labor Premier Michael Savage [7] died, and was

[6] Eric Estorick, in Walter Nash, *New Zealand,* p. 29.

[7] Michael J. Savage was born in Benalla, Australia, March 7, 1872. He left school at 14 years and worked as a clerk, as a laborer on a sheep ranch, and as a miner. In 1900 he became secretary of the Political Labor Council in Victoria and started the co-operative store. Seven years later he went to New Zealand and became an

succeeded on April 30, 1940, by Peter Fraser as Prime Minister, with Walter Nash as Deputy Prime Minister.[8]

On September 24, 1943, in the first national elections in five years, the Labor party was returned to power, although with a decreased majority. The party elected 45 representatives, a loss of 6, as compared with 34 for the National party and 1 for the Independents. In the Upper Chamber, the party continued with a representation of 27 out of 36. Following the elections Premier Fraser continued an all-Labor-party cabinet. In November, 1943, the party representatives urged a program of vacations with pay for all workers, equal pay for equal work, the establishment of a minimum family income, and greater socialization of industry.

---

active leader in the labor government. He was elected to the House of Representatives in 1919 and became leader of the Labor party in 1933 and Prime Minister in 1935. He died on March 26, 1940.

[8] Peter Fraser was born in Scotland in 1884. He joined the Independent Labor party at the age of 24, and in 1910 migrated to New Zealand. He became active in the labor and socialist movements and, prior to his election as Prime Minister, served as president of the Auckland General Laborers' Union, as member of the Wellington City Council (1919–23 and 1933–36), and as member of Parliament; and, from 1935 to 1940 as Minister of Education, of Health, of Marine, and of Police, and as Deputy Prime Minister.

Deputy Prime Minister Walter Nash, first New Zealand Minister to the United States, and President of the International Labor Organization Conference of 1944, was born in Kidderminster, England, February 12, 1882. After being graduated from school, he studied law, spent some time in the cycle manufacturing trade and in the wholesale mechandising business, and migrated to New Zealand in 1909. In 1919, after a decade in business in New Zealand, he joined the national executive of the Labor party. Three years later he became national secretary of the party. He was elected member of Parliament and in 1929, and, in 1935, was appointed Minister of Finance, Customs, and Marketing in the Labor government. In 1940, he became Deputy Prime Minister and from 1942 to 1944 served as New Zealand Minister to the United States.

CHAPTER 36

Socialism in South Africa and Asia

LABOR POLITICS IN SOUTH AFRICA

In South Africa until the beginning of the forties, labor political action was confined chiefly to the English-speaking industrial areas in South Africa. A small and active Labor party has, however, been in existence in South Africa since 1906. In 1913 and 1914 labor strikes and riots in the Rand, where labor was strong, resulted in the arrest of the chief labor leaders and their deportation without trial. The excuse for this action given by General Smuts, then Minister of the Interior in General Botha's Boer government, was that "the government could not run the ordinary risks of the law courts." The dissatisfaction resulting from the government's handling of this disturbance resulted in the increase of labor strength and in the succeeding elections for the Transvaal Provincial Council labor gained a majority.

Fresh stimulus was given to the activities of the Labor party in 1922, when 10,000 labor supporters were arrested during another violent strike in the Rand. As a result of the ensuing bitterness against General Smuts, then Prime Minister, the Labor party, at its conference at Durban in 1923, formed a pact with the Nationalist party led by General Hertzog and succeeded in defeating the Smuts' government in the 1924 elections. The Nationalist party elected that year 63 members of Parliament; the Labor party, 17; the South African party, led by General Smuts, 54; and other groups, 1. The Nationalist and Labor parties formed the government, and Labor was given 2 and subsequently 3 posts in a cabinet of 12. Colonel Cresswell, Laborite, became Minister of Defense and Labor. During the term of the pact, despite vigorous disagreement over international policy, the two parties combined to pass some important labor legislation.

The Labor party, however, soon became torn with internal dissensions, and in 1927 and 1928 its members found themselves divided into two camps, one led by Colonel Cresswell, who believed in supporting the nationalists and the other led by the National Council, which was opposed to the collaboration with the General Hertzog party. In the 1929 elections, labor's representation shrank to 8, 5 of whom were pledged to Colonel Cresswell and 3 to the National Council. General Hertzog assumed office with an absolute majority over all parties and independent of the Labor party.

Four years later, in 1933, the Nationalist and South African parties joined hands in the government of the country. For the next six years the Labor party, with a representation of 4 in Parliament, played a comparatively minor rôle in the political life of the country. The cabinet crisis of September 4, 1939, however, led to the dissolution of the past between the parties of General Smuts and General Hertzog over the question of neutrality and to the formation by General Smuts of a new cabinet, in which labor was given a seat, the Labor leader, Walter Madeley, becoming Secretary of Labor.

In the general elections of July, 1943, the Labor party increased its representation in the House to 9 out of 150 members. The party supported the war and exerted an influence on social legislation out of proportion to its numerical strength.

SOCIALIST AND COMMUNIST MOVEMENTS IN CHINA

Influence of Sun Yat-sen. During the revolution of 1911–12 many of those who took a prominent part in the overthrow of the Manchu dynasty and the establishment of the Chinese Republic were socialistic in their social outlook. Foremost among these was Dr. Sun Yat-sen, who was strongly influenced by the writings of an American socialist, Maurice Williams, author of *The Social Interpretation of History.* A distinctly socialist organization was formed in 1911. This group grew rapidly during the revolutionary period and elected some 30 Socialists to the Republican Parliament. The Kuomintang, or People's National party, at about the same time, incorporated in their platform the socialistic program of Dr. Sun on public ownership and agrarian reform, the latter along the lines laid down by Henry George.

In 1913, however, the Socialist party was dissolved by Marshal Yuan Shih-kai who, after receiving aid from foreign groups, destroyed the Republican regime. The dissolution of the Kuomintang followed in November, 1913.

Later, in the period of military chaos succeeding the collapse of the forces of Yuan Shih-kai, orderly social progress was difficult, if not impossible, except in such localities as Canton, where parliamentary leaders, ousted from Peking, set up a revolutionary government under the leadership of Dr. Sun Yat-sen. Dr. Sun was elected president of the Chinese republic in April, 1921. Canton soon became the center of the trade-union and the socialist movement in China.

Activities of Communist Party. In 1921 a Chinese Communist party was formed. Materially assisted from abroad, the communists soon became an influential force among large numbers of peasants and workers. In 1922 Dr. Sun was driven out of Canton and became a refugee in the French Concession in Shanghai where, early in 1923, he reached an agreement with the Soviet envoy to China that neither communism nor the Soviet system should be introduced into China. With this understanding, Dr. Sun agreed to communist co-operation in the reorganization of the Kuomintang.

In the winter of 1923–24 the Kuomintang was reorganized as a strictly disciplined party. The communists, while maintaining their own organization, entered the Kuomintang and helped to direct its policies. Dr. Sun died soon thereafter—March 12, 1925—leaving a last will and testament to the Chinese people in a book he had written, *San Min Chu I*. In this he urged a three-fold program: democratic government, a higher standard of living for the masses, and the recovery of the rights granted to foreigners; and stated that, pending the unification of the country, the full realization of democracy was to be postponed and the dictatorship of a single party, the Kuomintang, was to be substituted.

In 1927 a split occurred in the Kuomintang between the military and communist elements, after which the latter were "purged" by General Chiang Kai-shek and his associates, with the active support of the anti-Soviet powers.[1] The communists, though weakened, built up strength in the interior of China, and, by 1931, defeated Kuomintang forces sent against them in their main centers in South China, where they established the Chinese Soviet Republic. This new government, set up in the form of a dictatorship, distributed the land of the wealthier landlords among the poorer peasants and reorganized the taxation system, with a view to having the taxes rest primarily upon the more prosperous farmers. They established a state banking system, state trade controls, and communist-controlled co-operatives of a type similar to those in Russia.

The Chinese Soviet Republic steadily widened its territories until the

[1] Chiang Kai-shek that year married Soong Mayling, a sister of Madame Sun Yat-sen, and thereby strengthened his claim in the eyes of many to the inheritance of the leadership of the Kuomintang.

end of 1933, when it exercised its authority or leadership over more than 30,000,000 Chinese. The costly civil war between the Kuomintang and the communists was brought to a temporary end by an agreement reached at Sian in December, 1936, when General Chiang was under detention there.[2]

During the late twenties and thirties, little of democratic socialist organization was permitted by either the Kuomintang or the communists and no popular elections were held.

Formation of People's Political Council. In 1938, however, when the Kuomintang government was forced back by the Japanese army into the interior of China, it established a People's Political Council at Chungking. Though the Kuomintang retained control of the political administration, it appointed five members of "approved" parties to the People's Political Council, including Yang Kan-tao from the Social Democratic party and Carson Chang from the National Socialist party. Each member of a smaller party, however, attended the P. P. C. as an individual rather than as a party representative.

JAPANESE SOCIALIST MOVEMENT

Organization of Socialist League (1899). In 1897, when Professor Sen Katayama began his teaching of socialism and trade unionism in Japan, the socialist movement may be said to have begun.

In 1899 a group of young students organized a socialist league in Tokyo, which took on the nature of a debating society. Later the Railroad Workers' Union endorsed socialism as the final goal of the labor movement. Thus encouraged, the socialists formed a Japanese Socialist party in 1901, but the party was promptly dissolved by the police, and socialist newspapers, which had made occasional appearances, were likewise suppressed and their editors imprisoned. Trials of many prominent socialists, accused of entertaining anarchist views, were held behind closed doors, and twelve socialists were afterwards hanged. Socialists, however, continued to carry on educational work and launched a vigorous campaign against the war with Russia in 1904–5, in connection with which activity many arrests were made. The suppressions during these days led a number of radicals to resort to terror-

[2] Chang Hsüehliang, the leader of the communists, demanded of General Chiang during his detention the end of the civil war against the communists, a reorganization of the government with more toleration for the opposition, and a united front against Japan. Although Chiang Kai-shek was released without any public recognition that these concessions had been made, this incident proved to be a precursor of a co-operation between the communists and Chiang in the country's defense against Japan.

ism, and even to conspiracies against the life of the Emperor. Arrests, imprisonments, and executions followed the uncovering of these plots.

Developments during and since the First World War. During the First World War great industrial activity led to the growth of the labor movement and provided a wider field for socialist and radical activity. "Rice riots" and other disturbances, which culminated in pitched battles between the workers and police and later the regular army, broke out during the war. These signs of unrest led to the appointment of a civilian Premier and to concessions to labor, including the right to form unions and to go on strike. Labor and socialist influence increased. In 1921, 20,000 workers at the Kawasaki Dockyard in Kobe "occupied" the plant, but were soon driven out.

Socialist Gains in Elections 1928–1936. As a result, in part, of socialist education and agitation, universal manhood suffrage was granted in 1927. In the general election to the House of Representatives in February, 1928—the first to be held under the new law that increased the electorate from 3,000,000 to 11,000,000—five socialist and labor groups received 500,000 votes, or 10 per cent of the total, and elected several members to the Imperial Diet.[3]

In the election of 1930 the Social Democratic and the Japanese People's party, with a total of 170,000 and 165,000 votes respectively, each elected two representatives and the Farmer-Labor party, with a vote of 78,500, elected one representative to the Diet.

In 1932 the Social Democratic party, headed by the veteran socialist Isoh Abe, founder of the Japan Fabian Society, amalgamated with the Farmer-Labor party, the principal representative of organized labor and the peasant unions. In February, 1936, the unified Social Masses party, with a vote of more than a half million, elected 18 members to the Diet.

Domination of Japan by Army. This election, however, came at a time when the parliamentary system was in perilous straits in Japan. In 1931, after several years of encroaching control of governmental functions, the Japanese army came to the fore, launched their invasion of Manchuria, set up the puppet state of "Manchukuo" under Army control, and through military pressure, bribery, and assassination reestablished their old ascendancy over the Tokyo government.

The weakness and corruption of the old parties led to increasing

[3] The authorities in 1928 became alarmed at the spread of radicalism—the communists having agitated through numerous "front" organizations—and in March made an extensive "round-up" of communists, followed by widespread suppression and the execution of many of their leaders.

popular support of the socialists, and despite official interference the Socialist Masses party won 37 out of a total of 466 seats in the Diet (House of Representatives) in the 1937 elections. That year, the Kokumin Domei (Nationalists), the main fascist party, elected 11 representatives, as compared with 30 in 1932 and 15 in 1936.

In 1940, using the "war emergency" for this purpose, the Japanese militarists organized what was essentially a totalitarian corporative state side by side with the old "constitutional monarchy." A nominated Executive Council was to "convey the will and the ideas of those who govern to those who are governed." The political parties were called upon "voluntarily" to dissolve. Parliament was still permitted to vote on the budget, but its links with the electorate through party candidates and elections were ended.

CHAPTER 37

Socialism in the United States and Canada

IN CHAPTER 11 we mentioned a number of famous utopian socialists who contributed to the Brook Farm and other utopian experiments in the United States prior to the Civil War—among them Horace Greeley, Albert Brisbane, Robert Dale Owen, Charles A. Dana, George Ripley, Parke Godwin, Nathaniel Hawthorne, John S. Dwight, and Thomas Wentworth Higginson. These utopians preceded the modern socialist movements based on the principles of "scientific socialism."

LABOR AND SOCIALIST PARTIES IN THE UNITED STATES

Beginning of Modern Socialist Movement in the United States. The modern socialist movement of the United States may be said to have begun with the arrival of numbers of revolutionists from Germany, following the uprisings of 1830 and 1848. Among the early European socialists migrating to this country were Joseph Weydemeyer and F. A. Sorge, who had been in close contact with Marx and Engels before coming to this country in the fifties. Largely through the efforts of Weydemeyer, the New York German trade unionists established the American Workingmen's Alliance on March 21, 1853.[1] The object of this alliance was to build up an independent labor party and to support the trade unions. It organized German branches in New Jersey, Ohio, and Pennsylvania and an English local in Washington. Weydemeyer's paper, *Die Reform,* however, lasted less than a year, and the alliance exerted an influence for only a short period, many of those interested in the Alliance having turned their attention to the growing trade-union movement. The anti-slavery movement and the Civil War during the next decade absorbed the energies of the "forty-eighters," who had to begin their socialist activities over again after the war.

[1] Commons and Associates, *History of Labor in the United States,* Vol. I., p. 618.

First International Affiliates in the United States. In 1867 a group of Lassallean socialists united with a group of Marxians under F. A. Sorge, who had organized in the fifties, to form the General German Workingmen's Union. This union became affiliated in 1869 with the First International, which was organized in London in 1864. About the same time, Bohemian, French, and other German sections of the International were established in New York, Chicago, and San Francisco. In December, 1870, these sections united to form a provisional central committee of the International in the United States, with F. A. Sorge as corresponding secretary. The following year over 30 sections, having a combined membership of several thousand, were reported to be in existence.

Death of First International in America (1876). In the meanwhile a bitter controversy was taking place within the International in Europe between the socialist followers of Karl Marx and the anarchistic followers of Bakunin. In an effort to prevent the International from falling into the hands of the anarchists, as we have noted in our chapter on Karl Marx, Marx and his supporters secured at The Hague Congress of 1872 the transfer of the headquarters of the International to New York. Following this action, Sorge was made secretary of the governing body. For the next four years various sections engaged in vigorous controversy as to the proper tactics to pursue and, on July 15, 1876, at a meeting in Philadelphia, the First International was declared to be officially dead.

Organization of Illinois Labor Party by Lassallean Socialists (1874). During these years a number of other groups in the East and Middle West were active in the work of labor political action. In Chicago, in 1869, a group of German Lassalleans organized the Universal German Workingmen's Association, later the Socio-Political Workingmen's Association. Members of this group, in January, 1874, in the midst of the panic of the seventies, formed the Labor party of Illinois. This party, following the lead of the Lassallean socialists of Germany, laid emphasis in their platform on the establishment of workingmen's co-operatives, with state aid. It urged, among other things, the abolition of monopoly and public ownership of banks and of the means of transportation.

Recognizing that the farming population was a powerful factor in the economic life of the nation and that it was eminently desirable to develop a spirit of co-operation between the farmers and city workers, the party stressed the similarity of interests between farmers and industrial workers. "The union of the farmers with the industrial workers of the cities is necessary," declared the party platform, "for the latter are the major consumers of the products of the soil and they also suffer from the transportation monopoly. Only through common action will results be achieved." The socialists took the position that, if middlemen were wiped out, the worker could afford to pay the farmer a fair price.

In the fall of 1874 the Illinois Labor party entered the election campaign, but several of their candidates went over to their opponents, many votes cast for them were uncounted, and the next year they decided not to participate in elections until their ranks had been greatly strengthened.

Unity Convention of 1876 and Rise of Workingmen's Party of the United States. In May, 1874, a short time after the Illinois Labor party was formed, a Social Democratic Workingmen's party of North America was organized in the East along somewhat the same lines as those of the Chicago organization. In 1876 this organization joined with the Labor party of Illinois, the Socio-Political Labor-Union of Cincinnati, and the North American Federation of the International, with a combined membership of 3000, to call a unity convention in Philadelphia, July 19–22, 1876.

This convention gave birth to the Workingmen's party of the United States, committed to socialist principles. The delegates decided that the party should not enter a political campaign until it was strong enough to exercise a perceptible influence on the political scene and that before any section could take any political action it had to secure the consent of the Executive. "We can only become strong," declared Conrad Conzett of the Illinois Labor party, "when, instead of wasting our time and money at the ballot box, we devote ourselves with all our energy to the demands of the trade unions and bring material advantages to the workers." He maintained that a political movement would be developed if trade unions were first organized and their leaders educated in socialism. Philip Van Patten, an active member of the Knights of Labor, was chosen national secretary. In March, 1877, the party reported 35 German-speaking sections, 18 English, 6 Bohemian, 5 Scandinavian, and 2 French, in 44 cities and 19 states. Several sections during the next year were permitted to run candidates for offices and scored some successes.

Formation of Socialist Labor Party (1877) and Later Developments. On December 26, 1877, the Workingmen's party held a convention in Newark, New Jersey. At this convention the delegates repudiated the trade unionists, who felt that the party should devote primary attention to the economic side of the movement, and changed the party's name to the Socialist Labor party. The preamble of its new platform read:

"The industrial emancipation of labor, which must be achieved by the working classes themselves, independent of all political parties but their own, is . . . the great end to which every political movement should be subordinate as a means." The platform proper contained a long list of immediate demands to be emphasized in political campaigns.

During the next few years many controversies arose within the party over the value of independent political action, the advisability of organizing armed bodies of workers, and the relation between socialists and greenbackers, trade unionists and anarchists. In 1886 the Socialist Labor party endorsed Henry George, the single-tax candidate of the United Labor party, for mayor in the New York City elections.

DeLeon in Movement. One of the active supporters of Henry George in this campaign was Daniel DeLeon, later the outstanding leader of the Socialist Labor party. DeLeon was a native of the island of Curaçao, off the coast of Venezuela. Born on December 14, 1852, he received his education in Germany, and after coming to the United States in the early seventies studied law, and was granted a prize lectureship in international law at Columbia. In 1886 he joined with the United Labor party in the support of Henry George.

When the United Labor party, after the 1886 campaign, gradually faded out of the political picture, DeLeon joined the nationalists, formed following the publication of Edward Bellamy's popular novel *Looking Backward.* Later disagreeing with the policies of the nationalist clubs, which made no appeal to the organization of labor as such, DeLeon applied for membership in the Socialist Labor party and was admitted to that organization in 1890. Possessing a brilliant mind and an incisive pen, he quickly rose to the editorship of the official English organ, *The People,* in 1892. From that time to his death in 1914, a man of domineering personality who brooked no opposition, he maintained a position of unquestioned authority in the party.

DeLeon on New Trade Unionism. Soon after his rise to power in the party DeLeon began to preach what he called the new trade unionism. In this he was supported in his propaganda by Lucien Sanial, regarded as one of the party's scholars, and by Hugo Vogt. For some years DeLeon, Sanial, and Vogt worked together as the party's unofficial triumvirate.

The new trade unionist, according to DeLeon, is not after "groveling 'improvements' or hunger-aggravating crumbs" for labor, but urges labor to leave to their descendants "the heritage of the co-operative commonwealth and freedom." The old trade unionist, on the other hand, "grants the principle of private ownership in the means of production; grants the right of possessors of these means to keep their profits; talks about fair and legitimate profits; he is satisfied with wages."

DeLeon questioned whether under capitalism the workers in one trade or industry could, as a class, raise their wages or improve their conditions by the use of the economic weapon. "Nothing but the growing force of labor, exhibited by the socialist vote," declared Hugo Vogt, "can give the workers courage to persist in their organizing work and continue their unions for those favorable opportunities that sometimes offer for a successful economic contest with capital."[2] A close union between the party and the trade-union organization was, therefore, a necessity. "The membership would then be raised above the *paltry routine business of the unions* and brought to understand the broad questions that would inspire them with the requisite revolutionary spirit."[3]

In their campaign in behalf of this point of view the leaders of the Socialist Labor party assailed the "pure and simple trade-union" leaders with strong invective, characterizing them as "labor fakers." "Some are ignorant," declared DeLeon in 1893, "others are corrupt, all are unfit for leadership in the labor movement."

Organization of Socialist Trade and Labor Alliance (1895). DeLeon set out to capture and dominate the Knights of Labor, but, after a number of partial successes, was ousted from that body. On November 27, 1895, a few days after the announcement of this ouster, DeLeon called upon the Knights of Labor assemblies and all progressive organizations to join with the Socialist Labor party in the establishment of a national body "on the only national lines of the labor movement, the lines plainly marked out by the class struggle." In an ensuing meeting at Cooper Union on December 13, 1895, organized by the party, DeLeon and his followers secured the passage of a resolution calling upon the workers of the United States to join the Socialist Trade and Labor Alliance (S. T. L. A.), which the DeLeonites had just created, and to abandon the Knights of Labor and the American Federation of Labor. The new organization was to be formed along industrial lines.

The leading socialists within the American Federation of Labor (A. F. of L.) were not consulted on the advisability of forming the S. T. L. A. They were not convinced, as was DeLeon, that the days of the A. F. of L. were numbered. They felt that the trade unions were valuable agencies for improving labor conditions and that it was their

[2] Fine, *Labor and Farmer Parties,* p. 151. [3] *Ibid.,* pp. 151–2.

duty to remain inside the A. F. of L. unions, join with their fellows in fighting labor's immediate battles, and at the same time educate for socialism. They were convinced that the policy of organizing dual unions would greatly hinder the spread of socialistic ideas among the workers.

The Alliance fought vigorously for survival during the nineties. At first it controlled the Central Labor Federation of New York, and chartered some hundreds of locals, containing probably between 10,000 and 20,000 members. The Central Labor Federation, however, seceded from the Alliance in 1898. Likewise, offended by DeLeon's attempt to centralize all control in his hands even to the extent of unseating a general executive board not to his liking, some of DeLeon's ablest and most sincere followers soon left him. The Alliance gradually faded from the American scene.

The controversy over the S. T. L. A. had severe repercussions within the party. Numerous individuals and groups critical of DeLeon's policy of dual unionism were read out of the party by DeLeon, who took the position that it was necessary utterly to discredit his opponents in order to eliminate any threat to the party's principles.

Split in Socialist Labor Party (1899). The battle over ideas finally led to a rift between the Socialist Labor party and German, Jewish, and other socialist groups in New York and throughout the country, and to the organization of the opposition press. The fight between the DeLeon and the opposition group came to a head at the meeting of the general committee of Section Greater New York, on July 8, 1899, called, among other things, to select the national executive committee. The supporters of DeLeon were in charge of the meeting. No sooner had the meeting begun than a free-for-all fight developed over control. Each side claimed a majority of the general committee. Two days later, on July 10, the DeLeon opposition met and elected Julius Gerber, local secretary, Henry Slobodin, national secretary, and a national executive committee of seven, of which Morris Hillquit was one of the most outstanding. This group retained the name Socialist Labor party. In the ensuing battle over the control of the national headquarters the DeLeonites won out. They also kept the right to issue *The People* and to continue to function as the S. L. P.

DeLeon and his followers were less successful, however, in retaining their membership intact, and the split which followed left the old S. L. P. with less than half of its former membership and rendered it a party of little influence in the American labor movement.

Elimination of Immediate Demands by DeLeonites (1900). In the 1900 campaign, the DeLeon faction met in convention on June 28, and, among other things, struck out all immediate demands from their platform, declaring that such demands were "nonsense and untrue"; that they were "kangarooish" and belonged to the infancy of the movement. By formulating immediate demands which did not in any fundamental way affect the abolition of the wages system, "we [they declared] simply notified the freaks and capitalists through what doors they could get into our citadel and knock us out." The convention likewise threatened to expel from the party any member of the Socialist Labor party who accepted "office in a pure and simple trade or labor organization" and to refuse to accept into membership any officer of such a labor organization. In the 1900 elections their candidates for President and Vice-President of the United States secured 32,751 votes.

Entry of Debs into Socialist Movement. While the Socialist Laborites were engaged in a bitter internal struggle in the East, several other socialist groups were forging to the front in the Middle West. Principal among these groups was the Social Democracy, of which Eugene Victor Debs [4] of Terre Haute, Indiana, and Victor L. Berger of Milwaukee, Wisconsin, were outstanding.

[4] Debs was born in Terre Haute, Indiana, on November 5, 1855. He joined the Brotherhood of Locomotive Firemen at the age of 20 and five years later, in 1880, was selected secretary-treasurer of the national organization. At this post he remained until 1892, and for two years thereafter edited the official magazine of the Brotherhood. From 1879 to 1883 he served also as city clerk of Terra Haute and in 1885 was elected a Democratic member of the Indiana legislature. In 1892 Debs resigned from the Secretaryship of the Brotherhood, which yielded him a salary of $4000 a year, to accept a position at $900 a year with the American Railway Union—an all-inclusive railway employes' organization, containing skilled and unskilled men and women workers.

After winning a notable strike against the Great Northern Railway, the union voted in 1894 to support the strike of the Pullman Company employes by refusing to handle Pullman cars in the case the company refused to arbitrate. The company had contracts with 24 railroad companies, and the union soon found itself engaged in a struggle with the government and some of the most powerful organizations in the country. President Cleveland dispatched federal troops to Chicago against the protests of Governor Altgeld. The courts issued injunctions. Debs and his colleagues were arrested, and Debs later sentenced to six months in Woodstock jail in Illinois for contempt of court.

Debs entered jail a Democrat. In jail the labor leader read many socialist books and pamphlets, including the writings of Bellamy, Blatchford, Gronlund, and Kautsky. Victor L. Berger, prominent Milwaukee socialist, visited him and "delivered the first impassioned message of socialism" Debs had ever heard. The labor leader left prison with a socialistic philosophy.

In the 1896 campaign Debs supported William Jennings Bryan for President in the belief "that the triumph of Mr. Bryan and free silver would blunt the fangs of the

Birth of the Social Democracy of America (1897); Its Rise. The American Railway Union met in convention in Chicago June 15–18, 1897. At this meeting it wound up its affairs and merged in the convention of the Social Democracy, which opened on June 18.

At the Social Democratic convention there were present representatives of labor unions, various Socialist Labor party clubs, some religious organizations, and the Brotherhood of the Commonwealth, the latter a group interested in the organization of co-operative colonies. The convention elected an executive committee of five, with Debs as chairman. In its declaration of principles, it maintained that all of its efforts should be put forth "to secure the unemployed self-supporting employment. . . . For such purpose," it asserted, "one of the states of the Union, to be hereafter determined, shall be selected for the concentration of our supporters and the introduction of co-operative industry." Later the sphere of operations would be extended until a co-operative commonwealth would be established on a national scale.

"We call upon all honest citizens to unite under the banner of the Social Democracy of America," the declaration continued, "so that we may be ready to conquer capitalism by making use of our political liberty, and by taking possession of the public power."

The declaration, however, went further, and presented a number of immediate demands, among them recommendations for public ownership of monopolies, public utilities, and natural resources; public works for the unemployed; a reduction of hours; postal savings banks; "inventions to be free—the public to pay the inventor"; the initiative, referendum, and recall; and proportional representation.

The program of the Social Democracy was caustically attacked by DeLeon and his followers as "utopian." Other socialists, while critical of some of the proposals of the Social Democracy, saw in this organization an instrument for reaching the American people with the message of socialism.

Eastern Spread of Social Democracy. On July 31–August 2, 1897, soon after the convention of the Social Democracy, a group of Jewish socialists met in convention in New York, their 58 delegates claiming to represent 1,200 members of the Socialist Labor party and 10,000 trade unionists. Dr. I. A. Hourwich, later a prominent writer and statistician,

---

money power." Following this campaign, however, he declared himself a socialist, contending that there was "no hope for the toiling masses of my countrymen except by the pathways mapped out by socialists, the advocates of the co-operative commonwealth."

and Meyer London, afterwards socialist Congressman from New York City, speaking for local branch No. 1 of the Social Democracy, explained the purposes of the new organization and secured its approval by a four to one vote. The *Jewish Daily Forward,* of which Abraham Cahan was editor, established in April, 1897, as an independent socialist and labor paper, became, after this convention, the unofficial organ of this group.

ENTRANCE OF BERGER AND MILWAUKEE SOCIALISTS INTO SOCIAL DEMOCRACY. The Social Democracy also received the support of the Milwaukee socialists led by Victor L. Berger. Until his death Berger was the foremost leader of the Milwaukee socialist movement, largely composed of natives of Germany. Berger, who was a man of great energy and keen intelligence, a wide reader, and a forceful personality, was born in Austria-Hungary on February 28, 1860; he studied at the universities of Budapest and Vienna. On coming to the United States he worked at several trades. For a while he taught in the Milwaukee public schools. He joined the Socialist Labor party, but broke with the S. L. P. in 1889, later joining the Populist movement. From 1892 to 1898 he was editor of the *Milwaukee Daily Vorwaerts.* After helping to convert Debs to socialism, Berger joined the railway labor leader in the Social Democracy and sought to make that organization more realistic in its principles and program.

The Social Democracy held its second convention on June 7, 1898, with Debs as chairman. At this gathering a tense struggle for control took place between the colonizers and the anti-colonizers. Despite the vigorous opposition of Debs and Berger, the colonizers secured the adoption of their platform.

Formation of Social Democracy Party of America (1898). Following their defeat, the anti-colonizers, led by Debs, Berger, and others, bolted and met as a separate organization. They charged the colonizers with packing the convention and adopted a declaration of their own in which they maintained "the trade union movement and independent political action are the chief emancipating factors of the working class." Their immediate demands included five special measures for farmers. They elected an executive committee consisting of Jesse Cox as chairman, Seymour Stedman, Chicago lawyer, as secretary, and Eugene Victor Debs, Victor L. Berger, and Frederic Heath, the last-named a writer and editor. The convention proposed to enter the national field in the fall. It adopted as its official name the Social Democracy Party of America. The party that fall elected James F. Carey and Lewis H.

Scates to the Massachusetts legislature and John C. Chase as mayor of Haverhill, Massachusetts. The colonizers and their organization soon passed out of the field of action.

Mobilization of Anti-DeLeon Forces. Two years later, in the 1900 campaign, the Social Democratic party joined with the anti-DeLeon faction of the Socialist Labor party to nominate Eugene Victor Debs as Socialist candidate for President. Following the July, 1899, split between the two factions of the S. L. P., the anti-DeLeon group began to mobilize its forces. This group was led by Morris Hillquit, brilliant young socialist and attorney. Hillquit was born in Riga, Russia, on August 1, 1870 and came to this country at the age of 15. On his arrival, like Berger, he worked at various trades and at one time was secretary of the United Hebrew Trades of New York. While at his trade, he studied law at the New York University Law School and upon his graduation in 1893 started a legal career during which he became one of the most noted labor attorneys in the country and one of the most eminent socialist scholars, writers, and leaders. To him the opponents of DeLeon in the S. L. P. chiefly looked for leadership.

ROCHESTER CONVENTION OF ANTI-DELEON S. L. P. The opposition to the old Socialist Labor party assembled in its first national convention in Rochester, New York, in the early part of February, 1900, with 59 delegates. Following an address by N. I. Stone, editor of the *People,* the rival of the DeLeonite paper,[5] the convention repudiated the dual unionism of the old group in the Socialist Labor party and urged vigorous support of the trade-union movement. While fully recognizing, declared the convention resolution, "that the exploitation of labor will cease only when society takes possession of the means of production, we nevertheless declare it the duty of all socialists to participate in all struggles of organized labor to improve its conditions under the present system" and recommend "to all members of the party to join the organization of the trades to which they respectively belong."

In view of the coming national election, the delegates adopted a platform and nominated Job Harriman, a California lawyer, for President, and Max Hayes, a well-known Cleveland, Ohio, trade unionist, for Vice-President. In the hope that they would not have to wage the presidential campaign singlehanded, the delegates elected a committee of nine to confer with the Social Democratic party. Three members of this committee appeared before the Social Democratic party, which

[5] N. I. Stone years later served successively as Secretary of the U. S. Tariff Commission, labor arbitrator, business consultant, and one of the founders and later President of the National Bureau of Economic Research.

began its sessions on March 6, 1900, in Indianapolis. The delegates received them enthusiastically, and elected a committee of nine to confer with the Rochester group. They nominated Eugene V. Debs, as their most eloquent orator and magnetic personality, for President, and Job Harriman, the prominent anti-DeLeon S. L. P. spokesman, for Vice-President.

Debs and Harriman Social Democratic Nominees (1900). The joint committee on unity met in New York March 25, 1900, agreed on all important issues, established national headquarters at Springfield, Massachusetts, and arranged that a provisional national committee of ten be chosen from both parties. It likewise proposed to submit to a referendum vote of the membership of the two organizations the decision as to whether the name of the new party would be the Social Democratic party or the United Socialist party. A mass meeting in Cooper Union on March 28 celebrated the coming unity.

The unity proposals were overwhelmingly carried in the ensuing referendum vote, and the name Social Democratic party was selected as the name of the unified movement. Debs and Harriman were chosen the standard bearers of the 1900 campaign and after some delay the two groups co-operated in waging the campaign. Debs received 96,878 votes, about three times those of the candidate of DeLeon's Socialist Labor party.

The Unity Convention of 1901—Birth of Socialist Party. Following the campaign, the Social Democratic party of Chicago met in special convention on January 15, 1901, with 19 states represented, and declared for a general unity convention of the two groups. The unity convention was held July 29, 1901, in Indianapolis. The convention was composed to a large extent of young American-born delegates. Professor George D. Herron of Grinnell College was elected chairman at the opening session.

One of the most important questions brought before the convention was whether the party's platform should include immediate demands. After a vigorous debate, the delegates, by a large margin, voted in the affirmative, thus rejecting the position of the "impossibilists" of the old S. L. P. school. A second matter that divided the delegates was the party's position toward the American farmer. One group declared that farmers were essentially capitalists and belonged "by virtue of their economic position to the exploiting class." A second group, including Morris Hillquit, Seymour Stedman, and A. M. Simons, who had given particular study to the agricultural question, emphasized the economic dependence of the farmer upon the owners of transportation, machinery, storage facilities, and banks; maintained that the average farmer did not obtain "the product of his toil," and declared that it was ridiculous to hope that the party could ever accomplish anything without the farmers' votes.[6] The question was finally referred to a special committee for study and report. The party declared that it was the duty of socialists to urge trade unionists to join the Socialist party, but did not urge unions as such to join. The convention chose the Socialist party as its name, and selected St. Louis as its headquarters.

Growth of Socialist Party (1901–1912). From 1901 to 1912 the party grew steadily in membership and influence. The S. P. dues-paying membership from 1903 to 1912 inclusive was as follows:

1903	15,975	1908	41,751
1904	20,763	1909	41,479
1905	23,327	1910	58,011
1906	26,784	1911	84,116
1907	29,270	1912	118,045

In the presidential elections of 1904 and 1908 Debs and his running mate, Ben Hanford, received 402,400 and 420,820 votes, respectively, and in 1912 Debs and Emil Seidel, socialist mayor of Milwaukee, received 897,011. At the beginning of 1912 the party claimed 1,039 dues-paying members in public office, among whom were 56 mayors, over 300 aldermen, a number of state legislators, and one congressman, Victor L. Berger, first elected in 1910. Among the cities controlled by socialists the largest was Milwaukee, Wisconsin, where Emil Seidel, socialist, was elected mayor in 1910, and which remained in the socialist column, with Daniel W. Hoan as mayor from 1916 to 1938.

The party's influence in the trade unions during those years was considerable. Socialists played an active rôle at labor conventions. In 1912 Max Hayes, prominent Cleveland socialist, running for president of the American Federation of Labor against the veteran trade-union leader, Samuel Gompers, received one third of the total vote cast. "Socialist workingmen and intellectuals were everywhere in the forefront of all important labor struggles." [7]

Socialist Proponents before First World War Days. During and shortly following this period a flood of books, novels, plays, pamphlets, essays, poems, and cartoons presenting the socialistic point of view in various fields of thought and action issued from the pens and pencils of a host of American writers and artists.[8] Scores of magazines, weeklies,

[6] See Fine, *op. cit.*, p. 211.

[7] Fine, *op. cit.*, p. 215.

[8] Among them were Leonard D. Abbott, Sherwood Anderson, Charles A. Beard, Allan L. Benson, George Bellows, Victor L. Berger, Frank and William Bohn, Louis B. Boudin, Arthur Bullard, Berton Braley, Robert W. Bruere, Floyd Dell, John Dewey,

and dailies were being issued, the *Appeal to Reason,* a militant propaganda sheet published in Girard, Kansas, with a half-million subscribers, leading in circulation. The Rand School of Social Science and other schools were serving as educational centers for the movement, and the Intercollegiate Socialist Society, formed in 1905 "to promote an intelligent interest in socialism among college men and women," was spreading a knowledge of socialism among college and professional groups.

Socialist Party Condemnation of Sabotage. In 1912 much discussion arose within Socialist party ranks between William D. Haywood, leader of the Industrial Workers of the War, and the more moderate elements in the Socialist party over the advocacy of sabotage and direct action. The party finally took a position against their advocacy, maintaining that "the use of sabotage and violence made for guerilla warfare, demoralized those who employed these methods, and opened the door to the agent provocateur." [9] Haywood was expelled from membership on the party's Executive Committee in 1913, the year following the adoption of the direct action amendment, Article II, Section 6, to the party constitution.

The Socialist Party in the First World War. When war broke out in Europe in 1914, the Socialist party urged that the United States remain neutral. In 1916 the party, through a referendum vote—the only such vote on a party presidential candidate—nominated Allan L. Benson, an able and vigorous writer on social problems, and George R. Kirkpatrick, lecturer, former college teacher and ardent opponent of war, for President and Vice-President, respectively. The party candidates campaigned on a platform against war and militarism, and received a vote of 585,113, one-third smaller than in 1912.

Samuel A. DeWitt, Abraham Cahan, Eugene V. Debs, Charles W. Ervin, Max Eastman, August Claessens, Ira B. Cross, W. J. Ghent, Robert Herrick, Charlotte Perkins Gilman, Arturo Giovannitti, Laurence Gronlund, Ben Hanford, Morris Hillquit, Jessie W. Hughan, Robert Hunter, Inez Haynes Gillmore, William D. Haywood, Daniel W. Hoan, George D. Herron, Frederick C. Howe, William Dean Howells, Alexander Irvine, Helen Keller, Florence Kelley, Edmond Kelly, George R. Kirkpatrick, Harry W. Laidler, Arthur Morrow Lewis, Algernon Lee, Vachel Lindsay, Walter Lippmann, Jack London, James Mackaye, John Macy, William Mailly, Edwin Markham, James M. Maurer, Walter Thomas Mills, Gustavus Myers, Kate Richard O'Hare, Scott Nearing, James Oneal, James Oppenheim, Samuel P. Orth, David Graham Phillips, Ernest Poole, Walter Rauschenbusch, N. A. Richardson, Boardman Robinson, I. M. Rubinow, Charles Edward Russell, Carl Sandburg, Leroy Scott, Joseph Schlossberg, A. M. Simons, Upton Sinclair, John Sloan, John Spargo, Bishop J. L. Spaulding, Lincoln Steffens, Charles P. Steinmetz, Carl D. Thompson, Horace Traubel, Ernest Untermann, Charles H. Vail, Thorstein Veblen, Henry C. Vedder, Charney Vladeck, Louis Untermeyer, Mary Heaton Vorse, William English Walling, Lester F. Ward, Fred Warren, J. A. Wayland, Stitt Wilson, Clement Wood, John W. Work, Walter E. Weyl, Art Young, Charles Zueblin.

[9] Fine, *op. cit.*, p. 287.

In the spring of 1917, a few days after America's entrance into the First World War, the Socialist party met in St. Louis to consider their position toward the war. John Spargo introduced a resolution in support of the war; Louis B. Boudin, a resolution declaring that the party had opposed the war, that the war was now a fact, and that the party, recognizing that fact, should "force upon the government, through pressure of public opinion, a constructive program." That program should include protection of the rights of the people, the advancement of democratic collectivism, and the establishment of communication with the socialists within the enemy countries, "to the end that peace may be secured upon democratic terms at the earliest possible moment."

The majority report, introduced by Morris Hillquit, on the other hand, proclaimed "its unalterable opposition to the war just declared by the government of the United States" and called "upon the workers of all countries to refuse support to their governments in their wars." The practical course of action recommended included opposition to capitalistic wars "through demonstrations, mass petitions, and all other honorable and effective means within our power"; opposition to proposed legislation for militarism and industrial conscription; "vigorous resistance to all reactionary measures, such as censorship of the press and mails, restriction of the rights of free speech, free assemblage, and organization, or compulsory arbitration and limitation of the right to strike."

After the close of the convention many socialist headquarters were raided. The socialist press was, for the most part, suppressed, and numerous socialists were arrested. Eugene V. Debs was sentenced to the Federal penitentiary for an antiwar speech he delivered in Canton, Ohio. Leading members of the national executive committee were likewise convicted, although the United States Supreme Court later set their convictions aside.

In the fall of 1917, Morris Hillquit, nominated for mayor of New York City, waged a vigorous campaign in behalf of an early peace and received a record vote of 146,000, and in the same campaign seven socialist aldermen and ten socialist assemblymen were elected to office from New York City. The following year, with the coming of the Russian revolution, the wide acclaim of Wilson's Fourteen Points, and other developments, the position of the party shifted and war opposition by the socialists for the most part ceased.

In the meanwhile, following the St. Louis convention, a number of the "intellectuals" in the movement—John Spargo, J. G. Phelps Stokes, Rose Pastor Stokes, William English Walling, Charles Edward Russell,

Robert Hunter, among them—left the party because of its antiwar stand, formed the short-lived Social Democratic League of America, and conducted an intensive educational campaign in behalf of the war.

In the spring and fall of 1918 the socialist vote began to slump. Meyer London, elected to Congress in 1916, was defeated in his campaign for re-election, and only two assemblymen were re-elected from the socialist strongholds of New York City.[10] From 1912 to 1918, the Socialist party membership, under the stress and strain of war, gradually decreased. From the high level of 118,045 in 1912, it declined in 1918 to 82,344, as follows:

1913....95,957	1916....83,284
1914....93,579	1917....80,379
1915....79,374	1918....82,344

Left-Wing Split from Socialist Party (1919). The following year, 1919, there was, however, an upsurge of membership in the party to 108,504. The increase came largely from foreign-language federations, which had functioned practically independent of party control.

When the Communist or Third International was established in March, 1919, the left-wing elements of the American socialists, centered chiefly in the language federations, urged the Socialist party of the United States to affiliate with this international, and to condemn the Berne conference called for February, 1919, for the purpose of re-establishing an international socialist body. Instead of condemning it, however, the national executive committee sent delegates to the proposed conference.

Following this decision, the left-wing elements continued their agitation for affiliation with the Communist International. Many of them believed that the revolutionary outbreak in America was near at hand. The Socialist party, they contended, should thus give little or no attention to ameliorative measures, but should make their demand "the unconditional surrender of the capitalist class and the establishment of a proletarian state." The left-wingers on June 21, 1919, held a conference in New York. One faction at this Conference urged the immediate organization of a Communist party; another faction favored the continuance of the policy of boring from within the Socialist party until the next party convention, at which time they would seek to capture the party and, failing that, would split from it.

The language federations constituted the basis of the group favor-

[10] The defeat of socialist assemblymen, however, resulted largely from the fact that the Democratic and Republican parties in several districts combined to support the same candidates, with a view to defeating the socialists.

ing the formation of a Communist party. Upon their defeat they withdrew from the conference and issued a call for a convention at which a new party would be launched committed to a communist program. The left-wingers opposed to the language federation tactics likewise sent out a convention call. The Socialist party had already decided upon an emergency convention to be held in Chicago on August 30, 1919.

Formation of Communist Parties. All three conventions met in Chicago at the same time. The socialists were desirous of keeping the party intact and free from communistic control. The left-wingers opposed to dictation by the language federations were anxious to give birth to an "American" Communist party. The foreign-language groups, dominated by the Slavic federations, were intent on keeping the Communist party control in their own hands so as to "ensure its genuinely bolshevik character."

The result was the retention by the believers in democratic, peaceful progress in America of the control of the Socialist party; the organization by the language federations of the Communist party; and the formation by the non-federation left-wingers of the Communist Labor party. "The Communist party," declared its 1919 program, "shall keep in the foreground its consistent appeal for proletarian revolution, the overthrow of capitalism, and the establishment of the dictatorship of the proletariat. . . . Participation in parliamentary campaigns is for the purpose of revolutionary propaganda only. Parliamentary representatives of the Communist party shall not introduce or support reform measures . . . The state parliamentary representatives shall make clear how parliamentarism and parliamentary democracy deceive the workers."

No sooner had the Communist and Communist Labor parties organized than many of their members were arrested, imprisoned, and deported. Their headquarters were raided and they were driven underground.

The Communist Labor party soon died. A United Communist party came into being as an underground movement, and the U. C. P. and the C. P. continued as secret groups until 1921, when a Workers' party was formed as the legal and aboveground representative of the American communist movement. The underground Communist party continued for some time, but was finally liquidated on April 7, 1923. The Workers' party nominated William Z. Foster, an active labor leader, and Benjamin Gitlow for President and Vice-President, respectively, in 1924 and in 1928. In the former year these candidates received 33,361 votes; in the latter year, 48,228.

Communist Splits. In the late twenties bitter factional fights took place between the majority faction of the party, led by Jay Lovestone and Benjamin Gitlow, and the minority faction headed by William Z. Foster. The minority faction accused the majority of overestimating the prosperity and permanence of "American imperialism" and of underestimating the radical and revolutionary trends among the masses. The majority accused the minority of "ultra-leftism" and of failing to recognize the unevenness of capitalist development in various countries. The United States, it contended, was in no sense approaching an immediate revolutionary crisis. The Communist International sided with the minority group, and, upon their return from Moscow, Lovestone and Gitlow, together with a large number of their followers, were expelled from the party, which in 1929 changed its name from the Workers' to the Communist party. In July, 1929, those expelled formed the Communist party of the U. S. A. (Majority Group). The year before, James P. Cannon, Max Schachtman, and others were purged for their efforts to organize the Communist League of America (Opposition), a Trotskyite group. The Communist League demanded an entire reorganization of the C. P. control, including "genuine party democracy in place of the regime of administrative terror and suppression." The Lovestone and Cannon groups continued for a number of years as propaganda organizations, but, with rare exceptions, did not nominate candidates for political office.

Co operation of the Socialist Party with Labor Party Movements. As for the Socialist party, it emerged from the 1919 conflict with communist elements a greatly weakened organization, its membership having declined from 108,504 in 1919 to 26,766 in 1920 and to 13,484 in 1931. Despite the party's small membership, however, Eugene V. Debs, renominated in 1920 for President while he was still in prison for alleged antiwar activities, received a vote of 919,799, the largest vote accorded him during his four candidacies.

However, the structural weakness of the party led many of its members to turn their attention to the possible formation of a Labor party. After the war there was much unrest among the organized workers of the country and a definite trend toward progressive political and economic action. The railroad brotherhoods among other unions went on record in support of public ownership and democratic management of railroads and became actively interested in a new political alignment. The United Mine Workers of America, at its 1919 convention, declared itself in favor of the immediate formation of an American Labor party.[11]

[11] Trade unionists from various organizations also took part in the organization of a Labor party (later called the Farmer-Labor party) at a national convention on November 22, 1919. The F. L. P. adopted a platform that included a demand for public ownership of public utilities and natural resources, and nominated in 1929

A progressive movement during those years developed also among the farmers of the West under the leadership of the Nonpartisan League. This organization was first formed in North Dakota in 1915 by Arthur C. Townley, a former socialist, and others, and rapidly spread to several other western states. Through a concentration on the party primaries and electoral campaigns it secured the election of Republican and Democratic senators, congressmen, governors, and other officers friendly to progressive farmers. One of the most significant developments of this movement was the formation of the Farmer-Labor party of Minnesota, which for years wielded a powerful influence in that state.

THE CONFERENCE FOR PROGRESSIVE POLITICAL ACTION. Also during the early twenties labor gave birth to the Conference for Progressive Political Action. This organization was formed at a meeting in Chicago on February 20, 1922, called by William H. Johnston, president of the International Association of Machinists, and by the presidents of five powerful railway unions, with an aggregate membership of 1,500,000. The meeting was attended by Morris Hillquit, Victor L. Berger, Daniel W. Hoan, James Oneal, Otto Branstetter, and Bertha Hale White of the Socialist party; by representatives of 16 railway unions, of the United Mine Workers, of members of the needle trades, and of other labor and farmer groups. Morris Hillquit, socialist representative, was elected a member of the permanent committee of fifteen and played an active part in its affairs.

The constitution subsequently adopted limited the political support of the conference to such candidates as "are pledged to the interests of the producing classes and to the principles of genuine democracy in agriculture, industry, and government." It left the state conferences free to follow a non-partisan policy through the old-party primaries or to organize for independent political action, and directed that independent nominations be made when both old parties failed to name progressive candidates.

In February, 1924, the C. P. P. A. called a nationwide convention at Cleveland for July 4 "for the purpose of taking action on the nomination of candidates for the offices of President and Vice-President of the United States." Close to 600 delegates were present at this convention, representing trade-union, farmers', co-operative, and socialist groups. The Railroad Brotherhoods dominated. Socialists fought to have the convention vote for the establishment of a third party as a permanent

---

Parley Parker Christensen for President and Max Hayes for Vice-President. Christensen received 265,411 votes in the fall elections. Local labor parties also sprang up in various sections of the country.

party of opposition to the Republican and Democratic parties. The Brotherhoods, however, were unwilling to go so far. The convention endorsed Senator Robert M. La Follette for President, and authorized the national committee, on consultation with the presidential candidate, to pick his running mate. It likewise instructed the national committee to call a special national convention in late January, 1925, "to consider and pass upon the question of forming a permanent independent political party for national and local elections, upon the basis of the general principles laid down in the platform adopted by this Convention." [12]

In his convention speech Senator La Follette predicted that a new party would be born after the November elections because the people would "register their will and united purpose by a vote of such magnitude that a new political party" was inevitable. Socialists were of the opinion that the movement would give rise to an independent political party. In that belief, the Socialist party endorsed the candidacy of Robert M. La Follette, thus for the first time in its history departing from its established custom of supporting only socialist candidates. Senator La Follette and Senator Burton K. Wheeler, candidate for Vice-President, received in the November election 4,822,856 votes.[13]

Defeat of Mass Party Proposal (1925). The question whether, as a result of the showing during the campaign, a permanent Farmer-Labor or Progressive party should be launched was brought before a convention held in Chicago February 21–22, 1925. Socialists at this convention appealed for the organization of such a party. The Brotherhood representatives, on the other hand, declared that they had no mandate to commit their organizations to independent political action, and urged the continuation of the Conference for Progressive Political Action along non-partisan lines. No vote was taken on this motion. Instead, a motion was made to adjourn *sine die,* with the proviso that those wishing to organize a new party could reconvene individually. With that action, the C. P. P. A. passed out of existence.

Socialists refused to take part in the reconvened convention on the ground that the delegates constituted an entirely different body from that composing the original conference, and that the party it was thus proposed to organize "was far more likely to be a liberal party composed of the middle classes than a militant political organization of the toiling and producing masses of America." [14]

[12] See Hillquit, *Loose Leaves from a Busy Life,* p. 320.

[13] The Socialist Labor party that year received 38,958 votes; the Workers' party (Communist), 33,361 votes.

[14] *New Leader,* Feb. 28, 1925.

Norman Thomas and James H. Maurer, Standard-Bearers in 1928 and 1932. Following this episode, the Socialist party returned to its independent position, at the same time expressing its readiness "to merge its political functions in a genuine independent political party of American workers." In the 1928 campaign Norman Thomas, who joined the organization in 1917 during the Morris Hillquit campaign, was nominated as candidate for President, and James H. Maurer for Vice-President.[15] Eugene V. Debs, the standard-bearer of the party during five of the previous campaigns, had died in October, 1926.

Though running a vigorous campaign in that year (1928), Thomas and Maurer received but 267,420 votes. The Workers' party, with William Z. Foster as presidential candidate, received 48,770 votes that year; the Socialist Labor party, 21,603; the Farmer-Labor party, 6,390.

In 1932 Thomas and Maurer ran for the second time as candidates for President and Vice-President, and received a vote of 884,781. Foster, Communist party candidate, obtained that year 102,991 votes.

Conflicts within Socialist Party (1932–1936). The next four years were years of storm and stress within the Socialist party. During the

[15] Thomas was born in Marion, Ohio, November 20, 1884, the son of a Presbyterian minister. He was graduated from Princeton University—the valedictorian of his class—in 1905 and from Union Theological Seminary in 1911. While in the Seminary he served as assistant pastor of the Brick Presbyterian Church, New York, and from 1911 to 1918 as pastor of the East Harlem Church and Chairman of the American Parish, a New York settlement.

Thomas opposed American entrance into the First World War, and after the outbreak of the war joined the Socialist party, participated in the Hillquit campaign of 1917, and, resigning from his pastorate, became the editor of *The World Tomorrow* and secretary of the Fellowship of Reconciliation. In 1921 he became associate editor of *The Nation* and in 1922 was appointed co-Executive Director with Harry W. Laidler of the League for Industrial Democracy, which position he held until the mid-thirties. In this capacity he lectured extensively among college, labor, church, and civic groups throughout the country.

A brilliant scholar and orator, Thomas soon became an influential force in the Socialist party, was nominated for governor of New York in 1924, for mayor of New York City in 1925 and 1929, as well as for other offices, and for President of the United States in 1928, and subsequently in 1932, 1936, and 1940.

James H. Maurer, Thomas' running mate, was a veteran trade-unionist. He was born in Reading, Pennsylvania, April 15, 1864. At ten he became a factory hand; at 15, he was a machinist apprentice; at 16, a member of the Knights of Labor. Maurer joined the Socialist Labor party in 1898 and the Socialist party in 1902. From 1912 to 1928 he served as president of the Pennsylvania Federation of Labor. During these years he ran for many offices in Pennsylvania as Socialist party candidate, served in 1910, 1914, and 1916 as member of the Pennsylvania House of Representatives, where he introduced Workmen's Compensation and other labor legislation, and was a member for many years of the National Executive Committee of the Socialist party. For over a decade Maurer served as chairman of the Old-Age Pension Commission of Pennsylvania. He was one of the most popular and beloved leaders in the trade-union movement. He died in 1944. (See James H. Maurer, *It Can Be Done.*)

early days of the depression a young, active group, which maintained that the "old guard" was not taking full advantage of the opportunities afforded by the economic crisis to carry the socialist message to the masses, had entered the party. They believed that the party should help more vigorously in trade-union organization and, in regard to Russia, should not content itself with a mere demand for recognition by the United States. Many of them organized as "militants" and in the 1932 convention sought, though unsuccessfully, to secure the election of Daniel Hoan, Socialist mayor of Milwaukee, over Morris Hillquit, as chairman of the party's executive committee.[16]

Two years later, in 1934, a new declaration of principles was adopted at the Detroit convention in which the party declared, among other things, that, should the capitalist system collapse, it "will not shrink from the responsibility of organizing and maintaining a government under the workers' rule." Many of the older socialists in the Eastern states, among others, declared that this passage was communistic. Many proponents of the resolution pointed to that part of the declaration which stated that the party "seeks to attain its objectives by peaceful and orderly means" as proof of its democratic nature.[17] There was also a difference of opinion regarding conditions, if any, under which the party should hold united-front demonstrations with communists.

Formation of Social Democratic Federation (1936). The ensuing conflict of ideas, groups, and personalities finally led to a split in the party in the spring of 1936 and to the formation by the dissident group of the Social Democratic Federation, committed to a program of democratic socialism. Among the leaders of the new S. D. F. were Jasper McLevy, Socialist mayor of Bridgeport, Conn., first chairman of the group, Algernon Lee, President of the Rand School of Social Science, Louis Waldman, socialist attorney, Abraham Cahan, editor of the *Jewish Daily Forward,* James Oneal, former editor of *The New Leader,* August Claessens, former assemblyman, and Louis P. Goldberg, attorney.

16 This was the first convention since the beginning of the party in which Victor L. Berger, Milwaukee Socialist leader, did not play a prominent part, and the last convention participated in by Morris Hillquit before he passed away. Berger died August 2, 1929.

17 This paragraph was later somewhat modified and, as affirmed in the 1936 convention, read in part: "Capitalism is doomed, it must give way to a socialist order brought about by the socialization of the principal means of production and distribution. The Socialist party aims to accomplish this by peaceful and democratic means . . . If orderly and democratic means are completely denied us . . . the Socialist party with the aid of the economic organizations of the producing masses will rally all possible forces to organize and maintain a government of and for the working class." (See *Socialist Handbook,* 1937, p. 20.)

At the Federation's first convention in Pittsburgh, Pennsylvania, in May, 1937, it called upon labor and progressive elements to form a third party and voted to permit members of the federation to support candidates of state labor parties functioning as independent organs of political action. During the next few years it co-operated in New York State with the American Labor party. During the early forties it issued a postwar program calling for democratic socialization of industry. In May, 1944, the New York members voted to support the newly formed Liberal party. Its members, for the most part, supported President Roosevelt in his various candidacies from 1936 on.

Socialist Campaigns of 1936 and 1940. In the 1936 campaign Norman Thomas and George Nelson, a farm leader from Wisconsin, ran for President and Vice-President, respectively. The support given to Roosevelt as exponent of the New Deal, the socialist split, and other factors reduced the socialist presidential vote that year to 187,720. The vote for Earl Browder and James W. Ford, candidates for President and Vice-President on the Communist party ticket, was 80,159, and for the Socialist Labor party candidate, 12,777. In 1936 the Socialist party took in several hundred Trotskyites, whom, however, it expelled in 1937 for "disloyalty" and "disruptive activities." In the latter year it co-operated in many ways with the American Labor party and withdrew its candidate for mayor against Mayor La Guardia in New York City.

In 1939 an attempt was made to bring about unity between the S. P. and the S. D. F. The majority of the Socialist party, however, opposed America's entrance into the approaching war, whereas the Social Democratic Federation favored such entrance under certain circumstances. Differences over international policies led to the suspension of unity negotiations.

In the 1940 campaign the Socialist party nominated Norman Thomas for the fourth time as its presidential candidate and Maynard Krueger, assistant professor of economics at the University of Chicago, as its vice-presidential candidate. The party platform urged democratic socialization as the alternative to a drift to fascism. The candidates received a total of 116,796 votes as contrasted with a Communist party vote of 48,789 and a Socialist Labor vote of 14,861.

Socialists in the Second World War. Following the United States' entrance into the Second World War after the Japanese attack on Pearl Harbor, December 7, 1941, the party propagandized for the preservation of civil liberties and of social advances, the establishment of democratic controls over war and postwar collectivism, and the achievement of a permanent peace.

At the 1944 convention at Reading, Pennsylvania, Norman Thomas was nominated for President for the fifth time, and Darlington Hoopes, Reading attorney and former assemblyman, for Vice-President.

The platform called for (1) the winning of the earliest possible peace that will last, followed by the formation of an international organization from which no nation would be excluded and by co-operative action to remove the causes of war; (2) social ownership and democratic control of monopolies, semi-monopolies and other exploitive industries; (3) the establishment of equality of rights and obligations among all races; (4) "a democratic socialist party with mass support," similar to the Canadian C. C. F.

Developments in Communist Party (1932–1944). In the spring of 1941 many socialists not in sympathy with the party's antiwar stand, played a prominent part in the formation of the Union for Democratic Action, headed by Dr. Reinhold Niebuhr, Professor of Christian Ethics, Union Theological Seminary. The U. D. A., however, was not as an organization committed to a socialistic program.

During the thirties and early forties, as has been brought out, the Communist party frequently changed its tactics. William Z. Foster, the party's presidential candidate of 1932, declared that "in all its parliamentary activities the Communist party makes it clear to the workers that the capitalist democracy is a sham and that there must be no illusions about peacefully capturing the state for the working class." [18] It maintained that "progressivism is a grave danger to the working class" [19]; "that the Democratic party has ever more clearly exposed its big capitalist character" [20]; and that "the policy of the social democracy is basically that of fascism." [21]

In 1935, after the change in the tactics of the Comintern, the Communist party urged united action of all democratic groups in the fight against fascism.

Following the German-Russian non-aggression pact, August 23, 1939, the Communist party, U. S. A., began a vigorous campaign against America's participation in an "imperialistic war." Its 1940 platform, as has been noted in Chapter 29, urged that the people of the country combat "the imperialist policies and acts" of the administration, "to spread the war and involve the United States in it." [22] The communist candidates, Earl Browder and James W. Ford, fought the presidential campaign on these issues, among others. After the campaign, Browder was sentenced to prison for participation in a passport fraud. Before

[18] Foster, William J., *Toward Soviet America*, p. 255. For a further discussion of changes of communist tactics, see in this text pp. 463 ff.

[19] Foster, *op. cit.*, p. 239. [20] *Ibid.*, p. 236. [21] *Ibid.*, p. 177.

[22] See *New York Times*, June 2, 1940. See in this text, p. 464.

completing his sentence he was pardoned by President Franklin D. Roosevelt.

After the nazi invasion of Russia, June 22, 1941, the party reversed its stand, declaring that the struggle was no longer one "for supremacy between Britain and Germany, two imperialistic states," but that the issue at stake is "the democratic system and way of life." [23] During the Second World War, the party gave vigorous support to the war effort. In the spring of 1944 the party transformed itself into the American Communist Political Association, and its leader, Earl Browder, declared that in the war and immediate postwar period the party would regard "any plans for American postwar reconstruction which are based on the introduction of socialism" as, "in effect a repudiation" of the aim of American communists to unite the majority of the nation behind the Teheran policies. Communists would choose their associates on the bases of whether they were for or against the Teheran policy and the effectiveness of their support, regardless of class differences or past political divisions." [24]

Labor and Liberal Parties. During the thirties several attempts were made, some successful, others unsuccessful, to form labor parties in various parts of the country. In 1936 the American Labor party was organized in New York State largely with the view of mobilizing labor's full support in the state in behalf of the candidacy of President Roosevelt.

During the next eight years the party took an active part in city, state and national campaigns. In the city, it actively campaigned for Mayor Fiorello H. La Guardia, a registered member of the A. L. P., and elected several members of the City Council and of the State Assembly, among them, B. Charvey Vladeck. It supported in many instances Democratic and Republican candidates. In 1942 Dean Alfange, its candidate for Governor, polled 403,000 votes.

In 1944 the party split. The so-called right-wing groups, including the International Ladies' Garment Workers, led by President David Dubinsky, the Millinery Workers, the Social Democratic Federation, etc., left the party following the spring primaries which resulted in a victory for the "left-wing" slate. This slate contained both the names of officers of the Amalgamated Clothing Workers and other non-communist trade unions and those of trade-union officials and others who had closely followed Communist party policies.

The "right-wing" group, on June 20–1, 1944, formed the Liberal

[23] See statement of Robert Minor, acting secretary, Communist Party, U. S. A., *New York Times,* June 15, 1941.

[24] Browder, *Teheran and America,* pp. 19, 20, 21, 24, 41. See in this text, pp. 465–66.

party and elected Dr. John L. Childs, Professor of the Philosophy of Education of Teachers' College, Columbia University, chairman of the State Committee and Alexander Rose of the Millinery Workers, Chairman of the Administrative Committee. It likewise adopted a program calling for "full employment, full production, and a high standard of living," and favoring "public ownership of utilities, of natural resources, and of monopolistic enterprises, wherever this is necessary to maintain production or to serve other desirable social ends." The party declared that neither Republican nor Democratic party would be able to meet the challenge of the postwar world, and urged the building of a new party on a national scale.

The "left wing," following the primaries, elected Sidney Hillman, president of the Amalgamated Clothing Workers and head of the C. I. O. Political Action Committee, as chairman of the State A. L. P. and adopted a program calling for full employment and full utilization of the nation's productive capacity.

Both organizations voted support of President Roosevelt.

Other third party movements were initiated in 1943 and 1944 in Chicago, where an American Commonwealth Federation was formed, in Detroit, and also in other cities. The Farmer-Labor party of Minnesota merged with the Democratic party. The Progressive party of Wisconsin continued, with Senator Robert M. La Follette as its leading spokesman.

On May 20, 1944, the Communist party in a convention in New York voted to disband and to reorganize as the Communist Political Association. The Association pledged its support to President Roosevelt in the 1944 campaign.

CANADIAN LABOR IN POLITICS

Beginning of Socialism in Canada. During the early forties labor and socialism advanced steadily in Canada.

Before the turn of the twentieth century a few scattered attempts were made to educate Canadians along socialistic lines. In 1890 branches of the Socialist Labor party of the United States were organized in Montreal, Toronto, and Winnipeg. In 1899 a Canadian Socialist League was formed by those dissatisfied with the leadership of Daniel DeLeon, and this move was followed by the organization of other socialist groups. In 1905 all existing socialist organizations were united into the Socialist party of Canada, with the *Western Clarion* as the official party organ. The party membership increased from 3,507 in 1903 to 16,800 in 1915. The party, prior to the First World War, failed, however, to elect any representatives to the Federal Parliament, though succeeding in sending representatives to the Alberta and Manitoba provincial legislatures.

In 1911 a second socialist group, the Social Democratic party of Canada, came into existence and in 1915 claimed a membership in 230 locals of 5,380. The year after its formation, the S. D. P. joined the International Socialist Bureau, the Second International. The older and more radical of the parties had refused to unite with the International as long as the British and Australian Labor parties were affiliated with it.

During and immediately after the First World War much attention was given by Canadian laborites to the development of the One Big Union movement. This movement attracted wide attention in the spring of 1920 during the six weeks' general strike in Winnipeg, Manitoba.

Election of Labor Party Candidates (1920–1932). During these days, also, Labor parties sprang up in various parts of Canada and elected members to the Provincial legislatures and to the Federal Parliament, the first Labor party candidate to be elected to the Lower House in Ottawa being Angus McDonald, the successful candidate of the Labor party and the United Farmers of Ontario, in the April 7, 1920 elections. The following year the Labor party of Winnipeg Center, Manitoba, elected to Parliament J. S. Woodsworth, destined to become the leading spirit of the Canadian labor political forces for the next two decades.[25]

During the twenties labor and socialist groups functioned in various parts of Canada and elected many candidates to legislative and executive positions. Various communist groups were organized in 1920 and united the following year in the Communist party of Canada. The party was soon declared illegal.

[25] James Shaver Woodsworth was born July 29, 1874, in Etobicoke, Ontario, Canada, the son of a Methodist minister. He went west with his family, graduated in 1896 from the University of Manitoba, obtained the degree of Bachelor of Divinity from Victoria College, Toronto, in 1900, and then went to Oxford University, England, for two years of postgraduate work. Prior to his Oxford studies he had taught school and served in the mission fields of Manitoba. After his return to Canada he served as minister, social worker, university lecturer, longshoreman, and labor leader, and in 1916 became the Director of the Bureau of Social Research for the governments of Saskatchewan, Manitoba, and Alberta. His antiwar views forced him out of this position, and he resigned likewise from the church.

On a speaking tour through Canada in 1919 Mr. Woodsworth reached Winnipeg during an important strike and became editor of the *Western Labor News*, organ of the strikers. In 1920 he ran for the Provincial legislature in British Columbia as a Labor party candidate, and the following year was elected from Manitoba to the Federal Parliament. He served in Parliament until his death on March 21, 1942.

Organization and Development of Co-operative Commonwealth Federation. In the summer of 1932 a group of Canadian farm and labor leaders met in Calgary, Alberta, for the purpose of considering the organization of a more inclusive political party of the masses. The nucleus of this group were a number of members of Parliament, led by J. S. Woodsworth, who, because of their aggressive stand on social issues, had become known as the "Ginger Group." Though elected from widely separated labor and farm sections, these members had been able to act as a unified group in the Federal legislature and had felt it worth while exploring the possibilities of united action among similar groups, in one political organization. The outcome of the convention was the formation of the Cooperative Commonwealth Federation, a movement pledged to an intelligently planned social order in Canada.

At the first convention in Regina, Saskatchewan, in 1933, the delegates from farm, trade union, professional and other groups in eight provinces adopted a socialistic program, urging, among other things, the public ownership of industry in those cases where the power of the great monopolies operated against the national welfare.

During the thirties the C. C. F. grew slowly but steadily, and in 1940 was represented by eight members of Parliament. In the next few years of the Second World War its popularity rapidly increased. In the by-elections in February, 1942, Joseph Noseworthy, C. C. F., defeated former Prime Minister Arthur Meighan, leader of the Conservative party, for Parliament in the Toronto district.

Advances of C. C. F. in 1943 Elections. In the Ontario Provincial elections in August, 1943, the C. C. F. elected 34 members to the Provincial legislature, as against 38 members for the Conservatives and 15 for the Liberals. The C. C. F. received a popular vote of 400,000, 32.4 per cent of the total, as compared with 78,000 in 1937, when it failed to elect a single candidate. All of the industrial centers in that province went C. C. F. The campaign was waged on the basis of the need of "social and economic planning on a bold and comprehensive scale." In the succeeding by-elections for Parliament two western seats were captured by the C. C. F. candidates and one Quebec seat by a communist running as a candidate for the Labor-Progressives. The communists also won two seats in the Ontario elections.

In 1943 the C. C. F. members in the various provincial legislatures numbered 69. They were the official opposition in four Canadian provinces.

In June, 1944, at a provincial election in Saskatchewan, the C. C. F., formerly the chief opposition party, elected over 40 members to the provincial legislature out of a total of 55, and formed the first socialist provincial government in Canada. T. C. Douglas, a former minister and a former member of Parliament, was chosen Prime Minister of the province.

The leader of the C. C. F. parliamentary group since 1942 has been M. J. Coldwell, a native of England, and former president of the Canadian Federation of Teachers.[26]

[26] During his youth in Great Britain, Mr. Coldwell was active in the British Labor party. On arriving in Western Canada, he entered the teaching profession, and later became principal of a Regina school and president and secretary of the Canadian Teachers' Association. For ten years he served as a labor alderman in the City of Regina. He took part in the organization of the I. L. P. of Saskatchewan and was one of its principal officers and the head of the Saskatchewan C. C. F. until 1934. Because of his political activities, he was expelled from his post as principal, but the board that expelled him was later forced by popular pressure to reverse its decision. In the Federal election of 1935, Coldwell was sent to Parliament. That year he was appointed national secretary of the C. C. F., a post which he held until 1937 when he was elected national chairman, and his place as national secretary taken by David Lewis, a former Rhodes Scholar and brilliant young attorney. On the death of Mr. Woodsworth, Mr. Coldwell was elected parliamentary leader and, in 1942, was chosen national president of the C. C. F. Professor Frank R. Scott, Professor of Law, another former Rhodes Scholar, succeeded Coldwell as chairman.

The party from its inception received much help in the field of research and planning from the League for Social Reconstruction, of which Messrs. Woodsworth, Coldwell, and Lewis, Professor Frank H. Underhill, Canadian historian, J. King Gordon, at one time C. C. F. vice-chairman, Theodore Joliffe, Rhodes Scholar, lawyer, and later leader of the Ontario C. C. F., were among the moving spirits. An important contribution of this group was *Social Planning for Canada.*

CHAPTER 38

Labor and Socialist Thought in Latin America

MEXICO

DURING the Díaz regime in Mexico several groups of radicals conducted an ardent, though furtive propaganda campaign against the Díaz dictatorship. The socialistic groups centered around the newspaper, *El Obrero Socialista,* with headquarters in Guadalajara and in Yucatan. With the overthrow in 1910 of Porfirio Díaz, trade-union organizations and progressive political parties could, for the first time in years, work in the open.

The Yucatan Socialist Movement. The first powerful Socialist party was that in Yucatan, the scene of the worst exploitation among the peasants in all Mexico. In 1915 General Salvador Alvarado, a general of liberal sympathies, placed himself in power in that Mexican state. Upon achieving control, he confiscated much of the land in the large estates, freed the peons, and divided the seized land among them. He likewise proceeded to organize a Socialist party throughout Yucatan.

The overwhelming percentage of peasants and workers in the state joined the party, which soon boasted a membership of 100,000. Extensive propaganda was carried out, it was said, at the expense of the government, which also paid the dues of the party members.

Obregon as President (1920–1924). After the 1916 elections under the leadership of Felipe Carillo Huerto the party was reorganized along more orthodox socialist lines. In 1919–20 Alvarado united with Obregon, Calles, and other leaders to form an anti-Carranza army, which in 1920 took possession of the capital city and established under the presidency of Obregon what was widely heralded as a "labor government." During Obregon's regime, and until 1928, the aspirations of the workers on the political field were embodied to a large extent in the Mexican Labor party under Luis Morones, Secretary of the Mexican

Confederation of Labor (the C. R. O. M.). The Labor party was regarded as the political arm of the C. R. O. M. When the C. R. O. M. disintegrated, the Labor party lost strength. Its existence in the field precluded the development of a strong Socialist party, though socialist doctrines were advocated by many trade-union and governmental leaders. In the Obregon government Morones was appointed head of the national munitions factory, and numerous labor leaders were given positions of responsibility, some as governors of Mexican states.

Alignment of Calles with Labor (1924). In 1924 President Plutarco Elias Calles aligned himself much more definitely on the side of organized labor than had his predecessor, Obregon, who had been closer to the agrarian movement. Morones became the Minister of Labor.

In the meanwhile the Mexican Communist party, formed in 1919, was active in the country. In 1924–5 it was reorganized by an American, Bertram Wolfe, then of the Communist party of the United States, and did much propaganda work among the peasants. In 1929, with the advent of "the third period" of communism, it organized the Confederacion Sindical Unitaria Mexicana.

At the opening of Congress in 1928 President Calles announced that he would not run for re-election and asked for the formation of another political organization. As a result, the National Revolutionary party, a consolidation of many local and state groups, was formed. This party controlled the government, as there was no opposition party in Mexico, as that term is understood in other countries.

Assassination of Obregon; Gil as Successor (1928). On July 1, 1928, Obregon was again elected President, but a few days later, on July 17, he was killed by a religious opponent. In September the Congress elected Portes Gil as Provisional President. Gil was opposed by Morones and the C. R. O. M. because of the censorship prevailing in his administration and his threat to suppress the unions. As a result of this opposition, labor lost control of the municipal government of the capital and of all of its states' governorships.

During the next few years, the governments, influenced largely by Calles, who had become wealthy and conservative since the 1924 election, swung further to the right.

Liberal Government under Cárdenas (1934–1940). A shift to the left occurred again during the administration of President Cárdenas. Elected as a protégé of Calles in 1934, Cárdenas surprised many by enacting a definitely progressive program. When Calles and his followers threatened a revolt against the Cárdenas administration in the summer of 1935, a large section of organized labor warned the former President that it would not countenance a movement to establish an antilabor government. During the conference called to consider the national situation, a Pact of Solidarity was signed which laid the basis for a new labor federation. The conference was followed by a demand by the President for the resignation of his cabinet. Calles thereupon announced his retirement from politics and soon after left the country. A new cabinet from which the Callistas were purged was set up and met with popular support.

Under the new cabinet, labor was given a large share in the administration of the government. The labor movement received additional prestige when the government decided to take over the railroads and the oil industry and to allow labor to participate in their management. During these days the leadership of the organized labor movement was transferred from the C. R. O. M. to the C. T. M. (the Confederación de Trabajadores Mexicanas).

In 1937 President Cárdenas proposed in a special message that the National Revolutionary party be superseded by a more popular party to include workers, farmers, and soldiers. As a result, the Party of the Mexican Revolution was organized early in 1938 and soon occupied an important place in the government.

The communists under the Cárdenas regime were legalized as a movement, and its membership increased from about 2000 in 1936 to 17,000 in 1937. In the summer of 1940, after the assassination of Leon Trotsky, President Cárdenas accused the communists of responsibility for Trotsky's murder. The Communist party replied, charging that Cárdenas was betraying the revolution, whereupon the C. T. M. countered with a vigorous defense of the Cárdenas administration. These differences were followed by the expulsion of the secretary of the Communist party from the C. T. M.

The Camacho Government (1940). With the coming of the Avila Camacho government in 1940, labor's influence in politics was again weakened, though Camacho had received the support of labor. Somewhat more conservative influences began to take the leadership in the Party of the Mexican Revolution, and Lombardo Toledano, who was working closely with the communist movement, resigned from the secretaryship of the C. T. M. Control of the railroads was taken out of the hands of the railroad unions and vested in those of the state. The unions in general followed less aggressive policies than under Cárdenas.

In the early forties a small group that called itself socialist, functioned in Mexico. Although it advocates a socialist program, it is an educational and propaganda rather than a political group, and through its paper, *Acción Social,* has directed much attention to what it regards as the dangers of communist maneuvers within the Party of the Mexican Revolution.

ARGENTINA

Formation of Branches of First International. For many years the strongest socialist movement in Latin America was that of Argentina. Argentine utopian socialism started with the return from France of Esteban Echeverria and flourished when the collapse of the European revolution of 1848 led socialistic refugees to go to that country. During the early seventies several branches of the First International were established in various cities of the republic, but were taken over in 1879 by the followers of Bakunin.

The first Marxian group in this South American nation was organized by German immigrants in 1882 and christened *Vorwaerts.* This group published a newspaper, formed co-operatives, and in 1890 sponsored the first May-Day celebration.

In the meanwhile several Spanish- and French-speaking groups sprang up, and in 1895 met in convention with the German *Vorwaerts* group, drew up a minimum program, elected an executive, and decided to co-operate in the 1896 elections. At the second convention in 1896 they launched the Socialist Labor party under the leadership of Juan B. Justo, for many years the outstanding organizer and theoretician of the movement. Eight years later, in 1904, the party elected its first representative, Alfredo Palacios, to the Chamber of Deputies. Defeated in 1908, he was re-elected four years later, together with Justo. The following year the party elected two more representatives to the Lower House and one to the Senate, and won five additional seats in 1914 in the Chamber and several in the provincial legislatures. During these prewar years, many party members were prosecuted because of their participation in strikes.

Splits in Socialist Party. During the First World War Alfredo Palacios, who was expelled from the party on the charge of breaking its ban on dueling, formed the Socialist party of Argentina in competition with the Argentine Socialist party. A second split occurred over the war in 1917, when the party congress rejected the demand of the strong pro-Ally executive committee that Argentine merchant vessels be armed. Following the adoption by the congress of a resolution in favor of absolute neutrality, a small party group broke away and formed the International Socialist party. Despite these splits, however, the party continued to gain strength, and in the elections of 1916 polled a vote of 60,000 and seated 14 representatives.

After the war the party voted down the proposal to affiliate with the Third International and joined the Labor and Socialist International. The decision led to another party split and to the formation in 1920 of the Communist party. By the mid-twenties the communist vote had increased to more than 100,000, its representation in the Lower House to 18, and in the Senate to 2, and the party controlled about half of the vote in the larger cities.

In 1927 another serious split developed in the Socialist party, the dissenters maintaining that the party was not nationalist enough. For violation of discipline, Deputy Carballo and ten other deputies were expelled from the party. Those expelled formed the Independent Socialist party. In the 1929 elections the new party obtained 49,000 votes and elected eight of their members to Parliament, and the regulars secured only 44,500 votes and elected but two representatives. The Labor and Socialist International strove to compromise the differences between the two parties, but in vain. In the elections of 1930 the I. S. P. continued its lead over the Socialist party, polling 109,000 votes and electing ten deputies, as against 83,000 for the older group and a representation of one in the Chamber.

Socialist Co-operation with Progressive Republicans against Dictatorship (1931). The year 1930 saw the overthrow in Argentina of the Irigoyen government. The Independents joined with Irigoyen's opponents in demanding his ouster. The Socialist party, on the other hand, while objecting to many of the President's acts, suspected the motives of his opponents, and took no active part in his overthrow. Following the change in government, the Socialists declared that the new government exceeded their worst expectations and vigorously opposed the new regime, but the I. S. P. gave it their co-operation. In the next year the Independents supported a Conservative for President. The Socialists, feeling that it was essential to re-establish democratic political guarantees, joined with the Progressive Democratic party in supporting a Social Democrat for President and a Socialist for Vice-President. Their candidates received 126,000 votes as against 166,000 for the Conservatives. Because of the decision of the Civic Radical party to abstain from the elections, the Socialists were able to elect 44 of their number to the Chamber and to win control of five of the country's major cities. The party membership in that year was 21,000. The Independents co-operated ever more closely with the government after the elections, several entering the cabinet, and their party soon lost its identity.

With the decision in 1936 of the Civic Radicals again to participate in the parliamentary elections, the Socialists lost their large representation, winning only in Buenos Aires. The decline caused much dissatisfaction in the party. A considerable number of members who desired a united front with the communists withdrew from the party and organized the Socialist Labor party. In 1938–39 the Socialist party underwent a thorough reorganization. Its official organ, *La Vanguardia,* was technically improved and given a wider political scope. It aimed, among other things, to make a more effective appeal to the middle class. Following the reorganization of the movement, the Socialist vote increased from 99,000 in 1938 to 135,000 in 1940. The party in the 1940 elections, however, elected only five deputies and one senator, Alfredo Palacios (who rejoined the party in 1930). Two years later, that representation was increased to 17 deputies in a Lower House of 158.

Fight against Fascism. During these years the socialists were extremely active in fighting against fascistic forces and anti-American influences in the country. Throughout its career the Socialist party has taken an active part in the organized labor movement. It has been especially influential in the political life of Buenos Aires and other large cities. The party's minimum program for several years included demands for the liberalization of the constitution; direct election of senators; separation of church and state; division of large estates; nationalization of the oil resources and their exploitation by state or by mixed state and private enterprise; reduction of sales taxes and tariffs; land values taxation; legal recognition of trade unions; minimum wages; compulsory education to 18 years; insurance against illness and unemployment; old-age pensions; political rights of women; and a disarmament pact between the countries of America.

Its chief leaders in the early forties included Drs. Nicolás Repetto, Enrique Dickmann, Mario Bravo, Alfredo L. Palacios, Americo Ghioldi, and Juan Antonio Solari.

Repression by Ramirez after Coup d'État. When the Second World War broke out, the Socialist party urged hemispheric unity and a break with the Axis, and vigorously agitated against the infiltration of fascist ideas. The party, however, received a heavy blow as a result of the *coup d'état* of General Pedro P. Ramirez, Minister of War, who, backed by the army, forced the resignation of President Ramón S. Castillo on June 4, 1943, and established a fascistic form of government. The *coup d'état* was followed by the suppression of radical papers, the arrest and imprisonment of communist leaders, and increased restrictions on socialistic and non-fascist activities.

CHILE

Socialist Beginnings. The political life of Chile as well as that of its neighbor Argentina felt the effects of the defeat of the European revolution of 1848. Among the refugees from France going to Chile was Francisco Bilbao. In 1850 Bilbao organized the *Sociedad de la Igualdad,* a society composed of workers and artisans, which met in secret to discuss citizens' rights, labor banks, industrial schools, and the reform of usury laws. It was suppressed in 1851, accused of participating in an armed uprising against President Manuel Montt. During the quarter of a century following this suppression many of its former members took part in the Radical and Liberal parties, and were active in the organization of mutual aid societies, labor schools, musical societies and similar activities.

Various groups were brought together into one organization in 1887 with the founding of the Democratic party, the first avowedly socialistic political organization in Latin America. The new party held its first convention on July 14, 1889, the hundredth anniversary of the fall of the Bastille.

During the revolution of 1891 the party was dissolved, but was soon revived. It had its first electoral success in 1894, when it sent Angel Guarello, a Valparaiso lawyer, to the Chamber of Deputies. In 1897 five socialists were elected to the Valparaiso Municipal Council, giving the party control of the city government. In 1900 a split in the Valparaiso section of the party led to the defeat of Guarello and the five councilmen, though another socialist was elected from Concepción. By 1903 the democratic bloc in the Chamber consisted of four members; by 1912, of five.

Formation of Socialist Labor Party (1912). During these years, however, despite the efforts of the left-wing leader, Luis Recabarren, the party shifted increasingly to the right. In 1912 this shift resulted in the secession of the more militant elements from the Democratic party and the formation of the Socialist Labor party. Recabarren became secretary of the new organization, which was especially popular in the northern nitrate provinces. He was elected deputy that year, but was refused a seat in the Chamber. The following year the party elected five municipal councillors, and in 1915 it held its first convention and made *La Vanguardia* its official organ. In the meanwhile the Democratic party continued its conservative trend, and in 1917 Angel Guarello accepted a post in the Conservative cabinet.

During the First World War the Socialist Labor party was active in antimilitarist and anticlerical agitation and in the building of co-operatives and trade unions. It was supported by many trade unions. In 1919 the Socialist Labor party changed its program to conform with that of the Communist International and later, on joining that organization, changed its name to the Communist party.

The Alessandri Coalition Government (1920–1924). The elections of 1920, held in the midst of an economic depression, aftermath of the First World War, signalized a new era in the life of the labor and socialist movement. In that year Arturo Alessandri Palma was elected President by a coalition of Radicals, left-wing Liberals, Democrats, and Socialists. Alessandri was elected upon a program calling for the separation of church and state, woman suffrage, income taxes, labor legislation, and government control of the nitrate industry. As he did not have the support of the Senate, however, it was difficult for him during the next four years to put into effect much of his legislative program, though enacting legislation establishing sick and accident benefits, dismissal wages, and a special labor court.

The 1924 Coup d'État. In 1924 the government of Alessandri, unable sufficiently to improve conditions, was overthrown in a *coup d'état* on the part of officers of the army, who felt that the impasse between the government and the conservatives had prevented effective parliamentary action. The new regime, in an effort to win the support of labor, initiated a considerable amount of labor legislation. Unable to obtain labor support, however, it turned to the conservative elements of Chile for backing.

Following this turn in events, the Junta of Young Officers, who had engineered the former coup, became restless, and on January 23, 1925, a successful uprising took place, led by two young officers, Colonels Marmaduke Grove and Carlos Ibáñez. This group invited Alessandri to return to the presidency and fill out the rest of his term. Meanwhile, the regime launched an extensive program of housing and education for the workers.

Ibáñez Dictatorship (1927–1931). The second Alessandri administration accomplished in a few months what it had previously been unable to do in a number of years. One of its accomplishments was the adoption of a new constitution. After its adoption, Colonel Carlos Ibáñez, Minister of War, announced his candidacy for President after an unsuccessful attempt of various forces to agree on one candidate, thus disrupting the cabinet and forcing the resignation of President Allessandri. Alarmed at the prospect of military domination most of the political forces in the country arrived at a belated agreement upon Señor Emiliano Figueroa as a joint candidate.

Figueroa was elected and began to carry out a program of fiscal and social reform. Dissension, however, broke out in the cabinet and the legislature, and, following changes in the cabinet late in 1926, Colonel Ibáñez was made the head of that body, without being deprived of his military control. This new position made it possible for him to establish a veritable dictatorship. President Figueroa thereupon resigned.

Ibáñez, in full control, brooked no opposition either from labor or from the old agrarian aristocracy, and scores of conservatives, communists and liberals were exiled during his regime. In July, 1927, an election, which confirmed Ibáñez as President, was held. Dissatisfaction with his dictatorship increased with the depression of the early thirties. He was overthrown in the summer of 1931, when a student strike developed into a general demonstration against his rule.

Conservative Juan Esteban Montero was elected President in the elections of November, 1931, and the labor movement, though still persecuted by the government, ceased being a virtually underground movement. The *Federación Obrera Chilena* and the anarcho-syndicalist groups were revived, and the Communist party carried on vigorous propaganda.

Colonel Grove about this time became the center of a group of citizens disturbed over the return of the aristocracy of Chile to power. He resolved to overthrow the Montero regime, and in order to obtain sufficient force to succeed in this endeavor made an alliance with Carlos Davila, former Ambassador to the United States.

Grove-Davila Revolt; "Socialist Republic" (1932). The Grove-Davila group staged a successful revolt in June, 1932. Following this revolt, the new Junta proclaimed a "socialist republic." The government immediately published a program which, among other things, promised the dissolution of Congress and the calling of a constituent assembly to write a socialist constitution. It urged drastic taxation of large incomes; government monopoly of such articles as oil, matches, tobacco, and iodine; public control of foodstuffs; the division of large estates which paid no taxes; reorganization and reduction of armed forces; and socialization of credit. The government took immediate steps toward fixing prices and providing unemployment relief. In addition it set up a National Socialist Economic Council, made the national bank a government institution, and prohibited the exportation of foreign currency.

The "socialist republic" received support from many workers, who held mass meetings throughout the country. Democrats and communists, however, opposed the regime, the latter charging it with being a "tool of British capital." These two groups, together with a newly formed Radical Socialist group and certain army contingents, combined to overthrow the government on June 17, 1932, twelve days after it was inaugurated. They set up a new government under the leadership of Davila, who had worked actively for the overthrow of the Grove regime, although himself a member of the Grove government.

Davila, while insisting that his administration was also a socialist regime and calling for a new constituent assembly, passed rigorous laws against "agitating the masses," and sent Grove and numerous of his supporters to a prison colony. The regime was ended 100 days after its inception by a military coup, following the withdrawal of the support of the Radical Socialists and many of the Democrats.

The Second Alessandri Regime (1932–1938). In the November, 1932, elections Alessandri, who ran as a "moderate socialist" with the backing of one wing of the Democrats, was the successful candidate. The second Alessandri regime, which was a period of rebuilding both for Chile and for the labor and socialist movements, proposed, among other things, the nationalization of such British and American-owned industries as nitrates, electric power, oil, and air transport.

In April, 1933, the progressive and socialist groups that had supported the "socialist republic" of Grove came together and organized the Socialist party of Chile. In 1934 Grove, while still in prison, polled 60,000 votes in the presidential election of that year. He was, however, defeated by Alessandri, who with the help of the conservative elements was elected for the second time, on this occasion upon a frankly conservative platform. Alessandri re-established constitutional government and improved the country's credit. Despite the government's attempt to hinder trade-union activities, the labor movement grew during Alessandri's administration, and the socialists made considerable advances in the congressional elections of 1935 and 1937. In the latter elections 15 Socialists, 6 Communists, and one Radical Socialist were elected to the Lower Chamber, composed of 146 deputies in all.

Popular Front Control (1938). The dissatisfaction with Alessandri's regime led to a growth of the "Popular Front," composed of Socialist, Communist, Radical, Democratic, and Radical Socialist party elements. The Popular Front candidates won a number of victories between 1936 and 1938, and, in the latter year, opposed Gustavo Ross, finance minister of Alessandri, as candidate for President and threw their support to the Radical party leader, Pedro Aguirre Cerda. Cerda, after a close fight, won the election. The Popular Front government, elected for a six years' term, was inaugurated on December 24, 1938, and a cabinet was formed consisting of seven Radicals, one member of the Democratic party, and three Socialists, the latter serving as Ministers of Health, of Lands and Colonization, and of National Development.

Soon after the government came to power, a disastrous earthquake further complicated the already unsettled political situation and it became necessary to combine the government's program of social reform with an earthquake rehabilitation program. A corporation of Reconstruction and Assistance was instituted, which soon set about a program of housing, emergency public works, and general rebuilding. Numerous labor laws, which were passed despite an opposition Congress, provided for wage increases and the expansion of the system of family allowances to all manual workers.

During these years the Radical party became divided between those supporting and those opposing the continuance of the Popular Front. After the expulsion of Deputy César Godoy from the party and the resignation of five Socialist deputies, the Socialists split, these men forming another party, the Workers Socialist party. Much difference of opinion was voiced over the value to the workers of the Popular Front government.

The most important schism in the Popular Front in the early years of the Cerda regime developed in the fall of 1940 over the policy pursued by the Communist party. The communists at that time—during the life of the Nazi-Soviet Pact—were bitterly opposed to closer relations with North America and launched an attack against Minister Schnake on his visit to the United States to negotiate a trade treaty. Upon his return to Chile the socialist leader launched a counter-attack against the Communists, demanding that they be excluded from the Popular Front. The Radicals were unwilling, however, to concede this demand. This refusal led to the withdrawal from the Popular Front of the Socialist forces, although the Socialist ministers continued in the cabinet.

In the March, 1941 elections the left-wing forces gained control of both the Lower House and the Senate. The communists increased their representation, under the name of the National Democratic party, to 15 deputies and 4 senators. The Socialist representation in the Lower House advanced from 10 to 15 and in the Senate from 4 to 5. The party took a leading part during these years in the fight against fascism and in promoting friendly relations with the United States.

President Aguirre Cerda retired from office on account of illness, appointing the Minister of Interior, Gerónimo Mendez, as his successor, and died fifteen days after his retirement.

Co-operation of Socialists with Ríos Government. In the February, 1942, presidential elections, the Socialists first intended to run Oscar Schnake, chairman of their party, as their candidate. The decision of the conservatives, however, to nominate the former dictator, General Carlos Ibáñez, as their presidential candidate, led the party to support Juan Antonio Ríos, the candidate of the Radical party.

Ríos was elected, and the Socialist party had again to decide whether to accept positions of responsibility in the government. Immediately after the elections the Socialists held their national convention. At this gathering the general secretary, Marmaduke Grove, secured the reaffirmation of the party's coalition policy despite the opposition of what seemed to some to be a majority against its continuance.

Again the party secured three seats in the cabinet. The coalition policy, however, led to a vigorous controversy in the party convention in early 1943, and to a contemporary division of forces. In the summer the party convention decided to withdraw their representatives from the Ríos government, but in late May, 1944, party officials agreed again to join in the formation of a left coalition cabinet to include Radical, Socialist, and Democratic parties, subject to the confirmation of the party convention. The Communist party continued to remain outside of the cabinet.

BRAZIL

Founding of Socialist Party (1916). The Brazilian socialist movement was late in developing. At the turn of the twentieth century there existed in that country several scattered socialist groups, none of which possessed any considerable strength. With the arrival in Brazil of workers from Germany and Italy, numerous branches of the movement sprang into existence, and in 1916 the Socialist party of Brazil was founded. The next year it scored numerous successes in municipal elections.

After the First World War the socialist groups for the most part went over to the Third International and became members of the Communist party. This party existed during the twenties largely as an underground movement and became in 1927 a completely illegal party.

Formation of National Liberation Alliance (1934–1935). Two years later, in 1929, a Brazilian Labor party was organized and the following year claimed a membership of 130,000. This party and an independent

Socialist party in São Paulo later took part in the work of the National Liberation Alliance, organized with a view to opposing the increasing dictatorial tendency of Getulio Vargas. This Alliance, which developed during the years 1934–35, served as a co-ordinating body for left-wing elements that were critical of the Vargas regime. It carried on campaigns against fascistic Integralistas and took part in labor and agricultural disputes. Communists played a large part in the formulation of its policies.

On July 5, 1935, the Alliance issued a manifesto which called for the suspension of the payment of foreign debts, Brazilian control of public utilities, the separation of church and state, and the enactment of social insurance, minimum-wage, and eight-hour-day legislation.

Abolition of Political Parties (1935). In the fall of 1935 the Alliance took part in a general strike against the Vargas administration. Following this strike, which was unsuccessful, the Alliance disappeared as a public force. In the late thirties all political parties were abolished, a unitary state established, and the labor movement rendered comparatively impotent.

OTHER LATIN AMERICAN COUNTRIES

The socialist and communist forces until the mid-forties were weak in the other Latin American countries, many of which would not permit labor political organizations to exist as legal entities.

In Bolivia, in the mid-forties, several parties existed which included the name socialist in their titles, but socialist activities were strictly circumscribed by the government. In Colombia, while socialist and communist groups had occasional successes at the polls during the thirties and forties—the Communist party having elected one representative to the Lower Chamber in 1943—the principal political struggle during that period was between the Liberal and Conservative parties. The Liberal party, under the presidencies of Dr. Eduardo Santos and Alfonso Lopez, received during a number of these years the support of various left-wing groups, in return for its promulgation of a liberal program of social reform.

In Peru the Apra party was organized in the twenties as a radical, anti-imperialist party, which advocated close co-operation with Indo-American countries and on the domestic front aimed at the ultimate establishment of democratic collectivism, to be attained through the union of the middle class with the workers and peasants in one organic party. For some time this party exerted a considerable influence on the trade-union movement and among the middle class. In 1931, following the overthrow of the dictatorship of Leguia in 1930, Victor Raúl Hayo de la Torre, founder and chief theoretician of the movement, ran for President against General Luis M. Sanchez Cerro, the candidate of the army and of the conservative forces. De la Torre received 106,000 votes, as compared with 155,000 for Sanchez Cerro, the winning candidate, and the Apra won 51 seats in the Chamber of Deputies out of a total of 145. For the next year or two the parliamentary group of the party constituted the government's opposition and put up a vigorous fight in the field of civil liberties.

In 1933 Cerro was assassinated. His death was followed by the persecution of Apra party members, whose leaders went abroad or in hiding, and the party for the next decade or more was not permitted to run candidates.

In Uruguay, as a result of the 1942 elections, Socialists have been represented by one deputy in the Chamber of Deputies and the Communists by two. The party throughout its career has opposed anything smacking of dictatorship and, in its foreign policy during the Second World War favored hemispheric unity.

In Cuba the Socialists in the early forties, while influential in such economic organizations as the Maritime Workers' Union, had no representation in the House of Representatives. They joined with six other parties, including the Communists in 1940, in a coalition for the election of President Batista. Constitutional government was restored with the promulgation of a new constitution. In the early forties, the socialists published *Acción Socialista.*

In Central American countries, the socialist and communist movements, either because of government suppression or because of the character of the industrial and social development of the country, showed little vitality during the first four decades of the present century.

SUMMARY OF SOCIALIST MOVEMENTS IN VARIOUS LANDS

We have seen that, in Europe, the communist movement controls the republic of Russia, which with its immense territory occupies nearly one sixth of the land area of the world. At the beginning of the Second World War Labor and Socialist parties were in power in the three Scandinavian countries—Denmark, Sweden, and Norway—and in the British dominions of Australia and New Zealand, and were either the largest or the second largest parties in Great Britain, France, Belgium, Finland, Holland, Switzerland, having at times provided the country's prime ministers in each of the first four mentioned nations.

In Austria, Germany, Czechoslovakia, Spain, and Italy the socialist movements were powerful minority movements before their respective governments succumbed to the control of the Nazi or the Fascist parties. In Hungary, Communists were in control for a short period after the First World War, but the Hungarian Soviet government was soon succeeded by the Horthy dictatorship, and the socialist influence wiped out. The communist movement during the twenties and thirties was a strong one in Germany, France, and Czechoslovakia—though weaker than the socialist movement—and bitter controversies raged between Communist and Socialist parties for many years, resulting in sharp divisions within the ranks of labor.

On the American continent, the socialist movement, while an influential educational force, had not by the mid-forties become a significant political power on a national scale. In Canada, the Co-operative Commonwealth Federation had made large gains in the elections of 1942 and 1943 and had become in some of the Canadian provinces the first or second largest party.

In Latin America the Chilean socialists and communists were active in the mid-forties in the work of the popular front government. In most of the other Latin American countries, many of them suffering under undemocratic forms of government, the movement had gained little political strength. In many cases it had to operate as an underground movement.

With the defeat of fascism a renaissance in labor political action in many nations throughout the world seems inevitable.

PART SIX

Recent Socialist Thought

CHAPTER 39

Socialist Thought after the First World War

SINCE the First World War, aside from discussing the socialist versus the communist method of arriving at a co-operative system of industry, socialists have been giving much attention to the nature of the socialist state toward which the international labor movement is directing its forces.

Webb's Picture of a Socialist Society. One of the most thorough of the attempts made to picture a co-operative commonwealth, in the light of twentieth-century developments, is found in Sidney and Beatrice Webb's *A Constitution of the Socialist Commonwealth of Great Britain.* This volume, published in 1920, was written in response to a request of the International Socialist Bureau that the constituent socialist organizations submit to the International Congress a suggested constitution for a nation desirous of organizing its life upon socialist principles.

Fundamental to socialism, according to the Webbs, is democracy, which has for its object not merely the negative one of preventing individuals or classes from exercising powers contrary to the desires of the people at large, but also "the positive one of obtaining for all the people in the fullest degree practicable, that development of personality and that enlargement of faculty and desire dependent on the assumption of responsibility and the exercise of will."

"People," declared the Webbs, "have sometimes forgotten the spiritual values of democracy. The very necessity for obtaining that consciousness of consent involves the substitution of persuasion for force; implies, therefore, that those who are superior in will power or intelligence consent to forego the use of this force to compel other men to obey them and seek to convince the average sensual man so that he too may exercise his intellect and his will. The very consciousness of being engaged in co-operative enterprise, determined on and directed by common consent, is a stronger stimulus to self-activity, imperfect though it may be, than the docility of slavery. Hence there is, in all the armory of sociology, no such effective instrument of popular education, no such potent means of calling forth the latent powers of thought and feeling in the whole mass of citizens, as popular government. . . . The problem to be solved is how to remold the social institutions that have come into existence in such a way as to evoke, in all men and women, and not merely in a favored few, all their latent powers; to stimulate the whole population and not merely the exceptionally gifted or the exceptionally energetic, to the utmost possible exercise of their faculties; and at the same time to promote, throughout the whole mass and not alone in exceptionally altruistic or exceptionally enlightened individuals, the greatest attainable development of public spirit." [1]

The nature of the socialist commonwealth advocated by the authors, for Britain, has been mentioned earlier [2] in connection with our discussion of guild socialism. Politically, Great Britain, under a socialist regime, should have a two-chamber legislative body, the Webbs maintained, not as at present, representing the lords and the commons, but one chamber, the Political Parliament, in charge of such matters as the national defense, foreign affairs, and the policing of the country, and the other, the Social Parliament, with supervision over the economic resources, health, education, transport and communication, the organization of scientific research, the encouragement of art, literature, music and the drama, and control over finances. This Parliament would, in the nature of the case, not direct the state enterprises, but would appoint numerous committees whose duty it would be to supervise various industries and to see that the general policies of these industries conformed to the public welfare.

The Webbs believed that both Parliaments should be elected, not according to occupations, but according to geographical areas. "As it is the interests of the community as a whole that the Social Parliament is to safeguard, and not those of particular occupations or particular sets of consumers—and what has to be weighed in each case are the claims of the future against the insistent demands of the present—this Assembly, like the Political Parliament, must be elected by the citizens as such, whether old or young, well or ill, active or superannuated, home-keeping wives or vocational workers." [3]

1 Webb, Sidney and Beatrice, *A Constitution for the Socialist Commonwealth of Great Britain,* pp. 100–1.

2 See text, p. 341.

3 *Ibid.,* p. 120. This view is criticized by Harold J. Laski in his *Grammar of Politics* (p. 339). Professor Laski takes the point of view that if the upper chamber

In providing a scheme for the administration of industries under socialism, the Webbs again draw attention to the fact that all industry would not be uniform. While most of the industries would be socialized, there would be a number of "unsocialized" businesses, "such as the whole range of individual production in horticulture, peasant agriculture, and artistic handicrafts; the purely personal vocations of the poet and artist; the prosecution of many minor industries and services that may be most conveniently conducted on an individual basis; possibly the experimental promotion of some new inventions and devices, not to mention the co-operative organization of religious rites and observances. . . . And it must always be remembered that socialists accept, as one form of socialization, not only local government in all its manifestations, but also the free and voluntary association of groups of consumers for the production and distribution of those commodities and services for which they feel themselves to have an exceptional need, or for which they prefer this form." [4]

Workers, technicians, and consumers should, of course, all be adequately represented in the administration of the industry. The Webbs favored compensation for industries transformed into public property, such compensation to be raised largely by taxation imposed on those who have the ability to pay. Each owner should receive in compensation the fair market value of that of which he is compulsorily dispossessed. "Whether he is paid such a sum in cash, or in government securities at their own market value, or by an equivalent annuity for a term of years, or for life, is of no pecuniary importance. . . . As the socialist commonwealth will certainly . . . levy its revenue on the citizens in proportion to their relative 'ability to pay,' the burden of compensation for expropriation will fall, in effect, almost entirely on the property owners as a class. . . . No expropriation without full compensation; no payment of annuities, or of the interest and sinking fund thereby incurred, otherwise than from the taxes on property ownership." [5]

---

agreed with the lower, there was no need of it; if it obstructed the lower, its influence would often be disastrous, for the Webbs' proposed Social Parliament, possessing as it would taxing power, would gradually draw essential control to itself, and the Political Parliament would be left as a subordinate body. Nor could foreign policy, controlled by the Political Chamber, be divorced from economic policy, controlled by the Social Parliament. Joint committees of the two parliaments would have to be formed on every vital problem, and joint sessions of the two parliaments would probably be continually called for. "The making of policy, therefore, seems to involve a single assembly, charged with the oversight of the whole field of administration."

[4] Webb, *op. cit.*, pp. 147–8.

[5] *Ibid.*, pp. 334–5.

Kautsky on Methods of Socialization. In his *Labor Revolution* (1925) Karl Kautsky also discussed, among other things, the problem of compensating capitalists for the industries transferred to public ownership.

A reasonable compensation, he declared, ought to be paid "to those who have kept their undertakings in a state of efficiency and conducted them with good, commercial success. It ought not to be paid for obsolete, neglected, and badly managed undertakings, which as a rule only keep above water by the shameless exploitation of their workers.

"By this means only will it be possible to solve the process of socializing the means of production in those spheres where it has come up as a practicable question, whilst ensuring the continuance and energetic development of production upon a capitalist basis in those spheres where the conditions of socialization do not exist. . . .

"The most suitable means of compensating the expropriated capitalists will be to allot to them state bonds, the interest of which would be equal to the total former profits of the socialized undertakings. They could also be paid in cash from the proceeds of a loan which the state would raise."

Kautsky agreed with the Webbs that the money for the property socialized should be raised from taxation of large incomes, property, and inheritances. "This method, which affects the whole class and not a few individuals," concluded Kautsky, "remains the best under all circumstances, even after socialization has commenced. . . . This would be more rational from an economic standpoint, and more just according to our moral ideas than the plundering of a few capitalists who happen to be right in our path, whereby we should seriously obstruct and jeopardize the whole economic system."

Not only could the burden of payment be lightened by taxation, but by a redemption from time to time of state bonds, and their reconversion when the rate of interest is falling. "Thus capitalist exploitation will be steadily diminished until it finally disappears." [6]

Kautsky maintained that socialization must be gradual in its nature, and that it should begin where conditions are the most favorable, for instance, with railways, mines, and various municipal services. Fortified by experiences there acquired, socialization would then gradually extend its influence to more complicated and difficult provinces.[7]

The success of a socialized industry would depend in considerable part, he argued, on competent organizers. A socialist administration,

[6] Kautsky, Karl, *The Labor Revolution,* p. 141.
[7] *Ibid.,* p. 155.

therefore, must offer these organizers advantages equal at least to those of capitalistic business. "For this reason it is impossible to give effect to the demand . . . that nobody employed in the state services should receive a salary in excess of workers' wages. This principle may be in harmony with labor sensibilities and our socialist conceptions, but it is incompatible with economic requirements, which always enforce themselves. We shall do well to recognize this fact from the start and allow it to guide our actions, instead of becoming wise after bitter experience."

On the other hand, wrote Kautsky, "in a completely socialist society, where the socialized undertakings have no longer to compete with capital, the great organizers will find no other fields of activity than the service of society. Then they will be obliged to reconcile themselves to receiving no better pay than other intellectuals. Despite this, striking achievements will not be a thing of the past either in art or in science or the sphere of organization. The inner urge, ambition, delight in power, and reputation will be sufficient incentives to such achievements.

"But this will not apply to the period of transition from capitalist to socialist production. As long as capital is in a position to produce surplus value, it will try to attract great organizers by offering them important advantages, and thereby attain to a position of superiority over all undertakings that are not able to offer equal inducements. . . . There must be no hesitation about paying extraordinary remuneration if this is the only way to secure the services of capable organizers." [8]

In addition to securing able organizers, a state industry should be made independent of the state bureaucracy and should be invested with the self-governing attributes of an industrial democracy.

"On account of the widely extended division of labor, which renders special knowledge necessary for the most efficient organization and conduct of each trade," he wrote, "it would be well to establish each trade on as independent a basis as possible, to accord it the utmost freedom of self-government, and to create proper machinery to ensure that the consumer's interest is not lost sight of. Once the whole organism is functioning properly, the central committee would only have occasion to intervene when extraordinary and far-reaching innovations were projected, or when great disturbances and conflicts arise." [9]

More specifically, Kautsky believed that, as each branch of production is transferred from capitalist to state or municipal ownership, "a new

[8] *Ibid.*, pp. 164, 179.

[9] *Ibid.*, pp. 100–1, 205–6.

organization should be created, which would enable the workers and the consumers, as well as science, to exercise the necessary influence upon the adaptation of the processes of production. . . .

"The co-operation of these three factors would produce the happiest results. If every branch of industry were abandoned to its workers alone, there would be a danger that the workers would raise wages, reduce hours of labor, diminish the volume of production, and increase the prices of their products, without troubling about the community. The essential workers would be in a position to do this the soonest. The dispensable workers would soon find there was a limit to forcing up the prices of their products. The whole process would culminate in the domination of the essential workers over those who were at least temporarily dispensable, such as a domination of coal miners over textile workers, tailors, shoemakers, and joiners, a state of affairs which would be as intolerable as capitalist exploitation.

"But if the decisions respecting any branch of industry rested with the consumers alone, we should run the risk of their striving to force down prices at all costs, even at the expense of the workers.

"If workers and consumers were combined in an association in such wise that neither section could dominate the other, they would have to endeavor to overcome their antagonism by means which would be beneficial to both.

"To discover these means is the task of the men of science, whose services would be enlisted as the third party in the organization of economy. Their duty would be to ensure that the most perfect technical appliances and organization were adopted in the undertaking, so that the greatest possible result would be obtained with the smallest expenditure of energy."

Other German and Austrian Plans for Socialization. Numerous other plans of a suggestive and valuable nature for the socialization of industry were presented to the public during the early twenties. Among those put forward were the following: that by Rudolf Wissell and Dr. Otto Neurath—the so-called Economic Scheme; that by the First Socialization Commission of Germany, a plan drafted by Professor Lederer and supported by Kautsky, Hilferding, Dr. Adolph Braun, and prominent trade-unionists; that by the Second Nationalization Commission, composed of Rathenau and others; that by Heinrich Stroebel, prominent German social democrat; and that by Dr. Otto Bauer, a leader of the Austrian socialists. In the United States interesting proposals for the nationalization of the coal industry were made by the Nationalization Research Committee of the United Mine Workers, drawn up by John Brophy, chairman, Arthur Gleason, H. S. Raushenbush, and others.[10]

Psychological Approach to Socialism. With the development of social psychology an increasing number of socialists and social reformers have given attention to the psychological factors at work in society, particularly among the workers, that lead to a more democratic industrial society. The result has been the publication of such works as Graham Wallas' *Human Nature and Politics* and *The Great Society,* John A. Hobson's *Incentives and the New Industrial Order,* Walter Lippmann's *Drift and Mastery,* Seba Eldridge's *Political Action,* John Dewey's *Human Nature and Conduct,* Pitirim Sorokin's *Sociology of Revolution,* Henri De Man's *Psychology of Socialism,*[11] David Reisman's *The Lonely Crowd,* and Erich Fromm's *The Sane Society.*

Hobson on Industrial Incentives. A valuable contribution to the study of psychological forces now operative in industry and those that may be expected under a new social order is that of John A. Hobson's *Incentives in the New Industrial Order.* In this book the British economist showed how the old incentives are breaking down and analyzed various incentives that might supersede the profit motive under public ownership. Following his survey of the situation, Hobson concluded:

"While nothing can be more certain than that the old arrangements of incentives to efficient industry will no longer work, and need to be replaced by new ones, it is equally certain that the psychology of this reform must be adapted to the special technical and human conditions of the several industries, and the types of business in each industry, with close regard to the racial and other natural and educated characters of the employes. Finally, the pace and extent to which reformed industrial methods are capable of application will largely depend upon the education of the general body of citizen-consumers and their willingness to give serious attention to the central processes of industrial government through an intelligently ordered state." [12]

In a later book, *Free Thought in the Social Sciences,* he especially emphasized the waste of incentives under the present system.

[10] See R. Wissell, *Kritik und Auflau,* Berlin, 1921; Neurath, *Wesen und Weg Zur Sozialisierung,* Munich, 1919; Heinrich Stroebel, *Socialization in Theory and Practice,* London: King and Son: Otto Bauer, *Weg zum Sozialismus* (1919); Nationalization Research Committee of the U. M. W., *How to Run Coal* (1922); H. S. Raushenbush, *The Anthacite Question* (N. Y.: H. W. Wilson, 1924).

[11] De Man, Henri, *Psychology of Socialism* (N. Y.: Holt, 1928).

[12] Hobson, John A., *Incentives and the New Industrial Order* (N. Y.: Seltzer, 1922), pp. 159–60. See also Dell, Robert, *Socialism and Personal Liberty* (N. Y.: Seltzer, 1922), esp. ch. VIII; Keynes, J. M., *Laissez-Faire and Communism* (N. Y.: New Republic, 1926), pp. 103 ff.

"I hold," he declares, "that the true labor case lies, not in an insistence that labor is the sole source of wealth, still less in the narrow meaning of labor which excludes or disparages brain work, but in a clear, informed insistence upon the wasteful application of the incentives applied to evoke all the best physical and intellectual powers of production in their right proportions and combinations. This wasteful application of incentives arises from the unsatisfactory conditions of the 'markets' in which the various requisites of production are bought and sold, that is to say, in the bad conditions for the distribution of the economic product in the form of income. This, in its turn, is due to an inequality of bargaining power, which gives an unfair advantage at each stage to the buyer or the seller, resulting in a trebly wasteful apportionment of income. Those who get more than suffices to evoke the best use of their ability, labor, land, or other productive instrument they sell, tend to employ that 'surplus' wastefully, either in setting productive power to make luxuries for their consumption, or in enabling themselves to consume their share of work to the common stock, or else in selling productive power to make increased instruments of production in excess of possible demand. Those who get less than is required to support and evoke their best use of their labor, or other productive instrument, are thereby rendered less efficient producers. These two wastes of overpayment and underpayment are evidently the convex and the concave of the same fact. But this realization of the true origin and nature of 'waste' in our economic system involves a complicated analysis of many different sorts of bargain and is not easily accommodated to the needs of an inspiring myth." [13]

Hillquit on Waste. Hobson is not the only socialistic writer who emphasized waste, rather more than exploitation, during the years after the First World War, as an outstanding evil of capitalism. Thus the American Socialist, Morris Hillquit, maintained:

"The chief aim of the socialists, in fashioning the new social order, is not so much concerned with the re-distribution of wealth as with the elimination of the wastes of the present system.

"We object to the present inequitable distribution of wealth, but we are even more concerned with the anarchy of production that exists today. We know that the capitalist class does not take more than one-third of the total product. We know, also, that it does not itself consume this one third. It goes back into industry. If the workers were to receive 20 per cent more of the product than they receive today, there would not result any radical revolution in our present system. The

[13] Hobson, *Free Thought in the Social Sciences* (N. Y.: Macmillan, 1926), pp. 149–50.

ideal social order is primarily a system planfully, scientifically organized, without the wastes of today—the wastes of unemployment, of the middlemen, etc.

"The difference in systems would be primarily an increased productivity, followed by an equitable distribution of this increased product. There would then follow some very radical changes. While it is true that the ruling class does not itself consume the great wealth produced, it is nevertheless true that the possession and manipulation of this wealth by a ruling class undermines the foundation of the nation politically, morally and otherwise.

"Through this increase of wealth and its equitable distribution, we envisage a state of society in which political power, the arts, the sciences, and the general culture will also be heightened and diffused. Democracy will be diffused. To the masses will be brought for the first time the enjoyment of the benefits of modern civilization." [14]

This side of the socialist indictment was also emphasized during the twenties and thirties by Chase, Webb, Veblen, Chiozza-Money, the Committee of the British Labor party, and others.[15]

Tawney on the Functional Society. Following the First World War, R. H. Tawney attacked the social problem from another angle, that of function. Tawney vigorously criticized the present order on the ground that, under it, rewards and responsibility bore little relation to the function performed in industry.

"The first principle," declared Tawney, "is that industry should be subordinated to the community in such a way as to render the best service technically possible, that those who render that service faithfully should be honorably paid, and that those who render no service should not be paid at all, because it is of the essence of a function that it should find its meaning in the satisfaction, not of itself, but of the end which it serves. The second is that its direction and government should be in the hands of persons who are responsible to those who are directed and governed, because it is the condition of economic freedom that men should not be ruled by an authority which they cannot control. The industrial problem, in fact, is a problem of right, not merely of material misery, and because it is a problem of right it is most acute

[14] Bulletin, *League for Industrial Democracy,* May, 1926, p. 10.

[15] See Stuart Chase, *The Tragedy of Waste* (N. Y.: Macmillan, 1925); Sidney and Beatrice Webb, *The Decay of Capitalist Civilization* (N. Y.: Harcourt, Brace, 1923); Thorstein Veblen, *The Engineer and the Price System* (N. Y.: Huebsch, 1921); Laidler, *Socialism in Thought and Action* (N. Y.: Macmillan, 1920), ch. I; Federated Engineering Societies, *Waste in Industry* (N. Y.: McGraw-Hill, 1921); *The Waste of Capitalism* (London: National Joint Pub. Dept., 1924). A book written on this subject during the forties is John Putnam, *The Modern Case for Socialism* (Boston: Meador, 1943).

among those sections of the working classes whose material misery is least. It is a question, first of function, and secondly of freedom."[16]

"Today," he declared, "the enjoyment of property and the direction of industry are considered . . . to require no justification, because they are regarded as rights which stand by their own virtue, not functions to be judged by the success with which they contribute to a social purpose.

"What gives its special quality and character, its toughness and cohesion, to the industrial system built up in the last century and a half . . . is the doctrine that economic rights are anterior to, and independent of, economic functions, that they stand by their own virtue, and need adduce no higher credentials. The practical result of it is that economic rights remain, whether economic functions are performed or not. They remain today in a more menacing form than in the age of early industrialism, for those who control industry no longer compete but combine, and the rivalry between property in capital and property in land has long since ended.

"The basis of the New Conservatism appears to be a determination so to organize society, both by political and economic action, as to make it secure against every attempt to extinguish payments which are made, not for service, but because the owners possess a right to extract income from it. . . ."[17]

Tawney therefore urges that humanity reach forward to a functional society, that is, a society which aims at making the acquisitions of wealth contingent upon the discharge of social obligations, which seeks to proportion remuneration to service and denies it to those by whom no service is performed, which inquired first, not what men possess, but what they can make or create or achieve.[18]

Tawney took the older economists to task for failing to observe what incentives actually motivate mankind, and for assuming that fear of starvation, on the one hand, and profits, on the other, are the incentives that must be relied upon to gain the best results.[19]

[16] Tawney, R. H., *The Acquisitive Society* (London: Bell, 1924), pp. 7–8; also (N. Y.: Harcourt, Brace, 1924).

[17] *Ibid.*, pp. 27, 30–1.

[18] *Ibid.*, pp. 31–2. See also Joad, C. E. M., *Introduction to Modern Political Theory* (N. Y.: Oxford Univ. Press), esp. ch. VI.

[19] With the development of the great corporation, socialists and others are commenting to an increasing extent on the fact that the inactive stockholder has little if anything to do with management, and that the actual managers may or may not have any share in the ownership of industry; may, indeed, be uninfluenced by the profit incentive in the old sense in which this has been used. Thus, following an address by George Soule, an editor of the *New Republic,* on "Changing Relations between Property Ownership and Control," the Conference of the League for Industrial Democracy in June, 1926, resolved:

Wealth and Welfare. William A. Robson, a well-known Fabian socialist, in the period following the First World War, questioned the social efficiency of a system which leads to great economic inequalities, on the ground that, after an individual or a society receives a certain income, further increments to that income bear no necessary relation to increments in welfare. He also called into question the belief that a nation's real wealth can be calculated in monetary terms.

"Monetary wealth," declared Robson, "is a most inadequate index of wealth, since it not only ignores all moral or ethical values in reference to that wealth, but excludes from consideration all manner of things, such as, for example, the aesthetic sense, climatic conditions, etc., social harmony, the intellectual atmosphere, and so forth which may have but little relation to an ability to afford clothes of the best wool, or to satisfy carnivorous instincts three times a day. As Mr. Graham Wallas has said, 'two types of industrial organization might . . . be equally efficient in the production of wealth and yet life under one might be happy and under another unhappy.' "[20]

It is therefore necessary, concluded the author, to think of material well-being in terms of non-monetary individual welfare, actual and potential, of large numbers of men, women and children, if we are to move forward to the highest human destiny.

Veblen on Financiers versus Engineers. During these years certain socialistic economists in America developed the thesis that the financiers who were exercising a potent control over the system were throwing many obstacles in the path of the industrial engineers who were attempting to place industry on a more scientific basis. Thorstein Veblen thus put the case:

"Business enterprise may fairly be said to have shifted from the foot-

---

"Whereas, One of the fundamental justifications of profit and private enterprise has been that the owner of a business, who risks loss and seeks profit, is responsible for management, and thus is led to seek industrial expansion and efficient operation, with their benefits to society, and

"Whereas, It is neither possible nor desirable to restore control over management to millions of absentee owners . . .

"Resolved, That it is of great importance to recognize this fact in economic theory, popular discussion and public policy, and to inquire what other incentives can or do influence management."

20 See Wm. A. Robson, *The Relation of Wealth to Welfare* (N. Y.: Macmillan, 1925), p. 165. Also Roy Jenkins, "Equality," *New Fabian Essays* (London: Turnstile Press, 1952), pp. 69–91; John Wilson, *Equality* (London: Hutchinson, 1966).

20 See Robson, William A., *The Relation of Wealth to Welfare* (N. Y.: Macmillan, 1925), p. 165.

ing of free-swung competitive production to that of a 'conscientious withholding of efficiency,'" at least in large scale industry.

The modern financiers "are experts in prices and profits and financial manoeuvres; and yet the final discretion in all questions of industrial policy continues to rest in their hands. They are by training and interest captains of finance; and yet, with no competent grasp of the industrial arts, they continue to exercise a discretion as captains of industry. They are unremittingly engaged in a routine of acquisition, in which they habitually reach their ends by a shrewd restriction of output, and yet they continue to be entrusted with the community's industrial welfare, which calls for maximum production. . . .

"So it happens that the industrial system is deliberately handicapped with dissension, misdirection, and unemployment of material resources, equipment, and manpower, at every turn where the statesmen or the captains of finance can touch its mechanism; and all the civilized peoples are suffering privation together because their general staff of industrial experts are in this way required to take orders and submit to sabotage at the hands of the statesmen and the vested interests." [21]

Veblen urged the industrial engineers to organize to put an end to this domination, form a soviet of technicians, unite with labor, and assist in the great social change.[22]

Thomas on International Organization. Socialists have, since the First World War, increasingly realized that any scheme of socialization must, if not immediately, then ultimately, be considered in terms of a world, rather than a mere national, economy.

"These plans," declared Norman Thomas, socialist leader, in dealing with the problem of social ownership, "will doubtless begin with national boundaries—indeed they have begun—but unless they are backed up by a genuine internationalism of labor, and of consumers' co-operation, and are accompanied by a development of international machinery for the more equitable allocation of raw materials they will not solve the problems of social peace and well-being." [23]

[21] Veblen, Thorstein, *Engineers and the Price System,* pp. 36–8, 40–1, 54–5.

[22] See also Ward, Harry F., *The Profit Motive* (N. Y.: League of Industrial Democracy, 1924). For an engineers' point of view regarding methods of making socialism efficient, see MacKaye, James, *Americanized Socialism* (N. Y.: Boni and Liveright, 1918). See also Veblen, Thorstein, *The Theory of Business Enterprise* (N. Y.: Scribner's, 1912). Veblen, Thorstein, *The Instincts of Workmanship, Absentee Ownership,* etc. One of the most comprehensive attacks on the present order made since the First World War is *The Decay of Capitalist Civilization,* by Sidney and Beatrice Webb (N. Y.: Harcourt, Brace, 1923).

[23] Thomas, Norman, *What Is Industrial Democracy?* (N. Y.: League for Industrial Democracy, 1925), p. 54; see also Thomas' *What is Our Destiny?* (1944); Nearing, Scott,

Other Contributions to Socialist Thought. Finally socialists in the twenties began to evaluate the newer findings of educators, biologists, and anthropologists, as well as psychologists, in terms of the principles underlying the socialist movement and gave increasing attention to actual experiments in industrial democracy in the workshops and their effect on human motivation.[24]

The Next Step, 1922 (Ridgewood, N. J.: The Author); Russell, Bertrand, *Prospects of an Industrial Civilization.*

[24] See Dorsey, George A., *Why We Behave Like Human Beings* (N. Y.: Harper, 1926); Dewey, John, *Human Nature and Conduct;* Hocking, *Human Nature and Its Remaking;* Douglas, Paul H., *The Columbia Conserve Co.* (Indianapolis, Columbia Conserve Co., 1926); Myers, James, *Representative Government in Industry* (N. Y.: Doran, 1924); also publications of Russell Sage Foundation.

CHAPTER 40

Recent Programs for Reconstruction and a Socialized Society

PROBLEMS OF A SOCIALIZED ORDER

Price Fixing in a Socialist Society. During the thirties and forties various other trends have been noted in socialist thought and action. In the field of theory, besides the continuous discussion of the soundness of the Marxian theory of value and the theory of dialectical materialism, a battle royal has waged over the question as to whether a socialist society is practical from an economic standpoint; particularly, whether it would be possible under socialism to maintain a price system that would actually work.

Prior to the First World War, little thought was given to the economics of the socialist state. Even during the thirties it was possible for Professor Lippincott to declare that while "writers on history, sociology, and political science, like the Webbs, Tawney, and Laski, have done admirable work in constructing institutions for a socialist state, they have not pressed for an inquiry into the economics of such a state, even though the economics might vitally affect what they have constructed. They have not sufficiently considered the economic conditions that must be satisfied if a socialist state is to equal or to improve upon the standard of life provided by capitalism." [1]

Socialist writers, continued Dr. Lippincott, are not alone in this neglect. Orthodox economists with few exceptions have failed to consider whether their main theories would apply to socialist institutions equally with those of the capitalist structure. One of the main exceptions among the orthodox economists was Professor Ludwig von Mises, a Viennese economist, who asserted in 1920 that economic calculation is not possible in a socialist economy. Commodity prices, he declared, can be correctly arrived at only through the processes of competition

[1] Benjamin E. Lippincott, Editor, *On the Economic Theory of Socialism,* p. 4.

in the free market. There would be no such market under a socialistic system where the state owned the means of production and distribution. Without a workable price system the socialist economy would necessarily bog down.[2] Von Hayek and various other economists agreed with von Mises regarding the extreme difficulty or the impossibility of a sound price system under socialism.[3]

The essays of von Mises, von Hayek, and others led to a vigorous controversy among economists. Enrico Barone, entering the field of conflict, maintained that the accounting prices of a socialist economy would be as economically significant as the market prices of a competitive economy and that it would be possible for a socialist economy to provide for a rational allocation of resources.[4]

American Economists on Price System under Socialism. In the United States, leading economists have expressed their agreement with Barone. In his presidential address in 1928 before the American Economic Association, Professor Frederick M. Taylor, of the University of Michigan, declared that, in his opinion, there would be little difficulty in the way of a sound and sensible price system under socialism.[5]

Under a co-operative system, he asserted, the decisions as to what commodities would be produced would in fact be essentially the same as under a competitive economy. If a sound system of price fixing were to be arrived at in a co-operative economy, however, Professor Taylor maintained, certain procedures should be followed.

(1) A citizen under a co-operative system should be assured of an income upon condition that certain obligations fixed by the state had been fulfilled.

(2) An attempt should be made by the authorities to fix incomes on a socially sound basis.

(3) The citizen should have before his mind just what price he would be obliged to pay for the commodity he desires.

(4) In fixing the selling price of any particular commodity, the economic authorities would set that price at a point which fully covered the cost of producing said commodity.

(5) The citizen should be empowered to spend his income as he chose in buying commodities produced by the state—"a procedure which

2 F. A. von Hayek, editor, *Collectivist Economic Planning.* Essay by von Mises. See also von Mises' *Socialism* (1936).

3 Von Hayek admitted that it is theoretically possible to have a rational allocation of resources in a socialist state, but denied that it can be worked out practically.

4 See "Ministry of Production in a Collective Society," in *Collectivist Economic Planning,* by F. A. von Hayek, editor.

5 *American Economic Review,* Vol. 19, N. I., March, 1929. See also Lippincott, *op. cit.,* p. 42.

would virtually authorize the citizen to dictate just what commodities the economic authorities of the state should produce."

In arriving at the prices to be charged, the authorities, Professor Taylor continued, should discover the cost of the primary factors in the production of the commodity. They should multiply the valuation of each factor used in producing a commodity by the quantity of the factor so used and should add together these different products. If, after evaluating a certain factor, they found that some valuations appeared incorrect, they should then make the needed corrections in the factor tables.[6] A too high valuation would cause the stock of that factor to show a surplus at the end of the production period. If the valuation, on the other hand, appeared to be too low, there would be a deficit in the stock of that factor. "I find myself disposed to affirm rather dogmatically," concluded Professor Taylor, "that, if the economic authorities of a socialist state would recognize equality between cost of production, on the one hand, and the demand price of the buyer, on the other, as being the adequate and the only adequate proof that the commodity in question ought to be produced, they could, under all ordinary conditions, perform their duties as the persons who were immediately responsible for the guidance of production, with well-founded confidence that they would never make any other than the right use of the economic resources placed at their disposal." [7]

Professor Oscar Lange of the University of Chicago has joined Professor Taylor in his conviction regarding the practicability of the pricing process in a co-operative commonwealth. The "right" prices, he maintains, can be found through a process of trial and error, as in a capitalistic economy, and the prices of final consumption goods can be fixed through the operation of free consumers' choices, as in other systems. The pricing processes can, in fact, he contends, be made less complex and better adapted to desirable social ends than under a system of private ownership.[8]

In a later work Professor Joseph A. Schumpeter of Harvard Univer-

[6] H. D. Dickinson in his *Economics of Socialism* (pp. 194 ff.) in dealing with the correction in prices in a socialist society, declares, among other things: "Owing to variations in consumers' demand, goods may command a higher or lower price in the market than that accounted for in the plan. Some things may be all the rage, and the price will have to be raised in order to prevent their being sold out before new stock can be got ready, other things may have to be sold at a big reduction, in order to clear warehouse and shop space for other more urgently desired commodities. Price changes of this sort may be expected to cancel each other out, but there may be, at a given time, an appreciable balance one way or the other."

[7] Lippincott, *op. cit.*, p. 54.

[8] See Lippincott, *op. cit.*, essay by Oscar Lange.

sity has expressed his agreement with Professor Lange in his contention that such problems of a socialist management as pricing and production would be more easily solved than are those confronting capitalistic management. Following a detailed explanation of the manner in which a central board and the managements of particular industries under socialism might co-operate in the pricing process, Professor Schumpeter declares: "One of the most important difficulties of running a business [under capitalism]—the difficulties which absorb most of the energy of a successful business leader—consists in the uncertainties surrounding every decision. A very important class of these consists in turn in the uncertainties about the reaction of one's actual and potential competitors and about how general business situations are going to shape. Although other classes of uncertainties would undoubtedly persist in a socialist commonwealth, these two can reasonably be expected to vanish almost completely. The management of socialized industries and plants would be in a position to know exactly what the other fellow proposes to do and nothing would prevent them from getting together for concerted action. The central board could, and, to a certain extent, unavoidably would, act as a clearing house of information and as a co-ordinator of decisions—at least as much as an all-embracing cartel bureau would. This would immensely reduce the amount of work to be done in the workshops of managerial brains, and much less intelligence would be necessary to run such a system than is required to steer a concern of any importance through the waves and breakers of a capitalist sea." [9]

Practically all modern socialist writers agree with Professors Taylor, Lange, and Schumpeter that there must be freedom of consumer choice under a co-operative system if that system is to be both workable and truly democratic. "Over by far the greater part of the field of production," declares G. D. H. Cole, the British socialist economist, "the task of a planned economy will not be to dictate what is to be consumed, but to respond to the movements of consumers' demand. It will be for the consumers, and not for the planners, to express a preference for more gramophones as against more cigarettes, more commodious houses as against more motor cars, more mutton as against more bacon —in fact, more of any one thing as against everything else. . . . The planning authority will be endeavoring to anticipate correctly how much will be demanded at the prices at which it is proposed to sell,

[9] Joseph A. Schumpeter, *Capitalism, Socialism, and Democracy,* p. 186. See also A. P. Lerner in *Economic Journal,* September, 1937; Barbara Wootton, *Plan or No Plan;* Seba Eldridge, *New Social Horizons,* ch. IX; H. D. Dickinson, *Economics of Socialism,* ch. VIII.

and at producing just the quantity needed to satisfy the demand. If it proves to have overestimated the demand, it will have either to reduce its prices so as to clear its remaining stock, or, in the case of non-perishable goods, to hold the balance over and reduce its output to the desired extent in the next period of production. If the demand has been underestimated, either prices will have to be raised or, more probably, some people will have to manage with less than they would have been prepared to buy until there has been time to increase the supply." [10]

Extent of Socialization in a Co-operative Society. In the thirties and early forties, discussion continued in socialist circles as to what industries were ripe for socialization and what industries and services, at least for many years after the advent of a co-operative system, could safely be left to private ownership.

In its 1940 platform the Socialist party of the United States first gave definite content to the word socialization as they used it and then proceeded with their statement of conditions under which industry should be socialized. "Socialization," the party declared, "is social ownership and democratic control of industry, substituting the principles of public service or of social usefulness for the principle of private profit and preserving workers' free choice of occupation, consumers' free choice of goods, and freedom of association for all functional groups."

The party maintained that "wherever private exploitation of a limited natural resource is highly wasteful, as in the oil, coal, and timber industries, there socialization is required, in the interest of this as well as future generations.

"Wherever concentration of financial power leads to the restriction of the expansive forces of our economy, as in insurance and investment banking, we propose socialization.

"Wherever private monopoly, in the drive for monopoly profit, restricts production to less than is justified by the social usefulness of the product, as in the steel and cement industries, the principle of socialization should be applied.

"Wherever concentration of economic power creates a political interest which is too powerful for a democracy to tolerate in private hands, we would put this power in public hands.

"Wherever natural monopoly has consumers at its mercy, as in the aluminum industry, socialization is both practical and necessary.

[10] G. D. H. Cole, *Economic Planning,* p. 253. See also Sir William H. Beveridge, *Planning Under Socialism,* p. 13, in which the author declares that socialists would "seek to preserve, to the fullest possible extent, the freedom of the consumer in choosing how to spend his income."

"Wherever, as in the railroads, private operation cannot or will not undertake socially needed investment, socialization becomes the order of the day.

"Wherever, as in many large-scale corporations, ownership has lost its management function and the business is managed by hired men, these managers should be working for the public instead of for private owners.

"Wherever one or more of these conditions exist, it means that the private-profit principle is destroying the very basis of living; that business must be taken over by the public. This is a program of immediate socialization."

Similar analyses of what constitutes the socialization of industry and of what industries should be socialized appeared in the socialist literature of that period. In all that literature, a distinct place was left in socialized society for voluntary co-operatives and private industry under public regulation.[11]

[11] See Norman Thomas, *We Have A Future,* pp. 151–6, for an elaboration of the Socialist party statement. In reference to the continuance of private industry under socialism, Mr. Thomas declared (p. 156): "We contemplate a large area of action in which, subject to regulations in the interest of the workers, both as producers and consumers, private ownership and management may be effective, and profiteering prevented by the right sort of taxation, and the preservation of a genuine competition. Even in this field it may be necessary for the government to set up yardstick enterprises occasionally, as a check to what is going on. And if private enterprise is as slow as it has been these last years in undertaking new enterprises, it will be necessary to establish public corporations to do what private owners cannot or will not do. Already in the field of housing it has become a certainty that only public corporations can produce low-cost housing." See also Lewis Corey, *The Unfinished Task,* p. 133; Oscar Lange in Benjamin Lippincott, Editor, *On the Economy Theory of Socialism.* Professor Lange in this study differed from many in declaring that when socialists were placed in a position to carry out a program of socialization, their program should be achieved "at one stroke of the pen." He declared, however, that "absolute security of property and enterprise" should be given to those industries that were going to remain in private hands. In small-scale industry and farming "private enterprise may well continue to have a useful social function by being more efficient than a socialized industry may be" (pp. 120, 124, 125). Others urged the great extension of voluntary co-operation in agriculture, retail distribution, etc. See Laidler, *Socializing Our Democracy,* ch. VIII. Mr. Durbin, in his *Politics and Democratic Socialism,* contends that if we are to arrive at socialism peacefully and democratically, ameliorative measures should be placed after, not before the socialization of industry. The program of socialization should neither be so extreme that it drives the opposition to armed resistance or so emasculated that it fails to retain the active and loyal support of the reforming democratic party that is asked to advocate it (pp. 283, 298).

In Canada, M. J. Coldwell, leader of the Co-operative Commonwealth Federation in the Canadian Parliament, in defining the socialist aims of his party, declared: "The C. C. F. does not believe that everything should be owned and operated by the state. Indeed we distinguish clearly between two kinds of property: that upon which the life and general welfare of the community depends and which ought to

Democratic Techniques and Socialism. The rise of fascism in Europe and the continuance of the dictatorship in Russia also led many socialists during the thirties to give increasing attention to the techniques of democracy under a collectivist regime. While the socialist movement in general had for many years maintained that collectivism without democracy was a far cry from socialism, that there could be no socialism without the accompaniment of thorough-going democratic procedures in the economic, political, and social institutions of the country, there were many who took the position prior to the thirties that all that it was necessary to do was to transfer industry from private to public ownership and democracy would take care of itself. Experiments in state ownership and control in communist and fascist countries and even in lands with a democratic form of government, in times of peace and in times of war, proved a rude awakener to these students of the movement and caused large numbers within and without the socialist movement to think through ways and means of safeguarding and strengthening democratic processes under a co-operative system of industry. This examination caused them to lay increasing emphasis on:

1. The need for preserving and strengthening such democratic forces of the population as the trade- and industrial-union movement, the consumers' and producers' co-operatives, labor, socialist, and progressive political parties, and educational and cultural movements of the masses, and for endeavoring to make these movements thoroughly democratic.

2. The need for bringing about a close co-operation among industrial workers, the so-called middle class, and the farming population, in the struggle for better social arrangements.

3. The need for applying effective democratic techniques to local, state, and federal governments so as to make them thoroughly responsive to the will of the people.

4. The need for encouraging, under a co-operative system of industry, an extensive system of voluntary co-operative enterprises, as a supplement to publicly owned industries, especially in agriculture, the distributive trades, and in cultural activity.

---

be socially owned, and that which ministers to the welfare of the individual or family and does not interfere with the general economic plan, which ought to be individually owned. Thus we say that banks, investment trusts, nation-wide monopolistic enterprises, like oil, packing plants, and transportation, should be nationally owned, while others like telephone and hydro-electric power might be provincially owned. Others again ought to be municipal enterprises, while many industries and distributive services should be co-operatively owned. Thus it is that there are fields where private enterprise could perform a useful function. . . . We do not intend to socialize merely for the sake of socializing, but in order to secure efficiency and the greater satisfaction of social needs" (Coldwell, *Canadian Progress on the March,* League for Industrial Democracy Pamphlet).

5. The need for the establishment within each industry of procedures whereby consumer, worker, and technical and administrative groups would be adequately represented in the determination of policies.

6. The need for experimenting with the corporate form of public ownership of a semi-autonomous character, and of decentralizing the control and administration of public ownership as much as seemed compatible with social efficiency.

7. The need for developing administrative procedures directed toward efficient, honest, and democratic administration through sound systems of civil service, public accounting, collective bargaining, personnel relations, etc. Techniques should be devised for stimulating industrial incentives through a proper system of rewards for work well done.

8. The need for freedom of consumer choice.

9. The necessity of preserving civil liberties and preventing discriminatory practices against any portion of the population because of race, religion, color, or national origin.

10. The need for co-operating with other countries with a view of eliminating the causes of war, of abolishing imperialistic controls, and of raising living standards throughout the world.[12]

Social Planning and Freedom. The question of whether the type of social planning which democratic socialists aim to achieve is consistent with freedom has in recent years likewise occupied the thought of many progressive thinkers. Socialist writers of the type of Professor Laski, while acknowledging that such a planned society will inhibit certain kinds of liberty of action now enjoyed by members of the owning group, such as freedom to exploit the nation's workers, nevertheless contend that it will liberate men and women from the fear of insecurity and want, and "will enable men to think of the positive ends to which freedom can be devoted."[13] "And only," adds Professor Laski, "at the point where a positive freedom, in this sense, is possible can society provide with safety to itself for the expression of the whole individuality

[12] H. W. Laidler, *Socializing Our Democracy*, esp. chs. VII, VIII, IX, X, XIV; Lewis Corey, *Our Unfinished Task;* Alfred M. Bingham, *The Techniques of Democracy;* G. D. H. Cole, *The Simple Case for Socialism;* Ordway Tead, *New Adventures in Democracy;* Irving H. Flamm, *An Economic Program for a Living Democracy;* Wilbur C. Phillips, *Adventuring for Democracy;* Clinton Golden and Harold Ruttenberg, *The Dynamics of Industrial Democracy;* Eduard Heimann, *Communism, Fascism, or Democracy?* chs. III, VI; Charles E. Merriam, *On the Agenda of Democracy;* Arthur N. Holcombe, *The Middle Classes in American Politics;* Harold J. Laski, *Democracy in Crisis;* Seba Eldridge, *New Social Horizons,* ch. XII; George S. Counts, *Prospects of American Democracy;* Marshall E. Dimock, *British Public Utilities and National Development;* Terrence H. O'Brien, *British Experiments in Public Ownership and Control;* Max Ascoli and Fritz Lehmann, *Political and Economic Democracy.*

[13] Laski, *Reflections on the Revolution of Our Time,* p. 401.

of man. Until arrival at that point becomes a conscious, social purpose, which men are deliberately setting themselves, this expression is always purchased by some at the expense of others. Athenian democracy demands its slaves; the riches of the Roman aristocracy are built on the plundering of its conquered provinces; the luxury of the American millionaire does not, even when he has reached the level where convention demands philanthropy, conceal the broken lives of the steel worker in Pittsburgh or textile operative in Lowell. Fear is the price that freedom pays whenever its relations depend upon the security which private ownership is alone able to confer." Professor Laski, in comparing the present governments in capitalist democracies with the political structure under a socialist society, likewise maintains that freedom will be far better served under a socialist government than at present.[14]

An Economy of Abundance. The thirties and early forties likewise led many students of socialism and social change to contrast the poverty and insecurity of depression years with the possibilities of security and abundance if only our productive machinery and our human and material resources were fully utilized for the common good, and to enlarge upon these possibilities in a socialized order.[15]

At the May, 1944, Conference of the International Labor Organization, the delegates present adopted a charter, referred to as the Philadelphia Charter, which declared, among other things, that "poverty anywhere constitutes a danger to prosperity everywhere," and urged the carrying on of the war against want with unrelenting vigor.

The platforms of the Socialist party, the newly formed Liberal party,

[14] *Ibid.*, p. 407. See also George Soule in *The Future of Liberty*.

[15] See Stuart Chase, *The Economy of Abundance*. Mr. Chase contended that in the early nineteen thirties we had forty times the physical energy per capita at our disposal that the country had a hundred years before, a condition which has laid the technological foundation for the production of an abundance of material goods for the entire population (ch. I). See also Report of the Columbia University Commission, *Economic Reconstruction;* C. M. Hattersley, *This Age of Plenty;* Fred Henderson, *The Economic Consequences of Power Production;* J. A. Hobson, *Poverty in Plenty;* Ralph E. Flanders, *Taming Our Machines;* Maurice Levin and Others, *America's Capacity to Produce;* Harold Loeb and Associates, *The Chart of Plenty;* Ezekiel Mordecai, *"2500 a Year,"* and *Jobs for All;* Walter N. Polakov, *The Power Age;* The President's Research Committee, *Recent Economic Trends;* Harold Rugg, *The Great Technology;* Frederick Soddy, *Wealth, Virtual Wealth, and Debt.* These writers expressed their agreement with Dexter S. Kimball, Dean of the School of Engineering, Cornell University, that "never before has the human race made such progress in solving the problem of production. If poverty and industrial distress still exist, it is because of our inability to keep our industrial machine in operation and to distribute equitably the resulting products" (*Recent Economic Changes,* p. 82). There were numerous studies of the increase in productivity during this period, including that of Professor Frederic C. Mills, in *Economic Tendencies,* those of the W. P. A.; of Robert R. Nathan, in *Mobilizing for Abundance,* etc.

and the American Labor party in 1944 emphasized the fact that technological changes had made possible the inauguration of an age of plenty.

The Technocrats. Some of the writers of the depression era of the thirties confined their attention chiefly to an analysis of increasing productivity, while others laid down conditions under which, in their opinion, an economy of abundance could be attained. A school of thought which for a while attracted a good deal of attention was known as the Technocrats, led by Howard Scott. Scott and his associates maintained that if technicians, rather than financiers, ran the industrial system, then dangerously beset by a rising debt structure and increased unemployment, the average worker would need to work only a few hours a day to produce a standard of living several times as high as the average in 1929. The price system, they maintained, must go, and in its place a plan must be devised for trading goods and services on the basis of an energy determinant, possibly non-transferable tickets indicating the energy expended.[16]

The "Managerial Revolution." While Howard Scott and his followers maintained that the technicians should take the place of financiers and industrialists as the future ruling class, Professor James Burnham of the Department of Philosophy of New York University contended in the early forties that the managerial class, the class that makes the important decisions in the running of the industrial machine, would of necessity become the ruling class of the future; that the socialist goal of a classless society as the next step in industrial evolution was therefore not attainable. Burnham in his *Managerial Revolution* expressed agreement with the general socialist contention that capitalism contained within itself the seeds of its own destruction. Mass unemployment, recurring depressions, continuous agricultural crises, increasing national debt were weakening its superstructure. In addition, the area of free monetary exchanges on which the capitalist market depended was diminishing. Capitalism was no longer able to find uses for its available investments and failed to utilize fully its technological

[16] See Howard Scott, *Introduction to Technocracy;* Graham A. Laing, *Toward Technocracy;* Frank Arkwright, *A. B. C. of Technocracy;* J. George Frederick, Jr., Editor, *For and against Technocracy.* Socialists, while welcoming the educational work of the technocrats in bringing vividly to light the actual and potential increases in our industrial capacity, were critical of the technocrats on a number of counts. Chiefly they criticized the suggestion that the control of industry be placed in the hands of technicians, and their failure to emphasize the need of developing a democratic movement of the masses in bringing about a just and equitable social order. (See Paul Blanshard, *Technocracy and Socialism;* Lewis Corey, *The Decline of American Capitalism,* pp. 263, 287; and Stuart Chase, *Technocracy, An Interpretation.*)

possibilities. The great powers, furthermore, were "no longer able to manage the exploitation and development of backward sections of the world," and the "bourgeois ideologies" were "becoming increasingly impotent."

As a result of these defects in the present system, industry, Burnham maintained, would pass into the hands of the state while "within the new social structure a different social group or class—the managers—will be the dominant or ruling class." [17] This would occur because of the important function performed by managers under any advanced social order and because this class, on account of its strategic importance, would necessarily demand and receive under a system of state ownership, a relatively larger share of the products of economy than would the industrial workers. The receipt of such a large share would render the managerial class an exploiting class.[18] The "managerial revolution" would not lead, therefore, at least in the immediate future, to socialism and the abolition of exploitation, but to another class society.

Socialists have subjected Burnham's thesis, as they have that of the technocrats, to a barrage of criticisms. They admit that managers will occupy an important position in any conceivable new social order of the immediate future. However, they contend that this will not necessarily constitute them a new ruling group if democratic processes are maintained.

The trouble with Burnham, declares Lewis Corey, is that the chief "proof" which he adduces as to the impossibility of achieving socialism within the measurable future is the results of the bolshevik experiment, in which, he alleges, the managerial class rules. "Quite aside from the truth or falseness of this contention, it must be realized that the present rulers of Soviet Russia did not come into being following an attempt to achieve democratic socialism. Nor does the fact that 'workers' control of industry' as practised in Russia broke down, mean that socialism is impossible. It means that the bolshevik idea of management at the beginning of the Russian experiment was a primitive one, for management is a functional job that must be performed by special functional groups. What is wrong in Soviet Russia is not that managers manage, but that there is no economic or political freedom and no free labor unions." [19]

Socialism and Inequality of Income. Burnham, moreover, writes Corey, is wrong in assuming that socialists insist on absolute equality of income, and that any material deviation from equality would lead

[17] Burnham, *The Managerial Revolution,* p. 74. [18] *Ibid.,* p. 123.
[19] Corey, *The Unfinished Task,* p. 141n.

to a system of economic exploitation. Socialists have never objected to differences in compensation for services rendered if such inequalities are based on differences in ability and productivity and if they are necessary to bring about the best social and economic results. Absolute equality of income "fits what Marx called 'the higher state of communism'—of which Lenin wrote in *State and Revolution* that 'it has never entered the head of any socialist "to promise" that the higher stage of communism will actually arrive.' . . . Members of the new middle class," concludes Corey, "will occupy positions of privilege and power in any conceivable new social order of the immediate future. So be it. That is not dangerous if the basis is functional performance of useful services. The new middle class cannot become a new ruling class if democratic freedoms and rights flourish. The accent is on democracy." [20]

Incentives in a Socialized Society. Increased attention was given during the interwar days to the types of rewards that should be given to manual and intellectual workers under a co-operative social order with a view to maximizing their social efficiency. Many studies were made of the techniques employed in private, co-operative, publicly operated, and other forms of non-profit industries throughout the world and particularly to the application of non-profit incentives to collectivized industry in the Soviet Union.

In general the conclusions reached by advocates of a socialized order were summarized in the author's volume on *Socializing Our Democracy* (pp. 199–200) as follows:

"In deciding the question of awards [under a socialized order] we must have in mind both the problem of production and that of distribution. We must provide to the intellectual and manual workers such incentives, whether of money or of social recognition and appreciation, as will bring production to levels required for the living of the good life. We must also seek to give to the worker such monetary rewards as will permit him to develop his highest potentialities to the largest practicable extent.

"As society produces goods more and more abundantly and as living standards are increasingly raised, laborers with hand and brain will think less in terms of exact remuneration received and more in terms of needs. When water is abundant, each utilizes the supply according to his needs.

"The equality, the deeds, and the needs principles, however, should all find their place in a socialized order. That principle or combina-

[20] Corey, *op. cit.*, p. 142.

tion of principles should be applied, which seems most likely to stimulate the finest endeavor and promote the good and happiness of the greatest number." [21]

Socialist Planning and International Economic Relations. For many years socialist writers gave little attention to international economic relations under socialism. In more recent years, particularly with the advent of communism in Russia and the problem of international exchange between the Soviet Union and the other countries of the world, increasing speculation has arisen regarding the desirable type of international relationships.

One school of thought has conceived of the organization of a World Economic Planning Board as a regulator of trade, to which the various "national" planning boards would be subordinate. One of the main advocates of such a board during the thirties was Dr. F. M. Wibaut, who would give his board, or World Economic Council, as he called it, power to lay down the chief lines of economic development in the various countries of the world in accordance with consumers' needs and efficient production. The board would have supreme authority to arrange international exchanges of commodities and to allocate investments. It would co-operate with various national boards and with such organizations as the International Labor Office, the Bank of International Settlements, and the economic and financial sections of the League of Nations. It would gather statistical data and conduct researches. Its aim would be to improve living standards throughout the world, and to provide for an expanding economic order free from depressions, unemployment, and want.[22]

Numerous objections have been launched against this plan, the principal valid objections being directed "against the immediate possibility of putting the plan into effect and on the doubts that democracy could be preserved under such a plan." [23]

[21] See Laidler, *Socializing Our Democracy,* ch. X; also J. A. Hobson, *Economics and Ethics;* Harry F. Ward, *In Place of Profit;* Paul H. Douglas in Tugwell, Editor, *The Trend in Economics,* ch. V; Bernard Shaw, *An Intelligent Woman's Guide to Socialism and Capitalism;* also see text, pp. 214–16; 629–30.

[22] F. W. Wibaut, *A World Production Order* (London, 1935). See also for similar ideas F. E. Lawley, *The Growth of Collective Economy,* 2 vols. (London, 1938); L. Lorwin, *The Problem of Economic Planning* (Amsterdam, 1931), pp. 24–6; *The International Trade-Union Movement,* Vol. XII, No. 5, May 1932, p. 86; and for a criticism of the plan see Lionel Robbins, *Economic Planning and International Order* (London, 1937), pp. 187–220.

[23] Bert F. Hoselitz, on "Socialist Planning and International Economic Relations," in *The American Economic Review,* December, 1943, Vol. XXXIII, No. 4, p. 842.

A second group of proposals that have been made for the conduct of international trade under a co-operative system of society centers around the establishment of national foreign-trade monopolies which are in close touch with the national planning authorities and which arrange for the international exchange of commodities and the allocation of capital. G. D. H. Cole was the chief protagonist of this idea. He would have one centralized body take charge of the foreign trade of a country and determine the quantity of commodities to be imported and exported on the basis of the relative cost of production at home and abroad and the ability of a country to pay for its imports by exports.[24]

A third proposal is that of direct purchases and sales between plants and industries in different national economies, the various socialist countries practicing a policy of non-discrimination in the importation of goods.[25] It is the duty of managers of socialized plants, declare the advocates of this proposal, to see that the plants' products are turned out with maximum efficiency. To do this, they should be on the outlook for goods which, everything else being equal, may be obtained most cheaply. If domestic commodities are cheaper, they will buy them; if, on the other hand, foreign supplies are more inexpensive, they will seek imports.

This method of trading, its defenders declare, is superior to that of setting up export monopolies, because the latter scheme "would further bilateralism in international trade, with all the evil consequences of reduction of trade involved in bilateralism." [26] The proposal for government trade monopolies, declares Hoselitz, has been made largely because of the example set by Soviet Russia in establishing its foreign-trade monopoly. However, it should be realized that such an organization was established to meet an abnormal situation. "It was founded in 1918, being originally created out of necessity as an instrument dealing with a hostile world, with the internal breakdown of production and the hyper-inflation of the Russian currency. Later, especially after the introduction of the New Economic Policy, there arose the demand for free trade in bolshevik circles. . . . Krassin and his monopoly prevailed, however, mainly because of the fear that free trade between a socialist country which was primarily an exporter of raw materials and a capitalistic world which was still largely influenced

[24] See Cole, *Economic Planning* (New York, 1935), pp. 212–25; "Planning International Trade," *Foreign Affairs*, Vol. 12 (1933–34), pp. 231–43.

[25] See Abba P. Lerner, "Economic Liberalism in the Postwar World," in *Postwar Economic Problems* (New York, 1943), pp. 127–39.

[26] Hoselitz, *op. cit.*, p. 844.

by groups hostile to the USSR would seriously endanger the economic and political consolidation of the USSR."[27] There is no valid economic reason for placing control of international trade in other socialist states in the hands of a government monopoly. Free exchange, a policy of non-discrimination, "will secure the most economic allocation of resources and the most efficient division of labor internationally in accordance with the principles of comparative costs. Thus non-discrimination becomes the proper and effective supplement of a policy of national planning along socialist lines."[28] Undoubtedly the above and other proposals for international trade will be vigorously debated in socialist and non-socialist circles in the days ahead.

SOCIAL GROUPS IN THE TRANSITION FROM PRIVATE TO PUBLIC OWNERSHIP

Besides problems of the economic arrangements of a socialist society there have been discussed of late many problems relating to the transition from capitalism to socialism.

The Place of the Consumer in Advancing Collective Enterprise. One of the questions which has been much discussed in recent socialist literature has been the place of the consumer and general public in bringing about a collectivist industrial structure. Since the early days of scientific socialism, socialists have pointed to the working class as the group that could be relied upon primarily to bring the socialist state into being. They have, during the decades following the publication of the first classics of Marx and Engels, enlarged their interpretation of what constituted the working class, and have insisted that this class included brain workers as well as manual workers. They have also welcomed in their ranks members of the somewhat nebulous middle class—storekeepers, technicians, farmers, and others—but they have in general maintained that the industrial workers would prove the most dynamic force in the socialization process.

This view has of late been challenged by Professor Seba Eldridge of the University of Kansas after a careful empirical study of the main forces responsible for the advances toward collectivism that have thus far been made in the United States.[29] Including in collective enter-

[27] Hoselitz, *op. cit.*, p. 849. Leonid Krassin was the first People's Commissar for Foreign Trade. He urged a state monopoly, against the demand of Bukharin and others for a free trade policy. See Lubov Krassin, *Leonid Krassin, His Life and Work* (London, 1929), p. 163.

[28] Hoselitz, *op. cit.*, p. 851; see also Carl Landauer, "Literature on Economic Research," *Social Research*, Vol. 7 (1940), pp. 504–5; R. L. Hall, *The Economic System in a Socialist State;* Oscar Lange, *On the Economic Theory of Socialism.*

[29] Seba Eldridge and Associates, *Development of Collective Enterprise.*

prises those operated by public, co-operative, and non-profit groups, Professor Eldridge notes that at least ten major fields in the United States fall into this class. "These are (1) protection of person and property; (2) construction and upkeep of roads and streets; (3) development and maintenance of harbors and waterways; (4) the postal services; (5) water supply and sewage disposal; (6) land reclamation (irrigation, drainage, flood control); (7) education and research; (8) social work and institutional care; (9) social clubs and fraternal organizations; (10) libraries and museums. Major fields undergoing collectivization include (1) forestry; (2) rural resettlement; (3) electric power; (4) low-rent housing; (5) banking and credit; (6) property insurance; (7) life insurance; (8) minimum income insurance; (9) medical service and health care; (10) recreation and leisure-time activity."

Analyzing the forces back of collectivization in these fields, Eldridge and his fellow economists declare that their studies indicate that in a so-called capitalist democracy the factors in socialization "are to be found in the pressure of consumer and general public interests, not in the pressure applied by labor groups. Tax-supported schools were established with the interests of children and the community at large in view, not the interest of teachers (the labor group directly concerned); electric power is gradually being socialized in response to the interest of power users and general public, not in the interest of electric-power workers or of wage-earners in general. According to the record . . . consumers and citizens are slowly building a collective economy in this country, and one, as their own influence attests, that is essentially democratic in its foundations.[30] . . . The choices and convictions of the consumer-citizens govern the kinds, rates of growth, and amounts of public and collective enterprises. Negatively, this means that Marxians are all barking up the wrong tree. Labor and the labor movement have indispensable functions to serve, but socialization of industry happens not to be one of them. Managers also serve extremely important functions, but they are almost always found promoting the several kinds of enterprise in which they happen to be engaged, whether collective or capitalist." [31]

It is contended by some socialists, in reply to Professor Eldridge's analysis, that, while consumer pressures have undoubtedly been powerful in bringing about an increase of collectivism, more than "collec-

[30] Seba Eldridge, *op. cit.*, pp. 3, 4, 550. Professor Eldridge declares that he received his first impetus to his study by reading Sidney and Beatrice Webb's "Special Supplement on State and Municipal Enterprise," *The New Statesman* (London), May 8, 1915. See Webb's discussion in text, pp. 196–98, 218.

[31] *Ibid.*, p. 549.

tivism" of the type mentioned by Eldridge is needed to achieve socialism. A socialist society presupposes the control of the government by the masses together with the development of thoroughgoing democratic procedures in the administration of publicly owned industries. These, in turn, presuppose the effective organization of and pressures from the labor movement. Most collective controls in the United States have not as yet been democratized and socialized and are not likely to be socialized without the development of a powerful labor movement in the political and economic fields.

Professor Eldridge frankly admits that during the depression of the thirties the extension of collective controls through the public-works program of the government was due, to a very considerable extent, to the demand on the part of the workers for jobs.[32] After the Second World War a further extension of collective activities may be expected as the result, in considerable part, of the pressures of the millions of workers released in the postwar days from the military services and the war industries and in desperate need of work. Professor Eldridge and associates, however, have presented an analysis and challenge to social thought that those interested in a collectivist economy cannot afford to ignore.

The Entrepreneurial and Owning Class as a Force Making for Socialism. That socialism is being brought nearer to realization through the changes in the composition and functions of other groups than those of the workers and consumers, namely, the entrepreneurial and owning groups, has been the contention of other students of socialism, among them Professor Joseph A. Schumpeter of Harvard University. Professor Schumpeter sees the old type of entrepreneur disappearing. Before the days of our developed technology and giant corporations, he maintains, the entrepreneur was an adventurer whose success required a combination of talents of a high order. The giant corporation, however, is largely reducing industrial innovations to routine. "Technological progress is increasingly becoming the business of teams of trained specialists who turn out what is required and make it work in predictable ways. The romance of earlier commercial adventure is rapidly wearing away, because so many more things can be strictly calculated that had of old to be visualized in a flash of genius. . . . Bureau and committee work tends to replace individual action."[33] Entrepreneurs lose their prestige and their former functions. At the same time shareholders in the large corporations are far less willing

[32] *Ibid.*, p. 549.
[33] Schumpeter, *Capitalism, Socialism and Democracy*, pp. 132–3; see text, p. 200.

to fight for the continued possession of their private property than were the past owners of small one-man concerns.

"The capitalist process," Professor Schumpeter continues, "by substituting a mere parcel of shares for the walls and the machines in a factory, takes the life out of the idea of property. It loosens the grip that once was so strong—the grip in the sense of the legal right and the actual ability to do as one pleases with one's own; the grip also in the sense that the holder of the title loses the will to fight, economically, physically, politically, for 'his' factory and his control over it, to die if necessary on its steps. And this evaporation of what we may term the material substance of property—its visible and touchable reality—affects not only the attitude of holders but also that of the workmen and the public in general. Dematerialized, defunctionalized, and absentee ownership does not impress and call forth moral allegiance as the vital form of property did. Eventually there will be nobody left who really cares to stand for it—nobody within and nobody without the precincts of the big concerns." [34] One of the obstacles to the transference of industry from private to public ownership is thus gradually eliminated.

The Middle Class in Social Change. The importance of increased co-operation between labor and the so-called middle class as a means to peaceful and democratic change toward a socialized order was emphasized during the thirties and forties by many writers. The failure to bring about a co-operative arrangement with the middle class in Germany, according to Lewis Corey, was one of the factors leading to the success of fascism in that country. "As socialism approached political power, especially in Germany," declared Corey, "it was immobilized by failure to get the support of the non-proletarian groups necessary for a democratic majority. The emphasis on the proletariat alienated the middle classes and peasants, who saw in socialism an expression only of proletarian interests." Political necessity, it is true, Corey continued, "forced socialism to make an appeal to those groups. But

[34] *Ibid.*, p. 142. Prof. Schumpeter likewise declares that, as capitalism develops, the general atmosphere becomes increasingly hostile to its continuance, as a result of which the system begins to decompose. See also Laidler, *Socializing Our Democracy*, pp. 61 ff.; Berle and Means, *The Modern Corporation and Private Property*, p. 66. "In place of actual physical properties over which the owner could exert direction and for which he is responsible," declare Berle and Means, "the owner now holds a piece of paper representing a set of rights and expectations with respect to an enterprise. But over the enterprise and over the physical property—the instruments of production—in which he has an interest, the owner has little control. At the same time he bears no responsibility with respect to the enterprise or its physical property. . . . The owner is practically powerless through his own efforts, to affect the underlying property."

emphasis on the proletariat was not abandoned. . . . Socialism was watered down, virtually abandoned, to get the support of non-proletarian groups whose interests should have been inseparately identified with socialism and who should have been drawn into the struggle for socialism." [35]

Dr. Adolph Sturmthal maintained likewise that in Italy "the situation that nurtured fascism was characterized by a progressive disintegration of the nation due primarily to the stagnating equilibrium between the two main antagonists on the Italian social scene, the working class and the middle class." [36] The main reason for labor's failure in Europe to stem the fascist tide, however, according to Sturmthal, was that Labor and Socialist parties had too much the character of pressure groups intent on putting upon the statute books certain social reforms demanded by trade unions and democratic demands proclaimed by all democratic elements, and not enough concerned with basic social and economic reconstruction.[37]

In his challenge to the British Labor party to enlarge their appeal to the country, Professor Harold J. Laski joined with others in emphasizing the importance of an alliance between the working and the middle class. The Labor party, he declared, "has got to make the man of science, the technician, the managerial class, recognize that the kind of society for which it stands offers them an opportunity, a power, a security, which they cannot attain under the present order. It has got to win for a planned democracy groups that have so far largely failed to recognize its claims, groups, moreover, upon whose contribution the success of a planned democracy in large part depends." [38]

Planning for Security. As a practical means of interesting the middle class in forming an alliance with the working class in the work of social reconstruction, the Belgian Labor party, in late 1933, adopted a

[35] Lewis Corey, *The Unfinished Task,* p. 129. See also Corey, *Crisis of the Middle Class.*

[36] Sturmthal, *The Tragedy of European Labor,* p. 180. For an analysis of some of the difficulties that may be involved in securing the adherence of the middle class urbanite and the farmer to a socialist movement, see Reinhold Niebuhr, *Moral Man and Immoral Society,* ch. VII.

[37] Sturmthal, *op. cit.,* pp. 3–15.

[38] Laski, *Reflections on the Revolution of Our Time,* p. 224. In Canada, the Co-operative Commonwealth Federation was selected as the name of the labor-farmer-socialist party of that country rather than Farmer-Labor party, because the latter title "seemed to exclude the small but influential group of middle-class intellectuals and business men who were destined to give such valuable aid to the new party" (M. J. Coldwell in *Canadian Progressives on the March,* p. 8).

Plan du Travail, or an "Anti-Crisis Plan," as a basis for discussion throughout the country.[39]

The plan as presented to the Conference of the Belgian Labor party had as its ultimate objective the social ownership of industry, but it did not urge the socialization of all of the essential industries at once. Concretely it called for the nationalization of the key industries of the country and the banking system. Most non-monopolistic industries would, under the plan, be left for the time being in the hands of their present owners, while the private ownership of many of these industries would be, in fact, strengthened by liberal credits and other help from the state. This portion of the plan was formulated "to steal the fascist thunder"; to prevent the middle class from seeking its salvation in fascism; and to secure the alliance of the middle class and the workers so that, together, the industrial workers, the farmers, and the white-collar producers might win, as a united force, a parliamentary majority in Belgium.

The plan provided for the setting up of an Economic Council advisory to, and supervisory over, the various commissions in control of the national industries. With a view to bringing about business recovery through the enlargement of the domestic market, the plan proposed (1) security of investment and suppression of monetary speculation; (2) credit policies for specific branches of industry; (3) price control to prevent the exactions of private monopoly speculation in essential commodities and to stabilize agricultural, industrial, and commercial profits; (4) reduction of the working day; (5) standardization of wages by legal agreements; (6) recognition of trade unions; (7) the institution of joint boards of workers and employers in the working out of joint collective bargaining agreements; (8) increasing purchasing power of incomes derived from labor, while safeguarding gold reserves and the stability of exchange; (9) the development of foreign commerce and moderate retail prices by tariff reductions, recognition of the USSR, and the integration of the Congo into the Belgian economy; (10) lessening of the burden on production and trade; (11) taxation of land instead of homes and industrial buildings; and (12) the strengthening of the system of social insurance.

In order that these proposals might be carried out efficiently and democratically, a number of political reforms were urged, including universal suffrage, the strict observance of civil liberties, independence

[39] See *Planned Socialism,* published by the New Fabian Research Bureau, London, Pamphlet No. 25.

of the state from the money power, a unicameral Parliament, a consultative council of experts to assist Parliament, and the possession of executive power by economic commissions.

The plan thus sought both to improve conditions immediately by overcoming the crisis and to revolutionize the system. It was criticized by the left because of its alleged failure to recognize the class nature of the democratic state and because of the belief that many of its adherents seemed to harbor the conviction that the socialization of the banks and monopolized industries would in itself guarantee economic security.

The *Plan du Travail* was widely agitated in Belgium during the succeeding years prior to the Second World War. The Labor party, however, though at times represented prominently in the cabinet, was unable to secure the plan's adoption prior to the invasion of the country by the forces of the Third Reich.[40]

In the Western Hemisphere the Co-operative Commonwealth Federation of Canada issued, in 1933, its Regina Manifesto, in which it urged "the establishment of a planned, socialized, economic order," in which "transportation, communication, electric power, and all other industries and services essential to social planning" should be socially owned and operated. The first step in the direction of such an economic order, it declared, should be "the setting up of a National Planning Commission consisting of a small body of economists, engineers, and statisticians assisted by an appropriate technical staff." "The task of this Commission," the Manifesto continued, "will be to plan for the production, distribution, and exchange of all goods and services necessary to the efficient functioning of the economy; to co-ordinate the activities of the socialized industries; to provide for a satisfactory balance between the producing and consuming power; and to carry on continuous research into all branches of the national economy in order to acquire the detailed information necessary to efficient planning.

"The Commission will be responsible to the cabinet and will work in co-operation with the Managing Boards of the socialized industries.

"It is now certain that in every industrial country some form of planning will replace the disintegrating capitalist system. The C. C. F. will provide that in Canada the planning shall be done, not by a small group of capitalist magnates in their own interest but by public servants act-

[40] For other European plans, see *Proceedings of World Social Economic Congress*, Amsterdam, 1931. The Social Democratic Labor party of Holland and the International Federation of Trade Unions, among others, later favored somewhat similar plans.

ing in the public interest and responsible to the people as a whole." [41]

In the United States numerous plans for ridding the country of depressions and mass unemployment were evolved by labor, socialist, and progressive groups during the thirties. Some groups formulated numerous concrete proposals for the change of the country's economic structure somewhat along the lines of the *Plan du Travail;* some urged a complete change to a socialist order of society; others contented themselves with laying down certain general principles for a planned society, and suggesting the setting up of national planning boards for the purpose of accumulating and correlating economic information, working out general broad policies, and supervising the organization of productive and distributive industries, of banking, of agriculture, and of the labor market. "Every step in the direction of planning for social ends," declared George Soule, in suggesting an advance in social planning, starting with the organization of planning boards, "must be a step away from capitalism, no matter how that word is defined. The more advanced stages of a planned society must be something closely akin to the broad ambitions of socialism." [42]

The case for the socialization of the chief and controlling industries of the country as a means to effective social planning for the common good was presented by many socialists. "It is next to impossible," declared the author of this volume in 1936, "for society to make and carry out plans for industrial production, distribution, and investment, when industrial capital resides in the hands of hundreds of thousands of individuals intent on obtaining a maximum profit." Further, only under a system in which income is based on service rendered would the purchasing power of the masses be sufficient to keep the wheels of industry running smoothly.[43]

[41] David Lewis and Frank Scott, *Make This Your Canada,* p. 200; M. J. Coldwell, *Canadian Progressives on the March.*

[42] See George Soule, *A Planned Society,* pp. 277–8; see also Stuart Chase, *Idle Money, Idle Men.*

[43] *Survey Graphic,* April, 1936, p. 230, article by H. W. Laidler on "A Socialized Economy." See also G. D. H. Cole, *Economic Planning;* Barbara Wootton, *Plan or No Plan;* Norman Thomas, *After the New Deal, What?;* Laidler, *A Program for Modern America,* ch. XIX; Laidler, *Socializing Our Democracy,* chs. III, XIX; *Socialist Planning and a Socialist Program,* esp. ch. II, "American Proposals for Planning," by Pierce Williams and ch. XII, "A Proposed Socialist Blueprint," by Colston E. Warne; League for Social Reconstruction Research Committee, *Social Planning for Canada.* See likewise M. L. Fledderus, Editor, *World Social Economic Planning;* Fred Henderson, *Money Power.*

For plans involving a partial approach to socialism, see *Prosperity* (Harry W. Laidler, editor); *Challenge to the New Deal,* Alfred M. Bingham and S. Rodman, editors; British Economists, *The Next Five Years;* Stuart Chase, *The Economy of Abundance* and *Idle Money, Idle Men;* Columbia University Commission, *Economic Reconstruc-*

ECONOMIC FORCES UNDERMINING THE PROFIT SYSTEM

Concentration of Industrial Control and Socialism. As in former decades, many economists of recent years have been seeing in the shifts in business organization and in technology, forces making for the undermining of our capitalist order. One of these developments, according to many, is the continuous growth of giant corporations, trusts, monopolies, and quasi-monopolies. The development of great aggregations of capital, many declare, is producing a group of administrators who are depending for their chief incentive not on profit but on salaries for services rendered, and many of whom would be just as willing to work efficiently for a salary in a publicly owned concern as in a private corporation.[44] The big corporation is showing the possibility of administering entire industries under one corporate roof, and is thus greatly weakening, if not eliminating, the arguments used so frequently in the past against public ownership and operation on the ground of administrative difficulties. It is making it technically an easier job to transfer industry from private to public control. In many industries at the present time the transfer of the title to the ownership of one, two, three, or four corporations from private to public hands would bring the major part of the industry under public control. Under the present corporate set-up it would not, in many cases, be necessary, as in the past, to go into the industrial field and secure title to hundreds or thousands of separate concerns.[45]

The practices on the part of giant industry of sharing the market, of stabilizing prices, of resorting to price discrimination, of mobilizing public opinion through mass advertising, and of cornering patents and raw materials have likewise led toward a more rigid price structure, which has reduced the flexibility of the market place and almost entirely destroyed its effectiveness as an overall economic co-ordinator. Severe maladjustments, from a system of "monopolistic competition,"

---

tion; David C. Coyle, *Brass Tacks;* Harold Loeb and Associates, *The Chart of Plenty;* Sir Arthur Salter, *The Framework of an Ordered Society;* S. H. Schlecter, *Toward Stability;* Henry A. Wallace, *Democracy Reborn; Planned Society, Yesterday, Today, and Tomorrow,* Findlay Mackenzie, editor; *Plan Age,* Vol. I, No. 1, December 1934, to date; Earl R. Sikes, *Contemporary Economic System,* ch. XXIX; *America Faces the Future,* Charles A. Beard, editor; Lewis L. Lorwin, *Advisory Economic Councils;* the *Survey Graphic,* April, 1936; A. H. Hansen, *Economic Stabilization in an Unbalanced World; Annals,* July, 1932; Louis H. Pink, *Freedom from Fear.*

[44] See Laidler, *Socializing Our Democracy,* ch. X on "Incentives and a Socialized Society," esp. p. 189.

[45] See Laidler, *op. cit.,* pp. 49–66; Laidler, *Concentration of Control in American Industry;* see text, p. 201.

have resulted, tending "to impair or destroy the adjustibility of the economy." [46]

Under the resulting administered price system that is becoming an increasing feature of our economy, say McConnell and associates, "when demand at the prevailing price falls off, the manufacturer closes his plant, throws his workers out of employment, and attempts to wait until some time when demand will increase. But the fact that he does not have to lower his prices means that the disturbance is increased instead of being automatically corrected.

"If prices are flexible, demand would adjust itself to capacity, assuming some degree of elasticity in demand, and the plants would tend toward being fully used. The problem would simply be one of partial instead of general overproduction. But when prices can be controlled, production can be curtailed, and the losses involved may not be great enough to force a readjustment of productive resources.

"When curtailment of output and maintenance of prices are generally practiced, the effect upon the business economy as a whole may be very serious. Under these circumstances individual incomes are reduced to the point where people cannot afford to buy other products. There are no profitable alternative fields of enterprise or of employment. Overproduction and unemployment become general." [47] This

[46] *Industrial Prices and Their Relative Inflexibility*, Senate Document No. 13, 74th Congress, 1st Session; Laidler, *Socializing Our Democracy*, pp. 75–6.

[47] Donald W. McConnell and Associates, *Economic Behavior* (1939 edition), p. 402. See also George Soule, *The Coming American Revolution*, p. 116.

From 1929 to the spring of 1933, the drop in the price of agricultural implements, where there was a high degree of concentration, was only 6 per cent, while the drop in production during these depression years was 80 per cent. On the other hand, in the highly competitive farming industry, the drop in prices was 63 per cent, and in production only 6 per cent (*Industrial Prices and Their Relative Inflexibility;* McConnell and Associates, *op. cit.*, p. 369; Walton H. Hamilton and Associates, *Price and Price Policies.*) See Laidler, *Concentration of Control in American Industry.*

Numerous volumes were written during the thirties on the trust and combine movement and its economic significance, of which Berle and Means, *Private Property and the Modern Corporation* was among the most significant. These authors contended that, in 1930, 200 corporations, constituting seven-hundredths of one per cent of the total, owned 55 per cent of the wealth of the non-banking corporations of the country and did about two fifths of the business. They maintained that "approximately 2000 individuals out of a population of one hundred and twenty-five million are in a position to control and direct half of industry" (p. 33).

The Twentieth Century Fund studied concentration in banking as well as in industrial institutions and concluded: "Summaries of corporate income tax returns published by the Bureau of Internal Revenue of the U. S. Treasury Department show that the 549 largest corporations in all fields, or 0.15 per cent of the total number, owned approximately 53 per cent of total corporate assets in 1933. At the other extreme were 211,586 corporations with average total assets of less than $50,000 each. They comprised more than 54 per cent of the total number, but owned only

condition is likely to result in a demand for drastic change in our economic order.

Nor can the political consequences of concentration be ignored. "The political structure of the nation," declares Professor Joseph A. Schumpeter, of Harvard, "is profoundly affected by the elimination of a host of small and medium-sized firms the owner managers of which, together with their dependents, henchmen, and connections, count quantitatively at the polls and have a hold on what we may term the foreman class that no management of a large unit can ever have; the very foundation of private property and free contracting wears away in a nation in which its most vital, most concrete, most meaningful types disappear from the moral horizon of the people." [48] Other writers have brought out the fact that the movement toward giant corporations, trusts, and monopolies is preparing the way for a socialized order.

The Effect of Debts, Technological Change, and Unemployment. During the thirties and early forties numerous authors likewise pointed out what they regarded as the influence of the growing debt structure of the country—a structure which the economic crisis and, particularly, the Second World War developed to colossal proportions—on the weakening of the capitalistic organization of society.[49] Many socialist economists emphasized during the thirties the effect of technological advances and, in the United States, the closing of the frontier and the

---

1.4 per cent of the total corporate assets. Nearly 95 per cent of the total number of corporations had total assets averaging less than one million dollars each, but this great bulk of corporate enterprises owned less than 15 per cent of total assets of all corporations" (*Big Business: Its Growth and Its Place,* p. 5). This study did not include a study of unincorporated business concerns.

The most extensive studies during the thirties into industrial concentration were those made by the Temporary National Economic Committee and published in a series of 43 volumes under the title, *Investigation of Concentration of Economic Power.* Other studies include National Resources Committee, *The Structure of the American Economy—Part I—Basic Characteristics;* Anna Rochester, *Rulers of America;* Irving Lipkowitz, *Monopoly and Big Business* (L. I. D. Pamphlet); Ferdinand Lundberg, *America's 60 Families;* Alfred C. Neal, *Industrial Concentration and Price Inflexibility;* A. R. Burns, *The Decline of Competition;* Edward H. Chamberlin, *The Theory of Monopolistic Competition;* Joan Robinson, *The Economics of Imperfect Competition;* Frank A. Fetter, *The Masquerade of Monopoly;* Lewis Corey, *The House of Morgan.*

[48] Schumpeter, *Capitalism, Socialism and Democracy,* p. 141.

[49] See Laidler, *Socializing Our Democracy,* pp. 76–8; John Blair, *Seeds of Destruction;* Basset Jones, *Debts and Production;* Rautenstrauch, *Who Gets the Money?;* Evans Clark, editor, assisted by George B. Galloway, *The Internal Debt of the United States;* Lewis Corey, *The Decline in American Capitalism,* p. 291.

gradual leveling of population growth, on the increase in unemployment and the undermining of the capitalist system.[50]

Expansion of Collective Controls. Widespread unemployment and insecurity, these writers brought out, led the unemployed and other groups in the population during the thirties to demand extensive governmental action with a view to providing jobs, the extension of social insurance, public banking, public housing, the public generation and distribution of electric power, public works, the public distribution of food and relief, and the increased conservation by government of natural and human resources. Industrial stagnation and its consequences likewise tended to weaken the capitalist class through the reduction of profits and through the loss of popular loyalty. The owners of industry failed to receive the homage that was formerly theirs when they were able to point out that, despite many evils of capitalism, jobs were available to well-nigh all who were able and willing to work.[51]

[50] John A. Hobson in his *Rationalization and Unemployment,* in 1930, maintained that the evidence at hand showed that the recent development toward mechanization and combination "carries with it a net diminution of employment, the substitution of a large proportion of low-skilled for high-skilled workers, and a distribution of the product which increases the proportionate share of capital, reduces that of labor" (p. 90). See also Laidler, *Socializing Our Democracy,* pp. 66 ff.; Lewis Corey, *Decline in American Capitalism,* Part V; John Strachey, *The Nature of the Capitalist Crisis,* ch. XVIII; Stuart Chase, *Idle Money, Idle Men.*

[51] See George Soule, *The Coming Revolution,* p. 199. "Already the more sensitive of the writers and teachers have, with surprising unanimity," declared Soule, during the depression of the thirties, "ceased celebrating the virtues of the old order and embroidering its traditions, but rather have been busy exposing its failures and corruptions and ridiculing many of its leading figures." See Soule, *op. cit.,* esp. Parts II and IV, for a story of the forces making for social change in America. The Second World War likewise strengthened, at least temporarily, the control by the government of the economic life of the nation. The government became during the war the largest landowner and the greatest owner of manufacturing plants in the country, controlling no less than twenty billion dollars' worth of plants buying war materials. Moreover, it expanded its regulatory powers over every phase of the nation's economic life. By the middle of 1943 the Federal government had given nearly 11 billion dollars to the W. P. A.—largely in depression years—with the view to providing work for more than 8,500,000 persons. The Reconstruction Finance Corporation had committed itself to loans and investments in private and public agencies to the extent of 26 billion dollars and was operating many other financial agencies. As a result of its incursion into war industry, it was predicted in 1944 that "the end of the war will find the country with just a fifth of its productive capacity owned by the Federal government" (*Business Week,* June 19, 1943). See Stuart Chase, *Government in Business;* Leverett S. Lyons and Associates, *Government and Economic Life;* Harry W. Laidler, *The Federal Government and Functional Democracy;* Editorial Research Reports, Oct. 22, 1943, *Government War Plants.*

THE POSTWAR WORLD

Program of British Labor. With the progress of the Second World War and the prospects of a victory over fascism and nazism, socialists throughout the world began to give their attention increasingly to problems of postwar reconstruction. One of the most important programs of postwar reconstruction adopted by an important socialist body during the early forties was that presented by the party's executive to the 1942 conference of the British Labor party under the title, *The Old World and the New Society*.[52]

This pronouncement started with the assumption that, after the victory over the forces of nazism and fascism, "there can be no return to the prewar system" and that the basis of democracy in that period "is planned production for community consumption." The Labor party therefore urges, the report declared, "that the nation must own and operate the essential instruments of production; their power over our lives is too great for them to be left in private hands. This common ownership does not commit us to a regimented bureaucracy. It means, on the one hand, that the technical expert has his proper place in the direction of economic affairs, and, on the other hand, that the skill and experience of the workers are fully utilized in all branches of administration and management."

The party insisted that, during the changeover from a wartime to a peacetime economy, there is a "necessity of retaining the main wartime controls in industry and agriculture. . . . The vital lesson of the last [First World] war," it maintained, "is that, without them [postwar controls] the postwar scene becomes an ugly scramble for profit in which there is no serious attempt to assess, in any coherent way, the priorities of national need."

The program for the transitional period demands that jobs be provided for all; that special attention be given to the planning and rebuilding of urban areas; that the social insurance system be extended (the party later endorsed the Beveridge plan); that the socialization of medicine be an end deliberately kept in view; that minimum wages be guaranteed; that the rights of labor be given full and unfettered recognition; and that living standards be raised.

As a means of increased efficiency in the production and distribution of goods and services, the party urged the development of scientific research, the encouragement of consumers' co-operatives, and "the in-

[52] See Interim Report of the National Executive Committee of the British Labor Party, *Reconstruction in War and Peace*, or *The Old World and the New Society* (League for Industrial Democracy Pamphlet).

vestigation of the whole mechanism of distribution, its incoherence, its wasteful competition, its massive costs of advertising." Attention must be given likewise [the report continued] to modern systems of management and industrial welfare. "The possibilities of communal feeding in factories; the organization of medical inspection and care as part of the normal process of rational management; the growth of factory discipline built upon consultation from below rather than on coercion from above; the full use of industrial psychology, under proper control, and with effective safeguards for the workers, in testing fitness for the job; the importance of rest periods and of holidays with pay in securing the full effort of the worker; the provision of full opportunities for advanced training; the selection for executive posts in terms of tested competence rather than of nepotism; . . . the importance of relating managerial discretion to the trade-union function of protecting the workers' interest; on all these, a mass of important experience has been accumulated which the nation will neglect at its peril."

"A planned society," the party executive maintained, must be a free society, and it "can be a far more free society than the competitive laissez-faire order it has come to replace. Its greater freedom lies in its ability to offer those who work in it the sense, on the one hand, of continuous opportunity for the expression of capacity, and the power, on the other, to share fully in the making of the rules under which they work. . . . Justice is the parent of freedom."

The freedom and prosperity of British workers cannot be attained in isolation. They are bound up with the welfare of all other peoples It is, therefore, elementary common sense to relate the direction of British effort to the promotion of a higher international standard of living. "For this reason, the Labor party welcomes the recognition of this need in the Atlantic Charter. It applauds the determination of the International Labor Office to go on with its work."

British Labor on Socialist International Policy. Following a program for the further democratization of the state machinery, the party gave its attention [in this report] to international problems. In the field of imperial policies, it continued to affirm "that in all colonial territories the primary object of the administration must be the well being, education, and development of the native inhabitants and their training in every possible way so that they may be able in the shortest possible time to govern themselves." As far as India is concerned, Indian self-government, it contended, is to the interest of Great Britain as well as of India. Sooner or later Great Britain will have to concede the Indian demand. "It is more honorable and more just to act now with magnanimity than to wait until our admission of the Indian claim has lost all character of grace and generosity."

Dealing with the type of international organization which the world should seek to achieve after the war, the Labor party maintained that whatever international society was developed should have the power (a) "to complete the peaceful solution of international disputes; (b) to impose sanctions, both economic and military, against any nation state which rejects such a peaceful solution; (c) to promote common action upon matters of common concern and, especially in this realm, to protect the interests of minorities, both racial and religious, and of those people not able to stand alone; (d) to organize positive and continuous co-operation between states for the purpose of raising the international standard of economic life, and, particularly, of assisting, materially and technically, the less-developed nations to a higher level of well-being; (e) to promote international co-operation and understanding between states . . . ; (f) to safeguard and extend, directly and indirectly, the application of the Four Freedoms to the peoples of all lands, without discrimination in race or color or creed." The new international institutions, furthermore, must be founded upon the full application of democratic principles.

In making the peace, no attempt must be made, declared the party, to impose any peace of revenge, "nor to impose upon the defeated any terms which deprive them of the right to that well-being which is the due reward of capacity and energy exercised in a peaceful way for peaceful ends. . . . It would be a grave disservice to the future of the world to use the power of the victors . . . to promote in any country where revolution may occur, the claims of any privileged interest, whether of class, of religion, of dynasty, against which that revolution is a protest."

The report maintained that only the rapid socialization of the main instruments of production would make for the permanent maintenance of peace and would "enable us to move to that plane of common action where co-operation for abundance instead of division through scarcity is the chief motive in international effort." After the war, the party's report declared, "the economic system will have to lean heavily upon the support of the state. The central question this raises is whether this support is to be operated by the few, as in the past, or by the organized community in the interests of the community," whether it is to be democratic or fascistic.

In effecting such a program, it concludes, the Labor party seeks the support of the British people "not on the narrow ground of class or party." It asks "support from all citizens who are concerned to maintain in the peace that high place in the moral leadership of the world Great Britain has won in the years of conflict."

Numerous other postwar programs, more or less detailed in their nature, were formulated during the course of the war by socialists and progressives on the domestic and international fronts for the postwar period, with a view to full employment, economic and international security, democracy, and freedom.

In Great Britain the British Federation of Trade Unions, the Fabian Society, the Socialist Discussion Group, the Independent Labor party, and other socialist groups as well as individual socialists issued postwar programs. The P. E. P. (Political and Economic Planning) published much literature of a non-political nature on the subject of reconstruction after the war, as did economic, business, and professional groups outside of Great Britain. The International Labor Office formulated programs for the postwar period, as did active labor and socialist parties and the executives of parties in exile.

Other Postwar Programs. In Canada, the C. C. F. in its program, *For Victory and Reconstruction,* adopted at the July, 1942, convention, outlined a program for postwar Canada in which it maintained that the capitalist system in war and peace proved incapable of meeting the nation's needs.[53]

In the United States the Socialist party, the Social Democratic Federation, the American Labor Conference on International Affairs, the League for Industrial Democracy, the Union for Democratic Action, the Textile Workers Union of America, the United Automobile Workers, the C. I. O., the A. F. of L., the Liberal party, the American Labor party, and other labor groups tackled the problems of the postwar world. The International Labor Organization Conference meeting in Philadelphia on May, 1944, adopted an extensive program for the postwar period.[54]

[53] Lewis and Scott, *Make This Your Canada,* pp. 208–13.

[54] See Reports II, III, IV of International Labor Conference, 26th Session, on *Present and Postwar Social Policy, The Organization of Employment* and *Social Security* (Montreal: I. L. O., 1944); Lorwin, *Postwar Plans of the United Nations.*

For a list of governmental and non-governmental organizations which started shortly after the outbreak of the war to formulate postwar reconstruction programs see George B. Galloway, *American Postwar Planning,* and the United Nations Information Bureau. The reports of the National Resources Planning Board, published under the titles, *Security, Work, and Relief Policies, After the War—Full Employment, After the War—Toward Security,* etc., and the 1942, 1943 Reports of the Social Security Board were by 1943 among the most important governmental documents along these lines.

Stuart Chase, in *The Road We are Travelling* and *Goals for America* and other volumes sponsored by the Twentieth Century Fund, set forth postwar goals, proposing

Postwar Depressions and Social Change. Numerous students of social change during the Second World War expressed the viewpoint that the system of private enterprise would face one of its severest tests several years after the war, following a few years of peacetime expansion, during which domestic consumers would have satisfied their pent-up demand for goods, industry would have re-equipped its plants, and foreign nations would have become again able to produce most of what they desired.

Professor Wesley C. Mitchell, dean of American economists, asked the question whether, following such expansion, the people of the United States could "maintain a high level of employment, year in, year out?"

"Experience," he declared, "answers 'no.' Our business record has been one of alternating expansions and contractions. Only near the peak of our most vigorous expansions have we approximated full employment, and no approximation in peacetimes has been so close or lasted so long as the approximations achieved during major wars. Unless we can learn to manage our affairs more skillfully in the future, we

---

(1) full employment; (2) full and prudent use of material resources; (3) the guarantee of the five essentials to every citizen—food, housing, clothing, health services, education; (4) social insurance of all major exposed points in the social structure; and (5) minimum labor standards (*The Road We Are Travelling,* p. 92).

Planning for America, by George B. Galloway and Associates; the periodical literature of the National Planning Association, of the Committee for the Organization of Peace, and of the *New Republic* are especially significant. See also Norman Thomas, *We Have a Future* and *What is Our Destiny?*

One of the most prominent economic advisers of the Roosevelt administration during the Second World War was Professor Alvin H. Hansen of Harvard University. In his postwar program for full employment, Professor Hansen urges that, while retaining intact the system of private enterprise, the government should seek to aid in maintaining a system of full employment, among other things, through sufficient governmental expenditures "to provide a national minimum standard of public services in terms of health, education, and social security," and "an adequate volume of expenditures for urban redevelopment and resources development." The government, he maintains, should endeavor to see to it that, in an economy with a gross national product of 160–165 billion dollars (with a national income of 130 to 135 billion), construction should be stabilized at from 6 to 8 billion dollars for housing; at from 5 to 7 billions for business plant; and at from 5 to 7 billions for public works and improvement projects, federal, state, and local. "I should imagine," he declared, 'that satisfactory progress over the next two decades in terms of urban redevelopment, housing resource development, modernized and enlarged business and industrial facilities, and standard public works would require a volume of construction at around 18 billion. Thereafter we should gradually move toward a higher consumption economy with less emphasis on construction. A really advanced society is not a 'brick and mortar' society." See *New Republic,* Feb. 28, 1944, pp. 270–1. In same issue see postwar programs of Beardsley Ruml, with comments by George Soule and Oswald Knauth. See also Hansen, *Full Recovery or Stagnation.*

must look forward to an indefinite series of cyclical depressions, some relatively mild, some drastic."

During the war, he asserted, many Americans have been irked by government regulations and have looked forward to the return to the prewar economic system. "But if another severe depression occurs after a few years of peacetime expansion . . . , will not millions of people then recall the full employment and the high wages that prevailed under governmental supervision and argue that national planning brings better results than free enterprise? An economic organization that cannot use the most abundant resources in the world to make the goods its people are eager to produce and to consume will come in for heated condemnations and angry demands for drastic 'reforms.' People will listen sympathetically to advocates of over-all governmental planning in peace as well as in war." This advocacy of a collective economy, Professor Mitchell maintained, would be strengthened in their arguments by "the quite unexpected efficiency of the Russian economy." The fact would be stressed that Soviet Russia, after disastrous initial defeats, and after some of her most highly industrialized districts had been overrun by Germans, was able to put into the field an enormous and well-equipped army that expelled the invaders. . . . If the Russians hold to their modified form of communism after the war, and if it approximates the efficiency it is demonstrating now, critics will allege that Americans could maintain full employment of all their resources all the time if only they would stop producing for pecuniary profit and reorganize to produce for the common welfare.

"Thus one of the developments that peace seems likely to bring the United States is a fierce controversy over the fundamental character of economic organization." [55]

Laski on Concentration versus Democratization of Power. As a means of avoiding not only severe depressions after the war, but the undemocratic control of industry and politics by economic overlords, Professor Harold J. Laski urges the control by society of the sources of economic power at the earliest possible moment. "In modern society," he declares, "the large industrial corporations are controlled by a caste of economic directors, mainly remarkable for their skill in financial manipulation, who are masters alike of their shareholders and of the consumer, and are not seldom in a position to hold even the states to ransom. Their power is as massive in volume as it has largely been irresponsible in operation. We have reached a stage in historical evo-

[55] Twenty-fourth Annual Report of the National Bureau of Economic Research. *Economic Research and the Needs of Our Times* (1944), pp. 34–5.

lution where either their power must be subordinated to the interest of the community or the interest of the community will be a tragic pseudonym for their power."

It is for the democratization of economic power, declares Professor Laski, that the Second World War has, in the last analysis, been fought. While the defeat of Hitler "creates the opportunities required for the democratization of economic power," it is far from an assurance that it will be wisely used. We cannot achieve that democratization "if those who own and control property, especially in the era of the giant corporation, are in a position thereby either to acquire special privilege or to act in an arbitrary way. It is difficult to see how we can prevent the growth of these habits unless the vital instruments of production are owned and controlled by the community. . . . I do not think this means the necessity of taking over all industry and agriculture by the state. Rather, I think, it means that the fundamental basis of economic power shall be in the hands of the community. There are four bases of economic power, the supply of capital and credit, the ownership and control of land, the state control of the import and export trades, and the control of transport, fuel, and power. Upon the socialization of these resources it would be possible seriously to begin the process of democratizing economic powers."

The exact forms of nationalized industries, he declares, will differ in different industries. As for the relation of these publicly owned industries to Parliament, "that will . . . be effected through the Cabinet; and I believe that the Cabinet, in its turn, will find it necessary to set up a Committee of Ministers whose work is relevant to the field of production. The committee will need an expert staff, much like Gosplan in the Soviet Union, whose business it will be to prepare for it the material upon which it makes its final submission to the Cabinet which will, in its turn, obtain for them the general approval of Parliament. . . . I see no reason for the creation of an Economic General Staff in addition to these bodies; a new tier in the hierarchy of controls would detract from, rather than add to, its clarity and have the certain effect of delaying decisions which require speed not seldom as of their essence. The general layout of the plan, in a system of parliamentary democracy, is the clear responsibility of Ministers; and that responsibility is weakened, and not strengthened, by a conception like that of Sir William Beveridge, in which an Economic General Staff meditates generally upon planning without the power to decide upon the applicability of its meditations. The more clear the responsibility for decisions, the more direct is likely to be the judgment of their worth." [56]

Cole on the Necessity of Socialism to Avoid Third World War. Not only is an advance toward socialism necessary as a means of avoiding depressions and fascistic controls, but, according to numerous writers on this problem, it is the only alternative to a trend toward another war.

Prior to the Second World War, declared G. D. H. Cole,[57] industry in advanced countries became larger, more restrictive, more monopolistic. The free market gave way to the regulated market under state protection. There was a scramble to monopolize markets—home markets by tariffs, quotas, and the like, colonial markets by the policy of the "closed empire," foreign markets by political as well as economic pressure. "It became easier, in one trade after another, to make high profits by monopoly and low output than by competition to enlarge demand; and the growth of social legislation and collective bargaining actually helped on these monopolistic tendencies by reducing competition in the labor market and making costs more rigid and price-cutting therewith less worth-while."

Technological advance obscured this tendency. It is true that, with new inventions and the rapid improvement of technique, capitalism turned out an increasing quantity of goods. "But whereas capitalism in its earlier phases had, apart from its recurrent periods of crisis, turned out goods up to its maximum productive capacity, the newer capitalism dared not do this, for fear of glutting the market . . . The crises continued, and the epidemic of unemployment with them; but to this was added an inability of capitalism to find work for all willing hands, even at the top of a boom. In effect, underproduction—that is, a total output immensely below what was technically possible—became characteristic of world capitalism in its new, monopolistic forms.

"Such a situation was bound to lead to a violent recurrence of the disease of economic nationalism. It set each country at work on attempts to transfer its own economic misfortunes to its neighbors. . . . The economic nationalists . . . gave full support to political nationalism; and the political nationalists, in turn, became the faithful executants of nationalist economic policies. The result was impoverishment all round, and an economic structure in violent conflict with the basic necessities of modern productive technique.

"From this folly there can be no turning back to the old progressive capitalism of laissez faire. That form of capitalism was everywhere

[56] Laski, *Reflections on the Revolution of Our Time,* pp. 351–2.

[57] Cole, *Europe, Russia, and the Future,* pp. 48 ff.

dead or dying even before the last war." It cannot be revived because technological conditions have necessitated the organization of huge industrial units and "no power on earth can prevent these huge units from following restrictive and monopolistic policies. Indeed, attempts to prevent them are apt to make matters worse, by causing crises of 'underinvestment' and destroying that 'business confidence' without which a system dependent on the psychological reactions of business leaders cannot be made to work. . . . If, then, at the end of this war, we attempt to put the capitalist system back, the only form in which we can put it back is that of large-scale combinations with an inherent tendency towards restriction and monopoly. If it is attempted, and the new Europe is built on this foundation, it is safe to prophesy another great war within a generation, and, during the intervening years, a condition of economic chaos very much worse than that which existed between 1918 and 1939."

Three other alternatives are possible. One of them is to adopt a system closely akin to fascism, under which "the state will become the general planner and director of capitalist policies and programs," and the capitalists will do what the state tells them—on condition that they control the state and can use it as an instrument for keeping the working class in order. The other alternative is that the great capitalist groups will link up internationally under the aegis of American capitalism, and will force the various states to carry out their orders and the lesser capitalists to obey them—in effect, a kind of international capitalist feudalism under American leadership. The third alternative is democratic socialism.

If the various states endeavor to direct and plan capitalist policies, the states will have to take responsibility for the prevention of unemployment within their own frontiers. For a while it will be possible for these states to make a successful appeal for tax revenues as a means of providing work to rebuild the country. But when the period of reconstruction comes to an end, the capitalists will cry for a remission of the burdens of high taxation; and this action in turn will lead to a great increase in unemployment.

"The truth is that neither 'New Deal' work-finding nor nazi work-finding are workable as permanent solutions. The state cannot go on indefinitely with a grossly unbalanced budget, though it can go on much longer than orthodox financiers used to believe possible. The nazi economy worked only because it was meant to be temporary, and to end in war. The Roosevelt economy could work only as long as the American public were prepared to stand for a continuous piling up of the national debt.

"If, then, postwar Europe tries the nazi methods of 'national economy,' it will end up either in resorting to intensive rearmament to employ the peoples, or in a recurrence of mass-unemployment leading to economic and political collapse." [58]

If some sort of international feudal capitalism, on the other hand, is resorted to, "it will break down through inability to find markets for its products and under stress of the revolt its restrictionist policies will provoke. Finally, an attempt to extend international feudalism from the economic to the political sphere, by way of a capitalist super-state, will break upon the same rock of a limited market, and will end in war and revolution when the component capitalist groups fall out over the division of the spoils."

"What emerges from this analysis," declares Cole, "is that no capitalist solution of the European problem—that is, no solution which leaves the basic industries in private hands and continues to use private profit as an incentive to production—offers any prospect of permanence, or of escape from war." [59] The same general position was taken by the Executive Committee of the British Labor party in its report to the Labor Congress, in which it maintained that "war is inherent in the nature of a capitalist society."

Peaceful Progress toward World Socialism. The possibilities of a peaceful versus a violent transition to a socialized order in democratic capitalist countries after the defeat of Hitler were debated during the Second World War by numerous socialistic writers.

Dr. Paul M. Sweezy of the Department of Economics, Harvard University, in his *The Theory of Capitalist Development,* saw, following the war, the comparatively peaceful spread of socialism in Western continental Europe, the possible triumph of socialist forces in Great Britain, and the evolution of the entire Far East, including India, China, and Japan, in the socialist direction. The socialist sector, "with its stronger and more stable socialist system," would then, "it seems not unlikely . . . ," maintained Dr. Sweezy, "exercise a progressively disintegrating effect on the structure of the imperialist system, first paralyzing its capacity for aggression and then chipping out bit by bit the cement which holds it together as a cohesive social structure. Under these circumstances, paradoxically enough, a peaceful transition to socialism would for the first time become a genuine possibility. If—and

[58] *Ibid.*, p. 53.

[59] *Ibid.*, p. 57.

it seems by no means unthinkable—democratic forms in the Anglo-American countries were to survive even as great an upheaval as we have pictured, it would now be possible to fill them with a socialist content. Once socialism has had an opportunity to demonstrate its superiority on a large scale and under reasonably favorable conditions, the effect not only on the working class but also on the great majority of the middle classes still living under capitalist conditions can be counted upon to be unprecedentedly powerful. The adherents of socialism will multiply by leaps and bounds; the small oligarchy whose social existence is bound up with the old order will be weakened, deprived of its international support, and eventually rendered impotent. In the latter stages of the world revolution, democracy may at long last be able to fulfil the promises which have so far remained unhonored amid the frustrations of a self-contradictory economic system." [60]

Others during the war saw many violent upheavals taking place before a stable socialist society on a world scale was established, and still others, in view of the complexity of the all-over picture following the war, refused to hazard even a guess as to the probabilities of peaceful, as contrasted with violent progress toward a new social order.

Socialists and Post-Fascist Regimes. While socialists in democratic countries were engaged during the late thirties and early forties in working out future programs to end the depression or to reconstruct after the war their respective economies along democratic lines, socialists in exile or still living under the rule of fascist and nazi groups were formulating plans for a democratic society when, through defeat in civil or international war, their rulers were compelled to hand over the government machinery to the common people. In Germany especially, these groups agreed with H. N. Brailsford that, although many factors contributed to the rise of nazism, the republic fell, among other reasons, because, following the First World War, "its paper constitutions and its elaborate democratic mechanism left its enemies entrenched in the seats of power"—its Junkers still owned the broad acres of German land; its monarchist class supplied the judges who interpreted the new constitution; the old military class controlled the army; and large industrial magnates continued to control industry and used a part of their profits to buy the services of Hitler and equip his private army.[61] They agreed with the Executives of the German Social Democratic party at Prague in 1934 that the "great historical error committed by a German labor movement was that it should have taken over the old machinery of gov-

[60] Sweezy, *The Theory of Capitalist Development*, pp. 361–2.

[61] Miles, *Socialism's New Beginning*, p. 5.

ernment virtually unchanged."[62] The program of these groups was thus based upon the thesis that the first thing that a revolutionary government in Germany and other fascist countries should do would be to purge the government of all traces of nazism and of the reactionary movement and to fill all important posts with those having the confidence of the revolutionary movement. Its first act thus "must be to secure its existence against attack from within and without."[63] Its second act should be to take over "all the large-scale industrial enterprises which are politically or economically of social importance."[64]

Paul Hagen, a German socialist and an active worker for many years in the German underground movement, in his analysis of the situation during the Second World War, took the same general point of view. The Junkers and the big industrialists must go, following the defeat of Hitlerism, if nazism is not to regain power in Germany. "For more than a century the democratic movement in Germany," declared Hagen, "struggled vainly to break the privileged position and the virtual hegemony of the Junkers, a total of about 15,000 families among a people of 70,000,000. . . . To attempt to conserve economically privileged groups after the war in Germany, or to reopen the competitive fight between them would be to pronounce a death sentence on millions of Germans, and to endanger Europe's reconstruction. The rise of productivity would immediately be curtailed. Meanwhile the danger would exist that the traditional upper classes, thus bolstered, would prepare the ground for another aggressive venture. Therefore, the social program for a freedom movement [in Germany] had to be *a system of democratic planning, as against a restoration of profit capitalism*. . . . At the same time, the freedom movement will have to defend a liberal political program, guaranteeing political and personal liberty in a planned system, against any neo-totalitarian party or group."[65]

RECENT CRITIQUES OF MARXISM

Criticisms of Marxian Theories. In the interwar days there was far less discussion of such theoretical foundation stones of Marxism—the materialist conception of history, the class struggle, and surplus value—than in former decades, attention being turned to the more practical problems of socialization. A number of writers, however, continued the revision of Marxian doctrines during these years.

[62] See Laidler, *Socializing Our Democracy*, p. 86.

[63] Miles, *Socialism's New Beginning*, p. 63. This pamphlet was written by a New Beginning Group in Germany in late 1933.

[64] Miles, *op. cit.*, p. 63.

[65] Paul Hagen, *Germany After Hitler*, pp. 138, 146, 148 (N. Y.: Farrar and Rinehart, 1944).

Marxism as a Religion. One of the most vigorous criticisms against the Marxian system during this period was that of Max Eastman, who directed his attacks largely against Marx's dialectic materialism and against Marx's belief, based on his philosophical concepts, borrowed in modified form from Hegel, that the "materialistic universe" was making for the certain success of a socialist society.

The dialectic materialism of Marx, affirms Eastman, declares that "the world is essentially material and that mind evolved out of matter in connection with the complex organization of the central nervous system in animals and men." [66] Marx discarded Hegel's idealism, in so far as to assert that not thought, nor ideas, but "sense experience" was the real world. "But he retained in his conception of that sense-object the essential virtue that Hegel had attributed to his Idea, the property of purposive dialectic movement toward high ends. The only radical change was that, whereas Hegel's ideal reality was traveling toward an ideal goal in the being of God, Marx's sensible reality was traveling toward a sensible goal in the organization of the communist society. Marx thought that he had thus saved the 'rational kernel,' and got rid of the 'mystical shell' in the Hegelian philosophy. He even thought, and tried to keep on thinking, that he had achieved his aim to get rid of philosophy altogether and be scientific. But one does not get rid of philosophy by the simple device of turning an idealist philosophy the other side up. One does not get rid of philosophy without clearly understanding what one means by philosophy, and how it differs from the scientific point of view." [67]

Marxists, incorporating dialectic materialism in their beliefs, continues Eastman, acquired the belief that the external universe was "evolving with reliable, if not divine, necessity in exactly the direction which they want to go . . . This is not a scientific, but, in the most technical sense, a religious conception of the world." [68]

Marxists, Eastman argues, should abandon the dialectic religion and consciously substitute scientific skepticism for the Hegelian philosophy of Marx. Such abandonment might deprive them of "a religious certainty of success," but they would be "more than compensated by the advantages of a consciously practical and scientific attitude." [69] It would remove from them a certain fear of the developments of science, make possible a sensible policy toward other religions, and lead to the

[66] Eastman, *Marxism: Is It Science?* p. 251; see also Harry Paxton Howard in *Retort,* June, 1942.

[67] Eastman, *op. cit.,* p. 194.

[68] *Ibid.,* p. 15.

[69] *Ibid.,* p. 250.

discarding of "the irresponsible Marxian generalizations about morals," [70] and lessen the danger of bureaucratism and utopianism among Marxian leaders. Dialectic materialism, declares Eastman, is entirely unintelligible to simple men. It provides an "esoteric doctrine, property of the few who have learned to 'think dialectically' "; results in dividing the few from the common people, with their "vulgar gospel" and "militates directly against the formation of a radically democratic society." [71] Eastman might have added that there had been comparatively little discussion of "dialectic materialism" in the socialist movements of the world in the last few decades and that many who were active in the movement had little conception of the meaning of the term.

In the twenties and thirties, likewise, numerous criticisms were directed by progressive scholars against extreme applications of the economic interpretation of history,[72] the theory of class struggle,[73] and the Marxian theory of value.[74]

[70] *Ibid.*, p. 260.

[71] *Ibid.*, pp. 263–4, 267 ff. For an analysis made in the late thirties of dialectical materialism from a sympathetic viewpoint, see William J. Blake, *Marxian Economic Theory,* ch. XLI; also Sidney Hook, *Towards the Understanding of Karl Marx* (1933), chs. IX–XIII; see text, pp. 241–42.

[72] See Dr. Harry Elmer Barnes, Dr. Alexander Goldenweiser, Ernest Untermann, and others on "The Economic Interpretation of History" in Laidler and Thomas, *The Socialism of Our Times,* ch. XI; and also see M. M. Bober in *Karl Marx's Interpretation of History.*

[73] Dr. William Leiserson and others in Laidler and Thomas, *The Socialism of Our Times,* p. 244 ff. Dr. Leiserson maintains that the revision needed in the theory of the class struggle is "not in the theory of class struggles, but rather in the deduction from that theory of a simplified class struggle between capitalist and proletarian" (p. 247). See Louis B. Boudin's defense of the class struggle concept, *Ibid.*, p. 263 ff.

[74] See discussion on Marxian theory of value by Dr. N. I. Stone, Algernon Lee, and others, *ibid.*, pp. 344 ff. See likewise William J. Blake, *Marxian Economic Theory;* Sidney Hook, *Towards the Understanding of Karl Marx.*

William J. Blake, in chapter XXXVI of his *Marxian Economic Theory,* reviews the objections to the Marxian labor theory of value and other Marxian concepts by recent British critics. The criticisms are contained, among others, in H. W. B. Joseph's *Labor Theory of Value in Karl Marx,* A. D. Lindsay's *Karl Marx's Capital,* F. R. Salter's *Karl Marx and Modern Society,* and A. L. Rowse's *Criterion.* Among the British expositions of Marxism, mostly favorable, during the thirties were G. D. H. Cole's *What Marx Really Meant,* Maurice Dobb's *Political Economy and Capitalism,* and John Strachey's *Theory and Practice of Socialism;* text, pp. 241–42.

In Chapter XXXVII, Blake sets forth briefly such American criticisms as those found in O. D. Skelton's *Socialism, a Critical Analysis* and in the writings of Thorstein Veblen, A. S. Sachs, F. W. Taussig, E. R. A. Seligman, Lewis Corey, Paul H. Douglas, Howard Scott, Lewis H. Haney, John Dewey, J. R. Commons, Norman Thomas, Emil Lederer, I. M. Rubinow, and A. M. Bingham, Jr.

See also H. B. Parkes, *Marxism: An Autopsy.* In 1942, Paul M. Sweezy of Harvard University presented a comprehensive analysis of Marxian political economy in *The Theory of Capitalist Development.*

SUMMARY

It is thus seen that, since the war, socialists and other progressive thinkers have attacked the question of socialization of industry from various angles. They have given increased attention to the problem of securing an alliance between labor, middle class, professional, and managerial groups in the march toward a co-operative social order and in the operation of collectivized industry. They have studied the important problems of ensuring the application of democratic principles and procedures to the political, economic, and cultural sectors of society and of avoiding bureaucratic and dictatorial controls. They have made unique contributions to the problems of price-fixing and social planning under socialism and to the place of the consumer and producer in the industrial set-up.

They have given increased consideration to the questions of industrial incentives, to the problem of avoiding the unemployment and waste of the present economic order, to ways and means of undermining the forces that make for fascism, and of building nationally and internationally for a secure and abundant society, following the war against the fascist aggressors. And they have given much thought to the relative place of public, co-operative, and private enterprise in a co-operative social order.

They have also endeavored in recent years to relate the latest findings in social psychology, biology, and anthropology to human motivation under various types of social and economic systems, and have continued to debate the validity of Marxian economics.

In fascist countries, socialists, despite enormous difficulties, developed plans for the return of their respective countries to democratic forms of government and to the bringing about on a democratic basis of a collectivized order of industrial society.

PART SEVEN

Consumer Co-operation and Miscellaneous Movements

CHAPTER 41

The Co-operative Movement

IN THE preceding pages, we have discussed the thought life of socialism, and the efforts of socialists and of communists, through the control of the state, to put their theories into practice. While the socialist forces have been gathering strength, in their efforts to reconstruct industrial society, tens of thousands of workers, through the consumers' co-operative societies, have been quietly engaged in the practical work of building up an industrial democracy owned and controlled by working-class consumers within the framework of the capitalistic order.

CO-OPERATION IN GREAT BRITAIN

The Birth of the Consumers' Co-operative Movement. Various dates have been given for the birth of the modern consumers' co-operative movement. The first consumers' society of which definite records are available was that of the Fenwick Weavers, organized in Ayrshire, near Glasgow, Scotland, in 1769. During the next half century several other societies were founded in the Glasgow district, which may be regarded as the "cradle of the co-operative movement." [1]

The movement gained a new impetus during the twenties of the nineteenth century as a result of the agitation of Robert Owen in behalf of working-class communities. The communities, Owen urged, were, indeed, "as unlike the aims of the first co-operative societies as chalk is unlike cheese," but his propaganda popularized the notion of associated industry, and in time, "almost all poor workers who desired to escape from the slavery of the new factories and the horror of the new towns were convinced that if only they were to live together in a community, they would be as secure as any fugitive who ever sought sanctuary." [2]

[1] See Warbasse, James P., *Co-operative Democracy*, p. 379.

[2] T. W. Mercer, in "One Hundred Years Ago," *People's Year Book*, 1925, p. 13.

Starting out with a desire to organize such colonies, they soon came to the realization that they must have a certain initial capital to start with; that they had none; and that the rich and powerful had no wish to help them out. One plan of saving funds that suggested itself was that of co-operation in the buying and selling of necessities. They could put aside the amount that would be saved and use the accumulated funds for community purposes.

KING AND THE BRIGHTON PIONEERS. One of the most ardent co-operators of this period was Dr. William King, a physician of Brighton, who financed and edited *The Co-operator* (1828–30), a publication setting forth sound principles on which co-operative stores should be founded. A year previous to the issuance of this paper, a Brighton Society had been formed, with a capital of 100 pounds, and had opened a store for business. During the next few years some 300 co-operative stores sprang up in various parts of England. While most of these went out of existence, the movement did not die.

The Rochdale Experiment. It was not, however, until the forties that what might be called the standardized co-operative movement was born. In November, 1843, some twenty-eight flannel weavers, after an unsuccessful strike, met one afternoon in the Chartist Reading Room in Rochdale, England, near the great manufacturing center of Manchester, and discussed what could be done to better their condition. They finally agreed on a plan for starting a retail store to be owned and managed by the members, and to be run without profit. Twelve of the more opulent resolved to put aside a few pence a week toward the initial capital, and in the course of a year the weavers accumulated $140. They hired the ground floor of an old warehouse in Toad Lane, and, amid the derisive remarks of neighboring storekeepers, opened up the store December, 1844, for trade on Mondays and Saturday nights. "The objects and plans of this society," they wrote, "are to form arrangements for the pecuniary benefit and improvement of the social and domestic condition of its members."

Their first step was the sale of goods, but that was to be followed, they asserted in their rules, by the erection of houses, the manufacture of necessities, and the purchase of estates which might be cultivated by unemployed or poorly remunerated members. "As soon as practicable," they added, "this society shall proceed to arrange the powers of production, distribution, education, and government; or, in other words, to establish a self-supporting home colony of united interests, or assist other societies in establishing such colonies."

Rochdale Principles. They organized their society on principles which have been followed in general by the co-operative movement from that day to this. These principles were:

1. Each member of a society shall have one vote in such matters as the determination of policies and the election of officers, and one vote only.

2. Capital invested in the society shall receive a fixed rate of dividends, which shall be no more than the minimum commercial rate.

3. Any surplus accruing by virtue of the difference between the net cost and the net selling price of commodities and services—after meeting running expenses, paying interest, and setting aside a fund for depreciation, improvements, etc.—shall be returned to the members as savings-returns or "dividends" in proportion to their purchases, or spent for education or other social purposes.

In addition, the Rochdale pioneers decided (1) to sell goods on a cash basis; (2) to permit unlimited membership in the society; (3) preferably to charge the patrons prices similar to those charged by neighboring competitors in profit-making industry, rather than cost prices, so that they might accumulate capital and obviate hostile competition; (4) to insist on "supplying the purest provisions they could get, giving full weight and measure"; (5) to observe religious and political neutrality; (6) to expand co-operative services, in conjunction with other co-operatives, until these services included the control of raw materials and the production of certain necessities, and ultimately to form national and international organizations having a common aim; and (7) constantly to engage in educational work in the fields of co-operation and the social sciences in general.

Growth of the Rochdale Store. At the end of 1845 these Rochdale Pioneers, as they were called, had a membership of eighty, and a capital of $900. They early resolved to set aside from 2 to 5 per cent of their savings for educational purposes. They added commodity after commodity to their stock of merchandise, developed a reading room and library, and added recreational, banking, insurance, and other features. At its Fifty Year Jubilee, in 1894, this single society was able to report a membership of 12,000, funds of $2,000,000, and an annual business of $1,500,000. By 1939 its membership had reached about 40,000. Its accumulated sales by 1936 amounted to $150,000,000, and its savings during these years had amounted to about $20,000,000.

The Co-operative Union. The consumers' co-operative movement has steadily expanded in Great Britain from 1844 to the present time.

As the movement gained strength, the co-operators looked toward a federation of societies. Conferences were held in London in 1850, 1855, and, finally, 1869. In this latter year a federation was formed, which grew into the Co-operative Union, created for the purpose of education, propaganda, and protection.

This union now contains most of the British co-operative societies of Great Britain and "may be regarded as the soul of the British movement." [3] During its years of service it has published many dozens of tracts interpreting the work of the movement; has established scores of libraries and reading rooms; has conducted hundreds of courses on co-operation and civic problems; has organized lectures and entertainments; has given needed advice to struggling stores; has acted as arbitrator in times of disputes; has lessened the evil of overlapping; has defended the movement in Parliament; and, in many other ways, has helped to solidify the forces of co-operation and to bring before the membership the larger aims of the movement.

The Establishment of the Wholesale. Because of discrimination, the co-operative stores at first frequently found it difficult to obtain goods from wholesalers and, as isolated units, were often compelled to purchase goods in very small quantities. Agitation consequently arose for the establishment of a wholesale society owned by retail co-operative societies. In 1850 the Rochdale Pioneers set up a wholesale department of their own and in 1864, nearly twenty years after the establishment of the Rochdale store, a central wholesale—the Co-operative Wholesale Society at Manchester—began its remarkable career.

The headquarters of the wholesale appeared at first like "a gaunt spectre haunting certain rooms in Cooper Street and starving upon quarter rations." The wholesale, however, soon began to develop. During the first few years it confined its transactions and displays to groceries, boots, and shoes, but later added clothing, furniture, tea, printing, and various other services, and opened branches in London, Newcastle, and certain other cities. The Scottish co-operators began their wholesale in 1868.

Co-operative Factories. Following the development of the wholesale, the British co-operators decided, as their next step, to become their own brokers and to station purchasing agents in various parts of the world. Depots were established in Cork, New York, Hamburg, Copenhagen, Montreal, Freetown, South Africa, and other cities.

From becoming their own brokers, they soon took up the business of

[3] Warbasse, *op. cit.*, p. 389; see also Laidler, Harry W., *The British Co-operative Movement.*

manufacturing and established a number of factories for the preparation of such essential commodities as bread, flour, corn, cocoa, chocolate, lard, butter, jam, and tobacco. In this way only, they declared, could they assure the quality of their goods. Great factories were established, likewise, for the making of boots, shoes, and clothing. In 1874 they began the manufacture of soap and later organized a depot in Africa for the collection of palm oil and kernels, to be used for that purpose. By 1966 it operated more than 200 factories, mills and farms and produced a remarkably wide range of goods.

Land Purchases of Co-operatives. With the establishment of productive enterprises, the cry of "back to the land" was raised by numerous co-operators. These argued that the ideal of co-operation would not be reached until the movement owned some part of the soil and grew its own raw materials thereon. In accordance with this belief, the Co-operative Wholesale Society in 1896 purchased for $150,000 an estate of between 700 and 800 acres in the western part of England for the raising of fruits and vegetables. Eight years later it added another estate near Hereford, with great numbers of fruit trees. By the late thirties it had acquired about 50,000 acres of land in England.

In 1902 the English and Scottish wholesales purchased three large tea estates in Ceylon and at the outbreak of the Second World War carried in its own ships sufficient tea from its tea plantations to rank it far above the Lipton Company as the largest tea importer in England. In 1940 the English wholesale boasted a sale of over 60,000,000 pounds of that beverage.

In 1916 the Co-operative Wholesale Society obtained title to 10,000 acres of wheat land in Canada, and later bought palm oil estates in West Africa. It owns many steamships and possesses its own fishing fleet. It was long the largest single purchaser of Canadian wheat in the world, and its flour mills are the largest in Great Britain.

Entrance into Banking. The early co-operators soon saw the advantage of mobilizing their credit and conducting their own banking operations, and in 1872 the English wholesale opened a Deposit and Loan Department. This department, afterwards termed the Banking Department of the Co-operative Wholesale Society, received deposits from retail societies and loaned money to them in time of need. In the 1960's the C. W. S. Bank was one of the country's most important financial institutions. Interest rates on deposit accounts were higher than those offered by major banks. Most of England's retail societies and thousands of trade unions and friendly societies keep their accounts with this institution. The wholesale is now open for business to individual members who may deposit money with it through the retail co-operative stores, and borrow money from it for the purpose of building or purchasing their own homes. Its loans have facilitated building of working-class homes. Its municipal authority loans are large.

The Co-operative Insurance Business. Four years after the formation of the wholesale, the society entered the insurance business and handled its own fire insurance. It was, however, slow to realize the desirability of providing its members with industrial life insurance. Although the life insurance business was organized in 1886, it was not until 1900 that industrial insurance policies were offered its members. Since then, however, the progress of the department has been steady. At present practically every kind of industrial insurance is conducted by the Insurance Department—fire, accident, death, workingmen's compensation, employers' liability, burglary, and fidelity guaranty.

Perhaps the greatest achievement of the Co-operative Insurance Department is the so-called Collective Insurance Scheme, under which it is possible for retail co-operative stores to insure as societies. The retail long paid to the Wholesale Insurance Department two cents a year for each $5 of purchase made by members. By this means, all of the members of the co-operative are automatically insured. Insurance money is paid to the wife or husband on the basis of the average annual purchase made by the members during the three years prior to death. The expense of administering the plan is about 3 per cent of the premium paid in, only a small percentage of that incurred in administering the average industrial insurance company.

Between the First and Second World Wars, the C. I. S. made more progress than any other insurance company of Great Britain. Its total premium income in 1964 was around $220,000,000, and its funds were about $1,000,000,000.

Present Extent of the Movement. In 1961 co-operative societies had 29,396 retail establishments that conducted about 10.8 per cent (nearly $2.7 billion) of the total retail business, about one third of all dairy trade and one fifth of the grocery trade. In 1964, retail societies employed over 250,000 persons. The membership of the co-operatives was over 12,000,000. The movement possessed 25 factories and the largest wholesale organization in the country. The co-ops returned in dividends to purchasers an average of 4 per cent. In 1955, to increase the efficiency of the movement, it began the reorganization of the co-operative structure.[4]

[4] Prepared by the Central Office of Information, London, 1966, pp. 17, 18.

Control of Co-operatives. Any person of either sex can at any time join a consumers' co-operative society by purchasing a share of stock (in most of the societies the shares range from $5 to $10). As a rule, membership begins as soon as the first deposit on the share is paid to the society. The remainder of the stock is frequently paid for out of the dividends which would naturally accrue to the member through purchases at the store. All members are privileged to attend the quarterly meetings of the society and to vote on all issues. As has been before stated, each member has one vote and one vote only, irrespective of the number of shares owned.

"The poorest, youngest, humblest adult of either sex, who yesterday made his first purchase, if he pays up a single pound for his share," declared the Fabian Research Department, "is equally governor and controller of the whole colossal enterprise, and has an equal voice in the decisions of its most momentous issues with the man who has been a member since its establishment."

The membership elects the committee on store management, which ranges from 7 to 28 in number. Officers must possess a certain minimum of shares; in most societies employees are excluded from holding office. This democratically elected committee on management appoints the store manager, where he is not elected at meetings of the society, and has charge of the affairs of the society. The membership of the co-operative stores is overwhelmingly working class in its character—miners, weavers, artisans—and the management committee is, as a rule, very largely composed of manual workers. In many suburbs, however, professional and clerical groups exert an important influence.

The co-operative wholesale societies are managed in the same democratic fashion, from the standpoint of consumers, as are the retail societies. The large majority of the retail co-operatives in Great Britain are members of the English or Scottish wholesales. Each retail society, upon joining the wholesale, buys from the wholesale shares for every member it has enrolled. In England a society has one vote in the wholesale for every 500 of its members; in Scotland, voting power is proportionate to purchases from the wholesale. Delegate meetings, at which financial reports are presented and discussed and the general affairs of the society considered, are held by these wholesales twice yearly.

The management of the English wholesale is in the hands of thirty-odd directors elected by the delegates of retail societies to hold office for two years. These directors give their entire time to the business of the wholesale at a modest salary. The Scottish wholesale has a board of management of twelve. The majority of the boards of the English and Scottish wholesales is composed of workers. These two committees are proof of the capacity of the British workmen for industrial self-government.

The Co-operative party works closely with the Labor party, the local branches joining with labor in campaigns for local and parliamentary candidates. The aim of this party is both to make the mass of co-operators politically conscious and to permeate the Labor party with a knowledge of co-operative ideas and practices.

CO-OPERATION IN CONTINENTAL EUROPE

The above extensive review of the development of the British consumers' co-operative movement has been given because Great Britain was the "cradle of the Rochdale co-operative movement" and for years co-operators from other countries obtained their inspiration from British co-operative developments. The consumers' co-operative movement has spread throughout the world, and been particularly successful on the continent of Europe.

Belgium. In Belgium, consumers' co-operation took root in 1880, through the efforts of de Paepe, Anseele, Bertrand, Vandervelde, and others. The largest section of the Belgian movement until the Second World War differed from the British in several ways:

(1) It had always been an integral part of the trade-union and political labor movements. The ideal of the Belgian co-operators was to have the trade union, co-operative, and political wings of the labor movement work in complete harmony with each other and mutually to supplement each other. The co-operative store, declared Anseele years ago, is "a fortress whereby to bombard the capitalist society with potatoes and 4-lb. loaves of bread." [5] This unity was achieved to the advantage of all. Most of the workers in the Labor party were co-operators and trade-unionists. The headquarters of the three forms of working-class activity were usually in the same buildings and, directly and indirectly, the co-operative movement came to the assistance of the trade-union movement during economic crises and assisted in the propaganda of the political organization.

(2) The movement had its inception in co-operative bakeries rather than stores, and the importance of this phase of co-operation continued for three-score years.

(3) The movement laid little emphasis on the savings-return or "dividends" feature of co-operation. Rather than return a substantial

[5] Quoted in Warbasse, *op. cit.*, Gide, *Consumers' Co-operative Societies*, p. 39.

"dividend" to the member-purchaser at the end of each quarter, it sought to render the members certain social services that were performed in some other countries by the socialized state, such as old-age pensions, life, accident, unemployment, and maternity insurance, medical and nursing benefits, and educational services features. The "dividends" actually returned to the members were in the form of dockets which might be exchanged for goods at the co-operative store, rather than in the form of cash.

(4) It made a feature of the beautiful *Maison du Peuple* (House of the People) in each city and village, as a headquarters for co-operative, trade-union, and socialist purposes, for dramatic performances, lectures, library facilities, and recreation. The *Maison du Peuple* in Brussels and the *Voorhuit* in Ghent were famous throughout Europe as centers of the labor movement in its trade union, political, and co-operative aspects. Besides the socialist co-operatives there were the Catholic, Christian, Democratic, and Liberal groups of societies and also the neutral societies in which civil servants formed the majority of the membership. In 1963, consumers' societies, socialist and non-socialist, had a membership of 758,000, a more than 50 per cent increase over 1953.

A score or more of productive societies were affiliated with the *Société Générale Cooperative. La Prévoyance,* the insurance society of the co-operative and labor movement, was one of the largest insurance companies in the country.[6]

Sweden. Since the 1930's the most discussed co-operative movement in Europe was that in Sweden. While the Swedish co-operatives toward the end of the sixties were not the largest in Europe in proportion to the total retail trade in the country, they were in many ways one of the most imaginative and enterprising of the European movements, and were making remarkable strides with every passing year. The successful fight by the co-operatives against national and international monopolies, among other things, excited the admiration of students of co-operation throughout the world. In Sweden in the sixties the members of the co-operatives and their families constituted about 40 per cent of the Swedish population.

6 "The workman . . . willingly allows himself to be drawn into a network of schemes of insurance, providence, and mutual aids which surrounds him completely from his birth to his death, and follows him into all the actions of his domestic, working and political life. He is taught how to vote properly and not to drink alcohol. It is in order to keep in daily touch with him and to be able to control his actions more minutely that all Belgian co-operative societies make the selling of bread the basis of their operations." Gide, *op. cit.*, pp. 39–40.

The first concrete development of co-operation in this Scandinavian country was among farmers in the province of Uppland in 1850. However, until the turn of the century the Swedish movement, a victim of adverse legislation, of inefficient practices, and of generally unfavorable social conditions, was significant largely for its failures.

In 1899, however, despite these failures, about 300 co-operative stores were in existence. In that year a conference was called of representatives from existing co-operative societies. Forty-one societies responded to this call, and the conference resulted in the birth of the *Ko-operativa Forbundet,* or K. F., the co-ordinating agency. The co-operatives gained headway slowly until after the First World War.

Total sales volume of the societies was about $6,000,000 in 1912, nearly $30,000,000 six years later. The retail trade of the co-operative societies grew steadily during the following decades. After the Second World War and also during the fifties and sixties, the expansion accelerated, first through the self-service shops initiated by the co-ops, and later through even more competitive supermarkets and department stores. At the end of 1966 there were 297 consumer societies with approximately 36,000 employees and 1,356,000 members, with a total annual turnover of about $1,100,000 in their 3,450 outlets, of which 135 were department stores. The retail societies affiliated with K. F. accounted for 17 per cent of the total retail trade in Sweden, and for about 25 per cent of the foodstuffs trade. The largest Swedish co-operative society, and since 1962 the world's largest also, has been *Konsum* Stockholm. At the end of 1966 this society had 232,000 members and a turnover of more than $200,000,000.

Recent activity has been characterized by the amalgamation of societies, shops, factories, and regional warehouses to form larger units in order to achieve greater efficiency and thereby create the basis for an even more active price policy. The dividend returned to the members of the Swedish co-operative societies is relatively low, 3 to 4 per cent, a price policy that has favorably influenced the development of Swedish consumer co-operation.

As early as 1909 the co-operatives gave battle to the European margarine monopoly, acquiring their own margarine plant and greatly reducing prices to consumers throughout the country. In 1922, in protest against the high prices exacted by the flour trust, they bought a flour mill and modernized it. After acquiring another mill in 1925, K. F. became one of Sweden's largest millers. Bakeries followed. In 1925 K. F. bought a shoe factory. One year later it broke the grip of the rubber monopoly by manufacturing general rubber products, galoshes, and auto tires. It was able to reduce the price charged for galoshes by 56 per cent without reducing the wages of the workers.

The most spectacular fight against large combines of capital took place in the manufacture and sale of electric light bulbs. The international monopoly in this field was reaping large profits, and the consumers were paying 37 cents for a 60-watt lamp. The co-operatives entered the field, built a bulb factory, "Luma," which proved to be a model of efficiency, and sold Luma co-operative bulbs for 20 cents. Later, when a portion of its stock was purchased by the wholesales in Denmark, Norway, and Finland, the Luma factory became the first international co-operative factory.

In 1966 K. F.'s total sales amounted to about $825,000,000, a figure which made K. F. the largest enterprise in Scandinavia. The wholesale value of goods produced by fully integrated co-operative factories was approximately $380,000,000. K. F. thus carried on extensive industrial activities of its own. In addition, it held at least a 50 per cent interest in a number of companies, the output of which amounted to $55,000,000.

The co-operative movement in the cities was active during the thirties in the field of housing as well as in those of food and clothing. As a result of the remarkable development of the co-operative housing movement in Stockholm, at least 15 per cent of the population of the capital city at the outbreak of the Second World War lived in co-operative houses. This development added greatly to the beauty of the city and the quality of living of the working and middle classes.

Housing co-operation in Sweden is today represented by two national associations: HSB (National Association of Tenants' Savings and Building Societies) and SR (Co-operative Building Organization of the Swedish Trade Unions). In 1966, HSB and SR assisted in the construction of 23,750 new homes, about 27 per cent of the total.

Excellent relations have existed for many years between the consumers' movement and the agriculture wholesale. The latter supplies farmers' co-operative unions, to which 170,000 farmers belonged in the mid-sixties.

During the thirties, K. F. concluded an agreement with the farmers' wholesale providing a delimitation of the spheres of activity between the consumers' and agricultural movements. SL, the Federation of Swedish Farmers' Associations, with a membership of 250,000 farmers, acts as a supply and marketing organization. It co-operates with the K. F., among other things, in a jointly owned fertilizer factory, the output of which was valued in 1966 at some $20,000,000. The agricultural co-operative movement in 1966 had 40,000 employees and accounted for four fifths of the sales of agricultural products!

Denmark. To the south of Sweden, Denmark, one of the smallest countries in Europe, was, like Sweden, referred to for years prior to the nazi invasion as "the land of co-operation." Co-operation in this agrarian country was, in the nature of the case, predominantly agricultural. For decades it served the farmer as a powerful instrument of collective action for raising living standards and the improvement of agricultural production, processing, and marketing.

While the Danish agricultural co-operative societies dated back to 1769, the modern farmers' co-operative movement may be said to have begun in the eighties, originating in the dairy industry. In 1882 a group of farmers met to discuss how best they could supply the foreign market with butter shipments of high and standard grade. At this gathering, Stilling Anderson, a young dairy expert, suggested that they start a co-operative dairy association, and the others accepted his idea. The co-operative dairy which they built was an immediate success, and the movement quickly spread. In 1890, eight years after the opening of the first dairy, 675 dairy co-operatives had been formed. By the end of the thirties, practically the whole of the farming community in Denmark was co-operatively organized, and the co-operative movement had become one of the most important social and economic forces in the country. It processed more than 95 per cent of the milk yield, slaughtered 85 per cent of the livestock, and exported 50 per cent of the butter and 30 per cent of the eggs, and, in addition, supplied 45 per cent of the fodder and 40 per cent of the fertilizer.

The co-operative movement here as in other countries suffered greatly from nazi domination during the Second World War and was restricted on all sides by nazi regulations.

After the war, it revived, expanded its city consumer co-operatives and claimed one of the highest sales per member, as well as one of the largest memberships in proportion to the population, in the world.

Finland. In Sweden the co-operative movement developed largely as an industrial movement; in Denmark, as a movement of the farming population. In Finland, both industrial and agricultural co-operatives have shown great strength.

While numerous rural co-operatives were formed during the eighties of the last century, it was not until the establishment of the Pellervo Society in 1899 by Professor Hannes Gebhard and others that co-operatives began to take vigorous hold in Finland. During the next sixty years, the co-operative movement grew to such an extent that by the early 1960's it handled over a third of the wholesale trade of that country and about 37 per cent of the retail trade, a proportion unsurpassed by the co-operative movement in any other democratic country. In all there were 4,000 local co-operatives with a total membership of nearly 1,800,000 out of a population of 4,500,000.

In 1967, the country possessed two wholesale societies. The older, which went by the initials SOK, was established in 1904 and served largely the small towns and villages of Finland. It was a member of the so-called Neutral movement, and adhered strictly to the principle of political neutrality. The younger society, established in 1917, supplied, to a greater extent, the large cities, was connected with the Progressive co-operative movement, and was sympathetic to, although not affiliated with, the working-class political and economic movements of the country. Both societies possessed central unions, which acted as educational centers for the co-operatives.

In 1964, 515,000 members were associated with the KK, the educational center of the Progressive movement, and 512,000 members with the SOK co-operatives. The former had yearly sales of $331,-000,000; the latter, of $453,000,000.

The co-operators during the early sixties also showed great interest in co-operative housing. All told, the volume of business transacted in the local co-operatives in the early sixties amounted to more than 30 per cent of the net national income. The co-operatives' share of the national total in specific fields in 1961 was as follows: [7]

Wholesale trade of the consumer goods	35%
Retail trade of the consumer goods	37
Savings deposits	24
Export of eggs	74
Meat received by slaughterhouses	90
Milk received by dairies	98

Norway. The Norwegian co-operative movement developed later than those in the other Scandinavian countries. By the end of the thirties, however, it had become a strong factor in the economic life of the nation, having made particularly steady progress in the preceding decade.

The *Norges Ko-operative Landsforening*—the Co-operative Union and Wholesale Society of the consumers' movement—was organized in 1906. During the nazi invasion the co-operatives continued to function, although under great restrictions.

Reviving after the Second World War, the Co-operative Union in

[7] Finland, *The Land of Cooperatives* (Helsinki: Institute of Helsinki, 1963), p. 25.

1963 contained 971 societies with 327,000 individual members. The movement made a special effort to meet the needs not only of the capital city, but of the remote fishing villages, mountain valleys, and paper-mill towns. Paying low dividends on purchases, the amount of purchases per member was, as in Denmark, among the highest in the co-operative movement.

France. In France an incipient co-operative movement existed as far back as 1835. A number of producers' co-operatives were formed on the revolutionary wave that swept the country in 1848. The modern movement may be said to have begun at Nîmes in 1885. Professor Charles Gide soon joined and proved a tower of strength to it. For some time socialists showed considerable antagonism toward the movement, but, finally, in 1912, the two groups were brought into harmony, and a united French movement was established.

The movement grew rapidly during the First World War, when it acted as a public agency in the distribution of food.

In the thirties, the co-operative movement included many self-governing workshops and thousands of agricultural co-ops. In fact, up to the time of the nazi invasion, France was outstanding among the Western countries of Europe for the extent and quality of its self-governing workshops, or producers' co-operatives, but thereafter the movement was greatly crippled.

The Second World War subjected the French co-operative movement to the ordeal of enemy occupation. On the coming of peace, the movement emerged and remained prominent among the Continental co-operative movements in the democratic countries of Europe.

In 1964 the government reported the existence of some 10,000 retail stores in 500 consumer co-operative companies, with a membership of 3.5 million French families. One consumer out of every 7 belonged to the movement, while one grocery store in every 10 was a co-operative. A feature of the movement was a pioneer laboratory for analysis and research.

Holland. The consumer's co-operative movement before the Hitler invasion of Holland was organized in two unions—the Central Union of Dutch Consumers' Societies and the smaller Federation of Diocesan Unions of Catholic Co-operative Societies. Both of these unions were represented in the National Co-operative Council, which united all branches of consumers' and producers' co-operation for the defense of their common interests, especially in matters of legislation and taxation.

The Central Union, in April, 1940, after completing twenty years of activity, comprised 130 societies with 216,000 members. In the few years prior to the Hitler invasion, the union established an organization for financing and controlling societies when in difficulty or in the early stages of their development. Other auxiliary organizations formed during the thirties included one to administer a pension fund for the societies' employees and a Co-operative Employers' Association to deal with labor questions.

The Catholic Federation in 1940 contained 120 co-operative societies with a total membership of 40,000. The whole consumers' movement in 1964 had a membership of 280,000. Its societies through amalgamation had decreased from 350 in 1939 to 73. The Dutch movement in general was noted for its efficiency.

Switzerland. The Swiss co-operative movement in the sixties was the outstanding practitioner of co-operation in Southern Europe. In 1963 there were in the country 863 co-operative societies with an individual membership of 828,000. The movement was particularly strong in Basle. In addition to the principal union, there was a strong farmers' movement and a small Catholic federation.

Russia. The co-operative movement in Russia has undergone many changes since its inception. Before the First World War, consumers' co-operatives were discriminated against by the government at every turn. Despite this obstacle, however, the movement grew in membership from a quarter of a million in 1898 to nearly one-and-a-half million in 1914. During the First World War "co-operatives were the only structures that maintained any integrity and sustained in an orderly way the economy of a people betrayed by its government whose commanders were selling their armies into the hands of the enemy." [8] During the war the movement more than trebled in size. With the growth of the revolutionary movement, the co-operatives increased and, during the period of the Kerensky regime in 1917, became a powerful factor in the industrial life of the country.

When the bolsheviks came into power, the co-operatives were the chief instruments of production and distribution. In the decree of April, 1918, the bolsheviks ordered every consumer to become a member of a local consumers' co-operative.

In 1920 the co-operative movement was virtually nationalized and ceased to be of a voluntary character. Later it was again made an autonomous movement, and in 1930 the urban consumers' co-operatives controlled over one third of the total urban trade.

[8] *Report of the Inquiry in Co-operative Enterprise in Europe* (International Co-operative Alliance, 1967), p. 70.

In the decree of September 29, 1935, the government declared that the co-operatives "shall be transferred to the People's Commissariat of Internal Trade of the USSR." Thereafter the property of nearly 10,000,000 members of the co-operatives was transferred to state trusts.

The rural societies, however, remained in the field and, in 1963, the movement embraced 48,000,000 people organized in 16,000 societies. Co-operative stores near collective farms sold to the farmers articles of food, clothing, etc., which the farmers could not produce themselves. Co-operatives, in fact, were the sole means by which many necessities reached the rural consumer.

In 1946, co-operatives were invited to resume partial responsibility for the provisioning of the town workers. Their freedom of choice in the purchase of goods was, however, both in their rural and city trade, strictly limited.

Germany. Prior to the advent of Hitler the German co-operative movement was one of the most powerful in Europe. The German movement started as a middle-class institution. Its first form was a co-operative bank or credit union, organized about the year 1850. For nearly fifty years consumers' co-operation was frowned upon by the socialist movement in Germany largely in the belief that the only way of bettering the condition of the worker was to raise his income at the point of production and that "any reduction in the cost of living brings with it an equal reduction in the rate of wages."

This position was finally dropped by the socialists, and the co-operative societies for many years had the ardent support of the social democrats. The first distributive society was organized at Neustadt in 1864. In 1894, a co-operative wholesale was formed, and, in 1903, a Central Union of consumers' societies. By 1933, before the Hitler regime, one fourth of the population was included in the co-operative societies. The Central Union and their affiliated societies had over 50,000 employees. In addition to the consumers' societies there were over 20,000 co-operative banking societies; nearly 7,000 societies for the purchase of raw materials; over 4,000 home-building societies, and various other co-operatives, making up a total of over 50,000 organizations. With vigor they applied scientific efficiency.[9]

During the years before the rise of nazism, there were two co-operative movements—one of socialist leanings, the other under Roman Catholic control.

[9] Laidler and Campbell, *The Consumer Co-operative Movement,* p. 35; Arlette Schmetz, "Co-operative Movement in Federal Republic of Germany," in *Annals of Public and Co-operative Economy,* Jan.-March, 1965, pp. 15–38.

After 1933 the nazi authorities dissolved both federations and effected a compulsory amalgamation of the two wholesale consumer co-operatives. The individual societies of both associations were absorbed in the Labor Front and finally, in 1941, dissolved. By the end of the Second World War, nothing was left of the consumer co-operative movement.

Following the war, the movement in the Federal Republic of Germany (West Germany) revived. Its two opposing tendencies came together and, by the end of 1945, reconciled with one another, set up one wholesale organization, the G.E.G. In 1948 they established a single federation for the entire consumer movement—the Z.D.A. By 1963, the primary co-operative societies in West Germany were operating 8,628 stores and had a total membership of 2,500,000.

In the Schultze-Delitzsch sector of the co-operative movement there were in 1962 2,247 handicraft co-operatives and 713 people's banks, with their 2,603 branch establishments. The agricultural co-ops (credit, commercial, services) had a membership of over 4,000,000; the 1,568 housing co-ops, one of over 1,200,000.

Austria. Prior to World War II, the co-operative movement in Austria was strong and virile. The Vienna Co-operative Society controlled many stores, rented houses, conducted carpenter shops, laundries, bakeries, and dairies, and, in co-operation with the municipality, was the largest distributor of coal in Austria.[10]

Destroyed as an independent movement with the coming of the nazis to power, the movement revived after the war, and in the late sixties its membership was nearly 20 per cent of the population. The Vienna Co-operative Society, the largest society in the whole co-operative movement, possessed 180,000 members and nearly 300 stores. The co-operative educational, press, and productive activities were also significant.

Italy. While the first important distributive store in Italy was formed in 1850, Rochdale co-operatives were not developed there until thirty years later.

Prior to the fascist regime, the Co-operative League of Italy, established in 1886, had a membership of about 4,000 societies to which 1,000,000 individuals belonged. Besides consumers' societies, this organization included about an equal number of artisan co-partnership and agricultural producers' societies. Consumers' societies led in the number of members, agricultural societies in the volume of trade, and artisan unions in the number of societies. The artisan producers'

[10] Warbasse, *op. cit.*, p. 403.

groups specialized in such construction as that of roads, buildings, canals, and railroads. The Italian Co-operative Federation, with about 3,000 distributive societies, was the Catholic, or "white," co-operative movement.

Many of the Italian co-operatives were "liquidated" by the fascist forces. Stores were burned, plundered, and wrecked, and many co-operators were assaulted and killed. The co-operatives that remained were made into organs of the fascist regime.

In 1945, after World War II, a Directorate-General for Co-operation was established within the Ministry of Labor. One of the great leaders of the co-operative movement, Mr. Basevi, was placed in charge, and the free co-operative movement soon began to revive.

In 1962 the *Associazione generale delle Cooperative italiana* comprised consumer, agricultural production, housing, fishery, and other co-operatives as follows:

Kind	*Number*	*Membership (1000)*	*Turnover (000 million lire)*
Consumer	3,358	1,374	123
Agricultural	1,872	315	62
Production	1,251	83	80
Housing	600	87	5
Fisheries	87	15	
Mutual Aid	588	228	2
Mixed and Miscellaneous	102	19	4
Total	7,858	2,121	276

The consumer societies concentrated almost entirely on the sale of foodstuffs and handled between 5 and 6 per cent of all foodstuffs sold. Religious affiliations continued to lead to a divided movement.[11]

Czechoslovakia. For many years before the dismemberment of the Czechoslovakian Republic in 1937 and 1938, there was a strong co-operative movement in both the cities and the agricultural districts of that country. The societies were organized in the Central Union of Czechoslovak Co-operative Societies and in the Union of German Economic Co-operative Societies, with which was also affiliated a small group of Polish co-ops. The agricultural societies exercised a strong influence in rural districts where agricultural credit, the marketing of farm products, and the purchasing of agricultural supplies and electrical services were largely in co-operative hands.

11 See Ruggero Amaduzzi, "The New Co-operative Economy" in *Annals of Public and Co-operative Economy,* Jan.-March, 1964, pp. 57–67.

The Czechoslovak Union in 1937 had a membership of more than 400,000. In October, 1938, when the Sudetenland was annexed to Germany, the Czech co-ops were incorporated into the German economic system. Many of the German co-operative shops were closed and their stocks disposed of by the new administrators of the towns and districts. The co-operative officials were obliged to flee, and many of them went into exile abroad. The German Union and Wholesale were dissolved by public decree in July, 1939. Co-operatives, though of a different character, appeared again in many fields after the war.

Hungary. In Hungary in the early 1940's, the co-operative societies were centralized in the Union of Co-operative Societies, which had been established more than a generation before by Count Alexander von Karolyi. This was the only organization representative of the common interests of the whole movement and was recognized officially by the government.

This society not only supplied its affiliated organizations with a large part of their consumers' goods, but, through its marketing societies, played an important part in the export trade. During more than a quarter of a century of existence, the co-operative *Futura* took a leading part in the Hungarian wheat market.

Under the communist regime in Hungary, the co-operative movement has continued to grow and, in 1961, possessed 7,809 co-operatives and 3,172,042 members, over half of them in farmers' co-operatives.[12]

In 1960, the co-operative share of the retail trade in Hungary was 29.1 per cent; the state's, 69.7 per cent; and private, 1.2 per cent.

Poland. The Polish co-operative movement prior to the incorporation of Poland in the Reich and the Soviet Union was an influential one. At the beginning of 1939, co-operative organizations comprised about 3,500,000 members, representing, with their families, nearly 40 per cent of the population. Nearly 14,000 co-operative societies of all kinds were federated in Audit Unions. Of these, 5,600 credit societies formed the largest group, followed by about 5,400 agricultural and over 2,500 consumers' societies.

The Second World War broke out during a period of rapid co-operative development. Despite the cruelty and destruction of the war, a

[12] See Nyers, Rezso, *The Co-operative Movement in Hungary* (Budapest: Pannonia Press, 1963), p. 65. Dealing with the character of the Hungarian co-operative movement, the author states: "From November 4, 1956, onward, with the forming of the Workers' and Peasants' Revolutionary Government, the proper Leninistic principles have prevailed in the co-operative question, both in measures carried out by the state and in the development of the internal life of the co-operatives. The collective farming movement has developed on the basis of the voluntary principle."

majority of directors of the co-operative organizations remained at their posts. In the subsequent division of Poland among three states —Poland, Germany, and the USSR—the co-operative organizations, with their headquarters in Warsaw, lost the majority of their members.

After various transformations during the following decades, the Polish Central Statistical Office was able to report that Polish co-operatives numbered in 1966 some 10,500 units, with a membership of around 12,000,000.[13]

Other European Countries. Agricultural, consumers', credit and other co-operatives have existed for years in such other European countries as Turkey, Rumania, Yugoslavia, Estonia, Latvia and Lithuania during the century, in numerous instances exerting a powerful influence on the economic life of the country.

CO-OPERATION IN AUSTRALASIA

Australia. The co-operative movement in Australia before the Second World War was strongest in the producers' end. The consumers' movement had its greatest success in the eastern part of the country. Its stronghold was in New South Wales, where there were, at the beginning of the sixties (1963–4), about 320 societies with a membership of 277,000.

The producers' co-operative societies were strong chiefly in Western Australia, where a great number of farmers' purchasing and marketing societies controlled most of the agricultural business of the state. The movement maintained close relations with the English C. W. S.

New Zealand. In New Zealand, as in Australia, the co-operative movement was until the forties primarily an agricultural movement consisting of associations of dairy farmers, butter and cheese factories, societies for the purchase of farm equipment, and marketing boards. Dairy farmers were organized in the New Zealand Co-operative Dairy Company, which had in the beginning of the forties about 8,000 members and turned out 30 per cent of the dairy produce exported. The National Dairy Association, Limited, a co-operative organization, with which 200 dairies were closely affiliated, supplied in the early forties equipment to dairy factories and marketed their products.

Sales of New Zealand farm produce to Great Britain were made by the New Zealand Produce Association, owned and controlled jointly

[13] Over 2,500,000 of the 12,000,000 belonged to consumer co-ops; 4,000,000, to agricultural co-ops; 3,000,000, to savings and credit co-ops, and the remainder to co-ops in the fields of dairies, housing, labor, horticulture, handicrafts, farming, and publishing. The co-ops in Poland were not members of the International Co-operative Alliance. (*Concise Statistical Yearbook of Poland,* 1967, p. 267)

by the English C. W. S. and the New Zealand Co-operative Marketing Association.

CO-OPERATION IN ASIA

China. The Chinese co-operative movement was given a great impetus following the Japanese invasion of China. In September, 1938, the Chinese industrial co-operative movement launched its first units with the ambitious object of rebuilding the economic structure of the new China. The plan, which had the support of the government, visualized the establishment of a great network of some 30,000 small industrial producers' co-operative societies that would embrace all industrial processes from the producing of raw materials to the marketing of the finished product, and would, in addition, provide educational and cultural training. The difficulties of finance prevented the full realization of the plan, but considerable progress was made. By the middle of 1940, 1,780 societies, with a membership of over 20,000 and a paid-in capital of $500,000, were producing goods valued at about $10,000,000 a month.

After the proclamation of Communist China in 1949, the co-operative movement, closely linked to the government, steadily expanded. In 1958, the farming co-operatives counted about 30,000,000 members; the marketing and supply (consumers') societies, 158,000,000; and the craftsmen's co-operatives, 10,000,000 members.

A significant change took place in the Chinese movement at the end of 1958. Communes began to grow on a mass scale and soon covered the whole country. In 1959 there were 26,000 communes in China.[14]

Taiwan. In Taiwan, the Republic of China, the co-operatives movement first appeared in about 1910. In 1960 there were in the country nearly 2,000 single-purpose co-operatives—agricultural, industrial, marketing, insurance, credit, etc.—and multi-purpose co-operatives with a combined membership of nearly 1,600,000. In addition

14 Communes differed from the ordinary co-operative societies: (1) They combined within them the functions of agriculture and of industrial production, trade, transport, and finance; (2) their territorial dimensions were extremely great in comparison to those of earlier co-operatives; (3) the communes, in addition to their economic functions, also had public, administrative, financial, school, and educational functions; (4) within the communes, the various branches had special managerial organizations subordinated to the executive body of the commune; (5) the dwelling houses, however, as well as articles of use and movable property, bank deposits, simple equipment and small domestic animals, remain the personal property of the members (Nyers, Rezso, *The Co-operative Movement in Hungary,* pp. 45–6). Nor do the communes of China have the freedom of action vouchsafed to co-operatives in a democratic state.

there were some 40 co-operative federations throughout the country.

Japan. The first consumers' co-operative store in Japan was founded in Tokyo in 1879, and at the end of the century, some 65,000 were members of co-operatives, chiefly in Japanese farm villages. By 1909, as a result of government encouragement, the movement had increased to 380,000.

After the First World War, co-operatives of fishermen and workers' producers' co-operative societies showed considerable progress. By the Second World War, however, the Japanese co-operative movement had been virtually taken over by the state and had lost its independence.

Following the Second World War, the movement was again reorganized under new laws and in the early 1960's was dominant in agriculture and in the fishing industry. It had likewise made advances in industry, in commerce, and in the field of consumption. In 1963, in fact, over 6,000,000 members belonged to some 800 co-operatives.

India. The co-operative movement in India in the early forties was about 90 per cent a credit movement. One of the most important problems facing the co-operatives was agricultural indebtedness. Private banks in rural districts charged exorbitant rates of interest. The co-operative credit societies had been able, in many districts, to cut these rates from one third to one half of those charged by profit-making financial institutions.

After independence, the government sought to establish a co-operative in every village as a part of a national policy to assign an important role to co-operatives in achieving economic development. The second five-year plan called for the increase of the multi-purpose village societies from 5,000,000 to 15,000,000. The government likewise established a training program with a staff of technical advisers to work through the local co-operatives and the village schoolmasters. It utilized the Reserve Bank of India as an instrument for the distribution of agricultural credit, for organizing training programs, and for otherwise assisting the co-operative movement. Short-term credit was made available through 180,000 credit points. Production and marketing co-ops were widely organized for cottage industry, etc. In 1959 there were about 25,000,000 members in the country's 285,000 co-operative societies.

Other Asian Countries. In Pakistan at the end of 1957 there were 21,000 co-ops—chiefly agricultural credit societies—with a membership of a million. Credit societies were also actively promoted in **Ceylon, Burma, Malaysia,** and the **Philippines.** Consumer co-operatives were particularly active in Ceylon.

Israel. The co-operative movement in Israel is co-ordinated and guided by the General Co-operative Association of Jewish Workers in Israel (Hevrat Ovdim), organized in 1924 at the second convention of the Histadrut—the General Federation of Labor—with the provision that the membership of the two organizations—Histadrut and Hevrat Ovdim—would be co-extensive.

Under the supervision of Hevrat Ovdim, the co-operative movement in the early sixties in Israel constituted an important feature in the life of that country.

At the end of 1961, there were approximately 1,700 societies attached to the Hevrat Ovdim. Almost three quarters of the agricultural produce of Israel was produced and marketed by some 540 co-operative settlements linked to the general co-operative association. In the building industry, co-operation played a foremost role—in public works, industrial construction, and housing. In industry and manufacture, Hevrat Ovdim was responsible for 20 per cent of the output of the country operating in this sphere through a special holding company, Koor.

In commerce, almost 500,000 consumers were served by 1,200 branch stores of the central co-operative wholesale society and the co-operative retail societies.

Passenger transport by road was almost entirely conducted by co-operative organizations. Hevrat Ovdim also played a prominent part in the sphere of finance, mainly through the Workers' Bank, the second largest in the country. The above activities directly employed about one quarter of the working population, and at least the same proportion again indirectly owed its livelihood to the pioneering of Hevrat Ovdim.[15]

In agriculture, the main form of organization through which Hevrat entered the field in the sixties was the individual co-operative society in the form of the agricultural settlement, numbering about 540. About 70 of these settlements belonged within the orthodox religious workers' movement formally outside the framework of Hevrat Ovdim. The population of the co-operative villages was close to 10 per cent of the Jewish population.

In addition to conforming to the principles of nationally owned land and co-operative trading, all the settlements were bound by their rules to care for their members on the basis of mutual aid and to carry on their economic activities on the basis of their own labor.

The most communal of the three types of co-operative agricultural

[15] See Noah Malkosh, *Co-operation in Israel,* p. 24 (Tel Aviv: Histadrut, 1964).

settlements in Israel in the sixties was the *kibbutz,* or collective settlement. In the *kibbutz:*

(1) All the property of the group is collectively owned.

(2) All adult members work in collective undertakings without wages.

(3) All the needs of the members are supplied without charge, the community accepting full responsibility for members in times of sickness and other adversities.

(4) The communal dining hall, where members take their meals, is the social center of the settlements.

Kibbutz settlements number about 225 with a total population of some 80,000.

The second type of settlement is the *moshav.* In the *moshav,* all produce is marketed and all supplies are purchased co-operatively. In the *moshav,* however, in contrast to the *kibbutz,* each family farms its own allotment, its income depending on the quantity of produce it remits to the *moshav's* central marketing office.[16]

The third type of agricultural co-operative within the framework of Hevrat Ovdim is the *moshav shitufli,* a halfway house between the two others. Like the *moshav,* it is based on the family group, with the mother occupied mainly in domestic duties. Like the *kibbutz,* it is based on collective ownership of assets and communal farming. In the mid-sixties there were only about a score of this most recent type of agricultural co-operatives.

CO-OPERATION IN AFRICA

The co-operative movement in Africa grew rapidly after World War I, its object that of increasing the availability to agriculture of farm machinery, credit and marketing facilities, and education in new methods of production and distribution. For the most part, the movements followed the co-operative practices prevailing in the mother countries.

In the British territories the authorities actively assisted in the organization and supervision of co-operative societies. In Nigeria, cocoa marketing co-ops were first established in 1922, followed by credit, marketing and consumer societies. After World War II, membership in the British Eastern and Central African territories, formerly confined to people of European origin, was extended to the African population. Marketing societies added processing functions and began the operation of coffee-processing plants, cotton gins, etc.

16 Malkosh, *op. cit.,* ch. 4.

In FRENCH territories provident societies were turned into co-operatives. Following a number of failures, the authorities set up pilot marketing co-ops and rural producers' mutual societies. Co-operation in BELGIAN-controlled countries had a slower start.

SOUTH AFRICAN consumer and marketing institutions in the post-war years made marked advances. In NORTH AFRICA producers', handicraft, and farm-marketing co-ops also increased in strength.

As the African colonies obtained their independence from their European rulers, the co-operative movement continued to grow and join up with the world co-operative movement. In 1960 750,000 people belonged to co-operative societies in TANGANYIKA, NIGERIA, UGANDA, and GHANA. The year 1966 found co-operative unions from the African states of NIGERIA, TUNISIA, KENYA, UGANDA, and ZAMBIA active members of the International Co-operative Alliance.

CO-OPERATION IN THE AMERICAS

The United States. In striking contrast with the situation in numerous countries abroad, the consumers' co-operative movement in the United States for decades did not attract large numbers of consumers. The reasons for this failure are not far to seek. First, for generations the people of the United States were engaged in the gigantic task of exploring and settling a great continent, and centered their attention more on *production* than on *distribution*. Second, their philosophy was that of individualism. Third, the population came from many lands and co-operatives controlled by immigrant groups from one country were unable to cater successfully to working-class families with different national and racial backgrounds. There were also a number of other contributing factors.

At present the situation is for several reasons more favorable than formerly to the success of consumers' co-operation. The pioneer stage of the country's national development is now over, and problems of distribution are demanding and receiving far greater attention than in former days. With the rise of large scale industry the economic basis for the philosophy of individualism is rapidly narrowing. The immigrant population in the United States has drastically decreased, and working-class communities are tending to become more homogeneous. Further, co-operative education is advancing, and the movement is showing increased efficiency as the years advance. The bitter competition from chain stores remains, but the development of co-operative wholesales; the greater attention now paid in co-ops to scientific management; the tendency on the part of co-operatives to specialize, during their early stages, in the sale of those commodities where the margin of profit is large—all have placed the movement in a better position to compete against large private corporate units than in former days.

In the forties, besides its retail and wholesale stores, 116 mills, factories, refineries, and other productive works, the movement embraced 300 oil wells and one thousand miles of pipe lines. Agricultural co-operative purchasing societies handled feed, seed, fertilizer, farm machinery, and other farm necessities valued at 600 million dollars, a sum which represented about one fifth of all farm supply purchases. All told, in 1944 the co-operative movement as a whole contained a membership of 2,500,000 and the volume of consumers' co-operative business totaled over three quarters of a billion dollars.

One of the most significant developments in the thirties was the growth of the co-operative wholesales. By 1944 seven large grocery wholesales were serving 1150 retail co-operative stores. As a result of their uniform co-op label program the co-ops were given credit in the early forties for having done more than any other business in the field to introduce government grade labeling. In the mid-forties another conspicuous advance was made, this one in the field of co-operative factories, mills, and refineries, which were built and controlled by the consumer co-operative movement.

To meet the competition from the chain stores, the consumers' co-operatives have been content in the United States with lower dividends from the sale of groceries than from that of other articles on which the margin of profit was higher. Emphasis has been placed on the advantages of the quality of co-operative goods rather than on immediate cash returns. In many communities a co-operative store starts with the purchase of gas or oil or some other high-profit line, and later, when it has built up enough of a volume to meet chain-store competition, it adds groceries.[17]

Since the Second World War, notable progress has been made in the co-operative movement, in the credit-union movement, in insurance, in group health, in electric co-ops, in housing, in memorial societies, nursery schools, etc. In 1967, the number of members in various co-op undertakings and the annual business of the different types of co-ops were estimated as follows:

[17] See Laidler and Campbell, *The Consumer Co-operative Movement,* pp. 38–62.

Co-operatives and Mutual Organizations, 1967, U.S.A.*

Kind of Co-ops	*No. of Co-ops*	*Members*	*Annual Business*
Credit unions	22,796	18,007,000	$10,138,433,000
Co-op–oriented insurance companies	10	11,750,000	580,000,000
Group health plans	196	4,900,000	325,000,000
Farm purchasing	3,050	3,200,000	3,150,000,000
Farm marketing	5,100	3,700,000	12,750,000,000
Electric co-ops	993	5,600,000	1,021,904,409
Telephone co-ops	232	600,000	60,000,000
Farm Credit System			
Land bank assocs.	707	390,000	1,337,000,000
Production credit assocs.	466	545,000	4,813,000,000
Banks for co-operatives	13	2,972	1,664,000,000
Major consumer-goods centers	116	240,000	160,000,000
Housing co-ops	640	165,000	235,000,000
Student co-ops (rm. and bd.)	200	7,000	5,000,000
book stores	200	150,000	15,000,000
Memorial societies	90	135,000	900,000
Nursery school co-ops	1,440	72,000	6,840,000

* Estimates for latest available year in *Co-op Report, Co-operatives in the U.S.: Facts and Figures* (Annual Statistical Edition), Chicago: Cooperative League, U.S.A., 1967. The co-operative movement for rural electricity was greatly strengthened by the Congress' appropriation in 1936 for long-term, low-cost loans to electrify rural America.

Canada. In Canada, a large co-operative movement has developed during the past decades in the form of agricultural marketing and purchasing societies, which numbered over 1,100, in 1940, including nearly 500,000 members, and did a yearly business of around a quarter of a billion dollars. Membership and business transacted by marketing co-operatives were roughly ten times that of purchasing co-ops.

In 1964, 2,643 local co-operatives with a membership of 1,600,000 reported a total volume of $1,854,600,000 and assets of $818,000,000. The most extensive sales were in the fields of grain and seeds, dairy products and livestock. Numerous co-operative insurance companies, telephone, housing, hospitalization and medical plan groups, and several hundred retail societies were also being operated successfully in the sixties. Co-operative membership was greatest in the province of Saskatchewan.

Latin America. The co-operative movement in Latin America was organized at the turn of the century by European immigrants and received the financial help of the various states as a part of their agrarian reform programs. Through the years, among the chief types of societies that developed in the continent were agricultural, credit, housing and consumer co-operatives. By the early 1960's the Latin American co-operatives counted about 15,000 co-operative units with a membership of 5,000,000.

The consumers' movement has shown considerable strength over the years in Argentina, Brazil, and Chile. In these countries, many of the consumer co-ops were founded by business concerns or government departments with a view toward lower-priced and better-quality goods. They generally received tax exemptions.

Agricultural co-ops sprang up in every Latin American country during the century. ARGENTINA had six agricultural federations including the "Sancor" butter factories. BRAZIL in the 1960's possessed 1,300 agricultural productive co-operatives dealing with sugar cane, cocoa, bananas, coffee, timber, etc. About 300 of these were credit co-operatives. By 1965, the number of co-operatives in the country had increased to 5,893 with 2,899,372 members divided as follows: consumers, 1,278,979; credit, 620,920; production, 819,904; various, 179,569; total, 2,899,372. CHILE'S co-operatives gave much attention to dairy products, fruit, poultry, cattle and forestry. The URUGUAY movement dealt largely in livestock and cereal. Argentina and Chile likewise conducted many co-operative credit and insurance companies.

In COLOMBIA a special government agency, *Superintendencia de Co-operativas,* did much from the forties on in looking after the general interest of co-operative organizations. In ECUADOR an act passed in the late twenties empowered the Ministry of Social Welfare and its Department of Co-operation to supervise and encourage co-operative societies. In VENEZUELA a government decree in 1939 provided for the organization of co-operative distributive, producers', and housing societies. This decree provided that 25 per cent of the net profit of such societies be put aside for reserves, 25 per cent for social institutions, and 50 per cent for dividends to members in ratio purchases.

As for MEXICO the *ejidos* (land-owning villages) provide a system of co-operative farming and community improvements. There are also in the country co-operatives in forestry, fishing, transportation, mining and other services. The Mexican National Bank for the Development of Co-operatives, founded in 1944, extends credit to co-operatives and small businesses.

Numerous housing, student, and consumer societies also exist in the country, most of the latter established since 1934. The consumer co-ops include two types of co-operatives—the Syndical Co-operative Society, formed by members of a labor union or similar group, and the

Free Co-operative Society, which followed more closely the Rochdale principles. A National League of Co-operative Societies endeavors to coordinate the co-operative movement.

In 1959-61, the estimated membership of the co-operative movement in the countries of Latin America was as follows: [18]

Type of Co-operatives	*Number of Members*
Consumers	1,840,612
Credit Unions	796,808
Housing	65,571
Students	119,639
Electrification	395,489
Production and Auxiliary Services	909,957
	4,128,076

Nearly three out of four co-operators live in Argentina and Brazil.

The co-operative movement in Latin America has also in recent years been stimulated by the international organization, the Alliance for Progress.

In 1965, the Agency for International Development maintained that "in the first three years of the Alliance, 798 credit unions in 15 countries have been established." [19]

For this and other co-operative purposes, the A.I.D. called upon the experience gained by the U.S. co-operatives, labor unions, savings and loan institutions, credit unions, and educational institutions. Their experts, technicians, and advisers have gone to Latin America and have helped set up co-operative organizations.

. . . One of the brightest developments since the inception of the Alliance has been the mushrooming of savings and loan associations."

World Co-operative Membership. In general, co-operative membership throughout the world has continually expanded in the postwar years. From 1953 to 1963, the *membership* of the co-operative societies affiliated with the International Co-operative Alliance in 26 selected countries increased from 72,770,000 to 97,607,000, or 34 per cent. On the other hand, as a result of the co-operatives' efforts to rationalize the co-operative industry and merge many co-operative undertakings, the number of co-operative *societies* during the ten-year period has decreased from 67,000 to 47,000, or 30 per cent.

[18] See paper by Fernando Chaves on "The Agricultural Co-operative Movement in Latin America," published in 1962 by the Pan American Union.

[19] Agency of International Development, U. S. Dept. of State, *The Alliance for Progress—An American Partnership,* 1966, p. 20.

CHAPTER 42

Social Aspects of Consumers' Co-operatives

THE CO-OPERATIVE movement has been responsible for definite economic and psychological gains for its members and for society as a whole. Several of these gains are briefly summarized here.

Achievements of Consumers' Co-operation. 1. Consumers' co-operation has *reduced the cost of living* to large numbers of people by eliminating the profits of middlemen and by avoiding many of the wastes connected with the distribution of goods by small, inefficient private firms.

A report of retail prices in Denmark indicated that in the mid-thirties the prices charged for food in the co-operative stores in that country were 7 per cent lower than those charged in private stores, if patronage refunds were not taken into account, and 14 per cent lower, if those refunds were included.[1] In many countries, co-operatives, by setting lower prices, have forced down prices charged consumers as a whole by private merchants.

Of the Swedish co-operatives, President Roosevelt's Commission on Co-operation declared: "The Swedish co-operative movement is generally credited with lowering prices throughout the whole country; a group of Sweden's largest private business men not only said as much to us but added that this control has been very useful to the public." [2]

2. The co-operative movement has *raised the quality of goods* sold. Members of co-operative enterprises naturally wish to supply themselves with good quality goods in full weight and measure. They have no incentive to misrepresent the quality of the goods sold to themselves. "Many societies make a point of informing their members about the factors of value in goods they offer." In the Finnish wholesale co-operatives everything bought is tested. About 25 per cent of all goods examined is rejected because of inferior quality.[3]

[1] *Report of the Inquiry on Co-operative Enterprise in Europe,* p. 36.
[2] *Ibid.,* p. 36. [3] *Ibid.,* p. 27.

At times co-operatives have been induced to keep in stock advertised brands demanded by their members, even though tests have shown that these brands were not as represented. But in general the co-operator may be assured that the goods sold by co-ops are as represented.

3. The co-operative movement has *provided better conditions for its employes* than have comparable private establishments. The Report of the President Roosevelt Commission mentioned above again declared:

"Co-operative spokesmen claim that their workers are better paid and better treated than those of their private competitors. That seems to be true in all of the countries visited. In most of these countries, co-operative enterprise started as a labor movement. Co-operatives and labor unions are friendly and work together. Unions use co-operative labor standards to bring pressure on private employers. In many cases, co-operative enterprises operate on a closed shop basis, regardless of the attitude of their competitors. . . .

"Higher wages are particularly characteristic of employment in stores and offices. In manufacturing and transport, rates, in many cases, already are set by the unions, and co-operative wages tend to be approximately the same as those already paid, or only slightly higher. The co-operatives provide shorter hours, more generous vacations and pension arrangements, and tend to furnish more secure employment than is generally the case in private trade. There are some exceptions, but co-operatives are among the best employers from the point of view of the workers. In Sweden, according to a labor official, the 3,000 retail workers in Konsum in Stockholm average 10 per cent to 15 per cent higher wages per month than corresponding workers in private retail trade." [4]

Hours are usually somewhat shorter among co-operative employes. A survey made by the British Parliamentary Committee on Shop Assistants in 1931 indicated that actual hours worked by co-operative employes were appreciably lower than for other employes. Some co-operatives give to employes numerous other advantages not enjoyed by workers in private concerns. Thus in Finland employes of the consumer co-operative, *Elanto,* received during the thirties without charge, a small life insurance and free medical treatment for themselves and families. They were provided with a "recreation home" with supervision for children, and were entitled to attend educational classes and musical clubs free and to receive other free services.[5]

[4] *Ibid.*, p. 59.

[5] *Ibid.*, p. 61; see also Webb, Sidney and Beatrice, *The Consumers' Co-operative Movement,* p. 211.

The British co-operative movement provided during those years for retirement of employes on pension, usually at 65. In Sweden workers in co-operative stores obtained three months' free medical care in time of illness and annual vacations of 10 to 13 days with pay, with usual vacations in private trade being from 5 to 8 days. There was usually, moreover, a greater sense of security in co-operative than in private industry.

4. Consumers' co-operation is frequently of *material assistance to organized labor* in its struggle for better conditions.

In the 1920 transport strike of the National Union of Railwaymen of Great Britain the union was prevented by the bankers from utilizing its funds for the immediate payment of strike benefits. The Co-operative Wholesale issued checks payable at the co-operative societies, and the societies honored the vouchers issued by the local strike committee. "This prevented the government," declared a labor paper at that time, "from putting in operation a project to starve out the railwaymen's families by withdrawing their ration cards or withholding the food supplies under government control." [6]

Numerous other instances may be mentioned of vital assistance offered to the labor movement and to farm marketing co-ops by co-operatives in Great Britain and Belgium and in the Scandinavian and other countries.

5. Consumers' co-operation has provided to many a *valuable schooling in democracy in industry.* Each co-operative enterprise gives an opportunity to its members to participate on an equal basis with their fellow members in the conduct of its affairs. In the voluntary co-operative movement, as Sidney and Beatrice Webb have brought out, "the poorest, youngest, humblest adult of either sex, who yesterday made his first purchase, if he has paid his minimum share allotment, is equally governor and controller of the whole colossal enterprise, has equal vote and voice in the decision of its most momentous issues with the man who has been a member since its establishment and has accumulated in share and loan capital the very maximum that the rules permit." [7]

Consumers' co-operation has assisted the movement toward democracy in industry in other ways. It has given to millions of working-class consumers a realistic experience in the conduct of industry. It has whetted the appetite of the masses for further control of their in-

[6] See Warbasse, *Co-operative Democracy,* p. 197.

[7] Webb, *op. cit.,* p. 7.

dustrial life. It has strengthened their belief in the practicability of production and distribution for use and not for profit.

6. The co-operative movement has provided still another *example of the efficient working of non-profit incentives in industry.* "No private fortune has ever been made," as the Webbs declared, "out of co-operative administration." [8] J. T. W. Mitchell, who for over twenty years had served as chairman of the Co-operative Wholesale, received a salary of only about $2,000 a year at a time when the gross income of that organization amounted to over one hundred million dollars. "I enjoy the respect of my colleagues. I possess great power. I have a great faith in the co-operative ideal," he declared to John Graham Brooks. "These things satisfy me."

Similar non-profit incentives have motivated thousands of executives in the co-operative movement in all parts of Europe and America during the last few decades.

7. Consumers' co-operation, in practically every country, through its co-operative schools and colleges, its newspapers and periodicals, its thousands of lectures and classes has *performed an educational work of immense value* along social and economic lines.

8. The co-operative movement has *helped to lay the foundation for an extension of the co-operative commonwealth* in other ways: by delimiting, in many countries, the sphere of private enterprise and weakening the power of private capitalism to oppose the coming of a co-operative social order; by demonstrating what type of co-operative effort is likely to succeed, and what is likely to fail in different categories of industry; and in times of economic crisis, by helping to keep the lifeblood of industry flowing.

Consumers' co-operation has thus proved to be a movement of great value and is destined to become one of steadily increasing significance in the days ahead.

Consumers' Co-operation versus Private Capitalism. Consumers' co-operatives, as has been before indicated, differ in a number of respects from private corporations. (1) The private corporation is organized primarily for profit to the investing stockholders and to its promoters. The consumers' co-operative is formed to render service at cost to the purchasing consumer-members. The surplus in a private corporation is paid to the stockholders. The surplus in the consumers' co-operative is returned to the consumers in proportion to their purchases. A fixed rate of interest—the minimum for which capital can be obtained—is

[8] *Ibid.*, pp. 389–90.

paid to owners of capital. The rule that the profits belong to the consumer-purchaser, declares Professor Gide, is "a new and wholly revolutionary principle in our economic organization. . . . It amounts, in fact, to a decision that all of the profit which capital has regarded as its legitimate share should be restored to those from whom it was taken, and that share capital should be reduced to the position of debenture stock, with a rate of interest fixed at the minimum at which its services can be hired; that is to say, that it shall be treated exactly as capital itself has treated labor. . . .

"The transfer of profits from the capitalist to the consumer is actually the abolition of profits, because to say that profits shall be returned to those from whom they were taken is obviously abolishing them." [9]

(2) The private corporation gives a stockholder as many votes as he has stock. The co-operative society gives to its members one vote, and one vote only, thus introducing an industrial democracy of consumers into industry.

(3) No worker in the industry secures from it a profit. The reward for labor is a wage or a salary, promotion to a more responsible position, social prestige, joy in creative endeavor, and the feeling of comradeship in a great cause.

On the other hand, the consumers' co-operative societies, like private companies, do not as yet reach many who most need their aid. Frequently their members are motivated by little higher aims than that of securing a "dividend" at the end of the quarter.

"The essence of co-operation," declared Harold J. Laski in addressing the British co-operative movement, "is a denial that the profit-making motive can ever produce a just or humane society. My inference from this is the vital one that between co-operation and capitalism there can be no peace. They are mutually exclusive conceptions of society. The one seeks to end the exploitation of man by man; the life of the other is built upon that of exploitation. The one puts need where the other puts profit. The one thinks of the community as a great fellowship of consumers integrated into unity by common wants; the other thinks of it as an aggregate of individuals whose rights are measured only by the effective demand they embody. The one thinks of international trade as an exchange of goods and services to mutual advantage; how the other regards it is shown, dramatically enough, not merely by tariff and subsidy and quota, but, even more, by Japanese aggression in China, and Italian imperialism in Abyssinia. The co-operative movement is an exercise in fellowship, or it is nothing. Capi-

[9] Gide, *op. cit.*, p. 79.

talist society assumes that the individual's pursuit of his own gain is the inescapable condition of public well-being. There can be, as I say, no peace between co-operation and capitalism in the same world, there is no room for the ideologies of both." [10]

Co-operation and Socialism. Voluntary consumers' co-operatives and publicly owned industries are the only forms of socialized ownership that have been extensively applied in practice up to the present time and both forms of ownership are intermediate forms between private capitalism and socialism of great significance to the socialist movement.

While many socialists in the beginning of the co-operative movement —especially in Germany—regarded the co-operative store as of little value to labor, during the last generation the vast majority of socialists have looked upon it as an integral and important part of the movement toward a socialized society and as a valuable experimental school in industrial democracy.

They regret the defects of the movement—the fact that too many of the co-operators do not look beyond the dividend they receive and that many co-operators, particularly in the rural districts, have not as yet worked out an entirely satisfactory system of management-employe relationships. This, however, does not prevent them from seeing the positive values of the movement.

They also are coming increasingly to the belief that the field for voluntary co-operation will be a large one in a socialist society.

This does not mean that they agree with such consumerists as Dr. James P. Warbasse, former head of the Co-operative League of the U. S. A.[11] and Leonard S. Woolf, the British economist,[12] that voluntary co-operation will completely supplant both private ownership and state and municipal ownership. With the Webbs, socialists maintain that, while there is a very distinct field for the voluntary co-operative movement both now and under a socialistic regime, the voluntary co-operative movement has certain definite limits. Beyond these limits co-operative industry should give place to industry conducted by such "compulsory" organizations as the city and state.

"There seems no reason in the nature of things," declared the Webbs, "why the various forms of consumers' co-operation should not, in due course, eventually provide for the whole body of inhabitants, all the household requisites and objects of common expenditure not supplied

[10] Laski, Harold J., *The Spirit of Co-operation,* pp. 8–9.
[11] Warbasse, *op. cit.,* p. 140.
[12] Woolf, L. S., *Co-operation and the Future of Industry.*

by the national or municipal industries or services." The movement, as industry becomes increasingly socialized, will probably find a legitimate field of activity also in international trading, in agriculture, in certain educational experiments, in the publication of periodicals, etc.

Place for "Compulsory" Consumers' Organizations. On the other hand, there are many services which can be performed more efficiently by a "compulsory organization," such as the municipality or federal government, than by a voluntary co-operative group. "Experience has shown that voluntary associations of consumers cannot conveniently be made the basis of the government of industries and services in which use or consumption is essentially compulsory, or which involve risk or inconvenience not merely to the members, but to all citizens, as with the water supply or the paving, lighting, or drainage of a city. A like consideration applies to those branches of the administration in which it is found advantageous for the services to be supplied gratuitously on a communist basis, such as the public schools, libraries, museums, parks, and many other municipal enterprises. Moreover, there are some services in which the actual users or consumers form, owing to their wide dispersion or casual nature, an unfit unit of democratic government. The effective 'consumers' of the service of communication and transport are not restricted to those who actually send the letters and telegrams, or who travel and consign goods and parcels by railway, and there seems to be no possible form of democracy of consumers—as distinct from a democracy of citizens—to which we would entrust the supervision and control of the post office and the nationalized means of conveyance. There are plainly services of national importance in which, if we are to achieve the economy and efficiency of co-ordination, and anything like equality in the distribution of costs and benefits, administration has not only to be centralized, but also placed under the control of representatives of the community as a whole. . . . We cannot seriously anticipate that such industries as those already conducted by the Postmaster General; or of those of the railway and canal service; or, as we think, that of coal mining, will ever be wrested from the control of private capitalism, except for the purpose of being controlled and conducted by and for the whole community." [13]

The Webbs contended that many of the municipal services, such as street paving, cleaning, and lighting, were at first started by volunteer groups and were eventually taken over by the community because the control by these groups proved unsatisfactory. That the importance of public services cannot be ignored is indicated by the fact, they de-

[13] Webb, *op. cit.*, pp. 425–6.

clared, that "in Great Britain alone, the commodities and services . . . provided by the local authorities considerably exceed in annual cost of production, and, therefore, as we must assume, in value to the inhabitants, the whole of what is provided by the co-operative movement." And as for national property, they added, "Confining ourselves to Great Britain, we may point out that the Postmaster General is the most extensive banker and the principal agent for internal remittances, as well as the conductor of the most gigantic monopoly in the conveyance of letters and messages. The Minister of Health provides insurance for a far greater number of families than even the largest of the insurance companies; and is, in effect, the organizer and paymaster of the largest staff of medical practitioners in the world. The largest shipbuilder in the kingdom, although we often forget it, is the First Lord of the Admiralty, whilst the Controller of the Stationary Office is the most extensive of publishers, who is now beginning to be, not only his own bookseller, but also his own printer." [14]

These authors stated that in 1914 the property held by municipal and federal governments throughout the world was probably a hundred times as great as that held by the consumers' co-operative movement.

Leonard Woolf contended that public utilities could be satisfactorily controlled by the consumers' movement if, by some device, the citizens might be "universally" enrolled in local societies for the purpose of assisting in the administration of these services. In reply to this contention the Webbs, however, maintained that universal enrollment meant to all intents and purposes *compulsory* enrollment and that such enrollment did away with the voluntary nature of the co-operative movement, the only thing which distinguished it from public ownership.

The Place of the Employe in Co-operative Stores. One of the chief criticisms against consumers' co-operation is that, while the movement is thoroughly democratic as far as the consumer is concerned and while labor conditions are, as has been shown, generally better among employes of co-operative stores than they are in profit-making ventures, the movement differs in no fundamental respect from capitalist industry in its relation to the employe of the store and factory.

This criticism was at first raised by the advocates of the "self-governing workshop," a workshop whose ideal was to have each worker own a share in the shop and have a voice in the selection of management and the control of policies. These advocates contended that a co-

[14] *Ibid.*, pp. 432, 439–40.

operative society was worth but little unless complete control resided in the hands of the producer. The advocates of consumers' co-operation, however, for a while silenced these critics by pointing to the uniform failure of this form of co-operative effort. Although the experiments along these lines have been made in thousands of instances, extending over nearly a century, "in almost every occupation, in various countries, often under apparently most promising conditions, . . . the most enthusiastic believer in this form of democracy would be hard put to it to find," as the Webbs pointed out, "in all the range of industry and commerce, a single lasting success. . . . In the relatively few cases in which such enterprises have not eventually succumbed as business concerns," these authors continue, "they have ceased to be democracies of producers, themselves managing their own work; and have become, in effect, associations of capitalists on a small scale—some of them continuing also to work at their trade—making profit for themselves by the employment at wages of workers outside their association." [15]

The reasons for this failure are not far to seek. As these shops produced not for their own use, but for exchange, their members were continually tempted to charge all that the traffic would bear; to exclude new members from the privileges that the founders had acquired; to maintain existing processes unchanged; and to discourage innovations. Furthermore, the relationship set up in the self-governing workshop "between a foreman or manager, who has, throughout the working day, to be giving orders to his staff, and the members of that staff who, assembled in the evening as a general meeting or a committee, criticize his actions or give him direction, with the power of discharging him if he fails to conform to their desires, has always been found to be an impossible one." [16]

The advocates of consumers' co-operation, on the other hand, were able to point out that the simple devices which they adopted under the Rochdale plan of control by the consumer, one vote per man, and savings-returns on purchases, led naturally to a continuous growth of membership, and that the greater the number of buyers in a co-operative store, the greater were the economies effected. While, therefore, in a "self-governing workshop," it was to the economic interest of the founders to exclude newcomers from full membership in the consumers' co-operative, it was to their advantage to attract an ever-larger circle.

Trade Unions and the Co-operative Movement. In many countries considerable confusion has existed in regard to the desirable relationship between the trade-union movement and the co-operatives. This

[15] *Ibid.*, pp. 463–4. [16] *Ibid.*, p. 468.

relationship varies widely in the many countries in which the co-operative movement has gained a foothold. In Great Britain a large proportion of the employes of the co-operative movement are now organized in the Amalgamated Union of Co-operative Employes and an extensive machinery has been developed for the adjustment of disputes between the management and the employes. Under the agreement worked out by the movement, any dispute not settled by direct negotiations between a trade union and a co-operative body is referred to a National Conciliation Board.

No lockout or strike is to be declared unless the dispute has been referred to the Board and the Board has not succeeded in finding a satisfactory settlement. The organization of this machinery has met with considerable success. The proper relationships between the co-operatives and their employes are still to be effected in numerous co-operative undertakings in the United States where so many co-ops have been initiated by the farming population.[17]

Co-operatives and Politics. Most of the members and leaders of the co-operative movement in democratic countries have been also members of political parties of industrial workers and farmers. In Belgium before the Second World War, there was a definite official tie-up between the consumers' and the political movements. Officially many of the co-operative movements have, however, been politically neutral.

In Great Britain the co-operative movement at first eschewed politics. By 1902 the co-ops "learned the lesson that, in capitalist society, political action is dictated by economic power," and created a Joint-Parliamentary Committee of the Co-operative Congress to protect their general interests against the business groups in control of the machinery of government. Ten years later William Maxwell, head of the Scottish Wholesale, urged the Congress to effect a fusion of forces between the co-operative movement, the trade unions, and the Labor party, with a view "not to bring politics into co-operation, but to take co-operation into politics."

Five years later, in 1917, during the First World War, the government tried to impose the excess profits duty upon this non-profit organization. As a result, the co-operatives in their congress that year passed a resolution in which they declared that the time had arrived "for the co-operative movement to take the necessary steps to secure direct representation in Parliament as the only way of effectively voicing its demands and safeguarding its interests."

[17] See Laidler and Campbell, *The Consumer Co-operative Movement,* pp. 12–14; Percy Redfern, *The Story of the Co-operative Wholesale Society,* pp. 81, 228; Webb, *op. cit.,* p. 188; Joseph Hallsworth and Rhys J. Davies, *The Working Life of Shop Assistants.*

The resolution passed with a large majority. Six months later a special national conference approved a draft plan for securing co-operative representation in Parliament and on local municipal and administrative bodies. In 1918 the co-operative movement elected its first representative to Parliament. In 1937 it was represented in Parliament by nine members.

The Co-operative party works closely with the Labor party, the local branches joining with labor in joint campaigns for local and parliamentary candidates. Its aims are both to make the mass of co-operators politically conscious, and to permeate the Labor party with knowledge of co-operative ideas and practice.

During the Second World War A. V. Alexander, M. P., a member of the Co-operative party, was appointed First Lord of the Admiralty in Prime Minister Churchill's cabinet. The co-operative parliamentary group took an active part in such matters as opposing certain features of the purchase tax which they regarded as detrimental to consumers and urging a better system of rationing. The co-operative movement for the first time became officially associated (1941) with the National Council of Labor, representative of the Trade Union Congress, the Labor party, and the Parliamentary Labor party, and sent eight of its members to this Council. This move, the co-operative congress stated, "has strengthened the defensive, offensive, and exploratory links that should bind the workers' movements to each other," and has given practical expression to the principle of the unity of the working-class movements. The co-operatives throughout the war vigorously supported the government in its stand against nazism.

Some in Great Britain have maintained that the co-operators in that country should go deeper into politics than they have and ally themselves solely with the Labor party. To build up a separate Co-operative party, declared Professor Laski, is "a tragic waste of energy."

In the United States the co-operative movement has thus far given little attention to the field of politics.

The movement is faced in every country with grave problems—economic, political, cultural. Many of those problems are yet to be solved. The movement in many countries, after growing strong and influential, was temporarily overrun and destroyed by the forces of fascist reaction. In these countries it is bound sooner or later to strike roots again. In many other nations the consumers' co-operative movement continues as an increasingly powerful factor in the social and economic life of the nation, and its power for greatest social good is still before it.

CHAPTER 43

Variants of Socialism

WHILE the chief divisions in social-economic thought appearing during the nineteenth and twentieth centuries have been set forth in previous chapters, the student will from time to time be confronted with other schools of thought not already described, schools which, at certain periods, have exerted a considerable influence on the social life of their day. Among these are the Christian socialists, the socialists of the chair or academic socialists, and the state socialists, the last-named school differing but little from "the socialists of the chair."

CHRISTIAN SOCIALISM

During the last century numerous individuals and groups within and without the Christian Church, animated with a passion for social change, have assumed the name of Christian socialists. Some of these groups have been both ardent Christians and ardent socialists; others have been Christian, but only mildly socialistic; and still others—particularly among certain groups in Germany and Austria—have been primarily anti-Semitic in their aims, rather than Christian or socialist.

De Lamennais. Among the earliest of the church reformers who have gone by the designation of Christian socialist is De Lamennais, born in 1782. De Lamennais was for a time a French Catholic priest and an ardent defender of the faith. He aimed to bring about an alliance between the church and the masses in opposition to kings, whom he looked upon as oppressors of the people. The church was to become the soul of the economic, as well as of the religious world. And as a step in that direction, De Lamennais urged the formation by the church of a grand co-operative association of laborers, which should free them from the yoke of the capitalist and the tyranny of the landlord.[1]

He was received with open arms on the presentation of his views to

[1] Ely, *French and German Socialism*, p. 245.

Pope Leo XII. Later, however, he issued a paper, *L'Avenir,* on which was emblazoned the motto, "Separate yourselves from the king, extend your hand to the people," that urged Gregory XVI, Pope Leo's successor, to support him in this anti-monarchical propaganda, but he was unable to win over the hierarchy to his point of view. He thereupon resigned from the church in despair.[2]

He wrote in 1833 *The Words of a Believer,* describing therein, with poetry and beauty, the wrongs inflicted upon the laborer by rulers and capitalists and describing the condition of wage earners as in some respects worse than that of chattel slaves.

The Christian Socialists of England. Of far more significance, however, than the agitation of De Lamennais was the Christian socialist agitation of the middle of the last century in Great Britain, under the leadership of Frederick Denison Maurice and Charles Kingsley.[3]

MAURICE AND KINGSLEY. Frederick Denison Maurice, the most brilliant of the British proponents of Christian socialism, was born in 1805, the son of a Unitarian minister. From his youth he took an active interest in the philanthropic enterprises of his father and acquired an intimate knowledge of the destitution around him.

As a young man he joined a debating club, the outgrowth of an Owenite society, where the subject of co-operation was frequently discussed. He became a member of the faculty at King's College, and soon gained a reputation as a scholar, theologian, and historian.[4] His studies of medieval philosophy left a deep impression on his mind and predisposed him to look favorably on the socialist propagandists of the Chartist period. Indeed, in his economic philosophy he followed the Owenite school. However, he differed widely from the political Chartists, for he opposed their democratic philosophy and condemned the doctrine of the sovereignty of the people as atheistic and subversive. A visit to him by John M. Ludlow, while he was teaching in King's College, for the purpose of inducing him to aid in wiping out the terrible conditions prevailing in the neighborhood of the Inns of Court, marked a turning point in his life.

The other great leader of the movement was Charles Kingsley, a

[2] Quoted in *Lamennais and Kingsley, Contemporary Review,* April, 1882.

[3] See Seligman, E. R. A., *Owen and the Christian Socialists.* Reprinted from the *Political Science Quarterly,* Vol. I, No. 2, 1886.

[4] Maurice was ordained as a minister in 1834, but was drawn into the religious controversies of the day and soon broke with the Oxford school. After editing the *Educational Magazine* for a short period, he became Professor of Theology at King's College and Chaplain of Lincoln's Inn (1845). Following his Christian socialist activities, he published his great work, *Moral and Metaphysical Religion.* He died in 1872.

young minister of Eversley, 14 years Maurice's junior. Kingsley was a revolutionist in his economic convictions, but, with Maurice, a conservative politically. The two men were radically different in temperament. "Maurice was mild, unobtrusive, averse to undue opposition, convincing by his example and his earnest logic rather than by appeals to the feelings. Kingsley was ardent, aggressive, and enthusiastic, touching the heart rather than the head. Maurice had a deep, measured style; Kingsley wrote as he spoke, with sentences fervid, passionate, clear-cut. Both were men of transcendent ability, but Maurice was incomparably the superior in thoroughness of conviction, in repose of intellect, in talent for leadership." [5]

They held, however, the same views regarding the function of religion. The world, they claimed, was the manifestation of God's order, but the selfishness of man had induced a deviation from the original principles.[6]

The Belief of Early Christian Socialists. All that is good in the modern world, they believed, has come from the principles of self-sacrifice and fraternal co-operation as taught in Christian ethics. The reintroduction of a universal, practical Christianity in the best sense would check the downward tendency of the times and reintroduce peace and harmony.

"Vehemently opposing Calvinism and asceticism as removing mankind from a sense of its obligation in this world, asserting the moral impotence of the view that makes the hope of heaven or the fear of hell the sole determinants of human conduct, objecting equally to the Oxford Tractarianism, which they termed an aristocratic movement in the most carnal sense, 'a system for saving the souls of fine ladies and gentlemen in an easy and gentlemanlike way,' [7] they were reformers in the fullest sense of the word. . . . The Kingdom of Christ was to them no empty formula; they were thoroughly imbued with the belief that this kingdom, created through revelation, actually existed and was destined in time to subjugate all wickedness and misery. . . . The Christian socialists looked with consternation upon the growing cleft between rich and poor, upon the cynical indifference of the one class, and the brooding discontent of the other; they sternly took the clergy

[5] Seligman, E. R. A., in *Political Science Quarterly,* Vol. 1, No. 2, p. 219. Kingsley was the son of a country gentleman whose mismanaged fortune led him to the church. The tragic sight of riots and bloodshed during a strike, while he was a boy in school, he declared, made him a radical. He went to Cambridge, and later entered the ministry, where his brilliant preaching and robust personality made him exceedingly popular.

[6] Maurice, *Life,* Vol. II, p. 44.

[7] Kingsley, *Letters and Memories of His Life,* II, p. 250.

to task for their inactivity, for squandering time in doctrinal quibbles and neglecting the paramount issues of the day. They strongly protested against the notion of turning the Bible into a book for keeping the poor in order. The Bible they considered, on the contrary, the poor man's book, the voice of God against tyrants, idlers, and humbugs. It demands for the poor as much and more than they demand for themselves; it expresses the deepest yearnings of the poor man's heart far more nobly, more daringly, more eloquently, than any modern orator has done. 'Justice from God to those whom men oppress, glory from God to those whom men despise' is the thought which runs through the whole Bible. It is the poor man's comfort and the rich man's yearning." [8]

"We are teaching," writes Maurice, "true socialism, true liberty, brotherhood, and equality—not the carnal dead level equality of the communist, but the spiritual equality of the Church idea, which gives every man an equal chance of developing and rewards every man according to his work." [9]

Attack on Manchester School. To them the Manchester school, with its emphasis on laissez-faire industrialism, was an abomination. "Of all narrow, hypocritical, anarchic, and atheistic schemers of the universe," they held, "the Cobden and Bright one is exactly the worst." [10]

"I expect nothing," declared Kingsley, "from the advocates of laissez faire—the pedants whose glory is in the shame of society, who arrogantly talk of economics as of a science so completely perfected, so universal and all important that common humanity and morality, reason and religion must be pooh-poohed down, if they seem to interfere with its infallible conclusions and yet revile, as absurd and utopian, the slightest attempt to apply those conclusions to any practical purpose. The man who tells us that we ought to investigate nature, simply to sit still patiently under her, and let her freeze, and ruin, and starve, and stink us to death is a goose, whether he calls himself a chemist or a political economist." [11]

[8] Seligman, *op. cit.*, p. 221; see *Politics for the People*, May 21, 1848. Letter to the Chartists, by Kingsley; also Maurice, Letter to Kingsley, April 22, 1848.

[9] See Kingsley, *Letters*, Vol. I, p. 248.

[10] *Letters of Kingsley;* see Hughes, *Prefatory Memoir to Alton Locke*, p. 51. Writers for the Manchester School demanded the elimination of all government interference with economic life. They denounced not only protectionism but also the public care of the poor, protective labor legislation, compulsory education, and similar measures.

[11] *Thoughts on the Frimley Murder*, by Parson Lot. *The Christian Socialist*, Nov. 2, Nov. 16, 1850, Vol. I, pp. 3, 18; cf. Kingsley's criticism of the economists in *A Mad World, My Masters*, and in *New Miscellanies*, p. 6.

Maurice, Kingsley, and their school could not be included among the modern socialists, if socialism is regarded as a set of doctrines, rather than a spirit of brotherhood. "But if by socialism," declares Professor Seligman, "we mean that principle which looks upon human beings as members of one family and subject to one law, which regards the workingmen as endowed with the same possibilities, and worthy of the same opportunities as others, which sets up the idea of combination and universal co-operation in opposition to the anarchy of distribution and the shortcomings of competition, which, in short, seeks to develop those characteristics that bind mankind together and render them more conscious of reciprocal duties—then, in this wider sense, they are indeed the truest socialists of the century." [12]

THE CHRISTIAN SOCIALISTS AND THE CHARTISTS. The movement which Maurice and Kingsley represented began in 1848, the year of Marx and Engels' *Communist Manifesto,* of the culmination of the Chartist movement, of the French revolution—a year marked, incidentally, by a severe economic crisis. In February the French revolution broke out in Paris. John M. Ludlow, a lawyer and a friend of Maurice, who had been educated in Paris, returned to England with the impression that socialism had become a powerful factor in English life. He and Maurice felt that it must be Christianized, or it would shake Christianity to the foundation, as socialism appealed to the higher and not to the lower instincts in human life.[13]

On Ludlow's return the famous "five million" Chartist petition had been handed in, and the call issued for an immense mass meeting at Kennington Common for April 10. London was in a ferment, and had been placed under the military government of Wellington. Two hundred thousand special deputies had been sworn to protect the city against a possible outbreak, and trouble seemed imminent. Kingsley rushed down to London from Eversley in a state of intense excitement. At Maurice's house he met Ludlow, and together they walked to the Common, where the rain and the energy of O'Connor prevented an outbreak. The three decided to send placards broadcast, to allay the minds of the discontented workers. Kingsley wrote all night, and the next morning his appeal to the British workmen appeared on thousands of posters. He told the workmen that while many of them had been wronged, they had thousands of friends who loved them because they were brothers, and who would not neglect them. He declared that it would take more than the charter to make them free.

12 Seligman, *op. cit.,* pp. 221–2.
13 Correspondence with Ludlow; Maurice, *Life,* Vol. I, pp. 458 ff.

"When you cry for liberty . . . who would dare to refuse you freedom? But there will be no true freedom without virtue, no true science without religion, no true industry without the fear of God and love of your fellow-citizens. Workers of England, be wise, and then you *must* be free, for you will be *fit* to be free." [14]

The placard was signed, "A Working Parson," and produced a great impression. The danger of serious violence passed, but Maurice decided, at the suggestion of Ludlow, to start a penny weekly, which might show the workers the way out of their difficulties. The result was the *Politics of the People,* contributed to by a remarkable group of writers, including Maurice, Kingsley, Ludlow, Archdeacon Hare, Professor Connington, Sir Arthur Helps, Archbishop Whately, and others noted in the literary world of the day. The columns also contained many communications from the rank and file of the Chartists.

The paper, however, had to be discontinued after 17 issues for lack of funds, although it had attained a circulation of 2,000 and had won many workers to its point of view.

A group of friends continued their meetings at Maurice's house all winter, started night schools for workingmen and girls, and conducted weekly lectures. In 1849 Thomas Hughes, author of *Tom Brown's School Days,* joined the movement and became a tower of strength to it.

THE SWEATED INDUSTRIES. During these years a system of "sweating" that was horrible to contemplate had developed in the clothing industry. The ultimate victims of this system were the men and women employed by "sweaters," who had contracted to find workers for clothing merchants. These victims were forced to live in the sweaters' houses. "They were literally stripped," Professor Seligman maintains, "of everything, until it was common for half a dozen men to have only one coat between them—the so-called 'relieve' permitting only one to go out at a time. But the condition of most was still more horrible. As they fell into arrears they were cooped up, six and ten at a time, in a miserable dark hole which served both as work and bedroom, and in this fetid, reeking atmosphere, half-stifled and half-starved, thousands of these poor wretches endured a living death." [15] Kingsley's soul was stirred by this misery, and he wrote his famous pamphlet, *Cheap Clothes and Nasty,*[16] one of the most powerful indictments of the system of sweating in all literature.

Here Kingsley describes Mammon as pretending to hate cruelty and

[14] See Kingsley, *Letters,* Vol. I, p. 156.

[15] Seligman, *op. cit.,* p. 229.

[16] Reprinted as No. 5 of tracts of Christian Socialists and in Eversley's edition of *Alton Locke,* 1881, pp. 76–109.

shrieking benevolently when a drunken sailor is flogged, but trimming his paletot and adorning "his legs with the flesh of men and the skins of women, with degradation, pestilence, heathendom, and despair"; and then chuckling "complacently over the smallness of his tailor's bills." "What is flogging or hanging" . . . he asks, "to slavery, starvation, waste of life, year-long imprisonment in dungeons narrower and fouler than those of the Inquisition which goes on among thousands of free, English clothes-makers at this day?"

Birth of Co-operative Workshops. This essay and Maurice's article on labor conditions in *Fraser's Magazine* created intense excitement, and many reforms were suggested. Ludlow, having observed the co-operative workshops in operation in Paris, urged the establishment of similar co-operatives in England. He convinced Maurice of the desirability of such a venture, and the group decided to issue a number of pamphlets on the subject. It was at that time that the name Christian socialism was adopted. "That is the only name," they declared, "which will define our object and will commit us at once to the conflict we must engage in sooner or later with the unsocial Christians and the un-Christian socialists." [17]

Maurice wrote the first tract, in which he declared that anyone who recognized the principles of co-operation as stronger and truer than those of competition, was justly called a socialist, and admitted that Owen, Fourier, Louis Blanc, and others came within that definition. In later pamphlets he strove to disprove Owen's views regarding the all-inclusive influence of environment and endeavored to show that socialism and the church should work together. Many thousands of copies of these pamphlets were distributed.

The Christian socialists also rented a building in London and started a Working Tailors' Association, with 12 tailors, under the leadership of Walter Cooper, ex-Chartist. All monies loaned to this association were to be repaid in a fund to be used to start other co-operative workshops. Wages were apportioned according to work and talent, but profits were to be equally divided, provided that each did his utmost, the final decision on these questions to be in the hands of the workmen themselves. Other workmen applied for aid in developing co-operative shops, and in February, 1850, a Society for Promoting Workingmen Associations was organized. The promoters met weekly in Maurice's house. Before long some 17 co-operatives appeared in London. A

[17] *Life of Maurice,* Vol. II, p. 34. The name had first been used in Owen's *New Moral World,* Nov. 7, 1840, in a letter signed, Joseph Squiers Coventry. There were, however, several societies of Christian co-operators in 1830.

central board of delegates from various societies was formed, and later a central co-operative agency was organized, a forerunner of the Co-operative Wholesale Society.

"Competition," wrote Maurice at this time, "is put forth as the law of the universe. That is a lie. . . . The time is come to declare that it is a lie, by word and deed. I see no way but by association for work instead of for strikes." "That self-interest is the law of human nature," wrote Kingsley, "I know well. That it ought to be the root-law of human society, I deny, unless society is to sink down again into a Roman Empire and a cage of wild beasts." [18]

The society pursued its work with enthusiasm. Thomas Hughes was not alone at that time in believing that they had "nothing to do but just to announce it and found an association or two in order to convert all England and usher in the millennium at once, so plain did the whole thing seem." [19]

The success of the co-operative workshop idea was indeed at first remarkable. The members of the original society soon trebled in numbers. Interested friends were induced to give the society their custom and to get their friends to do likewise. The workers themselves were astonished at the interest of the upper classes. In the autumn of 1850 Cooper made two tours through the northern countries and Maurice, Hughes, and others followed. The idea was eagerly adopted in many large cities.

"THE CHRISTIAN SOCIALIST." In the autumn of 1850 the group founded the *Christian Socialist,* a weekly, under the editorship of Ludlow, to propagate their point of view. In this unique journal, the motives of the founders were thus expressed:

"A new idea has gone abroad into the world that socialism, the latest-born of the forces now at work in modern society, and Christianity, the eldest-born of those forces, are in their nature not hostile, but akin to each other; or rather that the one is but the development, the outgrowth, the manifestation of the other." The idea has grown that socialism without Christianity, on the one hand, is lifeless as the feathers without the bird, however skillfully the stuffer may dress them up into an artificial semblance of life. That every socialist system that has maintained itself, has stood upon the moral grounds of righteousness, self-sacrifice, mutual affection, and common brotherhood. . . . That Christianity, on the other hand, in this nineteenth century of ours, becomes in its turn chilly and helpless when stripped of its social influ-

[18] *Letters,* Vol. II, p. 37.

[19] *Memoir of a Brother,* p. 111.

ences; or in other words, when divorced from socialism. If it be given us," they continued, "to vindicate for Christianity its true authority over the realms of industry and trade, for socialism its true character as the great Christian revolution of the nineteenth century, so that the title of socialism shall be only a bugbear to the idle and to the wicked, and society from the highest rank to the lowest shall avowedly regulate itself upon the principle of co-operation, and not drift rudderless upon the sea of competition, as our let-alone political economists would have it do —then, indeed, we shall have achieved our task; and no amount of obloquy, ridicule, calumny, neglect, shall make us desert it, so long as we have strength and means to carry on the fight. For a fight it is; and a long one, and a deadly one—a fight against all the armies of Mammon." [20]

Developing Opposition. Kingsley had previously touched on some of the evils of "Mammonism" in his *The Saints' Tragedy,* as well as in his novel *Yeast* in which he set forth the poverty and the hopes of the farm workers. He followed this with his famous novel, *Alton Locke,* a fictitious biography of a tailor-poet who worked himself up from a lowly environment. *Alton Locke* was published just as the upper classes were beginning their bitter denunciations against the group, who were accused of suffering from a morbid craving for notoriety and a crazy straining after paradox. Advertisements were refused by the daily papers, booksellers did not dare sell copies of their publications, and the *Christian Socialist* was prohibited by the French government from circulating in France. A committee from King's College was selected to investigate Maurice's "dangerous schemes." The group replied to the attacks. Ludlow, who showed the best knowledge of the teachings of economists, issued at that time the first refutations of the wages-fund theory, now finally abandoned by English economists.

Partly as a result of the activity of Maurice, Kingsley, and others, the law regarding co-operative ventures was altered in 1852, and a more liberal law passed—"the first law in the civilized world that recognized and protected co-operative societies as separate entities." [21]

Thomas Hughes in the "Journal of Association." In January, 1852, the *Christian Socialist* was replaced by the *Journal of Association,* which Thomas Hughes undertook to edit. It excluded articles of a political or general nature, and devoted itself wholly to co-operation.

[20] "The New Idea," by Ludlow, *The Christian Socialist,* Vol. I, No. 1, Nov. 2, 1850; cf. *My Political Creed,* by Parson Lot, in Vol. I, p. 50.

[21] Seligman, *op. cit.,* p. 238.

The society modified its name (Society for Promoting Workingmen Associations) and was henceforth called the Association for Promoting Industrial and Provident Societies.

Wane of the Movement. During the engineers' strike of 1852 the society opposed the attacks against the workers and assisted in bringing before the public a better understanding of the aims of the trade-union movement. However, toward the close of 1853, defects found in productive co-operation began to come to the surface, and the producers' societies began to decline. Several were robbed of their funds; internal dissension and indifference destroyed some ventures; and rival ventures contributed to the general decline of the movement. E. Vansittart Neale, philanthropist, assisted many financially, but was soon compelled to stop his support.

Feeling that they were not able to cope with the practical details of co-operation, Maurice and Kingsley decided to form an institute to assist in educating the workers along the lines of broader social relationships. Early in 1854 the Workingmen's College was opened. A brilliant corps of instructors was secured, instruction was given in many branches of learning, and a periodical was published.

While the leaders of the movement kept up their enthusiastic teachings for many years, the Christian socialist movement as such, as an episode in the national life of England, practically ended in 1855.

The founders failed to accomplish many of their aims. Indirectly, however, they did much, through legislation and agitation, to stimulate the co-operative movement, to educate the economists to a different attitude toward the social problem, to call attention to the patent evils and abuses of unrestricted competition, and to develop a more sympathetic understanding of the labor movement.

It likewise, according to Vedder, "destroyed in England that hostility between advanced political and social ideas and established religion, which has prevailed on the Continent between socialism and Christianity to the mutual injury of both. Maurice and Kingsley introduced socialistic ideas among a wide circle of Christians, both clergy and laity, who but for them would never have listened to the new theories." [22]

Christian Socialism on the European Continent. In Germany in the middle and the latter part of the nineteenth century there were numerous attempts of ministers of the Protestant and Catholic churches to interest their respective churches in the problems of the working class.

Of the Catholic churchmen one of the foremost was Bishop of Mainz,

22 Vedder, Henry C., *Socialism and the Ethics of Business* (N. Y.: Macmillan, 1914).

Baron von Ketteler (1811–1877). Von Ketteler accepted the doctrine of the iron law of wages and assented to many of the teachings of the social democrats. He held that God, or the church, was the supreme owner of all property and advocated, besides labor legislation, the development of productive co-operative enterprises under Catholic auspices—but with state financial support—as the solution of the labor problem. The program was designed in part to weaken the state as a rival of the church, in part to help labor, in part to attract labor to the church. F. C. J. Moufang, Franze Hitze, Adolph Kolping, and others were also active in various movements of this order.

In Austria Karl Lueger (1844–1910) adopted the program of the German Catholic co-operators and organized the strong Austrian Christian Socialist party, which, however, became more anti-Semitic than either Christian or socialist. In France we find Albert de Mun (1841–1914) organizing the *Action Libérale Française,* virtually the Catholic Socialist party of France.

In more recent years Stöcker, the fanatical court preacher of the Hohenzollerns, organized what was called a Christian Social Workingmen's party. Like the Christian Socialist party of Austria, this party had little of Christianity or socialism in it as compared with its anti-Semitism. While Stöcker favored labor legislation, he wanted the monarch to be the leader in social reforms, and his prime interest was to bring the people back to the church. During the nineties Friedrich Naumann also made an unsuccessful effort to capture German Protestantism for a radical social reform policy.

The point of view of many of the so-called Christian socialists of the late nineteenth century on the Continent was expressed by the celebrated Belgian professor of Political Economy, de Laveleye:

"The proletarians have been detached from and will return to Christianity when they begin to understand that it brings to them freedom and equal rights, whereas atheistic materialism consecrates their slavery and sacrifices them to pretended natural laws. By a complete misapplication of ideas, the religion of Christ, transformed into a temporal and sacerdotal institution, has been called in as the ally of caste, despotism, and the ancient regime to sanction all inequalities. The Gospel, on the contrary, is the good news to the poor—the announcement of the advent of that kingdom when the humble shall be lifted up and the disinherited shall possess the earth." [23]

Later Christian Socialism in England. During the eighties in England the Rev. Stewart D. Headlam organized the Guild of St. Matthew,

[23] Quoted by Kaufmann, in *Contemporary Review,* April, 1882.

a high church organization. Headlam long edited the *Church Reformer,* the organ of the guild and an outspoken advocate of Christian socialism. In 1889 the Christian Social Union was founded under the leadership of the Bishop of Durham and embraced in its membership Bishop Gore, Bishop Stubbs, and many other churchmen. During this period a Christian Socialist Society, not confined to the Church of England, was also formed and, later, the Christian Socialist League, of which Dr. John Clifford was a leading spirit.

In the early twenties of the present century, the Socialist Christian League was established. Its members, "acknowledging the leadership of Jesus Christ," pledged themselves "to work and pray for the spiritual and economic emancipation of all people from the bondage of material things, and for the establishment of the Commonwealth of God on Earth."

The stated goal of the League was as follows:

"Recognizing that the present capitalist order of society of fundamentally anti-Christian, the League will strive for the creation of an international socialist order based on the communal control of the means of life and co-operation in freedom for the common weal.

"The League will work in close connection with the labor and socialist movements. It believes that the necessary transformation of our social order requires a change of heart and mind and will, and a corresponding change of political and industrial arrangements: substituting mutual service for exploitation, and a social democracy for the struggle of individuals and classes."

During the Second World War fourteen prominent British churchmen, led by the Bishop of Bradford, in a call to their fellow Christians to become active in the affairs of the League, issued the following manifesto:

"Capitalism has led to gross want, waste of material resources and human endowments, and spiritual and cultural enslavement, and has provoked those forces which have landed humanity in this present war.

"Because we are Christians we believe that it is the Divine intention that men should live together on this earth in brotherhood; we regard it as an offense against Almighty God that any should go hungry while others are over-fed, that the life of the family, hallowed by our Saviour and his Mother in the village home at Nazareth, should be robbed of decency and dignity, that there should be gross inequality of opportunity, and that men's spirits should be broken by standing, day after day, idle in the market-place with no opportunity to work.

"We are convinced that these evils must continue until the land and at least the key industries pass from private to common ownership and are used for the benefit of all and not of the few. Unless this Christian Revolution is effected, waste and want will continue, and war will follow war. Now is the time to act. Tomorrow may be too late. In self-defence the state has been compelled to restrict the capitalist and to appropriate some of his gains. What is necessary in war will be equally necessary in peace. We must unite *now* to defeat the efforts, already being planned and pursued, to bring the bad old times back again when the war is over.

"A Christian social order will not be built in a day; but we must begin to build. What should be demanded at once is the public ownership of land that good houses may be erected and public life freed from the heavy toll to the ground landlords, and that the land be no longer exploited but rightly and wisely used; the social ownership and control of banking, mines, transport, and power, with control of overseas trade and a transformed system of education that will abolish class schools and secure opportunity for all children to develop their innate capacities." [24]

In May, 1942, a number of clergy and ministers, objecting to the "vagueness" of the social pronouncements of the Malvern Conference of 1941, formed a Council of Clergy and Ministers for Common Ownership, with the Bishop of Bradford as president and the Dean of Canterbury and the Bishop of Malmesbury as vice-presidents.

"We believe," maintained the declaration of principles of this organization, written along lines similar to those of the basis of the Socialist Christian League, "that the private ownership of the great productive resources of the community is contrary to Divine Justice, and inevitably involves man in a self-centered way of life.

"We believe that the common ownership of these resources, with due regard for the freedom of the individual, more nearly expresses the will of God for man's life on earth as revealed by Jesus Christ. We pledge ourselves, as an essential part of our Christian duty, to work for this end.

"We affirm," it added, "that the road to common ownership lies through the increasing alliance of all sections of society with the working-class movement, and through victory over fascism abroad and at home." [25]

Another Christian socialist body that has functioned during the

[24] The League publishes a bulletin, *The Socialist Christian*, and pamphlet literature at 318, Almondbury Bank, Huddersfield, England.

[25] See other literature published by C. C. M. C. O., 28 Maypole Lane, Birmingham 14, England.

forties in England is the Catholic Crusade, which has maintained that the world was "split into two warring classes, rich and poor . . . the rich seeking to augment and maintain their power and riches, the poor to secure the necessities of life," and that "the first essential step towards the establishment of God's Kingdom on earth is that the sources of material wealth shall be in the hands of all, and not an owning class, and shall be used in co-operation for the common good." [26]

Christian Socialism in the United States. In the United States a Christian Labor Union was organized in 1872, and during the following years the Reverends Josiah Strong, George D. Herron, and Washington Gladden, Professor Richard T. Ely, and others presented through this and other organizations the social challenge to the Christian church. In 1889 the first strictly American Christian Socialist Society was organized by Rev. W. D. P. Bliss, an Episcopal clergyman.

The first quarter of the twentieth century witnessed the formation of several societies committed to socialism or to a new social order more in conformity with the principles of Jesus. Active organizations of that period included the Collectivist Society, of which Rufus W. Weeks, a vice-president of the New York Life Insurance Company, was a prominent member; the Christian Socialist League, the Church Socialist League, the Church League for Industrial Democracy, the Fellowship of Reconciliation, and the Fellowship for a Christian Social Order. Walter Rauschenbusch, for years Professor of Church History in Rochester Theological Seminary, during the years immediately before the First World War, did more than any other single individual to bring the social message before the church. His *Christianity and the Social Crisis, Christianizing the Social Order,* and other books were clarion calls to the church to uproot the commercialism of the day and work for an economic democracy.

"Christianity," declared Rauschenbusch, "makes the love of money the root of all evil and demands the exclusion of the covetous and extortioners from the Christian fellowship; capitalism cultivates the love of money for its own sake and gives its largest wealth to those who use monopoly for extortion. Thus two spirits are wrestling for the mastery in modern life, the spirit of Christ and the spirit of Mammon. . . . If the one is Christian, the other is anti-Christian. . . . Whoever declares that the law of Christ is impracticable in actual life and has to be superseded in business by the laws of capitalism, to that extent dethrones Christ and enthrones Mammon. . . . The most important advance in the knowledge of God that a modern man can make is to un-

[26] *The Catholic Crusade,* published c/o Christopher Cottage, Thaxted, Essex.

derstand that the Father of Jesus Christ does not stand for the permanence of the capitalistic system. . . .

"The most comprehensive and intensive act of love in which we could share would be a collective action of the community to change the present organization of the economic life into a new order that would rest on the Christian principles of equal rights, democratic distribution of economic power, the supremacy of the common good, the law of mutual dependence and service, and the uninterrupted flow of good will throughout the human family." [27]

Partly as a result of such teachings as those of Professor Rauschenbusch, Professor Harry F. Ward, Bishop Spaulding, Bishop Paul Jones, and a host of others, partly as a result of the larger social forces at work, the churches, in the first quarter of the twentieth century, organized various commissions on social service and formulated social creeds which, though not committed to a socialistic state, emphasize the need for more democracy and a more social motive in industry, and condemn many of the evils of our competitive system. The Encyclical on Labor of Leo XIII also had a profound effect on the clergy of the Catholic Church as far as the consideration of labor problems is concerned.

Socialist Christians in Recent Years. During the thirties and forties in the United States the main society around which the Christian socialists rallied was the Fellowship of Socialist Christians, of which Dr. Reinhold Niebuhr, Professor of Christian Ethics, Union Theological Seminary, was one of the moving spirits. In 1934 the Fellowship began the publication of *Radical Religion,* later named *Christianity and Society,* a quarterly publication "devoted to Christianity and social reconstruction." The principles enunciated by the society were as follows:

"The Fellowship of Socialist Christians accepts the Christian faith as the only adequate interpretation and rule of life. Within terms of this faith its members have arrived at socialist political and economic convictions. They see in the processes of decay and destruction in contemporary capitalist society the judgment of God upon a society which violates the law of God and of life by its injustices. They believe that modern society is involved in progressive tendencies of self-destruction because the very technical achievements of an industrial age, from which a more optimistic generation expected salvation, accentuate the anarchy of our common life.

"The Fellowship is committed to the belief that the social ownership and administration of natural resources and of basic means of pro-

[27] Rauschenbusch, Walter, *Christianizing the Social Order,* pp. 322–3.

duction is a primary requisite of justice in our technological age. It affirms and supports the efforts of those who seek a co-operative society along socialist lines, and it opposes those who seek to maintain the dominant contemporary system known as capitalism, which is characterized by private ownership of natural resources and the instruments of production. Capitalism, in its inevitable contracting phase, subordinates the needs of the masses to the preservation and enhancement of the privileges of a steadily narrowing class of owners. It destroys the opportunity of increasing numbers of people to earn a livelihood adequate for physical health, mental and moral development, and personal freedom. It thereby corrupts both culture and religion.

"The Fellowship believes that the workers of the world, who suffer most from the injustices of the present society, have a peculiar mission to be the instruments and heralds of this new society. It therefore seeks to associate those who are not engaged in manual toil with the interests of those who are striving to create political forces in which human need and moral decision will be united to bring in a new economic order.

"The Fellowship differs from doctrinaire collectivist philosophies not only in its adherence to the Christian faith but also on empirical grounds. It is aware of the danger of unnecessarily mutilating organic forms of social life by coercing them into mechanical moulds. It seeks a socialist society because of its intent to enrich human life in both its social and individual aspects. Whether collectivism best serves this purpose in certain types of agrarian production and retail distribution is a question which it leaves open advisedly, believing that more experimentation is required to determine this issue.

"The Fellowship believes that the process of change may involve conflict and destruction. It does not believe that good-will alone is a guarantee against the possibility of violent conflict. It does believe that the most certain way of mitigating conflict and violence is to enlist the largest number of the total community in the struggle for a new social order. The Fellowship does not share the optimism of those Marxists who imagine that a new mechanism of social ownership will eliminate all conflict in the world and solve all the problems of the human spirit. On the basis of its Christian convictions it recognizes the inevitability of the conflict of interests in society as one of the forms in which human sin will always express itself."

In 1944 a reformulation of the above principles was discussed, in which emphasis was placed on democracy as a means and as an end, and the members were asked to commit themselves only to as much government ownership and operation of the economic life of society as "seems necessary, to the end of substituting the goal of general human freedom and welfare for the goal of enhancing the income and wealth of individuals and corporations." [28]

During the early forties, the Church League for Industrial Democracy, formerly the Church Socialist League, made up of numerous religious groups, favored somewhat similar sets of social principles.

Catholic Criticism of the Economic System. For centuries leaders of the Catholic Church have condemned many social evils which have manifested themselves in the economic order. For centuries the Church has bitterly opposed the taking of interest, which it regarded as usury.

Since the famous Encyclical of Pope Leo XIII, *Rerum Novarum,* published in 1891, the Catholic Church has repeatedly called attention to the evils of the present industrial age, characterized by large-scale production, the concentration of economic power, and great inequalities in the distribution of wealth and income. In this Encyclical, Pope Leo XIII bluntly wrote:

> After the old trade guilds had been destroyed in the last century, and no protection was substituted in their place, and when public institutions and legislation had cast off traditional religious teaching, it gradually came about that the present age handed over the workers, each alone and defenseless, to the inhumanity of employers and the unbridled greed of competitors. A devouring usury, although often condemned by the Church, but practised nevertheless under another form by avaricious and grasping men, has increased the evil; and, in addition, the whole process of production as well as trade in every kind of goods has been brought almost entirely under the power of a few, so that a very few rich and exceedingly rich men have laid a yoke almost of slavery on the unnumbered masses of non-owning workers.

Forty years later, Pope Pius XI, in his Encyclical *Quadragesimo Anno,* noted the increased centralization of industrial power during the previous decades, and warned the nations of the menace that that centralization of power presented to the body politic.

Still later Pope Leo XIII declared:

> When we turn our attention . . . to the changes which this capitalistic economic order has undergone since the days of Leo XIII, we have regard to the interests, not of those only who live in countries where "capital" and industry prevail, but of the whole human race.
>
> In the first place, then, it is patent that in our days not alone is wealth

[28] See A. T. Mollegen on "The Common Convictions of the Fellowship of Socialist Christians," *Christianity and Society,* Spring, 1943, pp. 24, 27.

accumulated, but immense power and despotic economic domination is concentrated in the hands of a few, and that those few are for the most part not the owners, but only the trustees and directors of invested funds, who administered them at their good pleasure.

This power becomes particularly irresistible when exercised by those who, because they hold and control money, are able also to govern credit and determine its allotment, for that reason supplying, so to speak, the life-blood to the entire economic body, and grasping, as it were, in their hands the very soul of production, so that no one dare breathe against their will.

The Pope went on to explain that this condition resulted from the practice of unrestricted competition and that such competition favored the strongest or those paying least attention to the dictates of conscience.

While opposing "materialistic socialism," and expressing fear of too much concentration of power in the hands of the state, the Pope insisted that "the civil power is more than the mere guardian of law and order" and "that it must strive with all zeal to make sure that the laws and institutions, the general character and administration of the commonwealth, should be such as of themselves to realize public well-being and private prosperity." He praised those governments which were becoming aware of their obligation to see that justice was done to the working class, and that were engaged in promoting "a broader social policy." He recommended the new social legislation of the twenties and the work of the International Labor Office. He declared that both free competition and the economic despotism which supplanted it must be curbed by the state. "When we speak of the reform of the social order," he maintained, "it is principally the state we have in mind." Thus, while, like his predecessor, Pope Pius XI "wanted many details of economic life to be handled by organized economic groups," since such groups had been destroyed by individualistic capitalism, he believed that the state, "pending a more rational organization of economic life, was bound to intervene for the purpose of protecting the common good." [29]

In the middle of the forties, therefore, while the leaders of the Catholic Church still condemned what they conceived to be the social and philosophic teachings of socialism, they were one with the socialists in their demand for economic justice and the wide distribution of economic power, and in their belief that the community as well as voluntary co-operative groups should assume increasing functions and increasing controls over the economic life of the nation, if the great social evils of the day were to be eliminated.

[29] Benjamin L. Masse, *America,* April 8, 1944, p. 9.

Maynard C. Krueger (left), re-elected National Chairman of the Socialist party, in Reading, Pennsylvania, June, 1944, congratulating Norman Thomas (center), nominated for the fifth time as the party's Presidential candidate, and Darlington Hoopes (right), Reading lawyer, nominated for the Vice-Presidency. (Courtesy Wide World Photos)

(Left) Morris Hillquit (1869–1933), for many years leading socialist writer, labor attorney, and Chairman of the National Executive Committee, Socialist party. (Right) Eugene V. Debs (1855–1926), labor leader and five times Socialist party Presidential candidate, 1900–1920. (Courtesy Wide World Photos)

(Left) Thomas C. Douglas, Premier of Saskatchewan, Canadian Cooperative Commonwealth Federation Government, 1944–1961; Federal leader of the New Democratic party of Canada, 1961– ; leader of the N.D.P. Delegation in Canadian Parliament, 1961– . (Photo by Karsh, Ottawa, courtesy N.D.P.) (Right) M. J. Coldwell, former leader of C.C.F. of Canada and of C.C.F. group in the Canadian House of Commons; member of Canadian Commission on National Security. (Photo by Thomas Studio, Ottawa, courtesy N.D.P.)

Upton Sinclair (center), Pulitzer Prize-winning novelist and founder of the Intercollegiate Socialist Society, 1905, at meeting of League for Industrial Democracy on his 85th birthday in 1963. With him are (left to right) Nathaniel M. Minkoff, President, L.I.D.; Mark Starr, labor educator; Roger Baldwin, former Director, American Civil Liberties Union; Harry W. Laidler, Executive Director Emeritus, L.I.D.; Dr. Leroy E. Bowman, former Acting Chairman, New York Liberal party; Dr. Oscar Cargill, Chairman of Department of English, New York University. (Courtesy Alexander Archer)

Close-up of the windows of the original Rochdale co-operative Pioneers' store, Toad Lane, Rochdale, England, containing goods similar to those sold by the Pioneers on opening the store in 1844. (Courtesy Co-operative League, U.S.A.)

Farmers' Union co-operative oil refinery at Laurel, Montana. (Courtesy Co-operative League, U.S.A.)

Co-operative apartment houses, Zurich, Switzerland, erected with the financial assistance of the Zurich socialist city government.

(Left) The "Three Crowns" Flour Mill, Stockholm, Sweden, owned by the Co-operative Union of Sweden. One of the numerous large productive enterprises owned by the Swedish consumers' co-operative movement. (Courtesy American Swedish News Exchange)

Regional warehouse of OTK, wholesale society of the Finnish "Progressive" Co-operative movement, near Tampere. Completed in 1966, it is the second largest commercial building in Finland.

Summary. All types of Christian socialists have united in the belief that the application of Christianity to the social order would lead to the elimination of many of our social ills, but they have failed to agree regarding the remedies proposed and have been actuated by decidedly different motives. The early Christian socialists on the Continent and England had little conception of the doctrine of "scientific" socialism, as their educational work preceded the development of this school of socialist thought. For the most part, they urged a modification of conditions under the capitalist system rather than the overthrow of that system, and, in many instances, turned to the producers' co-operative movement—to the self-governing workshop—as the way out.

Back of much of the propaganda of the Christian socialists of that earlier day on the Continent was the desire to augment the prestige of the church and bring the masses within its membership. Maurice, Kingsley, and his followers, on the other hand, were more concerned in bringing the church nearer to an understanding of the masses than in bringing the masses to the church. The Christian socialist movement in Austria, which has been continued to this day, contained few of the elements either of Christianity or of socialism.

The later Christian socialist movements in England and America have been rather definitely committed to the tenets of modern socialism. Many of them have joined the Christian socialist movement in the belief that Christianity needs the socialist philosophy and that the socialist movement equally needs the spiritualizing influence of Christianity. They contend that, in addition to other reasons for working for socialism, they should strive for it as the logical application to industrial society of the Christian doctrine of the Fatherhood of God and the brotherhood of man.

On the whole, the propaganda of these movements has aided materially in bringing the ideals of socialism before tens of thousands who would otherwise be unaware of its existence and has brought into the socialist movement, especially in England, a group of earnest workers of no little value to the cause of socialism. Christian socialists have in general differed from the utopian socialists in refusing to construct the details of an ideal commonwealth which, in their opinion, should be superimposed upon society. They have laid more stress on ethical, emotional forces than on the power of logic and reason as a means of social salvation. With the utopians, however, they have, in numerous cases, refused to put their trust primarily in the workers as the economic group which would remedy injustices and have felt that the privileged groups in the community, if shown the light, would do their part to change the economic order. This attitude, however, applies to the earlier Christian socialist group more than to those of the present day.

SOCIALISM OF THE CHAIR; STATE SOCIALISM

The Origin of the Socialism of the Chair. Another form of so-called socialism that gained some vogue in Germany during the last half of the nineteenth century is professorial socialism or socialism of the chair. Precursors of this school were Karl Johann Rodbertus (1805–75) and the Frenchman, Charles Brook Dupont-White (1807–78). The scientific leader of this school, and its most advanced member, was Adolph Wagner, the Berlin professor. Gustav Schmoller, Brentano, Adolph Held, Schaeffle, and other scholars in German universities were likewise members. In 1871 Herr Offenheim, in the *National Zeitung,* dubbed a number of these professors *Katheder Sozialisten,* or socialists of the chair. This term was accepted by Professor Schmoller in his opening address at a gathering at Eisenach in 1872, which led to a considerable movement in Germany and to the formation of the Union for Social Politics.

The attitude of this school is thus expressed by Schmoller:

"We preach neither the upsetting of science nor the overthrow of the existing social order, and we protest against all socialistic experiments. But we do not wish, out of respect for abstract principles, to allow the most crying abuses to become daily worse, and to permit so-called freedom of contract to end in the actual exploitation of the laborer. We demand that it [the state] should concern itself, in an altogether new spirit, with his instruction and training, and should see that labor is not conducted under conditions which must have for their inevitable effect the degradation of the laborer."

Negatively, then, the German professorial socialists vigorously attacked the empty abstractions of the Manchester school of economics, declaring that this school had no appreciation of the higher duties of the state in the protection of the working class or of the ethical side of economic life. At the same time, they frowned upon the incipient socialist movement as being directed against the existing state and held that, if the just demands of the workers were satisfied by the state, the hold of the social democrats on the working class would be loosened.

The Professorial Socialists and the State. The state to them was, above all things, a moral person, arising out of the essential characteristics with which God had endowed humanity. State obligations, they held, are sacrosanct. The rights of the state spring from a higher source than a social contract of the citizens with one another. The state stands above the citizens as the church above its members. Humanity progresses, and ever must progress, through church and state. The state, in fact, according to Schmoller, is the grandest moral institution for the education and development of the human race.[30] In practical politics the Wagner-Schmoller school abjured violent or sudden change, and looked forward to a slow evolution toward improved labor conditions.

THE LAW OF GOVERNMENT. According to the law of government, as "discovered" by Wagner, the state was, in the nature of the case, bound to absorb an ever-larger number of functions. The development and operation by the state of railroads, the postal service, the telephone system, and the educational system was an illustration of this law. Governments were increasingly engaged with such responsibilities as passing sanitary legislation, inspecting buildings, and enacting wage and hour legislation. These matters are no longer left to individual initiative and private competition.

In commenting on this Wagnerian law, Professor Ely declares:

"Its operation would, of itself, establish the socialistic state, since, if government continually absorbs private business, there will, in the end, be only state business. In this socialistic state there would be the same difference in rank as at present between the different governmental employes. At the top of the social ladder there would still be an employer, and at the bottom ordinary laborers, steadily employed in the service of the state, as e.g., the workmen on the state railroads now." [31]

INFLUENCE ON BISMARCK. The socialists of the chair were no mere esoteric philosophers. They were vitally concerned with the problems of the Germany of their day, and they exerted a considerable influence on the outstanding statesman of Europe—Bismarck. Bismarck became a close student of this school and seized upon the program of Wagner, Schmoller, and others in attempting at one and the same time to strengthen the state, undermine the social democratic movement, and improve working conditions. The social legislation of the seventies and eighties in Germany was the result.

Social Legislation and State Socialism. The social legislation of Bismarck has been often referred to as state socialism. The term *state socialist* has had, however, during the last few decades, many connotations. It has been used to describe the social legislative program of Bismarck, which did not seek to reconstruct the present order, but merely to mitigate the evils of capitalism through social insurance

30 Ely, *French and German Socialism,* p. 242.

31 *Ibid.*, p. 243; see also in this text, p. 646.

against unemployment, sickness, and old age, through state ownership of such utilities as the railroads, and through public regulation. While Christian socialists hoped, through their program, to strengthen the church, the state socialists desired to increase the loyalty of workers to the state, and, at the same time, to weaken the revolutionary working-class party. Thus Bismarck declared: "Give the working man the right to employment as long as he has health. Assure him care when he is sick, and maintenance when he is old. If you will do that without fearing the sacrifice, or crying out 'state socialism' directly the words 'provision for old age' are uttered, . . . then I believe that the gentlemen of the Wyden [social democratic] program will sound their bird-call in vain; and as soon as the working men see that the government is earnestly concerned with their welfare, the thronging to them will cease."[32]

This general tendency toward state socialism has advanced to such an extent since the days of Bismarck that at present in most European and Australian countries, at least, the citizen receives his mail, his telegrams, and his telephone messages through public agencies. As Webb so well brought out, he walks along streets lit by the public gas or electric service, cleaned with brooms and water drawn from the public supply; he travels on public tramways or railroads. He sends his children to the public schools; many a leisure hour he spends engaged in sports in the public parks, swimming in the public pools, reading books loaned by the public library, and attending concerts or lectures or art exhibits arranged by public agencies.

He, perhaps, houses his family in a city-built cottage or tenement. If he chooses, he keeps his money in the public savings bank, and buys many of his supplies from the public market. When out of work or sick or old, he draws his allowance from the public insurance funds. He can at any time apply for treatment at the public hospital, and there secures the services of a physician paid from the public treasury. And when his life's work is over, he might be assured of a decent burial in a public cemetery with the competent assistance of a public undertaker.

In a thousand and one other ways he is constantly coming into vital touch with the industrial, financial, educational, and social agencies operated by local, provincial, or federal governments.

The impulse back of this movement has been varied. On the one hand, government ownership is advocated as a means of preserving the political or economic *status quo*. A certain amount of such ownership has been adopted with a view to making the state a more efficient mili-

32 Quoted in Hunter, Robert, *Socialists at Work*, p. 223.

tary power, ensuring additional revenues to the government, rendering business men needed assistance in their competition with foreign countries, taking "the wind out of the sails" of the socialist movement, and increasing the loyalty of the workers to the government.

Business interests have at times urged municipal ownership of utilities as a means of increasing the numerous revenues from them, with a consequent lowering of the tax rates, and, in addition, ownership of housing developments as a means of attracting outside industries through low gas and electric rates and better health and housing conditions.

The mass of the people have demanded public control in order to abolish the anti-social exploitation and tyranny of large corporations and monopolies; to promote the health and safety of the community; to increase educational and recreational opportunities; to encourage the use of certain services or commodities; to reduce the enormous wastes of individualistic competition; to decrease the high cost of living; to improve the condition of the workers; and to strengthen in general all those forces which are working for a more complete democracy and brotherhood.

The distinction between the motivating forces back of the socialist movement and those back of state socialism and certain kinds of government ownership was made by Morris Hillquit, leader of the American Socialist party:

"Government ownership [or state socialism] is often introduced not as a democratic measure for the benefit of the people, but as a fiscal measure to provide revenue for the government or to facilitate its military operations. In such cases government ownership may tend to strengthen rather than to loosen the grip of capitalist governments on the people, and its effect may be decidedly reactionary. Similarly government ownership is often advocated by middle-class 'reform' parties, with the main purpose of decreasing the rates of property owners and reducing the rates of freight, transportation, and communication for the smaller business men.

"The socialist demand for government ownership of industries of a public or quasi-public nature, springs from different motives and contemplates a different system than the similar demands of other parties. The socialists advocate government ownership primarily for the purpose of eliminating private profits from the operation of public utilities, and conferring the benefits of such industries on the employes and consumers. Their demand for national or municipal ownership of industries is always qualified by a provision for the democratic administration of such industries and for the application of the profits to the increase of the employes' wages and the improvement of the service. Furthermore, it must be borne in mind that when the socialist platform declares in favor of government ownership of certain industries, the Socialist party at the same time nominates candidates for public office pledged to carry out these measures in the spirit of that platform. In other words, what the socialists advocate is not government ownership under purely capitalistic administration, but collective ownership under a government controlled or at least strongly influenced by political representatives of the working class." [33]

Mr. Hillquit's distinction between government ownership and collective ownership as advocated by modern socialists was in general the distinction made between the state socialist and the democratic socialist approach. The distinction between state capitalism and state socialism made by the communists seems to be that state capitalism pre-supposes a considerable ownership of industry by the state—including public utilities, natural resources, etc.—and that state socialism presupposes the ownership by the state of practically all essential industries, accompanied, perhaps, by a much smaller spread between the minimum and maximum salaries paid than at present prevails in state industries. Beyond that stage they see communism.

There are, however, some who insist—the consumerists, syndicalists, and guild socialists among them—that all socialists who urge ownership of industry by the municipality, state and nation, are state socialists, even though such public ownership provides for a democratic administration and is operated by a government controlled or strongly influenced by labor. This, however, is not the generally accepted definition of state socialism in the working-class movement today.

OTHER SCHOOLS

At various stages in the socialist movement, socialists and social reformers have coined the names "constructive socialism," [34] "pragmatic socialism," [35] "practical socialism," [36] etc., and the opponents of "spu-

[33] Hillquit, Morris, *Socialism Summed Up*, pp. 73–4.

[34] H. G. Wells in his admirable book, *New Worlds for Old* (N. Y.: Macmillan, 1908), aligns himself with the "constructive" socialists, who believe that "unless you can change men's minds you cannot effect socialism, and when you have made clear and universal certain broad understandings, socialism becomes a mere matter of science and devices and applied intelligence."

[35] M. C. Rorty, vice-president of the International Telephone and Telegraph Corporation, at a dinner of the League for Industrial Democracy, December 29, 1926, defined "pragmatic socialism" as "that philosophy of human organization which seeks to promote the happiness, and the intellectual, scientific, and economic ad-

rious socialisms," have called their opponents by such names as "feudal" socialists, petty "bourgeois" socialists,[37] etc. None of these groups, however, have constituted a school of importance within the movement.

---

vancement, of a community as a whole, by utilizing the institutions of private and public property, and of individual and collective capital and enterprise in the most effective manner permitted at any given time by the existing character and capacity of the population involved."

[36] See Barnett, *Practicable Socialism;* see also Kelly, Edmond, *Twentieth Century Socialism* (N. Y.: Longmans, 1910).

[37] See *Communist Manifesto,* Part III.

PART EIGHT

Contributions of Various Social and Economic Movements

CHAPTER 44

Internationals: Socialist, Labor, and Communist

THE growth of the modern world is in many ways the growth of international relations; the relatively self-sufficient economies of the Middle Ages gave way to national, industrial economies, which, as they grew, developed complex sets of international relations. It is not surprising then that a social movement which sought either to transform capitalism or to reform its structure should find it expedient and necessary to develop international structures of its own. This chapter examines the history of Socialist Internationals, the Communist International, and Labor's International. Like the modern world which has undergone profound changes in economic, political, and international life, these internationals have similarly undergone marked changes.

SOCIALIST INTERNATIONALS

As previously stated,[1] the First International was organized in London in 1864 by Marx, Engels, and other revolutionists in a decade prior to any significant development in trade unionism, in labor legislation, or in working-class political parties; after a checkered career, it was declared officially dead at a meeting in its New York headquarters twelve years later. During the remainder of the seventies and eighties, socialist parties sprang into existence in numerous European countries, and the demand was increasingly heard for a revival of a socialist international.

In response to this demand, in late 1888, the German socialists issued an invitation to all socialist and labor movements to meet in

1 see *ante*, pp. 149, 154–5, 185, 192–3.

Paris on July 14, 1889, the one-hundredth anniversary of the Bastille.[2] Some 391 representatives of working class groups from twenty countries, including the United States, answered the call; many who later became central figures in the labor and socialist struggles of their countries in the decades ahead were present. Keir Hardie was there from Great Britain; the elder Liebknecht and Eduard Bernstein from Germany; Émile Vandervelde and Edouard Anseele from Belgium; Jules Guesde, Paul Lafargue, and Jean Longuet, the grandson of Marx, from France; Victor Adler from Austria, Plekhanov from Russia; Romela Nieuwenhuis from Holland; Pablo Iglesias from Spain; Andrea Costa from Italy, and many others.

The 1889 congress laid the foundation for the Second International as a loosely knit federation democratically controlled by its constituent parties. It formulated a program of international labor law, and, endorsing the suggestion of the A. F. of L. of the United States, decided to hold, on May 1, 1890, an "international manifestation" in favor of the eight-hour day, thus laying the foundation for subsequent international socialist (and later communist) May Day celebrations.

During the following years, sharp differences arose within the Second International over what labor's attitude should be toward the political state. A group of anarchists strove to obtain a foothold in the International. In order to prevent this, the 1896 congress passed a resolution excluding from subsequent congresses those who repudiated political action, thus ridding itself of the anarchist threat.

At its next congress in Paris in 1900, as a means of strengthening the organization's effectiveness, the delegates set up an International Socialist Bureau composed of permanent delegates from each country represented, and chose Brussels as the bureau's headquarters and Émile Vandervelde, Belgian scholar, socialist leader and statesman, as its president.

From its inception in 1889 to its death in 1914—a quarter of a century later—the Second International did much to advance labor and social legislation, coordinate and strengthen the democratic socialist movement, combat militarism, and avert local wars. In the Morocco crisis and in the disputes between Austria and Italy and Norway and Sweden, the huge demonstrations initiated by the International and its constituent parties were a potent force in keeping the peace.

[2] See Lewis L. Lorwin, *Labor and Internationalism* (N. Y.: Macmillan, 1929) p. 69; Lorwin, *The International Labor Movement* (N. Y.: Harper & Brothers, 1953), p. 7; see also *ante*, p. 518.

In the case of threatened war, it held that it was

"the duty of the working classes and their parliamentary representatives in the countries concerned, supported by the unifying activity of the International Socialist Bureau, to do everything possible to prevent the outbreak of war by whatever means seems to them the most effective, which will naturally differ according to the intensity of the class war and the general political situation.

"Should war break out in spite of all this, it is their duty to intercede for its speedy end, and to strive with all their might to make use of the severe economic and political crisis brought about by the war to rouse the people, and thereby to hasten the abolition of capitalist class rule." [3]

The International constantly urged that disputes between nations be submitted to arbitration by an international tribunal. Alarmed by the declaration of the first Balkan war in the summer of 1912, it called an extraordinary congress at Basle for November. The congress, when it convened, pledged the Balkan socialist parties to work for conciliation and the Austrian and Hungarian socialists to do their utmost to keep their countries from attacking Serbia.[4] The members of the Socialist International, therefore, found themselves in an unprecedented dilemma. As Julius Braunthal, later Secretary of the Socialist International, put it:

"In the minds of the rank and file of its member parties, the myth had grown during the decade prior to 1914 that the International was an invincible power to prevent war or stop it by revolutionary action, if war should occur. But in fact debates at its Congresses and the resolutions adopted left no doubt that the member parties did not feel strong enough to challenge the formidable power of the State in the emergency of war. Motions, submitted by the British and French parties proposing to answer the order for mobilization in case of war by a general strike, had been rejected by various Congresses of the International."

Thus, when World War I broke out, as Braunthal contended:

"the constellation of belligerent powers created a truly tragic situation for the Socialist parties. The German and Austrian parties felt impelled to cooperate in the war effort in order to repel the invasion of the armies of Czarist Russia, which they looked upon as the incarnation of reaction. The French and Belgian parties likewise rallied

3 Resolution of the Stuttgart congress, 1907.

4 See *ante,* p. 518.

without hesitation behind their governments in order to eject the German armies from their countries; and for the British Labor party, the issue was the defense of Western democracy against German militarism which, in breach of international treaties, had violated Belgium's neutrality." [5]

Minority socialist groups in the warring countries continued to oppose the prosecution of the war, but on the battlefronts and behind the lines great numbers of socialists in the Allied countries soon found themselves in deadly conflict with their erstwhile comrades of the Central Powers.

When the war clouds hovered over Europe during the summer of 1914, following the assassination of Archduke Ferdinand of Austria, the Bureau of the International, then a representative of twenty-seven Socialist and Labor parties in twenty-two countries, called a meeting in Brussels at the *Maison du Peuple* on July 29.

The Bureau appealed to socialists everywhere to help stem the tide of war. It advanced the date of its 1914 congress to August 9 from August 22 and changed the place of the meeting from Vienna to Paris. It was planned at the Vienna Congress to bring up again for discussion the question of whether the International should urge socialists to call general strikes as a means of preventing a threatened conflict.

That night its delegates attended a great *guerre à la guerre* meeting in Brussels and were addressed, among others, by Émile Vandervelde, Keir Hardie, Jean Jaurès, of France, Agnini of Italy, Pieter Troelstra of Holland, and Hugo Haase of Germany.

The next day the socialist leaders hurried back to their respective countries to use their influence to stop the threatened conflagration. Jaurès, socialism's most powerful orator, was assassinated on reaching Paris. Nation after nation, despite the socialists' appeal, soon called their people to arms.

International Socialist Conference (1915). Shortly after the declaration of war, various socialist groups called international conferences with a view to helping bring about a speedy and lasting peace.[6]

Socialists from the Allied countries and from the Central Powers met separately in Copenhagen, London, and Vienna in the early

[5] *Yearbook of the International Socialist Labour Movement,* edited by Julius Braunthal (London: Lincolns-Praeger International Yearbook Publishing Co., 1956–57), p. 30.

[6] See Harry W. Laidler, *Socialism in Thought and Action* (N. Y.: Macmillan, 1920), ch. X; Lorwin, *op. cit.,* ch. VII; William English Walling, *The Socialists and the War* (N. Y.: Holt, 1915), ch. XXIX.

months of 1915; in each case, with rare exceptions, only the conferees from nations on one side of the battle line were present.

Left-wing socialist groups began to confer, however, in the fall of 1915.[7] In response to a call issued by the Italian Socialist party, a number of left-wing socialists and syndicalists from France, Germany, Italy, Switzerland, Holland, Sweden, Norway, Poland, Rumania, Bulgaria, and Russia gathered secretly in a peasant's house in the village of Zimmerwald near Bern, Switzerland, on September 5, 1915. After a week's discussion, the Zimmerwald Conference issued a manifesto rebuking the socialists for straying from their principles and concluded with the slogan: "No annexations, no indemnities. Across frontiers, battlefields, devastated cities and countries—Workers Unite." They set up an international socialist commission which become known as the Zimmerwald Commission.

In April, 1916, the Zimmerwald Commission arranged a meeting in Kienthal, Switzerland, attended by 44 "delegates." The Kienthal meeting denounced the International Socialist Bureau for its failure to act; declared that a durable peace was impossible without "the complete triumph of the proletariat"; and urged socialists of all nations to make a concerted move for an immediate armistice.

The Stockholm Conference (1917). The above conferences were not, however, official meetings of the Second International. The International Socialist Bureau had made attempts in the beginning of 1915 to bring socialists from the warring nations to the conference table, but their attempts had failed, in no small measure because delegates were unable to obtain passports.

Early in 1917, however, in an effort to become a more effective force for peace, the Second International moved its headquarters to Stockholm and formed a Dutch-Scandinavian Committee of which Hjalmar Branting, later socialist Prime Minister of Sweden, was Chairman.

The Committee convened an informal meeting in Stockholm consisting of delegates from Holland and the Scandinavian countries, in addition to Huysmans of Belgium and Philip Scheidemann of Germany, and initiated a questionnaire among Socialist parties which indicated remarkable unanimity about the type of peace terms favored by the Socialist parties.[8]

[7] See *ante*, pp. 519, 539.

[8] The four principal socialist groups in the Central Powers stated that they desired substantially a peace without annexations and indemnities. They seemed to favor a "reestablishment of an independent Belgium," the restoration of Serbia and Montenegro, and the national independence of Russian Poland and Finland. All likewise

Following the Russian revolution of March, 1917, and America's entrance into the war in April of the same year, the International Socialist Bureau joined with the Dutch-Scandinavian Committee and the Petrograd soviets in issuing a joint invitation to a conference to be held at Stockholm on August 15, 1917, to discuss how best to arrive at a peaceful settlement. This invitation was accepted by many parties and groups, but the warring governments in Western Europe and the United States again refused to issue passports to delegates. Only delegates from the Central Powers, Russia, and the neutral countries arrived in Stockholm for the conference, and its purpose was defeated.

Spring 1918: The Inter-Allied Socialist and Labor Conference in London. In 1917 and 1918, the socialists in Allied countries organized two further conferences. In the spring of 1918, the Socialist and Labor Conference in London brought together delegates from all of the Allied socialist movements outside of the United States, Italy, and Russia.[9]

The conference outlined in some detail what should be done after the war to bring about lasting peace and prosperity. The nations of the world, the delegates declared, should, among other things, organize a league of nations, abolish colonial imperialism, co-operate in the development of the resources of the undeveloped nations, and avoid mass unemployment through large public works programs, etc.

Furthermore, within each country, governments should maintain control for some time over their most indispensable commodities, "in order to meet the most urgent needs of the whole community on the principle of 'no cake for anyone until all have bread.' "

To help make this program a reality, the conference recommended the inclusion of at least one representative of labor and socialism in the official delegation of every government conference.

The Bern Conference of the Second International, February 2–9, 1919—A Program for Permanent Peace. A few months later, on November 11, 1918, the Central Powers laid down their arms. Soon after the armistice the Second International began the task of preparing for a conference at Bern that would lay the foundations for a revitalized organization and would set forth what should be included

---

agreed to a program of disarmament, the abolition of secret diplomacy and of economic barriers, and seemed favorable to a court of international arbitration. They were considerably divided on the interpretation of indemnities and the disposal of Alsace-Lorraine, and other questions; see Laidler, *op. cit.*, ch. X; also Emily Balch, *Approaches to the Great Settlement*, pp. 172–94.

[9] The delegates from the U. S. A. were again refused passports as were those from Russia.

in the democratic terms of peace. One hundred delegates attended the conference from twenty-six countries. The Russians, who were invited, refused to attend on the ground that the Second International was opposed to dictatorship and was thus "a dangerous enemy to world revolution!"

The conference, when it was convened, repeated the socialist's belief in the need for a genuine democratic league of nations, based on a just peace. It endorsed President Wilson's Fourteen Points. It likewise contended that a peace treaty should set forth a plan for universal disarmament, provide for the world distribution of food stuffs and raw material, advance the cause of free trade, and include a labor charter.

The delegates hailed "with joy" the political revolutions which had overthrown the monarchies of Russia, Austria-Hungary, and Germany, while at the same denouncing the dictatorship and the suppression of free speech and press that existed in Russia. The reorganization of society along socialist lines, it contended, must be based "on the triumph of democracy, firmly rooted in the principles of liberty." In the belief that too little was known about events in Russia, it appointed a committee to bring pressure upon the official peace makers in Paris to visit Russia and report upon conditions in that country.

The conference also selected a "Commission for the Reconstitution of the International," containing two representatives from each of its affiliated organizations, and an Executive Committee consisting of Hjalmar Branting of Sweden, Chairman, Arthur Henderson of Great Britain, and Camille Huysmans of Belgium, the Commission's Secretary.

The Lucerne Debate Between Democracy and Dictatorship (August, 1919). At the next meeting in Lucerne, on August 2, 1919, the International denounced such "reactionary" developments as the re-establishment of a representative of the House of Hapsburg in Hungary, the blockading of Russia, and the attempt of Denikin and Kolchak to overthrow the Soviet government. As a means of universalizing the League of Nations, it urged that Germany, Russia, and Hungary be admitted to membership.

The Lucerne conference was also the scene of a sharp debate about the question of relations between the Second and the Third or Communist International—the latter founded in Moscow five months before.[10] Vandervelde, in the debate, declared that the Third International tended toward minority dictatorship contrary to the principles of democracy and that unity between the two internationals was thus im-

[10] *Ante*, pp. 519–20.

possible. With Bernstein of Germany and Louis De Brouckère of Belgium, among others, he contended that communism had nothing to do with Marxism, notwithstanding "its revolutionary verbiage." Troelstra of Holland, on the other hand, urged the conference to follow a clear policy of revolutionary action, not one of an exclusive parliamentary nature. The Vandervelde position carried the day.

Prior to adjournment on August 8, the conference decided to hold an International Socialist and Labor Conference in Geneva on February 2, 1920. The delegates expressed the hope that a vigorous international could soon be organized, pointing out that for the first time in history socialist or partly socialist governments had been formed in Germany, Austria, Czechoslovakia, Sweden, and several other countries; the organized labor movement in most European countries of Western Europe was giving its support to moderate socialist parties; and there was increasing need for an international organization to coordinate socialist and labor activities.

The Geneva Conference on Socialization (July 31, 1920). Wide differences of opinion regarding the future relations between democratic socialists and the recently organized Communist International necessitated the postponement of the proposed conference from February to July. It was finally convened in Geneva on July 31, 1920.

In attendance at the conference were representatives of the socialist parties and other labor groups from seventeen countries, prominent among them delegates from major working class organizations in Great Britain, Germany, Belgium, Denmark, Holland, and Sweden.

The Geneva conference reaffirmed the International's belief in democratic political action. It declared its belief that socialization of industry should proceed gradually from one industry to another, contrary to the bolshevik program of immediate collectivization of all important industries, and warned the workers not to destroy private enterprise in any industry until they were in a position to replace such enterprises with a more efficient form of organization.

It furthermore condemned the attempts of the followers of the Communist International to suppress "bourgeois" governments by force and to establish the "dictatorship of the proletariat," reminding the workers that it was the mission of socialism not to suppress democracy, but greatly to strengthen it.

The delegates appointed an executive committee of three to direct the future activities of the International and voted to move the organization's headquarters to London.

Vienna or Two-and-a-Half International (February, 1921). In the months immediately following the Geneva Conference, the Second International, now moved to London, was comparatively quiet. A number of minority center and left socialist groups had refused to attend the Geneva Conference—among them splinter parties in Austria, France, and Germany; the Independent Labor party of Great Britain; and the Swiss Social Democratic party.

These parties at first bent their efforts toward the creation of an international that would include both socialists and communists. As the months passed, however, many of the leaders of the movement became disillusioned with the Communist International, influenced in part by the highly critical report of the British Independent Labor Party (I. L. P.) on conditions in Russia, and by the communists' failure to win over the center and left socialists in Sweden, the United States, and other countries.

These center and left groups thus decided to form an organization that would be independent both of the Second and the Third International and called a conference in Vienna for February, 1920.

Some 80 delegates from thirteen countries responded to this invitation. Delegates at the conference in general took the position that other than parliamentary methods might be necessary to bring about the drastic social changes they envisaged, but strongly disapproved of any "mechanical imitation" of the methods of the Russian bolsheviks.

The Merger—Formation of Labor and Socialist International (May, 1923). As the forces of fascism, led by Mussolini, gained control of Italy, and as nazism obtained a foothold in Germany, leaders of the Second and Two-and-a-Half internationals became increasingly convinced that socialists should present a united front against reaction.[11]

At the initiation of British Labor, a "Unity Congress" was finally called in Hamburg for May, 1923. The response was enthusiastic. Over 400 delegates attended the congress from 43 parties in 30 countries, claiming a following of 6,700,000. The two internationals were merged into a new organization—the Labor and Socialist International (L. S. I.). The British Labor leader and later British Foreign Secretary, Arthur Henderson, was elected President of the L. S. I. and Tom Shaw of Britain and Friedrich Adler of Austria—son of the

[11] The main obstacle to the reconciliation of the two internationals was removed when the German Majority Socialists and the German Independent Socialists, in their reaction against the excesses of the German fascists and the assassination of Walter Rathenau, decided to bury their differences and form the United Socialist Democratic Party of Germany.

famous socialist statesman, Victor Adler—were chosen joint secretaries.

The aim of the organization, the congress asserted, was "to unify the activities of the affiliated parties, to arrange common action, and bring about the entire unification" of the labor and socialist movement. The international, its constitution read:

"is a union of such parties as accept the principle of the economic emancipation of the workers from capitalist domination and the establishment of the Socialist Commonwealth as their object, and the class struggle, which finds its expression in the independent political and industrial action of the workers' organizations, as a means of realizing that object."

The Labor and Socialist International was the main instrument of international political action from its formation in 1923 to its demise at the outbreak of World War II. During these years it functioned through its administrative staff, its executive committee of 40, which met four times a year, and its congresses which were convened in general every four years. Its party membership was chiefly confined to the powerful social and labor parties of Europe. It co-operated closely with the International Federation of Trade Unions with headquarters in Amsterdam. Its own headquarters were in London from 1923 to 1926, in Zurich from 1926 to 1935, and in Brussels from 1935 to 1940.

From its formation the L. S. I. was confronted with numerous and formidable problems. Prominent among them were the world economic crisis, the threat of fascism, and the communist struggle against democratic socialism. With the rise of Hitler, the International was occupied largely with the problem of how to avert a second world war. At every Congress, the problem of how best to deal with mass unemployment was also one of the main topics on the agenda. In 1931, in the early days of the world-wide crisis of the thirties, it issued a joint report with the International Confederation of Labor which contained a comprehensive plan for the dealing with this crisis.

"The basic fact of the crises," the report contended, "is the disproportion between productive capacity and consumption due to low wages." From this point of view, the crisis, it declared, could not be overcome by wage reductions. Unemployment should be met by reducing working time to a forty-hour, five-day week, by unemployment insurance, and by large expenditures by the state on public works.

The committee's report also recommended such anti-depression, international measures as: lower tariffs, the reduction of war debts, the restoration of economic relations with Soviet Russia, a more equitable distribution of gold to stabilize currencies, and the transformation of the Bank of International Settlements "into an organ of international credit policy."

While unemployment, maintained the committee, could be abolished only by the introduction of socialism, it could be reduced and the crisis shortened by the measures it proposed. A return to prosperity, the International believed, would strengthen democratic forces in their battle against fascism and war.

In its fight against fascism, the Labor and Socialist International also denounced Mussolini's destruction in Italy of free economic and political organizations of labor, his suppression of civil liberties, and his imprisonment and execution of many of his political opponents. In 1935, when the fascist army invaded Ethiopia, the L. S. I. urged the League of Nations to apply oil sanctions and other economic embargoes against Italy. During the following year, in conjunction with the International Federation of Labor, it held widely publicized protest meetings throughout Europe deploring the failure of the League to apply such sanctions.

Throughout Hitler's rise to power, it denounced Hitler's terroristic policies in Germany, and, in the late thirties, it vigorously protested his reoccupation of the Rhineland and his invasion of Czechoslovakia, of Austria, and other countries.

The L. S. I. exposed the evils of the communist as well as the fascist and nazi dictatorships in its further efforts in the twenties and thirties to promote peace and democracy. It worked for the limitation of German reparations, for equal cultural rights for national minorities, for the release of refugees from European dictatorships, for the support of the Loyalists in the Spanish Civil War, for the demilitarization and neutralization of certain frontier areas in Europe, and for the revision of frontiers through arbitration and by the holding of plebiscites. It likewise supported the movements for self-determination among the subject nations of Asia and Africa.

World War II—The Destruction of the Labor and Socialist International. As World War I led to the demise of the Second International (1889–1914), the invasion of the Western European democracies by the nazi armies in the fall of 1939—the outbreak of World War II—spelled the virtual destruction of the Labor and Socialist International. The only socialist parties of Europe that survived the war were the British Labor party and the Social Democratic parties of Sweden and Switzerland.

The Executive of the L. S. I. held its last meeting in Brussels in March of 1940. A few weeks later the International's headquarters was seized by the Gestapo following the march into Belgium of the German army. To escape with his life, Camille Huysmans, Belgian socialist statesman who had been elected President of the International at the Brussels meeting, left for London, while Friedrich Adler, Austrian Secretary of the L. S. I., fled to New York. Other members of the Executive were scattered throughout the world. It became impossible for the International to continue its pre-war services.

During the war national groups of exiled socialists met frequently in London under the auspices of the British Labor party. In 1944 the National Executive of these groups decided to study problems concerning "the future international association of democratic labor and socialist parties."

Birth of Socialist Information Liaison Office (1946). Following the conclusion of the war an informal international conference was convened at Clacton-on-Sea for May, 1946, "to reestablish contacts broken by the war, to exchange information and to work out, if possible, common policies on problems of common interest."

The conference, attended by representatives of nineteen Socialist parties, set up a Socialist Information and Liaison Office (S. I. L. O.), attached to the Secretariat of the British Labor party. Six months later, in November, 1946, a second conference was called for Bournemouth which established a Consultative Committee to act as a clearing house for information and to arrange for future conferences. These were followed by two further meetings held in Zurich in June, 1946, and in Antwerp in November, 1947, the latter of which transformed the Consultative Committee into a more representative body called the Committee of the International Socialist Conference (C. O. M. I. S. C. O.) composed of one representative from each member party.

C. O. M. I. S. C. O. C. O. M. I. S. C. O. held its first meeting in London in March, 1948, a meeting concerned chiefly with ways and means of stopping the expansion of communism in Eastern Europe. The delegates at the London gathering condemned the communist seizure of power in Czechoslovakia (February, 1948) and the absorption of Socialist parties in Eastern Europe by the Communist parties. They reaffirmed their belief in individual liberties as an essential principle of socialism and they expelled the former Social Democratic parties of Czechoslovakia, Bulgaria, Hungary, and Rumania which had merged with the Communist parties of their communist-dominated countries.

The London conference was succeeded by one held in Vienna during the same year. In this conference Pietro Nenni's influential Socialist party in Italy was likewise expelled because of its refusal to dissolve its pact with the communists, while the Unita Socialista, which had broken away from the Nenni party and later formed the Social Democratic party of Italy, was admitted to membership. The conference took a step toward the reconstitution of the International by its appointment of a subcommittee of five members under the chairmanship of Morgan Phillips, Secretary of the British Labor party, to function in the intervals between the C. O. M. I. S. C. O. conference.

Further steps toward the International's revival were taken in Paris in 1949 when Julius Braunthal was elected Secretary and a subcommittee was appointed to prepare a declaration of the basic principles of democratic socialism common to all members at the London conference of 1951.

Revival of the International—First Congress (1951). Finally, in 1951, at a London conference, a decision was reached to propose, at its next plenary session, the reconstruction of the International. The plenary session assembled in Frankfurt in July, 1951. The delegates voted to designate this assembly the First Congress of the International. They likewise adopted the now famous document, the "Aims and Tasks of Democratic Socialism," which set forth the common aims of the democratic socialists of the world in the middle of the century.

The declaration of aims, among other things, maintained that nationalization of industry was not an end in itself, but a means to an end—the satisfaction of human needs.

"Socialists," the declaration concluded, "work for a world of peace and freedom, for a world in which the exploitation and enslavement of men by men and peoples is unknown, for a world in which the development of the individual personality is the basis for the fruitful development of mankind."

The conference endorsed the principle of collective security and maintained that "free democracies cannot defend themselves against the threat of totalitarianism without arms," but insisted that arms themselves were not enough—democracies must have a constructive social and economic program aimed at the elimination of poverty, oppression, exploitation, and mass unemployment.

During the succeeding years of the fifties and sixties, it fought dictatorship and the suppression of civil liberties and it educated and propagandized for the elimination of poverty and the root causes of economic exploitation, unemployment, colonialism, imperialism, and war. It advocated regional, political, and economic integration; expanded East-West industrial and cultural relations; greater social and economic aid to the developing nations; democratic economic and social planning; and vastly increased health, educational, housing, and social security programs in the various countries of the world.

At its 1966 congress in Stockholm, the Socialist International declared its support of the United Nations "which is mankind's chief instrument for preserving the rule of law, fighting poverty, and promoting peaceful change"; advocated the seating of the People's Republic of China in the U. N.; urged the introduction of African majority rule in Rhodesia; condemned "the iniquitous system of apartheid in Africa"; and called for the convening of a peace conference to end the Vietnam conflict "under whatever auspices are most likely to lead to success and with access to the conference table guaranteed for all parties to the dispute."

CHANNELS OF COMMUNICATION. The international has sought to affect the social thinking and action of the times through its biennial congresses; the activities of its executive council and staff; its affiliated organizations, of socialist youth, women, parliamentarians, teachers, librarians, and members of the press; its regional conferences in Asia, Central Eastern Europe and Latin America; its close co-operation with the democratic trade union and co-operative internationals; and its fifty-odd political party affiliates with their membership of more than 10,000,000 and their voting strength of more than 60,000,000.[12]

In recent years the International has brought within its ranks as "observer members" numerous democratic, progressive political parties in the developing countries. While not strictly socialist in ideology, they embody, as in the case of Acción Democratica of Venezuela, perhaps the best expressions of democratic, progressive thought and action in their respective countries.

[12] In 1967 in Europe, socialists in parties affiliated with the Socialist International headed the governments of Great Britain, Denmark, Sweden and Finland and participated importantly in coalition governments in West Germany, Iceland, Italy, Luxembourg and Switzerland. Democratic socialist parties were the chief opposition parties in Austria, Belgium, Holland, and Norway and played an effective role in the political life of France. Outside Europe, affiliated parties dominated the government of Israel, Malagasy Republic (Madagascar), Singapore, Guyana, and Venezuela, and were the second largest parties in Australia, Belgium, Costa Rica, Holland, Jamaica, New Zealand, Japan, and Malta. A number of governments in the developing countries, including India, maintained that their aim in the far flung future was the attainment of a democratic socialist order and were considerably influenced by the policies and activities of the International.

REPRESENTATION IN PARLIAMENT OF AFFILIATES WITH SOCIALIST INTERNATIONAL, 1966

Country	*Name of Party*	*No. of Socialist Representatives*	*Total No. in Parliament*
Australia	Labor	41	124
Austria	Socialist	74	165
Belgium	Socialist	64	212
Canada	New Democratic	21	265
Chile	Socialist	15	147
Costa Rica	National Liberation	29 (?)	57
* Denmark	Social Democratic	69	179
† Finland	Social Democratic	55	200
France	Socialist	66	482
Germany	Social Democratic	202	496
Great Britain	Labor	363	630
‡ Holland	Labor	43	150
Iceland	Social Democrat	5	40
§ India	Praja Socialist	12	510
‖ Israel	Mapai and Achdut Ha'avoda-Poalei	45	120
Italy	Socialist	94	630
Jamaica	People's National	19	45
Japan	Socialist (145) Democratic Socialist Party (23)	168	467
Laos	Social Democrat	11	59
Luxembourg	Socialist	21	56
Malagasy Republic (Madagascar)	Social Democratic	104	107
Malta	Malta Labor	16	50
New Zealand	Labor	35	80
# Norway	Labor	68	150
Peru	Partido Aprista Peruano	56	140
Singapore	People's Action	38	51
Sweden	Social Democratic	113	233
Switzerland	Social Democratic	53	200
Northern Ireland	Labor	2	52
** Venezuela	Democratic Action	65	179

* Left-wing socialist party of Denmark has 20 seats.

† Social Democratic opposition in Finland has 2 seats.

‡ The Pacifist Socialist party in Holland has 4 seats.

§ The Congress party of India, the controlling party with 356 seats, declares that its ultimate aim is socialism, although it is not affiliated with the Socialist International.

‖ There is also Mapam, left-wing socialist, with 8 members of parliament. In 1968 Mapai, Achdut and Rafi merged into the Israel Labor party.

\# Also Socialist People's party of Norway has 2 seats.

** Admitted to International as an observer-member.

LABOR'S INTERNATIONALS

Throughout their histories, the modern democratic socialist and trade union movements have worked closely together in many of the democracies of Europe and other continents.

The Labor and Socialist Movements: Their Common Goal. Both movements have been dedicated to the abolition of ruthless exploitation and poverty, to advancement in the status and living standards of labor, to the strengthening of democracy in industry and of government, and to the bringing about of amity among the nations of the world.

The trade union movement has, in the nature of the case, functioned primarily in the industrial field; the socialist movement, in the realm of politics and government. Trade unions, however, have realized that success in achieving their aims has depended to no small extent on the strength of parties favorable to labor in the legislative, executive, and judicial branches of government, and many of them have become an organic part of labor and socialist parties.

Democratic socialist and labor parties have, in turn, realized the importance of strong trade and industrial unions with a social vision for the success of their electoral and legislative program, and have, in country after country, given powerful assistance to the rise and growth of the trade union movement.

Both movements have found strength in their co-operative efforts and in their myriad educational projects. Both, in this growingly interdependent world, have found increased strength in the development of international federations and in the co-operation of federations in the preservation of peace and democracy.

As has been said before, the socialists of the world founded their First International in London, in 1864—during the latter years of the American Civil War.

One of the prime movers of the conference, Karl Marx, drafted a constitution which threw open the membership of the association to local and national workers' societies.

The Socialist International and Organized Labor. Although, during the twelve years of its existence, the International's discussions and resolutions were widely diverse, it gave much attention to the demands which the emerging labor movement was voicing. At the First Congress of the First International in Geneva in 1866, its most important resolutions were those that favored a maximum eight-hour day, international protective legislation for women and children, and the abolition of night work for women.

In the strike movement of 1868, which followed the industrial uprising of that year, the International collected funds for strikers in London, Paris, Belgium, and Switzerland and aided in preventing the importation of strike-breakers.

As a result it gained in numbers and influence. In France its membership in 1869 was estimated at 200,000; here its membership comprised new trade unions which had experienced a dramatic growth in that year. In Belgium, Italy, Spain, and Portugal, incipient trade unions became members of the International. In the United States, the National Labor Union, under the leadership of William J. Sylvis, declared at its convention in 1870 its "adherence to the principles of the Working Men's Association" and its expectation to "join the Association in a short time." The attempt of Bakunin, with his doctrine of the abolition of the state, to capture the International, however, as has been stated,[13] led to the transfer by Marx and his followers of the headquarters to the United States in 1872 and to its demise in 1876.

The A. F. of L. Establishes International Contacts. Five years later, in 1881, the American Federation of Labor was organized. In the first years of its existence, the A. F. of L. followed the tradition established by the National Labor Union and maintained contacts between the United States and Europe. Between 1881 and 1889 it exchanged "fraternal greetings" with the British Trades Union Congress, corresponded with some French unions about holding a workingman's international exposition, and requested the international socialist congresses held in Paris in 1889 to support the movement for the eight-hour day—a request which the delegates of these gatherings (at which the Second International was born) enthusiastically endorsed.

Encouraged by these international congresses in Europe, Samuel Gompers, president of the A. F. of L., recommended the calling of an international congress of trade unions in Chicago in 1893, the year of the World's Fair. Supported by the Federation's conventions (1889 and 1890), Gompers issued invitations to "the organized workers of the world." The British Trades Union Congress, however, was the only body that agreed to attend.

Gompers dropped the plan, attributing the negative attitude of European labor to distance, lack of personal contacts, and, above all, to

[13] See *ante*, p. 192.

the "malicious" misrepresentation of the A. F. of L. by the Socialist Labor party of America. From that time on, the A. F. of L. President began to draw a sharp distinction between the trade unions and the socialist parties, and became eager to establish a trade union international organization distinct from, if not in opposition to, the Second International.

In 1894 the A. F. of L. began the practice of exchanging "fraternal delegates" with the British Trades Union Congress. Two years later the fraternal delegates suggested to the British Congress that a "bona fide trade union congress" be convened, but failed to win support for this suggestion.

Despite these setbacks, Gompers continued to take an interest in projects for international trade union organizations. He corresponded frequently with trade union labor abroad. He used the *American Federationist,* first published in 1894, to promote international exchanges and understanding. He collected funds for strikers in Great Britain and Germany.

From 1899 to 1904, however, big strikes and other important domestic problems absorbed most of the energies of American labor and little attention was given to international relations. After 1904, however, increasing immigration to the United States, the growth of trade secretariats, and the expanding interest in the problem of maintaining world peace led to greater intercourse with the trade union movement of Europe.

Gompers brought the subject of peace repeatedly before A. F. of L. conventions, maintaining that the growth of the international labor movement could be an important force in the preventing of international conflict.

AMERICAN LABOR JOINS INTERNATIONAL SECRETARIATS OF THEIR CRAFTS. Between 1904 and 1908, Gompers urged the American unions to attend the international conferences of their respective crafts and to join the trade secretariats. These recommendations were in no small degree responsible during these years for the American unions of miners, molders, painters, shoemakers, lithographers, bakers and brewers joining their respective international secretariats. In 1908, the A. F. of L. took another step forward toward international co-operation by accepting the invitation of the International Secretariat of National Trade Union Centers to attend its Congress in Paris in 1909, electing Gompers as its delegate.

A. F. OF L. JOINS INTERNATIONAL SECRETARIAT (1910). Gompers

had two objects in view in attending the Paris conferences. He was anxious, first, to counteract the unfavorable reports which had been circulated abroad about the American labor movement and, second, to promote the idea of an international federation of labor, which would leave the A. F. of L. on becoming a member, free to follow an independent course. The Executive Council of the A. F. of L. in 1909 voted in favor of submitting to the Paris conferences the proposal to establish an international federation of trade unions.

Gomper's reception at the Paris conference was not entirely friendly. In his conference speech he told the delegates that he was there not as a member but as an observer, and that the A. F. of L. would not join the international federation unless allowed to pursue its own ways. These remarks aroused considerable irritation. In turn Gompers was not pleased with the composition of the conference—with the "wholly socialist" character of the Austrian and Dutch delegates; with the "anarchistic" point of view of some delegates from France. Gompers, however, decided to overlook these "defects." The conference had adopted a provision that decisions of the international organization would be binding only if adopted unanimously, and that labor must be free in all countries to decide its own policy and methods.

In view of these provisions, Gompers on his return to the United States urged the A. F. of L. to affiliate with the international secretariats "in the best interest of the workers of America." The 1909 convention of the A. F. of L. voted to approve Gomper's recommendation and in 1910 the A. F. of L. became a member of the International Secretariat.

A.F. of L. Defeats I. W. W. (1911). A year later in 1911, at a conference of the International Secretariat at Budapest, William Z. Foster, representing the Industrial Workers of the World (I. W. W.), brought in a demand to expel the A. F. of L. and elect the I. W. W. as the Secretariat's American representative on the ground that the A. F. of L. was connected with the National Civic Federation and was therefore unfit to conduct a working class struggle. After a long and heated debate, the A. F. of L. won out and the I. W. W. was denied admission to the conference.

The A. F. of L. at that year's conference opposed the French federation's proposals to discuss militarism and the general strike. It helped defeat the proposal to hold the conferences of the International Secretariat every three years at the same time as the congresses of the Second International. It likewise introduced a resolution for the establishment of an international federation of labor, a resolution which the conference referred to the national trade union centers for their consideration.

International Secretariat Becomes International Federation of Labor (1913). At the Zurich conference in 1913 the name was changed from the International Secretariat to the International Federation of Labor, as the A. F. of L. had recommended. The delegates at the Zurich Conference accepted the American invitation to hold their 1915 conference in San Francisco in connection with the exposition to celebrate the opening of the Panama Canal. The A. F. of L. agreed to contribute $2,000 toward the costs.

From 1910 to 1914 the A. F. of L. used the International's office to obtain information on wages and labor conditions in Europe, while the International frequently applied to the A. F. of L. for aid during important strikes of European workers. The A. F. of L. paid its dues regularly, ranging from $600 to $2,000 a year.

On the eve of the First World War, the American organized workers were thus becoming actively interested in the international labor movement. A number of important American trade unions belonged to the International Trade Secretariat. The outbreak of the First World War, however, completely shattered labor's International.

A. F. of L. Retires from International Following First World War. Following the war when labor's International again became a functioning organization, a controversy arose between the A. F. of L. and the then International Federation of Trade Unions over the question that had been resolved temporarily when the A. F. of L. first joined the International as to whether each national affiliate should be bound by the resolutions that were passed by majority vote. The A. F. of L. was particularly anxious not to be pledged to support any resolution favoring the socialization of industry.

Failing to carry the I. F. T. U. with it, the A. F. of L. left the international and it was not until 1937, following the split between the A. F. of L. and the C. I. O., that the American Federation of Labor again affiliated itself with the I. F. T. U.

International Collapses with World War II—Emergency International Formed. Shortly thereafter World War II broke out; the international body was again disrupted. An emergency International Trade Union Council, however, was later formed and, at its September, 1942, meeting in London, decided to act during the remainder of the war as the "principal representative of international organized labor."

Emergence of World Federation of Trade Unions (1945). Meanwhile, Russia, following Hitler's invasion of the Soviet Union, urged the formation of a world trade union organization which would include all labor, communist and non-communist alike.

In Great Britain many labor leaders felt that cooperation with Russian unions would help the war effort, assist the Hitler-occupied countries in their fight for independence, and help to bring about a unified labor movement after the war. They first formed an Anglo-Soviet Trade Union Committee and later an Anglo-American Trade Union Committee, the latter to formulate peace objectives which the unions could advocate at the end of the conflict.

The British trade unionists requested the A. F. of L. to permit the Railroad Brotherhoods, and the C. I. O. to join this committee. The request was rejected by the A. F. of L. on the ground, among other things, that it was the custom of labor's internationals to recognize only one federation of labor in a country and that the C. I. O. was a "dual" union organized to duplicate the work of the already existing A. F. of L. The C. I. O. thereupon urged the British Trades Union Congress (T. U. C.) to take steps to form a wider international organization.

By the fall of 1943, the Soviet Union had, for the second time, taken the offensive against the nazis. Allied victory seemed in sight. Many union groups were envisioning a social order after the war where full employment and economic security would be the order of the day for the workers of the world.

Partly as a result of these developments, the British Trades Union Congress, in October, 1943, decided to call a world trade union congress to consider the problems of war and peace.

The A. F. of L., in the belief that such a conference should have been called by the I. F. T. U., that invitations should not have been sent to dual unions, and, primarily, that Soviet unions should not have been asked to participate, declined the invitation.

I. F. T. U. Dissolved (1945). After preliminary meetings a conference was held in Paris at the call of the British, Russians, and the C. I. O. on September 25, 1945. The gathering was attended by 250 delegates from 56 countries—the A. F. of L. being the only important national federation absent—and formed the World Federation of Trade Unions (W. F. T. U.). Two months later, on December 13, 1945, the general council of the I. F. T. U., met, and, by an overwhelming vote, decided to dissolve the Amsterdam International (I. F. T. U.).

W. F. T. U. Splits (1949). During the first years, the W. F. T. U., despite wide differences in the ideologies of its members, was able to maintain a precarious balance between the communist and non-communist forces that had founded the organization. Sir Walter Citrine of Great Britain and Sidney Hillman of the United States exerted much influence on the Executive Committee in behalf of the western type of trade unionism. The fact that the communists in France and Italy were working in coalition governments helped to lay a basis for a conciliatory policy on the part of the communists in union organizations.

From 1947 on, however, the organization of the Cominform; the controversy over the Marshall Plan; the bitter contests between communist and anti-communist unionists in the United States, France, Italy, Great Britain, Germany, and other countries; the activities of representatives of the A. F. of L. and other western union organizations against communist infiltration in the labor movements of Western Europe; the attempts of communists to dominate the international trade secretariats; and the increasing uses of the W. F. T. U. as an instrument for communist propaganda led to an ever-wider cleavage between the communists and the non-communists within the world body.

At the Rome meeting of the Executive Committee of the W. F. T. U. in May, 1948, the C. I. O. and the British T. U. C. representatives accused the secretary of the W. F. T. U., Louis Saillant, of being biased in action and inadequate as an administrator. They maintained that the *Information Bulletin* of the W. F. T. U. abounded in criticisms of Great Britain and the United States, while failing to criticize the Soviet Union and East Germany. Speaking for the C. I. O., James Carey declared that his organization was "sufficiently dissatisfied with the administration of the W. F. T. U. to withdraw from the international body." A successful attempt, however, was made at the meeting to prevent a split, and resolutions were passed which many hoped would prevent continued use of the W. F. T. U. for communist purposes.

However, these hopes were not realized, and in October, 1948, the General Council of the British T.U.C., declaring that the World Federation could not reach agreement on "real trade union tasks," proposed that the federation suspend its functions. If the W. F. T. U. refused to agree to its detailed plan for the dissolution of this world body, the T. U. C., it declared, would withdraw. A month later, the C. I. O.

convention rejected the proposals to "endorse the WFTU and make it effective in the UN," and authorized the Executive Council to take whatever action was required.

Two months thereafter, Arthur Deakin of the T. U. C. presented the British unions' proposal before the Executive Bureau of the W. F. T. U. in Paris (January 17–21, 1949) that the federation be suspended. Communists, he declared, had perverted the organization to serve their ends and communist and non-communist groups were split in two. "It's no use pretending," he declared, "that the WFTU is anything but a corpse. Let us bury it."

The communists proposed that discussion of the question of dissolution be postponed until the next congress of the W. F. T. U. This proposal the T. U. C. and C. I. O. refused to consider, demanding that the Executive Bureau unanimously favor the proposed suspension. When the Executive Bureau refused, Deakin, Carey, and Evert Kupers, the last from the Dutch trade union, walked out of the meeting. The split had taken place.

On June 29, 1949, in Milan, the W. F. T. U. opened its repeatedly postponed Second Congress. Delegates were present from France, Italy, Soviet-dominated countries, the Latin American Confederation of Labor, and various radical labor groups of Asia and Africa. The C. I. O., the T. U. C., and the unions of most of the democratic countries which had played such an important part in the organization of the W. F. T. U. in 1945, had left it; they proceeded to form a new world organization of free trade unions.

Birth of International Confederation of Free Trade Unions (1949). For several years before the rift in the W. F. T. U., the A. F. of L. had conducted vigorous activity against it and had engaged in numerous international labor services. It and other labor movements had obtained in the Economic and Social Council of the U. N. the same status as the W. F. T. U. It had opened a European bureau in Brussels, had consulted with European trade union leaders, had supplied relief to free labor movements in need, and had sought to combat communist influences in unions abroad. From 1947 it had agitated for the organization of an international of free trade unions.

Before the rift in the W. F. T. U., several labor federations abroad had also begun to lay plans for a new labor international. Soon after the split, Sir Vincent Tewson of the British unions and Leon Jouhaux of the French non-communist Force Ouvríere sent letters to William

Green, president of the A. F. of L., and Philip Murray, head of the C. I. O., suggesting the formation of a new international and expressing the hope that both the A. F. of L. and the C. I. O. would participate.

In April, Tewson reached an agreement in Washington with the two American bodies on calling for a preliminary conference in Geneva. At this meeting, it was agreed unanimously to establish a new international, and a preparatory committee was appointed to draft a constitution and convene an international congress.

The preparatory committee issued a call for a conference to be held in London from November 28 to December 9, 1949. In response to this call, which was not, in the nature of the case, sent to communist countries, 261 representatives from 59 national union centers and 28 other union organizations in 53 countries, claiming to represent 48,000,000 workers, assembled in the British capital. The delegates adopted a constitution, named the new labor body the International Confederation of Free Trade Unions (I. C. F. T. U.), and reconstituted the conference as the First Congress of the I. C. F. T. U.

Goals of the I. C. F. T. U. In the preamble of the constitution it was declared that the International stood for individual liberty, free labor, political democracy, and "the right of all peoples to full national freedom and sovereignty." It proclaimed the right of individuals to social justice, work, free choice of employment, security of employment and of their persons, protection of their industrial and economic interests through unions, and change of government by peaceful and democratic means. It maintained that unions must be free to bargain collectively and derive their authority from their own members, and pledged the new international organization to combat totalitarianism in every form. Unions under fascist, communist, or other totalitarian regimes, it declared, were not free democratic organizations, but "governmental instruments designed for the organized exploitation of workers for the benefit of a tyrannical state."

The I. C. F. T. U. conceived itself, as did the Socialist International, as a coordinating center for democratic national labor organizations and as an agency for the promotion of higher living standards, social security, and cultural advances. Its founders felt that, by advancing the cause of economic democracy and international economic co-operation, it would lay a firmer foundation for political democracy and for peace. Discrimination based on race, creed, color, or sex, it asserted, must be eliminated everywhere. As the workers were "the first victims of war," it demanded the right to participate in all international bodies concerned with economic and social co-operation.

On the final day of the congress, the I. C. F. T. U. issued a manifesto that set forth three basic goals: Bread—economic security and social justice for all. Freedom—through economic and political democracy. Peace—with liberty and dignity for all.

In conclusion the manifesto read:

"Workers of all countries, races and creeds: Join in this mighty movement of free and democratic labor.

"Together we can conquer poverty and exploitation and create a world of abundance and security. Together we can destroy tyranny and oppression and create a world of freedom and human dignity. Together we can defeat the forces of war and aggression, and create a world of peace and justice."

Following its organization, the I. C. F. T. U. grew in membership and influence, expanding particularly in the developing nations, and was able to report at its eighth world congress in 1965 the existence of 121 affiliated organizations in 96 countries with an individual membership of over 60 million.

During the intervening years, the International helped to unify and strengthen the free labor movement of the world through its daily research, publication, and administrative services in its Amsterdam headquarters; international congresses and executive council meetings; work of coordinating the activities of international craft organizations; and youth, women, and other affiliated groups.

In the developing countries in Asia, Africa, and Latin America it supplied labor organizers and consultants; conducted educational conferences and labor colleges; initiated regional labor councils; contributed to relief funds; combatted communist control of national trade unions; attacked dictatorships; and helped in the formulation of progressive labor legislation.

As a means of advancing the general welfare, its representatives participated actively in the specialized agencies of the U. N.; co-operated in specific projects with the Socialist International and International Cooperative Alliance; and were represented in the councils of world, educational, food, housing, human rights, international trade, and other organizations.

Its affiliations in 1965 can be seen in the following table.

MEMBERSHIP OF ORGANIZATIONS
AFFILIATED WITH THE
INTERNATIONAL CONFEDERATION OF
FREE TRADE UNIONS, JANUARY 1, 1965*

Europe

Austria	1,531,695	Grenada	2,373
Belgium	685,862	Iceland	30,370*
Cyprus	14,465	Italy	3,002,250
Denmark	818,077*	Luxembourg	28,000
Estonia (seamen's union in exile)	1,214	Malta	15,648*
Finland	226,927	Netherlands	525,000
France	1,000,000	Norway	567,223
Germany	6,430,978*	San Marino	1,629
Great Britain	8,325,790*	Sweden	1,970,525*
Greece	498,694*	Switzerland	451,102*

Near East

Aden	18,000	Turkey	476,000
Israel	800,000	Lebanon	18,000
Jordan	5,000		

Asia

Ceylon	315,079*	Japan	1,936,000
China	287,163	Korea	264,178
Fiji Islands	8,683*	Malaysia	230,000*
Hong Kong	125,885*	Okinawa	6,400
India	2,536,721	Pakistan	301,009*
Indonesia	59,530*	Philippines	80,000

Australasia

Australia	821,309*	New Zealand	220,000

Africa

Cameroon	45,000	Nigeria	250,000*
Congo (Brazzaville)	10,000*	Portuguese Guinea	1,821
Congo (Kinshasa)	15,000	Sierra Leone	12,000*
Ethiopia	28,000	Somalia	5,293*
Gabon	6,100	South Africa	570
Gambia	3,000	Spanish (in exile)	20,200
Liberia	4,000	St. Helena	1,995*
Malagasy Republic (Madagascar)	17,000*	Tunisia	155,000
Malawi	18,000*	Uganda	1,500*

* When figure is followed by asterisk, it relates to earlier date. No membership figures were available in connection with the unions of Angola, Aruba, Cameroon, Chad, Curaçao, Gambia, Indonesia, Kenya, Libya, Malawi, Mauritania, Morocco, Nepal, Paraguay, Rhodesia, Sudan, Surinam, Tanzania, Thailand, Upper Volta, Vietnam, Zambia.

Americas

Argentina	127,000	Guatemala	6,300*
Bahamas	6,091	Haiti	151
Barbados	10,000	Honduras	14,000*
Bermuda	153*	Jamaica	135,370
Bolivia	6,154	Mexico	1,400,000
Brazil	5,100,000	Montserrat	685*
British Guiana (Guyana)	45,000*	Nicaragua	9,000
British Honduras	3,000*	Panama	1,149*
Canada	1,100,000	Peru	1,250,000
Chile	82,000*	Puerto Rico	255,000*
Colombia	789,561*	St. Lucia	3,029
Costa Rica	12,000*	St. Vincent	2,160*
Dominica	3,000	Trinidad	36,000
Dominican Republic	80,000*	United States	13,049,344*
El Salvador	38,000*	Uruguay	62,420*
Falkland Islands	563*	Venezuela	700,000

THE COMMUNIST INTERNATIONAL

In the earlier pages of this book, we dealt with the bolshevik, or communist, revolution in Russia of November, 1917, and the first years of the Soviet government in the former land of the czars.[14]

Birth of Communist International (1919). With the establishment of the Soviet government, its leaders began the organization of a Third, or Communist, International, through which they hoped in part to channel communistic revolutionary propaganda and action throughout the world.[15]

At the first Congress of the Comintern or Communist International, held in Moscow in early March, 1919, the International represented hardly anything except the bolshevik regime in Russia. Its most important non-Russian section, the Spartacusbund in Germany, was practically nonexistent at the time of the Congress, since its leaders, Karl Liebknecht and Rosa Luxemburg, had been murdered two months before when attempting to seize German governmental power.

Second Congress—Call for Immediate World Revolution (1920). At the Comintern's Second Congress in Moscow from July 19 to August 7, 1920, however, it was in a position to start a frontal attack against the newly formed Vienna, or Two-and-a-Half, International by challenging that body to join its ranks, at the same time laying down such stringent conditions for admission as to guarantee that the invitation would be rejected.

14 See *ante*, Ch. 24, *et seq*.
15 See *ante*, p. 468 *et seq*. and 519–20.

When this Second Congress was held, the leaders of the International were determined to harness the unrest in Europe into an immediate "world revolution." Despite the suppression of the Spartacist uprising in Berlin in January, 1919, and the overthrow of the Bavarian and Hungarian Soviet republics and other reversals, the Third International claimed that "the world was hurrying towards proletarian revolution at breakneck speed."

The situation seemed to them to have become more revolutionary in 1920. Communist leaders pointed to general strikes in the Balkans, uprisings in the Ruhr, the seizure of factories in Italy, and the general strike for the nationalization of the railroads in France, among other things, as signs of the imminence of a general "social revolution."

By the spring of 1920, moreover, the Russian forces had beaten back or destroyed Kolchak, Yudinich, and Denikin. They had cleared Russia of foreign troops and were marching westward, aiming "to take Warsaw, march on Berlin, and join with the revolutionary groups of the west to establish a Soviet Europe."

It was in the midst of these events and future anticipations that the Third International held its second congress in Moscow from July 19 to August 7, 1920.

Several hundred delegates from thirty-seven countries crowded the halls of the Kremlin where the Second Congress was held. It was a motley gathering, representing a wide variety of ideologies and political and economic organizations.[16]

On the basis of their analysis of the international situation, the Russian communists summoned the assembled delegates to begin the work of the "world revolution" at once. "We are living in the epoch of civil war," declared the congress: "The critical hour has struck."

The congress adopted elaborate "theses" explaining the meaning of proletarian dictatorship and how communists could utilize various types of institutions in the developed and colonial countries for their purposes. It urged all in agreement with its views to break away from the socialists and to form independent communist parties.

It adopted twenty-one points which were conditions of admission to the Third International. According to these points, all those wishing to join the Third International had to accept fully the communist program, engage in illegal work, carry on propaganda in the army, sub-

16 Lewis L. Lorwin, *The International Labor Movement* (N. Y.: Harper & Brothers, 1953), p. 66.

mit to "iron discipline," and form "nuclei" in proletarian and "semi-proletarian organizations."

The purpose of these conditions was to break up socialist organizations and destroy their influence among the workers. The twenty-one points were also aimed at the destruction of "the Amsterdam International of yellow labor unions" and of the I. L. O. in the League of Nations. To promote this "struggle," trade unionists attending the Congress held a meeting and set up a Provisional International Council of Red Trade Unions.

Third Congress—Slowing Down of Revolutionary Developments (1921). Soon after the Congress, however, it became evident that the forces of world upheaval were spending themselves. The Red armies had been repulsed from Warsaw. The Italian strike of metal workers, during which the strikers had seized the factories, had been settled by a compromise. Other general strikes and uprisings had collapsed. Then at the end of the year came the world-wide industrial depression, and democratic governments began to give way to fascistic dictatorships in Italy, Spain, the Balkans, and elsewhere. Within Russia, the Kronstadt revolt of sailors and other developments had forced a retreat to the "New Economic Policy."

Outside of Russia, the German United Communist party, the largest non-Russian communist organization, had suffered a serious setback in its failure to carry to a successful conclusion its proposed general strikes and *putsch*.

It was these developments in the immediate past and the ominous specter of famine in the near future that confronted the delegates to the Third Congress in Moscow in June, 1921.

Lenin struck the keynote of the meeting with his admission that "revolutionary developments had slowed down" and that communists were mistaken in 1919–20 in believing that they could win with the help of a minority of organized workers.

Taking its cue from Lenin, the Congress approved the New Economic Policy (N. E. P.) in Russia and adopted a new slogan for the communists of all lands: "To the masses." In politics, this slogan meant that communists should still try to split and destroy socialist parties, but in other spheres they should remain within existing organizations and try to control them through "nuclei" or "cells." They were to make special efforts to control trade unions and other labor organizations from "works councils to sport clubs and musical circles."

On October 23, 1923, the communists in Hamburg gave the signal for the capture of mass organizations by declaring a general strike, starting with food riots, and attempting to seize city governments.

The undertaking, however, proved to be a complete failure. A few days later, on October 29, 1923, government troops marched into Dresden and overthrew the "workers' government" of Saxony composed of communists and left-socialists. Thousands of communists were arrested throughout Germany and communist papers were suppressed. On December 8, the Reichstag conferred dictatorial powers on President Ebert to deal with the situation. The failure of the "October uprising" marked a retreat for the Third International on many fronts.

Centralization of Stalin Control—Attempt to Capture Trade Unions. The next few years were years of intense struggle for control of the Russian Communist party and of the Third International by the opponents of Stalin—Trotsky, Zinoviev, Kamenev, Radek, and others. These years ended in the triumph of Stalin, the exclusion in 1928 of Trotsky and others from the executive committee of the Third International, the abandonment of the policy of the United Front, the rise of the Red International of Labor Unions, and the increased centralization of the Third International under the control of the Russian Communist party led by Stalin. The Soviet government during these years likewise spent much of its energy in carrying out its Five Year Plan to a successful conclusion.

In Central and Western Europe, the late twenties were years of continuous struggle for the control of the European trade union movement. On the one side of this struggle was the socialist-oriented Amsterdam International. On the other side was the Red International. The triumph of the one, communists believed, would mean the destruction of the other.

Communist parties in numerous European countries were weakened by the fight they had to wage on behalf of the Red International as well as by the dissensions within their ranks among the followers of Stalin, Trotsky and other Russian leaders. By 1929, therefore, the Communist International had made little headway outside of Russia, Germany, France, and Czechoslovakia. Russia, in that year, accounted for three-fourths of the Red International's estimated membership of 1,800,000.

Rising Fear of Nazism—Seventh Congress Urges Popular Front (1935). In the early thirties, the tactics of the Third International were drastically revised—communists became alarmed by the spread of nazism in Central Europe—Soviet Russia began to seek reconciliation with the democratic countries of the West. It sought and obtained recognition by the United States. It joined the League of Nations it had formerly vilified. It concluded an alliance with France.

In line with this new policy of conciliation by the Soviet government, the Communist International adopted a new line of propaganda and education. At the Seventh Congress held in Moscow in August, 1935, it declared that its future policy would be to organize "broad popular fronts" with socialist and liberal parties and "united action" with "reformist" trade unions. It admitted that it had misjudged the course of historic events and had committed many "errors" of strategy and tactics. Among other things it declared it had failed to foresee the menace of fascism, which it declared to be its chief enemy.

The "theses" of the Congress were ambiguous. They left room for the communists to continue their disruptive tactics against non-communist trade unions and against "labor governments" when the latter were in power. But the new, publicized communist slogans were "popular fronts," "united action," and "unity."

One of the results of this change in the economic field was the abandonment of the Red International of Labor Unions. While it was not formally dissolved, it was allowed to lapse into inactivity and became little more than a vessel for holding the Soviet unions. Of its membership of 20,000,000, 19,500,000 were reported to belong to the Soviet trade unions.

On the political field, under the "popular front" tactic, offers of cooperation were extended not only to the socialists, but to the "bourgeois" left and center. Thus the class struggle ceased for the time being to be a basic doctrine proclaimed by international communism. Communist programs and slogans became largely pragmatic, so that frequently the communists appeared to be more moderate than the socialists.

The Seventh and last world congress (1935) endorsed this policy which had its most conspicuous success in the victory in 1936 of the "Popular Front" movement in France. After this victory of the left-center forces and the selection of the socialist Léon Blum as Premier, the communists, however, refused to participate in the government and, from its inception, harassed it by organizing strikes, promoting an inflationary financial policy, and undermining the French socialist organizations.

Communist International and Spanish Civil War. The course pursued by the Soviet government and the Communist International at the outbreak of the Spanish Civil War also confronted the United Front government with a particularly grave difficulty.

The war was not anticipated by the communists who at the time had very few members in Spain. Once the war was started, however, the communists worked energetically to gain control of the republican camp, using as a means of pressure the military help sent it by the U. S. S. R.

When the communists obtained control of a large part of the police forces, they began an attack on the revolutionary left wing of the Spanish Republican government—the anarcho-syndicalists, left wing socialist and Trotskyites—whom they destroyed. They helped build up the new army and administration, thus gaining greater power. In view, however, of the sharp turn to the right in the U. S. S. R. and the international complications that a communist victory would involve, it is doubtful whether the non-Russian communists wanted fully to win the war.

Later they found themselves involved in a sharp controversy with the moderates in the republican camp who were opposed to foreign domination and to a dictatorial police regime. Ultimately various groups in that camp, together with the most important military leaders, rose against the communists in March, 1939, and capitulated to Francisco Franco.

The French communists, in the meanwhile, had attempted, without success, to push France into direct intervention with Spain. The French Popular Front government, however, was weakened by conflicts over foreign policy and inflation, and after several cabinet changes, it went out of office in April, 1938. In November, 1938, the communists pressured the French Confédération Général du Travail into a general strike which failed and led to the virtual collapse of the C. G. T.

The Popular Front had ended, but the French communists had greatly strengthened their position.

Reversal of Communist Internationalists after Nazis Invade Russia.

World War II. By this time Stalin had lost interest in co-operation with free nations or with democratic parties and was preparing his pact with Hitler. One of the unpublished stipulations of that pact seems to have been that the Communist party abroad should support the Nazi cause. The German Communist party-in-exile went to the point of supporting anti-Semitic and pro-Nazi propaganda, while the French and British communists attacked the French Allied effort in the first years of World War II. When Hitler invaded one western country after another, the communists joined in the nazi appeals for co-operation with the invader. Everywhere they tried to get control of the national trade union movement and as large a sector as possible of the government machinery.

This policy, however, was drastically reversed at the moment of the nazi invasion of the Soviet Union. The communists in the Western countries then adopted the slogans of the democratic struggle against fascism. In a repetition of the "Popular Front" phase, the communists continued to try to infiltrate governments and non-communist political parties and to undermine all non-communist political and economic leaderships. These tactics, together with the skilful foreign policy of Russia, helped to create an atmosphere of uncritical good will toward the Soviet regime—a prime factor in the post-war settlement favorable to the Russians.

During these years communists also engaged in guerrilla warfare in China and Yugoslavia, a tactic that greatly contributed to communist success while, in Eastern Europe, the Soviet armies installed friendly governments without the employment of this type of warfare.

On May 22, 1943, the Comintern, which had been removed to Ufa in the Urals, was officially dissolved. Actually its offices continued to function and returned to Moscow. In the meanwhile communists in various countries fought vigorously over whether the movement should strive for immediate revolution or should proceed along a more circuitous route to ultimate success. Stalin seemed to have sided with the party of caution.

Following the failure of attempts at direct capture of power in Belgium and Greece, the communist parties everywhere adopted the "patriotic-democratic" policy and in numerous continental countries joined in government coalitions.

The Cominform. The "patriotic-democratic" policy broke down with the ending of co-operative action between the Eastern and Western powers. At a conference at Wilcza, Gora in Poland in September, 1943, the communists set up a new official center of international control, described as the Communist Information Bureau, or Cominform.

Officially, the new body was composed of only the Communist parties of the U. S. S. R., of the Eastern European countries, and of France and Italy. Its jurisdiction, however, was more widespread than the Communist leaders admitted.

The formation of the Cominform initiated a phase in many countries of direct, revolutionary aggression. Communists everywhere left coalition governments. They helped stimulate revolutionary strikes in France and Italy. In February, 1948, they staged a *coup d'état* in Prague, thus completing the process of imposing communist regimes in countries originally occupied by the Soviet army.

The civil war in Greece, however, took a turn for the worse for the communists. In June, 1948, the dissidence of Tito, who had been one of the promoters of the Cominform, spelled the end of its policy of direct aggression. The Cominform's offices were transferred from Belgrade to more remote Bucharest.

Thereafter the Cominform largely confined its activity to issuing innocuous propaganda—the control over international communism in Europe was directed primarily from Moscow—while Mao Tse-tung, whose conquest of China (1948–50) had made him a world influence, was simultaneously lodging a claim to advise and control the communist movement in all the colonial, semi-colonial, and backward countries.

In the West, moreover, Moscow's control was increasingly hampered by the severe antagonisms besetting the Kremlin leadership immediately before Stalin's death. These antagonisms slowed down activity and interfered with the purge of the "Titoists." The widely publicized purge trials in Hungary, Bulgaria, and Czechoslovakia and the less spectacular trials in other Communist parties after Tito's defection may well have been connected with developments inside of the Kremlin.

Despite these hampering circumstances, however, Stalin, shortly before his death on March 5, 1953, was able to report that the Soviet Empire had grown during the forties and early fifties from a population of 170,000,000 to one of 700,000,000—through the use of Communist forces and the threat of force and of political, economic organization, propaganda, and manipulation.

Decades of the Fifties and Sixties. During the next decade from the early fifties to the early sixties, the following events had their impact on the world communist movement:

(1) Changes in Soviet Russia—Destalinization. Within the Soviet Union, the death of Stalin (1953); the regime of Nikita Khrushchev—flamboyant, erratic, more relaxed than Stalin; Khrushchev's sudden and dramatic denunciation (1957) of the "horrors and deg-

radation of Stalin's one-man leadership" followed by the de-Stalinization campaign; the rise of the more cautious leadership of Kosygin and Brezhnev; the gradual relaxation of restraints on personal liberty; the virtual disappearance of the revolutionists of 1917 from positions of power; the increasing power of the managerial class; the growth of consumer consciousness; and the increasing belief in the necessity of co-existence as an alternative to annihilation.

(2) DEMAND FOR GROWING INDEPENDENCE AMONG SATELLITE COUNTRIES. Outside the Soviet Union in the satellite countries of Eastern Europe, the decade witnessed bitter protests and rebellions against the rigid controls of the Soviet Union over their countries' political, economic, and social life, and the continued success of Tito's Yugoslavia in developing its particular brand of national communism.

(3) CO-EXISTENCE. In Central and Western Europe, the growing stability and strength of the democracies aided by N. A. T. O., the Common Market, and other projects designed to aid the movement toward integration, and continued weakness of Communist parties in most of the democracies, increasingly led the followers of Soviet communism during the decade to realize the futility of further communist attempts at military aggression on the Continent and to emphasize increasingly the need for "co-existence."

Communists began to urge improved trade and cultural relations between the East and West, more co-operation with progressive political fronts in democratic countries, and active co-operation with such international organizations as the U. N., U. N. E. S. C. O. and the I. L. O. as a means of strengthening communist influence in the west.

The comparative failure of world communism to dominate the governments of the developing nations of Asia, Africa, and Latin America through the use of arms, terrorism, infiltration, and political manipulation led the Soviet government to turn increasingly to granting economic and technological aid to countries as a means of advancing the communist cause. The Soviets, however, continued their military aid to communist governments engaged in battle with western democracies, as in the case of Vietnam, and the "cold war" between communists and Western democracies still continued on a lesser scale.

(4) INCREASING CONFLICTS BETWEEN SOVIET AND CHINESE COMMUNISTS. While these trends were observed in most Communist parties of the world under the leadership of Moscow, increasing differences in the theory and practice of communism were being voiced by the com-

munists of the People's Republic of China under the chairmanship of Mao Tse-tung and their followers.

Communists on all continents had rejoiced when, on October 1, 1949, the People's Republic of China—with the world's largest population, 750,000,000, and with its vast material and cultural resources—was born and joined the international communist movement.

This new giant in the communist world, which possessed many of the economic characteristics of the Soviet Union immediately after the bolshevik revolution, soon began to demand an equal status with Moscow in the leadership of international communism. In addition it became increasingly vocal with regard to its differences with Moscow's leadership, declaring that the Russians had turned their back on the Marxist-Leninist philosophy.

In the late fifties and early sixties, Mao began to assume the role of chief interpreter and theoretician of Marxist-Leninism. In the field of foreign affairs, he insisted that, according to the true communist philosophy, another world war between communist and capitalist nations was inevitable. In reply to the contention of Khrushchev that "we on our part must do everything possible to preclude war as a means of settling outstanding questions," Mao Tse-tung declared (in 1960 at Lenin's anniversary celebration): "We believe in the absolute correctness of Lenin's thinking; war is an inevitable outcome of systems of exploitation and the source of modern war is the imperialist system." "The imperialists," he declared, "will under no circumstances give up their policies of aggression and war"—a point of view which the Soviet communists attacked as "dogmatic and left-wing sectarian deviation from the Marxist-Leninist teaching."

In 1966 the total membership of all Communist parties, including splinter groups, was estimated at about 43,900,000, of which 41,300,000, or over 94 per cent, were in communist-controlled countries. Communist China accounted for 18,500,000, and the Soviet Union for 12,000,000, a total of about 7 out of every 10 members included in all the Communist parties of the world.

Communist membership in non-communist countries was sharply decreased in 1965 by the decimation of the Communist party of Indonesia, with its membership of 1,900,000, following an attempted *coup d'état* in which communists took a leading part.

In Europe, outside of the countries with Communist governments, the estimated party membership was 1,946,834, of which nearly three-fourths was in Italy and nearly nine-tenths were in Italy and France.

Austria	35,000	Iceland	975
Belgium	13,000	Ireland	125
Cyprus	10,000	Italy	1,350,000
Denmark	5,000	Luxembourg	500
Finland	50,000	The Netherlands	12,000
France	280,000	Norway	2,500
West Germany	10,000	Sweden	20,000
Greece	20,000	Switzerland	4,000
		United Kingdom	133,734
			1,946,834

As far as communist representation in national legislatures in the mid-sixties was concerned, the only democracies in Europe in which the Communist parties showed any significant strength were France, where Communists occupied about one-tenth of the parliamentary seats, and Finland and Italy, where they constituted about one-fourth of the total representation. No seats were held by communists in those years in the parliaments of Austria, Denmark, Great Britain, Ireland, Malta, Norway, or West Germany, while small delegations of from 4 to 8 communists were at work in the national legislative halls of Belgium, Cyprus, Holland, Luxembourg, Sweden, and Switzerland.[17]

In Asia, Communists controlled the governments of China, Outer Mongolia, North Korea, and North Vietnam. They held 29 seats in the Parliament of India, 4 each in Japan, Ceylon and Israel, and none in Indonesia, because of the outlawing of the Communist party following the unsuccessful *coup d'état* of 1965.[18]

At the beginning of 1966, the membership of Communist parties was estimated * (or claimed by the parties) to be as follows:

Membership of Communist Parties

Albania	53,000	Cambodia	100
Argentina	65,000	Canada	3,500
Australia	5,000	Ceylon	2,600
Austria	35,000	Chile	30,000
Belgium	13,000	China	18,500,000
Bolivia	4,500	Colombia	12,000
Brazil	23,000	Costa Rica	400
Bulgaria	550,384	Cuba	50,000
Burma	5,000	Cyprus	10,000

17 Communist front organizations in Greece and Iceland were represented by 22 and 6, respectively.

18 Soviet references to the Socialist Workers and Farmers party in Nigeria and the African Party of Independence in Senegal indicated in 1966 that they are regarded as pro-communist but not as full-fledged communist parties.

* Bureau of Intelligence and Research, U.S. Department of State, "World Strength of the Communist Party Organizations," January, 1966, pp. 1–8.

Czechoslovakia	684,416
Denmark	5,000
Dominican Republic	1,700
Ecuador	2,500
El Salvador	200
Finland	50,000
France	280,000
Germany, East	1,610,679
Germany, West	10,000
Greece	20,000
Guadeloupe	1,000
Guatemala	1,000
Honduras	1,300
Hungary	540,000
Iceland	975
India	125,000
Indonesia	100,000†
Iran	1,500
Iraq	2,000
Ireland	125
Israel	2,000
Italy	1,350,000
Japan	137,500
Jordan	500
Korea, North	1,600,000
Lebanon	4,000
Luxembourg	500
Malaysia	2,700
Martinique	700
Mexico	5,250
Mongolia, Outer	46,000
Morocco	500
Nepal	6,000
Netherlands	12,000
New Zealand	400
Nicaragua	200
Nigeria	500
Norway	2,500
Pakistan	3,250
Panama	500
Paraguay	5,000
Peru	5,000
Philippines	1,750
Poland	1,725,000
Portugal	2,000
Rumania	1,450,000
Singapore	200
South Africa	100
Spain	5,000
Sudan	8,000
Sweden	20,000
Switzerland	4,000
Syria	3,000
Tunisia	250
Turkey	1,250
U.S.S.R.	12,000,000
United Kingdom	33,734
Uruguay	10,000
Venezuela	20,000
Vietnam, North	700,000
Vietnam, South	31,000
Yugoslavia	1,030,041

† In some two score countries in 1966, the national laws declared the communist party illegal. For Indonesia an estimate has nevertheless been made above of the party's membership.

CHAPTER 45

Post-World War II European Socialist Developments

The history of socialism is never complete; its vast history suggests that it is subject to intense and sudden changes. Thus, it is impossible to have a full perspective on the most recent trends in socialism throughout the world. Yet it is important to establish the most recent developments in socialist history in various countries and the most recent trends in socialist thought in order that a fuller perspective may eventually be reached.

ENGLAND

The Attlee Labor Government (1945–51): Its Program of Social Control. Shortly after World War II was ended, the Labor members of the cabinet resigned their seats and asked for a new election. In the ensuing campaign, the party issued another manifesto, "Let Us Face the Future," which again called for a program of widespread social change.

In the June elections, to the surprise of members of all parties, the Laborites elected 393 of its candidates—over 60 per cent of the total parliamentary membership—as compared with 197 Conservatives. The elections marked the first time in British history that Labor had won a majority of seats in the House of Commons.

Following the balloting, Clement R. Attlee, the reserved and scholarly leader of the parliamentary party and a personality that differed sharply from the famous war Prime Minister, Winston Churchill, was called upon to form a Labor government.[1]

[1] Clement R. Attlee (1883–1967) was born at Putney, London, on January 3, 1883. He studied at Haileybury College and at University College, Oxford, and was called to the bar in the Inner Temple in 1905. In that year, shocked by the widespread poverty prevailing in the East End of London, he volunteered as a social worker and devoted much of his spare time to the building of boys clubs among the poor.

Following his acceptance, Attlee selected as Foreign Minister Ernest Bevin, powerful labor leader; as President of the Council, Herbert Morrison, veteran Laborite and former Chairman of the London County Council; and as President of the Board of Trade—and later as Chancellor of the Exchequer—Sir Stafford Cripps, one of Britain's most brilliant members of the bar.

During its next five years in office, the Labor party effected peacefully and democratically many fundamental and economic changes as "an essential part of a planned economy designed to help in promoting full employment, economic prosperity and justice for all." It nationalized the Bank of England, the coal mining industry, civil aviation, the cable and wireless services, inland transportation, the electricity and gas supply, atomic energy, and substantial firms in the iron and steel industry. The government paid a fair compensation for properties acquired by it from private enterprise.

The Attlee government established a national health service which provided free, comprehensive health services to all who earned or received an income. It regulated much of the country's investment, greatly expanded the educational and housing services, engaged in town and country planning, improved living conditions on the farms, and repealed the 1927 Trades Disputes and Trade Unions Act, enacted after the General Strike of 1926. It also established "working committees" in fifteen industries with a view to increasing their productivity and initiated steps toward over-all economic planning.

On the international front, Labor greatly narrowed the scope of the British Empire and delivered a blow to colonialism by granting independence to India, Pakistan, Burma, and Transjordan, and complete internal self-government to Ceylon. It also liberalized procedures in several of the African and Latin American colonies.

In the elections of 1950, the Conservatives fought the Labor party largely on the price and ration controls. When the votes were

---

In 1907, he became a convinced socialist and joined the Stepney Branch of the I. L. P., becoming its Secretary.

During World War I, Attlee served in France and the Near East, attaining the rank of major. He was elected to Parliament in 1922, was appointed Under-Secretary of War in the Labor government in 1929 and, in 1931, was appointed Postmaster General in Ramsay MacDonald's government and, following the resignation of Ramsay MacDonald, was chosen Leader of the party in 1935.

In World War II Attlee held high cabinet posts in the Churchill government and, following the sweeping victory of the Labor party in 1945, was asked to form a Labor government. After five years of his prime ministership, he was elected with a small majority, until the Conservative victory of 1951. In 1955, he became Earl Attlee and a member of the House of Lords. He died October 7, 1967.

counted, it was found that, while Labor won a larger number of parliamentary seats than the Conservatives (315 as compared with 297), its parliamentary representation had been reduced by 78.[2]

Because of Labor's slim parliamentary majority, Prime Minister Attlee in 1951 called for another election for October 25. The ensuing election resulted in a victory for the Conservatives who won 321 seats as compared with Labor's 294, though receiving a smaller popular vote than their defeated Labor opponents.

Labor as Opposition to Churchill Government (1951–64). Attlee was succeeded as Prime Minister by Winston Churchill; Labor returned to the status of "His Majesty's Loyal Opposition," which position it continued to hold until the elections of 1964.

On returning to the office of Prime Minister, Churchill declared that, while the government would denationalize steel, it could not attempt to turn back to private control other industries taken over by the Attlee government. Nor would the Conservatives abolish the National Health Service, which proved to be one of the most popular reforms effected during Labor's rule.

As the opposition party, Labor, on the domestic front during the fifties and early sixties, opposed the attempt of the Conservative government to charge for prescriptions, dental care, and some appliances in the National Health Service; urged the expansion of co-operative, municipal, and federal industries, of education and of the social services; proposed a plan for the acquisition by the government in 1957 of a portion of the stocks of several hundred of the larger firms of Great Britain; and urged the modernization of British methods of production and distribution, the establishment of a land commission, and an economic program to assure full employment.

In the international field, Labor opposed the landing of troops in Egypt in the Suez crisis and the government's South African policy; recommended the placing of Formosa under U. N. trusteeship and the admission of China to the U. N.; and favored a zone of military disengagement in Central Europe. It also opposed Britain's entrance into the Common Market unless greater provision was made to safeguard the living standards of the British farmers and to protect the markets of such members of the Commonwealth as Australia and New Zealand.

Within the Labor party during these years heated debates were con-

[2] Labor's popular vote, however, had increased from 11,963,000 to 13,241,077, an increase of 11 per cent.

tinuously being waged between the left-wing of the party led by Aneurin Bevan,[3] among others, and the moderates led by Attlee, Gaitskell, and many of the trade union leaders. In 1954 Bevan resigned from the "shadow cabinet" because of the party's failure, among other things, to oppose West Germany's rearmament.

In 1955, Attlee, on account of his age, resigned from the party's leadership. Hugh Gaitskell,[4] economist and Chancellor of the Exchequer in the Attlee cabinet, and a man of unusual ability and rare charm, was elected in Attlee's place. Four years later, following

[3] Aneurin Bevan (1897–1960), the most controversial figure in the British Labor party in the post-World War II period, was born in Tredegar, Wales, November 15, 1897, the son of a miner. He left school at thirteen to enter the mines, but he had to leave the mines at nineteen because of an eye disease.

After studying for two years in the Central Labor College in London, he entered local politics. He was elected to the House of Commons in 1929 and retained his seat until his death. In 1934 he was married to an attractive and talented fellow-member of Parliament, Jennie Lee.

He was expelled from the Labor party in 1939 for his Popular Front activities, but was readmitted the same year.

In the Attlee government he was appointed the Minister of Health and was in charge of the institution of the National Health Service. Long reputed one of the party's most incisive and effective speakers and debaters, as health minister, he also gained a wide reputation for his administrative ability.

Bevan opposed the imposition of charges for health services when Gaitskell was Chancellor of the Exchequer and, in 1951, some months after he had become Minister of Labor, he resigned from the cabinet.

After the war he opposed Labor's stand on German rearmament and in 1955 again narrowly escaped expulsion from the party. Later that year he contested the party's treasureship with Gaitskell, but lost heavily. After Attlee's retirement he likewise fought for leadership of the party against Gaitskell, but was again defeated.

Following these contests, Bevan's criticisms of the party became less sharp. He became Labor's spokesman for colonial affairs and for foreign affairs in 1956, and was widely regarded as Labor's choice for foreign minister in the next Labor cabinet. In 1959 he was elected deputy leader. He died July 6, 1960. (His autobiography, *In Place of Fear,* was published in 1952.)

[4] Hugh T. N. Gaitskell was born April 9, 1906, into a distinguished family of civil servants. He received his education at Winchester and New College, Oxford, from which he was graduated in 1927 with first class honors in philosophy, politics, and economics.

As a protest against class privileges, he joined the Labor party during his university days. He served during World War II in the Ministry of Economic Warfare and the Board of Trade.

When the war ended in 1945, Gaitskell was elected to Parliament on the Labor ticket (1945) and, in the Attlee government of 1945–51, served successively as Minister of Fuel and Power, Minister of State for Economic Affairs, and Chancellor of the Exchequer, holding the last post until the Labor government fell in 1951.

In 1954 and 1955, he was Treasurer of the Labor party and became its leader on the resignation of Attlee, and the next in line for Labor's premiership. He failed to recover from a severe virus attack in 1963.

Labor's defeat, Gaitskell's leadership was severely challenged, particularly as a result of disagreement over the party's defense policy, but his clarifying statement at the 1960 Labor party conference brought him an impressive victory.[5]

In the early sixties, a vigorous controversy waged in the party over the principle of collective security. At the 1960 party conference, the delegates voted by a narrow block vote majority in favor of unilateral disarmament. The moderate leadership of the party and the majority of the Parliamentary Labor party, however, refused to accept this conference decision, and it was reversed at the 1961 conference. In 1963, the party suffered a severe loss with the sudden death of its leader, Hugh Gaitskell.

After Gaitskell's death, Harold Wilson,[6] deputy leader of the party, a keen debater, and for years a Labor leftist and an economist, was elected as the party Leader.

In the next year, under the Wilson leadership, the party continued to emphasize the need for the modernization of the British economy, an expanded role for scientists and technologists in government, a fairer distribution of the national product, and a reduction in the gap in the balance of payments.

The Wilson Labor Government (1964–). At the end of its term in office, the Conservatives called Parliamentary elections to be held October 15, 1964. During the previous few years, the polls had indicated a gradual rise in Labor's popularity, and when the ballots were counted, Labor was found to be the victor, with the election of 315 members of Parliament as compared with 292 Conservatives, 10 Liberals, and 12 Ulster Unionists. The Labor popular vote was 12,205,576, about 200,500 above that of the Conservatives.

Harold Wilson, as Labor's Leader, was thereupon called by Queen Elizabeth to form the government. During the next 17 months of

[5] In the 1959 election Labor elected 258 parliamentary candidates, a loss of 19, while its popular vote dropped to 12,216,166, a decrease of 1.5 per cent.

[6] Harold Wilson was born in Huddersfield, Yorkshire, on March 11, 1916, and was educated at Jesus College, Oxford. He entered the public service during World War II and was elected as Labor candidate to the House of Commons in 1945. Two years later, in 1947, at the age of 31, he joined the Attlee cabinet as President of the Board of Trade, a post which he held until April, 1951.

During the next twelve years when the Labor party served as H. M. Opposition, Wilson was a leader of the left-wing of the party. He was elected the party's leader in 1963 following the death of Hugh Gaitskell, and as such, was called upon by Queen Elizabeth to form the government when the Labor party won a majority in the 1964 election.

office, the Labor party carried on a precarious existence—with its slight majority of from 2 to 4 representatives—under the steady hand of its Prime Minister.

It voted an increase in old age pensions; curbed the power of landlords; removed the charges on all prescriptions ordered by health service physicians; passed a tax bill which, among other things, taxed capital gains; abolished capital punishment; boycotted Rhodesia for its racial discrimination policy; and won the approval of Parliament for the support of the United States in South Vietnam. In the fight against inflation, it secured parliamentary approval for the submission of wage demands to a government board.

On March 5, 1965, the party lost, by death, Herbert Morrison, one of its most outstanding veteran leaders.

In the early spring of 1966, following a steady rise in Labor's popularity, new elections were called for March 31. The election resulted in the increase of Labor's seats in the House of Commons from 317 to 363 as compared with 253 for the Conservatives, and a growth in popular votes from 12, 205,576 to 13,064,951, or 47.9 per cent of the total (Conservatives, 11,418,433) votes.

Following the election leading to the larger and more comfortable Labor majority, Prime Minister Wilson decided that the Labor government in foreign affairs would continue to work for peace, disarmament, agreements on non-proliferation of nuclear weapons, the extension of the nuclear test ban treaty, a negotiated settlement of the conflict in Vietnam, and tariff reductions. It would continue to support N. A. T. O. and to promote the economic unity of Europe. It would also "be ready to enter the E. E. C. [Common Market] provided essential British and Commonwealth interests were safeguarded" and it would "pursue the policy of bringing the illegal regime in Rhodesia to an end."

In the succeeding months of 1966, in an attempt to "save the pound" and prevent spiraling inflation, Prime Minister Wilson obtained Parliament's approval—despite the opposition of some labor leaders—of a wage and price freeze, together with an increase in taxation.

He sought, through selected economic sanctions, to obtain the agreement of Rhodesia to extend the franchise to its majority African population. Parliament voted to renationalize the steel industry, and to increase the pay of physicians and dentists in the employ of the National Health Service.

In May, 1967, Prime Minister Wilson applied for Britain's entrance into the European Common Market. When President de Gaulle, later in the month, voiced his open opposition to Britain's request, Wilson declared that he would continue his bid for acceptance.

In April, Labor lost control of the Greater London Council for the first time in thirty years. In October 1967 former Prime Minister Attlee died. On November 18 the government devalued the pound from $2.80 to $2.40. In March, 1968, its parliamentary majority was 74.

FRANCE

Socialist Achievements in Post-War Governments, 1946–51. With the liberation of France and the end of war, the Socialist party took its place once again in French political life. The party participated in the first provisional government and, after the adoption of the constitution, it continued, up to the election of 1951, either to hold important cabinet posts or to lead the government.

The first elections to the National Assembly after the war were held in October, 1945, which resulted in the seating of 139 socialist representatives in the National Assembly. The party received six important posts in the subsequent coalition cabinet and, when General de Gaulle resigned from the presidency on January 20, 1946, Felix Gouin, Socialist leader, was elected President. Under his presidency, the Assembly enacted a far ranging program of public control—including the nationalization of the electrical and gas industries and insurance companies—following the collectivization of the mines, the Bank of France, and four principal deposit banks.

During the next few years, the party was a vital force in structural reforms in the field of security, workers' participation in industry, and public ownership. In 1946, Guy Mollet, later Prime Minister, was elected General Secretary of the party. The next year Vincent Auriol, Socialist leader, was elected President of the Republic for a term of seven years.[7]

As an opposition party in the early fifties, the Socialists denounced the war in Indo-China and the admission of Spain to

[7] Vincent Auriol (1884–1966). Socialist leader and the first President of the French Republic after World War II, was born at Revel, Haute-Garonne, on August 27, 1884. Lawyer and journalist, he became Secretary-General of the Socialist parliamentary group in 1919, was minister of finance, of justice, and of coordination in the Blum government; was arrested for his opposition to Petain in 1940, later escaping to London, joined the De Gaulle cabinet as Minister of State and was elected President of the first Constituent Assembly in 1946; and was first President of the Republic in 1947. He died on January 1, 1966.

U. N. E. S. C. O.; urged Allied control of nazi elements in West Germany, and advocated a conference of four or five powers, including China, "to achieve a settlement of European powers and restore an atmosphere of peace."

Socialists in Coalition Governments (1956–58). On January 2, 1956, in the general elections, the Socialists, left-wing Radicals led by Pierre Mendes-France, the U. D. S. R. (Union democratique et socialiste de la Résistance) and the more left-wing Gaullists formed an alliance—the Republican Front—and fought the elections in the belief that a non-Communist left-wing majority was possible.

The Socialists increased their votes (for the first time since 1956) from 14.5 per cent in 1951 to 15 per cent, and elected 94 members to the National Assembly. On January 26, Mollet,[8] as the leader of the most important non-Communist party in the opposition, was asked to form a cabinet, and organized a minority government of the Republican Front parties.

The coalition cabinet of Socialists and Radicals with Mollet as Premier was finally formed in January 31, 1956. In June Mollet signed an agreement with Adenauer on political integration of the Saar with the German Federal Republic. He condemned Nasser's seizure of the Suez Canal and urged a cease fire in Algeria to be followed within three months by free elections.

In domestic affairs, the government enacted legislation for the extension of paid holidays, the increase of old-age pensions, and the expansion and modernization of education. Much attention was given to the fight against inflation.

After sixteen months in office—the longest term for a French Premier since World War II—Mollet resigned (on May 21, 1957) under the pressure of the opposition which opposed his taxation, anti-inflation, and Algerian policies.[9]

[8] Guy A. Mollet (1905–). French Socialist statesman, was born at Flers, Orne, on December 31, 1905. He joined the Socialist party at the age of sixteen, entered the teaching profession, and was elected in 1932 secretary of a socialist teachers' trade union. Entering the army in August, 1939, at the outbreak of World War II, he was wounded and made a prisoner of war. Repatriated in 1942, he became a member of the Resistance movement and emerged as captain in the French Forces of the Interior.

In 1945, Mollet was elected Mayor of Arras and in September 1946, became Secretary-General of the French Socialist party. He was elected to the Constituent Assembly of 1945 and 1946, and, from 1946 sat in several successive National assemblies and French cabinets.

[9] On that date Mollet's financial program was defeated by a vote of 250 to 213 with 70 abstensions.

Following his resignation, several Socialists joined the succeeding Maurice Bourgès, Maunoury, and Gaillart governments.

Split in Socialist Party Following De Gaulle's Return (1958). When in the spring of 1958, with the worsening of the Algerian crisis, De Gaulle consented to head a government of national safety, the executive and parliamentary groups of the French Socialist party decided, by a vote of 77 to 74, in favor of his investiture.

This approval of De Gaulle's return to power led to a split in the Socialist party, followed by the formation of the group opposed to De Gaulle of an Autonomous Socialist party which joined with other leftist-oriented splinter groups to form the Unified Socialist party. At the Socialist party's annual conference in September, 1958, the delegates urged that a program be worked out for "the co-existence of Algeria," and, in domestic affairs, that the party re-examine the desirable limits of nationalized and private enterprises.

At first, Socialist leaders, including Mollet, accepted positions in the De Gaulle cabinet. Later the Socialists decided to work outside the cabinet as the government's "constructive opposition." In 1959 they campaigned for further progress toward the economic and political unity of democratic countries of Europe, the liberation of the peoples of the African community, and the control and suspension of nuclear tests for a two-year period.

In the following years the Socialists frequently attacked the De Gaulle government on domestic and international issues. Vincent Auriol, former Socialist President of France, resigned in 1960 from the constitutional council in protest against De Gaulle's attempt to create "a system of personal and arbitrary power in France." Auriol also declared that De Gaulle had violated the constitution by the large increase in state aid to church schools and his refusal to recall Parliament despite a request by a majority of deputies. Socialists likewise attacked his foreign policy as anti-European and overly nationalistic.

In the 1962 parliamentary elections the Socialists increased their representation in the National Assembly from 43 to 66. They became the second largest party in France in parliamentary strength, though their representation was a far cry from the 231 seats won by the De Gaullists. De Gaulle was in that year overwhelmingly elected President.

Socialists Enter Into Electoral Agreements with Communists and Left-of-Center Parties (1965 and 1967). In 1965, Socialists joined with Communists and some Radicals and left-of-center elements in support of François Mitterrand[10] for President of the Republic against President de Gaulle—the first election in the history of France in which a head of the state was elected by direct and universal suffrage. As De Gaulle failed to receive a majority of votes in the first balloting, a run-off election was held on December 19, in which Mitterrand received about 45 per cent of the votes and De Gaulle, 55 per cent, a much smaller proportion than the latter had anticipated.

Following the elections, the Socialists continued their activity in the Federation of Democratic Socialist Left which supported Mitterrand in the presidential campaign. In August, 1966, the Federation adopted a platform which urged a check on "the arbitrary and unconstitutional actions of the head of state" (De Gaulle), the strengthening of civil liberties, the end of the building of a nuclear striking force, long term economic planning, the expansion of the social services, equal opportunities for women, and an accelerated movement toward a peaceful Europe.

Prior to the March, 1967, elections for the National Assembly, in an effort to defeat the Gaullist candidates, the Socialists entered into an electoral agreement with left-of-center parties. Under the French voting system, if a candidate on the first round of balloting obtained a majority of all votes cast for the National Assembly, he would be declared elected. If he received less than a majority, he could appear under specified conditions on the list of candidates at a second election.

The parties of the left (including the Federation of Democratic and Socialist Left, the United Socialist party, and the Communists) agreed that, on the second round, they would withdraw their candidates in favor of those who seemed to have the best chance of election.

In the ensuing March election, as a result of this strategy, the

[10] François Mitterrand, candidate in 1965 for President of the Socialist Moscow-line Communists, and certain center groups, was born on October 16, 1916, at Jarnac, in southwestern France, one of eight children of a railroad worker. His industry and ready wit won him entry to France's outstanding schools and he earned degrees in law and political science.

In World War II, Sergeant Mitterrand was wounded and captured when France fell to the German army. On his third try, he escaped. He made his way to France to join the Resistance, and on his arrival founded the National Movement of War Prisoners and Deportees. In 1944, he first met General de Gaulle and was later made a cabinet officer responsible for returning deportees.

After the war, in the Fourth Republic, Mitterand became a left-wing Deputy and held cabinet posts under eleven coalition governments in nine years. He opposed General de Gaulle's 1958 return to power and was one of the General's severest critics in Parliament. He urged that France initiate steps toward disarmament, and advocated a United Europe with a political organization chosen by universal suffrage.

Gaullists lost many of their seats in the Assembly and won only a bare majority (244) out of 486. The number of seats won by the parties of the Left were: Democratic and Socialist Left, 116; Communists, 73; other left-wing groups including the Unified Socialist party, 10; Democratic Center, 27; and Independent Conservatives, 15.

In May, 1967, Socialists opposed President de Gaulle's request for special executive powers for a period of six months in the economic and social field. They vigorously supported the one-day general strike of the socialist-controlled Workers' Force and of the communist-dominated General Confederation of Labor in opposition to the government. The left-wing vote to censure the government failed by only 8 votes.

BELGIUM

The Van Acker and Huysmans Post-War Governments (1945–47). On February 11, 1945, following the return of the government, Achille Van Acker, a leading member of the underground, was asked to form a four-party cabinet, and Spaak became Foreign Minister. On March 31, 1946, Van Acker[11] organized a government of Socialists, Commu-

[11] Achille Van Acker, Belgian socialist, who headed four of his country's cabinets after the Germans had been driven from Belgium in 1944, was born in Bruges, April 8, 1898, son of a poor basket maker. At the age of ten he left school to go to work. He held a number of manual jobs, including that of a stevedore, and became interested in the trade union movement. Later young Van Acker sold books and operated a rare book and engraving shop in Bruges. In these years he educated himself through an extensive reading program. During World War I he served in the army.

Van Acker's first entrance into politics was in 1926 at the age of twenty-eight when he was elected to Bruges' municipal council. The next year he was chosen a socialist member of the House of Representatives. While there he took a prominent part in programs that supported labor and social legislation. In 1936 he was elected financial officer of the chamber.

During the German occupation in World War II, Van Acker lived clandestinely in Belgium and became a leader in the resistance movement. He helped to reorganize the Socialist party, which had been dissolved by the Germans, and negotiated an agreement with delegates of employers' and workers' groups for the enactment of social measures after the war.

In the reorganization of the Pierlot cabinet, on September 26, 1944, after the liberation, Van Acker was appointed Minister of Labor and Social Welfare, with Public Health added to his duties in later months. He began immediately to implement the social welfare program drafted during the occupation providing social security for all workers. The program was submitted to Prince Charles who signed it into law.

When Pierlot resigned on February 7, 1945, the Prince Regent called on Van Acker to form a new government. Accepting the call, he organized (on February 11) with difficulty a new ministry containing representatives of all four parties—Socialists, Catholics, Liberals, and Communists.

nists, and Liberals, with the Catholics as the government's chief opposition. During the Van Acker regime, controversy was widespread and bitter as to whether Belgium should invite King Leopold to return to the country; the Socialists and other left-wing groups opposed his return.

On August 2, the coalition government was reorganized, headed by Prime Minister Camille Huysmans,[12] veteran socialist, long Burgomaster of Antwerp.

The Spaak Government (1947–49). The Huysmans government lasted until March 19, 1947, when Paul-Henri Spaak,[13] Socialist Foreign Minister in various governments, became Prime Minister and pre-

---

Under his premiership, the House of Representatives voted overwhelmingly to bar the return of King Leopold to Belgium, without the consent of Parliament, on the ground that the King had not provided a maximum of resistance to the Germans in 1940. His regime witnessed a steady increase in the country's standard of living.

The first post-war elections were held on February 17, 1946, and led to the formation of a Socialist government, this time under Paul-Henri Spaak, in which Van Acker served as Minister of Economic Affairs. In succeeding Spaak cabinets he was Minister of Communications. He was Premier for three more terms during the forties and fifties, the last of which lasted from 1954 to 1958.

In 1957 Van Acker announced the relaxation of controls on trade with Communist China; in the previous year he had signed a cultural agreement with Soviet Russia. Following the Soviet interference in the Hungarian revolt, however, the U. S. S. R. was notified that the accord would not enter into force. In public life he was often referred to as "smiling Achille."

12 Camille Huysmans (1871–1968), Belgian Socialist leader and statesman, was born May 26, 1871, in Bilsen. After graduating at Liège, where he specialized in Germanic philosophy, he taught at the College Liberal of Ypres and then at the New University, Brussels. He entered the socialist movement early and wrote extensively for its press. He was elected a member of the Brussels City Council in 1905 and of the Belgian Parliament in 1910. From 1905 to 1922 he was the Secretary of the International Socialist Bureau.

After World War I, he became the chief organizer of the Labor party in Antwerp. In June, 1925, he became Minister of Science and Arts; in 1936, the President of the Chamber of Deputies; and from August, 1946, to March, 1947, Prime Minister. He was the author of several books.

13 Paul-Henri Spaak, Belgian socialist statesman, known to many as "Mr. Europe," was born in Schaerbeck, January 25, 1899. He came from a family prominent in the political and cultural life of Belgium. His father—lawyer, playwright and poet—was director of the Brussels' opera; his mother was active in the socialist movement, was elected in 1921 the first woman senator in Belgium; his grandfather was an outstanding Liberal leader; while his uncle, Paul-Emile Janson, was destined to become Belgium's Liberal Premier.

Spaak studied law at the University of Brussels, and soon took an active part in the socialist movement. After ten years of legal practice, he was elected a member of Parliament, representing the Belgian Labor party.

During his first year in Parliament, Spaak edited a left-wing socialist paper and was a strong critic of the "reformist" tendencies in his party. Three years later (in 1935), he was appointed Minister of Transport and Minister of Post, Telegraph and Telephone Services and, in 1936, having swung to a more moderate position, became Belgian Foreign Minister in a coalition cabinet headed by his uncle.

sided over a cabinet consisting of 8 Socialists, 9 Social Christians, and 2 Independents. One of the achievements of his administration was the preparation and signing of the Brussels treaty providing for mutual aid among the Benelux countries, Great Britain, and France. Belgian women during his premiership were granted the vote, a right they exercised on June 26, 1949, for the first time.

The Socialists in Opposition and in Coalition Governments (1950–66). In the 1949 elections Socialists won 66 parliamentary seats (a loss of 3) and came second to the Social Christians which elected 105 candidates. A Social Christian-Liberal government followed.

During the next year, as an opposition party, Socialists vigorously resisted the return of King Leopold, and on August 1, 1950, staged a march of protest on Brussels. The King gave heed to this and to other protests and decided to transfer his powers to his son, Prince Baudouin.

In 1954 Socialists increased their parliamentary representation to 86 (77 in 1950) and the Liberals from 20 to 25, while the Social Christians lost 10 seats. Socialists and Liberals thereupon formed a coalition gov-

---

In 1938, he succeeded his uncle Paul-Emile Janson, as Premier, becoming Belgium's youngest head of government in its history. He headed the cabinet from May, 1938, to February, 1939, and in September again assumed the post of Foreign Minister.

Following the invasion of Belgium by German troops in May, 1940, and a bitter eighteen-day battle, Spaak escaped from Belgium, and, on reaching London, was welcomed as the Foreign Minister of Belgium-in-exile. At the end of the war, he returned to Belgium where he served during the forties and fifties in several coalition governments as both Premier and Foreign Minister.

During these years he also became increasingly active in movements for international co-operation. In April, 1945, he headed the Belgian delegates to the U. N. Conference on International Organization in San Francisco. He was Second Vice-President of the Preparatory Commission of the U. N. in London, and, when the U. N. was finally established, was elected President of the U. N. General Assembly.

In the development of co-operative agencies among the nations of western Europe, he helped to form the Organization for European Economic Cooperation (O.E.E.C.) and was chairman of the Council from 1948 to 1950.

In the early fifties, Spaak served as President of the Council of the European Coal and Steel Community, and, as chairman of the Intergovernmental Committee, spent months in the drafting of the Rome Treaty which laid the foundation for the Common Market (the E. E. C.).

He was Secretary-General of N. A. T. O. from May, 1957, to March, 1961, and, to advance the cause of political co-operation, in 1949 he accepted, among other things, the presidency of the Consultative Assembly of the Council of Europe, and, in 1950, the chairmanship of the International Council of the European Movement, leaving that post in 1955.

On his resignation from N. A. T. O. in 1961, Spaak became deputy Prime Minister of Belgium, combining this post with Foreign Minister. His sixth term as Foreign Minister ended in May, 1965, when the Labor party went into opposition. On July 27, 1966, he resigned his parliamentary seat.

ernment, with Achille Van Acker, Socialist, as Prime Minister, and Spaak as foreign minister. During the next four years, the government reduced the term of compulsory military service from 21 to 18 months and expanded social services in the fields of old-age pensions, education, housing, employment, and obtained a shorter work week.

In 1955, the administration incurred the anger of the Catholic bishops by virtue of its decision to reduce state subsidies to Catholic schools and to impose restrictions on these funds. The bishops launched a vigorous campaign against the socialist movement. Partly as a result of this campaign, Socialists suffered a slight loss in the 1958 elections, dropping 2 seats (86 to 84). Van Acker resigned his premiership, and the Socialists again went into opposition. In 1959 they urged measures for the independence of the Congo with due safeguards for the protection of human rights.

They were again invited into a coalition government with the Christian Socialists in 1961, when in the elections of that year, they returned 84 representatives, while the Social Christians lost 10 parliamentary seats.

In the next Christian Social-Socialist coalition, Spaak was appointed deputy Prime Minister and Minister of Foreign Affairs. On February 10, 1966, however, the Socialists resigned from the coalition government because of the Social Christians' insistence that fees should be charged at seven clinics run by mutual insurance associations affiliated with the Socialist party.

During the fifties and sixties there were sharp differences within the party over language disputes between the French-speaking Walloons and the Germanic-speaking Flemish inhabitants of Belgium.

In 1966, Paul-Henri Spaak resigned from Parliament after forty-five years of noteworthy public service.

HOLLAND

Socialists in Post-War Coalitions. When the government-in-exile returned to Holland after the occupation, Queen Wilhelmina entrusted Willem Drees, leader of the Social Democratic party, and Willem Schermerhorn, Socialist, leader of the People's Movement—a former professor of geodesy—with the formation of the cabinet. Schermerhorn was appointed Premier.[14]

[14] Willem Schermerhorn, Dutch labor and socialist statesman and civil engineer, was born on December 17, 1894. From 1926 to 1945 he was Professor of Geodesy and Surveying at the Technical University of Delft. He served as scientific adviser

Dutch Labor Party Formed (1946). Following the formation of the cabinet, members of the People's Movement merged with the Socialists, the Liberal Democratic party, and progressive Catholic and Protestant groups, to form a Dutch Labor party. The party, in its inaugural program, expressed itself in favor of the nationalization of: mines, the Bank of the Netherlands, the nation's railroads, blast furnaces, and business monopolies. The government under Schermerhorn's premiership achieved important results in the fields of labor, finance, housing, old age pensions, and the social services.

In the first post-war elections, in May, 1946, the Labor party received the second largest vote, winning 29 parliamentary seats, compared with 32 for the Catholic People's party, which became the country's leading party. Professor Schermerhorn resigned as Premier and was succeeded by a liberal Catholic.

The Catholics asked Labor to form a coalition cabinet with them. Labor replied that it would join only if its conciliatory Indonesian policy were accepted and applied by persons acceptable to it. After several weeks of negotiations, Labor entered a cabinet containing 5 Catholics, 5 Laborites, and 3 non-political specialists. Schermerhorn was appointed the Commissioner General of the Netherland Indies.

In various coalition cabinets that followed, representatives of the Labor party succeeded in effecting important reforms. During 1947 and 1948, the future status of Indonesia led to intense discussion within the party. A comprehensive outline of the party's conception of society, in which planning for freedom was the central theme, was set forth in a report entitled "The Road to Freedom" at a special planing conference held by the party in 1951.

Controversy Between Archbishop of Utrecht and the Labor Party (1954). In May, 1954, a controversy between the Catholic Church and the Labor party again broke out. In May, 1954, the Archbishop of Utrecht issued a statement declaring that "it is not permissable for a Catholic to be a member of Socialist associations such

---

to the ministry of public works from 1931 to 1945; as president of the International Society of Photogrammetry from 1938 to 1948 and as President of the Anti-Fascist League from 1938 to 1940.

During World War II, the Germans held him as hostage in 1942 and 1943. During the next two years he was one of the Netherlands' Resistance leaders.

At the conclusion of the war, Dr. Schermerhorn was chosen Prime Minister of Holland, remaining in that position until the following year. In 1948 he became a member of the States Assembly and was a prominent member of that body for the next fifteen years.

as the Netherlands Federation of Trade Unions, or to visit socialist gatherings regularly, to read the socialist press regularly, or to listen to V. A. R. A. [Socialist radio networks] regularly."

Since the interdict against Catholics' joining the Socialist party had been removed at the end of World War II, this letter, reviving an old issue, caused heated discussion among Catholics and non-Catholics alike.

Labor Premier Drees attacked the Archbishop for his letter. The Catholic Workers' Group of the Labor party, in February, 1955, decided at the party congress to accept the party's tasks and responsibilities, and, within a few years, the Church reversed its position and announced that Catholics were free to use their own judgment in their socialist and trade union activities.

In the fifties and early sixties, the number of seats held by Labor party in Parliament ranged from 30 to 48 out of a possible 150—34 in 1956, 48 in 1959, and 43 in 1963; the Pacifist Socialist party elected 4 in 1963 and in 1967, they retained their representation of 4.

In 1965, the party entered a coalition government, which, however, was defeated on October 14, 1966, by a vote of Parliament on the ground that the country's next budget was not sufficiently geared to fight the inflation and that Socialists were exerting too great an influence on the government. Socialists maintained that in preparing the budget community institutions should be adequately financed. The party, the second largest in the nation, was not in the next two governments.

In the 1967 elections, some of the main planks in the Labor party's platform were the doubling of inheritance taxes and the doubling of aid to developing countries, nationalization of insurance companies, increased participation in gas and oil fuels in the North Sea, and the expulsion of Portugal from N. A. T. O.

Throughout this decade the Socialist party endeavored to reorganize the Dutch political parties which, they declared, were formed too closely along religious (denominational) lines. During these decades the Labor party supported N. A. T. O. and increased European integration. The Socialist Pacifist party opposed the government's support of N. A. T. O.

GERMANY

Social Democrats Reorganize (1945). After the collapse of nazism, members of the party who had worked underground came into the open; in May, 1945, political activity was resumed throughout the country under the leadership of Kurt Schumacher.[15] Many socialists were appointed by the occupying powers to important political offices.

The first Central Party Conference after the war was held in October, 1945, in Hanover.[16] At the 1946 Social Democratic party Congress in Hanover, Kurt Schumacher, socialist writer and former legislator, who had spent much of the war as a prisoner in a concentration camp, was elected party Chairman, retaining that position until his death in 1952.

Social Democrats as Chief Opposition. During the two decades following the war, the Social Democrats served as the chief opposition party in Germany. In the field of international relations they opposed the remilitarization of Western Germany; urged the establishment of a Central European zone that would exclude both conventional and nuclear armaments; and advocated the establishment of diplomatic and trade relations with Poland, Czechoslovakia, and the East European states. In domestic relations, they fought for land reforms, increased social services, the socialization of coal and steel, and a decentralized structure for public enterprise.

In the belief that its membership base should be broadened, its Executive Committee in the late fifties began the overhauling of the party organization, "with a view of drawing into work all sections of the population." The parliamentary election results indicated the gradually increasing popularity of the Social Democrats among the German people during the decade 1956–65, though it still remained a

15 Kurt Schumacher (1895–1952) was born in Kulm, West Prussia, October 13, 1895, son of a merchant, and was educated in several German universities. In World War I, he lost his right arm. After the war he served as socialist editor, state legislator, and member of the Reichstag (1930–33).

When the nazis came to power, he was arrested and spent the majority of the next eleven years in a concentration camp. Following the defeat of Hitler, he became active in reorganizing the Social Democratic party, and in 1946 presided over the first open meeting of the Socialists since 1933. In May, 1946, he was elected Chairman of the party in the three western zones.

During the next six years, as its leader, he sought to broaden the base of the party by appealing to the middle class and the religious, while refusing to compromise with the communists. A long illness, culminating in 1948 with the amputation of his left leg, further weakened his health and in those years he became increasingly bitter toward his political opponents. In 1949 he was elected Leader of the Opposition in the *Bundestag*. He died on August 20, 1952.

16 In 1946, the Social Democratic party in the Soviet-occupied zone of Germany was forced to join with the Communist party in the Socialist Unity party (S.E.D.). Those members who refused to submit were forced to go underground and were persecuted. In Berlin, thanks to the Four-Power Statute, it was possible to have a free vote. The merger with the communists was rejected by a large majority.

minority party at the end of this period. The results of the elections were as follows:

Year	*No. of members of the* Bundestag	*Proportion of the Popular Vote*
1949	131	28.2
1953	151	29.2
1957	169	31.8
1961	190	36.2
1965	202	39.3

In the meanwhile the Social Democrats showed much strength in municipal and provincial elections, particularly in West Berlin, where Mayor Ernest Reuter and later Mayor Willy Brandt were popular figures during the fifties and sixties.[17]

Social Democrats in Coalition Government (1966–). In 1966, Ludwig Erhard, Christian Democrat, under great political pressure, resigned his Chancellorship. In the state elections, the Free Democratic party, a member of Erhard's cabinet, had lost heavily to the National Democratic party, an ultra-conservative party, which many feared might develop into a neo-nazi party. At the same time the Social Democrats made distinct electoral gains.

This situation, among others, led many to demand the formation of another and more stable coalition government than the Christian Democrats and Free Democrats could provide. An increasing demand arose for a "grand coalition" participated in by the Christian Democratic Union, the Christian Social Union of Bavaria, and the

[17] Willy Brandt (1913–), Mayor of West Berlin, was born in Lübeck, December 18, 1913, as Herbert Frahm. Educated at the Lübeck Gymnasium, he was active in the Social Democratic youth movement and was a contributor to a local socialist newspaper. After Hitler's ascension to power, Brandt went to Norway to escape arrest. In that country, he changed his name to Willy Brandt, studied at the University of Oslo, and became a successful journalist, writing from Spain for a Swedish newspaper.

After the invasion of Norway by the Germans, Brandt proceeded to Sweden and, having been granted Norwegian citizenship, combined journalism with support of the Norwegian and German Resistance movements.

In 1945, Brandt returned to Germany as a Scandinavian newspaper correspondent and in 1946 was appointed press attaché with the Norwegian Military Mission in Berlin. Influenced by Ernest Reuter, popular Socialist Mayor of West Berlin and others, he regained in 1948 his German nationality. The next year he was elected to the *Bundestag* and was re-elected in 1952 and 1957. On October 3, 1957, he became the Mayor of West Berlin; in 1960 he was elected chairman of the Social Democratic party. In 1961 and 1965 he was chosen the party's candidate for the chancellorship.

Social Democrats—a coalition which would be backed in the *Bundestag* by 447 members out of a total of 496, 9 out of 10 in the Chamber. The Social Democratic party had not served in a coalition government since 1930. It had been a bitter opponent of the successive coalition governments. On account of these past inter-party relations, the "grand coalition" idea seemed to many to be unrealistic.

However, when Kurt Kiesinger of the Christian Social Union party asked the Social Democrats, through Willy Brandt, Social Democratic leader, to join the coalition government, the offer was accepted—though with numerous party dissenters partly because Kiesinger had, for a short time, been a member of the Nazi party. On December 1, the new government was formed with Kiesinger as Chancellor, Brandt as Vice-Chancellor and Foreign Minister, with the Social Democrats occupying 9 out of 19 seats in the cabinet.

AUSTRIA

Renner President after World War (1945). On April 29, 1945, when the defeat of Germany was imminent, provisional government was set up in Vienna under the leadership of Karl Renner. At the ensuing elections for the National and Provincial assemblies on November 25, 1945, the Social Democrats sent 76 representatives to the national legislature; the Catholic People's party, 84; and the Communists, 5.

The next month Dr. Renner was elected President; Leopold Figl, a member of the Catholic party, Chancellor; and Karl Gruber, a Social Democrat, Vice-Chancellor.

About that time the party changed its name from the Social Democratic to Austrian Socialist party. It rejected the proposal to merge with the Communist party and thus made possible the revival of the republic as an independent state; the coalition government then formed included the Austrian People's party, the Socialists, and the Communists.

At the initiation of the Socialists, the Austrian Parliament passed a law in 1946 that called for the nationalization of oil, shipping, electric power, metallurgy, and banking. The Soviet military authorities arrested several Austrians for attempting to carry out the nationalization decree, the Russians declaring that the property had been forceably Germanized and belonged to the Soviets as occupying forces. This issue led to much controversy and was only resolved with the formal re-establishment of the Austrian Republic in May, 1955, when

Austria agreed to buy back from the Administrator of Soviet Property in Austria many of the confiscated German assets.

Socialists in Coalition Governments (1947–1966). In November, 1947, the Communist minister resigned from the government in protest against a financial reform measure. Following his resignation, the coalition government consisted of Socialists and members of the Austrian People's party.

This coalition lasted, with but few interruptions, for the next twenty years, with the Socialists usually supplying the presidents of the Republic (elected by popular vote) and the Vice-Chancellor, and the People's Party supplying the Chancellor.

During the post-World War period, the Socialists gradually gave up certain extreme positions held in their earlier days. In May, 1958, they adopted a program which advanced them still further along the revisionist path. They discarded their old anti-religious attitude and stressed increasingly the duties as well as the rights of the individual.

During the years in the coalition government, frequent differences arose between the People's party and the Social Democratic party over social and labor legislation, the expansion of the public sector of the economy, the return to Austria of members of the House of Hapsburg —which the Socialists opposed—the abolition of the army, the relations of Austria to the E. E. C. and control by the two parties of the television and radio, among other issues.

The coalition government came to a temporary end in 1966, following the elections in which the Social Democrats lost 2 out of 76 of their parliamentary seats and decided that their future and that of the country would be better served if they changed their role—at that time—from a government party to that of the government's chief opposition.

SWITZERLAND

After increasing their parliamentary representation in 1943, the Social Democrats remained a part of the government until 1953, when the Social Democratic Party left the government and returned to the opposition in protest against the government's "reactionary" policies. During these years, the Social Democrats held to the program that had first been adopted at the 1943 party conference. Known as the New Switzerland, the program urged the extension of social security, a planned economy, and the transfer to public ownership of certain privately owned monopolies in key economic areas.

Soon after 1953 the Social Democrats returned to the government and, during the early sixties, were represented by 2 out of 7 members on the Federal Council. In 1963 one of their leaders, Willy Spühler, served as the Council's President. That same year the Social Democrats, in parliamentary elections, received the largest number of votes —26.7 per cent—compared with 23 per cent for the Radical Democrats, and won, as in the previous elections, 53 seats in the National Council (the Radical Democrats came in second with 51). Socialists during the sixties opposed Switzerland's participation in the atomic energy race, urged a progressive tax program, and advocated the employment of the popular initiative in federal legislation. In December, 1967, Dr. Spühler was again elected President for a year and continued in his post as Foreign Minister.

DENMARK

The Post-War Situation. A government under V. Buhl, which included members from a number of political parties and the Resistance was appointed on May 5, 1945, two days before the Germans surrendered. In an election held October 30, the Social Democrats lost 18 seats. The Buhl government resigned and the Liberals formed a minority government. In the late fall of 1946, following another election in which Socialists scored gains and the Liberals lost, the Liberal leader, Knud Kristensen, resigned and Social Democrat Hans Hedtoft [18] formed a new government.

Immediately after World War II, the government's problems were chiefly economic. Investment was necessary to bring production back to pre-war levels, and occupation costs had to be liquidated. The elections in 1950 did not decisively alter the strength of the parties, but soon thereafter Hedtoft resigned and was succeeded by a coalition of Liberals and Conservatives under Erik Eriksen.

In 1953, a new Constitution introducing a single-chamber system was passed and the Eriksen government gave way to the second Hed-

18 Hans Christian Hedtoft (1903–55), Danish Socialist statesman, was born in Aarhus, Jutland, April 21, 1903. He entered the trade of lithography. He began his socialist activities as a youth in the National Social Democratic Youth organization and was chosen President in 1928. As Secretary of the Social Democratic party, he was elected to the *Folketing* in 1935, remaining in that body until the Germans' invasion in 1940. He took an active part in the Resistance movement and returned as Minister of Labor and Social Affairs in 1945. He was Prime Minister from 1947 to 1950 and again from 1953. An advocate of a strong national defense and Scandinavian unity, he promoted the Nordic Council and urged Denmark's admission to N.A.T.O. He died January 29, 1955.

toft government. In 1955 Hedtoft died and was succeeded by H. C. Hansen.[19] Under Hansen's premiership, the old age pension system was further strengthened, trade with Russia was expanded, taxes were reduced, and price supports for agriculture were enacted. Other measures were passed with a view to guaranteeing full employment without inflation.

On February 19, 1960, in the midst of a period of prosperity and practically full employment, Prime Minister Hansen died. Two days later he was succeeded as Prime Minister and Chairman of the Social Democratic party by Viggo Kampmann, the Minister of Finance.

In the general election on November 15, 1960, the Social Democrats gained 6 seats (from 70 to 76), followed by the formation of a new coalition consisting of Social Democrats and Radicals; Viggo Kampmann retained his post as Prime Minister.

During the next few years Denmark reduced the voting age from 23 to 21 (1961), sought entrance to the Common Market on condition that Great Britain would be admitted, approved the establishment of a Danish–West German command, and ratified the convention on Nordic co-operation in economic, social, and cultural spheres. The government, however, was defeated in its legislative attempts to ensure the retention of Danish lands in Danish hands and to promote better city and recreational planning.

In the 1964 elections, the Social Democrats elected 76 representatives, the same as in 1960, followed by the formation under Prime Minister Krag[20] of an all-Social Democratic minority government.

In 1965 an exchange of heads of state of Russia and Denmark was arranged with a view toward increasing trade between the two countries.

In November, 1966, Prime Minister Krag called for a new election.

[19] H. C. Hansen (1906–1960), Socialist Premier, was born in Aarhus, February 19, 1906. In 1929 he became the Secretary of the Social Democratic party's youth movement and, in 1933, Chairman of the organization.

He was elected to the lower house of Parliament in 1936. During the Second World War, he was his party's Secretary and during the German occupation the publisher of an underground newspaper. From the end of the war until 1950 he was Minister of Finance and in that post established policies that led to a rapid economic recovery. In 1953 he became Minister of Foreign Affairs and retained that post when he was appointed Prime Minister in 1955. He died February 19, 1960.

[20] Jens Otto Krag, elected Prime Minister of Denmark in 1962, was born in Randers, September 15, 1914. He attended the University of Copenhagen. From 1947 he was in the public service as Minister of Commerce and Shipping (1947–50); Counsellor of the Danish embassy in Washington (1950–52); Minister of Economy and Labor (1953–57), and Minister of Foreign Economic Affairs (1957–58), and of foreign affairs (1958–62), when he was elected Prime Minister.

One of the issues was the advocacy by the Social Democrats of pay-as-you-go taxation. The election resulted in the decrease of 7 Social Democratic seats (from 76 to 69) out of a total of 179, but an increase of 10 members of parliament (from 10 to 20) representing the People's Socialist party, a socialist party of the left. With this net increase for the two socialist parties of three seats—to about half the seats—Prime Minister Krag again formed, and led, a new government. In the January, 1968, elections Socialists, owing to the protest against rising prices and taxes, lost 6 seats; Krag resigned his premiership; and a non-Socialist coalition was formed.

SWEDEN

The Post-War Period. After World War II, the Social Democrats dissolved the coalition and governed alone. The first post-War elections in 1948 confirmed that they were the strongest party. After unsuccessful attempts following the 1948 election to form a coalition with the Farmers' party, they decided to continue an all-Socialist government.

General European conditions and the Second World War had a disastrous effect on the Swedish economy. To aid in the revival of Europe, Sweden adopted a generous foreign credit policy. When the expected revival did not come, a serious economic crisis ensued in Sweden. Large cuts had to be made in imports and expenditures had to be reduced, although these reductions never affected social welfare or defense projects.

In 1951, Tage Erlander, Prime Minister after the death of Hansson, formed another coalition with the Farmers' party.[21] From then until 1953, the economic position gradually improved. Food prices, however, were high, and the country apparently blamed both parties of the coalition for this development. In the elections of 1952, the Social Democrats returned 110 representatives, a loss of 2; the Farmers, 26, a

[21] Tage Erlander, Prime Minister of Sweden, was born in Ransater, on June 13, 1901. He was educated at the University of Lund, from which institution he received his master's degree in 1928. Erlander began his career as a journalist, but soon entered politics, becoming successively a member of the Lund City Council (1931-38), of the Second Chamber of the Swedish *Riksdag* (1933-41), and of the First Chamber of Parliament, which he had entered in 1945.

While serving as a member of Parliament, Erlander was appointed (1938) Secretary of the Ministry of Social Affairs, which position he held for six years. In 1946, he became Sweden's Prime Minister, and, in the same year, the Chairman of the Social Democratic party, positions he retained almost continuously until present writing. In the thirties he served for many years as co-chairman of the encyclopedia, the *Svensk Uppslagsbok.*

loss of 6. The coalition with the Farmers after the election continued.

During the next fifteen years the Social Democratic party continued to dominate coalition and all-socialist governments; its parliamentary representations under the premiership of Erlander, changing from 110 in 1952 to 106 in 1956, to 114 in 1960, and to 113 in 1964. The Erlander government during this period enacted legislation providing for a three weeks' vacation for all workers and for an old age pension system which provided for a pension equal to approximately two-thirds of a person's average income in the most favorable 15 years of his working life.

Sweden in those years also entered the European Free Trade Association (E. F. T. A.) and played an active part in the Organization for Economic Cooperation (O. E. C.), though deciding against joining N. A. T. O. The Swedish government co-operated with Norway and Denmark in the research, power, and transportation fields, social security, trade, industrial projects, and cultural exchanges. In 1960 the Social Democratic party issued a comprehensive program for a new society in which equal opportunity would be the heritage of all.

In the early sixties, Sweden suffered a slight depression, but by 1964 it had been overcome and unemployment was just over 0.5 per cent of the total labor force. Wages had increased in the year ending May, 1964, by 8 per cent. Under the Social Democratic government, the country enjoyed marked prosperity, though the severe housing shortage continued.

In the parliamentary elections of September 20, 1964, the electorate returned the Social Democratic party to power after 32 years of unbroken rule, but without an absolute majority, electing 113 members to Parliament, a loss of 1, out of a total of 233. The Liberals came second with 43 representatives, and the Communists elected 8 parliamentary members, an increase from 3. Tage Erlander, Social Democratic Prime Minister, organized a new government. In the municipal elections in 1966, the Social Democrats again received the largest number of seats, although their vote decreased from 49 per cent to 42 per cent of the total.

NORWAY

Gerhardsen and Torp, Laborites, Head Post-War Governments (1945). In May, 1945, the Nygaardsvold government returned to Norway, and, in October, a general election was held, followed by municipal elections in December. The party's victory in both elections was striking; for the first time it had won an absolute majority in Parliament.

Another Labor government was formed following the elections, this time headed by the former General Secretary of the party, Einar Gerhardsen,[22] who had returned from a German concentration camp and had been elected Chairman of the party.

In 1949, the party conventions adopted a fundamental statement, *Principles and Programs,* based upon the experiences gained during the war and occupation. In 1951, Oscar Torp, for many years the party's Chairman, took over as Prime Minister, to be followed in 1953 by the former Prime Minister, Einar Gerhardsen. The party that year expressed their support of the U. N. and N. A. T. O.

In 1956, the government's plan for health insurance, which entitled all to free medical attention, medicine, and hospitalization, became operative. The next year, 1957, in the national elections, the party more than sustained its strength, electing 78 representatives out of 150, 1 more than in 1953. The popular vote registered 48.4 per cent, 17 per cent more than four years before.

In the general elections of September 11, 1961, the party, for the first time since 1946, failed to win more than half the seats in Parliament, electing only 74 out of 150, a loss of 4. The Communists lost their 1 seat.

A Left-Wing Party Formed (1961). The most interesting thing about this election was the success of the new left-wing Socialist party, which gained 2 seats and was largely responsible for the decrease in the Labor party's parliamentary strength. Formed in April, 1961, by a number of dissident Labor party members, the new party's program

[22] Einar Henry Gerhardsen, Prime Minister of Norway, was born in Oslo, on May 10, 1897. He received his education in the public schools, at a technical school, and at a socialist day school.

Employed from the ages of seventeen to twenty-five as a road laborer, Gerhardsen later served as a secretary of several workingmen's organizations, and spent 1929–30 on a scholarship studying the labor movements of Germany and Austria.

On returning to Norway, he was elected in 1932 to his first political office—to membership in Oslo's City Council. Four years later he was chosen Secretary of the Norwegian Labor party, and, in 1940, deputy Mayor of Oslo.

Following the German occupation of Norway, Gerhardsen was arrested by the invaders and held in prison from 1941 to 1945. With the coming of peace he was elected Prime Minister, at first presiding over a coalition cabinet; later over a Labor party cabinet. He remained head of the government until 1965. In the meanwhile, he assumed the office of Chairman of the Labor party and for some time presided over the Storting.

was based on a radical socialist domestic program and a foreign and defense policy involving withdrawal from N. A. T. O. There was general agreement that the voting figures showed no decisive trend, and Gerhardsen again continued as Prime Minister.

In 1963, the Labor party was severely criticized because of a fatal accident in the state-owned King's Bay Coal Company. When the question arose as to whether Parliament should give the government a vote of no confidence, the 2 parliamentary representatives of the left-wing Socialist party voted against the government, thus depriving it of its necessary majority. Thus the short-lived coalition government retired, and a new Labor government under the premiership of Gerhardsen was appointed.

In the following months, the government introduced a bill to extend annual paid vacations for workers from three to four weeks and recommended an inquiry about the question of reducing the work week. The following year, the *Storting* gave unanimous approval to a bill establishing a stand-by force of 1,250 men for use by the U. N.

Defeat of Labor Government (1965). The year 1965 witnessed the end of the Labor party rule which had held office continuously since 1945 except for a period of four weeks in 1963, and, before World War II, from 1935.

In the September 12/13, 1965, election, Labor lost 6 seats; its representation in the *Storting* was reduced to 68 out of 150. While remaining the largest single party, Labor found itself outnumbered by the combined vote of the four non-Socialist parties (Conservative, Center, Christian People's, and Liberal).

On October 11, 1965, Prime Minister Gerhardsen submitted his government's resignation and Per Borten, leader of the Center party, became his successor.

The adverse results of the election for Labor were ascribed to a number of things: partly to the feeling that, after 30 years of Labor rule, the complexion of the government "called for a change"; partly to the accusations concerning scandals in the Ministry of Industry; partly to the joint lists of candidates of some of the "bourgeois" parties; and partly to the competition of the newly formed Socialist People's party—a factor that the party's secretary, Haaken Lee, declared to have been the most important.

Despite these adverse factors, the results, however, were surprising to many. Norway was enjoying practically full employment. Production, consumption, and investment were high. The government had exerted great pressure against inflationary trends. Under Labor's rule living standards had significantly improved. These things, Labor felt, should have swept the party back into power.

This feeling was strengthened, in the months following the election, by the failure of the new government to attempt to rescind important legislation passed under the Labor government. What change, it was asked, did the anti-Labor parties think the times demanded?

FINLAND

Much controversy over Finland's relations with Russia took place within the Social Democratic party during the early forties. As a result, the Social Democratic vote shrank and, in March, 1945, in the national elections, the party returned to Parliament only 52 deputies, a loss of 28. Despite this loss, however, the Social Democrats constituted the country's largest party.

On March 24, 1946, on the resignation of Field Marshal Mannerheim from the presidency and the election of Premier Passikivi to the presidential post, M. Pekkala, Socialist, became Premier and presided over a coalition cabinet which was faced with such extremely difficult problems as the return of the evacuated population, reparations to Russia, reconstruction, and inflation.

In 1948 the Social Democrats formed a minority government under K. A. Fagerholm, comprising Social Democrats and some non-party men. In that year Communists were ousted from the government amid suspicion that they were planning to seize power.

The next eleven years (1948–1958) were marked by the inclusion of Social Democrats in coalition governments under the premiership of Social Democrat August Fagerholm and others; by splits in the party and in the trade unions; by the election of 53 Social Democratic representatives in the 1951 elections and 54 deputies in 1954; by conflicts with the Agrarian party on farmers' prices, wages, hours of labor, and social insurance; and by bitter opposition by the Soviet Union to the Social Democratic leadership, particularly to Väïno Tanner, labeled by Communists "an agent of American imperialism."

In 1958 Social Democratic Prime Minister Fagerholm resigned, partly as a result of Soviet opposition and veiled threats of the loss of Soviet trade. From his resignation until 1966, no Social Democrat was asked to serve as a member of a coalition cabinet.

In 1966, however, in the election of March 21, the Social Democrats added 17 parliamentary seats to the 38 they then held for a total of 55, with the left-wing socialists—a Social Democratic splinter group—capturing 6 seats, a gain of 2. The Communist party won 42 seats, a loss of 5. These three parties thus emerged from the election with 103 out of 201 representatives. Raphael Passio, Social Democratic leader, was thereupon called to form a government; he asked the participation in the ministry of the Social Democratic parties, the Communist party, and the Agrarian center party. A short time before the government was formed Väïno Tanner, one of the outstanding men in the party, former party leader and Finnish Premier and Minister of Finance, an uncompromising opponent of communism, died at the age of 81.

ITALY

The Socialists had been part of the Committee for National Liberation that had selected Ivanoe Bonomi as Premier in 1944. But in the fall of 1944 the Socialist party withdrew from the Bonomi cabinet, although it was later represented in the 1945 and 1946 Parri and De Gasperi governments. Divergencies of opinion over its future program led to vigorous debate at the meeting of the party council held in Rome on July 30, 1945. These differences and the fact that one section of the party became linked with the communists, led to a breakaway of the more moderate wing of the party which constituted itself the Social Democratic party. The Social Democrats, soon after its organization, became a member of the Socialist International. In the June, 1946, elections the Socialist party elected 115 deputies.

Split in Socialist Movement Following World War. For more than twenty years following the war, the socialist movement, split into a number of political parties, played an important part in the political and social life of Italy.

The largest of the socialist organizations during these years was the Socialist party led by Pietro Nenni. The Socialist party was a left-wing socialist organization which, in the first decade after the war, contended that the interests of the working class could best be served by the socialists supporting joint socialist-communist lists of candidates and, if successful, organizing united front local, provincial and national governments.

Nenni the leader of the party, was the recipient in 1952 of the Stalin Peace Prize. On his return from Moscow after receiving the prize, he was an exponent of much of the foreign policy of the Soviet government, and expressed strong opposition to Italy's joining N. A. T. O.

He was extremely critical, however, of Russia's action in 1956 in crushing the revolutionary movement in Hungary and from that year tended increasingly to restrict the Socialist party's political co-operation with Italian communists.

Socialists Join Coalition Government (1963). In the first eighteen years after the war, the Socialist party refused to join any center-left coalition cabinet. In 1963, however, the party voted to join the Aldo Moro left-of-center cabinet, with Nenni as Vice Premier.

A minority of the party, however, objected to this action, left the party, and formed a new party, known as the Party of Proletarian Unity. In that year's election (1963), the Socialist party won 62 parliamentary seats out of a total of 630, compared with 260 for the Christian Democrats, 166 for the Communists, 32 for the Democratic Socialists, and 25 for the party of Proletarian Unity.

The Democratic Socialist Party. The second largest socialist party during the post-World War II days was the Democratic Socialist party. This party had its origin in the withdrawal from the Socialist party of a minority group of delegates who opposed the party's "Unity of Action" pact with the Communist party.

Soon after leaving the Italian Socialist party, the group formed, under the leadership of Giuseppi Saragat, another political party at first called the Socialist Party of Italian Workers. At its organization meeting the Saragat party declared its independence from the Communists and its firm adherence to the principles of Western political democracy.

Four years later, in 1951, it merged with two other small socialist groups led by Ignazio Silone and Giuseppe Romita, respectively, which had also split with the Socialist party because of the close electoral connections with the Communists. The merged organization was named the Democratic Socialist party.

Although frequently expressing dissatisfaction with the lack of speed with which the moderate reforms were put into effect, members of this group participated in 1947 to 1951, before the merger, in all the De Gasperi center-left cabinets, and after unity was delivered, in the Moro, Scelba, Segni, and Fanfani governments. In these governments Saragat frequently served as Vice Premier and was elevated to the Presidency on December 28, 1964, for a seven-year term—the election marking the first time that a socialist had been elected as President of the Italian Republic. In 1966 the Democratic Socialist party was represented in the Chamber of Deputies by 32 members.

Merger of Socialist Parties (1966). For many years the Democratic Socialists had sought to bring about a merger with the larger Socialist party on a basis of democratic control of the united party, a policy of co-operation with the democratic countries of the West, and the rejection of all forms of popular front activity with the Communists.

A formula for unity was finally agreed to as the gap between the Italian Socialists and Communists widened and as the Socialist party shifted from being an opposition party to being a member in a coalition ministry in December, 1963. Finally, on October 30, 1966, at an enthusiastic congress in Rome, the Socialist parties merged into one organization, with Pietro Nenni—a unanimous choice—as President of the new party. The new party became the Italian member of the Socialist International.

In his address at the Foundation Congress, President Nenni declared that there remained in Italy the problems of rationalization and modernization of industry and of the development of the depressed areas of the South and of agriculture. Reforms in taxation, in the machinery of government, in the educational and medical services, in regional government, and in family law were all greatly needed.

GREECE

From 1900 to 1918, there existed in Greece several socialist groups which had received their socialist education largely from German socialist literature translated into Greek. In 1918, these socialist groups united to form the Socialist Labor party of Greece.

At the Second Congress held by the S. L. P. in 1920, the majority of the delegates voted to join the Third International. This decision led a large minority group, under the leadership of A. Sideris, to break away from the party and to set up the new Greek Socialist party, while the majority adopted the name of the Greek Communist party.

Following the split, the Socialists took an active part in the trade union movement, D. Stratis, a prominent member of the party, being elected General Secretary of the Greek Trade Union Confederation.

During World War II, when Greece was occupied by German, Italian and Bulgarian troops, the National Liberation Front was formed. Socialists joined the Front from its inception and held important positions in it. In the government set up by the Resistance movement in March, 1944, Professor Svolos, Socialist, served as President.

Socialists co-operated with the communists in the Liberation Front which aimed to regain the freedom of Greece. After Greece's liberation had been achieved however, they broke ties with the communists and the latter's tactics of violent revolt. In the 1950 election the party won 8 seats in Parliament, but was defeated in 1952.

The party in the early fifties decided to merge with the Democratic Party of the Working People. With a view of keeping their influence alive and vital in the merged party, a number of socialists met in Athens in 1953 and formed the Socialist League as a socialist educational and propaganda organization. The League in 1955 was admitted as an observer member of the Socialist International.

ICELAND

The Social Democratic party of Iceland was founded in 1916 and has been represented in the country's Parliament since 1921. The first chairman of the party, Jón Baldvinsson, died in 1938 and was succeeded as party chairman by Stefán Jón Stefansson.

Until 1940, the party was a member, with the trade unions, of a National Federation, which was the supreme Executive of both the party and the unions. In 1940, however, during the Second World War, the trade unions and the party separated.

Ten years before this separation, a group had broken from the party and formed the Communist party of Iceland. In 1938 the Social Democratic party was again split—this time over the question of collaboration with the Communists. The party had been in power, together with the Progressive party, at a difficult period and was constantly engaged in conflicts with conservatives on the right and communists on the left. Unsuccessful in the 1937 elections, it had been induced in 1938 to accept the communists' invitation to form a "popular front."

The party's Vice-President and numerous trade union leaders resigned and formed, together with the communists, a Socialist United People's party which was soon captured by the communists. The new party was the only government opposition during the war years 1939–41 when a national coalition government composed of representatives of the Independence party (Conservatives), Progressives, and Social Democrats, constituted the government.

In the next elections (1942) the United People's party received more votes than the Social Democrats and won 10 of the 52 seats in Parliament. Four years later, however, following the conclusion of World War II, the Social Democrats polled 40 per cent more votes and sent 9 of their representatives to Parliament as opposed to 10 for the United People's party (called by some the Labor Alliance). In 1953 each polled about the same percentage of the total vote—16 per cent.

Six years later, in 1959, the Social Democrats were included again in a coalition government with the Independence party. The Social Democrats in the mid-sixties had 5 representatives in Parliament out of a total of 40—the Independence party, 16—while the President of Parliament, the Minister of Foreign Affairs and the Minister of Education and Commerce in the coalition cabinet were party members. The party continued its support of N. A. T. O.

CHAPTER 46

Post-World War II Socialist Developments in Non-European Areas

Developments in North America

UNITED STATES

In 1948, the Socialist Party chose Norman Thomas as its nominee for the sixth and last time, with Tucker Smith, head of the Department of Economics, Olivet College, Michigan, and former labor organizer and educator, as his running mate. In the 1948 campaign, the A. F. of L. and the C. I. O. conducted an extremely active campaign for President Harry Truman, "the underdog" in the campaign; the left wing communist elements in the labor movement supported former Vice-President Henry Wallace on the Progressive ticket. The democratic socialists, backing Thomas, cast 139,414 votes, an increase of 75 per cent over 1944, but still a small number.

Following the 1948 campaign, Norman Thomas, increasingly disappointed by the number of socialist presidential votes, in a pamphlet written for circulation among party members, called upon the Socialist party to stop spending its "energy on political campaigns which gave us only a handful of votes." He urged instead that socialists work with liberals and unionists in the primaries and elections of various political parties, while constantly stressing socialist education.

"We do not advance the cause of socialism [he declared] when, by default, or sheer lack of resources, we become less and less able to put Socialist tickets in the field. In 1948 . . . faced with a tangle of state election laws increasingly intended to monopolize the ballot for the two Old Parties, we succeeded by Herculean efforts in putting our national ticket on the ballot in only 30 states which did not include California and Ohio.

"That isn't all the story. Almost without exception, the more dynamic younger people who at heart are Socialists are refusing to join us or, with important exceptions, to stay in the Socialist party. They want to be free to act in the political field with the great mass of liberals and labor . . .

"A party which does not see the magnificent job that can and must be done in constructive thinking and action for socialism outside of the nomination of candidates has lost what it takes to make socialism victorious. If we cannot convince the kind of people who are in farm organizations, labor unions, cooperatives, and the Americans for Democratic Action, of the necessity for democratic socialism, we shall never convince the American community as a whole."

A majority of the National Executive Committee of the Socialist party backed Thomas. But when the issue of nominating a presidential ticket came before the Detroit convention in June, 1950, the convention voted 64 to 42 for a resolution favoring continuation of straight Socialist electoral action on as broad a scale as possible.

Thomas predicted that "even if we should make an heroic effort and place a national ticket in the field in 1952, without a new miracle, the campaign would go almost unnoticed."

A new miracle did not occur. Darlington Hoopes and Samuel H. Friedman, long in the field of public relations, nominees for President and Vice President, respectively, polled but 20,203 votes and, in 1956, when they ran again, only 2,004 votes were counted for them.[1]

[1] Many things combined to prevent the Socialist party from attracting large numbers of votes for its ticket, despite its considerable impact on the social and economic life of America. Mr. Thomas above has already referred to some. Among them are the unlimited resources—material and human—of a comparatively new country, with pressures from organized labor, and the rapid development in technology, etc., resulting in a comparatively high standard of living for millions of workers; the fluidity of labor and the lack of working class consciousness; the weakness until fairly recently of the labor movement; the individualist philosophy of many trade union leaders, and the early antagonism between A. F. of L. and DeLeonites and I. W. W.'s; the recent pressures on trade unionists to engage in intensive political activity for "friends of labor" in the major parties; in New York State the rise of the Liberal party; the character of the electoral system under which a shift of a few votes in a given state might determine how an entire block of presidential electors would vote and in turn determine the results of the presidential election; and the two party system tradition in the U.S.A.

Other reasons for the failure of the party to achieve greater electoral success were (1) the splits resulting largely from developments originating abroad—the two world wars, the rise of syndicalism, communism, fascism, etc. (2) the personal popularity among the workers of such major party leaders as Theodore and Franklin D. Roosevelt, President Wilson and others (3) the taking over by the major parties of reforms first initiated by the socialists (4) the misunderstanding and misrepresentation

In 1957, when the party indicated that it would abandon the electoral field, the Social Democratic Federation merged with it, though many of its members remained outside of the party and formed the Democratic Socialist Federation. Soon after the Independent Socialist League, a group of ex-Trotskyites, led by Max Schactman, was dissolved and a number of its members became members of the S. P.

At present writing the party's role is educational and propagandist, rather than electoral. It is directing much attention to the ending of the war in Vietnam. It is taking an active part in the "war against poverty" which one of its prominent members, Michael Harrington, for some time editor of the party's organ, *The New America,* did much to initiate through his widely read book, *The Other America.* It is urging the adoption of the "A. Philip Randolph's Freedom Budget" of $100 billion in public funds to meet the needs of the poor. It is likewise advocating equality of racial opportunity, a massive housing program and economic and social planning in the cities, states, and nation.

Norman Thomas is continuing as Honorary Chairman of the party and Darlington Hoopes as Chairman; Dr. Ernst Papanek, psychologist and Professor of Education, Queens College, and Samuel H. Friedman, among others, are representing the party in the Socialist International.

The Socialist Labor party is still carrying on in the mid-sixties, as are the Socialist Workers Party, a left-wing (Trotskyite) organization, and the Communist party. The one party in the U. S. A. affiliated with the Socialist International is the Socialist party.

The New Left. During the sixties in the United States, many minority, civil liberties, peace and student groups who participated actively in behalf of racial equality, the ending of the Vietnam war, and in the war against poverty characterized themselves as members of the New Left.

Socialists gave support to specific antidiscrimination, antiwar, and other social demonstrations.

---

of the aims and ideals of socialism (5) the confusion as to whether the party should appeal for votes primarily on the basis of its demand for a socialist society or for immediate specified social reforms (6) the ever greater cost, with the new means of communication, of conducting an effective political campaign. (See Fleischman, *Norman Thomas—A Biography,* ch. XVIII, Harry W. Laidler, *Socialism in the U.S.* (League for Industrial Democracy Pamphlet), pp.19–22; Daniel Bell, *Socialism in American Life,* Vol. I., ch. VIII, p. 392; et seq; Norman Thomas, *Socialism Re-examined,* ch. VIII; David A. Shannon, *The Socialist Party of America.*)

While doing so, they criticized certain sections of the New Left for (1) their lack of consistent social philosophy and program; (2) their failure to urge the democratization of the economic order; (3) their failure to realize the vital importance of organized labor and consumer organizations in the battle for equal opportunity and international brotherhood; (4) their too great reliance on direct action and sabotage in the attainment of their goals; (5) their united front activities with communist and other nondemocratic forces; (6) their unconsidered enmity toward something vaguely called "The Establishment"; (7) their too great reliance on "youthfulness" "as if it were a moral good in its own right"; and (8) their inclination to view "the struggle for reform in the past as if it were dust and ashes" and "as if they could start afresh immaculately." [1a]

CANADA

During the late forties and the fifties, the Cooperative Commonwealth Federation (C. C. F.) was represented in the Dominion Parliament by some 13 to 28 members and, under the able leadership of M. J. Coldwell, played an important role in the fields of social security, labor legislation, economic planning, and international relations. It also sought vigorously to obtain the co-operation of the Canadian Labor Congress—the country's chief labor federation—in the formation of a new political party.

As a result of its efforts and those of progressive labor leaders, the Labor Congress, at its 1958 convention, instructed its Executive Committee to meet with the C. C. F. and interested farm, professional, and other liberal-minded groups to draft a constitution for a new party; the constitution was to be presented to a founding convention.

After much preliminary discussion, a convention was held in August, 1961—with delegates chiefly from the Labor Congress and the C. C. F. and with former C. C. F. Premier T. C. Douglas of Saskatchewan as Leader—at which a new party, the New Democratic party, was organized. Its program advocated the establishment of a planned economy; increased Canadian ownership and control of industry; greatly broadened social security benefits, including a national health

[1a] Irving Howe, *Steady Work* (N.Y.: Harcourt, 1966), pp. 41–6; Tom Kahn, *The Problem of the Left* (N.Y.: League for Industrial Democracy, 1966); Philip Luce, *A New Left* (N.Y.: David McKay, 1966); Paul Jacobs and Saul Landau, *The New Radicals* (N.Y.: Random House, 1966).

plan; jobs guaranteed by the government to all those willing and able to work; and large-scale construction of low rent housing.

In its agricultural program it urged guaranteed parity prices to farmers and the creation of national marketing boards to coordinate the work of provincial marketing boards and assist farmers in selling their products in national and international markets. It recommended governmental assistance to small businesses and public investment to increase productivity and reduce unemployment. In its international policy, it advocated more emphasis be placed on support of the U. N. and greater economic and technical assistance to the underdeveloped nations.

In the 1963 elections, the New Democratic party sent to Parliament 17 representatives; in the 1965 elections, 21, giving the N. D. P. the balance of power in that legislative body. Its popular vote increased from 1953 to 1955 by 300,000 to 1,347,459, 18 per cent of the total. T. C. Douglas remained as leader of the party and of N. D. P.'s Parliamentary delegation of 22.

During the early sixties, the New Democratic party delegation set forth a program for full employment, opposed the acquisition of nuclear weapons, and urged an "unremitting continuation of efforts to bring about negotiations and a negotiated settlement [in Vietnam] which will put an immediate end to hostilities." [2]

[2] Following the organization in 1961 of the New Democratic party, the members of the C. C. F. of Saskatchewan decided to retain its old name in provincial elections. The C. C. F., first elected to office in 1944, remained the government of this western province for the next twenty years (to 1964), seventeen of these years under the premiership of T. C. Douglas. He was succeeded by Woodrow Lloyd. In 1964, three years after Premier Douglas retired, the opposition Saskatchewan provincial parties combined in their electoral campaign to defeat the C. C. F. government, and were successful.

During its long tenure of office the C. C. F. instituted numerous, important social reforms. In 1947, it organized a province-wide hospital insurance plan, the first of its kind in North America. It established a Saskatchewan power corporation; a province-wide bus transportation system; a provincial telephone system; a Saskatchewan government insurance office, selling most types of insurance; and several crown companies in the fields of forest products, furs, and fishing, etc.

It likewise created Canada's first Department of Cooperation and Cooperative Development; organized a Bureau of Economic Planning with George W. Cadbury as director; enacted comprehensive trade union and anti-discrimination acts; and signed a collective bargaining agreement with unions representing its civil servants (the first such agreement in Canada). (See *Canadians Find Security* by T. C. Douglas [N.Y., L.I.D., 1949].) It later changed its name to New Democratic party.

The C. C. F. and New Democratic party were, for many years, particularly influential in the provinces of British Columbia and Ontario, among others.

Developments in South and Central America

In the latter part of the sixties, the democratic socialist and progressive movements in Central and South America and the West Indies, joined with the Socialist International; this had little impact on the political life of the larger and more powerful nations.

A democratic socialist party was the controlling force in Guyana (formerly British Guiana). A progressive democratic party affiliated with the Socialist International constituted the government of Venezuela. Socialist International affiliates varied from participants in government to chief opposition parties in Costa Rica, Jamaica, Trinidad, and Peru. Socialists held several seats in the Parliament in Chile, but in other countries they occupied few if any seats in the federal parliaments and in some authoritarian regimes were forbidden to run candidates for political office.

ARGENTINA

The Socialist party strongly opposed the 1943 military coup of General Pedro P. Ramirez which led to Perón's dictatorship. Their activities led to a long period of persecution, attacks on party premises, and the closing down of local associations. Many party members lost their possessions. In 1953 the People's House was attacked and set on fire; the labor library, the party headquarters, and the modern printing press of *La Vanguardia,* where nearly all trade union papers were printed before the dictatorship, were completely destroyed. Most of the Socialist party leaders were arrested. Perón substituted a puppet party—Movimiento Socialista—for the Socialist party, manning it with many whom the S. P. had expelled.

Following the overthrow of the Perón regime in September, 1955, Socialists accepted positions in the succeeding cabinet and assisted in wresting the trade unions from the control of the followers of Perón.

In its program the Socialist party reaffirmed its stand against a united front with the communists; protested against colonialism and imperialist exploitation in Asia, Africa and Latin America; urged cooperative action on the part of democratic countries in Europe; and advocated universal disarmament. In the 1957 elections—the first free elections since the beginning of the Perón dictatorship—it emerged as the third strongest party in the country.

At their forty-first congress in 1957, the Socialists pledged their support of the government's efforts to consolidate democracy and denounced any attempt to restore to private enterprise the German industrial undertakings taken over by the state after World War II. They likewise opposed public subsidies to denominational private schools.

In its 1965 congress, the party laid special emphasis on drastic agrarian reforms, urging the immediate abolition of large land holdings, "with the aim of finally doing away with feudalism" which, it contended, was created "by the landholding oligarchy."

Military Junta Takes Over—Abolishes Political Parties. In 1966 the party was again dealt a severe blow—this time by the coup of the military junta which, on June 28, took over the government and dissolved Congress, the Supreme Court, and *all* political parties. The socialists were informed that they would be dispossessed of all of their property. Although the party's property could be confiscated, declared the party Executive, "the people will never forget that it is to them [the socialists and their leaders] that we owe all our legislation concerned with cooperativism, working conditions, and the civil and political emancipation of women. What harsh irony that, on the one hundred and fiftieth anniversary of our Independence, our hard-won political freedom is being destroyed!"

BRAZIL

From the establishment of the unitary state in the late thirties until the middle of the sixties, the democratic socialist political activities were greatly restricted or prohibited. A possible, new beginning for the socialists was made in 1966 when a new Socialist party—committed to democratic socialism, freedom, and a better world—was formed. It advocated "an authentic cooperative system" and "profound banking reforms," which would eliminate the influence of "international bankers" and guarantee the "liberty and independence of trade unions." [3]

CHILE

In the 1958 elections, the socialists supported the Popular Action Front (F. R. A.) candidate, Salvador Allende, Socialist, for President of Chile, against Jorge Alessandri; the election resulted in a vote of 352,915 for Allende and 387,929 for Alessandri.

In 1964 the F. R. A. again nominated Allende for President. His

[3] See *Socialist International Information*, 1966, p. 113. Article by Aurelio Viana, Chairman of party.

chief opponent was Eduard Frei, a middle-of-the-road Christian Democrat.

In domestic affairs both candidates favored strengthened labor legislation and social reforms. Allende advocated complete nationalization of the copper industry, while Frei urged greater participation in the conduct of the industry.

In international affairs, Allende urged stronger ties with the Soviet Union and with Cuba. Frei remained quiet on this subject, although many of his followers expressed a fear, if Allende were elected, of Cuba's influence on Chile's policies. Some socialists broke with the party's policies and supported Frei, who received 56 per cent of the votes—1,404,800 compared with 975,210 for Allende—and was inaugurated President on November 4, 1964.

In the congressional election held in March, 1965, the Socialists elected 15 candidates, the Christian Democrats, 82, the Radicals 8; the Communists and three other parties, 12.

In general the socialists of Chile take a stand to the left of most of the parties associated with the Socialist International and are not at present affiliated with the international organization. They have, however, participated in Latin American conferences initiated by the Socialist International.

PERU

In Peru the Apra party (Partedo Aprista Peruano) was organized in the twenties as a radical, anti-imperialist party, which advocated close co-operation with Indian-oriented South American countries and, on the domestic front, aimed at the ultimate establishment of democratic collectivism, to be attained through the union of the "intellecual and manual" workers in one organic party. For some time this party exerted a considerable influence on the trade union movement and the middle class.

In 1931, following the overthrow of the dictatorship of Leguia in 1930, Victor Raúl Haya de la Torre, a founder and chief theoretician of the movement, ran for President against General Luis M. Sánchez Cerro, the candidate of the army and of the conservative forces. De la Torre received 106,000 votes, as compared with 155,000 for Sánchez Cerro, the winning candidate, and the Apra won 51 seats in the Chamber of Deputies out of a total of 145.

For the next year or two the parliamentary group of the party constituted the government's opposition and fought vigorously in the field of civil liberties. For his opposition to governmental policies, however, Haya de la Torre was jailed and his party outlawed in 1932 on the ground that he had been plotting against the government.

In 1933, President Sánchez Cerro was assassinated. His death was followed by further persecution of the Apra party members, whose leaders went abroad or into hiding. The party for the next ten or more years was not permitted to run candidates.

Shortly before the 1945 elections, Apra regained its legal status. In these elections Dr. José Luis Bustamente y Rivero won the presidency. He viewed his administration as one of "transition to democracy" and appointed several Apra members to the cabinet.

Bitter opposition to Apra, however, again developed, increased by an abortive naval revolt against the government; Apra was accused of supporting this and the party was again outlawed. In 1954, Haya de la Torre was expelled from the country after five years of asylum at the Colombian Embassy in Lima.

In the elections of 1956—the first really free elections since 1945—Dr. Manuel Prado, President, restored political freedom in Peru and Apra was again legalized.

In the national elections of June 10, 1962, the official result gave Haya de la Torre, Apra's presidential candidate, 32.97 per cent of the votes; Belaúnde Terry of the Popular Action party (P. A. P.), 32.13 per cent, and Odria of the Unión Nacionalista Odrista (U. N. O.), 28.45 per cent.

The army made it clear that whatever Haya de la Torre's vote might be, it would refuse to accept him as the chief of state. Haya de la Torre dropped out of the race, and the army feared that Odria would be elected by congress with Haya de la Torre's support. Thereupon, on July 18, the armed forces deposed President Prado and annulled the June 10 elections.

A junta composed of three generals and one admiral assumed power. Of these men General Pérez Godoy was on July 24 named provisional President. In March, 1963, Godoy was removed by the ruling junta, accused of "personalistic" politics; and General Nicholás Lindley López was chosen as the new President.

On June 9, 1963, Peru held a presidential election for the second time in two years. This time the vote was not so close as in 1962. Fernando Belaúnde Terry, representing the coalition composed of his Popular Action party and the Christian Democratic party, polled 708,662 votes; Haya de la Torre, 623,500; and Odria, 463,085. Many communists voted for Belaúnde who campaigned on a "progressive reform" platform, while a considerable number failed to vote for Haya de la Torre for fear that the army, as in 1962, would not permit him to assume office.

Belaúnde Terry was inaugurated President and, though his alliance was not in control of the Congress, considerable social and welfare legislation initiated by him was enacted. Apra, while favoring much of this legislation, voiced its criticism of the government for its alleged lack of planning, its "excessive" official expenditures, and "its inefficiency in dealing with small, communist-led armed bands in the Central Andes." It controlled, as a result of the 1963 elections, 56 seats out of 140 in the lower chamber, 10 more than President Belaúnde's alliance, and the largest bloc in that body. In the upper house, it occupied 15 seats out of 45, as compared with 19 held by the Popular Action–Democratic Christian Alliance. In the sixties, Apra became affiliated as observer with the Socialist International.

URUGUAY

The Uruguayan Socialist party was founded in Montevideo on December 12, 1910, by several socialist groups. In the elections of that year the Socialist party formed a coalition with the Liberal party on a platform demanding the separation of church and state, an eight-hour work day, a minimum wage, and the protection of women and children at work. The coalition received more votes than any of the other opposition parties and elected one representative, Emilio Frugoni, to the Chamber of Deputies.[4]

During the next decade, Socialists won several seats in the Montevideo Municipal Council and became an influential force in the trade union movement.

A split in this movement, however, took place in 1921 when a majority of the party's membership decided to break away and form the Communist party of Uruguay. Frugoni, remaining with the democratic Socialist party, resigned his seat in the Chamber. Alfred Caramilla, the first socialist representative in the Municipal Council, likewise resigned from that legislative body.

[4] Frugoni, who came from a well-known Montevideo family, was born in 1880, graduated in law, and joined the Socialist party at an early age. He taught at Montevideo University, was active as a journalist, and edited several socialist periodicals. He organized the Socialist Labor Center in 1904 and was a moving spirit in the formation six years later of the Socialist party.

During the early thirties, the economic crisis led to much agitation on the part of the workers for drastic social reform. On March 31, 1933, President Terra of Uruguay, fearing that this agitation might lead to civil strife, staged a *coup d'état* and declared himself a dictator. Frugoni denounced the dictatorship from the university and was banished from the country.

In the election of 1934, however, the party gained 2 seats in the Chamber and Frugoni was returned to that body. During the dictatorship which lasted until 1938, he led the opposition to the dictatorship in Parliament.

The party as a whole was also identified with the struggle against Terra, and, in the 1938 elections—when women voted for the first time —it won 3 seats in Parliament.

In 1942, the party's representation in the Chamber dropped to 1, but in the trade union movement it succeeded in setting up a trade union federation that was independent of the one controlled by the communists. In the 1954 elections, the seats occupied by the party in Parliament again were 3.

During the fifties and sixties the socialists remained a minor political force. In the 1962 elections they supported a leftist front called the Unión Popular, while the communists sponsored the Frente Izquierdista de Liberación.

VENEZUELA

In the sixties, the most powerful democratic party in Latin America affiliated with the Socialist International was the Democratic Action party (A. D.) of Venezuela, then head of the coalition government.

The Democratic Action party was founded in 1941 during World War II by Romulo Betancourt,[5] Raúl Leoni, and others as an alternative to the Communist party and to the parties and groups which were supporting the conservative governments of that period.

In 1945, after the Presidential regime of Isaias Medina had been

[5] Romulo Betancourt, President of Venezuela and leading Latin American democrat, was born in 1908. He began his political activities at an early age, celebrating his twentieth birthday in jail for leading a student rebellion.

When head of the provisional government from 1945 to 1948, he inaugurated universal suffrage and supervised the first free elections held in Venezuela.

Exiled when Marcos Pérez Jiménez seized control of the government, he returned to his country in 1958 to campaign and to win election as President. During his term of office he promulgated a new constitution and did much to strengthen the forces of democracy.

overthrown, a seven-man junta was set up consisting of three military officers and four political leaders, supplied by the Democratic Action party, with Betancourt as provisional President. The government fell in November, 1948, and its leaders went into exile.

A constitutional convention early in 1953 discarded the innovations introduced by the A. D. in 1947 and, on April 19, 1953, Col. Marcos Pérez Jiménez became the constitutional President.

In the elections of 1958, after the overthrow of the Jiménez government, Romulo Betancourt again ran for President as leader of the Democratic Action party, amassed 49.2 per cent of the popular vote, and was elected President.

President Betancourt, in accordance with a pre-election pact signed by three major parties, formed a coalition government with representatives of the Democratic Action party, the Democratic Republican Union, the Social Christian party, and the Independents.

On January 23, 1961, a new constitution was put into effect. Presidential elections were held on December 1, 1963. The Democratic Action party's candidate was Raúl Leoni, who had been a fellow student of President Betancourt at the University of Caracas, a cofounder of the A. D., a minister of labor in the short-lived A. D. government in 1945, and a senator in the second Betancourt ministry.

Leoni was elected President with the backing of 33 per cent of the voters—a sharp reduction from 1958—while the A. D. elected 65 representatives out of 179, as compared with 39 for the next largest group, the Social Christian party. This presidential transition was the first time in the country's history that a constitutional succession had been achieved.

Lacking a majority in each house of congress, President Leoni followed the lead of his predecessor in forming a coalition government. Leoni's cabinet included members from the Democratic Republic Union and Democratic National Front parties.

Both the Betancourt- and the Leoni-led coalition governments had to contend with terroristic activities allegedly initiated by the Cuban Castroites with a view to overthrowing the liberal-socialist governments. Betancourt, while President, barely escaped assassination.

Both governments helped to break up numerous large estates, distributing them among small owners, and gave much attention to the expansion of public education, health, housing, irrigation, and electric services. Leoni decided to make arrangements with foreign oil companies whereby they received grants on the basis of services rendered as a means of gradually increasing the government's participation in the country's petroleum industry.

COSTA RICA

Costa Rica, in Central America, had comparatively peaceful presidential successions, with the exception of 1917–1919, until 1948.

In that year Otilio Ulate Blanco defeated the government's candidate for President, Rafael Calderon Guardia. The elections were protested by the communist-oriented Calderonistas, upheld by the election jury, and then nullified by the National Assembly.

On March 12, Col. José Figueres, farmer, businessman, liberal, educated in Costa Rican and United States universities, led a revolt in support of Ulate. The revolt finally resulted in the organization of a governing junta in which Colonel Figueres was chosen provisional President.[6]

Constitutional government was restored in 1949. Figueres and his revolutionary government resigned and Ulate was inaugurated President. He gave Costa Rica four years of enlightened government.

In 1953, Figueres of the National Liberation party ran for President, with the support of President Ulate; and won the election, backed by a representation in the unicameral legislature that fell one short of two-thirds of the membership. During his term of office Figueres secured the enactment of increased income and inheritance taxes, initiated an extensive program of low-cost housing, and made a more favorable contract with the United Fruit Company. He likewise defended the country against raids from Nicaragua, stimulated, among others, by former President Calderon Picado, and fought communist efforts to foment strikes as a means of overthrowing the government.

In 1958, Figueres, who was not eligible for re-election as President, appealed to the people to elect Francisco Orlick of the National

[6] José Figueres, President of Costa Rica, was born in San Ramon, on September 25, 1906, the son of Dr. Mariano Figueres. He studied philosophy at the University of Mexico, electrical engineering at M. I. T., and languages at Columbia University, in New York.

Returning to Costa Rica from the United States, he spent the years 1929 to 1948 in farming and in business. When a communistic government obtained control in his native land, he led a revolt in March and April, 1948, which resulted in the government's overthrow. Following this successful revolt, Figueres was appointed provisional President, a position he held until the following year. In the elections of 1953, he was elected President, serving until 1957.

Liberation party (P. L. N.). Orlick, however, was defeated by a vote of 94,000 to 102,000 for Mario Echandi of the National Union party. The National Liberation party won 20 seats in the Assembly. The new president announced a program for restoring "private initiative" and denationalizing the four government banks.

In the 1962 presidential elections, the National Liberation party again won, and Francisco Orlick, the party's candidate, who polled more than 40 per cent of the total vote, was declared elected. Orlick's P. L. N. received a slight majority (29 out of 57) in the legislature.

President Orlick did much to expand industry during his term of office and completed plans for its first oil refinery. He urged stronger action in the Organization of American States (O. A. S.) against Castro's Cuba as well as other forms of dictatorship in the western continent and favored a long-overdue International Conference of American States to help settle questions of human rights.

The country played its role in the Central American Market, though its progress was hampered during these years by disastrous earthquakes and floods.

In the 1966 presidential election, the National Liberation party's candidate, Daniel Oduber Quiros, was narrowly defeated by 4,500 out of a total vote of 440,000 by José Trejos, candidate of the National Coalition, participated in by parties from the extreme left to the extreme right. During the campaign, its opponents crusaded against Oduber on the false charge of his being pro-communist.

The National Liberation party in the early sixties became an observer member of the Socialist International.

JAMAICA

The People's National party (P.N.P.) was founded in 1938 by Norman Washington Manley, Q.C., to give expression to the mounting dissatisfaction of thoughtful people about the crown colony status of Jamaica and its effect on the comparatively stagnant social and economic life of the island.

"Before 1938," declared the Socialist International Year Book, "Jamaican society consisted of the English Civil Service and the planter-merchant oligarchy at the top, an educated and socially aspiring Jamaican middle class and an economically depressed and under-educated peasantry and urban working class at the bottom; the second group was largely colored and the third group for the most part black.

"The hundred years since emancipation from slavery had been

marked by a growing resentment and suspicion between the two latter groups and the immediate objective of the People's National party was to bridge the gap between them."[7]

Jamaicans had been urging that they should be allowed self-determination under a government elected on the basis of universal adult suffrage. The leaders of the P.N.P. were socialist in their outlook and believed that, while universal suffrage was imperative, it was not enough. Sir Stafford Cripps who happened to be in Jamaica at the time of the founding conference of the party also voiced this belief. In 1940 the party formally declared its adherence to democratic socialism.

The party realized that it could not succeed unless it identified itself with the poorly paid and neglected urban and agricultural workers. Consequently, a Trade Union Congress was organized in 1939 as an association of almost all the existing trade unions in Jamaica and was affiliated with the party.

Between 1938 and 1944, the P.N.P. conducted an intensive educational campaign for self-government and political democracy. There followed, in 1944, the granting of a new constitution which went far toward vesting full responsibility in a parliament elected on the basis of universal suffrage.

In its first general election under universal suffrage, P.N.P. won only 5 out of 32 seats. The majority of seats went to the Jamaica Labor party led by Sir William Alexander Bustamante which had the support of the island's "establishment" together with considerable following from the masses.

From 1944 to 1949, the P.N.P. worked energetically for numerous other constitutional changes and in the second election in 1949 obtained a majority of the popular vote. However, the strength of the Labor party in the less-populated rural districts enabled it to retain its power with a narrow majority. In the following five years representatives of the P.N.P., though a minority, were instrumental in securing the enactment of many social reforms.

In 1952, some prominent figures in the party and the Trade Union Congress secretly organized a communist cell and planned to wrest control of the party from the socialist leadership. When this was discovered, leading members of the group were expelled, while the T. U. C. was disaffiliated. This internal struggle led to much bitterness and confusion, but the bulk of the membership of the party and the trade unions remained loyal. A new union—the National Workers'

[7] *Yearbook of the International Socialist Labour Movement,* 1956–7, p. 331.

Union—was formed and, by the end of 1953, the party was stronger and more united than ever.

The Manley P.N.P. Government (1955–62). In the general elections of 1955—the year the island celebrated its three hundredth year of association with the British crown—the party won 18 out of 32 seats and 50.5 per cent of the total vote and formed the government of the country; it was committed to a broad socialist program of planned agricultural and industrial development and social welfare.

Norman W. Manley, a Rhodes scholar and eloquent and dynamic leader of the People's National party, was chosen Chief Minister.[8] In 1959 the P.N.P. was returned to power with 30 out of 45 members of the House of Representatives. Manley was designated Prime Minister.

During Manley's term as leader of the government, a five-year agricultural development program was launched and numerous welfare measures were enacted.

Much of the government's time was spent throughout Manley's term of office in discussing the relation of Jamaica to the West Indies Federation formed in 1956. Much opposition soon arose as to whether Jamaica should continue as a member of the Federation. In a popular referendum held in 1961, a majority of voters cast their ballots against Jamaica's continuance despite the recommendation of Manley and the leaders of the P.N.P. Following the referendum, an application was made to admit Jamaica as an independent country into the Commonwealth. The application was granted and Manley called for a new election in April, 1962, to determine who should lead Jamaica into this body.

The election resulted in the defeat of Manley's party and the election of 26 out of 45 members of the National Labor party. Manley returned to leadership of the 19-member opposition in the House of Representatives. In 1967, the Labor party was re-elected, winning 33 seats, as compared with 20 for Manley's People's party.

[8] Norman Washington Manley was born in Roxburgh, Manchester, Jamaica, on July 4, 1893. He graduated from Jamaica College, was appointed a Rhodes Scholar, and studied at Jesus College, Oxford. In 1921 he was called to the bar at Gray's Inn and was admitted to practice in Jamaica the following year. In 1938 he founded the National People's party and was chosen its president.

Elected to the House of Representatives in Jamaica, he served as the leader of the opposition from 1949 to 1955. He was Chief Minister from 1955 to 1959, Prime Minister from 1959 to 1962, and, following his premiership, the opposition leader. When the British Caribbean Federation was formed in 1956, Manley was elected President of the Caribbean Federal Labor party.

Developments in Australia and Asia

AUSTRALIA

On July 5, 1945, Prime Minister John Curtin died and was succeeded by Joseph B. Chifley, Treasurer in the Curtin cabinet. In the ensuing years, the government created a national civil airline (T. A. A.), which operated independently of the private lines, and extended the public banking system. In the elections of September 29, 1946, Labor was again victorious, winning 44 seats, with the Liberals trailing behind with 17. In the U. N., Labor foreign minister Evatt and others served as powerful advocates of the rights of small nations.

The Chifley government remained in power until 1949. In the general election of December 10, 1949, Labor was defeated by a Liberal and Country party coalition and remained in opposition during the fifties and early sixties. In 1966 it won 41 seats out of a total of 124. In the 1966 campaign it urged the recall of Australian troops from South Vietnam. The party after a long delay became in the mid-sixties a member of the Socialist International. Of the general program sponsored by the Australian Labor party when in office, Lloyd Ross, Labor leader, declared: "We have accepted socialism as a goal, but we have seldom planned a legislative program of rapid and widespread steps toward socialism." [9]

NEW ZEALAND

The war placed a great strain on the budget, committed to maintaining the social services of a welfare state. The shortage of consumer services which occurred following the war weakened the stabilization measures. This situation irritated many and led to a demand for a change in government. As a result, in the 1949 elections the Labor party, after 14 years in office, received only 47.1 per cent of the votes and was defeated by the National party.

The Labor party functioned as the opposition party from 1949 until the elections of 1957, when it won power again by a small majority (41 deputies out of 80), under the leadership of Walter Nash. Nash, an extremely able and attractive personality, was selected Labor Prime Minister.[10]

[9] Ross, *Labor in Australia,* p. 17.

[10] Walter Nash was born in Kidderminster, England, February 12, 1882. After his graduation from St. John's Church School, Kidderminster, he studied law, spent

Following Labor's success in 1957, the party extended the existing social legislation, including a public development program for full employment; increased social security payments and government loans for housing at 3 per cent interest. It enacted import and exchange control to meet the balance-of-payment problem and increased the country's economic aid to developing countries. It abolished its system of compulsory military training and supported moves to prohibit by international agreement the use of weapons of mass destruction and to promote the peaceful uses of atomic energy.

When Labor came up for election again in November, 1960, however, despite a booming economy and a large surplus of exports over imports, it was defeated by the National party, Labor's opponents electing 45 deputies as against 35 for Labor. The party again went into opposition.

JAPAN

United Social Democratic Party Formed (1945). At the end of the Second World War the old Japanese ruling class was decimated and socialist parties again came into the open. Their leaders met in September, 1945, a few months after the Japanese surrender, to plan the creation of a unified socialist party. Invitations to the inaugural meeting were sent out in the names of the movement's senior leaders, Isoo Abe, Toyohiko Kagawa, and Iwasaburo Takano. The meeting was held in Tokyo on November 2, 1945, and resulted in the formation of the Social Democratic party of Japan. Tetsu Katayama was elected General Secretary and later, Chairman.

In its Declaration of Principles, the party declared that its main objectives were political freedom and democracy, the rejection of capitalism and the achievement of socialism as a means of raising the living standards of the people; a lasting peace through the co-operation of all nations; and the end of militarism in every form. In late December, 1945, the party demanded that the party of Shidehera resign

---

some time in the bicycle manufacturing trade and in the wholesale merchandising business and migrated to New Zealand in 1909. In 1919, after a decade in the business world in New Zealand, he joined the national Executive Committee of the Labor party. Three years later he became the party's secretary.

He was elected to Parliament in 1929 and, in 1935, under the Labor government, he was appointed Minister of Finance, Customs and Marketing. In 1940, he became deputy Prime Minister and from 1942 to 1944, served as New Zealand's first Minister to the United States. He was President of the International Labor Organization Conference in 1945.

en masse because the government had demonstrated that it lacked the power to meet the problems facing it.

At the first post-war elections, held in 1946—the first election in which Japanese women voted—socialists won over 90 seats out of 466 in the House of Representatives and became the third strongest party.

Katayama, Socialist Prime Minister (1947). In the general elections of April, 1947, the Socialist party gained the largest number of Diet seats (143) and, as a result, Socialist leader Tetsu Katayama became Prime Minister (May 30, 1947). Resigning in February, 1948, he was succeeded by Socialist Hitoshi Ashida, who, in turn, resigned in October, 1948, giving place to a Conservative government headed by Prime Minister Shigeru Yoshida.

In the meanwhile, bitter controversy waged within the party between followers of the extreme right-wing and followers of the extreme left, resulting in 1947—the same year as the Katayama government was formed—in the expulsion from the party of members of both extremes.

Following these expulsions, controversy continued among party members between followers of the more democratic and evolutionary Socialist doctrines of Moroto and the more revolutionary doctrines of Inamura.

Split in Party. This ideological struggle had its effect on the political prestige of the party and, in 1949, on account of these sharp intra-party differences and other factors, the party's representation in the Lower House shrank from 143 to 49.

At the Party congress the following year, in April, 1950, and at the extraordinary congress of October 23, 1951, called to discuss the United States–Japanese Security Peace Treaty, the controversy resulted, among other things, in widely different attitudes toward the treaty. The right-wing voted for the treaty despite its dissatisfaction with many of its features, while the left-wing denounced it. Both of them rejected the treaty under which the United States sought to maintain armed forces in post-war Japan. Party differences finally led to a split into the right-wing socialist party with Joraro Kawakami as chairman and the left-wing Socialist party led by Mosaburo Suzuki.

In the meantime the Conservative government which succeeded the Socialists following their resignation in October, 1948, enacted anti-democratic legislation and organized a military body in violation, Socialists contended, of the non-armament clause of the constitution. Both Socialist parties co-operated in their opposition to these actions.

Popular sentiment swung back to the Socialists and their electoral support increased, the two parties electing 111 members to the Lower House in 1952; 138 in 1953; and 155 in 1955. A demand for reunification of the parties increased and at a unification conference in Tokyo in October, 1955, following the election, the unified Social Democratic party of Japan was reconstituted.

In the triennial House of Counsellors' election of July, 1952, the left- and right-wing socialists won 71 and 66 seats, respectively. Two years later, on May 22, 1958, the representation of the two Socialist parties increased to 168, an increase of 31; in June 2, 1959, to 132 and 85, respectively, a total of 217. On October, 1959, another split occurred in the Socialist party and a part of the right-wing withdrew and formed the Democratic Socialist party. On November 20, 1960, another parliamentary election held after the resignation of the Ikeda cabinet following the approval of the United States–Japanese Military Security Pact, the representation of the two Socialist parties was again considerably reduced—to 145 seats for the Socialists and 17 for the Democratic Socialists. In 1963 the representation was practically the same, 145 and 23, respectively, over one-third of the total parliamentary number, and was outranked only by the Liberal-Democratic party with its representation of 282.

Both Socialist parties that year were members of the Socialist International; both urged a change into a socialist society by peaceful means. Both favored the abolition of the United States–Japanese Security Treaty, the Democratic Socialist party emphasizing the gradual character of this change. Both favored the admission of Communist China to the United Nations, the Democratic Socialist party urging a *two China policy*. Its program of public enterprise included the nationalization of a comparatively few giant industries.

INDIA

In the great and populous country of India, the ruling Congress Party has contended that the general, far-reaching aims of the Congress party were those of democratic socialism. The Congress party has initiated several national economic plans since India's independence.

Independent of the Congress party, however, have existed Socialist parties belonging to the Socialist International which maintain that they are the only true representatives of the world socialist movement.

Praja Socialist Party and Congress Socialist Party. The oldest of these parties is the Praja Socialist party. This party began as a socialist group inside of the Indian National Congress. In 1930, a mass civil disobedience movement developed in India and some of its younger members felt that a socialist orientation of the Congress would strengthen India in its fight for freedom. Socialist organizations were formed within the party in various parts of the country.

These groups came into close contact with each other inside of the prisons to which they had been sent in punishment for their participation in the civil disobedience movement. As a result, the Congress Socialist party (C. S. P.) was formed in 1934.

The Congress Socialist party played an important part in educating the members of the Congress party in the aims and program of socialism. In 1936 and 1937, it helped materially in obtaining the enactment in the party congress of a program for reorganizing Indian agriculture and for reaching the masses with the message of the need for political and social change. In the years 1936 to 1939 it sought to become a party of "socialist unity." When, however, the communists attempted to capture the party or to wreck it, the close alliance with the communists was ended.

With the declaration of war in Europe, the C. S. P. led the demand for opposition to the war until India was granted its freedom. The next year the Congress party as a whole announced its approval of this policy and the Congress socialists played a valuable role in the movement for national liberation that developed from 1942 to 1946.

Breakaway Parties of Congress Party. In 1952, following the achievement of independence and the death of Mahatma Gandhi, the leaders of the C. S. P., claiming that the Congress party was becoming too conservative, broke away and founded the Socialist party of India.

In its program the new party emphasized the need for both democracy and decentralization in a co-operative order. In the January, 1952, elections it obtained about 10,000,000 votes, 11 per cent of the total, and elected 12 representatives out of 489, with the Congress party winning the overwhelming majority of parliamentary seats.

In 1951 an influential group of Gandhian socialists had left the Congress party and founded the *Kisan Mazdoor Praja Party* (K.M.P.P.). The two parties resolved to merge and, in September, 1952, formed a new party, the Praja Socialist party. On December 28, 1955, Dr. Rammanohar Lohia formed a third Socialist party, called by that name.

Congress Party—Proclaims Its Socialistic Aims. In that year, the Congress party, India's ruling party led by Prime Minister Nehru, insisted that its aims, as well as that of the socialist parties, were socialistic. In its Madras meeting of 1955, it maintained that it favored social planning "with a view to the establishment of a socialistic pattern of society [in India] in which the principal means of production are under social ownership or control and there is an equitable distribution of the national wealth." On the other hand, it added that large sections of industry should remain private. Prime Ministers Jawaharlal Nehru, Lal Bahadur Shastri, and Indira Gandhi later proclaimed the socialistic nature of Congress party aims.

In 1958 numerous prominent members within the Congress party formed the Congress Socialist Forum with a view to educating the party membership about the aims and ideals of socialism.

Socialist Party Mergers. The Praja Socialist party merged with the Lohia Socialist party in 1964 to form the Samyukta Socialist party. Shortly thereafter a significant number of former Praja Socialist party members, declining to join the new Indian Socialist Party, followed Ashok Mehta into the Indian National Congress. In January, 1965, most of the remaining members of the Praja Socialist party revived the old party—their objective, the establishment of a democratic socialist society in India.

Decades of Fifties and Sixties. The Praja Socialists during the fifties and sixties voiced their protests against the "terroristic" attacks of communists on socialists and other non-communists in the state of Kerala, on China's "planned annihilation of the simple people" of Tibet, on Russian aggression in Hungary, and on colonialism of all types.

In the 1967 elections for Parliament, which led to a drastic reduction in the parliamentary representation of the ruling Congress party, the Praja Socialist party increased its representation in the lower house of Parliament from 9 to 14 seats, and, in the state legislatures, from 65 to 108. Various socialist groups joined successful anti-Congress coalitions in the states of Kerala and Madras. The Praja Socialists refrained from entering into electoral agreements in national parliamentary contests.

BURMA

In the fifties, the Burma Socialist party was a powerful influence in the political life of Burma and in Asian socialism. The movements which created the Burma Socialist party had their origin in the peasants' revolts of 1930.

At that time Burmese society consisted of (1) a class of foreign capitalists and the firms monopolizing foreign trade, (2) merchants who distributed foreign goods and absentee landlords who owned two-thirds of the land, and (3) the mass of poor peasants who constituted 85 per cent of the population.

The Thakin Party. The majority of the peasants were landless and were heavily burdened with rent, interest charges, and high prices. The trade depression of 1930 worsened their condition and a revolt broke out in the Tharrawaddy district, accompanied by strikes and racial riots in the towns. The revolt was ruthlessly suppressed, but a number of young people, particularly students inspired by the suffering of the peasants, formed the *Dobama Assi-a-yong,* or *Thakin* party. This was a left-wing, anti-imperialist organization which attacked the country's political leadership and strove to organize peasants and workers.

In 1938 strikes and demonstrations broke out among the oil workers, who were joined by the peasants in their marches on Rangoon. A conference in Shwe Dagon Pagoda passed a resolution to form the All-Burma Peasants' organization.

The conference resolved (1) to fight for national liberation, (2) to raise living standards, (3) to attack landlordism, (4) to work for land nationalization, and (5) to struggle for the attainment of a socialist state under the banner of workers and peasants.

The Burmese Revolutionary Party and Independence Army Formed During World War. When the Second World War broke out, one section of the Thakin party organized itself as the Burmese Revolutionary party with the object of creating an armed rebellion. In 1941, a conference of the All-Burma Peasants' Organization was held in Pegu at which a secret decision was made, in conjunction with the Burmese Revolutionary party, to send the famous "Thirty Comrades" for military training to Japan. The group later formed the Burma Independence Army in Thailand and fought with the Japanese army to defeat the British in Burma.

Formation of Anti-Fascist People's Freedom League. After the Independence Army served its purpose, steps were taken to dissolve it. The fascistic tactics of the Japanese led to disillusionment. A national front was formed, known as the *Anti-Fascist Peoples' Freedom League* (A. F. P. F. L.), consisting of the Burma Revolutionary party, the Communist party, and the Burmese Independence Army, later known as the Burma Defense Army.

On March 27, 1945, the A. F. P. F. L. organized a revolt against the Japanese and assisted the British forces in their fight to defeat them.

At first the Burma Revolutionary party aimed to organize an armed struggle to obtain independence from the British. Later they abandoned this course and decided to win their independence by peaceful means.

A. F. P. F. L. Governments (1947–58). Aung San, Socialist, became premier in all but name when, in September, 1946, he was given most of the seats on the governor's Executive Council as Leader of the A. F. P. F. L. and led that organization to an overwhelming victory in the April, 1947, elections. In October, 1946, the British authorities had asked the A. F. P. F. L. to form a government. By this time difficulties had arisen between Britain and the U. S. S. R.; the Burma Communist party had changed its attitude toward Britain and it was necessary to expel Communists from the A. F. P. F. L. This left the Burma Socialist party the leading group in the National Front.

U Nu succeeded his friend Aung San as Premier in July, 1947. His only experienced minister, Tin Tut, a former civil servant, was assassinated in September, 1948, by the supporters of rival ministers. Mutinies broke out in various parts of the country but Nu's conciliatory methods prevailed. In the Executive Committee of the A. F. P. F. L. under the leadership of U Nu, 8 of the 13, including the Vice-President and General Secretary, were socialists.

Lawlessness was still widespread in 1951 and 1952, but it was possible to hold elections in over 90 per cent of the constituencies. In the electoral campaign, the A. F. P. F. L. ran on a platform that included plans for drastic land reform, democratization of administration, the encouragement of unity among the various national groups, expansion of the nationalized and co-operative sectors of the economy, industrialization, and advanced social welfare legislation. Of the 375 members of both houses elected in May, 1952, 80 per cent were members of the A. F. P. F. L., 60 per cent of whom were socialists.

In the early fifties the government became a joint partner in the principal oil and mining companies. It decided on a course of "non-involvement" with other countries.

The Burma Socialist party, however, soon directed much of its attention to the formation of the Asian Socialist Conference. This conference, following numerous preliminary meetings, was organized in Rangoon, Burma, in January, 1953, at a gathering attended by delegates from Socialist parties of Burma, India, Indonesia, Israel, Japan, Lebanon, Malaya and Pakistan, and observers from numerous other groups and countries. The conference aimed to bring about closer relations with Asian democratic socialist parties and with the larger world of socialism. It established its headquarters in Burma and appointed U Ba Swe, General Secretary of the Burma Socialist party, as Chairman.

The Socialist government of the A. F. P. F. L. remained in power from 1947, the year before Burma's independence from Britain, to 1958, most of the time under the leadership of U Nu.

During U Nu's regime, the government suffered violent attacks from the communists, Karen rebels, bands of Chinese Nationalists, and others. Among its reforms were an eight-year economic plan and a ten-year plan of land nationalization. In 1956, U Nu left his office for a year to help strengthen the organization of the A. F. P. F. L.

Split in A. F. P. F. L. In May, 1958, the A. F. P. F. L. split into two factions. In the ensuing intra-party turmoil, General Ne Win, the Commander in Chief of the armed forces, served as Prime Minister, while retaining his army position.

In quick succession, the Revolutionary Government under Ne Win dissolved the Union Parliament, abolished the constitution, replaced the Supreme and High courts with a Chief Court, established the Burmese Socialist Program Party (B. S. P. P.) as the sole political party in Burma, took in custody the leaders of the U Nu government, and arrested top leaders of other Burmese parties and many other opposition elements.

The government proceeded to nationalize the banking industry, foreign trade, most of the wholesale and retail trade, the mining industry, some manufacturing industries, and several newspapers. Agricultural land continued to be operated on an individual basis, although land rent was abolished, and the government began the work of educating the peasants for some form of collectivization. The educational system was extensively reorganized along collectivist lines, and major private schools were nationalized. The B. S. P. P., organized in 1958, had no ties with the Socialist International.

SOUTH KOREA

The United Socialist party of Korea, an observer member of the Socialist International, was founded—at an inaugural congress—in Seoul, on September 20, 1966. The occasion marked the first organization of a progressive party in Korea since the military revolution of 1961. The congress called for immediate suspension of "governmental oppression of political freedom"; opposed the dispatch of combat troops in South Vietnam; urged the abrogation of the Korean–Japanese Normalization Treaty; and pledged its continued, unyielding dedication to Korea's movements "for freedom, progress, equality and complete independence and reunification of our fatherland."

VIETNAM

The socialist movement began in Vietnam in 1931 when the first Vietnamese socialists in the southern provinces joined the Saigon Federation of the French Socialist party.

From 1940 onward, during the occupation of Vietnam by Japan, many socialists joined the resistance movement against the invader. After the expulsion of the Japanese, many members of the local French socialist federation participated in the struggle for the independence of Vietnam. The socialists were thus represented in the nationalist movements during the period 1946–1951.

On September 12, 1952, the Vietnamese Socialist party was founded at a secret congress—public meetings at that time being banned. The party, which declared its independence from the French Socialist party, was officially recognized on July 20, 1953. A second congress was held on August 2 of that year.

The party was admitted as an observer to the Asian Socialist Congress in Rangoon in January, 1953, and to the Congress of the Socialist International in London in 1955.

During most of the sixties, because of the military situation, practically all party electoral activity on the part of the party was suspended.

Developments in the Middle East

ISRAEL

The one country in the Middle East in which a democratic socialist party in the post-war era played a leading political role was Israel. The party—affiliated with the Socialist International—was the Mapai party. Mapai was organized at a conference held at Tel Aviv on January 5–7, 1933, by David Ben-Gurion,[11] among others.

"Ideologically, the party was dedicated to a synthesis of national and

[11] David Ben-Gurion, one of the founders of Israel and for many years its Prime Minister, was born in Plonsk, Poland, in October, 1886. He was educated privately and at the University of Constantinople.

At the age of twenty he went to Palestine, then under Turkish rule, became active in the Palestine Labor party and, after a few years, was the editor of its journal.

socialist aspirations—the determination to rebuild the ancient homeland of the Jewish people as a foundation for a renewed and dignified national life and to develop there a Society of Labor based on social justice and equality." [12]

A major task of Mapai was to make the young socialists, who were its founders and members, into workers; to urge Jewish youth to migrate to Palestine and take part in the building of a nation; and to develop a labor commonwealth in a country held together within the framework of Histadrut—the General Federation of Labor founded in 1921.

The guiding principles of Mapai were that labor should form the vanguard of the nation "in its return to Zion" and that the new national life should be founded "on a sound economic and social basis."

Its first concern was settlement on the land—the "Return to the Soil"—which soon assumed the pattern of the collective (*Kibbutz*) and co-operative (*moshav ovdim*) village.

During those days, Histadrut, under Mapai guidance, played a large part in education and created a network of schools. It advanced modern Hebrew literature and art, and made Hebrew the language of the community. Later it developed independent labor economic enterprises in the form of producers', marketing, and consumers' co-operatives and organized Histadrut corporations in the building, insurance, and other industries.

Along with its work of developing autonomous labor institutions, Mapai participated extensively in the representative bodies of Palestine Jewry. It became a guiding force in Histadrut and the Zionist movement, and was largely responsible for the decision to declare the independence of Israel and to claim victory in the war that followed the invasion of the Arab states.

Exiled for his activities by the Turkish government, he went in 1915 to the United States and became active in the organization of the Pioneers for Settlement in Palestine. He became an effective force in the Jewish Legion for Service in World War I and entered war as a private, serving in British General Allenby's operations against the Turks.

When the war ended, Ben-Gurion became a member of the General Council of Zionist Organizations and in 1921 was elected Secretary of the General Federation of Labor, remaining in that office until 1935. In that year he was elected Chairman of the board of the Jewish Agency for Palestine and, thirteen years later, in 1948, he proclaimed the independence of Israel.

[12] Julius Braunthal in *Yearbook of the Interational Socialist Labour Movement, 1956–7*, p. 296.

Following the declaration of statehood, Mapai headed the provisional government and formed a coalition government with the United Religious front and smaller center parties with Ben-Gurion as Prime Minister.

In the first elections after independence, Mapai won the largest number of seats in the *Knesset*—46 out of a total of 120—while the left-wing socialist party—Mapai, won 19. Ben-Gurion was again called upon to head a coalition government.

During the years following independence, the Israeli government was forced to divide its attention between its many domestic problems and the preparation against threatened attack by the Arab world intent, it was stated, in many instances, on destroying it as a nation, or at least, on retarding the progress of the country.

One of the domestic problems with which the government was faced now was the question of the allocation of social services between the powerful federation of labor—the Histadrut—and public agencies. During the fifties the government assumed, at the request of Histadrut, the control over the water supply, the educational system, labor exchanges, etc.—formerly administered by Histadrut—while other services were transferred to the public domain during the succeeding decade.

In December, 1953, Ben-Gurion retired to a collective settlement in the Negev. He returned as Minister of Defense in March, 1955—the coalition government being headed in the meantime by Moshe Sharett, a member of the Mapai who had been Foreign Minister under Ben-Gurion. Sharett, like Ben-Gurion while Prime Minister, was the Premier as well as head of the foreign office.

Following the 1955 elections, Ben-Gurion again became Prime Minister and this time assembled a government which included representatives of the three labor parties as well as a member of the Progressives and of the religious parties. Sharett retired as Foreign Minister and was replaced by Golda Meir, Israel's Minister of Labor, a former school teacher from Milwaukee, Wisconsin.

In the late fifties, the Ben-Gurion government was attacked by left-wing parties for its sale of arms to West Germany. These attacks, among other things, led Ben-Gurion to resign his premiership on July 5, 1959. He consented, however, to head the coalition government until the fall elections, and, following the balloting, in which Mapai was returned with a larger plurality, formed another coalition government. He remained as head of the coalition government until the summer of 1963, when he unexpectedly resigned.

Following Ben-Gurion's resignation, Finance Minister Levi Eshkol was unanimously chosen (June 26, 1963) by Mapai to succeed Ben-Gurion with the latter's support.[13]

Late in 1964, former Prime Minister Ben-Gurion announced that he was preparing a detailed report on the ten-year old "Lavon affair"—a dispute over alleged blunders in espionage operations by former Defense Minister, and former General Secretary of the Federation of Labor (the Histadrut) Pinhas Lavon—with much new evidence that would need further investigation. During October he presented the result of this research to the Minister of Justice. The Attorney General supported Ben-Gurion's request for a full judicial inquiry into the alleged security mishap. Eshkol objected to this recommendation and carried the coalition cabinet with him.

Ben-Gurion then appealed to the central committee of the Mapai party, but, on December 14, before it could vote, Eshkol resigned with his cabinet. On December 27, however, the *Knesset* (Parliament) voted 59 to 36 to restore Eshkol to office. Eshkol's new cabinet refused to approve a new investigation into the Lavon affair.

Ben-Gurion, however, continued to press the issue. He and his supporters, moreover, opposed Premier Eshkol's plan for an "alignment" of the Mapai party with the much smaller and more doctrinaire socialist party, Achdut Avoda.

On February 23, 1965, at the tenth convention of the Mapai assembled, both issues reached a climax. Following presentation of the arguments on both sides, the convention voted to support Premier Eshkol both in the "Lavon affair" and on his "alignment" policy. The Mapai majority then refused to agree to a proportional representation of the minority on the governing bodies of the party.

The Ben-Gurion group thereupon set up its own organization and

13 Levi Eshkol was born in Oratova, in the Ukraine, on October 25, 1895. Because of a quota for educating Jews in Odessa, he attended school in Vilnius, Lithuania. There he became an agricultural worker. After serving two years with the Jewish Legion in the British army during World War I, he went to Palestine where, in 1920, he helped to found one of the first *Kibbutzim* and became an early member of the Mapai party and of its central committee.

Following the rise to power of Adolf Hitler, Eshkol devoted himself for three years to the transfer of immigrants and property to Israel. In 1942 he became director of the settlement department and a member of the Executive of the Jewish Agency.

Upon the founding of the state of Israel in 1948, Eshkol was made Director General of the Defense Ministry. In 1951 he was appointed Minister of Agriculture and Development, and, in the following year, was chosen Finance Minister. In this position he spent much time in the development of the oil industry, the chemical industry, and mineral resources. He also established a rehabilitation program for 20,000 returning Arab refugees. In 1958 he announced an eight-part program to consolidate the gains of the first ten years.

nominated its own candidates for the election of the governing body of the General Federation of Labor and of the *Knesset,* actions which led to the expulsion of the dissident group from the Mapai.

In the succeeding elections to the *Knesset* on November 2, 1965, the Mapai—Achdut Avoda alignment won a landslide victory, winning 45 seats in Parliament as compared with 10 seats for the newly formed Rafi party led by former Prime Minister Ben-Gurion. The results were (unexpectedly) decisive and Premier Eshkol proceeded with the formation of a broad coalition government that included parties represented by 73 out of 120 parliamentary seats. In the new cabinet, Abba Eban replaced Golda Meir as the Minister of Foreign Affairs. During 1965 normal relations were established with Germany.

Relations with Egypt and other members of the Arab world, however, became more strained. Cries in high Arab circles that Israel must be destroyed became more strident. In early June, 1967, Israel was forbidden access to an international waterway. Egyptian and other Arab military forces began the encirclement of Israel. On June 5 war broke out. Israeli forces during the next six days swept all before them and when the warring nations agreed to obey the cease-fire resolution of the U. N., the Arab armies, air forces, and navies were found to have been defeated on every front.

On June 8, during the war, an emergency meeting of the International Socialist Bureau was held. The meeting maintained that any permanent solution of the problems of the Middle East must take into account the following factors:

(a) The immediate right of Israel to exist as a foreign state;

(b) The recognition of the legitimate rights of the Arab peoples of the Middle East;

(c) The assertion and guarantee to all nations of right of passage on the international waterways of the Strait of Tiran and the Suez Canal.

(d) The need to find a humane and just solution to the problem of refugees in the Middle East;

(e) The establishment of effective means of international supervision to guarantee the maintenance of peace.

These questions and the question of whether Israel should remain in control of the Jordanian section of Jerusalem, were among the problems placed on the agenda for discussion at peace negotiations.

Following the war, renewed consideration was given to the question of unity between the powerful Mapai party led by Prime Minister

Eshkol and others, and the Rafi party founded by David Ben-Gurion. The membership in the latter party of Major General Moshe Dayan, newly created Minister of Defense during the war and an outstanding war hero, increased its prestige and led many to predict a bright future for the Rafi-ites. On January 21, 1968, Mapai, Rafi and Achdut Avoda merged into the Israel Labor party.

Developments in Africa

AFRICAN SOCIALISM

In Africa most of the countries which in the mid-twentieth century were tranformed from European colonies to independent republics developed marked socialist and communist trends, adapted to their particular traditions and states of economic, political, and cultural development.

The term "African socialism" has been applied to the social order which many of these African nations are striving to attain.

Fenner Brockway, former British Labor M. P., in his book, *African Socialism* [14] described "African Socialism" as a social order characterized by:

(1) A network of agricultural co-operatives and publicly initiated village industries;

(2) State ownership and management of important national projects in the fields of irrigation, electricity, transport, and shipping (dockyards);

(3) Partial state participation in the ownership and control of other industries;

(4) Incorporation in the administration of such industries of overall economic plans;

(5) The accompaniment, in the development of these plans, of rapid expansion in public education and health and housing services, and the employment of large armies of volunteer workers.

Brockway contends that, in the development of African socialism, different weights must be assigned to personal and political freedom than is given in the industrialized countries of the world.[15]

[14] Fenner Brockway, *African Socialism* (London: Bodley Head, 1963).

[15] The social organization contemplated by exponents of African socialism, Brockway continues, is one that evolves from African conditions and traditions. It is integrally socialist, he maintains, because it will progressively "give to the people the wealth they create, equality in everything which makes for human fulfillment," and

Kenya White Paper (1965). The Kenya government in 1965 issued a White Paper, largely drafted by Tom Mboya,[16] Minister of Economic Planning and Development, setting forth what it considered to be the essential conditions the system of African socialism should satisfy.

According to the White Paper African socialism must: draw on the best of African traditions; be adaptable to new and rapidly changing circumstances; must not rest for its success on the satellite relationship with any other country or group of countries.

1. African Traditions. There are two African traditions, declares the White Paper, which form an essential basis for African socialism. They are:

a) Political Democracy. "In African society [the White Paper elaborates] a man was born politically free and equal and his voice and counsel were heard and respected regardless of the economic wealth he possessed . . . African Socialism rests on full, equal and unfettered democracy. Thus African socialism differs politically from communism because it insures every mature citizen equal political rights, and from capitalism because it prevents the exercise of disproportionate political influence by economic power groups.

"Another fundamental force in African traditional life was religion which provided a strict moral code for the community. This will be a prominent feature of African socialism."

b) Mutual Social Responsibility. "Mutual social responsibility is also an extension of the African family spirit to the nation as a whole,

---

possesses the spirit of fraternity of a co-operative society. "How soon," he adds, "it will also embody all that we mean by liberty will depend upon the advance which is made in the coming together of conflicting elements and the sense of security that grows from stable conditions."

16 Tom Mboya was born on September 15, 1930, at Rusinga Island, Lake Victoria. He began his career in 1951 as a sanitary inspector for the Nairobi City Council and in 1953 became Secretary to the Kenya Local Government Workers' Union, later known as the Kenya Federation of Labor.

Awarded a scholarship, he studied at Oxford University for a year. On his return he was elected a member of the Colony's legislative council in 1957, but refused to take part in a proposed plan for multi-racial government, declaring his aim to be an "undiluted democracy," in effect, African rule in Kenya.

In 1958, Mboya was elected President of the Nairobi People's Convention. In 1960 he attended the constitutional conference on Kenya in London and was elected in May General Secretary of the newly formed Kenya African National Union (K. A. N. U.), which later announced its opposition to British bases in Kenya. He was also a supporter of an East African federation. After visiting the United States he was seriously injured in an automobile accident. In President Kenyatta's African Union Government, formed in 1963, he was selected Minister of Economic Planning and Development.

with the hope that ultimately the same spirit can be extended to ever larger areas. It implies a mutual responsibility by society and its members to do their very best for each other with the understanding that, if society prospers, its members will share in that prosperity, and that society cannot prosper without the full cooperation of its members. The state has an obligation to insure equal opportunities to all its citizens, eliminate exploitation and discrimination, and provide needed social services such as education, medical care and social security.

"Every member of African traditional society had a duty to work . . . African society had the power and duty to impose sanctions on those who refused to contribute their fair share of hard work to the common endeavor.

"Drawing on this background African socialism expects the members of the modern state to contribute willingly and without stint to the development of the nation. Society, in turn, will reward those efforts and at the same time will take measures against those who refuse to participate in the nation's efforts to grow."

2. ADAPTABILITY. African socialism must be adaptable and flexible because the problems it will confront will change often, quickly and substantially.

3. RELATIONSHIPS WITH OTHER COUNTRIES. A third conditional factor is the need to avoid making development depend on a satellite relationship with any country or group of countries. Such a relationship is abhorrent and a violation of the political and economic independence so close to the hearts of the people. Economic non-alignment does not mean a policy of isolation, any more than political non-alignment implies a refusal to participate in world affairs. On the contrary, it means a willingness and desire

a) to borrow technological knowledge and proven economic methods from any country—without commitment

b) to seek and accept technical and financial assistance from any source without strings

c) to participate fully in world trade—without political domination.

"To be consistent with the conditions specified, African socialism must be politically democratic, socially responsible, adaptable and independent. The system itself is based on the further idea that the nation's productive assets must be used in the interest of society and its members."

4. USE OF RESOURCES. Under African socialism the power to control resource use (land, etc.), continues the White Paper, resides with

the state. African socialism must rely on planning to determine the appropriate uses of productive resources. In order to control effectively and not excessively in each case, many types and degrees of state control are needed, ranging from none to absolute control represented by state ownership and operation. The degree and nature of controls can be modified over time. Another feature of the range of controls is that it permits a variety of forms of private participation, each of which can be utilized where it performs best. It also gives a substantial degree of freedom in attracting both private and public capital.

"The purpose of a range of controls and of planning is to insure that productive assets are used for the benefit of society. The holding of land for speculative purposes, the charging of exorbitant or discriminating prices, the abandonment of land and the production or sale of shoddy merchandise are all examples of violations of mutual social responsibility."

5. Class Problem. The White Paper, in dealing with the question of class divisions in Africa, declared that the class problem as it existed in Europe had no place in African socialism and no parallel in African society. The class problem in Africa was thus largely one of prevention, in particular

a) of eliminating the risk of foreign economic domination;

b) of planning the domestic economy so as to prevent the emergence of antagonistic classes.

Within the economy African socialism would use progressive taxation to prevent undue accumulation of wealth in the hands of the few. It would likewise diffuse the ownership of large-scale enterprises through the expansion of state ownership, joint ventures of the state and private investors, cooperatives, companies, and partnerships.

The main features of African socialism, the Kenya government White Paper declared in summary, "include 1) political democracy; 2) mutual social responsibility; 3) various forms of ownership; 4) a range of controls to insure that property is used in the mutual interest of society and its members; 5) progressive taxes to insure an equitable distribution of wealth and income." [17]

While declaring, however, that one of the essential features of African socialism was political democracy, many leaders of the Kenya

[17] See *Socialist International Information* (High St., London S.W. 8) June 5, 1965, Kenya's Government White Paper on "African Socialism and Its Application to Planning in Kenya." Mboya, chief drafter of the White Paper, later emphasized the need of African countries coming together to achieve greater rates of economic growth. (See *Socialist International Information,* December 18, 1966.)

government were not convinced that a multi-party system was an essential feature of a democratic form of government.

"The allegation that there can be no opposition in a one party system—and therefore no democracy," declared Mboya, "is misleading. There may be no paid opposition engaged to organize strikes and unrest and create confusion more than to further progress. But in countries such as mine, where Parliament makes the decisions, we are faced from our own ranks by significant and constructive criticism which is far from being timid or cautious. We think this kind of opposition has the genuine advantage of having to deal with given facts of a case or a bill instead of following party dogmas.

"True democracy can indeed exist in a form which does not necessitate a multi-party system . . . In the last two decades numerous newly-formed states in Asia and Africa have been trying to find compromise solutions for their own countries and institutions in order to blend attractive-looking ideas and methods with local traditions and opinions and to obtain in this way, as a final product, a special form of democracy which is understood and accepted by the people." [18]

In expressing the above opinion, Mboya differed from some other African socialist leaders, among them President Philibert Tsiranana of the Malagasy Republic, and from democratic socialists in developed countries.

MALAGASY REPUBLIC

From its independence in 1960 to the late sixties, Madagascar, or the Malagasy Republic, an island republic off the southeast coast of Africa and formerly a French colony, was controlled by a social democratic government committed to an African form of socialism.

In the elections of September, 1960, the Social Democratic party (P. S. D.), headed by Philibert Tsiranana, its founder, won 75 out of 98 seats in the lower chamber, with 5 other parties represented by 1 to 7 representatives each. Tsiranana was chosen President by an overwhelming vote.

Tsiranana's administration proved to be a popular one and five years later, on March 30, 1965, he was re-elected to a seven-year term by an astounding total of 2,451,441 out of 2,507,067 votes—nearly 98 per cent of the total!

In the August, 1965, parliamentary elections, the Social Democrats won another sweeping victory—electing 104 out of 107 members of the lower house and 52 out of 54 senators. The local elections also

[18] See *ibid.*, December 18, 1966, p. 254.

favored the Social Democrats with the election of 92 out of 94 candidates for local councils.

Following the elections, President Tsiranana, concerned about the weakness of the opposing parties, urged the opposition factions to unite into a single party, declaring, "I am against the one-party system, and I believe in the usefulness of constructive oppositions."

The Social Democratic party urges that the parties in the Vietnam conflict enter immediately into negotiations to put an end to the fighting, cease fire in the meanwhile, and effect the reunification of Vietnam "according to the democratic principles of self-determination." [19]

KENYA

Kenya, a former British colony with a population of less than ten million, achieved complete independence in December, 1963, and on December 12, 1964, became a republic with Jomo Kenyatta, advocate of African socialism, as President.[20]

Kenyatta was chosen as the first President of Kenya on December 12, 1964, when it became a republic while remaining a member of the British Commonwealth.

Kenyatta's party, K. A. N. U., held a majority of seats in both houses of Parliament at the time of independence. In 1964—the year of independence—the head of the African Democratic Union party (K. A. D. U.), Ronald Ngala, dissolved his party and joined Kenyatta's party, thus making Kenya—at least for the time being—a one-party state.

During the succeeding years, President Kenyatta, Tom Mboya,

[19] The Social Democratic party of Madagascar was the first party in Africa to be admitted as a full member of the Socialist International.

[20] Jomo Kenyatta, first Prime Minister of independent Kenya, was born in the Kikuyu tribal area, probably in 1893. He was educated at a Church of Scotland mission school and was for sometime employed as a clerk by the Nairobi municipality. In 1928 he became General Secretary of the Kikuyu Central Association and went to Britain in 1929, subsequently traveling in other parts of Europe and returning to Kenya in 1946.

Kenyatta first became widely known when, following the outbreak of Mau Mau disorders in 1952, he was arrested and sentenced (April, 1953) to seven years' imprisonment for managing an illegal society (Mau Mau) and for being a member of a prescribed cult. Six years later (1959), he was released under an order restricting his residence and was completely freed in August, 1961.

In October, 1961, he was elected President of the Kenya African National Union, Kenya's leading political party. Returned unopposed to Kenya's House of Representatives in April, 1963, Kenyatta led K. A. N. U. to a clear majority in the general elections in May.

Kenya's Minister of Economic Planning and Development, and others, sought through legislation to lead the country along the path of African socialism.

After three years of independence, Henry Reuter in *The New York Times*[21] wrote that the people of Kenya are "eating better, living in better homes and in cleaner villages," that Kenya has emerged as the most stable of all the new African countries, and as a country "in which a policy of non-racialism is working out as a living answer to apartheid.

"The Kenya story in all fields is one of unprecedented progress. Secondary school enrollment has been doubled.

"In the field of health, all children and out-patients now receive free treatment from a clinic and hospital system that is being expanded rapidly with the help of the World Health Organization.

"In the field of community development, more than 5,000 self-help groups have been formed since 1966. These have carried out thousands of local projects—roads, schools, hospitals, etc.

"Proof that the government can govern effectively," writes Reuter, has created a confidence that has led "to a great upsurge of investment and thereby of industrial expansion, an expansion that has been stimulated by the Development Finance Company of Kenya and the Commercial Development Company. The Government has entered into partnership with private investors from abroad in new industrial projects."

SENEGAL AND TANZANIA

Other political parties in Africa committed to the attainment of African socialism and affiliated in the late sixties to the Socialist International existed in:

1. **Senegal,** a former French colony in western Africa. The Republic of Senegal achieved independence August 20, 1960. A constitution adopted August 25 described the republic as secular, democratic, and social. On September 5, Leopold Sedar Senghor, Socialist, assumed the office of President and on December 1, 1963, was elected to that office for a four-year term. The first few years of Senghor's regime were devoted largely to the task of developing a spirit of co-operation between Senegal and African and Asian governments.

2. **Tanzania,** an East African member of the Commonwealth of na-

[21] *N. Y. Times,* Jan. 27, 1967.

tions, inaugurated April 26, 1964, when the former Republic of Tanganyika (independent since December 9, 1961) merged with the former sultanate of Zanzibar, a republic since January, 1964.

On the inauguration of Tanzania Dr. Julius Nyerere, head of the Tanganyika African National Union (T. A. N. U.), an advocate of the development of a democratic socialist state, was chosen President.

On assuming office, Nyerere gave much time to the preparation of a development plan for the country, to the unification of the republic, and the elimination of tensions with other African countries. He was re-elected for a five-year term in 1965.

While the republic was by law a one-party state, the constitution provided that the ruling party T. A. N. U. select two people in each constituency, among the aspiring candidates, to contest elections.

CHAPTER 47

Consumers' Co-operatives—Post-World War II Developments

As has been previously stated,[1] the modern consumers' co-operative movement had its birth in Rochdale, England, in 1843. It was on the twenty-first of December of that year that twenty-eight desperately poor flannel weavers, organized the Rochdale Equitable Pioneer Society, flung open the doors of their tiny shop in Toad Lane, Rochdale, and displayed for sale to their members their $70 stock of flour, oatmeal, butter, and sugar.

In the following decades, the store grew far beyond the expectations of their founders; co-operatives sprang up throughout Great Britain. The co-operatives formed regional centers; organized, in 1869, a national educational society—the Co-operative Union; began extensive trading with their counterparts that were developing on the European continent; and, in 1892, founded an international agency—the International Co-operative Alliance (I. C. A.)—which held its first congress in London three years later in 1895.

From that date on, co-operative societies from many lands sent their representatives every few years to I. C. A. congresses, and the I. C. A., with headquarters in London, devoted itself to the gathering of facts regarding co-operative developments, to the stimulation of international co-operative trade, to the advancement of co-operative education, and to the development of effective co-operative practices in many lands.

World War I had a devastating effect on the activities of the Alliance, but the international links of the co-operatives were soon restored with the coming of peace, and the First Congress of the I. C. A., held after the war, at Basle, Switzerland, in 1921, was attended by delegates from

[1] See *ante* p. 680.

co-operatives in twenty-one countries that reported a membership of 25,000,000.

Prior to 1940, the I. C. A. included among its affiliates only consumer co-operative societies. In that year, during World War II, however, the I. C. A. voted to include in its membership agricultural co-operatives.

Since World War II, the co-operative movement of the world has grown steadily in numbers and influence, and has developed along many lines. Noteworthy among its developments have been:

1. The Increase of Representation in the I. C. A.—Growth in the Developing Countries. Prior to World War II, the I. C. A. represented almost exclusively the co-operative movements in Europe and America. Few delegates from Asia or Africa could be seen on the floors of its congresses.

With the decline of colonialism in the East and other social and economic developments in Asia, Africa, and in Latin America, co-operators sought increasingly to establish links with the international co-operative movement. From 1963 to 1966, the I. C. A. admitted 19 new members, chiefly from co-operative societies in the industrially backward lands and, in 1966, 20 non-Europeans were elected by the I. C. A. congress to the Central Committee of the International as compared with 9 at the previous congress.[2]

The 1966 congress of the I. C. A. not only gave increasing recognition to co-operative representatives in non-industrial nations but also helped to finance these co-operatives through development funds—the I. C. A.'s and others. The International and its affiliates also sent to the Asian, African, and Latin American co-operatives its experts on housing, credit, and international trading co-operatives, as well as co-operators experienced in personnel administration, and in co-operatives devoted to the production of dairy products, tea, coffee, cocoa, wine, fruit, vegetables, and other commodities. They likewise ren-

[2] In most of the undeveloped nations of Southeast Asia, the Middle East, Africa, and Latin America, where farming was the chief occupation, the credit co-operative society in the late sixties was the most frequent form of co-operative undertaking. Many co-operative societies existed in parts of Africa in the handling and distribution of cotton, coffee, cocoa, and peanuts.

In addition to the agricultural societies, several other types of co-operatives were in operation: fishery societies in Malaysia, Mexico, and Peru; cottage weavers' societies in India; rural electrical societies in Brazil, etc. In India, co-operation held a significant place in the five-year plans, and, in 1965, the first co-operative department store, Super-Bazaar, was opened in New Delhi. In the Philippines, Pakistan, and Malaysia, co-operative housing began to make much progress in the sixties.

dered assistance to the co-operatives in non-industrialized countries through the International Co-operative Bank and the International Insurance Development Bureau.

As a result of post-war co-operative growth in many fields in the East and the West following the war, the co-operative movement approached the last third of this century with a world membership of 215,000,000, of which 66,000,000, resided in Asia. The co-operative society and individual membership as reported in 1964 by the International Co-operative Alliance was as follows:

CO-OPERATIVE SOCIETIES OF THE WORLD, 1964

Region	*Societies*	*Members*
Europe	111,099	118,054,213
Africa	4,570	1,133,693
Americas	35,892	27,981,190
Asia	421,531	66,388,685
Oceania	2,057	756,062
Total	575,149	214,313,843

2. The Expansion of Co-operative Activity into New Fields. In the early days of the consumers' co-operative movement, mention of co-operatives brought chiefly to mind small- and moderate-sized grocery stores run along co-operative lines, although wholesale enterprises, factories, banks, etc., were added to the co-operative empire within the first generation of the birth of the Rochdale co-operative.

In the years following World War II, the growth of the co-operative movement was accelerated in many fields. By 1963 co-operative credit unions were able to report a turnover of $30 billion a year; co-operative banking, a business of $137 billion. Sixty million policies had been issued by co-operative insurance companies. Co-operatives were owners and managers of tens of thousands of apartments. They were conducting a host of health centers, operating large numbers of electric plants, marketing and refining great quantities of oil for the running of automobiles, farm machinery, etc.; and engaging even more extensively in other kinds of co-operative efforts.

3. Modernization of Management. In the post-World War II years, ever greater attention was given to the rationalization and modernization of co-operative undertakings, with a view, among other things, to competing successfully with the modern, well-stocked, and attractive markets run in increasing numbers by commercial industry.

As a result of scientific analysis of economic trends in co-operative units, certain developments occurred:

a) Many inefficient, badly located co-ops were closed and merged with better located, larger, more efficient units, at times supermarkets in supermarket areas. The co-operative movements' success began no longer to be judged on the basis of the number of units it was operating. In many instances the number of co-operatives decreased, while the total volume of business increased and the co-ops became economically more secure.

b) Increasing use was made in the post-war period of experts in administration and technical skills, and greater effort was made to provide such financial and non-monetary awards to executives as to assure their continuance in the co-operative movement. The practice of many co-operatives of turning management over to co-operators on the basis of their availability and popularity rather than of skills and efficiency became less and less the order of the day. Training institutes for future members of the managerial staff constantly increased in number.

4. **Co-operation Increased among Co-operatives.** For decades, co-operators bemoaned the fact that many retail co-operatives bought but a small proportion of their supplies from the co-operative wholesalers and failed to utilize to the full co-operative warehouses, trading, banking, insurance, credit, educational and other co-operative agencies. As a result of this situation, the Co-operative League of the U. S. A. at its 1960 Congress called for the addition of a fifth principle to the movement, "Co-operation among Co-operatives." Throughout the international movement, attempts were made since the nineteen fifties to bring the various types of co-operatives into closer relation with each other.

A significant effort to bring about more meaningful coordination in the important field of co-operative information was made in the United States in 1958 at a conference of distinguished leaders in the fields of consumer co-operation, co-operative marketing, credit agencies, housing, insurance, health, farm supplies, etc.—a gathering referred to as a "consultation on Co-operation among Co-operators." [3] The conference was a fruitful one that led to meetings in the following years.

5. **The Raising of Increasing Capital.** As a means of financing the large better equipped co-operative stores, wholesales, and factories, and of obtaining adequate funds for the newer co-operative ventures in the fields of housing, health, recreation, banking, insurance, petro-

[3] See Jerry Voorhis, *American Co-operatives* (N. Y.: Harper & Row, 1961), pp. 206–207.

leum, and fertilizers, the co-operative movement in recent decades has required greatly increasing capital.

As a result of countless conferences on how best to raise these funds, the movement in many countries increased its initiation fee for new members; placed a larger amount of its yearly surplus in its capital reserves; issued bonds backed by its real estate holdings; encouraged its members and their families to place their savings in the co-operatives; organized an increasing number of co-operative banks; and obtained, as in the United States, grants and loans for co-operative housing undertakings from governments, foundations, labor unions, and other national and international institutions and interested individuals.

6. Up-dating Co-operative Principles and Practices—Credit Buying. The rapid changes in industrial and social conditions raised increasingly the question in the co-operative movement during the fifties and the sixties as to how far the basic principles and practices of consumers' co-operation were consistent with modern trading conditions and standards. As a result of this questioning, the twenty-second Congress of the I. C. A. in the early sixties appointed a special commission to examine whether co-operative principles should be changed to meet the prevailing situation.

One business practice of co-ops since the days of the Rochdale Pioneers had been that of selling their goods on a cash basis and refusing to extend credit to customers. The commission came to the conclusion that the greatly extended practice of private enterprise of granting credit to customers placed co-operatives at a competitive disadvantage especially in many new co-operative fields, if they continued to demand cash. It therefore recommended to the 1966 Congress of the I. C. A. that, when trading was carried on in a fair and equitable manner, the principles of "no credit" could be dispensed with by the co-ops.

The commission also examined the principle of democratic management and the provision of "one member one vote" to which the co-operative movement had adhered since its early days. The commission concluded in this field that, while the evolution of co-operative enterprises made continual modification inevitable, the co-operative movement had to remain true to its fundamental ideal of democracy. The movement had always held that each member should be given an equal opportunity to share in policy making. There was no way, the commission maintained, to assure that this would be the case, except by giving every member one vote and one vote only.

The commission therefore recommended to the congress of the

I. C. A. that this old practice of one member one vote should be continued. Its recommendation was adopted by the congress as well as that on the extension of credit—that the "no credit" principle be suspended.

The commission's full lists of recommendations for future standards for co-operative societies were as follows:

(1) Membership in a co-operative society should be voluntary and should be open, without social, political, racial, or religious discrimination to all persons willing to accept the responsibilities of membership.

(2) Co-operative societies are democratic organizations. Their affairs should be administered by persons elected or appointed by the members and accountable to them. Members of primary societies should enjoy equal rights of voting—one member one vote—and should participate in decisions affecting their societies.

(3) Share capital should receive only a strictly limited rate of interest, if any.

(4) Surplus or savings, if any, arising out of the operations of a society belong to the members and should be distributed in such a manner as would avoid one member's gaining at the expense of others.

(5) All co-operative societies should make provision for the education of their members, officers, and employees in the principles and techniques of education, both economic and political.[4]

7. **The Co-operatives, Labor, and the Public.** The co-operative movement associated itself extensively in the fifties and sixties with other community organizations, especially such undertakings as housing co-operatives. It sought increasingly to bring the advantages of the co-operative movement before the general public through advertising and public relations agencies and its own personnel. As a means of educating its members and the general public in the principles and achievements of the movement, it initiated an increasing number of conferences, institutes, co-operative tours at home and abroad, publications and broadcasts and became an increasingly active force within and without the U. N. agencies in the promotion of peace.

Many of its leaders maintained the ever greater need of underlining

[4] The standards of the commission, with the exception of that dealing with the extension of credit, adhered in general to those of past decades and received the approval of the congress. For recent co-operative developments in the United States see Voorhis, *American Co-operatives;* literature of the Co-operative League of America, 57 E. Van Buren St., Chicago 5, Ill., and of International Co-operative Alliance, 11 Upper Grosvenor St., London, W1, England.

the ethical as well as the economic aspects of the movement, especially in these decades of moral and world crises. They were critical of the passive role played by large sections of the co-operative membership in the movement which many regarded as primarily a means of reducing prices, and urged co-operative management to involve their members to an ever greater extent in the educational, cultural, economic, and community activities of the movement and to impress co-operators and the general public with the ethical values of the co-operative movement.

CHAPTER 48

Recent Socialist Thought

In the forties, there was a continuation in socialist and non-socialist literature of the controversy as to whether freedom and social planning were compatible. In 1944, the eminent Austrian economist, F. A. von Hayek, wrote a book, the *Road to Serfdom,* in which he maintained that freedom was impossible in a planned society.[1]

The following year Barbara Wootton, a British socialist economist, replied,[2] maintaining that, where the state was a political democracy in which cultural and civil freedoms were observed; where, under the economic plan there was freedom of consumer choice and of choice of work and freedom to bargain collectively; where there was a wise choice of planners, "a planned society can be a far freer society than the competitive *laissez-faire* order which it has come to replace. Its greater freedom lies in its ability to offer those who work in it the sense, on the one hand, of continuous opportunity for the expression of capacity, and the power, on the other hand, to share fully in making the rules under which they work. The failure of the pre-war order was the degree to which, in the daily economic life of the worker, it made freedom and security dependent on privilege . . . Justice is the parent of freedom."

The Frankfurt Declaration of International Socialism (1951). The most authoritative declaration of the world socialist movement on "The Aims and Tasks of Democratic Socialism" in the mid-twentieth century was the Frankfurt Declaration, issued by the constituent congress of the revivified Socialist International which met at Frankfurt, Germany, June 30–July 3, 1951.[3]

1 Published by University of Chicago Press.

2 See Barbara Wootton, *Freedom Under Planning* (Chapel Hill, 1945), pp. 16, 17.

3 See Norman Thomas, *Socialism Re-examined,* pp. 215–24.

The declaration was especially significant by virtue of the fact that its appeal was directed not to the working class as such, but to all men "who believe that the exploitation of man by man must be abolished"; that it emphasized the impossibility of socialism without political and economic democracy and world peace; that its economic aim was not public ownership of the principal means of production and distribution as such, but equal opportunity, freedom from exploitation, social security with increasingly high living standards, and such expansion of democratic public ownership as seemed necessary to attain these ends.

The principles proclaimed by the Frankfurt Declaration can be summarized in the following ten points:

1. Socialism is an international movement which does not demand a rigid uniformity of approach. Whether socialists build their faith on a Marxist or some other method of analyzing society, and whether they are inspired by religious or humanitarian principles, they all strive for the same goal—a system of social justice, better living, freedom, and world peace.

2. Without freedom there can be no socialism. Socialism can be achieved only through democracy. Democracy can be fully realized only through socialism.

3. Socialism seeks to replace capitalism by a system in which the public interest takes precedence over the interests of private profit. The immediate economic aims of socialist policy are full employment, higher production, a rising standard of life, social security, and a fair distribution of income and property.

4. Public ownership may take the form of nationalization of existing private concerns or the creation of new public concerns, municipal or regional enterprises, or consumers' or producers' co-operatives. These various forms of public ownership should be regarded not as ends in themselves, but as means of controlling the basic industries and services on which the economic life and welfare of the community depend, or as a means of nationalizing inefficient industries or preventing private monopolies and cartels from exploiting the public.

5. Trade unions and organizations of producers and consumers are necessary elements in a democratic society.

6. Socialist planning does not mean that all economic decisions are placed in the hands of the government or central authorities. Economic power should be decentralized wherever this is compatible with the aims of planning.

7. Socialists accept as self-evident the individual's right to be re-

warded according to his efforts. But they believe that there are other incentives, such as pride in work well done and a sense of solidarity and team spirit, which can be strengthened when men work for the common interest.

8. Socialists strive to abolish all legal, economic, and political discrimination between the sexes, between social groups, between town and countryside, between regional and racial groups.

9. Democratic socialism rejects every form of imperialism. It fights the oppression and exploitation of any people. Poverty in one part of the world is a threat to prosperity in other parts. There is a need for the redistribution of the world's wealth and for an increase in the productivity of the less developed countries.

10. The struggle for the preservation of peace is inseparably bound up with the struggle for freedom. It is the threat to the independence of free peoples which is directly responsible for the danger of war in our time.

The New Fabianism. In 1889, a number of brilliant members of the British Fabian Society, socialism's most distinguished educational institution, published a volume called *Fabian Essays,* a collection of lectures delivered the previous year before the London Fabian Society by George Bernard Shaw, Sidney Webb, Graham Wallas, William Clarke, Sidney Olivier, and Annie Besant.[4] The volume was edited by George Bernard Shaw. To the surprise of the authors, the book became a best seller and was eagerly read by socialists and students of social problems throughout the world.

The Fabian Essays, while not an official pronouncement of the Fabian Society, were long regarded as representing the best thought of that organization and had a significant impact on the thinking and action of the socialist movement in Great Britain and in other countries.

During the last few decades, leading members of the Society felt the rapidly changing world required new thinking in the realm of socialist philosophy and action and that the Society should prepare and publish a new series of essays.

"To the present generation of Socialists," declared R. H. S. Crossman and Margaret Cole (Mrs. G. D. H. Cole), historian of the Society, "the detailed proposals and formulations of the original *Fabian Essays* can mean little. Partly this is due to the achievements of the labor movement—Fabian blueprints for social welfare, redistributive taxation,

4 See *ante,* p. 238 *et seq.*

nationalization and national minima now form part of the law of the land; partly to changing conditions (the trade unions, for instance, have altered enormously since Annie Besant wrote about them—before the first great dock strike). But partly the outdatedness of *Fabian Essays* derives from inadequacies in the original analysis." Now, for example, "we realize that we cannot completely ignore the rest of the world—as our forebears did in 1889; nor can we accept the concept of a world automatically progressing toward expanding wealth and wider freedoms, which was so deeply rooted in Victorian thought that the first Fabians took it for granted without serious consideration." [5]

Clement Attlee wrote similarly, adding that at the time of the publication of *Fabian Essays,* there was an "underlying assumption that peace will continue and will allow the development of socialism to take place in country after country." [6]

It was not, however, until G. D. H. Cole, then chairman of the Fabian Society, persuaded a group of Fabians to spend a week-end at Buscot Park, in July, 1949, that a real start at a new series was made.

The July conference was the forerunner of many more long discussions and later of the publication in 1952 of the *New Fabian Essays,* written by Margaret Cole, former Prime Minister Attlee, and seven Labor M. P.'s and writers—H. S. Crossman, C. A. R. Crossland, Roy Jenkins, Austen Albu, Ian Mikardo, Denis Healey, and John Strachey.

Mr. Crossman attempted, in his essay, to define the nature of progress and asked what changes in socialist attitudes were required "in the century of totalitarianism." He examined what had happened since the middle of the nineteenth century in contrast with what Marx *said* would happen to western capitalism. Roy Jenkins, recognizing equality as the concept that differentiates socialism from both liberalism and communism, examined the extent to which the aim of economic equality could be further pursued.

Margaret Cole urged a reconstructed educational program, which she felt was essential to the foundation of any socialist society, "but which formed the most glaring gap in the Labor party's program of 1945, 1950 and 1951." Austen Albu dealt with the organization of industry, and, in particular, with methods of bringing the private sector of industry under democratic control, and Ian Mikardo dealt with the difficult issue of how the structure of trade unionism should be adapted to

5 *New Fabian Essays,* edited by R. H. S. Crossman (London: Turnstile Press, 1952) pp. x, xi.

6 *Ibid.,* p. vii.

the requirements of a new social system. In the concluding sections, Denis Healey contended that socialists in the past had failed to understand adequately the power element in politics and that such understanding was the first necessity for a sound foreign policy. The "Marxian Utopia," he declared, "exaggerated the influence of economic factors on human behavior." John Strachey, who combined socialist theory with cabinet experience, sought to assess the changes achieved by the Labor government as a basis on which to construct the next stage of socialism. In general they all agreed with Crossman that the early Fabians erred in not attempting to supply a theoretical basis for practical programs of action and in not fully realizing that economic justice does not automatically secure human freedom and that nothing but "human will and social conscience can liberate men from an historical process which, left to itself, leads to slavery, exploitation and war."

The authors of the essays believed, moreover, that socialists, in analyzing the forces leading to a democratic socialist society, should examine the effect on socialistic progress of developments which had hardly made their appearance when the original *Fabian Essays* was published. Among these developments were the powerful trade union, co-operative, and political labor movements; universal suffrage; mass education; the "welfare state"; giant corporations; the "managerial revolution"; mass communications; advanced industrial technology; the fluidity of labor; communism; fascism; atomic energy; wars, hot and cold; international economic and political organizations; the decline of colonialism; and the science of human behavior. In addition, they felt that it was impossible, as some Fabians and Marxists originally believed, to foretell with certainty, in the modern complex world, social developments of the future, but such analysis of present day trends would be of great value in estimating the road of the future and the things that must be done in helping to guide the future toward a democratic, and equitable, free society.[7]

[7] While preparing the *New Fabian Essays,* the Fabian Society continued its other valuable educational activities, including the issuance of its authoritative pamphlets on the social and international problems of the day; its researches extensively used by Labor members of Parliament and others; its summer schools; its international bureau; its youth section; its local societies, etc.

During the twenties and early thirties there were numerous controversies within the Fabian Society over labor and socialist tactics and in these decades many of the younger intellectuals left the Fabian Society to join the guild socialist movement and the New Fabian Research Bureau, formed during the period of the second Labor government.

Humanist Socialism. In recent years a school of socialist thought has arisen, which has taken the name "Humanist Socialism." Dr. Erich Fromm, prominent psychoanalyst and author, whose works in-

In 1939, a union of the New Fabian Research Bureau and the Fabian Society was effected. Following the amalgamation, the Society decided that its basis, adopted in the eighties of the last century and only slightly modified in 1929, was obsolete and to many unintelligible, and adopted another basis which read in part as follows:

"The Society consists of socialists. It therefore aims at the establishment of a society in which equality of opportunity will be assured, and the economic power and privileges of individuals and classes abolished through the collective ownership and democratic control of the economic resources of the community. It seeks to secure these ends by the methods of political democracy."

In a restatement of the nature of the Fabian Society made in 1942 after the amalgamation, G. D. H. Cole declared: "We believe there is need, somewhere in the socialist movement, for a body which is entirely free to think out and to give publicity to new ideas, even when they run counter to socialist orthodoxies inherited from the past. Socialism is not a set of fixed dogmas, always ready to be applied irrespective of time and place. It is a set of principles that need continual reinterpretations in the light of changing needs and conditions. There is always a danger of mistaking dogmas for principles, and of allowing policies and programs to become ossified, and this danger can be held off only by continual fresh thinking of an essentially objective sort." The Fabian Society is "organized for thought and discussion," Cole continued, "and not for electoral action which it leaves to other bodies, though it encourages its members in their individual capacities to play an active part in the work of these bodies."

In 1943 Cole expressed the opinion that as long as the Independent Labor party remained within the Labor party as a socialist propaganda group it was fitting that the Fabians should specialize in their chosen tasks, of writing and research. But now that no one was doing this wider job of socialist propaganda within the party, the Fabians would have to go out and preach socialism far and wide, if no one else would. (G. D. H. Cole, *Fabian Socialism,* p. 164.)

Among the Fabian developments in pursuance of this new policy, many local Fabian societies were formed throughout the country, these totaling in 1966 over 100.

For more than two score years after the Society's organization, the famous husband and wife team of socialist scholars, Sidney and Beatrice Webb, were the dominant figures in the Fabian Society. In the early 1930's, however, with their advancing age, declining health, and their intensive work on *Soviet Communism,* their activity in the Society waned, although Mrs. Webb remained President of the Fabians until 1941, when she reached the age of 83.

From the early thirties, G. D. H. Cole and Margaret Cole, another brilliant and dedicated team—both were economists and political scientists—succeeded the Webbs as its moving spirits. Professor Cole served either as Chairman or as President of the Society from 1939 until his death in 1959, and Margaret Cole, as President from 1963 until present writing. From the thirties, Clement Attlee, Hugh Gaitskell, Sir Stafford Cripps, Harold Laski, John Parker, John Strachey, and Harold Wilson were among the other distinguished socialists who served as officers of the Society. Included in its over 3,000 membership were scores of members of the House of Commons and many distinguished leaders in the fields of labor, education, and industry. (See Margaret Cole, *The Story of Fabian Socialism* [London: Heinemann, 1961], p. 366; G. D. H. Cole, *The Fabian Society, Past and Present* [The Fabian Society, 11 Dartmouth St., S.W.1, London], 1952.)

clude *Escape from Freedom* and *A Sane Society,* is one of the leading spirits.

Dr. Fromm maintains that every social and economic system is not only a specific system of relations between things and institutions, but a system of human relations.[8]

"The supreme value in all social and economic arrangements is man." The goal of society should be that of offering "the conditions for the full development of man's potentialities, his reason, his love, his creativity; all social arrangements must be conducive to overcoming the alienation of man and to achieve freedom and individuality."

Production and consumption must be subordinated to the needs of man's developments, not the reverse. As a consequence, all products must be directed by the principle of its social usefulness, and not by that of material profit for some individuals and corporations.

"In socialist industrialism the goal is not to achieve the highest *economic* productivity, but to achieve the highest human productivity . . . While, in order to live humanly, basic material needs must be satisfied, consumption must not be an aim in itself.

"Humanist socialism is a system in which man governs capital, not capital man. . . . It is the extension of the democratic process beyond the purely political realm into the economic sphere . . . the true participation of informed citizens in all decisions affecting them."

Humanist socialism, Fromm continues, is not primarily concerned with legal ownership, but with social control of the large and powerful industries: "Irresponsible control by bureaucratic management representing the profit interest of capital must be replaced by administration acting on behalf of, and controlled by, those who produce and consume."

Humanist socialism strives to build a world in which "the enrichment of life and the unfolding of the individual are the prime objects of society, while economics are reduced to their proper role as means for a humanly richer life."

RELIGION AND SOCIAL CHANGE

Following World War II, Protestant and Catholic churches and Jewish congregations laid increasing emphasis on the need of the commitment of religious groups in the fight against the social evils of the day. The battle for the redemption of the individual, they main-

[8] Erich Fromm, *Man, A Socialist Manifesto and Program* (N. Y.: Socialist Party, Third Printing, 1967), pp. 23–26.

tained, was not enough. The religious bodies must preach and practice the social gospel, as well as the gospel of individual redemption.

Churches and synagogues became increasingly active in the war against poverty, in the fight against racial discrimination, and against war. The words and deeds of Pope John XXIII during his reign from 1958 to 1963 greatly stimulated social action not only in the Roman Catholic Church, but throughout the religious world.

In Great Britain and other countries during the post-war days, the Christian socialist movement continued to furnish leaders in the continuing fight for a better social order. In the United States, on the other hand, Church socialist societies disappeared, the apostles of social change devoting their energies increasingly to projects originating in the social service commissions of the churches and in the peace, civil rights, community, labor, political, and other organizations that were springing up on all sides.

Most of the social efforts of the churches were directed to the uprooting of particular social ills; there was little debate on the wisdom of the social order as such. An exception was noted in the case, among others, of the publication of the bi-monthly periodical, *Christianity and Crisis.* Founded by Reinhold Neibuhr and John C. Bennett of Union Theological Seminary, formerly active members of the socialist movement, this magazine constantly called into question the moral nature of a society dominated primarily by profit and power motives.

CHAPTER 49

General Summary

In the previous pages we have traced socialist thinking through its various stages of development from utopianism to the present day.

In the utopian stage, as we have seen, numerous philosophers and humanitarians pictured an ideal commonwealth which needed but to be perceived to be accepted.

They were troubled not at all by the fear that society was not ready for the leap from private to common ownership of industry; that a privileged class could not, as a class, be depended upon to give up its privileges without pressure from below; and that no philosopher, however wise, could decide in detail the exact kind of industrial regime which a future social group would accept. But they performed a unique service in calling attention to the inadequacies of the industrial system and strove nobly to indicate how men and women should live on a more equitable and more brotherly basis.

During the middle of the nineteenth century utopian socialism began to give way to "scientific" or Marxian socialism. Marxian socialists refused to paint vivid word pictures of the coming order. They insisted that society changed from one stage of development to another not as a result of the imaginings of a few dreamers, but of the normal development of economic and social forces, accelerated by the pressure of the working class, conscious of its aims and determined to triumph over the capitalist class and do away with classes and class struggles. The economic interpretation of history, the theory of the class struggle, and the doctrine of surplus value were the cornerstones of the Marxian philosophy. Marx, applying his sociological doctrine to capitalist society, saw industry under capitalism concentrating in fewer and fewer hands; the working class, under unregulated capitalism, increasing in misery; crises becoming ever more extensive, and the industrial order finally collapsing, and giving place to a co-operative order. Marx and Engels believed that this collapse and the triumph of the workers would probably be attended by violence and civil war, although in their later writings they expressed the belief that a peaceful transition might be effected in some of the Western countries.

Some thirty-five years after the issuance of the *Communist Manifesto,* Fabian socialism made its appearance in England. The English Fabians based their economics on the Ricardian law of rent rather than on the labor theory of value. They realized the importance of the workers in bringing about social change, but they believed that other elements in the population besides the working class, namely the middle (professional) groups, could also be reached by the socialist challenge if it were properly presented to them. They set before themselves the task of "permeating" the middle class with the socialist message. They visualized the coming of socialism as a result of increasing municipal and federal ownership of industry, increasing power of labor in legislative and executive offices, increasing growth of the co-operative, trade-union, and educational movements, and the development of social consciousness; in short, through a gradual democratization of society on the political, economic, and intellectual fields. In this school of thought Sidney and Beatrice Webb and Bernard Shaw were the chief pioneers.

Allied with the Fabian school of England was the revisionist school, led by Eduard Bernstein, which originated in Germany. Revisionism was a more conscious attempt than was Fabianism to modify some of the tenets of the Marxian theory. Bernstein in particular saw the class struggle becoming less intense, the condition of the working class improving rather than becoming increasingly degraded, the middle class increasing in numbers, crises becoming less severe, and large areas of industry remaining under small-scale production. The most important thing to Bernstein about socialism was the *movement,* rather than the *ultimate ideal.* From the nineties, when the revisionist challenge was issued, until the First World War, socialism in Germany and other Continental countries was rent asunder in the realm of intellectual discussion if not in party organization by discussions over the issue of Marxism versus revisionism. The Marxian theories, ably defended by Kautsky, were still maintained as the official theories of the party, while revisionist tactics quietly won out in the actual day-to-day struggles of the movement.

In the meanwhile the "revisionism of the left," the syndicalist philosophy, was developing in France and other Latin countries and also making its appearance to some extent in the United States. The syndicalists accepted the class-struggle theory of Karl Marx; they preached the abolition of the political state, urged industrial action as the only effective means of bringing about a revolutionary change in society, looked to the general strike as a means of transforming industry from capitalist to workers' control, and visualized a social order in which all power would be given to the producer, and the trade and industrial union would serve as the economic framework of society.

Deriving their inspiration from the syndicalists, from the ancient guild system, and other sources, a new philosophy, known as guild socialism, endeavoring to combine the good points of socialism and syndicalism, grew up in England in the first quarter of the present century. Here we find, as in syndicalism, the Marxian emphasis on the class struggle, the abolition of the wage system, and the demand for representation of the workers in industrial control. We find also the old guildsman's emphasis on the need for the development of the creative instinct in industry, and the utopian's passion for visualizing in considerable detail the future socialist society.

The guild socialists, however, believed that the syndicalists had ridden one horse to death. The producer should have large control over the industries of the community, but the consumers should also have their say. The old state, used as an instrument of oppression, should be eliminated, but some organization must exist to take charge of the many civic activities necessary to the life of the community; the local control of industry in the bourses, suggested by the syndicalists, would, they believed, prove absolutely inadequate to modern industrial development.

The First World War came. Revolutions followed. Communism loomed up in the East, and the communist or bolshevik movement became the dominant political force throughout the vast Russian territory. Communism, however, failed to gain the adherence of any majority group of workers in any important country outside of Russia. The working class was badly split during the twenties and thirties by the bitter controversies that took place between the followers of the communist and socialist schools of thought. The fascist movement in Italy, Germany, Austria, Hungary, and Spain, among other countries, took advantage of the divisions in the ranks of labor and of the economic and international situation to sweep into power and crush the movements of the masses within their respective borders.

In the meanwhile, for many years before the Second World War, the labor and socialist movements of the Scandinavian countries and Australasia constituted the governments in their respective sectors of Europe and the Far East, and during the twenties and thirties labor alternated between the government and the chief opposition in Great Britain, France, Belgium, and other lands. As a result of the over-all political and international situation of these interwar days, the communist philosophy and policies were very considerably modified. They were further modified during the Second World War, in which period the Third or Communist International, organized originally to foster world revolution along Leninist lines, was finally liquidated, and communists, in such capitalist countries as the United States, declared a moratorium on the fight against the system of "free enterprise."

During these days, likewise, the socialist movement gave much attention to the economic and political problems of a co-operative social order, and to the problems of the transition along democratic lines from a capitalistic to a socialistic economy as well as to problems of postwar reconstruction.

Other social movements developed extensively during the years before the Second World War, notably the consumers' co-operative movement, which became a great economic force in scores of advanced industrial countries and served as a living example of the practicability of a democratic control of industry, with the aim of production for use and not for profit.

There have been other so-called socialist movements in the course of the last century—the school of Christian socialists, led by Charles Kingsley, Frederick Maurice, and others; the school of state socialism and of socialism of the chair of which Schmoller, Wagner, Bismarck, and others were representatives; nor do these exhaust the list.

Each school of thought has had its origin, as has been suggested, in political, economic, and psychical conditions of the period, and each has undergone an evolutionary process, making it at times almost indistinguishable from the school which it started out originally to oppose.

The modern socialist movement is in a sense an amalgam of the various schools of socialist thought which have preceded. The visions of utopian writers have been indelibly impressed on the minds of thousands of socialists and have aroused in them the first emotional impulse to join the host aiming at a reconstructed world. Marxism, with its emphasis on the importance of the economic factor in the progress of society and the part played by the class struggle in the fight to abolish class struggles; Fabianism and revisionism, with their insistence on the gradual development of society toward a new social order through democratic means, and the need of reaching non-proletarian forces with the socialist appeal; syndicalism and guild socialism, with their demand for adequate representation of the producer in the control of industry; communism, with its advocacy of proletarian dictatorship and its experiment in planned production—all are reflected to a greater or lesser extent in the various social movements of the present day. And all of these movements are united in the attainment of an industrial order whose aim is service rather than profit, based on public or co-operative ownership of the principal means of production and distribution. All desire the elimination of the waste, the gross inequality of wealth, and the insecurity of livelihood which, they insist, are inherent in the present organization of society. Yet it would be folly to gloss over the differences in the principles and tactics of the various movements, and especially the sharp conflicts between those who put their faith in democracy both as a method of progress and a goal to be achieved and those who would depend primarily on coercive means and dictatorial political institutions as a means to a socialized order.

A truly socialized system of industry has not as yet "arrived" in the nations of the world. But one cannot study the socialist and other social movements and philosophies which we have surveyed, and observe their effects on politics, on industry, on the social sciences, on literature, and on the ethical concepts of the age, without giving them a secure place among the most powerful influences of the last half-century and among those forces which seem destined fundamentally to shape our entire world economy in the years to come.

The foregoing summary of the history of socialism from utopianism to the early forties was written in the midst of World War II at a time when the socialist movements in nazi-dominated countries were suppressed, many of their leaders imprisoned or executed, and many engaged in a bitter, underground struggle against nazi-controlled governments. After the forces of nazism were defeated, the socialist, labor, and other democratic movements revived. In Great Britain, the Labor Party, under Clement Attlee, was swept into power and began a six-year term of office marked by far-reaching reforms in the fields of social security and nationalization, and the beginning of the dissolution of the Empire. The socialist parties on the continent began to function above ground, became important factors in the political and social life of their respective nations, and soon began to participate again in the international socialist movement.

With the Frankfurt Declaration, the publication of the *New Fabian Essays,* the rise of humanist socialism, democratic socialist thought was reaffirmed and strengthened. In the international field in the post-World War II decades, democratic socialists increasingly emphasized: (1) the need to strengthen the social, economic and peacekeeping services of the U. N.; (2) greater economic aid to the developing countries; (3) political and industrial integration of Europe and other continents; and (4) the expansion of cultural and trade relations with democratic nations and with specific communist countries as centralized controls in the communist bloc begin to weaken. Socialists continued to work for the end of colonialism, negotiations for peaceful settlements of existing wars, and for the uprooting of the causes of future wars. On the domestic front, Labor and Socialist parties, during the last half of the century, in a number of countries, entered coalition governments composed of center and the left-of-center parties to prevent extremist elements from acquiring political power and to press within the government for important social reforms. In France and Finland, where Communist parties were strong, socialists made electoral agreements in the mid-sixties with communists, although refusing in most other countries any voting arrangements with them, and, in Great Britain and other nations, refusing to consider any part in coalition cabinets.

In the belief that rapid technological advances made possible in many developed countries the total abolition of poverty, socialists formulated in the fifties and sixties comprehensive programs for the wiping out of this social evil. In the United States they helped to formulate and support the "Freedom Budget for All Americans," which, among other things, would assure a decent living standard to all.[1]

Socialists throughout the world continued with increasing vigor to attack racial and religious discrimination and to fight for adequate housing, education, health, social security, and recreational services, for the replanning of the cities, for the protection of agriculture, the conservation of natural resources, the preservation of civil liberties, and democratic economic planning for the common good. They co-operated increasingly with labor, cultural, and ethical forces in their respective nations in civil liberties, anti-poverty, anti-war, and other campaigns against the social injustices of the day. They emphasized increasingly the higher ethical, intellectual, and aesthetic values of a co-operative order of industrial society.

1 See *A Freedom Budget for all Americans,* A. Philip Randolph Institute, 127 W. 125 St., N. Y.; Michael Harrington, *The Other America.*

Selected References

PART ONE

Utopianism and Its Precursors

CHAPTER 1: The Social Prophets

BEER, M. *Social Struggles in Antiquity.* Boston: Small, Maynard, 1923.
THE BIBLE.
CRAWFORD, W. H. *Girolamo Savonarola.* N. Y.: Eaton and Mains, 1907.
HEADLAM, S. D. *Christian Socialism.* London: Fabian Tract No. 42, 1892.
HERTZLER, J. O. *The History of Utopian Thought.* N. Y.: Macmillan, 1923, chs. I, II.
HIGGER, MICHAEL. *The Jewish Utopia.* Baltimore: The Lord Baltimore Press, 1932.
HORSBURGH, E. L. S. *Girolamo Savonarola.* London: Methuen and Co., 1911.
MORLEY, HENRY. *Ideal Commonwealths.* N. Y.: Colonial Press, 1901.
OSMUN, G. W. *Augustine: The Thinker.* N. Y.: Eaton and Mains, 1906.
RAUSCHENBUSCH, W. *Christianity and the Social Crisis.* N. Y.: Macmillan, 1907, chs. I, II.
———. *Christianizing the Social Order.* N. Y.: Macmillan, 1912, Part II.
———. *The Social Principles of Jesus.* N. Y.: Association Press, 1916.
VEDDER, HENRY C. *Socialism and the Ethics of Jesus.* N. Y.: Macmillan, 1914, chs. IX, X.
VILLARI, LUIGI AND PASQUALE. "Girolamo Savonarola," *The Encyclopaedia Britannica,* 1940, Vol. XX, 21–24.
WESTMEYER, RUSSELL E. *Modern Economic and Social Systems.* N. Y.: Farrar and Rinehart, 1940, Part I.

CHAPTER 2: Plato's *Republic*

BARKER, ERNST. *Political Thought of Plato and Aristotle.* N. Y.: Holt, 1915.
DICKINSON, G. LOWES. *Plato and His Dialogues.* N. Y.: Norton, 1932.

HART, MADGE A. *Utopias—Old and New.* London: T. Nelson and Sons, 1932.
HERTZLER, J. O. *The History of Utopian Thought.* N. Y.: Macmillan, 1923, ch. III.
MUMFORD, LEWIS. *The Story of Utopias.* N. Y.: Boni & Liveright, 1922, ch. II.
The Republic of Plato. Translated by John Llewellyn Davies and David James Vaughan. N. Y.: A. J. Burt Co. See also Spen's translation in Everyman's Library.
TAYLOR, A. E. *Plato, the Man and His Work.* N. Y.: Dial Press, 1936; London: Constable, 1922.

CHAPTER 3: From Plato to Sir Thomas More

BEER, M. *History of British Socialism.* London: Bell, 1919, Vol. I, chs. I–IV.
———. *Social Struggles in the Middle Ages.* N. Y.: Small, Maynard, 1924.
HERTZLER, J. O. *The History of Utopian Thought.* N. Y.: Macmillan, 1923, ch. IV.
MUMFORD, LEWIS. *The Story of Utopias.* Boni & Liveright, 1922, ch. III.
OMAN, CH. W. C. *Great Revolt of 1381.* Oxford: Clarendon Press, 1906.
Piers Ploughman. N. Y.: Longmans, 1913.
TREVELYAN, G. M. *Age of Wycliffe.* N. Y.: Longmans, 1899.

CHAPTER 4: More's *Utopia*

BEER, M. *History of British Socialism.* London: Bell, 1919, Vol. I, ch. IV.
CHAMBERS, R. W. *Thomas More.* London: Jonathan Cape, 1935.
GUTHRIE, W. B. *Socialism before the French Revolution.* N. Y.: Macmillan, 1907, chs. II, III.
HART, MADGE A. *Utopias—Old and New.* London: T. Nelson, 1932.
HERTZLER, J. O. *The History of Utopian Thought.* N. Y.: Macmillan, 1923, ch. IV.
KAUTSKY, KARL. *Thomas More and His Utopia.* N. Y.: International Publishers, 1926.
LEE, SIDNEY. *Great Englishmen of the Sixteenth Century.* N. Y.: Scribner's, 1904.
MORE, SIR THOMAS. *Utopia.* N. Y.: Dutton, Everyman's Library.
MORLEY, HENRY, Editor. *Ideal Commonwealths.* Rev. ed. N. Y.: Colonial Press, 1901. Text of More's *Utopia.*
MUMFORD, LEWIS. *The Story of Utopias.* N. Y.: Boni & Liveright, 1922, ch. III.
ROUTH, E. M. G. *Sir Thomas More and His Friends.* London: Humphrey Milford, 1934.

STAPLETON, THOMAS. *The Life and Illustrious Martyrdom of Sir Thomas More.* London: Burns, Oates and Washbourne, Ltd., 1928. First published in 1588.

CHAPTER 5: Bacon's *New Atlantis*

ABBOTT, EDWIN A. *Francis Bacon.* London: Macmillan, 1885.

BEER, M. *History of British Socialism.* London: Bell, 1919, Vol. I, pp. 46–50.

CHURCH, R. W. *Bacon.* London: Macmillan, 1910.

GUTHRIE, W. B. *Socialism before the French Revolution.* N. Y.: Macmillan, 1907, pp. 183–7.

HERTZLER, J. O. *History of Utopian Thought.* N. Y.: Macmillan, 1923, pp. 146–53.

MORLEY, HENRY. *Ideal Commonwealths.* Rev. ed. N. Y.: Colonial Press, 1901.

MUMFORD, LEWIS. *The Story of Utopias.* N. Y.: Boni & Liveright, 1922, ch. V.

CHAPTER 6: German and Italian Utopias

ANDREAE, J. V. *Christianapolis.* Translated by Felix E. Held. Oxford University Press, 1916.

GUTHRIE, W. B. *Socialism before the French Revolution.* N. Y.: Macmillan, 1907, chs. IV, V.

HELD, FELIX E. *Christianapolis, an Ideal State of the Seventeenth Century.* Urbana, Ill.: University of Illinois Press, 1914. A translation of Andreae's text.

HERTZLER, J. O. *The History of Utopian Thought.* N. Y.: Macmillan, 1923, ch. IV.

MORLEY, HENRY. *Ideal Commonwealths.* Rev. ed. N. Y.: Colonial Press, 1901.

MUMFORD, L. *The Story of Utopias.* N. Y.: Boni & Liveright, 1922, ch. V.

CHAPTER 7: Social Thought through the Seventeenth Century

BEER, M. *History of British Socialism.* London: Bell, 1919, chs. V, VI.

CHAMBERLEN, P. *Poor Man's Advocate.* 1649.

HARRINGTON, JAMES. *The Commonwealth of Oceana.* London: Routledge, 1887.

HERTZLER, J. O. *History of Utopian Thought.* N. Y.: Macmillan, 1919, pp. 165–72.

Hobbes, Thomas. *Leviathan.* London: Routledge, 1886.
Locke, John. *Civil Government.* London: Dent, 1924.
Smith, H. F. R. *Harrington and His Oceana.* Cambridge: University Press, 1914, p. 5.
Winstanley, Gerrard. *The Law of Freedom in a Platform.* London: 1652; San Francisco: Sutro branch, California State Library. Occasional Papers. English Reprint Series. No. 3, 1939.

CHAPTER 8: The French Utopians

Beer, M. *Social Struggles and Thought.* Boston: Small, Maynard, chs. VII, X.
Booth, A. J. *Saint-Simon and Saint-Simonism.* London: Longmans, Green, Reader and Dyer, 1871.
Ely, Richard T. *French and German Socialism.* N. Y.: Harper, 1883, chs. I–VII.
Fourier, Charles. *Theory of Social Organization.* N. Y.: C. P. Somerby, 1876. 2 parts.
Hertzler, O. J. *History of Utopian Thought.* N. Y.: Macmillan, 1923, ch. V.
Kirkup, Thomas. *History of Socialism.* London: G. Black. Rev. and Enl., 1913, chs. II, III.
Mumford, Lewis. *The Story of Utopias.* N. Y.: Boni & Liveright, 1922, ch. VIII.
Reybaud, L. *Études sur les Réformateurs; ou Socialistes modernes.* Paris: Guillaumin, 1844–8.
Saint-Simon, C. H. *Œuvres.* Paris: Capelle, 1841.
———. *L'oeuvre d'Henri de Saint-Simon.* Paris: F. Alcan, 1925.
Wagner, Donald O. *Social Reformers.* N. Y.: Macmillan, 1934. Chapters on Fourier and Blanc.
Wilson, Edmund. *To the Finland Station.* N. Y.: Harcourt, Brace, 1940, pp. 71–98.

CHAPTER 9: The Forerunners of Robert Owen

Beer, M. *History of British Socialism.* London: Bell, 1919, Vol. I, Part II.
———. *The Pioneers of Land Reform.* London: Bell, 1920.
Burke, Edmund. *Vindication of Natural Society.* London: M. Cooper, 1756.
Coleridge, Samuel T. *Letters.* 2 vols. London: Heinemann, 1895.
Colquhoun, Patrick. *Treatise on the Wealth, Power, and Resources of the British Empire.* London: J. Mawman, 1815.
Godwin, William. *Enquiry Concerning Political Justice.* London: J. and J. Robinson, 1793; New York: Knopf, 1926.

HALL, CHARLES. *Effects of Civilization.* London, 1805.
OGILVIE, WILLIAM. *Essay on the Right of Property in Land.* London: J. Walter, 1782.
PAINE, THOMAS. *Life and Works.* New Rochelle: Thomas Paine National Historical Association, 1925.
PALEY, WILLIAM. *The Principles of Moral and Political Philosophy.* 1785, Book 3.
POPE, ALEXANDER. *Essay on Man.* London: J. and P. Knapton, 1748. Enlarged edition.
RICARDO, DAVID. *Principles of Political Economy.* N. Y.: Macmillan, 1909.
SHELLEY, PERCY B. *Poems.* Esp. *Queen Mab, Poems of the Times, Prometheus Unbound* in *The Complete Works of Percy B. Shelley.* London: Published for the Julian Editions by Ernest Benn, 1926–30.
SMITH, ADAM. *Wealth of Nations.* 1776; London: Methuen and Co., 1930.
SOUTHEY, ROBERT. *Letters from England.* N. Y.: Longworth, 1808.
WORDSWORTH, WILLIAM. *Prelude.* Book II.

CHAPTER 10: Robert Owen

BEER, M. *History of British Socialism.* London: Bell, 1919, Vol. I, Part II, ch. V.
COLE, G. D. H. *The Life of Robert Owen.* N. Y.: Macmillan, 1930.
HERTZLER, J. O. *History of Utopian Thought.* N. Y.: Macmillan, 1923, ch. V.
HILLQUIT, MORRIS. *History of Socialism in the United States.* N. Y.: Funk & Wagnalls, 1910, ch. II.
JONES, LLOYD. *The Life, Times, and Labors of Robert Owen.* London: Allen and Unwin, 1919.
KIRKUP, T. *History of Socialism.* London: G. Black, 1913, ch. VI.
LOCKWOOD, GEORGE B. *The New Harmony Movement.* N. Y.: Appleton, 1905.
OWEN, ROBERT. *New Moral World.* London, 1836.
———. *Life of Robert Owen by Himself,* with introduction by M. Beer. N. Y.: Knopf, 1920. Original autobiography from which references are made, published in 1857.
———. *Revolution in the Mind and Practice of the Human Race.* London, 1848.
PODMORE, FRANK. *Robert Owen.* A Biography. 2 vols. Hutchinson, 1906. London: Allen & Unwin, 1923.

CHAPTER 11: Utopianism in America

BRISBANE, ALBERT. *Association; or a Concise Exposition of the Practical Part of Fourier's Social Science.* N. Y.: Greeley & McElrath, 1843.

BROOKS, VAN WYCK. *The Flowering of New England.* N. Y.: Dutton, 1936.
HILLQUIT, MORRIS. *History of Socialism in the United States.* N. Y.: Funk & Wagnalls, 1910, Part I.
HINDS, W. A. *American Communities.* Chicago: Charles H. Kerr, 1902.
KENT, ALEXANDER. *Cooperative Communities in the United States.* In Bulletin of Dept. of Labor, No. 35, July, 1901.
LEOPOLD, RICHARD W. *Robert Dale Owen.* Cambridge, Mass.: Harvard University Press, 1940.
LOCKWOOD, G. B. *The New Harmony Movement.* N. Y.: Appleton, 1905.
NORDHOFF, CHARLES. *The Communistic Societies of the United States.* N. Y.: Harper, 1875.
NOYES, PIERREPONT. *My Father's House: An Oneida Boyhood.* N. Y.: Farrar and Rinehart, 1937.
SHAW, ALBERT. *Icaria; A Chapter in the History of Communism.* N. Y.: Putnam, 1884.
SOUTHERAN, CHARLES. *Horace Greeley and Other Pioneers of American Socialism.* N. Y.: Mitchell Kennerley, 1915.

CHAPTER 12: The Significance of Utopianism—Modern Utopian Writers

BELLAMY, EDWARD. *Looking Backward.* Boston: Houghton Mifflin, 1926. N. Y.: Vanguard Press.
———. *Equality.* N. Y.: Appleton, 1897.
BLOOMFIELD, PAUL. *Imaginary Worlds.* London: H. Hamilton, 1932.
BULWER-LYTTON, EDWARD. *The Coming Race.* London: Routledge. N. Y.: Felt & Co., 1871.
BUTLER, SAMUEL. *Erewhon.* N. Y.: E. P. Dutton, 1917.
ENGELS, FRIEDRICH. *Socialism, Utopian and Scientific.* N. Y.: International Publishers, 1935.
HERTZKA, THEODOR. *Freeland: A Social Anticipation.* Translation published London: British Freeland Association, 1894.
HERTZLER, J. O. *History of Utopian Thought.* N. Y.: Macmillan, 1923, Part II.
HILLQUIT, MORRIS. *History of Socialism in the United States.* N. Y.: Funk & Wagnalls, 1910, pp. 125–43.
HOWELLS, WILLIAM DEAN. *A Traveler from Altruria.*
HUDSON, W. H. *A Crystal Age.* N. Y.: Dutton, 1906.
MORRIS, WILLIAM. *News from Nowhere.* N. Y.: Vanguard Press, 1926.
———. *Stories in Prose.* N. Y.: Random House, 1934.
ROSS, HARRY. *Utopias Old and New.* London: Nicholson and Watson, 1938.
RUSSELL, FRANCES T. *Touring Utopia.* N. Y.: L. MacVeagh, Dial Press, 1932.

SOMBART, WERNER. *Socialism and the Social Movement.* N. Y.: Dutton, 1909, Part I, ch. II.

SPARGO, JOHN, AND ARNER, G. B. L. *Elements of Socialism.* N. Y.: Macmillan, 1912, ch. XVI.

WELLS, H. G. *A Modern Utopia.* N. Y.: Thomas Nelson, 1905.

———. *The Open Conspiracy.* N. Y.: Doubleday, Doran, 1928.

PART TWO

Marxism

CHAPTER 13: Beginnings of Marxism

ADAMS, HENRY. *Karl Marx and His Earlier Writings.* London: Allen and Unwin, 1940.

BEER, M. *The Life and Teaching of Karl Marx.* Boston: Small, Maynard, 1924.

COATES, ZELDA KAHAN. *The Life and Work of Friedrich Engels.* London: Communist Party, 1920.

COLE, G. D. H. *What Marx Really Meant.* N. Y.: Knopf, 1934.

CORNU, AUGUSTIN. *Karl Marx.* Paris: Felix Alcan, 1934 (In French).

ENGELS, FRIEDRICH. *Condition of the Working Class in 1844.* London: Sonnenschein, 1892.

GOLDENDACH, DAVID B. *Karl Marx, Man, Thinker and Revolutionist.* London: M. Lawrence, 1927.

HEGEL, G. W. H. *Science of Logic.* Part I. Oxford, 1894.

HOOK, SIDNEY. *Towards the Understanding of Karl Marx.* N. Y.: John Day, 1933.

KORSCH, KARL. *Karl Marx.* London: J. Wiley, 1938.

LEE, ALGERNON. *The Essentials of Marx.* N. Y.: Vanguard, 1926.

LORIA, ACHILLE. *Karl Marx.* N. Y.: Thomas Seltzer, 1920.

LOWENTHAL, E. *The Ricardian Socialists.* N. Y.: Columbia University Press, 1911.

MARX, KARL. *The Holy Family,* 1844.

———. *Poverty of Philosophy.* Chicago: C. H. Kerr, 1910 (originally published, 1847).

———, AND ENGELS, FRIEDRICH. *The Communist Manifesto.* London, 1848. There have been numerous editions.

MAYER, GUSTAV. *Friedrich Engels.* N. Y.: Knopf, 1936.

MEHRING, F. *Karl Marx: The Story of His Life.* N. Y.: Covici Friede, 1935.

Nicolaievsky, Boris, and Maenchen-Helfen, Otto. *Karl Marx, Man and Fighter.* N. Y.: Lippincott, 1936.
Riazanov, O. *Karl Marx and Friedrich Engels.* N. Y.: International Publishers, 1926.
Rühle, Otto. *Karl Marx.* N. Y.: Viking Press, 1929.
Spargo, John. *Karl Marx; His Life and Work.* N. Y.: Huebsch, 1910.

CHAPTER 14: The Communist Manifesto and the Revolutions of 1848

Beer, M. *History of British Socialism.* N. Y.: Harcourt, Brace, 1921, Vol. II, Part III.
———. *Life and Teaching of Karl Marx.* Boston: Small, Maynard, 1925, ch. III.
Hayes, C. J. H. *A Political and Social History of Modern Europe.* N. Y.: Macmillan, Vol. II.
Labor Research Study Group, Scott Nearing, Leader. *The Law of Social Revolution.* N. Y.: Social Science Pub., 1926, ch. VIII.
Laski, Harold J. *Karl Marx, An Essay.* With the *Communist Manifesto.* N. Y.: League for Industrial Democracy, 1933.
Lee, Algernon. *The Essentials of Marx.* N. Y.: Vanguard, 1926. Contains *The Communist Manifesto, Wage-Labor and Capital; Value, Price and Profit* and other selections by Karl Marx.
Marx, Karl. *Selections from "Capital," the "Communist Manifesto" and Other Writings.* N. Y.: Modern Library, 1932.
———. *The Civil War in France* (written 1871). Chicago: Chas. H. Kerr.
———. *Revolution and Counter-Revolution* (written 1851–2). Chicago: Chas. H. Kerr, 1914.
———. *The Eighteenth Brumaire of Louis Bonaparte.* 1852. American Edition. Chicago: Chas. H. Kerr, 1913.
Mehring, Franz. *Karl Marx.* N. Y.: Covici Friede, 1935.
Nicolaievsky, Boris, and Maenchen-Helfen, Otto. *Karl Marx, Man and Fighter.* N. Y.: Lippincott, 1936.
Postgate, R. W. *Revolution, from 1789 to 1906.* London: G. Richards, 1920.
Robinson, James Harvey, and Beard, Charles A. *Outlines of European History.* N. Y.: Ginn & Co., 1912, pp. 275–310.
Rosenberg, Arthur. *Democracy and Socialism.* N. Y.: Knopf, 1939.

CHAPTER 15: Marx's Career after 1848

Beer, M. *Life and Teaching of Karl Marx.* Boston: Small, Maynard, 1925.
Kirkup, Thomas. *History of Socialism.* N. Y.: Macmillan, 1892, ch. VII.

HOOK, SIDNEY. *Towards the Understanding of Karl Marx.* N. Y.: John Day, 1933.

LASKI, HAROLD, J. *Karl Marx,* with the *Communist Manifesto.* N. Y.: League for Industrial Democracy, 1933.

LEE, ALGERNON, Editor. *The Essentials of Marx.* N. Y.: Vanguard Press, 1926.

LIEBKNECHT, WILHELM. *Karl Marx, Biographical Memoirs.* Chicago: Kerr, 1901.

LAIDLER, HARRY W., AND THOMAS, NORMAN. *The Socialism of Our Times.* N. Y.: Vanguard, 1929.

LORIA, ACHILLE. *Karl Marx.* N. Y.: Seltzer, 1920.

MARX, KARL. *Eighteenth Brumaire of Louis Bonaparte.* (Originally written 1848.)

———. *Class Struggles in France.* N. Y.: Labor News Co. (Written 1848–50.)

———. *Revolution and Counter-Revolution.* (Originally written in the early fifties.)

———. *Critique of Political Economy.* Chicago: Kerr, 1913. (Originally written 1859.)

———. *Address and Provisional Rules of the International Working Men's Association.* London: Labor and Socialist International, 1924. (Originally delivered 1864.)

———. *Value, Price, and Profit.* Chicago: Kerr. (Originally published 1865.)

———. *Capital.* 3 volumes. Chicago: Kerr, 1907, 1909, London: Sonnenschein, 1903. (1st edition of 1st volume, 1867; 2nd and 3rd volumes not published until 1885 and 1894, respectively.)

———. *Capital, The Communist Manifesto and Other Writings,* edited by Max Eastman. N. Y.: Modern Library, 1932.

———. *The Civil War in France.* London: Labor Publishing Co., 1921. Chicago, Kerr (originally written 1871).

———. *The Gotha Program.* N. Y.: Socialist Labor Party, 1922 (originally written 1875).

MAYER, GUSTAV. *Friedrich Engels.* N. Y.: Knopf, 1936.

MEHRING, FRANZ. *Karl Marx, The Story of His Life.* N. Y.: Covici Friede, 1935.

NICOLAIEVSKY, BORIS, AND MAENCHEN-HELFEN, OTTO. *Karl Marx, Man and Fighter.* N. Y.: Lippincott, 1936.

RICARDO, DAVID. *Principles of Political Economy.* N. Y.: Macmillan, 1909.

ROSENBERG, ARTHUR. *Democracy and Socialism.* N. Y.: Knopf, 1939.

RÜHLE, OTTO. *Karl Marx.* N. Y.: Viking Press, 1929.

SPARGO, JOHN. *Karl Marx; His Life and Works.* N. Y.: Huebsch, 1910.

CHAPTER 16: Theoretical Foundation of Marxism

BEARD, CHAS. A. *An Economic Interpretation of the Constitution of the U. S.* N. Y.: Macmillan, 1913.

BEBER, M. M. *Karl Marx's Interpretation of History.* Cambridge, Mass.: Harvard University, 1927.

BERENBERG, DAVID P. *Socialist Fundamentals.* N. Y.: Rand School, 1932.

BLAKE, WILLIAM J. *Elements of Marxian Theory and Its Criticism.* N. Y.: Cordon Company, 1939.

BÖHM-BAWERK, E. V. *Karl Marx and the Close of His System.* N. Y.: 1898.

BOUDIN, LOUIS B. *Theoretical System of Karl Marx.* Chicago: Kerr, 1910.

BUKHARIN, NIKOLAI. *Historical Materialism.* N. Y.: International Publishers, 1925.

COLE, G. D. H. *What Marx Really Meant.* N. Y.: Knopf, 1934.

CROCE, B. *Historical Materialism and the Economics of Karl Marx.* N. Y.: Macmillan, 1914.

DOBB, MAURICE. *Capitalist Enterprise and Social Progress.* London: Routledge, 1925.

EASTMAN, MAX. *Marxism: Science or Religion?* N. Y.: W. W. Norton, 1940.

EMMET, W. H. *Marxian Economic Handbook.* N. Y.: International Publishers, 1925.

ENGELS, FRIEDRICH. *Socialism, Utopian and Scientific.* N. Y.: Scribner's, 1892.

———. *Origin of the Family.* Chicago: Kerr, 1902. (1st edition, 1884.)

———. *Landmarks of Scientific Socialism.* Chicago: Kerr, 1907.

GUEST, DAVID. *A Textbook of Dialectical Materialism.* N. Y.: International Publishers, 1939.

HILFERDING, R. *Böhm-Bawerk's Criticism of Marx.* Glasgow: 1920.

HILLQUIT, MORRIS. *Socialism in Theory and Practice.* N. Y.: Macmillan, 1909, Pt. I.

HOOK, SIDNEY. *Towards the Understanding of Karl Marx.* N. Y.: John Day Co., 1933.

HUGHAN, JESSIE W. *American Socialism of the Present Day.* N. Y.: Lane, 1911.

JACKSON, T. A. *Dialectics, the Logic of Marxism and Its Critics.* London: Lawrence and Wishart, 1936.

KAUTSKY, KARL. *The Economic Doctrines of Karl Marx.* London: A. and C. Black, 1925.

LABRIOLA, ANTONIO. *Essays on the Materialistic Conception of History.* Chicago: Kerr, 1912.

LAIDLER, HARRY W. *Socialism in Thought and Action.* N. Y.: Macmillan, 1920, chs. III, IV.

———, AND THOMAS, NORMAN, Editors. *The Socialism of Our Times.* N. Y.: Vanguard, 1929.

LEE, ALGERNON, Editor. *The Essentials of Marx.* Collection of Marx's Clas-

sics with an Introduction by Algernon Lee. N. Y.: Vanguard Press, 1926.
LeRossignol, James E. *From Marx to Stalin.* N. Y.: Thos. Y. Crowell, 1940.
Marx, Karl. *Value, Price, and Profit.* Chicago: Kerr.
———. *Critique of Political Economy.* Chicago: Kerr, 1913.
Mehring, Franz. *Karl Marx.* N. Y.: Covici Friede, 1935.
Murry, J. Middleton and Associates. *Marxism.* London: Chapman and Hall, 1935.
Parkes, Henry B. *Marxism: An Autopsy.* Boston: Houghton Mifflin, 1939.
Russell, Bertrand, Dewey, John, and Others. *The Meaning of Marx. A Symposium.* N. Y.: Farrar and Rinehart, 1934.
Sachs, A. S. *Basic Principles of Scientific Socialism.* N. Y.: Vanguard Press, 1926.
Seligman, E. R. A. *Economic Interpretation of History.* N. Y.: Columbia University, 1907.
Skelton, O. D. *Socialism, A Critical Analysis.* Boston: Houghton Mifflin, 1913.
Strachey, John. *The Nature of the Capitalist Crisis.* N. Y.: Covici Friede, 1935.
———. *Theory and Practice of Socialism.* London: Gollancz, 1936.
Sweezy, Paul M. *The Theory of Capitalist Development.* N. Y.: Oxford Press, 1942.
Tugan-Baranowski. *Modern Socialism and Its Historical Development.* London: S. Sonnenschein, 1910.

PART THREE

Other Schools of Thought

CHAPTER 17: Forerunners of the Fabians

Beer, M. *History of British Socialism.* N. Y.: Macmillan, Vol. II, ch. XII.
Cairns, John E. *Some Leading Principles of Political Economy.* N. Y.: Harper, 1874.
Carlyle, Thomas. *The Socialism and Unsocialism of Thomas Carlyle.* N. Y.: Humboldt Pub. Co., 1891.
———. *Past and Present, Chartism, Sartor Resartus.* N. Y.: Harper, 1848.
Engels, Friedrich. *Condition of the Working Class in England in 1844.* London: Sonnenschein, 1892. Preface.
Graham, William. *English Political Philosophy.* 1907. London: E. Arnold, 1899.
Laidler, H. W. *British Co-operative Movement.* N. Y.: Co-operative League, 1917.

MACCUNN, JOHN. *Six Radical Thinkers: Bentham, J. S. Mill, Cobden, Carlyle, Mazzini, T. H. Green.* London, Arnold, 1907.

MILL, JOHN STUART. *Autobiography.* N. Y.: Holt, 1873.

———. *Programme of the Land Tenure Reform Association.* London: 1871.

———. *Principles of Political Economy.* Book II, ch. 2, 1848.

———. *Socialism.* N. Y.: Humboldt, 1891.

PEASE, EDWARD. *History of the Fabian Society.* N. Y.: International Pub., 1925.

ROBINSON, J. H., AND BEARD, CHARLES A. *Outline of European History.* Part II, ch. XIX.

RUSKIN, JOHN. *Ruskin's Views of Social Justice.* Edited by James Fuchs. N. Y.: Vanguard Press, 1926.

WEBB, SIDNEY AND BEATRICE. *History of Trade Unionism.* London: Fabian Society, 1925. N. Y.: Longmans, Green, 1894, chs. IV–VII.

WEST, JULIUS. *John Stuart Mill.* London: Fabian Society. Fabian Tract 168, 1913.

CHAPTER 18: Fabianism

BEER, M. *History of British Socialism.* N. Y.: Harcourt, Brace, 1921, ch. XIV.

COLE, G. D. H. *Persons and Periods.* N. Y.: Macmillan, 1938.

———. *Fabian Socialism.* London: Allen and Unwin, 1943.

———. *The Fabian Society, Past and Present.* Tract 258. London: The Fabian Society, 1942.

Fabian Society. *Where Stands Democracy?* A series of essays by G. D. H. Cole, Harold J. Laski, and others. N. Y.: Macmillan, 1940.

Fabian Tracts. A volume of the Fabian Society pamphlets now in print. London: The Fabian Society.

HYNDMAN, HENRY M. *Economics of Socialism.* London: Twentieth Century Press, 1896.

———. *The Record of an Adventurous Life.* N. Y.: Macmillan, 1911.

MORRIS, WILLIAM. *Poems by the Way.* N. Y.: Longmans, 1920.

PEASE, EDWARD. *History of the Fabian Society.* N. Y.: International Publishers, 1925.

Report on Fabian Policy. Tract 70. London: Fabian Society, 1896.

SHAW, G. BERNARD. *Intelligent Women's Guide to Socialism and Capitalism.* N. Y.: Brentano, 1928.

———. *The Fabian Society, Its Early History.* Tract 41. London: Fabian Society, 1892.

———. *The Socialism of Shaw.* Edited by James Fuchs. N. Y.: Vanguard Press, 1927.

———, AND OTHERS. *Fabian Essays.* Boston: Ball Pub. Co.; also special edition of Fabian Society, 1920.

TROTSKY, LEON. *Whither England?* N. Y.: International Publishers, 1925, ch. IV.

WEBB, BEATRICE. *My Apprenticeship.* N. Y.: Longmans, 1926.

CHAPTER 19: Beginnings of German Social Democracy

BEBEL, AUGUST. *My Life.* Chicago: U. of Chicago Press, 1912.

BERNSTEIN, EDUARD. *Ferdinand Lassalle as Social Reformer.* London, 1893.

BRANDES, GEORGE. *Ferdinand Lassalle.* N. Y.: Bernard G. Richards, 1925.

DAWSON, W. H. *German Social Democracy and Ferdinand Lassalle.* N. Y.: Scribner's, 1899.

ELY, RICHARD T. *French and German Socialism.* N. Y.: Harper, 1883.

ENSOR, R. C. K. (ed.). *Modern Socialism.* N. Y.: Scribner's, 1908.

KAMPFFMEYER, PAUL. *Changes in the Theory and Tactics of the (German) Social Democracy.* Chicago: Kerr, 1908.

MARKHAM, S. F. *A History of Socialism.* N. Y.: Macmillan, 1930.

MAYER, GUSTAV. *Friedrich Engels.* N. Y.: Knopf, 1936.

MEHRING, FRANZ. *Geschichte der deutschen Sozial-Demokratie.* Stuttgart: Dietz, 1914.

———. *Karl Marx.* N. Y.: Covici Friede, 1935.

ORTH, S. P. *Socialism and Democracy in Europe.* N. Y.: Holt, 1913.

RUSSELL, BERTRAND. *German Social Democracy.* N. Y.: Longmans, 1896.

SANDERS, W. S. *Socialist Movement in Germany.* London: Fabian Society, 1913 (pamphlet).

CHAPTER 20: Eduard Bernstein and Revisionism

BERNSTEIN, EDUARD. *Evolutionary Socialism.* N. Y.: Huebsch (now Viking Press), 1909.

———. *My Life in Exile.* N. Y.: Harcourt, Brace, 1921.

BLAKE, WILLIAM J. *Marxian Economic Theory.* N. Y.: Cordon Co., 1939, ch. XXXIV.

BÖHM-BAWERK, E. V. *Karl Marx and the Close of His System.* N. Y.: 1898.

CROCE, BENEDETTO. *Historical Materialism and the Economics of Karl Marx.* N. Y.: Macmillan, 1914.

EASTMAN, MAX. *Marxism: Is It a Science?* N. Y.: Norton, 1940.

ENSOR, R. C. K. *Modern Socialism.* A Source Book. N. Y.: Scribner's, 1907

HOBSON, J. A. *The Industrial System.* N. Y.: Longmans, esp. chs. VIII, XIV

HOOK, SIDNEY. *Towards the Understanding of Karl Marx.* N. Y.: The John Day Co., 1933, ch. V.

HUGHAN, JESSIE W. *American Socialism of the Present Day.* N. Y.: Lane, 1911.

KAMPFFMEYER, PAUL. *Changes in the Theory and Tactics of the German Social Democracy.* Chicago: Kerr, 1908.

KAUTSKY, KARL. *Bernstein und das Sozial Democratische Programm.* Eine Antikritik. Stuttgart, 1899.

LASKI, HAROLD J. *Karl Marx.* With the *Communist Manifesto.* N. Y.: League for Industrial Democracy, 1933.

OPPENHEIMER, FRANZ. *The State.* N. Y.: Vanguard Press, 1926.

PEASE, EDWARD R. *History of the Fabian Society.* N. Y.: International Publishers, 1925, ch. XII.

SOMBART, WERNER. *Socialists and the Social Movement.* 1909, Part 1, ch. IV.

SIMKHOVITCH, V. G. *Marxism vs. Socialism.* N. Y.: Holt, 1913.

TUGAN-BARONOWSKY. *Modern Socialism in Its Historical Development.* London: Sonnenschein, 1910.

WEYL, W. E. *New Democracy.* N. Y.: Macmillan, 1912.

CHAPTER 21: Marxists' Reply to Revisionists

BLAKE, WILLIAM J. *Marxian Economic Theory.* N. Y.: Cordon, 1939.

BOUDIN, LOUIS B. *Theoretical System of Karl Marx.* Chicago: Kerr, 1910.

CAHN, HERMAN. *Capital Today.* Rev. Ed. N. Y.: Putnam, 1918.

EASTMAN, MAX. *Marxism: Is It a Science?* N. Y.: Norton, 1940.

HILFERDING, R. *Böhm-Bawerk's Criticism of Marx.* Glasgow, 1920.

HUGHAN, JESSIE W. *American Socialism of the Present Day.* N. Y.: Lane, 1911.

KAUTSKY, KARL. *Bernstein und das Sozial Democratische Programm.* Eine Antikritik. Stuttgart, 1899.

———. *The Labor Revolution.* London: George Allen and Unwin, 1925.

———. *Road to Power.* Chicago: Bloch, 1909.

———. *The Class Struggle.* Chicago: Kerr, 1910.

———. *The Social Revolution.* Chicago: Kerr, 1902.

———. *The Economic Doctrines of Karl Marx.* London: A. & C. Black, 1925.

LAIDLER, HARRY W., Editor. *The Socialism of Our Times.* N. Y.: Vanguard, 1929.

RUBINOW, I. M. *Was Marx Wrong?* N. Y.: Marx Institute, 1914.

SACHS, A. J. *Basic Principles of Scientific Socialism.* N. Y.: Vanguard Press, 1925.

SPARGO, JOHN, AND ARNER, G. B. L. *The Elements of Socialism.* N. Y.: Macmillan, 1912.

CHAPTER 22: French Syndicalism

BRISSENDEN, P. F. *The I. W. W., A Study in American Syndicalism.* N. Y.: Longmans, Green, 1919.

BROOKS, JOHN GRAHAM. *American Syndicalism.* N. Y.: Macmillan, 1913.

CLARK, MARJORIE R. *A History of the French Labor Movement (1910–1938)*. Berkeley, Calif.: University of California Press, 1930.

COLE, G. D..H. *World of Labor.* London: Bell, 1917.

———. *Self Government in Industry.* London: Bell, 1920, Appendix.

CROOK, W. WILFRED. *The General Strike.* Chapel Hill, N. Car.: University of North Carolina Press, 1931.

ESTEY, J. A. *Revolutionary Syndicalism, an Exposition and a Criticism.* London: P. S. King, 1913.

GAMBS, J. S. *The Decline of the I. W. W.* N. Y.: Columbia University Press, 1932.

HAYWOOD, WM. D., AND BOHN, FRANK. *Industrial Socialism.* Chicago: Chas. W. Kerr, 1911.

HOOK, SIDNEY. *Towards the Understanding of Karl Marx.* N. Y.: The John Day Co., 1933, ch. VI.

HUNTER, ROBERT. *Violence and the Labor Movement.* N. Y.: Macmillan, 1919.

JOUHAUX, LÉON. *Le Syndicalisme et la C. G. T.* Paris: Editions La Sirène, 1920.

———. *La C. G. T.* Paris: Gallimard, 1937.

LAGARDELLE, HUBERT, AND OTHERS. *Syndicalisme et Socialisme.* Paris: Librairie des sciences, politiques et sociales, 1908. (Bibliothéque du mouvement socialiste, no. 1.)

LAIDLER, HARRY W. *Socialism in Thought and Action.* N. Y.: Macmillan, 1920, ch. VI.

LEFRANC, GEORGES. *Histoire du Mouvement Syndical Français.* Paris: Librairie Syndicale, 1937.

LEVINE (LORWIN), LOUIS. *Syndicalism in France.* N. Y.: Longmans, Green, 1914.

———. *Development of Syndicalism in America.* N. Y.: Ginn & Co., 1913. Reprinted from Political Science Quarterly.

LOUIS, PAUL. *Histoire du Mouvement Syndical en France* (1789–1910). Paris: Librairie Felix Alcan, 1920.

———. *Histoire du Socialisme en France.* Paris: Librairie des Sciences Politiques et Sociales, 1937.

MARQUAND, H. A., AND OTHERS. *Organized Labor in Four Continents.* N. Y.: Longmans, Green, 1939, pp. 1–61.

MILLET, RAYMOND. *Jouhaux et la C. G. T.* Paris: Denoël et Steele.

MONATTE, PIERRE, AND OTHERS. *Left Wing Trade Unionism in France.* London: Labor Publishing Co., 1922.

PEASE, MARGARET. *Jean Jaurès.* N. Y.: Huebsch, 1917.

POUGET, EMILE. *Sabotage.* Chicago: Kerr, 1913.

PRELOT, MARCEL. *L'Evolution Politique du Socialisme Français,* 1789–1934. Paris: Editions Spes., 1939.

RUSSELL, BERTRAND. *Proposed Roads to Freedom.* N. Y.: Holt, 1919, pp. 56–85.

SAPOSS, DAVID. *Left-Wing Unionism.* N. Y.: International Publishers, 1926.

———. *Labor Movements in Post War France.* N. Y.: Columbia University Press, 1931.

SNOWDEN, PHILIP. *Socialism and Syndicalism.* London: Collins, 1913.

SOMBART, WERNER. *Socialism and the Social Movement.* N. Y.: Dutton, 1919.

SOREL, GEORGES. *Reflections on Violence.* N. Y.: Huebsch, 1916.

SPARGO, JOHN. *Syndicalism, Industrial Unionism and Socialism.* N. Y.: Huebsch, 1913.

WEBB, SIDNEY AND BEATRICE. *What Syndicalism Means.* London: The Crusade, 1912.

WESTMEYER, RUSSELL E. *Modern Economic and Social Systems,* 1940. Chs. XXI, XXII.

CHAPTER 23: Guild Socialism

BEER, M. *History of British Socialism.* N. Y.: Harcourt, Brace, 1921, Vol. II, chs. XV, XXI.

BELLOC, HILAIRE. *Servile State.* London: T. N. Foulis, 1912.

CARPENTER, NILES. *Guild Socialism.* N. Y.: Appleton, 1922.

COLE, G. D. H. *Economic Planning.* N. Y.: Knopf, 1935.

———. *The Essentials of Socialization.* London: New Fabian Research Bureau, 1932.

———. *The Simple Case for Socialism.* London: Gollancz, 1935.

———. *Guild Socialism Restated.* London: Parsons, 1920.

———. *Self Government in Industry.* London: Bell, 1920.

———. *Social Theory.* N. Y.: Stokes, 1920.

DOUGLAS, C. H. *Credit-Power and Democracy.* London: Cecil Palmer, 1920.

———. *Economic Democracy.* N. Y.: Harcourt, Brace, 1920.

DUGUIT, LEON. *Law and the Modern State.* N. Y.: Huebsch, 1919.

DURBIN, E. F. M. *Socialist Credit Policy.* London: New Fabian Research Bureau, 1934.

FIGGIS, J. N. *Churches in the Modern State.* London, 1914.

FOLLETT, M. P. *The New State.* N. Y.: Longmans, 1918.

HOBSON, S. G. *National Guilds.* London: G. Bell, 1919.

———. *National Guilds and the State.* N. Y.: Macmillan, 1919.

———. *Guild Principles in War and Peace.* N. Y.: Macmillan, 1919.

HODGES, FRANK. *Nationalization of the Mines.* N. Y.: Thomas Seltzer, 1920.

LABOR PARTY (Great Britain). *Socialism and "Social Credit."* London: The Labor Party, 1935.

LASKI, H. J. *Authority in the Modern State.* New Haven: Yale Univ., 1919.

MacDonald, J. Ramsay. *Socialism, Critical and Constructive.* Indianapolis: Bobbs Merrill, 1924.

MacIver, R. M. *The Modern State.* N. Y.: Oxford Press, 1926.

Maeztu, Ramiro de. *Authority, Liberty, and Function.* London: Allen and Unwin, 1916.

Orage, A. R. *An Alphabet of Economics.* London: T. Fisher Unwin, 1917.

Penty, A. J. *Old Worlds for New.* London: Allen and Unwin, 1917.

Reckitt, M. B., and Bechhofer, C. E. *Meaning of National Guilds.* N. Y.: Macmillan, 1920.

Russell, Bertrand. *Proposed Roads to Freedom.* N. Y.: Harcourt, 1919, pp. 80–5.

Tawney, R. H. *The Acquisitive Society.* N. Y.: Harcourt, 1920.

Webb, Sidney and Beatrice. *Constitution of a Socialist Commonwealth of Great Britain.* N. Y.: Longmans, 1920.

PART FOUR

Communism

CHAPTER 24: Russia to the Bolshevik Revolution

Alexinsky, G. *Modern Russia.* London: T. F. Unwin, 1913.

Antonelli, Etienne. *Bolshevik Russia.* N. Y.: Knopf, 1920.

Beatty, Bessie. *Red Heart of Soviet Russia.* N. Y.: Century, 1918.

Berdyaev, N. A. *The Origin of Russian Communism.* London: G. Bles; N. Y.: Scribner's, 1937.

Bloomfield, Daniel. *Modern Industrial Movements.* Bibliography on Bolshevism. N. Y.: H. W. Wilson, 1919.

Bryant, Louise. *Six Red Months in Russia.* N. Y.: Doran, 1918.

Bunyan, James. *The Bolshevik Revolution, 1917–1918.* Stanford, Cal.: Stanford University Press, 1934.

Chamberlin, William H. *The Russian Revolution, 1917–1921.* N. Y.: Macmillan, 1935.

Chernov, Victor. *The Great Russian Revolution.* New Haven: Yale University, 1936.

Coates, William P. *From Czardom to the Stalin Constitution.* London: Allen and Unwin, 1938.

Figner, Vera. *Memoirs of a Revolutionist.* London: Lawrence, 1925.

Ganken, H., and Fisher, H. H. *The Bolsheviks and the World War.* Stanford, Cal.: Hoover Library on War, Stanford University, 1940.

Gordon, Manya. *Workers Before and After Lenin.* N. Y.: Dutton, 1941.

HERZEN, ALEXANDER. *Memoirs.* London: Chatto and Windus, 1924. (6 vols.)
HINDUS, M. G. *Russian Peasant and the Revolution.* N. Y.: Holt, 1920.
JAMES, CYRIL L. R. *World Revolution, 1917–1936; The Rise and Fall of the Communist International.* London: M. Secker and Warburg, 1937.
KERENSKY, ALEX. *The Prelude to Bolshevism.* London: T. F. Unwin, 1919.
KORFF, SERGIUS A. *Autocracy and Revolution in Russia.* N. Y.: Macmillan, 1923.
KROPOTKIN, PETER. *Memoirs of a Revolutionist.* N. Y.: Houghton Mifflin, 1899.
LAIDLER, HARRY W. *Socialism in Thought and Action.* N. Y.: Macmillan, 1920, ch. XI.
LENIN, NIKOLAI. *Lessons of the Revolution.* Petrograd: Commissariat for Foreign Affairs, 1918.
———. *The Land Revolution in Russia.* London: Independent Labor Party, 1919.
———. *Will the Bolsheviks Maintain Power?* London: Labour Publishing Co.
———. *State and Revolution.* London: Allen & Unwin, 1917.
LEVIN, ALFRED. *The Second Duma.* London: H. Milford. N. Y: Oxford University Press, 1940.
LEVINE, ISAAC DON. *The Man Lenin.* N. Y.: Seltzer, 1924.
LORWIN, LEWIS L. *Labor and Internationalism.* N. Y.: Macmillan, 1929.
MAGNES, J. L. *Russia and Germany at Brest-Litovsk.* N. Y.: Rand School, 1920.
MARX-ENGELS-LENIN INSTITUTE. *Vladimir Lenin: A Political Biography.* N. Y.: International Publishers.
MASARYK, T. G. *The Spirit of Russia.* N. Y.: Macmillan, 1919. 2 vols.
MARCU, V. *Lenin.* N. Y.: Macmillan, 1928.
MILIUKOV, PAUL. *Russia Today and Tomorrow.* N. Y.: Macmillan, 1922.
———. *Outlines of Russian Culture.* Phila.: University of Pennsylvania Press, 1942.
OLGIN, M. J. *Soul of the Russian Revolution.* N. Y.: Holt, 1917.
PARES, BERNARD. *A History of Russia.* N. Y.: Knopf, 1928.
POOLE, ERNEST. *Dark People.* N. Y.: Macmillan, 1918.
POSTGATE, R. W. *Out of the Past.* N. Y.: Vanguard Press, 1926.
———. *Revolution from 1789 to 1906.* London: Richards, 1920.
PRATT, HELEN. *Russia: From Tsarist Empire to Socialism.* N. Y.: Institute of Pacific Relations, 1937.
PRICE, M. P. *My Reminiscences of the Russian Revolution.* London: Allen & Unwin, 1921.
REED, JOHN. *Ten Days that Shook the World.* N. Y.: Boni & Liveright, 1919.
RODIONOV, ALEKSEI T. *February, 1917.* N. Y.: Covici Friede, 1931.
ROSENBERG, ARTHUR. *A History of Bolshevism from Marx to the First Five-Year Plan.* London: Oxford Bookshelf. 1939.

ROSS, EDWARD A. *Russia in Upheaval.* N. Y.: Century, 1918.
RUSSELL, CHARLES E. *Unchained Russia.* N. Y.: Appleton, 1918.
SACK, A. J. *Birth of the Russian Democracy.* N. Y.: Russian Information Bureau, 1918.
SOUVARINE, BORIS. *Stalin, A Critical Survey of Bolshevism.* N. Y.: Longmans, Green, 1939.
SUMNER, B. H. *A Short History of Russia.* N. Y.: Reynal and Hitchcock, 1943.
STRONG, ANNA L. *The First Time in History.* N. Y.: Boni & Liveright, 1924.
TREVIRONUS, G. R. *Revolutions in Russia.* N. Y.: Harper, 1944.
TROTSKY, LEON. *Our Revolution.* N. Y.: Holt, 1918.
———. *Lenin.* N. Y.: Minton, Balch, 1925.
———. *The History of the Russian Revolution.* N. Y.: Simon and Schuster, 1937.
VANDERVELDE, EMILE. *Three Aspects of the Russian Revolution.* London: Allen & Unwin, 1918.
VERNADSKI, G. V. *A History of Russia.* New Haven: Yale University Press, 1943; London: H. Milford.
———. *Lenin.* New Haven: Yale University Press, 1931.
WILLIAMS, ALBERT R. *Lenin, the Man and His Work.* N. Y.: Seltzer, 1919.
———. *Through the Russian Revolution.* N. Y.: Boni & Liveright, 1921.
ZIMAND, SAVEL. *Modern Social Movements. Bibliography.* N. Y.: H. W. Wilson, 1921, pp. 227–253.

CHAPTER 25: Principles and Tactics of Communism

BORKENAU, F. *World Communism, A History of the Communist International.* N. Y.: W. W. Norton, 1939.
BROWDER, EARL R. *What Is Communism?* N. Y.: Vanguard, 1936.
BRAMELD, T. B. H. *A Philosophic Approach to Communism.* Chicago: University of Chicago Press, 1933.
BUKHARIN, N. *Imperialism and World Economy.* Introduction by Lenin. N. Y.: International Publishers, 1929.
———, AND OTHERS. *Marxism and Modern Thought.* N. Y.: Harcourt, 1935.
BURNS, EMILE. *Capitalism, Communism, and the Transition.* London: Gollancz, 1933.
COLTON, ETHAN T. *The XYZ of Communism.* N. Y.: Macmillan, 1931.
Communist Party. *History of the C. P. S. U.* N. Y.: International Publishers, 1939.
DAVIS, JEROME. *Contemporary Social Movements.* N. Y.: Century, 1930.
EASTMAN, MAX. *Marx, Lenin and the Science of Revolution.* London: Allen and Unwin, 1926.
FLORINSKI, M. T. *Toward an Understanding of the U. S. S. R.* N. Y.: Macmillan, 1939.

FOSTER, WILLIAM Z. *Toward Soviet America.* N. Y.: Coward-McCann, 1932.
GRAHAM, STEPHEN. *Stalin; an Impartial Study of the Life and Work of Joseph Stalin.* London: E. Benn, 1931.
GURIAN, WALDEMAR. *Bolshevism: Theory and Practice.* N. Y.: Macmillan, 1932.
HECKER, JULIUS F. *The Communists' Answer to the World's Needs.* N. Y.: Wiley, 1935.
HERMANN, EDUARD. *Communism, Fascism or Democracy?* N. Y.: Norton, 1938.
JAMES, C. L. P. *World Revolution, 1917–1936.* N. Y.: Pioneer Publishers, 1937.
LENIN, N. *Imperialism.* Detroit: Marxian Educational Society, 1924. Pamphlet.
———. *Left-Wing Communism.* London: Communist Party.
———. *The Proletarian Revolution.* London: British Socialist Party. Pamphlet.
———. *The State and Revolution.* N. Y.: Vanguard Press, 1926.
———. *The Letters of Lenin.* London: Chapman & Hall, 1937.
———. *Selected Works, V. 1–12.* N. Y.: International Publishers, 1935–1938.
———. *The Teachings of Karl Marx.* N. Y.: International Publishers, 1923.
Leningradski, Institute. *A Textbook of Marxist Philosophy.* London: V. Gollancz, 1939.
LE ROSSIGNOL, JAMES E. *From Marx to Stalin.* N. Y.: T. Y. Crowell, 1940.
LUNN, A. H. M. *Revolutionary Socialism in Theory and Practice.* London: The Right Book Club, 1939.
———. *Communism and Socialism.* London: Eyre and Spotteswoode, 1939.
MACMURRAY, JOHN. *The Philosophy of Communism.* London: Faber and Faber, 1933
NOUSSIMBAUM, LEO. *Stalin.* N. Y.: Viking Press, 1932.
PAUL, EDEN AND CEDAR. *Creative Revolution.* London: Allen and Unwin, 1920.
POSTGATE, R. W. *Bolshevik Theory.* N. Y.: Dodd, Mead, 1920.
ROSENBERG, ARTHUR. *A History of Bolshevism from Marx to the First Five Years' Plan.* London: Oxford University Press, 1934.
RUSSELL, BERTRAND. *Bolshevism: Practice and Theory.* N. Y.: Harcourt, 1920.
SIKES, EARL R. *Contemporary Economic Systems.* N. Y.: Holt, 1940.
SOUVARINE, BORIS. *Stalin.* N. Y.: Longmans, 1939.
STALIN, J. *Bolshevism.* London: Communist Party, 1925. Pamphlet.
———. *Leninism.* N. Y.: International Publishers, 2 vols.
———. *The Theory and Practice of Leninism.* London: Communist Party, 1925. Pamphlet.

Third International. *Theses and Statutes, Adopted 1920.* Moscow: Communist International, 1920.
TROTSKY, LEON. *Dictatorship vs. Democracy.* N. Y.: Workers' Party, 1922.
———. *In Defense of Marxism.* N. Y.: Pioneer Publishers, 1942.
———. *Lenin.* N. Y.: Minton, Balch and Co., 1925.
———. Edited by Olgin. *Our Revolution.* N. Y.: Holt, 1909.
WESTMEYER, RUSSELL E. *Modern Economic and Social Systems.* N. Y.: Farrar and Rinehart, 1940. Part IV.
ZINOVIEV, G. E., STALIN, J., AND KAMENEV, L. *Leninism or Trotskyism.* Chicago: Workers Party, 1925. Pamphlet.

CHAPTER 26: Soviet Russia through the Five-Year Plans

CHAPTER 27: The 1936 Soviet Constitution—Communist Party Controls

CHAPTER 28: Soviet Economic and Social Institutions and Policies

"American Russian Frontiers," *Survey Graphic,* Feb. 1944.
ARNOLD, A. Z. *Banks, Credit and Money in Soviet Russia.* N. Y.: Columbia University Press, 1937.
BAZILI, N. A. *Russia under Soviet Rule.* London: Allen and Unwin, 1938.
BEST, HARRY. *The Soviet Experiment.* N. Y.: R. R. Smith, 1941.
BIENSTOCK, GREGORY, AND SCHWARZ, SOLOMON M. *Management in Russian Industry and Agriculture.* N. Y.: Oxford Press, 1944.
BLODGETT, RALPH H. *Comparative Economic Systems.* N. Y.: Macmillan, 1944.
BRUTZKUS, BORIS. *Economic Planning in Soviet Russia.* London: Routledge, 1935.
CALLCOTT, MARY STEVENSON. *Russian Justice.* N. Y.: Macmillan, 1935.
CAMPBELL, J. *The Soviet Policy and Its Critics.* London: Gollancz, 1939.
CHAMBERLIN, WILLIAM H. *Russia's Iron Age.* Boston: Little Brown, 1934.
———. *The Russian Revolution.* 1917–1921. N. Y.: Macmillan, 1935.
———. *The Russian Enigma.* N. Y.: Scribner's, 1943.
CITRINE, SIR WALTER. *I Search for Truth in Russia.* London: George Routledge and Sons, 1936.
CLARK, C. *A Critique of Russian Statistics.* London: Macmillan, 1939.
COATES, WILLIAM P. *From Czardom to the Stalin Constitution.* London: Allen and Unwin, 1938.
COLE, G. D. H. *Economic Planning.* N. Y.: Knopf, 1935, ch. XI.

COLE, G. D. H. *Europe, Russia, and Future.* N. Y.: Macmillan, 1942.

COLE, MARGARET I. *Twelve Studies in Soviet Russia.* London: Gollancz, 1933.

"Collective Economy in Russia," in *Annals of Collective Economy,* Jan.–Aug., 1930 (Geneva).

DAVIES, JOSEPH E. *Mission to Moscow.* N. Y.: Simon and Schuster, 1941.

DAVIES, RAYMOND A., AND STEIGER, ANDREW J. *Soviet Asia.* N. Y.: Dial Press, 1942.

DAVIS, JEROME. *The New Russia.* N. Y.: John Day, 1933.

DIMITROV, GEORGI. *The United Front.* N. Y.: International Publishers, 1934.

DOBB, MAURICE. *Soviet Planning and Labor in Peace and War.* N. Y.: International Publishers, 1942.

———. *Soviet Economy and the War.* N. Y.: International Publishers.

DUNN, R. W., AND WALLACE, GEORGE. *Life and Labor in the Soviet Union.* N. Y.: International Publishers, 1937.

DURANTY, WALTER. *The Kremlin and the People.* N. Y.: Reynal and Hitchcock, 1941.

———. *USSR.* Phila.: Lippincott, 1944.

EASTMAN, MAX. *Stalin's Russia and the Crisis in Socialism.* N. Y.: Norton, 1940.

FISCHER, LOUIS. *Soviet Journey.* N. Y.: H. Smith and R. Haas, 1935.

FLORINSKI, M. T. *Toward an Understanding of the USSR.* N. Y.: Macmillan, 1939.

GIDE, ANDRÉ, P. N. *The Return from the USSR.* N. Y.: Knopf, 1937.

GORDON, MANYA. *Workers before and after Lenin.* N. Y.: Dutton, 1941.

GOURVITCH, ALEXANDER. "The Problem of Prices and Valuation," in *American Economic Review,* March, 1936.

GRAHAM, STEPHEN. *Stalin: An Impartial Study.* London: E. Benn, 1931.

GURIAN, WALDEMAR. *Bolshevism, Theory and Practice.* N. Y.: Macmillan, 1932.

HALL, R. L. *The Economic System in a Socialist State.* N. Y.: Macmillan, 1937.

Handbook of the Soviet Union. N. Y.: American-Russian Chamber of Commerce, 1936.

HAYEK, F. A. von (ed.) *Collectivist Economic Planning.* London: Routledge, 1935.

HELLER, A. A. *Industrial Revival in Russia.* N. Y.: Seltzer, 1924.

HINDUS, M. G. *The Great Offensive.* N. Y.: Smith and Haas, 1933.

———. *Hitler Cannot Conquer Russia.* N. Y.: Doubleday, Doran, 1941.

———. *Mother Russia.* N. Y.: Doubleday, Doran, 1943.

HOOVER, CALVIN B. *The Economic Life of Soviet Russia.* N. Y.: Macmillan, 1931.

HUBBARD, L. E. *The Economics of Soviet Agriculture.* London: Macmillan, 1939.

———. *Soviet Labor and Industry.* London: Macmillan, 1942.

———. *Soviet Money and Finance.* London: Macmillan, 1936.

———. *Soviet Trade and Distribution.* London: Macmillan, 1938.

ILIN, M. *New Russia's Primer.* Boston: Houghton Mifflin, 1931.

JAMES, C. L. R. *World Revolution.* N. Y.: Pioneer Publishers, 1937.

JOHNSON, HEWLETT. *The Soviet Power.* N. Y.: Modern Age Books, 1940.

———. *The Secret of Soviet Strength.* N. Y.: International Publishers, 1942.

KEYNES, JOHN M. *Laissez Faire and Communism.* N. Y.: New Republic, 1926.

KING, BEATRICE. *Changing Man: the Educational System in the USSR.* N. Y.: Viking Press, 1937.

KOURNAKOFF, SERGEI. *Russia's Fighting Forces.* N. Y.: Duell, Sloan and Pearce, 1942.

KRIVITSKI, WALTER G. *In Stalin's Secret Service.* N. Y.: Harper, 1939.

LADEJINSKY, W. "Collectivization of Agriculture in the Soviet Union." *Political Science Quarterly,* Mar., June, 1934.

LAMB, EDWARD. *The Planned Economy in Soviet Russia.* Philadelphia: Dorrance and Co., 1934.

LASKI, HAROLD J. *Reflections on the Revolution of Our Time.* N. Y.: Viking Press, 1943, ch. II.

LENIN, N. *State and Revolution.* N. Y.: Vanguard Press, 1926.

———. *Selected Works of V. I. Lenin.* N. Y.: International Publishers, 1930.

LESUEUR, LARRY. *Twelve Months That Changed the World.* N. Y.: Knopf, 1943.

LIPPINCOTT, B. E. (ed.). *On the Economic Theory of Socialism.* St. Paul, Minn.: University of Minnesota Press, 1938.

LITTLEPAGE, J. R., AND BESS D. *In Search of Soviet Gold.* N. Y.: Harcourt, Brace, 1937.

LORWIN, LEWIS L. *Labor and Internationalism.* N. Y.: Macmillan, 1929.

LOUCKS, W. N., AND HOOT, J. W. *Comparative Economic Systems.* N. Y.: Harper, 1938.

LYONS, EUGENE. *Assignment in Utopia.* N.Y.: Harcourt, Brace, 1937.

MOLOTOV, V. M. *Soviet Peace Policy.* London: Lawrence and Wishart, 1941.

MOSELEY, PHILIP E. "Freedom of Artistic Expressions and Scientific Inquiry in Russia." *Annals.* Nov., 1938.

The New Soviet Library (thirteen volumes, written by Soviet officials on various aspects of Soviet political, economic, social, and cultural life. London: 1934, 1935.

NOUSSIMBAUM, LEO. *Stalin.* N. Y.: Viking Press, 1932.

OBOLENSKI, V. V., AND OTHERS. *Socialist Planned Economy in the Soviet Union.* N. Y.: International Publishers, 1932.

PARES, BERNARD. *Russia.* N. Y.: Penguin Books, 1941.

PRATT, HELEN. *Russia: From Tsarist Empire to Socialism.* N. Y.: Institute of Pacific Relations, 1937.

REDDAWAY, WILLIAM B. *The Russian Financial System.* N. Y.: Macmillan, 1935.

Results of the Second Five-Year Plan and the Prospect of the Third Five-Year Plan. Birmingham University: Bureau of Research on Russian Economic Conditions, 1939.

ROSENBERG, ARTHUR. *A History of Bolshevism from Marx to the First Five-Year Plan.* London: Oxford Bookshelf, 1939.

RUSSELL, BERTRAND. *Bolshevism: Practice and Theory.* N. Y.: Harcourt, Brace, 1920.

Russian Economic Institute. *USSR Economy and the War.* N. Y.: Russian Economic Institute, 1943.

SCHACHTMAN, MAX. *Behind the Moscow Trials.* N. Y.: Pioneer Publishers, 1936.

SCOTT, JOHN. *Behind the Urals.* Boston: Houghton Mifflin, 1942.

The Second Five-Year Plan, State Planning Commission of the USSR. N. Y.: International Publishers, 1935.

SEMASHKO, N. A. *Health Protection in the USSR.* N. Y.: Putnam, 1935.

SERGE, VICTOR. *Russia Twenty Years After.* N. Y.: Hillman-Curl, 1937.

SIKES, EARL R. *Contemporary Economic Systems.* N. Y.: Holt, 1940, Part III.

SLOAN, PAT. *Soviet Democracy.* London: Gollancz, 1937.

SMITH, EDWIN C. *Organized Labor in the Soviet Union.* N. Y.: National Council of American Soviet Friendship, 1943.

SOUVARINE, BORIS. *Stalin, A Critical Survey of Bolshevism.* N. Y.: Longmans, 1939.

The Soviet Comes of Age by Twenty-Eight of the Foremost Citizens of the USSR. London: W. Hodge and Co., 1938.

The Soviet Union Today: An Outline Study. N. Y.: American Russian Institute, 1943.

STALIN, J. V. *The Stakhanov Movement in the Soviet Union.* N. Y.: Workers Library, 1935.

———. *The USSR in Home and Foreign Affairs.* London: The Anglo-Russian Parliamentary Committee, 1939.

———. *From Socialism to Communism in the Soviet Union.* N. Y.: International Publishers, 1939.

———. *Leninism.* N. Y.: International Publishers, 1929, 1933. Vols. I, II.

———. *The Soviet and the Individual.* N. Y.: International Publishers, 1935.

STALIN, MOLOTOV, KAGANOVICH, AND OTHERS. *Soviet Union, 1936.* London: Lawrence and Wishart, 1936.

———. A Collection of Addresses in 2 volumes. N. Y.: International Publishers.

———. *Stalin's Kampf: Joseph Stalin's Credo Written by Himself.* N. Y.: Howell, Soskin, 1940.

STRAUSS, E. *Soviet Russia, Anatomy of a Social History.* London: John Lane, 1941.

STRONG, ANNA LOUISE. *The Soviet World.* N. Y.: Holt, 1936.

———. *The Soviets Expected It.* N. Y.: Dial Press, 1941.

THOMAS, NORMAN, AND SEIDMAN, JOEL. *Russia—Democracy or Dictatorship?* N. Y.: League for Industrial Democracy, 1939.

TIMASHEFF, N. S. *Religion in Soviet Russia.* N. Y.: Sheed and Ward, 1942.

TROTSKY, LEON. *The History of the Russian Revolution.* Translated by Max Eastman. N. Y.: Simon and Schuster, 1932.

———. *The Revolution Betrayed.* N. Y.: Doubleday, Doran, 1937.

The USSR at War. N. Y.: American Russian Institute, 1943.

USSR Economy and the War (a symposium). N. Y.: Russian Economic Institute, 1943.

UTLEY, FREDA. *The Dream We Lost.* N. Y.: John Day, 1940.

VARGA, E. *Two Systems: Socialist Economy and Capitalist Economy.* N. Y.: International Publishers, 1939.

VOLIN, L. "Soviet Agriculture," *Journal of Political Economy.* Sept. and Dec., 1937.

VOSNESENSKY, N. *Economic Results of the USSR in 1940 and the Plan of National Economic Development for 1941.* Moscow: Foreign Language Publishing House, 1941.

VSESOYUZNAYA KOMMUNISTICHESKAYA. *The Land of Socialism Today and Tomorrow.* Moscow: Foreign Language Publishing House, 1939.

WARD, HARRY F. *In Place of Profit. Social Incentives in the Soviet Union.* N. Y.: Scribner's, 1933.

WEBB, SIDNEY AND BEATRICE. *The Future of Soviet Communism.* N. Y.: Macmillan, 1937.

———. *Soviet Communism* (2 vols.). N. Y.: Scribner's, 1936.

WESTMEYER, RUSSELL E. *Modern Economic and Social Systems.* N. Y.: Farrar and Rinehart, 1940, Part IV.

WILLIAMS, ALBERT RHYS. *The Russians; the Land, the People, and Why They Fight.* N. Y.: Harcourt, Brace, 1943.

———. *The Soviets.* N. Y.: Harcourt, Brace, 1937.

WOLFE, HENRY C. *The Imperial Soviets.* N. Y.: Doubleday, Doran, 1940.

WOOTTON, BARBARA. *Plan or No Plan.* N. Y.: Farrar and Rinehart, 1935.

YAGOW, A. *Russia's Economic Front for War and Peace.* N. Y.: Harper, 1942.

ZIMAND, SAVEL. *State Capitalism in Russia.* N. Y.: Foreign Policy Association, 1926.

CHAPTER 29: Criticisms of Early Communist Principles and Tactics

CHAPTER 30: Changes in Communist Tactics; Their Significance

ADLER, FRIEDRICH. *Democracy and Revolution.* N. Y.: Rand School, 1934.

ANGELL, NORMAN. *Must Britain Travel the Moscow Road?* London: Noel Douglas, 1926.

BORKENAU, F. *World Communism; a History of the Communist International.* N. Y.: Norton, 1939.

———. *The Totalitarian Enemy.* London: Faber and Faber, 1942.

BROOKS, ROBERT C. *Deliver Us from Dictators.* Philadelphia: University of Pennsylvania, 1935.

BROWDER, EARL. *Victory and After.* N. Y.: 1942.

———. *The People's Front.* N. Y.: International Publishers, 1938.

———. *Teheran and America.* N. Y.: Workers Library Publishers, 1944.

CHILDS, JOHN L., AND COUNTS, GEORGE C. *America, Russia and the Communist Party in the Postwar World.* N. Y.: 1943.

CHAMBERLIN, WILLIAM H. *Russia's Iron Age.* Boston: Little Brown, 1934.

COLE, G. D. H. *Europe, Russia and the Future.* N. Y.: Macmillan, 1942.

Communist International. *Program of the Communist International Together with Its Constitution.* N. Y.: Workers Library Publishers, 1936.

COREY, LEWIS. *The Unfinished Task.* N. Y.: Covici Friede, 1934.

DAVIES, JOSEPH E. *Mission to Moscow.* N. Y.: Simon and Schuster, 1941.

DIMITROV, GEORGI. *The People's Front against Fascism and War.* London: T. H. Wintringham, 1937.

DURBIN, E. F. M. *The Politics of Democratic Socialism.* London: Routledge, 1940.

EASTMAN, MAX. *Stalin's Russia and the Crisis in Socialism.* N. Y.: Norton, 1940.

EDWARDS, LYFORD P. *The Natural History of Revolution.* Chicago: University of Chicago Press, 1927.

FARBMAN, MICHAEL. *After Lenin.* London: L. Parsons, 1924.

FLORINSKI, MICHAEL T. *World Revolution and the USSR.* N. Y.: Macmillan, 1933.

FORD, G. S. (editor). *Dictatorship in the Modern World.* St. Paul: University of Minnesota, 1939.

FOSTER, WILLIAM J. *Toward Soviet America.* N. Y.: Coward, McCann, 1932.

GIBLOW, BENJ. *I Confess.* N. Y.: Dutton, 1940.

HEIMANN, EDWARD. *Communism, Fascism, or Democracy?* N. Y.: Norton, 1938.

JAMES, CYRIL L. R. *The Rise and Fall of the Communist International.* London: M. Secker and Warburg, 1937.

HILLQUIT, MORRIS. *From Marx to Lenin.* N. Y.: Hanford Press, 1922.

KAUTSKY, KARL. *Communism and Socialism.* N. Y.: American League for Democratic Socialism, 1932.

———. *Dictatorship of the Proletariat.* Manchester: National Labor Press, 1919.

———. *Labor Revolution.* London: George Allen and Unwin, 1925.

———. *Socialism at a Deadlock.* London: Allen and Unwin, 1931.

KELLETT, E. E. *The Story of Dictatorships.* N. Y.: Dutton & Co., 1937.

KOHN, HANS. *Nationalism in the Soviet Union.* London: Routledge, 1933.

LAIDLER, HARRY W. *Socializing Our Democracy.* N. Y.: Harper, 1935, ch. V.

———, AND THOMAS, N. *New Tactics in Social Conflict.* N. Y.: Vanguard, 1926.

LASKI, HAROLD J. *Karl Marx.* London: Fabian Society, 1924.

———. *Reflections on the Revolution of Our Time.* N. Y.: Viking, 1943.

LYONS, EUGENE. *Assignment in Utopia.* N. Y.: Harcourt, Brace, 1937.

MACDONALD, J. RAMSAY. *Dictatorship and Revolution.* N. Y.: Seltzer, 1920.

ONEAL, JAMES. *Socialism vs. Bolshevism.* N. Y.: Rand School Press, 1935.

PAGE, KIRBY. *Individualism and Socialism.* N. Y.: Farrar and Rinehart, 1933.

PARMELEE, MAURICE. *Bolshevism, Fascism, and the Liberal Democratic State.* N. Y.: Wiley, 1934.

POSTGATE, RAYMOND W. *How to Make a Revolution.* N. Y.: Vanguard, 1934.

ROSENBERG, ARTHUR. *A History of Bolshevism from Marx to the First Five-Year Plan.* London: Oxford Bookshelf, 1939.

RUSSELL, BERTRAND. *Bolshevism in Theory and Practice.* N. Y.: Harcourt, Brace, 1921.

———. *Power, A New Social Analysis.* N. Y.: Norton, 1938.

———, JOHN DEWEY, *et al.* *The Meaning of Marx* (a Symposium).

SCHUMPETER, JOSEPH A. *Capitalism, Socialism, and Democracy.* N. Y.: Harper, 1942, ch. XII.

SHAPLEN, JOSEPH (editor). *Socialism, Fascism, Communism.* N. Y.: American League for Democratic Socialism, 1934.

SIKES, EARL R. *Contemporary Economic Systems.* N. Y.: Holt, 1940.

SOULE, GEORGE. *The Coming American Revolution.* N. Y.: Macmillan, 1934.

SOUVARINE, BORIS. *Stalin.* N. Y.: Longmans, Green, 1939.

STRACHEY, JOHN. *The Theory and Practice of Socialism.* London: Gollancz, 1936.

STRASSER, OTTO. *Hitler and I.* N. Y.: Houghton Mifflin, 1940.

THOMAS, NORMAN, AND SEIDMAN, JOEL. *Russia—Democracy or Dictatorship?* N. Y.: League for Industrial Democracy, 1939.

UTLEY, FREDA. *The Dream We Lost.* N. Y.: John Day, 1940.

WEBB, SIDNEY AND BEATRICE. *Soviet Communism.* N. Y.: Macmillan, 1937.

PART FIVE

Socialist Movements in Various Lands

General

BEER, M. *Fifty Years of International Socialism.* N. Y.: Macmillan, 1935.

BORKENAU, F. *Socialism, National and International.* London: Routledge, 1942.

BRAATOY, BJARNE. *Labor and War.* London: G. Allen & Unwin, 1934.

BUELL, RAYMOND L. (ed.). *Democratic Governments in Europe.* N. Y.: T. Nelson & Sons, 1935.

GRAVES, SALLY. *A History of Socialism.* London: Hogarth Press, 1939.

HILLQUIT, MORRIS. *Socialism in Theory and Practice.* N. Y.: Macmillan, 1909.

HUNTER, ROBERT. *Revolution—Why? How? When?* N. Y.: Harper, 1940.

——— *Socialists at Work.* N. Y.: Macmillan, 1908.

Joint Legislative Committee, N. Y. State, 1920. *Revolutionary Radicalism.* Albany, N. Y.: J. B. Lyon, 1920.

Labor Research Department, Rand School of Social Science. *American Labor Year Books,* 1916–1932.

Labor and Socialist International. Reports and Proceedings of Second, Third, and Fourth Congresses, 1925, 1928, 1931, respectively. Published by British Labor Party, London, England.

LAIDLER, HARRY W. *Socialism in Thought and Action.* N. Y.: Macmillan, 1920.

LASSWELL, H. D., AND BLUMENSTOCK, DOROTHY. *World Revolutionary Propaganda.* N. Y.: Knopf, 1939.

LORWIN, LEWIS L. *Labor and Internationalism.* N. Y.: Macmillan, 1929.

MALLORY, WALTER H. (ed.). *Political Handbook of the World.* N. Y.: Harper. For *Council on Foreign Relations Annual.*

MARKHAM, S. F. *A History of Socialism.* London: A. & C. Black, 1930.

MARQUAND, H. A., AND OTHERS. *Organized Labor on Four Continents.* N. Y.: Longmans, 1939.

MICHELS, ROBERT. *Political Parties.* N. Y.: Hearst's International Library Co., 1915.

NOMAD, MAX. *Rebels and Renegades.* N. Y.: Macmillan, 1932.

ORTH, S. P. *Socialism and Democracy in Europe.* N. Y.: Holt, 1913.

RAPPARD, WILLIAM E., AND OTHERS. *Source Book on European Governments, Switzerland, France, Italy, Germany, the Soviet Union.* N. Y.: D. Van Nostrand Co., 1937.

Revolutionary Socialist Congress. *A New Hope for World Socialism.* Resolutions of R. S. C. in Paris, 1938. London: International Bureau for Revolutionary Socialist Unity, 1938.

ROSENBERG, ARTHUR. *Democracy and Socialism.* N. Y.: Knopf, 1939.

SCHUMPETER, JOSEPH A. *Capitalism, Socialism, and Democracy.* N. Y.: Harper, 1942, Part V.

The Second and Third Internationals and the Vienna Union. Official Report of the Conference between the Executives, April 2, 1922. London: Labor Publishing Co., 1922.

SOMBART, WERNER. *A New Social Philosophy.* Princeton, N. J.: Princeton, 1937.

———. *Socialism and the Socialist Movement.* N. Y.: Dutton, 1909.

SPARGO, JOHN, AND ARNER, G. B. L. *Elements of Socialism.* N. Y.: Macmillan, 1912.

STURMTHAL, ADOLF. *The Tragedy of European Labor.* N. Y.: Columbia University Press, 1943.

WALLING, WILLIAM ENGLISH. *Socialism as It Is.* N. Y.: Macmillan, 1912.

———, AND OTHERS. *The Socialism of Today.* N. Y.: Holt, 1916.

———. *Socialists and the War.* N. Y.: Holt, 1915.

Great Britain

Attlee, C. R., and Others. *Labor's Aims in War and Peace.* London: Lincolns-Prager; New York: Rand School, 1941.

Beer, M. *A History of British Socialism* (2 vols.). London: G. Bell, 1919–1920.

Bevin, Ernest. *The Balance Sheet of the Future.* N. Y.: McBride, 1941.

Blanshard, Paul. *An Outline of the British Labor Movement.* N. Y.: Doran, 1923.

Brand, Carl F. *British Labor's Rise to Power.* Stanford, Cal.: Stanford University Press, 1941.

British Labor Party. *Reports of the Annual Conferences.* London: British Labor Party.

———. *Interim Report on Reconstruction in War and Peace.* N. Y.: League for Industrial Democracy, 1942 (Pamphlet).

Brockway, A. Fenner. *The Next Step toward Working-Class Unity.* London: I. L. P., 1933.

Citrine, Walter M. *The Trade-Union Movement of Great Britain.* Amsterdam: International Federation of Trade Unions, 1926.

Cole, G. D. H. *The People's Front.* London: Gollancz, 1937.

———. *A Short History of the British Working-Class Movement, 1789–1937.* London: Allen and Unwin, 1938.

———. *British Trade-Unionism Today; A Survey with the Collaboration of Thirty Trade-Union Leaders and Other Experts.* London: Gollancz, 1939.

Crook, Wilfred H. *The General Strike.* Chapel Hill: University of No. Carolina, 1931, Part II.

Dalton, Hugh. *Practical Socialism for Britain.* London: Routledge, 1935.

Estorick, Eric. *Stafford Cripps.* N. Y.: John Day, 1941.

Fabian International Bureau. *Labor and Europe.* London: Fabian Society, 1943.

Gleason, Arthur. *What the Workers Want.* N. Y.: Harcourt, 1920.

Greenwood, Arthur. *Why We Fight Labor's Case.* London: Routledge, 1940.

Kellogg, Paul, and Gleason, Arthur. *British Labor and the War.* N. Y.: Boni and Liveright, 1919.

Laski, Harold J. *The Labor Party, the War, and the Future.* London: The Labor Party, 1939.

———. *Marx and Today.* London: Fabian Research Bureau, 1943.

———. *Reflections on the Revolution of Our Time.* N. Y.: Viking Press, 1943.

London Labor Party. *What Labor Has Done for London.* London: London Labor Publication, 1936.

MacDonald, J. Ramsay. *The Socialist Movement.* N. Y.: Holt, 1911.
McHenry, Dean E. *The Labor Party in Transition, 1931–38.* London: Routledge, 1938.
Mitchison, G. R. *The First Workers' Government.* London: Gollancz, 1934.
Morrison, Herbert. *Socialization and Transport.* London: Constable, 1933.
Murphy, John T. *Trade Unions and Socialism.* London: National Council of the Socialist League, 1936.
Nearing, Scott. *The British General Strike.* N. Y.: Vanguard, 1926.
Pease, E. R. *The History of the Fabian Society.* N. Y.: Dutton. Second Edition, London: Fabian Society, 1925.
Pipkin, Charles W. *The Idea of Social Justice; A Study of Legislation and Administration and the Labor Movement in England and France between 1900–1926.* N. Y.: Macmillan, 1927.
Publications of British Labor Party, Transport House, London; Fabian Society, 11 Dartmouth St, London; Independent Labor Party, 35 St. Bride St., London.
Strauss, Patricia. *Bevin and Co.* N. Y.: Putnam, 1941.
———. *Cripps, Advocate Extraordinary.* N. Y.: Duell, Sloan and Pearce, 1942.
Tawney, Richard H. *The British Labor Movement.* New Haven: Institute of Politics, 1925.
Tracey, Herbert. *Social-Democracy in Britain; Fifty Years of the Socialist Movement.* London: Social Democratic Federation, 1935.
Webb, Sidney and Beatrice. *The History of Trade Unionism.* New York: Longmans, 1920.
Webb, Beatrice. *My Apprenticeship.* Harmondsworth, England: Penguin Books, 1938.

France

Blum, Léon. *Les Radicaux et Nous (1932–1934).* Paris: Librairie Populaire, 1934.
———. *Le Socialisme devant la Crise.* Paris: Librairie Populaire du Parti Socialiste, 1933.
———. *L'Exercice du Pouvoir.* Paris: Librairie Gallimard, 1937.
Bourgin, Hubert. *De Jaurès à Léon Blum.* Paris: A. Fayard, 1938.
Brogan, D. W. *France under the Republic.* N. Y.: Harper, 1940.
Clark, Marjorie R. "A History of the French Labor Movement" (1910–1928). Berkeley, Cal.: University of California Press, 1930. *California University Publications: Economics.* Vol. 8, No. 1.
Dolléans, Edouard. *Histoire du Mouvement Ouvrier.* Paris: A. Cohm, 1936.
Ely, Richard T. *French and German Socialism.* N. Y.: Harper, 1898.

FAJON, ÉTIENNE. *Les Grands Problèmes de la Politique Contemporaine.* Paris: Bureau d'Éditions, 1938.

FAURE, PAUL. *Le Socialisme dans la Bataille Electorale.* Paris: Librairie Populaire 1936.

FOX, RALPH W. *France Faces the Future.* London: Lawrence and Wishart, 1936.

GAUCHER, FRANÇOIS. *Contributions à l'Histoire du Socialisme Français (1905–1933).* Paris: Les Presses Modernes, 1934.

HALE, RICHARD W., JR. *Democratic France.* N. Y.: Coward-McCann, 1941.

JACOBY, JEAN. *Le Front Populaire en France et les Égarements du Socialisme Moderne.* Paris: Les Libertés Françaises, 1937.

JAURÈS, JEAN LÉON. *Œuvres de Jean Jaurès.* Paris: Les Editions Rieder, 1931–39.

———. *Pages Choisis.* Paris: Rieder, 1922.

———. *Studies in Socialism.* N. Y.: Putnam, 1906.

Le Parti Socialiste. *Lettres à Brigitte.* Paris: Librairie Populaire, 1937.

LOUIS, PAUL. *Histoire du Socialisme en France, les Faits, les Idées de la Révolution à Nos Jours.* Paris: Marcel Rivière, 1937.

LEFRANC, GEORGES. *Histoire du Mouvement Syndical Français.* Paris: Librairie Syndicate, 1937.

MAUROIS, ANDRÉ. *Tragedy in France.* N. Y.: Harper, 1940.

MILLET, RAYMOND. *Jouhaux et la C G T.* Paris: Denoel et Steele, 1937.

Parti Socialiste. *Congrès National, 1938.* Paris: Librairie Populaire, 1938.

PEASE, MARGARET. *Jean Jaurès, Socialist and Humanitarian.* N. Y.: Huebsch, 1917.

PEIXOTTO, JESSICA B. *The French Revolution and Modern French Socialism.* N. Y.: Crowell, 1901.

PIPKIN, CHARLES W. *The Idea of Social Justice; A Study of Legislation and Administration and the Labor Movement in England and France: 1900–1926.* N. Y.: Macmillan, 1927.

POL, HEINZ. *Suicide of a Democracy.* N. Y.: Reynal and Hitchcock, 1940.

PRÉLOT, MARCEL. *L'Evolution Politique du Socialisme Français 1789–1934.* Paris: Editions Ipes, 1939.

SAPOSS, DAVID J. *The Labor Movement in Postwar France.* N. Y.: Columbia University, 1931.

THOREZ, MAURICE. *Son of the People.* London: Lawrence and Wishart, 1938.

TROTSKY, LEON. *Whither France?* N. Y.: Pioneer, 1936.

U. S. War Labor Policies Board. *Report on Labor and Socialism in France.* Washington: Government Printing Office, 1919.

VANDERVELDE, ÉMILE. *Jean L. Jaurès.* Paris: F. Alcan, 1929.

WALTER, GÉRARD. *Histoire du Communisme.* Paris: Payot, 1931.

WEILL, GEORGES J. *Histoire du Mouvement Social en France, 1852–1914.* Paris: F. Alcan, 1924.

WEINSTEIN, HAROLD R. *Jean Jaurès; A Study of Patriotism in the French Socialist Movement.* N. Y.: Columbia University Press, 1936.

WERTH, ALEXANDER. *France in Ferment.* London: Jarrolds, 1934.
———. *Which Way France?* N. Y.: Harper, 1937.
ZÉVAÈS, A. B. *Le Socialisme en France depuis 1904.* Paris: Fasquelle, 1934.

Scandinavia

ARNESON, BEN ALBERT. *The Democratic Monarchies of Scandinavia.* N. Y.: Van Nostrand, 1939.
BAKKEN, H. H. *Cooperation to the Finnish?* Madison, Wis.: Mimir, 1939.
BOHMAN, NILS. *Present Day Sweden.* Stockholm: Pope Förlag, 1937.
BRAATOY, BJARNE. *The New Sweden; a Vindication of Democracy.* New York: Thomas Nelson, 1939.
BULL, EDVARD. *Historie og Politikk.* Oslo: Tiden Norsh Forlag, 1933.
CHILDS, MARQUIS W. *Sweden: the Middle Way.* New Haven: Yale University Press, 1936.
———. *This Is Democracy.* New Haven: Yale University Press, 1938.
COLE, MARGARET, AND SMITH, CHARLES (Eds.). *Democratic Sweden.* London: New Fabian Research Bureau, Routledge, 1938.
Denmark. Copenhagen: Royal Danish Ministry for Foreign Affairs, 1937.
Finland American Scandinavian Review. N. Y.: A. S. R., 1940, Vol. 28, No. 1, pp. 8–67.
The Finland Year Book. Helsinki: Finnish Government.
GOLDMARK, JOSEPHINE. *Democracy in Denmark.* Washington: National Home Library Foundation, 1936.
GOODMAN, RAY. *The New Danish Constitution.* London: 1939, Vol. 4, pp. 124–38.
GRIMLEY, O. *The New Norway; A People with the Spirit of Co-operation.* Oslo: Griff-forlaget, 1937.
HACKETT, FRANCIS. *I Chose Denmark.* N. Y.: Doubleday, 1941.
HANSSON, PER ALBIN. *Demokrati.* Stockholm: Tidens Förlags, 1935.
HANSSON, SIGFRID. *The Trade Union Movement of Sweden.* Amsterdam: International Federation of Trade Unions, 1927.
HEBERLE, RUDOLF. *Zur Geschichte der Arbeiter-bewegrung in Schweden.* Jena: Fischer, 1925.
HOWE, FREDERIC C. *Denmark, the Land of Co-operation.* N. Y.: Coward-McCann, 1936.
JACKSON, JOHN H. *Finland.* London: G. Allen & Unwin, 1938.
JONES, HUGH. *Modern Denmark; Its Social, Economic, and Agricultural Life.* London: P. S. King, 1927.
LINDGREN, JOHN. *Från Per Götrek till Per Albin.* Stockholm: A. Bonnier, 1936.
MEYER, HÅKON. *Den Politske Arbeiderbevegelse i Norge.* Oslo: Det Norske Arbeiderpartis Förlag, 1931.
MOE, FINN. *Does Norwegian Labor Seek the Middle Way?* N. Y.: League for Industrial Democracy, 1937.

MYRDAL, ALVA. *Nation and Family; The Swedish Experiment in Democratic Family and Population Policy.* N. Y.: Harper, 1942.

NORDSKOG, JOHN E. *Social Reform in Norway; a Study of Nationalism and Social Democracy.* Los Angeles: U. of So. California Press, 1935.

Norway Does Not Yield. N. Y.: American Friends of German Freedom, 1941.

OAKLEY, AMY. *Scandinavia Beckons.* N. Y.: Appleton, 1938.

ODHE, THORSTEIN. *Finland, A Nation of Cooperators.* London: Williams and Norgate, 1931.

OHLIN, BERTIL (Ed.). "Social Problems and Policies in Sweden," *Annals of the American Academy of Political and Social Science.* Philadelphia: May, 1938, Vol. 197.

ROBBINS, JAMES J. *The Government of Labor Relations in Sweden.* Chapel Hill, No. Car.: Univ. of No. Carolina Press, 1942.

ROTHERY, AGNES E. *Norway, Changing and Changeless.* N. Y.: Viking Press, 1935.

Social Work and Legislation in Sweden. Stockholm: Royal Social Board, 1938.

Statement concerning Finnish-Russian Relations and the Circumstances Leading to the Invasion of Finland by the Union of Soviet Socialist Republics on November 30, 1939. Based on the official documents published.

STRODE, HUDSON, *Finland Forever.* N. Y.: Harcourt, 1941.

The Sweden Year Book: 1921. Stockholm: Almqvist & Wiksells.

U. S. Commission on Industrial Relations in Great Britain and Sweden. *Report of the Commission on Industrial Relations in Great Britain.* Washington: Government Printing Office, 1938.

VIDNES, JACOB. *Norway.* Oslo: M. Johansens, 1935.

WÜNBLAD, EMIL, AND ANDERSON, A. *Det Danske Socialdemokratis Historie, fra 1871 til 1921.* Copenhagen: Socialdemockrates Förlag Fremad, 1921.

Socialism in Other European Countries

Almanacco Socialista Italiano, 1921. Milan: Società Editrice Avanti, 1921.

BALABANOFF, ANGELICA. *My Life as a Rebel.* London: H. Hamilton, 1938.

BAUER, OTTO. "Tactical Lessons of the Austrian Catastrophe," *International Information* (Zurich), March 8, 1934; *New Leader* (N. Y.), Oct. 6, 1934.

BEVAN, EDWYN. *German Social Democracy during the War.* N. Y.: Dutton, 1919.

BORKENAU, F. *The Spanish Cockpit.* London: Faber and Faber, 1937.

BRENAN, GERALD. *The Spanish Labyrinth.* N. Y.: Macmillan, 1943.

BRETSCHER, W., AND OTHERS. *Die Sozialistische Bewegung in der Schwerz, 1848–1920.* Bern: G. Iseli, 1923.

Cěskoslovenská, Socíalne-demokratická Strana. *The Evolution of Socialism in Czechoslovakia.* Prague: The Czechoslovak Democratic Workers Party, 1924.

DE BROUCKÈRE, L. *Émile Vandervelde, L'homme et son œuvre.* Brussels: L'Eglantine.

del Vayo, J. Alvarez. *Freedom's Battle.* N. Y.: Knopf, 1940.

deMan, Hendrik. *Planned Socialism; 1935.* London: New Fabian Research Bureau Publication No. 25.

Devalte, Jos. *Histoire du Mouvement Socialiste Belge.* Brussels: Centrale d'Éducation Ouvrière de Belgique Publ., 1931.

Duchess of Atholl. *Searchlight on Spain.* London: Penguin Books, 1938.

Grimm, Robert. *Geschichte der Sozialistischen Ideen in der Schwerz.* Zurich: Verlag: dr. Oprecht & Helbing, 1931.

Hagen, Paul. *Will Germany Crack?* N. Y.: Harper, 1942.

Koster, F. *Het Socialisme in de Branding.* Bern: Hollandia-Drukkerij N. V., 1935.

Kull, Ernst. *Die Sozialreformerische Arbeiterbewegung in der Schwerz.* Zurich: O. Füssli, 1930.

LeGrande, Xavier. *Le Socialisme Belge et les Problemes d'aujourd'hui.* Brussels: L'Edition Universelle, 1935.

Mehring, Franz. *Geschichte der Deutschen Sozial-Demokratie.* Stuttgart: Dietz, 1941.

Mertens, Corneille. *The Trade-Union Movement in Belgium.* Amsterdam: International Federation of Trade Unions, 1925.

Miles. *Socialism's New Beginning.* N. Y.: League for Industrial Democracy, 1934.

Pierard, Louis. *Belgian Problems since the War.* New Haven: Institute of Politics, Yale University Press, 1929.

Rappard, William E. *The Government of Switzerland.* N. Y.: Van Nostrand, 1936.

Rosenberg, Arthur. *A History of the German Republic.* London: Methuen, 1936.

Schwechlers, K. *Die Oesterreichische Socialdemokratie.* Graz: Verlagsbuchhandlung "Styria," 1907.

Stewart, Margaret. *Reform under Fire—Social Progress in Spain 1931–1938.* London: New Fabian Research Bureau, 1938.

Troelstra, Pieter J. *Troelstra, de Ziener.* Amsterdam: N. V. E. Querido's Uitgevers Mij., 1935.

Vandervelde, Émile. *Le Parti Ouvrier Belge, 1885–1925.* Brusselles: L'Eglantine.

Warren, W. Preston. *Masaryk's Democracy.* Chapel Hill, No. Car.: University of North Carolina Press, 1941.

United States

Ameringer, Oscar. *If You Don't Weaken*—an Autobiography. N. Y.: Holt, 1940.

Benson, Allan L. *The Truth about Socialism.* N. Y.: Huebsch, 1913.

Berger, Victor L. *Voice and Pen of Victor L. Berger.* Milwaukee: Socialist Party, 1929.

BRISSENDEN, PAUL. *The I. W. W.* N. Y.: Columbia University Press, 1919.

BROWDER, EARL R. *The Communist Party of the U. S.; Its History, Role, and Organization.* N. Y.: Workers' Library Publishers, 1941.

———. *Victory and After.* N. Y.: John Day, 1942.

———. *The People's Front.* N. Y.: International Publishers, 1938.

———. *Teheran and America.* New York: Workers' Library Publishers, 1944.

BRYSON, LYMAN. *Which Way America? Communism—Fascism—Democracy?* N. Y.: Macmillan, 1939.

CARROLL, MOLLIE RAY. *Labor and Politics.* Boston: Houghton Mifflin, 1923.

CHAMBERLAIN, JOHN. *Farewell to Reform.* N. Y.: Liveright, 1932.

CHILDS, JOHN L., AND COUNTS, GEORGE S. *America, Russia, and the Communist Party in the Postwar World.* N. Y.: John Day, 1943.

COLEMAN, MCALISTER. *The Man Unafraid: Eugene V. Debs.* N. Y.: Greenberg Publishers, 1931.

COMMONS, JOHN R., AND ASSOCIATES. *History of Labor in the United States.* N. Y.: Macmillan, 1918.

DELEON, SOLON (Ed.). *American Labor's Who's Who.* N. Y.: Hanford Press, 1925.

FINE, NATHAN. *Labor and Farm Parties in the United States, 1828–1928.* N. Y.: Rand School of Social Service, 1928.

FOSTER, WILLIAM Z. *Toward Soviet America.* N. Y.: Coward-McCann, 1932.

GITLOW, BENJAMIN. *I Confess—The Truth about American Communism.* N. Y.: Dutton, 1940.

HARDMAN, J. B. S. (Ed.). *American Labor Dynamics.* N. Y.: Harcourt, 1928.

HAYNES, FRED E. *Social Politics in the United States.* Boston: Houghton Mifflin, 1924.

HILLQUIT, MORRIS. *History of Socialism in the United States.* N. Y.: Funk and Wagnalls, 1910.

———. *Loose Leaves from a Busy Life.* N. Y.: Macmillan, 1934.

HOAN, DANIEL W. *City Government.* N. Y.: Harcourt, 1936.

HUGHAN, JESSIE W. *American Socialism of the Present Day.* N. Y.: Lane, 1911.

JONES, ALFRED W. *Life, Liberty, and Property.* Philadelphia: Lippincott, 1941.

KELLY, EDMOND. *Twentieth-Century Socialism.* N. Y.: Longmans, 1916.

LAIDLER, HARRY W. *American Socialism.* N. Y.: Harper, 1937.

———. *The Federal Government and Functional Democracy.* N. Y.: League for Industrial Democracy, 1940.

———. *A Program for Modern America.* N. Y.: Crowell, 1936.

———. *Socialism in Thought and Action.* N. Y.: Macmillan, 1920.

———, *Toward a Farmer-Labor Party.* N. Y.: League for Industrial Democracy, 1938.

——— AND THOMAS, N. (Eds.). *The Socialism of Our Times.* N. Y.: Vanguard Press, 1929.

———. *Socialist Planning and a Socialist Program.* N. Y.: Falcon Press, 1932.

LAUCK, W. JETT. *Political and Industrial Democracy, 1776–1926.* N. Y.: Funk and Wagnalls, 1926.

LONDON, JACK. *Revolution and Other Essays.* N. Y.: Macmillan, 1910.

MACKAYE, JAMES. *Americanized Socialism.* N. Y.: Doubleday, Page, 1916.

MACY, JOHN. *Socialism in America.* N. Y.: Doubleday, Page, 1916.

MAURER, JAMES H. *It Can Be Done.* N. Y.: Rand School Press, 1938.

ONEAL, JAMES. *American Communism.* N. Y.: Rand School, 1927.

PETERSON, ARNOLD. *Daniel DeLeon.* N. Y.: New York Labor News, 1941.

RICE, STUART A. *Farmers and Workers in American Politics.* N. Y.: Columbia University, 1924.

ROGOFF, H. *An East Side Epic—Meyer London.* N. Y.: Vanguard Press, 1930.

RUSSELL, CHARLES EDWARD. *The Story of the Non-Partisan League.* N. Y.: Harper, 1920.

SCHLOSSBERG, JOSEPH. *The Workers and Their World.* N. Y.: A. L. P. Committee, 1935.

SINCLAIR, UPTON. *I, Candidate for Governor and How I Got Licked.* Pasadena: The Author, 1935.

SYMES, LILLIAN, AND CLEMENT, TRAVERS. *Rebel America.* N. Y.: Harper, 1934.

THOMAS, NORMAN. *America's Way Out.* N. Y.: Macmillan, 1932.

———. *As I See It.* N. Y.: Macmillan, 1932.

———. *Socialism on the Defensive.* N. Y.: Harper, 1938.

———. *We Have a Future.* Princeton, N. J.: Princeton University Press, 1941.

———. *What Is Our Destiny?* N. Y.: Doubleday, Doran, 1944.

WALKER, CHARLES R. *American City.* N. Y.: Farrar and Rinehart, 1937.

Labor and Socialism in Other Countries of the World

ALEXANDER, ROBERT. *Labor Parties in Latin America.* N. Y.: League for Industrial Democracy, 1942. (Pamphlet)

CLARK, MARJORIE. *Organized Labor in Mexico.* Chapel Hill, No. Car.: University of North Carolina, 1934.

COLDWELL, M. J. *Canadian Progressives on the March.* N. Y.: League for Industrial Democracy, 1944. (Pamphlet)

EVATT, HERBERT V. *Australian Labor Leader, the Story of W. A. Holman and the Labor Movement.* London, Sydney: Angus and Robertson, 1940.

GRATTAN, HARTLEY. *Introducing Australia.* N. Y.: John Day, 1942.

HUTCHINSON, ROBERT H. *The Socialism of New Zealand.* N. Y.: New Review Publishing Co., 1916.

LEE, JOHN A. *Socialism in New Zealand.* London: T. Werner Laurie, 1938.

LEWIS, DAVID, AND SCOTT, FRANK. *Make This Your Canada.* Toronto: Central Canada Publishing Co., 1943.

NASH, WALTER. *New Zealand—A Working Democracy.* N. Y.: Duell, Sloan and Pearce, 1943.

ODDONE, JACINTO. *Historia de Socialismo Argentine.* Buenos Aires: La Vanguardia, 1934.

Research Committee, League for Social Reconstruction. *Social Planning for Canada.* Toronto: Thomas Nelson, 1935.

ROSS, LLOYD. *Labor in Australia.* N. Y.: American Council, Institute of Pacific Relations, 1943.

SENIOR, CLARENCE O. *Mexico in Transition.* N. Y.: League for Industrial Democracy, 1939. (Pamphlet)

ST. LEDGER, A. J. *Australian Socialism.* London: Macmillan, 1919.

SUTCH, W. B. *New Zealand's Labor Government at Work.* N. Y.: League for Industrial Democracy, 1940.

Socialism's Struggle against Fascism and Nazism

ASCOLI, MAX, AND FEILER, ARTHUR. *Fascism for Whom?* N. Y.: Norton, 1938.

BORGESE, G. A. *Goliath, The March of Fascism.* N. Y.: Viking Press, 1938.

BORKENAU, F. *Austria and After.* London: Faber and Faber, 1938.

———. *The New German Empire.* N. Y.: Viking Press, 1939.

BRADY, ROBERT A. *The Spirit and Structure of German Fascism.* N. Y.: Viking; London: Gollancz, 1937.

BUTLER, ROHAN D' C. *The Roots of National Socialism.* N. Y.: Dutton, 1942.

DEAN, V. M. *The Economic Situation in Italy.* Foreign Policy Association, Jan. 16, 1935.

DEUTSCH, JULIUS. *The Civil War in Austria.* N. Y.: Socialist Party, 1934.

DEWILDE, J. C. *Building the Third Reich.* N. Y.: Foreign Policy Association, 1939.

DUTT, R. PALMER. *Fascism and Social Revolution.* N. Y.: International Publishers, 1935.

EBENSTEIN, WILLAM. *Fascist Italy.* N. Y.: American Book, 1939.

EINZIG, P. *The Economic Foundations of Fascism.* London: Macmillan, 1933.

FIELD, G. LOWELL. *The Syndical and Corporative Institutions of Fascism.* N. Y.: Columbia University, 1938.

FINER, HERMAN. *Mussolini's Italy.* N. Y.: Holt, 1935.

FLORINSKI, MICHAEL T. *Fascism and National Socialism.* N. Y.: Macmillan, 1938.

GOAD, H. E. *The Making of the Corporate State.* London: Christophers, 1932.

GUERIN, DANIEL. *Fascism and Big Business.* N. Y.: Pioneer, 1929.
HAIDER, C. *Capital and Labor under Fascism.* N. Y.: Columbia University Press, 1930.
HEIDEN, KONRAD. *A History of National Socialism.* N. Y.: Knopf, 1934.
HEIMANN, EDUARD. *Communism, Fascism, or Democracy?* N. Y.: Norton, 1938.
HOOVER, CALVIN B. *Germany Enters the Third Reich.* N. Y.: Macmillan, 1933.
LEND, EVELYN. *The Underground Struggle in Germany.* N. Y.: League for Industrial Democracy, 1938.
LOUCKS, J. W., AND HOOT, W. N. *Comparative Economic Systems.* N. Y.: Harper, 1938.
MEGARO, GAUDENS. *Mussolini in the Making.* Boston: Houghton Mifflin, 1938.
PARMELEE, MAURICE. *Bolshevism, Fascism, and the Liberal Democratic State.* N. Y.: Wiley, 1934.
RAUSHENBUSH, H. S. *The March of Fascism.* New Haven: Yale University Press, 1939.
ROBERTS, S. H. *The House That Hitler Built.* N. Y.: Harper, 1938.
SALVEMINI, GAETANO. *The Fascist Dictatorship in Italy.* N. Y.: Holt, 1927.
———. *Under the Axe of Fascism.* N. Y.: Viking Press, 1936.
SCHUMAN, FREDERICK L. *The Nazi Dictatorship.* N. Y.: Knopf, 1936.
SIKES, EARL R. *Contemporary Economic Systems.* N. Y.: Holt, 1940.
VAN DEN BRUCK. *Germany's Third Reich.* N. Y.: Europe, Verlog, 1940.
WESTMEYER, RUSSELL E. *Modern Economic and Social Systems.* N. Y.: Farrar and Rinehart, 1940.

PART SIX

Recent Socialist Thought

CHAPTER 39: Socialist Thought after the First World War

CHAPTER 40: Recent Programs for Reconstruction and a Socialized Society

General

ACLAND, SIR RICHARD. *The Forward March.* London: Allen & Unwin, 1941.
ADDISON, CHRISTOPHER, AND OTHERS. *Problems of a Socialist Government.* London: Gollancz, 1933.

Ascoli, Marx, and Lehmann, Fritz (Eds.). *Political and Economic Democracy.* N. Y.: Norton, 1937.

Attlee, Clement R. *The Will and the Way to Socialism.* London: Methuen, 1935.

Berle, A. A., and Means, Gardiner C. *Private Property and the Modern Corporation.* N. Y.: Macmillan, 1936.

Bingham, Alfred M. *Man's Estate.* N. Y.: Norton, 1939.

———. *The Techniques of Democracy.* N. Y.: Duell, Sloan, and Pearce, 1942.

Blair, John. *Seeds of Destruction: A Study of the Functional Weakness of Capitalism.* N. Y.: Covici Friede, 1938.

Brady, Robert. *Business as a System of Power.* N. Y.: Columbia University Press, 1943.

Brailsford, H. N. *Property or Peace.* N. Y.: Covici Friede, 1934.

———. *Why Capitalism Means War.* London: Gollancz, 1938.

British Labor Party, *Interim Report on Reconstruction in War and Peace.* N. Y.: League for Industrial Democracy, 1942.

Burnham, James. *The Managerial Revolution.* N. Y.: John Day, 1941.

Catlin, G. E. G. *New Trends in Socialism.* London: Lovat, Dickson and Thompson, 1935.

Chase, Stuart. *Technocracy, An Interpretation.* N. Y.: John Day, 1933.

———. *Tragedy of Waste.* N. Y.: Macmillan, 1925.

Claessens, August. *The Democratic Way of Life.* N. Y.: Rand School, 1940.

Coldwell, M. J. *Canadian Progressives on the March.* N. Y.: League for Industrial Democracy, 1944.

Cole, G. D. H. *The Simple Case for Socialism.* London: Gollancz, 1935.

Corey, Lewis. *The Decline of American Capitalism.* N. Y.: Covici Friede, 1934.

———. *The Unfinished Task.* N. Y.: Viking Press, 1942.

Counts, George S. *Prospects of American Democracy.* N. Y.: John Day, 1938.

Cripps, Sir Stafford. *Democracy Up-to-Date.* London: Allen and Unwin, 1939.

———. *Why This Socialism?* London: Gollancz, 1934.

Dell, Robert. *Socialism and Personal Liberty.* N. Y.: Seltzer, 1922.

De Man, Henri. *The Psychology of Socialism.* N. Y.: Holt, 1928.

Davis, Jerome. *Capitalism and Its Culture.* N. Y.: Farrar and Rinehart, 1935.

Dewey, John. *Freedom and Culture.* N. Y.: Putnam, 1939.

Douglas Social Credit Movement. *Manifesto of.* Leicester, Eng.: The Minerva Co., 1933.

Drucker, Peter F. *The End of Economic Man.* N. Y.: John Day, 1939.

Durbin, E. F. M. *The Politics of Democratic Socialism.* London: Routledge, 1940.

ELDRIDGE, SEBA, AND ASSOCIATES. *Development of Collective Enterprise.* Lawrence, Kansas: University of Kansas Press, 1943.

———. *New Social Horizons.* N. Y.: Appleton, 1941.

———. *Political Action.* Philadelphia: Lippincott, 1924.

FAIRCHILD, HENRY PRATT. *Economics for the Millions.* N. Y.: Modern Age, 1940.

FENN, L. ANDERSON, CLAY, HAROLD E., COLE, G. D. H., AND OTHERS. *Problems of the Socialist Transition.* London: Gollancz, 1934.

FLAMM, IRVING H. *An Economic Program for a Living Democracy.* N. Y.: Liveright, 1942.

FODOR, M. W. *The Revolution Is On.* Boston: Houghton Mifflin, 1940.

FOLLETT, M. P. *The New State.* N. Y.: Longmans, 1918.

HEIMANN, EDUARD. *Communism, Fascism, or Democracy?* N. Y.: Norton, 1938.

HENDERSON, FRED. *The Case for Socialism.* N. Y.: Socialist Party, 1934.

HILLQUIT, MORRIS. *Socialism in Theory and Practice.* N. Y.: Macmillan, 1909.

HOBSON, JOHN A. *Confessions of an Economic Heretic.* London: Allen and Unwin, 1938.

———. *Economics and Ethics.* Boston: Heath, 1929.

———. *Free Thought in the Social Sciences.* N. Y.: Macmillan, 1926.

———. *Incentives and the New Industrial Order.* N. Y.: Seltzer, 1922.

HUGHAN, JESSIE W. *What Is Socialism?* N. Y.: Vanguard, 1928.

HUMPHREY, A. W. *The Modern Case for Socialism.* London: Allen and Unwin, 1928.

HURD, ARCHIBALD S. *State Socialism in Practice.* London: Allan and Co., 1925.

JAY, DOUGLAS. *The Socialist Case.* London: Faber and Faber, 1937.

KANTOROVITCH, HAIM. *Problems of Revolutionary Socialism.* N. Y.: American Socialist Monthly, 1936.

KAUTSKY, KARL. *The Labor Revolution.* London: Allen and Unwin, 1925.

KEYNES, JOHN MAYNARD. *The End of Laissez Faire.* London: L. & V. Wolff, 1926.

———. *Laissez Faire and Communism.* N. Y.: New Republic, 1926.

LAIDLER, H. W. *Concentration of Control in American Industry.* N. Y.: Crowell, 1930.

———. *A Program for Modern America.* N. Y.: Crowell, 1936.

———. *Socialism in Thought and Action.* N. Y.: Macmillan, 1920.

———. *Socializing Our Democracy.* N. Y.: Harper, 1935.

———, AND THOMAS, NORMAN (eds.). *The Socialism of Our Times.* N. Y.: Vanguard, 1929.

——— (eds.). *New Tactics in Social Conflict.* A Symposium. N. Y.: Vanguard Press, 1926.

Lamont, Corliss. *You Might Like Socialism.* N. Y.: Modern Age Books, 1939.

Laski, Harold J. *Democracy in Crisis.* Chapel Hill, No. Car.: U. of North Carolina Press, 1933.

———. *Faith, Reason and Civilization.* N. Y.: Viking, 1944.

———. *A Grammar of Politics.* New Haven: Yale University Press, 1925.

———. *Reflections on the Revolution of Our Time.* N. Y.: Viking, 1943.

Laurat, Lucien. *Marxism and Democracy.* London: Gollancz, 1940.

Lederer, Emil. *State of the Masses.* N. Y.: Norton, 1940.

Lerner, Max. *Ideas for the Ice Age.* N. Y.: Viking, 1941.

———. *It Is Later Than You Think.* N. Y.: Viking, 1938.

Lewis, David, and Scott, Frank. *Make This Your Canada.* Toronto: Central Canada Publishing Co., 1943.

Lippmann, Walter. *Drift and Mastery.* N. Y.: Mitchell Kennerley, 1914.

Loucks, William N., and Hoot, J. W. *Comparative Economic Systems.* N. Y.: Harper, 1938.

Lunn, A. H. M. *The Science of World Revolution.* N. Y.: Sheed and Ward, 1938.

MacDonald, J. R. *Socialism: Critical and Constructive.* Indianapolis: Bobbs-Merrill, 1924.

MacKaye, James. *Americanized Socialism.* N. Y.: Boni and Liveright, 1918.

Miles. *Socialism's New Beginning.* N. Y.: League for Industrial Democracy, 1934.

Morrison, Herbert. *Socialization of Transport.* London: Constable, 1933.

Mumford, Lewis. *Technics and Civilization.* N. Y.: Harcourt, 1934.

Niebuhr, Reinhold. *Moral Man and Immoral Society.* N. Y.: Scribner, 1933.

———. *Reflections on the End of an Era.* N. Y.: Scribner, 1934.

Osbert, Reuben. *Freud and Marx.* N. Y.: Equinox Co-operative Press, 1937.

Overstreet, Harry A. *A Declaration of Interdependence.* N. Y.: Norton, 1937.

Page, Kirby. *A New Economic Order.* N. Y.: Harcourt, 1930.

Putnam, John. *The Modern Case for Socialism.* Boston: Meador Publishing Co., 1943.

Raushenbush, H. S. *The March of Fascism.* New Haven: Yale University Press, 1939.

Rautenstrauch, Walter. *Who Gets the Money?* N. Y.: Harper, 1934.

Rosenberg, Arthur. *Democracy and Socialism.* N. Y.: Knopf, 1939.

Russell, Bertrand. *Freedom vs. Organization,* N. Y.: Norton, 1934.

———. *Power: A New Social Analysis.* N. Y.: Norton, 1938.

———. *Proposed Roads to Freedom.* N. Y.: Harcourt, Brace, 1919.

———, and Others. *Dare We Look Ahead?* N. Y.: Macmillan, 1938.

Ryan, John A. *Distributive Justice.* N. Y.: Macmillan, 1942.

SCHUMPETER, JOSEPH A. *Capitalism, Socialism, and Democracy.* N. Y.: Harper, 1942.

SHAW, G. BERNARD. *The Intelligent Women's Guide to Socialism and Capitalism.* N. Y.: Brentano, 1928.

SIKES, EARL R. *Contemporary Economic Systems.* N. Y.: Holt, 1940.

SINCLAIR, UPTON. *The Ways Out: What Lies Ahead for America.* N. Y.: Farrar and Rinehart, 1933.

SOMBART, WERNER. *A New Social Philosophy.* London: H. Milford, Oxford University Press, 1937.

SOROKIN, PITIRIM A. *The Sociology of Revolution.* Philadelphia: Lippincott, 1925.

SOULE, GEORGE H. *The Coming American Revolution.* N. Y.: Macmillan, 1934.

———. *An Economic Constitution for Democracy.* New Haven: Yale University Press, 1939.

———. *The Future of Liberty.* N. Y.: Macmillan, 1936.

———. *The Strength of Nations,* 1942. N. Y.: Macmillan, 1942.

STEINMETZ, CHARLES P. *America and the New Epoch.* N. Y.: Harper, 1916.

STRACHEY, JOHN. *A Program for Progress.* London: Gollancz, 1940.

———. *How Socialism Works.* N. Y.: Modern Age Books, 1939.

———. *A Faith to Fight For.* London: Gollancz, 1941.

STRAIGHT, MICHAEL. *Make This the Last War.* N. Y.: Harcourt, Brace, 1943.

STROEBEL, HEINRICH. *Socialization in Theory and Practice.* London: King and Son, 1922.

STURMTHAL, ADOLPH. *The Tragedy of European Labor.* N. Y.: Columbia University Press, 1943.

TAWNEY, R. W. *The Acquisitive Society.* N. Y.: Harcourt, 1920.

TEAD, ORDWAY. *The Case for Democracy.* N. Y.: Association Press, 1938.

THOMAS, NORMAN. *America's Way Out.* Macmillan, 1931.

———. *As I See It.* Macmillan, 1932.

———. *The Choice Before Us.* N. Y.: Macmillan, 1934.

———. *Socialism on the Defensive.* N. Y.: Harper, 1938.

———. *We Have a Future.* N. J.: Princeton University Press, 1941.

———. *What Is Our Destiny?* N. Y.: Doubleday, Doran, 1944.

VANDERVELDE, ÉMILE. *L'Alternative: Capitalisme d'État ou Socialisme Démocratique.* Paris: L'Églantine, 1933.

———. *Études Marxistes.* Brussels: L'Églantine, 1930.

VAN KLEECK, MARY. *Creative America.* N. Y.: Covici Friede, 1936.

VEBLEN, THORSTEIN. *The Engineers and the Price System.* N. Y.: Huebsch, 1921.

———. *The Theory of Business Enterprise.* N. Y.: Scribner, 1912.

WARD, HARRY F. *In Place of Profit.* N. Y.: Scribner, 1933.

WEBB, SIDNEY AND BEATRICE. *A Constitution for the Socialist Commonwealth of Great Britain.* N. Y.: Longmans, 1921.

WESTMEYER, RUSSELL E. *Modern Economic and Social Systems.* N. Y.: Farrar and Rinehart, 1940.

WIBAUT, F. M. *A World Production Order.* London: Allen and Unwin, 1935.

WILSON, EDMUND. *To the Finland Station.* N. Y.: Harcourt, 1940.

Economics of Socialism

BLAKE, WILLIAM J. *Marxian Economic Theory.* N. Y.: Cordon Co., 1939.

BOBER, M. M. *Karl Marx's Interpretation of History.* Cambridge, Mass.: Harvard University, 1927.

CHANG, S. H. M. *The Marxian Theory of the State.* Phila.: Univ. of Pennsylvania, 1931.

COLE, G. D. H. *What Marx Really Meant.* N. Y.: Knopf, 1934.

DICKINSON, HENRY D. *Economics of Socialism.* London: Oxford Univ. Press, 1939.

DICKINSON, ZENAS C. *Economic Motives.* Cambridge: Harvard Univ. Press, 1924.

DOBB, MAURICE. *Political Economy and Capitalism.* N. Y.: International Publishers, 1937.

EASTMAN, MAX. *Marxism: Is It a Science?* N. Y.: Norton, 1940.

HALL, ROBERT L. *The Economic System in a Socialist State.* London: Macmillan, 1937.

HAYEK, FRIEDRICH A. VON. *Collectivist Economic Planning.* London: Routledge, 1935.

HOOK, SIDNEY. *Towards the Understanding of Karl Marx.* N. Y.: John Day, 1933.

JACKSON, T. A. *Dialectics.* London: Lawrence and Wishart, 1936.

JOSEPH, H. W. B. *The Labor Theory of Value in Karl Marx.* London: Oxford University Press, 1923.

KNIGHT, F. H. "The Place of Marginal Economics in a Collectivist System," *American Economic Review,* Supplement to Vol. XXVI (March, 1936).

LANGE, OSCAR. "Marxian Economics and Modern Economic Theory," *Review of Economic Studies,* June, 1935.

LERNER, A. P. "Economic Theory and Socialist Economy," *Review of Economic Studies,* Vol. II (Oct., 1934).

LINDSAY, A. D. *Karl Marx's Capital.* London: Oxford University Press, 1931.

LIPPINCOTT, BENJAMIN E. (ed.). *On the Economic Theory of Socialism,* by Oscar Lange and Fred M. Taylor. Minneapolis, Minn.: The University of Minnesota Press, 1938.

MEYER, GERHARD. "A Contribution to the Theory of Socialist Planning," *Plan Age,* Vol. III (Oct., 1937).

MISES, LUDWIG VON. "Economic Calculation in the Socialist Commonwealth." Reprinted in *Collectivist Economic Planning* (F. A. von Hayek, ed.). London: Routledge, 1935.

———. *Socialism: An Economic and Sociological Analysis* (translated by J. Kahane). London: J. Cape.

PARKES, H. B. *Marxism: An Autopsy.* Boston: Houghton Mifflin, 1939.

PORTUS, G. W. *Marx and Modern Thought.* Sydney, Australia: Macmillan, 1921.

ROBBINS, L. C. *Economic Basis of Class Conflict.* N. Y.: Macmillan, 1939.

ROPER, W. CROSBY. *The Problem of Pricing in a Socialist State.* Cambridge, Mass., Harvard University Press, 1929.

SACHS, A. S. *Basic Principles of Scientific Socialism.* N. Y.: Vanguard Press, 1923.

SALTER, F. R. *Karl Marx and Modern Socialism.* London: Macmillan, 1921.

STRACHEY, JOHN. *Theory and Practice of Socialism.* London: Gollancz, 1936.

SWEEZY, A. R. "The Economist's Place Under Socialism," in *Explorations in Economics.* Cambridge, Mass.: Harvard University Press, 1937.

SWEEZY, PAUL M. *The Theory of Capitalist Development.* N. Y.: Oxford Press, 1942.

VEBLEN, THORSTEIN. *The Place of Science in Modern Civilization.* N. Y.: Huebsch, 1919.

Economic Planning and Socialism

BEVERIDGE, SIR WILLIAM H. *Planning under Socialism.* N. Y.: Longmans, 1936.

COLE, G. D. H. *Economic Planning.* N. Y.: Knopf, 1935.

DEMAN, HENRI. *Planned Socialism.* London: Gollancz, 1935.

DOOB, LEONARD W. *The Plans of Men.* New Haven: Yale University Press, 1940.

FLEDDERUS, MARY, AND VAN KLEECK, MARY (Eds.). *On Economic Planning.* N. Y.: Covici Friede, 1935.

HOLCOMBE, A. N. *Government in a Planned Democracy.* Norton, 1935.

International Federation of Trade Unions. *Economic Planning and Labor Plans.* London: I. F. T. U., 1935.

LAIDLER, HARRY W. (Ed.). *Socialist Planning and a Socialist Program.* N. Y.: Falcon Press, 1932.

League for Social Reconstruction. *Social Planning for Canada.* Toronto: T. Nelson and Co., 1935.

LORWIN, LEWIS L. *Postwar Plans of the United Nations.* N. Y.: Twentieth Century Fund, 1943.

SOULE, GEORGE H. *A Planned Society.* N. Y.: Macmillan, 1932.

WOOTTON, BARBARA. *Plan or No Plan.* N. Y.: Farrar and Rinehart, 1935.

———. *End Social Inequality.* London: K. Paul, Trench, Trubner & Co., 1941.

Full Employment—Toward Partial or Complete Socialization

BAUER, JOHN. *National Welfare and Business Stability.* N. Y.: Harper, 1940.

BERLE, ADOLPH A., Jr. *New Directions in the New World.* N. Y.: Harper, 1941.

BEVERIDGE, WILLIAM H. *The Pillars of Security.* N. Y.: Macmillan, 1943.

CHAMBERLIN, JOHN. *The American Stakes.* N. Y.: Carrick and Evans, 1940.

CHASE, STUART. *The Economy of Abundance.* N. Y.: Macmillan, 1934.

———. *Goals for America.* N. Y.: Twentieth Century Fund, 1942.

———. *Idle Money, Idle Men.* N. Y.: Harcourt, 1940.

———. *Where's the Money Coming From?* N. Y.: Twentieth Century Fund, 1944.

COYLE, DAVID C. *Roads to a New America.* Boston: Little Brown, 1938.

DOUGLAS, PAUL H. *Controlling Depressions.* N. Y.: Norton, 1935.

EZEKIEL, MORDECAI. *Jobs for All.* N. Y.: Knopf, 1939.

FAIRCHILD, HENRY PRATT. *This Way Out.* N. Y.: Harper, 1936.

GALLOWAY, GEORGE B., AND ASSOCIATES. *Planning for America.* N. Y.: Holt, 1941.

GILBERT, RICHARD V., AND SIX OTHER HARVARD AND TUFTS ECONOMISTS. *Economic Program for American Democracy.* N. Y.: Vanguard, 1938.

HANSEN, ALVIN H. *Full Recovery or Stagnation?* N. Y.: Norton, 1938.

International Labor Conference. *The Organization of Employment in the Transition from War to Peace.* Montreal: I. L. O., 1944.

KEYNES, J. M. *The General Theory of Employment, Interest and Money.* N. Y.: Harcourt, 1936.

LEWIS, ALFRED BAKER. *Labor, Machines, and Depressions.* N. Y.: League for Industrial Democracy, 1938.

LOEB, HAROLD. *The Chart of Plenty.* N. Y.: Viking Press, 1935.

NATHAN, ROBERT R. *Mobilizing for Abundance.* N. Y.: McGraw-Hill, 1944.

National Resources Planning Board Publications.

RUGG, HAROLD J. *The Great Technology.* N. Y.: John Day, 1933.

PINK, LOUIS H. *Freedom from Want.* N. Y.: Harper, 1944.

SINCLAIR, UPTON. *The Epic Plan for California.* N. Y.: Farrar and Rinehart, 1934.

WALLACE, HENRY A. *Democracy Reborn.* N. Y.: Reynal and Hitchcock, 1944.

WITHERS, WILLIAM. *Financing Economic Security in the United States.* N. Y.: Columbia University Press, 1939.

PART SEVEN

Consumer Co-operation and Miscellaneous Movements

CHAPTER 41: The Co-operative Movement

CHAPTER 42: Social Aspects of Consumers' Co-operatives

BAKER, JACOB. *Co-operative Enterprise.* N. Y.: Vanguard Press, 1937.

BAKKEN, H. H., AND SHAARS, M. A. *The Economics of Co-operative Marketing.* N. Y.: McGraw-Hill, 1937.

BARNETT, JAMES D. *A More Co-operative Democracy.* N. Y.: R. R. Smith, 1941.

BARON, N. *Co-operative Banking.* London: P. S. King, 1932.

BERGENGREN, ROY F. *Credit Union of North America.* Madison: Credit Union National Association, 1941.

BOLLES, JOSHUA K. *The People's Business.* N. Y.: Harper, 1942.

BOYLE, GEORGE. *Democracy's Second Chance.* N. Y.: Sheed and Ward, 1941.

BRAINERD, G. G. (ed.) "Consumers' Co-operation." *Annals* of the American Academy of Political and Social Science, Vol. 191, 1937.

British Co-operation Today. London: Co-operative Union, 1934.

BROUCKÈRE, LOUIS DE. *Les Aspects Politiques du Mouvement Cooperatif.* Brussels: Brussels University, 1938.

CAMPBELL, WALLACE J., AND LAIDLER, HARRY W. *The Consumer Co-operative Movement.* N. Y.: League for Industrial Democracy, 1940 (Pamphlet).

CARR-SAUNDERS, A. M., *et al. Consumer Co-operation in Great Britain.* N. Y.: Harper, 1938.

CASSAN, T. O. *Consumers' Co-operative Movement in Germany* (trans. by J. F. Mills). London: Allen and Unwin, 1935.

CHILDS, MARQUIS. *Sweden: The Middle Way.* New Haven: Yale University Press, 1936.

COADY, M. M. *Masters of Their Own Destiny.* N. Y.: Harper, 1939.

Co-operative Enterprise in Europe. Report of the Inquiry on Co-operative Enterprise in Europe. Washington: Superintendent of Documents, 1937.

Co-operative League, U. S. A., publications. New York.

"Co-operative Societies throughout the World," *Annals of Collective Economy,* Geneva, 1940.

Co-operative Union Publications. Manchester, England.

COWLING, ELLIS. *Co-operatives in America.* N. Y.: Coward McCann, 1939.

FABER, HAROLD. *Co-operation in Danish Agriculture.* London: Longmans, 1931.

ELLIOTT, SYDNEY. *The English Co-operatives.* New Haven: Yale University Press, 1938.

ELLSWORTH, R. H. *Statistics of Farmers' Marketing and Purchasing Co-operatives: 1937–1938 Marketing Season.* Washington: Farm Credit Association. Misc. Rep. No. 18, Feb., 1939.

FAY, CHARLES R. *Co-operation at Home and Abroad.* London: P. S. King, Vol. I (1908–1918); Vol. II (1908–1938).

GIDE, CHARLES. *Consumers' Co-operative Societies.* N. Y.: Knopf, 1922.

GJOERES, AXEL. *Co-operation in Sweden* (trans. by John Downie). Manchester: Co-operative Union, 1927.

GRIMLEY, O. *The New Norway.* Oslo: Graff-Forlaget, 1939.

HALL, L., AND WATKINS, W. P. *Co-operation.* Manchester, England: Co-operative Union, 1934.

HOLYOKE, GEORGE J. *History of Co-operation.* N. Y.: Dutton, 1906.

HUTCHINSON, CARL R. *Seeking a New World through Co-operation.* N. Y.: Methodist Book Concern, 1935.

International Labor Office. *Co-operative Organizations and Postwar Relief.* Montreal, Can.: I. L. O., 1944; N. Y.: Co-operative League, U. S. A.

JACOBSON, DOROTHY H. *Our Interests as Consumers.* N. Y.: Harper, 1941.

KALLEN, HORACE M. *The Decline and Rise of the Consumer.* N. Y.: Appleton-Century, 1936.

KERCHER, LEONARD C. *Consumers' Co-operatives in the North Central States.* Minneapolis: University of Minnesota, 1941.

KRESS, ANDREW J. *Introduction to the Co-operative Movement.* N. Y.: Harper, 1941.

LAIDLER, HARRY W. *Socializing Our Democracy.* N. Y.: Harper, 1935, ch. VIII.

LANDIS, BENSON Y. *Manual on the Church and Co-operatives.* N. Y.: Federal Council of Churches, 1941.

———. *A Co-operative Economy.* N. Y.: Harper, 1943.

LOUCKS, WILLIAM N., AND HOOT, J. W. *Comparative Economic Systems.* N. Y.: Harper, 1938.

MOONEY, GEORGE S. *Co-operatives Today and Tomorrow: A Canadian Survey.* Montreal: The Survey Committee, 1938.

MYERS, JAMES. *Organized Labor and Consumer Co-operatives.* N. Y.: Co-operative League of U. S. A., 1940.

ODHE, THORSTEIN. *Finland, A Nation of Co-operators* (trans. by John Downie). London: Williams and Norgate, 1931.

NEIFELD, M. R. *Co-operative Consumer Credit.* N. Y.: Harper, 1936.

OSTERGAARD, SOREN K. *Into Abundance.* N. Y.: Willett, Clark, 1940.

PALMER, R. A. *World Co-operation: History of Co-operative International Relations,* 1937.

PARKER, FLORENCE E. *Consumer Co-operation in the United States, 1936.* Washington, D. C.: Department of Labor, Bull. No. 659, 1939.

PAUL, L. A. *Co-operation in the USSR.* London: Gollancz, 1934.

People's Year Book. Manchester: Co-operative Wholesale Society. Annual.

REDFERN, PERCY. *The New History of the C. W. S.* London: J. M. Dent & Sons, 1938.

Report of the Proceedings of the Fifteenth Congress of the I. C. A., 1937. London: International Co-operative Alliance, 1938.

RUSSELL, GEORGE (A. E.). *The National Being.* N. Y.: Macmillan, 1916.

SCHMALZ, CARL N. *Operating Results of Consumer Co-operatives in the U. S. in 1937.* Boston: Harvard University, 1939.

SCHMIEDELER, EDGAR. *Co-operation—A Christian Mode of Industry.* Ozone Park, N. Y.: Catholic Literary Guild, 1941.

SIKES, EARL R. *Contemporary Economic Systems.* N. Y.: Holt, 1940.

Statistical Handbook of Farmers' Co-operatives. Washington, D. C.: Farm Credit Administration Bull. No. 26. Nov., 1938.

STEWART, MAXWELL S. *Co-operatives in the U. S.—A Balance Sheet.* N. Y.: Public Affairs Pamphlets, 1941.

TWIGG, H. J. *The Economic Advance of British Co-operation, 1913–1934.* Manchester, England: Co-operative Union, 1934.

VOORHIS, JERRY. *The Morale of Democracy.* N. Y.: Greystone Press, 1941.

WARBASSE, JAMES P. *Co-operative Democracy.* N. Y.: Harper, 1942.

WARD, LEO R. *Nova Scotia: Land of Co-operatives.* N. Y.: Sheed and Ward, 1942.

WEBB, SIDNEY AND BEATRICE. *The Consumers' Co-operative Movement.* N. Y.: Longmans, 1915.

WOOLF, LEONARD. *Socialism and Co-operatives.* London: Allen and Unwin, 1921.

CHAPTER 43: Variants of Socialism

Christian Socialism

BEER, M. *History of British Socialism.* N. Y.: Harcourt, 1921, Vol. II, pp. 180–7.

BENNETT, JOHN C. *Social Salvation.* N. Y. and London: Scribner, 1935.

BLISS, W. D. P. *Encyclopaedia of Social Reform.* N. Y.: Funk and Wagnalls, 1907. See Index.

BRADFORD, THE LORD BISHOP OF. *The Gospel of Dives.* London: Industrial Christian Fellowship, 1942.

BREHME, ROBERT G., JR. *Social Doctrines of the Catholic Church.* N. Y.: Putnam, 1936.

BRUEHL, CHARLES P. *The Pope's Plan for Social Reconstruction.* N. Y.: Devin-Adair Co., 1939.

CLIFFORD, JOHN. *Socialism and the Teaching of Christ.* London: Fabian Society, 1897. Fabian Tract No. 78.

COPE, GILBERT. *Christians in the Class Struggle.* Birmingham: Council of Clergy and Ministers for Common Ownership, 1942.

DAVIS, JEROME. *Christianity and Social Adventuring.* N. Y.: Century, 1927.

DEARMER, PERCY. *Socialism and Christianity.* London: Fabian Society, 1907. Fabian Tract No. 133.

DEXTER, ROBERT C. *The Social Obligation of Liberal Religion.* Boston: American Unitarian Association, 1939.

DOMBROWSKI, JAMES. *The Early Days of Christian Socialism in America.* N. Y.: Columbia University, 1935.

EDDY, GEORGE SHERWOOD. *Revolutionary Christianity.* N. Y.: Willett, Clark, 1939.

ELY, RICHARD T. *French and German Socialism.* N. Y.: Harper, 1883, ch. XVI.

FIGGIS, J. N. *Churches in the Modern State.* London, N. Y.: Longmans, 1913.

FITZPATRICK, PAUL J. *Bibliography of Economic Books and Pamphlets by Catholic Authors, 1891–1941.* Washington, D. C.: The Catholic University of America Press, 1941.

FRANKLIN, J. E. *The Relation of Christianity to Socialism.* N. Y.: American Baptist Pub. Society, 1914.

GLADDEN, WASHINGTON. *Christianity and Socialism.* N. Y.: Eaton & Means, 1905.

HEADLAM, STEWART P. *Christian Socialism.* London: Fabian Society, 1897. Fabian Tract No. 42.

HIGGINSON, JOHN H. *New Testament Economics.* London: Wyman, 1938.

HILLQUIT, MORRIS, AND RYAN, JOHN A. *Socialism: Promise or Menace.* N. Y.: Macmillan, 1914.

HOLMES, JOHN HAYNES. *The Revolutionary Function of the Modern Church.* N. Y.: Putnam, 1912.

HOLT, ARTHUR E. *Christian Roots of Democracy in America.* N. Y.: Friendship Press, 1941.

HOPKINS, CHARLES H. *The Rise of the Social Gospel in American Protestantism, 1865–1915.* New Haven: Yale University Press, 1940.

HUGHES, PHILIP. *The Pope's New Order.* N. Y.: Macmillan, 1944.

HUGHES, THOMAS. *Memoir of a Brother.* London: Macmillan, 1874.

HUTCHINSON, PAUL. *World Revolution and Religion.* N. Y.: Abingdon Press, 1931.

INGE, BISHOP WILLIAM R. *The Social Teaching of the Church.* London: Epworth League Press, 1930.

JOHNSON, F. ERNEST. *Religion and the World Order.* N. Y.: Harper, 1944.

———. *The Social Gospel Re-examined.* N. Y.: Harper, 1940.

JOHNSON, HEWLETT. *Religion Interferes.* London: E. Benn, 1928.

KAUFMANN, M. *Christian Socialism.* London: Paul, 1888.

KAUTSKY, KARL. *Foundations of Christianity.* N. Y.: International Publishers, 1925.

KINGSLEY, CHARLES. *Alton Locke.* London: Macmillan, 1881.

———. *Letters and Memories.* Philadelphia: J. D. Morris, 1899.

———. *Yeast.* London: Macmillan, 1883.

LANDIS, BENSON Y., Editor. *Religion and the Good Society. An Introduction to Social Teachings of Judaism, Catholicism, and Protestantism.* N. Y.: National Conference of Christians and Jews, 1943.

MCCONNELL, BISHOP FRANCIS J. *Human Needs and World Christianity.* N. Y.: Friendship Press, 1929.

MCGOWAN, RAYMOND A. *Toward Social Justice.* N. Y.: Paulist Press, 1933.

MACINTOSH, DOUGLAS C. *Social Religion.* N. Y.: Scribner, 1939.

MAURICE, FREDERICK. *The Life of Frederick Maurice* (2 vols.). N. Y.: 1884.

MELISH, HOWARD. *Bishop J. L. Spaulding.* N. Y.: Macmillan, 1917.

MEYEROWITZ, ARTHUR. *Social Ethics of the Jews.* N. Y.: Bloch Publishing Co., 1935.

MILLER, SPENCER, JR. *The Church and Industry.* N. Y.: Longmans, 1930.

MORRISON, CHARLES C. *The Social Gospel and the Christian Cults.* N. Y.: Harper, 1933.

MYERS, JAMES. *Churches in Social Action.* N. Y.: Federal Council of Churches, 1943.

———. *Religion Lends a Hand.* N. Y.: Harper, 1929.

National Catholic Welfare Conference. *The Church and the Social Order.* Washington, D. C.: Press of Randsdell, 1940.

NIEBUHR, REINHOLD. *Reflections on the End of an Era.* N. Y.: Scribner, 1934.

NITTI, SIGNOR F. S. *Catholic Socialism.* London: 1895.

NOEL, CONRAD. *Socialism in Church History.* London: Palmer, 1910.

PAGE, KIRBY (ed.). *Christianity and Economic Problems.* N. Y.: Young Men's Christian Association Press, 1922.

———, *et al. Christianity and Economic Problems.* N. Y.: Young Men's Christian Association Press, 1922.

PEABODY, FRANCIS G. *Jesus Christ and the Social Question.* N. Y.: Macmillan, 1900.

RAUSCHENBUSCH, WALTER. *Christianity and the Social Crisis.* N. Y.: Macmillan, 1907.

——— *Christianizing the Social Order.* N. Y.: Macmillan, 1912.

RAUSCHENBUSCH, WALTER. *The Social Principles of Jesus.* N. Y.: Young Men's Christian Association Press, 1916.

RECKETT, MAURICE B. *A Christian Sociology for Today.* N. Y.: Longmans, 1934.

ROWNTREE, MAURICE L. *Mankind Set Free,* with an Introduction by George Lansbury. London: J. Cape, 1939.

RYAN, RT. REV. MSGR. JOHN A. *A Better Economic Order.* N. Y.: Harper, 1935.

———. *Catholic Principles of Politics.* N. Y.: Macmillan, 1940.

———. *Relation of Catholicism to Fascism, Communism, and Democracy.* Washington, D. C.: National Catholic Welfare Conference, 1938.

SCUDDER, VIDA D. *Socialism and Character.* Boston: Houghton Mifflin, 1912.

SEARLE, ROBERT W. *Contemporary Religious Thinking.* N. Y.: Falcon Press, 1933.

SELIGMAN, E. R. A. "Robert Owen and Christian Socialism," *Political Science Quarterly,* Vols. I, II, 1883.

SHARPE, D. R. *Walter Rauschenbusch.* N. Y.: Macmillan, 1942.

SINGER, ISIDORE. *Social Justice.* N. Y.: I. Goldmann Co., 1923.

SMYTH, JAMES P. *Our Present Discontent. With a Foreword by the Most Reverend Richard Downey.* London: Burns, Oates and Washbourne, 1941.

Social Ideals of the Churches. N. Y.: Federal Council of Churches of Christ, 1933.

SPARGO, JOHN. *Marxian Socialism and Religion.* N. Y.: Huebsch, 1915.

———. *The Spiritual Significance of Modern Socialism.* N. Y.: Huebsch, 1908.

STEAD, FRANCIS H. *The Story of Social Christianity* (2 vols.). London: J. Clarke and Co., 1924.

SWIFT, ARTHUR L. *New Frontiers of Religion.* N. Y.: Macmillan, 1938.

TAWNEY, R. H. *Religion and the Rise of Capitalism.* N. Y.: Harcourt, 1926.

TEMPLE, WILLIAM (Archbishop of Canterbury). *The Christian and the World Situation.* London: New Commonwealth, 1937.

Toward Social Christianity. N. Y.: Young Men's Christian Association Press, 1939.

VAN DUSEN, HENRY P. *For the Healing of the Nations.* N. Y.: Scribner, 1940.

VAUGHAN, BERNARD. *Socialism from the Christian Standpoint.* N. Y.: Macmillan, 1912.

VEDDER, HENRY C. *Socialism and the Ethics of Jesus.* N. Y.: Macmillan, 1912.

VUILLIAMY, B. COLWYN. *Charles Kingsley and Christian Socialism.* London: Fabian Society, 1924. Fabian Tract No. 174.

WARD, HARRY F. *Democracy and Social Change.* N. Y.: Modern Age Books, 1940.

———. *The New Social Order.* N. Y.: Macmillan, 1920.

———. *On Economic Morality and the Ethics of Jesus.* N. Y.: Macmillan, 1929.

WESTCOTT, B. F. (BISHOP OF DURHAM). *Social Aspects of Christianity.* N. Y.: Macmillan, 1900.

———. *Socialism.* London: Guild of St. Matthew, 1890.

WILLIGAN, WALTER L., AND O'CONNOR, JOHN L. *The Social Order.* N. Y.: Longmans, 1941.

State Socialism and Socialism of the Chair

BIRD, FREDERICK L., AND RYAN, FRANCES M. *Public Ownership on Trial,* New Republic, 1930.

BLISS, W. D. P. *New Encyclopaedia of Social Reform.* N. Y.: Funk and Wagnalls, 1897. See Index.

CHASE, STUART. *Government in Business.* N. Y.: Macmillan, 1935.

COLE, G. D. H. *Self-Government in Industry.* London: Bell, 1918.

COREY, LEWIS. *The Unfinished Task.* N. Y.: Funk and Wagnalls, 1897.

DAVIES, EMIL. *The Case for Nationalization.* London: Allen and Unwin, 1920.

———. *The Collectivist State in the Making.* London: Bell, 1913.

DIMOCK, MARSHALL E. *British Public Utilities and National Development.* London: Allen and Unwin, 1933.

ELDRIDGE, SEBA, AND ASSOCIATES. *Development of Collective Enterprise.* Lawrence, Kans.: University of Kansas, 1943.

ELY, RICHARD T. *French and German Socialism.* N. Y.: Harper, 1884, ch. XV.

HILLQUIT, MORRIS. *Socialism Summed Up.* N. Y.: Rand Book Store, 1913.

———. *Socialism in Theory and Practice.* N. Y.: Macmillan, 1909, pp. 284–8.

HOWE, FRED C. *European Cities at Work.* N. Y.: Scribner, 1913.

LAIDLER, HARRY W. *A Program for Modern America.* N. Y.: Crowell, 1936, chs. VII–XIV.

———. *Public Ownership Here and Abroad.* N. Y.: League for Industrial Democracy, 1924.

———. *Socializing Our Democracy.* N. Y.: Harper, 1935.

LILIENTHAL, DAVID. *TVA—Democracy on the March.* N. Y.: Harper, 1940.

LYON, L. S., ABRAMSON, V., AND ASSOCIATES. *Government and Economic Life.* Washington: Brookings, 1940.

O'BRIEN, TERENCE H. *British Experiments in Public Ownership and Control.* N. Y.: Norton, 1938.

ROBERTS, ELMER. *Monarchial Socialism in Germany.* N. Y.: Scribner, 1913.

SHAW, BERNARD. *Common Sense of Municipal Trading.* N. Y.: Dodd, Mead, 1911. Also London: Fabian Socialist Series No. 5, 1908.

"State and Municipal Enterprise," *New Statesman.* London: May 5, 1915.

SUTHERS, R. B. *Mind Your Own Business.* London: Allen and Unwin, 1929.

SWENSON, RINEHART J. *The National Government and Business.* N. Y.: Century, 1924.

THOMPSON, CARL D. *Public Ownership.* N. Y.: Crowell, 1925.

VANDERVELDE, ÉMILE. *The State vs. Socialism.* Chicago: Kerr, 1919.

WALLING, E. E., AND LAIDLER, H. W. *State Socialism—Pro and Con.* N. Y.: Holt, 1917.

WARBASSE, JAMES P. *Co-operative Democracy.* N. Y.: Macmillan, 1924.

WEBB, SIDNEY AND BEATRICE. *The Consumers' Co-operative Movement.* N. Y.: Longmans, 1915.

———. *Constitution for the Socialist Commonwealth of Great Britain.* N. Y.: Longmans, 1921.

PART EIGHT

Contributions of Various Social and Economic Movements

Bibliography

EGBERT, DONALD DREW, and PERSONS, STOW (Eds.). *Socialism and American Life.* 2 vols. Princeton: Princeton University Press, 1952. Volume II is an analytic bibliography of socialism in its every aspect—the most extensive bibliography on this movement extant.

General Histories

BRAUNTHAL, JULIUS (Ed.). *Yearbook of the International Socialist Labour Movement, 1956–7.* London: Lincolns-Praeger International Yearbook Publishing Co., or Socialist International, 8, Motcomb St., London, S.W. 1. Short histories of socialism in practically every country.

———. *History of the International,* vol. 1, 1864–1914. N. Y.: Praeger, 1967.

COLE, G. D. H. *A History of Socialist Thought.* London: Macmillan; New York: St. Martin's Press. 1953–60. 5 vols. Most comprehensive history of socialism from Utopianism to the 1950's.

———. *World Socialism Restated.* London: Turnstile Press, 1956.

GRAY, ALEXANDER. *The Socialist Tradition.* London: Longmans, 1946.

LAIDLER, HARRY W. *Labor Governments at Work.* N. Y.: League for Industrial Democracy, 1948. Pamphlet.

LORWIN, LEWIS L. *The International Labor Movement.* N. Y.: Harper & Brothers, 1953.

MALLORY, WALTER H. (Ed.). *Political Handbook and Atlas of the World, Parliaments, Parties and Press.* N. Y., Harper & Row, year books.

Fabianism

ATTLEE, CLEMENT R. *The Labour Party in Perspective and Twelve Years Later.* London: Gollancz, 1949.

COLE, G. D. H. *Second International, 1889–1914.* History of Socialist Thought Series. Vol. III. London: Macmillan; N. Y.: St. Martin's Press, 1956.

COLE, MARGARET. *Beatrice Webb.* London: Longmans, 1945; N. Y.: Harcourt, Brace, 1946.

———. *The Fabian Society.* Rev. London: Fabian Society, 1952.

———. *Growing Up Into Revolution.* London, 1949. Autobiography.

———. *The Story of Fabian Socialism.* London: Heinemann, 1961.

CROSSMAN, R. H. S. (Ed.). *The New Fabian Essays.* London: Turnstile Press, 1952.

Fabian Tracts. Several hundred published by the Fabian Society, 11 Dartmouth St., S.W. 1, London.

FREMANTLE, ANNE. *This Little Band of Prophets—The British Fabians.* N. Y.: New American Library, 1960.

GRANT, ANDREW. *Socialism and the Middle Class*. London: Lawrence and Wishart, 1958.

JONES, ARTHUR CREECH. *New Fabian Colonial Essays*. London: Hogarth Press, 1959.

MCBRIAR, A. *Fabian Socialism and English Politics, 1884–1918*. Cambridge: Cambridge University Press, 1962.

TAWNEY, R. H. *Equality*. (4th ed. rev.) with an Introduction by Richard M. Titmuss. N. Y.: Barnes and Noble, 1965.

———. *The Webbs and Their Work*. London: Fabian Society, 1947.

WEBB, BEATRICE, *Diaries, 1912–24* and *Diaries, 1924–32*. Edited and with an Introduction by Margaret Cole. London and Toronto: Longmans, 1952.

———. *Our Partnership*. Edited by Margaret M. Cole and Barbara Draker. N. Y.: Longmans, 1948.

Marxism

BECKWITH, BURNHAM P. *The Economic Theory of a Socialist Economy*. Stanford: Stanford University Press, 1949.

BOBER, MANDELL M. *Karl Marx's Interpretation of History*. Cambridge: Harvard University Press, 1949.

CHRISTMAN, HENRY M. (Editor). *The American Journalism of Marx and Engels*. N. Y.: New American Library, 1966.

COLE, G. D. H. *Socialist Economics*. London: Gollancz, 1950.

DOBB, MAURICE H. *On Economic Theory and Socialism*. London: Routledge, 1955.

EASTMAN, MAX. *Reflections on the Failure of Socialism*. N. Y.: Devin Adair, 1955.

FRIED, ALBERT, and SANDERS, RONALD (Eds.). *Socialist Thought: A Documentary History*. Garden City, L. I.: Doubleday, 1964.

LE ROSSIGNOL, JAMES E. *From Marx to Stalin*. N. Y.: Thomas Y. Crowell Company, 1950.

LEWIS, JOHN. *Marxism and Modern Socialism*. London: Lawrence and Wishart, 1944.

LICHTHEIM, GEORGE. *Marxism: An Historical and Critical Study*. London: Routledge, 1961.

MAYO, HENRY B., *Introduction to Marxist Theory*. N. Y.: Oxford University Press, 1960.

MENDEL, ARTHUR P. *Essential Works of Marxism*. N. Y.: Bantam Books, 1961.

NEARING, SCOTT. *Economics for the Power Age*. N. Y.: John Day Co., 1952.

NOVA, FRITZ. *Friedrich Engels: His Contributions to Political Theory*. N. Y.: Philosophical Library, 1968.

SCHLESINGER, RUDOLF. *Marx: His Time and Ours*. N. Y.: Kelley, 1950.

VON MISES, LUDWIG. *Socialism: An Economic and Sociological Analysis.* Trans. by J. Kahane. New Haven: Yale University Press, 1951.

WOLFE, BERTRAM D. *Marxism: One Hundred Years in the Life of a Doctrine.* N. Y.: Dial Press, 1965.

Humanist Socialism

COLTON, JOEL. *Leon Blum: Humanist in Politics.* N. Y.: Knopf, 1966.

FROMM, ERICH. *The Art of Loving.* N. Y.: Harper & Brothers, 1956.

———. *Beyond the Chains of Illusion: My Encounter With Marx and Freud.* N. Y.: Simon & Schuster, 1962.

———. *Escape from Freedom.* N. Y.: Rinehart, 1960.

———. *Marx's Concept of Man.* N. Y.: Frederick Ungar, 1961.

———. *The Sane Society.* N. Y.: Rinehart, 1955.

———. *Socialist Humanism: An International Symposium.* N. Y.: Doubleday, 1965.

Religion and Social Thought

BENNETT, JOHN C. *Christian Ethics and Social Policy.* N. Y.: Scribner, 1946.

———. *Christianity and Communism.* N. Y.: Association Press, 1948.

BENNETT, JOHN C., and Others. *Christian Values and Economic Life.* N. Y.: Harper & Brothers, 1954.

CALLAHAN, DANIEL. *The New Church—Essays in Catholic Reform.* N. Y.: Scribner, 1966.

CALVEZ, JEAN-YVES. *The Social Thought of John XXIII.* Chicago: Regnery, 1965. Sequel to *The Church and Social Justice from Leo XIII to Pius XII* by Calvez and J. Perrin. Chicago: Regnery, 1961.

Christian Socialist. Official organ of Christian Socialist Movement of England. Issues of 1960–64.

Christianity and Crisis. 1941 to present-day issues.

COWAN, WAYNE H. (Ed.). *Witness to a Generation.* Writings from *Christianity and Crisis.* N. Y.: Bobbs-Merrill Co., 1967.

CRONBACH, ABRAHAM. *Religion and Its Social Setting.* Cincinnati: The Social Press (Hebrew Union College), 1933.

CRONIN, JOHN F. *The Social Teaching of John XXIII.* Milwaukee: Bruce Publishing, 1963.

DOMENOCH, JEAN-MARIE, and Others (Ed.). *The Catholic Avant-Garde.* N. Y.: Rinehart, 1967. French Catholicism since World War II.

EGBERT, DONALD DREW, and PERSONS, STOW (Eds.).*Socialism and American Life.* Vol. I, Ch. 4, Albert T. Mollegan, "The Religious Basis of Western Socialism." In Vol. II are bibliography and index. Princeton: Princeton University Press, 1952.

FROMM, ERICH. *You Shall Be As Gods: A Radical Interpretation of the Old Testament and Its Tradition.* N. Y.: Rinehart, 1966.

JOHN XXIII. *The Encyclicals and Other Messages of John XXIII, With Commentaries.* Washington: T.P.S. Press, 1964.

National Council of Churches of Christ in the United States of America. *The Christian Conscience and an Economy of Abundance.* Published for the Department of the Church and Economic Life. N. Y.: National Council of Churches, 1958.

———. *Christian Principles and Assumptions on Economic Life.* N. Y.: National Council of Churches, 1954.

NIEBUHR, REINHOLD. *Man's Nature and His Communities.* N. Y.: Scribner, 1965.

VORSPAN, ALBERT, and LIPMAN, EUGENE J. *Justice and Judaism: The Work of Social Action.* N. Y.: Union of American Hebrew Congregation, 1956.

Utopian Socialism

AMES, R. A. *Citizen Thomas More and His Utopia.* Princeton: Princeton University Press, 1949.

BUBER, MARTIN. *Paths in Utopia.* London: Routledge, 1949.

COLE, G. D. H. *Socialist Thought: The Forerunners, 1789–1850.* History of Socialist Thought Series. Vol. I. London: Macmillan; N. Y.: St. Martin's Press, 1953.

EGBERT, DONALD DREW, and PERSONS, STOW (Eds.). *Socialism and American Life.* 2 Vols. Princeton: Princeton University Press, 1952. See Vol. II.

MORGAN, A. E., *Nowhere Was Somewhere.* Chapel Hill, N. C.: University of North Carolina Press, 1946.

United States and Canada

ADAMS, GEORGE PLIMPTON. *Competitive Economic Systems.* N. Y.: Thomas Y. Crowell Co., 1955.

BELL, DANIEL. "The Background and Development of Marxian Socialism in the U.S." in Egbert and Persons' *Socialism and American Life,* Vol. I, pp. 213–405.

———. *The End of Ideology: On the Exhaustion of Political Ideas in the Fifties.* Glencoe, Ill.: Free Press, 1960.

———. *Work and Its Discontents.* Boston: Beacon Press, 1956.

BENDINER, ROBERT. *Just Around the Corner.* N. Y.: Harper & Row, 1967.

CHASE, STUART. *The Most Probable World.* N. Y.: Harper & Row, 1968.

COLDWELL, M. J. *Canadian Progressives on the March.* N. Y.: League for Industrial Democracy, 1944.

Conference on Economic Progress, Poverty and Deprivation in the United States. Washington, D. C.: Conference on Economic Progress, 1962.

COOK, FRED J. *The Corrupted Land: The Social Morality of Modern America.* N. Y.: Macmillan, 1966.

CROSSER, PAUL K. *State Capitalism in the Economy of the United States.* N. Y.: Bookman Assoc., 1962.

DIAMOND, MARTIN. *Socialism and the Decline of the American Socialist Party.* Chicago: University of Chicago Press, 1956.

Dissent. Bi-monthly journal devoted to ideas and values of democratic socialism. N. Y.: 509 Fifth Avenue.

Echoes of Revolt: The Masses, 1911–1917. Edited by William L. O'Neill. Introduction by Irving Howe. Chicago: Quadrangle Books, 1966.

EGBERT, DONALD D. and PERSONS, STOW. *Socialism in American Life.* 2 Vols. Princeton: Princeton University Press, 1952. Vol. I contains a series of studies on various aspects of American socialism and their background. Vol. II is a bibliography on socialism throughout the world.

FINER, HERMAN. *Road to Reaction.* Boston: Little Brown, 1945.

FLEISCHMAN, HARRY. *Norman Thomas, a Biography.* N. Y.: Norton, 1964.

FONER, PHILIP S. (Ed.). *Jack London American Rebel.* N. Y.: Citadel Press, 1947.

GALBRAITH, JOHN KENNETH. *The Affluent Society.* Boston: Houghton, Mifflin, 1958.

———. *American Capitalism: The Concept of Countervailing Power.* 2d ed. rev. Boston: Houghton, Mifflin, 1956.

———. *The New Industrial State.* Boston: Houghton, Mifflin, 1967.

GAY, PETER. *The Dilemma of Democratic Socialism.* N. Y.: Columbia University Press, 1952.

GINGER, RAYMOND. *The Age of Excess.* N. Y.: Macmillan, 1965. American Life from the Age of Reconstruction to World War I.

———. (Ed.). *American Social Thought.* American Century Series. N. Y.: Hill and Wang, 1961.

———.*The Bending Cross: A Biography of Eugene Victor Debs.* N. Y.: Rutgers University Press, 1949.

GINSBERG, ELI, and Others. *The Pluralistic Economy.* N. Y.: McGraw-Hill, 1965.

GORDAN, MANYA. *How to Tell Progress from Reaction.* N. Y.: Dutton, 1944.

HARRINGTON, MICHAEL. *The Accidental Century.* N. Y.: Macmillan, 1965.

———. *The Other America.* N. Y.: Macmillan, 1962.

HEILBRONER, ROBERT. *The Limits of American Capitalism.* N. Y.: Harper & Row, 1966.

HOOK, SIDNEY. *From Hegel to Marx: Studies in the Intellectual Development of Karl Marx.* Ann Arbor: University of Michigan Press, 1962.

———. *Political Power and Personal Freedom.* N. Y.: Criterion Books, 1959.

HOOVER, CALVIN B. *The Economy, Liberty and the State.* N. Y.: Twentieth Century Fund, 1959.

HOWE, IRVING (Ed.). *The Radical Imagination.* N. Y.: New American Library, 1967.

——. *The Radical Papers,* N. Y.: Doubleday, 1966.

——. *Steady Work: Essays in the Politics of Democratic Radicalism, 1953–1966.* N. Y.: Harcourt, 1966.

HUSS, JOHN DAVID. *Socialism in the U.S.: An Inquiry into Its Lack of Success.* Durham, N. C.: Duke University Press, 1960.

KIPNIS, IRA. *The American Socialist Movement, 1897–1912.* N. Y.: Columbia University Press, 1952.

LAIDLER, HARRY W. *Our Changing Industrial Incentives.* N. Y.: League for Industrial Democracy, 1949. Pamphlet.

——. *Socialism in the United States: A Brief History.* N. Y.: League for Industrial Democracy, 1952. Pamphlet.

LANDAUER, CARL. *Theory of National Economic Theory.* Berkeley: University of California Press, 1944.

LASCH, CHRISTOPHER. *The New Radicalism in America, 1889–1963.* N. Y.: Alfred A. Knopf and Random House (Vintage Books), 1965. Studies of the intellectual as a political type.

LEKACHMAN, ROBERT. *The Age of Keynes.* N. Y.: Random House, 1966.

LENS, SIDNEY. *Radicalism in America.* N. Y.: Thomas Y. Crowell Company, 1966.

LEVENSTEIN, AARON. *The Atomic Age: Suicide, Slavery or Social Planning.* N. Y. League for Industrial Democracy, 1946.

——. *Why People Work.* N. Y.: Crowell-Collier, 1962.

LEWIS, DAVID, and SCOTT, FRANK. *Make This Your Canada.* Toronto: Central Canada Publishing Co., 1943.

LIPSET, SEYMOUR M. *Agrarian Socialism.* Berkeley: University of California Press, 1950.

LORWIN, L. L. *The International Labor Movement.* N. Y.: Harper & Brothers, 1953.

MILLER, HERMAN P. *Rich Man, Poor Man.* N. Y.: Thomas Y. Crowell Company, 1966.

MILLS, C. WRIGHT. *The Power Elite.* N. Y.: Oxford University Press, 1956.

MYRDAL, GUNNAR. *Challenge to Affluence.* N. Y.: Random House, 1963.

NATHAN, ROBERT R. *Mobilizing for Abundance.* N. Y.: McGraw-Hill, 1944.

NEARING, SCOTT. *Economics for the Power Age.* N. Y.: John Day, 1952.

New America. Semi-monthly–official organ of American Socialist Party. N. Y.: 1182 Broadway.

NEWFIELD, JACK. *A Prophetic Minority.* Introduction by Michael Harrington. N. Y.: New American Library, 1966. About the "New Radicals."

New Politics. Quarterly–journal of socialist thought.

QUINT, HOWARD H. *The Forging of American Socialism.* Columbia, S. C.: University of South Carolina Press, 1953.

RIESMAN, DAVID. *Individualism Reconsidered.* Chicago: The Free Press, 1954.

——, and others. *The Lonely Crowd.* New Haven: Yale University Press, 1950.

A. PHILIP RANDOLPH INSTITUTE. *A "Freedom Budget" for All Americans.* N. Y.: A. Philip Randolph Institute, 1966.

SEIDLER, MURRAY B. *Norman Thomas; Respectable Rebel.* Syracuse: Syracuse University Press, 1961.

SELVIN, DAVID F. *Eugene Debs.* N. Y.: Lothrop, Lee and Shepard Co., 1967.

SHANNON, DAVID A. *The Socialist Party of America.* N. Y.: Macmillan, 1955.

SINCLAIR, UPTON. *The Autobiography of Upton Sinclair.* N. Y.: Harcourt, Brace & World, 1962.

——. *The Jungle.* N. Y.: Viking Press, 1946.

SOULE, GEORGE. *Planning U.S.A.* N. Y.: Viking Press, 1967.

STONE, IRVING. *Adversary in the House.* N. Y.: Doubleday, 1947. A fictionalized biography of Eugene Victor Debs.

SWEEZY, PAUL M. *Socialism.* N. Y.: McGraw-Hill, 1949.

THEOBALD, ROBERT. *The Guaranteed Income.* N. Y.: Doubleday, 1966.

THOMAS, NORMAN. *A Socialist's Faith.* N. Y.: Norton, 1951.

——. *Democratic Socialism—A New Appraisal.* Pamphlet. N. Y., League for Industrial Democracy.

——. *Socialism Re-examined.* N. Y.: Norton, 1963.

WARREN, FRANK A. *Liberals and Communism: The 'Reed Decade' Revisited.* Bloomington: Indiana University Press, 1966.

WILSON, JOHN. *Equality.* N. Y.: Harcourt, Brace & World, 1966.

WITHERS, WILLIAM. *Freedom Through Power.* N. Y., John Day, 1965.

Europe and Other Lands

ANDERSON, PERRY, and BLACKBURN, ROBIN. Introduction by Andrew Hacker. *Toward Socialism.* Ithaca: Cornell University, 1966. Essays by prominent British socialists.

ATTLEE, CLEMENT R. *The Labor Party in Perspective and Twelve Years Later.* London: Gollancz, 1949.

BEVERIDGE, SIR. WILLIAM H. *Full Employment in a Free Society.* London: Allen and Unwin, 1945.

BLUM, LEON. *For All Mankind.* N. Y.: Viking Press, 1946.

BROCKWAY, A. FENNER. *African Socialism.* Chester Springs, Pa.: Dufour, 1963.

COLE, G. D. H. *The Case for Industrial Partnership.* N. Y.: St. Martin's Press, 1957.

——. *A History of the Labour Party from 1914; British Working Class Politics, 1832–1914.* London: Routledge, 1941 and 1949.

CONNERY, DONALD S. *The Scandinavian.* N. Y.: Simon and Schuster, 1966.

COWLES, VIRGINIA. *No Cause for Alarm: The Story of the Labor Government.* N. Y.: Harper, 1940.

CROSSMAN, R. H. S. *Socialist Values in a Changing Civilization.* London: Fabian Society, 1950.

DURBIN, E. F. M. *Problems of Economic Planning.* With a Foreword by Clement R. Attlee. London: Routledge, 1949.

EATON, JOHN. *Marx Against Keynes.* London: Lawrence and Wishart, 1951.

———. *Socialism in the Nuclear Age.* London: Lawrence and Wishart, 1961.

GANDHI, M. K. *Towards Non-Violent Socialism.* Ahmadabad Navajivan Publishing House, 1951.

GROSS, FELIKS. *The Polish Worker.* N. Y.: Roy Publishers, 1945.

———. *World Politics and Tension Areas.* N. Y.: New York University Press, 1966.

HOBSON, JOHN A. *Imperialism, a Study.* New introduction by Philip Siegelman. Ann Arbor: University of Michigan Press, 1965.

HUTCHINSON, KEITH. *The Decline and Fall of British Capitalism.* N. Y.: Scribners, 1958.

JAY, DOUGLAS. *Socialism and the New Society.* London: Longmans, 1962.

LAIDLER, HARRY W. *British Labor As Government and Opposition.* N. Y.: The League for Industrial Democracy, 1946. Pamphlet.

———. *British Labor's Rise to Power.* N. Y.: League for Industrial Democracy, 1945. Pamphlet

LANDAUER, CARL. *European Socialism.* 2 Vols. Berkeley: University of California Press, 1959.

LASKI, HAROLD J. *Faith, Reason and Civilization.* N. Y.: Viking, 1944.

LINDBOM, TAGE. *Sweden's Labor Program.* N. Y.: League for Industrial Democracy, 1948. Pamphlet.

MANSON, JULIUS. *The British Health Service.* N. Y.: League for Industrial Democracy, 1952. Pamphlet.

MORRISON, HERBERT. *Forward from Victory.* London: Gollancz, 1946.

MOULIN, LEO. *Socialism of the West.* London: Gollancz, 1945.

SCHAPIRO, JACOB S. *Movements of Social Dissent in Modern Europe.* N. Y.: Anvil, 1962.

SELSAM, HOWARD. *Socialism and Ethics.* London: Lawrence and Wishart, 1947.

SHAW, GEORGE BERNARD. *Everybody's Political What's What.* N. Y.: Dodd, Mead, 1944.

Socialist Union. *Twentieth Century Socialism.* London; Baltimore: Penguin, 1956.

STRACHEY, JOHN. *Socialism Looks Forward.* N. Y.: Philosophical Library, 1945.

STURMTHAL, ADOLPH. *The Tragedy of European Labor.* N. Y.: Columbia University Press, 1943.

Swedish Social Welfare Board. *Social Sweden.* Stockholm: Gernandts Boktryckeri, 1952.

TAWNEY, R. H. *The Radical Tradition.* Twelve essays edited by Rita Hinden. N. Y.: Pantheon Books, 1964; London: Allen and Unwin, 1964.

TEGNER, G. *Security in Sweden.* Stockholm: The Swedish Institute, 1956.

TRACEY, HERBERT (Ed.). *British Labor Party.* 3 vols. London: Caxton, 1948.

WARBEY, WILLIAM, and Others. *Modern Norway: A Study in Social Democracy.* London: Fabian Society, 1953.

WILLIAMS, FRANCOIS. *Fifty Years March—The Rise of the Labor Party.* London: Odhams Press, 1949.

———. *Socialist Britain.* N. Y.: Viking Press, 1949.

WOOTTON, BARBARA. *Freedom Under Planning.* London: Allen and Unwin, 1945; Chapel Hill: University of North Carolina Press, 1945.

Communism

ALEXANDER, ROBERT J. *Communism in Latin America.* New Brunswick, N. J.: Rutgers University Press, 1958.

ANDERSON, THORNTON. *Russian Political Thought.* Ithaca: Cornell University Press, 1967.

BALDWIN, ROGER N. (Ed.). *A New Slavery: The Communist Betrayal of Human Rights.* N. Y.: Oceana Publishers, 1953.

BELOV, FEDOR. *A History of a Soviet Collective Farm.* N. Y.: Praeger, 1955.

BORKENAU, FRANZ. *European Communism.* N. Y.: Harper, 1953.

CHAMBERLAIN, WILLIAM H. *The Russian Enigma.* N. Y.: Scribner, 1943.

COLE, G. D. H. *A History of Socialist Thought.* Vol. IV, "Communism and Social Democracy, 1914–1931." London: Macmillan; N. Y.: St. Martin's Press, 1955.

CONWAY, JOHN (Trans.). *The Path to Dictatorship, 1918–13.* N. Y.: Praeger, 1966. Ten essays by German scholars.

COUNTS, GEORGE S. *The Challenge of Soviet Education.* N. Y.: McGraw-Hill, 1957.

DALLIN, DAVID J. *The Real Soviet Russia.* New Haven: Yale University Press, 1944.

DEUTSCHER, ISAAC. *Stalin: A Political Biography.* N. Y.: Oxford University Press, 1967.

———. *The Unfinished Revolution, Russia, 1917–1967.* N. Y.: Oxford University Press, 1967.

DJILAS, MILOVAN. *The New Class.* N. Y.: Praeger, 1957.

DRAPER, THEODORE. *The Roots of American Communism.* N. Y.: Viking, 1957.

EPSTEIN, MELECH. *The Jew and Communism.* N. Y.: Trade Union Sponsoring Committee, 1959.

FAINSOD, MERLE. *How Russia Is Ruled.* Cambridge: Harvard University Press, 1954.

FISCHER, LOUIS. *The Life and Death of Stalin.* N. Y.: Harper & Brothers, 1962.

———. *The Life of Lenin.* N. Y.: Harper & Row, 1964.

Foreign Affairs (quarterly), "The Russian Revolution—Fifty Years After," Oct. 1967.

FOSTER, WILLIAM Z. *History of the Three Internationals.* N. Y.: International Publishers, 1955.

———. *Outline History of the World Trade Union Movement.* N. Y.: International Publishers, 1956.

FRANKLAND, MARK. *Khrushchev.* N. Y.: Stein and Day, 1967.

GREY, IAN. *The First Fifty Years.* N. Y.: Coward-McCann, 1967.

GROSS, FELIKS. *The Seizure of Political Power.* N. Y.: Philosophical Library, 1958.

HALL, GUS. *For A Radical Change—The Communist View.* N. Y.: New Outlook Publishers, 1966.

HINDUS, MAURICE. *The House Without a Roof: Russia After Forty-Three Years of Revolution.* Garden City: Doubleday, 1961.

HOOK, SIDNEY. *Heresy, Yes—Conspiracy, No.* N. Y.: John Day, 1953.

HUNT, R. N. CAREW. *The Theory and Practice of Communism.* N. Y.: Macmillan, 1957.

KAUTSKY, KARL. *Social Democracy vs. Communism.* N. Y.: Rand School Press, 1946.

KHRUSHCHEV, NIKITA S. *Crimes of the Stalin Era: Special Report to the 20th Congress of the Communist Party of the Soviet Union.* Annotated for the *New Leader,* N. Y., by Boris I. Nicolaevsky.

LENIN, NIKOLAI. *Marx, Engels, Marxism.* Moscow: Foreign Languages Publishing House, 1947.

LYONS, EUGENE. *Worker's Paradise Lost.* N. Y.: Funk & Wagnalls, 1967.

MOORE, BARRINGTON, JR. *Social Origins of Dictatorship and Democracy.* Boston: Beacon Press, 1966.

NOVE, ALEC. *The Soviet Economy.* N. Y.: Frederick A. Praeger, 1966.

OVERSTREET, HARRY and BONARO. *What We Must Know About Communism.* N. Y.: Norton, 1958.

PETERSON, ARNOLD. *Marxism vs. Soviet Despotism.* N. Y.: Labor News Co., 1958.

Royal Institute of International Affairs. *The Impact of the Russian Revolution, 1917–67.* London: The Institute, 1967.

SALISBURY, HARRISON (Ed.). *The Soviet Union: The Fifty Years.* N. Y.: Harcourt, Brace & World, 1967.

SETON-WATSON, HUGH. *The East European Revolution.* N. Y.: Praeger, 1951.

———. *From Lenin to Malenkov: The History of World Communism.* N. Y.: Praeger, 1953.

SHUB, DAVID. *Lenin: A Biography*. N. Y.: Doubleday, 1948.

WOLFE, BERTRAM D. *Communist Totalitarianism*. Boston: Beacon Press, 1961.

———. *Six Keys to the Soviet System*. Boston: Beacon Press, 1956.

Consumers' Co-operation

AMES, J. W. *Co-operative Sweden Today*. Manchester: Co-operative Union, 1956.

Co-operative League of the U.S.A. 57 E. Van Buren St., Chicago, Ill. Publications of this League.

Co-operative Union. *The Co-operative Movement in a Collective Economy*. Manchester: British Co-operative Union, 1950. Various publications on Co-operative Movement.

DIGBY, MARGARET. *The World Co-operative Movement*. London: Hutchinson University Library, 1960.

GORST, SHEILA. *Co-operative Organizations in Tropical Countries*. London: Oxford, 1959.

International Co-operative Alliance, 11 Upper Grosvenor, London, S.W. 1.

POLLARD, SIDNEY. *The Co-operative Movement at the Crossroads*. London: Fabian Society, 1965.

VOORHIS, JERRY. *American Cooperatives*. N. Y.: Harper & Row, 1961.

Index